Contents

A Note from the Peterson's Editors

For more than forty years, Peterson's has given students and parents the most comprehensive, up-to-date information on undergraduate institutions in the United States. *Peterson's College & University Almanac* features advice and tips on the college search and selection process, such as how to consider the factors that truly make a difference during your college search and how to file for financial aid. Peterson's researches the data published in *Peterson's College & University Almanac* each year. The information is furnished by the colleges and is accurate at the time of publishing.

- For advice and guidance in the college search and selection process, just turn the page for our **Your College: Picking It and Paying for It** section, with information on choosing a high-quality school and what "quality" really means, using the Web to further research your choices, and how to fund a college education.

- Next, you'll want to read through "How to Use This Guide," which explains the information presented in the individual college profiles, how we collect our data, and how we determine eligibility for inclusion in this guide. Following that are the **Profiles of Four-Year Colleges.** Here you'll find the college descriptions, arranged alphabetically by state. They provide need-to-know information about accredited four-year colleges—including total enrollment, application deadlines, expenses, and most frequently chosen baccalaureate fields. And if you still thirst for even more information, nearly 100 narrative descriptions appear in the **College Close-Ups** section of the book. These descriptions are written by college officials and provide great detail about each college. They are edited to provide a consistent format across entries for your ease of comparison. Lastly, you'll find an **Index** of an Alphabetical Listing of Four-Year Colleges, useful in quickly finding a particular school.

Peterson's publishes a full line of resources to help guide you through the admission process. Peterson's publications can be found at your local bookstore or library and at your high school guidance office; you can access us online at www.petersons.com.

We welcome any comments or suggestions you may have about this publication and invite you to complete our online survey at **www.petersons.com/booksurvey.**

Your feedback will help us make your education dreams come true.

Colleges will be pleased to know that Peterson's helped you in your selection. Admissions staff members are more than happy to answer questions, address specific problems, and help in any way they can. The editors at Peterson's wish you great success in your college search!

YOUR COLLEGE: PICKING IT AND PAYING FOR IT

PETERSON'S COLLEGE & UNIVERSITY ALMANAC

2009

PETERSON'S
A nelnet COMPANY

About Peterson's, a Nelnet company

Peterson's (www.petersons.com) is a leading provider of education information and advice, with books and online resources focusing on education search, test preparation, and financial aid. Its Web site offers searchable databases and interactive tools for contacting educational institutions, online practice tests and instruction, and planning tools for securing financial aid. Peterson's serves 110 million education consumers annually.

For more information, contact Peterson's, 2000 Lenox Drive, Lawrenceville, NJ 08648; 800-338-3282; or find us on the World Wide Web at www.petersons.com/about.

Stephen Clemente, President; Fern A. Oram, Content Director; Bernadette Webster, Operations Director; Roger S. Williams, Sales and Marketing; Mark D. Snider, Production Editor; Bret Bollman, Pam Sullivan, Copy Editors; Daniel Margolin, Research Project Manager; Cathleen Fee, Research Associate; Phyllis Johnson, Programmer; Ray Golaszewski, Manufacturing Manager; Linda M. Williams, Composition Manager

ISSN 1523-9128
ISBN-13: 978-0-7689-2547-0
ISBN-10: 0-7689-2547-9

Printed in the United States of America

10 9 8 7 6 5 4 3 2 1 10 09 08

Eleventh Edition

A Guide to Good Four-Year Colleges

Ernest L. Boyer
edited by Paul Boyer

When you think of college, perhaps you imagine the cliché or Hollywood image: a campus filled with ivy-covered buildings, students socializing in the academic quad, and the faint sounds of a professor's voice coming from an open window. Despite this stereotypical picture of what college might look like on the surface, there is no single model of a "good college." Missions and circumstances vary greatly from one campus to another. Each four-year college and university has something different to offer its students. And with increased college costs, you want to be assured that you will get the best value out of the college investment. This makes choosing the right college even more difficult. It may help to know that despite all of the differences among colleges, there are characteristics commonly shared by reputable schools that you should consider in your search.

Although these standards can be used to evaluate any college, you should narrow your list prior to the "test of quality" and put these questions to the schools on your final list. As you work through the list, you will find that a great deal of this information can be uncovered by reading material in print and online, as well as by reading literature from individual colleges. In order to come up with the most complete review of a particular school, though, you will need to discuss these items with your guidance counselor, representatives from the colleges, and other advisers.

Some Common Measures of Quality

Every college should be guided by a clear and vital mission. It should understand its unique role in higher education and present itself honestly to prospective students through its literature and other information outlets. An institution cannot be all things to all people, so choices must be made and priorities assigned. What shows the strength of an institution is whether it has clearly defined its focus and, beyond that, whether it has successfully turned those goals into a living purpose for the campus. Of course, you also need to determine if the college's mission matches up with your own goals and values. At the very least, you need to know that you will be comfortable at a college and that it will deliver the type of educational experience you are seeking.

The quality of the undergraduate college is measured largely by the extent of its cooperation with high schools and by its willingness to smooth the transition of students into college. The way you are recruited by a college helps to shape your expectations of that college. A good college conducts its recruitment and selection with the best interests of the student in mind and should, therefore, try to learn more about you than simply your test scores and class rank.

Beyond the admissions process, it is important for a college to continue to demonstrate commitment to you by taking steps to make you feel at home. The first few weeks on campus are a major rite of passage and may have a significant influence on your entire undergraduate experience. In short, you will want to determine whether the freshman year is viewed as something special and whether the college has a well-planned orientation program that addresses the particular concerns of new students.

Since students need guidance throughout their entire education, a college of quality has a year-round program of academic advising and personal counseling, structured to serve all undergraduates, including part-time and commuting students. You will want to find out if faculty members are available to freshmen to talk about their disciplines and whether or not faculty members give guidance in considering career choices. A college worthy of commendation works as hard at holding students as it does at getting them to the campus in the first place. You may wish to investigate a college's retention rate over the past five years and find out whether or not it offers guidance programs for students who are having trouble. These are all measures of a college's dedication to its students.

A Planned, Yet Flexible, Curriculum

At a good college, the academic major will broaden rather than restrict the student's perspective, presenting, in effect, an enriched major. An enriched major will answer three essential questions: What are the history and traditions of the field to be examined? What are the social and economic implications to be pursued? What are the ethical and moral issues within the specialty that need to be confronted? Rather than dividing the undergraduate experience into separate camps—general versus specialized education—the curriculum at a college of high quality will bring the two together. Therefore, it is important to determine if the college has a coherent general education sequence—an integrated core—rather than a more loosely connected distribution arrangement. This core academic program should provide not only for an integration of the separate academic principles but also for their application and relationship to life. All colleges impose requirements for graduation, including a set number of credits and some predetermined courses within a major. But within this set of general expectations, there is also room for flexibility. Increasingly, innovative colleges are recognizing the needs and skills of older students, encouraging individual learning, giving credit for experience, and helping students craft their own unique majors. Students should not have to march on to graduation in four years if they have interests, skills, and needs that are not acknowledged by a traditional degree program. New types of students are enrolling, and the location of learning has moved beyond the campus—to the home, the workplace, and around the world. In recognition of this trend, an effective college designs programs that meet new patterns and creates ways to both extend and encourage diversity on the campus.

The Classroom Climate

The undergraduate experience, at its best, encourages students to be active, rather than passive, learners. In measuring the quality of a college, students should ask if the institution has a climate that encourages independent, self-directed study, where teaching is perceived as more than just lecturing. If a college encourages small discussion sessions in which students work together on group assignments, it may indicate dedication to the undergraduate curriculum. In addition, if undergraduate courses are taught by the most respected and most gifted teachers on campus, it speaks further to this commitment.

Indeed, the strength of the faculty plays a leading role in determining the quality of the undergraduate experience. Students and parents have become increasingly concerned with the balance of time that faculty members spend on research and publishing requirements versus lecturing or advising. To uncover how an institution views this balance, you should ask if good teaching is valued equally with research and if it is an important criterion for tenure and promotion. It is important to know if the college recognizes that some faculty members are great teachers, others great researchers, and still others a blend of both. The central qualities that make for successful teaching are the ones that can be simply stated: command of the material to be taught; a contagious enthusiasm for the play of ideas; optimism about the potential of one's students; and sensitivity, integrity, and warmth as a human being. At a good college, this combination is present in the classroom.

Devoting Resources to Learning

An institution of high quality is one that supports its mission of learning both financially and philosophically. In doing so, a college should allot ample funds to its library and other educational resources. In terms of its use, one should determine if the library is more than just a study hall and if students are encouraged to spend at least as much time with library resources as they spend in classes. These resources should primarily serve the interests of undergraduate research and not be dominated by narrow scholarly interests of faculty members or graduate students. In addition, computers offer great potential for learning on campus. Most colleges now require that you purchase a computer before coming to campus. Some make terminals available to all students in common areas. Particularly if you are looking to advance in computer-related fields, or if you are inclined toward furthering your computer skills, you will want to know if campus terminals are linked to the Internet and if the college connects technology, the library, and the classroom.

The Campus Culture

A college campus is also a community. A high-quality college will work to make the time spent outside of the classroom as meaningful as the time spent in class. The high-quality college sees academic and nonacademic functions as related and arranges events ranging from lecture series and concerts to sports and student organizations to reinforce the curriculum. These campuswide activities, intended for both faculty members and students, should encourage community, sustain college traditions, and stimulate both social and cultural interaction. Because much learning occurs outside the classroom, it is important to know how accessible faculty members are to their students—not only through office hours, but also elsewhere on the campus, at social or extracurricular functions. In this setting, the academic campus transcends the classroom and is viewed as a place for learning. Beyond the structured programs, the campus culture extends into the residence halls and other social areas on campus. Residential living can be one of the most chaotic parts of campus life, yet it also has the potential of being one of the most rewarding. It is a good idea to find out if residence halls also promote a sense of community through organized activities and informal learning.

A Final Word of Advice

In the end, a high-quality college is concerned about outcomes. It asks questions about student development that go beyond the evaluation of skill. But a good college will avoid measuring that which matters least and will focus on the need for students to think clearly, be well informed, integrate their knowledge, and apply what they have learned.

The impact of college extends beyond graduation, and a college of quality will provide placement guidance to its students and follow their careers. These students will be well equipped to put their work in context and prepared to move from one intellectual challenge to another. The undergraduate experience will also have shown students how to see beyond the narrow boundaries of their own interests and discover global connections. The college succeeds as its graduates are inspired by a larger vision, using their newfound knowledge to form values and advance the common good.

When you make your college contacts and campus visits, you now know what questions to ask and what to look for in order to make an informed decision. In doing so, however, you should always take into account your specific goals. In the end, the important thing to remember is that a college of high quality is one that will prepare you for a productive career, but will also offer you values and principles that you can apply *beyond* graduation day.

Choosing Your Top Ten Colleges

By using all the information in the various sections of this guide, you will find the colleges worthy of the most important top-ten list on the planet—yours.

The first thing you will need to do is decide what type of institution of higher learning you want to attend. Each of the thousands of four-year colleges and universities in the United States is as unique as the people applying to it. Although listening to the voices and media hype around you can make it sound as though there are only a few elite schools worth attending, this simply is not true. By considering some of the following criteria, you will soon find that the large pool of interesting colleges can be narrowed down to a more reasonable number.

Size and Category

Schools come in all shapes and sizes, from tiny rural colleges of 400 students to massive state university systems serving 100,000 students or more. If you are coming from a small high school, a college with 3,500 students may seem large to you. If you are currently attending a high school with 3,000 students, selecting a college of a similar size may not feel like a new enough experience. Some students coming from very large impersonal high schools are looking for a place where they will be recognized from the beginning and offered a more personal approach. If you don't have a clue about what size might feel right to you, try visiting a couple of nearby colleges of varying sizes. You do not have to be seriously interested in them; just feel what impact the number of students on campus has on you.

Large Universities

Large universities offer a wide range of educational, athletic, and social experiences. Universities offer a full scope of undergraduate majors and award master's and doctoral degrees as well. Universities are usually composed of several smaller colleges. Depending on your interest in a major field or area of study, you would likely apply to a specific college within the university. Each college has the flexibility to set its own standards for admission, which may differ from the overall average of the university. The colleges within a university system also set their own course requirements for earning a degree.

Universities may be public or private. Some large private universities, such as Harvard, Yale, Princeton, University of Pennsylvania, New York University, Northwestern, and Stanford, are well-known for their high entrance standards, the excellence of their education, and the success rates of their graduates. These institutions place a great deal of emphasis on research and compete aggressively for grants from the federal government to fund these projects. Large public universities, such as the State University of New York (SUNY) System, University of Michigan, University of Texas, University of Illinois, University of Washington, and University of North Carolina, also support excellent educational programs, compete for and win research funding, and have successful graduates. Public universities usually offer substantially lower tuition rates to in-state students, although their tuition rates for out-of-state residents are often comparable to those of private institutions.

At many large universities, sports play a major role on campus. Athletics can dominate the calendar and set the tone year-round at some schools. Alumni travel from far and wide to attend their alma mater's football or basketball games, and the campus, and frequently the entire town, grinds to a halt when there is a home game. Athletes are heroes and dominate campus social life.

What are some other features of life on a university campus? Every kind of club imaginable, from literature to bioengineering and chorus to politics, can be found on most college campuses. You will be able to play the intramural version of almost every sport in which the university fields interscholastic teams and join fraternities, sororities, and groups dedicated to social action. You can become a member of a band, an orchestra, or perhaps a chamber music group or work on the newspaper, the literary magazine, or the Web site. The list can go on and on. You may want to try out a new interest or two or pursue what you have always been interested in and make like-minded friends along the way.

Take a look at the size of the classrooms in the larger universities and envision yourself sitting in that atmosphere. Would this offer a learning environment that would benefit you?

Liberal Arts Colleges

If you have considered large universities and come to the conclusion that all that action could be a distraction, a small liberal arts college might be right for you. Ideally tucked away on a picture-perfect campus, a liberal arts college generally has fewer than 5,000 students. The mission of most liberal arts schools is learning for the sake of learning, with a strong emphasis on creating lifelong learners who will be able to apply their education to any number of careers. This contrasts with objectives of the profession-based preparation of specialized colleges.

Liberal arts colleges cannot offer the breadth of courses provided by the large universities. As a result, liberal arts colleges try to create a niche for themselves. For instance, a college may place its emphasis on its humanities departments, whose professors are all well-known published authors and international presenters in their areas of expertise. A college may highlight its science departments by providing state-of-the-art facilities where undergraduates conduct research side by side with top-notch professors and copublish their findings in the most prestigious scientific journals in the country. The personal approach is very important at liberal arts colleges. Whether in advisement, course selection, athletic programs tailored to students' interests, or dinner with the department head at her home, liberal arts colleges emphasize that they get to know their students.

If they are so perfect, why doesn't everyone choose a liberal arts college? Well, the small size limits options. Fewer people may mean less diversity. The fact that many of these colleges encourage a study-abroad option (a student elects to spend a semester or a year studying in another country) reduces the number of students on campus even further. Some liberal arts colleges have a certain reputation that does not appeal to some students. You should ask yourself questions about the campus life that most appeals to you. Will you fit in with the campus culture? Will the small size mean that you go through your social options quickly? Check out the activities listed on the Student Center bulletin board. Does the student body look diverse enough for you? Will what is happening keep you busy and interested? Do the students have input into decision making? Do they create the social climate of the school?

Small Universities

Smaller universities often combine stringent admissions policies, handpicked faculty members, and attractive scholarship packages. These institutions generally have undergraduate enrollments of about 4,000 students. Some are more famous for their graduate and professional schools but have also established strong undergraduate colleges. Smaller universities balance the great majors options of large universities with a smaller campus community. They offer choices but not to the same extent as large universities. On the other hand, by limiting admissions and enrollment, they manage to cultivate some of the characteristics of a liberal arts college. Like a liberal arts college, a small university may emphasize a particular program and go out of its way to draw strong candidates in a specific area, such as premed, to its campus. Universities such as The Johns Hopkins University, University of Notre Dame, Vanderbilt University, Washington University in St. Louis, and Wesleyan University in Connecticut are a few examples of this category.

Technical or Specialized Colleges

Another alternative to the liberal arts college or large university is the technical or otherwise specialized college. Their goal is to offer a specialized and saturated experience in a particular field of study. Such an institution might limit its course offerings to engineering and science, the performing or fine arts, or business. Schools such as California Institute of Technology, Carnegie Mellon University, Massachusetts Institute of Technology, and Rensselaer Polytechnic Institute concentrate on attracting the finest math and science students in the country. At other schools, like Bentley College in Massachusetts or Bryant College in Rhode Island, students eat, sleep, and breathe business. These institutions are purists at heart and strong believers in the necessity of focused, specialized study to produce excellence in their graduates' achievements. If you are certain about your chosen path in life and want to immerse yourself in subjects such as math, music, or business, you will fit right in.

Religious Colleges

Many private colleges have religious origins, and many of these have become secular institutions with virtually no trace of their religious roots. Others remain dedicated to a religious way of education. What sets religious colleges apart is the way they combine faith, learning, and student life. Faculty members and administrators are hired with faith as a criterion as much as their academic credentials.

Single-Gender Colleges

There are strong arguments that being able to pursue one's education without the distraction, competition, and stress caused by the presence of the opposite sex helps a student evolve a stronger sense of her or his self-worth; achieve more academically; have a more fulfilling, less pressured social life; and achieve more later in life. For various historic, social, and psychological reasons, there are many more all-women than all-men colleges. A strict single-sex environment is rare. Even though the undergraduate day college adheres to an all-female or all-male admissions policy, coeducational evening classes or graduate programs and coordinate facilities and classes shared with nearby coed or opposite-sex institutions can result in a good number of students of the opposite sex being found on campus. If you want to concentrate on your studies and hone your leadership qualities, a single-gender school is an option.

Location

Location and distance from home are two other important considerations. If you have always lived in the suburbs, choosing an urban campus can be an adventure, but after a week of the urban experience, will you long for a grassy campus and open space? On the other hand, if you choose a college in a rural area, will you run screaming into the Student Center some night looking for noise, lights, and people? The location—urban, rural, or suburban—can directly affect how easy or how difficult adjusting to college life will be for you.

Don't forget to factor in distance from home. Everyone going off to college wants to think he or she won't be homesick, but sometimes it's nice to get a home-cooked meal or to do the laundry in a place that does not require quarters. Even your kid sister may seem like less of a nuisance after a couple of months away.

Here are some questions you might ask yourself as you go through the selection process: In what part of the country do I want to be? How far away from home do I want to be? What is the cost of returning home? Do I need to be close to a city? How close? How large of a city? Would city life distract me? Would I concentrate better in a setting that is more rural or more suburban?

Entrance Difficulty

Many students will look at a college's entrance difficulty as an indicator of whether or not they will be admitted. For instance, if you have an excellent academic record, you might wish to primarily consider those colleges that are highly competitive. Although entrance difficulty does not translate directly to quality of education, it indicates which colleges are attracting large numbers of high-achieving students. A high-achieving student body usually translates into prestige for the college and its graduates. Prestige has some advantages but should definitely be viewed as a secondary factor that might tip the scales when all the other important factors are equal. Never base your decision on prestige alone!

The other principle to keep in mind when considering this factor is to not sell yourself short. If everything else tells you that a college might be right for you, but your numbers just miss that college's average range, apply there anyway. Your numbers—grades and test scores—are undeniably important in the admissions decision, but there are other considerations. First, lower grades in honors or AP courses will impress colleges more than top grades in regular-track courses because they demonstrate that you are the kind of student willing to accept challenges. Second, admissions directors are looking for different qualities in students that can be combined to create a multifaceted class. For example, if you did poorly in your freshman and sophomore years but made a great improvement in your grades in later years, this usually will impress a college. If you are likely to contribute to your class because of your special personal qualities, a strong sense of commitment and purpose, unusual and valuable experiences, or special interests and talents, these factors can outweigh numbers that are weaker than average. Nevertheless, be practical. Overreach yourself in a few applications, but put the bulk of your effort into gaining admission to colleges where you have a realistic chance for admission.

The Price of an Education

The price tag for higher education continues to rise, and it has become an increasingly important factor for people. While it is necessary to consider your family's resources when choosing a list of colleges to which you might apply, never eliminate a college solely because of cost. There are many ways to pay for college, including loans, and a college education will never depreciate in value, unlike other purchases. It is an investment in yourself and will pay back the expense many times over in your lifetime.

Financing a College Education

Don M. Betterton

Former Director of Undergraduate Aid, Princeton University

Given the lifelong benefit of a college degree (college graduates are projected to earn in a lifetime $1 million more than those with only a high school diploma), higher education is a worthwhile investment. However, it is also an expensive one made even harder to manage by cost increases that have outpaced both inflation and gains in family income. This reality of higher education economics means that parental concern about how to pay for a child's college education is a dilemma that shows no sign of getting easier.

Because of the high cost involved (even the most inexpensive four-year education at a public institution costs about $10,000 a year), good information about college budgets and strategies for reducing the "sticker price" is essential. In the pages that follow, you will find valuable information about the four main sources of aid—federal, state, institutional, and private. Before you learn about the various programs, however, it will be helpful if you have an overview of how the college financial aid system operates and what long-range financing strategies are available.

Financial Aid

Financial aid refers to money that is awarded to a student, usually in a "package" that consists of gift aid (commonly called a scholarship or grant), a student loan, and a campus job.

College Costs

The starting point for organizing a plan to pay for your child's college education is to make a good estimate of the yearly cost of attendance. You can use the **College Cost Worksheet** on page 17 to do this.

To estimate your college costs for 2009–10, refer to the Tuition and Room & Board figures under **Expenses** in the **Profiles of Four-Year**

Colleges. If your child will commute from your home, use $2500 instead of the college's room and board charges and $900 for transportation. We have used $800 for books and $1300 for personal expenses. Finally, estimate the cost of two round trips if your home is more than a few hundred miles from the college. Add the items to calculate the total budget. You should now have a reasonably good estimate of college costs for 2009–10. (To determine the costs for later years, adding 5 percent per year will probably give you a fairly accurate estimate.)

Do You Qualify for Need-Based Aid?

The next step is to evaluate whether or not you are likely to qualify for financial aid based on need. This step is critical, since more than 90 percent of the yearly total of $128 billion in student aid is awarded only after a determination is made that the family lacks sufficient financial resources to pay the full cost of college on its own. To judge your chance of receiving need-based aid, it is necessary to estimate an Expected Family Contribution (EFC) according to a government formula known as the Federal Methodology (FM). You can do so by referring to the **Approximate Expected Family Contribution Chart** on page 18.

Applying for Need-Based Aid

Because the federal government provides about 67 percent of all aid awarded, the application and need evaluation process is controlled by Congress and the U.S. Department of Education. The application is the Free Application for Federal Student Aid, or FAFSA. In addition, nearly every state that offers student assistance uses the federal government's system to award its own aid. Furthermore, in addition to arranging for the payment of federal and state aid, many colleges use the FAFSA to award their own funds to eligible students. (*Note:* In addition to the FAFSA, some colleges also ask the family to complete the CSS/PROFILE® application.)

The FAFSA is your "passport" to receiving your share of the billions of dollars awarded annually in need-based aid. Even if you're uncertain as to whether or not you qualify for need-based aid, everyone who might need assistance in financing an education should pick up a FAFSA from the high school guidance office after mid-November 2008. This form will ask for 2008 financial data, and it should be filed after January 1, 2009, in time to meet the earliest college or state scholarship deadline. Within

College Cost Worksheet				
	College 1	College 2	College 3	Commuter College
Tuition and Fees	______	______	______	______
Room and Board	______	______	______	$2,500
Books	$ 800	$ 800	$ 800	$ 750
Personal Expenses	$1,300	$1,300	$1,300	$1,300
Travel	______	______	______	$ 900
Total Budget	______	______	______	______

two to four weeks after you submit the form, you will receive a summary of the FAFSA information, called the Student Aid Report, or SAR. The SAR will give you the EFC and also allow you to make corrections to the data you submitted.

You can also apply for federal student aid via the Internet using FAFSA on the Web. FAFSA on the Web can be accessed at

How Need Is Calculated and Aid Is Awarded		
	College 1	College 2
Total Cost of Attendance	$ 10,000	$ 24,000
− Expected Family Contribution	−5,500	−5,500
= Financial Need	$ 4,500	$ 18,500
− Grant Aid Awarded	−675	−14,575
− Campus Job (Work-Study) Awarded	−1,400	−1,300
− Student Loan Awarded	−2,425	−2,625
= Unmet Need	0	0

Note: Sometimes an institution is unable to meet all need. The amount of unmet need is called "the gap."

Approximate Expected Family Contribution Chart

	Assets	Income Before Taxes								
		$20,000	30,000	40,000	50,000	60,000	70,000	80,000	90,000	100,000
	$20,000									
Family Size	3	$ 0	160	1,800	3,500	5,800	9,100	12,600	14,100	17,400
	4	0	0	850	2,500	4,400	7,100	10,600	12,000	15,300
	5	0	0	0	1,600	3,300	5,500	8,600	10,100	13,400
	6	0	0	0	600	2,200	4,100	6,600	7,900	11,200
	$30,000									
Family Size	3	$ 0	160	1,800	3,500	5,800	9,100	12,600	14,100	17,400
	4	0	0	850	2,500	4,400	7,100	10,600	12,000	15,300
	5	0	0	0	1,600	3,300	5,500	8,600	10,100	13,400
	6	0	0	0	600	2,200	4,100	6,600	7,900	11,200
	$40,000									
Family Size	3	$ 0	160	1,800	3,500	5,800	9,100	12,600	14,100	17,400
	4	0	0	850	2,500	4,400	7,100	10,600	12,000	15,300
	5	0	0	0	1,600	3,300	5,500	8,600	10,100	13,400
	6	0	0	0	600	2,200	4,100	6,600	7,900	11,200
	$50,000									
Family Size	3	$ 0	340	2,000	3,800	6,200	9,500	13,000	14,500	17,800
	4	0	0	1,100	2,700	4,700	7,400	11,000	12,400	15,700
	5	0	0	0	1,800	3,500	5,800	9,000	10,400	13,750
	6	0	0	0	800	2,400	4,300	6,900	8,300	11,600
	$60,000									
Family Size	3	$ 0	600	2,300	4,100	6,600	10,000	13,600	15,000	18,300
	4	0	0	1,300	3,000	5,000	8,000	11,500	13,000	16,300
	5	0	0	400	2,050	3,800	6,200	9,600	11,000	14,300
	6	0	0	0	1,000	2,700	4,600	7,400	8,800	12,150
	$80,000									
Family Size	3	$ 0	1,130	2,800	4,800	7,600	11,200	14,700	16,150	19,500
	4	0	170	1,800	3,600	5,900	9,100	9,600	14,100	17,400
	5	0	0	900	2,600	4,500	7,200	10,700	12,100	15,450
	6	0	0	0	1,600	3,200	5,400	8,500	10,000	13,300
	$100,000									
Family Size	3	$ 0	1,660	3,400	5,600	8,800	12,300	15,900	17,300	20,600
	4	0	700	2,400	4,200	6,800	10,250	13,800	15,200	18,500
	5	0	0	1,400	3,100	5,300	8,300	11,800	13,300	16,600
	6	0	0	400	2,100	3,900	6,300	9,700	11,100	14,400
	$120,000									
Family Size	3	$ 0	2,190	4,000	6,500	9,900	13,400	17,000	18,400	21,700
	4	0	1,220	3,000	4,900	7,800	11,400	14,900	16,350	19,650
	5	0	310	2,000	3,700	6,100	9,500	13,000	14,400	17,700
	6	0	0	1,000	2,600	4,600	7,300	10,800	12,200	15,550
	$140,000									
Family Size	3	$ 0	2,700	4,700	7,500	11,000	13,400	18,100	19,500	22,850
	4	0	1,750	3,500	5,700	9,000	12,500	16,000	17,750	20,800
	5	0	850	2,500	4,400	7,100	10,500	14,100	15,500	18,850
	6	0	0	1,500	3,200	5,300	8,400	11,900	13,350	16,650

This chart makes the following assumptions:

- $20,000 income files 1040A or 1040EZ, all other incomes file regular 1040
- Age of older parent is 45+
- No parental untaxed income reported
- Estimated federal income tax for incomes $20,000 to $80,000 is 10 percent
- Estimated federal income tax for incomes $90,000 to $100,000 is 15 percent
- One student in college, two parent family
- No student income or assets reported

Comparing Financial Aid Awards and Family Contribution Worksheet			
	College 1	**College 2**	**College 3**
Cost of Attendance	______	______	______
Aid Awarded	______	______	______
Grant/Scholarship	______	______	______
Loan	______	______	______
Job	______	______	______
Total Aid	______	______	______
Expected Family Contribution	______	______	______
Student Contribution	______	______	______
Parent Contribution	______	______	______

www.fafsa.ed.gov. Both the student and at least one parent should apply for a federal PIN number at www.pin.ed.gov. The PIN number serves as your electronic signature when applying for aid on the Web. (*Note:* Many colleges provide the option to apply for early decision or early action admission. If you apply for this before January 1, 2009, which is prior to when the FAFSA can be used, follow the college's instructions. Many colleges use either PROFILE or their own application form for early admission candidates.)

Awarding Aid

About the same time you receive the SAR, the colleges you list will receive your FAFSA information so they can calculate a financial aid award in a package that typically includes aid from at least one of the major sources—federal, state, college, or private. In addition, the award will probably consist of a combination of a scholarship or a grant, a loan, and a campus job. These last two pieces—loan and job—are called self-help aid because they require effort on your child's part (that is, the aid must be either earned through work or paid back later). Scholarships or grants are outright gifts that have no such obligation.

It is important that you understand each part of the package. You'll want to know, for example, how much is gift aid, the interest rate and repayment terms of the student loan, and how many hours per week the campus job requires. There should be an enclosure with the award letter that answers these questions. If not, make a list of your questions and call or visit the financial aid office.

Once you understand the terms of each item in the award letter, you should turn your attention to the "bottom line"—how much you will have to pay at each college where your child was accepted. In addition to understanding the aid award, this means having a good estimate of the college budget so you can accurately calculate how much you and your child will have to contribute. (Often, an aid package does not cover the entire need.) Colleges follow different practices in how much detail they include in their award notifications. Many colleges provide full information—types and amounts of aid, yearly costs, and the EFC divided into the parent and student shares. If these important items are missing or incomplete, you can do the work on your own. (See the **Comparing Financial Aid Awards and Family Contribution Worksheet** on page 19.) For example, if only the college's direct charges for tuition, room, and board are shown on the award letter, make your own estimate of indirect costs like books, personal expenses, and travel. Then subtract the total aid awarded from the yearly cost to get the EFC. A portion of that amount may be your child's contribution (20 percent of student assets and 50 percent of student earnings over $3000) and the remainder is the parental share. If you can afford this amount at your child's first-choice college, the financial aid system has worked well for you, and your child's college enrollment plans can go forward.

But if you think your EFC is too high, you should contact the college's financial aid office and ask whether additional aid is available. Many colleges, private high-cost colleges in particular, are enrollment-oriented—they are willing to work with families to help make attendance at their institutions possible. Most colleges also allow applicants to appeal their financial aid awards, the budget used for you, or any of the elements used to determine the family contribution, especially if there are extenuating circumstances or if the information has changed since the application was submitted. Some colleges may also reconsider an award based on a "competitive appeal," the submission of a more favorable award letter from another college.

If your appeal is unsuccessful and there is still a gap between the expected family contribution and what you feel you can pay from income and savings, you are left with two choices. One option is for your child to attend a college where paying your share of the bill will not be a problem. (This assumes that an affordable option was included on your child's original list of colleges, a wise admission application strategy.) The second is to look into alternate methods of financing. At this stage, parental loans and tuition payment plans are the best financing options. A parental loan can bring the yearly cost down to a manageable level by spreading payments over a number of years. This is the type of financing that families use when purchasing a home or automobile. A tuition payment plan is essentially a short-term loan and allows you to pay the costs over ten to twelve months. It is an option for families who have the resources available but need help with managing their cash flow.

Non-Need-Based Aid

Regardless of whether you might qualify for a need-based award, it is always worthwhile to look into merit, or non-need, scholarships from sources such as foundations, agencies, religious groups, and service organizations. For a family that isn't eligible for need-based aid, merit scholarships are the only form of gift aid available. If your child later qualifies for a need-based award, a merit scholarship can be quite helpful in providing additional resources if the aid does not fully cover the costs. Even if the college meets 100 percent of need, a merit scholarship reduces the self-help (loan and job) portion of an award.

In searching for merit-based scholarships, keep in mind that there are relatively few awards (compared to those that are need-based), and most of them are highly competitive. Follow these guidelines when investigating merit scholarships.

- Take advantage of any scholarships for which your child is automatically eligible based on parents' employer benefits, military service, association or church membership, other affiliations, or student or parent attributes (ethnic background, nationality, etc.). Company or union tuition remissions are the most common examples of these awards.

- Look for other awards for which your child might be eligible based on the previous characteristics and affiliations but where there is a selection process and an application is required. Free computerized searches are available on the Internet. (You should not pay a fee for a scholarship search.) Peterson's free scholarship search can

What Is CSS/PROFILE®?

There are many complexities in the financial aid process: knowing which aid is merit-based and which aid is need-based; understanding the difference between grants, loans, and work-study; and determining whether funds are from federal, state, institutional, or private sources.

In addition, the aid application process itself can be confusing. It can involve more than the Free Application for Federal Student Aid (FAFSA) and the Federal Methodology (FM). Many colleges feel that the federal aid system (FAFSA and FM) does not collect or evaluate information thoroughly enough for them to award their own institutional funds. These colleges have made an arrangement with the College Scholarship Service, a branch of the College Board, to establish a separate application system.

The application is called the CSS/PROFILE®, and the need-analysis formula is referred to as the Institutional Methodology (IM). If you apply for financial aid at one of the colleges that uses PROFILE, the admission material will state that PROFILE is required in addition to the FAFSA. You should read the information carefully and file PROFILE to meet the earliest college deadline. Before you can receive PROFILE, however, you must register, either by phone or through the Web (https://profileonline.collegeboard.com/index.jsp), providing enough basic information so the PROFILE package can be designed specifically for you. The FAFSA is free, but there is a charge for PROFILE. As with the FAFSA, PROFILE can be submitted via the Internet.

In addition to the requirement by certain colleges that you submit both the FAFSA and PROFILE (when used, PROFILE is always in addition to the FAFSA; it does not replace it), you should understand that each system has its own method for analyzing a family's ability to pay for college. The main differences between PROFILE's Institutional Methodology and the FAFSA's Federal Methodology are

- PROFILE includes equity in the family home as an asset; the FAFSA doesn't.
- PROFILE takes a broader look at assets not included on the FAFSA.
- PROFILE expects a minimum student contribution, usually in the form of summer earnings; the FAFSA has no such minimum.
- PROFILE may collect information on the noncustodial parent; the FAFSA does not.

- PROFILE allows for more professional judgment than the FAFSA. Medical expenses, private secondary school costs, and a variety of special circumstances are considered under PROFILE, subject to the discretion of the aid counselor on campus.
- PROFILE includes information on assets not reported on the FAFSA, including life insurance, annuities, retirement plans, etc.

To summarize: PROFILE's Institutional Methodology tends to be both more complete in its data collection and more rigorous in its analysis than the FAFSA's Federal Methodology. When IM results are compared to FM results for thousands of applicants, IM will usually come up with a somewhat higher expected parental contribution than FM.

be accessed by logging on to www.petersons.com/finaid. Scholarship directories, such as *Peterson's Scholarships, Grants & Prizes*, which details more than 4,000 scholarship programs, are useful resources and can be found in bookstores, high school guidance offices, or public libraries.

- See if your state has a merit scholarship program.
- Look into national scholarship competitions. High school guidance counselors usually know about these scholarships. Examples of these awards are the National Merit Scholarship, the Coca-Cola Scholarship, Gates Millennium Scholars, Intel Science Talent Search, and the U.S. Senate Youth Program.
- ROTC (Reserve Officers' Training Corps) scholarships are offered by the Army, Navy, Air Force, and Marine Corps. A full ROTC scholarship covers tuition, fees, textbook costs and, in some cases, a stipend. Acceptance of an ROTC scholarship entails a commitment to take military science courses and to serve for a specific number of years as an officer in the sponsoring branch of the service. Competition is heavy, and preference may be given to students in certain fields of study, such as engineering, languages, science, and health professions. Application procedures vary by service. Contact an armed services recruiter or high school guidance counselor for further information.

Creditworthiness

If you will be borrowing to pay for your child's college education, making sure you qualify for a loan is critical. For the most part, that means your credit record must be free of default or delinquency. You can check your credit history with one or more of the following three major credit bureaus and clean up any adverse information that appears. The numbers below will offer specific information on what you need to provide to obtain a report. All of the credit bureaus accept credit report requests over their Web sites. You will usually be asked to provide your full name, phone number, social security number, birth date, and addresses for the last five years. You are entitled to a free report from each bureau.

Equifax
P.O. Box 740241
Atlanta, GA 30374
800-685-1111
www.equifax.com

Trans Union
877-322-8228
www.transunion.com

Experian
888-397-3742
www.experian.com

- Investigate community scholarships. High school guidance counselors usually have a list of these awards, and announcements are published in local newspapers. Most common are awards given by service organizations like the American Legion, Rotary International, and the local women's club.
- If your child is strong academically (for example, a National Merit® Commended Student or better) or is very talented in fields such as athletics or performing/creative arts, you may want to consider colleges that offer their own merit awards to gifted students they wish to enroll. Refer to the Non-Need Scholarships for Undergraduates index.

In addition to merit scholarships, there are loan and job opportunities for students who do not qualify for need-based aid. Federal loan programs include the unsubsidized federal Stafford and Direct loans. Some of the organizations that sponsor scholarships—for example, the Air Force Aid Society—also provide loans.

Work opportunities during the academic year are another type of assistance that is not restricted to aid recipients. Many colleges will, after assigning jobs to students on aid, open campus positions to all students looking for work. In addition, there are usually off-campus employment opportunities available to everyone.

Note on Savings

A point of clarification about whether to put college savings in your name or your child's: If you are certain that your child will not be a candidate for need-based aid, there may be a tax advantage to accumulating money in his or her name. However, when it comes to maximizing aid eligibility, it is important to understand that student assets are assessed at a 20 percent rate and parental assets at about 5 percent. Therefore, if your college savings are in your child's name, it may be wise to reestablish title to these funds before applying for financial aid. You should contact your financial planner or accountant before making any modifications to your asset structure.

Financing Your Child's College Education

"Financing" means putting together resources to pay the balance due the college over and above payments from the primary sources of aid—grants, scholarships, student loans, and jobs. Financing strategies are important because the high cost of a college education today often requires a family, whether or not it receives aid, to think about stretching its college payment beyond the four-year period of enrollment. For high-cost colleges, it is not unreasonable to think about a 10-4-10 plan: ten years of saving; four years of paying college bills out of current income, savings, and borrowing; and ten years to repay a parental loan.

Savings

Although saving for college is always a good idea, many families are unclear about its advantages. Some families do not save because after normal living expenses have been covered, they do not have much money to set aside. An affordable but regular savings plan through a payroll deduction is usually the answer to the problem of spending your entire paycheck every month.

The second reason why saving for college is not a high priority is the belief that the financial aid system penalizes a family by lowering aid eligibility. The Federal Methodology of need determination is very kind to savers. In fact, savings are ignored completely for most families that earn less than $50,000. Savings in the form of home equity, retirement plans, and most annuities are excluded from the calculation. And even when savings are counted, a maximum of 5 percent of the total is expected each year. In other words, if a family has $40,000 in savings after an asset protection allowance is considered, the contribution is no greater than $2000. Given the impact of compound interest it is easy to see that a long-term savings plan can make paying for college much easier.

A sensible savings plan is important because of the financial advantage of saving compared to borrowing. The amount of money students borrow for college is now greater than the amount they receive in grants and scholarships. With loans becoming so widespread, savings should be carefully considered as an alternative to borrowing. Your incentive for saving is that a dollar saved is a dollar not borrowed.

Borrowing

Once you've calculated your "bottom-line" parental contribution and determined that the amount is not affordable out of your current income and assets, the most likely alternative is borrowing. First determine if your child is eligible for a larger subsidized federal Stafford or Direct loan. Because no interest is due while your child attends college, these are the most favorable loans. If this is not possible, look into the unsubsidized Stafford or Direct loan, which is not based on need but the interest accrues each year. The freshman year limit (either subsidized or unsubsidized) is $3500.

After your child has taken out the maximum amount of student loans, the next step is to look into parental loans. The federal government's parent loan program is called PLUS and is the standard against which other loans should be judged. A local bank that participates in the PLUS program can give you a schedule of monthly repayments per $1000 borrowed. Use this repayment figure to compare other parental loans available from commercial lenders (including home equity loans), state programs, or colleges themselves. Choose the one that offers the best terms after all up-front costs, tax advantages, and the amount of monthly payments are considered. Be sure to check with your financial aid office before making a final decision. Often, the financial aid office will have reviewed the various programs that are available and can help direct you to the best choice.

Make Financial Aid Work for You

If you are like millions of families that benefit from financial aid, it is likely that your child's college plans can go forward without undue worry about the costs involved. The key is to understand the financial aid system and to follow the best path for your family. The result of good information and good planning should be that you will receive your fair share of the billions of dollars available each year and that the cost of college will not prevent your child from attending.

Federal Financial Aid Programs

There are a number of sources of financial aid available to students: federal and state governments, private agencies, and the colleges themselves. In addition, there are three different forms of aid: grants, earnings, and loans.

The federal government is the single largest source of financial aid for students. For the 2005–06 academic year, the U.S. Department of Education's student financial aid programs made an estimated $94 billion available in loans, grants, and other aid to nearly 10 million students, while 11 million families benefited from various education tax cuts and deductions. At present, there are four federal grant programs—Federal Pell Grant, Federal Supplemental Educational Opportunity Grant (FSEOG), Academic Competitiveness Grant (ACG), and National Smart Grant (SMART). There are three federal loan programs: Federal Perkins Loan Program, Direct Loan Program, and Federal Family Education Loan Program (FFELP). The federal government also has a job program, Federal Work-Study Program (FWS), which helps colleges provide employment for students. In addition to the student aid programs, there are also tuition tax credits and deductions. They are the Hope Credit for freshmen and sophomores, the Lifetime Learning Credit for undergraduate students after their second year, and the Tuition and Fees Tax Deduction.

The majority of federal higher education loans are made either in the Direct Loan Program or the FFELP. The difference between these loans is the lending source, but, for the borrower, the terms and conditions are essentially the same. Both Direct and FFEL programs make available two kinds of loans: loans to students and PLUS loans to parents or to graduate or professional students. These loans are either subsidized or unsubsidized. Subsidized loans are made on the basis of demonstrated student need, and the interest is paid by the government during the time the student is in school. For the unsubsidized (non-need-based) loans and PLUS loans, interest begins to accrue as funds are disbursed.

To qualify for the Federal Pell Grant, ACG, SMART, FSEOG, Federal Work-Study Program, and Federal Perkins Loan Program and the subsidized Stafford loan, you must demonstrate financial need.

Pell Grant

The Federal Pell Grant is the largest grant program; more than 6 million students receive Pell Grants annually. This grant is intended to be the starting point of assistance for lower-income families. Eligibility for a Pell Grant is based on the Expected Family Contribution. The amount you receive will depend on your EFC and the cost of education at the college you will attend. The highest award depends on how much funding the program receives from the government. The maximum for 2008–09 is $4731.

To give you some idea of your possible eligibility for a Pell Grant, the table on page 31 may be helpful. The amounts shown are based on a family of four, with one student in college, no emergency expenses, no contribution from student income or assets, and college costs of at least $4050 per year. Pell Grants range from $890 to $4731.

Federal Supplemental Educational Opportunity Grant (FSEOG)

As its name implies, Federal Supplemental Educational Opportunity Grants provide additional need-based federal grant money to supplement the Federal Pell Grant Program. Each participating college is given funds to award to especially needy students. The maximum award is $4000 per year, but the amount you receive depends on the college's awarding policy, the availability of FSEOG funds, the total cost of education, and the amount of other aid awarded.

Academic Competitiveness Grant

U.S. citizens who are Pell Grant–eligible and who attended a "rigorous" high school program, as defined by the U.S. Secretary of Education, can receive up to $750 in their first year and $1300 in their second year if they have a minimum 3.0 GPA. More information about this program is available from the high school or college financial aid office.

National Smart Grant

Third- and fourth-year undergraduates who are Pell Grant–eligible and major in math, science, technology, or certain foreign languages and

Federal Financial Aid Programs		
Name of Program	**Type of Program**	**Maximum Award Per Year**
Federal Pell Grant	need-based grant	$4731
Federal Supplemental Educational Opportunity Grant (FSEOG)	need-based grant	$4000
Academic Competitiveness Grant (ACG)	need/merit	$750 (freshman) $1300 (sophomore)
National Smart Grant (SMART)	need/merit/program	up to $4000 (third- and fourth-year undergraduate)
Federal Work-Study Program	need-based part-time job	no maximum
Federal Perkins Loan Program	need-based loan	$4000
Subsidized Stafford/ Direct Loan	need-based student loan	$3500 (first year)
Unsubsidized Stafford/ Direct Loan	non-need-based student loan	$3500 (first year, dependent student)

have a minimum 3.0 in their major can qualify for a grant of up to $4000. More information about this program is available from the high school or college financial aid office.

Federal Work-Study Program (FWS)

This program provides jobs for students who demonstrate need. Salaries are paid by funds from the federal government as well as the college. Students work on an hourly basis on or off campus and must be paid at least the federal minimum wage. Students may earn only up to the amount awarded in the financial aid package.

Federal Perkins Loan Program

This is a low-interest (5 percent) loan for students with exceptional financial need. Perkins Loans are made through the college's financial aid office with the college as the lender. Students can borrow a maximum of $4000 per year for up to five years of undergraduate study. Borrowers may take up to ten years to repay the loan, beginning nine months after they graduate, leave school, or drop below half-time status. No interest accrues while they are in school, and, under certain conditions (e.g., they teach in low-income areas, work in law enforcement, are full-time nurses or medical technicians, serve as Peace Corps or VISTA volunteers, etc.), some or all of the loan can be cancelled. In addition, payments can be deferred under certain conditions such as unemployment.

Federal Stafford and Direct Loan

Federal Stafford and Direct loans generally have the same interest rates, loan maximums, deferments, and cancellation benefits. A Stafford loan may be borrowed from a commercial lender, such as a bank or a credit union. A Direct loan is borrowed directly from the U.S. Department of Education through the college's financial aid office.

The unsubsidized Direct and federal Stafford loan programs carry a fixed 6.8 percent interest rate. If a student qualifies for a need-based subsidized Stafford or Direct loan, the interest is paid by the federal government while he or she is enrolled in college during grace, and during periods of deferment. Over a four-year period beginning July 1, 2008, the fixed interest rate on subsidized Direct and federal Stafford loans made to undergraduate students will be reduced in phases. For loans first disbursed on or after

- July 1, 2008, and before July 1, 2009, the interest rate will be fixed at 6.00 percent;
- July 1, 2009, and before July 1, 2010, the interest rate will be fixed at 5.60 percent;
- July 1, 2010, and before July 1, 2011, the interest rate will be fixed at 4.50 percent;
- July 1, 2011, and before July 1, 2012, the interest rate will be fixed at 3.40 percent.

Interest rates for subsidized Direct and federal Stafford loans made to undergraduate borrowers first disbursed on or after July 1, 2012, will revert to 6.80 percent.

The maximum amount dependent students may borrow in any one year is $3500 for freshmen, $4500 for sophomores, and $5500 for juniors and seniors, with a maximum of $23,000 for the total undergraduate program. The maximum amount independent students can borrow is $7500 for freshmen (of which no more than $3500 can be subsidized), $8500 for sophomores (of which no more than $4500 can be subsidized), and $10,500 for juniors and seniors (of which no more than $5500 can be subsidized). Independent students can borrow up to $46,000 (of which no more than $23,000 can be subsidized) for the total undergraduate program. Borrowers may be charged a small origination fee, which is deducted from the loan proceeds. Some lenders offer reduced or no-fee loans.

To apply for a Stafford loan, you must first complete the FAFSA to determine eligibility for a subsidized loan and then complete a separate loan application that is submitted to a lender. The financial aid office can help in selecting a lender, but students are free to select any lender they choose. The lender will send a master promissory for completion. The proceeds of the loan, less the origination fee, will be sent to the college to be either credited to your account or released to you directly. Direct loans are processed by the financial aid office as part of the overall financial aid package.

Once the repayment period starts, borrowers of both subsidized and unsubsidized Stafford or Direct loans have to pay a combination of interest and principal monthly for up to a ten-year period. There are a number of repayment options as well as opportunities to consolidate federal loans. There are also provisions for extended repayments, deferments, and repayment forbearance, if needed.

Federal PLUS and Direct PLUS Loan

PLUS loans are for parents of dependent students to help families with the cost of education. There is no needs test to qualify. A Federal PLUS loan has a fixed interest rate of 8.5 percent. A Direct PLUS loan has a fixed interest rate of 7.9 percent. There is no yearly limit; you can borrow up to the cost of your child's education, less other financial aid received. Repayment begins sixty days after the funds are disbursed. A small origination fee (usually about 3 percent or less) may be subtracted from the proceeds. Parent borrowers must generally have a good credit record to qualify. PLUS may be processed under either the Direct loan or FFELP system, depending on the type of loan program for which the college has contracted.

Tuition Tax Credit

Tuition tax credits allow families to reduce their tax bill by the out-of-pocket college tuition expense. Unlike a tax deduction, which is modified according to your tax bracket, a tax credit is a dollar-for-dollar reduction in taxes paid.

There are two programs: the Hope Credit and the Lifetime Learning Credit. As is true of many federal programs, there are numerous rules and restrictions that apply. You should check with your tax preparer, financial advisor, or IRS Publication 970 for information about your own particular situation.

Hope Credit

The Hope Credit offsets some of the expense for the first two years of college or vocational school. Students or the parents of dependent students can claim an annual income tax credit of up to $1650—100 percent of the first $1100 of tuition and required fees and 50 percent of the second $1100. Grants, scholarships, and other tax-free educational assistance must be deducted from the total tuition and fee payments.

This credit can be claimed for students who are in their first two years of college and who are enrolled on at least a half-time basis in a degree or certificate program for any portion of the year. This credit phases out for joint filers who have an income between $94,000 and $114,000 and for single filers who have between $47,000 and $57,000 of income. Parents may claim credits for more than one qualifying student. (The income figures are subject to change and can be found in each year's IRS Publication 970.)

Lifetime Learning Credit

The Lifetime Learning Credit is the counterpart of the Hope Credit; it is for college juniors, seniors, graduate students, and part-time students pursuing lifelong learning to improve or upgrade their job skills. The qualifying taxpayer can claim an annual tax credit of up to $2000—20 percent of the first $10,000 of tuition. The credit is available for net tuition and fees, less grant aid. The total credit available is limited to $2000 per year per taxpayer (or joint-filing couple), and is phased out at the same income levels as the Hope Credit. (The income figures are subject to change and can be found in each year's IRS Publication 970.)

Tuition and Fees Tax Deduction

The Tuition and Fees Tax Deduction could reduce taxable income by as much as $4000. This deduction is taken as an adjustment to income, which means you can claim this deduction even if you do not itemize deductions on Schedule A of Form 1040. This deduction may benefit taxpayers who do not qualify for either the Hope Credit or Lifetime Learning Credit.

Up to $4000 may be deducted for tuition and fees required for enrollment or attendance at an eligible postsecondary institution. Personal living and family expenses, including room and board, insurance, medical, and transportation, are not deductible expenses.

The exact amount of the Tuition and Fees Tax Deduction depends on the amount of qualified tuition and related expenses paid for one's self, spouse, or dependents, and your Adjusted Gross Income. Consult the IRS or your tax preparer for more information.

Student Loan Interest Tax Deduction

If you made student loan interest payments in 2007, you may be able to reduce your taxable income by up to $2500. You should check with your lender with regards to the amount of interest you paid if you did not receive an IRS Form 1098-E and your tax preparer or IRS Publication 970 for additional information.

AmeriCorps

AmeriCorps is a national umbrella group of service programs for students. Participants work in a public or private nonprofit agency and provide service to the community in one of four priority areas: education, human services, the environment, and public safety. In exchange, they earn a stipend (for living expenses) of between $7400 and $14,800 a year, health insurance coverage, and $4725 per year for up to two years to apply toward college expenses. Many student-loan lenders will postpone the repayment of student loans during service in AmeriCorps, and AmeriCorps will pay the interest that is accrued on qualified student loans for members who complete the service program. Participants can work before, during, or after college and can use the funds to either pay current educational expenses or repay federal student loans. For more information, visit www.americorps.org.

Searching for Four-Year Colleges Online

The Internet can be a great tool for gathering information about four-year colleges and universities. There are many worthwhile sites that are ready to help guide you through the various aspects of the selection process, including Peterson's College Search at www.petersons.com/colleges.

How Peterson's College Search Can Help

Peterson's College Search is a comprehensive information resource that will help you make sense of the college admissions process and is a great place to start your college search-and-selection journey—it's as easy as these three steps:

1. Decide what's important
2. Define your criteria
3. Get results

Decide What's Important

There's no such thing as a best college—there's only the best college *for you*! Peterson's College Search site is organized into various sections and offers you enhanced search criteria—and it's easy to use! You can find colleges by name or keyword for starters, or do a detailed search based on the following:

- The Basics (location, setting, size, cost, type, religious and ethnic affiliation)
- Student Body (male-female ratio, diversity, in-state vs. out-of-state)
- Getting In (selectivity, GPA)
- Academics (degree type, majors, special programs and services)
- Campus Life (sports, clubs, fraternities and sororities, housing)

Define Your Criteria

Now it's time to take to define your criteria by taking a closer look at some more specific details. Here you are able to answer questions about what is important to you, skip questions that aren't important, and click for instant results. You'll be prompted to think about criteria:

- Where do you want to study?
- What range of tuition are you willing to consider?
- How many people do you want to go to school with?

Get Results

Once you have gotten your results, simply click on any school to get information about the institution, including school type, setting, degrees offered, comprehensive cost, entrance difficulty, application deadline, undergraduate student population, minority breakdown, international population, housing info, freshman details, faculty, majors, academic programs, student life, athletics, facilities/endowments, costs, financial aid, and applying. Keep reading but take a peek at all the great info you'll see on Petersons.com on the next page!

Get Free Info

If, after looking at the information provided on Peterson's College Search, you still have questions, you can send an e-mail directly to the admissions department of the school. Just click on the "Get Free Info" button and send your message!

Visit School Site

For institutions that have provided information about their Web sites, simply click on the "Visit School Site" button and you will be taken directly to that institution's Web page. Once you arrive at the school's Web site, look around and get a feel for the place. Often, schools offer virtual tours of the campus, complete with photos and commentary.

College Close-Up

If the schools you are interested in have provided Peterson's with a **College Close-Up,** you can do a keyword search on that description. Here, schools are given the opportunity to communicate unique features of their programs to prospective students.

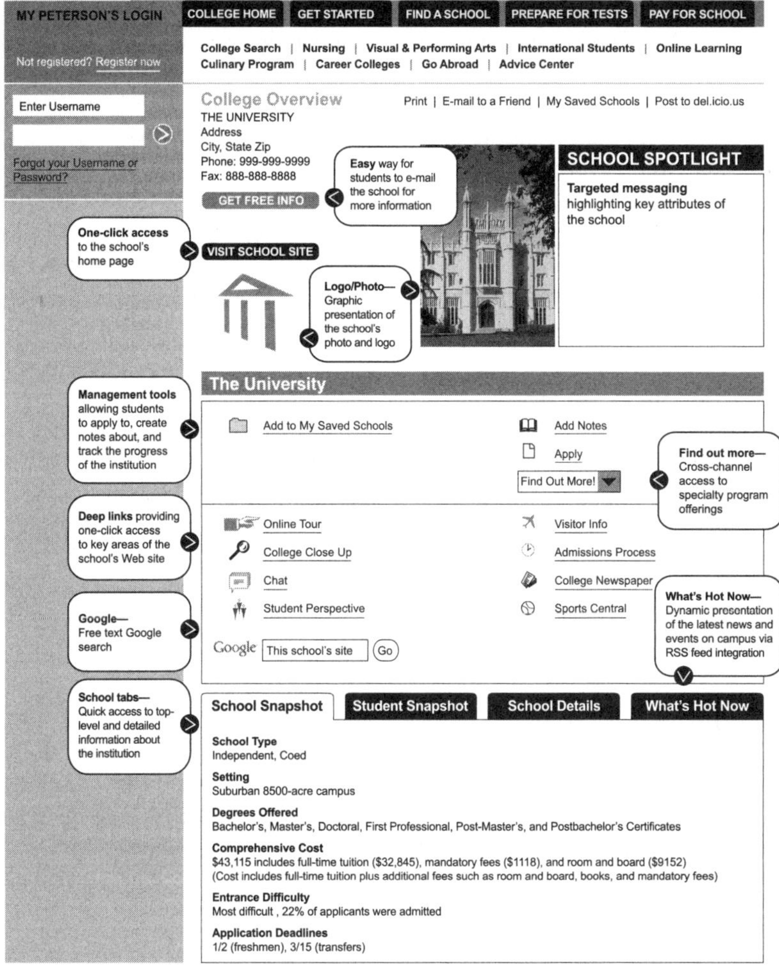

Add to My Saved Schools/Add Notes/Apply

The "Add to My Saved Schools" features are designed to help you with your college planning with management tools to create notes about and track the school. The Apply link gives you the ability to directly apply to the school online.

Write Admissions Essays

This year, 500,000 college applicants will write 500,000 different admissions essays. Half will be rejected by their first-choice school, while only 11 percent will gain admission to the nation's most selective colleges. With acceptance rates at all-time lows, setting yourself apart requires more than just blockbuster SAT scores and impeccable transcripts—it requires the perfect application essay. Named "the world's premier application essay editing service" by the *New York Times* Learning Network and "one of the best essay services on the Internet" by the *Washington Post*, EssayEdge (www.essayedge.com) has helped more applicants write successful personal statements than any other company in the world. Learn more about EssayEdge and how it can give you an edge over hundreds of applicants with comparable academic credentials.

Practice for Your Test

At Peterson's, we understand that the college admissions process can be very stressful. With the stakes so high and the competition getting tighter every year, it's easy to feel like the process is out of your control. Fortunately, preparing for college admissions tests, like the PSAT, SAT, and ACT, helps you exert some control over the options you will have available to you. You can visit Peterson's Prep Central (click on the "Prepare for Tests" tab at the top of the screen) to learn more about how Peterson's can help you maximize your scores—and your options.

Use the Tools to Your Advantage

Choosing a college is an involved and complicated process. The tools available to you on www.petersons.com can help you to be more productive in this process. So, what are you waiting for? Fire up your computer; your future alma mater may be just a click away!

How to Use This Guide

Profiles of Four-Year Colleges

The **Profiles of Four-Year Colleges** contain basic data for quick review and comparison. The following outline of the **Profile** format shows the section headings and the items that each section covers. Any item that does not apply to a particular college or for which no information was supplied is omitted from that college's **Profile.**

General: The first category noted is *Institutional control.* Private institutions are designated as independent (nonprofit), proprietary (profit-making), or independent with a specific religious denomination or affiliation. Nondenominational or interdenominational religious orientation is possible and would be indicated. Public institutions are designated by the source of funding. Designations include federal, state, province, commonwealth (Puerto Rico), territory (U.S. territories), county, district (an educational administrative unit often having boundaries different from units of local government), city, state and local (local may refer to county, district, or city), or state-related (funded primarily by the state but administratively autonomous). *Religious affiliation* is then noted, followed by *Institutional type.* Each institution is classified as one of the following:

- Four-year college: Awards baccalaureate degrees; may also award associate degrees; does not award graduate (postbaccalaureate) degrees.
- Five-year college: Awards a five-year baccalaureate in a professional field such as architecture or pharmacy; does not award graduate degrees.
- Upper-level institution: Awards baccalaureate degrees, but entering students must have at least two years of previous college-level credit; may also offer graduate degrees.

- Comprehensive institution: Awards baccalaureate degrees; may also award associate degrees; offers graduate degree programs, primarily at the master's, specialist's, or professional level, although one or two doctoral programs may be offered.
- University: Offers four years of undergraduate work, plus graduate degrees through the doctorate in more than two academic or professional fields.

The last category noted is *System or administrative affiliation.* Any coordinate institutions or system affiliations are indicated. An institution that has separate colleges or campuses for men and women but shares facilities and courses is termed a coordinate institution. A formal administrative grouping of institutions, either private or public, of which the college is a part, or the name of a single institution with which the college is administratively affiliated, is a system.

Entrance: The five levels of entrance difficulty (*most difficult, very difficult, moderately difficult, minimally difficult,* and *noncompetitive*) are based on the percentage of applicants who were accepted for fall 2007 freshman admission (or, in the case of upper-level schools, for entering-class admission) and on the high school class rank and standardized test scores of the accepted freshmen who actually enrolled in fall 2007. The colleges were asked to select the level that most closely corresponds to their entrance difficulty, according to these guidelines, to assist prospective students in assessing their chances for admission.

Setting: Designated as *urban* (located within a major city), *suburban* (a residential area within commuting distance of a major city), *small town* (a small but compactly settled area not within commuting distance of a major city), or *rural* (a remote and sparsely populated area).

Total enrollment: The number of undergraduate and (if applicable) graduate students, both full-time and part-time, as of fall 2007.

Student-faculty ratio: The school's estimate of the ratio of undergraduate students to faculty members teaching undergraduate courses.

Application deadline: Deadlines and dates for notification of acceptance or rejection are given either as specific dates or as rolling or continuous. *Rolling* means that applications are processed as they are received and qualified students are accepted as long as there are openings. *Continuous notification* means that applicants are notified of acceptance or rejection as applications are processed up until the date indicated or the actual beginning of classes.

Freshmen: Figures are given for the percentage of applicants who were accepted.

Housing: Indicates whether or not on-campus housing is available.

Expenses: Tuition is the average basic tuition for an academic year presented as a dollar amount. Room & Board is the average yearly room and board cost presented as a dollar amount.

Undergraduates: Percentages of undergraduates who are women, part-time students, 25 years or older, Native American (Indian, Eskimo, Polynesian), Hispanic, African American, and Asian American are given.

Most frequently chosen baccalaureate fields: The most popular majors of the 2005 graduating class.

Academic program includes the following offerings:

- English as a second language: A course of study designed specifically for students whose native language is not English.
- Advanced placement: Credit toward a degree awarded for acceptable scores on some or all College Board Advanced Placement tests.
- Accelerated degree program: Students may earn a bachelor's degree in three academic years.
- Self-designed majors: Students may design their own program of study based on individual interests.
- Honors program: Unusually challenging academic program for superior students.
- Summer session: Summer courses through which students may make up degree work or accelerate their program.
- Adult/continuing education programs: Courses offered for nontraditional students who are currently working or are returning to formal education.
- Internships: College-arranged work experience for which students earn academic credit.

Contact: The name, title, mailing address, and telephone number of the person to contact for further information are given at the end of the profile. Toll-free telephone numbers may also be included. The admission office fax number, e-mail address, and Web site may be provided.

College Close-Ups

Nearly 100 narrative descriptions provide an inside look at colleges and universities appearing in this section, shifting the focus to a variety of other factors that should also be considered. The descriptions presented in this section provide information on crucial components in the college decision-making equation—components such as student life, academic programs, and financial aid. Prepared exclusively by college officials, the descriptions are designed to help give students a better sense of the individuality of each institution. The absence from this section of any college or university does not constitute an editorial decision on the part of Peterson's. In essence, this section is an open forum for colleges and universities, on a voluntary basis, to communicate their particular message to prospective college students. The colleges included have paid a fee to Peterson's to provide this information. The descriptions are edited to provide a consistent format across entries for your ease of comparison and are presented alphabetically by the official name of the institution.

Index

The Alphabetical Listing of Four-Year Colleges lists the schools contained in the almanac. Page numbers refer to each college's **Profile;** page numbers in **bold-faced** text refer to **College Close-Ups.**

Data Collection Procedures

The **Profiles** of the colleges and universities include all four-year colleges in the United States that appear in *Peterson's Four-Year Colleges 2009.* The data contained in the **Profiles of Four-Year Colleges** were researched between fall 2007 and spring 2008 through *Peterson's Annual Survey of Undergraduate Institutions.* Questionnaires were sent to the more than 2,100 colleges and universities that met the outlined inclusion criteria. All data included in this edition have been submitted by officials (usually admissions officers, registrars, or institutional research personnel) at the colleges. In addition, many of the institutions that submitted data were contacted directly by the Peterson's research staff to verify unusual figures, resolve discrepancies, or obtain additional data. All usable information received in time for publication has been included. The omission of any particular item from the **Profiles of Four-Year Colleges** listing signifies that the information is either not applicable to that institution or not available. Because of Peterson's comprehensive editorial review and because all material comes directly from college officials, we believe that the information presented in this guide is accurate. You should check with a specific college or university at the time of application to verify such figures as tuition and fees, which may have changed since the publication of this volume.

Criteria for Inclusion in This Book

The term "four-year college" is the commonly used designation for institutions that grant the baccalaureate degree. Four years is the expected amount of time required to earn this degree, although some bachelor's degree programs may be completed in three years, others require five years, and part-time programs may take considerably longer. Upper-level institutions offer only the junior and senior years and accept only students with two years of college-level credit. Therefore, "four-year college" is a conventional term that accurately describes most of the institutions included in this guide, but should not be taken literally in all cases.

To be included in this guide, an institution must have full accreditation or be a candidate for accreditation (preaccreditation) status by an institutional or specialized accrediting body recognized by the U.S. Department of Education or the Council for Higher Education Accreditation (CHEA). Institutional accrediting bodies, which review each institution as a whole, include the six regional associations of schools and colleges (Middle States, New England, North Central, Northwest, Southern, and Western), each of which is responsible for a specified portion of the United States and its territories. Other institutional accrediting bodies are national in scope and accredit specific kinds of institutions (e.g., Bible colleges, independent colleges, and rabbinical and Talmudic schools). Program registration by the New York State Board of Regents is considered to be the equivalent of institutional accreditation, since the board requires that all programs offered by an institution meet its standards before recognition is granted. There are recognized specialized or professional accrediting bodies in more than forty different fields, each of which is authorized to accredit institutions or specific programs in its particular field. For specialized institutions that offer programs in one field only, we designate this to be the equivalent of institutional accreditation. A full explanation of the accrediting process and complete information on recognized, institutional (regional and national) and specialized accrediting bodies can be found online at www.chea.org or at www.ed.gov/admins/finaid/accred/index.html.

PROFILES OF FOUR-YEAR COLLEGES

ALABAMA

ALABAMA AGRICULTURAL AND MECHANICAL UNIVERSITY
HUNTSVILLE, ALABAMA

General State-supported, university, coed **Entrance** Minimally difficult **Setting** 2,001-acre suburban campus **Total enrollment** 5,706 **Student-faculty ratio** 14:1 **Application deadline** 7/15 (freshmen), rolling (transfer) **Freshmen** 32% were admitted **Housing** Yes **Expenses** Tuition $3432; Room & Board $4770 **Undergraduates** 53% women, 7% part-time, 13% 25 or older, 0.1% Native American, 0.4% Hispanic American, 95% African American, 0.1% Asian American/Pacific Islander **The most frequently chosen baccalaureate fields are** business/marketing, education, public administration and social services **Academic program** Advanced placement, honors program, summer session, adult/continuing education programs **Contact** Dr. Evelyn Ellis, Interim Director of Admissions, Alabama Agricultural and Mechanical University, 4900 Meridian Street, Huntsville, AL 35811. Phone: 256-372-5245 or toll-free 800-553-0816. Fax: 256-851-9747. E-mail: admissions@aamu.edu. Web site: http://www.aamu.edu/.

ALABAMA STATE UNIVERSITY
MONTGOMERY, ALABAMA

General State-supported, comprehensive, coed **Entrance** Minimally difficult **Setting** 172-acre urban campus **Total enrollment** 5,608 **Student-faculty ratio** 15:1 **Application deadline** 7/30 (freshmen), 7/30 (transfer) **Freshmen** 37% were admitted **Housing** Yes **Expenses** Tuition $4508; Room & Board $4150 **Undergraduates** 60% women, 10% part-time, 12% 25 or older, 0.3% Hispanic American, 98% African American, 0.1% Asian American/Pacific Islander **The most frequently chosen baccalaureate fields are** business/marketing, computer and information sciences, education **Academic program** Advanced placement, self-designed majors, honors program, summer session, adult/continuing education programs, internships **Contact** Dr. Martha Pettway, Director of Admissions and Recruitment, Alabama State University, PO Box 271, Montgomery, AL 36101-0271. Phone: 334-229-4291 or toll-free 800-253-5037. Fax: 334-229-4984. E-mail: mpettway@alasu.edu. Web site: http://www.alasu.edu/.

AMRIDGE UNIVERSITY
MONTGOMERY, ALABAMA

General Independent, university, coed, affiliated with Church of Christ **Contact** Mr. Rick Johnson, Director of Enrollment Management, Amridge University, 1200 Taylor Road, Montgomery, AL 36117. Phone: 334-387-3877 Ext. 7513 or toll-free 800-351-4040 Ext. 213. Fax: 334-387-3878. E-mail: admissions@regions.edu. Web site: http://www.amridgeuniversity.edu/.

ANDREW JACKSON UNIVERSITY
BIRMINGHAM, ALABAMA

General Private, comprehensive, coed **Contact** Tammy Kassner, Senior Admissions Representative, Andrew Jackson University, 2919 John Hawkins Parkway, Birmingham, AL 35244. Phone: 205-871-9288. Fax: 800-321-9694. E-mail: info@aju.edu. Web site: http://www.aju.edu/.

ATHENS STATE UNIVERSITY
ATHENS, ALABAMA

General State-supported, upper-level, coed **Entrance** Noncompetitive **Setting** 45-acre small-town campus **Total enrollment** 3,072 **Student-faculty ratio** 23:1 **Application deadline** Rolling (freshmen), rolling (transfer) **Housing** No **Expenses** Tuition $3240 **Undergraduates** 67% women, 56% part-time, 91% 25 or older, 3% Native American, 1% Hispanic American, 11% African American, 1% Asian American/Pacific Islander **The most frequently chosen baccalaureate fields are** business/marketing, engineering, library science **Academic program** Advanced placement, summer session, adult/continuing education programs, internships **Contact** Ms. Necedah Henderson, Coordinator of Admissions, Athens State University, 300 North Beaty Street, Athens, AL 35611. Phone: 256-233-8217 or toll-free 800-522-0272. Fax: 256-233-6565. E-mail: necedah.henderson@athens.edu. Web site: http://www.athens.edu/.

AUBURN UNIVERSITY
AUBURN UNIVERSITY, ALABAMA

General State-supported, university, coed **Entrance** Moderately difficult **Setting** 1,875-acre small-town campus **Total enrollment** 24,137 **Student-faculty ratio** 18:1 **Application deadline** Rolling (freshmen), rolling (transfer) **Freshmen** 69% were admitted **Housing** Yes **Expenses** Tuition $5834; Room only $3200 **Undergraduates** 49% women, 8% part-time, 4% 25 or older, 1% Native American, 2% Hispanic American, 9% African American, 2% Asian American/Pacific Islander **The most frequently chosen baccalaureate fields are** business/marketing, education, engineering **Academic program** English as a second language, advanced placement, accelerated degree program, honors program, summer session, adult/continuing education programs, internships **Contact** Mr. Michael

Auburn University *(continued)*

M. Waldrop, Associate Director, Marketing and Recruitment, Auburn University, 202 Mary Martin Hall, Auburn, AL 36849-5145. Phone: 334-844-6406 or toll-free 800-AUBURN9. E-mail: admissions@auburn.edu. Web site: http://www.auburn.edu/.

AUBURN UNIVERSITY MONTGOMERY

MONTGOMERY, ALABAMA

General State-supported, comprehensive, coed **Entrance** Moderately difficult **Setting** 500-acre suburban campus **Total enrollment** 5,117 **Student-faculty ratio** 15:1 **Application deadline** Rolling (freshmen), rolling (transfer) **Freshmen** 92% were admitted **Housing** Yes **Expenses** Tuition $5280; Room & Board $3050 **Undergraduates** 64% women, 36% part-time, 29% 25 or older, 0.5% Native American, 1% Hispanic American, 32% African American, 2% Asian American/Pacific Islander **The most frequently chosen baccalaureate fields are** business/marketing, education, health professions and related sciences **Academic program** English as a second language, advanced placement, accelerated degree program, honors program, summer session, adult/continuing education programs, internships **Contact** Mr. Ronnie McKinney, Assistant Director of Admissions, Auburn University Montgomery, PO Box 244023, Montgomery, AL 36124-4023. Phone: 334-244-3667 or toll-free 800-227-2649. Fax: 334-244-3795. E-mail: rmckinne@aum.edu. Web site: http://www.aum.edu/.

BIRMINGHAM-SOUTHERN COLLEGE

BIRMINGHAM, ALABAMA

General Independent Methodist, comprehensive, coed **Entrance** Moderately difficult **Setting** 196-acre urban campus **Total enrollment** 1,389 **Student-faculty ratio** 12:1 **Application deadline** Rolling (freshmen), rolling (transfer) **Freshmen** 66% were admitted **Housing** Yes **Expenses** Tuition $25,586; Room & Board $9105 **Undergraduates** 51% women, 2% part-time, 2% 25 or older, 1% Native American, 1% Hispanic American, 8% African American, 3% Asian American/Pacific Islander **The most frequently chosen baccalaureate fields are** biological/life sciences, business/marketing, visual and performing arts **Academic program** Advanced placement, self-designed majors, honors program, summer session, internships **Contact** Ms. Sheri E. Salmon, Dean of Enrollment Management, Birmingham-Southern College, Box 549008, Birmingham, AL 35254. Phone: 205-226-4696 or toll-free 800-523-5793. Fax: 205-226-3074. E-mail: admitme@bsc.edu. Web site: http://www.bsc.edu/.

COLUMBIA SOUTHERN UNIVERSITY

ORANGE BEACH, ALABAMA

General Proprietary, comprehensive, coed **Entrance** Noncompetitive **Setting** small-town campus **Total enrollment** 10,817 **Application deadline** Rolling (freshmen), rolling (transfer) **Freshmen** 37% were admitted **Housing** No **Expenses** Tuition $4714 **Undergraduates** 99% 25 or older **The most frequently chosen baccalaureate fields are** business/marketing, natural resources/environmental science, security and protective services **Academic program** Adult/continuing education programs **Contact** Ms. Kathy Cole, Director of Admissions, Columbia Southern University, 25326 Canal Road, Orange Beach, AL 36561. Phone: 251-981-3771 Ext. 120 or toll-free 800-977-8449. Fax: 251-981-3815. E-mail: kathy@columbiasouthern.edu. Web site: http://www.columbiasouthern.edu/.

CONCORDIA COLLEGE

SELMA, ALABAMA

Contact Ms. Phyllis Richardson, Director, STARS, Concordia College, 1804 Green Street, PO Box 1329, Selma, AL 36701. Phone: 334-874-5700 Ext. 171. Fax: 334-874-5755. E-mail: prichrdson@concordiaselma.edu. Web site: http://www.concordiaselma.edu/.

FAULKNER UNIVERSITY

MONTGOMERY, ALABAMA

General Independent, comprehensive, coed, affiliated with Church of Christ **Entrance** Minimally difficult **Setting** 75-acre urban campus **Total enrollment** 2,963 **Student-faculty ratio** 19:1 **Application deadline** Rolling (freshmen), rolling (transfer) **Freshmen** 59% were admitted **Housing** Yes **Expenses** Tuition $12,720; Room & Board $6350 **Undergraduates** 60% women, 26% part-time, 48% 25 or older, 0.4% Native American, 1% Hispanic American, 45% African American, 0.5% Asian American/Pacific Islander **Academic program** Advanced placement, accelerated degree program, honors program, summer session, adult/continuing education programs, internships **Contact** Mr. Keith Mock, Director of Admissions, Faulkner University, 5345 Atlanta Highway, Montgomery, AL 36109. Phone: 334-386-7200 or toll-free 800-879-9816. Fax: 334-386-7137. E-mail: admissions@faulkner.edu. Web site: http://www.faulkner.edu/.

HERITAGE CHRISTIAN UNIVERSITY

FLORENCE, ALABAMA

General Independent, comprehensive, coed, primarily men, affiliated with Church of Christ **Entrance** Noncompetitive **Setting** 43-acre small-town campus **Total enrollment** 112 **Student-faculty ratio** 9:1 **Application deadline** Rolling (freshmen), rolling (transfer) **Freshmen** 56% were admitted **Housing** Yes **Expenses** Tuition $9660; Room & Board $3300 **Undergraduates** 18% women, 55% part-time, 57% 25 or older, 12% African American, 1% Asian American/Pacific Islander **The most frequently chosen baccalaureate field is** philosophy and religious studies **Academic program** Accelerated degree program, summer session, adult/continuing education programs, internships **Contact** Mr. Travis Harmon, Dean of Students, Heritage Christian University, PO Box HCU, Florence, AL 35630. Phone: 256-766-6610 or toll-free 800-367-3565. Fax: 256-766-9289. E-mail: tharmon@hcu.edu. Web site: http://www.hcu.edu/.

HUNTINGDON COLLEGE

MONTGOMERY, ALABAMA

General Independent United Methodist, 4-year, coed **Entrance** Moderately difficult **Setting** 71-acre suburban campus **Total enrollment** 954 **Student-faculty ratio** 15:1 **Application deadline** Rolling (freshmen), rolling (transfer) **Freshmen** 66% were admitted **Housing** Yes **Expenses** Tuition $20,020; Room & Board $6950 **Undergraduates** 49% women, 18% part-time, 19% 25 or older, 1% Native American, 1% Hispanic American, 15% African American, 1% Asian American/Pacific Islander **The most frequently chosen baccalaureate fields are** business/marketing, biological/life sciences, parks and recreation **Academic program** Advanced placement, accelerated degree program, self-designed majors, honors program, summer session, adult/continuing education programs, internships **Contact** Office of Admission, Huntingdon College, 1500 East Fairview Avenue, Montgomery, AL 36106-2148. Phone: 334-833-4497 or toll-free 800-763-0313. Fax: 334-833-4347. E-mail: admiss@huntingdon.edu. Web site: http://www.huntingdon.edu/.

JACKSONVILLE STATE UNIVERSITY

JACKSONVILLE, ALABAMA

General State-supported, comprehensive, coed **Entrance** Minimally difficult **Setting** 459-acre small-town campus **Total enrollment** 9,077 **Student-faculty ratio** 20:1 **Application deadline** Rolling (freshmen), rolling (transfer) **Freshmen** 86% were admitted **Housing** Yes **Expenses** Tuition $5070; Room & Board $3763 **Undergraduates** 58% women, 22% part-time, 23% 25 or older, 1% Native American, 1% Hispanic American, 26% African American, 1% Asian American/Pacific Islander **The most frequently chosen baccalaureate fields are** business/marketing, education, health professions and related sciences **Academic program** Advanced placement, accelerated degree program, honors program, summer session, adult/continuing education programs, internships **Contact** Ms. Martha Mitchell, Director of Admission, Jacksonville State University, 700 Pelham Road North, Jacksonville, AL 36265. Phone: 256-782-5363 or toll-free 800-231-5291. Fax: 256-782-5291. E-mail: info@jsu.edu. Web site: http://www.jsu.edu/.

JUDSON COLLEGE

MARION, ALABAMA

General Independent Baptist, 4-year, women only **Entrance** Moderately difficult **Setting** 80-acre rural campus **Total enrollment** 311 **Student-faculty ratio** 9:1 **Application deadline** Rolling (freshmen), rolling (transfer) **Freshmen** 80% were admitted **Housing** Yes **Expenses** Tuition $11,120; Room & Board $7120 **Undergraduates** 23% part-time, 26% 25 or older, 0.3% Native American, 1% Hispanic American, 15% African American, 0.3% Asian American/Pacific Islander **The most frequently chosen baccalaureate fields are** education, biological/life sciences, psychology **Academic program** Advanced placement, accelerated degree program, self-designed majors, summer session, adult/continuing education programs, internships **Contact** Mrs. Charlotte Clements, Vice President for Admissions and Financial Aid, Judson College, 302 Bibb Street, Marion, AL 36756. Phone: 334-683-5110 or toll-free 800-447-9472. Fax: 334-683-5282. E-mail: admissions@judson.edu. Web site: http://www.judson.edu/.

MILES COLLEGE

FAIRFIELD, ALABAMA

General Independent Christian Methodist Episcopal, 4-year, coed **Entrance** Noncompetitive **Setting** 76-acre suburban campus **Total enrollment** 1,738 **Student-faculty ratio** 14:1 **Application deadline** 8/23 (freshmen), rolling (transfer) **Freshmen** 26% were admitted **Housing** Yes **Expenses** Tuition $7051; Room & Board $5356 **Undergraduates** 54% women, 9% part-time, 20% 25 or older, 95% African American **The most frequently chosen baccalaureate fields are** business/marketing, foreign languages and literature, public administration and social services **Academic program** Accelerated degree program, honors program, summer session, adult/continuing education programs, internships **Contact** Mr. Christopher Robertson, Director of Admissions and Recruitment, Miles College, 5500 Myron Massey Boulevard, Bell Building, Fairfield, AL 35064. Phone: 205-929-1657 or toll-free 800-445-0708. Fax: 205-929-1627. E-mail: admissions@miles.edu. Web site: http://www.miles.edu/.

OAKWOOD COLLEGE
HUNTSVILLE, ALABAMA

General Independent Seventh-day Adventist, upper-level, coed **Entrance** Minimally difficult **Setting** 1,200-acre campus **Total enrollment** 1,824 **Student-faculty ratio** 14:1 **Application deadline** Rolling (freshmen), rolling (transfer) **First-year students** 57% were admitted **Housing** Yes **Expenses** Tuition $13,174; Room & Board $7458 **Undergraduates** 58% women, 6% part-time, 13% 25 or older, 0.1% Native American, 1% Hispanic American, 89% African American, 0.2% Asian American/Pacific Islander **The most frequently chosen baccalaureate fields are** biological/life sciences, business/marketing, psychology **Academic program** Advanced placement, honors program, internships **Contact** Mr. Jason McCracken, Director of Enrollment Management, Oakwood College, 7000 Adventist Boulevard, NW, Huntsville, AL 35896. Phone: 256-726-7354 or toll-free 800-358-3978. Fax: 256-726-7154. E-mail: admission@oakwood.edu. Web site: http://www.oakwood.edu/.

SAMFORD UNIVERSITY
BIRMINGHAM, ALABAMA

General Independent Baptist, university, coed **Entrance** Moderately difficult **Setting** 180-acre suburban campus **Total enrollment** 4,485 **Student-faculty ratio** 12:1 **Application deadline** 12/15 (freshmen), 8/15 (transfer) **Freshmen** 92% were admitted **Housing** Yes **Expenses** Tuition $17,920; Room & Board $6320 **Undergraduates** 64% women, 6% part-time, 0.2% Native American, 1% Hispanic American, 6% African American, 1% Asian American/Pacific Islander **The most frequently chosen baccalaureate fields are** business/marketing, communications/journalism, health professions and related sciences **Academic program** Advanced placement, accelerated degree program, honors program, summer session, adult/continuing education programs, internships **Contact** Dr. Phil Kimrey, Dean of Admissions and Financial Aid, Samford University, 800 Lakeshore Drive, Samford Hall, Birmingham, AL 35229-0002. Phone: 205-726-3673 or toll-free 800-888-7218. Fax: 205-726-2171. E-mail: admiss@samford.edu. Web site: http://www.samford.edu/.

►**For more information, see page 488.**

SOUTHEASTERN BIBLE COLLEGE
BIRMINGHAM, ALABAMA

General Independent nondenominational, 4-year, coed **Entrance** Moderately difficult **Setting** 10-acre suburban campus **Total enrollment** 220 **Student-faculty ratio** 11:1 **Application deadline** 8/1 (freshmen), 8/1 (transfer) **Freshmen** 96% were admitted **Housing** Yes **Expenses** Tuition $9490; Room only $2200 **Undergraduates** 40% women, 28% part-time, 45% 25 or older, 0.5% Native American, 28% African American **The most frequently chosen baccalaureate field is** theology and religious vocations **Academic program** Advanced placement, summer session, adult/continuing education programs, internships **Contact** Mrs. Katy Holmes, Admissions Counselor, Southeastern Bible College, 2545 Valleydale Road, Birmingham, AL 35244. Phone: 205-970-9218 or toll-free 800-749-8878. Fax: 205-970-9207. E-mail: kholmes@sebc.edu. Web site: http://www.sebc.edu/.

SOUTH UNIVERSITY
MONTGOMERY, ALABAMA

General Proprietary, comprehensive, coed **Setting** urban campus **Contact** Director of Admissions, South University, 5355 Vaughn Road, Montgomery, AL 36116-1120. Phone: 334-395-8800 or toll-free 800-688-0932. Fax: 334-395-8859. Web site: http://www.southuniversity.edu/.

SPRING HILL COLLEGE
MOBILE, ALABAMA

General Independent Roman Catholic (Jesuit), comprehensive, coed **Entrance** Moderately difficult **Setting** 450-acre suburban campus **Total enrollment** 1,538 **Student-faculty ratio** 13:1 **Application deadline** 7/15 (freshmen), rolling (transfer) **Freshmen** 66% were admitted **Housing** Yes **Expenses** Tuition $23,100; Room & Board $8700 **Undergraduates** 67% women, 11% part-time, 8% 25 or older, 1% Native American, 6% Hispanic American, 16% African American, 1% Asian American/Pacific Islander **The most frequently chosen baccalaureate fields are** biological/life sciences, business/marketing, communications/journalism **Academic program** Advanced placement, accelerated degree program, self-designed majors, honors program, summer session, adult/continuing education programs, internships **Contact** Admissions Office, Spring Hill College, 4000 Dauphin Street, Mobile, AL 36608-1791. Phone: 251-380-3030 or toll-free 800-SHC-6704. Fax: 251-460-2186. E-mail: admit@shc.edu. Web site: http://www.shc.edu/.

STILLMAN COLLEGE
TUSCALOOSA, ALABAMA

General Independent, 4-year, coed, affiliated with Presbyterian Church (U.S.A.) **Entrance** Minimally difficult **Setting** 100-acre urban campus **Total enrollment** 915 **Student-faculty ratio** 16:1 **Application deadline** Rolling (freshmen), rolling (transfer) **Freshmen** 37% were admitted **Housing** Yes **Expenses** Tuition $12,185; Room & Board

$5775 **Undergraduates** 54% women, 3% part-time, 19% 25 or older, 0.4% Hispanic American, 91% African American, 0.1% Asian American/Pacific Islander **The most frequently chosen baccalaureate fields are** biological/life sciences, business/marketing, education **Academic program** Advanced placement, honors program, summer session, internships **Contact** Monica Finch, Director of Admissions, Stillman College, PO Drawer 1430, 3600 Stillman Boulevard, Tuscaloosa, AL 35403-9990. Phone: 205-366-8837 or toll-free 800-841-5722. Fax: 205-366-8941. E-mail: mfinch@stillman.edu. Web site: http://www.stillman.edu/.

TALLADEGA COLLEGE
TALLADEGA, ALABAMA

General Independent, 4-year, coed **Contact** Mr. Monroe Thornton, Director of Admissions, Talladega College, 627 West Battle Street, Talladega, AL 35160-2354. Phone: 256-761-6219 or toll-free 800-762-2468 (in-state); 800-633-2440 (out-of-state). Fax: 205-362-0274. E-mail: admissions@talladega.edu. Web site: http://www.talladega.edu/.

TROY UNIVERSITY
TROY, ALABAMA

General State-supported, comprehensive, coed **Entrance** Moderately difficult **Setting** 512-acre small-town campus **Total enrollment** 28,953 **Student-faculty ratio** 21:1 **Application deadline** Rolling (freshmen), rolling (transfer) **Freshmen** 64% were admitted **Housing** Yes **Expenses** Tuition $4264; Room & Board $5718 **Undergraduates** 56% women, 53% part-time, 60% 25 or older, 1% Native American, 4% Hispanic American, 37% African American, 1% Asian American/Pacific Islander **The most frequently chosen baccalaureate fields are** business/marketing, education, security and protective services **Academic program** English as a second language, advanced placement, accelerated degree program, honors program, summer session, adult/continuing education programs, internships **Contact** Mr. Buddy Starling, Dean of Enrollment Management, Troy University, 134 Adams Administration Building, Troy, AL 36082. Phone: 334-670-3243 or toll-free 800-551-9716. Fax: 334-670-3733. E-mail: bstar@troy.edu. Web site: http://www.troy.edu/.

TUSKEGEE UNIVERSITY
TUSKEGEE, ALABAMA

General Independent, comprehensive, coed **Entrance** Moderately difficult **Setting** 4,390-acre small-town campus **Total enrollment** 2,936 **Student-faculty ratio** 11:1 **Application deadline** 4/15 (freshmen), 4/15 (transfer) **Freshmen** 58% were admitted **Housing** Yes **Expenses** Tuition $15,450; Room & Board $7130 **Undergraduates** 55% women, 3% part-time, 5% 25 or older, 0.2% Native American, 0.1% Hispanic American, 86% African American **The most frequently chosen baccalaureate fields are** business/marketing, engineering, social sciences **Academic program** English as a second language, honors program, summer session, internships **Contact** Mr. Robert Laney Jr., Admissions, Tuskegee University, 102 Old Administration Building, Tuskegee, AL 36088. Phone: 334-727-8500 or toll-free 800-622-6531. Web site: http://www.tuskegee.edu/.

UNITED STATES SPORTS ACADEMY
DAPHNE, ALABAMA

Contact United States Sports Academy, One Academy Drive, Daphne, AL 36526-7055. Web site: http://www.ussa.edu/.

THE UNIVERSITY OF ALABAMA
TUSCALOOSA, ALABAMA

General State-supported, university, coed **Entrance** Moderately difficult **Setting** 1,000-acre suburban campus **Total enrollment** 25,544 **Student-faculty ratio** 19:1 **Application deadline** 2/1 (freshmen) **Freshmen** 64% were admitted **Housing** Yes **Expenses** Tuition $5700; Room & Board $5868 **Undergraduates** 53% women, 8% part-time, 8% 25 or older, 1% Native American, 2% Hispanic American, 11% African American, 1% Asian American/Pacific Islander **The most frequently chosen baccalaureate fields are** business/marketing, communications/journalism, health professions and related sciences **Academic program** English as a second language, advanced placement, accelerated degree program, self-designed majors, honors program, summer session, adult/continuing education programs, internships **Contact** Ms. Mary K. Spiegel, Executive Director of Undergraduate Admissions, The University of Alabama, Box 870132, 203 Student Services Center, Tuscaloosa, AL 35487-0132. Phone: 205-348-5666 or toll-free 800-933-BAMA. Fax: 205-348-9046. E-mail: admissions@ua.edu. Web site: http://www.ua.edu/.

THE UNIVERSITY OF ALABAMA AT BIRMINGHAM
BIRMINGHAM, ALABAMA

General State-supported, university, coed **Entrance** Moderately difficult **Setting** 265-acre urban campus **Total enrollment** 16,246 **Student-faculty ratio** 18:1 **Application deadline** 3/1 (freshmen), 5/1 (transfer) **Freshmen** 77% were admitted **Housing** Yes **Expenses** Tuition $4208;

The University of Alabama at Birmingham *(continued)*

Room & Board $7640 **Undergraduates** 60% women, 27% part-time, 27% 25 or older, 0.3% Native American, 1% Hispanic American, 29% African American, 4% Asian American/Pacific Islander **The most frequently chosen baccalaureate fields are** business/marketing, biological/life sciences, health professions and related sciences **Academic program** Advanced placement, self-designed majors, honors program, summer session, adult/continuing education programs, internships **Contact** Ms. Chenise Ryan, Director of Undergraduate Admissions, The University of Alabama at Birmingham, 1530 3rd Avenue South, HUC 260, Birmingham, AL 35294-1150. Phone: 205-934-8221 or toll-free 800-421-8743. Fax: 205-975-7114. E-mail: undergradadmit@uab.edu. Web site: http://main.uab.edu/.

THE UNIVERSITY OF ALABAMA IN HUNTSVILLE
HUNTSVILLE, ALABAMA

General State-supported, university, coed **Entrance** Moderately difficult **Setting** 400-acre suburban campus **Total enrollment** 7,264 **Student-faculty ratio** 16:1 **Application deadline** 8/15 (freshmen) **Freshmen** 88% were admitted **Housing** Yes **Expenses** Tuition $5216; Room & Board $6290 **Undergraduates** 48% women, 26% part-time, 25% 25 or older, 2% Native American, 2% Hispanic American, 15% African American, 3% Asian American/Pacific Islander **The most frequently chosen baccalaureate fields are** business/marketing, engineering, health professions and related sciences **Academic program** English as a second language, advanced placement, honors program, summer session, adult/continuing education programs, internships **Contact** Ms. Sandra Patterson, Director of Admissions, The University of Alabama in Huntsville, Enrollment Services, 301 Sparkman Drive, Huntsville, AL 35899. Phone: 256-824-6070 or toll-free 800-UAH-CALL. Fax: 256-824-6073. E-mail: admitme@email.uah.edu. Web site: http://www.uah.edu/.

UNIVERSITY OF ATLANTA
MOBILE, ALABAMA

Contact Admissions Office, University of Atlanta, 801 Executive Park Drive, #204, Mobile, AL 36606. Phone: 251-471-9977 or toll-free 800-533-3378. Fax: 888-368-8667. E-mail: info@uofa.edu. Web site: http://www.uofa.edu/.

UNIVERSITY OF MOBILE
MOBILE, ALABAMA

General Independent Southern Baptist, comprehensive, coed **Entrance** Moderately difficult **Setting** 830-acre suburban campus **Total enrollment** 1,639 **Student-faculty ratio** 14:1 **Application deadline** Rolling (freshmen), rolling (transfer) **Freshmen** 80% were admitted **Housing** Yes **Expenses** Tuition $13,390; Room & Board $7140 **Undergraduates** 66% women, 14% part-time, 22% 25 or older, 2% Native American, 1% Hispanic American, 23% African American, 1% Asian American/Pacific Islander **The most frequently chosen baccalaureate fields are** education, business/marketing, interdisciplinary studies **Academic program** English as a second language, advanced placement, accelerated degree program, honors program, summer session, adult/continuing education programs, internships **Contact** Mrs. Kathy Lee, Assistant Director of Admissions, University of Mobile, 5735 College Parkway, Mobile, AL 36613-2842. Phone: 251-442-2290 or toll-free 800-946-7267. Fax: 251-442-2498. E-mail: adminfo@umobile.edu. Web site: http://www.umobile.edu/.

UNIVERSITY OF MONTEVALLO
MONTEVALLO, ALABAMA

General State-supported, comprehensive, coed **Entrance** Moderately difficult **Setting** 106-acre small-town campus **Total enrollment** 2,948 **Student-faculty ratio** 16:1 **Application deadline** 8/1 (freshmen), rolling (transfer) **Freshmen** 78% were admitted **Housing** Yes **Expenses** Tuition $6080; Room & Board $4360 **Undergraduates** 67% women, 10% part-time, 12% 25 or older, 0.3% Native American, 2% Hispanic American, 14% African American, 1% Asian American/Pacific Islander **The most frequently chosen baccalaureate fields are** business/marketing, education, visual and performing arts **Academic program** Advanced placement, accelerated degree program, honors program, summer session, internships **Contact** Mr. Lynn Gurganus, Director of Admissions, University of Montevallo, Station 6030, Montevallo, AL 35115-6030. Phone: 205-665-6030 or toll-free 800-292-4349. Fax: 205-665-6032. E-mail: admissions@montevallo.edu. Web site: http://www.montevallo.edu/.

UNIVERSITY OF NORTH ALABAMA
FLORENCE, ALABAMA

General State-supported, comprehensive, coed **Entrance** Minimally difficult **Setting** 125-acre urban campus **Total enrollment** 7,097 **Student-faculty ratio** 21:1 **Application deadline** Rolling (freshmen), rolling (transfer) **Freshmen** 85% were admitted **Housing** Yes **Expenses** Tuition $5393;

Room & Board $4460 **Undergraduates** 56% women, 11% part-time, 19% 25 or older, 1% Native American, 1% Hispanic American, 10% African American, 1% Asian American/Pacific Islander **The most frequently chosen baccalaureate fields are** business/marketing, education, health professions and related sciences **Academic program** English as a second language, advanced placement, accelerated degree program, self-designed majors, honors program, summer session, adult/continuing education programs, internships **Contact** Mrs. Kim O. Mauldin, Director of Admissions, University of North Alabama, Office of Admissions, Box 5011, Florence, AL 35632-0001. Phone: 256-765-4316 or toll-free 800-TALKUNA. Fax: 256-765-4329. E-mail: admissions@una.edu. Web site: http://www.una.edu/.

UNIVERSITY OF SOUTH ALABAMA
MOBILE, ALABAMA

General State-supported, university, coed **Entrance** Moderately difficult **Setting** 1,225-acre suburban campus **Total enrollment** 13,779 **Student-faculty ratio** 16:1 **Application deadline** 7/15 (freshmen), 8/10 (transfer) **Freshmen** 90% were admitted **Housing** Yes **Expenses** Tuition $4822; Room & Board $4820 **Undergraduates** 60% women, 27% part-time, 30% 25 or older, 1% Native American, 2% Hispanic American, 19% African American, 3% Asian American/Pacific Islander **The most frequently chosen baccalaureate fields are** business/marketing, education, health professions and related sciences **Academic program** English as a second language, advanced placement, accelerated degree program, self-designed majors, summer session, adult/continuing education programs, internships **Contact** Mr. Christopher A. Lynch, Director, New Student Recruitment, University of South Alabama, 307 University Boulevard, Mobile, AL 36688-0002. Phone: 251-460-7725 or toll-free 800-872-5247. Fax: 251-460-7876. E-mail: admiss@usouthal.edu. Web site: http://www.usouthal.edu/.

THE UNIVERSITY OF WEST ALABAMA
LIVINGSTON, ALABAMA

General State-supported, comprehensive, coed **Entrance** Minimally difficult **Setting** 595-acre small-town campus **Total enrollment** 4,011 **Student-faculty ratio** 28:1 **Application deadline** Rolling (freshmen), rolling (transfer) **Freshmen** 75% were admitted **Housing** Yes **Expenses** Tuition $4608; Room & Board $3624 **Undergraduates** 57% women, 17% part-time, 21% 25 or older, 0.4% Native American, 1% Hispanic American, 49% African American, 0.4% Asian American/Pacific Islander **The most frequently chosen baccalaureate fields are** business/marketing, education, engineering technologies **Academic program** Advanced placement, accelerated degree program, honors program, summer session, internships **Contact** Mr. Danny Buckalew, The University of West Alabama, Station 4, Livingston, AL 35470. Phone: 205-652-3400 Ext. 3578 or toll-free 800-621-7742 (in-state); 800-621-8044 (out-of-state). Fax: 205-652-3522. E-mail: db@uwa.edu. Web site: http://www.uwa.edu/.

VIRGINIA COLLEGE AT BIRMINGHAM
BIRMINGHAM, ALABAMA

Contact Joe Rogalski, Director of Admissions, Virginia College at Birmingham, 65 Bagby Drive, Birmingham, AL 35209. Phone: 205-802-1200. Fax: 205-802-7045. E-mail: bibbie@vc.edu. Web site: http://www.vc.edu/.

ALASKA

ALASKA BIBLE COLLEGE
GLENNALLEN, ALASKA

General Independent nondenominational, 4-year, coed **Contact** Mrs. Carol C. Ridley, Director of Admissions, Alaska Bible College, Box 289, 200 College Road, Glennallen, AK 99588-0289. Phone: 907-822-3201 or toll-free 800-478-7884. Fax: 907-822-5027. E-mail: info@akbible.edu. Web site: http://www.akbible.edu/.

ALASKA PACIFIC UNIVERSITY
ANCHORAGE, ALASKA

General Independent, comprehensive, coed **Entrance** Moderately difficult **Setting** 170-acre suburban campus **Total enrollment** 719 **Student-faculty ratio** 7:1 **Application deadline** 8/15 (freshmen), 8/15 (transfer) **Freshmen** 93% were admitted **Housing** Yes **Expenses** Tuition $21,010; Room & Board $7600 **Undergraduates** 68% women, 41% part-time, 54% 25 or older, 16% Native American, 5% Hispanic American, 6% African American, 2% Asian American/Pacific Islander **The most frequently chosen baccalaureate fields are** business/marketing, education, parks and recreation **Academic program** Advanced placement, accelerated degree program, self-designed majors, summer session, adult/continuing education programs, internships **Contact** Mr. Michael Warner, Director of Admissions, Alaska Pacific University, 4101 University Drive, Anchorage, AK 99508. Phone: 907-564-8248 or toll-free 800-252-7528. Fax: 907-564-

Alaska Pacific University *(continued)*

8317. E-mail: admissions@alaskapacific.edu. Web site: http://www.alaskapacific.edu/.

UNIVERSITY OF ALASKA ANCHORAGE
ANCHORAGE, ALASKA

General State-supported, comprehensive, coed **Contact** Enrollment Services, University of Alaska Anchorage, PO Box 141629, 3901 Old Seward Highway, Anchorage, AK 99508-8046. Phone: 907-786-1558. Fax: 907-786-4888. E-mail: enroll@uaa.alaska.edu. Web site: http://www.uaa.alaska.edu/.

UNIVERSITY OF ALASKA FAIRBANKS
FAIRBANKS, ALASKA

General State-supported, university, coed **Entrance** Minimally difficult **Setting** 2,250-acre small-town campus **Total enrollment** 8,627 **Student-faculty ratio** 10:1 **Application deadline** 8/1 (freshmen), 8/1 (transfer) **Freshmen** 78% were admitted **Housing** Yes **Expenses** Tuition $4756; Room & Board $6030 **Undergraduates** 59% women, 56% part-time, 34% 25 or older, 19% Native American, 3% Hispanic American, 3% African American, 4% Asian American/Pacific Islander **The most frequently chosen baccalaureate fields are** biological/life sciences, business/marketing, engineering **Academic program** Advanced placement, accelerated degree program, self-designed majors, honors program, summer session, internships **Contact** Tim Stickel, Acting Director, Admissions, University of Alaska Fairbanks, PO Box 757480, Fairbanks, AK 99775-7480. Phone: 907-474-7500 or toll-free 800-478-1823. Fax: 907-474-5379. E-mail: admissions@uaf.edu. Web site: http://www.uaf.edu/.

UNIVERSITY OF ALASKA SOUTHEAST
JUNEAU, ALASKA

General State-supported, comprehensive, coed **Entrance** Noncompetitive **Setting** 198-acre small-town campus **Total enrollment** 2,955 **Student-faculty ratio** 11:1 **Application deadline** Rolling (freshmen), rolling (transfer) **Freshmen** 50% were admitted **Housing** Yes **Expenses** Tuition $4636; Room & Board $6714 **Undergraduates** 65% women, 73% part-time, 47% 25 or older, 15% Native American, 2% Hispanic American, 1% African American, 3% Asian American/Pacific Islander **The most frequently chosen baccalaureate fields are** business/marketing, biological/life sciences, liberal arts/general studies **Academic program** Advanced placement, self-designed majors, summer session, adult/continuing education programs, internships **Contact** Ms. Deema Ferguson, Admissions Clerk, University of Alaska Southeast, 11120 Glacier Highway, Juneau, AK 99801-8625. Phone: 907-796-6294 or toll-free 877-796-4827. Fax: 907-796-6365. E-mail: admissions@uas.alaska.edu. Web site: http://www.uas.alaska.edu/.

ARIZONA

AMERICAN INDIAN COLLEGE OF THE ASSEMBLIES OF GOD, INC.
PHOENIX, ARIZONA

Contact Ms. Sandy Ticeahkie, Director of Admissions, American Indian College of the Assemblies of God, Inc., 10020 North Fifteenth Avenue, Phoenix, AZ 85021-2199. Phone: 602-944-3335 Ext. 235 or toll-free 800-933-3828. Fax: 602-943-8299. E-mail: aicadm@aicag.edu. Web site: http://www.aicag.edu/.

ARGOSY UNIVERSITY, PHOENIX
PHOENIX, ARIZONA

General Proprietary, university, coed **Setting** urban campus **Contact** Director of Admissions, Argosy University, Phoenix, 2233 West Dunlap Avenue, Phoenix, AZ 85021. Phone: 602-216-2600 or toll-free 866-216-2777. Fax: 602-216-2601. Web site: http://www.argosy.edu/locations/phoenix/.

ARIZONA STATE UNIVERSITY
TEMPE, ARIZONA

General State-supported, university, coed **Entrance** Moderately difficult **Setting** 814-acre suburban campus **Total enrollment** 51,481 **Student-faculty ratio** 22:1 **Application deadline** Rolling (freshmen), rolling (transfer) **Freshmen** 95% were admitted **Housing** Yes **Expenses** Tuition $5661; Room & Board $8797 **Undergraduates** 50% women, 27% part-time, 14% 25 or older, 2% Native American, 13% Hispanic American, 4% African American, 6% Asian American/Pacific Islander **The most frequently chosen baccalaureate fields are** business/marketing, communications/journalism, interdisciplinary studies **Academic program** Advanced placement, accelerated degree program, honors program, summer session, adult/continuing education programs, internships **Contact** Martha Byrd, Dean of Undergraduate Admissions, Arizona State University, PO Box 870113, Tempe, AZ 85287-0112. Phone: 480-965-7788. Fax: 480-965-3610. E-mail: ugradinq@asu.edu. Web site: http://www.asu.edu/.

ARIZONA STATE UNIVERSITY AT THE DOWNTOWN PHOENIX CAMPUS
PHOENIX, ARIZONA

Contact Arizona State University at the Downtown Phoenix Campus, 411 N. Central Avenue, Phoenix, AZ 85004. Web site: http://www.asu.edu/downtownphoenix/.

ARIZONA STATE UNIVERSITY AT THE POLYTECHNIC CAMPUS
MESA, ARIZONA

General State-supported, comprehensive, coed **Entrance** Moderately difficult **Setting** 600-acre suburban campus **Total enrollment** 8,756 **Application deadline** Rolling (freshmen), rolling (transfer) **Freshmen** 75% were admitted **Housing** Yes **Expenses** Tuition $4768; Room & Board $7320 **Undergraduates** 52% women, 79% part-time, 32% 25 or older, 2% Native American, 13% Hispanic American, 4% African American, 5% Asian American/Pacific Islander **The most frequently chosen baccalaureate fields are** business/marketing, agriculture, education **Academic program** Advanced placement, accelerated degree program, self-designed majors, honors program, summer session, internships **Contact** Matthew Engel, Arizona State University at the Polytechnic Campus, 7001 East Williams Field Road #350, Mesa, AZ 85212. Phone: 480-727-1041. Fax: 480-727-1008. E-mail: poly@au.edu. Web site: http://www.poly.asu.edu/.

ARIZONA STATE UNIVERSITY AT THE WEST CAMPUS
PHOENIX, ARIZONA

General State-supported, comprehensive, coed **Entrance** Moderately difficult **Setting** 300-acre urban campus **Total enrollment** 8,664 **Student-faculty ratio** 21:1 **Application deadline** Rolling (freshmen), rolling (transfer) **Freshmen** 93% were admitted **Housing** Yes **Expenses** Tuition $4766; Room & Board $7320 **Undergraduates** 64% women, 26% part-time, 34% 25 or older, 3% Native American, 20% Hispanic American, 5% African American, 5% Asian American/Pacific Islander **The most frequently chosen baccalaureate fields are** business/marketing, education, security and protective services **Academic program** Advanced placement, self-designed majors, honors program, summer session, adult/continuing education programs, internships **Contact** Mr. Thomas Cabot, Registrar, Arizona State University at the West campus, PO Box 37100, 4701 West Thunderbird Road, Phoenix, AZ 85069-7100. Phone: 602-543-8134. Fax: 602-543-8312. E-mail: cabot@asu.edu. Web site: http://www.west.asu.edu/.

THE ART CENTER DESIGN COLLEGE
TUCSON, ARIZONA

Contact Ms. Colleen Gimbel-Froebe, Director of Enrollment Management, The Art Center Design College, 2525 North Country Club Road, Tucson, AZ 85716-2505. Phone: 520-325-0123 or toll-free 800-825-8753. Fax: 520-325-5535. E-mail: cgf@theartcenter.edu. Web site: http://www.theartcenter.edu/.

THE ART INSTITUTE OF PHOENIX
PHOENIX, ARIZONA

General Proprietary, 4-year, coed **Setting** suburban campus **Contact** Director of Admissions, The Art Institute of Phoenix, 2233 West Dunlap Avenue, Phoenix, AZ 85021. Phone: 602-331-7500 or toll-free 800-474-2479. Web site: http://www.artinstitutes.edu/phoenix/.

THE ART INSTITUTE OF TUCSON
TUCSON, ARIZONA

General Proprietary, 4-year, coed **Contact** Director of Admissions, The Art Institute of Tucson, 5099 E. Grant Road, Tucson, AZ 85712. Phone: 520-318-2700 or toll-free 866-690-8850. Fax: 520-881-4234. E-mail: 5099 East Grant Road, Suite 100. Web site: http://www.artinstitutes.edu/tucson/.

BROWN MACKIE COLLEGE–TUCSON
TUCSON, ARIZONA

General Proprietary, 4-year, coed **Setting** suburban campus **Contact** Director of Admissions, Brown Mackie College–Tucson, 4585 East Speedway, No 204, Tucson, AZ 85712. Phone: 520-327-6866. Web site: http://www.brownmackie.edu/tucson/.

COLLEGE OF THE HUMANITIES AND SCIENCES, HARRISON MIDDLETON UNIVERSITY
TEMPE, ARIZONA

General Independent, comprehensive, coed **Contact** College of the Humanities and Sciences, Harrison Middleton University, 1105 East Broadway, Tempe, AZ 85282. Phone: toll-free 877-248-6724. Web site: http://www.chumsci.edu/.

COLLINS COLLEGE: A SCHOOL OF DESIGN AND TECHNOLOGY
TEMPE, ARIZONA

General Proprietary, 4-year, coed **Setting** 3-acre urban campus **Total enrollment** 1,287 **Student-**

Collins College: A School of Design and Technology *(continued)*

faculty ratio 30:1 **Application deadline** Rolling (freshmen), rolling (transfer) **Expenses** Tuition $39,146; Room only $4860 **Undergraduates** 23% women, 26% 25 or older, 5% Native American, 9% Hispanic American, 6% African American, 2% Asian American/Pacific Islander **Contact** Admissions Department, Collins College: A School of Design and Technology, 1140 South Priest, Tempe, AZ 85281. Phone: 480-966-3000 or toll-free 800-876-7070. Fax: 480-966-2599. E-mail: contact@collinscollege.edu. Web site: http://www.collinscollege.edu/.

DeVRY UNIVERSITY
MESA, ARIZONA

Contact DeVry University, 1201 South Alma School Road, Mesa, AZ 85210-2011. Web site: http://www.devry.edu/.

DeVRY UNIVERSITY
PHOENIX, ARIZONA

General Proprietary, comprehensive, coed **Entrance** Minimally difficult **Setting** 18-acre urban campus **Total enrollment** 1,217 **Student-faculty ratio** 20:1 **Application deadline** Rolling (freshmen), rolling (transfer) **Housing** No **Expenses** Tuition $13,810 **Undergraduates** 21% women, 29% part-time, 38% 25 or older, 7% Native American, 19% Hispanic American, 9% African American, 6% Asian American/Pacific Islander **The most frequently chosen baccalaureate fields are** business/marketing, computer and information sciences, engineering technologies **Academic program** Advanced placement, accelerated degree program, summer session, adult/continuing education programs **Contact** Admissions Office, DeVry University, 2149 West Dunlap Avenue, Phoenix, AZ 85021-2995. Web site: http://www.devry.edu/.

EMBRY-RIDDLE AERONAUTICAL UNIVERSITY
PRESCOTT, ARIZONA

General Independent, comprehensive, coed **Entrance** Moderately difficult **Setting** 547-acre suburban campus **Total enrollment** 1,707 **Student-faculty ratio** 14:1 **Application deadline** Rolling (freshmen), rolling (transfer) **Freshmen** 85% were admitted **Housing** Yes **Expenses** Tuition $26,130; Room & Board $7214 **Undergraduates** 17% women, 8% part-time, 7% 25 or older, 1% Native American, 8% Hispanic American, 3% African American, 7% Asian American/Pacific Islander **The most frequently chosen baccalaureate fields are** engineering, social sciences, transport and materials moving, visual and performing arts **Academic program** English as a second language, advanced placement, accelerated degree program, self-designed majors, honors program, summer session, adult/continuing education programs, internships **Contact** Mr. Bill Thompson, Director of Admissions, Embry-Riddle Aeronautical University, 3700 Willow Creek Road, Prescott, AZ 86301-3720. Phone: 928-777-6600 or toll-free 800-888-3728. Fax: 928-777-6606. E-mail: pradmit@erau.edu. Web site: http://www.embryriddle.edu/.

GRAND CANYON UNIVERSITY
PHOENIX, ARIZONA

General Independent Southern Baptist, comprehensive, coed **Entrance** Moderately difficult **Setting** 90-acre urban campus **Total enrollment** 13,415 **Student-faculty ratio** 13:1 **Application deadline** Rolling (freshmen), rolling (transfer) **Freshmen** 73% were admitted **Housing** Yes **Expenses** Tuition $16,030; Room & Board $7896 **Undergraduates** 71% women, 64% part-time, 78% 25 or older, 0.2% Native American, 3% Hispanic American, 3% African American, 1% Asian American/Pacific Islander **The most frequently chosen baccalaureate fields are** health professions and related sciences, education, interdisciplinary studies **Academic program** English as a second language, advanced placement, accelerated degree program, honors program, summer session, adult/continuing education programs, internships **Contact** Enrollment, Grand Canyon University, 3300 West Camelback Road, PO Box 11097, Phoenix, AZ 86017-3030. Phone: 800-486-7085 or toll-free 800-800-9776. Fax: 602-589-2580. E-mail: admissionsonline@gcu.edu. Web site: http://www.gcu.edu/.

INTERNATIONAL BAPTIST COLLEGE
TEMPE, ARIZONA

Contact Ms. Rebecca M. Stertzbach, Director of Recruitment, International Baptist College, 2150 East Southern Avenue, Tempe, AZ 85282. Phone: 480-838-7070 Ext. 262 or toll-free 800-422-4858. Fax: 480-505-3299. E-mail: jeff.caupp@ibconline.edu. Web site: http://www.tri-citybaptist.org/ibc/.

INTERNATIONAL IMPORT-EXPORT INSTITUTE
PHOENIX, ARIZONA

Contact Dr. Donald N. Burton, International Import-Export Institute, 2432 West Peoria Avenue, Suite 1026, Phoenix, AZ 85029. Phone: 602-648-5750 or toll-free 800-474-8013. Fax: 602-648-5755. E-mail: director@expandglobal.com. Web site: http://www.iiei.edu/.

ITT TECHNICAL INSTITUTE
TEMPE, ARIZONA

General Proprietary, 4-year **Application deadline** Rolling (freshmen), rolling (transfer) **Contact** Ms. Patti Moberly, Director of Recruitment, ITT Technical Institute, 5005 S. Wendler Drive, Tempe, AZ 85282. Phone: 602-437-7500 or toll-free 800-879-4881. Fax: 602-437-7505. Web site: http://www.itt-tech.edu/.

MIDWESTERN UNIVERSITY, GLENDALE CAMPUS
GLENDALE, ARIZONA

Contact Mr. James Walter, Director of Admissions, Midwestern University, Glendale Campus, 19555 North 59th Avenue, Glendale, AZ 85308. Phone: 623-572-3340 or toll-free 888-247-9277 (in-state); 888-247-9271 (out-of-state). Fax: 623-572-3229. E-mail: admissionaz@midwestern.edu. Web site: http://www.midwestern.edu/.

NORTHCENTRAL UNIVERSITY
PRESCOTT VALLEY, ARIZONA

General Proprietary, comprehensive, coed **Entrance** Minimally difficult **Total enrollment** 6,578 **Student-faculty ratio** 16:1 **Application deadline** Rolling (freshmen), rolling (transfer) **Housing** No **Expenses** Tuition $8340 **Undergraduates** 49% women, 92% 25 or older, 1% Native American, 6% Hispanic American, 12% African American, 3% Asian American/Pacific Islander **The most frequently chosen baccalaureate fields are** business/marketing, psychology **Academic program** Advanced placement, accelerated degree program, summer session **Contact** Mr. Brent Passey, Director of Admissions, Northcentral University, 10000 East University Drive, Prescott Valley, AZ 86314. Phone: 866-776-0331 Ext. 8085 or toll-free 888-327-2877. Fax: 928-541-7817. E-mail: info@ncu.edu. Web site: http://www.ncu.edu/.

NORTHERN ARIZONA UNIVERSITY
FLAGSTAFF, ARIZONA

General State-supported, university, coed **Entrance** Moderately difficult **Setting** 730-acre small-town campus **Total enrollment** 21,352 **Student-faculty ratio** 17:1 **Application deadline** Rolling (freshmen), rolling (transfer) **Freshmen** 75% were admitted **Housing** Yes **Expenses** Tuition $4844; Room & Board $6572 **Undergraduates** 60% women, 18% part-time, 24% 25 or older, 6% Native American, 12% Hispanic American, 3% African American, 2% Asian American/Pacific Islander **The most frequently chosen baccalaureate fields are** business/marketing, education, liberal arts/general studies **Academic program** English as a second language, advanced placement, accelerated degree program, honors program, summer session, internships **Contact** James E. Casebeer, Associate Director, Northern Arizona University, PO Box 4084, Flagstaff, AZ 86011. Phone: 928-523-6053 or toll-free 888-MORE-NAU. Fax: 928-523-1230. E-mail: undergraduate.admissions@nau.edu. Web site: http://www.nau.edu/.

NORTHERN ARIZONA UNIVERSITY–YUMA
YUMA, ARIZONA

Contact Northern Arizona University–Yuma, 2020 South Avenue 8E, PO Box 6236, Yuma, AZ 85365. Phone: toll-free 888-NAU-Yuma. Web site: http://yuma.nau.edu/.

PRESCOTT COLLEGE
PRESCOTT, ARIZONA

General Independent, comprehensive, coed **Entrance** Moderately difficult **Setting** 4-acre small-town campus **Total enrollment** 1,007 **Student-faculty ratio** 9:1 **Application deadline** 8/15 (freshmen), 8/15 (transfer) **Freshmen** 83% were admitted **Housing** Yes **Expenses** Tuition $20,180; Room only $3120 **Undergraduates** 59% women, 13% part-time, 40% 25 or older, 1% Native American, 6% Hispanic American, 1% African American, 1% Asian American/Pacific Islander **The most frequently chosen baccalaureate fields are** education, psychology, visual and performing arts **Academic program** Advanced placement, self-designed majors, summer session, adult/continuing education programs, internships **Contact** Mr. Timothy Robison, Director of Resident Degree Program Admissions, Prescott College, 220 Grove Avenue, Prescott, AZ 86301. Phone: 800-628-6364 or toll-free 800-628-6364. Fax: 928-776-5242. E-mail: admissions@prescott.edu. Web site: http://www.prescott.edu/.

SOUTHWESTERN COLLEGE
PHOENIX, ARIZONA

General Independent Conservative Baptist, 4-year, coed **Entrance** Minimally difficult **Setting** 19-acre urban campus **Total enrollment** 361 **Student-faculty ratio** 17:1 **Application deadline** 8/1 (freshmen), 8/1 (transfer) **Freshmen** 48% were admitted **Housing** Yes **Expenses** Tuition $13,764; Room & Board $5004 **Academic program** Advanced placement, summer session, adult/continuing education programs, internships **Contact** Rebekah Dubina, Admissions Advisor, Southwestern College, 2625 E. Cactus Road, Phoenix, AZ 85032. Phone: 602-386-4114 or toll-

Southwestern College *(continued)*

free 800-247-2697. Fax: 602-404-2159. E-mail: rebekah@swcaz.edu. Web site: http://www.swcaz.edu/.

UNIVERSITY OF ADVANCING TECHNOLOGY
TEMPE, ARIZONA

General Proprietary, comprehensive, coed, primarily men **Setting** urban campus **Total enrollment** 1,250 **Student-faculty ratio** 19:1 **Application deadline** Rolling (freshmen) **Housing** Yes **Expenses** Tuition $17,300; Room & Board $7140 **Undergraduates** 8% women, 26% 25 or older, 0.4% Native American, 6% Hispanic American, 4% African American, 2% Asian American/Pacific Islander **Academic program** Summer session, internships **Contact** Admissions Office, University of Advancing Technology, 2625 West Baseline Road, Tempe, AZ 85283-1042. Phone: 602-383-8228 or toll-free 602-383-8228 (in-state); 800-658-5744 (out-of-state). Fax: 602-383-8222. E-mail: admissions@uat.edu. Web site: http://www.uat.edu/.

►**For more information, see page 496.**

THE UNIVERSITY OF ARIZONA
TUCSON, ARIZONA

General State-supported, university, coed **Entrance** Moderately difficult **Setting** 362-acre urban campus **Total enrollment** 37,217 **Student-faculty ratio** 18:1 **Application deadline** 4/1 (freshmen), 6/1 (transfer) **Freshmen** 80% were admitted **Housing** Yes **Expenses** Tuition $5048; Room & Board $7370 **Undergraduates** 53% women, 13% part-time, 8% 25 or older, 2% Native American, 16% Hispanic American, 3% African American, 6% Asian American/Pacific Islander **The most frequently chosen baccalaureate fields are** business/marketing, education, social sciences **Academic program** English as a second language, advanced placement, honors program, summer session, adult/continuing education programs, internships **Contact** Ms. Kasey Urquidez, Director of Recruitment, Admissions, The University of Arizona, Tucson, AZ 85721. Phone: 520-621-3237. Fax: 520-621-9799. E-mail: appinfo@arizona.edu. Web site: http://www.arizona.edu/.

UNIVERSITY OF PHOENIX
PHOENIX, ARIZONA

General Proprietary, comprehensive, coed **Contact** Ms. Evelyn Gaskin, Registrar/Executive Director, University of Phoenix, 4615 East Elwood Street, Mail Stop AA-K101, Phoenix, AZ 85040-1958. Phone: 480-557-3301 or toll-free 800-776-4867 (in-state); 800-228-7240 (out-of-state). Fax: 480-643-1020. E-mail: evelyn.gaskin@phoenix.edu. Web site: http://www.uopxonline.com/.

UNIVERSITY OF PHOENIX–PHOENIX CAMPUS
PHOENIX, ARIZONA

General Proprietary, comprehensive, coed **Contact** Ms. Evelyn Gaskin, Registrar/Executive Director, University of Phoenix–Phoenix Campus, 4615 East Elwood Street, Mail Stop AA-K101, Phoenix, AZ 85040-1958. Phone: 480-557-3301 or toll-free 800-776-4867 (in-state); 800-228-7240 (out-of-state). Fax: 480-643-1020. E-mail: evelyn.gaskin@phoenix.edu. Web site: http://www.phoenix.edu/.

UNIVERSITY OF PHOENIX–SOUTHERN ARIZONA CAMPUS
TUCSON, ARIZONA

General Proprietary, comprehensive, coed **Contact** Ms. Evelyn Gaskin, Registrar/Executive Director, University of Phoenix–Southern Arizona Campus, 4615 East Elwood Street, Mail Stop AA-K101, Phoenix, AZ 85040-1958. Phone: 480-557-3301 or toll-free 800-776-4867 (in-state); 800-228-7240 (out-of-state). Fax: 480-643-1020. E-mail: evelyn.gaskin@phoenix.edu. Web site: http://www.phoenix.edu/.

WESTERN INTERNATIONAL UNIVERSITY
PHOENIX, ARIZONA

General Proprietary, comprehensive, coed **Entrance** Moderately difficult **Setting** 4-acre urban campus **Total enrollment** 2,687 **Student-faculty ratio** 10:1 **Application deadline** Rolling (freshmen), rolling (transfer) **Freshmen** 79% were admitted **Housing** No **Expenses** Tuition $8400 **Undergraduates** 66% women, 90% 25 or older, 3% Native American, 12% Hispanic American, 8% African American, 2% Asian American/Pacific Islander **The most frequently chosen baccalaureate fields are** business/marketing, computer and information sciences, liberal arts/general studies **Academic program** English as a second language, advanced placement, accelerated degree program, honors program, summer session, adult/continuing education programs **Contact** Ms. Karen Janitell, Executive Director of Enrollment, Western International University, 9215 North Black Canyon Highway, Phoenix, AZ 85021-2718. Phone: 602-943-2311 Ext. 1081. E-mail: karen.janitell@apollogrp.edu. Web site: http://www.wintu.edu/.

ARKANSAS

ARKANSAS BAPTIST COLLEGE
LITTLE ROCK, ARKANSAS

General Independent Baptist, 4-year, coed **Entrance** Minimally difficult **Setting** urban campus **Total enrollment** 521 **Student-faculty ratio** 9:1 **Application deadline** Rolling (freshmen) **Housing** Yes **Expenses** Tuition $5250; Room & Board $6392 **Undergraduates** 38% women, 7% part-time, 99% African American **Academic program** Accelerated degree program, summer session, adult/continuing education programs **Contact** Mrs. Jamesetta Ballard, Director of Admissions and Enrollment, Arkansas Baptist College, 1600 Bishop Street, Little Rock, AR 72202-6067. Phone: 501-374-7856 Ext. 5124. Web site: http://www.arkansasbaptist.edu/.

ARKANSAS STATE UNIVERSITY
JONESBORO, ARKANSAS

General State-supported, university, coed **Entrance** Minimally difficult **Setting** 2,008-acre small-town campus **Total enrollment** 10,869 **Student-faculty ratio** 17:1 **Application deadline** Rolling (freshmen), rolling (transfer) **Freshmen** 80% were admitted **Housing** Yes **Expenses** Tuition $6010; Room & Board $4710 **Undergraduates** 60% women, 21% part-time, 26% 25 or older, 0.4% Native American, 1% Hispanic American, 17% African American, 1% Asian American/Pacific Islander **The most frequently chosen baccalaureate fields are** business/marketing, education, health professions and related sciences **Academic program** Advanced placement, accelerated degree program, honors program, summer session, internships **Contact** Ms. Tammy Fowler, Director of Admissions, Arkansas State University, PO Box 1630, State University, AR 72467. Phone: 870-972-3024 or toll-free 800-382-3030. Fax: 870-910-3406. E-mail: admissions@astate.edu. Web site: http://www.astate.edu/.

ARKANSAS TECH UNIVERSITY
RUSSELLVILLE, ARKANSAS

General State-supported, comprehensive, coed **Entrance** Moderately difficult **Setting** 516-acre small-town campus **Total enrollment** 7,476 **Student-faculty ratio** 18:1 **Freshmen** 91% were admitted **Housing** Yes **Expenses** Tuition $5120; Room & Board $4640 **Undergraduates** 53% women, 17% part-time, 21% 25 or older, 2% Native American, 3% Hispanic American, 6% African American, 1% Asian American/Pacific Islander **The most frequently chosen baccalaureate fields are** business/marketing, education, health professions and related sciences **Academic program** Advanced placement, honors program, summer session, adult/continuing education programs, internships **Contact** Ms. Shauna Donnell, Director of Enrollment Management, Arkansas Tech University, L.L. "Doc" Bryan Student Services Building, Suite 141, Russellville, AR 72801-2222. Phone: 479-968-0343 or toll-free 800-582-6953. Fax: 479-964-0522. E-mail: tech.enroll@atu.edu. Web site: http://www.atu.edu/.

CENTRAL BAPTIST COLLEGE
CONWAY, ARKANSAS

General Independent Baptist, 4-year, coed **Contact** Ms. Lindsay Watson, Admissions Counselor, Central Baptist College, 1501 College Avenue, Conway, AR 72034. Phone: 501-329-6872 Ext. 167 or toll-free 800-205-6872. Fax: 501-329-2941. E-mail: lwatson@cbc.edu. Web site: http://www.cbc.edu/.

HARDING UNIVERSITY
SEARCY, ARKANSAS

General Independent, comprehensive, coed, affiliated with Church of Christ **Entrance** Moderately difficult **Setting** 215-acre small-town campus **Total enrollment** 6,139 **Student-faculty ratio** 17:1 **Freshmen** 80% were admitted **Housing** Yes **Expenses** Tuition $12,360; Room & Board $5578 **Undergraduates** 55% women, 6% part-time, 6% 25 or older, 1% Native American, 2% Hispanic American, 4% African American, 1% Asian American/Pacific Islander **The most frequently chosen baccalaureate fields are** business/marketing, education, health professions and related sciences **Academic program** English as a second language, advanced placement, accelerated degree program, honors program, summer session, adult/continuing education programs, internships **Contact** Mr. Glenn Dillard, Assistant Vice President for Enrollment Management, Harding University, Box 12255, Searcy, AR 72149-2255. Phone: 501-279-4407 or toll-free 800-477-4407. Fax: 501-279-4129. E-mail: admissions@harding.edu. Web site: http://www.harding.edu/.

HENDERSON STATE UNIVERSITY
ARKADELPHIA, ARKANSAS

General State-supported, comprehensive, coed **Entrance** Moderately difficult **Setting** 139-acre small-town campus **Total enrollment** 3,603 **Student-faculty ratio** 17:1 **Application deadline** 7/15 (freshmen), rolling (transfer) **Freshmen** 66% were admitted **Housing** Yes **Expenses** Tuition $4939; Room & Board $4860 **Undergraduates** 54% women, 11% part-time, 22% 25

Henderson State University *(continued)*

or older, 1% Native American, 2% Hispanic American, 20% African American, 0.5% Asian American/Pacific Islander **The most frequently chosen baccalaureate fields are** business/marketing, education, health professions and related sciences **Academic program** Advanced placement, honors program, summer session, internships **Contact** Ms. Vikita Hardwrick, Director of University Relations/Admissions, Henderson State University, 1100 Henderson Street, PO Box 7560, Arkadelphia, AR 71999-0001. Phone: 870-230-5028 or toll-free 800-228-7333. Fax: 870-230-5066. E-mail: hardwrv@hsu.edu. Web site: http://www.hsu.edu/.

HENDRIX COLLEGE
CONWAY, ARKANSAS

General Independent United Methodist, comprehensive, coed **Entrance** Very difficult **Setting** 158-acre suburban campus **Total enrollment** 1,195 **Student-faculty ratio** 11:1 **Application deadline** 8/1 (freshmen), 8/1 (transfer) **Freshmen** 83% were admitted **Housing** Yes **Expenses** Tuition $24,498; Room & Board $7200 **Undergraduates** 55% women, 1% part-time, 1% Native American, 3% Hispanic American, 4% African American, 3% Asian American/Pacific Islander **The most frequently chosen baccalaureate fields are** biological/life sciences, psychology, social sciences **Academic program** Advanced placement, self-designed majors, honors program, internships **Contact** Ms. Laura E. Martin, Director of Admission, Hendrix College, 1600 Washington Avenue, Conway, AR 72032. Phone: 501-450-1362 or toll-free 800-277-9017. Fax: 501-450-3843. E-mail: martinl@hendrix.edu. Web site: http://www.hendrix.edu/.

JOHN BROWN UNIVERSITY
SILOAM SPRINGS, ARKANSAS

General Independent interdenominational, comprehensive, coed **Entrance** Moderately difficult **Setting** 200-acre small-town campus **Total enrollment** 2,061 **Student-faculty ratio** 13:1 **Application deadline** Rolling (freshmen), rolling (transfer) **Freshmen** 76% were admitted **Housing** Yes **Expenses** Tuition $18,066; Room & Board $6580 **Undergraduates** 53% women, 5% part-time, 5% 25 or older, 2% Native American, 3% Hispanic American, 3% African American, 1% Asian American/Pacific Islander **The most frequently chosen baccalaureate fields are** business/marketing, education, visual and performing arts **Academic program** English as a second language, advanced placement, honors program, adult/continuing education programs, internships **Contact** Mr. Don Crandall, Vice President for Enrollment Management, John Brown University, 2000 West University Street, Siloam Springs, AR 72761-2121. Phone: 479-524-7150 or toll-free 877-JBU-INFO. Fax: 479-524-4196. E-mail: dcrandal@jbu.edu. Web site: http://www.jbu.edu/.

LYON COLLEGE
BATESVILLE, ARKANSAS

General Independent Presbyterian, 4-year, coed **Entrance** Moderately difficult **Setting** 136-acre small-town campus **Total enrollment** 495 **Student-faculty ratio** 10:1 **Application deadline** Rolling (freshmen), rolling (transfer) **Freshmen** 69% were admitted **Housing** Yes **Expenses** Tuition $15,960; Room & Board $6644 **Undergraduates** 54% women, 6% part-time, 8% 25 or older, 2% Native American, 2% Hispanic American, 3% African American, 1% Asian American/Pacific Islander **The most frequently chosen baccalaureate fields are** biological/life sciences, business/marketing, history **Academic program** Advanced placement, accelerated degree program, self-designed majors, summer session, internships **Contact** Mrs. Anne Woodbury, Director of Admission Operations, Lyon College, PO Box 2317, Batesville, AR 72503-2317. Phone: 870-307-7250 or toll-free 800-423-2542. Fax: 870-793-1791. E-mail: admissions@lyon.edu. Web site: http://www.lyon.edu/.

OUACHITA BAPTIST UNIVERSITY
ARKADELPHIA, ARKANSAS

General Independent Baptist, 4-year, coed **Entrance** Moderately difficult **Setting** 84-acre small-town campus **Total enrollment** 1,448 **Student-faculty ratio** 11:1 **Application deadline** 8/15 (freshmen), 8/15 (transfer) **Freshmen** 69% were admitted **Housing** Yes **Expenses** Tuition $18,400; Room & Board $5530 **Undergraduates** 55% women, 4% part-time, 4% 25 or older, 1% Native American, 2% Hispanic American, 7% African American, 1% Asian American/Pacific Islander **The most frequently chosen baccalaureate fields are** business/marketing, theology and religious vocations, visual and performing arts **Academic program** English as a second language, advanced placement, accelerated degree program, honors program, summer session, internships **Contact** Ms. Keisha Pittman, Director of Admissions Counseling, Ouachita Baptist University, OBU Box 3776, Arkadelphia, AR 71998-0001. Phone: 870-245-5578 or toll-free 800-342-5628. Fax: 870-245-5500. E-mail: pittmank@obu.edu. Web site: http://www.obu.edu/.

PHILANDER SMITH COLLEGE
LITTLE ROCK, ARKANSAS

General Independent United Methodist, 4-year, coed **Contact** Mr. George Gray, Director of

Recruitment and Admissions, Philander Smith College, 812 West 13th Street, Little Rock, AR 72202-3799. Phone: 501-370-5310 or toll-free 800-446-6772. Fax: 501-370-5225. E-mail: ggray@philander.edu. Web site: http://www.philander.edu/.

SOUTHERN ARKANSAS UNIVERSITY–MAGNOLIA

MAGNOLIA, ARKANSAS

General State-supported, comprehensive, coed **Entrance** Moderately difficult **Setting** 781-acre small-town campus **Total enrollment** 3,147 **Student-faculty ratio** 16:1 **Application deadline** 8/27 (freshmen), 8/27 (transfer) **Freshmen** 73% were admitted **Housing** Yes **Expenses** Tuition $5646; Room & Board $4250 **Undergraduates** 59% women, 18% part-time, 24% 25 or older, 1% Native American, 1% Hispanic American, 31% African American, 1% Asian American/Pacific Islander **The most frequently chosen baccalaureate fields are** business/marketing, education, security and protective services **Academic program** Advanced placement, accelerated degree program, honors program, summer session, adult/continuing education programs, internships **Contact** Ms. Sarah Jennings, Dean of Enrollment Services, Southern Arkansas University–Magnolia, 100 East University, Magnolia, AR 71753. Phone: 870-235-4040 or toll-free 800-332-7286. Fax: 870-235-5005. E-mail: addanne@saumag.edu. Web site: http://www.saumag.edu/.

UNIVERSITY OF ARKANSAS

FAYETTEVILLE, ARKANSAS

General State-supported, university, coed **Entrance** Moderately difficult **Setting** 410-acre suburban campus **Total enrollment** 18,648 **Student-faculty ratio** 17:1 **Application deadline** 8/15 (freshmen), 8/15 (transfer) **Freshmen** 62% were admitted **Housing** Yes **Expenses** Tuition $6038; Room & Board $7017 **Undergraduates** 49% women, 15% part-time, 12% 25 or older, 2% Native American, 3% Hispanic American, 5% African American, 3% Asian American/Pacific Islander **The most frequently chosen baccalaureate fields are** business/marketing, education, engineering **Academic program** English as a second language, advanced placement, accelerated degree program, honors program, summer session, internships **Contact** Dawn Medley, Director, University of Arkansas, 232 Silas H. Hunt Hall, Office of Admissions, Fayetteville, AR 72701-1201. Phone: 479-575-5346 or toll-free 800-377-5346 (in-state); 800-377-8632 (out-of-state). Fax: 479-575-7515. E-mail: uofa@uark.edu. Web site: http://www.uark.edu/.

UNIVERSITY OF ARKANSAS AT FORT SMITH

FORT SMITH, ARKANSAS

General State and locally supported, 4-year, coed **Entrance** Minimally difficult **Setting** 120-acre suburban campus **Total enrollment** 6,641 **Student-faculty ratio** 18:1 **Application deadline** Rolling (freshmen), rolling (transfer) **Freshmen** 67% were admitted **Housing** Yes **Undergraduates** 59% women, 38% part-time, 35% 25 or older, 5% Native American, 4% Hispanic American, 4% African American, 4% Asian American/Pacific Islander **The most frequently chosen baccalaureate fields are** business/marketing, communication technologies, education **Academic program** English as a second language, advanced placement, accelerated degree program, honors program, summer session, adult/continuing education programs, internships **Contact** Office of Admissions and School Relations, University of Arkansas at Fort Smith, 5210 Grand Avenue, PO Box 3649, Fort Smith, AR 72913-3649. Phone: 479-788-7121 or toll-free 888-512-5466. Fax: 479-788-7016. E-mail: information@uafortsmith.edu. Web site: http://www.uafortsmith.edu/.

UNIVERSITY OF ARKANSAS AT LITTLE ROCK

LITTLE ROCK, ARKANSAS

General State-supported, university, coed **Contact** Ms. Tammy Harrison, Director of Admissions, University of Arkansas at Little Rock, 2801 South University Avenue, Little Rock, AR 72204-1099. Phone: 501-569-3127 or toll-free 800-482-8892. Fax: 501-569-8956. E-mail: twharrison@ualn.edu. Web site: http://www.ualr.edu/.

UNIVERSITY OF ARKANSAS AT MONTICELLO

MONTICELLO, ARKANSAS

General State-supported, comprehensive, coed **Entrance** Noncompetitive **Setting** 1,600-acre small-town campus **Total enrollment** 3,187 **Student-faculty ratio** 17:1 **Application deadline** 8/1 (freshmen), 8/1 (transfer) **Freshmen** 60% were admitted **Housing** Yes **Expenses** Tuition $4300; Room & Board $3690 **Undergraduates** 59% women, 27% part-time, 28% 25 or older, 1% Native American, 1% Hispanic American, 32% African American, 0.3% Asian American/Pacific Islander **The most frequently chosen baccalaureate fields are** business/marketing, education, health professions and related sciences **Academic program** Advanced placement, accelerated degree program, summer session **Contact** Ms. Mary Whiting, Director of Admissions, University of Arkansas at Monticello, Monticello,

University of Arkansas at Monticello *(continued)*

AR 71656. Phone: 870-460-1026 or toll-free 800-844-1826. Fax: 870-460-1321. E-mail: admissions@uamont.edu. Web site: http://www.uamont.edu/.

UNIVERSITY OF ARKANSAS AT PINE BLUFF
PINE BLUFF, ARKANSAS

General State-supported, comprehensive, coed **Setting** 327-acre urban campus **Total enrollment** 3,200 **Student-faculty ratio** 18:1 **Application deadline** Rolling (freshmen) **Freshmen** 64% were admitted **Housing** Yes **Expenses** Tuition $4499; Room & Board $6070 **Undergraduates** 58% women, 13% part-time, 19% 25 or older, 0.3% Hispanic American, 96% African American, 0.2% Asian American/Pacific Islander **The most frequently chosen baccalaureate fields are** business/marketing, liberal arts/general studies, security and protective services **Academic program** Advanced placement, accelerated degree program, honors program, summer session, adult/continuing education programs, internships **Contact** Mrs. Erica W. Fulton, Director of Admissions and Academic Records, University of Arkansas at Pine Bluff, 1200 North University Drive, Pine Bluff, AR 71601-2799. Phone: 870-575-8487 or toll-free 800-264-6585. Fax: 870-543-8014. E-mail: fulton_e@uapb.edu. Web site: http://www.uapb.edu/.

UNIVERSITY OF ARKANSAS FOR MEDICAL SCIENCES
LITTLE ROCK, ARKANSAS

General State-supported, upper-level, coed **Setting** 5-acre urban campus **Total enrollment** 2,549 **Housing** Yes **Undergraduates** 81% women, 27% part-time, 42% 25 or older, 1% Native American, 2% Hispanic American, 15% African American, 2% Asian American/Pacific Islander **Contact** Ms. Mona Stiles, Admissions Officer, University of Arkansas for Medical Sciences, 4301 West Markham, Little Rock, AR 72205-7199. Phone: 501-686-5730. Web site: http://www.uams.edu/.

UNIVERSITY OF CENTRAL ARKANSAS
CONWAY, ARKANSAS

General State-supported, comprehensive, coed **Entrance** Moderately difficult **Setting** 365-acre small-town campus **Total enrollment** 12,619 **Student-faculty ratio** 18:1 **Application deadline** Rolling (freshmen), rolling (transfer) **Freshmen** 49% were admitted **Housing** Yes **Expenses** Tuition $6205; Room & Board $4600 **Undergraduates** 58% women, 16% part-time, 9% 25 or older, 1% Native American, 2% Hispanic American, 15% African American, 1% Asian American/Pacific Islander **The most frequently chosen baccalaureate fields are** business/marketing, education, health professions and related sciences **Academic program** English as a second language, advanced placement, accelerated degree program, honors program, summer session, internships **Contact** Ms. Melissa Goff, Director of Institutional Research and Admissions, University of Central Arkansas, 201 Donaghey Avenue, Conway, AR 72035. Phone: 501-450-5371 or toll-free 800-243-8245. Fax: 501-450-5228. E-mail: mgoff@uca.edu. Web site: http://www.uca.edu/.

UNIVERSITY OF PHOENIX–LITTLE ROCK CAMPUS
LITTLE ROCK, ARKANSAS

General Proprietary, comprehensive, coed **Contact** Ms. Evelyn Gaskin, Registrar/Executive Director, University of Phoenix–Little Rock Campus, 4615 East Elwood Street, Mail Stop AA-K101, Phoenix, AZ 85040-1958. Phone: 480-557-3301 or toll-free 800-776-4867 (in-state); 800-228-7240 (out-of-state). Fax: 480-643-1020. E-mail: evelyn.gaskin@phoenix.edu. Web site: http://www.phoenix.edu/.

UNIVERSITY OF THE OZARKS
CLARKSVILLE, ARKANSAS

General Independent Presbyterian, 4-year, coed **Entrance** Moderately difficult **Setting** 56-acre small-town campus **Total enrollment** 622 **Student-faculty ratio** 11:1 **Application deadline** Rolling (freshmen), rolling (transfer) **Freshmen** 97% were admitted **Housing** Yes **Expenses** Tuition $16,110; Room & Board $5475 **Undergraduates** 54% women, 6% part-time, 5% 25 or older, 4% Native American, 5% Hispanic American, 4% African American, 3% Asian American/Pacific Islander **The most frequently chosen baccalaureate fields are** biological/life sciences, business/marketing, education **Academic program** English as a second language, advanced placement, summer session, internships **Contact** Ms. Kimberly Myrick, Dean of Enrollment, University of the Ozarks, 415 North College Avenue, Clarksville, AR 72830-2880. Phone: 479-979-1227 or toll-free 800-264-8636. Fax: 479-979-1417. E-mail: admiss@ozarks.edu. Web site: http://www.ozarks.edu/.

WILLIAMS BAPTIST COLLEGE
WALNUT RIDGE, ARKANSAS

General Independent Southern Baptist, 4-year, coed **Contact** Mrs. Angela Flippo, Vice President for Enrollment, Williams Baptist College, 60 West Fulbright Avenue, Walnut Ridge, AR 72476. Phone: 870-759-4117 or toll-free 800-722-4434. Fax: 870-886-3924. E-mail: admissions@wbcoll.edu. Web site: http://www.wbcoll.edu/.

CALIFORNIA

ACADEMY OF ART UNIVERSITY
SAN FRANCISCO, CALIFORNIA

General Proprietary, comprehensive, coed **Entrance** Noncompetitive **Setting** 3-acre urban campus **Total enrollment** 11,334 **Student-faculty ratio** 21:1 **Application deadline** Rolling (freshmen), rolling (transfer) **Freshmen** 100% were admitted **Housing** Yes **Expenses** Tuition $16,360; Room & Board $13,500 **Undergraduates** 53% women, 36% part-time, 37% 25 or older, 1% Native American, 9% Hispanic American, 5% African American, 12% Asian American/Pacific Islander **The most frequently chosen baccalaureate fields are** communication technologies, computer and information sciences, visual and performing arts **Academic program** English as a second language, summer session, adult/continuing education programs, internships **Contact** Academy of Art University, 79 New Montgomery Street, San Francisco, CA 94105. Phone: 800-544-2787 Ext. 5518 or toll-free 800-544-ARTS. Fax: 415-618-6287. E-mail: info@academyart.edu. Web site: http://www.academyart.edu/.

ALLIANT INTERNATIONAL UNIVERSITY
SAN DIEGO, CALIFORNIA

General Independent, university, coed **Setting** 60-acre suburban campus **Total enrollment** 3,690 **Student-faculty ratio** 15:1 **Application deadline** Rolling (freshmen) **Housing** Yes **Expenses** Tuition $15,220 **Undergraduates** 61% women, 23% part-time, 30% 25 or older, 15% Hispanic American, 8% African American, 5% Asian American/Pacific Islander **Academic program** English as a second language, advanced placement, honors program, summer session, adult/continuing education programs, internships **Contact** Mr. Louis Cruz, Alliant International University, 10455 Pomerado Road, San Diego, CA 92131-1799. Phone: 858-635-4772 or toll-free 866-825-5426. Fax: 858-635-4739. E-mail: admissions@alliant.edu. Web site: http://www.alliant.edu/.

AMERICAN JEWISH UNIVERSITY
BEL AIR, CALIFORNIA

General Independent Jewish, comprehensive, coed **Entrance** Moderately difficult **Setting** 28-acre suburban campus **Total enrollment** 291 **Student-faculty ratio** 7:1 **Application deadline** Rolling (freshmen), rolling (transfer) **Housing** Yes **Expenses** Tuition $21,300; Room & Board $10,890 **Undergraduates** 49% women, 5% 25 or older **Academic program** Advanced placement, self-designed majors, summer session, internships **Contact** Ms. Julie Brydon, Undergraduate Admissions Administrative Assistant, American Jewish University, 15600 Mulholland Drive, Los Angeles, CA 90077-1519. Phone: 310-440-1250 or toll-free 888-853-6763. Fax: 310-471-3657. E-mail: admissions@ajula.edu. Web site: http://www.ajula.edu/.

AMERICAN MUSICAL AND DRAMATIC ACADEMY, LOS ANGELES
LOS ANGELES, CALIFORNIA

Contact American Musical and Dramatic Academy, Los Angeles, 6305 Yucca Street, Los Angeles, CA 90028. Phone: toll-free 866-374-5300. Web site: http://www.amda.edu/.

ANTIOCH UNIVERSITY LOS ANGELES
CULVER CITY, CALIFORNIA

General Independent, upper-level, coed **Contact** Admissions, Antioch University Los Angeles, 400 Corporate Pointe, Culver City, CA 90230. Phone: 310-578-1080 Ext. 217 or toll-free 800-7ANTIOCH. Fax: 310-822-4824. E-mail: admissions@antiochla.edu. Web site: http://www.antiochla.edu/.

ANTIOCH UNIVERSITY SANTA BARBARA
SANTA BARBARA, CALIFORNIA

General Independent, upper-level, coed **Setting** small-town campus **Total enrollment** 347 **Student-faculty ratio** 15:1 **Application deadline** Rolling (transfer) **Housing** No **Expenses** Tuition $14,696 **Undergraduates** 75% women, 71% part-time, 86% 25 or older, 4% Native American, 33% Hispanic American, 1% African American, 1% Asian American/Pacific Islander **The most frequently chosen baccalaureate field is** liberal arts/general studies **Academic program** Accelerated degree program, self-designed majors, summer session, adult/continuing education programs, internships **Contact** Director of Admissions, Antioch University Santa Barbara, 801 Garden Street, Suite 101, Santa Barbara, CA 93101-1580. Phone: 805-962-8179. Fax: 805-962-4786. E-mail: admissions@antiochsb.edu. Web site: http://www.antiochsb.edu/.

ARGOSY UNIVERSITY, INLAND EMPIRE
SAN BERNARDINO, CALIFORNIA

General Proprietary, university, coed **Contact** Director of Admissions, Argosy University, Inland

Argosy University, Inland Empire *(continued)*

Empire, 636 East Brier Drive, Suite 235, San Bernardino, CA 92408. Phone: toll-free 866-217-9075. Web site: http://www.argosy.edu/locations/los-angeles-inland-empire/.

ARGOSY UNIVERSITY, LOS ANGELES

SANTA MONICA, CALIFORNIA

General Proprietary, university, coed **Contact** Director of Admissions, Argosy University, Los Angeles, 2950 31st Street, Santa Monica, CA 90405. Phone: 310-866-4000 or toll-free 866-505-0332. Web site: http://www.argosy.edu/locations/los-angeles/.

ARGOSY UNIVERSITY, ORANGE COUNTY

SANTA ANA, CALIFORNIA

General Proprietary, university, coed **Setting** urban campus **Contact** Director of Admissions, Argosy University, Orange County, 3501 West Sunflower Avenue, Suite 110, Santa Ana, CA 92704. Phone: 714-338-6200 or toll-free 800-716-9598. Web site: http://www.argosy.edu/locations/los-angeles-orange-county/.

ARGOSY UNIVERSITY, SAN DIEGO

SAN DIEGO, CALIFORNIA

General Proprietary, university, coed **Contact** Director of Admissions, Argosy University, San Diego, 1615 Murray Canyon Road, Suite 100, San Diego, CA 92108. Phone: toll-free 866-505-0333. Web site: http://www.argosy.edu/locations/san-diego/.

ARGOSY UNIVERSITY, SAN FRANCISCO BAY AREA

ALAMEDA, CALIFORNIA

General Proprietary, university, coed **Setting** urban campus **Contact** Director of Admissions, Argosy University, San Francisco Bay Area, 1005 Atlantic Avenue, Alameda, CA 94501. Phone: 510-217-4700 or toll-free 866-215-2777. Fax: 510-217-4800. Web site: http://www.argosy.edu/locations/san-francisco/.

ART CENTER COLLEGE OF DESIGN

PASADENA, CALIFORNIA

General Independent, comprehensive, coed **Entrance** Very difficult **Setting** 175-acre suburban campus **Total enrollment** 1,832 **Student-faculty ratio** 12:1 **Application deadline** Rolling (freshmen), rolling (transfer) **Freshmen** 71% were admitted **Housing** No **Expenses** Tuition $29,579 **Undergraduates** 43% women, 21% part-time, 40% 25 or older, 1% Native American, 11% Hispanic American, 2% African American, 37% Asian American/Pacific Islander **Academic program** Advanced placement, accelerated degree program, summer session, adult/continuing education programs, internships **Contact** Ms. Kit Baron, Vice President, Admissions and Enrollment Management, Art Center College of Design, 1700 Lida Street, Pasadena, CA 91103-1999. Phone: 626-396-2373. Fax: 626-795-0578. E-mail: admissions@artcenter.edu. Web site: http://www.artcenter.edu/.

THE ART INSTITUTE OF CALIFORNIA–HOLLYWOOD

LOS ANGELES, CALIFORNIA

General Proprietary, 4-year, coed **Setting** urban campus **Contact** Director of Admissions, The Art Institute of California–Hollywood, 3440 Wilshire Boulevard, Tenth Floor, Los Angeles, CA 90010. Phone: 213-251-3636 Ext. 153 or toll-free 877-468-6232. Fax: 213-385-3545. E-mail: aicdcinfo@aii.edu. Web site: http://www.cdc.edu/.

THE ART INSTITUTE OF CALIFORNIA–INLAND EMPIRE

SAN BERNARDINO, CALIFORNIA

General Proprietary, 4-year, coed **Setting** suburban campus **Contact** Director of Admissions, The Art Institute of California–Inland Empire, 630 East Brier Drive, San Bernadino, CA 92408. Phone: 909-915-2100 or toll-free 800-353-0812. Web site: http://www.artinstitutes.edu/inlandempire/.

THE ART INSTITUTE OF CALIFORNIA–LOS ANGELES

SANTA MONICA, CALIFORNIA

General Proprietary, 4-year, coed **Entrance** Noncompetitive **Setting** urban campus **Total enrollment** 2,068 **Student-faculty ratio** 19:1 **Application deadline** Rolling (freshmen), rolling (transfer) **Freshmen** 56% were admitted **Housing** Yes **Expenses** Tuition $21,840; Room only $10,652 **Undergraduates** 34% women, 27% 25 or older, 1% Native American, 19% Hispanic American, 6% African American, 9% Asian American/Pacific Islander **The most frequently chosen baccalaureate fields are** personal and culinary services, visual and performing arts **Academic program** Advanced placement, honors program, summer session, adult/continuing education programs, internships **Contact** Assistant Director of Admissions, The Art Institute of California–Los Angeles, 2900 31st Street, Santa Monica, CA 90405-3035. Phone: 310-752-4700 or toll-free 888-646-4610. Fax: 310-752-4708.

E-mail: ailaadm@aii.edu. Web site: http://www.artinstitutes.edu/losangeles/.

THE ART INSTITUTE OF CALIFORNIA–ORANGE COUNTY

SANTA ANA, CALIFORNIA

General Proprietary, 4-year, coed **Setting** urban campus **Contact** Director of Admissions, The Art Institute of California–Orange County, 3601 West Sunflower Avenue, Santa Ana, CA 92704. Phone: 714-830-0200 or toll-free 888-549-3055. E-mail: aicaocadm@aii.edu. Web site: http://www.artinstitutes.edu/orangecounty/.

THE ART INSTITUTE OF CALIFORNIA–SACRAMENTO

SACRAMENTO, CALIFORNIA

General Proprietary, 4-year, coed **Contact** Director of Admissions, The Art Institute of California–Sacramento, 2850 Gateway Oaks Drive, Suite 100, Sacramento, CA 95833. Phone: 916-830-6320 or toll-free 800-477-1957. Fax: 916-830-6344. Web site: http://www.artinstitutes.edu/sacramento/.

THE ART INSTITUTE OF CALIFORNIA–SAN DIEGO

SAN DIEGO, CALIFORNIA

General Proprietary, 4-year, coed **Setting** urban campus **Contact** Director of Admission, The Art Institute of California–San Diego, 7650 Mission Valley Road, San Diego, CA 92108. Phone: 858-598-1200 or toll-free 866-275-2422. Fax: 619-291-3206. Web site: http://www.artinstitutes.edu/sandiego/.

THE ART INSTITUTE OF CALIFORNIA–SAN FRANCISCO

SAN FRANCISCO, CALIFORNIA

General Proprietary, comprehensive, coed **Setting** urban campus **Contact** Director of Admissions, The Art Institute of California–San Francisco, 1170 Market Street, San Francisco, CA 94102. Phone: 415-865-1025 or toll-free 888-493-3261. Fax: 415-863-6344. Web site: http://www.artinstitutes.edu/sanfrancisco.

THE ART INSTITUTE OF CALIFORNIA–SUNNYVALE

SUNNYVALE, CALIFORNIA

Contact Director of Admissions, The Art Institute of California–Sunnyvale, 1120 Kifer Road, Sunnyvale, CA 94086. Phone: 408-962-6400 or toll-free 866-583-7961. Fax: 408-962-6498. Web site: http://www.artinstitutes.edu/sunnyvale/.

AZUSA PACIFIC UNIVERSITY

AZUSA, CALIFORNIA

General Independent nondenominational, comprehensive, coed **Entrance** Moderately difficult **Setting** 60-acre small-town campus **Total enrollment** 8,084 **Application deadline** 6/1 (freshmen), 6/1 (transfer) **Freshmen** 73% were admitted **Housing** Yes **Expenses** Tuition $25,130; Room & Board $7518 **Undergraduates** 63% women, 15% part-time, 15% 25 or older, 0.5% Native American, 14% Hispanic American, 5% African American, 7% Asian American/Pacific Islander **The most frequently chosen baccalaureate fields are** business/marketing, liberal arts/general studies, philosophy and religious studies **Academic program** English as a second language, advanced placement, accelerated degree program, honors program, summer session, adult/continuing education programs, internships **Contact** Ms. Lynnette Barnes, Processing Coordinator, Azusa Pacific University, 901 East Alosta Avenue, PO Box 7000, Undergraduate Admissions - 7221, Azusa, CA 91702-7000. Phone: 626-812-3016 or toll-free 800-TALK-APU. E-mail: admissions@apu.edu. Web site: http://www.apu.edu/.

BETHANY UNIVERSITY

SCOTTS VALLEY, CALIFORNIA

General Independent Assemblies of God, comprehensive, coed **Entrance** Minimally difficult **Setting** 40-acre small-town campus **Total enrollment** 546 **Student-faculty ratio** 11:1 **Application deadline** 7/31 (freshmen), 7/31 (transfer) **Freshmen** 51% were admitted **Housing** Yes **Expenses** Tuition $18,150; Room & Board $7050 **Undergraduates** 59% women, 17% part-time, 37% 25 or older, 1% Native American, 15% Hispanic American, 9% African American, 6% Asian American/Pacific Islander **Academic program** Advanced placement, accelerated degree program, summer session, adult/continuing education programs, internships **Contact** Ms. Gretchen Mineni, Director of Admissions, Bethany University, 800 Bethany Drive, Scotts Valley, CA 95066-2820. Phone: 831-438-3800 Ext. 3900 or toll-free 800-843-9410. Fax: 831-438-4517. E-mail: info@bethany.edu. Web site: http://www.bethany.edu/.

BETHESDA CHRISTIAN UNIVERSITY

ANAHEIM, CALIFORNIA

Contact Jacquie Ha, Director of Admission, Bethesda Christian University, 730 North Euclid Street, Anaheim, CA 92801. Phone: 714-517-

Bethesda Christian University *(continued)*

1945. Fax: 714-517-1948. E-mail: admission@bcu.edu. Web site: http://www.bcu.edu/.

BIOLA UNIVERSITY
LA MIRADA, CALIFORNIA

General Independent interdenominational, university, coed **Entrance** Moderately difficult **Setting** 95-acre suburban campus **Total enrollment** 5,858 **Student-faculty ratio** 17:1 **Application deadline** 3/1 (freshmen), 3/1 (transfer) **Freshmen** 82% were admitted **Housing** Yes **Expenses** Tuition $26,424 **Undergraduates** 3% 25 or older, 1% Native American, 12% Hispanic American, 4% African American, 10% Asian American/Pacific Islander **The most frequently chosen baccalaureate fields are** business/marketing, communications/journalism, theology and religious vocations **Academic program** English as a second language, advanced placement, accelerated degree program, honors program, summer session, adult/continuing education programs, internships **Contact** Mr. Andre Stephens, Director of Enrollment Management, Biola University, 13800 Biola Avenue, La Mirada, CA 90639. Phone: 562-903-4752 or toll-free 800-652-4652. Fax: 562-903-4709. E-mail: admissions@biola.edu. Web site: http://www.biola.edu/.

BROOKS INSTITUTE OF PHOTOGRAPHY
SANTA BARBARA, CALIFORNIA

Contact Ms. Inge B. Kautzmann, Director of Admissions, Brooks Institute of Photography, 801 Alston Road, Santa Barbara, CA 93108-2399. Phone: 805-966-3888 Ext. 4601 or toll-free 888-304-3456. Fax: 805-564-1475. E-mail: admissions@brooks.edu. Web site: http://www.brooks.edu/.

CALIFORNIA BAPTIST UNIVERSITY
RIVERSIDE, CALIFORNIA

General Independent Southern Baptist, comprehensive, coed **Entrance** Minimally difficult **Setting** 110-acre suburban campus **Total enrollment** 3,775 **Student-faculty ratio** 17:1 **Application deadline** Rolling (freshmen), rolling (transfer) **Freshmen** 72% were admitted **Housing** Yes **Expenses** Tuition $20,640; Room & Board $7510 **Undergraduates** 64% women, 14% part-time, 21% 25 or older, 1% Native American, 17% Hispanic American, 8% African American, 3% Asian American/Pacific Islander **The most frequently chosen baccalaureate fields are** business/marketing, liberal arts/general studies, psychology **Academic program** English as a second language, advanced placement, accelerated degree program, honors program, summer session, adult/continuing education programs, internships **Contact** Mr. Allen Johnson, Director, Undergraduate Admissions, California Baptist University, 8432 Magnolia Avenue, Riverside, CA 92504-3297. Phone: 951-343-4212 or toll-free 877-228-8866. Fax: 951-343-4525. E-mail: admissions@calbaptist.edu. Web site: http://www.calbaptist.edu/.

CALIFORNIA CHRISTIAN COLLEGE
FRESNO, CALIFORNIA

General Independent religious, 4-year, coed **Entrance** Noncompetitive **Setting** 5-acre urban campus **Total enrollment** 28 **Student-faculty ratio** 6:1 **Application deadline** Rolling (freshmen), rolling (transfer) **Housing** Yes **Expenses** Tuition $7100; Room & Board $3740 **Undergraduates** 36% women, 11% part-time, 28% 25 or older, 54% Hispanic American, 7% African American, 4% Asian American/Pacific Islander **The most frequently chosen baccalaureate field is** theology and religious vocations **Academic program** Accelerated degree program, summer session **Contact** Mrs. Phyllis LoForti, Director of Admissions and Recruitment, California Christian College, 4881 East University Avenue, Fresno, CA 93703-3533. Phone: 559-251-4215 Ext. 5571. Fax: 559-251-4231. E-mail: cccfresno@aol.com. Web site: http://www.calchristiancollege.org/.

CALIFORNIA COAST UNIVERSITY
SANTA ANA, CALIFORNIA

Contact Dr. William L. Barcroft, Dean of Admissions, California Coast University, 700 North Main Street, Santa Ana, CA 92701. Phone: toll-free 888-CCU-UNIV. Fax: 714-547-5777. E-mail: admissions@calcoast.edu. Web site: http://www.calcoast.edu/.

CALIFORNIA COLLEGE
SAN DIEGO, CALIFORNIA

Contact California College, 2820 Camino del Rio South, Suite 300, San Diego, CA 92108. Web site: http://www.cc-sd.edu.

CALIFORNIA COLLEGE OF THE ARTS
SAN FRANCISCO, CALIFORNIA

General Independent, comprehensive, coed **Entrance** Moderately difficult **Setting** 4-acre urban campus **Total enrollment** 1,614 **Student-faculty ratio** 14:1 **Application deadline** 2/1 (freshmen), rolling (transfer) **Freshmen** 78% were admitted **Housing** Yes **Expenses** Tuition $31,382; Room only $6600 **Undergraduates** 61% women, 10% part-time, 29% 25 or older, 1% Native American, 10% Hispanic American, 3% African

American, 14% Asian American/Pacific Islander **The most frequently chosen baccalaureate fields are** architecture, English, visual and performing arts **Academic program** Advanced placement, self-designed majors, honors program, summer session, internships **Contact** Ms. Robynne Royster, Director of Admissions, California College of the Arts, 1111 Eighth Street at 16th and Wisconsin, San Francisco, CA 94107. Phone: 415-703-9523 Ext. 9535 or toll-free 800-447-1ART. Fax: 415-703-9539. E-mail: enroll@cca.edu. Web site: http://www.cca.edu/.

►**For more information, see page 446.**

CALIFORNIA INSTITUTE OF INTEGRAL STUDIES

SAN FRANCISCO, CALIFORNIA

Contact Admissions Department/Student Worker, California Institute of Integral Studies, 1453 Mission Street, San Francisco, CA 94103. Phone: 415-575-6100 Ext. 156. Fax: 415-575-1268. E-mail: info@ciis.edu. Web site: http://www.ciis.edu/.

CALIFORNIA INSTITUTE OF TECHNOLOGY

PASADENA, CALIFORNIA

General Independent, university, coed **Entrance** Most difficult **Setting** 124-acre suburban campus **Total enrollment** 2,133 **Student-faculty ratio** 3:1 **Application deadline** 1/1 (freshmen), 2/15 (transfer) **Freshmen** 17% were admitted **Housing** Yes **Expenses** Tuition $34,515; Room & Board $10,146 **Undergraduates** 31% women, 1% 25 or older, 0.3% Native American, 5% Hispanic American, 1% African American, 38% Asian American/Pacific Islander **The most frequently chosen baccalaureate fields are** engineering, mathematics, physical sciences **Academic program** English as a second language, self-designed majors **Contact** Mr. Rick T. Bischoff, Director of Admissions, California Institute of Technology, 1200 East California Boulevard, Pasadena, CA 91125-0001. Phone: 626-395-6341. Fax: 626-683-3026. E-mail: ugadmissions@caltech.edu. Web site: http://www.caltech.edu/.

CALIFORNIA INSTITUTE OF THE ARTS

VALENCIA, CALIFORNIA

General Independent, comprehensive, coed **Entrance** Very difficult **Setting** 60-acre suburban campus **Total enrollment** 1,324 **Student-faculty ratio** 7:1 **Application deadline** 1/5 (freshmen), 1/5 (transfer) **Freshmen** 32% were admitted **Housing** Yes **Expenses** Room & Board $8648 **Undergraduates** 46% women, 1% part-time, 18% 25 or older, 1% Native American, 12% Hispanic American, 9% African American, 9% Asian American/Pacific Islander **The most frequently chosen baccalaureate field is** visual and performing arts **Academic program** Advanced placement, self-designed majors, internships **Contact** Director of Admissions, California Institute of the Arts, 24700 McBean Parkway, Valencia, CA 91355. Phone: 661-255-1050 or toll-free 800-545-2787. Fax: 661-253-7710. E-mail: admiss@calarts.edu. Web site: http://www.calarts.edu/.

CALIFORNIA LUTHERAN UNIVERSITY

THOUSAND OAKS, CALIFORNIA

General Independent Lutheran, comprehensive, coed **Entrance** Moderately difficult **Setting** 290-acre suburban campus **Total enrollment** 3,411 **Student-faculty ratio** 15:1 **Application deadline** 3/15 (freshmen) **Freshmen** 68% were admitted **Housing** Yes **Expenses** Tuition $27,850; Room & Board $9650 **Undergraduates** 57% women, 11% part-time, 1% Native American, 17% Hispanic American, 4% African American, 5% Asian American/Pacific Islander **The most frequently chosen baccalaureate fields are** business/marketing, communications/journalism, psychology **Academic program** Advanced placement, accelerated degree program, self-designed majors, honors program, summer session, adult/continuing education programs, internships **Contact** Mr. Matthew Ward, Dean of Undergraduate Enrollment, California Lutheran University, Office of Admission, #1350, Thousand Oaks, CA 91360. Phone: 805-493-3135 or toll-free 877-258-3678. Fax: 805-493-3114. E-mail: cluadm@clunet.edu. Web site: http://www.callutheran.edu/.

CALIFORNIA MARITIME ACADEMY

VALLEJO, CALIFORNIA

General State-supported, 4-year, coed **Entrance** Moderately difficult **Setting** 64-acre suburban campus **Total enrollment** 865 **Student-faculty ratio** 22:1 **Freshmen** 79% were admitted **Housing** Yes **Expenses** Tuition $3836; Room & Board $8830 **Undergraduates** 17% women **Academic program** Advanced placement, summer session, internships **Contact** Marc McGee, Director of Admission and Enrollment Services, California Maritime Academy, 200 Maritime Academy Drive, Vallejo, CA 94590. Phone: 707-654-1330 or toll-free 800-561-1945. Fax: 707-654-1336. E-mail: admission@csum.edu. Web site: http://www.csum.edu/.

CALIFORNIA NATIONAL UNIVERSITY FOR ADVANCED STUDIES

NORTHRIDGE, CALIFORNIA

Contact Ms. Stephanie Smith, Registrar, California National University for Advanced Studies,

California National University for Advanced Studies *(continued)*

California National University Admissions, 8550 Balboa Boulevard, Suite 210, Northridge, CA 91325. Phone: 818-830-2411 or toll-free 800-744-2822 (in-state); 800-782-2422 (out-of-state). Fax: 818-830-2418. E-mail: cnuadms@mail.cnuas.edu. Web site: http://www.cnuas.edu/.

CALIFORNIA POLYTECHNIC STATE UNIVERSITY, SAN LUIS OBISPO

SAN LUIS OBISPO, CALIFORNIA

General State-supported, comprehensive, coed **Entrance** Moderately difficult **Setting** 6,000-acre small-town campus **Total enrollment** 19,777 **Student-faculty ratio** 20:1 **Application deadline** 11/30 (freshmen), 11/30 (transfer) **Freshmen** 45% were admitted **Housing** Yes **Expenses** Tuition $4689; Room & Board $8817 **Undergraduates** 43% women, 5% part-time, 1% Native American, 11% Hispanic American, 1% African American, 11% Asian American/Pacific Islander **The most frequently chosen baccalaureate fields are** business/marketing, agriculture, engineering **Academic program** English as a second language, advanced placement, honors program, summer session, internships **Contact** Mr. James Maraviglia, Director of Admissions and Evaluations, California Polytechnic State University, San Luis Obispo, 1 Grand Avenue, San Luis Obispo, CA 93407. Phone: 805-756-2311. Fax: 805-756-5400. E-mail: admissions@calpoly.edu. Web site: http://www.calpoly.edu/.

CALIFORNIA STATE POLYTECHNIC UNIVERSITY, POMONA

POMONA, CALIFORNIA

General State-supported, comprehensive, coed **Entrance** Moderately difficult **Setting** 1,400-acre urban campus **Total enrollment** 21,477 **Student-faculty ratio** 23:1 **Application deadline** 11/30 (freshmen), 11/30 (transfer) **Freshmen** 69% were admitted **Housing** Yes **Expenses** Tuition $3279; Room & Board $8493 **Undergraduates** 43% women, 17% part-time, 16% 25 or older, 0.4% Native American, 29% Hispanic American, 4% African American, 29% Asian American/Pacific Islander **The most frequently chosen baccalaureate fields are** business/marketing, engineering, liberal arts/general studies **Academic program** English as a second language, advanced placement, honors program, summer session, adult/continuing education programs, internships **Contact** Mr. Scott J. Duncan, Director, Admissions, California State Polytechnic University, Pomona, 3801 West Temple Avenue, Pomona, CA 91768-2557. Phone: 909-869-3258. Fax: 909-869-4529. E-mail: admissions@csupomona.edu. Web site: http://www.csupomona.edu/.

CALIFORNIA STATE UNIVERSITY, BAKERSFIELD

BAKERSFIELD, CALIFORNIA

Contact Dr. Kendyl Magnuson, Associate Dean of Admissions and Records, California State University, Bakersfield, 9001 Stockdale Highway, Balersfield, CA 93311-1099. Phone: 661-654-3036 or toll-free 800-788-2782. E-mail: admissions@csub.edu. Web site: http://www.csubak.edu/.

CALIFORNIA STATE UNIVERSITY CHANNEL ISLANDS

CAMARILLO, CALIFORNIA

General State-supported, comprehensive, coed **Contact** Ms. Ginger Reyes, California State University Channel Islands, One University Drive, Camarillo, CA 93012. Phone: 805-437-8500. Fax: 805-437-8519. E-mail: prospective.student@csuci.edu. Web site: http://www.csuci.edu/.

CALIFORNIA STATE UNIVERSITY, CHICO

CHICO, CALIFORNIA

General State-supported, comprehensive, coed **Entrance** Moderately difficult **Setting** 119-acre small-town campus **Total enrollment** 17,034 **Student-faculty ratio** 22:1 **Application deadline** 11/30 (freshmen), 11/30 (transfer) **Freshmen** 95% were admitted **Housing** Yes **Undergraduates** 52% women, 9% part-time, 13% 25 or older, 1% Native American, 12% Hispanic American, 2% African American, 6% Asian American/Pacific Islander **The most frequently chosen baccalaureate fields are** business/marketing, liberal arts/general studies, social sciences **Academic program** English as a second language, advanced placement, self-designed majors, honors program, summer session, adult/continuing education programs, internships **Contact** Rocky Raquel, Interim Director of Admissions, California State University, Chico, 400 West First Street, Chico, CA 95929-0722. Phone: 530-898-4428 or toll-free 800-542-4426. Fax: 530-898-6456. E-mail: info@csuchico.edu. Web site: http://www.csuchico.edu/.

CALIFORNIA STATE UNIVERSITY, DOMINGUEZ HILLS

CARSON, CALIFORNIA

General State-supported, comprehensive, coed **Entrance** Moderately difficult **Setting** 350-acre urban campus **Total enrollment** 12,149 **Student-faculty ratio** 17:1 **Application deadline** Rolling (freshmen), rolling (transfer) **Freshmen** 12% were admitted **Housing** Yes **Expenses** Tuition $3377; Room & Board $8690 **Undergraduates** 68% women, 39% part-time, 44% 25 or older, 0.3% Native American, 38% Hispanic American, 28% African American, 8% Asian American/Pacific Islander **The most frequently chosen baccalaureate fields are** business/marketing, liberal arts/general studies, public administration and social services **Academic program** English as a second language, advanced placement, self-designed majors, honors program, summer session, adult/continuing education programs, internships **Contact** Information Center, California State University, Dominguez Hills, 1000 East Victoria Street, Carson, CA 90747-0001. Phone: 310-243-3645. Fax: 310-243-3609. E-mail: lwise@csudeh.edu. Web site: http://www.csudh.edu/.

CALIFORNIA STATE UNIVERSITY, EAST BAY

HAYWARD, CALIFORNIA

General State-supported, comprehensive, coed **Entrance** Moderately difficult **Setting** 343-acre suburban campus **Total enrollment** 13,124 **Student-faculty ratio** 23:1 **Application deadline** 3/1 (freshmen), 8/31 (transfer) **Freshmen** 70% were admitted **Housing** Yes **Expenses** Room & Board $4942 **Undergraduates** 61% women, 19% part-time, 39% 25 or older **The most frequently chosen baccalaureate fields are** business/marketing, liberal arts/general studies, social sciences **Academic program** English as a second language, advanced placement, accelerated degree program, self-designed majors, honors program, summer session, adult/continuing education programs, internships **Contact** Mr. Dave Vasquez, Director of Admissions, California State University, East Bay, 25800 Carlos Bee Boulevard, Hayward, CA 94542-3035. Phone: 510-885-3000. Fax: 510-885-4059. E-mail: admissions@csueeastbay.edu. Web site: http://www.csueastbay.edu/.

CALIFORNIA STATE UNIVERSITY, FRESNO

FRESNO, CALIFORNIA

General State-supported, comprehensive, coed **Entrance** Minimally difficult **Setting** 1,410-acre urban campus **Total enrollment** 22,383 **Student-faculty ratio** 20:1 **Application deadline** 4/1 (freshmen) **Freshmen** 69% were admitted **Housing** Yes **Expenses** Tuition $3299; Room & Board $7053 **Undergraduates** 58% women, 19% part-time, 24% 25 or older, 1% Native American, 33% Hispanic American, 6% African American, 15% Asian American/Pacific Islander **The most frequently chosen baccalaureate fields are** business/marketing, education, liberal arts/general studies **Academic program** English as a second language, advanced placement, accelerated degree program, self-designed majors, honors program, summer session, adult/continuing education programs, internships **Contact** Ms. Yolanda Deleon, Admissions Officer, California State University, Fresno, 5150 North Maple Avenue, M/S JA 57, Fresno, CA 93740-8026. Phone: 559-278-2261. Fax: 559-278-4812. E-mail: yolandad@csufresno.edu. Web site: http://www.csufresno.edu/.

CALIFORNIA STATE UNIVERSITY, FULLERTON

FULLERTON, CALIFORNIA

General State-supported, comprehensive, coed **Entrance** Moderately difficult **Setting** 225-acre suburban campus **Total enrollment** 37,130 **Student-faculty ratio** 23:1 **Application deadline** 11/30 (freshmen), rolling (transfer) **Freshmen** 61% were admitted **Housing** Yes **Expenses** Room & Board $9035 **Undergraduates** 58% women, 28% part-time, 26% 25 or older, 1% Native American, 30% Hispanic American, 4% African American, 22% Asian American/Pacific Islander **The most frequently chosen baccalaureate fields are** business/marketing, communications/journalism, education **Academic program** English as a second language, advanced placement, self-designed majors, honors program, summer session, adult/continuing education programs, internships **Contact** Ms. Nancy J. Dority, Assistant Vice President of Enrollment Services, California State University, Fullerton, Office of Admissions and Records, PO Box 6900, 800 North State College Boulevard, Fullerton, CA 92834-6900. Phone: 714-278-2370. Fax: 714-278-2356. E-mail: admissions@fullerton.edu. Web site: http://www.fullerton.edu/.

CALIFORNIA STATE UNIVERSITY, LONG BEACH

LONG BEACH, CALIFORNIA

General State-supported, comprehensive, coed **Entrance** Moderately difficult **Setting** 320-acre suburban campus **Total enrollment** 36,868 **Student-faculty ratio** 20:1 **Application deadline** 11/30 (freshmen), 11/30 (transfer) **Freshmen** 47% were admitted **Housing** Yes **Expenses** Room & Board $7940 **Undergraduates** 60% women, 21% part-time, 19% 25 or older, 1% Native American, 27% Hispanic American, 6% African American, 23% Asian American/Pacific Islander **The most frequently chosen baccalaureate fields are** business/marketing, English, visual and performing arts **Academic program** English as a second language, advanced placement, accelerated degree program, self-designed majors, honors program, summer session, adult/continuing educa-

California State University, Long Beach *(continued)*

tion programs, internships **Contact** Mr. Thomas Enders, Director of Enrollment Services, California State University, Long Beach, Brotman Hall, 1250 Bellflower Boulevard, Long Beach, CA 90840. Phone: 562-985-4641. Web site: http://www.csulb.edu/.

CALIFORNIA STATE UNIVERSITY, LOS ANGELES

LOS ANGELES, CALIFORNIA

General State-supported, comprehensive, coed **Entrance** Moderately difficult **Setting** 173-acre urban campus **Total enrollment** 21,051 **Student-faculty ratio** 21:1 **Application deadline** 6/15 (freshmen), 6/15 (transfer) **Freshmen** 63% were admitted **Housing** Yes **Expenses** Tuition $3377; Room & Board $8406 **Undergraduates** 61% women, 26% part-time, 34% 25 or older, 0.4% Native American, 46% Hispanic American, 8% African American, 19% Asian American/Pacific Islander **The most frequently chosen baccalaureate fields are** business/marketing, security and protective services, social sciences **Academic program** English as a second language, advanced placement, accelerated degree program, self-designed majors, honors program, summer session, adult/continuing education programs, internships **Contact** Mr. Vince Lopez, Director of Outreach and Recruitment, California State University, Los Angeles, 5151 State University Drive, Los Angeles, CA 90032-8530. Phone: 323-343-3940. E-mail: admission@calstatela.edu. Web site: http://www.calstatela.edu/.

CALIFORNIA STATE UNIVERSITY, MONTEREY BAY

SEASIDE, CALIFORNIA

General State-supported, comprehensive, coed **Entrance** Minimally difficult **Setting** 1,500-acre small-town campus **Total enrollment** 4,080 **Student-faculty ratio** 22:1 **Application deadline** 7/15 (freshmen), 8/4 (transfer) **Freshmen** 69% were admitted **Housing** Yes **Expenses** Tuition $3000; Room & Board $9152 **Undergraduates** 56% women, 10% part-time, 19% 25 or older, 1% Native American, 28% Hispanic American, 4% African American, 7% Asian American/Pacific Islander **The most frequently chosen baccalaureate fields are** business/marketing, liberal arts/general studies, social sciences **Academic program** Self-designed majors, summer session, adult/continuing education programs, internships **Contact** Admissions and Recruitment, California State University, Monterey Bay, 100 Campus Center, Seaside, CA 93955-8001. Phone: 831-582-3905. Fax: 831-582-3783. E-mail: admissions@csumb.edu. Web site: http://csumb.edu/.

CALIFORNIA STATE UNIVERSITY, NORTHRIDGE

NORTHRIDGE, CALIFORNIA

General State-supported, comprehensive, coed **Contact** Ms. Mary Baxton, Associate Director of Admissions and Records, California State University, Northridge, 18111 Nordhoff Street, Northridge, CA 91330-8207. Phone: 818-677-3700. Fax: 818-677-3766. E-mail: admissions.records@csun.edu. Web site: http://www.csun.edu/.

CALIFORNIA STATE UNIVERSITY, SACRAMENTO

SACRAMENTO, CALIFORNIA

General State-supported, comprehensive, coed **Entrance** Moderately difficult **Setting** 300-acre urban campus **Total enrollment** 28,829 **Student-faculty ratio** 21:1 **Application deadline** 8/1 (freshmen), 7/1 (transfer) **Freshmen** 67% were admitted **Housing** Yes **Expenses** Tuition $4752; Room & Board $8598 **Undergraduates** 57% women, 24% part-time, 23% 25 or older, 1% Native American, 14% Hispanic American, 8% African American, 19% Asian American/Pacific Islander **The most frequently chosen baccalaureate fields are** business/marketing, communication technologies, public administration and social services **Academic program** English as a second language, advanced placement, accelerated degree program, self-designed majors, honors program, summer session, internships **Contact** Mr. Emiliano Diaz, Director of University Outreach Services, California State University, Sacramento, 6000 J Street, Lassen Hall, Sacramento, CA 95819-6048. Phone: 916-278-7362. Fax: 916-278-5603. E-mail: admissions@csus.edu. Web site: http://www.csus.edu/.

CALIFORNIA STATE UNIVERSITY, SAN BERNARDINO

SAN BERNARDINO, CALIFORNIA

General State-supported, comprehensive, coed **Entrance** Moderately difficult **Setting** 430-acre suburban campus **Total enrollment** 17,066 **Student-faculty ratio** 21:1 **Application deadline** Rolling (freshmen), rolling (transfer) **Freshmen** 61% were admitted **Housing** Yes **Expenses** Tuition $3398; Room & Board $7517 **Undergraduates** 65% women, 17% part-time, 23% 25 or older, 1% Native American, 37% Hispanic American, 12% African American, 8% Asian American/Pacific Islander **The most**

frequently chosen baccalaureate fields are business/marketing, liberal arts/general studies, social sciences **Academic program** Accelerated degree program, self-designed majors, honors program, summer session, adult/continuing education programs, internships **Contact** Ms. Cynthia Olivo, Associate Director, California State University, San Bernardino, 5500 University Parkway, University Hall, Room 107, San Bernardino, CA 92407-2397. Phone: 909-537-5188. Fax: 909-537-7034. E-mail: moreinfo@mail.csusb.edu. Web site: http://www.csusb.edu/.

CALIFORNIA STATE UNIVERSITY, SAN MARCOS

SAN MARCOS, CALIFORNIA

General State-supported, comprehensive, coed **Entrance** Moderately difficult **Setting** 304-acre suburban campus **Total enrollment** 6,956 **Student-faculty ratio** 24:1 **Application deadline** 11/30 (freshmen), 11/30 (transfer) **Freshmen** 44% were admitted **Housing** Yes **Expenses** Tuition $3092; Room only $5600 **Undergraduates** 61% women, 26% part-time, 30% 25 or older, 1% Native American, 21% Hispanic American, 3% African American, 11% Asian American/Pacific Islander **Academic program** English as a second language, advanced placement, self-designed majors, summer session, adult/continuing education programs, internships **Contact** Ms. Cherine Heckman, Director of Admissions, California State University, San Marcos, 333 South Twin Oaks Valley Road, San Marcos, CA 92096-0001. Phone: 760-750-4848. Fax: 760-750-3248. E-mail: apply@csusm.edu. Web site: http://www.csusm.edu/.

CALIFORNIA STATE UNIVERSITY, STANISLAUS

TURLOCK, CALIFORNIA

General State-supported, comprehensive, coed **Setting** 228-acre small-town campus **Total enrollment** 8,836 **Student-faculty ratio** 19:1 **Application deadline** 2/1 (freshmen), rolling (transfer) **Freshmen** 65% were admitted **Housing** Yes **Expenses** Tuition $3307; Room & Board $7707 **Undergraduates** 65% women, 30% part-time, 26% 25 or older, 1% Native American, 30% Hispanic American, 4% African American, 12% Asian American/Pacific Islander **The most frequently chosen baccalaureate fields are** business/marketing, liberal arts/general studies, social sciences **Academic program** English as a second language, advanced placement, self-designed majors, honors program, summer session, adult/continuing education programs, internships **Contact** Student Outreach, California State University, Stanislaus, 801 West Monte Vista Avenue, Turlock, CA 95382. Phone: 209-667-3152 or toll-free 800-300-7420. Fax: 209-667-3788. E-mail: outreach_help_desk@csustan.edu. Web site: http://www.csustan.edu/.

CHAPMAN UNIVERSITY

ORANGE, CALIFORNIA

General Independent, comprehensive, coed, affiliated with Christian Church (Disciples of Christ) **Entrance** Moderately difficult **Setting** 76-acre suburban campus **Total enrollment** 6,022 **Student-faculty ratio** 14:1 **Application deadline** 1/15 (freshmen), 3/15 (transfer) **Freshmen** 49% were admitted **Housing** Yes **Expenses** Tuition $34,700; Room & Board $11,315 **Undergraduates** 59% women, 5% part-time, 5% 25 or older, 1% Native American, 10% Hispanic American, 2% African American, 8% Asian American/Pacific Islander **The most frequently chosen baccalaureate fields are** business/marketing, communications/journalism, visual and performing arts **Academic program** English as a second language, advanced placement, self-designed majors, honors program, summer session, adult/continuing education programs, internships **Contact** Mr. Michael Drummy, Assistant Vice President of Enrollment Services and Chief Admission Officer, Chapman University, One University Drive, Orange, CA 92866. Phone: 714-997-6711 or toll-free 888-CUAPPLY. Fax: 714-997-6713. E-mail: admit@chapman.edu. Web site: http://www.chapman.edu/.

▶**For more information, see page 449.**

CHARLES R. DREW UNIVERSITY OF MEDICINE AND SCIENCE

LOS ANGELES, CALIFORNIA

Contact Ms. Maranda Montgomery, Director, Student Affairs, Charles R. Drew University of Medicine and Science, 1731 East 120th Street, Keck Building, Los Angeles, CA 90059. Phone: 323-563-5886. Fax: 323-563-4923. E-mail: mmmontgo@cdrewu.edu. Web site: http://www.cdrewu.edu/.

CLAREMONT McKENNA COLLEGE

CLAREMONT, CALIFORNIA

General Independent, 4-year, coed **Entrance** Most difficult **Setting** 50-acre small-town campus **Total enrollment** 1,135 **Student-faculty ratio** 9:1 **Application deadline** 1/2 (freshmen), 4/1 (transfer) **Freshmen** 18% were admitted **Housing** Yes **Expenses** Tuition $34,980; Room & Board $10,536 **Undergraduates** 46% women, 0.1% 25 or older, 0.2% Native American, 13% Hispanic American, 4% African American, 13% Asian American/Pacific Islander **The most frequently chosen baccalaureate fields are** psychology,

Claremont McKenna College *(continued)*

interdisciplinary studies, social sciences **Academic program** Advanced placement, accelerated degree program, self-designed majors, honors program, internships **Contact** Mr. Richard C. Vos, Vice President/Dean of Admission and Financial Aid, Claremont McKenna College, 890 Columbia Avenue, Claremont, CA 91711. Phone: 909-621-8088. Fax: 909-621-8516. E-mail: admission@claremontmckenna.edu. Web site: http://www.claremontmckenna.edu/.

CLEVELAND CHIROPRACTIC COLLEGE–LOS ANGELES CAMPUS
LOS ANGELES, CALIFORNIA

General Independent, upper-level, coed **Entrance** Minimally difficult **Setting** urban campus **Total enrollment** 372 **Student-faculty ratio** 7:1 **Application deadline** 8/29 (freshmen), 9/29 (transfer) **First-year students** 51% were admitted **Housing** No **Expenses** Tuition $6358 **Undergraduates** 38% women, 24% part-time, 54% 25 or older, 14% Hispanic American, 5% African American, 15% Asian American/Pacific Islander **The most frequently chosen baccalaureate field is** health professions and related sciences **Academic program** Advanced placement, accelerated degree program, summer session, adult/continuing education programs **Contact** Ms. Norma Ngiramolan, Cleveland Chiropractic College–Los Angeles Campus, 590 North Vermont Avenue, Los Angeles, CA 90004-2196. Phone: 323-906-2031 or toll-free 800-446-CCLA. Fax: 323-906-2094. E-mail: la.admissions@cleveland.edu. Web site: http://www.clevelandchiropractic.edu/.

COGSWELL POLYTECHNICAL COLLEGE
SUNNYVALE, CALIFORNIA

General Independent, 4-year, coed, primarily men **Entrance** Moderately difficult **Setting** 2-acre suburban campus **Total enrollment** 230 **Student-faculty ratio** 7:1 **Application deadline** 3/1 (freshmen), 3/1 (transfer) **Freshmen** 61% were admitted **Housing** Yes **Expenses** Tuition $17,268; Room only $3500 **Undergraduates** 18% women, 52% part-time, 51% 25 or older, 9% Hispanic American, 3% African American, 11% Asian American/Pacific Islander **The most frequently chosen baccalaureate fields are** security and protective services, engineering, visual and performing arts **Academic program** Advanced placement, summer session, adult/continuing education programs, internships **Contact** Mr. Bill Souza, Admissions Coordinator, Cogswell Polytechnical College, 1175 Bordeaux Drive, Sunnyvale, CA 94089. Phone: 408-541-0100 Ext. 136 or toll-free 800-264-7955. Fax: 408-747-0764. E-mail: info@cogswell.edu. Web site: http://www.cogswell.edu/.

THE COLBURN SCHOOL CONSERVATORY OF MUSIC
LOS ANGELES, CALIFORNIA

General Independent, 4-year, coed **Entrance** Most difficult **Setting** urban campus **Total enrollment** 96 **Student-faculty ratio** 6:1 **Application deadline** 1/15 (freshmen), 1/15 (transfer) **Freshmen** 19% were admitted **Housing** Yes **Expenses** Tuition $1400 **Undergraduates** 57% women **The most frequently chosen baccalaureate field is** visual and performing arts **Academic program** English as a second language **Contact** Ms. Agnieszka Laskus, Assistant for Admissions and Records, The Colburn School Conservatory of Music, 200 South Grand Avenue, Los Angeles, CA 90012. Phone: 213-621-4545. Fax: 213-625-0371. E-mail: admissions@colburnschool.edu. Web site: http://www.colburnschool.edu/.

COLEMAN COLLEGE
SAN DIEGO, CALIFORNIA

Contact Admissions Department, Coleman College, 7380 Parkway Drive, La Mesa, CA 91942-1532. Phone: 619-465-3990 Ext. 109. Fax: 619-463-0162. E-mail: jschafer@cts.com. Web site: http://www.coleman.edu/.

COLUMBIA COLLEGE HOLLYWOOD
TARZANA, CALIFORNIA

General Independent, 4-year, coed **Entrance** Minimally difficult **Setting** 1-acre urban campus **Total enrollment** 301 **Application deadline** Rolling (freshmen) **Freshmen** 60% were admitted **Housing** Yes **Expenses** Tuition $15,300 **Undergraduates** 26% women, 10% 25 or older **Academic program** Accelerated degree program, summer session, adult/continuing education programs **Contact** Carmen Munoz, Admissions Director, Columbia College Hollywood, 18618 Oxnard Street, Tarzana, CA 91356. Phone: 818-345-8414 Ext. 203 or toll-free 800-785-0585. Fax: 818-345-9053. E-mail: admissions@columbiacollege.edu. Web site: http://www.columbiacollege.edu/.

CONCORDIA UNIVERSITY
IRVINE, CALIFORNIA

General Independent, comprehensive, coed, affiliated with Lutheran Church–Missouri Synod **Entrance** Moderately difficult **Setting** 70-acre suburban campus **Total enrollment** 2,392 **Student-faculty ratio** 14:1 **Application deadline** Rolling (freshmen), rolling (transfer) **Freshmen** 67% were admitted **Housing** Yes **Expenses** Tuition $22,380; Room & Board $7480 **Undergraduates** 61% women, 4% part-time, 10% 25 or older, 1% Native American, 13% Hispanic

American, 4% African American, 4% Asian American/Pacific Islander **The most frequently chosen baccalaureate fields are** business/marketing, education, liberal arts/general studies **Academic program** English as a second language, advanced placement, accelerated degree program, self-designed majors, honors program, summer session, adult/continuing education programs, internships **Contact** Ms. Lori McDonald, Executive Director of Enrollment Services, Concordia University, 1530 Concordia West, Irvine, CA 92612-3299. Phone: 949-854-8002 Ext. 1419 or toll-free 800-229-1200. Fax: 949-854-6894. E-mail: admission@cui.edu. Web site: http://www.cui.edu/.

DESIGN INSTITUTE OF SAN DIEGO
SAN DIEGO, CALIFORNIA

Contact Ms. Paula Parrish, Director of Admissions, Design Institute of San Diego, 8555 Commerce Avenue, San Diego, CA 92121-2685. Phone: 858-566-1200 or toll-free 800-619-4337. Fax: 858-566-2711. E-mail: admissions@disd.edu. Web site: http://www.disd.edu/.

DEVRY UNIVERSITY
ELK GROVE, CALIFORNIA

Contact DeVry University, Sacramento Center, 2218 Kausen Drive, Elk Grove, CA 95758. Phone: toll-free 866-573-3879. Web site: http://www.devry.edu/.

DEVRY UNIVERSITY
FREMONT, CALIFORNIA

General Proprietary, comprehensive, coed **Entrance** Minimally difficult **Setting** 17-acre suburban campus **Total enrollment** 1,577 **Student-faculty ratio** 18:1 **Application deadline** Rolling (freshmen), rolling (transfer) **Housing** No **Expenses** Tuition $14,660 **Undergraduates** 30% women, 35% part-time, 40% 25 or older, 1% Native American, 18% Hispanic American, 10% African American, 26% Asian American/Pacific Islander **The most frequently chosen baccalaureate fields are** business/marketing, computer and information sciences, engineering technologies **Academic program** Advanced placement, accelerated degree program, summer session, adult/continuing education programs **Contact** Director of Admissions, DeVry University, 6600 Dumbarton Circle, Fremont, CA 94555. Web site: http://www.devry.edu/.

DEVRY UNIVERSITY
IRVINE, CALIFORNIA

Contact DeVry University, 3333 Michelson Drive, Suite 420, Irvine, CA 92612-1682. Web site: http://www.devry.edu/.

DEVRY UNIVERSITY
LONG BEACH, CALIFORNIA

General Proprietary, comprehensive, coed **Entrance** Minimally difficult **Setting** 23-acre urban campus **Total enrollment** 1,064 **Student-faculty ratio** 17:1 **Application deadline** Rolling (freshmen), rolling (transfer) **Housing** No **Expenses** Tuition $13,990 **Undergraduates** 32% women, 51% part-time, 53% 25 or older, 0.4% Native American, 38% Hispanic American, 13% African American, 24% Asian American/Pacific Islander **The most frequently chosen baccalaureate fields are** business/marketing, computer and information sciences, engineering technologies **Academic program** Advanced placement, accelerated degree program, summer session, adult/continuing education programs **Contact** Admissions Office, DeVry University, 3880 Kilroy Airport Way, Long Beach, CA 90806. Web site: http://www.devry.edu/.

DEVRY UNIVERSITY
PALMDALE, CALIFORNIA

Contact Admissions Office, DeVry University, 38256 Sierra Highway, Suite D, Palmdale, CA 93550. Phone: toll-free 866-986-9388. Web site: http://www.devry.edu/.

DEVRY UNIVERSITY
POMONA, CALIFORNIA

General Proprietary, comprehensive, coed **Entrance** Minimally difficult **Setting** 15-acre urban campus **Total enrollment** 1,717 **Student-faculty ratio** 25:1 **Application deadline** Rolling (freshmen), rolling (transfer) **Housing** No **Expenses** Tuition $13,990 **Undergraduates** 28% women, 51% part-time, 53% 25 or older, 1% Native American, 41% Hispanic American, 9% African American, 17% Asian American/Pacific Islander **The most frequently chosen baccalaureate fields are** business/marketing, computer and information sciences, engineering technologies **Academic program** Advanced placement, accelerated degree program, summer session, adult/continuing education programs **Contact** Admissions Office, DeVry University, 901 Corporate Center Drive, Pomona, CA 91768-2642. Web site: http://www.devry.edu/.

DEVRY UNIVERSITY
SAN DIEGO, CALIFORNIA

Contact DeVry University, 2655 Camino Del Rio North, Suite 201, San Diego, CA 92108-1633. Web site: http://www.devry.edu/.

DeVRY UNIVERSITY
SAN FRANCISCO, CALIFORNIA

Contact DeVry University, 455 Market Street, Suite 1650, San Francisco, CA 94105-2472. Web site: http://www.devry.edu/.

DeVRY UNIVERSITY
SHERMAN OAKS, CALIFORNIA

General Proprietary, comprehensive, coed **Total enrollment** 581 **Student-faculty ratio** 10:1 **Application deadline** Rolling (freshmen), rolling (transfer) **Expenses** Tuition $13,990 **Undergraduates** 29% women, 53% part-time, 52% 25 or older, 2% Native American, 32% Hispanic American, 7% African American, 20% Asian American/Pacific Islander **The most frequently chosen baccalaureate fields are** business/marketing, computer and information sciences, engineering technologies **Academic program** Accelerated degree program **Contact** Admissions Office, DeVry University, 15301 Ventura Boulevard, D-100, Sherman Oaks, CA 91403. Phone: toll-free 888-610-0800. Web site: http://www.devry.edu/.

DOMINICAN SCHOOL OF PHILOSOPHY AND THEOLOGY
BERKELEY, CALIFORNIA

General Independent Roman Catholic, upper-level, coed **Contact** Mr. John D. Knutsen, Director of Admissions, Dominican School of Philosophy and Theology, 2301 Vine Street, Berkeley, CA 94708. Phone: 510-883-2073. Fax: 510-849-1372. E-mail: admissions@dspt.edu. Web site: http://www.dspt.edu/.

DOMINICAN UNIVERSITY OF CALIFORNIA
SAN RAFAEL, CALIFORNIA

General Independent, comprehensive, coed, affiliated with Roman Catholic Church **Entrance** Moderately difficult **Setting** 80-acre suburban campus **Total enrollment** 2,125 **Student-faculty ratio** 11:1 **Application deadline** 8/1 (freshmen), rolling (transfer) **Freshmen** 56% were admitted **Housing** Yes **Expenses** Tuition $32,360; Room & Board $12,560 **Undergraduates** 76% women, 22% part-time, 26% 25 or older, 1% Native American, 16% Hispanic American, 7% African American, 21% Asian American/Pacific Islander **The most frequently chosen baccalaureate fields are** business/marketing, health professions and related sciences, psychology **Academic program** English as a second language, advanced placement, self-designed majors, honors program, summer session, adult/continuing education programs, internships **Contact** Ms. Rebecca Finn Kenney, Director of Undergraduate Admissions, Dominican University of California, 50 Acacia Avenue, San Rafael, CA 94901-2298. Phone: 415-485-3204 or toll-free 888-323-6763. Fax: 415-485-3214. E-mail: enroll@dominican.edu. Web site: http://www.dominican.edu/.

►**For more information, see page 455.**

EMMANUEL BIBLE COLLEGE
PASADENA, CALIFORNIA

Contact Mr. Hovel Babikian, President, Emmanuel Bible College, 1605 East Elizabeth Street, Pasadena, CA 91104. Phone: 626-791-2575. Fax: 626-398-2424. Web site: http://www.emmanuelbiblecollege.edu/.

FRESNO PACIFIC UNIVERSITY
FRESNO, CALIFORNIA

General Independent, comprehensive, coed, affiliated with Mennonite Brethren Church **Entrance** Moderately difficult **Setting** 42-acre suburban campus **Total enrollment** 2,353 **Student-faculty ratio** 11:1 **Application deadline** Rolling (freshmen), rolling (transfer) **Freshmen** 68% were admitted **Housing** Yes **Expenses** Tuition $21,796; Room & Board $6600 **Undergraduates** 69% women, 15% part-time, 1% Native American, 29% Hispanic American, 4% African American, 4% Asian American/Pacific Islander **The most frequently chosen baccalaureate fields are** business/marketing, education, psychology **Academic program** English as a second language, advanced placement, accelerated degree program, self-designed majors, summer session, adult/continuing education programs, internships **Contact** Fresno Pacific University, 1717 South Chestnut Avenue, #2005, Fresno, CA 93727. Phone: 800-660-6089 or toll-free 800-660-6089. Fax: 559-453-2007. E-mail: ugadmis@fresno.edu. Web site: http://www.fresno.edu/.

GOLDEN GATE UNIVERSITY
SAN FRANCISCO, CALIFORNIA

General Independent, university, coed **Entrance** Moderately difficult **Setting** urban campus **Total enrollment** 3,891 **Student-faculty ratio** 16:1 **Application deadline** Rolling (freshmen), rolling (transfer) **Housing** No **Expenses** Tuition $12,240 **Undergraduates** 53% women, 76% part-time, 76% 25 or older, 1% Native American, 11% Hispanic American, 9% African American, 17% Asian American/Pacific Islander **The most frequently chosen baccalaureate fields are** business/marketing, computer and information sciences, liberal arts/general studies **Academic program** English as a second language, advanced placement, accelerated degree program, summer session, adult/continuing education programs, internships **Contact** Mr. Louis D. Riccardi Jr., Director of Enrollment Services, Golden Gate University, 536 Mission Street, San Francisco, CA 94105-2968. Phone: 415-442-7800 or toll-free 800-448-3381. Fax: 415-442-7807. E-mail: info@ggu.edu. Web site: http://www.ggu.edu/.

HARVEY MUDD COLLEGE
CLAREMONT, CALIFORNIA

General Independent, 4-year, coed **Entrance** Most difficult **Setting** 33-acre suburban campus **Total enrollment** 735 **Student-faculty ratio** 9:1 **Application deadline** 1/2 (freshmen), 4/1 (transfer) **Freshmen** 28% were admitted **Housing** Yes **Expenses** Tuition $34,891; Room & Board $11,415 **Undergraduates** 33% women, 1% Native American, 8% Hispanic American, 1% African American, 20% Asian American/Pacific Islander **The most frequently chosen baccalaureate fields are** engineering, computer and information sciences, mathematics **Academic program** Advanced placement, self-designed majors, internships **Contact** Mr. Peter Osgood, Director of Admissions, Harvey Mudd College, 301 Platt Boulevard, Claremont, CA 91711. Phone: 909-621-8011. Fax: 909-607-7046. E-mail: admission@hmc.edu. Web site: http://www.hmc.edu/.

HOLY NAMES UNIVERSITY
OAKLAND, CALIFORNIA

General Independent Roman Catholic, comprehensive, coed, primarily women **Entrance** Moderately difficult **Setting** 60-acre urban campus **Total enrollment** 1,114 **Student-faculty ratio** 12:1 **Application deadline** 8/1 (freshmen), 8/1 (transfer) **Freshmen** 27% were admitted **Housing** Yes **Expenses** Tuition $25,060; Room & Board $8400 **Undergraduates** 72% women, 23% part-time, 37% 25 or older, 1% Native American, 16% Hispanic American, 30% African American, 13% Asian American/Pacific Islander **The most frequently chosen baccalaureate fields are** business/marketing, health professions and related sciences, liberal arts/general studies **Academic program** English as a second language, advanced placement, accelerated degree program, self-designed majors, summer session, adult/continuing education programs, internships **Contact** Marcia Nance, Holy Names University, 3500 Mountain Boulevard, Oakland, CA 94619-1699. Phone: 510-436-1351 or toll-free 800-430-1321. Fax: 510-436-1325. E-mail: admissions@hnu.edu. Web site: http://www.hnu.edu/.

HOPE INTERNATIONAL UNIVERSITY
FULLERTON, CALIFORNIA

General Independent, comprehensive, coed, affiliated with Christian Churches and Churches of Christ **Entrance** Moderately difficult **Setting** 16-acre suburban campus **Total enrollment** 948 **Student-faculty ratio** 8:1 **Application deadline** 5/1 (freshmen), 6/1 (transfer) **Freshmen** 71% were admitted **Housing** Yes **Expenses** Tuition $22,761; Room & Board $8230 **Undergraduates** 60% women, 17% part-time, 35% 25 or older, 1% Native American, 15% Hispanic American, 5% African American, 5% Asian American/Pacific Islander **The most frequently chosen baccalaureate fields are** business/marketing, family and consumer sciences, theology and religious vocations **Academic program** English as a second language, advanced placement, accelerated degree program, summer session, adult/continuing education programs, internships **Contact** Ms. Midge Madden, Office Manager, Hope International University, 2500 East Nutwood Avenue, Fullerton, CA 92831-3138. Phone: 714-879-3901 Ext. 2215 or toll-free 800-762-1294. Fax: 714-681-7423. E-mail: mfmadden@hiu.edu. Web site: http://www.hiu.edu/.

HUMBOLDT STATE UNIVERSITY
ARCATA, CALIFORNIA

General State-supported, comprehensive, coed **Entrance** Moderately difficult **Setting** 161-acre rural campus **Total enrollment** 7,773 **Student-faculty ratio** 19:1 **Application deadline** 1/1 (freshmen), 6/1 (transfer) **Freshmen** 82% were admitted **Housing** Yes **Expenses** Room & Board $8522 **Undergraduates** 53% women, 10% part-time, 22% 25 or older, 2% Native American, 11% Hispanic American, 4% African American, 5% Asian American/Pacific Islander **The most frequently chosen baccalaureate fields are** social sciences, liberal arts/general studies, visual and performing arts **Academic program** English as a second language, advanced placement, self-designed majors, honors program, summer session, adult/continuing education programs, internships **Contact** Ms. Rebecca Kalal, Assistant Director of Admissions, Humboldt State University, 1 Harpst Street, Arcata, CA 95521-8299. Phone: 707-826-6221. Fax: 707-826-6190. E-mail: hsuinfo@humboldt.edu. Web site: http://www.humboldt.edu/.

HUMPHREYS COLLEGE
STOCKTON, CALIFORNIA

Contact Ms. Wilma Okamoto Vaughn, Dean of Administration, Humphreys College, 6650 Inglewood Avenue, Stockton, CA 95207-3896. Phone: 209-478-0800. Fax: 209-478-8721. Web site: http://www.humphreys.edu/.

INTERIOR DESIGNERS INSTITUTE
NEWPORT BEACH, CALIFORNIA

Contact Interior Designers Institute, 1061 Camelback Road, Newport Beach, CA 92660.

Interior Designers Institute *(continued)*

Fax: 949-759-0667. E-mail: contact@idi.edu. Web site: http://www.idi.edu/.

INTERNATIONAL TECHNOLOGICAL UNIVERSITY
SANTA CLARA, CALIFORNIA

Contact Chun Mou Peng, Director of Operations, International Technological University, 1650 Warburton Avenue, Santa Clara, CA 95050. Phone: 408-556-9027. E-mail: chunmou@itu.edu. Web site: http://www.itu.edu/.

ITT TECHNICAL INSTITUTE
CLOVIS, CALIFORNIA

General Proprietary, 4-year, coed **Contact** Ms. Linda Stolling, Director of Recruitment, ITT Technical Institute, 362 North Clovis Avenue, Clovis, NM 93612. Phone: 559-325-5400 or toll-free 800-564-9771. Fax: 559-325-5499. Web site: http://www.itt-tech.edu/campus/school.cfm?lloc_num=61.

JOHN F. KENNEDY UNIVERSITY
PLEASANT HILL, CALIFORNIA

General Independent, upper-level, coed **Entrance** Noncompetitive **Setting** 5-acre suburban campus **Total enrollment** 1,565 **Student-faculty ratio** 9:1 **Application deadline** Rolling (transfer) **Housing** No **Expenses** Tuition $12,408 **Undergraduates** 71% women, 83% part-time, 89% 25 or older, 2% Native American, 9% Hispanic American, 9% African American, 8% Asian American/Pacific Islander **The most frequently chosen baccalaureate fields are** business/marketing, liberal arts/general studies, psychology **Academic program** Advanced placement, self-designed majors, summer session, adult/continuing education programs **Contact** Ms. Jen Miller-Hogg, Director of Admissions, John F. Kennedy University, 100 Ellinwood Way, Pleasant Hill, CA 94523-4817. Phone: 925-969-3584 or toll-free 800-696-JFKU. Fax: 925-969-3328. E-mail: proginfo@jfku.edu. Web site: http://www.jfku.edu/.

THE KING'S COLLEGE AND SEMINARY
VAN NUYS, CALIFORNIA

Contact Mrs. Marilyn J. Chappell, Director of Admissions, The King's College and Seminary, 14800 Sherman Way, Van Nuys, CA 91405-8040. Phone: 818-779-8040 or toll-free 888-779-8040. Fax: 818-779-8429. E-mail: mchappell@kingscollege.edu. Web site: http://www.kingscollege.edu/.

LA COLLEGE INTERNATIONAL
LOS ANGELES, CALIFORNIA

General Proprietary, 4-year, coed **Entrance** Noncompetitive **Setting** urban campus **Total enrollment** 85 **Student-faculty ratio** 5:1 **Housing** No **Expenses** Tuition $19,575 **Undergraduates** 44% women, 49% 25 or older, 61% Hispanic American, 20% African American, 9% Asian American/Pacific Islander **The most frequently chosen baccalaureate fields are** business/marketing, computer and information sciences **Academic program** Advanced placement, internships **Contact** Shavonne Turner, Director of Admissions, LA College International, 3200 Wilshire Boulevard, # 400, Los Angeles, CA 90010-1308. Phone: 213-381-3333 or toll-free 800-57 GO ICT. Fax: 213-383-9369. E-mail: sturner@lac.edu. Web site: http://www.lac.edu/.

LAGUNA COLLEGE OF ART & DESIGN
LAGUNA BEACH, CALIFORNIA

General Independent, 4-year, coed **Entrance** Very difficult **Setting** 9-acre small-town campus **Total enrollment** 310 **Student-faculty ratio** 10:1 **Freshmen** 88% were admitted **Housing** No **Expenses** Tuition $20,600 **Undergraduates** 47% women, 22% 25 or older, 1% Native American, 9% Hispanic American, 2% African American, 15% Asian American/Pacific Islander **Academic program** English as a second language, advanced placement, summer session, adult/continuing education programs, internships **Contact** Mike Rivas, Vice President of Enrollment, Laguna College of Art & Design, 2222 Laguna Canyon Road, Laguna Beach, CA 92651-1136. Phone: 949-376-6000 Ext. 232 or toll-free 800-255-0762. Fax: 949-376-6009. E-mail: admissions@lagunacollege.edu. Web site: http://www.lagunacollege.edu/.

LA SIERRA UNIVERSITY
RIVERSIDE, CALIFORNIA

General Independent Seventh-day Adventist, comprehensive, coed **Entrance** Moderately difficult **Setting** 100-acre suburban campus **Total enrollment** 1,749 **Student-faculty ratio** 13:1 **Application deadline** Rolling (freshmen), rolling (transfer) **Freshmen** 45% were admitted **Housing** Yes **Expenses** Tuition $23,154; Room & Board $6711 **Undergraduates** 59% women, 12% part-time, 12% 25 or older, 0.5% Native American, 26% Hispanic American, 8% African American, 25% Asian American/Pacific Islander **The most frequently chosen baccalaureate fields are** biological/life sciences, business/marketing, liberal arts/general studies **Academic program** English as a second language, advanced placement, accelerated degree program, self-designed majors, honors program, summer session, adult/continuing education programs, internships **Contact** Faye Swayze, Director of Admissions and Registrar, La Sierra University, 4500 Riverwalk Parkway, Riverside, CA 92515. Phone: 951-785-2176 or toll-free 800-874-5587. Fax: 951-785-2477. E-mail: admissions@lasierra.edu. Web site: http://www.lasierra.edu/.

LIFE PACIFIC COLLEGE
SAN DIMAS, CALIFORNIA

Contact Ms. Gina Nicodemus, Director of Admissions, Life Pacific College, 1100 Covina Boulevard, San Dimas, CA 91773-3298. Phone: 909-599-5433 Ext. 314 or toll-free 877-886-5433 Ext. 314. Fax: 909-706-3070. E-mail: adm@lifepacific.edu. Web site: http://www.lifepacific.edu/.

LINCOLN UNIVERSITY
OAKLAND, CALIFORNIA

General Independent, comprehensive, coed **Entrance** Minimally difficult **Setting** 2-acre urban campus **Total enrollment** 319 **Student-faculty ratio** 14:1 **Application deadline** 8/22 (freshmen), 8/22 (transfer) **Freshmen** 93% were admitted **Housing** No **Expenses** Tuition $8230 **Undergraduates** 65% women, 11% part-time, 20% 25 or older **Academic program** English as a second language, advanced placement, summer session, internships **Contact** Ms. Helen Zhou, Admissions Officer, Lincoln University, 401 15th Street, Oakland, CA 94612. Phone: 510-628-8010. Fax: 510-628-8012. E-mail: adminofficer@lincolnuca.edu. Web site: http://www.lincolnuca.edu/.

LOMA LINDA UNIVERSITY
LOMA LINDA, CALIFORNIA

General Independent Seventh-day Adventist, upper-level, coed **Setting** small-town campus **Total enrollment** 4,270 **Student-faculty ratio** 8:1 **Housing** Yes **Expenses** Tuition $27,320; Room only $2460 **Undergraduates** 72% women, 28% part-time, 50% 25 or older, 1% Native American, 17% Hispanic American, 7% African American, 23% Asian American/Pacific Islander **The most frequently chosen baccalaureate field is** health professions and related sciences **Academic program** English as a second language, internships **Contact** Admissions Office, Loma Linda University, Loma Linda, CA 92350. Phone: 909-558-1000. Web site: http://www.llu.edu/.

LOYOLA MARYMOUNT UNIVERSITY
LOS ANGELES, CALIFORNIA

General Independent Roman Catholic, comprehensive, coed **Entrance** Very difficult **Setting** 128-acre suburban campus **Total enrollment** 8,977 **Student-faculty ratio** 13:1 **Application deadline** 1/15 (freshmen), 6/1 (transfer) **Freshmen** 52% were admitted **Housing** Yes **Expenses** Tuition $31,914; Room & Board $11,145 **Undergraduates** 58% women, 5% part-time, 2% 25 or older, 1% Native American, 20% Hispanic American, 8% African American, 13% Asian American/Pacific Islander **The most frequently chosen baccalaureate fields are** business/marketing, communications/journalism, visual and performing arts **Academic program** Advanced placement, accelerated degree program, self-designed majors, honors program, summer session, adult/continuing education programs, internships **Contact** Mr. Matthew X. Fissinger, Director of Admissions, Loyola Marymount University, One LMU Drive, Los Angeles, CA 90045-2659. Phone: 310-338-2750 or toll-free 800-LMU-INFO. E-mail: admissions@lmu.edu. Web site: http://www.lmu.edu/.

THE MASTER'S COLLEGE AND SEMINARY
SANTA CLARITA, CALIFORNIA

General Independent nondenominational, comprehensive, coed **Entrance** Moderately difficult **Setting** 110-acre suburban campus **Total enrollment** 1,516 **Student-faculty ratio** 16:1 **Application deadline** 3/2 (transfer) **Freshmen** 84% were admitted **Housing** Yes **Expenses** Tuition $23,120; Room & Board $7250 **Undergraduates** 51% women, 16% part-time, 18% 25 or older, 1% Native American, 7% Hispanic American, 2% African American, 5% Asian American/Pacific Islander **The most frequently chosen baccalaureate fields are** business/marketing, liberal arts/general studies, philosophy and religious studies **Academic program** Advanced placement, accelerated degree program, summer session, adult/continuing education programs, internships **Contact** Ms. Hollie Gorsh, Director of Admissions, The Master's College and Seminary, 21726 Placerita Canyon Road, Santa Clarita, CA 91321. Phone: 661-259-3540 Ext. 3369 or toll-free 800-568-6248. Fax: 661-288-1037. E-mail: admissions@masters.edu. Web site: http://www.masters.edu/.

MENLO COLLEGE
ATHERTON, CALIFORNIA

General Independent, 4-year, coed **Contact** Mr. Ken Bowman, Director of Admission, Menlo College, 1000 El Camino Real, Atherton, CA 94027. Phone: 650-543-3932 or toll-free 800-556-3656. Fax: 650-543-4496. E-mail: admissions@menlo.edu. Web site: http://www.menlo.edu/.

MILLS COLLEGE
OAKLAND, CALIFORNIA

General Independent, comprehensive, undergraduate: women only; graduate: coed **Entrance** Moderately difficult **Setting** 135-acre urban campus **Total enrollment** 1,446 **Student-faculty ratio** 11:1 **Application deadline** 5/1 (freshmen), 3/1 (transfer) **Freshmen** 64% were admitted **Housing** Yes **Expenses** Tuition $35,432; Room & Board $10,820 **Undergraduates** 6% part-time, 20% 25 or older, 1% Native American, 15% Hispanic American, 10% African American, 8% Asian American/Pacific Islander **The most frequently chosen baccalaureate fields are** English, social sciences, visual and performing arts **Academic program** Advanced placement, self-designed majors, honors program, adult/continuing education programs, internships **Contact** Ms. Giulietta Aquino, Vice President of Enrollment Management, Mills College, 5000 MacArthur Boulevard, Oakland, CA 94613-1301. Phone: 510-430-2135 or toll-free 800-87-MILLS. Fax: 510-430-3314. E-mail: admission@mills.edu. Web site: http://www.mills.edu/.

▶**For more information, see page 475.**

MOUNT ST. MARY'S COLLEGE
LOS ANGELES, CALIFORNIA

General Independent Roman Catholic, comprehensive, coed, primarily women **Entrance** Moderately difficult **Setting** 71-acre suburban campus **Total enrollment** 2,366 **Student-faculty ratio** 14:1 **Application deadline** 2/15 (freshmen), 3/15 (transfer) **Freshmen** 86% were admitted **Housing** Yes **Expenses** Tuition $25,358; Room & Board $9620 **Undergraduates** 93% women, 25% part-time, 28% 25 or older, 0.5% Native American, 45% Hispanic American, 9% African American, 24% Asian American/Pacific Islander **The most frequently chosen baccalaureate fields are** health professions and related sciences, business/marketing, social sciences **Academic program** English as a second language, advanced placement, accelerated degree program, self-designed majors, honors program, summer session, adult/continuing education programs, internships **Contact** Ms. Shannon Shank, Interim Director of Admissions, Mount St. Mary's College, 12001 Chalon Road, Los Angeles, CA 90049-1599. Phone: 310-954-4252 or toll-free 800-999-9893. Fax: 310-954-4259. E-mail: admissions@msmc.la.edu. Web site: http://www.msmc.la.edu/.

MT. SIERRA COLLEGE
MONROVIA, CALIFORNIA

Contact Kimberly Rodriguez-Delaney, Director of Admissions, Mt. Sierra College, 101 East Huntington Drive, Monrovia, CA 91016. Phone: 626-873-2100 Ext. 213 or toll-free 888-828-8800.. Fax: 626-359-5528. E-mail: krodriguez@mtsierra.edu. Web site: http://www.mtsierra.edu/.

MUSICIANS INSTITUTE
HOLLYWOOD, CALIFORNIA

Contact Mr. Steve Lunn, Admissions Representative, Musicians Institute, 1655 North McCadden Place, Hollywood, CA 90028. Phone: 323-462-1384 Ext. 156 or toll-free 800-255-PLAY. E-mail: admissions@mi.edu. Web site: http://www.mi.edu/.

THE NATIONAL HISPANIC UNIVERSITY
SAN JOSE, CALIFORNIA

Contact Ms. Pamela Bustillo, Director of Office of Admissions/Registrar, The National Hispanic University, 14271 Story Road, San Jose, CA 95127-3823. Phone: 408-254-6900. Web site: http://www.nhu.edu/.

NATIONAL UNIVERSITY
LA JOLLA, CALIFORNIA

General Independent, comprehensive, coed **Entrance** Minimally difficult **Setting** urban campus **Total enrollment** 26,363 **Student-faculty ratio** 17:1 **Application deadline** Rolling (freshmen), rolling (transfer) **Freshmen** 100% were admitted **Housing** No **Expenses** Tuition $9780 **Undergraduates** 60% women, 69% part-time, 75% 25 or older, 1% Native American, 16% Hispanic American, 11% African American, 9% Asian American/Pacific Islander **The most frequently chosen baccalaureate fields are** business/marketing, computer and information sciences, law/legal studies **Academic program** English as a second language, advanced placement, accelerated degree program, summer session, adult/continuing education programs, internships **Contact** Mr. Dominick Giovanniello, Associate Regional Dean, San Diego, National University, 11255 North Torrey Pines Road, La Jolla, CA 92037. Phone: 858-628-8648 Ext. 7701 or toll-free 800-NAT-UNIV. Fax: 858-541-7792. E-mail: dgiovann@nu.edu. Web site: http://www.nu.edu/.

NEWSCHOOL OF ARCHITECTURE & DESIGN
SAN DIEGO, CALIFORNIA

Contact Ms. Lexi Rogers, Director of Admissions, Newschool of Architecture & Design, 1249 F Street, San Diego, CA 92101-6634. Phone: 619-235-4100 Ext. 104. E-mail: admissions@newschoolarch.edu. Web site: http://www.newschoolarch.edu/.

NORTHWESTERN POLYTECHNIC UNIVERSITY
FREMONT, CALIFORNIA

General Independent, comprehensive, coed **Contact** Ms. Catherine Meng, Admission Officer, Northwestern Polytechnic University, 47671 Westinghouse Drive, Fremont, CA 94539. Phone: 510-248-4584. Fax: 510-657-8975. E-mail: admission@npu.edu. Web site: http://www.npu.edu/.

NOTRE DAME DE NAMUR UNIVERSITY
BELMONT, CALIFORNIA

General Independent Roman Catholic, comprehensive, coed **Entrance** Minimally difficult **Setting** 80-acre suburban campus **Total enrollment** 1,491 **Student-faculty ratio** 11:1 **Application deadline** Rolling (freshmen), rolling (transfer) **Freshmen** 99% were admitted **Housing** Yes **Expenses** Tuition $25,570; Room & Board $10,680 **Undergraduates** 67% women, 30% part-time, 21% 25 or older, 1% Native American, 20% Hispanic American, 5% African American, 15% Asian American/Pacific Islander **The most frequently chosen baccalaureate fields are** business/marketing, psychology, public administration and social services **Academic program** English as a second language, advanced placement, accelerated degree program, self-designed majors, summer session, adult/continuing education programs, internships **Contact** Mr. Brian O'Rourke, Associate Director for Undergraduate Admission, Notre Dame de Namur University, 1500 Ralston Avenue, Belmont, CA 94002-1908. Phone: 650-508-3525 or toll-free 800-263-0545. Fax: 650-508-3426. E-mail: Borourke@ndnu.edu. Web site: http://www.ndnu.edu/.

OCCIDENTAL COLLEGE
LOS ANGELES, CALIFORNIA

General Independent, comprehensive, coed **Entrance** Very difficult **Setting** 120-acre urban campus **Total enrollment** 1,877 **Student-faculty ratio** 10:1 **Application deadline** 1/10 (freshmen), 3/15 (transfer) **Freshmen** 44% were admitted **Housing** Yes **Expenses** Tuition $37,093; Room & Board $10,270 **Undergraduates** 56% women, 1% part-time, 1% 25 or older, 1% Native American, 15% Hispanic American, 6% African American, 13% Asian American/Pacific Islander **The most frequently chosen baccalaureate fields are** history, social sciences, visual and performing arts **Academic program** Advanced placement, self-designed majors, honors program, summer session, internships **Contact** Mr. Vince Cuseo, Dean of Admission, Occidental College, 1600 Campus Road, Los Angeles, CA 90041. Phone: 323-259-2700 or toll-free 800-825-5262. Fax: 323-341-4875. E-mail: admission@oxy.edu. Web site: http://www.oxy.edu/.

OTIS COLLEGE OF ART AND DESIGN
LOS ANGELES, CALIFORNIA

General Independent, comprehensive, coed **Entrance** Moderately difficult **Setting** 5-acre urban campus **Total enrollment** 1,177 **Student-faculty ratio** 9:1 **Application deadline** Rolling (freshmen), rolling (transfer) **Freshmen** 42% were admitted **Housing** Yes **Expenses** Tuition $28,946 **Undergraduates** 68% women, 2% part-time, 18% 25 or older, 1% Native American, 14% Hispanic American, 3% African American, 28% Asian American/Pacific Islander **The most frequently chosen baccalaureate fields are** architecture, visual and performing arts **Academic program** English as a second language, advanced placement, honors program, summer session, adult/continuing education programs, internships **Contact** Mr. Marc D. Meredith, Dean of Admissions, Otis College of Art and Design, 9045 Lincoln Boulevard, Los Angeles, CA 90045-9785. Phone: 310-665-6820 or toll-free 800-527-OTIS. Fax: 310-665-6821. E-mail: admissions@otis.edu. Web site: http://www.otis.edu/.

PACIFIC OAKS COLLEGE
PASADENA, CALIFORNIA

General Independent, upper-level, coed, primarily women **Contact** Ms. Augusta Pickens, Office of Admissions, Pacific Oaks College, 5 Westmoreland Place, Pasadena, CA 91103. Phone: 626-397-4945 or toll-free 800-684-0900. Fax: 626-666-1220. E-mail: admissions@pacificoaks.edu. Web site: http://www.pacificoaks.edu/.

PACIFIC STATES UNIVERSITY
LOS ANGELES, CALIFORNIA

General Independent, comprehensive, coed **Entrance** Minimally difficult **Setting** 1-acre urban campus **Total enrollment** 68 **Student-faculty ratio** 20:1 **Application deadline** 9/21 (freshmen), 10/27 (transfer) **Freshmen** 100% were admitted **Housing** No **Expenses** Tuition $8860 **Undergraduates** 100% 25 or older, 100% Asian American/Pacific Islander **Academic program** English as a second language, accelerated degree program, self-designed majors, summer session, adult/continuing education programs **Contact** Ms. Marina Miller, Assistant Director of Admissions, Pacific States University, 1516 South Western Avenue, Los Angeles, CA 90006. Phone: 323-731-2383 or toll-free 888-200-0383. Fax: 323-731-7276. E-mail: admission@psuca.edu. Web site: http://www.psuca.edu/.

PACIFIC UNION COLLEGE
ANGWIN, CALIFORNIA

General Independent Seventh-day Adventist, 4-year, coed **Entrance** Moderately difficult **Setting** 200-acre rural campus **Total enrollment** 1,375 **Student-faculty ratio** 15:1 **Application deadline** Rolling (freshmen), rolling (transfer) **Freshmen** 75% were admitted **Housing** Yes **Expenses** Tuition $21,435; Room & Board $5955 **Undergraduates** 54% women, 11% part-time, 11% 25 or older, 0.4% Native American, 15% Hispanic American, 3% African American, 26% Asian American/Pacific Islander **The most frequently chosen baccalaureate fields are** business/marketing, health professions and related sciences, physical sciences **Academic program** Advanced placement, self-designed majors, honors program, summer session, adult/continuing education programs, internships **Contact** Mr. Darren Hagen, Director of Enrollment Services, Pacific Union College, Enrollment Services, One Angwin Avenue, Angwin, CA 94508. Phone: 707-965-6425 or toll-free 800-862-7080. Fax: 707-965-6432. E-mail: enroll@puc.edu. Web site: http://www.puc.edu/.

PATTEN UNIVERSITY
OAKLAND, CALIFORNIA

General Independent interdenominational, comprehensive, coed **Entrance** Noncompetitive **Setting** 5-acre urban campus **Total enrollment** 791 **Student-faculty ratio** 14:1 **Application deadline** Rolling (freshmen), rolling (transfer) **Housing** Yes **Expenses** Tuition $12,480; Room & Board $6980 **Undergraduates** 39% women, 67% part-time, 59% 25 or older, 1% Native American, 9% Hispanic American, 16% African American, 10% Asian American/Pacific Islander **The most frequently chosen baccalaureate fields are** psychology, business/marketing, theology and religious vocations **Academic program** Advanced placement, accelerated degree program, honors program, summer session, adult/continuing education programs, internships **Contact** Ms. Kim Guerra, Patten University, 2433 Coolidge Avenue, Oakland, CA 94601-2699. Phone: 510-261-8500 Ext. 7763. Fax: 510-534-4344. E-mail: kim.guerra@patten.edu. Web site: http://www.patten.edu/.

PEPPERDINE UNIVERSITY
MALIBU, CALIFORNIA

General Independent, university, coed, affiliated with Church of Christ **Entrance** Very difficult **Setting** 830-acre small-town campus **Total enrollment** 7,582 **Student-faculty ratio** 13:1 **Application deadline** 1/15 (freshmen), 1/15 (transfer) **Freshmen** 35% were admitted **Housing** Yes **Expenses** Tuition $34,700; Room & Board $9930 **Undergraduates** 55% women, 14% part-time, 1% Native American, 10% Hispanic American, 7% African American, 10% Asian American/Pacific Islander **The most frequently chosen baccalaureate fields are** business/marketing, communications/journalism, social sciences **Academic program** Advanced placement, self-designed majors, honors program, summer session, internships **Contact** Mr. Paul A. Long, Dean of Admission and Enrollment Management, Pepperdine University, 24255 Pacific Coast Highway, Malibu, CA 90263. Phone: 310-506-4392. Fax: 310-506-4861. E-mail: admission-seaver@pepperdine.edu. Web site: http://www.pepperdine.edu/.

PITZER COLLEGE
CLAREMONT, CALIFORNIA

General Independent, 4-year, coed **Entrance** Moderately difficult **Setting** 35-acre suburban campus **Total enrollment** 999 **Student-faculty ratio** 12:1 **Application deadline** 1/1 (freshmen), 4/15 (transfer) **Freshmen** 26% were admitted **Housing** Yes **Expenses** Tuition $35,912; Room & Board $10,212 **Undergraduates** 59% women, 4% part-time, 6% 25 or older, 0.3% Native American, 14% Hispanic American, 6% African American, 10% Asian American/Pacific Islander **The most frequently chosen baccalaureate fields are** interdisciplinary studies, psychology, social sciences **Academic program** English as a second language, advanced placement, self-designed majors, honors program, summer session, adult/continuing education programs, internships **Contact** Angel Perez, Director of Admission, Pitzer College, 1050 North Mills Avenue, Claremont, CA 91711-6101. Phone: 909-621-8129 or toll-free 800-748-9371. Fax: 909-621-8770. E-mail: admission@pitzer.edu. Web site: http://www.pitzer.edu/.

POINT LOMA NAZARENE UNIVERSITY
SAN DIEGO, CALIFORNIA

General Independent Nazarene, comprehensive, coed **Entrance** Moderately difficult **Setting** 88-acre suburban campus **Total enrollment** 3,404 **Student-faculty ratio** 16:1 **Application deadline** 3/1 (freshmen), 3/1 (transfer) **Freshmen** 73% were admitted **Housing** Yes **Expenses** Tuition $24,820; Room & Board $8170 **Undergraduates** 61% women, 3% part-time, 2% 25 or older, 1% Native American, 11% Hispanic American, 2% African American, 6% Asian American/Pacific Islander **The most frequently chosen baccalaureate fields are** business/marketing, health professions and related sciences, psychology **Academic program** Advanced placement, honors program, summer session, internships **Contact** Mr. Chip Killingsworth, Director of Admissions, Point Loma Nazarene University, 3900 Lomaland Drive, San Diego, CA 92106. Phone: 619-849-2273 or toll-free 800-733-7770. Fax: 619-849-2601. E-mail: admissions@pointloma.edu. Web site: http://www.pointloma.edu/.

POMONA COLLEGE
CLAREMONT, CALIFORNIA

General Independent, 4-year, coed **Entrance** Most difficult **Setting** 140-acre suburban campus **Total enrollment** 1,522 **Student-faculty ratio** 8:1 **Application deadline** 1/2 (freshmen), 3/15 (transfer) **Freshmen** 16% were admitted **Housing** Yes **Expenses** Tuition $33,932; Room & Board $11,748 **Undergraduates** 50% women, 1% 25 or older, 0.3% Native American, 11% Hispanic American, 8% African American, 14% Asian American/Pacific Islander **Academic program** Advanced placement, self-designed majors, internships **Contact** Mr. Bruce Poch, Vice President and Dean of Admissions, Pomona College, 333 North College Way, Claremont, CA 91711. Phone: 909-621-8134. Fax: 909-621-8952. E-mail: admissions@pomona.edu. Web site: http://www.pomona.edu/.

REMINGTON COLLEGE–SAN DIEGO CAMPUS
SAN DIEGO, CALIFORNIA

General Proprietary, 4-year **Setting** 2-acre campus **Contact** April Webb, Director of Recruitment, Remington College–San Diego Campus, 123 Camino de la Reina, North Building, Suite 100, San Diego, CA 92108. Phone: 619-686-8600 or toll-free 800-214-7001. Fax: 619-686-8684. E-mail: april.webb@remingtoncollege.edu. Web site: http://www.remingtoncollege.edu/.

SAINT MARY'S COLLEGE OF CALIFORNIA
MORAGA, CALIFORNIA

General Independent Roman Catholic, comprehensive, coed **Entrance** Moderately difficult **Setting** 420-acre suburban campus **Total enrollment** 3,809 **Student-faculty ratio** 12:1 **Application deadline** 2/1 (freshmen), 7/1 (transfer) **Freshmen** 82% were admitted **Housing** Yes **Expenses** Tuition $31,080; Room & Board $11,090 **Undergraduates** 62% women, 11% part-time, 2% 25 or older, 1% Native American, 20% Hispanic American, 6% African American, 10% Asian American/Pacific Islander **The most frequently chosen baccalaureate fields are** business/marketing, communications/journalism, social sciences **Academic program** Advanced placement, self-designed majors, honors program, adult/continuing education programs, internships **Contact** Ms. Dorothy Jones, Dean of Admissions, Saint Mary's College of California, PO Box 4800, Moraga, CA 94556-4800. Phone: 925-631-4224 or toll-free 800-800-4SMC. Fax: 925-376-7193. E-mail: smcadmit@stmarys-ca.edu. Web site: http://www.stmarys-ca.edu/.

SAMUEL MERRITT COLLEGE
OAKLAND, CALIFORNIA

General Independent, upper-level, coed, primarily women **Entrance** Moderately difficult **Setting** 1-acre urban campus **Total enrollment** 1,278 **Student-faculty ratio** 9:1 **Application deadline** 3/1 (transfer) **Housing** Yes **Expenses** Tuition $30,974; Room only $6858 **Undergraduates** 88% women, 13% part-time, 65% 25 or older, 1% Native American, 10% Hispanic American, 6% African American, 27% Asian American/Pacific Islander **The most frequently chosen baccalaureate field is** health professions and related sciences **Academic program** Advanced placement, accelerated degree program, summer session, internships **Contact** Ms. Anne Seed, Director of Admissions, Samuel Merritt College, 570 Hawthorne Avenue, Oakland, CA 94609. Phone: 510-869-6610 or toll-free 800-607-MERRITT. Fax: 510-869-6525. E-mail: admission@samuelmerritt.edu. Web site: http://www.samuelmerritt.edu/.

SAN DIEGO CHRISTIAN COLLEGE
EL CAJON, CALIFORNIA

General Independent nondenominational, 4-year, coed **Entrance** Moderately difficult **Setting** 55-acre suburban campus **Total enrollment** 488 **Student-faculty ratio** 8:1 **Application deadline** 7/1 (freshmen), 7/1 (transfer) **Freshmen** 71% were admitted **Housing** Yes **Expenses** Tuition $20,480; Room & Board $7540 **Undergraduates** 54% women, 11% part-time, 18% 25 or older, 2% Native American, 14% Hispanic American, 7% African American, 5% Asian American/Pacific Islander **The most frequently chosen baccalaureate fields are** family and consumer sciences, interdisciplinary studies, psychology **Academic program** English as a second language, advanced placement, self-designed majors, honors program, summer session, adult/continuing education programs, internships **Contact** Candace Del Giudice, San Diego Christian College, 2100 Greenfield Drive, El Cajon, CA 92019-1157. Phone: 619-588-7747 or toll-free 800-676-2242. Fax: 619-590-1739. E-mail: cdelgiudice@sdcc.edu. Web site: http://www.sdcc.edu/.

SAN DIEGO STATE UNIVERSITY
SAN DIEGO, CALIFORNIA

General State-supported, university, coed **Entrance** Moderately difficult **Setting** 300-acre urban campus **Total enrollment** 36,559 **Student-faculty ratio** 20:1 **Application deadline** 11/30 (freshmen), 11/30 (transfer) **Freshmen** 44% were admitted **Housing** Yes **Expenses** Tuition $3428; Room & Board $10,904 **Undergraduates** 57% women, 17% part-time, 14% 25 or older, 1% Native American, 23% Hispanic American, 4% African American, 16% Asian American/Pacific Islander **The most frequently chosen baccalaureate fields are** business/marketing, psychology, social sciences **Academic program** English as a second language, advanced placement, self-designed majors, honors program, summer session, internships **Contact** Ms. Beverly Arata, Director of Admissions, San Diego State University, 5500 Campanile Drive, San Diego, CA 92182-0771. Phone: 619-594-6336. E-mail: admissions@sdsu.edu. Web site: http://www.sdsu.edu/.

SAN DIEGO STATE UNIVERSITY–IMPERIAL VALLEY CAMPUS
CALEXICO, CALIFORNIA

Contact San Diego State University–Imperial Valley Campus, 720 Heber Avenue, Calexico, CA 92231. Web site: http://www.ivcampus.sdsu.edu/.

SAN FRANCISCO ART INSTITUTE
SAN FRANCISCO, CALIFORNIA

General Independent, comprehensive, coed **Contact** Office of Admissions, San Francisco Art Institute, 800 Chestnut Street, San Francisco, CA 94133. Phone: 415-749-4580 or toll-free 800-345-SFAI. E-mail: admissions@sfai.edu. Web site: http://www.sfai.edu/.

SAN FRANCISCO CONSERVATORY OF MUSIC
SAN FRANCISCO, CALIFORNIA

General Independent, comprehensive, coed **Entrance** Moderately difficult **Setting** 2-acre urban campus **Total enrollment** 406 **Student-faculty ratio** 7:1 **Application deadline** 12/1 (freshmen), 12/1 (transfer) **Freshmen** 52% were admitted **Housing** No **Expenses** Tuition $29,980 **Undergraduates** 46% women, 6% part-time, 18% 25 or older, 6% Hispanic American, 2% African American, 13% Asian American/Pacific Islander **The most frequently chosen baccalaureate field is** visual and performing arts **Academic program** Advanced placement, internships **Contact** Mr. Alexander Brose, Director of Admissions, San Francisco Conservatory of Music, 50 Oak Street, San Francisco, CA 94102. Phone: 415-503-6231. Fax: 415-503-6299. E-mail: admit@sfcm.edu. Web site: http://www.sfcm.edu/.

SAN FRANCISCO STATE UNIVERSITY
SAN FRANCISCO, CALIFORNIA

General State-supported, comprehensive, coed **Setting** 90-acre urban campus **Total enrollment** 30,125 **Student-faculty ratio** 22:1 **Application deadline** 1/15 (freshmen), 3/3 (transfer) **Freshmen** 67% were admitted **Housing** Yes **Expenses** Room & Board $9896 **Undergraduates** 58% women, 20% part-time, 23% 25 or older, 1% Native American, 16% Hispanic American, 6% African American, 31% Asian American/Pacific Islander **The most frequently chosen baccalaureate fields are** business/marketing, social sciences, visual and performing arts **Academic program** English as a second language, advanced placement, accelerated degree program, self-designed majors, honors program, summer session, adult/continuing education programs, internships **Contact** Admissions Officer, San Francisco State University, 1600 Holloway Avenue, San Francisco, CA 94132-1722. Phone: 415-338-3111. Fax: 415-338-7196. E-mail: ugadmit@sfsu.edu. Web site: http://www.sfsu.edu/.

SAN JOSE STATE UNIVERSITY
SAN JOSE, CALIFORNIA

General State-supported, comprehensive, coed **Contact** San Jose State University, One Washington Square, San Jose, CA 95192-0001. Phone: 408-283-7500. Fax: 408-924-2050. E-mail: contact@sjsu.edu. Web site: http://www.sjsu.edu/.

SANTA CLARA UNIVERSITY
SANTA CLARA, CALIFORNIA

General Independent Roman Catholic (Jesuit), university, coed **Entrance** Moderately difficult **Setting** 106-acre suburban campus **Total enrollment** 8,248 **Student-faculty ratio** 12:1 **Application deadline** 1/7 (freshmen), 5/1 (transfer) **Freshmen** 60% were admitted **Housing** Yes **Expenses** Tuition $33,000; Room & Board $10,644 **Undergraduates** 53% women, 2% part-time, 3% 25 or older, 0.5% Native American, 13% Hispanic American, 3% African American, 17% Asian American/Pacific Islander **The most frequently chosen baccalaureate fields are** business/marketing, communications/journalism, social sciences **Academic program** Advanced placement, self-designed majors, honors program, summer session, internships **Contact** Ms. Sandra Hayes, Dean of Undergraduate Admissions, Santa

Clara University, 500 El Camino Real, Santa Clara, CA 95053. Phone: 408-554-4700. Fax: 408-554-5255. E-mail: ugadmissions@scu.edu. Web site: http://www.scu.edu/.

SCRIPPS COLLEGE
CLAREMONT, CALIFORNIA

General Independent, 4-year, women only **Entrance** Very difficult **Setting** 30-acre suburban campus **Total enrollment** 917 **Student-faculty ratio** 11:1 **Application deadline** 1/1 (freshmen), 4/1 (transfer) **Freshmen** 43% were admitted **Housing** Yes **Expenses** Tuition $35,850; Room & Board $10,800 **Undergraduates** 1% part-time, 1% Native American, 8% Hispanic American, 4% African American, 13% Asian American/Pacific Islander **The most frequently chosen baccalaureate fields are** area and ethnic studies, social sciences, visual and performing arts **Academic program** Advanced placement, accelerated degree program, self-designed majors, internships **Contact** Ms. Patricia F. Goldsmith, Dean of Admission and Financial Aid, Scripps College, 1030 Columbia Avenue, Claremont, CA 91711. Phone: 909-621-8149 or toll-free 800-770-1333. Fax: 909-607-7508. E-mail: admission@scrippscollege.edu. Web site: http://www.scrippscollege.edu/.

SHASTA BIBLE COLLEGE
REDDING, CALIFORNIA

General Independent nondenominational, comprehensive, coed **Entrance** Noncompetitive **Setting** 25-acre small-town campus **Total enrollment** 90 **Student-faculty ratio** 5:1 **Application deadline** 8/25 (freshmen), 8/25 (transfer) **Freshmen** 85% were admitted **Housing** Yes **Expenses** Tuition $7670; Room only $1650 **Undergraduates** 33% 25 or older, 3% Hispanic American, 1% African American, 1% Asian American/Pacific Islander **Academic program** Accelerated degree program, summer session, adult/continuing education programs **Contact** Mr. Mark A. Mueller, Registrar, Shasta Bible College, 2951 Goodwater Avenue, Redding, CA 96002. Phone: 530-221-4275 Ext. 205 or toll-free 800-800-45BC (in-state); 800-800-6929 (out-of-state). Fax: 530-221-6929. E-mail: admissions@shasta.edu. Web site: http://www.shasta.edu/.

SILICON VALLEY UNIVERSITY
SAN JOSE, CALIFORNIA

Contact Silicon Valley University, 2160 Lundy Avenue, Suite 110, San Jose, CA 95131. Web site: http://www.svuca.edu/.

SIMPSON UNIVERSITY
REDDING, CALIFORNIA

General Independent, comprehensive, coed, affiliated with The Christian and Missionary Alliance **Entrance** Moderately difficult **Setting** 92-acre suburban campus **Total enrollment** 1,076 **Student-faculty ratio** 15:1 **Application deadline** Rolling (freshmen), rolling (transfer) **Freshmen** 61% were admitted **Housing** Yes **Expenses** Tuition $19,500; Room & Board $6700 **Undergraduates** 67% women, 1% part-time, 24% 25 or older, 1% Native American, 6% Hispanic American, 3% African American, 6% Asian American/Pacific Islander **The most frequently chosen baccalaureate fields are** business/marketing, liberal arts/general studies, psychology **Academic program** Advanced placement, accelerated degree program, self-designed majors, honors program, summer session, adult/continuing education programs, internships **Contact** Mr. James Herberger, Director of Enrollment Management, Simpson University, 2211 College View Drive, Redding, CA 96003-8606. Phone: 530-226-5600 or toll-free 800-598-2493. Fax: 530-226-4861. E-mail: admissions@simpsonuniversity.edu. Web site: http://www.simpsonuniversity.edu/.

SOKA UNIVERSITY OF AMERICA
ALISO VIEJO, CALIFORNIA

General Independent, 4-year, coed **Entrance** Moderately difficult **Setting** 103-acre suburban campus **Total enrollment** 367 **Student-faculty ratio** 9:1 **Application deadline** 1/15 (freshmen) **Freshmen** 26% were admitted **Housing** Yes **Expenses** Tuition $24,180; Room & Board $9000 **Undergraduates** 63% women, 4% 25 or older **The most frequently chosen baccalaureate field is** liberal arts/general studies **Academic program** Internships **Contact** Ms. Marilyn Grove, Director of Student Recruitment Programs, Soka University of America, Enrollment Services, 1 University Drive, Aliso Viejo, CA 92656. Phone: 949-480-4010 or toll-free 949-480-4150 (in-state); 888-600-SOKA (out-of-state). Fax: 949-480-4151. E-mail: admission@soka.edu. Web site: http://www.soka.edu/.

SONOMA STATE UNIVERSITY
ROHNERT PARK, CALIFORNIA

General State-supported, comprehensive, coed **Entrance** Moderately difficult **Setting** 280-acre small-town campus **Total enrollment** 8,586 **Student-faculty ratio** 23:1 **Application deadline** Rolling (freshmen), rolling (transfer) **Freshmen** 73% were admitted **Housing** Yes **Expenses** Tuition $3946; Room & Board $8820 **Undergraduates** 62% women, 4% part-time, 11%

Sonoma State University *(continued)*

25 or older, 1% Native American, 11% Hispanic American, 2% African American, 5% Asian American/Pacific Islander **The most frequently chosen baccalaureate fields are** business/marketing, psychology, social sciences **Academic program** English as a second language, advanced placement, accelerated degree program, self-designed majors, honors program, summer session, adult/continuing education programs, internships **Contact** Mr. Gustavo Flores, Director of Admissions, Sonoma State University, 1801 East Cotati Avenue, Rohnert Park, CA 94928-3609. Phone: 707-664-2846. Fax: 707-664-2060. E-mail: gustavo.flores@sonoma.edu. Web site: http://www.sonoma.edu/.

SOUTHERN CALIFORNIA INSTITUTE OF ARCHITECTURE

LOS ANGELES, CALIFORNIA

General Independent, comprehensive, coed **Contact** Mr. J.J. Jackman, Admissions Director, Southern California Institute of Architecture, 960 East Third Street, Los Angeles, CA 90013. Phone: 213-613-2200 Ext. 321 or toll-free 800-774-7242. Fax: 213-613-2260. E-mail: jj@sciarc.edu. Web site: http://www.sciarc.edu/.

SOUTHERN CALIFORNIA SEMINARY

EL CAJON, CALIFORNIA

General Independent interdenominational, comprehensive, coed, primarily men **Entrance** Moderately difficult **Total enrollment** 283 **Student-faculty ratio** 10:1 **Application deadline** 8/13 (freshmen) **Freshmen** 88% were admitted **Expenses** Tuition $7112 **Undergraduates** 60% 25 or older **The most frequently chosen baccalaureate field is** theology and religious vocations **Contact** Mr. Steve Perdue, Director of Admissions, Southern California Seminary, 2075 East Madison Avenue, El Cajon, CA 92019. Phone: 619-442-9841. Fax: 619-442-4510. E-mail: sperdue@socalsem.edu. Web site: http://www.socalsem.edu/.

STANFORD UNIVERSITY

STANFORD, CALIFORNIA

General Independent, university, coed **Entrance** Most difficult **Setting** 8,180-acre suburban campus **Total enrollment** 19,782 **Student-faculty ratio** 6:1 **Application deadline** 1/1 (freshmen), 3/15 (transfer) **Freshmen** 10% were admitted **Housing** Yes **Expenses** Tuition $34,800; Room & Board $10,808 **Undergraduates** 48% women, 1% part-time, 1% 25 or older, 2% Native American, 12% Hispanic American, 9% African American, 24% Asian American/Pacific Islander **The most frequently chosen baccalaureate fields are** inter-disciplinary studies, engineering, social sciences **Academic program** Advanced placement, self-designed majors, honors program, summer session, internships **Contact** Rick Shaw, Dean of Undergraduate Admission and Financial Aid, Stanford University, Montag Hall, 355 Galvez Street, Stanford, CA 94305-3020. Phone: 650-723-2091. Fax: 650-725-2846. E-mail: admission@stanford.edu. Web site: http://www.stanford.edu/.

THOMAS AQUINAS COLLEGE

SANTA PAULA, CALIFORNIA

General Independent Roman Catholic, 4-year, coed **Entrance** Very difficult **Setting** 170-acre rural campus **Total enrollment** 360 **Student-faculty ratio** 11:1 **Application deadline** Rolling (freshmen) **Freshmen** 60% were admitted **Housing** Yes **Expenses** Tuition $21,400; Room & Board $6950 **Undergraduates** 49% women, 3% 25 or older, 0.3% Native American, 6% Hispanic American, 0.3% African American, 3% Asian American/Pacific Islander **The most frequently chosen baccalaureate field is** liberal arts/general studies **Contact** Mr. Jonathan P. Daly, Director of Admissions, Thomas Aquinas College, 10000 North Ojai Road, Santa Paula, CA 93060-9621. Phone: 805-525-4417 Ext. 5901 or toll-free 800-634-9797. Fax: 805-525-9342. E-mail: admissions@thomasaqinas.edu. Web site: http://www.thomasaquinas.edu/.

TRINITY LIFE BIBLE COLLEGE

SACRAMENTO, CALIFORNIA

Contact Ms. Kathy Clarke, Registrar, Trinity Life Bible College, 5225 Hillsdale Boulevard, Sacramento, CA 95842. Phone: 916-348-4689. E-mail: kclarke@tlbc.edu. Web site: http://www.tlbc.edu/.

TUI UNIVERSITY

CYPRESS, CALIFORNIA

General Independent, university, coed **Entrance** Minimally difficult **Total enrollment** 5,300 **Student-faculty ratio** 18:1 **Application deadline** Rolling (freshmen) **Freshmen** 71% were admitted **Housing** No **Expenses** Tuition $8000 **Undergraduates** 32% women, 45% part-time, 85% 25 or older **The most frequently chosen baccalaureate fields are** business/marketing, health professions and related sciences **Academic program** Summer session, adult/continuing education programs **Contact** Wei Ren-Finaly, Registrar, TUI University, 5336 Plaza Drive, 3rd Floor, Cypress, CA 90630. Phone: 714-816-0366. Fax: 714-827-7407. E-mail: registration@tuiu.edu. Web site: http://www.tuiu.edu/.

UNIVERSITY OF CALIFORNIA, BERKELEY
BERKELEY, CALIFORNIA

General State-supported, university, coed **Entrance** Very difficult **Setting** 1,232-acre urban campus **Total enrollment** 34,953 **Student-faculty ratio** 15:1 **Application deadline** 11/30 (freshmen), 11/30 (transfer) **Freshmen** 23% were admitted **Housing** Yes **Expenses** Tuition $7164; Room & Board $13,848 **Undergraduates** 54% women, 3% part-time, 7% 25 or older, 1% Native American, 12% Hispanic American, 3% African American, 42% Asian American/Pacific Islander **The most frequently chosen baccalaureate fields are** biological/life sciences, engineering, social sciences **Academic program** English as a second language, advanced placement, accelerated degree program, self-designed majors, honors program, summer session, adult/continuing education programs, internships **Contact** Mr. Walter Robinson, Director of Undergraduate Admissions, University of California, Berkeley, Berkeley, CA 94720-1500. Phone: 510-642-2316. Fax: 510-642-7333. E-mail: ouars@uclink.berkeley.edu. Web site: http://www.berkeley.edu/.

UNIVERSITY OF CALIFORNIA, DAVIS
DAVIS, CALIFORNIA

General State-supported, university, coed **Entrance** Moderately difficult **Setting** 5,993-acre suburban campus **Total enrollment** 29,796 **Student-faculty ratio** 19:1 **Application deadline** 11/30 (freshmen), 11/30 (transfer) **Freshmen** 59% were admitted **Housing** Yes **Expenses** Room & Board $11,533 **Undergraduates** 56% women, 1% part-time, 6% 25 or older, 1% Native American, 12% Hispanic American, 3% African American, 41% Asian American/Pacific Islander **The most frequently chosen baccalaureate fields are** biological/life sciences, psychology, social sciences **Academic program** English as a second language, advanced placement, self-designed majors, honors program, summer session, adult/continuing education programs, internships **Contact** Pamela Burnett, Director of Undergraduate Admissions, University of California, Davis, Undergraduate Admission and Outreach Services, 178 Mrak Hall, Davis, CA 95616. Phone: 530-752-3018. Fax: 530-752-1280. E-mail: freshmanadmissions@ucdavis.edu. Web site: http://www.ucdavis.edu/.

UNIVERSITY OF CALIFORNIA, IRVINE
IRVINE, CALIFORNIA

General State-supported, university, coed **Setting** 1,477-acre suburban campus **Total enrollment** 26,483 **Student-faculty ratio** 19:1 **Application deadline** 11/30 (freshmen), 11/30 (transfer) **Freshmen** 56% were admitted **Housing** Yes **Expenses** Tuition $8276; Room & Board $10,547 **Undergraduates** 52% women, 2% part-time, 5% 25 or older, 0.4% Native American, 12% Hispanic American, 2% African American, 51% Asian American/Pacific Islander **The most frequently chosen baccalaureate fields are** biological/life sciences, psychology, social sciences **Academic program** English as a second language, accelerated degree program, honors program, summer session, internships **Contact** Ms. Marguerite Bonous-Hammarth, Director of Admissions and Relations with Schools, University of California, Irvine, Irvine, CA 92697. Phone: 949-824-6703. Web site: http://www.uci.edu/.

UNIVERSITY OF CALIFORNIA, LOS ANGELES
LOS ANGELES, CALIFORNIA

General State-supported, university, coed **Entrance** Very difficult **Setting** 419-acre urban campus **Total enrollment** 38,896 **Student-faculty ratio** 16:1 **Application deadline** 11/30 (freshmen), 11/30 (transfer) **Freshmen** 24% were admitted **Housing** Yes **Expenses** Tuition $7038; Room & Board $12,420 **Undergraduates** 55% women, 4% part-time, 6% 25 or older, 0.4% Native American, 15% Hispanic American, 3% African American, 38% Asian American/Pacific Islander **The most frequently chosen baccalaureate fields are** biological/life sciences, psychology, social sciences **Academic program** English as a second language, advanced placement, self-designed majors, honors program, summer session, adult/continuing education programs, internships **Contact** Dr. Vu T. Tran, Director of Undergraduate Admissions, University of California, Los Angeles, 405 Hilgard Avenue, Box 951436, Los Angeles, CA 90095-1436. Phone: 310-825-3101. E-mail: ugadm@saonet.ucla.edu. Web site: http://www.ucla.edu/.

UNIVERSITY OF CALIFORNIA, RIVERSIDE
RIVERSIDE, CALIFORNIA

General State-supported, university, coed **Entrance** Very difficult **Setting** 1,200-acre urban campus **Total enrollment** 17,187 **Student-faculty ratio** 19:1 **Application deadline** 11/30 (freshmen), 11/30 (transfer) **Freshmen** 82% were admitted **Housing** Yes **Expenses** Tuition $7355; Room & Board $10,800 **Undergraduates** 52% women, 3% part-time, 5% 25 or older, 0.4% Native American, 26% Hispanic American, 7% African American, 42% Asian American/Pacific Islander **The most frequently chosen baccalaureate fields are** business/marketing, biological/life sciences, social sciences **Academic program** English as a second language, advanced placement, accelerated degree program, self-designed majors, honors program, summer session, adult/

University of California, Riverside *(continued)*

continuing education programs, internships **Contact** Emily Engelschall, Director, Undergraduate Recruitment, University of California, Riverside, 1120 Hinderaker Hall, Riverside, CA 92521. Phone: 951-827-3411. Fax: 951-827-6344. E-mail: discover@ucr.edu. Web site: http://www.ucr.edu/.

UNIVERSITY OF CALIFORNIA, SAN DIEGO

LA JOLLA, CALIFORNIA

General State-supported, university, coed **Entrance** Very difficult **Setting** 1,976-acre suburban campus **Total enrollment** 27,144 **Student-faculty ratio** 19:1 **Application deadline** 11/30 (freshmen), 11/30 (transfer) **Freshmen** 40% were admitted **Housing** Yes **Expenses** Tuition $7509; Room & Board $10,237 **Undergraduates** 51% women, 4% 25 or older, 0.01% Native American, 12% Hispanic American, 1% African American, 44% Asian American/Pacific Islander **The most frequently chosen baccalaureate fields are** biological/life sciences, engineering, social sciences **Academic program** English as a second language, advanced placement, accelerated degree program, self-designed majors, honors program, summer session, internships **Contact** Ms. Mae Brown, Assistant Vice Chancellor, Admissions and Relations with Schools, University of California, San Diego, 9500 Gilman Drive, 0021, La Jolla, CA 92093-0021. Phone: 858-534-4831. E-mail: admissionsinfo@ucsd.edu. Web site: http://www.ucsd.edu/.

UNIVERSITY OF CALIFORNIA, SANTA BARBARA

SANTA BARBARA, CALIFORNIA

General State-supported, university, coed **Entrance** Very difficult **Setting** 989-acre suburban campus **Total enrollment** 21,410 **Student-faculty ratio** 17:1 **Application deadline** 11/30 (freshmen), 11/30 (transfer) **Freshmen** 54% were admitted **Housing** Yes **Expenses** Tuition $7896; Room & Board $11,604 **Undergraduates** 55% women, 2% part-time, 3% 25 or older, 1% Native American, 19% Hispanic American, 3% African American, 16% Asian American/Pacific Islander **The most frequently chosen baccalaureate fields are** business/marketing, biological/life sciences, social sciences **Academic program** English as a second language, advanced placement, accelerated degree program, self-designed majors, honors program, summer session, internships **Contact** Office of Admissions, University of California, Santa Barbara, 1210 Cheadle Hall, Santa Barbara, CA 93106-2014. Phone: 805-893-3641. Fax: 805-893-2676. E-mail: admissions@sa.ucsb.edu. Web site: http://www.ucsb.edu/.

UNIVERSITY OF CALIFORNIA, SANTA CRUZ

SANTA CRUZ, CALIFORNIA

General State-supported, university, coed **Entrance** Very difficult **Setting** 2,000-acre small-town campus **Total enrollment** 15,825 **Student-faculty ratio** 19:1 **Application deadline** 11/30 (freshmen), 11/30 (transfer) **Freshmen** 82% were admitted **Housing** Yes **Expenses** Tuition $9534; Room & Board $12,831 **Undergraduates** 54% women, 3% part-time, 4% 25 or older, 1% Native American, 16% Hispanic American, 3% African American, 21% Asian American/Pacific Islander **The most frequently chosen baccalaureate fields are** biological/life sciences, social sciences, visual and performing arts **Academic program** English as a second language, advanced placement, self-designed majors, summer session, adult/continuing education programs, internships **Contact** Michael McCawley, Interim/Acting Director of Admissions and University Registrar, University of California, Santa Cruz, 1156 High Street, Santa Cruz, CA 95064. Phone: 831-459-5779. Fax: 831-459-4452. E-mail: admissions@ucsc.edu. Web site: http://www.ucsc.edu/.

UNIVERSITY OF LA VERNE

LA VERNE, CALIFORNIA

General Independent, university, coed **Entrance** Moderately difficult **Setting** 38-acre suburban campus **Total enrollment** 3,907 **Student-faculty ratio** 12:1 **Application deadline** 2/1 (freshmen), 4/1 (transfer) **Freshmen** 65% were admitted **Housing** Yes **Expenses** Tuition $26,910; Room & Board $10,460 **Undergraduates** 64% women, 5% part-time, 2% 25 or older, 1% Native American, 39% Hispanic American, 7% African American, 4% Asian American/Pacific Islander **The most frequently chosen baccalaureate fields are** business/marketing, liberal arts/general studies, social sciences **Academic program** English as a second language, advanced placement, accelerated degree program, self-designed majors, honors program, summer session, adult/continuing education programs, internships **Contact** Ms. Ana Liza V. Zell, Associate Dean of Undergraduate Admissions, University of La Verne, 1950 Third Street, La Verne, CA 91750. Phone: 909-593-3511 Ext. 4035 or toll-free 800-876-4858. Fax: 909-392-2714. E-mail: admissions@ulv.edu. Web site: http://www.ulv.edu/.

UNIVERSITY OF PHOENIX–BAY AREA CAMPUS
PLEASANTON, CALIFORNIA

General Proprietary, comprehensive, coed **Contact** Ms. Evelyn Gaskin, Registrar/Executive Director, University of Phoenix–Bay Area Campus, 4615 East Elwood Street, Mail Stop AA-K101, Phoenix, AZ 85040-1958. Phone: 480-557-3301 or toll-free 877-4-STUDENT. Fax: 480-643-1020. E-mail: evelyn.gaskin@phoenix.edu. Web site: http://www.phoenix.edu/.

UNIVERSITY OF PHOENIX–CENTRAL VALLEY CAMPUS
FRESNO, CALIFORNIA

General Proprietary, comprehensive, coed **Contact** Ms. Evelyn Gaskin, Registrar/Executive Director, University of Phoenix–Central Valley Campus, 4615 East Elwood Street, Mail Stop AA-K101, Phoenix, AZ 85040-1958. Phone: 480-557-3301 or toll-free 888-776-4867 (in-state); 888-228-7240 (out-of-state). Fax: 480-643-1020. E-mail: evelyn.gaskin@phoenix.edu. Web site: http://www.phoenix.edu/.

UNIVERSITY OF PHOENIX–SACRAMENTO VALLEY CAMPUS
SACRAMENTO, CALIFORNIA

General Proprietary, comprehensive, coed **Contact** Ms. Evelyn Gaskin, Registrar/Executive Director, University of Phoenix–Sacramento Valley Campus, 4615 East Elwood Street, Mail Stop AA-K101, Phoenix, AZ 85040-1958. Phone: 480-557-3301 or toll-free 800-776-4867 (in-state); 800-228-7240 (out-of-state). Fax: 480-643-1020. E-mail: evelyn.gaskin@phoenix.edu. Web site: http://www.phoenix.edu/.

UNIVERSITY OF PHOENIX–SAN DIEGO CAMPUS
SAN DIEGO, CALIFORNIA

General Proprietary, comprehensive, coed **Contact** Ms. Evelyn Gaskin, Registrar/Executive Director, University of Phoenix–San Diego Campus, 4615 East Elwood Street, Mail Stop AA-K101, Phoenix, AZ 85040-1958. Phone: 480-557-3301 or toll-free 888-776-4867 (in-state); 888-228-7240 (out-of-state). Fax: 480-643-1020. E-mail: evelyn.gaskin@phoenix.edu. Web site: http://www.phoenix.edu/.

UNIVERSITY OF PHOENIX–SOUTHERN CALIFORNIA CAMPUS
COSTA MESA, CALIFORNIA

General Proprietary, comprehensive, coed **Contact** Ms. Evelyn Gaskin, Registrar/Executive Director, University of Phoenix–Southern California Campus, 4615 East Elwood Street, Mail Stop AA-K101, Phoenix, AZ 85040-1958. Phone: 480-557-3301 or toll-free 800-776-4867 (in-state); 800-228-7240 (out-of-state). Fax: 480-643-1020. E-mail: evelyn.gaskin@phoenix.edu. Web site: http://www.phoenix.edu/.

UNIVERSITY OF REDLANDS
REDLANDS, CALIFORNIA

General Independent, comprehensive, coed **Entrance** Moderately difficult **Setting** 140-acre small-town campus **Total enrollment** 2,445 **Application deadline** 4/1 (freshmen), 5/1 (transfer) **Freshmen** 67% were admitted **Housing** Yes **Expenses** Tuition $30,626; Room & Board $9782 **Undergraduates** 57% women, 1% part-time, 1% 25 or older, 0.3% Native American, 12% Hispanic American, 3% African American, 6% Asian American/Pacific Islander **The most frequently chosen baccalaureate fields are** business/marketing, liberal arts/general studies, social sciences **Academic program** Advanced placement, self-designed majors, honors program, adult/continuing education programs, internships **Contact** Mr. Paul Driscoll, Dean of Admissions, University of Redlands, PO Box 3080, Redlands, CA 92373-0999. Phone: 909-748-8159 or toll-free 800-455-5064. Fax: 909-335-4089. E-mail: admissions@redlands.edu. Web site: http://www.redlands.edu/.

UNIVERSITY OF SAN DIEGO
SAN DIEGO, CALIFORNIA

General Independent Roman Catholic, university, coed **Entrance** Very difficult **Setting** 180-acre urban campus **Total enrollment** 7,504 **Student-faculty ratio** 15:1 **Application deadline** 1/15 (freshmen), 3/1 (transfer) **Freshmen** 48% were admitted **Housing** Yes **Expenses** Tuition $34,264; Room & Board $11,870 **Undergraduates** 58% women, 4% part-time, 4% 25 or older, 1% Native American, 14% Hispanic American, 2% African American, 10% Asian American/Pacific Islander **The most frequently chosen baccalaureate fields are** business/marketing, communications/journalism, social sciences **Academic program** English as a second language, advanced placement, honors program, summer session, internships **Contact** Mr. Stephen Pultz, Director of Admission, University of San Diego, 5998 Alcala Park, San Diego, CA 92110. Phone: 619-260-4506 or toll-free 800-248-4873. Fax: 619-260-6836. E-mail: admissions@sandiego.edu. Web site: http://www.sandiego.edu/.

UNIVERSITY OF SAN FRANCISCO
SAN FRANCISCO, CALIFORNIA

General Independent Roman Catholic (Jesuit), university, coed **Contact** Mr. Michael Hughes,

University of San Francisco *(continued)*

Director, University of San Francisco, 2130 Fulton Street, San Francisco, CA 94117-1080. Phone: 415-422-6563 or toll-free 415-422-6563 (in-state); 800-CALL USF (out-of-state). Fax: 415-422-2217. E-mail: admissions@usfca.edu. Web site: http://www.usfca.edu/.

UNIVERSITY OF SOUTHERN CALIFORNIA
LOS ANGELES, CALIFORNIA

General Independent, university, coed **Entrance** Most difficult **Setting** 155-acre urban campus **Total enrollment** 33,408 **Student-faculty ratio** 9:1 **Application deadline** 1/10 (freshmen), 2/1 (transfer) **Freshmen** 25% were admitted **Housing** Yes **Expenses** Tuition $35,810; Room & Board $10,858 **Undergraduates** 50% women, 4% part-time, 5% 25 or older, 1% Native American, 13% Hispanic American, 6% African American, 22% Asian American/Pacific Islander **The most frequently chosen baccalaureate fields are** business/marketing, social sciences, visual and performing arts **Academic program** English as a second language, advanced placement, accelerated degree program, self-designed majors, honors program, summer session, internships **Contact** Katharine L. Harrington, Dean/Director of Admission, University of Southern California, University Park Campus, Los Angeles, CA 90089. Phone: 213-740-1111. Fax: 213-740-6364. E-mail: admitusc@usc.edu. Web site: http://www.usc.edu/.

UNIVERSITY OF THE PACIFIC
STOCKTON, CALIFORNIA

General Independent, university, coed **Entrance** Moderately difficult **Setting** 175-acre suburban campus **Total enrollment** 6,235 **Student-faculty ratio** 13:1 **Application deadline** 1/15 (freshmen), 6/1 (transfer) **Freshmen** 69% were admitted **Housing** Yes **Expenses** Tuition $28,980; Room & Board $9210 **Undergraduates** 55% women, 3% part-time, 5% 25 or older, 1% Native American, 10% Hispanic American, 3% African American, 32% Asian American/Pacific Islander **The most frequently chosen baccalaureate fields are** biological/life sciences, business/marketing, social sciences **Academic program** English as a second language, advanced placement, accelerated degree program, self-designed majors, honors program, summer session, adult/continuing education programs, internships **Contact** Mr. Rich Toledo, Director of Admissions, University of the Pacific, 3601 Pacific Avenue, Stockton, CA 95211-0197. Phone: 209-946-2211 or toll-free 800-959-2867. Fax: 209-946-2413. E-mail: admissions@pacific.edu. Web site: http://www.pacific.edu/.

UNIVERSITY OF THE WEST
ROSEMEAD, CALIFORNIA

General Independent, comprehensive, coed **Setting** 10-acre suburban campus **Total enrollment** 79 **Application deadline** 6/1 (freshmen) **Freshmen** 97% were admitted **Housing** Yes **Expenses** Tuition $7470; Room & Board $5430 **Undergraduates** 52% women, 6% part-time, 19% 25 or older, 6% Hispanic American **The most frequently chosen baccalaureate fields are** business/marketing, English, liberal arts/general studies **Academic program** English as a second language, accelerated degree program, summer session, adult/continuing education programs, internships **Contact** Ms. Grace Hsiao, Admissions Officer, University of the West, 1409 North Walnut Grove Avenue, Rosemead, CA 91770. Phone: 626-571-8811 Ext. 120. Fax: 626-571-4413. E-mail: graceh@uwest.edu. Web site: http://www.uwest.edu/.

VANGUARD UNIVERSITY OF SOUTHERN CALIFORNIA
COSTA MESA, CALIFORNIA

General Independent, comprehensive, coed, affiliated with Assemblies of God **Entrance** Moderately difficult **Setting** 38-acre suburban campus **Total enrollment** 2,251 **Student-faculty ratio** 28:1 **Application deadline** 1/15 (freshmen), 12/1 (transfer) **Freshmen** 82% were admitted **Housing** Yes **Expenses** Tuition $24,310; Room only $3804 **Undergraduates** 65% women, 22% part-time, 17% 25 or older, 2% Native American, 17% Hispanic American, 3% African American, 5% Asian American/Pacific Islander **The most frequently chosen baccalaureate fields are** business/marketing, communications/journalism, psychology **Academic program** Advanced placement, accelerated degree program, summer session, adult/continuing education programs, internships **Contact** Amberley Wolf, Director of Undergraduate Admissions, Vanguard University of Southern California, 55 Fair Drive, Costa Mesa, CA 92626. Phone: 714-556-3610 Ext. 4240 or toll-free 800-722-6279. Fax: 714-966-5471. E-mail: admissions@vanguard.edu. Web site: http://www.vanguard.edu/.

WESTMONT COLLEGE
SANTA BARBARA, CALIFORNIA

General Independent nondenominational, 4-year, coed **Entrance** Moderately difficult **Setting** 133-acre suburban campus **Total enrollment** 1,337 **Student-faculty ratio** 12:1 **Application deadline** 2/20 (freshmen), 3/1 (transfer) **Freshmen** 73% were admitted **Housing** Yes **Expenses** Tuition $31,212; Room & Board $9622 **Undergraduates** 61% women, 2% part-time, 1%

25 or older, 2% Native American, 10% Hispanic American, 2% African American, 9% Asian American/Pacific Islander **The most frequently chosen baccalaureate fields are** business/ marketing, communications/journalism, English **Academic program** Advanced placement, accelerated degree program, self-designed majors, honors program, summer session, internships **Contact** Mrs. Joyce Luy, Dean of Admission, Westmont College, 955 La Paz Road, Santa Barbara, CA 93108. Phone: 805-565-6200 or toll-free 800-777-9011. Fax: 805-565-6234. E-mail: admissions@westmont.edu. Web site: http://www.westmont.edu/.

WHITTIER COLLEGE
WHITTIER, CALIFORNIA

General Independent, comprehensive, coed **Entrance** Moderately difficult **Setting** 95-acre suburban campus **Total enrollment** 1,962 **Student-faculty ratio** 13:1 **Application deadline** Rolling (freshmen), rolling (transfer) **Freshmen** 67% were admitted **Housing** Yes **Expenses** Tuition $32,470; Room & Board $9050 **Undergraduates** 55% women, 2% part-time, 3% 25 or older, 1% Native American, 30% Hispanic American, 3% African American, 8% Asian American/Pacific Islander **The most frequently chosen baccalaureate fields are** business/ marketing, biological/life sciences, social sciences **Academic program** Advanced placement, accelerated degree program, self-designed majors, summer session, adult/continuing education programs, internships **Contact** Ms. Lisa Meyer, Vice President for Enrollment, Whittier College, 13406 E Philadelphia Street, Whittier, CA 90608-0634. Phone: 562-907-4238. Fax: 562-907-4870. E-mail: admission@whittier.edu. Web site: http://www.whittier.edu/.

WILLIAM JESSUP UNIVERSITY
ROCKLIN, CALIFORNIA

General Independent nondenominational, 4-year, coed **Entrance** Noncompetitive **Setting** 156-acre suburban campus **Total enrollment** 515 **Student-faculty ratio** 9:1 **Application deadline** 8/1 (freshmen), 8/1 (transfer) **Freshmen** 57% were admitted **Housing** Yes **Expenses** Tuition $18,790; Room & Board $7118 **Undergraduates** 59% women, 16% part-time, 10% 25 or older, 2% Native American, 8% Hispanic American, 6% African American, 5% Asian American/Pacific Islander **The most frequently chosen baccalaureate fields are** business/marketing, psychology, theology and religious vocations **Academic program** Advanced placement, accelerated degree program, summer session, adult/continuing education programs, internships **Contact** Mr. Vance Pascua, Director of Admission, William Jessup University, 333 Sunset Boulevard, Rocklin, CA 95765. Phone: 916-577-2222 or toll-free 800-355-7522. Fax: 916-577-2220. E-mail: admissions@jessup.edu. Web site: http://www.jessup.edu/.

WOODBURY UNIVERSITY
BURBANK, CALIFORNIA

General Independent, comprehensive, coed **Entrance** Moderately difficult **Setting** 22-acre suburban campus **Total enrollment** 1,539 **Student-faculty ratio** 12:1 **Application deadline** Rolling (freshmen), rolling (transfer) **Freshmen** 81% were admitted **Housing** Yes **Expenses** Tuition $25,198; Room & Board $8510 **Undergraduates** 56% women, 19% part-time, 28% 25 or older, 0.2% Native American, 32% Hispanic American, 6% African American, 11% Asian American/Pacific Islander **The most frequently chosen baccalaureate fields are** architecture, business/marketing, visual and performing arts **Academic program** Advanced placement, accelerated degree program, summer session, adult/continuing education programs, internships **Contact** Ms. Sabrina Taylor, Woodbury University, 7500 Glenoaks Boulevard, Burbank, CA 91510-7846. Phone: 800-784-9663 or toll-free 800-784-WOOD. Fax: 818-767-0032. E-mail: admissions@woodbury.edu. Web site: http://www.woodbury.edu/.

YESHIVA OHR ELCHONON CHABAD/ WEST COAST TALMUDICAL SEMINARY
LOS ANGELES, CALIFORNIA

Contact Rabbi Ezra Binyomin Schochet, Dean, Yeshiva Ohr Elchonon Chabad/West Coast Talmudical Seminary, 7215 Waring Avenue, Los Angeles, CA 90046-7660. Phone: 323-937-3763.

COLORADO

ADAMS STATE COLLEGE
ALAMOSA, COLORADO

General State-supported, comprehensive, coed **Entrance** Moderately difficult **Setting** 90-acre small-town campus **Total enrollment** 4,674 **Student-faculty ratio** 14:1 **Application deadline** 8/1 (freshmen), 8/1 (transfer) **Freshmen** 58% were admitted **Housing** Yes **Expenses** Tuition $3464; Room & Board $6410 **Undergraduates** 56% women, 23% part-time, 24% 25 or older, 2% Native American, 27% Hispanic American, 8% African American, 2% Asian American/ Pacific Islander **The most frequently chosen baccalaureate fields are** business/marketing,

Adams State College *(continued)*

liberal arts/general studies, visual and performing arts **Academic program** Advanced placement, accelerated degree program, self-designed majors, summer session, adult/continuing education programs, internships **Contact** Mr. Eric Carpio, Director of Admissions, Adams State College, 208 Edgemont Boulevard, Alamosa, CO 81102. Phone: 719-587-7712 or toll-free 800-824-6494. Fax: 719-587-7522. E-mail: ascadmit@adams.edu. Web site: http://www.adams.edu/.

AMERICAN SENTINEL UNIVERSITY
ENGLEWOOD, COLORADO

Contact American Sentinel University, 385 Inverness Parkway, Englewood, CO 80112. Web site: http://www.americansentinel.edu/.

ARGOSY UNIVERSITY, DENVER
DENVER, COLORADO

General Proprietary, university, coed **Contact** Director of Admissions, Argosy University, Denver, 1200 Lincoln Street, Denver, CO 80203. Phone: toll-free 866-431-5981. Fax: 303-248-2800. E-mail: 1200 Lincoln Street. Web site: http://www.argosy.edu/locations/denver/.

THE ART INSTITUTE OF COLORADO
DENVER, COLORADO

General Proprietary, 4-year, coed **Entrance** Minimally difficult **Setting** urban campus **Total enrollment** 2,765 **Student-faculty ratio** 19:1 **Application deadline** Rolling (freshmen), rolling (transfer) **Housing** Yes **Expenses** Tuition $20,928; Room only $9000 **Undergraduates** 51% women, 32% part-time, 1% Native American, 10% Hispanic American, 4% African American, 3% Asian American/Pacific Islander **The most frequently chosen baccalaureate fields are** education, personal and culinary services **Academic program** Advanced placement, adult/continuing education programs, internships **Contact** Mr. Brian Parker, Director of Admissions, The Art Institute of Colorado, 1200 Lincoln Street, Denver, CO 80203. Phone: 303-837-0825 Ext. 4729 or toll-free 800-275-2420. Fax: 303-860-8520. E-mail: aicadm@aii.edu. Web site: http://www.artinstitutes.edu/denver/.

ASPEN UNIVERSITY
DENVER, COLORADO

Contact Admissions, Aspen University, 501 South Cherry Street, Suite 350, Denver, CO 80246. Phone: 303-333-4224 Ext. 177 or toll-free 800-441-4746 Ext. 177. Fax: 303-336-1144. E-mail: info@aspen.edu. Web site: http://www.aspen.edu/.

COLORADO CHRISTIAN UNIVERSITY
LAKEWOOD, COLORADO

General Independent interdenominational, comprehensive, coed **Contact** Mr. Jeff Cazer, Associate, Colorado Christian University, 8787 W Alameda Avenue, Lakewood, CO 80226. Phone: 303-963-3163 or toll-free 800-44-FAITH. Fax: 303-963-3201. E-mail: admission@ccu.edu. Web site: http://www.ccu.edu/.

THE COLORADO COLLEGE
COLORADO SPRINGS, COLORADO

General Independent, comprehensive, coed **Entrance** Very difficult **Setting** 90-acre urban campus **Total enrollment** 2,075 **Student-faculty ratio** 11:1 **Application deadline** 1/15 (freshmen), 3/1 (transfer) **Freshmen** 32% were admitted **Housing** Yes **Expenses** Tuition $33,972; Room & Board $8498 **Undergraduates** 54% women, 1% part-time, 1% 25 or older, 1% Native American, 7% Hispanic American, 2% African American, 5% Asian American/Pacific Islander **The most frequently chosen baccalaureate fields are** biological/life sciences, social sciences, visual and performing arts **Academic program** English as a second language, advanced placement, self-designed majors, summer session, internships **Contact** Mr. Matt Bonser, Associate Director of Admission, The Colorado College, 14 East Cache La Poudre, Colorado Springs, CO 80903-3294. Phone: 719-389-6344 or toll-free 800-542-7214. Fax: 719-389-6816. E-mail: admission@coloradocollege.edu. Web site: http://www.coloradocollege.edu/.

COLORADO SCHOOL OF MINES
GOLDEN, COLORADO

General State-supported, university, coed **Entrance** Very difficult **Setting** 373-acre small-town campus **Total enrollment** 4,268 **Student-faculty ratio** 15:1 **Application deadline** 6/1 (freshmen), 6/1 (transfer) **Freshmen** 85% were admitted **Housing** Yes **Expenses** Tuition $10,154; Room & Board $7350 **Undergraduates** 22% women, 18% part-time, 5% 25 or older, 1% Native American, 6% Hispanic American, 2% African American, 5% Asian American/Pacific Islander **The most frequently chosen baccalaureate fields are** engineering, computer and information sciences, physical sciences **Academic program** English as a second language, advanced placement, accelerated degree program, honors program, summer session, internships **Contact** Ms. Heather Boyd, Associate Director of Enrollment Management, Colorado School of Mines, Student Center, 1600 Maple Street, Golden, CO 80401. Phone: 303-273-3227 or toll-free 800-446-9488 Ext. 3220. Fax: 303-273-3509. E-mail: admit@mines.edu. Web site: http://www.mines.edu/.

COLORADO STATE UNIVERSITY
FORT COLLINS, COLORADO

General State-supported, university, coed **Entrance** Moderately difficult **Setting** 579-acre urban campus **Total enrollment** 27,569 **Student-faculty ratio** 17:1 **Application deadline** 7/1 (freshmen), 7/1 (transfer) **Freshmen** 86% were admitted **Housing** Yes **Expenses** Tuition $5419; Room & Board $7382 **Undergraduates** 52% women, 12% part-time, 8% 25 or older, 2% Native American, 7% Hispanic American, 2% African American, 3% Asian American/Pacific Islander **The most frequently chosen baccalaureate fields are** business/marketing, family and consumer sciences, social sciences **Academic program** English as a second language, advanced placement, accelerated degree program, honors program, summer session, internships **Contact** Ms. Mary Ontiveros, Associate Vice President for Enrollment and Access and Executive Director of Admissions, Colorado State University, Spruce Hall, Fort Collins, CO 80523-0015. Phone: 970-491-6909. Fax: 970-491-7799. E-mail: admissions@colostate.edu. Web site: http://www.colostate.edu/.

COLORADO STATE UNIVERSITY–PUEBLO
PUEBLO, COLORADO

General State-supported, comprehensive, coed **Entrance** Moderately difficult **Setting** 275-acre suburban campus **Total enrollment** 5,903 **Student-faculty ratio** 17:1 **Application deadline** 8/1 (freshmen), 8/1 (transfer) **Freshmen** 97% were admitted **Housing** Yes **Expenses** Tuition $3343; Room & Board $8092 **Undergraduates** 58% women, 36% part-time, 33% 25 or older, 2% Native American, 25% Hispanic American, 6% African American, 3% Asian American/Pacific Islander **The most frequently chosen baccalaureate fields are** business/marketing, health professions and related sciences, social sciences **Academic program** English as a second language, advanced placement, accelerated degree program, honors program, summer session, adult/continuing education programs, internships **Contact** Ms. Jennifer Jensen, Associate Director of Admissions and Records, Colorado State University–Pueblo, 2200 Bonforte Blvd., Pueblo, CO 81001. Phone: 719-549-2434. Fax: 719-549-2419. E-mail: jennifer.jensen@colostate-pueblo.edu. Web site: http://www.colostate-pueblo.edu/.

COLORADO TECHNICAL UNIVERSITY COLORADO SPRINGS
COLORADO SPRINGS, COLORADO

General Proprietary, comprehensive, coed **Entrance** Minimally difficult **Setting** 14-acre suburban campus **Total enrollment** 26,375 **Application deadline** Rolling (freshmen), rolling (transfer) **Housing** No **Academic program** Advanced placement, accelerated degree program, summer session, adult/continuing education programs, internships **Contact** Chief Admission Officer, Colorado Technical University Colorado Springs, 4435 North Chestnut Street, Colorado Springs, CO 80907-3896. Phone: 719-598-0200. Fax: 719-598-3740. Web site: http://www.coloradotech.edu/.

COLORADO TECHNICAL UNIVERSITY DENVER
GREENWOOD VILLAGE, COLORADO

General Proprietary, comprehensive, coed **Entrance** Minimally difficult **Setting** 1-acre urban campus **Total enrollment** 26,375 **Application deadline** Rolling (freshmen), rolling (transfer) **Housing** No **Academic program** Advanced placement, summer session, adult/continuing education programs **Contact** Director of Admissions, Colorado Technical University Denver, 5775 Denver Tech Center Boulevard, Greenwood Village, CO 80111. Phone: 303-694-6600. Fax: 303-694-6673. E-mail: ctudenver@coloradotech.edu. Web site: http://www.coloradotech.edu/.

COLORADO TECHNICAL UNIVERSITY ONLINE
COLORADO SPRINGS, COLORADO

General Proprietary, comprehensive, coed **Total enrollment** 26,375 **Contact** Chief Admission Officer, Colorado Technical University Online, 4435 West Chestnut Street, Suite E, Colorado Springs, CO 80907. Phone: 866-813-1836. Web site: http://www.coloradotech.edu/.

DEVRY UNIVERSITY
COLORADO SPRINGS, COLORADO

Contact Admissions Office, DeVry University, 225 South Union Boulevard, Colorado Springs, CO 80910. Phone: toll-free 866-338-7934. Fax: 719-632-1909. Web site: http://www.devry.edu/.

DEVRY UNIVERSITY
WESTMINSTER, COLORADO

General Proprietary, comprehensive, coed **Entrance** Noncompetitive **Setting** 3-acre urban

DeVry University *(continued)*

campus **Total enrollment** 669 **Student-faculty ratio** 19:1 **Application deadline** Rolling (freshmen), rolling (transfer) **Housing** No **Expenses** Tuition $13,990 **Undergraduates** 36% women, 51% part-time, 60% 25 or older, 1% Native American, 12% Hispanic American, 7% African American, 4% Asian American/Pacific Islander **The most frequently chosen baccalaureate fields are** business/marketing, computer and information sciences, engineering technologies **Academic program** Accelerated degree program, summer session, adult/continuing education programs **Contact** Admissions Office, DeVry University, 1870 West 122nd Avenue, Westminster, CO 80234-2010. Web site: http://www.devry.edu/.

FORT LEWIS COLLEGE
DURANGO, COLORADO

General State-supported, 4-year, coed **Entrance** Moderately difficult **Setting** 350-acre small-town campus **Total enrollment** 3,935 **Student-faculty ratio** 17:1 **Application deadline** 8/1 (freshmen), rolling (transfer) **Freshmen** 72% were admitted **Housing** Yes **Expenses** Tuition $6464; Room & Board $6876 **Undergraduates** 48% women, 10% part-time, 15% 25 or older, 20% Native American, 6% Hispanic American, 1% African American, 1% Asian American/Pacific Islander **The most frequently chosen baccalaureate fields are** business/marketing, liberal arts/general studies, social sciences **Academic program** English as a second language, advanced placement, accelerated degree program, self-designed majors, honors program, summer session, adult/continuing education programs, internships **Contact** Mr. Andrew Burns, Director of Admissions, Fort Lewis College, 1000 Rim Drive, Durango, CO 81301-3999. Phone: 970-247-7184. Fax: 970-247-7179. E-mail: admission@fortlewis.edu. Web site: http://www.fortlewis.edu/.

JOHNSON & WALES UNIVERSITY
DENVER, COLORADO

General Independent, 4-year, coed **Entrance** Minimally difficult **Setting** small-town campus **Total enrollment** 1,466 **Student-faculty ratio** 19:1 **Application deadline** Rolling (freshmen), rolling (transfer) **Freshmen** 76% were admitted **Housing** Yes **Expenses** Tuition $22,585; Room & Board $7956 **Undergraduates** 52% women, 3% part-time, 8% 25 or older, 1% Native American, 11% Hispanic American, 5% African American, 4% Asian American/Pacific Islander **The most frequently chosen baccalaureate fields are** family and consumer sciences, history, parks and recreation **Academic program** Advanced placement, accelerated degree program, honors program, summer session, adult/continuing education programs, internships **Contact** Kim Ostrowski, Director of Admissions, Johnson & Wales University, 7150 Montview Boulevard, Denver, CO 80220. Phone: 977-598-3368 or toll-free 877-598-3368. Fax: 303-256-9333. E-mail: den.admissions@jwu.edu. Web site: http://www.jwu.edu/.

JONES INTERNATIONAL UNIVERSITY
CENTENNIAL, COLORADO

Contact Ms. Candace Morrissey, Associate Director of Admissions, Jones International University, 9697 East Mineral Avenue, Centennial, CO 80112. Phone: toll-free 800-811-5663. Fax: 303-799-0966. E-mail: admissions@international.edu. Web site: http://www.jonesinternational.edu/.

MESA STATE COLLEGE
GRAND JUNCTION, COLORADO

General State-supported, comprehensive, coed **Entrance** Minimally difficult **Setting** 42-acre small-town campus **Total enrollment** 6,151 **Student-faculty ratio** 17:1 **Application deadline** Rolling (freshmen), rolling (transfer) **Freshmen** 82% were admitted **Housing** Yes **Expenses** Tuition $4064; Room & Board $7077 **Undergraduates** 59% women, 26% part-time, 27% 25 or older, 2% Native American, 9% Hispanic American, 2% African American, 3% Asian American/Pacific Islander **The most frequently chosen baccalaureate fields are** business/marketing, health professions and related sciences, parks and recreation **Academic program** Advanced placement, accelerated degree program, self-designed majors, honors program, summer session, adult/continuing education programs, internships **Contact** Mr. Rance Larsen, Director of Admission, Mesa State College, 1100 North Avenue, Grand Junction, CO 81501. Phone: 970-248-1802 or toll-free 800-982-MESA. Fax: 970-248-1973. E-mail: rlarsen@mesastate.edu. Web site: http://www.mesastate.edu/.

METROPOLITAN STATE COLLEGE OF DENVER
DENVER, COLORADO

Contact Ms. Miriam Tapia, Associate Director, Metropolitan State College of Denver, PO Box 173362, Denver, CO 80217-3362. Phone: 303-556-3058. Fax: 303-556-6345. Web site: http://www.mscd.edu/.

NAROPA UNIVERSITY
BOULDER, COLORADO

General Independent, comprehensive, coed **Entrance** Moderately difficult **Setting** 12-acre urban campus **Total enrollment** 1,104 **Student-faculty ratio** 9:1 **Application deadline** 1/15 (freshmen), rolling (transfer) **Freshmen** 93% were admitted **Housing** Yes **Expenses** Tuition $20,814; Room & Board $6501 **Undergraduates** 63% women, 9% part-time, 33% 25 or older, 0.4% Native American, 4% Hispanic American, 1% African American, 2% Asian American/Pacific Islander **The most frequently chosen baccalaureate fields are** psychology, English, visual and performing arts **Academic program** Advanced placement, self-designed majors, summer session, adult/continuing education programs, internships **Contact** Ms. Amy Kopkin, Associate Director of Admissions, Naropa University, 2130 Arapahoe Avenue, Boulder, CO 80302. Phone: 303-546-3572 or toll-free 800-772-0410. Fax: 303-546-3583. E-mail: admissions@naropa.edu. Web site: http://www.naropa.edu/.

NATIONAL AMERICAN UNIVERSITY
COLORADO SPRINGS, COLORADO

Contact Ms. Markita McKamie, Director of Admissions, National American University, 5125 North Academy Boulevard, Colorado Springs, CO 80918. Phone: 719-277-0588. Fax: 719-277-0589. E-mail: mmckamie@national.edu. Web site: http://www.national.edu/.

NATIONAL AMERICAN UNIVERSITY
DENVER, COLORADO

General Proprietary, 4-year, coed **Contact** Jacklyn Haack, Director of Admissions, National American University, 1325 South Colorado Blvd, Suite 100, Denver, CO 80222. Phone: 303-876-7112. Fax: 303-876-7105. E-mail: jhaack@national.edu. Web site: http://www.national.edu/.

NAZARENE BIBLE COLLEGE
COLORADO SPRINGS, COLORADO

General Independent, 4-year, coed, affiliated with Church of the Nazarene **Entrance** Noncompetitive **Setting** 64-acre urban campus **Total enrollment** 808 **Student-faculty ratio** 10:1 **Application deadline** 7/31 (freshmen), 7/31 (transfer) **Freshmen** 20% were admitted **Housing** No **Expenses** Tuition $8400 **Undergraduates** 37% women, 82% part-time, 89% 25 or older, 1% Native American, 3% Hispanic American, 3% African American, 1% Asian American/Pacific Islander **The most frequently chosen baccalaureate field is** theology and religious vocations **Academic program** Summer session, internships **Contact** Dr. Laurel Matson, Director of Admissions/Public Relations, Nazarene Bible College, 1111 Academy Park Loop, Colorado Springs, CO 80910-3704. Phone: 719-884-5061 or toll-free 800-873-3873. Fax: 719-884-5199. Web site: http://www.nbc.edu/.

REGIS UNIVERSITY
DENVER, COLORADO

General Independent Roman Catholic (Jesuit), comprehensive, coed **Entrance** Moderately difficult **Setting** 90-acre suburban campus **Total enrollment** 15,740 **Student-faculty ratio** 14:1 **Application deadline** Rolling (freshmen), rolling (transfer) **Freshmen** 25% were admitted **Housing** Yes **Expenses** Tuition $28,700; Room & Board $8982 **Undergraduates** 63% women, 66% part-time, 67% 25 or older, 1% Native American, 10% Hispanic American, 5% African American, 4% Asian American/Pacific Islander **The most frequently chosen baccalaureate fields are** business/marketing, interdisciplinary studies, social sciences **Academic program** Advanced placement, accelerated degree program, self-designed majors, honors program, summer session, adult/continuing education programs, internships **Contact** Mr. Vic Davolt, Director of Admission, Regis University, 3333 Regis Boulevard, Denver, CO 80221-1099. Phone: 303-458-4905 or toll-free 800-388-2366 Ext. 4900. Fax: 303-964-5534. E-mail: regisadm@regis.edu. Web site: http://www.regis.edu/.

REMINGTON COLLEGE–COLORADO SPRINGS CAMPUS
COLORADO SPRINGS, COLORADO

General Proprietary, 4-year **Setting** 3-acre urban campus **Housing** No **Contact** Ms. Shirley McCray, Campus President, Remington College–Colorado Springs Campus, 6050 Erin Park Drive, #250, Colorado Springs, CO 80918. Phone: 719-532-1234 Ext. 202. Fax: 719-264-1234. E-mail: larry.schafer@remingtoncollege.edu. Web site: http://www.remingtoncollege.edu/.

ROCKY MOUNTAIN COLLEGE OF ART + DESIGN
LAKEWOOD, COLORADO

General Proprietary, 4-year, coed **Entrance** Moderately difficult **Setting** 23-acre suburban campus **Total enrollment** 498 **Student-faculty ratio** 12:1 **Application deadline** Rolling (freshmen), rolling (transfer) **Freshmen** 99% were admitted **Expenses** Tuition $19,752; Room & Board $8440 **Undergraduates** 58% women, 13% part-time, 17% 25 or older, 1% Native American, 12% Hispanic American, 2% African American, 2% Asian American/Pacific Islander **The most frequently chosen baccalaureate fields are** communication technologies, education, visual and performing arts **Academic program**

Rocky Mountain College of Art + Design *(continued)*

Advanced placement, accelerated degree program, summer session, internships **Contact** Ms. Angela Carlson, Vice President of Admissions and Marketing, Rocky Mountain College of Art + Design, 1600 Pierce Street, Lakewood, CO 80214. Phone: 303-753-6046 or toll-free 800-888-ARTS. Fax: 303-759-4970. E-mail: admit@rmcad.edu. Web site: http://www.rmcad.edu/.

TEIKYO LORETTO HEIGHTS UNIVERSITY
DENVER, COLORADO

Contact Teikyo Loretto Heights University, 3001 South Federal Boulevard, Denver, CO 80236-2711. Web site: http://www.tlhu.edu/.

UNITED STATES AIR FORCE ACADEMY
COLORADO SPRINGS, COLORADO

General Federally supported, 4-year, coed, primarily men **Entrance** Most difficult **Setting** 18,000-acre suburban campus **Total enrollment** 4,461 **Student-faculty ratio** 8:1 **Application deadline** 1/31 (freshmen), 1/31 (transfer) **Freshmen** 14% were admitted **Housing** Yes **Undergraduates** 19% women, 1% 25 or older, 2% Native American, 7% Hispanic American, 5% African American, 8% Asian American/Pacific Islander **The most frequently chosen baccalaureate fields are** engineering, business/marketing, social sciences **Academic program** English as a second language, advanced placement, self-designed majors, summer session, internships **Contact** Mr. Rolland Stoneman, Associate Director of Admissions/Selections, United States Air Force Academy, HQ USAFA/RR, 2304 Cadet Drive, Suite 2400, USAF Academy, CO 80840-5025. Phone: 719-333-2520 or toll-free 800-443-9266. Fax: 719-333-3012. E-mail: rr_webmail@usafa.af.mil. Web site: http://www.usafa.edu/.

UNIVERSITY OF COLORADO AT BOULDER
BOULDER, COLORADO

General State-supported, university, coed **Entrance** Moderately difficult **Setting** 600-acre suburban campus **Total enrollment** 31,470 **Student-faculty ratio** 16:1 **Application deadline** 1/15 (freshmen), 4/1 (transfer) **Freshmen** 82% were admitted **Housing** Yes **Expenses** Tuition $7278; Room & Board $9860 **Undergraduates** 47% women, 9% part-time, 7% 25 or older, 1% Native American, 6% Hispanic American, 2% African American, 6% Asian American/Pacific Islander **The most frequently chosen baccalaureate fields are** business/marketing, biological/life sciences, social sciences **Academic program** English as a second language, advanced placement, accelerated degree program, self-designed majors, honors program, summer session, adult/continuing education programs, internships **Contact** Admissions Office, University of Colorado at Boulder, Regent Administrative Center 125, 552 UCB, Boulder, CO 80309. Phone: 303-492-6301. Fax: 303-492-7115. E-mail: apply@colorado.edu. Web site: http://www.colorado.edu/.

UNIVERSITY OF COLORADO AT COLORADO SPRINGS
COLORADO SPRINGS, COLORADO

General State-supported, comprehensive, coed **Contact** Mr. James Tidwell, Assistant Admissions Director, University of Colorado at Colorado Springs, 1420 Austin Bluffs Parkway, PO Box 7150, Colorado Springs, CO 80933-7150. Phone: 719-262-3375 or toll-free 800-990-8227 Ext. 3383. Fax: 719-262-3116. E-mail: admrec@mail.uccs.edu. Web site: http://www.uccs.edu/.

UNIVERSITY OF COLORADO DENVER
DENVER, COLORADO

General State-supported, university, coed **Entrance** Moderately difficult **Setting** 171-acre urban campus **Total enrollment** 20,162 **Student-faculty ratio** 15:1 **Application deadline** 7/22 (freshmen), 7/22 (transfer) **Freshmen** 68% were admitted **Housing** Yes **Expenses** Tuition $5932; Room & Board $9990 **Undergraduates** 56% women, 44% part-time, 33% 25 or older, 1% Native American, 11% Hispanic American, 4% African American, 9% Asian American/Pacific Islander **The most frequently chosen baccalaureate fields are** business/marketing, health professions and related sciences, social sciences **Academic program** English as a second language, advanced placement, accelerated degree program, self-designed majors, honors program, summer session, adult/continuing education programs, internships **Contact** Ms. Barbara Edwards, Director of Admissions, University of Colorado Denver, PO Box 173354, Campus Box 167, Denver, CO 80217. Phone: 303-556-3287. Fax: 303-556-4838. E-mail: admissions@castle.cudenver.edu. Web site: http://www.cudenver.edu/.

UNIVERSITY OF DENVER
DENVER, COLORADO

General Independent, university, coed **Entrance** Moderately difficult **Setting** 125-acre suburban campus **Total enrollment** 11,053 **Student-faculty ratio** 10:1 **Application deadline** 1/15 (freshmen), rolling (transfer) **Freshmen** 74% were admitted **Housing** Yes **Expenses** Tuition $32,232;

Room & Board $9678 **Undergraduates** 55% women, 9% part-time, 10% 25 or older, 1% Native American, 7% Hispanic American, 3% African American, 5% Asian American/Pacific Islander **The most frequently chosen baccalaureate fields are** business/marketing, communications/journalism, social sciences **Academic program** English as a second language, advanced placement, accelerated degree program, self-designed majors, honors program, summer session, adult/continuing education programs, internships **Contact** Mr. Todd Rinehart, Assistant Vice Chancellor for Enrollment, University of Denver, University Park, Denver, CO 80208. Phone: 303-871-3383 or toll-free 800-525-9495. Fax: 303-871-3301. E-mail: admission@du.edu. Web site: http://www.du.edu/.

UNIVERSITY OF NORTHERN COLORADO

GREELEY, COLORADO

General State-supported, university, coed **Entrance** Moderately difficult **Setting** 240-acre suburban campus **Total enrollment** 12,219 **Student-faculty ratio** 22:1 **Application deadline** 8/1 (freshmen), rolling (transfer) **Freshmen** 91% were admitted **Housing** Yes **Expenses** Tuition $4313; Room & Board $7342 **Undergraduates** 61% women, 9% part-time, 9% 25 or older, 1% Native American, 8% Hispanic American, 3% African American, 3% Asian American/Pacific Islander **The most frequently chosen baccalaureate fields are** business/marketing, health professions and related sciences, interdisciplinary studies **Academic program** English as a second language, advanced placement, self-designed majors, honors program, summer session, adult/continuing education programs, internships **Contact** Mr. Chris Dowen, Director of Admissions, University of Northern Colorado, Campus Box 10, Carter Hall 3006, Greeley, CO 80639. Phone: 970-351-2881 or toll-free 888-700-4UNC. Fax: 970-351-2984. E-mail: admissions.help@unco.edu. Web site: http://www.unco.edu/.

UNIVERSITY OF PHOENIX–DENVER CAMPUS

LONE TREE, COLORADO

General Proprietary, comprehensive, coed **Contact** Ms. Evelyn Gaskin, Registrar/Executive Director, University of Phoenix–Denver Campus, 4615 East Elmwood Street, Mail Stop AA-KK101, Phoenix, AZ 85040-1958. Phone: 480-557-3301 or toll-free 800-776-4867 (in-state); 800-228-7240 (out-of-state). Fax: 480-643-1020. E-mail: evelyn.gaskin@phoenix.edu. Web site: http://www.phoenix.edu/.

UNIVERSITY OF PHOENIX–SOUTHERN COLORADO CAMPUS

COLORADO SPRINGS, COLORADO

General Proprietary, comprehensive, coed **Contact** Ms. Evelyn Gaskin, Registrar/Executive Director, University of Phoenix–Southern Colorado Campus, 4615 East Elwood Street, Mail Stop AA-K101, Phoenix, AZ 85040-1958. Phone: 480-557-3301 or toll-free 800-776-4867 (in-state); 800-228-7240 (out-of-state). Fax: 480-643-1020. E-mail: evelyn.gaskin@phoenix.edu. Web site: http://www.phoenix.edu/.

WESTERN STATE COLLEGE OF COLORADO

GUNNISON, COLORADO

General State-supported, 4-year, coed **Entrance** Moderately difficult **Setting** 381-acre small-town campus **Total enrollment** 2,064 **Student-faculty ratio** 16:1 **Application deadline** 8/1 (freshmen) **Freshmen** 91% were admitted **Housing** Yes **Expenses** Tuition $3586; Room & Board $7226 **Undergraduates** 38% women, 10% part-time, 9% 25 or older, 1% Native American, 5% Hispanic American, 2% African American, 1% Asian American/Pacific Islander **The most frequently chosen baccalaureate fields are** business/marketing, parks and recreation, psychology **Academic program** Advanced placement, accelerated degree program, self-designed majors, honors program, summer session, adult/continuing education programs, internships **Contact** Mr. Timothy Albers, Director of Admissions, Western State College of Colorado, 6 Admission Office, Gunnison, CO 81231. Phone: 970-943-2119 or toll-free 800-876-5309. Fax: 970-943-2212. E-mail: discover@western.edu. Web site: http://www.western.edu/.

YESHIVA TORAS CHAIM TALMUDICAL SEMINARY

DENVER, COLORADO

Contact Rabbi Israel Kagan, Dean, Yeshiva Toras Chaim Talmudical Seminary, 1400 Quitman Street, Denver, CO 80204-1415. Phone: 303-629-8200. Fax: 303-623-5949.

CONNECTICUT

ALBERTUS MAGNUS COLLEGE

NEW HAVEN, CONNECTICUT

General Independent Roman Catholic, comprehensive, coed **Entrance** Moderately difficult **Setting** 55-acre suburban campus **Total enroll-**

Albertus Magnus College *(continued)*

ment 2,034 **Student-faculty ratio** 16:1 **Application deadline** 8/20 (freshmen), rolling (transfer) **Freshmen** 82% were admitted **Housing** Yes **Expenses** Tuition $21,074; Room & Board $8907 **Undergraduates** 68% women, 6% part-time, 37% 25 or older, 0.3% Native American, 10% Hispanic American, 27% African American, 1% Asian American/Pacific Islander **The most frequently chosen baccalaureate fields are** business/marketing, psychology, social sciences **Academic program** English as a second language, advanced placement, accelerated degree program, self-designed majors, honors program, summer session, adult/continuing education programs, internships **Contact** Ms. Jessica Van Deren, Dean of Admissions, Albertus Magnus College, 700 Prospect Street, New Haven, CT 06511-1189. Phone: 203-773-8501 or toll-free 800-578-9160. Fax: 203-773-5248. E-mail: admissions@albertus.edu. Web site: http://www.albertus.edu/.

BETH BENJAMIN ACADEMY OF CONNECTICUT

STAMFORD, CONNECTICUT

Contact Rabbi David Mayer, Director of Admissions, Beth Benjamin Academy of Connecticut, 132 Prospect Street, Stamford, CT 06901-1202. Phone: 203-325-4351.

CENTRAL CONNECTICUT STATE UNIVERSITY

NEW BRITAIN, CONNECTICUT

General State-supported, comprehensive, coed **Entrance** Moderately difficult **Setting** 294-acre suburban campus **Total enrollment** 12,106 **Student-faculty ratio** 16:1 **Application deadline** 6/1 (freshmen), 6/1 (transfer) **Freshmen** 61% were admitted **Housing** Yes **Expenses** Tuition $6734; Room & Board $8146 **Undergraduates** 49% women, 21% part-time, 16% 25 or older, 0.4% Native American, 6% Hispanic American, 8% African American, 3% Asian American/Pacific Islander **The most frequently chosen baccalaureate fields are** business/marketing, education, social sciences **Academic program** English as a second language, advanced placement, self-designed majors, honors program, summer session, adult/continuing education programs, internships **Contact** Mr. Richard Bishop, Interim Director of Admissions, Central Connecticut State University, 1615 Stanley Street, New Britain, CT 06050. Phone: 860-832-2285 or toll-free 888-733-2278. Fax: 860-832-2522. E-mail: admissions@ccsu.edu. Web site: http://www.ccsu.edu/.

CHARTER OAK STATE COLLEGE

NEW BRITAIN, CONNECTICUT

General State-supported, 4-year, coed **Entrance** Noncompetitive **Setting** small-town campus **Total enrollment** 1,577 **Student-faculty ratio** 11:1 **Application deadline** Rolling (transfer) **Housing** No **Undergraduates** 60% women, 95% part-time, 90% 25 or older, 1% Native American, 6% Hispanic American, 13% African American, 2% Asian American/Pacific Islander **The most frequently chosen baccalaureate field is** liberal arts/general studies **Academic program** Advanced placement, accelerated degree program, self-designed majors, summer session, adult/continuing education programs **Contact** Ms. Lori Pendleton, Director of Admissions, Charter Oak State College, 55 Paul J. Manafort Drive, New Britain, CT 06053-2150. Phone: 860-832-3858. Fax: 860-832-3999. E-mail: info@charteroak.edu. Web site: http://www.charteroak.edu/.

CONNECTICUT COLLEGE

NEW LONDON, CONNECTICUT

General Independent, comprehensive, coed **Entrance** Very difficult **Setting** 702-acre suburban campus **Total enrollment** 1,869 **Student-faculty ratio** 9:1 **Application deadline** 1/1 (freshmen), 4/1 (transfer) **Freshmen** 35% were admitted **Housing** Yes **Expenses** Tuition $46,675 **Undergraduates** 60% women, 3% part-time, 2% 25 or older, 0.1% Native American, 5% Hispanic American, 4% African American, 4% Asian American/Pacific Islander **The most frequently chosen baccalaureate fields are** social sciences, biological/life sciences, visual and performing arts **Academic program** Advanced placement, self-designed majors, honors program, summer session, adult/continuing education programs, internships **Contact** Ms. Martha Merrill, Dean of Admissions and Financial Aid, Connecticut College, 270 Mohegan Avenue, New London, CT 06320-4196. Phone: 860-439-2200. Fax: 860-439-4301. E-mail: admission@conncoll.edu. Web site: http://www.conncoll.edu/.

EASTERN CONNECTICUT STATE UNIVERSITY

WILLIMANTIC, CONNECTICUT

General State-supported, comprehensive, coed **Entrance** Moderately difficult **Setting** 179-acre small-town campus **Total enrollment** 5,137 **Student-faculty ratio** 16:1 **Application deadline** Rolling (freshmen), rolling (transfer) **Freshmen** 58% were admitted **Housing** Yes **Expenses** Tuition $6692; Room & Board $8377 **Undergraduates** 55% women, 18% part-time, 15% 25 or older, 1% Native American, 5% Hispanic American, 7% African American, 2%

Asian American/Pacific Islander **The most frequently chosen baccalaureate fields are** business/marketing, psychology, social sciences **Academic program** Advanced placement, self-designed majors, honors program, summer session, adult/continuing education programs, internships **Contact** Ms. Kimberly M. Crone, Director of Admissions and Enrollment Management, Eastern Connecticut State University, 83 Windham Street, Willimantic, CT 06226. Phone: 860-465-5286 or toll-free 877-353-3278. Fax: 860-465-5544. E-mail: admissions@easternct.edu. Web site: http://www.easternct.edu/.

FAIRFIELD UNIVERSITY
FAIRFIELD, CONNECTICUT

General Independent Roman Catholic (Jesuit), comprehensive, coed **Entrance** Moderately difficult **Setting** 200-acre suburban campus **Total enrollment** 5,024 **Student-faculty ratio** 13:1 **Application deadline** 1/15 (freshmen), 6/1 (transfer) **Freshmen** 55% were admitted **Housing** Yes **Expenses** Tuition $33,905; Room & Board $10,430 **Undergraduates** 58% women, 14% part-time, 0.2% Native American, 6% Hispanic American, 3% African American, 3% Asian American/Pacific Islander **The most frequently chosen baccalaureate fields are** business/marketing, communications/journalism, social sciences **Academic program** Advanced placement, self-designed majors, honors program, summer session, adult/continuing education programs, internships **Contact** Ms. Karen Pellegrino, Director of Admission, Fairfield University, 1073 North Benson Road, Fairfield, CT 06824-5195. Phone: 203-254-4100. Fax: 203-254-4199. E-mail: admis@mail.fairfield.edu. Web site: http://www.fairfield.edu/.

HOLY APOSTLES COLLEGE AND SEMINARY
CROMWELL, CONNECTICUT

General Independent Roman Catholic, comprehensive, coed, primarily men **Entrance** Noncompetitive **Setting** 17-acre suburban campus **Total enrollment** 284 **Student-faculty ratio** 11:1 **Application deadline** Rolling (freshmen), rolling (transfer) **Freshmen** 100% were admitted **Housing** No **Expenses** Tuition $7800 **Undergraduates** 35% women, 63% part-time, 71% 25 or older, 9% Hispanic American, 2% African American, 4% Asian American/Pacific Islander **The most frequently chosen baccalaureate fields are** philosophy and religious studies, social sciences **Academic program** English as a second language, summer session, adult/continuing education programs **Contact** Mr. Mark Azzara, Holy Apostles College and Seminary, 33 Prospect Hill Road, Cromwell, CT 06416-2005. Phone: 860-632-3010 or toll-free 800-330-7272. Fax: 860-632-3075. E-mail: recruitment@holyapostles.edu. Web site: http://www.holyapostles.edu/.

LYME ACADEMY COLLEGE OF FINE ARTS
OLD LYME, CONNECTICUT

General Independent, 4-year, coed **Entrance** Moderately difficult **Setting** 3-acre small-town campus **Total enrollment** 160 **Student-faculty ratio** 7:1 **Application deadline** Rolling (freshmen), rolling (transfer) **Freshmen** 89% were admitted **Housing** No **Expenses** Tuition $20,245 **Undergraduates** 66% women, 56% part-time, 55% 25 or older, 1% Native American, 5% Hispanic American **Academic program** Summer session **Contact** Ms. Debra Sigmon, Director of Admission, Lyme Academy College of Fine Arts, 84 Lyme Street, Old Lyme, CT 06371. Phone: 860-434-5232 Ext. 119. Fax: 860-434-8725. E-mail: desigmon@lymeacademy.edu. Web site: http://www.lymeacademy.edu/.

MITCHELL COLLEGE
NEW LONDON, CONNECTICUT

General Independent, 4-year, coed **Entrance** Minimally difficult **Setting** 67-acre suburban campus **Total enrollment** 894 **Student-faculty ratio** 12:1 **Application deadline** Rolling (freshmen), rolling (transfer) **Freshmen** 58% were admitted **Housing** Yes **Expenses** Tuition $24,358; Room & Board $10,977 **Undergraduates** 51% women, 16% part-time, 4% 25 or older, 3% Native American, 8% Hispanic American, 12% African American, 1% Asian American/Pacific Islander **The most frequently chosen baccalaureate fields are** business/marketing, liberal arts/general studies, psychology **Academic program** English as a second language, advanced placement, summer session, adult/continuing education programs, internships **Contact** Ms. Kimberly Hodges, Director of Admissions, Mitchell College, 437 Pequot Avenue, New London, CT 06320. Phone: 860-701-5038 or toll-free 800-443-2811. Fax: 860-444-1209. E-mail: admissions@mitchell.edu. Web site: http://www.mitchell.edu/.

PAIER COLLEGE OF ART, INC.
HAMDEN, CONNECTICUT

General Proprietary, 4-year, coed **Entrance** Minimally difficult **Setting** 3-acre suburban campus **Total enrollment** 249 **Student-faculty ratio** 7:1 **Application deadline** Rolling (freshmen), rolling (transfer) **Freshmen** 78% were admitted **Housing** No **Expenses** Tuition $12,385 **Undergraduates** 68% women, 33% part-time, 21% 25 or older, 0.4% Native American, 2% Hispanic American, 4% African American, 2% Asian American/

Paier College of Art, Inc. *(continued)*

Pacific Islander **The most frequently chosen baccalaureate field is** visual and performing arts **Academic program** Advanced placement, summer session **Contact** Ms. Lynn Pascale, Secretary to Admissions, Paier College of Art, Inc., 20 Gorham Avenue, Hamden, CT 06514-3902. Phone: 203-287-3031. Fax: 203-287-3021. E-mail: paier.admission@snet.net. Web site: http://www.paiercollegeofart.edu/.

POST UNIVERSITY
WATERBURY, CONNECTICUT

Contact Mr. Jay Murray, Director of Admissions, Post University, PO Box 2540, Waterbury, CT 06723. Phone: 203-596-4630 or toll-free 800-345-2562. Fax: 203-756-5810. E-mail: admiss@post.edu. Web site: http://www.post.edu/.

QUINNIPIAC UNIVERSITY
HAMDEN, CONNECTICUT

General Independent, comprehensive, coed **Entrance** Moderately difficult **Setting** 500-acre suburban campus **Total enrollment** 7,216 **Student-faculty ratio** 15:1 **Application deadline** 2/1 (freshmen), 4/1 (transfer) **Freshmen** 47% were admitted **Housing** Yes **Expenses** Tuition $30,900; Room & Board $11,800 **Undergraduates** 62% women, 5% part-time, 5% 25 or older, 0.2% Native American, 5% Hispanic American, 3% African American, 2% Asian American/Pacific Islander **The most frequently chosen baccalaureate fields are** business/marketing, communications/journalism, health professions and related sciences **Academic program** Advanced placement, self-designed majors, honors program, summer session, adult/continuing education programs, internships **Contact** Ms. Joan Isaac Mohr, Vice President and Dean of Admissions, Quinnipiac University, 275 Mount Carmel Avenue, Hamden, CT 06518. Phone: 203-582-8600 or toll-free 800-462-1944. Fax: 203-582-8906. E-mail: admissions@quinnipiac.edu. Web site: http://www.quinnipiac.edu/.

SACRED HEART UNIVERSITY
FAIRFIELD, CONNECTICUT

General Independent Roman Catholic, comprehensive, coed **Entrance** Moderately difficult **Setting** 65-acre suburban campus **Total enrollment** 5,756 **Student-faculty ratio** 13:1 **Freshmen** 62% were admitted **Housing** Yes **Expenses** Tuition $27,150; Room & Board $11,346 **Undergraduates** 62% women, 19% part-time, 7% 25 or older, 0.2% Native American, 6% Hispanic American, 5% African American, 2% Asian American/Pacific Islander **The most frequently chosen baccalaureate fields are** business/marketing, health professions and related sciences, psychology **Academic program** English as a second language, advanced placement, accelerated degree program, self-designed majors, honors program, summer session, adult/continuing education programs, internships **Contact** Ms. Karen N. Guastelle, Dean of Undergraduate Admissions, Sacred Heart University, 5151 Park Avenue, Fairfield, CT 06825-1000. Phone: 203-365-4763. Fax: 203-365-7607. E-mail: enroll@sacredheart.edu. Web site: http://www.sacredheart.edu/.

SAINT JOSEPH COLLEGE
WEST HARTFORD, CONNECTICUT

General Independent Roman Catholic, comprehensive, undergraduate: women only; graduate: coed **Setting** 84-acre suburban campus **Total enrollment** 1,773 **Student-faculty ratio** 10:1 **Application deadline** Rolling (freshmen), rolling (transfer) **Freshmen** 83% were admitted **Housing** Yes **Expenses** Tuition $24,690; Room & Board $11,880 **Undergraduates** 26% part-time, 27% 25 or older, 0.2% Native American, 9% Hispanic American, 12% African American, 3% Asian American/Pacific Islander **The most frequently chosen baccalaureate fields are** health professions and related sciences, psychology, public administration and social services **Academic program** English as a second language, advanced placement, accelerated degree program, self-designed majors, honors program, summer session, adult/continuing education programs, internships **Contact** Office of Admissions, Saint Joseph College, Saint Joseph College, 1678 Asylum Avenue, West Hartford, CT 06117. Phone: 866-442-8752 or toll-free 866-442-8752. Fax: 860-231-5744. E-mail: admissions@sjc.edu. Web site: http://www.sjc.edu/.

SOUTHERN CONNECTICUT STATE UNIVERSITY
NEW HAVEN, CONNECTICUT

General State-supported, comprehensive, coed **Entrance** Moderately difficult **Setting** 168-acre urban campus **Total enrollment** 11,930 **Student-faculty ratio** 15:1 **Application deadline** 4/1 (freshmen), 7/15 (transfer) **Freshmen** 52% were admitted **Housing** Yes **Expenses** Tuition $7179; Room & Board $8966 **Undergraduates** 62% women, 16% part-time, 16% 25 or older, 0.2% Native American, 7% Hispanic American, 12% African American, 2% Asian American/Pacific Islander **The most frequently chosen baccalaureate fields are** business/marketing, education, psychology **Academic program** Advanced placement, accelerated degree program, self-designed majors, honors program, summer session, adult/

continuing education programs, internships **Contact** Ms. Paula Kennedy, Associate Director of Admissions, Southern Connecticut State University, Admissions House, 131 Farnham Avenue, New Haven, CT 06515-1202. Phone: 203-392-5651. Fax: 203-392-5727. Web site: http://www.southernct.edu/.

TRINITY COLLEGE
HARTFORD, CONNECTICUT

General Independent, comprehensive, coed **Entrance** Most difficult **Setting** 100-acre urban campus **Total enrollment** 2,564 **Student-faculty ratio** 10:1 **Application deadline** 1/1 (freshmen), 4/1 (transfer) **Freshmen** 34% were admitted **Housing** Yes **Expenses** Tuition $36,870; Room & Board $9420 **Undergraduates** 50% women, 7% part-time, 0.2% Native American, 6% Hispanic American, 7% African American, 5% Asian American/Pacific Islander **The most frequently chosen baccalaureate fields are** area and ethnic studies, English, social sciences **Academic program** Advanced placement, accelerated degree program, self-designed majors, honors program, summer session, adult/continuing education programs, internships **Contact** Mr. Larry Dow, Dean of Admissions and Financial Aid, Trinity College, 300 Summit Street, Hartford, CT 06106-3100. Phone: 860-297-2180. Fax: 860-297-2287. E-mail: admissions.office@trincoll.edu. Web site: http://www.trincoll.edu/.

UNITED STATES COAST GUARD ACADEMY
NEW LONDON, CONNECTICUT

General Federally supported, 4-year, coed **Entrance** Very difficult **Setting** 110-acre suburban campus **Total enrollment** 963 **Student-faculty ratio** 9:1 **Application deadline** 2/1 (freshmen) **Freshmen** 27% were admitted **Housing** Yes **Undergraduates** 27% women, 0.4% Native American, 6% Hispanic American, 3% African American, 4% Asian American/Pacific Islander **The most frequently chosen baccalaureate fields are** business/marketing, engineering, social sciences **Academic program** Honors program, summer session, internships **Contact** Capt. Susan Bibeau, Director of Admissions, United States Coast Guard Academy, 31 Mohegan Avenue, New London, CT 06320-4195. Phone: 860-444-8500 or toll-free 800-883-8724. Fax: 860-701-6700. E-mail: admissions@uscga.edu. Web site: http://www.uscga.edu/.

UNIVERSITY OF BRIDGEPORT
BRIDGEPORT, CONNECTICUT

General Independent, comprehensive, coed **Entrance** Moderately difficult **Setting** 86-acre urban campus **Total enrollment** 4,752 **Student-faculty ratio** 12:1 **Application deadline** Rolling (freshmen), rolling (transfer) **Freshmen** 57% were admitted **Housing** Yes **Expenses** Tuition $22,860; Room & Board $10,000 **Undergraduates** 68% women, 32% part-time, 37% 25 or older, 0.3% Native American, 13% Hispanic American, 33% African American, 3% Asian American/Pacific Islander **The most frequently chosen baccalaureate fields are** business/marketing, liberal arts/general studies, social sciences **Academic program** English as a second language, advanced placement, accelerated degree program, self-designed majors, honors program, summer session, adult/continuing education programs, internships **Contact** Ms. Barbara Maryak, Associate Vice President Admissions, University of Bridgeport, 126 Park Avenue, Bridgeport, CT 06604. Phone: 203-576-4552 or toll-free 800-EXCEL-UB (in-state); 800-243-9496 (out-of-state). Fax: 203-576-4941. E-mail: admit@bridgeport.edu. Web site: http://www.bridgeport.edu/.

UNIVERSITY OF CONNECTICUT
STORRS, CONNECTICUT

General State-supported, university, coed **Entrance** Moderately difficult **Setting** 4,104-acre rural campus **Total enrollment** 23,692 **Student-faculty ratio** 17:1 **Application deadline** 2/1 (freshmen), 4/1 (transfer) **Freshmen** 49% were admitted **Housing** Yes **Expenses** Tuition $9338; Room & Board $9300 **Undergraduates** 51% women, 4% part-time, 3% 25 or older, 0.4% Native American, 5% Hispanic American, 5% African American, 7% Asian American/Pacific Islander **The most frequently chosen baccalaureate fields are** business/marketing, health professions and related sciences, social sciences **Academic program** English as a second language, advanced placement, accelerated degree program, self-designed majors, honors program, summer session, adult/continuing education programs, internships **Contact** Mr. Brian Usher, Associate Director of Admissions, University of Connecticut, 2131 Hillside Road, U-88, Storrs, CT 06269. Phone: 860-486-3137. Fax: 860-486-1476. E-mail: beahusky@uconnvm.uconn.edu. Web site: http://www.uconn.edu/.

UNIVERSITY OF HARTFORD
WEST HARTFORD, CONNECTICUT

General Independent, comprehensive, coed **Entrance** Moderately difficult **Setting** 320-acre suburban campus **Total enrollment** 7,290 **Student-faculty ratio** 14:1 **Application deadline** Rolling (freshmen), rolling (transfer) **Freshmen** 54% were admitted **Housing** Yes **Expenses** Tuition $28,172; Room & Board $10,876 **Undergraduates** 52% women, 15% part-

University of Hartford *(continued)*

time, 12% 25 or older, 0.2% Native American, 6% Hispanic American, 11% African American, 3% Asian American/Pacific Islander **The most frequently chosen baccalaureate fields are** business/marketing, education, visual and performing arts **Academic program** English as a second language, advanced placement, self-designed majors, honors program, summer session, adult/continuing education programs, internships **Contact** Mr. Richard Zeiser, Dean of Admissions, University of Hartford, 200 Bloomfield Avenue, West Hartford, CT 06117. Phone: 860-768-4296 or toll-free 800-947-4303. Fax: 860-768-4961. E-mail: admissions@hartford.edu. Web site: http://www.hartford.edu/.

UNIVERSITY OF NEW HAVEN
WEST HAVEN, CONNECTICUT

General Independent, comprehensive, coed **Entrance** Moderately difficult **Setting** 78-acre suburban campus **Total enrollment** 4,774 **Student-faculty ratio** 14:1 **Application deadline** Rolling (freshmen), rolling (transfer) **Freshmen** 73% were admitted **Housing** Yes **Expenses** Tuition $26,868; Room & Board $10,581 **Undergraduates** 48% women, 14% part-time, 4% 25 or older, 0.4% Native American, 8% Hispanic American, 9% African American, 3% Asian American/Pacific Islander **The most frequently chosen baccalaureate fields are** business/marketing, security and protective services, visual and performing arts **Academic program** Advanced placement, accelerated degree program, honors program, summer session, adult/continuing education programs, internships **Contact** Mr. Kevin Phillips, Director of Undergraduate Admissions, University of New Haven, Bayer Hall, 300 Boston Post Road, West Haven, CT 06516. Phone: 203-932-7318 or toll-free 800-DIAL-UNH. Fax: 203-931-6093. E-mail: adminfo@newhaven.edu. Web site: http://www.newhaven.edu/.

WESLEYAN UNIVERSITY
MIDDLETOWN, CONNECTICUT

General Independent, university, coed **Entrance** Most difficult **Setting** 240-acre small-town campus **Total enrollment** 3,222 **Student-faculty ratio** 9:1 **Application deadline** 1/1 (freshmen), 3/15 (transfer) **Freshmen** 27% were admitted **Housing** Yes **Expenses** Tuition $36,806; Room & Board $10,130 **Undergraduates** 50% women, 1% part-time, 1% Native American, 8% Hispanic American, 7% African American, 11% Asian American/Pacific Islander **The most frequently chosen baccalaureate fields are** area and ethnic studies, social sciences, visual and performing arts **Academic program** English as a second language, advanced placement, accelerated degree program, self-designed majors, honors program, summer session, adult/continuing education programs, internships **Contact** Ms. Nancy Meislahn, Dean of Admission and Financial Aid, Wesleyan University, Stewart M Reid House, 70 Wyllys Avenue, Middletown, CT 06459-0265. Phone: 860-685-3000. Fax: 860-685-3001. E-mail: admissions@wesleyan.edu. Web site: http://www.wesleyan.edu/.

WESTERN CONNECTICUT STATE UNIVERSITY
DANBURY, CONNECTICUT

General State-supported, comprehensive, coed **Entrance** Moderately difficult **Setting** 340-acre urban campus **Total enrollment** 6,211 **Student-faculty ratio** 15:1 **Freshmen** 58% were admitted **Housing** Yes **Expenses** Tuition $6624; Room & Board $8400 **Undergraduates** 55% women, 21% part-time, 15% 25 or older, 0.2% Native American, 7% Hispanic American, 7% African American, 4% Asian American/Pacific Islander **The most frequently chosen baccalaureate fields are** business/marketing, education, security and protective services **Academic program** English as a second language, advanced placement, accelerated degree program, self-designed majors, honors program, summer session, internships **Contact** Office of University Admissions, Western Connecticut State University, 181 White Street, Danbury, CT 06810. Phone: 203-837-9000 or toll-free 877-837-WCSU. E-mail: admissions@wcsu.edu. Web site: http://www.wcsu.edu/.

YALE UNIVERSITY
NEW HAVEN, CONNECTICUT

General Independent, university, coed **Entrance** Most difficult **Setting** 200-acre urban campus **Total enrollment** 11,350 **Student-faculty ratio** 6:1 **Application deadline** 12/31 (freshmen), 3/1 (transfer) **Freshmen** 10% were admitted **Housing** Yes **Expenses** Tuition $34,530; Room & Board $10,470 **Undergraduates** 49% women, 0.4% part-time, 1% 25 or older, 1% Native American, 8% Hispanic American, 9% African American, 14% Asian American/Pacific Islander **The most frequently chosen baccalaureate fields are** history, interdisciplinary studies, social sciences **Academic program** English as a second language, advanced placement, accelerated degree program, self-designed majors, honors program, summer session, internships **Contact** Admissions Director, Yale University, PO Box 208234, New Haven, CT 06520. Phone: 203-432-9316. Fax: 203-432-9392. E-mail: undergraduate.admissions@yale.edu. Web site: http://www.yale.edu/.

DELAWARE

DELAWARE STATE UNIVERSITY

DOVER, DELAWARE

General State-supported, comprehensive, coed **Entrance** Moderately difficult **Setting** 400-acre small-town campus **Total enrollment** 3,756 **Student-faculty ratio** 14:1 **Application deadline** 4/1 (freshmen), 4/1 (transfer) **Freshmen** 43% were admitted **Housing** Yes **Expenses** Tuition $6146; Room & Board $9006 **Undergraduates** 59% women, 11% part-time, 24% 25 or older, 0.1% Native American, 2% Hispanic American, 77% African American, 1% Asian American/Pacific Islander **The most frequently chosen baccalaureate fields are** business/marketing, public administration and social services, social sciences **Academic program** English as a second language, advanced placement, accelerated degree program, honors program, summer session, adult/continuing education programs, internships **Contact** Mrs. Lawita Cheatham, Executive Director for Admissions, Delaware State University, 1200 North DuPont Highway, Dover, DE 19901-2277. Phone: 302-857-6103 or toll-free 800-845-2544. Fax: 302-857-6908. E-mail: gcheatha@desu.edu. Web site: http://www.desu.edu/.

GOLDEY-BEACOM COLLEGE

WILMINGTON, DELAWARE

General Independent, comprehensive, coed **Entrance** Moderately difficult **Setting** 27-acre suburban campus **Total enrollment** 1,208 **Student-faculty ratio** 24:1 **Application deadline** Rolling (freshmen), rolling (transfer) **Housing** Yes **Expenses** Tuition $18,840; Room only $4982 **Undergraduates** 54% women, 31% part-time **Academic program** Advanced placement, accelerated degree program, honors program, summer session, internships **Contact** Corinne Clemetsen, Admissions Representative, Goldey-Beacom College, 4701 Limestone Road, Wilmington, DE 19808. Phone: 302-225-6289 Ext. 289 or toll-free 800-833-4877. Fax: 302-996-5408. E-mail: clemetc@gbc.edu. Web site: http://www.gbc.edu/.

UNIVERSITY OF DELAWARE

NEWARK, DELAWARE

General State-related, university, coed **Entrance** Moderately difficult **Setting** 1,000-acre small-town campus **Total enrollment** 19,677 **Student-faculty ratio** 12:1 **Application deadline** 1/15 (freshmen), 5/1 (transfer) **Freshmen** 56% were admitted **Housing** Yes **Expenses** Tuition $8150; Room & Board $7948 **Undergraduates** 58% women, 11% part-time, 4% 25 or older, 0.4% Native American, 5% Hispanic American, 5% African American, 4% Asian American/Pacific Islander **The most frequently chosen baccalaureate fields are** business/marketing, education, social sciences **Academic program** English as a second language, advanced placement, accelerated degree program, self-designed majors, honors program, summer session, adult/continuing education programs, internships **Contact** Mr. Lou Hirsh, Director of Admissions, University of Delaware, 116 Hullihen Hall, Newark, DE 19716. Phone: 302-831-8123. Fax: 302-831-6905. E-mail: admissions@udel.edu. Web site: http://www.udel.edu/.

WESLEY COLLEGE

DOVER, DELAWARE

General Independent United Methodist, comprehensive, coed **Entrance** Moderately difficult **Setting** 40-acre small-town campus **Total enrollment** 1,871 **Student-faculty ratio** 17:1 **Application deadline** Rolling (freshmen), rolling (transfer) **Freshmen** 67% were admitted **Housing** Yes **Expenses** Tuition $17,579; Room & Board $7800 **Undergraduates** 52% women, 17% part-time, 6% 25 or older, 0.2% Native American, 2% Hispanic American, 19% African American, 2% Asian American/Pacific Islander **The most frequently chosen baccalaureate fields are** business/marketing, education, psychology **Academic program** English as a second language, advanced placement, summer session, adult/continuing education programs, internships **Contact** Mr. Arthur Jacobs, Director of Undergraduate Admissions, Wesley College, 120 North State Street, Dover, DE 19901-3875. Phone: 302-736-2400 or toll-free 800-937-5398 Ext. 2400. Fax: 302-736-2382. E-mail: admissions@wesley.edu. Web site: http://www.wesley.edu/.

WILMINGTON UNIVERSITY

NEW CASTLE, DELAWARE

General Independent, comprehensive, coed **Entrance** Noncompetitive **Setting** 17-acre suburban campus **Total enrollment** 8,496 **Student-faculty ratio** 17:1 **Application deadline** Rolling (freshmen), rolling (transfer) **Freshmen** 100% were admitted **Housing** No **Expenses** Tuition $8450 **Undergraduates** 65% women, 48% part-time, 52% 25 or older, 0.2% Native American, 2% Hispanic American, 17% African American, 1% Asian American/Pacific Islander **The most frequently chosen baccalaureate fields are** business/marketing, education, liberal arts/general studies **Academic program** Accelerated degree program, summer session, adult/continuing education programs, internships **Contact** Mr. Christopher Ferguson, Director of Admissions, Wilmington University, 320 North

Wilmington University *(continued)*

DuPont Highway, New Castle, DE 19720-6491. Phone: 302-356-6745 or toll-free 877-967-5464. Fax: 302-328-5902. E-mail: inquire@wilmcoll.edu. Web site: http://www.wilmu.edu/.

DISTRICT OF COLUMBIA

AMERICAN UNIVERSITY
WASHINGTON, DISTRICT OF COLUMBIA

General Independent Methodist, university, coed **Entrance** Very difficult **Setting** 84-acre suburban campus **Total enrollment** 11,450 **Student-faculty ratio** 14:1 **Application deadline** 1/15 (freshmen), 7/1 (transfer) **Freshmen** 53% were admitted **Housing** Yes **Expenses** Tuition $33,283; Room & Board $12,418 **Undergraduates** 62% women, 4% part-time, 3% 25 or older, 1% Native American, 5% Hispanic American, 5% African American, 5% Asian American/Pacific Islander **The most frequently chosen baccalaureate fields are** business/marketing, communications/journalism, social sciences **Academic program** Advanced placement, accelerated degree program, self-designed majors, honors program, summer session, adult/continuing education programs, internships **Contact** Director of Admissions, American University, 4400 Massachusetts Avenue, NW, Washington, DC 20016-8001. Phone: 202-885-6000. Fax: 202-885-6014. E-mail: admissions@american.edu. Web site: http://www.american.edu/.

►**For more information, see page 439.**

THE CATHOLIC UNIVERSITY OF AMERICA
WASHINGTON, DISTRICT OF COLUMBIA

General Independent, university, coed, affiliated with Roman Catholic Church **Entrance** Moderately difficult **Setting** 193-acre urban campus **Total enrollment** 6,440 **Student-faculty ratio** 10:1 **Application deadline** 2/15 (freshmen), 7/15 (transfer) **Freshmen** 80% were admitted **Housing** Yes **Expenses** Tuition $28,990; Room & Board $10,808 **Undergraduates** 54% women, 8% part-time, 9% 25 or older, 0.2% Native American, 6% Hispanic American, 5% African American, 3% Asian American/Pacific Islander **The most frequently chosen baccalaureate fields are** architecture, social sciences, visual and performing arts **Academic program** English as a second language, advanced placement, accelerated degree program, honors program, summer session, adult/continuing education programs, internships **Contact** Ms. Christine Mica, Director of University Admissions, The Catholic University of America, 102 McMahon Hall, 620 Michigan Avenue, NE, Washington, DC 20064. Phone: 202-319-5305 or toll-free 202-319-5305 (in-state); 800-673-2772 (out-of-state). Fax: 202-319-6533. E-mail: cua-admissions@cua.edu. Web site: http://www.cua.edu/.

CORCORAN COLLEGE OF ART AND DESIGN
WASHINGTON, DISTRICT OF COLUMBIA

General Independent, comprehensive, coed **Entrance** Moderately difficult **Setting** 7-acre urban campus **Total enrollment** 698 **Student-faculty ratio** 4:1 **Application deadline** Rolling (freshmen), rolling (transfer) **Freshmen** 64% were admitted **Housing** Yes **Expenses** Tuition $27,380; Room & Board $12,154 **Undergraduates** 70% women, 34% part-time, 7% 25 or older, 0.4% Native American, 6% Hispanic American, 8% African American, 9% Asian American/Pacific Islander **The most frequently chosen baccalaureate field is** visual and performing arts **Academic program** Advanced placement, summer session, adult/continuing education programs, internships **Contact** Ms. Elizabeth Smith Paladino, Director of Admissions, Corcoran College of Art and Design, 500 17th Street, NW, Washington, DC 20006-4804. Phone: 202-639-1814 or toll-free 888-CORCORAN. Fax: 202-639-1830. E-mail: admissions@corcoran.org. Web site: http://www.corcoran.edu/.

GALLAUDET UNIVERSITY
WASHINGTON, DISTRICT OF COLUMBIA

Contact Ms. Charity Reedy-Hines, Director of Admissions, Gallaudet University, 800 Florida Avenue, NE, Washington, DC 20002-3625. Phone: 202-651-5750 or toll-free 800-995-0550. Fax: 202-651-5744. E-mail: admissions.studentvisits@gallaudet.edu. Web site: http://www.gallaudet.edu/.

GEORGETOWN UNIVERSITY
WASHINGTON, DISTRICT OF COLUMBIA

General Independent Roman Catholic (Jesuit), university, coed **Entrance** Most difficult **Setting** 110-acre urban campus **Total enrollment** 14,826 **Student-faculty ratio** 11:1 **Application deadline** 1/10 (freshmen), 3/1 (transfer) **Freshmen** 21% were admitted **Housing** Yes **Expenses** Tuition $35,568; Room & Board $12,146 **Undergraduates** 54% women, 4% part-time, 4% 25 or older, 0.1% Native American, 7% Hispanic American, 7% African American, 9% Asian American/Pacific Islander **The most frequently chosen baccalaureate fields are** business/marketing, English, social sciences **Academic**

program English as a second language, advanced placement, self-designed majors, honors program, summer session, adult/continuing education programs, internships **Contact** Mr. Charles A. Deacon, Dean of Undergraduate Admissions, Georgetown University, 37th and O Street, NW, Washington, DC 20057. Phone: 202-687-3600. Fax: 202-687-5084. Web site: http://www.georgetown.edu/.

THE GEORGE WASHINGTON UNIVERSITY
WASHINGTON, DISTRICT OF COLUMBIA

General Independent, university, coed **Entrance** Very difficult **Setting** 36-acre urban campus **Total enrollment** 25,078 **Student-faculty ratio** 13:1 **Application deadline** 1/15 (freshmen), rolling (transfer) **Freshmen** 37% were admitted **Housing** Yes **Expenses** Tuition $40,437; Room & Board $9920 **Undergraduates** 55% women, 10% part-time, 6% 25 or older, 0.3% Native American, 6% Hispanic American, 6% African American, 10% Asian American/Pacific Islander **The most frequently chosen baccalaureate fields are** business/marketing, psychology, social sciences **Academic program** English as a second language, advanced placement, accelerated degree program, self-designed majors, honors program, summer session, adult/continuing education programs, internships **Contact** Dr. Kathryn M. Napper, Director of Admission, The George Washington University, 2121 Eye Street, NW, Washington, DC 20052. Phone: 202-994-6040. Fax: 202-994-0325. E-mail: gwadm@gwu.edu. Web site: http://www.gwu.edu/.

HOWARD UNIVERSITY
WASHINGTON, DISTRICT OF COLUMBIA

Contact Interim Director of Admissions, Howard University, 2400 Sixth Street, NW, Washington, DC 20059-0002. Phone: 202-806-2700 or toll-free 800-HOWARD-U. Fax: 202-806-4462. E-mail: admissions@howard.edu. Web site: http://www.howard.edu/.

POTOMAC COLLEGE
WASHINGTON, DISTRICT OF COLUMBIA

Contact Asha Ellison, Assistant to the President, Potomac College, 4000 Chesapeake Street, NW, Washington, DC 20016. Phone: 202-686-0876 Ext. 203 or toll-free 888-686-0876. Fax: 202-686-0818. E-mail: info@potomac.edu. Web site: http://www.potomac.edu/.

SOUTHEASTERN UNIVERSITY
WASHINGTON, DISTRICT OF COLUMBIA

General Independent, 4-year, coed, primarily women **Entrance** Noncompetitive **Setting** 1-acre urban campus **Total enrollment** 813 **Student-faculty ratio** 7:1 **Application deadline** Rolling (freshmen), rolling (transfer) **Freshmen** 36% were admitted **Housing** No **Expenses** Tuition $10,230 **Undergraduates** 79% 25 or older, 0.4% Native American, 1% Hispanic American, 71% African American, 1% Asian American/Pacific Islander **The most frequently chosen baccalaureate fields are** business/marketing, computer and information sciences, law/legal studies **Academic program** English as a second language, advanced placement, accelerated degree program, honors program, summer session, adult/continuing education programs, internships **Contact** Ms. Halima Griffin, Recruitment Officer, Southeastern University, 501 I Street, SW, Washington, DC 20024. Phone: 202-478-8200 Ext. 255. Fax: 202-488-8093. E-mail: admissions@seu.edu. Web site: http://www.seu.edu/.

STRAYER UNIVERSITY
WASHINGTON, DISTRICT OF COLUMBIA

Contact Ms. Deepali Kala, Director of Student Enrollment, Strayer University, 1025 15th Street, NW, Washington, DC 20005-2603. Phone: 703-339-1850 or toll-free 888-4-STRAYER. Fax: 202-419-1425. E-mail: mzm@strayer.edu. Web site: http://www.strayer.edu/.

TRINITY (WASHINGTON) UNIVERSITY
WASHINGTON, DISTRICT OF COLUMBIA

Contact Ms. Marien Noblitt, Vice President for Marketing, Recruiting, and Admissions, Trinity (Washington) University, 125 Michigan Avenue, NE, Washington, DC 20017-1094. Phone: 800-492-6882 or toll-free 800-IWANTTC. Fax: 202-884-9403. E-mail: admissions@trinitydc.edu. Web site: http://www.trinitydc.edu/.

UNIVERSITY OF THE DISTRICT OF COLUMBIA
WASHINGTON, DISTRICT OF COLUMBIA

General District-supported, comprehensive, coed **Entrance** Noncompetitive **Setting** 28-acre urban campus **Total enrollment** 5,371 **Student-faculty ratio** 13:1 **Application deadline** 8/1 (freshmen), 8/1 (transfer) **Freshmen** 85% were admitted **Housing** No **Expenses** Tuition $5040 **Undergraduates** 60% women, 53% part-time, 55% 25 or older, 0.1% Native American, 6% Hispanic American, 71% African American, 3% Asian American/Pacific Islander **The most frequently chosen baccalaureate fields are** business/marketing, health professions and related sciences, security and protective services **Academic program** English as a second language, accelerated degree program, honors program, summer session, adult/continuing education

University of the District of Columbia *(continued)*

programs, internships **Contact** Mrs. LaVerne Hill Flannigan, Director of Admission/Recruitment/ Registrar, University of the District of Columbia, 4200 Connecticut Avenue NW, Building 39, Level A, Washington, DC 20008. Phone: 202-274-6110. Fax: 202-274-5553. Web site: http://www.udc.edu/.

FLORIDA

AMERICAN INTERCONTINENTAL UNIVERSITY

WESTON, FLORIDA

General Proprietary, comprehensive, coed **Entrance** Minimally difficult **Setting** 3-acre suburban campus **Total enrollment** 26,686 **Application deadline** Rolling (freshmen), rolling (transfer) **Academic program** Advanced placement, summer session, adult/continuing education programs **Contact** Vice President of Admissions, American InterContinental University, 2250 North Commerce Parkway, Suite 100, Weston, FL 33326. Phone: 954-446-6100 or toll-free 888-603-4888. Fax: 954-233-8127. Web site: http://www.aiuniv.edu/.

ARGOSY UNIVERSITY, SARASOTA

SARASOTA, FLORIDA

General Proprietary, university, coed **Contact** Director of Admissions, Argosy University, Sarasota, 5250 17th Street, Sarasota, FL 34235. Phone: toll-free 800-331-5995. Web site: http://www.argosy.edu/locations/sarasota/.

ARGOSY UNIVERSITY, TAMPA

TAMPA, FLORIDA

General Proprietary, university, coed **Setting** urban campus **Contact** Director of Admissions, Argosy University, Tampa, 4401 North Himes Avenue, Suite 150, Tampa, FL 33614. Phone: 813-393-5290 or toll-free 800-850-6488. Web site: http://www.argosy.edu/locations/tampa/.

THE ART INSTITUTE OF FORT LAUDERDALE

FORT LAUDERDALE, FLORIDA

General Proprietary, 4-year, coed **Entrance** Minimally difficult **Setting** urban campus **Total enrollment** 3,121 **Student-faculty ratio** 19:1 **Application deadline** Rolling (freshmen), rolling (transfer) **Freshmen** 57% were admitted **Housing** Yes **Expenses** Tuition $20,700; Room only $5880 **Undergraduates** 55% women, 49% part-time, 21% 25 or older, 0.2% Native American, 36% Hispanic American, 18% African American, 2% Asian American/Pacific Islander **The most frequently chosen baccalaureate fields are** computer and information sciences, architecture, visual and performing arts **Academic program** English as a second language, advanced placement, accelerated degree program, honors program, summer session, adult/continuing education programs, internships **Contact** Ms. Kim Moss, The Art Institute of Fort Lauderdale, 1799 Southeast 17th Street, Fort Lauderdale, FL 33316. Phone: 954-308-2148 or toll-free 800-275-7603. Fax: 954-728-8637. E-mail: kmoss@aii.edu. Web site: http://www.artinstitutes.edu/fortlauderdale/.

THE ART INSTITUTE OF JACKSONVILLE

JACKSONVILLE, FLORIDA

General Proprietary, 4-year, coed **Setting** suburban campus **Contact** Director of Admissions, The Art Institute of Jacksonville, 8775 Baypine Road, Jacksonville, FL 32256. Phone: 904-486-3002 or toll-free 800-924-1589. Fax: 904-732-9423. Web site: http://www.artinstitutes.edu/jacksonville/.

THE ART INSTITUTE OF TAMPA

TAMPA, FLORIDA

General Proprietary, 4-year, coed **Entrance** Moderately difficult **Setting** suburban campus **Total enrollment** 881 **Student-faculty ratio** 12:1 **Application deadline** 10/9 (freshmen), rolling (transfer) **Freshmen** 56% were admitted **Housing** Yes **Undergraduates** 46% women, 28% part-time, 29% 25 or older, 18% Hispanic American, 12% African American, 2% Asian American/Pacific Islander **The most frequently chosen baccalaureate fields are** computer and information sciences, visual and performing arts **Academic program** Advanced placement, summer session, adult/continuing education programs, internships **Contact** Mr. Joe Mure, Director of Admissions, The Art Institute of Tampa, 4401 North Himes Avenue, Suite 150, Tampa, FL 33614. Phone: 813-873-2112 or toll-free 866-703-3277. Fax: 813-873-2171. E-mail: aitainformation@aii.edu. Web site: http://www.artinstitutes.edu/tampa/.

AVE MARIA UNIVERSITY

AVE MARIA, FLORIDA

General Independent Roman Catholic, comprehensive, coed **Entrance** Moderately difficult **Setting** suburban campus **Total enrollment** 421 **Student-faculty ratio** 8:1 **Application deadline** Rolling (freshmen), 12/1 (transfer) **Freshmen**

55% were admitted **Housing** Yes **Expenses** Tuition $16,900; Room & Board $7600 **Undergraduates** 54% women, 2% part-time, 6% 25 or older **Academic program** Summer session **Contact** Mr. Michael C. Williams, Associate Director of Admissions, Ave Maria University, 5050 Ave Maria Boulevard, Ave Maria, FL 34142. Phone: 239-280-2556 or toll-free 877-283-8648. Fax: 239-280-2559. E-mail: admissions@avemaria.edu. Web site: http://www.avemaria.edu/.

THE BAPTIST COLLEGE OF FLORIDA
GRACEVILLE, FLORIDA

General Independent Southern Baptist, 4-year, coed **Entrance** Noncompetitive **Setting** 165-acre small-town campus **Total enrollment** 564 **Student-faculty ratio** 12:1 **Application deadline** 8/11 (freshmen), 8/11 (transfer) **Freshmen** 73% were admitted **Housing** Yes **Expenses** Tuition $7850; Room & Board $3736 **Undergraduates** 36% women, 32% part-time, 43% 25 or older, 1% Native American, 3% Hispanic American, 4% African American, 1% Asian American/Pacific Islander **Academic program** Advanced placement, summer session, internships **Contact** Mrs. Sandra Richards, Director of Marketing, The Baptist College of Florida, 5400 College Drive, Graceville, FL 32440-1898. Phone: 850-263-3261 Ext. 460 or toll-free 800-328-2660 Ext. 460. Fax: 850-263-9026. E-mail: admissions@baptistcollege.edu. Web site: http://www.baptistcollege.edu/.

BARRY UNIVERSITY
MIAMI SHORES, FLORIDA

General Independent Roman Catholic, university, coed **Entrance** Moderately difficult **Setting** 122-acre suburban campus **Total enrollment** 8,733 **Student-faculty ratio** 13:1 **Application deadline** Rolling (freshmen), rolling (transfer) **Freshmen** 57% were admitted **Housing** Yes **Expenses** Tuition $24,500; Room & Board $8200 **Undergraduates** 68% women, 20% part-time, 27% 25 or older, 0.3% Native American, 29% Hispanic American, 22% African American, 1% Asian American/Pacific Islander **The most frequently chosen baccalaureate fields are** business/marketing, education, liberal arts/general studies **Academic program** English as a second language, advanced placement, accelerated degree program, honors program, summer session, adult/continuing education programs, internships **Contact** Ms. Laura Antczak, Director of Undergraduate Admission, Barry University, 11300 Northeast Second Avenue, Miami Shores, FL 33161-6695. Phone: 305-899-3138 or toll-free 800-695-2279. Fax: 305-899-2971. E-mail: admissions@mail.barry.edu. Web site: http://www.barry.edu/.

BEACON COLLEGE
LEESBURG, FLORIDA

General Independent, 4-year, coed **Entrance** Minimally difficult **Setting** 12-acre small-town campus **Total enrollment** 116 **Student-faculty ratio** 8:1 **Freshmen** 71% were admitted **Housing** Yes **Expenses** Tuition $25,150; Room & Board $7400 **Undergraduates** 43% women, 18% 25 or older, 5% Hispanic American, 14% African American, 3% Asian American/Pacific Islander **Academic program** Advanced placement, self-designed majors **Contact** Dr. Johnny Good, Vice President - Institutional Effectiveness, Beacon College, 105 East Main Street, Leesburg, FL 34748. Phone: 352-315-9269. Fax: 352-787-0721. E-mail: jgood@beaconcollege.edu. Web site: http://www.beaconcollege.edu/.

BELHAVEN COLLEGE
MAITLAND, FLORIDA

Contact Belhaven College, Maitland 200 Suite 165, 2301 Maitland Center Parkway, Maitland, FL 32751. Phone: toll-free 888-421-0280. Web site: http://www.belhaven.edu/.

BETHUNE-COOKMAN UNIVERSITY
DAYTONA BEACH, FLORIDA

General Independent Methodist, comprehensive, coed **Entrance** Minimally difficult **Setting** 60-acre urban campus **Total enrollment** 3,433 **Student-faculty ratio** 17:1 **Application deadline** 6/30 (freshmen), 6/30 (transfer) **Freshmen** 28% were admitted **Housing** Yes **Expenses** Tuition $12,382; Room & Board $7378 **Undergraduates** 58% women, 6% part-time, 7% 25 or older, 0.2% Native American, 2% Hispanic American, 94% African American, 0.2% Asian American/Pacific Islander **The most frequently chosen baccalaureate fields are** business/marketing, education, psychology **Academic program** Advanced placement, accelerated degree program, honors program, summer session, adult/continuing education programs, internships **Contact** Mr. Les Ferrier, Executive Director of Admissions, Bethune-Cookman University, 640 Dr. Mary McLeod Bethune Boulevard, Daytona Beach, FL 32114-3099. Phone: 386-481-2600 or toll-free 800-448-0228. Fax: 386-481-2601. E-mail: admissions@cookman.edu. Web site: http://www.bethune.cookman.edu/.

CARLOS ALBIZU UNIVERSITY, MIAMI CAMPUS
MIAMI, FLORIDA

General Independent, comprehensive, coed, primarily women **Entrance** Minimally difficult **Setting** 2-acre urban campus **Total enrollment**

Carlos Albizu University, Miami Campus *(continued)*

1,092 **Student-faculty ratio** 10:1 **Application deadline** 9/10 (freshmen), rolling (transfer) **Freshmen** 100% were admitted **Housing** No **Expenses** Tuition $11,724 **Undergraduates** 81% women, 58% part-time, 70% 25 or older, 64% Hispanic American, 6% African American, 0.2% Asian American/Pacific Islander **The most frequently chosen baccalaureate fields are** business/marketing, education, psychology **Academic program** English as a second language, advanced placement, accelerated degree program, summer session, adult/continuing education programs, internships **Contact** Ms. Barbara De la Cruz, Admissions Officer, Carlos Albizu University, Miami Campus, Carlos Albizu University, 2173 N.W. 99th Avenue, Miami, FL 33172. Phone: 305-593-1223 Ext. 136 or toll-free 888-672-3246. Fax: 305-593-1854. E-mail: bdelacruz@albizu.edu. Web site: http://www.mia.albizu.edu/.

CLEARWATER CHRISTIAN COLLEGE
CLEARWATER, FLORIDA

General Independent nondenominational, 4-year, coed **Entrance** Minimally difficult **Setting** 138-acre suburban campus **Total enrollment** 594 **Student-faculty ratio** 15:1 **Application deadline** Rolling (freshmen), rolling (transfer) **Freshmen** 93% were admitted **Housing** Yes **Expenses** Tuition $13,160; Room & Board $5610 **Undergraduates** 50% women, 5% part-time, 4% 25 or older, 0.3% Native American, 5% Hispanic American, 3% African American, 2% Asian American/Pacific Islander **The most frequently chosen baccalaureate fields are** biological/life sciences, business/marketing, education **Academic program** Advanced placement, summer session, internships **Contact** Dr. Keith Hutchison, Director of Admissions, Clearwater Christian College, 3400 Gulf-to-Bay Boulevard, Clearwater, FL 33759-4595. Phone: 727-726-1153 or toll-free 800-348-4463. Fax: 813-726-8597. E-mail: admissions@clearwater.edu. Web site: http://www.clearwater.edu/.

DeVRY UNIVERSITY
MIAMI, FLORIDA

Contact DeVry University, 200 South Biscayne Boulevard, Suite 500, Miami, FL 33131-5351. Web site: http://www.devry.edu/.

DeVRY UNIVERSITY
MIRAMAR, FLORIDA

General Proprietary, comprehensive, coed **Entrance** Minimally difficult **Total enrollment** 1,024 **Student-faculty ratio** 17:1 **Application deadline** Rolling (freshmen), rolling (transfer) **Housing** No **Expenses** Tuition $13,990 **Undergraduates** 37% women, 50% part-time, 55% 25 or older, 0.3% Native American, 45% Hispanic American, 36% African American, 2% Asian American/Pacific Islander **The most frequently chosen baccalaureate fields are** business/marketing, computer and information sciences, engineering technologies **Academic program** Advanced placement, accelerated degree program **Contact** Admissions Office, DeVry University, 2300 Southwest 145th Avenue, Miramar, FL 33027-4150. Web site: http://www.devry.edu/.

DeVRY UNIVERSITY
ORLANDO, FLORIDA

General Proprietary, comprehensive, coed **Entrance** Minimally difficult **Setting** 10-acre urban campus **Total enrollment** 1,408 **Student-faculty ratio** 19:1 **Application deadline** Rolling (freshmen), rolling (transfer) **Housing** No **Expenses** Tuition $13,990 **Undergraduates** 35% women, 48% part-time, 53% 25 or older, 0.3% Native American, 23% Hispanic American, 27% African American, 3% Asian American/Pacific Islander **The most frequently chosen baccalaureate fields are** business/marketing, computer and information sciences, engineering technologies **Academic program** Advanced placement, accelerated degree program, summer session, adult/continuing education programs **Contact** Admissions Office, DeVry University, 4000 Millenia Boulevard, Orlando, FL 32839. Web site: http://www.devry.edu/.

DeVRY UNIVERSITY
TAMPA, FLORIDA

Contact DeVry University, 3030 North Rocky Point Drive West, Suite 100, Tampa, FL 33607-5901. Web site: http://www.devry.edu/.

ECKERD COLLEGE
ST. PETERSBURG, FLORIDA

General Independent Presbyterian, 4-year, coed **Entrance** Moderately difficult **Setting** 188-acre suburban campus **Total enrollment** 1,835 **Student-faculty ratio** 14:1 **Application deadline** Rolling (freshmen), rolling (transfer) **Freshmen** 67% were admitted **Housing** Yes **Expenses** Tuition $30,590; Room & Board $8754 **Undergraduates** 58% women, 1% part-time, 1% 25 or older, 0.3% Native American, 4% Hispanic American, 3% African American, 2% Asian American/Pacific Islander **The most frequently chosen baccalaureate fields are** biological/life sciences, business/marketing, social sciences **Academic program** English as a second language, advanced placement, accelerated degree program, self-designed majors, honors program, summer session, adult/continuing education programs, internships **Contact** Ms. Donna Grosso, Eckerd College, 4200 54th Avenue South, St. Petersburg, FL 33711. Phone: 727-864-8331 or toll-free 800-456-9009. Fax: 727-866-2304. E-mail: admissions@eckerd.edu. Web site: http://www.eckerd.edu/.

EDWARD WATERS COLLEGE
JACKSONVILLE, FLORIDA

General Independent African Methodist Episcopal, 4-year, coed **Contact** Mr. Lonnie Morris, Director of Admissions, Edward Waters College, 1658 Kings Road, Jacksonville, FL 32209-6199. Phone: 904-470-8202 or toll-free 888-898-3191. E-mail: Lmorris@ewc.edu. Web site: http://www.ewc.edu/.

EMBRY-RIDDLE AERONAUTICAL UNIVERSITY
DAYTONA BEACH, FLORIDA

General Independent, comprehensive, coed **Entrance** Moderately difficult **Setting** 178-acre suburban campus **Total enrollment** 4,978 **Student-faculty ratio** 16:1 **Application deadline** Rolling (freshmen), 5/1 (transfer) **Freshmen** 78% were admitted **Housing** Yes **Expenses** Tuition $26,496; Room & Board $9150 **Undergraduates** 16% women, 10% part-time, 8% 25 or older, 0.3% Native American, 8% Hispanic American, 6% African American, 5% Asian American/Pacific Islander **The most frequently chosen baccalaureate fields are** engineering, business/marketing, transportation and materials moving **Academic program** English as a second language, advanced placement, summer session, adult/continuing education programs, internships **Contact** Mr. Richard Clarke, Director of Admissions, Embry-Riddle Aeronautical University, 600 South Clyde Morris Boulevard, Daytona Beach, FL 32114-3900. Phone: 386-226-6100 or toll-free 800-862-2416. Fax: 386-226-7070. E-mail: dbadmit@erau.edu. Web site: http://www.embryriddle.edu/.

►**For more information, see page 458.**

EMBRY-RIDDLE AERONAUTICAL UNIVERSITY WORLDWIDE
DAYTONA BEACH, FLORIDA

General Independent, comprehensive, coed **Entrance** Minimally difficult **Total enrollment** 16,353 **Application deadline** Rolling (freshmen), rolling (transfer) **Housing** No **Expenses** Tuition $4968 **Undergraduates** 12% women, 83% part-time, 1% Native American, 8% Hispanic American, 9% African American, 3% Asian American/Pacific Islander **The most frequently chosen baccalaureate fields are** business/marketing, transportation and materials moving **Academic program** Advanced placement, adult/continuing education programs **Contact** Mrs. Pam Thomas, Director of Admissions, Records and Registration, Embry-Riddle Aeronautical University Worldwide, 600 South Clyde Morris Boulevard, Daytona Beach, FL 32114-3900. Phone: 386-226-7610 or toll-free 800-522-6787. Fax: 386-226-6984. E-mail: ecinfo@erau.edu. Web site: http://www.embryriddle.edu/.

EVEREST UNIVERSITY
CLEARWATER, FLORIDA

Contact Mr. Kevin Buskirk, Director of Admissions, Everest University, 2471 McMullen Road, Clearwater, FL 33759. Phone: 727-725-2688 Ext. 116 or toll-free 800-353-FMUS. Fax: 727-796-3406. E-mail: kbuskirk@cci.edu. Web site: http://www.everest.edu/.

EVEREST UNIVERSITY
JACKSONVILLE, FLORIDA

Contact Mr. Robin Manning, Admissions Director, Everest University, 8226 Phillips Highway, Jacksonville, FL 32256. Phone: 904-731-4949 or toll-free 888-741-4270. E-mail: rmanning@cci.edu. Web site: http://www.everest.edu/.

EVEREST UNIVERSITY
LAKELAND, FLORIDA

General Proprietary, comprehensive, coed **Contact** Ms. Patricia Sabol, Director of Student Services, Everest University, 995 East Memorial Boulevard, Suite 110, Lakeland, FL 33801. Phone: 863-686-1444 or toll-free 877-225-0014. Fax: 863-688-9881. E-mail: psabol@cci.edu. Web site: http://www.everest.edu/.

EVEREST UNIVERSITY
MELBOURNE, FLORIDA

Contact Mr. Timothy Alexander, Director of Admissions, Everest University, 2401 North Harbor City Boulevard, Melbourne, FL 32935-6657. Phone: 321-253-2929 Ext. 121. Web site: http://www.everest.edu/.

EVEREST UNIVERSITY
ORLANDO, FLORIDA

Contact Joann Derosa-Weber, Director of Admissions, Everest University, 5421 Diplomat Circle, Orlando, FL 32810-5674. Phone: 407-628-5870

Everest University *(continued)*

Ext. 108 or toll-free 800-628-5870. Fax: 407-628-1344. Web site: http://www.everest.edu/.

EVEREST UNIVERSITY
ORLANDO, FLORIDA

Contact Ms. Annette Cloin, Director of Admissions, Everest University, 9200 South Park Center Loop, Orlando, FL 32819. Phone: 407-851-2525 Ext. 111 or toll-free 407-851-2525 (in-state); 888-471-4270 (out-of-state). Fax: 407-851-1477. Web site: http://www.everest.edu/.

EVEREST UNIVERSITY
POMPANO BEACH, FLORIDA

General Proprietary, comprehensive, coed **Contact** Ms. Fran Heaston, Director of Admissions, Everest University, 225 North Federal Highway, Pompano Beach, FL 33062. Phone: 954-783-7339 Ext. 139 or toll-free 800-468-0168. Fax: 954-783-7964. E-mail: fheaston@cci.edu. Web site: http://www.everest.edu/.

EVEREST UNIVERSITY
TAMPA, FLORIDA

General Proprietary, comprehensive, coed **Entrance** Minimally difficult **Setting** 4-acre urban campus **Total enrollment** 1,320 **Student-faculty ratio** 20:1 **Application deadline** Rolling (freshmen), rolling (transfer) **Housing** No **Undergraduates** 51% 25 or older **Academic program** English as a second language, advanced placement, accelerated degree program, self-designed majors, summer session, adult/continuing education programs, internships **Contact** Mr. Donnie Broughton, Director of Admissions, Everest University, 3319 West Hillsborough Avenue, Tampa, FL 33614-5899. Phone: 813-879-6000 Ext. 129. Fax: 813-871-2483. Web site: http://www.everest.edu/.

EVEREST UNIVERSITY
TAMPA, FLORIDA

General Proprietary, comprehensive, coed **Entrance** Minimally difficult **Setting** 5-acre urban campus **Total enrollment** 972 **Student-faculty ratio** 17:1 **Application deadline** Rolling (freshmen), rolling (transfer) **Housing** No **Expenses** Tuition $15,360 **Undergraduates** 0.4% Native American, 18% Hispanic American, 29% African American, 1% Asian American/Pacific Islander **The most frequently chosen baccalaureate fields are** business/marketing, personal and culinary services, security and protective services **Academic program** English as a second language, accelerated degree program, summer session, adult/continuing education programs **Contact** Ms. Shandretta Pointer, Director of Admissions, Everest University, 3924 Coconut Palm Drive, Tampa, FL 33619. Phone: 813-621-0041 Ext. 106 or toll-free 877-338-0068. Fax: 813-628-0919. E-mail: spointer@cci.edu. Web site: http://www.everest.edu/.

EVERGLADES UNIVERSITY
ALTAMONTE SPRINGS, FLORIDA

Contact Everglades University, 887 East Altamonte Drive, Altamonte Springs, FL 32701. Web site: http://www.evergladesuniversity.edu/.

EVERGLADES UNIVERSITY
BOCA RATON, FLORIDA

General Independent, comprehensive, coed **Contact** Ms. Jean Graham, Everglades University, 5002 T-Rex Avenue, Suite 100, Boca Raton, FL 33431. Phone: 561-912-1211 or toll-free 888-772-6077. Fax: 561-912-1191. E-mail: admissions-boca@evergladesuniversity.edu. Web site: http://www.evergladesuniversity.edu/.

EVERGLADES UNIVERSITY
SARASOTA, FLORIDA

Contact Mr. Brad Brewer, Campus President, Everglades University, 6151 Lake Osprey Drive, Sarasota, FL 34240. Phone: 941-907-2262 or toll-free 866-907-2262. Fax: 941-907-6634. E-mail: bbrewer@evergladesuniversity.edu. Web site: http://www.evergladesuniversity.edu/.

FLAGLER COLLEGE
ST. AUGUSTINE, FLORIDA

General Independent, 4-year, coed **Entrance** Moderately difficult **Setting** 42-acre small-town campus **Total enrollment** 2,537 **Student-faculty ratio** 21:1 **Application deadline** 3/1 (freshmen), 3/1 (transfer) **Freshmen** 40% were admitted **Housing** Yes **Expenses** Tuition $13,600; Room & Board $6900 **Undergraduates** 61% women, 3% part-time, 3% 25 or older, 0.3% Native American, 3% Hispanic American, 1% African American, 1% Asian American/Pacific Islander **The most frequently chosen baccalaureate fields are** business/marketing, communications/journalism, visual and performing arts **Academic program** Advanced placement, summer session, internships **Contact** Mr. Marc Williar, Director of Admissions, Flagler College, PO Box 1027, St. Augustine, FL 32085-1027. Phone: 904-819-6220 or toll-free 800-304-4208. Fax: 904-819-6466. E-mail: admiss@flagler.edu. Web site: http://www.flagler.edu/.

FLORIDA AGRICULTURAL AND MECHANICAL UNIVERSITY
TALLAHASSEE, FLORIDA

General State-supported, university, coed **Entrance** Moderately difficult **Setting** 419-acre urban campus **Total enrollment** 11,587 **Student-faculty ratio** 18:1 **Application deadline** 5/9 (freshmen), 5/1 (transfer) **Freshmen** 63% were admitted **Housing** Yes **Expenses** Tuition $4220; Room & Board $5956 **Undergraduates** 58% women, 12% part-time, 9% 25 or older, 0.2% Native American, 1% Hispanic American, 93% African American, 1% Asian American/Pacific Islander **The most frequently chosen baccalaureate fields are** business/marketing, health professions and related sciences, security and protective services **Academic program** Advanced placement, accelerated degree program, honors program, summer session, adult/continuing education programs, internships **Contact** Office of Admissions, Florida Agricultural and Mechanical University, Office of the University Registrar, Tallahassee, FL 32307. Phone: 850-599-3866. Fax: 850-599-3069. E-mail: admission@famu.edu. Web site: http://www.famu.edu/.

FLORIDA ATLANTIC UNIVERSITY
BOCA RATON, FLORIDA

General State-supported, university, coed **Entrance** Moderately difficult **Setting** 850-acre suburban campus **Total enrollment** 26,275 **Student-faculty ratio** 18:1 **Application deadline** 6/1 (freshmen) **Freshmen** 57% were admitted **Housing** Yes **Expenses** Tuition $3367; Room & Board $8610 **Undergraduates** 59% women, 42% part-time, 32% 25 or older, 0.4% Native American, 19% Hispanic American, 18% African American, 5% Asian American/Pacific Islander **The most frequently chosen baccalaureate fields are** business/marketing, education, social sciences **Academic program** English as a second language, advanced placement, accelerated degree program, honors program, summer session, adult/continuing education programs, internships **Contact** Assistant Director, Florida Atlantic University, 777 Glades Road, PO Box 3091, Boca Raton, FL 33431-0991. Phone: 561-297-3040 Ext. 3031 or toll-free 800-299-4FAU. Fax: 561-297-2758. E-mail: admisweb@fau.edu. Web site: http://www.fau.edu/.

FLORIDA CHRISTIAN COLLEGE
KISSIMMEE, FLORIDA

Contact Mr. Terry Davis, Admissions Director, Florida Christian College, 1011 Bill Beck Boulevard, Kissimmee, FL 34744-5301. Phone: 407-847-8966 Ext. 305 or toll-free 888-GO-TO-FCC. Web site: http://www.fcc.edu/.

FLORIDA COLLEGE
TEMPLE TERRACE, FLORIDA

General Independent, 4-year, coed **Entrance** Moderately difficult **Setting** 95-acre small-town campus **Total enrollment** 524 **Student-faculty ratio** 15:1 **Application deadline** 8/1 (freshmen), 8/1 (transfer) **Freshmen** 85% were admitted **Housing** Yes **Expenses** Tuition $11,700; Room & Board $5640 **Undergraduates** 54% women, 5% part-time, 4% Hispanic American, 2% African American, 1% Asian American/Pacific Islander **The most frequently chosen baccalaureate fields are** liberal arts/general studies, philosophy and religious studies, visual and performing arts **Academic program** Advanced placement **Contact** Mrs. Shay Angelo, Assistant Director of Admissions, Florida College, 119 North Glen Arven Avenue, Temple Terrace, FL 33617. Phone: 813-988-5131 Ext. 6716 or toll-free 800-326-7655. Fax: 813-899-6772. E-mail: admissions@floridacollege.edu. Web site: http://www.floridacollege.edu/.

FLORIDA GULF COAST UNIVERSITY
FORT MYERS, FLORIDA

General State-supported, comprehensive, coed **Entrance** Moderately difficult **Setting** 760-acre suburban campus **Total enrollment** 9,358 **Student-faculty ratio** 18:1 **Application deadline** 6/1 (freshmen), 6/1 (transfer) **Freshmen** 76% were admitted **Housing** Yes **Expenses** Tuition $5699; Room & Board $8267 **Undergraduates** 60% women, 23% part-time, 18% 25 or older, 0.3% Native American, 11% Hispanic American, 4% African American, 2% Asian American/Pacific Islander **The most frequently chosen baccalaureate fields are** business/marketing, education, liberal arts/general studies **Academic program** Advanced placement, accelerated degree program, honors program, summer session, internships **Contact** Mr. Marc Laviolette, Director of Admissions, Florida Gulf Coast University, 10501 FGCU Boulevard South, Fort Meyers, FL 33965-6565. Phone: 239-590-7878 or toll-free 888-889-1095. Fax: 239-590-7894. E-mail: admissions@fgcu.edu. Web site: http://www.fgcu.edu/.

FLORIDA INSTITUTE OF TECHNOLOGY
MELBOURNE, FLORIDA

General Independent, university, coed **Entrance** Moderately difficult **Setting** 130-acre small-town campus **Total enrollment** 5,118 **Student-faculty ratio** 13:1 **Application deadline** Rolling (freshmen), rolling (transfer) **Freshmen** 81% were admitted **Housing** Yes **Expenses** Tuition $28,920; Room & Board $7770 **Undergraduates** 30% women, 7% part-time, 6% 25 or older, 1% Native American, 6% Hispanic American, 3% African

Florida Institute of Technology *(continued)*

American, 2% Asian American/Pacific Islander **The most frequently chosen baccalaureate fields are** engineering, biological/life sciences, transportation and materials moving **Academic program** English as a second language, advanced placement, summer session, adult/continuing education programs, internships **Contact** Michael J. Perry, Director of Undergraduate Admission, Florida Institute of Technology, 150 West University Boulevard, Melbourne, FL 32901-6975. Phone: 321-674-8030 or toll-free 800-888-4348. Fax: 321-723-9468. E-mail: admission@fit.edu. Web site: http://www.fit.edu/.

FLORIDA INTERNATIONAL UNIVERSITY
MIAMI, FLORIDA

General State-supported, university, coed **Entrance** Moderately difficult **Setting** 573-acre urban campus **Total enrollment** 38,290 **Student-faculty ratio** 21:1 **Application deadline** Rolling (freshmen), rolling (transfer) **Freshmen** 47% were admitted **Housing** Yes **Expenses** Tuition $3414; Room & Board $10,608 **Undergraduates** 23% 25 or older, 0.2% Native American, 64% Hispanic American, 13% African American, 4% Asian American/Pacific Islander **The most frequently chosen baccalaureate fields are** business/marketing, health professions and related sciences, psychology **Academic program** English as a second language, advanced placement, accelerated degree program, honors program, summer session, adult/continuing education programs, internships **Contact** Ms. Carmen Brown, Director of Admissions, Florida International University, 11200 SW Eighth Street, PC 140, Miami, FL 33199. Phone: 305-348-3675. Fax: 305-348-3648. E-mail: admiss@fiu.edu. Web site: http://www.fiu.edu/.

FLORIDA MEMORIAL UNIVERSITY
MIAMI-DADE, FLORIDA

General Independent, 4-year, coed, affiliated with Baptist Church **Entrance** Noncompetitive **Setting** 77-acre suburban campus **Total enrollment** 1,750 **Student-faculty ratio** 12:1 **Application deadline** 7/1 (freshmen), 7/1 (transfer) **Freshmen** 39% were admitted **Housing** Yes **Expenses** Tuition $12,254; Room & Board $5340 **Undergraduates** 62% women, 9% part-time, 30% 25 or older, 3% Hispanic American, 84% African American **The most frequently chosen baccalaureate fields are** business/marketing, education, law/legal studies **Academic program** English as a second language, honors program, summer session, internships **Contact** Mrs. Peggy Murray Martin, Director of Admissions and International Student Advisor, Florida Memorial University, 15800 NW 42nd Avenue, Miami-Dade, FL 33054. Phone: 305-626-3147 or toll-free 800-822-1362. Web site: http://www.fmuniv.edu/.

FLORIDA SOUTHERN COLLEGE
LAKELAND, FLORIDA

General Independent, comprehensive, coed, affiliated with United Methodist Church **Entrance** Moderately difficult **Setting** 100-acre suburban campus **Total enrollment** 1,818 **Student-faculty ratio** 13:1 **Application deadline** 3/1 (freshmen), rolling (transfer) **Freshmen** 58% were admitted **Housing** Yes **Expenses** Tuition $22,145; Room & Board $7850 **Undergraduates** 60% women, 4% part-time, 4% 25 or older, 0.3% Native American, 6% Hispanic American, 7% African American, 1% Asian American/Pacific Islander **The most frequently chosen baccalaureate fields are** business/marketing, education, visual and performing arts **Academic program** Advanced placement, honors program, summer session, adult/continuing education programs, internships **Contact** Mr. Bill C. Langston, Director of Admissions, Florida Southern College, 111 Lake Hollingsworth Drive, Lakeland, FL 33801-5698. Phone: 863-680-4131 or toll-free 800-274-4131. Fax: 863-680-4120. E-mail: fscadm@flsouthern.edu. Web site: http://www.flsouthern.edu/.

FLORIDA STATE UNIVERSITY
TALLAHASSEE, FLORIDA

General State-supported, university, coed **Entrance** Very difficult **Setting** 451-acre suburban campus **Total enrollment** 40,555 **Student-faculty ratio** 24:1 **Application deadline** 2/14 (freshmen), 7/1 (transfer) **Freshmen** 55% were admitted **Housing** Yes **Expenses** Tuition $3355; Room & Board $8000 **Undergraduates** 56% women, 11% part-time, 8% 25 or older, 1% Native American, 11% Hispanic American, 11% African American, 3% Asian American/Pacific Islander **The most frequently chosen baccalaureate fields are** business/marketing, family and consumer sciences, social sciences **Academic program** English as a second language, advanced placement, accelerated degree program, honors program, summer session, adult/continuing education programs, internships **Contact** Ms. Janice Finney, Director of Admissions, Florida State University, PO Box 3062400, Tallahassee, FL 32306-2400. Phone: 850-644-6200. Fax: 850-644-0197. E-mail: admissions@admin.fsu.edu. Web site: http://www.fsu.edu/.

FULL SAIL UNIVERSITY
WINTER PARK, FLORIDA

General Proprietary, comprehensive, coed, primarily men **Entrance** Noncompetitive **Setting**

suburban campus **Total enrollment** 5,867 **Student-faculty ratio** 9:1 **Application deadline** Rolling (freshmen) **Freshmen** 71% were admitted **Housing** Yes **Undergraduates** 12% women, 12% 25 or older **Academic program** Summer session, internships **Contact** Ms. Mary Beth Plank, Director of Admissions, Full Sail University, 3300 University Boulevard, Winter Park, FL 32792-7437. Phone: 407-679-0100 Ext. 2122 or toll-free 800-226-7625. E-mail: admissions@fullsail.com. Web site: http://www.fullsail.com/.

HOBE SOUND BIBLE COLLEGE
HOBE SOUND, FLORIDA

Contact Mrs. Ann French, Director of Admissions, Hobe Sound Bible College, PO Box 1065, Hobe Sound, FL 33475-1065. Phone: 772-546-5534 Ext. 1015 or toll-free 800-881-5534. Fax: 772-545-1422. E-mail: hsbcuwin@aol.com. Web site: http://www.hsbc.edu/.

HODGES UNIVERSITY
NAPLES, FLORIDA

General Independent, comprehensive, coed **Entrance** Minimally difficult **Setting** suburban campus **Total enrollment** 1,699 **Student-faculty ratio** 17:1 **Application deadline** Rolling (freshmen), rolling (transfer) **Freshmen** 79% were admitted **Housing** No **Expenses** Tuition $15,680 **Undergraduates** 68% women, 24% part-time, 65% 25 or older, 0.2% Native American, 24% Hispanic American, 16% African American, 2% Asian American/Pacific Islander **The most frequently chosen baccalaureate fields are** business/marketing, interdisciplinary studies, public administration and social services **Academic program** English as a second language, advanced placement, accelerated degree program, summer session, adult/continuing education programs, internships **Contact** Ms. Rita Lampus, Vice President of Student Enrollment Management, Hodges University, 2655 Northbrooke Drive, Naples, FL 34119. Phone: 239-513-1122 Ext. 104 or toll-free 800-466-8017. Fax: 239-598-6254. E-mail: admit@internationalcollege.edu. Web site: http://www.hodges.edu/.

INTERNATIONAL ACADEMY OF DESIGN & TECHNOLOGY
TAMPA, FLORIDA

General Proprietary, comprehensive, coed **Entrance** Noncompetitive **Setting** 1-acre urban campus **Student-faculty ratio** 16:1 **Application deadline** Rolling (freshmen), rolling (transfer) **Housing** Yes **Academic program** Advanced placement, accelerated degree program, summer session, internships **Contact** Mr. Jonathan Morris, Vice President of Admissions and Marketing, International Academy of Design & Technology, 5104 Eisenhower Boulevard, Tampa, FL 33634-7350. Phone: 813-227-4161 or toll-free 800-ACADEMY. Fax: 813-881-0008. E-mail: admissions@academy.edu. Web site: http://www.academy.edu/.

JACKSONVILLE UNIVERSITY
JACKSONVILLE, FLORIDA

General Independent, comprehensive, coed **Entrance** Moderately difficult **Setting** 198-acre suburban campus **Total enrollment** 3,436 **Student-faculty ratio** 14:1 **Application deadline** Rolling (freshmen), rolling (transfer) **Freshmen** 40% were admitted **Housing** Yes **Expenses** Tuition $23,900; Room & Board $8760 **Undergraduates** 59% women, 28% part-time, 15% 25 or older, 1% Native American, 5% Hispanic American, 21% African American, 2% Asian American/Pacific Islander **The most frequently chosen baccalaureate fields are** business/marketing, health professions and related sciences, visual and performing arts **Academic program** Advanced placement, accelerated degree program, self-designed majors, honors program, summer session, adult/continuing education programs, internships **Contact** Ms. Lisa Hannasch, Director of First-Year Student Admission and Enrollment, Jacksonville University, 2800 University Boulevard North, Office of Admissions, Jacksonville, FL 32211. Phone: 904-256-7000 or toll-free 800-225-2027. Fax: 904-256-7012. E-mail: admissions@ju.edu. Web site: http://www.ju.edu/.

JOHNSON & WALES UNIVERSITY
NORTH MIAMI, FLORIDA

General Independent, 4-year, coed **Entrance** Minimally difficult **Setting** 8-acre suburban campus **Total enrollment** 1,955 **Student-faculty ratio** 28:1 **Application deadline** Rolling (freshmen), rolling (transfer) **Freshmen** 63% were admitted **Housing** Yes **Expenses** Tuition $22,585; Room & Board $7956 **Undergraduates** 53% women, 6% part-time, 11% 25 or older, 0.4% Native American, 21% Hispanic American, 27% African American, 1% Asian American/Pacific Islander **The most frequently chosen baccalaureate fields are** business/marketing, family and consumer sciences, security and protective services **Academic program** English as a second language, advanced placement, accelerated degree program, honors program, summer session, internships **Contact** Mr. Jeff Greenip, Director of Admissions, Johnson & Wales University, 1701 Northeast 127th Street, North Miami, FL 33181. Phone: 305-892-7002 or toll-free 800-232-2433. Fax: 305-892-7020. E-mail: admissions.mia@jwu.edu. Web site: http://www.jwu.edu/.

JONES COLLEGE
JACKSONVILLE, FLORIDA

General Independent, 4-year, coed **Entrance** Noncompetitive **Setting** 5-acre urban campus **Total enrollment** 647 **Student-faculty ratio** 12:1 **Application deadline** Rolling (freshmen) **Housing** No **Expenses** Tuition $6690 **Undergraduates** 79% women, 58% part-time, 77% 25 or older **The most frequently chosen baccalaureate fields are** business/marketing, computer and information sciences, law/legal studies **Academic program** Advanced placement, accelerated degree program, self-designed majors, summer session, adult/continuing education programs, internships **Contact** Linda Vaughn, Director of Admissions, Jones College, 555 Arlington Expressway, Jacksonville, FL 32211-5588. Phone: 904-743-1122 Ext. 141. Fax: 904-743-4446. E-mail: bdurden@jones.edu. Web site: http://www.jones.edu/.

JONES COLLEGE
MIAMI, FLORIDA

General Independent, 4-year, coed **Setting** suburban campus **Total enrollment** 650 **Student-faculty ratio** 12:1 **Housing** No **Expenses** Tuition $6690 **Undergraduates** 79% women, 58% part-time, 77% 25 or older, 0.3% Native American, 15% Hispanic American, 58% African American, 1% Asian American/Pacific Islander **The most frequently chosen baccalaureate fields are** business/marketing, computer and information sciences, law/legal studies **Contact** Frank McCafferty, Director of Admissions, Jones College, 11430 North Kendall Drive, Suite 200, Miami, FL 33176. Phone: 904-743-1122 Ext. 141. E-mail: lvaughn@jones.edu. Web site: http://www.jones.edu/.

KEISER UNIVERSITY
FORT LAUDERDALE, FLORIDA

General Proprietary, comprehensive, coed **Entrance** Minimally difficult **Setting** urban campus **Total enrollment** 11,548 **Student-faculty ratio** 11:1 **Application deadline** Rolling (freshmen), rolling (transfer) **Freshmen** 54% were admitted **Housing** No **Undergraduates** 0.5% Native American, 23% Hispanic American, 26% African American, 2% Asian American/Pacific Islander **Academic program** Adult/continuing education programs **Contact** LaFrawn Mays, Admissions Director, Keiser University, 1900 W. Commercial Boulevard, Fort Lauderdale, FL 33309. Phone: 954-776-4456 or toll-free 888-KEISER-9. Fax: 954-771-4894. E-mail: admissions@keisercollege.edu. Web site: http://www.keiseruniversity.edu/.

LYNN UNIVERSITY
BOCA RATON, FLORIDA

General Independent, comprehensive, coed **Entrance** Moderately difficult **Setting** 123-acre suburban campus **Total enrollment** 2,549 **Student-faculty ratio** 17:1 **Application deadline** Rolling (freshmen), rolling (transfer) **Freshmen** 68% were admitted **Housing** Yes **Expenses** Tuition $29,300; Room & Board $10,900 **Undergraduates** 49% women, 11% part-time, 13% 25 or older, 0.1% Native American, 6% Hispanic American, 4% African American, 1% Asian American/Pacific Islander **The most frequently chosen baccalaureate fields are** business/marketing, communications/journalism, security and protective services **Academic program** English as a second language, advanced placement, accelerated degree program, honors program, summer session, adult/continuing education programs, internships **Contact** Dr. Brett Ormandy, Director of Admissions, Lynn University, 3601 North Military Trail, Boca Raton, FL 33431-5598. Phone: 561-237-7304 or toll-free 800-888-LYNN (in-state); 800-888-5966 (out-of-state). Fax: 561-237-7100. E-mail: bormandy@lynn.edu. Web site: http://www.lynn.edu/.

►**For more information, see page 474.**

MIAMI INTERNATIONAL UNIVERSITY OF ART & DESIGN
MIAMI, FLORIDA

General Proprietary, comprehensive, coed **Setting** 4-acre urban campus **Contact** Mr. Kevin Ryan, Director of Admissions, Miami International University of Art & Design, 1501 Biscayne Boulevard, Suite 100, Miami, FL 33132. Phone: 305-428-5700 or toll-free 800-225-9023. Fax: 305-374-5933. Web site: http://www.artinstitutes.edu/miami.

NEW COLLEGE OF FLORIDA
SARASOTA, FLORIDA

General State-supported, 4-year, coed **Entrance** Very difficult **Setting** 144-acre suburban campus **Total enrollment** 767 **Student-faculty ratio** 10:1 **Application deadline** 4/15 (freshmen), 4/15 (transfer) **Freshmen** 57% were admitted **Housing** Yes **Expenses** Tuition $3772; Room & Board $7035 **Undergraduates** 61% women, 4% 25 or older, 0.4% Native American, 9% Hispanic American, 2% African American, 2% Asian American/Pacific Islander **The most frequently chosen baccalaureate fields are** interdisciplinary studies, area and ethnic studies, psychology **Academic program** Self-designed majors, honors program, internships **Contact** Office of Admissions, New College of Florida, 5800 Bay Shore Road, Sarasota, FL 34243-2109. Phone: 941-487-

5000. Fax: 941-487-5010. E-mail: admissions@ncf.edu. Web site: http://www.ncf.edu/.

NEW WORLD SCHOOL OF THE ARTS
MIAMI, FLORIDA

General State-supported, 4-year, coed **Entrance** Noncompetitive **Setting** 5-acre urban campus **Total enrollment** 416 **Student-faculty ratio** 5:1 **Application deadline** Rolling (freshmen) **Freshmen** 52% were admitted **Housing** No **Expenses** Tuition $3000 **Undergraduates** 58% women, 53% Hispanic American, 12% African American, 3% Asian American/Pacific Islander **The most frequently chosen baccalaureate field is** visual and performing arts **Academic program** English as a second language, advanced placement, summer session **Contact** Ms. Pamela Neumann, Recruitment and Admissions Coordinator, New World School of the Arts, 300 NE Second Avenue, Miami, FL 33132. Phone: 305-237-3472. Fax: 305-237-3794. E-mail: nwsaadm@mdc.edu. Web site: http://www.mdc.edu/nwsa.

NORTHWOOD UNIVERSITY, FLORIDA CAMPUS
WEST PALM BEACH, FLORIDA

General Independent, 4-year, coed **Entrance** Moderately difficult **Setting** 90-acre suburban campus **Total enrollment** 675 **Student-faculty ratio** 21:1 **Application deadline** Rolling (freshmen), rolling (transfer) **Freshmen** 59% were admitted **Housing** Yes **Expenses** Tuition $16,710; Room & Board $7194 **Undergraduates** 38% women, 3% part-time, 8% 25 or older, 0.1% Native American, 10% Hispanic American, 11% African American, 1% Asian American/Pacific Islander **The most frequently chosen baccalaureate fields are** business/marketing, communications/journalism, parks and recreation **Academic program** Advanced placement, accelerated degree program, honors program, summer session, adult/continuing education programs, internships **Contact** Mr. John (Jack) M. Letvinchuck, Director of Admissions, Northwood University, Florida Campus, 2600 North Military Trail, West Palm Beach, FL 33409-2911. Phone: 989-837-4237 or toll-free 800-458-8325. Fax: 561-640-3328. E-mail: fladmit@northwood.edu. Web site: http://www.northwood.edu/.

NOVA SOUTHEASTERN UNIVERSITY
FORT LAUDERDALE, FLORIDA

General Independent, university, coed **Entrance** Moderately difficult **Setting** 300-acre suburban campus **Total enrollment** 27,353 **Student-faculty ratio** 17:1 **Application deadline** Rolling (freshmen), rolling (transfer) **Freshmen** 51% were admitted **Housing** Yes **Expenses** Tuition $19,450; Room & Board $7742 **Undergraduates** 74% women, 36% part-time, 50% 25 or older, 0.4% Native American, 25% Hispanic American, 25% African American, 6% Asian American/Pacific Islander **The most frequently chosen baccalaureate fields are** biological/life sciences, business/marketing, health professions and related sciences **Academic program** English as a second language, advanced placement, accelerated degree program, honors program, summer session, adult/continuing education programs, internships **Contact** Ms. Maria Dillard, Director of Enrollment Management, Nova Southeastern University, Enrollment Processing Services, 3301 College Avenue, Ft. Lauderdale, FL 33329-9905. Phone: 954-262-8000 or toll-free 800-541-NOVA. Fax: 954-262-3811. E-mail: nsuinfo@nova.edu. Web site: http://www.nova.edu/.

PALM BEACH ATLANTIC UNIVERSITY
WEST PALM BEACH, FLORIDA

General Independent nondenominational, comprehensive, coed **Entrance** Moderately difficult **Setting** 25-acre urban campus **Total enrollment** 3,291 **Student-faculty ratio** 15:1 **Application deadline** Rolling (freshmen) **Freshmen** 78% were admitted **Housing** Yes **Expenses** Tuition $20,210; Room & Board $8086 **Undergraduates** 62% women, 9% part-time, 19% 25 or older, 1% Native American, 10% Hispanic American, 15% African American, 2% Asian American/Pacific Islander **The most frequently chosen baccalaureate fields are** business/marketing, communications/journalism, psychology **Academic program** Advanced placement, accelerated degree program, self-designed majors, honors program, summer session, adult/continuing education programs, internships **Contact** Mr. Rod Sullivan, Vice President of Enrollment Services, Palm Beach Atlantic University, PO Box 24708, West Palm Beach, FL 33416-4708. Phone: 561-803-2102 or toll-free 800-238-3998. Fax: 561-803-2115. E-mail: admit@pba.edu. Web site: http://www.pba.edu/.

POLYTECHNIC UNIVERSITY OF THE AMERICAS–MIAMI CAMPUS
MIAMI, FLORIDA

Contact Ernesto Castro, Admissions Department, Polytechnic University of the Americas–Miami Campus, 8180 NW 36th Street, Suite 401, Miami, FL 33166. Phone: 305-418-4220 Ext. 206 or toll-free 888-729-7659. Fax: 305-418-4325. E-mail: ecastro@pupr.edu. Web site: http://www.pupr.edu/miami/.

POLYTECHNIC UNIVERSITY OF THE AMERICAS–ORLANDO CAMPUS
WINTER PARK, FLORIDA

Contact Office of Admissions, Polytechnic University of the Americas–Orlando Campus, 4800 Howell Branch Road, Winter Park, FL 32792. Phone: 407-677-5661. Fax: 407-677-5082. Web site: http://www.pupr.edu/orlando/.

RINGLING COLLEGE OF ART AND DESIGN
SARASOTA, FLORIDA

General Independent, 4-year, coed **Entrance** Moderately difficult **Setting** 34-acre small-town campus **Total enrollment** 1,199 **Student-faculty ratio** 13:1 **Application deadline** Rolling (freshmen), rolling (transfer) **Freshmen** 73% were admitted **Housing** Yes **Expenses** Tuition $24,725; Room & Board $10,000 **Undergraduates** 54% women, 4% part-time, 11% 25 or older, 1% Native American, 11% Hispanic American, 3% African American, 6% Asian American/Pacific Islander **The most frequently chosen baccalaureate field is** visual and performing arts **Academic program** Advanced placement, internships **Contact** Ms. Amy Fischer, Associate Dean of Admissions, Ringling College of Art and Design, 2700 North Tamiami Trail, Sarasota, FL 34234-5895. Phone: 941-359-7525 or toll-free 800-255-7695. Fax: 941-359-7517. E-mail: admissions@ringling.edu. Web site: http://www.ringling.edu/.

ROLLINS COLLEGE
WINTER PARK, FLORIDA

General Independent, comprehensive, coed **Entrance** Very difficult **Setting** 70-acre suburban campus **Total enrollment** 2,532 **Student-faculty ratio** 10:1 **Application deadline** 2/15 (freshmen), 4/15 (transfer) **Freshmen** 58% were admitted **Housing** Yes **Expenses** Tuition $32,640; Room & Board $10,200 **Undergraduates** 58% women, 1% 25 or older, 0.5% Native American, 10% Hispanic American, 4% African American, 4% Asian American/Pacific Islander **The most frequently chosen baccalaureate fields are** psychology, business/marketing, social sciences **Academic program** Advanced placement, accelerated degree program, self-designed majors, honors program, adult/continuing education programs, internships **Contact** Mr. David Erdmann, Dean of Admission and Enrollment, Rollins College, 1000 Holt Avenue, Winter Park, FL 32789-4499. Phone: 407-646-2161. Fax: 407-646-1502. E-mail: admission@rollins.edu. Web site: http://www.rollins.edu/.

ST. JOHN VIANNEY COLLEGE SEMINARY
MIAMI, FLORIDA

Contact Br. Edward Van Merrienboer, Academic Dean, St. John Vianney College Seminary, 2900 Southwest 87th Avenue, Miami, FL 33165-3244. Phone: 305-223-4561. Fax: 305-223-0650. E-mail: academic@sjvcs.edu. Web site: http://www.sjvcs.edu/.

SAINT LEO UNIVERSITY
SAINT LEO, FLORIDA

General Independent Roman Catholic, comprehensive, coed **Entrance** Moderately difficult **Setting** 186-acre rural campus **Total enrollment** 3,033 **Student-faculty ratio** 15:1 **Application deadline** 8/15 (freshmen), 8/1 (transfer) **Freshmen** 71% were admitted **Housing** Yes **Expenses** Tuition $17,150; Room & Board $8430 **Undergraduates** 54% women, 5% part-time, 7% 25 or older, 1% Native American, 10% Hispanic American, 9% African American, 1% Asian American/Pacific Islander **The most frequently chosen baccalaureate fields are** business/marketing, education, security and protective services **Academic program** Advanced placement, honors program, summer session, adult/continuing education programs, internships **Contact** Mr. Martin Smith, Assistant Vice President for Enrollment, Saint Leo University, MC 2008, PO Box 6665, Saint Leo, FL 33574-6665. Phone: 352-588-8283 or toll-free 800-334-5532. Fax: 352-588-8257. E-mail: admissions@saintleo.edu. Web site: http://www.saintleo.edu/.

ST. PETERSBURG THEOLOGICAL SEMINARY
ST. PETERSBURG, FLORIDA

Contact Ms. Carol Cagwin, Director of Admissions, St. Petersburg Theological Seminary, 10830 Navajo Drive, St. Petersburg, FL 33708. Phone: 727-399-0276. Fax: 727-399-1324. E-mail: c.cagwin@sptseminary.edu. Web site: http://www.sptseminary.edu/.

ST. THOMAS UNIVERSITY
MIAMI GARDENS, FLORIDA

General Independent Roman Catholic, comprehensive, coed **Entrance** Moderately difficult **Setting** 140-acre suburban campus **Total enrollment** 2,407 **Application deadline** Rolling (freshmen), rolling (transfer) **Freshmen** 65% were admitted **Housing** Yes **Expenses** Tuition $19,680; Room & Board $6206 **Undergraduates** 57% women, 5% part-time, 24% 25 or older, 0.1% Native American, 47% Hispanic American, 27% African American, 1% Asian American/Pacific Islander **The most frequently chosen baccalau-**

reate fields are business/marketing, education, psychology **Academic program** Advanced placement, honors program, summer session, adult/continuing education programs **Contact** Mr. Andre Lightbourne, Director of Admissions, St. Thomas University, 16401 Northwest 37th Avenue, Miami Gardens, FL 33054-6459. Phone: 305-628-6712 or toll-free 800-367-9010. Fax: 305-628-6591. E-mail: signup@stu.edu. Web site: http://www.stu.edu/.

SCHILLER INTERNATIONAL UNIVERSITY
LARGO, FLORIDA

General Independent, comprehensive, coed **Entrance** Minimally difficult **Setting** 4-acre suburban campus **Total enrollment** 535 **Student-faculty ratio** 10:1 **Application deadline** Rolling (freshmen), rolling (transfer) **Freshmen** 79% were admitted **Housing** Yes **Expenses** Tuition $17,530; Room only $3800 **Undergraduates** 90% 25 or older **Academic program** English as a second language, advanced placement, accelerated degree program, self-designed majors, summer session, adult/continuing education programs, internships **Contact** Ms. Stephanie Givens, Associate Director of Admissions, Schiller International University, 300 East Bay Drive, Largo, FL 33770. Phone: 727-736-5082 Ext. 237 or toll-free 800-336-4133. Fax: 727-734-0436. E-mail: admissions@schiller.edu. Web site: http://www.schiller.edu/.

SOUTHEASTERN UNIVERSITY
LAKELAND, FLORIDA

General Independent, 4-year, coed, affiliated with Assemblies of God **Entrance** Minimally difficult **Setting** 62-acre suburban campus **Total enrollment** 3,069 **Student-faculty ratio** 24:1 **Application deadline** 5/1 (freshmen), 5/1 (transfer) **Freshmen** 78% were admitted **Housing** Yes **Expenses** Tuition $14,470; Room & Board $7000 **Undergraduates** 58% women, 14% part-time, 21% 25 or older, 0.2% Native American, 11% Hispanic American, 7% African American, 1% Asian American/Pacific Islander **Academic program** Advanced placement, accelerated degree program, summer session, adult/continuing education programs, internships **Contact** Mr. Omar Rashed, Executive Director, Enrollment Management, Southeastern University, 1000 Longfellow Boulevard, Lakeland, FL 33801. Phone: 800-500-8760 or toll-free 800-500-8760. Fax: 863-667-5200. E-mail: admission@seuniversity.edu. Web site: http://www.seuniversity.edu/.

SOUTH UNIVERSITY
TAMPA, FLORIDA

General Proprietary, 4-year, coed **Setting** urban campus **Contact** Admissions, South University, 4401 North Himes Avenue, Tampa, FL 33614. Phone: 813-393-3800 or toll-free 800-846-1472. Fax: 813-874-1989. E-mail: tampa@southuniversity.edu. Web site: http://www.southuniversity.edu/.

SOUTH UNIVERSITY
WEST PALM BEACH, FLORIDA

General Proprietary, comprehensive, coed **Setting** suburban campus **Contact** Director of Admissions, South University, 1760 North Congress Avenue, West Palm Beach, FL 33409. Phone: toll-free 866-688-0932. Fax: 561-697-9944. Web site: http://www.southuniversity.edu/.

STETSON UNIVERSITY
DELAND, FLORIDA

General Independent, comprehensive, coed **Entrance** Moderately difficult **Setting** 170-acre small-town campus **Total enrollment** 3,721 **Student-faculty ratio** 11:1 **Application deadline** 3/15 (freshmen), rolling (transfer) **Freshmen** 64% were admitted **Housing** Yes **Expenses** Tuition $30,216; Room & Board $8436 **Undergraduates** 59% women, 4% part-time, 5% 25 or older, 0.4% Native American, 9% Hispanic American, 5% African American, 2% Asian American/Pacific Islander **The most frequently chosen baccalaureate fields are** business/marketing, education, visual and performing arts **Academic program** Advanced placement, accelerated degree program, self-designed majors, honors program, summer session, adult/continuing education programs, internships **Contact** Ms. Deborah Thompson, Vice President for Enrollment Management and Campus Life, Stetson University, Unit 8378, Griffith Hall, DeLand, FL 32723. Phone: 386-822-7100 or toll-free 800-688-0101. Fax: 386-822-7112. E-mail: admissions@stetson.edu. Web site: http://www.stetson.edu/.

TALMUDIC COLLEGE OF FLORIDA
MIAMI BEACH, FLORIDA

General Independent Jewish, comprehensive, men only **Entrance** Moderately difficult **Setting** urban campus **Total enrollment** 35 **Student-faculty ratio** 5:1 **Application deadline** Rolling (freshmen) **Freshmen** 80% were admitted **Housing** Yes **Expenses** Tuition $7500; Room & Board $5000 **Undergraduates** 1% 25 or older, 17% Hispanic American **Academic program** English as a second language, honors program, summer session, adult/continuing education programs **Contact** Peggy Loewy Wellisch, Admissions Director, Talmudic College of Florida, 1910 Alton Road, Miami Beach, FL 33139. Phone: 305-534-7050 Ext. 11 or toll-free 888-825-6834.

Talmudic College of Florida *(continued)*

Fax: 305-534-8444. E-mail: plw@talmudicu.edu. Web site: http://www.talmudicu.edu/.

TRINITY BAPTIST COLLEGE
JACKSONVILLE, FLORIDA

General Independent Baptist, comprehensive, coed **Contact** Mr. Larry Appleby, Administrative Dean, Trinity Baptist College, 800 Hammond Boulevard, Jacksonville, FL 32221. Phone: 904-596-2538 or toll-free 800-786-2206. Fax: 904-596-2531. E-mail: trinity@tbc.edu. Web site: http://www.tbc.edu/.

TRINITY COLLEGE OF FLORIDA
NEW PORT RICHEY, FLORIDA

General Independent nondenominational, 4-year, coed **Entrance** Minimally difficult **Setting** 40-acre small-town campus **Total enrollment** 180 **Student-faculty ratio** 14:1 **Application deadline** 8/8 (freshmen), 8/8 (transfer) **Freshmen** 69% were admitted **Housing** Yes **Expenses** Tuition $10,550; Room & Board $5940 **Undergraduates** 39% women, 34% part-time, 39% 25 or older, 7% Hispanic American, 6% African American, 2% Asian American/Pacific Islander **The most frequently chosen baccalaureate fields are** education, theology and religious vocations **Academic program** Advanced placement, accelerated degree program, self-designed majors, honors program, summer session, adult/continuing education programs, internships **Contact** Mark A. Sawyer, Interim Director of Admissions, Trinity College of Florida, 24300 Welbilt Boulevard, Trinity, FL 34655. Phone: 727-376-6911 Ext. 309 or toll-free 800-388-0869. Fax: 727-569-1410. E-mail: msawyer@trinitycollege.edu. Web site: http://www.trinitycollege.edu/.

UNIVERSIDAD FLET
MIAMI, FLORIDA

General Independent religious, comprehensive, coed **Setting** urban campus **Total enrollment** 977 **Student-faculty ratio** 36:1 **Housing** No **Expenses** Tuition $1820 **Undergraduates** 40% women, 100% part-time, 70% 25 or older, 100% Hispanic American **The most frequently chosen baccalaureate field is** theology and religious vocations **Academic program** Adult/continuing education programs **Contact** Ms. Lourdes Ramirez, Director of Admissions, Universidad FLET, 14540 SW 136th Street, Suite 200, Miami, FL 33186. Phone: 305-378-8700 or toll-free 888-376-3538. Fax: 305-232-5832. E-mail: admisiones@flet.edu. Web site: http://www.flet.edu/.

UNIVERSITY OF CENTRAL FLORIDA
ORLANDO, FLORIDA

General State-supported, university, coed **Entrance** Moderately difficult **Setting** 1,415-acre suburban campus **Total enrollment** 48,497 **Student-faculty ratio** 29:1 **Application deadline** 3/1 (freshmen), 5/1 (transfer) **Freshmen** 50% were admitted **Housing** Yes **Expenses** Tuition $3620; Room & Board $8164 **Undergraduates** 54% women, 25% part-time, 17% 25 or older, 0.4% Native American, 13% Hispanic American, 9% African American, 5% Asian American/Pacific Islander **The most frequently chosen baccalaureate fields are** business/marketing, education, health professions and related sciences **Academic program** English as a second language, advanced placement, honors program, summer session, adult/continuing education programs, internships **Contact** Dr. Gordon Chavis, Assistant Vice President, University of Central Florida, PO Box 160111, Orlando, FL 32816-0111. Phone: 407-823-3000. Fax: 407-823-5625. E-mail: admission@mail.ucf.edu. Web site: http://www.ucf.edu/.

UNIVERSITY OF FLORIDA
GAINESVILLE, FLORIDA

General State-supported, university, coed **Entrance** Very difficult **Setting** 2,000-acre suburban campus **Total enrollment** 51,725 **Student-faculty ratio** 22:1 **Application deadline** 11/1 (freshmen) **Freshmen** 42% were admitted **Housing** Yes **Expenses** Tuition $3257; Room & Board $7020 **Undergraduates** 54% women, 8% part-time, 5% 25 or older, 0.3% Native American, 14% Hispanic American, 10% African American, 8% Asian American/Pacific Islander **The most frequently chosen baccalaureate fields are** business/marketing, engineering, social sciences **Academic program** English as a second language, advanced placement, accelerated degree program, self-designed majors, honors program, summer session, adult/continuing education programs, internships **Contact** Office of Admissions, University of Florida, PO Box 114000, Gainesville, FL 32611-4000. Phone: 352-392-1365. E-mail: ourwebrequests@registrar.ufl.edu. Web site: http://www.ufl.edu/.

UNIVERSITY OF MIAMI
CORAL GABLES, FLORIDA

General Independent, university, coed **Entrance** Very difficult **Setting** 230-acre suburban campus **Total enrollment** 15,462 **Student-faculty ratio** 12:1 **Application deadline** 1/15 (freshmen), 3/1 (transfer) **Freshmen** 38% were admitted **Housing** Yes **Expenses** Tuition $33,118; Room & Board

$9606 **Undergraduates** 54% women, 7% part-time, 6% 25 or older, 0.3% Native American, 23% Hispanic American, 8% African American, 5% Asian American/Pacific Islander **The most frequently chosen baccalaureate fields are** business/marketing, biological/life sciences, visual and performing arts **Academic program** English as a second language, advanced placement, accelerated degree program, self-designed majors, honors program, summer session, adult/continuing education programs, internships **Contact** Mr. Edward M. Gillis, Associate Dean of Enrollment and Director of Admission, University of Miami, PO Box 248025, Ashe Building Room 132, Coral Gables, FL 33146-4616. Phone: 305-284-4472. Fax: 305-284-2507. E-mail: admission@miami.edu. Web site: http://www.miami.edu/.

UNIVERSITY OF NORTH FLORIDA
JACKSONVILLE, FLORIDA

General State-supported, comprehensive, coed **Entrance** Very difficult **Setting** 1,300-acre urban campus **Total enrollment** 16,406 **Student-faculty ratio** 22:1 **Application deadline** 7/2 (freshmen), 7/2 (transfer) **Freshmen** 66% were admitted **Housing** Yes **Expenses** Tuition $3491; Room & Board $7071 **Undergraduates** 57% women, 28% part-time, 21% 25 or older, 0.5% Native American, 7% Hispanic American, 10% African American, 5% Asian American/Pacific Islander **The most frequently chosen baccalaureate fields are** business/marketing, education, health professions and related sciences **Academic program** English as a second language, advanced placement, accelerated degree program, self-designed majors, honors program, summer session, adult/continuing education programs, internships **Contact** Mr. John Yancey, Director of Admissions, University of North Florida, 4567 St. Johns Bluff Road South, Jacksonville, FL 32224. Phone: 904-620-2624. Fax: 904-620-2014. E-mail: admissions@unf.edu. Web site: http://www.unf.edu/.

UNIVERSITY OF PHOENIX–CENTRAL FLORIDA CAMPUS
MAITLAND, FLORIDA

General Proprietary, comprehensive, coed **Contact** Ms. Evelyn Gaskin, Registrar/Executive Director, University of Phoenix–Central Florida Campus, 4615 East Elwood Street, Mail Stop AA-K101, Phoenix, AZ 85040-1958. Phone: 480-557-3301 or toll-free 800-776-4867 (in-state); 800-228-7240 (out-of-state). Fax: 480-643-1020. E-mail: evelyn.gaskin@phoenix.edu. Web site: http://www.phoenix.edu/.

UNIVERSITY OF PHOENIX–FORT LAUDERDALE CAMPUS
FORT LAUDERDALE, FLORIDA

General Proprietary, comprehensive, coed **Contact** Ms. Evelyn Gaskin, Registrar/Executive Director, University of Phoenix–Fort Lauderdale Campus, 4615 East Elwood Street, Mail Stop AA-K101, Phoenix, AZ 85040-1958. Phone: 480-557-3301 or toll-free 800-228-7240. Fax: 480-643-1020. E-mail: evelyn.gaskin@phoenix.edu. Web site: http://www.phoenix.edu/.

UNIVERSITY OF PHOENIX–NORTH FLORIDA CAMPUS
JACKSONVILLE, FLORIDA

General Proprietary, comprehensive, coed **Contact** Ms. Evelyn Gaskin, Registrar/Executive Director, University of Phoenix–North Florida Campus, 4615 East Elwood Street, Mail Stop AA-K101, Phoenix, AZ 85040-1958. Phone: 480-557-3301 or toll-free 800-776-4867 (in-state); 800-894-1758 (out-of-state). Fax: 480-643-1020. E-mail: evelyn.gaskin@phoenix.edu. Web site: http://www.phoenix.edu/.

UNIVERSITY OF PHOENIX–WEST FLORIDA CAMPUS
TEMPLE TERRACE, FLORIDA

General Proprietary, comprehensive, coed **Contact** Ms. Evelyn Gaskin, Registrar/Executive Director, University of Phoenix–West Florida Campus, 4615 East Elwood Street, Mail Stop AA-K101, Phoenix, AZ 85040-1958. Phone: 480-557-3301 or toll-free 800-776-4867 (in-state); 800-228-7240 (out-of-state). Fax: 480-643-1020. E-mail: evelyn.gaskin@phoenix.edu. Web site: http://www.phoenix.edu/.

UNIVERSITY OF SOUTH FLORIDA
TAMPA, FLORIDA

General State-supported, university, coed **Entrance** Moderately difficult **Setting** 1,913-acre urban campus **Total enrollment** 44,870 **Application deadline** 4/15 (freshmen), 4/15 (transfer) **Freshmen** 50% were admitted **Housing** Yes **Expenses** Tuition $3457; Room & Board $7590 **Undergraduates** 59% women, 30% part-time, 18% 25 or older, 0.5% Native American, 13% Hispanic American, 13% African American, 6% Asian American/Pacific Islander **The most frequently chosen baccalaureate fields are** business/marketing, education, social sciences **Academic program** Advanced placement, accelerated degree program, self-designed majors, honors program, summer session, adult/continuing education programs, internships **Contact**

University of South Florida *(continued)*

Ms. Alicia Kormowa, Undergraduate Admissions and Recruitment, University of South Florida, Office of Undergraduate Admissions, 4202 East Fowler Avenue, SVC 1036, Tampa, FL 33620-9951. Phone: 813-974-3350 or toll-free 877-USF-BULLS. Fax: 813-974-9689. E-mail: bullseye@admin.usf.edu. Web site: http://www.usf.edu/.

THE UNIVERSITY OF TAMPA

TAMPA, FLORIDA

General Independent, comprehensive, coed **Setting** 90-acre urban campus **Total enrollment** 5,628 **Student-faculty ratio** 15:1 **Application deadline** 5/1 (freshmen), rolling (transfer) **Freshmen** 49% were admitted **Housing** Yes **Expenses** Tuition $20,682; Room & Board $7616 **Undergraduates** 59% women, 8% part-time, 9% 25 or older, 0.4% Native American, 10% Hispanic American, 6% African American, 2% Asian American/Pacific Islander **The most frequently chosen baccalaureate fields are** business/marketing, communications/journalism, social sciences **Academic program** English as a second language, advanced placement, honors program, summer session, adult/continuing education programs, internships **Contact** Mrs. Barbara Strickler, Vice President for Enrollment, The University of Tampa, 401 West Kennedy Boulevard, Tampa, FL 33606-1480. Phone: 813-253-6211 or toll-free 888-646-2438 (in-state); 888-MINARET (out-of-state). Fax: 813-258-7398. E-mail: admissions@ut.edu. Web site: http://www.ut.edu/.

UNIVERSITY OF WEST FLORIDA

PENSACOLA, FLORIDA

General State-supported, comprehensive, coed **Entrance** Moderately difficult **Setting** 1,600-acre suburban campus **Total enrollment** 10,358 **Student-faculty ratio** 19:1 **Application deadline** 6/30 (freshmen), 6/30 (transfer) **Freshmen** 70% were admitted **Housing** Yes **Expenses** Tuition $3467; Room & Board $6600 **Undergraduates** 60% women, 29% part-time, 30% 25 or older, 1% Native American, 5% Hispanic American, 10% African American, 5% Asian American/Pacific Islander **The most frequently chosen baccalaureate fields are** business/marketing, communications/journalism, education **Academic program** English as a second language, advanced placement, honors program, summer session, internships **Contact** Director of Admissions, University of West Florida, Admissions, 11000 University Parkway, Pensacola, FL 32514. Phone: 850-474-2230 or toll-free 800-263-1074. Fax: 850-474-3460. E-mail: admissions@uwf.edu. Web site: http://uwf.edu/.

WARNER SOUTHERN COLLEGE

LAKE WALES, FLORIDA

Contact Mr. Jason Roe, Director of Admissions, Warner Southern College, Warner Southern Center, 13895 Highway 27, Lake Wales, FL 33859. Phone: 863-638-7212 Ext. 7213 or toll-free 800-949-7248. Fax: 863-638-1472. E-mail: admissions@warner.edu. Web site: http://www.warner.edu/.

WEBBER INTERNATIONAL UNIVERSITY

BABSON PARK, FLORIDA

General Independent, comprehensive, coed **Entrance** Moderately difficult **Setting** 110-acre small-town campus **Total enrollment** 596 **Student-faculty ratio** 18:1 **Application deadline** 8/1 (freshmen), 8/1 (transfer) **Freshmen** 57% were admitted **Housing** Yes **Expenses** Tuition $16,760; Room & Board $5960 **Undergraduates** 39% women, 11% part-time, 15% 25 or older, 0.4% Native American, 9% Hispanic American, 23% African American, 1% Asian American/Pacific Islander **The most frequently chosen baccalaureate fields are** business/marketing, computer and information sciences, parks and recreation **Academic program** Advanced placement, accelerated degree program, summer session, adult/continuing education programs, internships **Contact** Ms. Julie Ragans, Director of Admissions, Webber International University, 1201 Scenic Highway, North, PO Box 96, Babson Park, FL 33827. Phone: 863-638-2910 or toll-free 800-741-1844. Fax: 863-638-1591. E-mail: admissions@webber.edu. Web site: http://www.webber.edu/.

►**For more information, see page 500.**

YESHIVA GEDOLAH RABBINICAL COLLEGE

MIAMI BEACH, FLORIDA

Contact Yeshiva Gedolah Rabbinical College, 1140 Alton Road, Miami Beach, FL 33139.

GEORGIA

AGNES SCOTT COLLEGE

DECATUR, GEORGIA

General Independent, comprehensive, undergraduate: women only; graduate: coed, affiliated with Presbyterian Church (U.S.A.) **Entrance** Very difficult **Setting** 100-acre urban campus **Total enrollment** 892 **Student-faculty ratio** 9:1 **Application deadline** 3/1 (freshmen), 3/1 (transfer) **Freshmen** 45% were admitted **Housing** Yes

Expenses Tuition $28,200; Room & Board $9850 **Undergraduates** 3% part-time, 6% 25 or older, 0.2% Native American, 4% Hispanic American, 21% African American, 5% Asian American/Pacific Islander **The most frequently chosen baccalaureate fields are** English, psychology, social sciences **Academic program** Advanced placement, accelerated degree program, self-designed majors, summer session, adult/continuing education programs, internships **Contact** Ms. Stephanie Balmer, Dean of Admission, Agnes Scott College, 141 East College Avenue, Decatur, GA 30030-3797. Phone: 404-471-6285 or toll-free 800-868-8602. Fax: 404-471-6414. E-mail: admission@agnesscott.edu. Web site: http://www.agnesscott.edu/.

ALBANY STATE UNIVERSITY

ALBANY, GEORGIA

General State-supported, comprehensive, coed **Entrance** Minimally difficult **Setting** 232-acre urban campus **Total enrollment** 3,927 **Student-faculty ratio** 19:1 **Application deadline** 7/1 (freshmen), 7/1 (transfer) **Freshmen** 29% were admitted **Housing** Yes **Expenses** Tuition $3470; Room & Board $4914 **Undergraduates** 67% women, 15% part-time, 0.1% Native American, 0.3% Hispanic American, 95% African American, 0.3% Asian American/Pacific Islander **The most frequently chosen baccalaureate fields are** business/marketing, education, security and protective services **Academic program** Advanced placement, honors program, summer session, adult/continuing education programs, internships **Contact** Office of Recruitment and Admissions, Albany State University, 504 College Drive, Albany, GA 31705-2717. Phone: 229-430-4646 or toll-free 800-822-RAMS. Fax: 229-430-3936. E-mail: admissions@asurams.edu. Web site: http://www.asurams.edu/.

AMERICAN INTERCONTINENTAL UNIVERSITY BUCKHEAD CAMPUS

ATLANTA, GEORGIA

General Proprietary, comprehensive, coed **Entrance** Minimally difficult **Setting** 3-acre urban campus **Total enrollment** 26,686 **Application deadline** Rolling (freshmen), rolling (transfer) **Academic program** Advanced placement, accelerated degree program, summer session, adult/continuing education programs, internships **Contact** John Payton, Senior Director of Admissions, American InterContinental University Buckhead Campus, 3300 Peachtree Road, NE, Atlanta, GA 30326-1016. Phone: 404-965-5953 or toll-free 888-591-7888. Fax: 404-965-5701. E-mail: john.payton@buckhead.aiuniv.edu. Web site: http://www.aiuniv.edu/.

AMERICAN INTERCONTINENTAL UNIVERSITY DUNWOODY CAMPUS

ATLANTA, GEORGIA

General Proprietary, comprehensive, coed **Entrance** Minimally difficult **Setting** 2-acre urban campus **Total enrollment** 26,686 **Application deadline** Rolling (freshmen), rolling (transfer) **Freshmen** 80% were admitted **Contact** Director of Admissions, American InterContinental University Dunwoody Campus, 6600 Peachtree-Dunwoody Road, 500 Embassy Row, Atlanta, GA 30328. Phone: 404-965-6500 or toll-free 800-353-1744. E-mail: info@aiuniv.edu. Web site: http://www.aiuniv.edu/.

ARGOSY UNIVERSITY, ATLANTA

ATLANTA, GEORGIA

General Proprietary, university, coed **Setting** suburban campus **Contact** Director of Admissions, Argosy University, Atlanta, 980 Hammond Drive, Suite 100, Atlanta, GA 30328. Phone: 770-671-1200 or toll-free 888-671-4777. Web site: http://www.argosy.edu/locations/atlanta/.

ARMSTRONG ATLANTIC STATE UNIVERSITY

SAVANNAH, GEORGIA

General State-supported, comprehensive, coed **Entrance** Minimally difficult **Setting** 250-acre suburban campus **Total enrollment** 6,831 **Student-faculty ratio** 17:1 **Application deadline** 6/30 (freshmen), 6/30 (transfer) **Freshmen** 60% were admitted **Housing** Yes **Expenses** Tuition $3424; Room only $5000 **Undergraduates** 67% women, 35% part-time, 36% 25 or older, 0.5% Native American, 4% Hispanic American, 23% African American, 3% Asian American/Pacific Islander **The most frequently chosen baccalaureate fields are** education, health professions and related sciences, liberal arts/general studies **Academic program** Advanced placement, honors program, summer session, adult/continuing education programs, internships **Contact** Mr. Craig Morrison, Assistant Registrar, Armstrong Atlantic State University, 11935 Abercom Street, Savannah, GA 31419. Phone: 912-344-5425 or toll-free 800-633-2349. Fax: 912-921-5462. E-mail: craig.morrison@armstrong.edu. Web site: http://www.armstrong.edu/.

THE ART INSTITUTE OF ATLANTA

ATLANTA, GEORGIA

General Proprietary, 4-year, coed **Entrance** Moderately difficult **Setting** 7-acre suburban campus **Total enrollment** 3,187 **Student-faculty ratio** 22:1 **Application deadline** Rolling

The Art Institute of Atlanta *(continued)*

(freshmen), rolling (transfer) **Freshmen** 46% were admitted **Housing** Yes **Expenses** Tuition $20,880; Room only $9075 **Undergraduates** 46% women, 16% part-time, 37% 25 or older, 0.5% Native American, 4% Hispanic American, 39% African American, 2% Asian American/Pacific Islander **The most frequently chosen baccalaureate fields are** computer and information sciences, communications/journalism, visual and performing arts **Academic program** Advanced placement, honors program, summer session, adult/continuing education programs, internships **Contact** Mr. Newton Myvett, Vice President/ Director of Admissions, The Art Institute of Atlanta, 6600 Peachtree Dunwoody Road, 100 Embassy Row, Atlanta, GA 30328. Phone: 770-394-8300 or toll-free 800-275-4242. Fax: 770-394-0008. E-mail: aidadm@aii.edu. Web site: http://www.artinstitutes.edu/atlanta.

THE ART INSTITUTE OF ATLANTA–DECATUR

DECATUR, GEORGIA

General Proprietary, 4-year, coed **Contact** Ms. Jennifer Ramey, Director of Admissions, The Art Institute of Atlanta–Decatur, One West Court Square, Suite 1, Decatur, GA 30030. Phone: 404-942-1807 or toll-free 866-856-6203. Fax: 404-942-1818. E-mail: jramey@aii.edu. Web site: http://www.artinstitutes.edu/decatur.

ATLANTA CHRISTIAN COLLEGE

EAST POINT, GEORGIA

Contact Ms. Sarah Huxford, Director of Admissions, Atlanta Christian College, 2605 Ben Hill Road, East Point, GA 30344-1999. Phone: 404-761-8861 or toll-free 800-776-1ACC. Fax: 404-669-2024. E-mail: admissions@acc.edu. Web site: http://www.acc.edu/.

AUGUSTA STATE UNIVERSITY

AUGUSTA, GEORGIA

General State-supported, comprehensive, coed **Entrance** Minimally difficult **Setting** 72-acre urban campus **Total enrollment** 6,588 **Student-faculty ratio** 18:1 **Application deadline** 7/21 (freshmen), rolling (transfer) **Freshmen** 53% were admitted **Housing** Yes **Expenses** Tuition $3728; Room & Board $9600 **Undergraduates** 64% women, 30% part-time, 59% 25 or older, 0.3% Native American, 3% Hispanic American, 27% African American, 3% Asian American/Pacific Islander **The most frequently chosen baccalaureate fields are** business/marketing, education, psychology **Academic program** English as a second language, advanced placement, honors program, summer session, adult/continuing education programs, internships **Contact** Ms. Jody Wilson, Coordinator of Publications and Marketing, Augusta State University, 2500 Walton Way, Augusta, GA 30904-2200. Phone: 706-737-1632 or toll-free 800-341-4373. Fax: 706-667-4355. E-mail: admissions@aug.edu. Web site: http://www.aug.edu/.

BAUDER COLLEGE

ATLANTA, GEORGIA

Contact Ms. Lillie Lanier, Admissions Representative, Bauder College, Phipps Plaza, 3500 Peachtree Rd, NE, Atlanta, GA 30326. Phone: 404-443-1793 or toll-free 404-237-7573 (in-state); 800-241-3797 (out-of-state). Fax: 404-237-1642. E-mail: admissions@bauder.edu. Web site: http://www.bauder.edu/.

BEACON UNIVERSITY

COLUMBUS, GEORGIA

General Independent religious, comprehensive, coed **Contact** Dr. James Cornett, Dean of Student Services, Beacon University, 6003 Veterans Parkway, Columbus, GA 31909. Phone: 706-323-5364. Fax: 706-323-5891. E-mail: james.cornett@beacon.edu. Web site: http://www.beacon.edu/.

BERRY COLLEGE

MOUNT BERRY, GEORGIA

General Independent interdenominational, comprehensive, coed **Entrance** Moderately difficult **Setting** 28,000-acre suburban campus **Total enrollment** 1,858 **Student-faculty ratio** 12:1 **Application deadline** 7/25 (freshmen), 7/25 (transfer) **Freshmen** 70% were admitted **Housing** Yes **Expenses** Tuition $20,570; Room & Board $7626 **Undergraduates** 66% women, 2% part-time, 1% 25 or older, 0.2% Native American, 2% Hispanic American, 3% African American, 2% Asian American/Pacific Islander **The most frequently chosen baccalaureate fields are** business/marketing, education, social sciences **Academic program** Advanced placement, accelerated degree program, self-designed majors, honors program, summer session, adult/continuing education programs, internships **Contact** Mr. Timothy Tarpley, Associate Director of Admissions and Financial Aid, Berry College, PO Box 490159, 2277 Martha Berry Highway, NW, Mount Berry, GA 30149-0159. Phone: 706-236-2215 or toll-free 800-237-7942. Fax: 706-290-2178. E-mail: admissions@berry.edu. Web site: http://www.berry.edu/.

BEULAH HEIGHTS UNIVERSITY

ATLANTA, GEORGIA

General Independent Pentecostal, 4-year, coed **Entrance** Noncompetitive **Setting** 10-acre urban campus **Total enrollment** 620 **Student-faculty ratio** 17:1 **Application deadline** Rolling (freshmen), rolling (transfer) **Housing** Yes **Expenses** Tuition $5600; Room & Board $9000 **Undergraduates** 57% women, 59% part-time, 90% 25 or older, 1% Hispanic American, 77% African American, 1% Asian American/Pacific Islander **Academic program** Advanced placement, accelerated degree program, summer session, adult/continuing education programs, internships **Contact** Ms. Jacquelyn B. Armstrong, Registrar/Director of Admissions, Beulah Heights University, 892 Berne Street, SE, PO Box 18145, Atlanta, GA 30316. Phone: 404-627-2681 Ext. 104 or toll-free 888-777-BHBC. Fax: 404-627-0702. E-mail: admissions@beulah.org. Web site: http://www.beulah.org/.

BRENAU UNIVERSITY
GAINESVILLE, GEORGIA

General Independent, comprehensive, women only **Entrance** Moderately difficult **Setting** 57-acre small-town campus **Total enrollment** 916 **Student-faculty ratio** 10:1 **Application deadline** Rolling (freshmen), rolling (transfer) **Freshmen** 40% were admitted **Housing** Yes **Expenses** Tuition $18,800; Room & Board $9487 **Undergraduates** 8% part-time, 17% 25 or older, 0.2% Native American, 3% Hispanic American, 19% African American, 2% Asian American/Pacific Islander **The most frequently chosen baccalaureate fields are** health professions and related sciences, education, visual and performing arts **Academic program** Advanced placement, accelerated degree program, self-designed majors, honors program, internships **Contact** Ms. Christina White, Assistant Vice President of Enrollment Management and Dean of Admissions, Brenau University, Admissions, 500 Washington Street, SE, Gainesville, GA 30501. Phone: 770-531-6100 or toll-free 800-252-5119. Fax: 770-538-4701. E-mail: wcadmissions@brenau.edu. Web site: http://www.brenau.edu/.

BREWTON-PARKER COLLEGE
MT. VERNON, GEORGIA

General Independent Southern Baptist, 4-year, coed **Entrance** Minimally difficult **Setting** 280-acre rural campus **Total enrollment** 1,034 **Student-faculty ratio** 7:1 **Application deadline** Rolling (freshmen), rolling (transfer) **Freshmen** 97% were admitted **Housing** Yes **Expenses** Tuition $14,050; Room & Board $5470 **Undergraduates** 62% women, 30% part-time, 37% 25 or older, 0.3% Native American, 2% Hispanic American, 25% African American, 1% Asian American/Pacific Islander **The most frequently chosen baccalaureate fields are** business/marketing, education, liberal arts/general studies **Academic program** Advanced placement, accelerated degree program, honors program, summer session, adult/continuing education programs, internships **Contact** Mr. Ken Wuerzberger, Director of Admissions, Brewton-Parker College, PO Box 197, Mount Vernon, GA 30445. Phone: 912-583-3245 or toll-free 800-342-1087 Ext. 245. Fax: 912-583-3598. E-mail: kwuerzberger@bpc.edu. Web site: http://www.bpc.edu/.

CARVER BIBLE COLLEGE
ATLANTA, GEORGIA

Contact Ms. Patsy S. Singh, Director of Admissions, Carver Bible College, 437 Nelson Street, Atlanta, GA 30313. Phone: 404-527-4520. Web site: http://www.carver.edu/.

CLARK ATLANTA UNIVERSITY
ATLANTA, GEORGIA

General Independent United Methodist, university, coed **Entrance** Moderately difficult **Setting** 126-acre urban campus **Total enrollment** 4,271 **Student-faculty ratio** 15:1 **Application deadline** 6/1 (freshmen), 6/1 (transfer) **Freshmen** 66% were admitted **Housing** Yes **Expenses** Tuition $17,038; Room & Board $7044 **Undergraduates** 73% women, 4% part-time, 4% 25 or older, 0.1% Native American, 0.4% Hispanic American, 87% African American, 0.1% Asian American/Pacific Islander **The most frequently chosen baccalaureate fields are** business/marketing, communications/journalism, psychology **Academic program** English as a second language, advanced placement, accelerated degree program, honors program, summer session, adult/continuing education programs, internships **Contact** Office of Admissions, Clark Atlanta University, 223 James P. Brawley Drive, SW, Atlanta, GA 30314. Phone: 404-880-8000 Ext. 8021 or toll-free 800-688-3228. Fax: 404-880-6174. E-mail: cauadmissions@cau.edu. Web site: http://www.cau.edu/.

CLAYTON STATE UNIVERSITY
MORROW, GEORGIA

General State-supported, comprehensive, coed **Entrance** Minimally difficult **Setting** 163-acre suburban campus **Total enrollment** 6,043 **Student-faculty ratio** 21:1 **Application deadline** 7/17 (freshmen) **Freshmen** 55% were admitted **Housing** No **Expenses** Tuition $3354 **Undergraduates** 71% women, 44% part-time, 48% 25 or older, 0.2% Native American, 3% Hispanic American, 56% African American, 5% Asian American/Pacific Islander **The most frequently chosen baccalaureate fields are** business/marketing, health professions and related sciences, psychology **Academic program** English

Clayton State University *(continued)*

as a second language, advanced placement, self-designed majors, honors program, summer session, adult/continuing education programs, internships **Contact** Ms. Carol S. Montgomery, Admissions, Clayton State University, 2000 Clayton State Boulevard, Morrow, GA 30260-0285. Phone: 678-466-4115. Fax: 678-466-4149. E-mail: csc-info@clayton.edu. Web site: http://www.clayton.edu/.

COLUMBUS STATE UNIVERSITY
COLUMBUS, GEORGIA

General State-supported, comprehensive, coed **Entrance** Minimally difficult **Setting** 132-acre suburban campus **Total enrollment** 7,590 **Student-faculty ratio** 19:1 **Application deadline** 7/1 (freshmen), 7/1 (transfer) **Freshmen** 56% were admitted **Housing** Yes **Expenses** Tuition $3514; Room & Board $6220 **Undergraduates** 61% women, 31% part-time, 25% 25 or older, 0.3% Native American, 3% Hispanic American, 32% African American, 2% Asian American/Pacific Islander **The most frequently chosen baccalaureate fields are** business/marketing, education, health professions and related sciences **Academic program** English as a second language, advanced placement, honors program, summer session, adult/continuing education programs, internships **Contact** Ms. Susan Lovell, Director of Admissions, Columbus State University, 4225 University Avenue, Columbus, GA 31907-5645. Phone: 706-507-8806 or toll-free 866-264-2035. Fax: 706-568-5091. E-mail: admissions@colstate.edu. Web site: http://www.colstate.edu/.

COVENANT COLLEGE
LOOKOUT MOUNTAIN, GEORGIA

General Independent, comprehensive, coed, affiliated with Presbyterian Church in America **Entrance** Moderately difficult **Setting** 250-acre suburban campus **Total enrollment** 1,063 **Student-faculty ratio** 14:1 **Application deadline** Rolling (freshmen), rolling (transfer) **Freshmen** 65% were admitted **Housing** Yes **Expenses** Tuition $22,840; Room & Board $6490 **Undergraduates** 56% women, 4% part-time, 2% 25 or older, 0.2% Native American, 1% Hispanic American, 3% African American, 2% Asian American/Pacific Islander **The most frequently chosen baccalaureate fields are** business/marketing, education, social sciences **Academic program** Advanced placement, self-designed majors, summer session, adult/continuing education programs, internships **Contact** Mrs. Jan Weaver, Assistant Director of Admissions, Covenant College, 14049 Scenic Highway, Lookout Mountain, GA 30750. Phone: 706-419-1127 or toll-free 888-451-2683. Fax: 706-419-2255. E-mail: admissions@covenant.edu. Web site: http://www.covenant.edu/.

DALTON STATE COLLEGE
DALTON, GEORGIA

General State-supported, 4-year, coed **Contact** Dr. Angela Harris, Director of Admissions, Dalton State College, 650 College Drive, Dalton, GA 30720-3797. Phone: 706-272-4436 or toll-free 800-829-4436. Fax: 706-272-2530. E-mail: aharris@daltonstate.edu. Web site: http://www.daltonstate.edu/.

DEVRY UNIVERSITY
ALPHARETTA, GEORGIA

General Proprietary, comprehensive, coed **Entrance** Minimally difficult **Setting** 9-acre suburban campus **Total enrollment** 797 **Student-faculty ratio** 10:1 **Application deadline** Rolling (freshmen), rolling (transfer) **Housing** No **Expenses** Tuition $13,990 **Undergraduates** 45% women, 56% part-time, 69% 25 or older, 0.3% Native American, 4% Hispanic American, 44% African American, 3% Asian American/Pacific Islander **The most frequently chosen baccalaureate fields are** business/marketing, computer and information sciences, engineering technologies **Academic program** Advanced placement, accelerated degree program, summer session, adult/continuing education programs **Contact** Admissions Office, DeVry University, 2555 Northwinds Parkway, Alpharetta, GA 30004. Phone: toll-free 800-346-5420. Web site: http://www.devry.edu/.

DEVRY UNIVERSITY
ATLANTA, GEORGIA

Contact DeVry University, Fifteen Piedmont Center, Plaza Level 100, Atlanta, GA 30305-1543. Web site: http://www.devry.edu/.

DEVRY UNIVERSITY
DECATUR, GEORGIA

General Proprietary, comprehensive, coed **Entrance** Minimally difficult **Setting** 21-acre suburban campus **Total enrollment** 2,391 **Student-faculty ratio** 21:1 **Application deadline** Rolling (freshmen), rolling (transfer) **Housing** No **Expenses** Tuition $13,990 **Undergraduates** 50% women, 46% part-time, 63% 25 or older, 0.2% Native American, 2% Hispanic American, 71% African American, 2% Asian American/Pacific Islander **The most frequently chosen baccalaureate fields are** business/marketing, computer and information sciences, engineering technologies **Academic program** Advanced placement, accelerated degree program, summer session, adult/continuing education programs **Contact** Admissions Department, DeVry University, 250 North Arcadia Avenue, Decatur, GA 30030-2198. Web site: http://www.devry.edu/.

DeVRY UNIVERSITY
DULUTH, GEORGIA

Contact DeVry University, 3505 Koger Boulevard, Suite 170, Duluth, GA 30096-7671. Web site: http://www.devry.edu/.

EMMANUEL COLLEGE
FRANKLIN SPRINGS, GEORGIA

General Independent, 4-year, coed, affiliated with Pentecostal Holiness Church **Entrance** Minimally difficult **Setting** 90-acre rural campus **Total enrollment** 658 **Student-faculty ratio** 11:1 **Application deadline** 8/1 (freshmen), 8/1 (transfer) **Freshmen** 41% were admitted **Housing** Yes **Expenses** Tuition $12,260; Room & Board $5584 **Undergraduates** 54% women, 12% part-time, 10% 25 or older, 0.5% Native American, 3% Hispanic American, 15% African American, 1% Asian American/Pacific Islander **The most frequently chosen baccalaureate fields are** business/marketing, education, theology and religious vocations **Academic program** Advanced placement, accelerated degree program, honors program, summer session, internships **Contact** Ms. Jessica Dunning, Admissions Assistant, Emmanuel College, PO Box 129, 181 Spring Street, Franklin Springs, GA 30639-0129. Phone: 706-245-7226 Ext. 2873 or toll-free 800-860-8800. Fax: 706-245-4424. E-mail: admissions@ec.edu. Web site: http://www.ec.edu/.

EMORY UNIVERSITY
ATLANTA, GEORGIA

General Independent Methodist, university, coed **Entrance** Most difficult **Setting** 634-acre suburban campus **Total enrollment** 10,921 **Student-faculty ratio** 7:1 **Application deadline** 1/15 (freshmen), 6/1 (transfer) **Freshmen** 27% were admitted **Housing** Yes **Expenses** Tuition $36,286; Room & Board $11,572 **Undergraduates** 56% women, 1% part-time, 3% 25 or older, 0.2% Native American, 3% Hispanic American, 9% African American, 18% Asian American/Pacific Islander **The most frequently chosen baccalaureate fields are** business/marketing, psychology, social sciences **Academic program** English as a second language, advanced placement, accelerated degree program, honors program, summer session, internships **Contact** Ms. Jean Jordan, Interim Dean of Admission, Emory University, 200 Boisfeuillet Jones Center, Atlanta, GA 30322-1100. Phone: 404-727-6036 or toll-free 800-727-6036. E-mail: admiss@learnlink.emory.edu. Web site: http://www.emory.edu/.

FORT VALLEY STATE UNIVERSITY
FORT VALLEY, GEORGIA

Contact Mr. Donald Moore, Director of Admissions and Recruitment, Fort Valley State University, 1005 State University Drive, Fort Valley, GA 31030. Phone: 478-825-6307 or toll-free 800-248-7343. Fax: 478-825-6169. E-mail: admissap@fvsu.edu. Web site: http://www.fvsu.edu/.

GEORGIA COLLEGE & STATE UNIVERSITY
MILLEDGEVILLE, GEORGIA

General State-supported, comprehensive, coed **Entrance** Moderately difficult **Setting** 590-acre small-town campus **Total enrollment** 6,249 **Student-faculty ratio** 17:1 **Application deadline** 4/1 (freshmen), 7/1 (transfer) **Freshmen** 59% were admitted **Housing** Yes **Expenses** Tuition $5066; Room & Board $7380 **Undergraduates** 60% women, 9% part-time, 3% 25 or older, 0.3% Native American, 2% Hispanic American, 6% African American, 1% Asian American/Pacific Islander **The most frequently chosen baccalaureate fields are** business/marketing, education, psychology **Academic program** English as a second language, advanced placement, accelerated degree program, self-designed majors, honors program, summer session, internships **Contact** Mr. Mike Augustine, Director of Admissions, Georgia College & State University, CPO Box 023, Milledgeville, GA 31061. Phone: 478-445-1283 or toll-free 800-342-0471. Fax: 478-445-3653. E-mail: info@gcsu.edu. Web site: http://www.gcsu.edu/.

GEORGIA INSTITUTE OF TECHNOLOGY
ATLANTA, GEORGIA

General State-supported, university, coed, primarily men **Entrance** Very difficult **Setting** 400-acre urban campus **Total enrollment** 18,742 **Student-faculty ratio** 14:1 **Application deadline** 1/15 (freshmen), 2/1 (transfer) **Freshmen** 63% were admitted **Housing** Yes **Expenses** Tuition $5642; Room & Board $7328 **Undergraduates** 30% women, 7% part-time, 4% 25 or older, 0.3% Native American, 5% Hispanic American, 7% African American, 16% Asian American/Pacific Islander **The most frequently chosen baccalaureate fields are** business/marketing, computer and information sciences, engineering **Academic program** English as a second language, advanced placement, accelerated degree program, self-designed majors, honors program, summer

Georgia Institute of Technology *(continued)*

session, internships **Contact** Ms. Ingrid Hayes, Director of Admissions (Undergraduate), Georgia Institute of Technology, Georgia Institute of Technology, Office of Undergraduate Admission, Atlanta, GA 30332-0320. Phone: 404-894-4154. Fax: 404-894-9511. E-mail: admission@gatech.edu. Web site: http://www.gatech.edu/.

GEORGIA SOUTHERN UNIVERSITY

STATESBORO, GEORGIA

General State-supported, university, coed **Entrance** Moderately difficult **Setting** 634-acre small-town campus **Total enrollment** 16,841 **Student-faculty ratio** 19:1 **Application deadline** 5/1 (freshmen), 8/1 (transfer) **Freshmen** 45% were admitted **Housing** Yes **Expenses** Tuition $4082; Room & Board $6860 **Undergraduates** 49% women, 11% part-time, 8% 25 or older, 0.3% Native American, 2% Hispanic American, 22% African American, 1% Asian American/Pacific Islander **The most frequently chosen baccalaureate fields are** business/marketing, education, engineering technologies **Academic program** English as a second language, advanced placement, honors program, summer session, adult/continuing education programs, internships **Contact** Mrs. Susan Davies, Director, Georgia Southern University, PO Box 8055, Statesboro, GA 30460. Phone: 912-681-5391. Fax: 912-486-7240. E-mail: admissions@georgiasouthern.edu. Web site: http://www.georgiasouthern.edu/.

GEORGIA SOUTHWESTERN STATE UNIVERSITY

AMERICUS, GEORGIA

General State-supported, comprehensive, coed **Entrance** Moderately difficult **Setting** 255-acre small-town campus **Total enrollment** 2,405 **Student-faculty ratio** 18:1 **Application deadline** 7/21 (freshmen), 7/21 (transfer) **Freshmen** 79% were admitted **Housing** Yes **Expenses** Tuition $3526; Room & Board $5274 **Undergraduates** 65% women, 24% part-time, 29% 25 or older, 0.4% Native American, 1% Hispanic American, 31% African American, 1% Asian American/Pacific Islander **The most frequently chosen baccalaureate fields are** business/marketing, education, psychology **Academic program** English as a second language, advanced placement, honors program, summer session, internships **Contact** Mr. David Jenkins, Assistant Director of Admissions, Georgia Southwestern State University, 800 Wheatley Street, Americus, GA 31709. Phone: 229-928-1273 or toll-free 800-338-0082. Fax: 229-931-2983. E-mail: gswapps@canes.gsw.edu. Web site: http://www.gsw.edu/.

GEORGIA STATE UNIVERSITY

ATLANTA, GEORGIA

General State-supported, university, coed **Entrance** Moderately difficult **Setting** 48-acre urban campus **Total enrollment** 27,137 **Student-faculty ratio** 17:1 **Application deadline** 3/1 (freshmen), 6/1 (transfer) **Freshmen** 53% were admitted **Housing** Yes **Expenses** Tuition $5485; Room & Board $9230 **Undergraduates** 61% women, 27% part-time, 26% 25 or older, 0.3% Native American, 5% Hispanic American, 29% African American, 11% Asian American/Pacific Islander **The most frequently chosen baccalaureate fields are** business/marketing, psychology, social sciences **Academic program** English as a second language, advanced placement, accelerated degree program, honors program, summer session, internships **Contact** Daniel Niccum, Associate Director of Admissions, Georgia State University, PO Box 4009, Atlanta, GA 30302-4009. Phone: 404-651-2365. Fax: 404-651-4811. E-mail: dniccum@gsu.edu. Web site: http://www.gsu.edu/.

KENNESAW STATE UNIVERSITY

KENNESAW, GEORGIA

General State-supported, comprehensive, coed **Entrance** Moderately difficult **Setting** 240-acre suburban campus **Total enrollment** 20,603 **Student-faculty ratio** 23:1 **Application deadline** 5/16 (freshmen), 6/30 (transfer) **Freshmen** 59% were admitted **Housing** Yes **Expenses** Tuition $3806; Room only $4599 **Undergraduates** 61% women, 27% part-time, 31% 25 or older, 0.4% Native American, 3% Hispanic American, 9% African American, 3% Asian American/Pacific Islander **The most frequently chosen baccalaureate fields are** business/marketing, education, health professions and related sciences **Academic program** English as a second language, advanced placement, honors program, summer session, adult/continuing education programs, internships **Contact** Admissions Office, Kennesaw State University, 1000 Chastain Road, Campus Box #0115, Kennesaw, GA 30144-5591. Phone: 770-423-6300. Fax: 770-420-4435. E-mail: ksuadmit@ksumail.kennesaw.edu. Web site: http://www.kennesaw.edu/.

LAGRANGE COLLEGE

LAGRANGE, GEORGIA

General Independent United Methodist, comprehensive, coed **Entrance** Moderately difficult **Setting** 120-acre small-town campus **Total enrollment** 1,091 **Student-faculty ratio** 12:1 **Application deadline** Rolling (freshmen), rolling (transfer) **Freshmen** 57% were admitted **Housing** Yes **Expenses** Tuition $18,575; Room & Board

$7598 **Undergraduates** 55% women, 9% part-time, 19% 25 or older, 1% Native American, 2% Hispanic American, 21% African American, 2% Asian American/Pacific Islander **The most frequently chosen baccalaureate fields are** business/marketing, health professions and related sciences, visual and performing arts **Academic program** Advanced placement, summer session, adult/continuing education programs, internships **Contact** Mr. Dana Paul, Vice President of Enrollment Management, LaGrange College, 601 Broad Street, LaGrange, GA 30240-2999. Phone: 706-880-8253 or toll-free 800-593-2885. Fax: 706-880-8010. E-mail: lgcadmis@lagrange.edu. Web site: http://www.lagrange.edu/.

►**For more information, see page 470.**

LIFE UNIVERSITY
MARIETTA, GEORGIA

General Independent, comprehensive, coed **Entrance** Minimally difficult **Setting** 96-acre suburban campus **Total enrollment** 1,908 **Student-faculty ratio** 15:1 **Application deadline** 9/1 (freshmen) **Freshmen** 30% were admitted **Housing** Yes **Expenses** Tuition $7605; Room & Board $12,000 **Undergraduates** 49% women, 27% part-time, 47% 25 or older, 1% Native American, 5% Hispanic American, 21% African American, 5% Asian American/Pacific Islander **The most frequently chosen baccalaureate fields are** biological/life sciences, business/marketing, health professions and related sciences **Academic program** English as a second language, advanced placement, accelerated degree program, summer session, internships **Contact** Dr. Deb Heairlston, Office of New Student Development, Life University, 1269 Barclay Circle, Marietta, GA 30067. Phone: 800-543-3202 or toll-free 800-543-3202. Fax: 770-426-2895. E-mail: admissions@life.edu. Web site: http://www.life.edu/.

LUTHER RICE UNIVERSITY
LITHONIA, GEORGIA

Contact Mr. Steve Pray, Admissions Counselor, Luther Rice University, 3038 Evans Mill Road, Lithonia, GA 30038-2454. Phone: 770-484-1204 Ext. 231 or toll-free 800-442-1577. E-mail: admissions@lru.edu. Web site: http://www.lru.edu/.

MACON STATE COLLEGE
MACON, GEORGIA

General State-supported, 4-year, coed **Contact** Mr. Ryan Tucker, Admissions Representative, Macon State College, 100 College Station Drive, Macon, GA 31206. Phone: 478-471-2800 Ext. 2854 or toll-free 800-272-7619 Ext. 2800. Fax: 478-471-5343. E-mail: mscinfo@mail.maconstate.edu. Web site: http://www.maconstate.edu/.

MEDICAL COLLEGE OF GEORGIA
AUGUSTA, GEORGIA

General State-supported, upper-level, coed **Entrance** Moderately difficult **Setting** 100-acre urban campus **Total enrollment** 2,392 **Student-faculty ratio** 6:1 **First-year students** 50% were admitted **Housing** Yes **Expenses** Tuition $4775; Room only $2734 **Undergraduates** 88% women, 14% part-time, 40% 25 or older, 2% Hispanic American, 17% African American, 4% Asian American/Pacific Islander **The most frequently chosen baccalaureate field is** health professions and related sciences **Academic program** Summer session **Contact** Ms. Carol S. Nobles, Director of Student Recruitment and Admissions, Medical College of Georgia, 1120 Fifteenth Street, Augusta, GA 30912. Phone: 706-721-2725 or toll-free 800-519-3388. Fax: 706-721-7279. E-mail: underadm@mail.mcg.edu. Web site: http://www.mcg.edu/.

MERCER UNIVERSITY
MACON, GEORGIA

General Independent Baptist, comprehensive, coed **Entrance** Moderately difficult **Setting** 150-acre suburban campus **Total enrollment** 5,253 **Student-faculty ratio** 13:1 **Application deadline** 7/1 (freshmen), rolling (transfer) **Freshmen** 60% were admitted **Housing** Yes **Expenses** Tuition $26,960; Room & Board $8015 **Undergraduates** 53% women, 3% part-time, 3% 25 or older, 0.2% Native American, 3% Hispanic American, 17% African American, 7% Asian American/Pacific Islander **The most frequently chosen baccalaureate fields are** business/marketing, engineering, psychology **Academic program** English as a second language, advanced placement, accelerated degree program, self-designed majors, honors program, summer session, adult/continuing education programs, internships **Contact** Mr. Terry Whittum, Senior Vice President, Enrollment Management, Mercer University, 1400 Coleman Avenue, Macon, GA 31207-0003. Phone: 478-301-2650 or toll-free 800-840-8577. Fax: 478-301-2828. E-mail: admissions@mercer.edu. Web site: http://www.mercer.edu/.

MOREHOUSE COLLEGE
ATLANTA, GEORGIA

General Independent, 4-year, men only **Entrance** Moderately difficult **Setting** 61-acre urban campus **Total enrollment** 2,810 **Student-faculty ratio** 15:1 **Application deadline** 2/15 (freshmen), 2/15 (transfer) **Freshmen** 59% were admitted **Housing** Yes **Expenses** Tuition $17,982; Room & Board $9928 **Undergraduates** 5% part-time, 4% 25 or older, 0.04% Native American, 0.3% Hispanic

Morehouse College *(continued)*

American, 95% African American **The most frequently chosen baccalaureate fields are** business/marketing, biological/life sciences, social sciences **Academic program** Advanced placement, honors program, summer session, internships **Contact** Mr. Terrance Dixon, Associate Dean for Admissions and Recruitment, Morehouse College, 830 Westview Drive, SW, Atlanta, GA 30314. Phone: 404-215-2632 or toll-free 800-851-1254. Fax: 404-524-5635. E-mail: janderso@morehouse.edu. Web site: http://www.morehouse.edu/.

NORTH GEORGIA COLLEGE & STATE UNIVERSITY

DAHLONEGA, GEORGIA

General State-supported, comprehensive, coed **Entrance** Moderately difficult **Setting** 140-acre small-town campus **Total enrollment** 5,227 **Student-faculty ratio** 16:1 **Application deadline** 7/1 (freshmen), rolling (transfer) **Freshmen** 62% were admitted **Housing** Yes **Expenses** Tuition $3810; Room & Board $5142 **Undergraduates** 60% women, 18% part-time, 18% 25 or older, 0.4% Native American, 3% Hispanic American, 3% African American, 1% Asian American/Pacific Islander **The most frequently chosen baccalaureate fields are** business/marketing, education, social sciences **Academic program** Advanced placement, honors program, summer session, adult/continuing education programs, internships **Contact** Jennifer Collins, Director of Admissions, North Georgia College & State University, Admissions Center, Dahlonega, GA 30533. Phone: 706-864-2885 or toll-free 800-498-9581. Fax: 706-864-1478. E-mail: admissions@ngcsu.edu. Web site: http://www.ngcsu.edu/.

OGLETHORPE UNIVERSITY

ATLANTA, GEORGIA

General Independent, comprehensive, coed **Entrance** Very difficult **Setting** 102-acre suburban campus **Total enrollment** 1,020 **Student-faculty ratio** 13:1 **Application deadline** Rolling (freshmen), rolling (transfer) **Freshmen** 48% were admitted **Housing** Yes **Expenses** Tuition $25,580; Room & Board $9500 **Undergraduates** 61% women, 13% part-time, 6% 25 or older, 1% Native American, 3% Hispanic American, 23% African American, 5% Asian American/Pacific Islander **The most frequently chosen baccalaureate fields are** business/marketing, English, social sciences **Academic program** Advanced placement, accelerated degree program, self-designed majors, honors program, summer session, adult/continuing education programs, internships **Contact** Ms. Lucy Leusch, Vice President for Enrollment and Financial Aid, Oglethorpe University, 4484 Peachtree Road, NE, Atlanta, GA 30319. Phone: 404-364-8307 or toll-free 800-428-4484. Fax: 404-364-8491. E-mail: admission@oglethorpe.edu. Web site: http://www.oglethorpe.edu/.

PAINE COLLEGE

AUGUSTA, GEORGIA

General Independent Methodist, 4-year, coed **Entrance** Minimally difficult **Setting** 55-acre urban campus **Total enrollment** 917 **Student-faculty ratio** 11:1 **Application deadline** 8/1 (freshmen), 8/1 (transfer) **Freshmen** 37% were admitted **Housing** Yes **Expenses** Tuition $10,694; Room & Board $5216 **Undergraduates** 67% women, 7% part-time, 8% 25 or older, 0.2% Hispanic American, 97% African American, 0.2% Asian American/Pacific Islander **The most frequently chosen baccalaureate fields are** psychology, business/marketing, social sciences **Academic program** Advanced placement, accelerated degree program, honors program, summer session, internships **Contact** Mr. Joseph Tinsley, Director of Admissions, Paine College, 1235 15th Street, Augusta, GA 30901-3182. Phone: 706-821-8320 or toll-free 800-476-7703. Fax: 706-821-8691. E-mail: tinsleyj@mail.paine.edu. Web site: http://www.paine.edu/.

PIEDMONT COLLEGE

DEMOREST, GEORGIA

General Independent, comprehensive, coed, affiliated with United Church of Christ **Entrance** Moderately difficult **Setting** 115-acre rural campus **Total enrollment** 2,283 **Student-faculty ratio** 13:1 **Application deadline** 7/1 (freshmen), 7/1 (transfer) **Freshmen** 44% were admitted **Housing** Yes **Expenses** Tuition $18,000; Room & Board $6000 **Undergraduates** 67% women, 15% part-time, 36% 25 or older, 0.3% Native American, 2% Hispanic American, 8% African American, 1% Asian American/Pacific Islander **The most frequently chosen baccalaureate fields are** business/marketing, education, social sciences **Academic program** Advanced placement, accelerated degree program, self-designed majors, honors program, summer session, adult/continuing education programs, internships **Contact** Ms. Cynthia L. Peterson, Director of Undergraduate Admissions, Piedmont College, PO Box 10, 165 Central Avenue, Demorest, GA 30535. Phone: 706-776-0103 Ext. 1188 or toll-free 800-277-7020. Fax: 706-776-6635. E-mail: cpeterson@piedmont.edu. Web site: http://www.piedmont.edu/.

REINHARDT COLLEGE
WALESKA, GEORGIA

General Independent, 4-year, coed, affiliated with United Methodist Church **Contact** Ms. Julie Fleming, Director of Admissions, Reinhardt College, 7300 Reinhardt College Circle, Waleska, GA 30183-0128. Phone: 770-720-5526 or toll-free 87-REINHARDT. Fax: 770-720-5602. E-mail: admissions@mail.reinhardt.edu. Web site: http://www.reinhardt.edu/.

SAVANNAH COLLEGE OF ART AND DESIGN
SAVANNAH, GEORGIA

General Independent, comprehensive, coed **Entrance** Moderately difficult **Setting** urban campus **Total enrollment** 8,966 **Student-faculty ratio** 17:1 **Application deadline** Rolling (freshmen), rolling (transfer) **Freshmen** 54% were admitted **Housing** Yes **Expenses** Tuition $26,465; Room & Board $10,015 **Undergraduates** 55% women, 10% part-time, 5% 25 or older, 0.3% Native American, 3% Hispanic American, 5% African American, 2% Asian American/Pacific Islander **The most frequently chosen baccalaureate fields are** communication technologies, architecture, visual and performing arts **Academic program** English as a second language, advanced placement, summer session, internships **Contact** Ms. Ginger Hansen, Executive Director of Recruitment, Savannah College of Art and Design, 342 Bull Street, PO Box 3146, Savannah, GA 31402-3146. Phone: 912-525-5100 or toll-free 800-869-7223. Fax: 912-525-5983. E-mail: admission@scad.edu. Web site: http://www.scad.edu/.

►**For more information, see page 489.**

SAVANNAH STATE UNIVERSITY
SAVANNAH, GEORGIA

General State-supported, comprehensive, coed **Contact** Mrs. Gwendolyn J. Moore, Associate Director of Admissions, Savannah State University, PO Box 20209, Savannah, GA 31404. Phone: 912-356-2181 or toll-free 800-788-0478. Fax: 912-356-2256. E-mail: mooreg@savstate.edu. Web site: http://www.savstate.edu/.

SHORTER COLLEGE
ROME, GEORGIA

General Independent Baptist, comprehensive, coed **Entrance** Moderately difficult **Setting** 155-acre small-town campus **Total enrollment** 1,394 **Student-faculty ratio** 11:1 **Application deadline** 8/25 (freshmen), 8/25 (transfer) **Freshmen** 65% were admitted **Housing** Yes **Expenses** Tuition $15,160; Room & Board $7000 **Undergraduates** 49% women, 4% part-time, 5% 25 or older, 1% Native American, 3% Hispanic American, 12% African American, 1% Asian American/Pacific Islander **The most frequently chosen baccalaureate fields are** business/marketing, biological/life sciences, visual and performing arts **Academic program** Advanced placement, self-designed majors, honors program, summer session, adult/continuing education programs, internships **Contact** Mr. John Head, Vice President for Enrollment Management, Shorter College, 315 Shorter Avenue, Rome, GA 30165. Phone: 706-233-7342 or toll-free 800-868-6980. Fax: 706-233-7224. E-mail: admissions@shorter.edu. Web site: http://www.shorter.edu/.

SOUTHERN POLYTECHNIC STATE UNIVERSITY
MARIETTA, GEORGIA

General State-supported, comprehensive, coed **Entrance** Moderately difficult **Setting** 200-acre suburban campus **Total enrollment** 4,460 **Student-faculty ratio** 18:1 **Application deadline** 8/1 (freshmen), 8/1 (transfer) **Freshmen** 61% were admitted **Housing** Yes **Expenses** Tuition $3872; Room & Board $5780 **Undergraduates** 18% women, 31% part-time, 30% 25 or older, 0.4% Native American, 4% Hispanic American, 20% African American, 5% Asian American/Pacific Islander **The most frequently chosen baccalaureate fields are** business/marketing, computer and information sciences, engineering technologies **Academic program** Advanced placement, self-designed majors, honors program, summer session, adult/continuing education programs, internships **Contact** Ms. Virginia Head, Director of Admissions, Southern Polytechnic State University, 1100 South Marietta Parkway, Marietta, GA 30060-2896. Phone: 678-915-4188 or toll-free 800-635-3204. Fax: 678-915-7292. E-mail: admissions@spsu.edu. Web site: http://www.spsu.edu/.

SOUTH UNIVERSITY
SAVANNAH, GEORGIA

General Proprietary, comprehensive, coed **Setting** urban campus **Contact** Director of Admissions, South University, 709 Mall Boulevard, Savannah, GA 31406. Phone: 912-201-8000 or toll-free 800-688-0932. Fax: 912-201-8070. Web site: http://www.southuniversity.edu/.

SPELMAN COLLEGE
ATLANTA, GEORGIA

General Independent, 4-year, women only **Entrance** Very difficult **Setting** 32-acre urban campus **Total enrollment** 2,343 **Student-faculty ratio** 12:1 **Application deadline** 2/1

Spelman College *(continued)*

(freshmen), 4/1 (transfer) **Freshmen** 33% were admitted **Housing** Yes **Expenses** Tuition $17,005; Room & Board $8750 **Undergraduates** 5% part-time, 4% 25 or older, 0.04% Native American, 0.1% Hispanic American, 96% African American, 0.04% Asian American/Pacific Islander **The most frequently chosen baccalaureate fields are** psychology, biological/life sciences, social sciences **Academic program** Advanced placement, self-designed majors, honors program, adult/continuing education programs, internships **Contact** Ms. Arlene Cash, Vice President for Admissions and Orientation, Spelman College, 350 Spelman Lane, SW, Atlanta, GA 30314-4399. Phone: 404-681-3643 or toll-free 800-982-2411. Fax: 404-270-5201. E-mail: admiss@spelman.edu. Web site: http://www.spelman.edu/.

THOMAS UNIVERSITY
THOMASVILLE, GEORGIA

General Independent, comprehensive, coed **Entrance** Noncompetitive **Setting** 24-acre small-town campus **Total enrollment** 684 **Student-faculty ratio** 12:1 **Application deadline** Rolling (freshmen), rolling (transfer) **Freshmen** 63% were admitted **Housing** Yes **Expenses** Tuition $11,040; Room only $2626 **Undergraduates** 74% women, 34% part-time, 60% 25 or older, 1% Native American, 2% Hispanic American, 36% African American, 1% Asian American/Pacific Islander **The most frequently chosen baccalaureate fields are** education, business/marketing, law/legal studies **Academic program** Advanced placement, accelerated degree program, summer session, adult/continuing education programs, internships **Contact** Thomas University Office of Admission, Thomas University, 1501 Millpond Road, Thomasville, GA 31792. Phone: 229-226-1621 Ext. 181 or toll-free 800-538-9784. Fax: 229-227-6919. E-mail: hmueller@thomasu.edu. Web site: http://www.thomasu.edu/.

TOCCOA FALLS COLLEGE
TOCCOA FALLS, GEORGIA

General Independent interdenominational, 4-year, coed **Entrance** Moderately difficult **Setting** 500-acre small-town campus **Total enrollment** 924 **Student-faculty ratio** 7:1 **Application deadline** Rolling (freshmen), rolling (transfer) **Freshmen** 51% were admitted **Housing** Yes **Expenses** Tuition $14,625; Room & Board $5350 **Undergraduates** 56% women, 6% part-time, 8% 25 or older, 2% Hispanic American, 2% African American, 7% Asian American/Pacific Islander **The most frequently chosen baccalaureate fields are** psychology, area and ethnic studies, theology and religious vocations **Academic program** Advanced placement, accelerated degree program, summer session, internships **Contact** John Gailer, Director of Admissions, Toccoa Falls College, Office of Admissions, PO Box 800899, Toccoa Falls, GA 30598-1000. Phone: 888-785-5624. Fax: 706-282-6012. E-mail: admissions@tfc.edu. Web site: http://www.tfc.edu/.

TRUETT-McCONNELL COLLEGE
CLEVELAND, GEORGIA

General Independent Baptist, 4-year, coed **Entrance** Minimally difficult **Setting** 310-acre rural campus **Total enrollment** 468 **Student-faculty ratio** 15:1 **Application deadline** 8/1 (freshmen), 8/1 (transfer) **Freshmen** 42% were admitted **Housing** Yes **Expenses** Tuition $14,000; Room & Board $5100 **Undergraduates** 50% women, 19% part-time, 5% 25 or older, 4% Hispanic American, 14% African American, 0.3% Asian American/Pacific Islander **The most frequently chosen baccalaureate field is** visual and performing arts **Academic program** Advanced placement, accelerated degree program, honors program, summer session **Contact** Mr. Mike W. Davis, Dean of Enrollment Services, Truett-McConnell College, 100 Alumni Drive, Cleveland, GA 30528-9799. Phone: 706-865-2134 Ext. 210 or toll-free 800-226-8621. Fax: 706-865-7615. E-mail: admissions@truett.edu. Web site: http://www.truett.edu/.

UNIVERSITY OF GEORGIA
ATHENS, GEORGIA

General State-supported, university, coed **Entrance** Moderately difficult **Setting** 1,289-acre suburban campus **Total enrollment** 33,831 **Student-faculty ratio** 18:1 **Application deadline** 1/15 (freshmen), 4/1 (transfer) **Freshmen** 55% were admitted **Housing** Yes **Expenses** Tuition $5622; Room & Board $7292 **Undergraduates** 58% women, 8% part-time, 6% 25 or older, 0.3% Native American, 2% Hispanic American, 6% African American, 6% Asian American/Pacific Islander **The most frequently chosen baccalaureate fields are** business/marketing, education, social sciences **Academic program** Advanced placement, accelerated degree program, self-designed majors, honors program, summer session, adult/continuing education programs, internships **Contact** Mr. Patrick Winter, Associate Director of Admissions, University of Georgia, Terrel Hall, Athens, GA 30602. Phone: 706-542-8776. Fax: 706-542-1466. E-mail: undergrad@admissions.uga.edu. Web site: http://www.uga.edu/.

UNIVERSITY OF PHOENIX–ATLANTA CAMPUS

SANDY SPRINGS, GEORGIA

General Proprietary, comprehensive, coed **Contact** Ms. Evelyn Gaskin, Registrar/Executive Director, University of Phoenix–Atlanta Campus, 4615 East Elwood Street, Mail Stop AA-K101, Phoenix, AZ 85040-1958. Phone: 480-557-3301 or toll-free 800-776-4867 (in-state); 800-228-7240 (out-of-state). Fax: 480-643-1020. E-mail: evelyn.gaskin@phoenix.edu. Web site: http://www.phoenix.edu/.

UNIVERSITY OF PHOENIX–COLUMBUS GEORGIA CAMPUS

COLUMBUS, GEORGIA

General Proprietary, comprehensive, coed **Contact** Ms. Evelyn Gaskin, Registrar/Executive Director, University of Phoenix–Columbus Georgia Campus, 4747 Hamilton Road, Suite E, Columbus, GA 31904-6321. Phone: 480-557-3301 or toll-free 800-776-4867 (in-state); 800-228-7240 (out-of-state). Fax: 480-643-1020. E-mail: evelyn.gaskin@phoenix.edu. Web site: http://www.phoenix.edu/.

UNIVERSITY OF WEST GEORGIA

CARROLLTON, GEORGIA

General State-supported, comprehensive, coed **Entrance** Minimally difficult **Setting** 395-acre small-town campus **Total enrollment** 10,677 **Student-faculty ratio** 18:1 **Application deadline** 6/1 (freshmen), 6/1 (transfer) **Freshmen** 53% were admitted **Housing** Yes **Expenses** Tuition $3918; Room & Board $5406 **Undergraduates** 60% women, 16% part-time, 15% 25 or older, 0.3% Native American, 2% Hispanic American, 25% African American, 2% Asian American/Pacific Islander **The most frequently chosen baccalaureate fields are** business/marketing, education, health professions and related sciences **Academic program** Advanced placement, accelerated degree program, honors program, summer session, adult/continuing education programs, internships **Contact** Dr. Robert Johnson, Director of Admissions, University of West Georgia, 1601 Maple Street, Carrollton, GA 30118. Phone: 678-839-4000. Fax: 678-839-4747. E-mail: admiss@westga.edu. Web site: http://www.westga.edu/.

VALDOSTA STATE UNIVERSITY

VALDOSTA, GEORGIA

General State-supported, university, coed **Entrance** Moderately difficult **Setting** 178-acre small-town campus **Total enrollment** 11,280 **Student-faculty ratio** 20:1 **Application deadline** 7/1 (freshmen), 7/1 (transfer) **Freshmen** 63% were admitted **Housing** Yes **Expenses** Tuition $4038; Room & Board $5990 **Undergraduates** 59% women, 15% part-time, 14% 25 or older, 0.3% Native American, 2% Hispanic American, 25% African American, 1% Asian American/Pacific Islander **The most frequently chosen baccalaureate fields are** business/marketing, education, health professions and related sciences **Academic program** English as a second language, advanced placement, accelerated degree program, honors program, summer session, internships **Contact** Mr. Walter Peacock, Director of Admissions, Valdosta State University, 1500 North Patterson Street, Valdosta, GA 31698. Phone: 229-333-5791 or toll-free 800-618-1878 Ext. 1. Fax: 229-333-5482. E-mail: admissions@valdosta.edu. Web site: http://www.valdosta.edu/.

WESLEYAN COLLEGE

MACON, GEORGIA

General Independent United Methodist, comprehensive, undergraduate: women only; graduate: coed **Entrance** Moderately difficult **Setting** 200-acre suburban campus **Total enrollment** 691 **Student-faculty ratio** 7:1 **Application deadline** 4/1 (freshmen), rolling (transfer) **Freshmen** 49% were admitted **Housing** Yes **Expenses** Tuition $16,500; Room & Board $7600 **Undergraduates** 36% part-time, 37% 25 or older, 1% Native American, 4% Hispanic American, 22% African American, 1% Asian American/Pacific Islander **The most frequently chosen baccalaureate fields are** business/marketing, education, psychology **Academic program** Advanced placement, self-designed majors, honors program, summer session, adult/continuing education programs, internships **Contact** Ms. Patricia Gibbs, Vice President for Enrollment Services and Student Affairs, Wesleyan College, 4760 Forsyth Road, Macon, GA 31210-4462. Phone: 478-757-5206 or toll-free 800-447-6610. Fax: 478-757-4030. E-mail: admission@wesleyancollege.edu. Web site: http://www.wesleyancollege.edu/.

WESTWOOD COLLEGE–ATLANTA NORTHLAKE

ATLANTA, GEORGIA

General Proprietary, 4-year, coed **Total enrollment** 336 **Undergraduates** 2% Hispanic American, 80% African American, 2% Asian American/Pacific Islander **Contact** Westwood College–Atlanta Northlake, 2220 Parklake Drive, Suite 175, Atlanta, GA 30345. Web site: http://www.westwood.edu/.

HAWAII

ARGOSY UNIVERSITY, HAWAI'I
HONOLULU, HAWAII

General Proprietary, university, coed **Contact** Director of Admissions, Argosy University, Hawai'i, 400 ASBTower, 1001 Bishop Street, Honolulu, HI 96813. Phone: 808-536-5555 or toll-free 888-323-2777. Fax: 808-536-5505. Web site: http://www.argosy.edu/locations/hawaii/.

BRIGHAM YOUNG UNIVERSITY–HAWAII
LAIE, HAWAII

General Independent Latter-day Saints, 4-year, coed **Contact** Mr. Arapata P. Meha, Brigham Young University–Hawaii, 55-220 Kulanui Street, Laie, HI 96762-1294. Phone: 808-293-3731. Fax: 808-293-3741. E-mail: admissions@byuh.edu. Web site: http://www.byuh.edu/.

CHAMINADE UNIVERSITY OF HONOLULU
HONOLULU, HAWAII

General Independent Roman Catholic, comprehensive, coed **Entrance** Minimally difficult **Setting** 62-acre urban campus **Total enrollment** 2,685 **Student-faculty ratio** 12:1 **Application deadline** Rolling (freshmen), rolling (transfer) **Freshmen** 94% were admitted **Housing** Yes **Expenses** Tuition $16,140; Room & Board $10,420 **Undergraduates** 64% women, 34% part-time, 17% 25 or older, 1% Native American, 9% Hispanic American, 7% African American, 48% Asian American/Pacific Islander **The most frequently chosen baccalaureate fields are** education, business/marketing, security and protective services **Academic program** Advanced placement, accelerated degree program, self-designed majors, summer session, adult/continuing education programs, internships **Contact** Martin Motooka, Assistant Director, Chaminade University of Honolulu, 3140 Waialae Avenue, Honolulu, HI 96816-1578. Phone: 808-735-4735 or toll-free 800-735-3733. Fax: 808-739-4647. E-mail: admissions@chaminade.edu. Web site: http://www.chaminade.edu/.

HAWAI'I PACIFIC UNIVERSITY
HONOLULU, HAWAII

General Independent, comprehensive, coed **Entrance** Moderately difficult **Setting** 140-acre urban campus **Total enrollment** 7,943 **Student-faculty ratio** 16:1 **Application deadline** Rolling (freshmen), rolling (transfer) **Freshmen** 82% were admitted **Housing** Yes **Expenses** Tuition $13,080; Room & Board $10,560 **Undergraduates** 61% women, 39% part-time, 40% 25 or older, 1% Native American, 7% Hispanic American, 6% African American, 39% Asian American/Pacific Islander **The most frequently chosen baccalaureate fields are** business/marketing, communications/journalism, health professions and related sciences **Academic program** English as a second language, advanced placement, accelerated degree program, self-designed majors, honors program, summer session, adult/continuing education programs, internships **Contact** Mr. Scott Stensrud, Vice President Enrollment Management, Hawai'i Pacific University, 1164 Bishop Street, Honolulu, HI 96813-2785. Phone: 808-544-0238 or toll-free 866-225-5478. Fax: 808-544-1136. E-mail: admissions@hpu.edu. Web site: http://www.hpu.edu/.

▶**For more information, see page 466.**

REMINGTON COLLEGE–HONOLULU CAMPUS
HONOLULU, HAWAII

General Proprietary, 4-year, coed **Contact** Louis LaMair, Director of Recruitment, Remington College–Honolulu Campus, 1111 Bishop Street, Suite 400, Honolulu, HI 96813. Phone: 808-942-1000. Fax: 808-533-3064. E-mail: louis.lamair@remingtoncollege.edu. Web site: http://www.remingtoncollege.edu/.

UNIVERSITY OF HAWAII AT HILO
HILO, HAWAII

General State-supported, comprehensive, coed **Entrance** Moderately difficult **Setting** 115-acre small-town campus **Total enrollment** 3,573 **Student-faculty ratio** 14:1 **Application deadline** 7/1 (freshmen), 7/1 (transfer) **Freshmen** 56% were admitted **Housing** Yes **Expenses** Tuition $3676; Room & Board $6850 **Undergraduates** 60% women, 19% part-time, 23% 25 or older, 1% Native American, 3% Hispanic American, 1% African American, 43% Asian American/Pacific Islander **Academic program** English as a second language, advanced placement, self-designed majors, honors program, summer session, internships **Contact** Mr. James Cromwell, Student Services Specialist/Director of Admissions, University of Hawaii at Hilo, 200 West Kawili Street, Hilo, HI 96720-4091. Phone: 808-974-7414 or toll-free 808-974-7414 (in-state); 800-897-4456 (out-of-state). Fax: 808-933-0861. E-mail: uhhao@hawaii.edu. Web site: http://www.uhh.hawaii.edu/.

UNIVERSITY OF HAWAII AT MANOA
HONOLULU, HAWAII

General State-supported, university, coed **Entrance** Moderately difficult **Setting** 300-acre urban campus **Total enrollment** 20,357 **Student-faculty ratio** 11:1 **Application deadline** 5/1 (freshmen), 5/1 (transfer) **Freshmen** 68% were admitted **Housing** Yes **Expenses** Tuition $5390; Room & Board $7185 **Undergraduates** 55% women, 18% part-time, 17% 25 or older, 1% Native American, 2% Hispanic American, 1% African American, 63% Asian American/Pacific Islander **The most frequently chosen baccalaureate fields are** business/marketing, education, social sciences **Academic program** English as a second language, advanced placement, accelerated degree program, self-designed majors, honors program, summer session, internships **Contact** Ms. Janice Heu, Interim Director of Admissions and Records, University of Hawaii at Manoa, 2600 Campus Road, Room 001, Honolulu, HI 96822. Phone: 808-956-8975 or toll-free 800-823-9771. Fax: 808-956-4148. E-mail: ar-info@hawaii.edu. Web site: http://www.uhm.hawaii.edu/.

UNIVERSITY OF HAWAII–WEST OAHU

PEARL CITY, HAWAII

General State-supported, upper-level, coed **Entrance** Moderately difficult **Setting** small-town campus **Total enrollment** 940 **Student-faculty ratio** 12:1 **Application deadline** 8/1 (freshmen), 8/1 (transfer) **First-year students** 89% were admitted **Housing** No **Expenses** Tuition $3706 **Undergraduates** 69% women, 65% part-time, 68% 25 or older, 1% Native American, 2% Hispanic American, 2% African American, 62% Asian American/Pacific Islander **The most frequently chosen baccalaureate fields are** business/marketing, psychology, social sciences **Academic program** Advanced placement, summer session **Contact** Robyn Oshiro, University of Hawaii–West Oahu, 96-129 Ala Ike Street, Pearl City, HI 96782. Phone: 808-454-4700. Fax: 808-453-6075. E-mail: robyno@hawaii.edu. Web site: http://www.uhwo.hawaii.edu/.

UNIVERSITY OF PHOENIX–HAWAII CAMPUS

HONOLULU, HAWAII

General Proprietary, comprehensive, coed **Contact** Ms. Evelyn Gaskin, Registrar/Executive Director, University of Phoenix–Hawaii Campus, 4615 East Elwood Street, Mail Stop AA-K101, Phoenix, AZ 85040-1958. Phone: 480-557-3301 or toll-free 800-776-4867 (in-state); 800-228-7240 (out-of-state). Fax: 480-643-1020. E-mail: evelyn.gaskin@phoenix.edu. Web site: http://www.phoenix.edu/.

IDAHO

BOISE BIBLE COLLEGE

BOISE, IDAHO

General Independent nondenominational, 4-year, coed **Contact** Mr. Martin Flaherty, Director of Admissions, Boise Bible College, 8695 West Marigold Street, Boise, ID 83714-1220. Phone: 208-376-7731 or toll-free 800-893-7755. Fax: 208-376-7743. E-mail: martinf@boisebible.edu. Web site: http://www.boisebible.edu/.

BOISE STATE UNIVERSITY

BOISE, IDAHO

General State-supported, university, coed **Entrance** Minimally difficult **Setting** 175-acre urban campus **Total enrollment** 19,540 **Student-faculty ratio** 18:1 **Application deadline** 7/12 (freshmen), 7/12 (transfer) **Freshmen** 89% were admitted **Housing** Yes **Expenses** Tuition $4410; Room & Board $5938 **Undergraduates** 54% women, 37% part-time, 42% 25 or older, 1% Native American, 6% Hispanic American, 1% African American, 3% Asian American/Pacific Islander **The most frequently chosen baccalaureate fields are** business/marketing, education, health professions and related sciences **Academic program** English as a second language, advanced placement, self-designed majors, honors program, summer session, adult/continuing education programs, internships **Contact** Ms. Jenny Cardenas, Dean of Admissions, Boise State University, Enrollment Services, 1910 University Drive, Boise, ID 83725. Phone: 208-426-1177 or toll-free 800-632-6586 (in-state); 800-824-7017 (out-of-state). E-mail: bsuinfo@boisestate.edu. Web site: http://www.boisestate.edu/.

THE COLLEGE OF IDAHO

CALDWELL, IDAHO

General Independent, comprehensive, coed **Entrance** Very difficult **Setting** 50-acre suburban campus **Total enrollment** 840 **Student-faculty ratio** 9:1 **Application deadline** 6/1 (freshmen), rolling (transfer) **Freshmen** 81% were admitted **Housing** Yes **Expenses** Tuition $18,990; Room & Board $6567 **Undergraduates** 61% women, 6% part-time, 4% 25 or older, 0.4% Native American, 7% Hispanic American, 1% African American, 3% Asian American/Pacific Islander **The most frequently chosen baccalaureate fields are** business/marketing, psychology, visual and performing arts **Academic program** Advanced placement, self-designed majors, honors program, internships **Contact** Ms. Charlene Brown, Director of Admissions, The College of Idaho, 2112 Cleveland Boulevard, Caldwell, ID

The College of Idaho *(continued)*

83605-4494. Phone: 208-459-5689 or toll-free 800-244-3246. Fax: 208-459-5151. E-mail: admission@collegeofidaho.edu. Web site: http://www.collegeofidaho.edu/.

IDAHO STATE UNIVERSITY
POCATELLO, IDAHO

General State-supported, university, coed **Entrance** Minimally difficult **Setting** 972-acre small-town campus **Total enrollment** 13,208 **Student-faculty ratio** 14:1 **Application deadline** 8/1 (freshmen), 8/1 (transfer) **Freshmen** 80% were admitted **Housing** Yes **Expenses** Tuition $4400; Room & Board $4950 **Undergraduates** 57% women, 37% part-time, 39% 25 or older, 2% Native American, 5% Hispanic American, 1% African American, 2% Asian American/Pacific Islander **The most frequently chosen baccalaureate fields are** education, business/marketing, health professions and related sciences **Academic program** English as a second language, advanced placement, self-designed majors, honors program, summer session, adult/continuing education programs, internships **Contact** Mr. Scott Teichert, Director, Admissions and Recruitment, Idaho State University, Campus Box 8270, 741 South 7th Avenue, Pocatello, ID 83209. Phone: 208-282-2475. Fax: 208-282-4511. E-mail: info@isu.edu. Web site: http://www.isu.edu/.

LEWIS-CLARK STATE COLLEGE
LEWISTON, IDAHO

General State-supported, 4-year, coed **Entrance** Minimally difficult **Setting** 44-acre small-town campus **Total enrollment** 3,612 **Student-faculty ratio** 14:1 **Application deadline** Rolling (freshmen), rolling (transfer) **Freshmen** 59% were admitted **Housing** Yes **Expenses** Tuition $4092; Room & Board $5100 **Undergraduates** 60% women, 37% part-time, 4% Native American, 6% Hispanic American, 1% African American, 1% Asian American/Pacific Islander **The most frequently chosen baccalaureate fields are** business/marketing, education, health professions and related sciences **Academic program** English as a second language, advanced placement, accelerated degree program, self-designed majors, honors program, summer session, adult/continuing education programs, internships **Contact** Soo Lee Bruce-Smith, Coordinator of New Student Recruitment, Lewis-Clark State College, 500 Eighth Avenue, Lewiston, ID 83501-2698. Phone: 208-792-2210 or toll-free 800-933-5272. Fax: 208-792-2876. E-mail: admissions@lcsc.edu. Web site: http://www.lcsc.edu/.

NEW SAINT ANDREWS COLLEGE
MOSCOW, IDAHO

General Proprietary, 4-year, coed **Entrance** Moderately difficult **Setting** small-town campus **Total enrollment** 163 **Student-faculty ratio** 10:1 **Application deadline** 2/15 (freshmen), 2/15 (transfer) **Freshmen** 75% were admitted **Housing** No **Expenses** Tuition $8500 **Undergraduates** 56% women, 10% part-time, 4% 25 or older, 1% Native American, 3% Hispanic American, 3% Asian American/Pacific Islander **The most frequently chosen baccalaureate field is** liberal arts/general studies **Academic program** Advanced placement, summer session **Contact** Mr. Aaron Rench, Director of Admissions, New Saint Andrews College, PO Box 9025, Moscow, ID 83843. Phone: 208-882-1566 Ext. 100. Fax: 208-882-4293. E-mail: info@nsa.edu. Web site: http://www.nsa.edu/.

NORTHWEST NAZARENE UNIVERSITY
NAMPA, IDAHO

General Independent, comprehensive, coed, affiliated with Church of the Nazarene **Entrance** Moderately difficult **Setting** 85-acre rural campus **Total enrollment** 1,857 **Student-faculty ratio** 12:1 **Application deadline** 8/15 (freshmen), 8/15 (transfer) **Freshmen** 70% were admitted **Housing** Yes **Expenses** Tuition $21,170; Room & Board $5520 **Undergraduates** 60% women, 9% part-time, 10% 25 or older, 1% Native American, 2% Hispanic American, 1% African American, 1% Asian American/Pacific Islander **The most frequently chosen baccalaureate fields are** business/marketing, education, health professions and related sciences **Academic program** Advanced placement, accelerated degree program, self-designed majors, honors program, summer session, adult/continuing education programs, internships **Contact** Stacey Berggren, Director of Admissions, Northwest Nazarene University, 623 Holly Street, Nampa, ID 83686-5897. Phone: 208-467-8648 or toll-free 877-668-4968. Fax: 208-467-8645. E-mail: admissions@nnu.edu. Web site: http://www.nnu.edu/.

STEVENS-HENAGER COLLEGE
BOISE, IDAHO

Contact Stevens-Henager College, 730 Americana Boulevard, Boise, ID 83702. Web site: http://www.stevenshenager.edu/.

UNIVERSITY OF IDAHO
MOSCOW, IDAHO

General State-supported, university, coed **Entrance** Moderately difficult **Setting** 1,450-acre small-town campus **Total enrollment** 11,636

Student-faculty ratio 16:1 **Application deadline** 8/1 (freshmen), rolling (transfer) **Freshmen** 77% were admitted **Housing** Yes **Expenses** Tuition $4410; Room & Board $6424 **Undergraduates** 46% women, 11% part-time, 14% 25 or older, 1% Native American, 5% Hispanic American, 1% African American, 2% Asian American/Pacific Islander **The most frequently chosen baccalaureate fields are** business/marketing, education, engineering **Academic program** Advanced placement, accelerated degree program, self-designed majors, honors program, summer session, adult/continuing education programs, internships **Contact** Mr. Dan Davenport, Director of Admissions, University of Idaho, PO Box 444264, Moscow, ID 83844-4264. Phone: 208-885-6326 or toll-free 888-884-3246. Fax: 208-885-9119. E-mail: admissions@uidaho.edu. Web site: http://www.uidaho.edu/.

UNIVERSITY OF PHOENIX–IDAHO CAMPUS
MERIDIAN, IDAHO

General Proprietary, comprehensive, coed **Contact** Ms. Evelyn Gaskin, Registrar/Executive Director, University of Phoenix–Idaho Campus, 4615 East Elwood Street, Mail Stop AA-K101, Phoenix, AZ 85040-1958. Phone: 480-557-3301 or toll-free 800-776-4867 (in-state); 800-228-7240 (out-of-state). Fax: 480-643-1020. E-mail: evelyn.gaskin@phoenix.edu. Web site: http://www.phoenix.edu/.

ILLINOIS

AMERICAN ACADEMY OF ART
CHICAGO, ILLINOIS

Contact Mr. Stuart Rosenbloom, Director of Admissions, American Academy of Art, 332 South Michigan Avenue, Suite 300, Chicago, IL 60604-4302. Phone: 312-461-0600 Ext. 159. E-mail: srosenbloom@aaart.edu. Web site: http://www.aaart.edu/.

AMERICAN INTERCONTINENTAL UNIVERSITY ONLINE
HOFFMAN ESTATES, ILLINOIS

General Proprietary, comprehensive, coed **Entrance** Minimally difficult **Setting** 1-acre suburban campus **Total enrollment** 26,686 **Application deadline** Rolling (freshmen), rolling (transfer) **Contact** Senior Vice President of Admissions and Marketing, American InterContinental University Online, 5550 Prairie Stone Parkway, Suite 400, Hoffman Estates, IL 60192. Phone: toll-free 877-701-3800. E-mail: info@aiu-online.com. Web site: http://www.aiuniv.edu/.

ARGOSY UNIVERSITY, CHICAGO
CHICAGO, ILLINOIS

General Proprietary, university, coed **Setting** urban campus **Contact** Director of Admissions, Argosy University, Chicago, 350 North Orleans Street, Chicago, IL 60654. Phone: toll-free 800-626-4123. Web site: http://www.argosy.edu/locations/chicago-downtown/.

ARGOSY UNIVERSITY, SCHAUMBURG
SCHAUMBURG, ILLINOIS

General Proprietary, university, coed **Setting** suburban campus **Contact** Director of Admissions, Argosy University, Schaumburg, 999 North Plaza Drive, Suite 111, Schaumburg, IL 60173-5403. Phone: 847-969-4900 or toll-free 866-290-2777. Fax: 847-969-4998. Web site: http://www.argosy.edu/locations/chicago-schaumburg/.

AUGUSTANA COLLEGE
ROCK ISLAND, ILLINOIS

General Independent, 4-year, coed, affiliated with Evangelical Lutheran Church in America **Entrance** Moderately difficult **Setting** 115-acre suburban campus **Total enrollment** 2,537 **Student-faculty ratio** 12:1 **Application deadline** Rolling (freshmen), rolling (transfer) **Freshmen** 73% were admitted **Housing** Yes **Expenses** Tuition $26,484; Room & Board $7233 **Undergraduates** 57% women, 1% part-time, 1% 25 or older, 1% Native American, 4% Hispanic American, 2% African American, 2% Asian American/Pacific Islander **The most frequently chosen baccalaureate fields are** biological/life sciences, business/marketing, social sciences **Academic program** Advanced placement, accelerated degree program, honors program, summer session, internships **Contact** Megan Cooley, Director of Admissions, Augustana College, 639 38th Street, Rock Island, IL 61201-2296. Phone: 309-794-7341 or toll-free 800-798-8100. Fax: 309-794-7422. E-mail: admissions@augustana.edu. Web site: http://www.augustana.edu/.

AURORA UNIVERSITY
AURORA, ILLINOIS

General Independent, comprehensive, coed **Contact** Mr. James Lancaster, Director, Freshman Admission, Aurora University, 347 South Gladstone Avenue, Aurora, IL 60506-4892. Phone: 630-844-5533 or toll-free 800-742-5281. Fax: 630-844-5535. E-mail: admission@aurora.edu. Web site: http://www.aurora.edu/.

BENEDICTINE UNIVERSITY
LISLE, ILLINOIS

General Independent Roman Catholic, comprehensive, coed **Entrance** Moderately difficult **Setting** 108-acre suburban campus **Total enrollment** 4,573 **Student-faculty ratio** 13:1 **Application deadline** Rolling (freshmen), rolling (transfer) **Freshmen** 79% were admitted **Housing** Yes **Expenses** Tuition $21,310; Room & Board $6955 **Undergraduates** 57% women, 35% part-time, 38% 25 or older, 0.2% Native American, 6% Hispanic American, 10% African American, 12% Asian American/Pacific Islander **The most frequently chosen baccalaureate fields are** business/marketing, education, health professions and related sciences **Academic program** Advanced placement, accelerated degree program, honors program, summer session, adult/continuing education programs, internships **Contact** Ms. Kari Gibbons, Dean of Enrollment, Benedictine University, 5700 College Road, Lisle, IL 60532-0900. Phone: 630-829-6300 or toll-free 888-829-6363. Fax: 630-829-6301. E-mail: admissions@ben.edu. Web site: http://www.ben.edu/.

►**For more information, see page 441.**

BLACKBURN COLLEGE
CARLINVILLE, ILLINOIS

General Independent Presbyterian, 4-year, coed **Entrance** Moderately difficult **Setting** 80-acre small-town campus **Total enrollment** 617 **Student-faculty ratio** 13:1 **Application deadline** Rolling (freshmen), rolling (transfer) **Freshmen** 61% were admitted **Housing** Yes **Expenses** Tuition $11,130; Room & Board $4363 **Undergraduates** 55% women, 2% part-time, 4% 25 or older, 0.3% Native American, 1% Hispanic American, 8% African American, 1% Asian American/Pacific Islander **Academic program** Advanced placement, self-designed majors, honors program, summer session, internships **Contact** Ron Bryan, Director of Admission, Blackburn College, 700 College Avenue, Carlinville, IL 62626-1498. Phone: 217-854-3231 Ext. 4252 or toll-free 800-233-3550. Fax: 217-854-3713. E-mail: admit@mail.blackburn.edu. Web site: http://www.blackburn.edu/.

BLESSING-RIEMAN COLLEGE OF NURSING
QUINCY, ILLINOIS

General Independent, 4-year, coed, primarily women **Entrance** Moderately difficult **Setting** 1-acre small-town campus **Total enrollment** 219 **Student-faculty ratio** 12:1 **Application deadline** Rolling (freshmen), rolling (transfer) **Freshmen** 77% were admitted **Housing** Yes **Expenses** Tuition $19,114; Room & Board $7502 **Undergraduates** 92% women, 6% part-time, 41% 25 or older, 0.5% Native American, 1% Hispanic American, 4% African American, 3% Asian American/Pacific Islander **The most frequently chosen baccalaureate field is** health professions and related sciences **Academic program** Advanced placement, honors program, summer session, adult/continuing education programs, internships **Contact** Ms. Heather Mutter or Ms. Kate Boster, Admissions Counselors, Blessing-Rieman College of Nursing, PO Box 7005, Quincy, IL 62305-7005. Phone: 217-228-5520 Ext. 6984 or toll-free 800-877-9140 Ext. 6964. Fax: 217-223-4661. E-mail: admissions@brcn.edu. Web site: http://www.brcn.edu/.

BRADLEY UNIVERSITY
PEORIA, ILLINOIS

General Independent, comprehensive, coed **Entrance** Moderately difficult **Setting** 85-acre suburban campus **Total enrollment** 6,053 **Student-faculty ratio** 14:1 **Application deadline** Rolling (freshmen) **Freshmen** 83% were admitted **Housing** Yes **Expenses** Tuition $21,360; Room & Board $7050 **Undergraduates** 55% women, 6% part-time, 6% 25 or older, 0.4% Native American, 3% Hispanic American, 6% African American, 4% Asian American/Pacific Islander **The most frequently chosen baccalaureate fields are** business/marketing, education, engineering **Academic program** Advanced placement, accelerated degree program, self-designed majors, honors program, summer session, adult/continuing education programs, internships **Contact** Mr. Rodney San Jose, Director of Admissions, Bradley University, 1501 West Bradley Avenue, 100 Swords Hall, Peoria, IL 61625-0002. Phone: 309-677-3144 or toll-free 800-447-6460. Fax: 309-677-2797. E-mail: admissions@bradley.edu. Web site: http://www.bradley.edu/.

CHICAGO STATE UNIVERSITY
CHICAGO, ILLINOIS

General State-supported, comprehensive, coed **Entrance** Minimally difficult **Setting** 161-acre urban campus **Total enrollment** 6,810 **Student-faculty ratio** 13:1 **Freshmen** 57% were admitted **Housing** Yes **Expenses** Tuition $8878; Room & Board $7250 **Undergraduates** 72% women, 37% part-time, 52% 25 or older, 0.2% Native American, 7% Hispanic American, 85% African American, 1% Asian American/Pacific Islander **The most frequently chosen baccalaureate fields are** health professions and related sciences, education, liberal arts/general studies **Academic program** Advanced placement, accelerated degree program, self-designed majors, honors program, summer session, adult/continuing education programs, internships **Contact** Ms. Addie Epps,

Director of Admissions, Chicago State University, 95th Street at King Drive, ADM 200, Chicago, IL 60628. Phone: 773-995-2513. Fax: 773-995-3820. E-mail: ug-admissions@csu.edu. Web site: http://www.csu.edu/.

CHRISTIAN LIFE COLLEGE
MOUNT PROSPECT, ILLINOIS

Contact Mr. Jim Spenner, Director of Admissions, Christian Life College, 400 East Gregory Street, Mount Prospect, IL 60056. Phone: 847-259-1840 Ext. 17. E-mail: jspenner@christianlifecollege.edu. Web site: http://www.christianlifecollege.edu/.

COLUMBIA COLLEGE CHICAGO
CHICAGO, ILLINOIS

General Independent, comprehensive, coed **Entrance** Noncompetitive **Setting** urban campus **Total enrollment** 11,499 **Student-faculty ratio** 14:1 **Application deadline** Rolling (freshmen), rolling (transfer) **Freshmen** 95% were admitted **Housing** Yes **Expenses** Tuition $17,634; Room & Board $12,018 **Undergraduates** 14% 25 or older **The most frequently chosen baccalaureate fields are** liberal arts/general studies, communications/journalism, visual and performing arts **Academic program** English as a second language, advanced placement, self-designed majors, summer session, internships **Contact** Mr. Murphy Monroe, Executive Director of Admissions, Columbia College Chicago, 600 South Michigan Avenue, Chicago, IL 60605-1996. Phone: 312-344-7133 or toll-free 312-663-1600 Ext. 7130. Fax: 312-344-8024. E-mail: admissions@colum.edu. Web site: http://www.colum.edu/.

▶**For more information, see page 452.**

CONCORDIA UNIVERSITY CHICAGO
RIVER FOREST, ILLINOIS

General Independent, comprehensive, coed, affiliated with Lutheran Church–Missouri Synod **Entrance** Moderately difficult **Setting** 40-acre suburban campus **Total enrollment** 4,126 **Student-faculty ratio** 17:1 **Application deadline** Rolling (freshmen), rolling (transfer) **Freshmen** 84% were admitted **Housing** Yes **Expenses** Tuition $22,390; Room & Board $7350 **Undergraduates** 62% women, 13% part-time, 16% 25 or older, 10% Hispanic American, 12% African American, 1% Asian American/Pacific Islander **The most frequently chosen baccalaureate fields are** business/marketing, education, theology and religious vocations **Academic program** Advanced placement, accelerated degree program, honors program, summer session, adult/continuing education programs, internships **Contact** Dr. Evelyn Burdick, Vice President for Enrollment Services, Concordia University Chicago, 7400 Augusta Street, River Forest, IL 60305. Phone: 708-209-3100 or toll-free 800-285-2668. Fax: 708-209-3473. E-mail: crfadmis@cuchicago.edu. Web site: http://www.cuchicago.edu/.

DEPAUL UNIVERSITY
CHICAGO, ILLINOIS

General Independent Roman Catholic, university, coed **Entrance** Moderately difficult **Setting** 36-acre urban campus **Total enrollment** 23,401 **Student-faculty ratio** 17:1 **Application deadline** Rolling (freshmen), rolling (transfer) **Freshmen** 63% were admitted **Housing** Yes **Expenses** Tuition $24,394; Room & Board $9955 **Undergraduates** 56% women, 20% part-time, 23% 25 or older, 0.3% Native American, 12% Hispanic American, 9% African American, 9% Asian American/Pacific Islander **The most frequently chosen baccalaureate fields are** business/marketing, liberal arts/general studies, social sciences **Academic program** English as a second language, advanced placement, accelerated degree program, self-designed majors, honors program, summer session, adult/continuing education programs, internships **Contact** Carlene Klaas, Undergraduate Admissions, DePaul University, 1 East Jackson Boulevard, Suite 9100, Chicago, IL 60604. Phone: 312-362-8650. E-mail: admitdpu@depaul.edu. Web site: http://www.depaul.edu/.

DEVRY UNIVERSITY
ADDISON, ILLINOIS

General Proprietary, 4-year, coed **Entrance** Minimally difficult **Setting** 14-acre suburban campus **Total enrollment** 1,321 **Student-faculty ratio** 15:1 **Application deadline** Rolling (freshmen), rolling (transfer) **Housing** No **Expenses** Tuition $13,990 **Undergraduates** 27% women, 40% part-time, 51% 25 or older, 0.1% Native American, 14% Hispanic American, 10% African American, 12% Asian American/Pacific Islander **The most frequently chosen baccalaureate fields are** business/marketing, computer and information sciences, engineering technologies **Academic program** Advanced placement, accelerated degree program, summer session, adult/continuing education programs **Contact** Admissions Office, DeVry University, 1221 North Swift Road, Addison, IL 60101-6106. Phone: toll-free 800-346-5420. Web site: http://www.devry.edu/.

DEVRY UNIVERSITY
CHICAGO, ILLINOIS

General Proprietary, 4-year, coed **Entrance** Minimally difficult **Setting** 17-acre urban campus **Total**

DeVry University *(continued)*

enrollment 1,896 **Student-faculty ratio** 22:1 **Application deadline** Rolling (freshmen), rolling (transfer) **Housing** No **Expenses** Tuition $13,990 **Undergraduates** 41% women, 48% part-time, 48% 25 or older, 1% Native American, 32% Hispanic American, 37% African American, 6% Asian American/Pacific Islander **The most frequently chosen baccalaureate fields are** business/marketing, computer and information sciences, engineering technologies **Academic program** Advanced placement, accelerated degree program, summer session, adult/continuing education programs **Contact** Admissions Office, DeVry University, 3300 North Campbell Avenue, Chicago, IL 60618-5994. Web site: http://www.devry.edu/.

DeVRY UNIVERSITY
ELGIN, ILLINOIS

Contact DeVry University, 385 Airport Road, Elgin, IL 60123-9341. Web site: http://www.devry.edu/.

DeVRY UNIVERSITY
GURNEE, ILLINOIS

Contact DeVry University, 1075 Tri-State Parkway, Suite 800, Gurnee, IL 60031-9126. Phone: toll-free 866-563-3879. Web site: http://www.devry.edu/.

DeVRY UNIVERSITY
NAPERVILLE, ILLINOIS

General Proprietary, comprehensive, coed **Contact** Admissions Office, DeVry University, 2056 Westings Avenue, Suite 40, Naperville, IL 60563-2361. Phone: toll-free 877-496-9050. Web site: http://www.devry.edu/.

DeVRY UNIVERSITY
OAKBROOK TERRACE, ILLINOIS

Contact DeVry University, One Tower Lane, Oakbrook Terrace, IL 60181. Web site: http://www.devry.edu/.

DeVRY UNIVERSITY
TINLEY PARK, ILLINOIS

General Proprietary, comprehensive, coed **Entrance** Minimally difficult **Setting** 12-acre suburban campus **Total enrollment** 1,312 **Student-faculty ratio** 14:1 **Application deadline** Rolling (freshmen), rolling (transfer) **Housing** No **Expenses** Tuition $13,990 **Undergraduates** 29% women, 40% part-time, 45% 25 or older, 0.5% Native American, 8% Hispanic American, 34% African American, 2% Asian American/Pacific Islander **The most frequently chosen baccalaureate fields are** business/marketing, computer and information sciences, engineering technologies **Academic program** Advanced placement, accelerated degree program, summer session, adult/continuing education programs **Contact** Admissions Office, DeVry University, 18624 West Creek Drive, Tinley Park, IL 60477. Web site: http://www.devry.edu/.

DeVRY UNIVERSITY ONLINE
OAKBROOK TERRACE, ILLINOIS

General Proprietary, comprehensive, coed **Total enrollment** 12,276 **Student-faculty ratio** 6:1 **Application deadline** Rolling (freshmen), rolling (transfer) **Expenses** Tuition $14,560 **Undergraduates** 49% women, 69% part-time, 76% 25 or older, 1% Native American, 7% Hispanic American, 24% African American, 2% Asian American/Pacific Islander **The most frequently chosen baccalaureate fields are** business/marketing, computer and information sciences **Contact** Admissions Office, DeVry University Online, One Tower Lane, Suite 1000, Oakbrook Terrace, IL 60181. Phone: toll-free 866-338-7934. Web site: http://online.devry.edu/.

DOMINICAN UNIVERSITY
RIVER FOREST, ILLINOIS

General Independent Roman Catholic, comprehensive, coed **Entrance** Moderately difficult **Setting** 30-acre suburban campus **Total enrollment** 3,338 **Student-faculty ratio** 12:1 **Application deadline** Rolling (freshmen), rolling (transfer) **Freshmen** 85% were admitted **Housing** Yes **Expenses** Tuition $22,450; Room & Board $7000 **Undergraduates** 70% women, 13% part-time, 12% 25 or older, 22% Hispanic American, 7% African American, 3% Asian American/Pacific Islander **The most frequently chosen baccalaureate fields are** business/marketing, psychology, social sciences **Academic program** English as a second language, advanced placement, accelerated degree program, self-designed majors, honors program, summer session, adult/continuing education programs, internships **Contact** Mr. Glenn Hamilton, Director of Freshman Admission, Dominican University, 7900 West Division Street, River Forest, IL 60305. Phone: 708-524-6800 or toll-free 800-828-8475. Fax: 708-524-6864. E-mail: domadmis@dom.edu. Web site: http://www.dom.edu/.

EASTERN ILLINOIS UNIVERSITY
CHARLESTON, ILLINOIS

General State-supported, comprehensive, coed **Entrance** Moderately difficult **Setting** 320-acre

small-town campus **Total enrollment** 12,179 **Student-faculty ratio** 15:1 **Application deadline** Rolling (freshmen), rolling (transfer) **Freshmen** 71% were admitted **Housing** Yes **Expenses** Tuition $7990; Room & Board $7124 **Undergraduates** 58% women, 10% part-time, 12% 25 or older, 0.4% Native American, 3% Hispanic American, 9% African American, 1% Asian American/Pacific Islander **The most frequently chosen baccalaureate fields are** business/marketing, education, English **Academic program** Advanced placement, honors program, summer session, adult/continuing education programs, internships **Contact** Brenda Major, Director of Admissions, Eastern Illinois University, 600 Lincoln Avenue, Charleston, IL 61920-3099. Phone: 217-581-2223 or toll-free 800-252-5711. Fax: 217-581-7060. E-mail: admissions@eiu.edu. Web site: http://www.eiu.edu/.

EAST-WEST UNIVERSITY
CHICAGO, ILLINOIS

General Independent, 4-year, coed **Entrance** Minimally difficult **Setting** urban campus **Total enrollment** 1,150 **Student-faculty ratio** 15:1 **Application deadline** Rolling (freshmen), rolling (transfer) **Freshmen** 91% were admitted **Housing** No **Expenses** Tuition $13,480 **Undergraduates** 65% women, 1% part-time, 24% 25 or older, 0.2% Native American, 12% Hispanic American, 70% African American, 2% Asian American/Pacific Islander **Academic program** Summer session, internships **Contact** Mr. William Link, Director of Admissions, East-West University, 816 South Michigan Avenue, Chicago, IL 60605-2103. Phone: 312-939-0111 Ext. 1830. Fax: 312-939-0083. E-mail: williaml@eastwest.edu. Web site: http://www.eastwest.edu/.

ELMHURST COLLEGE
ELMHURST, ILLINOIS

General Independent, comprehensive, coed, affiliated with United Church of Christ **Contact** Mrs. Stephanie Levenson, Director of Admission, Elmhurst College, Elmhurst College Admission Office, 190 South Prospect Avenue, Elmhurst, IL 60126-3296. Phone: 630-617-3400 or toll-free 800-697-1871. Fax: 630-617-5501. E-mail: admit@elmhurst.edu. Web site: http://www.elmhurst.edu/.

EUREKA COLLEGE
EUREKA, ILLINOIS

Contact Dr. Brian Sajko, Dean of Admissions and Financial Aid, Eureka College, 300 East College Avenue, Eureka, IL 61530-1500. Phone: 309-467-6350 or toll-free 888-4-EUREKA. Fax: 309-467-6576. E-mail: admissions@eureka.edu. Web site: http://www.eureka.edu/.

GOVERNORS STATE UNIVERSITY
UNIVERSITY PARK, ILLINOIS

Contact Mr. Randall Tumblin, Director of Admissions, Governors State University, One University Parkway, University Park, IL 60466. Phone: 708-534-4490. Fax: 708-534-1640. E-mail: gsunow@govst.edu. Web site: http://www.govst.edu/.

GREENVILLE COLLEGE
GREENVILLE, ILLINOIS

General Independent Free Methodist, comprehensive, coed **Entrance** Moderately difficult **Setting** 12-acre small-town campus **Total enrollment** 1,528 **Student-faculty ratio** 16:1 **Application deadline** 8/1 (freshmen), 8/1 (transfer) **Freshmen** 81% were admitted **Housing** Yes **Expenses** Tuition $18,672; Room & Board $6348 **Undergraduates** 54% women, 3% part-time, 1% 25 or older, 1% Native American, 2% Hispanic American, 7% African American, 1% Asian American/Pacific Islander **The most frequently chosen baccalaureate fields are** business/marketing, biological/life sciences, education **Academic program** Advanced placement, accelerated degree program, self-designed majors, honors program, summer session, adult/continuing education programs, internships **Contact** Mr. Michael Ritter, Director of Admissions, Greenville College, 315 East College Avenue, Greenville, IL 62246. Phone: 618-664-7100 or toll-free 800-345-4440. Fax: 618-664-9841. E-mail: admissions@greenville.edu. Web site: http://www.greenville.edu/.

HARRINGTON COLLEGE OF DESIGN
CHICAGO, ILLINOIS

General Proprietary, 4-year, coed, primarily women **Contact** Ms. Melissa Laurentius, Director of Admissions, Harrington College of Design, 200 West Madison, Chicago, IL 60606. Phone: toll-free 877-939-4975. Fax: 312-939-8032. E-mail: barrington@interiordesign.edu. Web site: http://www.interiordesign.edu/.

HEBREW THEOLOGICAL COLLEGE
SKOKIE, ILLINOIS

Contact Rabbi Berish Cardash, Hebrew Theological College, 7135 North Carpenter Road, Skokie, IL 60077-3263. Phone: 847-982-2500. Web site: http://www.htc.edu/.

ILLINOIS COLLEGE
JACKSONVILLE, ILLINOIS

General Independent interdenominational, 4-year, coed **Entrance** Moderately difficult **Setting** 62-acre small-town campus **Total enrollment** 1,014 **Student-faculty ratio** 13:1 **Application deadline** 7/1 (freshmen), 7/1 (transfer) **Freshmen** 91% were admitted **Housing** Yes **Expenses** Tuition $18,800; Room & Board $6970 **Undergraduates** 52% women, 3% part-time, 2% 25 or older, 1% Native American, 2% Hispanic American, 3% African American, 1% Asian American/Pacific Islander **The most frequently chosen baccalaureate fields are** biological/life sciences, business/marketing, education **Academic program** Advanced placement, accelerated degree program, summer session, internships **Contact** Mr. Rick Bystry, Associate Director of Admission, Illinois College, 1101 West College, Jacksonville, IL 62650. Phone: 217-245-3030 or toll-free 866-464-5265. Fax: 217-245-3034. E-mail: admissions@ic.edu. Web site: http://www.ic.edu/.

THE ILLINOIS INSTITUTE OF ART–CHICAGO
CHICAGO, ILLINOIS

General Proprietary, 4-year, coed **Setting** urban campus **Contact** Director of Admissions, The Illinois Institute of Art–Chicago, 350 North Orleans Street, Chicago, IL 60654. Phone: 312-280-3500 or toll-free 800-351-3450. Fax: 312-280-8562. Web site: http://www.artinstitutes.edu/chicago.

THE ILLINOIS INSTITUTE OF ART–SCHAUMBURG
SCHAUMBURG, ILLINOIS

General Proprietary, 4-year, coed **Entrance** Minimally difficult **Setting** suburban campus **Contact** Admissions, The Illinois Institute of Art–Schaumburg, 1000 Plaza Drive, Schaumburg, IL 60173. Phone: 847-619-3450 or toll-free 800-314-3450. Fax: 847-619-3064. Web site: http://www.artinstitutes.edu/schaumburg.

ILLINOIS INSTITUTE OF TECHNOLOGY
CHICAGO, ILLINOIS

General Independent, university, coed **Entrance** Very difficult **Setting** 120-acre urban campus **Total enrollment** 7,409 **Student-faculty ratio** 8:1 **Application deadline** 8/1 (freshmen), rolling (transfer) **Freshmen** 56% were admitted **Housing** Yes **Expenses** Tuition $25,746; Room & Board $8618 **Undergraduates** 27% women, 10% part-time, 13% 25 or older, 0.4% Native American, 7% Hispanic American, 4% African American, 14% Asian American/Pacific Islander **The most frequently chosen baccalaureate fields are** architecture, computer and information sciences, engineering **Academic program** English as a second language, advanced placement, summer session, internships **Contact** Mr. Gerald Doyle, Associate Vice President, Undergraduate Admissions, Illinois Institute of Technology, Office of Undergraduate Admission, Perlstein 101, 10 West 33rd Street, Chicago, IL 60616. Phone: 312-567-3025 or toll-free 800-448-2329. Fax: 312-567-6939. E-mail: admission@iit.edu. Web site: http://www.iit.edu/.

ILLINOIS STATE UNIVERSITY
NORMAL, ILLINOIS

General State-supported, university, coed **Entrance** Moderately difficult **Setting** 850-acre urban campus **Total enrollment** 20,274 **Student-faculty ratio** 19:1 **Application deadline** 3/1 (freshmen), rolling (transfer) **Freshmen** 67% were admitted **Housing** Yes **Expenses** Tuition $9019; Room & Board $6848 **Undergraduates** 57% women, 6% part-time, 7% 25 or older, 0.3% Native American, 4% Hispanic American, 6% African American, 2% Asian American/Pacific Islander **The most frequently chosen baccalaureate fields are** business/marketing, education, social sciences **Academic program** English as a second language, advanced placement, accelerated degree program, self-designed majors, honors program, summer session, adult/continuing education programs, internships **Contact** Ms. Molly Arnold, Director of Admissions, Illinois State University, Campus Box 2200, Normal, IL 61790-2200. Phone: 309-438-2181 or toll-free 800-366-2478. Fax: 309-438-3932. E-mail: admissions@ilstu.edu. Web site: http://www.ilstu.edu/.

ILLINOIS WESLEYAN UNIVERSITY
BLOOMINGTON, ILLINOIS

General Independent, 4-year, coed **Entrance** Very difficult **Setting** 79-acre suburban campus **Total enrollment** 2,094 **Student-faculty ratio** 11:1 **Application deadline** Rolling (freshmen), 8/15 (transfer) **Freshmen** 57% were admitted **Housing** Yes **Expenses** Tuition $30,750; Room & Board $7030 **Undergraduates** 58% women, 0.3% part-time, 0.4% Native American, 3% Hispanic American, 5% African American, 4% Asian American/Pacific Islander **The most frequently chosen baccalaureate fields are** business/marketing, biological/life sciences, visual and performing arts **Academic program** Advanced placement, self-designed majors, honors program, internships **Contact** Mr. Tony Bankston, Dean of Admissions, Illinois Wesleyan University, PO Box 2900, Bloomington, IL 61702-2900. Phone: 309-556-3031 or toll-free 800-332-2498. Fax:

309-556-3820. E-mail: iwuadmit@iwu.edu. Web site: http://www.iwu.edu/.

INTERNATIONAL ACADEMY OF DESIGN & TECHNOLOGY

CHICAGO, ILLINOIS

General Proprietary, 4-year, coed, primarily women **Entrance** Minimally difficult **Setting** 1-acre urban campus **Total enrollment** 2,335 **Student-faculty ratio** 15:1 **Application deadline** Rolling (freshmen), rolling (transfer) **Freshmen** 27% were admitted **Housing** No **Expenses** Tuition $23,640 **Undergraduates** 66% women, 13% part-time, 31% 25 or older, 0.5% Native American, 20% Hispanic American, 36% African American, 4% Asian American/Pacific Islander **The most frequently chosen baccalaureate fields are** business/marketing, computer and information sciences, visual and performing arts **Academic program** Advanced placement, summer session, adult/continuing education programs, internships **Contact** Suzanne Reichart, Director of Student Management, International Academy of Design & Technology, One North State Street, Suite 500, Chicago, IL 60602. Phone: 312-980-9200 or toll-free 877-ACADEMY. Fax: 312-541-3929. E-mail: sreichart@iadtchicago.edu. Web site: http://www.iadtchicago.edu/.

JUDSON UNIVERSITY

ELGIN, ILLINOIS

General Independent Baptist, comprehensive, coed **Entrance** Moderately difficult **Setting** 80-acre suburban campus **Total enrollment** 1,230 **Student-faculty ratio** 14:1 **Application deadline** Rolling (freshmen), rolling (transfer) **Freshmen** 73% were admitted **Housing** Yes **Expenses** Tuition $20,420; Room & Board $7200 **Undergraduates** 61% women, 19% part-time, 33% 25 or older, 0.1% Native American, 6% Hispanic American, 4% African American, 1% Asian American/Pacific Islander **The most frequently chosen baccalaureate fields are** business/marketing, education, public administration and social services **Academic program** Advanced placement, accelerated degree program, honors program, adult/continuing education programs, internships **Contact** Mr. William W. Dean, Director of Enrollment Management, Judson University, 1151 North State Street, Elgin, IL 60123-1498. Phone: 847-628-2522 or toll-free 800-879-5376. Fax: 847-628-2526. E-mail: bdean@judsoncollege.edu. Web site: http://www.judsonu.edu/.

KENDALL COLLEGE

CHICAGO, ILLINOIS

General Independent United Methodist, 4-year, coed **Contact** Susanne Noel, Vice President of Admissions, Kendall College, 900 N North Branch Street, Chicago, IL 60622. Phone: 312-752-2252 or toll-free 866-667-3344 (in-state); 877-588-8860 (out-of-state). Fax: 312-752-2021. E-mail: admissions@kendall.edu. Web site: http://www.kendall.edu/.

KNOX COLLEGE

GALESBURG, ILLINOIS

General Independent, 4-year, coed **Entrance** Very difficult **Setting** 82-acre small-town campus **Total enrollment** 1,371 **Student-faculty ratio** 12:1 **Application deadline** 2/1 (freshmen), 4/1 (transfer) **Freshmen** 61% were admitted **Housing** Yes **Expenses** Tuition $30,507; Room & Board $6726 **Undergraduates** 58% women, 1% part-time, 2% 25 or older, 1% Native American, 5% Hispanic American, 4% African American, 7% Asian American/Pacific Islander **The most frequently chosen baccalaureate fields are** English, education, social sciences **Academic program** Advanced placement, self-designed majors, honors program, internships **Contact** Mr. Paul Steenis, Director of Admissions, Knox College, Box K-148, Galesburg, IL 61401. Phone: 309-341-7100 or toll-free 800-678-KNOX. Fax: 309-341-7070. E-mail: admission@knox.edu. Web site: http://www.knox.edu/.

LAKE FOREST COLLEGE

LAKE FOREST, ILLINOIS

General Independent, comprehensive, coed **Entrance** Very difficult **Setting** 110-acre suburban campus **Total enrollment** 1,456 **Student-faculty ratio** 13:1 **Application deadline** 2/15 (freshmen), rolling (transfer) **Freshmen** 61% were admitted **Housing** Yes **Expenses** Tuition $30,964; Room & Board $7326 **Undergraduates** 59% women, 1% part-time, 1% 25 or older, 0.3% Native American, 6% Hispanic American, 4% African American, 5% Asian American/Pacific Islander **The most frequently chosen baccalaureate fields are** communications/journalism, business/marketing, social sciences **Academic program** Advanced placement, accelerated degree program, self-designed majors, honors program, summer session, adult/continuing education programs, internships **Contact** Mr. William Motzer, Vice President for Admissions and Career Services, Lake Forest College, 555 North Sheridan Road, Lake Forest, IL 60045-2399. Phone: 847-735-5000 or toll-free 800-828-4751. Fax: 847-735-6271. E-mail: admissions@lakeforest.edu. Web site: http://www.lakeforest.edu/.

LAKEVIEW COLLEGE OF NURSING

DANVILLE, ILLINOIS

Contact Amy McFadden, Recruiter, Lakeview College of Nursing, 903 North Logan Avenue,

Lakeview College of Nursing *(continued)*

Danville, IL 61832. Phone: 217-554-6899 or toll-free 217-443-5238 Ext. 5454. Fax: 217-442-2279. E-mail: amcfadden@lakeviewcol.edu. Web site: http://www.lakeviewcol.edu/.

LEWIS UNIVERSITY

ROMEOVILLE, ILLINOIS

General Independent, comprehensive, coed, affiliated with Roman Catholic Church **Entrance** Moderately difficult **Setting** 375-acre suburban campus **Total enrollment** 5,327 **Student-faculty ratio** 13:1 **Application deadline** 8/1 (freshmen), rolling (transfer) **Freshmen** 68% were admitted **Housing** Yes **Expenses** Tuition $20,450; Room & Board $7800 **Undergraduates** 61% women, 23% part-time, 28% 25 or older, 0.1% Native American, 11% Hispanic American, 11% African American, 4% Asian American/Pacific Islander **The most frequently chosen baccalaureate fields are** business/marketing, health professions and related sciences, security and protective services **Academic program** English as a second language, advanced placement, accelerated degree program, self-designed majors, honors program, summer session, adult/continuing education programs, internships **Contact** Mr. Ryan Cockerill, Director of Freshman Admission, Lewis University, Box 297, One University Parkway, Romeoville, IL 60446. Phone: 815-838-0500 Ext. 5684 or toll-free 800-897-9000. Fax: 815-836-5002. E-mail: admissions@lewisu.edu. Web site: http://www.lewisu.edu/.

LEXINGTON COLLEGE

CHICAGO, ILLINOIS

General Independent, 4-year, women only **Entrance** Noncompetitive **Setting** urban campus **Total enrollment** 57 **Student-faculty ratio** 6:1 **Application deadline** Rolling (freshmen), rolling (transfer) **Freshmen** 47% were admitted **Housing** No **Expenses** Tuition $20,550 **Undergraduates** 14% part-time, 28% 25 or older, 2% Native American, 18% Hispanic American, 25% African American, 4% Asian American/Pacific Islander **Academic program** Advanced placement, adult/continuing education programs, internships **Contact** Ms. Nina Pelligrino, Freshman Admissions Representative, Lexington College, 310 South Peoria Street, Chicago, IL 60607-3534. Phone: 312-226-6294 Ext. 228. Fax: 312-226-6405. E-mail: admissions@lexingtoncollege.edu. Web site: http://lexingtoncollege.edu/general-education.htm.

LINCOLN CHRISTIAN COLLEGE

LINCOLN, ILLINOIS

Contact Mrs. Mary K. Davis, Assistant Director of Admissions, Lincoln Christian College, 100 Campus View Drive, Lincoln, IL 62656. Phone: 217-732-3168 Ext. 2367 or toll-free 888-522-5228. Fax: 217-732-4199. E-mail: coladmis@lccs.edu. Web site: http://www.lccs.edu/.

LOYOLA UNIVERSITY CHICAGO

CHICAGO, ILLINOIS

General Independent Roman Catholic (Jesuit), university, coed, primarily women **Entrance** Moderately difficult **Setting** 105-acre urban campus **Total enrollment** 15,545 **Student-faculty ratio** 14:1 **Application deadline** 4/1 (freshmen), 7/1 (transfer) **Freshmen** 73% were admitted **Housing** Yes **Expenses** Tuition $29,486; Room & Board $10,490 **Undergraduates** 65% women, 8% part-time, 9% 25 or older, 0.3% Native American, 10% Hispanic American, 5% African American, 12% Asian American/Pacific Islander **The most frequently chosen baccalaureate fields are** business/marketing, biological/life sciences, social sciences **Academic program** English as a second language, advanced placement, accelerated degree program, honors program, summer session, adult/continuing education programs, internships **Contact** Ms. April Hansen, Director of Admission, Loyola University Chicago, 820 North Michigan Avenue, Suite 613, Chicago, IL 60611-9810. Phone: 773-508-3079 or toll-free 800-262-2373. Fax: 312-508-8926. E-mail: admission@luc.edu. Web site: http://www.luc.edu/.

MacMURRAY COLLEGE

JACKSONVILLE, ILLINOIS

General Independent United Methodist, 4-year, coed **Contact** Ms. Rhonda Cors, Vice President for Enrollment, MacMurray College, 447 East College Avenue, Jacksonville, IL 62650. Phone: 217-479-7056 or toll-free 800-252-7485. Fax: 217-291-0702. E-mail: admiss@mac.edu. Web site: http://www.mac.edu/.

McKENDREE UNIVERSITY

LEBANON, ILLINOIS

General Independent, comprehensive, coed, affiliated with United Methodist Church **Entrance** Moderately difficult **Setting** 80-acre small-town campus **Total enrollment** 3,393 **Student-faculty ratio** 13:1 **Application deadline** Rolling (freshmen), rolling (transfer) **Freshmen** 71% were admitted **Housing** Yes **Expenses** Tuition $20,150; Room & Board $7660 **Undergraduates** 56% women, 31% part-time, 34% 25 or older, 0.3% Native American, 2% Hispanic American, 13% African American, 1% Asian American/Pacific Islander **The most frequently chosen baccalaureate fields are** business/marketing, education, health professions and related sciences **Academic**

program Advanced placement, accelerated degree program, self-designed majors, honors program, summer session, internships **Contact** Chris Hall, Vice President for Admissions and Financial Aid, McKendree University, 701 College Road, Lebanon, IL 62254. Phone: 618-537-6833 or toll-free 800-232-7228 Ext. 6831. Fax: 618-537-6496. E-mail: inquiry@mckendree.edu. Web site: http://www.mckendree.edu/.

MIDSTATE COLLEGE
PEORIA, ILLINOIS

Contact Ms. Jessica Hancock, Director of Admissions, Midstate College, 411 West Northmoor Road, Peoria, IL 61614. Phone: 309-692-4092. Fax: 309-692-3893. E-mail: jhancock2@midstate.edu. Web site: http://www.midstate.edu/.

MILLIKIN UNIVERSITY
DECATUR, ILLINOIS

General Independent, comprehensive, coed, affiliated with Presbyterian Church (U.S.A.) **Entrance** Moderately difficult **Setting** 70-acre suburban campus **Total enrollment** 2,376 **Student-faculty ratio** 12:1 **Application deadline** Rolling (freshmen), rolling (transfer) **Freshmen** 68% were admitted **Housing** Yes **Expenses** Tuition $23,845; Room & Board $7210 **Undergraduates** 61% women, 6% part-time, 16% 25 or older, 0.3% Native American, 3% Hispanic American, 9% African American, 1% Asian American/Pacific Islander **The most frequently chosen baccalaureate fields are** business/marketing, education, visual and performing arts **Academic program** Advanced placement, accelerated degree program, self-designed majors, honors program, summer session, adult/continuing education programs, internships **Contact** Mr. Joe Havis, Assistant Director of Admission, Millikin University, 1184 West Main Street, Decatur, IL 62522-2084. Phone: 217-424-6210 or toll-free 800-373-7733. Fax: 217-425-4669. E-mail: admis@millikin.edu. Web site: http://www.millikin.edu/.

MONMOUTH COLLEGE
MONMOUTH, ILLINOIS

General Independent, 4-year, coed, affiliated with Presbyterian Church **Entrance** Moderately difficult **Setting** 80-acre small-town campus **Total enrollment** 1,343 **Student-faculty ratio** 13:1 **Application deadline** Rolling (freshmen), rolling (transfer) **Freshmen** 78% were admitted **Housing** Yes **Expenses** Tuition $24,000; Room & Board $7000 **Undergraduates** 55% women, 1% part-time, 3% 25 or older, 1% Native American, 3% Hispanic American, 5% African American, 1% Asian American/Pacific Islander **The most frequently chosen baccalaureate fields are** business/marketing, biological/life sciences, education **Academic program** Advanced placement, self-designed majors, honors program, internships **Contact** Ms. Christine Johnston, Dean of Admission, Monmouth College, 700 East Broadway, Monmouth, IL 61462-1988. Phone: 309-457-2131 or toll-free 800-747-2687. Fax: 309-457-2141. E-mail: admit@monm.edu. Web site: http://www.monm.edu/.

MOODY BIBLE INSTITUTE
CHICAGO, ILLINOIS

Contact Mrs. Marthe Campa, Application Coordinator, Moody Bible Institute, 820 North LaSalle Boulevard, Chicago, IL 60610. Phone: 312-329-4267 or toll-free 800-967-4MBI. Fax: 312-329-8987. E-mail: admissions@moody.edu. Web site: http://www.moody.edu/.

NATIONAL-LOUIS UNIVERSITY
CHICAGO, ILLINOIS

General Independent, university, coed **Entrance** Minimally difficult **Setting** 12-acre urban campus **Total enrollment** 6,950 **Application deadline** Rolling (freshmen), rolling (transfer) **Housing** No **Expenses** Tuition $18,075 **Undergraduates** 76% women, 30% part-time, 83% 25 or older, 0.4% Native American, 12% Hispanic American, 32% African American, 3% Asian American/Pacific Islander **The most frequently chosen baccalaureate fields are** business/marketing, education, interdisciplinary studies **Academic program** English as a second language, advanced placement, accelerated degree program, honors program, summer session, adult/continuing education programs, internships **Contact** Dr. Larry Poselli, Vice President of Enrollment and Student Services, National-Louis University, 1000 Capitol Drive, Wheeling, IL 60090. Phone: 888-NLU-TODAY or toll-free 888-NLU-TODAY (in-state); 800-443-5522 (out-of-state). Web site: http://www.nl.edu/.

NORTH CENTRAL COLLEGE
NAPERVILLE, ILLINOIS

General Independent United Methodist, comprehensive, coed **Entrance** Moderately difficult **Setting** 56-acre suburban campus **Total enrollment** 2,559 **Student-faculty ratio** 15:1 **Application deadline** Rolling (freshmen), rolling (transfer) **Freshmen** 69% were admitted **Housing** Yes **Expenses** Tuition $24,564; Room & Board $7677 **Undergraduates** 57% women, 9% part-time, 8% 25 or older, 0.4% Native American, 4% Hispanic American, 3% African American, 3% Asian American/Pacific Islander **The most frequently chosen baccalaureate fields are** business/marketing, education, social sciences

North Central College *(continued)*

Academic program English as a second language, advanced placement, accelerated degree program, self-designed majors, honors program, summer session, adult/continuing education programs, internships **Contact** Ms. Martha Stolze, Director of Freshman Admission, North Central College, 30 North Brainard Street, PO Box 3063, Naperville, IL 60566-7063. Phone: 630-637-5800 or toll-free 800-411-1861. Fax: 630-637-5819. E-mail: admissions@noctrl.edu. Web site: http://www.noctrl.edu/.

NORTHEASTERN ILLINOIS UNIVERSITY
CHICAGO, ILLINOIS

General State-supported, comprehensive, coed **Entrance** Minimally difficult **Setting** 67-acre urban campus **Total enrollment** 11,644 **Student-faculty ratio** 16:1 **Application deadline** 7/1 (freshmen), 7/1 (transfer) **Freshmen** 68% were admitted **Housing** No **Expenses** Tuition $7050 **Undergraduates** 60% women, 44% part-time, 39% 25 or older, 0.4% Native American, 29% Hispanic American, 10% African American, 11% Asian American/Pacific Islander **The most frequently chosen baccalaureate fields are** business/marketing, education, liberal arts/general studies **Academic program** English as a second language, advanced placement, honors program, summer session, adult/continuing education programs, internships **Contact** Ms. Zarrin Kerwell, Admissions Counselor, Northeastern Illinois University, 5500 North St. Louis Avenue, Chicago, IL 60625. Phone: 773-442-4026. Fax: 773-794-6243. E-mail: admrec@neiu.edu. Web site: http://www.neiu.edu/.

NORTHERN ILLINOIS UNIVERSITY
DE KALB, ILLINOIS

General State-supported, university, coed **Entrance** Moderately difficult **Setting** 589-acre small-town campus **Total enrollment** 25,254 **Student-faculty ratio** 17:1 **Application deadline** 8/1 (freshmen), 8/1 (transfer) **Freshmen** 61% were admitted **Housing** Yes **Expenses** Tuition $7455; Room & Board $7568 **Undergraduates** 52% women, 10% part-time, 12% 25 or older, 0.2% Native American, 7% Hispanic American, 12% African American, 5% Asian American/ Pacific Islander **The most frequently chosen baccalaureate fields are** business/marketing, education, social sciences **Academic program** Advanced placement, accelerated degree program, self-designed majors, honors program, summer session, adult/continuing education programs, internships **Contact** Dr. Robert Burk, Director of Admissions, Northern Illinois University, Office of Admissions, DeKalb, IL 60445-257. Phone: 815-753-0446 or toll-free 800-892-3050. E-mail: admission-info@niu.edu. Web site: http://www.niu.edu/.

NORTH PARK UNIVERSITY
CHICAGO, ILLINOIS

Contact Office of Admissions, North Park University, 3225 West Foster Avenue, Chicago, IL 60625-4895. Phone: 773-244-5500 or toll-free 800-888-NPC8. Fax: 773-583-0858. E-mail: afao@northpark.edu. Web site: http://www.northpark.edu/.

NORTHWESTERN UNIVERSITY
EVANSTON, ILLINOIS

General Independent, university, coed **Entrance** Most difficult **Setting** 250-acre suburban campus **Total enrollment** 18,028 **Student-faculty ratio** 7:1 **Application deadline** 1/1 (freshmen), 5/1 (transfer) **Freshmen** 27% were admitted **Housing** Yes **Expenses** Tuition $37,125; Room & Board $11,295 **Undergraduates** 53% women, 2% part-time, 1% 25 or older, 0.1% Native American, 7% Hispanic American, 6% African American, 17% Asian American/Pacific Islander **The most frequently chosen baccalaureate fields are** communications/journalism, engineering, social sciences **Academic program** Advanced placement, accelerated degree program, self-designed majors, honors program, summer session, adult/ continuing education programs, internships **Contact** Mr. Christopher Watson, Dean of Undergraduate Admission, Northwestern University, PO Box 3060, Evanston, IL 60204-3060. Phone: 847-491-7271. E-mail: ug-admission@northwestern.edu. Web site: http://www.northwestern.edu/.

OLIVET NAZARENE UNIVERSITY
BOURBONNAIS, ILLINOIS

Contact Ms. Mary Cary, Applicant Coordinator, Olivet Nazarene University, One University Avenue, Bourbonnais, IL 60914-2271. Phone: 815-939-5203 or toll-free 800-648-1463. Fax: 815-935-4998. E-mail: admissions@olivet.edu. Web site: http://www.olivet.edu/.

PRINCIPIA COLLEGE
ELSAH, ILLINOIS

Contact Mrs. Martha Quirk, Dean of Admissions, Principia College, One Maybeck Place, Elsah, IL 62028. Phone: 618-374-5180 or toll-free 800-277-4648 Ext. 2802. Fax: 618-374-4000. E-mail: collegeadmissions@prin.edu. Web site: http://www.prin.edu/college/.

QUINCY UNIVERSITY
QUINCY, ILLINOIS

General Independent Roman Catholic, comprehensive, coed **Entrance** Moderately difficult **Setting** 75-acre small-town campus **Total enrollment** 1,323 **Student-faculty ratio** 13:1 **Application deadline** Rolling (freshmen), rolling (transfer) **Freshmen** 96% were admitted **Housing** Yes **Expenses** Tuition $20,790; Room & Board $7900 **Undergraduates** 57% women, 15% part-time, 15% 25 or older, 3% Hispanic American, 7% African American, 1% Asian American/Pacific Islander **The most frequently chosen baccalaureate fields are** business/marketing, education, health professions and related sciences **Academic program** English as a second language, advanced placement, accelerated degree program, self-designed majors, honors program, summer session, adult/continuing education programs, internships **Contact** Mrs. Syndi Peck, Director of Admissions, Quincy University, Admissions Office, Quincy, IL 62301. Phone: 217-228-5210 or toll-free 800-688-4295. E-mail: admissions@quincy.edu. Web site: http://www.quincy.edu/.

ROBERT MORRIS COLLEGE
CHICAGO, ILLINOIS

General Independent, comprehensive, coed **Entrance** Minimally difficult **Setting** urban campus **Total enrollment** 4,824 **Student-faculty ratio** 23:1 **Application deadline** Rolling (freshmen), rolling (transfer) **Freshmen** 81% were admitted **Housing** Yes **Expenses** Tuition $16,800; Room only $7500 **Undergraduates** 62% women, 5% part-time, 35% 25 or older, 0.3% Native American, 23% Hispanic American, 34% African American, 3% Asian American/Pacific Islander **The most frequently chosen baccalaureate fields are** business/marketing, computer and information sciences, visual and performing arts **Academic program** Advanced placement, accelerated degree program, honors program, summer session, adult/continuing education programs, internships **Contact** Ms. Connie Esparza, Vice President for Marketing, Robert Morris College, 401 South State Street, Chicago, IL 60605. Phone: 312-935-6640 or toll-free 800-RMC-5960. Fax: 312-935-4440. E-mail: cesparza@robertmorris.edu. Web site: http://www.robertmorris.edu/.

ROBERT MORRIS COLLEGE–DuPAGE
AURORA, ILLINOIS

Contact Robert Morris College–DuPage, 905 Meridian Lake Drive, Aurora, IL 60504. Web site: http://www.robertmorris.edu/.

ROBERT MORRIS COLLEGE–ORLAND PARK
ORLAND PARK, ILLINOIS

Contact Robert Morris College–Orland Park, 43 Orland Square, Orland Park, IL 60462. Web site: http://www.robertmorris.edu/.

ROCKFORD COLLEGE
ROCKFORD, ILLINOIS

General Independent, comprehensive, coed **Entrance** Moderately difficult **Setting** 130-acre suburban campus **Total enrollment** 1,566 **Student-faculty ratio** 11:1 **Application deadline** 8/15 (freshmen), 8/15 (transfer) **Freshmen** 51% were admitted **Housing** Yes **Expenses** Tuition $23,500; Room & Board $6750 **Undergraduates** 63% women, 15% part-time, 28% 25 or older, 0.2% Native American, 6% Hispanic American, 7% African American, 2% Asian American/Pacific Islander **The most frequently chosen baccalaureate fields are** business/marketing, education, health professions and related sciences **Academic program** English as a second language, advanced placement, accelerated degree program, honors program, summer session, adult/continuing education programs, internships **Contact** Ms. Kerry Fink, Director of Recruiting, Rockford College, 5050 East State Street, Rockford, IL 61108-2393. Phone: 815-226-4050 or toll-free 800-892-2984. Fax: 815-226-2822. E-mail: rcadmissions@rockford.edu. Web site: http://www.rockford.edu/.

ROOSEVELT UNIVERSITY
CHICAGO, ILLINOIS

General Independent, comprehensive, coed **Entrance** Moderately difficult **Setting** urban campus **Total enrollment** 7,163 **Student-faculty ratio** 13:1 **Application deadline** 9/1 (freshmen), rolling (transfer) **Freshmen** 43% were admitted **Housing** Yes **Expenses** Tuition $16,980; Room & Board $9848 **Undergraduates** 66% women, 44% part-time, 54% 25 or older, 0.2% Native American, 11% Hispanic American, 22% African American, 5% Asian American/Pacific Islander **The most frequently chosen baccalaureate fields are** business/marketing, education, psychology **Academic program** English as a second language, advanced placement, accelerated degree program, self-designed majors, honors program, summer session, adult/continuing education programs, internships **Contact** Ms. Gwen Kanelos, Assistant Vice President for Enrollment Services, Roosevelt University, 430 South Michigan Avenue, Chicago, IL 60605-1394. Phone: 847-619-8620 or toll-free 877-APPLYRU. Fax: 847-619-8636. E-mail: applyru@roosevelt.edu. Web site: http://www.roosevelt.edu/.

RUSH UNIVERSITY
CHICAGO, ILLINOIS

General Independent, upper-level, coed **Entrance** Moderately difficult **Setting** 35-acre urban campus **Total enrollment** 1,362 **Student-faculty ratio** 8:1 **Application deadline** Rolling (transfer) **First-year students** 54% were admitted **Housing** Yes **Expenses** Tuition $20,352; Room & Board $9960 **Undergraduates** 86% women, 8% part-time, 5% Hispanic American, 7% African American, 11% Asian American/Pacific Islander **The most frequently chosen baccalaureate field is** health professions and related sciences **Academic program** Accelerated degree program **Contact** Ms. Hicela Castruita Woods, Director of College Admission Services, Rush University, 600 S. Paulina - Suite 440, Chicago, IL 60612. Phone: 312-942-7100. Fax: 312-942-2219. E-mail: rush_admissions@rush.edu. Web site: http://www.rushu.rush.edu/.

SAINT ANTHONY COLLEGE OF NURSING
ROCKFORD, ILLINOIS

General Independent Roman Catholic, upper-level, coed, primarily women **Contact** Ms. Nancy Sanders, Assistant Dean for Admissions and Student Affairs, Saint Anthony College of Nursing, 5658 East State Street, Rockford, IL 61108-2468. Phone: 815-227-2141. Fax: 815-395-2275. E-mail: info@sacn.edu. Web site: http://www.sacn.edu/.

ST. AUGUSTINE COLLEGE
CHICAGO, ILLINOIS

General Independent, 4-year, coed **Contact** Ms. Gloria Quiroz, Director of Recruitment, St. Augustine College, 1333-1345 West Argyle, Chicago, IL 60640-3501. Phone: 773-878-3256. Fax: 773-728-7067. E-mail: info@staugustine.edu. Web site: http://www.staugustinecollege.edu/.

SAINT FRANCIS MEDICAL CENTER COLLEGE OF NURSING
PEORIA, ILLINOIS

General Independent Roman Catholic, upper-level, coed, primarily women **Contact** Mrs. Janice Farquharson, Director of Admissions and Registrar, Saint Francis Medical Center College of Nursing, 511 NE Greenleaf Street, Peoria, IL 61603-3783. Phone: 309-624-8980. Fax: 309-624-8973. E-mail: janice.farquharson@osfhealthcare.org. Web site: http://www.sfmccon.edu/.

ST. JOHN'S COLLEGE
SPRINGFIELD, ILLINOIS

Contact Ms. Beth Beasley, Student Development Officer, St. John's College, 421 North Ninth Street, Springfield, IL 62702-5317. Phone: 217-525-5628 Ext. 45468. Fax: 217-757-6870. E-mail: college@st-johns.org. Web site: http://www.st-johns.org/education/schools/nursing/.

SAINT XAVIER UNIVERSITY
CHICAGO, ILLINOIS

General Independent Roman Catholic, comprehensive, coed **Entrance** Moderately difficult **Setting** 70-acre urban campus **Total enrollment** 5,675 **Student-faculty ratio** 15:1 **Application deadline** Rolling (freshmen), rolling (transfer) **Freshmen** 77% were admitted **Housing** Yes **Expenses** Tuition $21,236; Room & Board $7626 **Undergraduates** 71% women, 22% part-time, 24% 25 or older, 0.4% Native American, 14% Hispanic American, 18% African American, 3% Asian American/Pacific Islander **The most frequently chosen baccalaureate fields are** business/marketing, education, health professions and related sciences **Academic program** English as a second language, advanced placement, accelerated degree program, self-designed majors, honors program, summer session, adult/continuing education programs, internships **Contact** Ms. Elizabeth A. Gierach, Assistant Vice President, Saint Xavier University, 3700 West 103rd Street, Chicago, IL 60655-3105. Phone: 773-298-3063 or toll-free 800-462-9288. Fax: 773-298-3076. E-mail: admissions@sxu.edu. Web site: http://www.sxu.edu/.

SCHOOL OF THE ART INSTITUTE OF CHICAGO
CHICAGO, ILLINOIS

General Independent, comprehensive, coed **Entrance** Moderately difficult **Setting** 1-acre urban campus **Total enrollment** 3,006 **Student-faculty ratio** 11:1 **Application deadline** 6/1 (freshmen), 8/15 (transfer) **Freshmen** 80% were admitted **Housing** Yes **Expenses** Tuition $31,020; Room only $8900 **Undergraduates** 64% women, 9% part-time, 17% 25 or older, 1% Native American, 8% Hispanic American, 3% African American, 11% Asian American/Pacific Islander **The most frequently chosen baccalaureate field is** visual and performing arts **Academic program** English as a second language, advanced placement, self-designed majors, summer session, internships **Contact** Mr. Scott Ramon, Director, Undergraduate Admissions, School of the Art Institute of Chicago, 36 South Wabash, Chicago, IL 60603. Phone: 312-629-6100 or toll-free 800-232-SAIC. Fax: 312-629-6101. E-mail: admiss@saic.edu. Web site: http://www.artic.edu/saic/.

SHIMER COLLEGE
CHICAGO, ILLINOIS

General Independent, 4-year, coed **Entrance** Moderately difficult **Setting** 3-acre urban campus **Total enrollment** 90 **Application deadline** 7/31 (freshmen), rolling (transfer) **Freshmen** 69% were admitted **Housing** Yes **Expenses** Tuition $24,845; Room & Board $8618 **Undergraduates** 41% women, 36% part-time, 15% 25 or older, 4% Hispanic American, 12% African American, 4% Asian American/Pacific Islander **Academic program** Self-designed majors, summer session, adult/continuing education programs, internships **Contact** Ms. Elaine Vincent, Director of Admission, Shimer College, 3424 South State Street, Chicago, IL 60616. Phone: 312-235-3504 or toll-free 800-215-7173. Fax: 847-249-8798. E-mail: e.vincent@shimer.edu. Web site: http://www.shimer.edu/.

SOUTHERN ILLINOIS UNIVERSITY CARBONDALE
CARBONDALE, ILLINOIS

General State-supported, university, coed **Entrance** Moderately difficult **Setting** 1,133-acre rural campus **Total enrollment** 20,983 **Student-faculty ratio** 17:1 **Application deadline** Rolling (freshmen), rolling (transfer) **Freshmen** 71% were admitted **Housing** Yes **Expenses** Tuition $8899; Room & Board $6666 **Undergraduates** 43% women, 11% part-time, 23% 25 or older, 0.5% Native American, 4% Hispanic American, 18% African American, 2% Asian American/Pacific Islander **The most frequently chosen baccalaureate fields are** business/marketing, education, engineering technologies **Academic program** English as a second language, advanced placement, honors program, summer session, adult/continuing education programs, internships **Contact** Katharine Suski, Associate Director, Undergraduate Admissions, Southern Illinois University Carbondale, Carbondale, IL 62901-4701. Phone: 618-536-4405. Fax: 618-453-4609. E-mail: joinsiuc@siu.edu. Web site: http://www.siu.edu/siuc/.

SOUTHERN ILLINOIS UNIVERSITY EDWARDSVILLE
EDWARDSVILLE, ILLINOIS

General State-supported, comprehensive, coed **Entrance** Moderately difficult **Setting** 2,660-acre suburban campus **Total enrollment** 13,298 **Student-faculty ratio** 17:1 **Application deadline** 5/1 (freshmen), 7/21 (transfer) **Freshmen** 84% were admitted **Housing** Yes **Expenses** Tuition $7118; Room & Board $6750 **Undergraduates** 54% women, 15% part-time, 16% 25 or older, 0.2% Native American, 2% Hispanic American, 10% African American, 2% Asian American/Pacific Islander **The most frequently chosen baccalaureate fields are** business/marketing, education, health professions and related sciences **Academic program** English as a second language, advanced placement, accelerated degree program, self-designed majors, honors program, summer session, adult/continuing education programs, internships **Contact** Mr. Todd Burrell, Director of Admissions, Southern Illinois University Edwardsville, Campus Box 1600, Rendleman Hall, Edwardsville, IL 62026-1600. Phone: 618-650-3705 or toll-free 800-447-SIUE. Fax: 618-650-5013. E-mail: admissions@siue.edu. Web site: http://www.siue.edu/.

TELSHE YESHIVA–CHICAGO
CHICAGO, ILLINOIS

Contact Rosh Hayeshiva, Telshe Yeshiva–Chicago, 3535 West Foster Avenue, Chicago, IL 60625-5598. Phone: 773-463-7738.

TRINITY CHRISTIAN COLLEGE
PALOS HEIGHTS, ILLINOIS

General Independent Christian Reformed, 4-year, coed **Entrance** Moderately difficult **Setting** 53-acre suburban campus **Total enrollment** 1,367 **Student-faculty ratio** 12:1 **Application deadline** Rolling (freshmen) **Freshmen** 89% were admitted **Housing** Yes **Expenses** Tuition $19,046; Room & Board $7120 **Undergraduates** 69% women, 20% part-time, 20% 25 or older, 0.1% Native American, 6% Hispanic American, 8% African American, 1% Asian American/Pacific Islander **The most frequently chosen baccalaureate fields are** business/marketing, education, health professions and related sciences **Academic program** Advanced placement, honors program, adult/continuing education programs, internships **Contact** Mr. Jeremy Klyn, Director of Admissions, Trinity Christian College, 6601 West College Drive, Palos Heights, IL 60463. Phone: 708-239-4708 or toll-free 800-748-0085. Fax: 708-239-4826. E-mail: admissions@trnty.edu. Web site: http://www.trnty.edu/.

TRINITY COLLEGE OF NURSING AND HEALTH SCIENCES
ROCK ISLAND, ILLINOIS

General Independent, 4-year, coed **Contact** Ms. Barbara Kimpe, Admissions Representative, Trinity College of Nursing and Health Sciences, 2122-25th Avenue, Rock Island, IL 61201. Phone: 309-779-7812. Fax: 309-779-7748. E-mail: con@trinityqc.com. Web site: http://www.trinitycollegeqc.edu/.

TRINITY INTERNATIONAL UNIVERSITY
DEERFIELD, ILLINOIS

General Independent, university, coed, affiliated with Evangelical Free Church of America **Entrance** Moderately difficult **Setting** 108-acre suburban campus **Total enrollment** 2,939 **Student-faculty ratio** 12:1 **Application deadline** Rolling (freshmen), rolling (transfer) **Freshmen** 48% were admitted **Housing** Yes **Expenses** Tuition $21,020; Room & Board $6800 **Undergraduates** 59% women, 21% part-time, 27% 25 or older, 0.5% Native American, 3% Hispanic American, 13% African American, 3% Asian American/Pacific Islander **The most frequently chosen baccalaureate fields are** education, business/marketing, theology and religious vocations **Academic program** Advanced placement, honors program, adult/continuing education programs, internships **Contact** Mr. Aaron Mahl, Director of Undergraduate Admissions, Trinity International University, 2065 Half Day Road, Deerfield, IL 60015-1284. Phone: 847-317-7000 or toll-free 800-822-3225. Fax: 847-317-8097. E-mail: tcadmissions@tiu.edu. Web site: http://www.tiu.edu/.

UNIVERSITY OF CHICAGO
CHICAGO, ILLINOIS

General Independent, university, coed **Entrance** Most difficult **Setting** 211-acre urban campus **Total enrollment** 12,336 **Student-faculty ratio** 6:1 **Application deadline** 1/2 (freshmen), 4/1 (transfer) **Freshmen** 35% were admitted **Housing** Yes **Expenses** Tuition $37,632; Room & Board $11,697 **Undergraduates** 50% women, 1% part-time, 1% 25 or older, 0.3% Native American, 8% Hispanic American, 5% African American, 13% Asian American/Pacific Islander **The most frequently chosen baccalaureate fields are** biological/life sciences, mathematics, social sciences **Academic program** Advanced placement, accelerated degree program, self-designed majors, summer session, adult/continuing education programs, internships **Contact** Mr. Theodore O'Neill, Dean of Admissions, University of Chicago, Rosenwald Hall, 1101 East 58th Street, Suite 105, Chicago, IL 60637-1513. Phone: 773-702-8650. Fax: 773-702-4199. E-mail: questions@phoenix.uchicago.edu. Web site: http://www.uchicago.edu/.

UNIVERSITY OF ILLINOIS AT CHICAGO
CHICAGO, ILLINOIS

General State-supported, university, coed **Entrance** Moderately difficult **Setting** 240-acre urban campus **Total enrollment** 25,747 **Student-faculty ratio** 15:1 **Application deadline** 1/15 (freshmen), 3/1 (transfer) **Freshmen** 64% were admitted **Housing** Yes **Expenses** Tuition $10,546; Room & Board $7818 **Undergraduates** 53% women, 8% part-time, 12% 25 or older, 0.2% Native American, 16% Hispanic American, 9% African American, 23% Asian American/Pacific Islander **The most frequently chosen baccalaureate fields are** biological/life sciences, business/marketing, psychology **Academic program** English as a second language, advanced placement, accelerated degree program, self-designed majors, honors program, summer session, internships **Contact** Mr. Thomas E. Glenn, Executive Director of Admissions, University of Illinois at Chicago, Box 5220, Chicago, IL 60680-5220. Phone: 312-996-4350. Fax: 312-413-7628. E-mail: uic.admit@uic.edu. Web site: http://www.uic.edu/.

UNIVERSITY OF ILLINOIS AT SPRINGFIELD
SPRINGFIELD, ILLINOIS

General State-supported, comprehensive, coed **Entrance** Moderately difficult **Setting** 746-acre suburban campus **Total enrollment** 4,855 **Student-faculty ratio** 12:1 **Application deadline** Rolling (freshmen), rolling (transfer) **Freshmen** 62% were admitted **Housing** Yes **Expenses** Tuition $9069; Room & Board $8840 **Undergraduates** 56% women, 41% part-time, 45% 25 or older, 1% Native American, 3% Hispanic American, 11% African American, 3% Asian American/Pacific Islander **The most frequently chosen baccalaureate fields are** business/marketing, liberal arts/general studies, psychology **Academic program** Advanced placement, self-designed majors, honors program, summer session, internships **Contact** Dr. Marya Leatherwood, Associate Vice Chancellor and Director of Enrollment Management, University of Illinois at Springfield, One University Plaza, Room 1015, Springfield, IL 62703. Phone: 217-206-7288 or toll-free 888-977-4847. Fax: 217-206-6048. E-mail: admissions@uis.edu. Web site: http://www.uis.edu/.

UNIVERSITY OF ILLINOIS AT URBANA–CHAMPAIGN
CHAMPAIGN, ILLINOIS

General State-supported, university, coed **Entrance** Very difficult **Setting** 1,470-acre urban campus **Total enrollment** 42,326 **Student-faculty ratio** 17:1 **Application deadline** 1/2 (freshmen), 3/1 (transfer) **Freshmen** 71% were admitted **Housing** Yes **Expenses** Tuition $11,130; Room & Board $8196 **Undergraduates** 47% women, 2% part-time, 2% 25 or older, 0.3% Native American, 7% Hispanic American, 7% African American, 13% Asian American/Pacific Islander **The most frequently chosen baccalau-**

reate fields are business/marketing, engineering, social sciences **Academic program** English as a second language, advanced placement, accelerated degree program, self-designed majors, honors program, summer session, internships **Contact** Mrs. Stacey Kostell, Director of Admissions, University of Illinois at Urbana–Champaign, 901 West Illinois, Urbana, IL 61801. Phone: 217-333-0302. Fax: 217-244-4614. E-mail: ugradadmissions@uiuc.edu. Web site: http://www.uiuc.edu/.

UNIVERSITY OF PHOENIX–CHICAGO CAMPUS

SCHAUMBURG, ILLINOIS

General Proprietary, comprehensive, coed **Contact** Ms. Evelyn Gaskin, Registrar/Executive Director, University of Phoenix–Chicago Campus, 4615 East Elwood Street, Mail Stop AA-K101, Phoenix, AZ 85040-1958. Phone: 480-557-3301 or toll-free 800-776-4867 (in-state); 800-228-7240 (out-of-state). Fax: 480-643-1020. E-mail: evelyn.gaskin@phoenix.edu. Web site: http://www.phoenix.edu/.

UNIVERSITY OF ST. FRANCIS

JOLIET, ILLINOIS

General Independent Roman Catholic, comprehensive, coed **Entrance** Moderately difficult **Setting** 22-acre suburban campus **Total enrollment** 2,143 **Student-faculty ratio** 13:1 **Application deadline** 8/1 (freshmen) **Freshmen** 67% were admitted **Housing** Yes **Expenses** Tuition $20,830; Room & Board $7610 **Undergraduates** 69% women, 6% part-time, 19% 25 or older, 0.1% Native American, 8% Hispanic American, 10% African American, 5% Asian American/Pacific Islander **The most frequently chosen baccalaureate fields are** business/marketing, education, health professions and related sciences **Academic program** Advanced placement, accelerated degree program, self-designed majors, honors program, summer session, adult/continuing education programs, internships **Contact** Ms. Meghan Connolly, Director of Undergraduate Admissions, University of St. Francis, 500 North Wilcox Street, Joliet, IL 60435-6188. Phone: 800-735-7500 or toll-free 800-735-3500 (in-state); 800-735-7500 (out-of-state). Fax: 815-740-5032. E-mail: mconnolly1@stfrancis.edu. Web site: http://www.stfrancis.edu/.

VANDERCOOK COLLEGE OF MUSIC

CHICAGO, ILLINOIS

General Independent, comprehensive, coed **Entrance** Moderately difficult **Setting** 1-acre urban campus **Total enrollment** 320 **Student-faculty ratio** 8:1 **Application deadline** Rolling (freshmen), rolling (transfer) **Freshmen** 98% were admitted **Housing** Yes **Expenses** Tuition $18,800; Room & Board $8830 **Undergraduates** 47% women, 34% part-time, 6% 25 or older, 14% Hispanic American, 16% African American, 7% Asian American/Pacific Islander **The most frequently chosen baccalaureate field is** education **Academic program** Advanced placement, internships **Contact** Ms. Tamara V. Trutwin, Student Recruiter, VanderCook College of Music, 3140 South Federal Street, Chicago, IL 60616-3731. Phone: toll-free 800-448-2655. Fax: 312-225-5211. E-mail: admissions@vandercook.edu. Web site: http://www.vandercook.edu/.

WESTERN ILLINOIS UNIVERSITY

MACOMB, ILLINOIS

General State-supported, comprehensive, coed **Entrance** Moderately difficult **Setting** 1,050-acre small-town campus **Total enrollment** 13,331 **Student-faculty ratio** 15:1 **Application deadline** 5/15 (freshmen), rolling (transfer) **Freshmen** 70% were admitted **Housing** Yes **Expenses** Tuition $8272; Room & Board $7210 **Undergraduates** 47% women, 9% part-time, 12% 25 or older, 0.5% Native American, 5% Hispanic American, 7% African American, 1% Asian American/Pacific Islander **The most frequently chosen baccalaureate fields are** business/marketing, education, security and protective services **Academic program** English as a second language, advanced placement, self-designed majors, honors program, summer session, adult/continuing education programs, internships **Contact** Mr. Eric Campbell, Director of Admissions, Western Illinois University, 1 University Circle, 115 Sherman Hall, Macomb, IL 61455-1390. Phone: 309-298-3157 or toll-free 877-742-5948. Fax: 309-298-3111. E-mail: admissions@wiu.edu. Web site: http://www.wiu.edu/.

WEST SUBURBAN COLLEGE OF NURSING

OAK PARK, ILLINOIS

General Independent, upper-level, coed **Entrance** Moderately difficult **Setting** 10-acre suburban campus **Total enrollment** 214 **Application deadline** Rolling (freshmen), rolling (transfer) **First-year students** 35% were admitted **Housing** No **Expenses** Tuition $20,270 **Undergraduates** 85% women, 19% part-time, 70% 25 or older, 13% Hispanic American, 16% African American, 30% Asian American/Pacific Islander **The most frequently chosen baccalaureate field is** history **Academic program** Advanced placement, accelerated degree program, summer session, adult/continuing education programs **Contact** Ms. Cynthia Valdez, Director of Enrollment Management, West Suburban College of Nursing, 3 Erie

West Suburban College of Nursing *(continued)*

Court, Oak Park, IL 60302. Phone: 708-763-6530. Fax: 708-763-1531. Web site: http://www.wscn.edu/.

WESTWOOD COLLEGE–CHICAGO DU PAGE
WOODRIDGE, ILLINOIS

Contact Mr. Scott Kawall, Director of Admissions, Westwood College–Chicago Du Page, 7155 Janes Avenue, Woodridge, IL 60517. Phone: 630-434-8244 or toll-free 888-721-7646. Fax: 630-434-8255. E-mail: info@westwood.edu. Web site: http://www.westwood.edu/.

WHEATON COLLEGE
WHEATON, ILLINOIS

General Independent nondenominational, comprehensive, coed **Entrance** Very difficult **Setting** 80-acre suburban campus **Total enrollment** 2,895 **Student-faculty ratio** 12:1 **Application deadline** 1/10 (freshmen), 3/1 (transfer) **Freshmen** 55% were admitted **Housing** Yes **Expenses** Tuition $23,730; Room & Board $7252 **Undergraduates** 51% women, 4% part-time, 1% 25 or older, 0.3% Native American, 4% Hispanic American, 3% African American, 7% Asian American/Pacific Islander **The most frequently chosen baccalaureate fields are** social sciences, English, theology and religious vocations **Academic program** Advanced placement, self-designed majors, summer session, internships **Contact** Ms. Shawn Leftwich, Director of Admissions, Wheaton College, 501 East College Avenue, Wheaton, IL 60187-5593. Phone: 630-752-5011 or toll-free 800-222-2419. Fax: 630-752-5285. E-mail: admissions@wheaton.edu. Web site: http://www.wheaton.edu/.

INDIANA

ANDERSON UNIVERSITY
ANDERSON, INDIANA

General Independent, comprehensive, coed, affiliated with Church of God **Entrance** Moderately difficult **Setting** 100-acre suburban campus **Total enrollment** 2,707 **Student-faculty ratio** 14:1 **Application deadline** 7/1 (freshmen), rolling (transfer) **Freshmen** 67% were admitted **Housing** Yes **Expenses** Tuition $21,920; Room & Board $7600 **Undergraduates** 57% women, 9% part-time, 7% 25 or older, 0.4% Native American, 1% Hispanic American, 6% African American, 1% Asian American/Pacific Islander **The most frequently chosen baccalaureate fields are** business/marketing, education, health professions and related sciences **Academic program** Advanced placement, accelerated degree program, self-designed majors, honors program, summer session, adult/continuing education programs, internships **Contact** Mr. Jim King, Director of Admissions, Anderson University, 1100 East 5th Street, Anderson, IN 46012-3495. Phone: 765-641-4080 or toll-free 800-421-3014 (in-state); 800-428-6414 (out-of-state). Fax: 765-641-3851. E-mail: info@anderson.edu. Web site: http://www.anderson.edu/.

THE ART INSTITUTE OF INDIANAPOLIS
INDIANAPOLIS, INDIANA

General Proprietary, 4-year, coed **Setting** suburban campus **Contact** Director of Admissions, The Art Institute of Indianapolis, 3500 Depauw Boulevard, Suite 1010, Indianapolis, IN 46268. Phone: 317-613-4821. Fax: 317-613-4808. Web site: http://www.artinstitutes.edu/indianapolis/.

BALL STATE UNIVERSITY
MUNCIE, INDIANA

General State-supported, university, coed **Entrance** Moderately difficult **Setting** 955-acre suburban campus **Total enrollment** 19,849 **Student-faculty ratio** 16:1 **Application deadline** 8/15 (freshmen), rolling (transfer) **Freshmen** 72% were admitted **Housing** Yes **Expenses** Tuition $7148; Room & Board $7240 **Undergraduates** 52% women, 8% part-time, 5% 25 or older, 0.3% Native American, 2% Hispanic American, 7% African American, 1% Asian American/Pacific Islander **The most frequently chosen baccalaureate fields are** business/marketing, education, liberal arts/general studies **Academic program** English as a second language, advanced placement, accelerated degree program, honors program, summer session, adult/continuing education programs, internships **Contact** Mr. Christopher Munchel, Associate Director of Admissions, Ball State University, 2000 University Avenue, Muncie, IN 47306-1099. Phone: 765-285-8300 or toll-free 800-482-4BSU. Fax: 765-285-1632. E-mail: askus@bsu.edu. Web site: http://www.bsu.edu/.

BETHEL COLLEGE
MISHAWAKA, INDIANA

Contact Randy Beachy, Assistant Vice President for Enrollment/Marketing, Bethel College, 1001 West McKinley Avenue, Mishawaka, IN 46545-5591. Phone: 574-257-3319 or toll-free 800-422-

4101. Fax: 574-257-3335. E-mail: admissions@bethelcollege.edu. Web site: http://www.bethelcollege.edu.

BROWN MACKIE COLLEGE–FORT WAYNE
FORT WAYNE, INDIANA

General Proprietary, 4-year, coed **Contact** Director of Admissions, Brown Mackie College–Fort Wayne, 3000 East Coliseum Boulevard, Suite 100, Fort Wayne, IN 46805. Phone: 260-484-4400. Web site: http://www.brownmackie.edu/fortwayne.

BROWN MACKIE COLLEGE–INDIANAPOLIS
INDIANAPOLIS, INDIANA

General Proprietary, 4-year, coed **Contact** Director of Admissions, Brown Mackie College–Indianapolis, 1200 North Meridian Street, Suite 100, Indianapolis, IN 46204. Phone: 317-554-8301 or toll-free 866-255-0279. E-mail: bmcindadm@brownmackie.edu. Web site: http://www.brownmackie.edu/Indianapolis/.

BUTLER UNIVERSITY
INDIANAPOLIS, INDIANA

General Independent, comprehensive, coed **Entrance** Moderately difficult **Setting** 290-acre urban campus **Total enrollment** 4,479 **Student-faculty ratio** 11:1 **Application deadline** Rolling (freshmen), 8/15 (transfer) **Freshmen** 76% were admitted **Housing** Yes **Expenses** Tuition $26,806; Room & Board $8960 **Undergraduates** 61% women, 2% part-time, 2% 25 or older, 0.3% Native American, 2% Hispanic American, 3% African American, 2% Asian American/Pacific Islander **The most frequently chosen baccalaureate fields are** business/marketing, education, health professions and related sciences **Academic program** Advanced placement, self-designed majors, honors program, summer session, adult/continuing education programs, internships **Contact** Mr. Scott McIntyre, Director of Admissions, Butler University, 4600 Sunset Avenue, Indianapolis, IN 46208-3485. Phone: 317-940-8100 or toll-free 888-940-8100. Fax: 317-940-8150. E-mail: admission@butler.edu. Web site: http://www.butler.edu/.

CALUMET COLLEGE OF SAINT JOSEPH
WHITING, INDIANA

General Independent Roman Catholic, comprehensive, coed **Entrance** Noncompetitive **Setting** 25-acre urban campus **Total enrollment** 1,238 **Student-faculty ratio** 13:1 **Application deadline** Rolling (freshmen), rolling (transfer) **Freshmen** 47% were admitted **Housing** No **Expenses** Tuition $11,650 **Undergraduates** 55% women, 59% part-time, 64% 25 or older, 1% Native American, 23% Hispanic American, 27% African American, 1% Asian American/Pacific Islander **The most frequently chosen baccalaureate fields are** business/marketing, education, security and protective services **Academic program** Advanced placement, accelerated degree program, summer session, adult/continuing education programs, internships **Contact** Mr. Chuck Walz, Director of Admissions, Calumet College of Saint Joseph, 2400 New York Avenue, Whiting, IN 46394. Phone: 219-473-4215 Ext. 379 or toll-free 877-700-9100. Fax: 219-473-4259. E-mail: admissions@ccsj.edu. Web site: http://www.ccsj.edu/.

CROSSROADS BIBLE COLLEGE
INDIANAPOLIS, INDIANA

Contact Nathan McGuire, Director of Admissions, Crossroads Bible College, 601 North Shortridge Road, Indianapolis, IN 46219. Phone: 317-352-8736 Ext. 230 or toll-free 800-273-2224 Ext. 230. Fax: 317-352-9145. E-mail: admissions@crossroads.edu. Web site: http://www.crossroads.edu/.

DePAUW UNIVERSITY
GREENCASTLE, INDIANA

General Independent, 4-year, coed, affiliated with United Methodist Church **Entrance** Moderately difficult **Setting** 655-acre small-town campus **Total enrollment** 2,398 **Student-faculty ratio** 10:1 **Application deadline** 2/1 (freshmen), 3/1 (transfer) **Freshmen** 69% were admitted **Housing** Yes **Expenses** Tuition $29,700; Room & Board $8100 **Undergraduates** 56% women, 2% part-time, 0.2% 25 or older, 0.3% Native American, 3% Hispanic American, 6% African American, 3% Asian American/Pacific Islander **The most frequently chosen baccalaureate fields are** biological/life sciences, English, social sciences **Academic program** Advanced placement, self-designed majors, honors program, internships **Contact** Brett Kennedy, Senior Associate Director of Admission, DePauw University, 313 South Locust Street, Greencastle, IN 46135-0037. Phone: 765-658-4006 or toll-free 800-447-2495. Fax: 765-658-4007. E-mail: admission@depauw.edu. Web site: http://www.depauw.edu/.

DeVRY UNIVERSITY
INDIANAPOLIS, INDIANA

General Proprietary, comprehensive, coed **Entrance** Minimally difficult **Total enrollment** 291 **Student-faculty ratio** 38:1 **Application deadline** Rolling (freshmen), rolling (transfer)

DeVry University *(continued)*

Housing No **Expenses** Tuition $13,890 **Undergraduates** 56% women, 74% part-time, 74% 25 or older, 1% Native American, 2% Hispanic American, 39% African American, 2% Asian American/Pacific Islander **The most frequently chosen baccalaureate fields are** business/ marketing, computer and information sciences **Academic program** English as a second language, advanced placement, accelerated degree program, summer session, adult/continuing education programs **Contact** Admissions Office, DeVry University, 9100 Keystone Crossing, Suite 350, Indianapolis, IN 46240-2158. Web site: http:// www.devry.edu/.

DeVRY UNIVERSITY
MERRILLVILLE, INDIANA

Contact DeVry University, Twin Towers, 1000 East 80th Place, Suite 222 Mall, Merrillville, IN 46410-5673. Web site: http://www.devry.edu/.

EARLHAM COLLEGE
RICHMOND, INDIANA

General Independent, comprehensive, coed, affiliated with Society of Friends **Entrance** Very difficult **Setting** 800-acre small-town campus **Total enrollment** 1,360 **Student-faculty ratio** 12:1 **Application deadline** 2/15 (freshmen), 4/1 (transfer) **Freshmen** 69% were admitted **Housing** Yes **Expenses** Tuition $31,514; Room & Board $6504 **Undergraduates** 55% women, 2% part-time, 2% 25 or older, 0.3% Native American, 3% Hispanic American, 6% African American, 2% Asian American/Pacific Islander **The most frequently chosen baccalaureate fields are** interdisciplinary studies, social sciences, visual and performing arts **Academic program** Advanced placement, accelerated degree program, self-designed majors, internships **Contact** Mr. Jeff Rickey, Dean of Admissions and Financial Aid, Earlham College, 801 National Road West, Richmond, IN 47374. Phone: 765-983-1600 or toll-free 800-327-5426. Fax: 765-983-1560. E-mail: admission@earlham.edu. Web site: http://www.earlham.edu/.

FRANKLIN COLLEGE
FRANKLIN, INDIANA

General Independent, 4-year, coed, affiliated with American Baptist Churches in the U.S.A. **Entrance** Moderately difficult **Setting** 74-acre small-town campus **Total enrollment** 1,130 **Student-faculty ratio** 12:1 **Application deadline** Rolling (freshmen) **Freshmen** 66% were admitted **Housing** Yes **Expenses** Tuition $21,325; Room & Board $6390 **Undergraduates** 49% women, 10% part-time, 2% 25 or older, 0.2% Native American, 1% Hispanic American, 3% African American, 1% Asian American/Pacific Islander **The most frequently chosen baccalaureate fields are** communications/journalism, business/marketing, education **Academic program** Advanced placement, summer session, internships **Contact** Ms. Jacqueline Acosta, Director of Admissions, Franklin College, 101 Branigin Boulevard, Franklin, IN 46131-2623. Phone: 317-738-8062 or toll-free 800-852-0232. Fax: 317-738-8274. E-mail: jacosta@franklincollege.edu. Web site: http://www.franklincollege.edu/.

GOSHEN COLLEGE
GOSHEN, INDIANA

General Independent Mennonite, comprehensive, coed **Entrance** Moderately difficult **Setting** 135-acre small-town campus **Total enrollment** 955 **Student-faculty ratio** 10:1 **Application deadline** 8/15 (freshmen), 8/15 (transfer) **Freshmen** 76% were admitted **Housing** Yes **Expenses** Tuition $22,300; Room & Board $7450 **Undergraduates** 60% women, 8% part-time, 8% 25 or older, 0.3% Native American, 6% Hispanic American, 3% African American, 2% Asian American/Pacific Islander **The most frequently chosen baccalaureate fields are** business/ marketing, biological/life sciences, health professions and related sciences **Academic program** Advanced placement, accelerated degree program, self-designed majors, honors program, summer session, adult/continuing education programs, internships **Contact** Ms. Lynn Jackson, Vice President for Enrollment Management, Goshen College, 1700 South Main Street, Goshen, IN 46526-4794. Phone: 574-535-7535 or toll-free 800-348-7422. Fax: 574-535-7609. E-mail: lynnj@goshen.edu. Web site: http://www.goshen.edu/.

GRACE COLLEGE
WINONA LAKE, INDIANA

General Independent, comprehensive, coed, affiliated with Fellowship of Grace Brethren Churches **Entrance** Moderately difficult **Setting** 160-acre small-town campus **Total enrollment** 1,403 **Student-faculty ratio** 17:1 **Application deadline** 8/1 (freshmen), 8/1 (transfer) **Freshmen** 56% were admitted **Housing** Yes **Expenses** Tuition $19,224; Room & Board $6360 **Undergraduates** 49% women, 9% part-time, 26% 25 or older, 1% Native American, 2% Hispanic American, 11% African American, 1% Asian American/ Pacific Islander **The most frequently chosen baccalaureate fields are** business/marketing, education, psychology **Academic program** Advanced placement, accelerated degree program, honors program, summer session, adult/continuing education programs, internships **Contact** Mr. Mark D. Weinstein, Dean of Enrollment and Marketing, Grace College, Admissions Office, 200 Seminary Drive, Winona Lake, IN 46590. Phone: 574-372-5100 Ext. 6004 or toll-free 800-54-GRACE Ext. 6412 (in-state); 800-54 GRACE Ext. 6412 (out-of-state). Fax: 574-372-5120. E-mail: enroll@grace.edu. Web site: http://www.grace.edu/.

HANOVER COLLEGE
HANOVER, INDIANA

General Independent Presbyterian, 4-year, coed **Entrance** Moderately difficult **Setting** 630-acre rural campus **Total enrollment** 929 **Student-faculty ratio** 10:1 **Application deadline** 3/1 (freshmen), rolling (transfer) **Freshmen** 66% were admitted **Housing** Yes **Expenses** Tuition $24,220; Room & Board $7150 **Undergraduates** 54% women, 1% part-time, 1% 25 or older, 1% Native American, 1% Hispanic American, 1% African American, 2% Asian American/Pacific Islander **The most frequently chosen baccalaureate fields are** business/marketing, English, social sciences **Academic program** Advanced placement, self-designed majors, internships **Contact** Mr. Bill Preble, Dean of Admission and Financial Assistance, Hanover College, PO Box 108, Hanover, IN 47243-0108. Phone: 812-866-7021 or toll-free 800-213-2178. Fax: 812-866-7098. E-mail: admission@hanover.edu. Web site: http://www.hanover.edu/.

HUNTINGTON UNIVERSITY
HUNTINGTON, INDIANA

General Independent, comprehensive, coed, affiliated with Church of the United Brethren in Christ **Entrance** Moderately difficult **Setting** 170-acre small-town campus **Total enrollment** 1,152 **Student-faculty ratio** 12:1 **Application deadline** 8/1 (freshmen), rolling (transfer) **Freshmen** 86% were admitted **Housing** Yes **Expenses** Tuition $19,430; Room & Board $6730 **Undergraduates** 55% women, 8% part-time, 4% 25 or older, 0.1% Native American, 1% Hispanic American, 0.5% African American, 1% Asian American/Pacific Islander **The most frequently chosen baccalaureate fields are** business/marketing, education, theology and religious vocations **Academic program** Advanced placement, summer session, adult/continuing education programs, internships **Contact** Mr. Jeff Berggren, Vice President of Enrollment Management and Marketing, Huntington University, 2303 College Avenue, Huntington, IN 46750-1299. Phone: 260-356-6000 Ext. 4016 or toll-free 800-642-6493. Fax: 260-356-9448. E-mail: admissions@huntington.edu. Web site: http://www.huntington.edu/.

INDIANA STATE UNIVERSITY
TERRE HAUTE, INDIANA

General State-supported, university, coed **Entrance** Moderately difficult **Setting** 91-acre small-town campus **Total enrollment** 10,543 **Student-faculty ratio** 17:1 **Application deadline** 8/15 (freshmen) **Freshmen** 70% were admitted **Housing** Yes **Expenses** Tuition $7148 **Undergraduates** 51% women, 14% part-time, 20% 25 or older, 0.4% Native American, 1% Hispanic American, 13% African American, 1% Asian American/Pacific Islander **The most frequently chosen baccalaureate fields are** business/marketing, education, social sciences **Academic program** English as a second language, advanced placement, accelerated degree program, honors program, summer session, adult/continuing education programs, internships **Contact** Mr. Richard Toomey, Director of Admissions, Indiana State University, 218 North Sixth Street, Erickson Hall, Terre Haute, IN 47809-9989. Phone: 812-237-2121 or toll-free 800-742-0891. Fax: 812-237-8023. E-mail: ADMISU@isugw.indstate.edu. Web site: http://web.indstate.edu/.

INDIANA TECH
FORT WAYNE, INDIANA

General Independent, comprehensive, coed **Entrance** Moderately difficult **Setting** 25-acre urban campus **Total enrollment** 3,408 **Student-faculty ratio** 21:1 **Freshmen** 65% were admitted **Housing** Yes **Expenses** Tuition $19,480; Room & Board $7300 **Undergraduates** 53% women, 41% part-time, 68% 25 or older, 0.3% Native American, 2% Hispanic American, 20% African American, 1% Asian American/Pacific Islander **The most frequently chosen baccalaureate fields are** business/marketing, computer and information sciences, engineering **Academic program** Advanced placement, accelerated degree program, self-designed majors, summer session, adult/continuing education programs, internships **Contact** Ms. Monica Ladig, Director of Admissions for Day Division, Indiana Tech, 1600 East Washington Boulevard, Fort Wayne, IN 46803. Phone: 260-422-5561 Ext. 2206 or toll-free 800-937-2448 (in-state); 888-666-TECH (out-of-state). Fax: 260-422-7696. E-mail: admissions@indianatech.edu. Web site: http://www.indianatech.edu.

INDIANA UNIVERSITY BLOOMINGTON
BLOOMINGTON, INDIANA

General State-supported, university, coed **Entrance** Moderately difficult **Setting** 1,933-acre small-town campus **Total enrollment** 38,990 **Student-faculty ratio** 18:1 **Application deadline** Rolling (freshmen), rolling (transfer)

Indiana University Bloomington *(continued)*

Freshmen 70% were admitted **Housing** Yes **Expenses** Tuition $7837; Room & Board $6676 **Undergraduates** 51% women, 5% part-time, 4% 25 or older, 0.3% Native American, 2% Hispanic American, 4% African American, 4% Asian American/Pacific Islander **The most frequently chosen baccalaureate fields are** business/marketing, communications/journalism, education **Academic program** English as a second language, advanced placement, accelerated degree program, self-designed majors, honors program, summer session, adult/continuing education programs, internships **Contact** Ms. Mary Ellen Anderson, Director of Admissions, Indiana University Bloomington, 300 North Jordan Avenue, Bloomington, IN 47405-1106. Phone: 812-855-0661. Fax: 812-855-5102. E-mail: iuadmit@indiana.edu. Web site: http://www.iub.edu/.

INDIANA UNIVERSITY EAST
RICHMOND, INDIANA

General State-supported, 4-year, coed **Entrance** Moderately difficult **Setting** 174-acre small-town campus **Total enrollment** 2,266 **Student-faculty ratio** 14:1 **Application deadline** Rolling (freshmen), rolling (transfer) **Freshmen** 82% were admitted **Housing** No **Expenses** Tuition $5292 **Undergraduates** 67% women, 44% part-time, 48% 25 or older, 0.3% Native American, 2% Hispanic American, 4% African American, 0.5% Asian American/Pacific Islander **The most frequently chosen baccalaureate fields are** liberal arts/general studies, health professions and related sciences, philosophy and religious studies **Academic program** Advanced placement, summer session, adult/continuing education programs, internships **Contact** Ms. Molly Vanderpool, Admissions Counselor, Indiana University East, 2325 Chester Boulevard, WZ 116, Richmond, IN 47374-1289. Phone: 765-973-8415 or toll-free 800-959-EAST. Fax: 765-973-8288. E-mail: eaadmit@indiana.edu. Web site: http://www.iu.edu/.

INDIANA UNIVERSITY KOKOMO
KOKOMO, INDIANA

General State-supported, comprehensive, coed **Entrance** Minimally difficult **Setting** 51-acre small-town campus **Total enrollment** 2,835 **Student-faculty ratio** 16:1 **Application deadline** Rolling (freshmen) **Freshmen** 83% were admitted **Housing** No **Expenses** Tuition $5325 **Undergraduates** 70% women, 49% part-time, 44% 25 or older, 1% Native American, 2% Hispanic American, 4% African American, 1% Asian American/Pacific Islander **The most frequently chosen baccalaureate fields are** health professions and related sciences, business/marketing, liberal arts/general studies **Academic program** Advanced placement, accelerated degree program, honors program, summer session, adult/continuing education programs, internships **Contact** Mr. David Campbell, Admissions Director, Indiana University Kokomo, PO Box 9003, Kelley Student Center 230A, Kokomo, IN 46904-9003. Phone: 765-455-9217 or toll-free 888-875-4485. Fax: 765-455-9537. E-mail: iuadmis@iuk.edu. Web site: http://www.iuk.edu/.

INDIANA UNIVERSITY NORTHWEST
GARY, INDIANA

General State-supported, comprehensive, coed **Entrance** Minimally difficult **Setting** 38-acre urban campus **Total enrollment** 4,790 **Student-faculty ratio** 14:1 **Application deadline** Rolling (freshmen), rolling (transfer) **Freshmen** 78% were admitted **Housing** No **Expenses** Tuition $5398 **Undergraduates** 69% women, 41% part-time, 43% 25 or older, 0.4% Native American, 12% Hispanic American, 22% African American, 2% Asian American/Pacific Islander **The most frequently chosen baccalaureate fields are** health professions and related sciences, business/marketing, liberal arts/general studies **Academic program** Advanced placement, accelerated degree program, self-designed majors, honors program, summer session, adult/continuing education programs, internships **Contact** Dr. Linda B. Templeton, Director of Admissions, Indiana University Northwest, 3400 Broadway, Gary, IN 46408-1197. Phone: 219-980-6767 or toll-free 800-968-7486. Fax: 219-981-4219. E-mail: admit@iun.edu. Web site: http://www.iun.edu/.

INDIANA UNIVERSITY–PURDUE UNIVERSITY FORT WAYNE
FORT WAYNE, INDIANA

General State-supported, comprehensive, coed **Entrance** Minimally difficult **Setting** 643-acre urban campus **Total enrollment** 11,943 **Student-faculty ratio** 17:1 **Application deadline** 8/1 (freshmen), 8/1 (transfer) **Freshmen** 97% were admitted **Housing** Yes **Expenses** Tuition $5681; Room only $5140 **Undergraduates** 56% women, 34% part-time, 32% 25 or older, 0.4% Native American, 3% Hispanic American, 5% African American, 2% Asian American/Pacific Islander **The most frequently chosen baccalaureate fields are** business/marketing, education, liberal arts/general studies **Academic program** English as a second language, advanced placement, accelerated degree program, self-designed majors, honors program, summer session, adult/continuing education programs, internships **Contact** Ms. Carol Isaacs, Director of Admissions, Indiana

University–Purdue University Fort Wayne, 2101 East Coliseum Boulevard, Fort Wayne, IN 46805-1499. Phone: 260-481-6812 or toll-free 800-324-4739. Fax: 260-481-6880. E-mail: Ask@ipfw.edu. Web site: http://www.ipfw.edu/.

INDIANA UNIVERSITY–PURDUE UNIVERSITY INDIANAPOLIS

INDIANAPOLIS, INDIANA

General State-supported, university, coed **Entrance** Moderately difficult **Setting** 509-acre urban campus **Total enrollment** 29,854 **Student-faculty ratio** 17:1 **Application deadline** 6/1 (freshmen), rolling (transfer) **Freshmen** 71% were admitted **Housing** Yes **Expenses** Tuition $6851; Room & Board $5100 **Undergraduates** 59% women, 32% part-time, 36% 25 or older, 0.3% Native American, 3% Hispanic American, 10% African American, 3% Asian American/Pacific Islander **The most frequently chosen baccalaureate fields are** business/marketing, health professions and related sciences, liberal arts/general studies **Academic program** English as a second language, advanced placement, accelerated degree program, honors program, summer session, adult/continuing education programs, internships **Contact** Mr. Chris J. Foley, Director of Admissions, Indiana University–Purdue University Indianapolis, Cavanaugh Hall 129, 425 University Boulevard, Indianapolis, IN 46202-5143. Phone: 317-274-4591. Fax: 317-278-1862. E-mail: apply@iupui.edu. Web site: http://www.iupui.edu/.

INDIANA UNIVERSITY SOUTH BEND

SOUTH BEND, INDIANA

General State-supported, comprehensive, coed **Entrance** Moderately difficult **Setting** 80-acre suburban campus **Total enrollment** 7,517 **Student-faculty ratio** 14:1 **Application deadline** Rolling (freshmen), rolling (transfer) **Freshmen** 83% were admitted **Housing** No **Expenses** Tuition $5491 **Undergraduates** 62% women, 43% part-time, 26% 25 or older, 0.5% Native American, 4% Hispanic American, 7% African American, 1% Asian American/Pacific Islander **The most frequently chosen baccalaureate fields are** business/marketing, health professions and related sciences, liberal arts/general studies **Academic program** English as a second language, accelerated degree program, honors program, summer session, adult/continuing education programs, internships **Contact** Mr. Jeff Johnston, Director of Recruitment/Admissions, Indiana University South Bend, 1700 Mishawaka Avenue, PO Box 7111, South Bend, IN 46634-7111. Phone: 574-237-4480 or toll-free 877-GO-2-IUSB. Fax: 574-237-4834. E-mail: admissio@iusb.edu. Web site: http://www.iusb.edu/.

INDIANA UNIVERSITY SOUTHEAST

NEW ALBANY, INDIANA

General State-supported, comprehensive, coed **Entrance** Minimally difficult **Setting** 177-acre suburban campus **Total enrollment** 6,241 **Student-faculty ratio** 16:1 **Application deadline** Rolling (freshmen), rolling (transfer) **Freshmen** 89% were admitted **Housing** No **Expenses** Tuition $5376 **Undergraduates** 62% women, 39% part-time, 37% 25 or older, 0.5% Native American, 2% Hispanic American, 5% African American, 1% Asian American/Pacific Islander **The most frequently chosen baccalaureate fields are** business/marketing, education, liberal arts/general studies **Academic program** Advanced placement, accelerated degree program, self-designed majors, summer session, adult/continuing education programs, internships **Contact** Ms. Anne Skuce, Director of Admissions, Indiana University Southeast, University Center Building, Room 100, 4201 Grant Line Road, New Albany, IN 47150. Phone: 812-941-2212 or toll-free 800-852-8835. Fax: 812-941-2595. E-mail: admissions@ius.edu. Web site: http://www.ius.edu/.

INDIANA WESLEYAN UNIVERSITY

MARION, INDIANA

General Independent Wesleyan, comprehensive, coed **Entrance** Moderately difficult **Setting** 132-acre small-town campus **Total enrollment** 3,050 **Student-faculty ratio** 15:1 **Application deadline** Rolling (freshmen), rolling (transfer) **Freshmen** 81% were admitted **Housing** Yes **Expenses** Tuition $19,376; Room & Board $6564 **Undergraduates** 63% women, 8% part-time, 4% 25 or older, 0.2% Native American, 1% Hispanic American, 1% African American, 1% Asian American/Pacific Islander **The most frequently chosen baccalaureate fields are** education, health professions and related sciences, theology and religious vocations **Academic program** Advanced placement, accelerated degree program, self-designed majors, honors program, summer session, adult/continuing education programs, internships **Contact** Mr. Daniel Solms, Director of Admissions, Indiana Wesleyan University, 4201 South Washington Street, Marion, IN 46953-4974. Phone: 765-677-2138 or toll-free 800-332-6901. Fax: 765-677-2333. E-mail: admissions@indwes.edu. Web site: http://www.indwes.edu/.

MANCHESTER COLLEGE

NORTH MANCHESTER, INDIANA

General Independent, 4-year, coed, affiliated with Church of the Brethren **Entrance** Moderately difficult **Setting** 125-acre small-town campus **Total enrollment** 1,036 **Student-faculty ratio**

Manchester College *(continued)*

13:1 **Application deadline** Rolling (freshmen), rolling (transfer) **Freshmen** 73% were admitted **Housing** Yes **Expenses** Tuition $22,025; Room & Board $8200 **Undergraduates** 50% women, 3% part-time, 2% 25 or older, 1% Native American, 2% Hispanic American, 4% African American, 1% Asian American/Pacific Islander **The most frequently chosen baccalaureate fields are** business/marketing, education, health professions and related sciences **Academic program** Advanced placement, self-designed majors, honors program, summer session, adult/continuing education programs, internships **Contact** Mr. Adam Hohman, Assistant Director of Admissions, Manchester College, 604 East College Avenue, North Manchester, IN 46962-1225. Phone: 260-982-5055 or toll-free 800-852-3648. Fax: 260-982-5239. E-mail: admitinfo@manchester.edu. Web site: http://www.manchester.edu/.

MARIAN COLLEGE
INDIANAPOLIS, INDIANA

General Independent Roman Catholic, comprehensive, coed **Entrance** Moderately difficult **Setting** 114-acre suburban campus **Total enrollment** 2,043 **Student-faculty ratio** 15:1 **Application deadline** 8/1 (freshmen), 8/1 (transfer) **Freshmen** 62% were admitted **Housing** Yes **Expenses** Tuition $20,800; Room & Board $7400 **Undergraduates** 68% women, 29% part-time, 43% 25 or older **Academic program** English as a second language, advanced placement, accelerated degree program, honors program, summer session, adult/continuing education programs, internships **Contact** Ms. Luann Brames, Marian College, 3200 Cold Spring Road, Indianapolis, IN 46222-1997. Phone: 317-955-6016 or toll-free 800-772-7264. Fax: 317-955-6401. E-mail: admissions@marian.edu. Web site: http://www.marian.edu/.

MARTIN UNIVERSITY
INDIANAPOLIS, INDIANA

General Independent, comprehensive, coed **Entrance** Noncompetitive **Setting** 5-acre urban campus **Total enrollment** 571 **Student-faculty ratio** 20:1 **Application deadline** Rolling (freshmen), rolling (transfer) **Housing** No **Expenses** Tuition $7080 **Undergraduates** 76% women, 53% part-time, 80% 25 or older, 0.2% Native American, 0.2% Hispanic American, 92% African American **Academic program** Advanced placement, accelerated degree program, self-designed majors, honors program, summer session, adult/continuing education programs, internships **Contact** Ms. Brenda Shaheed, Director of Enrollment Management, Martin University, 2171 Avondale Place, PO Box 18567, Indianapolis, IN 46218-3867. Phone: 317-543-3237. Fax: 317-543-4790. Web site: http://www.martin.edu/.

OAKLAND CITY UNIVERSITY
OAKLAND CITY, INDIANA

General Independent General Baptist, comprehensive, coed **Entrance** Minimally difficult **Setting** 20-acre rural campus **Total enrollment** 2,007 **Student-faculty ratio** 14:1 **Application deadline** Rolling (freshmen), rolling (transfer) **Freshmen** 56% were admitted **Housing** Yes **Expenses** Tuition $14,820; Room & Board $5800 **Undergraduates** 55% women, 24% part-time, 52% 25 or older, 0.5% Native American, 0.2% Hispanic American, 11% African American, 1% Asian American/Pacific Islander **The most frequently chosen baccalaureate fields are** business/marketing, education, liberal arts/general studies **Academic program** Advanced placement, accelerated degree program, summer session, adult/continuing education programs **Contact** Mr. Brian Baker, Director of Admissions, Oakland City University, 138 North Lucretia Street, Oakland City, IN 47660. Phone: 812-749-1222 or toll-free 800-737-5125. Web site: http://www.oak.edu/.

PURDUE UNIVERSITY
WEST LAFAYETTE, INDIANA

General State-supported, university, coed **Entrance** Moderately difficult **Setting** 2,307-acre suburban campus **Total enrollment** 39,102 **Student-faculty ratio** 14:1 **Application deadline** 3/1 (freshmen), rolling (transfer) **Freshmen** 79% were admitted **Housing** Yes **Expenses** Tuition $7750; Room & Board $7530 **Undergraduates** 42% women, 5% part-time, 4% 25 or older, 0.5% Native American, 3% Hispanic American, 4% African American, 6% Asian American/Pacific Islander **The most frequently chosen baccalaureate fields are** business/marketing, engineering, engineering technologies **Academic program** English as a second language, advanced placement, accelerated degree program, honors program, summer session, adult/continuing education programs, internships **Contact** Ms. Pamela T. Horne, Assistant Vice President for Enrollment Management and Dean of Admissions, Purdue University, 475 Stadium Mall Drive, Schleman Hall, West Lafayette, IN 47907-2050. Phone: 765-494-1776. Fax: 765-494-0544. E-mail: admissions@purdue.edu. Web site: http://www.purdue.edu/.

PURDUE UNIVERSITY CALUMET
HAMMOND, INDIANA

General State-supported, comprehensive, coed **Entrance** Moderately difficult **Setting** 167-acre

urban campus **Total enrollment** 9,607 **Student-faculty ratio** 17:1 **Application deadline** Rolling (freshmen), rolling (transfer) **Freshmen** 79% were admitted **Housing** Yes **Expenses** Tuition $5757; Room & Board $6155 **Undergraduates** 56% women, 37% part-time, 20% 25 or older, 0.4% Native American, 14% Hispanic American, 18% African American, 1% Asian American/Pacific Islander **The most frequently chosen baccalaureate fields are** business/marketing, engineering technologies, social sciences **Academic program** English as a second language, advanced placement, accelerated degree program, honors program, summer session, adult/continuing education programs, internships **Contact** Mr. Paul McGuinness, Director of Admissions, Purdue University Calumet, 2200-169th Street, Hammond, IN 46323-2094. Phone: 219-989-2213 or toll-free 800-447-8738. E-mail: adms@calumet.purdue.edu. Web site: http://www.calumet.purdue.edu/.

PURDUE UNIVERSITY NORTH CENTRAL

WESTVILLE, INDIANA

General State-supported, comprehensive, coed **Entrance** Minimally difficult **Setting** 305-acre rural campus **Total enrollment** 3,904 **Student-faculty ratio** 17:1 **Application deadline** 8/15 (freshmen), 8/15 (transfer) **Freshmen** 87% were admitted **Housing** No **Expenses** Tuition $6080 **Undergraduates** 59% women, 39% part-time, 37% 25 or older, 1% Native American, 5% Hispanic American, 5% African American, 1% Asian American/Pacific Islander **The most frequently chosen baccalaureate fields are** business/marketing, engineering technologies, liberal arts/general studies **Academic program** Advanced placement, self-designed majors, honors program, summer session, adult/continuing education programs, internships **Contact** Mr. Anthony Cardenas, Director of Admissions, Purdue University North Central, 1401 South U.S. Highway 421, Westville, IN 46391. Phone: 219-785-5283 or toll-free 800-872-1231. Fax: 219-785-5538. E-mail: acardenas@pnc.edu. Web site: http://www.pnc.edu/.

ROSE-HULMAN INSTITUTE OF TECHNOLOGY

TERRE HAUTE, INDIANA

General Independent, comprehensive, coed, primarily men **Entrance** Very difficult **Setting** 200-acre suburban campus **Total enrollment** 1,936 **Student-faculty ratio** 12:1 **Application deadline** 3/1 (freshmen) **Freshmen** 70% were admitted **Housing** Yes **Expenses** Tuition $30,768; Room & Board $8343 **Undergraduates** 21% women, 1% part-time, 0.3% 25 or older, 0.2% Native American, 2% Hispanic American, 2% African American, 5% Asian American/Pacific Islander **The most frequently chosen baccalaureate fields are** computer and information sciences, engineering, mathematics **Academic program** Advanced placement, accelerated degree program, summer session, adult/continuing education programs **Contact** Mr. James Goecker, Dean of Admissions and Financial Aid, Rose-Hulman Institute of Technology, 5500 Wabash Avenue, CM 1, Terre Haute, IN 47803-3920. Phone: 812-877-8894 or toll-free 800-248-7448. Fax: 812-877-8941. E-mail: admissions@rose-hulman.edu. Web site: http://www.rose-hulman.edu/.

SAINT JOSEPH'S COLLEGE

RENSSELAER, INDIANA

General Independent Roman Catholic, comprehensive, coed **Entrance** Moderately difficult **Setting** 180-acre small-town campus **Total enrollment** 1,070 **Student-faculty ratio** 15:1 **Application deadline** Rolling (freshmen), rolling (transfer) **Freshmen** 75% were admitted **Housing** Yes **Expenses** Tuition $21,880; Room & Board $6940 **Undergraduates** 60% women, 5% part-time, 14% 25 or older, 4% Hispanic American, 8% African American, 0.5% Asian American/Pacific Islander **The most frequently chosen baccalaureate fields are** business/marketing, education, security and protective services **Academic program** Advanced placement, accelerated degree program, self-designed majors, honors program, summer session, internships **Contact** Ms. Karen Raftus, Director of Admissions, Saint Joseph's College, PO Box 815, Rensselaer, IN 47978-0850. Phone: 219-866-6170 or toll-free 800-447-8781. Fax: 219-866-6122. E-mail: admissions@saintjoe.edu. Web site: http://www.saintjoe.edu/.

SAINT MARY-OF-THE-WOODS COLLEGE

SAINT MARY-OF-THE-WOODS, INDIANA

General Independent Roman Catholic, comprehensive, coed, primarily women **Entrance** Moderately difficult **Setting** 67-acre rural campus **Total enrollment** 1,677 **Student-faculty ratio** 11:1 **Application deadline** 8/1 (freshmen), 8/1 (transfer) **Housing** Yes **Expenses** Tuition $20,180; Room & Board $7380 **Undergraduates** 96% women, 70% part-time, 60% 25 or older, 0.5% Native American, 1% Hispanic American, 2% African American, 0.1% Asian American/Pacific Islander **The most frequently chosen baccalaureate fields are** agriculture, business/marketing, education **Academic program** Advanced placement, accelerated degree program, self-designed majors, summer session, adult/continuing education programs, internships **Contact** Mr. Bryan Michel, Associate Director of Admission, Saint Mary-of-the-Woods College, Guerin Hall, Saint

Saint Mary-of-the-Woods College *(continued)*

Mary-of-the-Woods, IN 47876. Phone: 812-535-5106 or toll-free 800-926-SMWC. Fax: 812-535-5010. E-mail: smwcadms@smwc.edu. Web site: http://www.smwc.edu/.

SAINT MARY'S COLLEGE
NOTRE DAME, INDIANA

General Independent Roman Catholic, 4-year, women only **Entrance** Moderately difficult **Setting** 75-acre suburban campus **Total enrollment** 1,604 **Student-faculty ratio** 10:1 **Application deadline** 2/15 (freshmen), rolling (transfer) **Freshmen** 81% were admitted **Housing** Yes **Expenses** Tuition $26,875; Room & Board $8675 **Undergraduates** 2% part-time, 1% 25 or older, 0.4% Native American, 6% Hispanic American, 1% African American, 2% Asian American/Pacific Islander **The most frequently chosen baccalaureate fields are** business/marketing, education, health professions and related sciences **Academic program** Advanced placement, accelerated degree program, self-designed majors, summer session, internships **Contact** Mona Bowe, Director of Admission, Saint Mary's College, Notre Dame, IN 46558. Phone: 574-284-4587 or toll-free 800-551-7621. Fax: 574-284-4841. E-mail: admission@saintmarys.edu. Web site: http://www.saintmarys.edu/.

TAYLOR UNIVERSITY
UPLAND, INDIANA

General Independent interdenominational, comprehensive, coed **Entrance** Moderately difficult **Setting** 950-acre rural campus **Total enrollment** 1,879 **Student-faculty ratio** 13:1 **Application deadline** Rolling (freshmen), rolling (transfer) **Freshmen** 91% were admitted **Housing** Yes **Expenses** Tuition $24,546; Room & Board $6352 **Undergraduates** 55% women, 3% part-time, 1% 25 or older, 2% Hispanic American, 2% African American, 2% Asian American/Pacific Islander **The most frequently chosen baccalaureate fields are** business/marketing, education, psychology **Academic program** English as a second language, advanced placement, self-designed majors, honors program, summer session, internships **Contact** Mrs. Kathy Thornburgh, Visit Coordinator, Taylor University, 236 West Reade Avenue, Upland, IN 46989-1001. Phone: 765-998-5206 or toll-free 800-882-3456. Fax: 765-998-4925. E-mail: admissions@taylor.edu. Web site: http://www.taylor.edu/.

TAYLOR UNIVERSITY FORT WAYNE
FORT WAYNE, INDIANA

General Independent interdenominational, comprehensive, coed **Entrance** Moderately difficult **Setting** 32-acre urban campus **Total enrollment** 964 **Student-faculty ratio** 13:1 **Application deadline** Rolling (freshmen), rolling (transfer) **Freshmen** 68% were admitted **Housing** Yes **Expenses** Tuition $21,164; Room & Board $5610 **Undergraduates** 62% women, 68% part-time, 18% 25 or older, 1% Hispanic American, 4% African American, 0.1% Asian American/Pacific Islander **The most frequently chosen baccalaureate fields are** education, English, theology and religious vocations **Academic program** Advanced placement, accelerated degree program, self-designed majors, summer session, adult/continuing education programs, internships **Contact** Mr. Leo Gonot, Associate Vice President for Enrollment Management, Taylor University Fort Wayne, 1025 West Rudisill Boulevard, Fort Wayne, IN 46807-2197. Phone: 260-744-8689 or toll-free 800-233-3922. Fax: 260-744-8850. E-mail: admissions@fw.taylor.edu. Web site: http://www.tayloru.edu/.

TRI-STATE UNIVERSITY
ANGOLA, INDIANA

General Independent, comprehensive, coed **Entrance** Moderately difficult **Setting** 400-acre small-town campus **Total enrollment** 1,337 **Student-faculty ratio** 13:1 **Application deadline** 8/1 (freshmen), 8/1 (transfer) **Freshmen** 74% were admitted **Housing** Yes **Expenses** Tuition $23,450; Room & Board $6700 **Undergraduates** 32% women, 10% part-time, 8% 25 or older, 2% Hispanic American, 3% African American, 1% Asian American/Pacific Islander **The most frequently chosen baccalaureate fields are** business/marketing, mathematics, security and protective services **Academic program** Advanced placement, honors program, summer session, adult/continuing education programs, internships **Contact** Mr. Scott Goplin, Dean of Admission, Tri-State University, 1 University Avenue, Angola, IN 46703. Phone: 260-665-4365 or toll-free 800-347-4TSU. Fax: 260-665-4578. E-mail: admit@tristate.edu. Web site: http://www.tristate.edu/.

UNIVERSITY OF EVANSVILLE
EVANSVILLE, INDIANA

General Independent, comprehensive, coed, affiliated with United Methodist Church **Entrance** Moderately difficult **Setting** 75-acre urban campus **Total enrollment** 2,898 **Student-faculty ratio** 13:1 **Application deadline** 2/1 (freshmen), rolling (transfer) **Freshmen** 89% were admitted **Housing** Yes **Expenses** Tuition $24,340; Room & Board $7650 **Undergraduates** 60% women, 13% part-time, 4% 25 or older, 0.2% Native American, 2% Hispanic American, 3% African American, 1% Asian American/Pacific Islander **The most**

frequently chosen baccalaureate fields are education, health professions and related sciences, visual and performing arts **Academic program** English as a second language, advanced placement, accelerated degree program, self-designed majors, honors program, summer session, adult/continuing education programs, internships **Contact** Don Vos, Dean of Admission, University of Evansville, 1800 Lincoln Avenue, Evansville, IN 47722. Phone: 812-488-2468 or toll-free 800-423-8633 Ext. 2468. Fax: 812-488-4076. E-mail: admission@evansville.edu. Web site: http://www.evansville.edu/.

UNIVERSITY OF INDIANAPOLIS

INDIANAPOLIS, INDIANA

General Independent, comprehensive, coed, affiliated with United Methodist Church **Entrance** Moderately difficult **Setting** 65-acre urban campus **Total enrollment** 4,598 **Student-faculty ratio** 12:1 **Application deadline** Rolling (freshmen), rolling (transfer) **Freshmen** 82% were admitted **Housing** Yes **Expenses** Tuition $19,730; Room & Board $7560 **Undergraduates** 67% women, 25% part-time, 23% 25 or older, 0.2% Native American, 2% Hispanic American, 10% African American, 1% Asian American/Pacific Islander **The most frequently chosen baccalaureate fields are** business/marketing, education, health professions and related sciences **Academic program** English as a second language, advanced placement, accelerated degree program, self-designed majors, honors program, summer session, adult/continuing education programs, internships **Contact** Mr. Ronald Wilks, Director of Admissions, University of Indianapolis, 1400 East Hanna Avenue, Indianapolis, IN 46227-3697. Phone: 317-788-3216 or toll-free 800-232-8634 Ext. 3216. Fax: 317-788-3300. E-mail: admissions@uindy.edu. Web site: http://www.uindy.edu/.

UNIVERSITY OF NOTRE DAME

NOTRE DAME, INDIANA

General Independent Roman Catholic, university, coed **Entrance** Most difficult **Setting** 1,250-acre suburban campus **Total enrollment** 11,733 **Student-faculty ratio** 11:1 **Application deadline** 12/31 (freshmen), 4/15 (transfer) **Freshmen** 24% were admitted **Housing** Yes **Expenses** Tuition $35,187; Room & Board $9290 **Undergraduates** 47% women, 0.1% part-time, 1% Native American, 9% Hispanic American, 4% African American, 7% Asian American/Pacific Islander **The most frequently chosen baccalaureate fields are** business/marketing, engineering, social sciences **Academic program** Advanced placement, accelerated degree program, self-designed majors, honors program, summer session, internships **Contact** Office of Undergraduate Admissions, University of Notre Dame, 220 Main Building, Notre Dame, IN 46556-5612. Phone: 574-631-7505. Fax: 574-631-8865. E-mail: admissions@nd.edu. Web site: http://www.nd.edu/.

UNIVERSITY OF PHOENIX–INDIANAPOLIS CAMPUS

INDIANAPOLIS, INDIANA

General Proprietary, comprehensive, coed **Contact** Ms. Evelyn Gaskin, Registrar/Executive Director, University of Phoenix–Indianapolis Campus, 4615 East Elwood Street, Mail Stop AA-K101, Phoenix, AZ 85040-1958. Phone: 480-557-3301 or toll-free 800-776-4867 (in-state); 800-228-7240 (out-of-state). Fax: 480-643-1020. E-mail: evelyn.gaskin@phoenix.edu. Web site: http://www.phoenix.edu/.

UNIVERSITY OF SAINT FRANCIS

FORT WAYNE, INDIANA

General Independent Roman Catholic, comprehensive, coed **Entrance** Moderately difficult **Setting** 74-acre suburban campus **Total enrollment** 2,135 **Student-faculty ratio** 12:1 **Application deadline** Rolling (freshmen), rolling (transfer) **Freshmen** 55% were admitted **Housing** Yes **Expenses** Tuition $19,570; Room & Board $6006 **Undergraduates** 69% women, 20% part-time, 23% 25 or older, 0.4% Native American, 2% Hispanic American, 5% African American, 1% Asian American/Pacific Islander **Academic program** Advanced placement, honors program, summer session, adult/continuing education programs, internships **Contact** Mr. Ron Schumacher, Vice President for Enrollment Management, University of Saint Francis, 2701 Spring Street, Fort Wayne, IN 46808. Phone: 260-434-3264 or toll-free 800-729-4732. Fax: 260-434-7590. E-mail: admis@sf.edu. Web site: http://www.sf.edu/.

UNIVERSITY OF SOUTHERN INDIANA

EVANSVILLE, INDIANA

General State-supported, comprehensive, coed **Entrance** Moderately difficult **Setting** 330-acre suburban campus **Total enrollment** 9,939 **Student-faculty ratio** 18:1 **Application deadline** 8/15 (freshmen) **Freshmen** 90% were admitted **Housing** Yes **Expenses** Tuition $5219; Room & Board $6542 **Undergraduates** 59% women, 17% part-time, 17% 25 or older, 0.4% Native American, 1% Hispanic American, 5% African American, 1% Asian American/Pacific Islander **The most frequently chosen baccalaureate fields are** business/marketing, education, health professions and related sciences **Academic**

University of Southern Indiana *(continued)*

program English as a second language, advanced placement, honors program, summer session, adult/continuing education programs, internships **Contact** Mr. Eric Otto, Director of Admission, University of Southern Indiana, 8600 University Boulevard, Evansville, IN 47712-3590. Phone: 812-464-1765 or toll-free 800-467-1965. Fax: 812-465-7154. E-mail: enroll@usi.edu. Web site: http://www.usi.edu/.

VALPARAISO UNIVERSITY
VALPARAISO, INDIANA

General Independent, comprehensive, coed, affiliated with Lutheran Church **Entrance** Moderately difficult **Setting** 310-acre small-town campus **Total enrollment** 3,872 **Student-faculty ratio** 12:1 **Application deadline** 8/15 (freshmen) **Freshmen** 90% were admitted **Housing** Yes **Expenses** Tuition $25,200; Room & Board $7150 **Undergraduates** 52% women, 6% part-time, 3% 25 or older, 0.3% Native American, 4% Hispanic American, 4% African American, 1% Asian American/Pacific Islander **The most frequently chosen baccalaureate fields are** business/marketing, engineering, social sciences **Academic program** English as a second language, advanced placement, accelerated degree program, self-designed majors, honors program, summer session, adult/continuing education programs, internships **Contact** Office of Admission, Valparaiso University, Kretzmann Hall, 1700 Chapel Drive, Valparaiso, IN 46383-6493. Phone: 219-464-5011 or toll-free 888-GO-VALPO. Fax: 219-464-6898. E-mail: undergrad.admissions@valpo.edu. Web site: http://www.valpo.edu/.

WABASH COLLEGE
CRAWFORDSVILLE, INDIANA

General Independent, 4-year, men only **Entrance** Moderately difficult **Setting** 50-acre small-town campus **Total enrollment** 917 **Student-faculty ratio** 10:1 **Application deadline** Rolling (freshmen), 3/15 (transfer) **Freshmen** 47% were admitted **Housing** Yes **Expenses** Tuition $26,350; Room & Board $7700 **Undergraduates** 0.4% part-time, 0.1% Native American, 5% Hispanic American, 6% African American, 2% Asian American/Pacific Islander **The most frequently chosen baccalaureate fields are** English, psychology, social sciences **Academic program** Advanced placement, internships **Contact** Mr. Steve Klein, Dean of Admissions, Wabash College, PO Box 362, Crawfordsville, IN 47933-0352. Phone: 765-361-6225 or toll-free 800-345-5385. Fax: 765-361-6437. E-mail: admissions@wabash.edu. Web site: http://www.wabash.edu/.

IOWA

AIB COLLEGE OF BUSINESS
DES MOINES, IOWA

General Independent, 4-year, coed **Entrance** Minimally difficult **Setting** 20-acre urban campus **Total enrollment** 965 **Student-faculty ratio** 24:1 **Application deadline** Rolling (freshmen), rolling (transfer) **Freshmen** 87% were admitted **Housing** Yes **Expenses** Tuition $12,120; Room & Board $4311 **Undergraduates** 71% women, 40% part-time, 34% 25 or older, 1% Native American, 3% Hispanic American, 2% African American, 1% Asian American/Pacific Islander **Academic program** Summer session, adult/continuing education programs, internships **Contact** Mr. Tim Hauber, Vice President of Enrollment, AIB College of Business, 2500 Fleur Drive, Des Moines, IA 50321. Phone: 515-244-4221 or toll-free 800-444-1921. Fax: 515-244-6773. E-mail: haubert@aib.edu. Web site: http://www.aib.edu/.

ALLEN COLLEGE
WATERLOO, IOWA

General Independent, comprehensive, coed, primarily women **Entrance** Moderately difficult **Setting** 20-acre suburban campus **Total enrollment** 462 **Student-faculty ratio** 14:1 **Application deadline** 7/1 (freshmen), 7/1 (transfer) **Freshmen** 76% were admitted **Housing** Yes **Expenses** Tuition $14,895; Room & Board $6178 **Undergraduates** 96% women, 14% part-time, 22% 25 or older, 1% Native American, 1% Hispanic American, 1% African American, 0.3% Asian American/Pacific Islander **The most frequently chosen baccalaureate field is** health professions and related sciences **Academic program** Advanced placement, internships **Contact** Dina Dowden, Education Secretary-Student Services, Allen College, Barrett Forum, 1825 Logan Avenue, Waterloo, IA 50703. Phone: 319-226-2002. Fax: 319-226-2051. E-mail: allencollegeadmissions@ihs.org. Web site: http://www.allencollege.edu/.

ASHFORD UNIVERSITY
CLINTON, IOWA

General Proprietary, comprehensive, coed **Entrance** Minimally difficult **Setting** 24-acre small-town campus **Total enrollment** 10,568 **Student-faculty ratio** 37:1 **Application deadline** Rolling (freshmen), rolling (transfer) **Housing** Yes **Expenses** Tuition $15,980; Room & Board $5800 **Undergraduates** 77% women, 1% part-time, 1% Native American, 7% Hispanic American, 23% African American, 2% Asian American/Pacific Islander **Academic program**

Advanced placement, honors program, summer session, internships **Contact** Ms. Waunita M. Sullivan, Director of Enrollment, Ashford University, 400 North Bluff Boulevard, PO Box 2967, Clinton, IA 52733-2967. Phone: 563-242-4023 Ext. 3401 or toll-free 800-242-4153. Fax: 563-243-6102. E-mail: admissions@ashford.edu. Web site: http://www.ashford.edu/.

BRIAR CLIFF UNIVERSITY
SIOUX CITY, IOWA

General Independent Roman Catholic, comprehensive, coed **Contact** Briar Cliff Admissions, Briar Cliff University, 3303 Rebecca Street, Sioux City, IA 51104. Phone: 712-279-1628 or toll-free 800-662-3303 Ext. 5200. Fax: 712-279-1632. E-mail: admissino@briarcliff.edu. Web site: http://www.briarcliff.edu/.

BUENA VISTA UNIVERSITY
STORM LAKE, IOWA

General Independent, comprehensive, coed, affiliated with Presbyterian Church (U.S.A.) **Entrance** Moderately difficult **Setting** 60-acre small-town campus **Total enrollment** 1,131 **Student-faculty ratio** 11:1 **Freshmen** 74% were admitted **Housing** Yes **Expenses** Tuition $23,842; Room & Board $6712 **Undergraduates** 53% women, 2% part-time, 4% 25 or older, 0.2% Native American, 3% Hispanic American, 4% African American, 1% Asian American/Pacific Islander **The most frequently chosen baccalaureate fields are** business/marketing, education, interdisciplinary studies **Academic program** English as a second language, advanced placement, self-designed majors, honors program, summer session, adult/continuing education programs, internships **Contact** Alan Coheley, Vice President for Enrollment Management, Buena Vista University, 610 West Fourth Street, Storm Lake, IA 50588. Phone: 712-749-2235 or toll-free 800-383-9600. E-mail: admissions@bvu.edu. Web site: http://www.bvu.edu/.

CENTRAL COLLEGE
PELLA, IOWA

General Independent, 4-year, coed, affiliated with Reformed Church in America **Entrance** Moderately difficult **Setting** 133-acre small-town campus **Total enrollment** 1,605 **Student-faculty ratio** 13:1 **Application deadline** Rolling (freshmen), rolling (transfer) **Freshmen** 79% were admitted **Housing** Yes **Expenses** Tuition $23,944; Room & Board $8006 **Undergraduates** 54% women, 3% part-time, 3% 25 or older, 0.3% Native American, 2% Hispanic American, 1% African American, 1% Asian American/Pacific Islander **The most frequently chosen baccalaureate fields are** business/marketing, education, parks and recreation **Academic program** English as a second language, self-designed majors, honors program, summer session, internships **Contact** Ms. Carol Williamson, Dean of Admission and Student Enrollment Services, Central College, 812 University Street, Pella, IA 50219-1999. Phone: 641-628-7600 or toll-free 877-462-3687 (in-state); 877-462-3689 (out-of-state). Fax: 641-628-5316. E-mail: admissions@central.edu. Web site: http://www.central.edu/.

CLARKE COLLEGE
DUBUQUE, IOWA

General Independent Roman Catholic, comprehensive, coed **Entrance** Moderately difficult **Setting** 55-acre urban campus **Total enrollment** 1,230 **Student-faculty ratio** 11:1 **Application deadline** Rolling (freshmen), rolling (transfer) **Freshmen** 62% were admitted **Housing** Yes **Expenses** Tuition $21,312; Room & Board $6574 **Undergraduates** 71% women, 13% part-time, 22% 25 or older, 0.2% Native American, 2% Hispanic American, 2% African American, 0.5% Asian American/Pacific Islander **The most frequently chosen baccalaureate fields are** business/marketing, education, health professions and related sciences **Academic program** English as a second language, advanced placement, accelerated degree program, self-designed majors, honors program, summer session, adult/continuing education programs, internships **Contact** Mr. Andy Shroeder, Director of Admissions, Clarke College, 1550 Clarke Drive, Dubuque, IA 52001-3198. Phone: 563-588-6316 or toll-free 800-383-2345. Fax: 563-588-6789. E-mail: admissions@clarke.edu. Web site: http://www.clarke.edu/.

COE COLLEGE
CEDAR RAPIDS, IOWA

General Independent, comprehensive, coed, affiliated with Presbyterian Church **Contact** Mr. John Grundig, Dean of Admission, Coe College, 1220 1st Avenue, NE, Cedar Rapids, IA 52402-5070. Phone: 319-399-8500 or toll-free 877-225-5263. Fax: 319-399-8816. E-mail: admission@coe.edu. Web site: http://www.coe.edu/.

CORNELL COLLEGE
MOUNT VERNON, IOWA

General Independent Methodist, 4-year, coed **Entrance** Moderately difficult **Setting** 129-acre small-town campus **Total enrollment** 1,083 **Student-faculty ratio** 11:1 **Application deadline** 3/1 (freshmen), 3/1 (transfer) **Freshmen** 45% were admitted **Housing** Yes **Expenses** Tuition $26,280; Room & Board $6970 **Undergradu-**

Cornell College *(continued)*

ates 51% women, 1% part-time, 1% 25 or older, 1% Native American, 3% Hispanic American, 3% African American, 2% Asian American/ Pacific Islander **The most frequently chosen baccalaureate fields are** biological/life sciences, social sciences, visual and performing arts **Academic program** English as a second language, advanced placement, self-designed majors, internships **Contact** Todd White, Director of Admissions, Cornell College, 600 First Street West, Mount Vernon, IA 52314-1098. Phone: 319-895-4477 or toll-free 800-747-1112. Fax: 319-895-4451. E-mail: twhite@cornellcollege.edu. Web site: http://www.cornellcollege.edu/.

DIVINE WORD COLLEGE
EPWORTH, IOWA

Contact Vice President of Recruitment/Director of Admissions, Divine Word College, 102 Jacoby Drive SW, Epworth, IA 52045-0380. Phone: 563-876-3332 or toll-free 800-553-3321. Fax: 319-876-3407. E-mail: svdalum@mwci.net. Web site: http://www.dwci.edu/.

DORDT COLLEGE
SIOUX CENTER, IOWA

General Independent Christian Reformed, comprehensive, coed **Entrance** Moderately difficult **Setting** 100-acre small-town campus **Total enrollment** 1,376 **Student-faculty ratio** 15:1 **Application deadline** 8/1 (transfer) **Freshmen** 88% were admitted **Housing** Yes **Expenses** Tuition $19,900; Room & Board $5460 **Undergraduates** 49% women, 5% part-time, 5% 25 or older, 1% Hispanic American, 0.4% African American, 0.5% Asian American/Pacific Islander **The most frequently chosen baccalaureate fields are** business/marketing, education, engineering **Academic program** English as a second language, advanced placement, self-designed majors, honors program, internships **Contact** Mr. Quentin Van Essen, Executive Director of Admissions, Dordt College, 498 4th Avenue, NE, Sioux Center, IA 51250-1697. Phone: 712-722-6080 or toll-free 800-343-6738. Fax: 712-722-1967. E-mail: admissions@dordt.edu. Web site: http://www.dordt.edu/.

DRAKE UNIVERSITY
DES MOINES, IOWA

General Independent, university, coed **Entrance** Moderately difficult **Setting** 120-acre suburban campus **Total enrollment** 5,617 **Student-faculty ratio** 14:1 **Application deadline** 3/1 (freshmen), rolling (transfer) **Freshmen** 78% were admitted **Housing** Yes **Expenses** Tuition $23,692; Room & Board $6920 **Undergraduates** 57% women, 7% part-time, 7% 25 or older, 0.1% Native American, 2% Hispanic American, 3% African American, 5% Asian American/Pacific Islander **The most frequently chosen baccalaureate fields are** business/marketing, communications/journalism, education **Academic program** English as a second language, advanced placement, accelerated degree program, self-designed majors, honors program, summer session, internships **Contact** Ms. Laura Linn, Director of Admission, Drake University, 2507 University Avenue, Des Moines, IA 50311. Phone: 515-271-3181 Ext. 3182 or toll-free 800-44DRAKE Ext. 3181. Fax: 515-271-2831. E-mail: admission@drake.edu. Web site: http://www.drake.edu/.

EMMAUS BIBLE COLLEGE
DUBUQUE, IOWA

Contact Mr. Steve Schimpf, Enrollment Services Manager, Emmaus Bible College, 2570 Asbury Road, Dubuque, IA 52001-3097. Phone: 563-588-8000 Ext. 1310 or toll-free 800-397-2425. Fax: 563-557-0573. E-mail: admissions@emmaus.edu. Web site: http://www.emmaus.edu/.

FAITH BAPTIST BIBLE COLLEGE AND THEOLOGICAL SEMINARY
ANKENY, IOWA

General Independent, comprehensive, coed, affiliated with General Association of Regular Baptist Churches **Entrance** Minimally difficult **Setting** 52-acre small-town campus **Total enrollment** 389 **Student-faculty ratio** 14:1 **Application deadline** 8/1 (freshmen), 8/1 (transfer) **Freshmen** 86% were admitted **Housing** Yes **Expenses** Tuition $12,706; Room & Board $5010 **Undergraduates** 52% women, 13% part-time, 6% 25 or older, 0.3% Native American, 2% Hispanic American, 1% African American, 1% Asian American/ Pacific Islander **The most frequently chosen baccalaureate fields are** education, philosophy and religious studies, theology and religious vocations **Academic program** Advanced placement, summer session, adult/continuing education programs, internships **Contact** Admissions Secretary, Faith Baptist Bible College and Theological Seminary, 1900 NW 4th Street, Ankeny, IA 50023. Phone: 515-964-0601 Ext. 238 or toll-free 888-FAITH 4U. Fax: 515-964-1638. E-mail: admissions@faith.edu. Web site: http://www.faith.edu/.

GRACELAND UNIVERSITY
LAMONI, IOWA

General Independent Community of Christ, comprehensive, coed **Contact** Mr. Greg Sutherland, Interim Vice President for Enrollment, and Dean of Admission, Graceland University, 1 University Place, Lamoni, IA 50140. Phone: 641-784-5110 or toll-free 866-GRACELAND. Fax: 641-784-5480. E-mail: sutherla@graceland.edu. Web site: http://www.graceland.edu/.

GRAND VIEW COLLEGE

DES MOINES, IOWA

General Independent, 4-year, coed, affiliated with Evangelical Lutheran Church in America **Entrance** Minimally difficult **Setting** 25-acre urban campus **Total enrollment** 1,748 **Student-faculty ratio** 13:1 **Application deadline** 8/15 (freshmen), 8/15 (transfer) **Freshmen** 98% were admitted **Housing** Yes **Expenses** Tuition $18,554; Room & Board $6164 **Undergraduates** 68% women, 23% part-time, 33% 25 or older, 0.2% Native American, 2% Hispanic American, 5% African American, 3% Asian American/Pacific Islander **The most frequently chosen baccalaureate fields are** business/marketing, education, health professions and related sciences **Academic program** Advanced placement, accelerated degree program, self-designed majors, honors program, summer session, adult/continuing education programs, internships **Contact** Ms. Diane Schaefer, Director of Admissions, Grand View College, 1200 Grandview Avenue, Des Moines, IA 50316-1599. Phone: 515-263-2810 or toll-free 800-444-6083 Ext. 2810. Fax: 515-263-2974. E-mail: admissions@gvc.edu. Web site: http://www.gvc.edu/.

GRINNELL COLLEGE

GRINNELL, IOWA

General Independent, 4-year, coed **Entrance** Very difficult **Setting** 120-acre small-town campus **Total enrollment** 1,654 **Student-faculty ratio** 9:1 **Application deadline** 1/20 (freshmen), 5/1 (transfer) **Freshmen** 50% were admitted **Housing** Yes **Expenses** Tuition $34,392; Room & Board $8030 **Undergraduates** 53% women, 2% part-time, 0.4% Native American, 5% Hispanic American, 5% African American, 7% Asian American/Pacific Islander **The most frequently chosen baccalaureate fields are** foreign languages and literature, biological/life sciences, social sciences **Academic program** Advanced placement, accelerated degree program, self-designed majors, internships **Contact** Mr. Seth Allen, Dean for Admission and Financial Aid, Grinnell College, 1103 Park Street, Grinnell, IA 50112. Phone: 641-269-3600 or toll-free 800-247-0113. Fax: 641-269-4800. E-mail: askgrin@grinnell.edu. Web site: http://www.grinnell.edu/.

HAMILTON TECHNICAL COLLEGE

DAVENPORT, IOWA

Contact Mr. Scott Ervin, Director of Admissions, Hamilton Technical College, 1011 East 53rd Street, Davenport, IA 52807-2653. Phone: 563-386-3570. Fax: 563-386-6756. E-mail: servin@hamiltontechcollege.com. Web site: http://www.hamiltontechcollege.com/.

IOWA STATE UNIVERSITY OF SCIENCE AND TECHNOLOGY

AMES, IOWA

General State-supported, university, coed **Entrance** Moderately difficult **Setting** 1,788-acre suburban campus **Total enrollment** 26,160 **Student-faculty ratio** 16:1 **Application deadline** 7/1 (freshmen), 7/1 (transfer) **Freshmen** 89% were admitted **Housing** Yes **Expenses** Tuition $6360 **Undergraduates** 43% women, 6% part-time, 7% 25 or older, 0.3% Native American, 3% Hispanic American, 3% African American, 3% Asian American/Pacific Islander **The most frequently chosen baccalaureate fields are** business/marketing, agriculture, engineering **Academic program** English as a second language, advanced placement, accelerated degree program, self-designed majors, honors program, summer session, adult/continuing education programs, internships **Contact** Mr. Phil Caffrey, Associate Director for Freshman Admissions, Iowa State University of Science and Technology, 100 Alumni Hall, Ames, IA 50011-2010. Phone: 515-294-0815 or toll-free 800-262-3810. Fax: 515-294-2592. E-mail: admissions@iastate.edu. Web site: http://www.iastate.edu/.

IOWA WESLEYAN COLLEGE

MOUNT PLEASANT, IOWA

General Independent United Methodist, 4-year, coed **Entrance** Moderately difficult **Setting** 60-acre small-town campus **Total enrollment** 833 **Student-faculty ratio** 14:1 **Application deadline** 8/15 (freshmen), 8/15 (transfer) **Freshmen** 60% were admitted **Housing** Yes **Expenses** Tuition $18,870; Room & Board $5880 **Undergraduates** 61% women, 24% part-time, 36% 25 or older **Academic program** English as a second language, advanced placement, self-designed majors, summer session, adult/continuing education programs, internships **Contact** Mr. Mark T. Petty, Dean of Admissions, Iowa Wesleyan College, 601 North Main Street, Mount Pleasant, IA 52641-1398. Phone: 319-385-6230 or toll-free 800-582-2383 Ext. 6231. Fax: 319-385-6240. E-mail: mpetty@iwc.edu. Web site: http://www.iwc.edu/.

KAPLAN UNIVERSITY–CEDAR FALLS

CEDAR FALLS, IOWA

Contact Ms. Jill Lines, Director of Admissions, Kaplan University–Cedar Falls, 7009 Nordic Drive, Cedar Falls, IA 50613. Phone: 319-277-

Kaplan University–Cedar Falls *(continued)*

0220 or toll-free 800-728-1220. Web site: http://www.kucampus.edu/kucampusPortal/kucampusCampuses/Iowa/CedarFalls/.

KAPLAN UNIVERSITY–COUNCIL BLUFFS

COUNCIL BLUFFS, IOWA

General Proprietary, 4-year, coed **Contact** Kate Packard, Director of Admissions, Kaplan University–Council Bluffs, 1751 Madison Avenue, Council Bluffs, IA 51503. Phone: 712-328-4212 or toll-free 800-518-4212. Web site: http://www.kucampus.edu/kucampusPortal/kucampusCampuses/Iowa/CouncilBluffs/.

KAPLAN UNIVERSITY–DAVENPORT

DAVENPORT, IOWA

General Proprietary, 4-year, coed **Contact** Jason Wilebski, Director of Campus Admissions, Kaplan University–Davenport, 1801 East Kimberly Road, Suite 1, Davenport, IA 52807-2095. Phone: 563-355-3500 or toll-free 800-747-1035. Fax: 563-355-1320. E-mail: infoke@kaplancollege.edu. Web site: http://www.kucampus.edu/kucampusPortal/default.htm.

LORAS COLLEGE

DUBUQUE, IOWA

General Independent Roman Catholic, comprehensive, coed **Entrance** Moderately difficult **Setting** 60-acre suburban campus **Total enrollment** 1,591 **Student-faculty ratio** 11:1 **Application deadline** Rolling (freshmen), rolling (transfer) **Freshmen** 74% were admitted **Housing** Yes **Expenses** Tuition $23,330; Room & Board $6500 **Undergraduates** 48% women, 3% part-time, 3% 25 or older, 0.1% Native American, 2% Hispanic American, 1% African American, 1% Asian American/Pacific Islander **The most frequently chosen baccalaureate fields are** business/marketing, education, social sciences **Academic program** English as a second language, advanced placement, self-designed majors, honors program, summer session, adult/continuing education programs, internships **Contact** Ms. Sharon Lyons, Director of Admissions, Loras College, 1450 Alta Vista, Dubuque, IA 52004-0178. Phone: 563-588-7829 or toll-free 800-245-6727. Fax: 563-588-7119. E-mail: adms@loras.edu. Web site: http://www.loras.edu/.

LUTHER COLLEGE

DECORAH, IOWA

General Independent, 4-year, coed, affiliated with Evangelical Lutheran Church in America **Entrance** Moderately difficult **Setting** 200-acre small-town campus **Total enrollment** 2,476 **Student-faculty ratio** 12:1 **Freshmen** 83% were admitted **Housing** Yes **Expenses** Tuition $28,840; Room & Board $4660 **Undergraduates** 57% women, 2% part-time, 2% 25 or older, 0.2% Native American, 2% Hispanic American, 1% African American, 2% Asian American/Pacific Islander **The most frequently chosen baccalaureate fields are** business/marketing, biological/life sciences, visual and performing arts **Academic program** Advanced placement, self-designed majors, honors program, summer session, internships **Contact** Kirk Neubauer, Director of Recruiting Services, Luther College, 700 College Drive, Decorah, IA 52101. Phone: 563-387-1430 or toll-free 800-458-8437. Fax: 563-387-2159. E-mail: admissions@luther.edu. Web site: http://www.luther.edu/.

►**For more information, see page 473.**

MAHARISHI UNIVERSITY OF MANAGEMENT

FAIRFIELD, IOWA

General Independent, university, coed **Entrance** Moderately difficult **Setting** 272-acre small-town campus **Total enrollment** 948 **Student-faculty ratio** 16:1 **Application deadline** 8/1 (freshmen), 8/1 (transfer) **Freshmen** 41% were admitted **Housing** Yes **Expenses** Tuition $24,430; Room & Board $6000 **Undergraduates** 43% women, 7% part-time, 32% 25 or older, 7% Hispanic American, 2% African American, 4% Asian American/Pacific Islander **The most frequently chosen baccalaureate fields are** liberal arts/general studies, natural resources/environmental science, visual and performing arts **Academic program** Advanced placement, self-designed majors, honors program, adult/continuing education programs, internships **Contact** Ms. Barbara Rainbow, Associate Dean of Admissions, Maharishi University of Management, Office of Admissions, Fairfield, IA 52557. Phone: 641-472-1110 or toll-free 800-369-6480. Fax: 641-472-1179. E-mail: admissions@mum.edu. Web site: http://www.mum.edu/.

MERCY COLLEGE OF HEALTH SCIENCES

DES MOINES, IOWA

General Independent, 4-year, coed, primarily women, affiliated with Roman Catholic Church **Setting** 5-acre urban campus **Total enrollment** 680 **Student-faculty ratio** 9:1 **Application deadline** Rolling (freshmen) **Housing** No **Expenses** Tuition $13,000 **Undergraduates** 91% women, 38% part-time, 1% Native American, 3% Hispanic American, 2% African American, 3% Asian American/Pacific Islander **The most frequently chosen baccalaureate field is** health professions and related sciences **Academic program**

Advanced placement, accelerated degree program, summer session **Contact** Susan Hill/Sandi Nagel, Admissions Representative, Mercy College of Health Sciences, 928 Sixth Avenue, Des Moines, IA 50309-1239. Phone: 515-643-3180 or toll-free 800-637-2994. Fax: 515-643-6698. E-mail: shill@mercydesmoines.org or snagel@mercydesmoines.org. Web site: http://www.mchs.edu/.

MORNINGSIDE COLLEGE
SIOUX CITY, IOWA

General Independent, comprehensive, coed, affiliated with United Methodist Church **Entrance** Moderately difficult **Setting** 68-acre suburban campus **Total enrollment** 1,798 **Student-faculty ratio** 17:1 **Application deadline** Rolling (freshmen), rolling (transfer) **Freshmen** 79% were admitted **Housing** Yes **Expenses** Tuition $20,164; Room & Board $6166 **Undergraduates** 55% women, 4% part-time, 6% 25 or older, 1% Native American, 3% Hispanic American, 1% African American, 2% Asian American/Pacific Islander **The most frequently chosen baccalaureate fields are** business/marketing, education, visual and performing arts **Academic program** English as a second language, advanced placement, self-designed majors, honors program, summer session, adult/continuing education programs, internships **Contact** Ms. Stephanie Peters, Ms. Amy Williams, Co-Directors of Admissions, Morningside College, 1501 Morningside Avenue, Sioux City, IA 51106. Phone: 712-274-5111 or toll-free 800-831-0806 Ext. 5111. Fax: 712-274-5101. E-mail: mscadm@morningside.edu. Web site: http://www.morningside.edu/.

MOUNT MERCY COLLEGE
CEDAR RAPIDS, IOWA

General Independent Roman Catholic, 4-year, coed **Entrance** Moderately difficult **Setting** 40-acre suburban campus **Total enrollment** 1,506 **Student-faculty ratio** 11:1 **Application deadline** 8/15 (freshmen), 8/15 (transfer) **Freshmen** 72% were admitted **Housing** Yes **Expenses** Tuition $20,070; Room & Board $6270 **Undergraduates** 72% women, 38% part-time, 40% 25 or older, 0.4% Native American, 1% Hispanic American, 2% African American, 1% Asian American/Pacific Islander **The most frequently chosen baccalaureate fields are** business/marketing, education, health professions and related sciences **Academic program** Advanced placement, accelerated degree program, honors program, summer session, adult/continuing education programs, internships **Contact** Ms. Beth Tjelle, Assistant Director of Admissions, Mount Mercy College, 1330 Elmhurst Drive, NE, Cedar Rapids, IA 52402. Phone: 319-368-6460 or toll-free 800-248-4504. Fax: 319-363-5270. E-mail: btjelle@metmercy.edu. Web site: http://www.mtmercy.edu/.

NORTHWESTERN COLLEGE
ORANGE CITY, IOWA

General Independent, 4-year, coed, affiliated with Reformed Church in America **Entrance** Moderately difficult **Setting** 45-acre rural campus **Total enrollment** 1,315 **Student-faculty ratio** 15:1 **Application deadline** Rolling (freshmen), rolling (transfer) **Freshmen** 79% were admitted **Housing** Yes **Expenses** Tuition $21,648; Room & Board $6302 **Undergraduates** 61% women, 3% part-time, 3% 25 or older, 0.2% Native American, 1% Hispanic American, 1% African American, 1% Asian American/Pacific Islander **The most frequently chosen baccalaureate fields are** business/marketing, biological/life sciences, education **Academic program** English as a second language, advanced placement, self-designed majors, honors program, summer session, internships **Contact** Mr. Mark Bloemendaal, Director of Admissions, Northwestern College, 101 7th Street SW, Orange City, IA 51041-1996. Phone: 712-737-7130 or toll-free 800-747-4757. Fax: 712-707-7164. E-mail: admissions@nwciowa.edu. Web site: http://www.nwciowa.edu/.

PALMER COLLEGE OF CHIROPRACTIC
DAVENPORT, IOWA

General Independent, comprehensive, coed **Entrance** Moderately difficult **Setting** urban campus **Total enrollment** 1,480 **Application deadline** Rolling (freshmen) **Housing** No **Expenses** Tuition $6850 **Undergraduates** 51% women, 7% part-time, 1% Hispanic American, 4% African American, 3% Asian American/Pacific Islander **The most frequently chosen baccalaureate field is** biological/life sciences **Academic program** Summer session, internships **Contact** Ms. Karen Eden, Director of Admissions, Palmer College of Chiropractic, 1000 Brady Street, Davenport, IA 52803-5287. Phone: 563-884-5656 or toll-free 800-722-3648. Fax: 563-884-5414. E-mail: pcadmit@palmer.edu. Web site: http://www.palmer.edu/.

ST. AMBROSE UNIVERSITY
DAVENPORT, IOWA

General Independent Roman Catholic, comprehensive, coed **Entrance** Moderately difficult **Setting** 50-acre urban campus **Total enrollment** 3,870 **Student-faculty ratio** 11:1 **Application deadline** Rolling (freshmen), rolling (transfer) **Freshmen** 70% were admitted **Housing** Yes **Expenses** Tuition $21,610; Room & Board $7825 **Undergraduates** 63% women, 19% part-time,

St. Ambrose University *(continued)*

21% 25 or older, 1% Native American, 3% Hispanic American, 3% African American, 1% Asian American/Pacific Islander **The most frequently chosen baccalaureate fields are** business/marketing, education, psychology **Academic program** Advanced placement, accelerated degree program, self-designed majors, summer session, adult/continuing education programs, internships **Contact** Ms. Meg Halligan, Director of Admissions, St. Ambrose University, 518 West Locust Street, Davenport, IA 52803-2898. Phone: 563-333-6300 Ext. 6311 or toll-free 800-383-2627. Fax: 563-333-6297. E-mail: halliganmegf@sau.edu. Web site: http://www.sau.edu/.

SIMPSON COLLEGE
INDIANOLA, IOWA

General Independent United Methodist, 4-year, coed **Entrance** Moderately difficult **Setting** 75-acre small-town campus **Total enrollment** 2,039 **Student-faculty ratio** 16:1 **Application deadline** 8/15 (freshmen), 8/15 (transfer) **Freshmen** 88% were admitted **Housing** Yes **Expenses** Tuition $24,771; Room & Board $6988 **Undergraduates** 58% women, 26% part-time, 2% 25 or older, 0.5% Native American, 2% Hispanic American, 2% African American, 1% Asian American/Pacific Islander **The most frequently chosen baccalaureate fields are** business/marketing, education, social sciences **Academic program** Advanced placement, honors program, summer session, adult/continuing education programs, internships **Contact** Ms. Deborah Tierney, Vice President for Enrollment, Simpson College, 701 North C Street, Indianola, IA 50125. Phone: 515-961-1624 or toll-free 800-362-2454 (in-state); 800-362-2454 Ext. 1624 (out-of-state). Fax: 515-961-1870. E-mail: admiss@simpson.edu. Web site: http://www.simpson.edu/.

►**For more information, see page 491.**

UNIVERSITY OF DUBUQUE
DUBUQUE, IOWA

Contact Mr. Jesse James, Director of Admissions, University of Dubuque, 2000 University Avenue, Dubuque, IA 52001-5099. Phone: 563-589-3214 or toll-free 800-722-5583. Fax: 563-589-3690. E-mail: admissns@dbq.edu. Web site: http://www.dbq.edu/.

THE UNIVERSITY OF IOWA
IOWA CITY, IOWA

General State-supported, university, coed **Entrance** Moderately difficult **Setting** 1,900-acre small-town campus **Total enrollment** 29,117 **Student-faculty ratio** 15:1 **Application deadline** 4/1 (freshmen), 4/1 (transfer) **Freshmen** 83% were admitted **Housing** Yes **Expenses** Tuition $6544; Room & Board $7673 **Undergraduates** 53% women, 11% part-time, 9% 25 or older, 0.5% Native American, 3% Hispanic American, 2% African American, 4% Asian American/Pacific Islander **The most frequently chosen baccalaureate fields are** business/marketing, communications/journalism, social sciences **Academic program** English as a second language, advanced placement, accelerated degree program, self-designed majors, honors program, summer session, adult/continuing education programs, internships **Contact** Mr. Michael Barron, Assistant Provost for Enrollment Services and Director of Admissions, The University of Iowa, 107 Calvin Hall, Iowa City, IA 52242. Phone: 319-335-3847 or toll-free 800-553-4692. Fax: 319-335-1535. E-mail: admissions@uiowa.edu. Web site: http://www.uiowa.edu/.

UNIVERSITY OF NORTHERN IOWA
CEDAR FALLS, IOWA

General State-supported, comprehensive, coed **Entrance** Moderately difficult **Setting** 916-acre small-town campus **Total enrollment** 12,692 **Student-faculty ratio** 16:1 **Application deadline** 8/15 (freshmen), 8/15 (transfer) **Freshmen** 80% were admitted **Housing** Yes **Expenses** Tuition $7084; Room & Board $6280 **Undergraduates** 57% women, 11% part-time, 9% 25 or older, 0.3% Native American, 2% Hispanic American, 3% African American, 1% Asian American/Pacific Islander **The most frequently chosen baccalaureate fields are** business/marketing, communications/journalism, education **Academic program** English as a second language, advanced placement, accelerated degree program, self-designed majors, honors program, summer session, adult/continuing education programs, internships **Contact** Mr. Philip Patton, Interim Director of Admissions, University of Northern Iowa, 120 Gilchrist Hall, Cedar Falls, IA 50614-0018. Phone: 319-273-2281 or toll-free 800-772-2037. Fax: 319-273-2885. E-mail: admissions@uni.edu. Web site: http://www.uni.edu/.

UPPER IOWA UNIVERSITY
FAYETTE, IOWA

General Independent, comprehensive, coed **Contact** Ms. Jobyna Johnston, Interim Director of Admissions, Upper Iowa University, 605 Washington Street, Box 1857, Fayette, IA 52142-1857. Phone: 563-425-5393 or toll-free 800-553-4150 Ext. 2. Fax: 563-425-5323. E-mail: admission@uiu.edu. Web site: http://www.uiu.edu/.

VENNARD COLLEGE
UNIVERSITY PARK, IOWA

General Independent interdenominational, 4-year, coed **Entrance** Moderately difficult **Setting** 70-acre small-town campus **Total enrollment** 72 **Student-faculty ratio** 9:1 **Freshmen** 55% were admitted **Housing** Yes **Expenses** Tuition $9200; Room & Board $4600 **Undergraduates** 49% women, 7% part-time, 10% 25 or older, 1% Asian American/Pacific Islander **The most frequently chosen baccalaureate fields are** psychology, interdisciplinary studies, theology and religious vocations **Academic program** Advanced placement, self-designed majors, summer session, internships **Contact** Ms. Rikki Huggett, Administrative Assistance for Admissions, Vennard College, PO Box 29, University Park, IA 52595. Phone: 641-673-8391 or toll-free 800-686-8391. Fax: 641-673-8365. E-mail: rikki.huggett@vennard.edu. Web site: http://www.vennard.edu/.

WALDORF COLLEGE
FOREST CITY, IOWA

General Independent Lutheran, 4-year, coed **Contact** Mr. Steve Hall, Assistant Dean of Admission, Waldorf College, 106 South 6th Street, Forest City, IA 50436-1713. Phone: 641-585-8112 or toll-free 800-292-1903. Fax: 641-585-8125. E-mail: admissions@waldorf.edu. Web site: http://www.waldorf.edu/.

WARTBURG COLLEGE
WAVERLY, IOWA

General Independent Lutheran, 4-year, coed **Entrance** Moderately difficult **Setting** 118-acre small-town campus **Total enrollment** 1,810 **Student-faculty ratio** 12:1 **Application deadline** Rolling (freshmen), rolling (transfer) **Freshmen** 84% were admitted **Housing** Yes **Expenses** Tuition $24,300; Room & Board $6985 **Undergraduates** 52% women, 4% part-time, 1% 25 or older, 0.4% Native American, 2% Hispanic American, 3% African American, 2% Asian American/Pacific Islander **The most frequently chosen baccalaureate fields are** business/marketing, biological/life sciences, education **Academic program** Advanced placement, accelerated degree program, self-designed majors, honors program, summer session, internships **Contact** Mr. Todd Coleman, Assistant Vice President for Admissions, Wartburg College, 100 Wartburg Boulevard, PO Box 1003, Waverly, IA 50677-0903. Phone: 319-352-8264 or toll-free 800-772-2085. Fax: 319-352-8579. E-mail: admissions@wartburg.edu. Web site: http://www.wartburg.edu/.

WILLIAM PENN UNIVERSITY
OSKALOOSA, IOWA

General Independent, 4-year, coed, affiliated with Society of Friends **Contact** John Ottosson, Vice President for Enrollment Management, William Penn University, 201 Trueblood Avenue, Oskaloosa, IA 52577-1799. Phone: 641-673-1012 or toll-free 800-779-7366. Fax: 641-673-2113. E-mail: admissions@wmpenn.edu. Web site: http://www.wmpenn.edu/.

KANSAS

BAKER UNIVERSITY
BALDWIN CITY, KANSAS

General Independent United Methodist, comprehensive, coed **Entrance** Moderately difficult **Setting** 26-acre small-town campus **Total enrollment** 942 **Student-faculty ratio** 10:1 **Application deadline** Rolling (freshmen), rolling (transfer) **Freshmen** 63% were admitted **Housing** Yes **Expenses** Tuition $18,750; Room & Board $6150 **Undergraduates** 54% women, 4% part-time, 2% 25 or older, 0.4% Native American, 3% Hispanic American, 8% African American, 1% Asian American/Pacific Islander **The most frequently chosen baccalaureate fields are** business/marketing, biological/life sciences, education **Academic program** Advanced placement, self-designed majors, honors program, summer session, internships **Contact** Mr. Daniel McKinney, Director of Admissions, Baker University, PO Box 65, Baldwin City, KS 66006-0065. Phone: 785-594-8307 or toll-free 800-873-4282. Fax: 785-594-8372. E-mail: admissions@bakeru.edu. Web site: http://www.bakeru.edu/.

BARCLAY COLLEGE
HAVILAND, KANSAS

General Independent, 4-year, coed, affiliated with Society of Friends **Entrance** Minimally difficult **Setting** 13-acre rural campus **Total enrollment** 129 **Student-faculty ratio** 10:1 **Application deadline** 9/1 (freshmen), 9/1 (transfer) **Freshmen** 86% were admitted **Housing** Yes **Expenses** Tuition $12,300; Room & Board $6000 **Undergraduates** 49% women, 20% part-time, 26% 25 or older, 6% Hispanic American, 2% African American, 2% Asian American/Pacific Islander **The most frequently chosen baccalaureate fields are** security and protective services, business/marketing, theology and religious vocations **Academic program** Advanced placement, accelerated degree program, self-designed majors, adult/continuing education programs, internships

Barclay College *(continued)*

Contact Mr. Justin Kendall, Admissions Recruiter, Barclay College, 607 North Kingman, Haviland, KS 67059. Phone: 620-862-5252 Ext. 21 or toll-free 800-862-0226. Fax: 620-862-5242. E-mail: jkendall@barclaycollege.edu. Web site: http://www.barclaycollege.edu/.

BENEDICTINE COLLEGE
ATCHISON, KANSAS

General Independent Roman Catholic, comprehensive, coed **Entrance** Moderately difficult **Setting** 225-acre small-town campus **Total enrollment** 1,833 **Student-faculty ratio** 15:1 **Freshmen** 27% were admitted **Housing** Yes **Expenses** Tuition $17,700; Room & Board $6210 **Undergraduates** 50% women, 24% part-time, 3% 25 or older, 0.5% Native American, 6% Hispanic American, 5% African American, 1% Asian American/Pacific Islander **The most frequently chosen baccalaureate fields are** business/marketing, philosophy and religious studies, social sciences **Academic program** English as a second language, advanced placement, self-designed majors, summer session, internships **Contact** Mr. Pete A. Helgesen, Dean of Enrollment Management, Benedictine College, 1020 North 2nd Street, Atchison, KS 66002. Phone: 913-367-5340 Ext. 2476 or toll-free 800-467-5340. Fax: 913-367-5462. E-mail: bcadmiss@benedictine.edu. Web site: http://www.benedictine.edu/.

BETHANY COLLEGE
LINDSBORG, KANSAS

General Independent Lutheran, 4-year, coed **Entrance** Moderately difficult **Setting** 80-acre small-town campus **Total enrollment** 537 **Student-faculty ratio** 9:1 **Application deadline** Rolling (freshmen), rolling (transfer) **Freshmen** 61% were admitted **Housing** Yes **Expenses** Tuition $18,124; Room & Board $5650 **Undergraduates** 49% women, 5% part-time, 4% 25 or older, 1% Native American, 6% Hispanic American, 10% African American, 1% Asian American/Pacific Islander **The most frequently chosen baccalaureate fields are** business/marketing, education, visual and performing arts **Academic program** Advanced placement, accelerated degree program, self-designed majors, honors program, summer session, internships **Contact** Mrs. Tricia Hawk, Dean of Admissions and Financial Aid, Bethany College, 335 East Swensson Street, Lindsborg, KS 67456. Phone: 785-227-3311 Ext. 8344 or toll-free 800-826-2281. Fax: 785-227-8993. E-mail: admissions@bethanylb.edu. Web site: http://www.bethanylb.edu/.

BETHEL COLLEGE
NORTH NEWTON, KANSAS

General Independent, 4-year, coed, affiliated with Mennonite Church USA **Entrance** Moderately difficult **Setting** 60-acre small-town campus **Total enrollment** 541 **Student-faculty ratio** 9:1 **Application deadline** Rolling (freshmen), rolling (transfer) **Freshmen** 75% were admitted **Housing** Yes **Expenses** Tuition $17,800; Room & Board $6400 **Undergraduates** 50% women, 5% part-time, 16% 25 or older, 1% Native American, 4% Hispanic American, 6% African American, 2% Asian American/Pacific Islander **The most frequently chosen baccalaureate fields are** business/marketing, education, health professions and related sciences **Academic program** Advanced placement, summer session, internships **Contact** Mr. Allan Bartel, Vice President for Admissions, Bethel College, 300 East 27th Street, North Newton, KS 67117-0531. Phone: 316-284-5230 or toll-free 800-522-1887 Ext. 230. Fax: 316-284-5870. E-mail: admissions@bethelks.edu. Web site: http://www.bethelks.edu/.

CENTRAL CHRISTIAN COLLEGE OF KANSAS
McPHERSON, KANSAS

General Independent Free Methodist, 4-year, coed **Entrance** Minimally difficult **Setting** 16-acre small-town campus **Total enrollment** 362 **Student-faculty ratio** 16:1 **Application deadline** Rolling (freshmen), rolling (transfer) **Freshmen** 99% were admitted **Housing** Yes **Expenses** Tuition $16,000; Room & Board $5500 **Undergraduates** 48% women, 16% part-time, 10% 25 or older, 2% Native American, 5% Hispanic American, 13% African American, 1% Asian American/Pacific Islander **The most frequently chosen baccalaureate fields are** business/marketing, liberal arts/general studies, theology and religious vocations **Academic program** Advanced placement, self-designed majors, adult/continuing education programs, internships **Contact** Dr. David Ferrell, Dean of Admissions, Central Christian College of Kansas, PO Box 1403, McPherson, KS 67460. Phone: 620-241-0723 Ext. 380 or toll-free 800-835-0078 Ext. 337. Fax: 620-241-6032. E-mail: admissions@centralchristian.edu. Web site: http://www.centralchristian.edu/.

CLEVELAND CHIROPRACTIC COLLEGE–KANSAS CITY CAMPUS
OVERLAND PARK, KANSAS

General Independent, upper-level, coed **Entrance** Noncompetitive **Setting** 10-acre urban campus **Total enrollment** 502 **Student-faculty ratio** 11:1 **Application deadline** 8/28 (freshmen) **Housing**

No **Expenses** Tuition $6245 **Undergraduates** 32% women, 24% part-time, 52% 25 or older, 2% Native American, 2% African American **The most frequently chosen baccalaureate field is** biological/life sciences **Academic program** Advanced placement, accelerated degree program, summer session, internships **Contact** Ms. Melissa Denton, Director of Admissions, Cleveland Chiropractic College–Kansas City Campus, 10850 Lowell Avenue, Overland Park, KS 66210. Phone: 913-234-0750 or toll-free 800-467-2252. Fax: 913-234-0912. E-mail: kc.admissions@cleveland.edu. Web site: http://www.cleveland.edu/.

EMPORIA STATE UNIVERSITY
EMPORIA, KANSAS

General State-supported, comprehensive, coed **Entrance** Noncompetitive **Setting** 207-acre small-town campus **Total enrollment** 6,354 **Student-faculty ratio** 18:1 **Application deadline** Rolling (freshmen), rolling (transfer) **Freshmen** 87% were admitted **Housing** Yes **Expenses** Tuition $3926; Room & Board $5581 **Undergraduates** 62% women, 11% part-time, 16% 25 or older, 1% Native American, 4% Hispanic American, 4% African American, 1% Asian American/Pacific Islander **The most frequently chosen baccalaureate fields are** business/marketing, education, social sciences **Academic program** English as a second language, advanced placement, accelerated degree program, honors program, summer session, adult/continuing education programs, internships **Contact** Ms. Laura Eddy, Director of Admissions, Emporia State University, 1200 Commercial Street, Campus Box 4034, Emporia, KS 66801-5087. Phone: 620-341-5465 or toll-free 877-GOTOESU (in-state); 877-468-6378 (out-of-state). Fax: 620-341-5599. E-mail: go2esu@emporia.edu. Web site: http://www.emporia.edu/.

FORT HAYS STATE UNIVERSITY
HAYS, KANSAS

General State-supported, comprehensive, coed **Contact** Ms. Susan Cochran, Office Manager/Campus Visit Coordinator, Office of Admissions, Fort Hays State University, 600 Park Street, Hays, KS 67601-4099. Phone: 785-628-4091 or toll-free 800-628-FHSU. Fax: 800-432-0248. E-mail: tigers@fhsu.edu. Web site: http://www.fhsu.edu/.

FRIENDS UNIVERSITY
WICHITA, KANSAS

Contact Marla Sexson, Director of Admissions, Friends University, 2100 West University Street, Wichita, KS 67213. Phone: 316-295-5100 or toll-free 800-577-2233. Fax: 316-262-5027. E-mail: tmyers@friends.edu. Web site: http://www.friends.edu/.

HASKELL INDIAN NATIONS UNIVERSITY
LAWRENCE, KANSAS

Contact Ms. Patty Grant, Recruitment Officer, Haskell Indian Nations University, 155 Indian Avenue, #5031, Lawrence, KS 66046-4800. Phone: 785-749-8454 Ext. 456. Fax: 785-749-8429. Web site: http://www.haskell.edu/.

KANSAS STATE UNIVERSITY
MANHATTAN, KANSAS

General State-supported, university, coed **Entrance** Noncompetitive **Setting** 668-acre suburban campus **Total enrollment** 22,530 **Student-faculty ratio** 20:1 **Application deadline** Rolling (freshmen), rolling (transfer) **Freshmen** 95% were admitted **Housing** Yes **Expenses** Tuition $6235; Room & Board $6084 **Undergraduates** 48% women, 12% part-time, 13% 25 or older, 1% Native American, 3% Hispanic American, 3% African American, 1% Asian American/Pacific Islander **The most frequently chosen baccalaureate fields are** agriculture, business/marketing, social sciences **Academic program** English as a second language, advanced placement, accelerated degree program, honors program, summer session, adult/continuing education programs, internships **Contact** Ms. Christy Crenshaw, Associate Director of Admissions, Kansas State University, 119 Anderson Hall, Manhattan, KS 66506. Phone: 785-532-6250 or toll-free 800-432-8270. Fax: 785-532-6393. E-mail: kstate@ksu.edu. Web site: http://www.ksu.edu/.

KANSAS WESLEYAN UNIVERSITY
SALINA, KANSAS

General Independent United Methodist, comprehensive, coed **Entrance** Moderately difficult **Setting** 28-acre urban campus **Total enrollment** 864 **Student-faculty ratio** 15:1 **Application deadline** Rolling (freshmen), rolling (transfer) **Freshmen** 61% were admitted **Housing** Yes **Expenses** Tuition $18,200; Room & Board $6400 **Undergraduates** 57% women, 17% part-time, 17% 25 or older, 1% Native American, 7% Hispanic American, 7% African American, 1% Asian American/Pacific Islander **The most frequently chosen baccalaureate fields are** business/marketing, psychology, security and protective services **Academic program** English as a second language, advanced placement, self-designed majors, summer session, adult/continuing education programs, internships **Contact** Mr. Jim Allen, Director of Admissions, Kansas

Kansas Wesleyan University *(continued)*

Wesleyan University, 100 East Claflin Avenue, Salina, KS 67401-6196. Phone: 785-827-5541 Ext. 1283 or toll-free 800-874-1154 Ext. 1285. Fax: 785-827-0927. E-mail: admissions@kwu.edu. Web site: http://www.kwu.edu/.

MANHATTAN CHRISTIAN COLLEGE
MANHATTAN, KANSAS

Contact Director of Admissions, Manhattan Christian College, 1415 Anderson Avenue, Manhattan, KS 66502-4081. Phone: 785-539-3571 or toll-free 877-246-4622. Fax: 785-776-9251. E-mail: admit@mccks.edu. Web site: http://www.mccks.edu/.

McPHERSON COLLEGE
McPHERSON, KANSAS

Contact Ms. Carol L. Williams, Director of Admissions and Financial Aid, McPherson College, 1600 East Euclid, PO Box 1402, McPherson, KS 67460-1402. Phone: 620-241-0731 Ext. 1270 or toll-free 800-365-7402. Fax: 620-241-8443. E-mail: admiss@mcpherson.edu. Web site: http://www.mcpherson.edu/.

MIDAMERICA NAZARENE UNIVERSITY
OLATHE, KANSAS

General Independent, comprehensive, coed, affiliated with Church of the Nazarene **Entrance** Minimally difficult **Setting** 105-acre suburban campus **Total enrollment** 1,720 **Student-faculty ratio** 20:1 **Application deadline** 8/1 (freshmen), 8/1 (transfer) **Housing** Yes **Expenses** Tuition $18,216; Room & Board $6180 **Undergraduates** 56% women, 11% part-time, 28% 25 or older, 1% Native American, 4% Hispanic American, 7% African American, 1% Asian American/Pacific Islander **The most frequently chosen baccalaureate fields are** business/marketing, education, health professions and related sciences **Academic program** Advanced placement, accelerated degree program, summer session, adult/continuing education programs, internships **Contact** Ms. Brigit Mattix, Associate Director of Admissions, MidAmerica Nazarene University, 2030 East College Way, Olathe, KS 66062-1899. Phone: 913-791-3380 or toll-free 800-800-8887. Fax: 913-791-3481. E-mail: admissions@mnu.edu. Web site: http://www.mnu.edu/.

NEWMAN UNIVERSITY
WICHITA, KANSAS

General Independent Roman Catholic, comprehensive, coed **Entrance** Minimally difficult **Setting** 61-acre urban campus **Total enrollment** 2,166 **Student-faculty ratio** 14:1 **Application deadline** Rolling (freshmen), rolling (transfer) **Freshmen** 64% were admitted **Housing** Yes **Expenses** Tuition $18,874; Room & Board $6500 **Undergraduates** 63% women, 39% part-time, 24% 25 or older, 2% Native American, 8% Hispanic American, 6% African American, 4% Asian American/Pacific Islander **The most frequently chosen baccalaureate fields are** education, business/marketing, health professions and related sciences **Academic program** Advanced placement, accelerated degree program, summer session, adult/continuing education programs, internships **Contact** Jann Reusser, Admissions Recruitment, Newman University, 3100 McCormick Avenue, Wichita, KS 67213. Phone: 316-942-4291 Ext. 2233 or toll-free 877-NEWMANU Ext. 2144. Fax: 316-942-4483. E-mail: admissions@newmanu.edu. Web site: http://www.newmanu.edu/.

OTTAWA UNIVERSITY
OTTAWA, KANSAS

General Independent American Baptist Churches in the USA, comprehensive, coed **Contact** Ms. Fola Akande, Director of Admissions, Ottawa University, 1001 South Cedar #17, Ottawa, KS 66067-3399. Phone: 785-242-5200 Ext. 5561 or toll-free 800-755-5200 Ext. 5559. Fax: 785-229-1008. E-mail: admiss@ottawa.edu. Web site: http://www.ottawa.edu/.

PITTSBURG STATE UNIVERSITY
PITTSBURG, KANSAS

General State-supported, comprehensive, coed **Entrance** Minimally difficult **Setting** 233-acre small-town campus **Total enrollment** 7,087 **Student-faculty ratio** 18:1 **Application deadline** Rolling (freshmen), rolling (transfer) **Freshmen** 88% were admitted **Housing** Yes **Expenses** Tuition $4060; Room & Board $5088 **Undergraduates** 48% women, 9% part-time, 16% 25 or older, 2% Native American, 2% Hispanic American, 3% African American, 1% Asian American/Pacific Islander **The most frequently chosen baccalaureate fields are** business/marketing, biological/life sciences, education **Academic program** English as a second language, advanced placement, self-designed majors, honors program, summer session, adult/continuing education programs, internships **Contact** Director of Admission and Enrollment Services, Pittsburg State University, 1701 S. Broadway, Pittsburg, KS 66762. Phone: 620-235-4251 or toll-free 800-854-7488 Ext. 1. Fax: 620-235-6003. E-mail: psuadmit@pittstate.edu. Web site: http://www.pittstate.edu/.

SOUTHWESTERN COLLEGE
WINFIELD, KANSAS

General Independent United Methodist, comprehensive, coed **Entrance** Moderately difficult **Setting** 70-acre small-town campus **Total enrollment** 1,703 **Student-faculty ratio** 9:1 **Application deadline** 8/25 (freshmen), 8/25 (transfer) **Freshmen** 91% were admitted **Housing** Yes **Expenses** Tuition $17,820; Room & Board $5622 **Undergraduates** 47% women, 63% part-time, 55% 25 or older, 2% Native American, 5% Hispanic American, 10% African American, 1% Asian American/Pacific Islander **The most frequently chosen baccalaureate fields are** business/marketing, computer and information sciences, security and protective services **Academic program** Self-designed majors, honors program, adult/continuing education programs, internships **Contact** Mr. Todd Moore, Director of Admission, Southwestern College, 100 College Street, Winfield, KS 67156. Phone: 620-229-6236 or toll-free 800-846-1543. Fax: 620-229-6344. E-mail: scadmit@sckans.edu. Web site: http://www.sckans.edu/.

STERLING COLLEGE
STERLING, KANSAS

General Independent Presbyterian, 4-year, coed **Entrance** Minimally difficult **Setting** 46-acre rural campus **Total enrollment** 603 **Student-faculty ratio** 13:1 **Application deadline** 7/15 (freshmen), rolling (transfer) **Freshmen** 58% were admitted **Housing** Yes **Expenses** Tuition $15,500; Room & Board $6230 **Undergraduates** 44% women, 9% part-time, 5% 25 or older, 2% Native American, 7% Hispanic American, 10% African American, 1% Asian American/Pacific Islander **The most frequently chosen baccalaureate fields are** business/marketing, education, visual and performing arts **Academic program** Advanced placement, self-designed majors, honors program, internships **Contact** Mr. Dennis Dutton, Vice President for Enrollment Services, Sterling College, PO Box 98, Sterling, KS 67579-0098. Phone: 620-278-4364 Ext. 364 or toll-free 800-346-1017. Fax: 620-278-4416. E-mail: admissions@sterling.edu. Web site: http://www.sterling.edu/.

TABOR COLLEGE
HILLSBORO, KANSAS

General Independent Mennonite Brethren, comprehensive, coed **Entrance** Moderately difficult **Setting** 26-acre small-town campus **Total enrollment** 574 **Student-faculty ratio** 10:1 **Application deadline** 8/1 (freshmen), 8/1 (transfer) **Freshmen** 100% were admitted **Housing** Yes **Expenses** Tuition $18,710; Room & Board $6750 **Undergraduates** 50% women, 18% part-time, 4% 25 or older, 1% Native American, 4% Hispanic American, 7% African American, 1% Asian American/Pacific Islander **The most frequently chosen baccalaureate fields are** business/marketing, health professions and related sciences, theology and religious vocations **Academic program** Advanced placement, accelerated degree program, self-designed majors, honors program, adult/continuing education programs, internships **Contact** Mr. Rusty Allen, Dean of Enrollment Management, Tabor College, 400 South Jefferson, Hillsboro, KS 67063. Phone: 620-947-3121 Ext. 1727 or toll-free 800-822-6799. Fax: 620-947-6276. E-mail: rustya@tabor.edu. Web site: http://www.tabor.edu/.

UNIVERSITY OF KANSAS
LAWRENCE, KANSAS

General State-supported, university, coed **Entrance** Moderately difficult **Setting** 1,100-acre suburban campus **Total enrollment** 28,569 **Student-faculty ratio** 19:1 **Application deadline** 4/1 (freshmen), 5/1 (transfer) **Freshmen** 92% were admitted **Housing** Yes **Expenses** Tuition $7146; Room & Board $6144 **Undergraduates** 50% women, 11% part-time, 8% 25 or older, 1% Native American, 4% Hispanic American, 4% African American, 4% Asian American/Pacific Islander **The most frequently chosen baccalaureate fields are** business/marketing, health professions and related sciences, social sciences **Academic program** English as a second language, advanced placement, accelerated degree program, honors program, summer session, internships **Contact** Ms. Lisa Pinamonti Kress, Director of Admissions and Scholarships, University of Kansas, KU Visitor Center, 1502 Iowa Street, Lawrence, KS 66045-7576. Phone: 785-864-3911 or toll-free 888-686-7323. Fax: 785-864-5006. E-mail: adm@ku.edu. Web site: http://www.ku.edu.

UNIVERSITY OF PHOENIX–WICHITA CAMPUS
WICHITA, KANSAS

General Proprietary, comprehensive, coed **Contact** Ms. Evelyn Gaskin, Registrar/Executive Director, University of Phoenix–Wichita Campus, 4615 East Elwood Street, Mail Stop AA-K101, Phoenix, AZ 85040-1958. Phone: 480-557-3301 or toll-free 800-776-4867 (in-state); 800-228-7240 (out-of-state). Fax: 480-643-1020. E-mail: evelyn.gaskin@phoenix.edu. Web site: http://www.phoenix.edu/.

UNIVERSITY OF SAINT MARY
LEAVENWORTH, KANSAS

General Independent Roman Catholic, comprehensive, coed **Entrance** Moderately difficult

University of Saint Mary *(continued)*

Setting 240-acre small-town campus **Total enrollment** 882 **Student-faculty ratio** 10:1 **Application deadline** Rolling (freshmen), rolling (transfer) **Freshmen** 61% were admitted **Housing** Yes **Expenses** Tuition $17,270; Room & Board $6400 **Undergraduates** 62% women, 31% part-time, 28% 25 or older, 1% Native American, 8% Hispanic American, 12% African American, 1% Asian American/Pacific Islander **The most frequently chosen baccalaureate fields are** business/marketing, psychology, social sciences **Academic program** Advanced placement, self-designed majors, honors program, summer session, adult/continuing education programs, internships **Contact** Ms. Jessica Goffinet, Director of Admissions, University of Saint Mary, 4100 South Fourth Street, Leavenworth, KS 66048. Phone: 913-682-5151 Ext. 6118 or toll-free 800-752-7043. Fax: 913-758-6140. E-mail: admiss@stmary.edu. Web site: http://www.stmary.edu/.

WASHBURN UNIVERSITY
TOPEKA, KANSAS

General City-supported, comprehensive, coed **Entrance** Noncompetitive **Setting** 160-acre urban campus **Total enrollment** 6,901 **Student-faculty ratio** 16:1 **Application deadline** 8/1 (freshmen), 8/1 (transfer) **Freshmen** 98% were admitted **Housing** Yes **Expenses** Tuition $5636; Room & Board $5281 **Undergraduates** 61% women, 32% part-time, 32% 25 or older **The most frequently chosen baccalaureate fields are** business/marketing, health professions and related sciences, security and protective services **Academic program** English as a second language, advanced placement, self-designed majors, honors program, summer session, adult/continuing education programs, internships **Contact** Mr. Kirk R. Haskins, Director of Admission, Washburn University, 1700 SW College Avenue, Topeka, KS 66621. Phone: 785-670-1812 or toll-free 800-332-0291. Fax: 785-670-1089. E-mail: admissions@washburn.edu. Web site: http://www.washburn.edu/.

WICHITA STATE UNIVERSITY
WICHITA, KANSAS

General State-supported, university, coed **Entrance** Noncompetitive **Setting** 335-acre urban campus **Total enrollment** 14,442 **Student-faculty ratio** 18:1 **Application deadline** Rolling (freshmen), rolling (transfer) **Freshmen** 85% were admitted **Housing** Yes **Expenses** Tuition $4770; Room & Board $5580 **Undergraduates** 55% women, 34% part-time, 29% 25 or older, 1% Native American, 5% Hispanic American, 6% African American, 6% Asian American/Pacific Islander **The most frequently chosen baccalaureate fields are** business/marketing, engineering, health professions and related sciences **Academic program** English as a second language, advanced placement, accelerated degree program, self-designed majors, honors program, summer session, internships **Contact** Mr. Bobby Gandu, Director of Admissions, Wichita State University, 1845 Fairmount Street, Wichita, KS 67260-0124. Phone: 316-978-3085 or toll-free 800-362-2594. Fax: 316-978-3174. E-mail: admissions@wichita.edu. Web site: http://www.wichita.edu/.

KENTUCKY

ALICE LLOYD COLLEGE
PIPPA PASSES, KENTUCKY

General Independent, 4-year, coed **Entrance** Moderately difficult **Setting** 175-acre rural campus **Total enrollment** 621 **Student-faculty ratio** 18:1 **Application deadline** Rolling (freshmen), rolling (transfer) **Freshmen** 47% were admitted **Housing** Yes **Expenses** Tuition $0 **Undergraduates** 52% women, 5% part-time, 3% 25 or older, 0.2% Hispanic American, 1% African American, 1% Asian American/Pacific Islander **The most frequently chosen baccalaureate fields are** biological/life sciences, business/marketing, education **Academic program** Advanced placement, self-designed majors, internships **Contact** Mr. Bryan Swafford, Director of Admissions, Alice Lloyd College, 100 Purpose Road, Pippa Passes, KY 48144. Phone: 606-368-6036. Fax: 606-368-6215. E-mail: bryanswafford@alc.edu. Web site: http://www.alc.edu/.

ASBURY COLLEGE
WILMORE, KENTUCKY

General Independent nondenominational, comprehensive, coed **Entrance** Moderately difficult **Setting** 400-acre small-town campus **Total enrollment** 1,391 **Student-faculty ratio** 11:1 **Application deadline** Rolling (freshmen), rolling (transfer) **Freshmen** 63% were admitted **Housing** Yes **Expenses** Tuition $22,413; Room & Board $5414 **Undergraduates** 57% women, 7% part-time, 5% 25 or older, 0.4% Native American, 2% Hispanic American, 2% African American, 1% Asian American/Pacific Islander **The most frequently chosen baccalaureate fields are** communication technologies, English, theology and religious vocations **Academic program** English as a second language, advanced placement, summer session, adult/continuing education programs, internships **Contact** Ronald

Anderson, Director of Enrollment Management, Asbury College, 1 Macklem Drive, Wilmore, KY 40390. Phone: 859-858-3511 Ext. 2142 or toll-free 800-888-1818. Fax: 859-858-3921. E-mail: admissions@asbury.edu. Web site: http://www.asbury.edu/.

BELLARMINE UNIVERSITY

LOUISVILLE, KENTUCKY

General Independent Roman Catholic, comprehensive, coed **Entrance** Moderately difficult **Setting** 144-acre suburban campus **Total enrollment** 3,001 **Student-faculty ratio** 13:1 **Application deadline** 8/15 (freshmen), 8/15 (transfer) **Freshmen** 63% were admitted **Housing** Yes **Expenses** Tuition $28,230; Room & Board $8406 **Undergraduates** 64% women, 18% part-time, 9% 25 or older, 0.3% Native American, 2% Hispanic American, 3% African American, 2% Asian American/Pacific Islander **The most frequently chosen baccalaureate fields are** business/marketing, education, health professions and related sciences **Academic program** Advanced placement, accelerated degree program, self-designed majors, honors program, summer session, adult/continuing education programs, internships **Contact** Mr. Timothy A. Sturgeon, Dean of Admission, Bellarmine University, 2001 Newburg Road, Louisville, KY 40205-0671. Phone: 502-452-8131 or toll-free 800-274-4723 Ext. 8131. Fax: 502-452-8002. E-mail: admissions@bellarmine.edu. Web site: http://www.bellarmine.edu/.

BEREA COLLEGE

BEREA, KENTUCKY

General Independent, 4-year, coed **Entrance** Very difficult **Setting** 140-acre small-town campus **Total enrollment** 1,582 **Student-faculty ratio** 11:1 **Application deadline** 4/30 (freshmen), rolling (transfer) **Freshmen** 29% were admitted **Housing** Yes **Expenses** Tuition $790; Room & Board $5492 **Undergraduates** 60% women, 3% part-time, 5% 25 or older, 1% Native American, 2% Hispanic American, 17% African American, 2% Asian American/Pacific Islander **The most frequently chosen baccalaureate fields are** business/marketing, engineering technologies, social sciences **Academic program** Advanced placement, self-designed majors, honors program, summer session, internships **Contact** Ms. Erika Smith, Director of Admissions, Berea College, CPO 2220, Berea, KY 40404. Phone: 859-985-3500 or toll-free 800-326-5948. Fax: 859-985-3512. E-mail: admissions@berea.edu. Web site: http://www.berea.edu/.

BRESCIA UNIVERSITY

OWENSBORO, KENTUCKY

Contact Sr. Mary Austin Blank, Dean of Enrollment, Brescia University, 717 Frederica Street, Owensboro, KY 42301-3023. Phone: 270-686-4241 Ext. 241 or toll-free 877-273-7242. Fax: 270-686-4201. E-mail: admissions@brescia.edu. Web site: http://www.brescia.edu/.

CAMPBELLSVILLE UNIVERSITY

CAMPBELLSVILLE, KENTUCKY

General Independent, comprehensive, coed, affiliated with Kentucky Baptist Convention **Contact** Mr. David Walters, Vice President for Admissions and Student Services, Campbellsville University, 1 University Drive, Campbellsville, KY 42718-2799. Phone: 270-789-5220 Ext. 5007 or toll-free 800-264-6014. Fax: 270-789-5071. E-mail: admissions@campbellsville.edu. Web site: http://www.campbellsville.edu/.

CENTRE COLLEGE

DANVILLE, KENTUCKY

General Independent, 4-year, coed, affiliated with Presbyterian Church (U.S.A.) **Entrance** Very difficult **Setting** 100-acre small-town campus **Total enrollment** 1,189 **Student-faculty ratio** 11:1 **Application deadline** 2/1 (freshmen), 6/1 (transfer) **Freshmen** 61% were admitted **Housing** Yes **Expenses** Tuition $35,000 **Undergraduates** 55% women, 0.3% part-time, 0.3% Native American, 2% Hispanic American, 3% African American, 2% Asian American/Pacific Islander **The most frequently chosen baccalaureate fields are** foreign languages and literature, English, social sciences **Academic program** Advanced placement, self-designed majors, internships **Contact** Mr. Bob Nesmith, Director of Admission, Centre College, 600 West Walnut Street, Danville, KY 40422-1394. Phone: 859-238-5350 or toll-free 800-423-6236. Fax: 859-238-5373. E-mail: admission@centre.edu. Web site: http://www.centre.edu/.

CLEAR CREEK BAPTIST BIBLE COLLEGE

PINEVILLE, KENTUCKY

General Independent Southern Baptist, 4-year, coed, primarily men **Entrance** Noncompetitive **Setting** 700-acre rural campus **Total enrollment** 166 **Student-faculty ratio** 13:1 **Application deadline** 7/15 (freshmen), 7/15 (transfer) **Housing** Yes **Expenses** Tuition $5262; Room & Board $3310 **Undergraduates** 19% women, 30% part-time, 72% 25 or older **Academic program** Summer session **Contact** Mr. Billy Howell, Clear Creek Baptist Bible College, 300 Clear Creek Road, Pineville, KY 40977-9754. Phone: 606-337-

Clear Creek Baptist Bible College *(continued)*

3196 Ext. 103. Fax: 606-337-1631. E-mail: bhowell@ccbbc.edu. Web site: http://www.ccbbc.edu/.

EASTERN KENTUCKY UNIVERSITY
RICHMOND, KENTUCKY

General State-supported, comprehensive, coed **Entrance** Noncompetitive **Setting** 500-acre small-town campus **Total enrollment** 15,839 **Student-faculty ratio** 17:1 **Application deadline** 8/1 (freshmen), rolling (transfer) **Freshmen** 69% were admitted **Housing** Yes **Expenses** Tuition $5682; Room & Board $5478 **Undergraduates** 59% women, 19% part-time, 24% 25 or older, 0.3% Native American, 1% Hispanic American, 5% African American, 1% Asian American/Pacific Islander **The most frequently chosen baccalaureate fields are** health professions and related sciences, education, security and protective services **Academic program** English as a second language, advanced placement, accelerated degree program, self-designed majors, honors program, summer session, adult/continuing education programs, internships **Contact** Mr. Stephen Byrn, Director of Admissions, Eastern Kentucky University, SSB CPO 54, 521 Lancaster Avenue, Richmond, KY 40475-3102. Phone: 859-622-2106 or toll-free 800-465-9191. Fax: 859-622-8024. E-mail: admissions@eku.edu. Web site: http://www.eku.edu/.

GEORGETOWN COLLEGE
GEORGETOWN, KENTUCKY

General Independent, comprehensive, coed, affiliated with Baptist Church **Entrance** Moderately difficult **Setting** 110-acre suburban campus **Total enrollment** 1,903 **Student-faculty ratio** 12:1 **Application deadline** 8/1 (freshmen), rolling (transfer) **Freshmen** 85% were admitted **Housing** Yes **Expenses** Tuition $22,360; Room & Board $6380 **Undergraduates** 57% women, 4% part-time, 2% 25 or older, 0.1% Native American, 1% Hispanic American, 4% African American, 1% Asian American/Pacific Islander **The most frequently chosen baccalaureate fields are** business/marketing, communications/journalism, psychology **Academic program** Advanced placement, self-designed majors, honors program, summer session, internships **Contact** Mr. Johnnie Johnson, Director of Admissions, Georgetown College, 400 East College Street, Georgetown, KY 40324. Phone: 502-863-8009 or toll-free 800-788-9985. Fax: 502-868-7733. E-mail: admissions@georgetowncollege.edu. Web site: http://www.georgetowncollege.edu/.

ITT TECHNICAL INSTITUTE
LEXINGTON, KENTUCKY

General Proprietary, 4-year, coed **Application deadline** Rolling (freshmen), rolling (transfer) **Contact** Mr. George Nosko, Director of Recruitment, ITT Technical Institute, 2473 Fortune Drive, Suite 180, Lexington, KY 40509. Phone: 859-246-3300 or toll-free 800-519-8151. Web site: http://www.itt-tech.edu/.

KENTUCKY CHRISTIAN UNIVERSITY
GRAYSON, KENTUCKY

General Independent, comprehensive, coed, affiliated with Christian Churches and Churches of Christ **Entrance** Moderately difficult **Setting** 124-acre rural campus **Total enrollment** 632 **Student-faculty ratio** 12:1 **Application deadline** Rolling (freshmen), rolling (transfer) **Freshmen** 66% were admitted **Housing** Yes **Expenses** Tuition $11,850; Room & Board $4992 **Undergraduates** 51% women, 9% part-time, 9% 25 or older, 0.3% Native American, 1% Hispanic American, 6% African American, 0.3% Asian American/Pacific Islander **The most frequently chosen baccalaureate fields are** education, health professions and related sciences, theology and religious vocations **Academic program** Advanced placement, accelerated degree program, summer session, internships **Contact** Mr. Brandon Dulaney, Director of Admissions, Kentucky Christian University, 100 Academic Parkway, Grayson, KY 41143. Phone: 606-474-3281 or toll-free 800-522-3181. Fax: 606-474-3155. E-mail: bdulaney@kcu.edu. Web site: http://www.kcu.edu/.

KENTUCKY MOUNTAIN BIBLE COLLEGE
VANCLEVE, KENTUCKY

Contact Mr. Jay Wisler, Director of Recruiting, Kentucky Mountain Bible College, PO Box 10, 855 Route 41, Vancleve, KY 41385. Phone: 606-693-5000 Ext. 138 or toll-free 800-879-KMBC Ext. 130 (in-state); 800-879-KMBC Ext. 136 (out-of-state). Fax: 606-693-4884. E-mail: jnelson@kmbc.edu. Web site: http://www.kmbc.edu/.

KENTUCKY STATE UNIVERSITY
FRANKFORT, KENTUCKY

General State-related, comprehensive, coed **Entrance** Minimally difficult **Setting** 818-acre small-town campus **Total enrollment** 2,696 **Student-faculty ratio** 13:1 **Application deadline** Rolling (freshmen), rolling (transfer) **Freshmen** 37% were admitted **Housing** Yes **Expenses** Tuition $5320; Room & Board $6340 **Undergraduates** 58% women, 25% part-time,

30% 25 or older, 0.1% Native American, 0.3% Hispanic American, 60% African American, 1% Asian American/Pacific Islander **Academic program** English as a second language, advanced placement, accelerated degree program, self-designed majors, honors program, summer session, adult/continuing education programs, internships **Contact** Mr. James Burrell, Director of Admission, Kentucky State University, 400 East Main Street, Frankfort, KY 40601-9957. Phone: 502-597-6322 or toll-free 800-633-9415 (in-state); 800-325-1716 (out-of-state). Fax: 502-597-5814. E-mail: james.burrell@kysu.edu. Web site: http://www.kysu.edu/.

KENTUCKY WESLEYAN COLLEGE
OWENSBORO, KENTUCKY

General Independent Methodist, 4-year, coed **Entrance** Moderately difficult **Setting** 52-acre suburban campus **Total enrollment** 956 **Student-faculty ratio** 15:1 **Freshmen** 78% were admitted **Housing** Yes **Expenses** Tuition $14,550; Room & Board $5950 **Undergraduates** 47% women, 6% part-time, 9% 25 or older, 0.4% Native American, 1% Hispanic American, 10% African American, 0.4% Asian American/Pacific Islander **The most frequently chosen baccalaureate fields are** business/marketing, biological/life sciences, education **Academic program** Advanced placement, summer session, internships **Contact** Mr. Clayton Daniels, Dean of Admission and Financial Aid, Kentucky Wesleyan College, 3000 Frederica Street, Owensboro, KY 42301. Phone: 270-852-3120 or toll-free 800-999-0592 (in-state); 800-990-0592 (out-of-state). Fax: 270-852-3133. E-mail: admitme@kwc.edu. Web site: http://www.kwc.edu/.

LINDSEY WILSON COLLEGE
COLUMBIA, KENTUCKY

General Independent United Methodist, comprehensive, coed **Entrance** Minimally difficult **Setting** 45-acre rural campus **Total enrollment** 1,893 **Student-faculty ratio** 23:1 **Application deadline** Rolling (freshmen), rolling (transfer) **Freshmen** 79% were admitted **Housing** Yes **Expenses** Tuition $15,806; Room & Board $6540 **Undergraduates** 66% women, 9% part-time, 27% 25 or older, 0.4% Native American, 1% Hispanic American, 7% African American, 0.4% Asian American/Pacific Islander **The most frequently chosen baccalaureate fields are** business/marketing, communications/journalism, public administration and social services **Academic program** English as a second language, advanced placement, accelerated degree program, self-designed majors, summer session, adult/continuing education programs, internships **Contact** Ms. Charity Ferguson, Assistant Director of Admissions, Lindsey Wilson College, 210 Lindsey Wilson Street, Columbia, KY 42728-1298. Phone: 270-384-8100 or toll-free 800-264-0138. Fax: 270-384-8591. E-mail: poolert@lindsey.edu. Web site: http://www.lindsey.edu/.

MID-CONTINENT UNIVERSITY
MAYFIELD, KENTUCKY

General Independent Southern Baptist, 4-year, coed **Entrance** Minimally difficult **Setting** 60-acre small-town campus **Total enrollment** 1,541 **Student-faculty ratio** 16:1 **Application deadline** Rolling (freshmen), rolling (transfer) **Freshmen** 83% were admitted **Housing** Yes **Expenses** Tuition $12,050; Room & Board $6000 **Undergraduates** 61% women, 14% part-time, 78% 25 or older, 0.3% Native American, 1% Hispanic American, 13% African American, 0.2% Asian American/Pacific Islander **The most frequently chosen baccalaureate fields are** business/marketing, psychology, theology and religious vocations **Academic program** Advanced placement, accelerated degree program, self-designed majors, summer session **Contact** Ms. Debbie Smith, Acting Director of Admissions, Mid-Continent University, 99 Powell Road East, Mayfield, KY 42066-9007. Phone: 270-247-8521 Ext. 244. Fax: 270-247-3115. E-mail: admissions@midcontinent.edu. Web site: http://www.midcontinent.edu/.

MIDWAY COLLEGE
MIDWAY, KENTUCKY

General Independent, 4-year, coed, primarily women, affiliated with Christian Church (Disciples of Christ) **Entrance** Minimally difficult **Setting** 105-acre small-town campus **Total enrollment** 1,422 **Student-faculty ratio** 15:1 **Application deadline** Rolling (freshmen), rolling (transfer) **Freshmen** 79% were admitted **Housing** Yes **Expenses** Tuition $15,900; Room & Board $6400 **Undergraduates** 91% women, 27% part-time, 46% 25 or older, 0.3% Native American, 1% Hispanic American, 7% African American, 0.4% Asian American/Pacific Islander **The most frequently chosen baccalaureate fields are** business/marketing, agriculture, education **Academic program** Advanced placement, honors program, summer session, adult/continuing education programs, internships **Contact** Dr. Jim Wombles, Vice President of Admissions, Chief Enrollment Officer, Midway College, 512 East Stephens Street, Midway, KY 40347-1120. Phone: 859-846-5799 or toll-free 800-755-0031. Fax: 859-846-5823. E-mail: admissions@midway.edu. Web site: http://www.midway.edu/.

MOREHEAD STATE UNIVERSITY
MOREHEAD, KENTUCKY

General State-supported, comprehensive, coed **Entrance** Minimally difficult **Setting** 1,016-acre small-town campus **Total enrollment** 8,966 **Student-faculty ratio** 16:1 **Application deadline** Rolling (freshmen), rolling (transfer) **Freshmen** 71% were admitted **Housing** Yes **Expenses** Tuition $5280; Room & Board $5620 **Undergraduates** 61% women, 24% part-time, 16% 25 or older, 0.4% Native American, 1% Hispanic American, 3% African American, 0.3% Asian American/Pacific Islander **The most frequently chosen baccalaureate fields are** business/marketing, education, liberal arts/general studies **Academic program** Advanced placement, accelerated degree program, self-designed majors, honors program, summer session, adult/continuing education programs, internships **Contact** Mr. Jeffrey Liles, Associate Vice President for Enrollment Services, Morehead State University, 100 Admissions Center, Morehead, KY 40351. Phone: 606-783-2000 or toll-free 800-585-6781. Fax: 606-783-5038. E-mail: admissions@moreheadstate.edu. Web site: http://www.moreheadstate.edu/.

MURRAY STATE UNIVERSITY
MURRAY, KENTUCKY

General State-supported, comprehensive, coed **Entrance** Moderately difficult **Setting** 238-acre small-town campus **Total enrollment** 10,149 **Student-faculty ratio** 16:1 **Freshmen** 85% were admitted **Housing** Yes **Expenses** Tuition $5748; Room & Board $6004 **Undergraduates** 58% women, 16% part-time, 17% 25 or older, 0.4% Native American, 1% Hispanic American, 6% African American, 1% Asian American/Pacific Islander **The most frequently chosen baccalaureate fields are** business/marketing, education, health professions and related sciences **Academic program** English as a second language, advanced placement, accelerated degree program, honors program, summer session, adult/continuing education programs, internships **Contact** Ms. Stacy Bell, Undergraduate Admissions Specialist, Murray State University, 113 Sparks Hall, Murray, KY 42701-0009. Phone: 270-809-6831 or toll-free 800-272-4678. Fax: 270-809-3050. E-mail: admissions@murraystate.edu. Web site: http://www.murraystate.edu/.

NORTHERN KENTUCKY UNIVERSITY
HIGHLAND HEIGHTS, KENTUCKY

General State-supported, comprehensive, coed **Contact** Ms. Melissa Gorbandt, Director of Admissions and Outreach, Northern Kentucky University, Administrative Center 400, Highland Heights, KY 41099-7010. Phone: 859-572-5220 Ext. 5744 or toll-free 800-637-9948. Fax: 859-572-6665. E-mail: admitnku@nku.edu. Web site: http://www.nku.edu/.

PIKEVILLE COLLEGE
PIKEVILLE, KENTUCKY

General Independent, comprehensive, coed, affiliated with Presbyterian Church (U.S.A.) **Entrance** Noncompetitive **Setting** 25-acre small-town campus **Total enrollment** 1,100 **Student-faculty ratio** 11:1 **Application deadline** 8/15 (freshmen), 8/15 (transfer) **Freshmen** 100% were admitted **Housing** Yes **Expenses** Tuition $13,750; Room & Board $5250 **Undergraduates** 52% women, 9% part-time, 14% 25 or older, 1% Hispanic American, 9% African American, 1% Asian American/Pacific Islander **The most frequently chosen baccalaureate fields are** business/marketing, education, psychology **Academic program** Advanced placement, self-designed majors, summer session, internships **Contact** Ms. Melinda Lynch, Dean of Enrollment Management, Pikeville College, 147 Sycamore Street, Pikeville, KY 41501. Phone: 606-218-5251 or toll-free 866-232-7700. Fax: 606-218-5255. E-mail: wewantyou@pc.edu. Web site: http://www.pc.edu/.

SOUTHERN BAPTIST THEOLOGICAL SEMINARY
LOUISVILLE, KENTUCKY

General Independent Southern Baptist, comprehensive, coed **Total enrollment** 3,190 **Application deadline** 7/15 (freshmen), 7/15 (transfer) **Freshmen** 71% were admitted **Housing** Yes **Expenses** Tuition $5736; Room & Board $3500 **Undergraduates** 29% women, 38% part-time, 63% 25 or older, 0.5% Native American, 2% Hispanic American, 3% African American, 6% Asian American/Pacific Islander **Contact** Dr. Daniel DeWitt, Southern Baptist Theological Seminary, 2825 Lexington Road, Louisville, KY 40280-0004. Phone: 502-897-4011 Ext. 4617. Web site: http://www.sbts.edu/.

SPALDING UNIVERSITY
LOUISVILLE, KENTUCKY

Contact Mr. Chris Hart, Assistant Director of Admissions, Spalding University, 851 South Fourth Street, Louisville, KY 40203. Phone: 502-585-9911 Ext. 2111 or toll-free 800-896-8941 Ext. 2111. Fax: 502-992-2418. E-mail: admissionsW@spalding.edu. Web site: http://www.spalding.edu/.

SULLIVAN UNIVERSITY
LOUISVILLE, KENTUCKY

General Proprietary, comprehensive, coed **Entrance** Minimally difficult **Setting** 10-acre suburban campus **Total enrollment** 4,538 **Student-faculty ratio** 20:1 **Application deadline** Rolling (freshmen), rolling (transfer) **Housing** Yes **Expenses** Tuition $14,940; Room only $4320 **Undergraduates** 53% women, 15% part-time, 68% 25 or older, 1% Native American, 2% Hispanic American, 18% African American, 2% Asian American/Pacific Islander **Academic program** Advanced placement, accelerated degree program, summer session, adult/continuing education programs **Contact** Ms. Terri Thomas, Director of Admissions, Sullivan University, 3101 Bardstown Road, Louisville, KY 40205. Phone: 502-456-6505 Ext. 370 or toll-free 800-844-1354. Fax: 502-456-0040. E-mail: admissions@sullivan.edu. Web site: http://www.sullivan.edu/.

THOMAS MORE COLLEGE
CRESTVIEW HILLS, KENTUCKY

General Independent Roman Catholic, comprehensive, coed **Entrance** Moderately difficult **Setting** 100-acre suburban campus **Total enrollment** 1,645 **Student-faculty ratio** 14:1 **Application deadline** 8/15 (freshmen), 8/15 (transfer) **Freshmen** 83% were admitted **Housing** Yes **Expenses** Tuition $21,220; Room & Board $6250 **Undergraduates** 52% women, 24% part-time, 32% 25 or older, 1% Native American, 1% Hispanic American, 4% African American, 1% Asian American/Pacific Islander **The most frequently chosen baccalaureate fields are** biological/life sciences, business/marketing, education **Academic program** Advanced placement, accelerated degree program, self-designed majors, honors program, summer session, adult/continuing education programs, internships **Contact** Mr. Billy Sarge, Associate Director of Admissions, Thomas More College, 333 Thomas More Parkway, Crestview Hills, KY 41017-3495. Phone: 859-344-3332 or toll-free 800-825-4557. Fax: 859-344-3444. E-mail: admissions@thomasmore.edu. Web site: http://www.thomasmore.edu/.

TRANSYLVANIA UNIVERSITY
LEXINGTON, KENTUCKY

General Independent, 4-year, coed, affiliated with Christian Church (Disciples of Christ) **Entrance** Very difficult **Setting** 40-acre urban campus **Total enrollment** 1,153 **Student-faculty ratio** 13:1 **Application deadline** 2/1 (freshmen), rolling (transfer) **Freshmen** 80% were admitted **Housing** Yes **Expenses** Tuition $23,810; Room & Board $7450 **Undergraduates** 1% 25 or older, 0.3% Native American, 1% Hispanic American, 3% African American, 1% Asian American/Pacific Islander **The most frequently chosen baccalaureate fields are** business/marketing, biological/life sciences, social sciences **Academic program** Advanced placement, self-designed majors, summer session, internships **Contact** Mr. Bradley Goan, Director of Admissions, Transylvania University, 300 North Broadway, Lexington, KY 40508-1797. Phone: 859-233-8242 or toll-free 800-872-6798. Fax: 859-281-3642. E-mail: admissions@transy.edu. Web site: http://www.transy.edu/.

UNION COLLEGE
BARBOURVILLE, KENTUCKY

General Independent United Methodist, comprehensive, coed **Entrance** Moderately difficult **Setting** 110-acre small-town campus **Total enrollment** 1,420 **Student-faculty ratio** 10:1 **Application deadline** 8/1 (freshmen), 8/31 (transfer) **Freshmen** 70% were admitted **Housing** Yes **Expenses** Tuition $16,020; Room & Board $5000 **Undergraduates** 47% women, 8% part-time, 21% 25 or older, 1% Native American, 2% Hispanic American, 9% African American, 0.1% Asian American/Pacific Islander **The most frequently chosen baccalaureate fields are** business/marketing, education, history **Academic program** Advanced placement, accelerated degree program, self-designed majors, summer session, internships **Contact** Mr. Jerry Jackson, Dean for Enrollment Management, Union College, 310 College Street, Barbourville, KY 40906. Phone: 606-546-1222 or toll-free 800-489-8646. Fax: 606-546-1667. E-mail: enroll@unionky.edu. Web site: http://www.unionky.edu/.

UNIVERSITY OF KENTUCKY
LEXINGTON, KENTUCKY

General State-supported, university, coed **Entrance** Moderately difficult **Setting** 685-acre urban campus **Total enrollment** 25,856 **Student-faculty ratio** 17:1 **Application deadline** 2/15 (freshmen), 8/1 (transfer) **Freshmen** 77% were admitted **Housing** Yes **Expenses** Tuition $7096; Room & Board $7973 **Undergraduates** 51% women, 11% part-time, 10% 25 or older, 0.2% Native American, 1% Hispanic American, 6% African American, 2% Asian American/Pacific Islander **The most frequently chosen baccalaureate fields are** business/marketing, communications/journalism, social sciences **Academic program** English as a second language, advanced placement, accelerated degree program, self-designed majors, honors program, summer session, adult/continuing education programs, internships **Contact** Ms. Michelle Nordin, Associate Director of Admissions, University of

University of Kentucky *(continued)*

Kentucky, 100 W.D. Funkhouser Building, Lexington, KY 40506-0054. Phone: 859-257-2000 or toll-free 800-432-0967. E-mail: admissio@uky.edu. Web site: http://www.uky.edu/.

UNIVERSITY OF LOUISVILLE
LOUISVILLE, KENTUCKY

General State-supported, university, coed **Entrance** Moderately difficult **Setting** 169-acre urban campus **Total enrollment** 20,592 **Student-faculty ratio** 18:1 **Application deadline** Rolling (freshmen) **Freshmen** 70% were admitted **Housing** Yes **Expenses** Tuition $7564; Room & Board $6058 **Undergraduates** 52% women, 22% part-time, 20% 25 or older, 0.3% Native American, 2% Hispanic American, 12% African American, 3% Asian American/Pacific Islander **The most frequently chosen baccalaureate fields are** business/marketing, psychology, social sciences **Academic program** English as a second language, advanced placement, accelerated degree program, self-designed majors, honors program, summer session, adult/continuing education programs, internships **Contact** Ms. Jenny L. Sawyer, Executive Director for Admissions, University of Louisville, 2211 South Brook, Louisville, KY 40292. Phone: 502-852-6531 or toll-free 502-852-6531 (in-state); 800-334-8635 (out-of-state). Fax: 502-852-4776. E-mail: admitme@gwise.louisville.edu. Web site: http://www.louisville.edu/.

UNIVERSITY OF THE CUMBERLANDS
WILLIAMSBURG, KENTUCKY

General Independent Kentucky Baptist, comprehensive, coed **Entrance** Moderately difficult **Setting** 60-acre rural campus **Total enrollment** 1,884 **Student-faculty ratio** 14:1 **Application deadline** Rolling (freshmen) **Freshmen** 83% were admitted **Housing** Yes **Expenses** Tuition $13,658; Room & Board $6626 **Undergraduates** 53% women, 12% part-time, 12% 25 or older, 0.3% Native American, 2% Hispanic American, 6% African American, 1% Asian American/Pacific Islander **The most frequently chosen baccalaureate fields are** business/marketing, biological/life sciences, education **Academic program** English as a second language, advanced placement, accelerated degree program, self-designed majors, honors program, summer session, adult/continuing education programs, internships **Contact** Mrs. Erica Harris, Director of Admissions, University of the Cumberlands, 6178 College Station Drive, Williamsburg, KY 40769. Phone: 606-539-4201 or toll-free 800-343-1609. Fax: 606-539-4303. E-mail: admiss@ucumberlands.edu. Web site: http://www.ucumberlands.edu/.

WESTERN KENTUCKY UNIVERSITY
BOWLING GREEN, KENTUCKY

General State-supported, comprehensive, coed **Entrance** Moderately difficult **Setting** 223-acre suburban campus **Total enrollment** 19,258 **Student-faculty ratio** 18:1 **Application deadline** 8/1 (freshmen), 8/1 (transfer) **Freshmen** 95% were admitted **Housing** Yes **Expenses** Tuition $6416; Room & Board $5704 **Undergraduates** 58% women, 20% part-time, 19% 25 or older, 0.3% Native American, 1% Hispanic American, 10% African American, 1% Asian American/Pacific Islander **The most frequently chosen baccalaureate fields are** business/marketing, communications/journalism, education **Academic program** English as a second language, advanced placement, accelerated degree program, self-designed majors, honors program, summer session, adult/continuing education programs, internships **Contact** Mr. Scott S. Gordon, Director of Admissions and Academic Services, Western Kentucky University, Potter Hall 117, 1906 College Heights Blvd., Bowling Green, KY 42101-3576. Phone: 270-745-2551 or toll-free 800-495-8463. Fax: 270-745-6133. E-mail: admission@wku.edu. Web site: http://www.wku.edu/.

LOUISIANA

CENTENARY COLLEGE OF LOUISIANA
SHREVEPORT, LOUISIANA

General Independent United Methodist, comprehensive, coed **Entrance** Moderately difficult **Setting** 65-acre suburban campus **Total enrollment** 938 **Student-faculty ratio** 10:1 **Application deadline** 8/1 (freshmen), 8/15 (transfer) **Freshmen** 62% were admitted **Housing** Yes **Expenses** Tuition $22,000; Room & Board $7330 **Undergraduates** 58% women, 2% part-time, 2% 25 or older, 0.2% Native American, 4% Hispanic American, 7% African American, 3% Asian American/Pacific Islander **The most frequently chosen baccalaureate fields are** biological/life sciences, business/marketing, visual and performing arts **Academic program** Advanced placement, self-designed majors, honors program, summer session, adult/continuing education programs, internships **Contact** Mr. Tim Crowley, Director of Admissions, Centenary College of Louisiana, Office of Admissions, Centenary College of Louisiana, 2911 Centenary Boulevard, PO Box 41188, Shreveport, LA 71134-1188. Phone: 318-869-5104 or toll-free 800-234-4448. Fax: 318-869-5005. E-mail: dcolson@centenary.edu. Web site: http://www.centenary.edu/.

DILLARD UNIVERSITY
NEW ORLEANS, LOUISIANA

General Independent interdenominational, 4-year, coed **Entrance** Moderately difficult **Setting** 55-acre urban campus **Total enrollment** 956 **Student-faculty ratio** 9:1 **Application deadline** 7/1 (freshmen), 7/1 (transfer) **Freshmen** 46% were admitted **Housing** Yes **Expenses** Tuition $12,240; Room & Board $5364 **Undergraduates** 69% women, 8% part-time, 6% 25 or older, 0.4% Hispanic American, 97% African American, 1% Asian American/Pacific Islander **The most frequently chosen baccalaureate fields are** business/marketing, biological/life sciences, health professions and related sciences **Academic program** Advanced placement, honors program, summer session, adult/continuing education programs, internships **Contact** Ms. Meredith Reed, Director of Admissions, Dillard University, 2601 Gentilly Boulevard, New Orleans, LA 70122-3097. Phone: 504-816-4670 or toll-free 800-716-8353 (in-state); 800-216-6637 (out-of-state). Fax: 504-816-4895. E-mail: mreed@dillard.edu. Web site: http://www.dillard.edu/.

GRAMBLING STATE UNIVERSITY
GRAMBLING, LOUISIANA

General State-supported, university, coed **Entrance** Noncompetitive **Setting** 380-acre small-town campus **Total enrollment** 5,161 **Student-faculty ratio** 17:1 **Application deadline** 6/30 (freshmen), 6/30 (transfer) **Freshmen** 30% were admitted **Housing** Yes **Expenses** Tuition $3622; Room & Board $5072 **Undergraduates** 55% women, 8% part-time, 13% 25 or older, 0.2% Native American, 0.4% Hispanic American, 88% African American, 1% Asian American/Pacific Islander **The most frequently chosen baccalaureate fields are** business/marketing, health professions and related sciences, security and protective services **Academic program** Advanced placement, honors program, summer session, adult/continuing education programs, internships **Contact** Ms. Annie Moss, Acting Director of Admissions, Grambling State University, PO Box 607, Grambling, LA 71245. Phone: 318-274-6183. E-mail: mossa@gram.edu. Web site: http://www.gram.edu/.

LOUISIANA COLLEGE
PINEVILLE, LOUISIANA

General Independent Southern Baptist, 4-year, coed **Entrance** Moderately difficult **Setting** 81-acre small-town campus **Total enrollment** 1,056 **Student-faculty ratio** 13:1 **Application deadline** 8/15 (freshmen) **Freshmen** 78% were admitted **Housing** Yes **Expenses** Tuition $11,490; Room & Board $4256 **Undergraduates** 52% women, 19% part-time, 16% 25 or older, 1% Native American, 2% Hispanic American, 13% African American, 1% Asian American/Pacific Islander **The most frequently chosen baccalaureate fields are** education, biological/life sciences, health professions and related sciences **Academic program** Advanced placement, accelerated degree program, self-designed majors, honors program, summer session, adult/continuing education programs, internships **Contact** Mr. Byron McGee, Director of Enrollment Management, Louisiana College, LC Box 566, Pineville, LA 71359. Phone: 318-487-7439 or toll-free 800-487-1906. Fax: 318-487-7550. E-mail: admissions@lacollege.edu. Web site: http://www.lacollege.edu/.

LOUISIANA STATE UNIVERSITY AND AGRICULTURAL AND MECHANICAL COLLEGE
BATON ROUGE, LOUISIANA

General State-supported, university, coed **Entrance** Moderately difficult **Setting** 2,000-acre urban campus **Total enrollment** 28,628 **Student-faculty ratio** 20:1 **Application deadline** 4/15 (freshmen), 4/15 (transfer) **Freshmen** 73% were admitted **Housing** Yes **Expenses** Tuition $4543; Room & Board $6852 **Undergraduates** 51% women, 7% part-time, 6% 25 or older, 0.4% Native American, 3% Hispanic American, 9% African American, 3% Asian American/Pacific Islander **The most frequently chosen baccalaureate fields are** business/marketing, biological/life sciences, education **Academic program** English as a second language, advanced placement, accelerated degree program, self-designed majors, honors program, summer session, adult/continuing education programs, internships **Contact** Ms. Mary G. Parker, Executive Director of Undergraduate Admissions and Student Aid, Louisiana State University and Agricultural and Mechanical College, Baton Rouge, LA 70803. Phone: 225-578-1175. Fax: 225-578-4433. E-mail: admissions@lsu.edu. Web site: http://www.lsu.edu/.

LOUISIANA STATE UNIVERSITY HEALTH SCIENCES CENTER
NEW ORLEANS, LOUISIANA

General State-supported, university, coed **Setting** 80-acre urban campus **Total enrollment** 2,233 **Application deadline** 3/1 (transfer) **Housing** Yes **Expenses** Tuition $4577; Room & Board $4470 **Undergraduates** 85% women, 49% part-time, 29% 25 or older **The most frequently chosen baccalaureate field is** health professions and related sciences **Academic program** Advanced placement, accelerated degree program, summer session, internships **Contact** Mr. W. Bryant Faust

Louisiana State University Health Sciences Center *(continued)*

IV, Acting Registrar, Louisiana State University Health Sciences Center, 433 Bolivar Street, New Orleans, LA 70112-2223. Phone: 504-568-4829. Fax: 504-568-5545. Web site: http://www.lsuhsc.edu/no/.

LOUISIANA STATE UNIVERSITY IN SHREVEPORT

SHREVEPORT, LOUISIANA

General State-supported, comprehensive, coed **Entrance** Moderately difficult **Setting** 200-acre urban campus **Total enrollment** 3,960 **Student-faculty ratio** 18:1 **Application deadline** 8/1 (freshmen) **Freshmen** 76% were admitted **Housing** Yes **Expenses** Tuition $3521 **Undergraduates** 64% women, 33% part-time, 34% 25 or older, 1% Native American, 2% Hispanic American, 22% African American, 2% Asian American/Pacific Islander **The most frequently chosen baccalaureate fields are** business/marketing, education, liberal arts/general studies **Academic program** Advanced placement, accelerated degree program, self-designed majors, honors program, summer session, adult/continuing education programs, internships **Contact** Mr. Mickey Diez, Dean of Enrollment Services and Registrar, Louisiana State University in Shreveport, 1 University Place, Shreveport, LA 71115-2399. Phone: 318-797-5063 or toll-free 800-229-5957. Fax: 318-797-5286. E-mail: admissions@pilot.lsus.edu. Web site: http://www.lsus.edu/.

LOUISIANA TECH UNIVERSITY

RUSTON, LOUISIANA

General State-supported, university, coed **Entrance** Moderately difficult **Setting** 247-acre small-town campus **Total enrollment** 10,564 **Student-faculty ratio** 18:1 **Application deadline** 7/31 (freshmen), rolling (transfer) **Freshmen** 66% were admitted **Housing** Yes **Expenses** Tuition $4548; Room & Board $4740 **Undergraduates** 48% women, 20% part-time, 19% 25 or older, 0.4% Native American, 2% Hispanic American, 16% African American, 1% Asian American/Pacific Islander **The most frequently chosen baccalaureate fields are** business/marketing, engineering, liberal arts/general studies **Academic program** English as a second language, advanced placement, honors program, summer session, adult/continuing education programs, internships **Contact** Mrs. Jan B. Albritton, Director of Admissions, Louisiana Tech University, PO Box 3168, Ruston, LA 71272. Phone: 318-257-3036 or toll-free 800-528-3241. Fax: 318-257-2499. E-mail: bulldog@latech.edu. Web site: http://www.latech.edu/.

LOYOLA UNIVERSITY NEW ORLEANS

NEW ORLEANS, LOUISIANA

General Independent Roman Catholic (Jesuit), comprehensive, coed **Entrance** Moderately difficult **Setting** 26-acre urban campus **Total enrollment** 4,360 **Student-faculty ratio** 11:1 **Application deadline** 1/15 (freshmen), rolling (transfer) **Freshmen** 61% were admitted **Housing** Yes **Expenses** Tuition $28,044; Room & Board $9394 **Undergraduates** 59% women, 11% part-time, 4% 25 or older, 1% Native American, 12% Hispanic American, 12% African American, 4% Asian American/Pacific Islander **The most frequently chosen baccalaureate fields are** business/marketing, communications/journalism, visual and performing arts **Academic program** Advanced placement, accelerated degree program, self-designed majors, honors program, summer session, adult/continuing education programs, internships **Contact** Ms. Deborah C. Stieffel, Dean of Admission and Enrollment Management, Loyola University New Orleans, 6363 Saint Charles Avenue, New Orleans, LA 70118-6195. Phone: 504-865-3240 or toll-free 800-4-LOYOLA. Fax: 504-865-3383. E-mail: admit@loyno.edu. Web site: http://www.loyno.edu/.

►**For more information, see page 472.**

McNEESE STATE UNIVERSITY

LAKE CHARLES, LOUISIANA

General State-supported, comprehensive, coed **Entrance** Moderately difficult **Setting** 766-acre suburban campus **Total enrollment** 8,095 **Student-faculty ratio** 20:1 **Application deadline** Rolling (freshmen), rolling (transfer) **Freshmen** 78% were admitted **Housing** Yes **Expenses** Tuition $3262; Room & Board $3460 **Undergraduates** 61% women, 18% part-time, 20% 25 or older, 1% Native American, 1% Hispanic American, 18% African American, 1% Asian American/Pacific Islander **The most frequently chosen baccalaureate fields are** business/marketing, health professions and related sciences, liberal arts/general studies **Academic program** English as a second language, advanced placement, accelerated degree program, honors program, summer session, adult/continuing education programs, internships **Contact** Ms. Kara Smith, Director of Admissions, McNeese State University, Box 91740, Lake Charles, LA 70609. Phone: 337-475-5146 or toll-free 800-622-3352. Fax: 337-475-5151. E-mail: info@mcneese.edu. Web site: http://www.mcneese.edu/.

NEW ORLEANS BAPTIST THEOLOGICAL SEMINARY
NEW ORLEANS, LOUISIANA

Contact Dr. Paul E. Gregoire Jr., Registrar/ Director of Admissions, New Orleans Baptist Theological Seminary, 3939 Gentilly Boulevard, New Orleans, LA 70126-4858. Phone: 504-282-4455 Ext. 3337 or toll-free 800-662-8701. Web site: http://www.nobts.edu/.

NICHOLLS STATE UNIVERSITY
THIBODAUX, LOUISIANA

General State-supported, comprehensive, coed **Entrance** Noncompetitive **Setting** 210-acre small-town campus **Total enrollment** 6,865 **Student-faculty ratio** 20:1 **Application deadline** Rolling (freshmen), rolling (transfer) **Freshmen** 84% were admitted **Housing** Yes **Expenses** Tuition $3623; Room & Board $4556 **Undergraduates** 62% women, 21% part-time, 3% 25 or older, 2% Native American, 2% Hispanic American, 18% African American, 1% Asian American/Pacific Islander **The most frequently chosen baccalaureate fields are** business/marketing, education, health professions and related sciences **Academic program** English as a second language, advanced placement, accelerated degree program, honors program, summer session, adult/continuing education programs, internships **Contact** Mrs. Becky L. Durocher, Director of Admissions, Nicholls State University, PO Box 2004-NSU, Thibodaux, LA 70310. Phone: 985-448-4507 or toll-free 877-NICHOLLS. Fax: 985-448-4929. E-mail: nicholls@nicholls.edu. Web site: http://www.nicholls.edu.

NORTHWESTERN STATE UNIVERSITY OF LOUISIANA
NATCHITOCHES, LOUISIANA

General State-supported, comprehensive, coed **Entrance** Moderately difficult **Setting** 916-acre small-town campus **Total enrollment** 9,037 **Student-faculty ratio** 17:1 **Application deadline** 7/6 (freshmen), 7/6 (transfer) **Freshmen** 82% were admitted **Housing** Yes **Expenses** Tuition $3528; Room & Board $5850 **Undergraduates** 68% women, 29% part-time, 31% 25 or older, 2% Native American, 2% Hispanic American, 29% African American, 1% Asian American/ Pacific Islander **The most frequently chosen baccalaureate fields are** business/marketing, health professions and related sciences, liberal arts/general studies **Academic program** Advanced placement, honors program, summer session, adult/continuing education programs, internships **Contact** Ms. Jana Lucky, Director of University Recruiting, Northwestern State University of Louisiana, South Hall, Natchitoches, LA 71497. Phone: 318-357-4078 or toll-free 800-327-1903. Fax: 318-357-5567. E-mail: recruiting@nsula.edu. Web site: http://www.nsula.edu/.

OUR LADY OF HOLY CROSS COLLEGE
NEW ORLEANS, LOUISIANA

Contact Ms. Kristine Hatfield Kopecky, Vice President for Enrollment Services, Our Lady of Holy Cross College, 4123 Woodland Drive, New Orleans, LA 70131-7399. Phone: 504-394-7744 Ext. 185 or toll-free 800-259-7744 Ext. 175. Fax: 504-391-2421. E-mail: admissions@olhcc.edu. Web site: http://www.olhcc.edu/.

OUR LADY OF THE LAKE COLLEGE
BATON ROUGE, LOUISIANA

General Independent Roman Catholic, 4-year, coed, primarily women **Entrance** Minimally difficult **Setting** 5-acre suburban campus **Total enrollment** 2,103 **Student-faculty ratio** 11:1 **Application deadline** Rolling (freshmen), rolling (transfer) **Freshmen** 78% were admitted **Housing** No **Expenses** Tuition $6984 **Undergraduates** 83% women, 67% part-time, 49% 25 or older, 1% Native American, 2% Hispanic American, 22% African American, 3% Asian American/ Pacific Islander **The most frequently chosen baccalaureate fields are** health professions and related sciences, biological/life sciences, public administration and social services **Academic program** Advanced placement, summer session, adult/continuing education programs **Contact** Director of Admissions, Our Lady of the Lake College, 7434 Perkins Road, Baton Rouge, LA 70808. Phone: 225-768-1718 or toll-free 877-242-3509. E-mail: admission@ololcollege.edu. Web site: http://www.ololcollege.edu/.

SAINT JOSEPH SEMINARY COLLEGE
SAINT BENEDICT, LOUISIANA

General Independent Roman Catholic, 4-year, men only **Entrance** Minimally difficult **Setting** 1,300-acre rural campus **Total enrollment** 171 **Student-faculty ratio** 3:1 **Application deadline** Rolling (freshmen), rolling (transfer) **Housing** Yes **Expenses** Tuition $12,600; Room & Board $5392 **Undergraduates** 55% part-time, 25% 25 or older, 1% Native American, 14% Hispanic American, 4% African American, 6% Asian American/ Pacific Islander **The most frequently chosen baccalaureate field is** philosophy and religious studies **Academic program** English as a second language, advanced placement, adult/continuing education programs **Contact** George J. Binder Jr., Registrar, Saint Joseph Seminary College, 75376 River Road, St. Benedict, LA 70457.

Saint Joseph Seminary College *(continued)*

Phone: 985-867-2225. Fax: 985-327-1085. E-mail: gbinder@sjasc.edu. Web site: http://www.sjasc.edu/.

SOUTHEASTERN LOUISIANA UNIVERSITY

HAMMOND, LOUISIANA

General State-supported, comprehensive, coed **Entrance** Moderately difficult **Setting** 375-acre small-town campus **Total enrollment** 14,757 **Student-faculty ratio** 25:1 **Application deadline** 8/1 (freshmen), 8/1 (transfer) **Freshmen** 88% were admitted **Housing** Yes **Expenses** Tuition $3561; Room & Board $5990 **Undergraduates** 62% women, 17% part-time, 17% 25 or older, 0.4% Native American, 2% Hispanic American, 18% African American, 1% Asian American/Pacific Islander **The most frequently chosen baccalaureate fields are** business/marketing, health professions and related sciences, liberal arts/general studies **Academic program** English as a second language, advanced placement, honors program, summer session, adult/continuing education programs, internships **Contact** Director of Admissions, Southeastern Louisiana University, SLU 10752, Hammond, LA 70402. Phone: 985-549-2066 or toll-free 800-222-7358. Fax: 985-549-5632. E-mail: admissions@selu.edu. Web site: http://www.selu.edu/.

SOUTHERN UNIVERSITY AND AGRICULTURAL AND MECHANICAL COLLEGE

BATON ROUGE, LOUISIANA

General State-supported, university, coed **Entrance** Moderately difficult **Setting** 964-acre suburban campus **Total enrollment** 8,179 **Student-faculty ratio** 16:1 **Application deadline** 7/1 (freshmen), 7/1 (transfer) **Freshmen** 56% were admitted **Housing** Yes **Expenses** Tuition $3706; Room & Board $6504 **Undergraduates** 61% women, 11% part-time, 80% 25 or older, 0.03% Native American, 0.1% Hispanic American, 95% African American, 0.4% Asian American/Pacific Islander **The most frequently chosen baccalaureate fields are** business/marketing, health professions and related sciences, security and protective services **Academic program** Advanced placement, honors program, summer session, adult/continuing education programs, internships **Contact** Ms. Tracie Abraham, Director of Admissions, Southern University and Agricultural and Mechanical College, PO Box 9901, Baton Rouge, LA 70813. Phone: 225-771-2430 or toll-free 800-256-1531. Fax: 225-771-2500. E-mail: tracie_abraham@subr.edu. Web site: http://www.subr.edu/.

SOUTHERN UNIVERSITY AT NEW ORLEANS

NEW ORLEANS, LOUISIANA

General State-supported, comprehensive, coed **Entrance** Noncompetitive **Setting** 17-acre campus **Total enrollment** 2,648 **Student-faculty ratio** 19:1 **Application deadline** 7/1 (freshmen), 7/1 (transfer) **Freshmen** 79% were admitted **Housing** No **Expenses** Tuition $2970 **Undergraduates** 73% women, 23% part-time, 46% 25 or older, 0.1% Native American, 1% Hispanic American, 96% African American, 0.5% Asian American/Pacific Islander **The most frequently chosen baccalaureate fields are** business/marketing, liberal arts/general studies, security and protective services **Academic program** Adult/continuing education programs **Contact** Ms. Rene Gill Pratt, Acting Director of Admissions, Recruitment, and Retention, Southern University at New Orleans, 6400 Press Drive, New Orleans, LA 70126-1009. Phone: 504-286-5033. Fax: 504-284-5481. E-mail: rgpratt@suno.edu. Web site: http://www.suno.edu/.

TULANE UNIVERSITY

NEW ORLEANS, LOUISIANA

General Independent, university, coed **Entrance** Very difficult **Setting** 110-acre urban campus **Total enrollment** 10,519 **Student-faculty ratio** 9:1 **Application deadline** 1/15 (freshmen), 6/1 (transfer) **Freshmen** 44% were admitted **Housing** Yes **Expenses** Tuition $36,610; Room & Board $8940 **Undergraduates** 54% women, 21% part-time, 13% 25 or older, 2% Native American, 4% Hispanic American, 9% African American, 5% Asian American/Pacific Islander **The most frequently chosen baccalaureate fields are** business/marketing, engineering, social sciences **Academic program** English as a second language, advanced placement, accelerated degree program, self-designed majors, honors program, summer session, adult/continuing education programs, internships **Contact** Mr. Earl Retif, Vice President for Enrollment Management and University Registrar, Tulane University, Office of Admissions, 210 Gibson Hall, New Orleans, LA 70118. Phone: 504-865-5731 or toll-free 800-873-9283. Fax: 504-862-8715. E-mail: undergrad.admission@tulane.edu. Web site: http://www.tulane.edu/.

►**For more information, see page 494.**

UNIVERSITY OF LOUISIANA AT LAFAYETTE

LAFAYETTE, LOUISIANA

General State-supported, university, coed **Entrance** Moderately difficult **Setting** 1,375-

acre urban campus **Total enrollment** 16,345 **Student-faculty ratio** 23:1 **Application deadline** Rolling (freshmen), rolling (transfer) **Freshmen** 70% were admitted **Housing** Yes **Expenses** Tuition $3402; Room & Board $3820 **Undergraduates** 58% women, 16% part-time, 17% 25 or older, 0.5% Native American, 2% Hispanic American, 18% African American, 2% Asian American/Pacific Islander **The most frequently chosen baccalaureate fields are** engineering, communications/journalism, visual and performing arts **Academic program** Advanced placement, accelerated degree program, self-designed majors, honors program, summer session, adult/continuing education programs, internships **Contact** Mr. Leroy Broussard Jr., Admissions Director, University of Louisiana at Lafayette, PO Drawer 41210, Lafayette, LA 70504. Phone: 337-482-5912 or toll-free 800-752-6553. Fax: 337-482-1317. E-mail: admissions@louisiana.edu. Web site: http://www.louisiana.edu/.

UNIVERSITY OF LOUISIANA AT MONROE

MONROE, LOUISIANA

General State-supported, university, coed **Entrance** Noncompetitive **Setting** 238-acre urban campus **Total enrollment** 8,549 **Student-faculty ratio** 17:1 **Application deadline** Rolling (freshmen), rolling (transfer) **Freshmen** 84% were admitted **Housing** Yes **Expenses** Tuition $3607; Room & Board $3750 **Undergraduates** 63% women, 20% part-time, 23% 25 or older, 0.3% Native American, 1% Hispanic American, 26% African American, 2% Asian American/Pacific Islander **The most frequently chosen baccalaureate fields are** business/marketing, health professions and related sciences, liberal arts/general studies **Academic program** English as a second language, advanced placement, honors program, summer session, internships **Contact** Ms. Susan Duggins, Director, Recruitment and Admissions, University of Louisiana at Monroe, Sandel Hall, Monroe, LA 71209. Phone: 318-342-5272 or toll-free 800-372-5272 (in-state); 800-372-5127 (out-of-state). Fax: 318-342-1915. E-mail: admissions@ulm.edu. Web site: http://www.ulm.edu/.

UNIVERSITY OF NEW ORLEANS

NEW ORLEANS, LOUISIANA

General State-supported, university, coed **Entrance** Moderately difficult **Setting** 345-acre urban campus **Total enrollment** 11,363 **Student-faculty ratio** 18:1 **Application deadline** Rolling (freshmen), 7/1 (transfer) **Freshmen** 81% were admitted **Housing** Yes **Expenses** Tuition $3984; Room & Board $5240 **Undergraduates** 53% women, 25% part-time, 27% 25 or older, 1% Native American, 7% Hispanic American, 20% African American, 6% Asian American/Pacific Islander **The most frequently chosen baccalaureate fields are** business/marketing, communications/journalism, psychology **Academic program** English as a second language, advanced placement, self-designed majors, honors program, summer session, adult/continuing education programs, internships **Contact** Mr. Andy Benoit, Director of Admissions, University of New Orleans, Lake Front, New Orleans, LA 70148. Phone: 504-280-7013 or toll-free 800-256-5866. Fax: 504-280-5522. E-mail: admissions@uno.edu. Web site: http://www.uno.edu/.

UNIVERSITY OF PHOENIX–LOUISIANA CAMPUS

METAIRIE, LOUISIANA

Contact Ms. Evelyn Gaskin, Registrar/Executive Director, University of Phoenix–Louisiana Campus, 4615 East Elwood Street, Mail Stop AA-K101, Phoenix, AZ 85040-1958. Phone: 480-557-3301 or toll-free 800-776-4867 (in-state); 800-228-7240 (out-of-state). Fax: 480-643-1020. E-mail: evelyn.gaskin@phoenix.edu. Web site: http://www.phoenix.edu/.

XAVIER UNIVERSITY OF LOUISIANA

NEW ORLEANS, LOUISIANA

General Independent Roman Catholic, comprehensive, coed **Entrance** Moderately difficult **Setting** 23-acre urban campus **Total enrollment** 3,088 **Student-faculty ratio** 15:1 **Application deadline** 7/1 (freshmen), 6/1 (transfer) **Freshmen** 59% were admitted **Housing** Yes **Expenses** Tuition $14,700; Room & Board $6975 **Undergraduates** 72% women, 4% part-time, 6% 25 or older, 0.1% Native American, 1% Hispanic American, 75% African American, 7% Asian American/Pacific Islander **The most frequently chosen baccalaureate fields are** biological/life sciences, physical sciences, psychology **Academic program** Advanced placement, accelerated degree program, honors program, summer session, adult/continuing education programs, internships **Contact** Mr. Winston Brown, Dean of Admissions, Xavier University of Louisiana, 7325 Palmetto Street, New Orleans, LA 70125. Phone: 504-520-7388 or toll-free 877-XAVIERU. Fax: 504-520-7941. E-mail: apply@xula.edu. Web site: http://www.xula.edu/.

MAINE

BATES COLLEGE

LEWISTON, MAINE

General Independent, 4-year, coed **Entrance** Most difficult **Setting** 109-acre small-town

Bates College *(continued)*

campus **Total enrollment** 1,660 **Student-faculty ratio** 10:1 **Application deadline** 1/1 (freshmen), 3/1 (transfer) **Freshmen** 30% were admitted **Housing** Yes **Expenses** Tuition $46,800 **Undergraduates** 52% women, 0.1% 25 or older, 0.5% Native American, 2% Hispanic American, 3% African American, 6% Asian American/Pacific Islander **The most frequently chosen baccalaureate fields are** biological/life sciences, English, social sciences **Academic program** Advanced placement, accelerated degree program, self-designed majors, honors program, internships **Contact** Mr. Wylie Mitchell, Dean of Admissions, Bates College, 23 Campus Avenue, Lewiston, ME 04240-6028. Phone: 207-786-6000. Fax: 207-786-6025. E-mail: admissions@bates.edu. Web site: http://www.bates.edu/.

BOWDOIN COLLEGE
BRUNSWICK, MAINE

General Independent, 4-year, coed **Entrance** Most difficult **Setting** 205-acre small-town campus **Total enrollment** 1,716 **Student-faculty ratio** 10:1 **Application deadline** 1/1 (freshmen), 3/1 (transfer) **Freshmen** 19% were admitted **Housing** Yes **Expenses** Tuition $36,370; Room & Board $9890 **Undergraduates** 52% women, 0.4% part-time, 1% 25 or older, 1% Native American, 7% Hispanic American, 6% African American, 13% Asian American/Pacific Islander **The most frequently chosen baccalaureate fields are** foreign languages and literature, social sciences, visual and performing arts **Academic program** Advanced placement, accelerated degree program, self-designed majors **Contact** Peter T. Wiley, Associate Dean of Admissions, Bowdoin College, 5000 College Station, Brunswick, ME 04011-8411. Phone: 207-725-3190. Fax: 207-725-3101. E-mail: admissions@bowdoin.edu. Web site: http://www.bowdoin.edu/.

COLBY COLLEGE
WATERVILLE, MAINE

General Independent, 4-year, coed **Entrance** Most difficult **Setting** 714-acre small-town campus **Total enrollment** 1,867 **Student-faculty ratio** 10:1 **Application deadline** 1/1 (freshmen), 3/1 (transfer) **Freshmen** 32% were admitted **Housing** Yes **Expenses** Tuition $46,100 **Undergraduates** 55% women, 0.5% Native American, 3% Hispanic American, 2% African American, 8% Asian American/Pacific Islander **The most frequently chosen baccalaureate fields are** English, area and ethnic studies, social sciences **Academic program** Advanced placement, self-designed majors, honors program, internships **Contact** Mr. Steve Thomas, Director of Admissions, Colby College, Mayflower Hill, Waterville, ME 04901-8840. Phone: 207-859-4802 or toll-free 800-723-3032. Fax: 207-859-4828. E-mail: admissions@colby.edu. Web site: http://www.colby.edu/.

COLLEGE OF THE ATLANTIC
BAR HARBOR, MAINE

General Independent, comprehensive, coed **Entrance** Very difficult **Setting** 35-acre small-town campus **Total enrollment** 349 **Student-faculty ratio** 11:1 **Application deadline** 2/15 (freshmen), 4/1 (transfer) **Freshmen** 77% were admitted **Housing** Yes **Expenses** Tuition $29,970; Room & Board $8190 **Undergraduates** 64% women, 5% part-time, 3% 25 or older, 1% Hispanic American, 0.3% African American, 1% Asian American/Pacific Islander **The most frequently chosen baccalaureate field is** liberal arts/general studies **Academic program** Advanced placement, accelerated degree program, self-designed majors, internships **Contact** Ms. Sarah Baker, Director of Admission, College of the Atlantic, 105 Eden Street, Bar Harbor, ME 04609-1198. Phone: 207-288-5015 Ext. 233 or toll-free 800-528-0025. Fax: 207-288-4126. E-mail: inquiry@coa.edu. Web site: http://www.coa.edu/.

HUSSON COLLEGE
BANGOR, MAINE

General Independent, comprehensive, coed **Entrance** Moderately difficult **Setting** 170-acre suburban campus **Total enrollment** 2,350 **Student-faculty ratio** 19:1 **Application deadline** 9/1 (freshmen), 9/1 (transfer) **Freshmen** 91% were admitted **Housing** Yes **Expenses** Tuition $12,250; Room & Board $6500 **Undergraduates** 59% women, 19% part-time, 13% 25 or older, 1% Native American, 1% Hispanic American, 4% African American, 2% Asian American/Pacific Islander **The most frequently chosen baccalaureate fields are** business/marketing, health professions and related sciences, security and protective services **Academic program** English as a second language, advanced placement, self-designed majors, summer session, adult/continuing education programs, internships **Contact** Mrs. Jane Goodwin, Director of Admissions, Husson College, One College Circle, Bangor, ME 04401-2999. Phone: 207-941-7100 or toll-free 800-4-HUSSON. Fax: 207-941-7935. E-mail: admit@husson.edu. Web site: http://www.husson.edu/.

MAINE COLLEGE OF ART
PORTLAND, MAINE

General Independent, comprehensive, coed **Entrance** Moderately difficult **Setting** urban campus **Total enrollment** 377 **Student-faculty ratio** 9:1 **Application deadline** Rolling (freshmen), rolling (transfer) **Freshmen** 82% were admitted **Housing** Yes **Expenses** Tuition $27,740; Room & Board $9400 **Undergraduates** 69% women, 6% part-time, 10% 25 or older, 1% Native American, 1% Hispanic American, 1% African American, 1% Asian American/Pacific Islander **The most frequently chosen baccalaureate field is** visual and performing arts **Academic program** Advanced placement, self-designed majors, adult/continuing education programs, internships **Contact** Ms. Blaise MacCarrone, Admissions Coordinator, Maine College of Art, 97 Spring Street, Portland, ME 04101-3987. Phone: 207-879-5742 Ext. 721 or toll-free 800-639-4808. Fax: 207-871-1349. E-mail: admissions@meca.edu. Web site: http://www.meca.edu/.

MAINE MARITIME ACADEMY

CASTINE, MAINE

General State-supported, comprehensive, coed, primarily men **Entrance** Moderately difficult **Setting** 35-acre small-town campus **Total enrollment** 860 **Student-faculty ratio** 12:1 **Application deadline** 7/1 (freshmen), 7/1 (transfer) **Freshmen** 65% were admitted **Housing** Yes **Expenses** Tuition $8805; Room & Board $7400 **Undergraduates** 16% women, 2% part-time, 18% 25 or older, 1% Native American, 1% Hispanic American, 0.5% African American, 0.3% Asian American/Pacific Islander **The most frequently chosen baccalaureate fields are** engineering, engineering technologies, transportation and materials moving **Academic program** Advanced placement, self-designed majors, adult/continuing education programs, internships **Contact** Mr. Jeffery Wright, Director of Admissions, Maine Maritime Academy, Castine, ME 04420. Phone: 207-326-2215 or toll-free 800-464-6565 (in-state); 800-227-8465 (out-of-state). Fax: 207-326-2515. E-mail: admissions@mma.edu. Web site: http://www.mainemaritime.edu/.

NEW ENGLAND SCHOOL OF COMMUNICATIONS

BANGOR, MAINE

General Independent, 4-year, coed, primarily men **Entrance** Minimally difficult **Setting** 200-acre small-town campus **Total enrollment** 393 **Student-faculty ratio** 15:1 **Application deadline** Rolling (freshmen), rolling (transfer) **Freshmen** 66% were admitted **Housing** Yes **Expenses** Tuition $10,680; Room & Board $6725 **Undergraduates** 24% women, 5% part-time, 5% 25 or older, 1% Native American, 3% Hispanic American, 2% African American, 1% Asian American/Pacific Islander **The most frequently chosen baccalaureate field is** communication technologies **Academic program** English as a second language, advanced placement, self-designed majors, summer session, adult/continuing education programs, internships **Contact** Ms. Louise Grant, Director of Admissions, New England School of Communications, 1 College Circle, Bangor, ME 04401. Phone: 207-941-7176 Ext. 1093 or toll-free 888-877-1876. Fax: 207-947-3987. E-mail: info@nescom.edu. Web site: http://www.nescom.edu/.

SAINT JOSEPH'S COLLEGE OF MAINE

STANDISH, MAINE

General Independent, comprehensive, coed, affiliated with Roman Catholic Church **Contact** Mr. Vincent J. Kloskowski, Dean of Admission, Saint Joseph's College of Maine, 278 Whites Bridge Road, Standish, ME 04084-5263. Phone: 207-893-7746 or toll-free 800-338-7057. Fax: 207-893-7862. E-mail: admission@sjcme.edu. Web site: http://www.sjcme.edu/.

THOMAS COLLEGE

WATERVILLE, MAINE

General Independent, comprehensive, coed **Entrance** Minimally difficult **Setting** 70-acre small-town campus **Total enrollment** 975 **Student-faculty ratio** 18:1 **Application deadline** Rolling (freshmen), rolling (transfer) **Freshmen** 81% were admitted **Housing** Yes **Expenses** Tuition $18,710; Room & Board $7780 **Undergraduates** 49% women, 17% part-time, 14% 25 or older, 0.3% Native American, 1% Hispanic American, 2% African American, 1% Asian American/Pacific Islander **The most frequently chosen baccalaureate fields are** business/marketing, computer and information sciences, security and protective services **Academic program** Advanced placement, summer session, adult/continuing education programs, internships **Contact** Mr. James Love, Dean of Admissions, Thomas College, 180 West River Road, Waterville, ME 04901. Phone: 207-859-1101 or toll-free 800-339-7001. Fax: 207-859-1114. E-mail: admiss@thomas.edu. Web site: http://www.thomas.edu/.

UNITY COLLEGE

UNITY, MAINE

General Independent, 4-year, coed **Contact** Mr. Gary Zane, Dean of Students, Unity College, 90 Quaker Hill Rd., Unity, MO 04988. Phone: 207-948-3131 Ext. 275. Fax: 207-948-6277. E-mail: gzane@unity.edu. Web site: http://www.unity.edu/.

UNIVERSITY OF MAINE
ORONO, MAINE

General State-supported, university, coed **Entrance** Moderately difficult **Setting** 3,300-acre small-town campus **Total enrollment** 11,912 **Student-faculty ratio** 16:1 **Application deadline** Rolling (freshmen), rolling (transfer) **Freshmen** 77% were admitted **Housing** Yes **Expenses** Tuition $8330; Room & Board $7484 **Undergraduates** 51% women, 18% part-time, 11% 25 or older, 2% Native American, 1% Hispanic American, 1% African American, 1% Asian American/Pacific Islander **The most frequently chosen baccalaureate fields are** business/marketing, education, engineering **Academic program** English as a second language, advanced placement, accelerated degree program, self-designed majors, honors program, summer session, adult/continuing education programs, internships **Contact** Ms. Sharon Oliver, Director of Admissions, University of Maine, 5713 Chadbourne Hall, Orono, ME 04469-5713. Phone: 207-581-1561 or toll-free 877-486-2364. Fax: 207-581-1213. E-mail: um-admit@maine.edu. Web site: http://www.umaine.edu/.

THE UNIVERSITY OF MAINE AT AUGUSTA
AUGUSTA, MAINE

General State-supported, 4-year, coed **Entrance** Noncompetitive **Setting** 159-acre small-town campus **Total enrollment** 5,101 **Student-faculty ratio** 18:1 **Application deadline** 8/31 (freshmen), rolling (transfer) **Freshmen** 57% were admitted **Housing** No **Expenses** Tuition $5985 **Undergraduates** 74% women, 70% part-time, 63% 25 or older, 3% Native American, 1% Hispanic American, 1% African American, 0.5% Asian American/Pacific Islander **The most frequently chosen baccalaureate fields are** business/marketing, health professions and related sciences, library science **Academic program** Advanced placement, self-designed majors, honors program, summer session, adult/continuing education programs, internships **Contact** Jonathan Henry, Director of Admissions and Advising, The University of Maine at Augusta, 46 University Drive, Robinson Hall, Augusta, ME 04330. Phone: 207-621-3465 or toll-free 877-862-1234 Ext. 3185. Fax: 207-621-3333. E-mail: umaadm@maine.edu. Web site: http://www.uma.maine.edu/.

UNIVERSITY OF MAINE AT FARMINGTON
FARMINGTON, MAINE

General State-supported, 4-year, coed **Entrance** Moderately difficult **Setting** 50-acre small-town campus **Total enrollment** 2,265 **Student-faculty ratio** 14:1 **Application deadline** Rolling (freshmen) **Freshmen** 71% were admitted **Housing** Yes **Expenses** Tuition $7343; Room & Board $6722 **Undergraduates** 67% women, 10% part-time, 12% 25 or older, 1% Native American, 1% Hispanic American, 1% African American, 1% Asian American/Pacific Islander **The most frequently chosen baccalaureate fields are** education, English, interdisciplinary studies **Academic program** Advanced placement, accelerated degree program, self-designed majors, honors program, summer session, internships **Contact** Mr. James G. Collins, Associate Director of Admissions, University of Maine at Farmington, 246 Main Street, Farmington, ME 04938-1994. Phone: 207-778-7087. Fax: 207-778-8182. E-mail: umfadmit@maine.edu. Web site: http://www.umf.maine.edu/.

UNIVERSITY OF MAINE AT FORT KENT
FORT KENT, MAINE

General State-supported, 4-year, coed **Entrance** Moderately difficult **Setting** 52-acre rural campus **Total enrollment** 1,269 **Student-faculty ratio** 17:1 **Application deadline** Rolling (freshmen), rolling (transfer) **Freshmen** 81% were admitted **Housing** Yes **Expenses** Tuition $5753; Room & Board $6620 **Undergraduates** 67% women, 42% part-time, 36% 25 or older, 1% Native American, 1% Hispanic American, 1% African American, 0.3% Asian American/Pacific Islander **The most frequently chosen baccalaureate fields are** education, biological/life sciences, health professions and related sciences **Academic program** English as a second language, advanced placement, accelerated degree program, self-designed majors, honors program, summer session, internships **Contact** Mrs. Jill B. Cairns, Acting Director of Admissions, University of Maine at Fort Kent, 23 University Drive, Fort Kent, ME 04743-1292. Phone: 207-834-7600 or toll-free 888-TRY-UMFK. Fax: 207-834-7609. E-mail: umfkadm@maine.maine.edu. Web site: http://www.umfk.maine.edu/.

UNIVERSITY OF MAINE AT MACHIAS
MACHIAS, MAINE

General State-supported, 4-year, coed **Entrance** Moderately difficult **Setting** 42-acre rural campus **Total enrollment** 1,093 **Student-faculty ratio** 16:1 **Application deadline** 8/15 (freshmen), rolling (transfer) **Freshmen** 92% were admitted **Housing** Yes **Expenses** Tuition $5100 **Undergraduates** 72% women, 60% part-time, 24% 25 or older, 4% Native American, 2% Hispanic American, 1% African American, 1% Asian American/Pacific Islander **The most frequently chosen baccalaureate fields are** business/marketing, education, interdisciplinary studies

Academic program Advanced placement, self-designed majors, honors program, summer session, internships **Contact** Mr. Stewart Bennett, Director of Admissions, University of Maine at Machias, 9 O'Brien Avenue, Machias, ME 04654. Phone: 207-255-1318 or toll-free 888-GOTOUMM (in-state); 888-468-6866 (out-of-state). Fax: 207-255-1363. E-mail: ummadmissions@maine.edu. Web site: http://www.umm.maine.edu/.

UNIVERSITY OF MAINE AT PRESQUE ISLE
PRESQUE ISLE, MAINE

General State-supported, 4-year, coed **Contact** Ms. Erin V. Benson, Director of University Relations and Student Enrollment Services, University of Maine at Presque Isle, 181 Main Street, Presque Isle, ME 04769. Phone: 207-768-9453. Fax: 207-768-9777. E-mail: adventure@umpi.maine.edu. Web site: http://www.umpi.maine.edu/.

UNIVERSITY OF NEW ENGLAND
BIDDEFORD, MAINE

General Independent, comprehensive, coed **Entrance** Moderately difficult **Setting** 410-acre small-town campus **Total enrollment** 3,792 **Student-faculty ratio** 9:1 **Application deadline** 2/15 (freshmen), rolling (transfer) **Freshmen** 76% were admitted **Housing** Yes **Expenses** Tuition $25,330; Room & Board $9860 **Undergraduates** 73% women, 12% part-time, 12% 25 or older, 0.3% Native American, 1% Hispanic American, 1% African American, 1% Asian American/Pacific Islander **The most frequently chosen baccalaureate fields are** biological/life sciences, health professions and related sciences, psychology **Academic program** Advanced placement, accelerated degree program, summer session, internships **Contact** Mr. Robert J. Pecchia, Associate Dean of Admissions, University of New England, Hills Beach Road, Biddeford, ME 04005-9526. Phone: 207-283-0170 Ext. 2297 or toll-free 800-477-4UNE. Fax: 207-602-5900. E-mail: admissions@une.edu. Web site: http://www.une.edu/.

UNIVERSITY OF SOUTHERN MAINE
PORTLAND, MAINE

General State-supported, comprehensive, coed **Entrance** Moderately difficult **Setting** 144-acre suburban campus **Total enrollment** 10,453 **Student-faculty ratio** 13:1 **Application deadline** 2/15 (freshmen), 2/15 (transfer) **Freshmen** 80% were admitted **Housing** Yes **Expenses** Tuition $6866; Room & Board $8038 **Undergraduates** 58% women, 42% part-time, 1% Native American, 1% Hispanic American, 2% African American, 2% Asian American/Pacific Islander **The most frequently chosen baccalaureate fields are** business/marketing, health professions and related sciences, social sciences **Academic program** English as a second language, advanced placement, accelerated degree program, self-designed majors, honors program, summer session, adult/continuing education programs, internships **Contact** Mr. Jonathan Barker, Associate Director, University of Southern Maine, 37 College Avenue, Gorham, ME 04038. Phone: 207-780-5670 or toll-free 800-800-4USM Ext. 5670. Fax: 207-780-5640. E-mail: usmadm@usm.maine.edu. Web site: http://www.usm.maine.edu/.

MARYLAND

BALTIMORE HEBREW UNIVERSITY
BALTIMORE, MARYLAND

Contact Ms. Essie Keyser, Director of Admissions, Baltimore Hebrew University, 5800 Park Heights Avenue, Baltimore, MD 21215-3996. Phone: 410-578-6967 or toll-free 888-248-7420. Fax: 410-578-6940. E-mail: bhu@bhu.edu. Web site: http://www.bhu.edu/.

BOWIE STATE UNIVERSITY
BOWIE, MARYLAND

General State-supported, comprehensive, coed **Contact** Don Kiah, Director of Admissions, Bowie State University, Administration Building, 1st Floor, Bowie, MD 20715-9465. Phone: 301-860-3427 or toll-free 877-772-6943. Fax: 301-860-3438. E-mail: sholt@bowiestate.edu. Web site: http://www.bowiestate.edu/.

►**For more information, see page 443.**

CAPITOL COLLEGE
LAUREL, MARYLAND

Contact Mr. Darnell Edwards, Director of Admissions, Capitol College, 11301 Springfield Road, Laurel, MD 20708-9759. Phone: 301-953-3200 Ext. 3032 or toll-free 800-950-1992. E-mail: admissions@capitol-college.edu. Web site: http://www.capitol-college.edu/.

COLLEGE OF NOTRE DAME OF MARYLAND
BALTIMORE, MARYLAND

Contact Dr. Jennifer Blair, Vice President for Enrollment Management, College of Notre Dame

College of Notre Dame of Maryland *(continued)*

of Maryland, 4701 North Charles Street, Baltimore, MD 21210-2476. Phone: 410-532-5330 or toll-free 800-435-0200 (in-state); 800-435-0300 (out-of-state). Fax: 410-532-6287. E-mail: admiss@ndm.edu. Web site: http://www.ndm.edu/.

COLUMBIA UNION COLLEGE
TAKOMA PARK, MARYLAND

General Independent Seventh-day Adventist, comprehensive, coed **Entrance** Moderately difficult **Setting** 19-acre suburban campus **Total enrollment** 1,069 **Student-faculty ratio** 12:1 **Application deadline** 8/1 (freshmen), 8/1 (transfer) **Housing** Yes **Expenses** Tuition $19,375; Room & Board $6559 **Undergraduates** 62% women, 29% part-time **The most frequently chosen baccalaureate fields are** business/marketing, health professions and related sciences, psychology **Academic program** English as a second language, advanced placement, accelerated degree program, self-designed majors, honors program, summer session, adult/continuing education programs, internships **Contact** Elaine Oliver, Associate Vice President, Enrollment Services, Columbia Union College, 7600 Flower Avenue, Takoma Park, MD 20912. Phone: 301-891-4502 or toll-free 800-835-4212. Fax: 301-971-4230. E-mail: enroll@cuc.edu. Web site: http://www.cuc.edu/.

COPPIN STATE UNIVERSITY
BALTIMORE, MARYLAND

Contact Ms. Michelle Gross, Director of Admissions, Coppin State University, 2500 West North Avenue, Baltimore, MD 21216-3698. Phone: 410-951-3600 or toll-free 800-635-3674. Fax: 410-523-7351. E-mail: mgross@coppin.edu. Web site: http://www.coppin.edu/.

DeVRY UNIVERSITY
BETHESDA, MARYLAND

General Proprietary, comprehensive, coed **Entrance** Minimally difficult **Total enrollment** 99 **Student-faculty ratio** 26:1 **Application deadline** Rolling (freshmen), rolling (transfer) **Housing** No **Expenses** Tuition $14,560 **Undergraduates** 40% women, 71% part-time, 67% 25 or older, 27% Hispanic American, 49% African American **The most frequently chosen baccalaureate field is** business/marketing **Academic program** Advanced placement, accelerated degree program, summer session, adult/continuing education programs **Contact** Admissions Office, DeVry University, 4550 Montgomery Avenue. Suite 100 North, Bethesda, MD 20814-3304. Web site: http://www.devry.edu/.

FROSTBURG STATE UNIVERSITY
FROSTBURG, MARYLAND

General State-supported, comprehensive, coed **Entrance** Moderately difficult **Setting** 260-acre small-town campus **Total enrollment** 4,993 **Student-faculty ratio** 17:1 **Application deadline** Rolling (freshmen), rolling (transfer) **Freshmen** 63% were admitted **Housing** Yes **Expenses** Tuition $6614; Room & Board $6746 **Undergraduates** 49% women, 6% part-time, 6% 25 or older, 0.4% Native American, 2% Hispanic American, 20% African American, 2% Asian American/Pacific Islander **The most frequently chosen baccalaureate fields are** business/marketing, education, liberal arts/general studies **Academic program** Advanced placement, honors program, summer session, adult/continuing education programs, internships **Contact** Ms. Trish Gregory, Director of Admissions, Frostburg State University, 101 Braddock Road, Pullen Hall, Frostburg, MD 21532-1099. Phone: 301-687-4201. Fax: 301-687-7074. E-mail: fsuadmissions@frostburg.edu. Web site: http://www.frostburg.edu/.

GEORGE MEANY CENTER FOR LABOR STUDIES–THE NATIONAL LABOR COLLEGE
SILVER SPRING, MARYLAND

Contact Carrie Spruill, Acting Chief Financial Aid Officer/Student Services, George Meany Center for Labor Studies–The National Labor College, 10000 New Hampshire Avenue, Silver Spring, MD 20903. Phone: 301-431-5404 or toll-free 800-GMC-4CDP. E-mail: cspruill@georgemeany.org. Web site: http://www.georgemeany.org/.

GOUCHER COLLEGE
BALTIMORE, MARYLAND

General Independent, comprehensive, coed **Entrance** Moderately difficult **Setting** 287-acre suburban campus **Total enrollment** 2,362 **Student-faculty ratio** 9:1 **Application deadline** 2/1 (freshmen), 5/1 (transfer) **Freshmen** 66% were admitted **Housing** Yes **Expenses** Tuition $31,082; Room & Board $9840 **Undergraduates** 67% women, 2% part-time, 1% 25 or older, 0.4% Native American, 4% Hispanic American, 5% African American, 3% Asian American/Pacific Islander **The most frequently chosen baccalaureate fields are** psychology, social sciences, visual and performing arts **Academic program**

Advanced placement, self-designed majors, adult/continuing education programs, internships **Contact** Mr. Carlton Surbeck III, Director of Admissions, Goucher College, 1021 Dulaney Valley Road, Baltimore, MD 21204-2794. Phone: 410-337-6100 or toll-free 800-468-2437. Fax: 410-337-6354. E-mail: admissions@goucher.edu. Web site: http://www.goucher.edu/.

GRIGGS UNIVERSITY
SILVER SPRING, MARYLAND

General Independent Seventh-day Adventist, 4-year, coed **Contact** Ms. Marilyn Riley, Enrollment Officer, Griggs University, PO Box 4437, Silver Spring, MD 20914-4437. Phone: 301-680-6579 or toll-free 800-782-4769. Fax: 301-680-6577. E-mail: 74617.74@compuserve.com. Web site: http://www.griggs.edu/.

HOOD COLLEGE
FREDERICK, MARYLAND

General Independent, comprehensive, coed **Entrance** Moderately difficult **Setting** 50-acre suburban campus **Total enrollment** 2,522 **Student-faculty ratio** 13:1 **Application deadline** 2/15 (freshmen), 8/10 (transfer) **Freshmen** 71% were admitted **Housing** Yes **Expenses** Tuition $25,076; Room & Board $8542 **Undergraduates** 71% women, 12% part-time, 14% 25 or older, 0.3% Native American, 3% Hispanic American, 9% African American, 3% Asian American/Pacific Islander **The most frequently chosen baccalaureate fields are** business/marketing, biological/life sciences, psychology **Academic program** Advanced placement, accelerated degree program, self-designed majors, honors program, summer session, adult/continuing education programs, internships **Contact** Mr. David Adams, Director of Admissions, Hood College, 401 Rosemont Avenue, Frederick, MD 21701. Phone: 301-696-3400 or toll-free 800-922-1599. Fax: 301-696-3819. E-mail: admissions@hood.edu. Web site: http://www.hood.edu/.

THE JOHNS HOPKINS UNIVERSITY
BALTIMORE, MARYLAND

General Independent, university, coed **Entrance** Most difficult **Setting** 140-acre urban campus **Total enrollment** 6,257 **Application deadline** 1/1 (freshmen), 3/15 (transfer) **Freshmen** 24% were admitted **Housing** Yes **Expenses** Tuition $35,900; Room & Board $11,092 **Undergraduates** 47% women, 1% part-time, 1% 25 or older, 1% Native American, 7% Hispanic American, 6% African American, 25% Asian American/Pacific Islander **The most frequently chosen baccalaureate fields are** engineering, health professions and related sciences, social sciences **Academic program** Advanced placement, accelerated degree program, self-designed majors, honors program, summer session, adult/continuing education programs, internships **Contact** Dr. John Latting, Dean of Undergraduate Admissions, The Johns Hopkins University, Mason Hall, 3400 North Charles Street, Baltimore, MD 21218-2699. Phone: 410-516-8341. Fax: 410-516-6025. E-mail: gotojhu@jhu.edu. Web site: http://www.jhu.edu/.

LOYOLA COLLEGE IN MARYLAND
BALTIMORE, MARYLAND

General Independent Roman Catholic (Jesuit), comprehensive, coed **Entrance** Moderately difficult **Setting** 89-acre urban campus **Total enrollment** 6,028 **Student-faculty ratio** 12:1 **Application deadline** 2/1 (freshmen), 7/15 (transfer) **Freshmen** 60% were admitted **Housing** Yes **Undergraduates** 58% women, 1% part-time, 1% 25 or older, 0.1% Native American, 3% Hispanic American, 5% African American, 3% Asian American/Pacific Islander **The most frequently chosen baccalaureate fields are** business/marketing, communications/journalism, social sciences **Academic program** Advanced placement, accelerated degree program, honors program, summer session, internships **Contact** Ms. Elena Hicks, Director of Undergraduate Admissions, Loyola College in Maryland, 4501 North Charles Street, Baltimore, MD 21210-2699. Phone: 410-617-2323 or toll-free 800-221-9107 Ext. 2252. Fax: 410-617-2176. Web site: http://www.loyola.edu/.

MAPLE SPRINGS BAPTIST BIBLE COLLEGE AND SEMINARY
CAPITOL HEIGHTS, MARYLAND

Contact Ms. Mazie Murphy, Assistant Director of Admissions and Records, Maple Springs Baptist Bible College and Seminary, 4130 Belt Road, Capitol Heights, MD 20743. Phone: 301-736-3631. Fax: 301-735-6507. E-mail: percy.coker@msbbcs.edu. Web site: http://www.msbbcs.edu/.

MARYLAND INSTITUTE COLLEGE OF ART
BALTIMORE, MARYLAND

General Independent, comprehensive, coed **Entrance** Very difficult **Setting** 12-acre urban campus **Total enrollment** 1,899 **Student-faculty ratio** 10:1 **Application deadline** 2/15 (freshmen), 3/3 (transfer) **Freshmen** 37% were admitted **Housing** Yes **Expenses** Tuition $30,680; Room & Board $8390 **Undergraduates** 66% women, 1% part-time, 3% 25 or older, 0.2% Native American, 4% Hispanic American, 4% African American, 10% Asian American/Pacific Islander **The most frequently chosen baccalau-**

Maryland Institute College of Art *(continued)*

reate fields are education, visual and performing arts **Academic program** Advanced placement, accelerated degree program, self-designed majors, summer session, adult/continuing education programs, internships **Contact** Ms. Christine Seese, Director of Undergraduate Admission, Maryland Institute College of Art, 1300 Mount Royal Avenue, Baltimore, MD 21217. Phone: 410-225-2222. Fax: 410-225-2337. E-mail: cgyland@mica.edu. Web site: http://www.mica.edu/.

McDANIEL COLLEGE

WESTMINSTER, MARYLAND

General Independent, comprehensive, coed **Entrance** Moderately difficult **Setting** 160-acre suburban campus **Total enrollment** 3,642 **Student-faculty ratio** 12:1 **Application deadline** 2/1 (freshmen), 4/1 (transfer) **Freshmen** 73% were admitted **Housing** Yes **Expenses** Tuition $28,940; Room & Board $5900 **Undergraduates** 56% women, 3% part-time, 4% 25 or older, 1% Native American, 2% Hispanic American, 5% African American, 3% Asian American/Pacific Islander **The most frequently chosen baccalaureate fields are** psychology, business/marketing, social sciences **Academic program** Advanced placement, self-designed majors, honors program, summer session, adult/continuing education programs, internships **Contact** Ms. Florence Hines, Vice President for Enrollment Management and Dean of Admissions, McDaniel College, 2 College Hill, Westminster, MD 21157-4390. Phone: 410-857-2230 or toll-free 800-638-5005. Fax: 410-857-2757. E-mail: admissions@mcdaniel.edu. Web site: http://www.mcdaniel.edu/.

MORGAN STATE UNIVERSITY

BALTIMORE, MARYLAND

General State-supported, university, coed **Entrance** Moderately difficult **Setting** 143-acre urban campus **Total enrollment** 6,847 **Application deadline** 5/1 (freshmen), rolling (transfer) **Freshmen** 34% were admitted **Housing** Yes **Expenses** Tuition $6318; Room & Board $7620 **Undergraduates** 55% women, 11% part-time **Academic program** Advanced placement, accelerated degree program, honors program, summer session, adult/continuing education programs, internships **Contact** Mr. Edwin T. Johnson, Director of Admissions and Recruitment, Morgan State University, 1700 East Cold Spring Lane, Baltimore, MD 21251. Phone: 443-885-3000 or toll-free 800-332-6674. E-mail: ejohnson@moac.morgan.edu. Web site: http://www.morgan.edu/.

MOUNT ST. MARY'S UNIVERSITY

EMMITSBURG, MARYLAND

General Independent Roman Catholic, comprehensive, coed **Entrance** Moderately difficult **Setting** 1,400-acre rural campus **Total enrollment** 2,157 **Student-faculty ratio** 13:1 **Application deadline** Rolling (freshmen), 6/1 (transfer) **Freshmen** 80% were admitted **Housing** Yes **Expenses** Tuition $25,890; Room & Board $9130 **Undergraduates** 60% women, 8% part-time, 2% 25 or older, 0.4% Native American, 5% Hispanic American, 6% African American, 3% Asian American/Pacific Islander **The most frequently chosen baccalaureate fields are** business/marketing, education, social sciences **Academic program** Advanced placement, accelerated degree program, self-designed majors, honors program, summer session, adult/continuing education programs, internships **Contact** Mr. Stephen Neitz, Dean of Admissions and Enrollment Management, Mount St. Mary's University, 16300 Old Emmitsburg Road, Emmitsburg, MD 21727. Phone: 301-447-5214 or toll-free 800-448-4347. Fax: 301-447-5860. E-mail: admissions@msmary.edu. Web site: http://www.msmary.edu/.

NER ISRAEL RABBINICAL COLLEGE

BALTIMORE, MARYLAND

Contact Rabbi Berel Weisbord, Dean of Admissions, Ner Israel Rabbinical College, 400 Mount Wilson Lane, Baltimore, MD 21208. Phone: 410-484-7200.

PEABODY CONSERVATORY OF MUSIC OF THE JOHNS HOPKINS UNIVERSITY

BALTIMORE, MARYLAND

General Independent, comprehensive, coed **Entrance** Very difficult **Setting** 1-acre urban campus **Total enrollment** 676 **Student-faculty ratio** 4:1 **Application deadline** 12/1 (freshmen), 12/1 (transfer) **Freshmen** 40% were admitted **Housing** Yes **Expenses** Tuition $33,000; Room & Board $10,200 **Undergraduates** 48% women, 3% part-time, 2% 25 or older, 4% Hispanic American, 4% African American, 7% Asian American/Pacific Islander **The most frequently chosen baccalaureate fields are** education, visual and performing arts **Academic program** English as a second language, advanced placement, accelerated degree program, honors program, internships **Contact** Mr. David Lane, Director of Admissions, Peabody Conservatory of Music of The Johns Hopkins University, Peabody Conservatory Admissions Office, One East Mount Vernon Place, Baltimore, MD 21202-2397. Phone: 410-659-8110 or toll-free 800-368-2521. Web site: http://www.peabody.jhu.edu/.

ST. JOHN'S COLLEGE
ANNAPOLIS, MARYLAND

General Independent, comprehensive, coed **Entrance** Moderately difficult **Setting** 36-acre small-town campus **Total enrollment** 563 **Student-faculty ratio** 8:1 **Application deadline** Rolling (freshmen), rolling (transfer) **Freshmen** 81% were admitted **Housing** Yes **Expenses** Tuition $36,596; Room & Board $8684 **Undergraduates** 47% women, 0.2% part-time, 3% 25 or older, 0.2% Native American, 3% Hispanic American, 1% African American, 3% Asian American/Pacific Islander **The most frequently chosen baccalaureate field is** liberal arts/general studies **Academic program** Internships **Contact** Mr. John Christensen, Director of Admissions, St. John's College, PO Box 2800, 60 College Avenue, Annapolis, MD 21404. Phone: 410-626-2522 or toll-free 800-727-9238. Fax: 410-269-7916. E-mail: admissions@sjca.edu. Web site: http://www.stjohnscollege.edu/.

ST. MARY'S COLLEGE OF MARYLAND
ST. MARY'S CITY, MARYLAND

General State-supported, 4-year, coed **Entrance** Very difficult **Setting** 319-acre rural campus **Total enrollment** 2,002 **Student-faculty ratio** 12:1 **Application deadline** 1/15 (freshmen), 2/15 (transfer) **Freshmen** 55% were admitted **Housing** Yes **Expenses** Tuition $12,604; Room & Board $9225 **Undergraduates** 57% women, 4% part-time, 2% 25 or older, 1% Native American, 5% Hispanic American, 8% African American, 4% Asian American/Pacific Islander **The most frequently chosen baccalaureate fields are** psychology, English, social sciences **Academic program** Advanced placement, self-designed majors, honors program, summer session, internships **Contact** Mr. Richard Edgar, Director of Admissions, St. Mary's College of Maryland, 18952 East Fisher Road, St. Mary's City, MD 20686-3001. Phone: 240-895-5000 or toll-free 800-492-7181. Fax: 240-895-5001. E-mail: admissions@smcm.edu. Web site: http://www.smcm.edu/.

▶**For more information, see page 487.**

SALISBURY UNIVERSITY
SALISBURY, MARYLAND

General State-supported, comprehensive, coed **Entrance** Moderately difficult **Setting** 154-acre small-town campus **Total enrollment** 7,581 **Student-faculty ratio** 18:1 **Application deadline** 1/15 (freshmen), rolling (transfer) **Freshmen** 56% were admitted **Housing** Yes **Expenses** Tuition $6412; Room & Board $7601 **Undergraduates** 55% women, 8% part-time, 8% 25 or older, 1% Native American, 2% Hispanic American, 11% African American, 3% Asian American/Pacific Islander **The most frequently chosen baccalaureate fields are** business/marketing, communications/journalism, education **Academic program** English as a second language, advanced placement, self-designed majors, honors program, summer session, adult/continuing education programs, internships **Contact** Ms. Laura Thorpe, Director of Admissions, Salisbury University, Admissions House, 1101 Camden Avenue, Salisbury, MD 21801. Phone: 410-543-6161 or toll-free 888-543-0148. Fax: 410-546-6016. E-mail: admissions@salisbury.edu. Web site: http://www.ssu.edu/.

SOJOURNER-DOUGLASS COLLEGE
BALTIMORE, MARYLAND

Contact Ms. Diana Samuels, Manager, Office of Admissions, Sojourner-Douglass College, 500 North Caroline Street, Baltimore, MD 21205-1814. Phone: 410-276-0306 Ext. 251. Fax: 410-675-1810. Web site: http://sdc.edu/.

TOWSON UNIVERSITY
TOWSON, MARYLAND

General State-supported, university, coed **Entrance** Moderately difficult **Setting** 321-acre suburban campus **Total enrollment** 19,758 **Student-faculty ratio** 18:1 **Application deadline** 2/15 (freshmen), 2/15 (transfer) **Freshmen** 60% were admitted **Housing** Yes **Expenses** Tuition $7234; Room & Board $7986 **Undergraduates** 60% women, 13% part-time, 11% 25 or older, 0.4% Native American, 2% Hispanic American, 11% African American, 4% Asian American/Pacific Islander **The most frequently chosen baccalaureate fields are** business/marketing, education, public administration and social services **Academic program** English as a second language, advanced placement, accelerated degree program, self-designed majors, honors program, summer session, adult/continuing education programs, internships **Contact** Ms. Louise Shulack, Director of Admissions, Towson University, 8000 York Road, Towson, MD 21252. Phone: 410-704-3687 or toll-free 888-4TOWSON. Fax: 410-704-3030. E-mail: admissions@towson.edu. Web site: http://www.towson.edu/.

UNITED STATES NAVAL ACADEMY
ANNAPOLIS, MARYLAND

General Federally supported, 4-year, coed, primarily men **Entrance** Very difficult **Setting** 329-acre small-town campus **Total enrollment** 4,443 **Student-faculty ratio** 8:1 **Application deadline** 1/31 (freshmen) **Freshmen** 10% were admitted **Housing** Yes **Undergraduates** 21% women, 2% 25 or older, 1% Native American, 10% Hispanic

United States Naval Academy *(continued)*

American, 4% African American, 3% Asian American/Pacific Islander **The most frequently chosen baccalaureate fields are** engineering, physical sciences, social sciences **Academic program** English as a second language, advanced placement, honors program, summer session **Contact** Dean of Admissions, United States Naval Academy, 117 Decatur Road, United States Naval Academy, Annapolis, MD 21402. Phone: 410-293-4361. Fax: 410-293-4348. E-mail: webmail@usna.edu. Web site: http://www.usna.edu/.

UNIVERSITY OF BALTIMORE
BALTIMORE, MARYLAND

General State-supported, upper-level, coed **Entrance** Minimally difficult **Setting** 49-acre urban campus **Total enrollment** 5,414 **Student-faculty ratio** 16:1 **Application deadline** 2/15 (freshmen), 6/1 (transfer) **First-year students** 34% were admitted **Housing** Yes **Expenses** Tuition $6130 **Undergraduates** 58% women, 48% part-time, 61% 25 or older, 0.5% Native American, 2% Hispanic American, 35% African American, 4% Asian American/Pacific Islander **The most frequently chosen baccalaureate fields are** business/marketing, computer and information sciences, security and protective services **Academic program** Advanced placement, accelerated degree program, self-designed majors, honors program, summer session, adult/continuing education programs, internships **Contact** Jenifer Blair, University of Baltimore, 1420 North Charles Street, Baltimore, MD 21201. Phone: 410-837-4777 or toll-free 877-APPLYUB. Fax: 410-837-4793. E-mail: admissions@ubalt.edu. Web site: http://www.ubalt.edu/.

UNIVERSITY OF MARYLAND, BALTIMORE COUNTY
BALTIMORE, MARYLAND

General State-supported, university, coed **Entrance** Moderately difficult **Setting** 530-acre suburban campus **Total enrollment** 12,041 **Student-faculty ratio** 18:1 **Application deadline** 2/1 (freshmen), 5/31 (transfer) **Freshmen** 69% were admitted **Housing** Yes **Expenses** Tuition $8708; Room & Board $8658 **Undergraduates** 46% women, 16% part-time, 12% 25 or older, 1% Native American, 4% Hispanic American, 16% African American, 21% Asian American/Pacific Islander **The most frequently chosen baccalaureate fields are** communication technologies, biological/life sciences, social sciences **Academic program** English as a second language, advanced placement, self-designed majors, honors program, summer session, adult/continuing education programs, internships **Contact** Mr. Dale Bittinger, Director of Admissions, University of Maryland, Baltimore County, 1000 Hilltop Circle, Baltimore, MD 21250. Phone: 410-455-2291 or toll-free 800-UMBC-4U2 (in-state); 800-862-2402 (out-of-state). Fax: 410-455-1094. E-mail: admissions@umbc.edu. Web site: http://www.umbc.edu/.

UNIVERSITY OF MARYLAND, COLLEGE PARK
COLLEGE PARK, MARYLAND

General State-supported, university, coed **Entrance** Moderately difficult **Setting** 3,688-acre suburban campus **Total enrollment** 35,970 **Student-faculty ratio** 18:1 **Application deadline** 1/20 (freshmen), 6/1 (transfer) **Freshmen** 47% were admitted **Housing** Yes **Expenses** Tuition $7969; Room & Board $8854 **Undergraduates** 48% women, 8% part-time, 6% 25 or older, 0.4% Native American, 6% Hispanic American, 13% African American, 14% Asian American/Pacific Islander **The most frequently chosen baccalaureate fields are** business/marketing, biological/life sciences, social sciences **Academic program** English as a second language, advanced placement, accelerated degree program, self-designed majors, honors program, summer session, adult/continuing education programs, internships **Contact** Ms. Barbara Gill, Director of Undergraduate Admissions, University of Maryland, College Park, College Park, MD 20742. Phone: 301-314-8385 or toll-free 800-422-5867. Fax: 301-314-9693. E-mail: um-admit@uga.umd.edu. Web site: http://www.maryland.edu/.

UNIVERSITY OF MARYLAND EASTERN SHORE
PRINCESS ANNE, MARYLAND

General State-supported, university, coed **Entrance** Moderately difficult **Setting** 700-acre rural campus **Total enrollment** 3,762 **Student-faculty ratio** 20:1 **Application deadline** 7/15 (freshmen), rolling (transfer) **Freshmen** 58% were admitted **Housing** Yes **Expenses** Tuition $5988; Room & Board $6580 **Undergraduates** 59% women, 13% part-time, 13% 25 or older, 0.4% Native American, 1% Hispanic American, 76% African American, 2% Asian American/Pacific Islander **Academic program** Advanced placement, accelerated degree program, self-designed majors, honors program, summer session, adult/continuing education programs, internships **Contact** Tyrone Young, Director of Admissions, University of Maryland Eastern Shore, Princess Anne, MD 21853-1299. Phone: 410-651-8410. Fax: 410-651-7922. E-mail: umesadmissions@mail.umes.edu. Web site: http://www.umes.edu/.

UNIVERSITY OF MARYLAND UNIVERSITY COLLEGE

ADELPHI, MARYLAND

General State-supported, comprehensive, coed **Entrance** Noncompetitive **Setting** suburban campus **Total enrollment** 32,540 **Student-faculty ratio** 19:1 **Application deadline** Rolling (freshmen), rolling (transfer) **Freshmen** 100% were admitted **Housing** No **Expenses** Tuition $5640 **Undergraduates** 58% women, 86% part-time, 83% 25 or older, 1% Native American, 5% Hispanic American, 29% African American, 4% Asian American/Pacific Islander **The most frequently chosen baccalaureate fields are** business/marketing, computer and information sciences, interdisciplinary studies **Academic program** Advanced placement, accelerated degree program, summer session, adult/continuing education programs **Contact** Ms. Jessica Sadaka, Director of Admissions, University of Maryland University College, 3501 University Boulevard East, Adelphi, MD 20783. Phone: 800-885-UMUC or toll-free 800-888-8682. Fax: 301-985-7364. E-mail: admissions@umuc.edu. Web site: http://www.umuc.edu/.

UNIVERSITY OF PHOENIX–MARYLAND CAMPUS

COLUMBIA, MARYLAND

General Proprietary, comprehensive, coed **Contact** Ms. Evelyn Gaskin, Registrar/Executive Director, University of Phoenix–Maryland Campus, 4615 East Elwood Street, Mail Stop AA-K101, Phoenix, AZ 85040-1958. Phone: 480-557-3301 or toll-free 800-776-4867 (in-state); 800-228-7240 (out-of-state). Fax: 480-643-1020. E-mail: evelyn.gaskin@phoenix.edu. Web site: http://www.phoenix.edu/.

VILLA JULIE COLLEGE

STEVENSON, MARYLAND

General Independent, comprehensive, coed **Entrance** Moderately difficult **Setting** 150-acre suburban campus **Total enrollment** 3,304 **Student-faculty ratio** 14:1 **Application deadline** Rolling (freshmen), rolling (transfer) **Freshmen** 82% were admitted **Housing** Yes **Expenses** Tuition $17,944; Room & Board $8900 **Undergraduates** 70% women, 17% part-time, 17% 25 or older, 0.4% Native American, 1% Hispanic American, 15% African American, 3% Asian American/Pacific Islander **The most frequently chosen baccalaureate fields are** business/marketing, health professions and related sciences, visual and performing arts **Academic program** Advanced placement, accelerated degree program, self-designed majors, honors program, summer session, adult/continuing education programs, internships **Contact** Mr. Mark Hergan, Vice President, Enrollment Management, Villa Julie College, 1525 Greenspring Valley Road, Stevenson, MD 21153. Phone: 410-486-7001 or toll-free 877-468-6852 (in-state); 877-468-3852 (out-of-state). Fax: 410-352-4440. E-mail: admissions@vjc.edu. Web site: http://www.vjc.edu/.

WASHINGTON BIBLE COLLEGE

LANHAM, MARYLAND

General Independent nondenominational, 4-year, coed **Entrance** Moderately difficult **Setting** 63-acre suburban campus **Total enrollment** 616 **Student-faculty ratio** 13:1 **Application deadline** 1/9 (freshmen), rolling (transfer) **Freshmen** 65% were admitted **Housing** Yes **Expenses** Tuition $9700; Room & Board $6450 **Undergraduates** 46% women, 50% part-time, 57% 25 or older, 1% Native American, 3% Hispanic American, 44% African American, 7% Asian American/Pacific Islander **The most frequently chosen baccalaureate field is** theology and religious vocations **Academic program** English as a second language, advanced placement, accelerated degree program, summer session, adult/continuing education programs, internships **Contact** Mr. Mark D. Johnson, Director of Admissions, Washington Bible College, 6511 Princess Garden Parkway, Lanham, MD 20706. Phone: 877-793-7227 or toll-free 877-793-7227 Ext. 1212. Fax: 301-552-2775. E-mail: admissions@bible.edu. Web site: http://www.bible.edu/.

WASHINGTON COLLEGE

CHESTERTOWN, MARYLAND

General Independent, comprehensive, coed **Entrance** Moderately difficult **Setting** 140-acre small-town campus **Total enrollment** 1,289 **Student-faculty ratio** 10:1 **Application deadline** 3/1 (freshmen), 6/1 (transfer) **Freshmen** 64% were admitted **Housing** Yes **Expenses** Tuition $34,005; Room & Board $7180 **Undergraduates** 61% women, 5% part-time, 2% 25 or older, 0.4% Native American, 0.1% Hispanic American, 5% African American, 1% Asian American/Pacific Islander **The most frequently chosen baccalaureate fields are** business/marketing, English, social sciences **Academic program** English as a second language, advanced placement, self-designed majors, internships **Contact** Mr. Kevin Coveney, Vice President for Admissions and Enrollment Management, Washington College, 300 Washington Avenue, Chesterton, MD 21620. Phone: 410-778-7700 or toll-free 800-422-1782. Fax: 410-778-7287. E-mail: admissions_office@washcoll.edu. Web site: http://www.washcoll.edu/.

►**For more information, see page 499.**

YESHIVA COLLEGE OF THE NATION'S CAPITAL
SILVER SPRING, MARYLAND

Contact Yeshiva College of the Nation's Capital, 1216 Arcola Avenue, Silver Spring, MD 20902. Web site: http://www.yeshiva.edu/default.shtml.

MASSACHUSETTS

AMERICAN INTERNATIONAL COLLEGE
SPRINGFIELD, MASSACHUSETTS

General Independent, comprehensive, coed **Entrance** Moderately difficult **Setting** 58-acre urban campus **Total enrollment** 2,678 **Student-faculty ratio** 17:1 **Application deadline** Rolling (freshmen), rolling (transfer) **Freshmen** 80% were admitted **Housing** Yes **Expenses** Tuition $24,100; Room & Board $10,150 **Undergraduates** 61% women, 12% part-time, 20% 25 or older, 1% Native American, 9% Hispanic American, 27% African American, 3% Asian American/Pacific Islander **The most frequently chosen baccalaureate fields are** business/marketing, health professions and related sciences, security and protective services **Academic program** English as a second language, advanced placement, accelerated degree program, honors program, summer session, adult/continuing education programs, internships **Contact** Mr. Peter Miller, Dean of Admissions, American International College, 1000 State Street, Springfield, MA 01109-3189. Phone: 413-205-3201. Fax: 413-205-3051. E-mail: inquiry@aic.edu. Web site: http://www.aic.edu/.

AMHERST COLLEGE
AMHERST, MASSACHUSETTS

General Independent, 4-year, coed **Entrance** Most difficult **Setting** 1,020-acre small-town campus **Total enrollment** 1,686 **Student-faculty ratio** 8:1 **Application deadline** 1/1 (freshmen), 2/1 (transfer) **Freshmen** 18% were admitted **Housing** Yes **Expenses** Tuition $36,232; Room & Board $9420 **Undergraduates** 50% women, 1% 25 or older, 0.4% Native American, 9% Hispanic American, 10% African American, 12% Asian American/Pacific Islander **The most frequently chosen baccalaureate fields are** foreign languages and literature, psychology, public administration and social services **Academic program** Self-designed majors, honors program **Contact** Mr. Thomas H. Parker, Dean of Admission and Financial Aid, Amherst College, PO Box 5000, Amherst, MA 01002-5000. Phone: 413-542-2328. Fax: 413-542-2040. E-mail: admission@amherst.edu. Web site: http://www.amherst.edu/.

ANNA MARIA COLLEGE
PAXTON, MASSACHUSETTS

General Independent Roman Catholic, comprehensive, coed **Entrance** Minimally difficult **Setting** 180-acre rural campus **Total enrollment** 1,244 **Student-faculty ratio** 9:1 **Application deadline** Rolling (freshmen), rolling (transfer) **Freshmen** 89% were admitted **Housing** Yes **Expenses** Tuition $24,617; Room & Board $8915 **Undergraduates** 56% women, 23% part-time, 20% 25 or older, 0.2% Native American, 4% Hispanic American, 5% African American, 1% Asian American/Pacific Islander **The most frequently chosen baccalaureate fields are** health professions and related sciences, public administration and social services, security and protective services **Academic program** Advanced placement, accelerated degree program, self-designed majors, summer session, adult/continuing education programs, internships **Contact** Mr. Tim Donahue, Director of Recruitment and Admission, Anna Maria College, Box O, Sunset Lane, Paxton, MA 01612. Phone: 508-849-3491 or toll-free 800-344-4586 Ext. 360. Fax: 508-849-3362. E-mail: admission@annamaria.edu. Web site: http://www.annamaria.edu/.

THE ART INSTITUTE OF BOSTON AT LESLEY UNIVERSITY
BOSTON, MASSACHUSETTS

General Independent, comprehensive, coed **Entrance** Moderately difficult **Setting** 1-acre urban campus **Total enrollment** 6,474 **Student-faculty ratio** 9:1 **Application deadline** Rolling (freshmen), rolling (transfer) **Freshmen** 86% were admitted **Housing** Yes **Expenses** Tuition $25,635; Room & Board $12,000 **Undergraduates** 75% women, 6% part-time, 6% 25 or older, 0.4% Native American, 5% Hispanic American, 5% African American, 4% Asian American/Pacific Islander **The most frequently chosen baccalaureate fields are** liberal arts/general studies, psychology, visual and performing arts **Academic program** English as a second language, advanced placement, accelerated degree program, self-designed majors, honors program, summer session, adult/continuing education programs, internships **Contact** Bob Gielow, Director of Admission, The Art Institute of Boston at Lesley University, 700 Beacon Street, Boston, MA 02215-2598. Phone: 617-585-6710 or toll-free 800-773-0494. Fax: 617-585-6720. E-mail: admissions@aiboston.edu. Web site: http://www.aiboston.edu/.

ASSUMPTION COLLEGE
WORCESTER, MASSACHUSETTS

General Independent Roman Catholic, comprehensive, coed **Entrance** Moderately difficult **Setting** 180-acre suburban campus **Total enrollment** 2,649 **Student-faculty ratio** 12:1 **Application deadline** 2/15 (freshmen), 5/1 (transfer) **Freshmen** 67% were admitted **Housing** Yes **Expenses** Tuition $27,485; Room & Board $5977 **Undergraduates** 59% women, 2% part-time, 1% 25 or older, 0.1% Native American, 3% Hispanic American, 2% African American, 1% Asian American/Pacific Islander **The most frequently chosen baccalaureate fields are** business/marketing, communications/journalism, psychology **Academic program** Advanced placement, self-designed majors, honors program, summer session, adult/continuing education programs, internships **Contact** Ms. Kathleen Murphy, Dean of Enrollment, Assumption College, 500 Salisbury Street, Worcester, MA 01609-1296. Phone: 508-767-7286 or toll-free 888-882-7786. Fax: 508-799-4412. E-mail: admiss@assumption.edu. Web site: http://www.assumption.edu/.

ATLANTIC UNION COLLEGE
SOUTH LANCASTER, MASSACHUSETTS

General Independent Seventh-day Adventist, comprehensive, coed **Entrance** Moderately difficult **Setting** 314-acre small-town campus **Total enrollment** 497 **Student-faculty ratio** 11:1 **Application deadline** 8/1 (freshmen), 8/1 (transfer) **Freshmen** 43% were admitted **Housing** Yes **Expenses** Tuition $17,640; Room & Board $5000 **Undergraduates** 63% women, 17% part-time, 17% Hispanic American, 45% African American, 3% Asian American/Pacific Islander **Academic program** English as a second language, advanced placement, honors program, summer session, adult/continuing education programs, internships **Contact** Mrs. Rosita Lashley, Director for Admissions, Atlantic Union College, PO Box 1000, South Lancaster, MA 01561-1000. Phone: 978-368-2239 or toll-free 800-282-2030. Fax: 978-368-2015. E-mail: rosita.lashley@auc.edu. Web site: http://www.auc.edu/.

BABSON COLLEGE
WELLESLEY, MASSACHUSETTS

General Independent, comprehensive, coed **Entrance** Very difficult **Setting** 370-acre suburban campus **Total enrollment** 3,434 **Student-faculty ratio** 16:1 **Application deadline** 1/15 (freshmen), 4/1 (transfer) **Freshmen** 38% were admitted **Housing** Yes **Expenses** Tuition $34,112; Room & Board $11,670 **Undergraduates** 41% women, 2% 25 or older, 0.2% Native American, 8% Hispanic American, 4% African American, 11% Asian American/Pacific Islander **The most frequently chosen baccalaureate field is** business/marketing **Academic program** Advanced placement, accelerated degree program, self-designed majors, honors program, summer session, internships **Contact** Ms. Adrienne Fowkes, Assistant Director of Undergraduate Admission, Babson College, Lunder Undergraduate Admission Center, Babson Park, MA 02457-0310. Phone: 781-239-5522 or toll-free 800-488-3696. Fax: 781-239-4135. E-mail: ugradadmission@babson.edu. Web site: http://www.babson.edu/.

BARD COLLEGE AT SIMON'S ROCK
GREAT BARRINGTON, MASSACHUSETTS

General Independent, 4-year, coed **Entrance** Very difficult **Setting** 275-acre rural campus **Total enrollment** 408 **Student-faculty ratio** 8:1 **Application deadline** 5/31 (freshmen), 7/15 (transfer) **Freshmen** 84% were admitted **Housing** Yes **Expenses** Tuition $37,130; Room & Board $9730 **Undergraduates** 58% women, 1% part-time, 1% Native American, 6% Hispanic American, 7% African American, 4% Asian American/Pacific Islander **The most frequently chosen baccalaureate fields are** area and ethnic studies, English, visual and performing arts **Academic program** Self-designed majors, adult/continuing education programs, internships **Contact** Barbara Shultis, Assistant to the Director of Admissions, Bard College at Simon's Rock, 84 Alford Road, Great Barrington, MA 01230-9702. Phone: 413-528-7312 or toll-free 800-235-7186. Fax: 413-528-7334. E-mail: admit@simons-rock.edu. Web site: http://simons-rock.edu/.

BAY PATH COLLEGE
LONGMEADOW, MASSACHUSETTS

General Independent, comprehensive, undergraduate: women only; graduate: coed **Entrance** Moderately difficult **Setting** 48-acre suburban campus **Total enrollment** 1,603 **Student-faculty ratio** 17:1 **Application deadline** Rolling (freshmen), rolling (transfer) **Freshmen** 76% were admitted **Housing** Yes **Expenses** Tuition $22,073; Room & Board $9200 **Undergraduates** 22% part-time, 54% 25 or older, 0.4% Native American, 11% Hispanic American, 11% African American, 1% Asian American/Pacific Islander **The most frequently chosen baccalaureate fields are** business/marketing, liberal arts/general studies, psychology **Academic program** English as a second language, advanced placement, self-designed majors, honors program, summer session, adult/continuing education programs, internships **Contact** Julie Richardson, Dean of Enrollment Management, Traditional Program,

Bay Path College *(continued)*

Bay Path College, 588 Longmeadow Street, Longmeadow, MA 01106-2292. Phone: 413-565-1000 Ext. 1331 or toll-free 800-782-7284 Ext. 1331. Fax: 413-565-1105. E-mail: admiss@baypath.edu. Web site: http://www.baypath.edu/.

BECKER COLLEGE
WORCESTER, MASSACHUSETTS

General Independent, 4-year, coed **Entrance** Minimally difficult **Setting** 100-acre rural campus **Total enrollment** 1,660 **Student-faculty ratio** 15:1 **Application deadline** Rolling (freshmen), rolling (transfer) **Freshmen** 70% were admitted **Housing** Yes **Expenses** Tuition $25,668; Room & Board $9300 **Undergraduates** 80% women, 45% part-time, 23% 25 or older, 0.3% Native American, 3% Hispanic American, 5% African American, 1% Asian American/Pacific Islander **Academic program** Advanced placement, accelerated degree program, summer session, adult/continuing education programs, internships **Contact** Admissions Receptionist, Becker College, 61 Sever Street, Worcester, MA 01609. Phone: 508-373-9400 or toll-free 877-5BECKER Ext. 245. Fax: 508-890-1500. E-mail: admissions@beckercollege.edu. Web site: http://www.beckercollege.edu/.

BENTLEY COLLEGE
WALTHAM, MASSACHUSETTS

General Independent, comprehensive, coed **Entrance** Very difficult **Setting** 163-acre suburban campus **Total enrollment** 5,593 **Student-faculty ratio** 12:1 **Application deadline** 1/15 (freshmen), rolling (transfer) **Freshmen** 38% were admitted **Housing** Yes **Expenses** Tuition $32,896; Room & Board $10,940 **Undergraduates** 40% women, 6% part-time, 5% 25 or older, 0.02% Native American, 4% Hispanic American, 3% African American, 8% Asian American/Pacific Islander **The most frequently chosen baccalaureate fields are** business/marketing, computer and information sciences, interdisciplinary studies **Academic program** English as a second language, advanced placement, accelerated degree program, self-designed majors, honors program, summer session, adult/continuing education programs, internships **Contact** Erika Vardaro, Director of Undergraduate Admission, Bentley College, 175 Forest Street, Waltham, MA 02452. Phone: 781-891-2244 or toll-free 800-523-2354. Fax: 781-891-3414. E-mail: ugadmission@bentley.edu. Web site: http://www.bentley.edu.

BERKLEE COLLEGE OF MUSIC
BOSTON, MASSACHUSETTS

General Independent, 4-year, coed **Entrance** Moderately difficult **Setting** urban campus **Total enrollment** 4,090 **Student-faculty ratio** 8:1 **Application deadline** 2/1 (freshmen), 2/1 (transfer) **Freshmen** 32% were admitted **Housing** Yes **Expenses** Tuition $28,200; Room & Board $14,960 **Undergraduates** 28% women, 9% part-time, 17% 25 or older **The most frequently chosen baccalaureate fields are** business/marketing, education, visual and performing arts **Academic program** English as a second language, advanced placement, accelerated degree program, self-designed majors, summer session, internships **Contact** Mr. Damien Bracken, Director of Admissions, Berklee College of Music, 1140 Boylesto Street, Boston, MA 02215-3693. Phone: 617-747-2222 or toll-free 800-BERKLEE. Fax: 617-747-2047. E-mail: admissions@berklee.edu. Web site: http://www.berklee.edu/.

BOSTON ARCHITECTURAL COLLEGE
BOSTON, MASSACHUSETTS

General Independent, comprehensive, coed **Entrance** Noncompetitive **Setting** 1-acre urban campus **Total enrollment** 1,017 **Student-faculty ratio** 4:1 **Application deadline** Rolling (freshmen), rolling (transfer) **Freshmen** 88% were admitted **Housing** No **Expenses** Tuition $10,580 **Undergraduates** 36% women, 3% part-time, 48% 25 or older, 0.4% Native American, 12% Hispanic American, 5% African American, 6% Asian American/Pacific Islander **Academic program** Advanced placement, summer session, adult/continuing education programs, internships **Contact** Richard Moyer, Director of Admission, Boston Architectural College, 320 Newbury Street, Boston, MA 02115-2795. Phone: 617-585-0256 or toll-free 877-585-0100. Fax: 617-585-0121. E-mail: admissions@the-bac.edu. Web site: http://www.the-bac.edu/.

BOSTON BAPTIST COLLEGE
BOSTON, MASSACHUSETTS

General Independent Baptist, 4-year, coed **Entrance** Moderately difficult **Setting** 8-acre suburban campus **Total enrollment** 149 **Student-faculty ratio** 6:1 **Application deadline** Rolling (freshmen), rolling (transfer) **Housing** Yes **Expenses** Tuition $8765; Room & Board $6992 **Undergraduates** 40% women, 26% part-time, 8% 25 or older, 1% Native American, 2% Hispanic American, 7% African American, 4% Asian American/Pacific Islander **The most frequently chosen baccalaureate field is** theology and religious vocations **Academic program** Honors program, summer session, internships **Contact** Mrs. Karen Fox, Director of Admissions, Boston Baptist College, 950 Metropolitan Avenue, Boston, MA 02136. Phone: 617-364-3510 Ext. 217 or toll-free 888-235-2014. Fax: 775-522-4803. E-mail: kfox@boston.edu. Web site: http://www.boston.edu/.

BOSTON COLLEGE

CHESTNUT HILL, MASSACHUSETTS

General Independent Roman Catholic (Jesuit), university, coed **Entrance** Very difficult **Setting** 379-acre suburban campus **Total enrollment** 13,723 **Student-faculty ratio** 13:1 **Application deadline** 1/1 (freshmen), 4/1 (transfer) **Freshmen** 27% were admitted **Housing** Yes **Expenses** Tuition $35,674; Room & Board $12,053 **Undergraduates** 52% women, 0.4% Native American, 8% Hispanic American, 6% African American, 10% Asian American/Pacific Islander **The most frequently chosen baccalaureate fields are** business/marketing, communications/journalism, social sciences **Academic program** Advanced placement, accelerated degree program, self-designed majors, honors program, summer session, adult/continuing education programs, internships **Contact** Office of Undergraduate Admissions, Boston College, 140 Commonwealth Avenue, Devlin 208, Chestnut Hill, MA 02467-3809. Phone: 617-552-3100 or toll-free 800-360-2522. Fax: 617-552-0798. E-mail: ugadmis@bc.edu. Web site: http://www.bc.edu/.

THE BOSTON CONSERVATORY

BOSTON, MASSACHUSETTS

General Independent, comprehensive, coed **Entrance** Moderately difficult **Setting** urban campus **Total enrollment** 560 **Student-faculty ratio** 4:1 **Application deadline** 12/1 (freshmen), 12/1 (transfer) **Freshmen** 34% were admitted **Housing** Yes **Expenses** Tuition $30,099; Room & Board $15,640 **Undergraduates** 63% women, 12% 25 or older, 0.2% Native American, 6% Hispanic American, 3% African American, 6% Asian American/Pacific Islander **Academic program** English as a second language, advanced placement, summer session, adult/continuing education programs **Contact** Ms. Halley Shefler, Dean of Enrollment, The Boston Conservatory, 8 The Fenway, Boston, MA 02215. Phone: 617-912-9153. Fax: 617-536-3176. E-mail: admissions@bostonconservatory.edu. Web site: http://www.bostonconservatory.edu/.

BOSTON UNIVERSITY

BOSTON, MASSACHUSETTS

General Independent, university, coed **Entrance** Very difficult **Setting** 132-acre urban campus **Total enrollment** 32,053 **Student-faculty ratio** 14:1 **Application deadline** 1/1 (freshmen), 4/1 (transfer) **Freshmen** 59% were admitted **Housing** Yes **Expenses** Tuition $37,050; Room & Board $11,418 **Undergraduates** 59% women, 8% part-time, 3% 25 or older, 0.3% Native American, 7% Hispanic American, 3% African American, 13% Asian American/Pacific Islander **The most frequently chosen baccalaureate fields are** business/marketing, communications/journalism, social sciences **Academic program** English as a second language, advanced placement, accelerated degree program, self-designed majors, honors program, summer session, adult/continuing education programs, internships **Contact** Ms. Kelly Walter, Director of Undergraduate Admissions, Boston University, 121 Bay State Road, Boston, MA 02215. Phone: 617-353-2300. Fax: 617-353-9695. E-mail: admissions@bu.edu. Web site: http://www.bu.edu/.

BRANDEIS UNIVERSITY

WALTHAM, MASSACHUSETTS

General Independent, university, coed **Entrance** Most difficult **Setting** 235-acre suburban campus **Total enrollment** 5,333 **Student-faculty ratio** 8:1 **Application deadline** 1/15 (freshmen), 4/1 (transfer) **Freshmen** 34% were admitted **Housing** Yes **Expenses** Tuition $35,702; Room & Board $9908 **Undergraduates** 56% women, 1% part-time, 0.2% Native American, 4% Hispanic American, 4% African American, 9% Asian American/Pacific Islander **The most frequently chosen baccalaureate fields are** area and ethnic studies, biological/life sciences, social sciences **Academic program** English as a second language, advanced placement, self-designed majors, honors program, summer session, adult/continuing education programs, internships **Contact** Mr. Gil J. Villanueva, Dean of Admissions, Brandeis University, 415 South Street, Waltham, MA 02254-9110. Phone: 781-736-3500 or toll-free 800-622-0622. Fax: 781-736-3536. E-mail: admissions@brandeis.edu. Web site: http://www.brandeis.edu/.

BRIDGEWATER STATE COLLEGE

BRIDGEWATER, MASSACHUSETTS

General State-supported, comprehensive, coed **Entrance** Moderately difficult **Setting** 235-acre suburban campus **Total enrollment** 9,934 **Student-faculty ratio** 20:1 **Application deadline** 2/15 (freshmen), 6/1 (transfer) **Freshmen** 69% were admitted **Housing** Yes **Expenses** Tuition $6033; Room & Board $6852 **Undergraduates** 59% women, 17% part-time, 13% 25 or older, 0.4% Native American, 2% Hispanic American, 6% African American, 2% Asian American/Pacific Islander **The most frequently chosen baccalaureate fields are** business/marketing, education, psychology **Academic program** English as a second language, advanced placement, accelerated degree program, honors program, summer session, adult/continuing education programs, internships **Contact** Mr. Gregg Meyer, Director of Admissions, Bridgewater State College, Bridgewater State College, Bridgewater,

Bridgewater State College *(continued)*

MA 02325-0001. Phone: 508-531-1237. Fax: 508-531-1746. E-mail: admission@bridgew.edu. Web site: http://www.bridgew.edu/.

CAMBRIDGE COLLEGE

CAMBRIDGE, MASSACHUSETTS

General Independent, comprehensive, coed **Entrance** Minimally difficult **Setting** urban campus **Total enrollment** 5,086 **Student-faculty ratio** 11:1 **Application deadline** Rolling (freshmen), rolling (transfer) **Housing** No **Expenses** Tuition $10,480 **Undergraduates** 69% women, 73% part-time, 65% 25 or older, 1% Native American, 22% Hispanic American, 35% African American, 3% Asian American/Pacific Islander **The most frequently chosen baccalaureate fields are** business/marketing, interdisciplinary studies, psychology **Academic program** English as a second language, accelerated degree program, summer session, adult/continuing education programs, internships **Contact** Undergraduate Admissions, Cambridge College, 1000 Massachusetts Avenue, Cambridge, MA 02138. Phone: 617-868-1000 Ext. 1124 or toll-free 800-877-4723. Fax: 617-349-3545. E-mail: admit@cambridgecollege.edu. Web site: http://www.cambridgecollege.edu/.

CLARK UNIVERSITY

WORCESTER, MASSACHUSETTS

General Independent, university, coed **Entrance** Moderately difficult **Setting** 50-acre urban campus **Total enrollment** 3,210 **Student-faculty ratio** 10:1 **Application deadline** 1/15 (freshmen), 4/15 (transfer) **Freshmen** 56% were admitted **Housing** Yes **Expenses** Tuition $32,865; Room & Board $6300 **Undergraduates** 60% women, 6% part-time, 1% 25 or older, 0.3% Native American, 2% Hispanic American, 2% African American, 4% Asian American/Pacific Islander **The most frequently chosen baccalaureate fields are** psychology, social sciences, visual and performing arts **Academic program** English as a second language, advanced placement, accelerated degree program, self-designed majors, honors program, summer session, adult/continuing education programs, internships **Contact** Mr. Harold Wingood, Dean of Admissions, Clark University, Admissions House, 950 Main Street, Worcester, MA 01610. Phone: 508-793-7431 or toll-free 800-GO-CLARK. Fax: 508-793-8821. E-mail: admissions@clarku.edu. Web site: http://www.clarku.edu/.

COLLEGE OF THE HOLY CROSS

WORCESTER, MASSACHUSETTS

General Independent Roman Catholic (Jesuit), 4-year, coed **Entrance** Very difficult **Setting** 174-acre suburban campus **Total enrollment** 2,846 **Student-faculty ratio** 11:1 **Application deadline** 1/15 (freshmen), 5/1 (transfer) **Freshmen** 33% were admitted **Housing** Yes **Expenses** Tuition $37,242; Room & Board $10,260 **Undergraduates** 56% women, 1% part-time, 0.5% Native American, 5% Hispanic American, 4% African American, 5% Asian American/Pacific Islander **The most frequently chosen baccalaureate fields are** psychology, history, social sciences **Academic program** Advanced placement, accelerated degree program, self-designed majors, honors program, internships **Contact** Ms. Ann Bowe McDermott, Director of Admissions, College of the Holy Cross, 105 Fenwick Hall, 1 College Street, Worcester, MA 01610-2395. Phone: 508-793-2443 or toll-free 800-442-2421. Fax: 508-793-3888. E-mail: admissions@holycross.edu. Web site: http://www.holycross.edu/.

CURRY COLLEGE

MILTON, MASSACHUSETTS

General Independent, comprehensive, coed **Entrance** Moderately difficult **Setting** 131-acre suburban campus **Total enrollment** 3,183 **Student-faculty ratio** 12:1 **Application deadline** 4/1 (freshmen), 7/1 (transfer) **Freshmen** 66% were admitted **Housing** Yes **Expenses** Tuition $25,925; Room & Board $10,290 **Undergraduates** 58% women, 28% part-time, 25% 25 or older, 0.2% Native American, 2% Hispanic American, 7% African American, 1% Asian American/Pacific Islander **The most frequently chosen baccalaureate fields are** health professions and related sciences, business/marketing, security and protective services **Academic program** Advanced placement, accelerated degree program, self-designed majors, honors program, summer session, adult/continuing education programs, internships **Contact** Ms. Jane P. Fidler, Dean of Admission, Curry College, 1071 Blue Hill Avenue, Milton, MA 02186. Phone: 617-333-2210 or toll-free 800-669-0686. Fax: 617-333-2114. E-mail: curryadm@curry.edu. Web site: http://www.curry.edu/.

EASTERN NAZARENE COLLEGE

QUINCY, MASSACHUSETTS

General Independent, comprehensive, coed, affiliated with Church of the Nazarene **Entrance** Moderately difficult **Setting** 15-acre suburban campus **Total enrollment** 762 **Student-faculty ratio** 11:1 **Application deadline** 9/1 (freshmen), 9/1 (transfer) **Freshmen** 57% were admitted **Housing** Yes **Expenses** Tuition $22,014; Room & Board $7913 **Undergraduates** 59% women, 4% part-time, 4% 25 or older, 0.1% Native American, 4% Hispanic American, 11% African

American, 2% Asian American/Pacific Islander **The most frequently chosen baccalaureate fields are** business/marketing, liberal arts/general studies, psychology **Academic program** Advanced placement, accelerated degree program, honors program, summer session, adult/continuing education programs, internships **Contact** Mr. Jeffrey Wells, Vice President of Enrollment Management, Eastern Nazarene College, 23 East Elm Avenue, Quincy, MA 02170-2999. Phone: 617-745-3732 or toll-free 800-88-ENC88. Fax: 617-745-3992. E-mail: admissions@enc.edu. Web site: http://www.enc.edu/.

ELMS COLLEGE
CHICOPEE, MASSACHUSETTS

Contact Mr. Joseph Wagner, Director of Admissions, Elms College, 291 Springfield Street, Chicopee, MA 01013-2839. Phone: 413-592-3189 Ext. 350 or toll-free 800-255-ELMS. Fax: 413-594-2781. E-mail: admissions@elms.edu. Web site: http://www.elms.edu/.

EMERSON COLLEGE
BOSTON, MASSACHUSETTS

General Independent, comprehensive, coed **Entrance** Very difficult **Setting** urban campus **Total enrollment** 4,380 **Student-faculty ratio** 14:1 **Application deadline** 1/5 (freshmen), 3/15 (transfer) **Freshmen** 45% were admitted **Housing** Yes **Expenses** Tuition $26,880; Room & Board $11,376 **Undergraduates** 56% women, 7% part-time, 4% 25 or older, 1% Native American, 7% Hispanic American, 3% African American, 5% Asian American/Pacific Islander **The most frequently chosen baccalaureate fields are** communications/journalism, English, visual and performing arts **Academic program** Advanced placement, self-designed majors, honors program, summer session, adult/continuing education programs, internships **Contact** Ms. Sara S. Ramirez, Director of Undergraduate Admission, Emerson College, 120 Boylston Street, Boston, MA 02116-4624. Phone: 617-824-8600. Fax: 617-824-8609. E-mail: admission@emerson.edu. Web site: http://www.emerson.edu/.

►**For more information, see page 459.**

EMMANUEL COLLEGE
BOSTON, MASSACHUSETTS

General Independent Roman Catholic, comprehensive, coed **Entrance** Moderately difficult **Setting** 17-acre urban campus **Total enrollment** 2,467 **Student-faculty ratio** 15:1 **Application deadline** 3/1 (freshmen), 4/1 (transfer) **Freshmen** 61% were admitted **Housing** Yes **Expenses** Tuition $26,250; Room & Board $11,200 **Undergraduates** 73% women, 27% part-time, 18% 25 or older, 0.3% Native American, 4% Hispanic American, 6% African American, 2% Asian American/Pacific Islander **The most frequently chosen baccalaureate fields are** business/marketing, health professions and related sciences, psychology **Academic program** Advanced placement, accelerated degree program, self-designed majors, honors program, summer session, adult/continuing education programs, internships **Contact** Ms. Sandra Robbins, Dean for Enrollment, Emmanuel College, Admissions Office, 400 The Fenway, Boston, MA 02115. Phone: 617-735-9715. Fax: 617-735-9801. E-mail: enroll@emmanuel.edu. Web site: http://www.emmanuel.edu/.

ENDICOTT COLLEGE
BEVERLY, MASSACHUSETTS

General Independent, comprehensive, coed **Entrance** Moderately difficult **Setting** 240-acre suburban campus **Total enrollment** 3,970 **Student-faculty ratio** 16:1 **Application deadline** 2/15 (freshmen), 2/15 (transfer) **Freshmen** 48% were admitted **Housing** Yes **Expenses** Tuition $24,530; Room & Board $11,380 **Undergraduates** 57% women, 8% part-time, 0.3% Native American, 2% Hispanic American, 1% African American, 1% Asian American/Pacific Islander **The most frequently chosen baccalaureate fields are** business/marketing, parks and recreation, visual and performing arts **Academic program** English as a second language, advanced placement, accelerated degree program, self-designed majors, honors program, summer session, adult/continuing education programs, internships **Contact** Mr. Thomas J. Redman, Vice President of Admission and Financial Aid, Endicott College, 376 Hale Street, Beverly, MA 01915. Phone: 978-921-1000 or toll-free 800-325-1114. Fax: 978-232-2520. E-mail: admissio@endicott.edu. Web site: http://www.endicott.edu/.

FITCHBURG STATE COLLEGE
FITCHBURG, MASSACHUSETTS

General State-supported, comprehensive, coed **Entrance** Moderately difficult **Setting** 45-acre suburban campus **Total enrollment** 6,692 **Student-faculty ratio** 16:1 **Freshmen** 66% were admitted **Housing** Yes **Expenses** Tuition $5992; Room & Board $6632 **Undergraduates** 55% women, 17% part-time, 14% 25 or older, 0.3% Native American, 3% Hispanic American, 3% African American, 2% Asian American/Pacific Islander **The most frequently chosen baccalaureate fields are** business/marketing, education, visual and performing arts **Academic program** Advanced placement, accelerated degree program, self-designed majors, honors program, summer session, adult/continuing education programs,

Fitchburg State College *(continued)*

internships **Contact** Director of Admissions, Fitchburg State College, 160 Pearl Street, Fitchburg, MA 01420-2697. Phone: 978-665-3140 or toll-free 800-705-9692. Fax: 978-665-4540. E-mail: admissions@fsc.edu. Web site: http://www.fsc.edu/.

FRAMINGHAM STATE COLLEGE
FRAMINGHAM, MASSACHUSETTS

General State-supported, comprehensive, coed **Entrance** Moderately difficult **Setting** 73-acre suburban campus **Total enrollment** 5,903 **Student-faculty ratio** 16:1 **Application deadline** 5/15 (freshmen), 5/1 (transfer) **Freshmen** 56% were admitted **Housing** Yes **Expenses** Tuition $5799; Room & Board $7127 **Undergraduates** 64% women, 18% part-time, 17% 25 or older, 0.4% Native American, 4% Hispanic American, 4% African American, 2% Asian American/Pacific Islander **The most frequently chosen baccalaureate fields are** business/marketing, family and consumer sciences, social sciences **Academic program** English as a second language, advanced placement, honors program, summer session, adult/continuing education programs, internships **Contact** Ms. Elizabeth J. Canella, Associate Dean of Admissions, Framingham State College, PO Box 9101, Dwight Hall, Room 209, 100 State Street, Framingham, MA 01701-9101. Phone: 508-626-4500. Fax: 508-626-4017. E-mail: admiss@frc.mass.edu. Web site: http://www.framingham.edu/.

FRANKLIN W. OLIN COLLEGE OF ENGINEERING
NEEDHAM, MASSACHUSETTS

General Independent, 4-year, coed **Entrance** Very difficult **Total enrollment** 296 **Student-faculty ratio** 9:1 **Application deadline** 12/1 (freshmen) **Freshmen** 11% were admitted **Housing** Yes **Expenses** Tuition $35,025; Room & Board $11,800 **Undergraduates** 42% women, 4% Hispanic American, 2% African American, 11% Asian American/Pacific Islander **Academic program** Self-designed majors, internships **Contact** Mr. Charles Nolan, Vice President for External Relations and Dean of Admission, Franklin W. Olin College of Engineering, Olin Way, Needham, MA 02492-1200. Phone: 781-292-2201. Fax: 781-292-2310. E-mail: info@olin.edu. Web site: http://www.olin.edu/.

GORDON COLLEGE
WENHAM, MASSACHUSETTS

General Independent nondenominational, comprehensive, coed **Entrance** Moderately difficult **Setting** 500-acre suburban campus **Total enrollment** 1,645 **Student-faculty ratio** 12:1 **Application deadline** Rolling (freshmen), rolling (transfer) **Freshmen** 71% were admitted **Housing** Yes **Expenses** Tuition $27,294; Room & Board $7424 **Undergraduates** 63% women, 2% part-time, 1% 25 or older, 0.3% Native American, 3% Hispanic American, 2% African American, 1% Asian American/Pacific Islander **The most frequently chosen baccalaureate fields are** English, business/marketing, social sciences **Academic program** Advanced placement, self-designed majors, honors program, internships **Contact** Barbara Layne, Associate Vice President for Enrollment, Gordon College, 255 Grapevine Road, Wenham, MA 01984-1899. Phone: 978-867-4034 or toll-free 866-464-6736. Fax: 978-867-4682. E-mail: admissions@gordon.edu. Web site: http://www.gordon.edu/.

HAMPSHIRE COLLEGE
AMHERST, MASSACHUSETTS

General Independent, 4-year, coed **Entrance** Very difficult **Setting** 800-acre small-town campus **Total enrollment** 1,431 **Student-faculty ratio** 12:1 **Application deadline** 1/15 (freshmen), 3/1 (transfer) **Freshmen** 55% were admitted **Housing** Yes **Expenses** Tuition $36,545; Room & Board $9545 **Undergraduates** 57% women, 2% 25 or older, 1% Native American, 6% Hispanic American, 4% African American, 4% Asian American/Pacific Islander **The most frequently chosen baccalaureate fields are** social sciences, English, visual and performing arts **Academic program** Advanced placement, accelerated degree program, self-designed majors, internships **Contact** Ms. Karen S. Parker, Director of Admissions, Hampshire College, 893 West Street, Amherst, MA 01002. Phone: 413-559-5471 or toll-free 877-937-4267. Fax: 413-559-5631. E-mail: admissions@hampshire.edu. Web site: http://www.hampshire.edu/.

HARVARD UNIVERSITY
CAMBRIDGE, MASSACHUSETTS

General Independent, university, coed **Entrance** Most difficult **Setting** 380-acre urban campus **Total enrollment** 19,257 **Student-faculty ratio** 7:1 **Application deadline** 1/1 (freshmen), 2/1 (transfer) **Freshmen** 9% were admitted **Housing** Yes **Expenses** Tuition $34,998; Room & Board $10,622 **Undergraduates** 50% women, 0.1% part-time, 0.2% 25 or older, 1% Native American, 7% Hispanic American, 8% African American, 16% Asian American/Pacific Islander **The most frequently chosen baccalaureate fields are** biological/life sciences, history, social sciences **Academic program** English as a second language, advanced placement, accelerated degree program, self-designed majors, honors program, summer session, adult/continuing education programs, internships **Contact** Dr. William R. Fitzsimmons, Office of Admissions and Financial Aid, Harvard University, Byerly Hall, 8 Garden Street, Cambridge, MA 02138. Phone: 617-495-1551. E-mail: college@harvard.edu. Web site: http://www.harvard.edu/.

HEBREW COLLEGE

NEWTON CENTRE, MASSACHUSETTS

General Independent Jewish, comprehensive, coed **Entrance** Minimally difficult **Setting** 3-acre suburban campus **Total enrollment** 6 **Application deadline** Rolling (freshmen), 4/15 (transfer) **Housing** No **Undergraduates** 83% women, 17% part-time, 99% 25 or older **Academic program** Summer session, adult/continuing education programs, internships **Contact** Ms. Kate Nachman, Admissions, Hebrew College, Hebrew College, 160 Herreck Road, Newton, MA 02459. Phone: 617-559-8619 or toll-free 800-866-4814 Ext. 8619. Fax: 617-559-8601. E-mail: admissions@lhebrewcollege.edu. Web site: http://www.hebrewcollege.edu/.

HELLENIC COLLEGE

BROOKLINE, MASSACHUSETTS

General Independent Greek Orthodox, 4-year, coed **Entrance** Minimally difficult **Setting** 52-acre suburban campus **Total enrollment** 187 **Student-faculty ratio** 9:1 **Application deadline** Rolling (freshmen), rolling (transfer) **Freshmen** 36% were admitted **Housing** Yes **Expenses** Tuition $17,325; Room & Board $10,890 **Undergraduates** 32% women, 10% 25 or older, 1% Native American, 1% African American **The most frequently chosen baccalaureate field is** liberal arts/general studies **Academic program** Advanced placement, summer session, internships **Contact** Ms. Sonia Daly, Director of Admissions, Hellenic College, 50 Goddard Avenue, Brookline, MA 02445-7496. Phone: 617-731-3500 Ext. 1285 or toll-free 866-424-2338. Fax: 617-850-1460. E-mail: admissions@hchc.edu. Web site: http://www.hchc.edu/.

LASELL COLLEGE

NEWTON, MASSACHUSETTS

Contact Mr. James Tweed, Director of Undergraduate Admission, Lasell College, 1844 Commonwealth Avenue, Newton, MA 02468. Phone: 617-243-2225 or toll-free 888-LASELL-4. Fax: 617-243-2380. E-mail: info@lasell.edu. Web site: http://www.lasell.edu/.

LESLEY UNIVERSITY

CAMBRIDGE, MASSACHUSETTS

General Independent, comprehensive, coed **Entrance** Moderately difficult **Setting** 5-acre urban campus **Total enrollment** 6,474 **Student-faculty ratio** 9:1 **Application deadline** Rolling (transfer) **Freshmen** 86% were admitted **Housing** Yes **Expenses** Tuition $27,510; Room & Board $12,000 **Undergraduates** 75% women, 6% part-time, 6% 25 or older, 0.4% Native American, 5% Hispanic American, 5% African American, 4% Asian American/Pacific Islander **The most frequently chosen baccalaureate fields are** liberal arts/general studies, psychology, visual and performing arts **Academic program** Advanced placement, accelerated degree program, self-designed majors, honors program, summer session, adult/continuing education programs, internships **Contact** Ms. Deborah Kocar, Director of Lesley College Admissions, Lesley University, 29 Everett Street, Cambridge, MA 02138-2790. Phone: 617-349-8800 or toll-free 800-999-1959 Ext. 8800. Fax: 617-349-8810. E-mail: ugadm@mail.lesley.edu. Web site: http://www.lesley.edu/.

MASSACHUSETTS COLLEGE OF ART AND DESIGN

BOSTON, MASSACHUSETTS

General State-supported, comprehensive, coed **Entrance** Very difficult **Setting** 5-acre urban campus **Total enrollment** 2,315 **Application deadline** 2/15 (freshmen), 3/15 (transfer) **Freshmen** 56% were admitted **Housing** Yes **Expenses** Tuition $7450; Room & Board $10,900 **Undergraduates** 67% women, 30% part-time, 15% 25 or older, 1% Native American, 6% Hispanic American, 3% African American, 6% Asian American/Pacific Islander **The most frequently chosen baccalaureate fields are** education, architecture, visual and performing arts **Academic program** Self-designed majors, summer session, internships **Contact** Ms. Lydia Polanco-Pena, Director of Admissions Operations, Massachusetts College of Art and Design, 621 Huntington Avenue, Boston, MA 02115. Phone: 617-879-7250. Fax: 617-879-7250. E-mail: admissions@massart.edu. Web site: http://www.massart.edu/.

MASSACHUSETTS COLLEGE OF LIBERAL ARTS

NORTH ADAMS, MASSACHUSETTS

General State-supported, comprehensive, coed **Entrance** Moderately difficult **Setting** 80-acre small-town campus **Total enrollment** 1,841 **Student-faculty ratio** 12:1 **Application deadline** Rolling (freshmen), rolling (transfer)

Massachusetts College of Liberal Arts *(continued)*

Freshmen 71% were admitted **Housing** Yes **Expenses** Tuition $6168; Room & Board $6804 **Undergraduates** 60% women, 14% part-time, 16% 25 or older, 0.1% Native American, 4% Hispanic American, 4% African American, 1% Asian American/Pacific Islander **The most frequently chosen baccalaureate fields are** business/marketing, English, social sciences **Academic program** Advanced placement, self-designed majors, honors program, summer session, internships **Contact** Mr. Steve King, Assistant Dean of Enrollment Services/Director of Admission, Massachusetts College of Liberal Arts, 375 Church Street, North Adams, MA 01247-4100. Phone: 413-662-5410 or toll-free 800-292-6632. Fax: 413-662-5179. E-mail: admissions@mcla.edu. Web site: http://www.mcla.edu/.

MASSACHUSETTS COLLEGE OF PHARMACY AND HEALTH SCIENCES

BOSTON, MASSACHUSETTS

General Independent, university, coed **Entrance** Moderately difficult **Setting** 3-acre urban campus **Total enrollment** 3,626 **Student-faculty ratio** 19:1 **Application deadline** 2/1 (freshmen), 2/1 (transfer) **Freshmen** 65% were admitted **Housing** Yes **Expenses** Tuition $22,700; Room & Board $11,800 **Undergraduates** 68% women, 4% part-time, 12% 25 or older, 0.2% Native American, 3% Hispanic American, 5% African American, 28% Asian American/Pacific Islander **The most frequently chosen baccalaureate field is** health professions and related sciences **Academic program** English as a second language, advanced placement, accelerated degree program, summer session, adult/continuing education programs, internships **Contact** Mr. Jim Zarakas, Admissions Assistant, Massachusetts College of Pharmacy and Health Sciences, 179 Longwood Avenue, Boston, MA 02115. Phone: 617-732-2850 or toll-free 617-732-2850 (in-state); 800-225-5506 (out-of-state). Fax: 617-732-2118. E-mail: admissions@mphs.edu. Web site: http://www.mcphs.edu/.

MASSACHUSETTS INSTITUTE OF TECHNOLOGY

CAMBRIDGE, MASSACHUSETTS

General Independent, university, coed **Entrance** Most difficult **Setting** 168-acre urban campus **Total enrollment** 10,220 **Student-faculty ratio** 6:1 **Application deadline** 1/1 (freshmen), 3/15 (transfer) **Freshmen** 12% were admitted **Housing** Yes **Expenses** Tuition $34,986; Room & Board $10,400 **Undergraduates** 45% women, 1% part-time, 1% 25 or older, 1% Native American, 12% Hispanic American, 7% African American, 26% Asian American/Pacific Islander **The most frequently chosen baccalaureate fields are** computer and information sciences, engineering, physical sciences **Academic program** English as a second language, advanced placement, internships **Contact** Admissions Counselors, Massachusetts Institute of Technology, Building 3-108, 77 Massachusetts Avenue, Cambridge, MA 02139-4307. Phone: 617-253-3400. Fax: 617-258-8304. E-mail: admissions@mit.edu. Web site: http://web.mit.edu/.

MASSACHUSETTS MARITIME ACADEMY

BUZZARDS BAY, MASSACHUSETTS

General State-supported, 4-year, coed, primarily men **Entrance** Moderately difficult **Setting** 55-acre small-town campus **Total enrollment** 1,134 **Student-faculty ratio** 15:1 **Application deadline** Rolling (freshmen), rolling (transfer) **Freshmen** 33% were admitted **Housing** Yes **Expenses** Tuition $7966; Room & Board $7812 **Undergraduates** 9% women, 6% part-time, 3% 25 or older, 0.3% Native American, 1% Hispanic American, 1% African American, 1% Asian American/Pacific Islander **The most frequently chosen baccalaureate fields are** engineering, natural resources/environmental science, transportation and materials moving **Academic program** Advanced placement, summer session, adult/continuing education programs, internships **Contact** Roy Fulgueras, Director of Admissions, Massachusetts Maritime Academy, 101 Academy Drive, Blinn Hall, Buzzards Bay, MA 02532. Phone: 508-830-6441 or toll-free 800-544-3411. Fax: 508-830-5077. E-mail: admissions@maritime.edu. Web site: http://www.maritime.edu/.

MERRIMACK COLLEGE

NORTH ANDOVER, MASSACHUSETTS

General Independent Roman Catholic, comprehensive, coed **Entrance** Moderately difficult **Setting** 220-acre suburban campus **Total enrollment** 2,131 **Student-faculty ratio** 12:1 **Application deadline** 2/1 (freshmen), 12/30 (transfer) **Freshmen** 71% were admitted **Housing** Yes **Expenses** Tuition $29,810; Room & Board $10,705 **Undergraduates** 51% women, 13% part-time, 5% 25 or older, 0.2% Native American, 4% Hispanic American, 2% African American, 2% Asian American/Pacific Islander **The most frequently chosen baccalaureate fields are** business/marketing, psychology, social sciences **Academic program** English as a second language, advanced placement, self-designed majors, honors program, summer session, adult/continuing education programs, internships **Contact** Director of Admissions, Merrimack College, Austin Hall, A22, North Andover, MA 01845. Phone: 978-837-

5100. Fax: 978-837-5133. E-mail: admission@merrimack.edu. Web site: http://www.merrimack.edu/.

MONTSERRAT COLLEGE OF ART
BEVERLY, MASSACHUSETTS

General Independent, 4-year, coed **Entrance** Moderately difficult **Setting** 10-acre suburban campus **Total enrollment** 285 **Student-faculty ratio** 12:1 **Application deadline** 8/15 (freshmen), 8/15 (transfer) **Freshmen** 68% were admitted **Housing** Yes **Expenses** Tuition $22,300; Room only $5800 **Undergraduates** 68% women, 9% part-time, 5% 25 or older, 2% Hispanic American, 1% African American, 1% Asian American/Pacific Islander **The most frequently chosen baccalaureate field is** visual and performing arts **Academic program** English as a second language, advanced placement, self-designed majors, adult/continuing education programs, internships **Contact** Mr. Brian Bicknell, Dean of Students, Montserrat College of Art, 23 Essex Street, PO Box 26, Beverly, MA 01915. Phone: 978-921-4242 Ext. 1153 or toll-free 800-836-0487. Fax: 978-921-4241. E-mail: bbicknell@montserrat.edu. Web site: http://www.montserrat.edu/.

MOUNT HOLYOKE COLLEGE
SOUTH HADLEY, MASSACHUSETTS

General Independent, comprehensive, women only **Entrance** Very difficult **Setting** 800-acre small-town campus **Total enrollment** 2,204 **Student-faculty ratio** 10:1 **Application deadline** 1/15 (freshmen), 5/15 (transfer) **Freshmen** 52% were admitted **Housing** Yes **Expenses** Tuition $35,940; Room & Board $10,520 **Undergraduates** 2% part-time, 6% 25 or older, 1% Native American, 5% Hispanic American, 5% African American, 12% Asian American/Pacific Islander **The most frequently chosen baccalaureate fields are** English, social sciences, visual and performing arts **Academic program** Advanced placement, self-designed majors, honors program, adult/continuing education programs, internships **Contact** Ms. Diane Anci, Dean of Admission, Mount Holyoke College, 50 College Street, South Hadley, MA 01075. Phone: 413-538-2023. Fax: 413-538-2409. E-mail: admission@mtholyoke.edu. Web site: http://www.mtholyoke.edu/.

MOUNT IDA COLLEGE
NEWTON, MASSACHUSETTS

General Independent, 4-year, coed **Entrance** Moderately difficult **Setting** 72-acre suburban campus **Total enrollment** 1,430 **Student-faculty ratio** 13:1 **Application deadline** Rolling (freshmen), rolling (transfer) **Freshmen** 78% were admitted **Housing** Yes **Expenses** Tuition $22,500; Room & Board $11,000 **Undergraduates** 67% women, 7% part-time, 9% 25 or older, 0.4% Native American, 6% Hispanic American, 9% African American, 2% Asian American/Pacific Islander **Academic program** English as a second language, accelerated degree program, self-designed majors, honors program, adult/continuing education programs, internships **Contact** Jay Titus MS, Dean of Admissions, Mount Ida College, 777 Dedham Street, Newton, MA 02459-3310. Phone: 617-928-4553. Fax: 617-928-4507. E-mail: admissions@mountida.edu. Web site: http://www.mountida.edu/.

NEWBURY COLLEGE
BROOKLINE, MASSACHUSETTS

General Independent, 4-year, coed **Entrance** Minimally difficult **Setting** 10-acre suburban campus **Total enrollment** 1,202 **Student-faculty ratio** 15:1 **Application deadline** Rolling (freshmen), rolling (transfer) **Freshmen** 66% were admitted **Housing** Yes **Expenses** Tuition $22,000; Room & Board $10,700 **Undergraduates** 63% women, 23% part-time, 10% 25 or older **Academic program** English as a second language, advanced placement, accelerated degree program, honors program, summer session, adult/continuing education programs, internships **Contact** Mr. Ken Sawada, Interim Director of Admission, Newbury College, 129 Fisher Avenue, Brookline, MA 02445-5796. Phone: 617-730-7007 or toll-free 800-NEWBURY. Fax: 617-731-9618. E-mail: info@newbury.edu. Web site: http://www.newbury.edu/.

NEW ENGLAND CONSERVATORY OF MUSIC
BOSTON, MASSACHUSETTS

General Independent, comprehensive, coed **Entrance** Very difficult **Setting** 2-acre urban campus **Total enrollment** 795 **Student-faculty ratio** 6:1 **Application deadline** 12/1 (freshmen), 12/3 (transfer) **Freshmen** 29% were admitted **Housing** Yes **Expenses** Tuition $33,325; Room & Board $11,600 **Undergraduates** 44% women, 7% part-time, 3% 25 or older, 0.3% Native American, 5% Hispanic American, 3% African American, 9% Asian American/Pacific Islander **The most frequently chosen baccalaureate field is** visual and performing arts **Academic program** English as a second language, advanced placement, summer session, adult/continuing education programs, internships **Contact** Ms. Christina Daly, Dean of Admissions, New England Conservatory of Music, 290 Huntington Avenue, Boston, MA 02115-5000. Phone: 617-585-1103. Fax: 617-585-1115. E-mail: admissions@

New England Conservatory of Music *(continued)*

newenglandconservatory.edu. Web site: http://www.newenglandconservatory.edu/.

THE NEW ENGLAND INSTITUTE OF ART
BROOKLINE, MASSACHUSETTS

General Proprietary, 4-year, coed **Setting** urban campus **Contact** Second Director of Admissions, The New England Institute of Art, 10 Brookline Place West, Brookline, MA 02445. Phone: 617-739-1700 or toll-free 800-903-4425. Fax: 617-582-4500. Web site: http://www.artinstitutes.edu/boston.

NICHOLS COLLEGE
DUDLEY, MASSACHUSETTS

General Independent, comprehensive, coed **Entrance** Moderately difficult **Setting** 210-acre suburban campus **Total enrollment** 1,500 **Student-faculty ratio** 18:1 **Application deadline** Rolling (freshmen), rolling (transfer) **Freshmen** 77% were admitted **Housing** Yes **Expenses** Tuition $25,700; Room & Board $8960 **Undergraduates** 40% women, 17% part-time, 30% 25 or older, 0.4% Native American, 3% Hispanic American, 4% African American, 1% Asian American/Pacific Islander **The most frequently chosen baccalaureate fields are** business/marketing, liberal arts/general studies **Academic program** Advanced placement, accelerated degree program, honors program, summer session, adult/continuing education programs, internships **Contact** Ms. Marie Keegan, Admissions Assistant, Nichols College, PO Box 5000, Dudley, MA 01571-5000. Phone: 508-213-2203 or toll-free 800-470-3379. Fax: 508-943-9885. E-mail: admissions@nichols.edu. Web site: http://www.nichols.edu/.

NORTHEASTERN UNIVERSITY
BOSTON, MASSACHUSETTS

General Independent, university, coed **Entrance** Very difficult **Setting** 67-acre urban campus **Total enrollment** 20,593 **Student-faculty ratio** 16:1 **Application deadline** 1/15 (freshmen), 5/1 (transfer) **Freshmen** 39% were admitted **Housing** Yes **Expenses** Tuition $31,899; Room & Board $11,420 **Undergraduates** 51% women, 4% 25 or older, 0.4% Native American, 5% Hispanic American, 6% African American, 8% Asian American/Pacific Islander **The most frequently chosen baccalaureate fields are** business/marketing, engineering, social sciences **Academic program** English as a second language, advanced placement, accelerated degree program, self-designed majors, honors program, summer session, adult/continuing education programs, internships **Contact** Ronne Turner, Director of Admissions, Northeastern University, 360 Huntington Avenue, 150 Richards Hall, Boston, MA 02115. Phone: 617-373-2200. Fax: 617-373-8780. E-mail: admissions@neu.edu. Web site: http://www.northeastern.edu/.

PINE MANOR COLLEGE
CHESTNUT HILL, MASSACHUSETTS

General Independent, 4-year, women only **Contact** Mr. Robin Engel, Dean of Admissions and Financial Aid, Pine Manor College, 400 Heath Street, Chestnut Hill, MA 02467-2332. Phone: 617-731-7104 or toll-free 800-762-1357. Fax: 617-731-7102. E-mail: admisson@pmc.edu. Web site: http://www.pmc.edu/.

REGIS COLLEGE
WESTON, MASSACHUSETTS

General Independent Roman Catholic, comprehensive, coed **Entrance** Moderately difficult **Setting** 131-acre small-town campus **Total enrollment** 1,511 **Student-faculty ratio** 14:1 **Application deadline** Rolling (freshmen), rolling (transfer) **Freshmen** 77% were admitted **Housing** Yes **Expenses** Tuition $25,900; Room & Board $11,600 **Undergraduates** 91% women, 22% part-time, 9% 25 or older, 0.3% Native American, 9% Hispanic American, 19% African American, 6% Asian American/Pacific Islander **The most frequently chosen baccalaureate fields are** health professions and related sciences, communications/journalism, social sciences **Academic program** Advanced placement, accelerated degree program, self-designed majors, honors program, summer session, adult/continuing education programs, internships **Contact** Ms. Emily Keily, Director of Admission, Regis College, 235 Wellesley Street, Weston, MA 02493. Phone: 781-768-7100 or toll-free 866-438-7344. Fax: 781-768-7071. E-mail: admission@regiscollege.edu. Web site: http://www.regiscollege.edu/.

SALEM STATE COLLEGE
SALEM, MASSACHUSETTS

General State-supported, comprehensive, coed **Entrance** Minimally difficult **Setting** 62-acre suburban campus **Total enrollment** 10,085 **Student-faculty ratio** 17:1 **Application deadline** Rolling (freshmen), rolling (transfer) **Freshmen** 60% were admitted **Housing** Yes **Expenses** Tuition $6210; Room only $5545 **Undergraduates** 62% women, 19% part-time, 21% 25 or older, 0.4% Native American, 7% Hispanic American, 8% African American, 3% Asian American/Pacific Islander **The most frequently chosen baccalaureate fields are** business/marketing, education, health professions and related sciences **Academic program** English as a second language, advanced placement, honors program, summer session, adult/continuing education programs, internships **Contact** Mr. Nate Bryant, Dean of Student Development, Salem State College, 352 Lafayette Street, Salem, MA 01970. Phone: 978-542-6200. Fax: 978-542-6893. E-mail: admissions@salemstate.edu. Web site: http://www.salemstate.edu/.

SCHOOL OF THE MUSEUM OF FINE ARTS, BOSTON
BOSTON, MASSACHUSETTS

General Independent, comprehensive, coed **Entrance** Moderately difficult **Setting** 14-acre urban campus **Total enrollment** 797 **Student-faculty ratio** 10:1 **Application deadline** 2/1 (freshmen), 3/1 (transfer) **Freshmen** 82% were admitted **Housing** Yes **Expenses** Tuition $27,970; Room only $11,600 **Undergraduates** 69% women, 12% part-time, 18% 25 or older, 1% Native American, 5% Hispanic American, 2% African American, 4% Asian American/Pacific Islander **The most frequently chosen baccalaureate fields are** education, visual and performing arts **Academic program** English as a second language, self-designed majors, summer session, adult/continuing education programs, internships **Contact** Jesse Tarantino, Assistant Dean of Admissions, School of the Museum of Fine Arts, Boston, 230 The Fenway, Boston, MA 02115. Phone: 617-369-3626 or toll-free 800-643-6078. Fax: 617-369-4264. E-mail: admissions@smfa.edu. Web site: http://www.smfa.edu/.

SIMMONS COLLEGE
BOSTON, MASSACHUSETTS

General Independent, university, undergraduate: women only; graduate: coed **Entrance** Moderately difficult **Setting** 12-acre urban campus **Total enrollment** 4,733 **Student-faculty ratio** 13:1 **Application deadline** 2/1 (freshmen), 4/1 (transfer) **Freshmen** 57% were admitted **Housing** Yes **Expenses** Tuition $28,302; Room & Board $11,138 **Undergraduates** 10% part-time, 9% 25 or older, 0.3% Native American, 4% Hispanic American, 5% African American, 8% Asian American/Pacific Islander **The most frequently chosen baccalaureate fields are** health professions and related sciences, communications/journalism, social sciences **Academic program** English as a second language, advanced placement, accelerated degree program, self-designed majors, honors program, summer session, adult/continuing education programs, internships **Contact** Ms. Catherine Childs-Capolupo, Director of Undergraduate Admissions, Simmons College, 300 The Fenway, Boston, MA 02115. Phone: 617-521-2057 or toll-free 800-345-8468. Fax: 617-521-3190. E-mail: ugadm@simmons.edu. Web site: http://www.simmons.edu/.

SMITH COLLEGE
NORTHAMPTON, MASSACHUSETTS

General Independent, comprehensive, undergraduate: women only; graduate: coed **Entrance** Very difficult **Setting** 125-acre small-town campus **Total enrollment** 3,065 **Student-faculty ratio** 9:1 **Application deadline** 1/15 (freshmen), 5/15 (transfer) **Freshmen** 52% were admitted **Housing** Yes **Expenses** Tuition $34,186; Room & Board $11,420 **Undergraduates** 1% part-time, 7% 25 or older, 1% Native American, 6% Hispanic American, 7% African American, 12% Asian American/Pacific Islander **The most frequently chosen baccalaureate fields are** area and ethnic studies, foreign languages and literature, social sciences **Academic program** Advanced placement, accelerated degree program, self-designed majors, honors program, adult/continuing education programs, internships **Contact** Ms. Debra Shaver, Director of Admissions, Smith College, 7 College Lane, Northampton, MA 01063. Phone: 413-585-2500 or toll-free 800-383-3232. Fax: 413-585-2527. E-mail: admission@smith.edu. Web site: http://www.smith.edu/.

SPRINGFIELD COLLEGE
SPRINGFIELD, MASSACHUSETTS

Contact Ms. Mary DeAngelo, Director of Undergraduate Admissions, Springfield College, 263 Alden Street, Box M, Springfield, MA 01109. Phone: 413-748-3136 or toll-free 800-343-1257. Fax: 413-748-3694. E-mail: admissions@spfldcol.edu. Web site: http://www.spfldcol.edu/.

►**For more information, see page 492.**

STONEHILL COLLEGE
EASTON, MASSACHUSETTS

General Independent Roman Catholic, comprehensive, coed **Entrance** Very difficult **Setting** 375-acre suburban campus **Total enrollment** 2,450 **Student-faculty ratio** 13:1 **Application deadline** 1/15 (freshmen), 4/1 (transfer) **Freshmen** 52% were admitted **Housing** Yes **Expenses** Tuition $30,150; Room & Board $11,830 **Undergraduates** 61% women, 4% part-time, 3% 25 or older, 0.2% Native American, 4% Hispanic American, 2% African American, 2% Asian American/Pacific Islander **The most frequently chosen baccalaureate fields are** business/marketing, psychology, social sciences **Academic program** Advanced placement, self-designed majors, honors program, summer session, adult/continuing education programs, internships **Contact** Mr. Brian P. Murphy, Dean

Stonehill College *(continued)*

of Admissions and Enrollment, Stonehill College, 320 Washington Street, Easton, MA 02357-5610. Phone: 508-565-1373. Fax: 508-565-1545. E-mail: admissions@stonehill.edu. Web site: http://www.stonehill.edu/.

SUFFOLK UNIVERSITY
BOSTON, MASSACHUSETTS

General Independent, comprehensive, coed **Entrance** Moderately difficult **Setting** 2-acre urban campus **Total enrollment** 9,083 **Student-faculty ratio** 12:1 **Application deadline** 3/1 (freshmen), 3/15 (transfer) **Freshmen** 80% were admitted **Housing** Yes **Expenses** Tuition $24,250; Room & Board $13,300 **Undergraduates** 57% women, 12% part-time, 7% 25 or older, 0.3% Native American, 5% Hispanic American, 3% African American, 6% Asian American/Pacific Islander **The most frequently chosen baccalaureate fields are** business/marketing, communications/journalism, social sciences **Academic program** English as a second language, advanced placement, accelerated degree program, honors program, summer session, adult/continuing education programs, internships **Contact** Undergraduate Admissions, Suffolk University, 8 Ashburton Place, Boston, MA 02108. Phone: 617-573-8460 or toll-free 800-6-SUFFOLK. Fax: 617-742-4291. E-mail: admission@suffolk.edu. Web site: http://www.suffolk.edu/.

TUFTS UNIVERSITY
MEDFORD, MASSACHUSETTS

General Independent, university, coed **Entrance** Most difficult **Setting** 150-acre suburban campus **Total enrollment** 9,758 **Student-faculty ratio** 7:1 **Application deadline** 1/1 (freshmen), 3/1 (transfer) **Freshmen** 28% were admitted **Housing** Yes **Expenses** Tuition $36,700; Room & Board $10,160 **Undergraduates** 51% women, 1% part-time, 1% 25 or older, 0.2% Native American, 6% Hispanic American, 6% African American, 12% Asian American/Pacific Islander **The most frequently chosen baccalaureate fields are** engineering, social sciences, visual and performing arts **Academic program** Advanced placement, self-designed majors, honors program, summer session, adult/continuing education programs, internships **Contact** Mr. Lee Coffin, Office of Undergraduate Admissions, Tufts University, Bendetson Hall, Medford, MA 02155. Phone: 617-627-3170. Fax: 617-627-3860. E-mail: admissions.inquiry@ase.tufts.edu. Web site: http://www.tufts.edu/.

UNIVERSITY OF MASSACHUSETTS AMHERST
AMHERST, MASSACHUSETTS

General State-supported, university, coed **Entrance** Moderately difficult **Setting** 1,463-acre small-town campus **Total enrollment** 25,873 **Student-faculty ratio** 17:1 **Application deadline** 1/15 (freshmen), 4/15 (transfer) **Freshmen** 66% were admitted **Housing** Yes **Expenses** Tuition $10,417; Room & Board $8114 **Undergraduates** 50% women, 7% part-time, 7% 25 or older, 0.3% Native American, 4% Hispanic American, 5% African American, 8% Asian American/Pacific Islander **The most frequently chosen baccalaureate fields are** business/marketing, communications/journalism, social sciences **Academic program** English as a second language, advanced placement, self-designed majors, honors program, summer session, adult/continuing education programs, internships **Contact** Mr. Kevin Kelly, Director, Undergraduate Admissions, University of Massachusetts Amherst, 37 Mather Drive, Amherst, MA 01003. Phone: 413-545-0222. Fax: 413-545-4312. E-mail: mail@admissions.umass.edu. Web site: http://www.umass.edu/.

UNIVERSITY OF MASSACHUSETTS BOSTON
BOSTON, MASSACHUSETTS

General State-supported, university, coed **Entrance** Moderately difficult **Setting** 177-acre urban campus **Total enrollment** 13,433 **Student-faculty ratio** 16:1 **Application deadline** 6/1 (freshmen), rolling (transfer) **Freshmen** 61% were admitted **Housing** No **Expenses** Tuition $8837 **Undergraduates** 57% women, 34% part-time, 35% 25 or older, 0.5% Native American, 8% Hispanic American, 16% African American, 13% Asian American/Pacific Islander **The most frequently chosen baccalaureate fields are** business/marketing, health professions and related sciences, social sciences **Academic program** English as a second language, advanced placement, accelerated degree program, self-designed majors, honors program, summer session, adult/continuing education programs, internships **Contact** Mrs. Liliana Mickle, Director of Undergraduate Admissions, University of Massachusetts Boston, 100 Morrissey Boulevard, Boston, MA 02125-3393. Phone: 617-287-6100. Fax: 617-287-5999. E-mail: undergrad@umb.edu. Web site: http://www.umb.edu/.

UNIVERSITY OF MASSACHUSETTS DARTMOUTH
NORTH DARTMOUTH, MASSACHUSETTS

General State-supported, university, coed **Entrance** Moderately difficult **Setting** 710-acre suburban campus **Total enrollment** 9,080 **Student-faculty ratio** 17:1 **Application deadline** Rolling (freshmen), rolling (transfer) **Freshmen** 66% were admitted **Housing** Yes **Expenses** Tuition $8592; Room & Board $8432 **Undergraduates** 49% women, 14% part-time, 10% 25 or older, 1% Native American, 2% Hispanic American, 7% African American, 3% Asian American/Pacific Islander **The most frequently chosen baccalaureate fields are** business/marketing, social sciences, visual and performing arts **Academic program** Advanced placement, self-designed majors, honors program, summer session, adult/continuing education programs, internships **Contact** Mr. Steven Briggs, Director of Admissions, University of Massachusetts Dartmouth, 285 Old Westport Road, North Dartmouth, MA 02747-2300. Phone: 508-999-8605. Fax: 508-999-8755. E-mail: admissions@umassd.edu. Web site: http://www.umassd.edu/.

▶**For more information, see page 497.**

UNIVERSITY OF MASSACHUSETTS LOWELL

LOWELL, MASSACHUSETTS

General State-supported, university, coed **Entrance** Moderately difficult **Setting** 100-acre urban campus **Total enrollment** 11,635 **Student-faculty ratio** 17:1 **Application deadline** Rolling (freshmen), rolling (transfer) **Freshmen** 69% were admitted **Housing** Yes **Expenses** Tuition $8731; Room & Board $6978 **Undergraduates** 40% women, 32% part-time, 13% 25 or older, 0.2% Native American, 5% Hispanic American, 4% African American, 8% Asian American/Pacific Islander **The most frequently chosen baccalaureate fields are** business/marketing, engineering, security and protective services **Academic program** Advanced placement, accelerated degree program, honors program, summer session, adult/continuing education programs, internships **Contact** Ms. Kerri Mead, Associate Director of Admissions, University of Massachusetts Lowell, 883 Broadway Street, Room 110, Lowell, MA 01854-5104. Phone: 978-934-3944 or toll-free 800-410-4607. Fax: 978-934-3086. E-mail: admissions@umi.edu. Web site: http://www.uml.edu/.

UNIVERSITY OF PHOENIX–BOSTON CAMPUS

BRAINTREE, MASSACHUSETTS

General Proprietary, comprehensive, coed **Contact** Ms. Evelyn Gaskin, Registrar/Executive Director, University of Phoenix–Boston Campus, 4615 East Elwood Street, Mail Stop AA-K101, Phoenix, AZ 85040-1958. Phone: 480-557-3301 or toll-free 800-228-7240. Fax: 480-643-1020. E-mail: evelyn.gaskin@phoenix.edu. Web site: http://www.phoenix.edu/.

UNIVERSITY OF PHOENIX–CENTRAL MASSACHUSETTS CAMPUS

WESTBOROUGH, MASSACHUSETTS

General Proprietary, comprehensive, coed **Contact** Ms. Evelyn Gaskin, Registrar/Executive Director, University of Phoenix–Central Massachusetts Campus, 4615 East Elwood Street, Mail Stop AA-K101, Phoenix, AZ 85040-1958. Phone: 480-557-3301 or toll-free 800-776-4867 (in-state); 800-228-7240 (out-of-state). Fax: 480-643-1020. E-mail: evelyn.gaskin@phoenix.edu. Web site: http://www.phoenix.edu/.

WELLESLEY COLLEGE

WELLESLEY, MASSACHUSETTS

General Independent, 4-year, women only **Entrance** Most difficult **Setting** 500-acre suburban campus **Total enrollment** 2,380 **Student-faculty ratio** 9:1 **Application deadline** 1/15 (freshmen), 3/1 (transfer) **Freshmen** 36% were admitted **Housing** Yes **Expenses** Tuition $34,994; Room & Board $10,826 **Undergraduates** 6% part-time, 3% 25 or older, 0.5% Native American, 7% Hispanic American, 6% African American, 26% Asian American/Pacific Islander **The most frequently chosen baccalaureate fields are** foreign languages and literature, psychology, social sciences **Academic program** Advanced placement, self-designed majors, honors program, summer session, adult/continuing education programs, internships **Contact** Ms. Heather Ayres, Director of Admission, Wellesley College, 106 Central Street, Wellesley, MA 02481. Phone: 781-283-2273. Fax: 781-283-3678. E-mail: admission@wellesley.edu. Web site: http://www.wellesley.edu/.

WENTWORTH INSTITUTE OF TECHNOLOGY

BOSTON, MASSACHUSETTS

General Independent, 4-year, coed **Entrance** Moderately difficult **Setting** 35-acre urban campus **Total enrollment** 3,728 **Student-faculty ratio** 24:1 **Application deadline** Rolling (freshmen), rolling (transfer) **Freshmen** 80% were admitted **Housing** Yes **Expenses** Tuition $20,150; Room & Board $9650 **Undergraduates** 20% women, 11% part-time, 12% 25 or older, 0.1% Native American, 3% Hispanic American, 3% African American, 5% Asian American/Pacific Islander **The most frequently chosen baccalaureate fields are** business/marketing, construction trades, engineering technologies **Academic program** English as a second language, advanced place-

Wentworth Institute of Technology *(continued)*

ment, accelerated degree program, summer session, internships **Contact** Admissions Office, Wentworth Institute of Technology, 550 Huntington Avenue, Boston, MA 02115-5998. Phone: 617-989-4009 or toll-free 800-556-0610. Fax: 617-989-4010. E-mail: admissions@wit.edu. Web site: http://www.wit.edu/.

►**For more information, see page 501.**

WESTERN NEW ENGLAND COLLEGE
SPRINGFIELD, MASSACHUSETTS

General Independent, comprehensive, coed **Entrance** Moderately difficult **Setting** 215-acre suburban campus **Total enrollment** 3,657 **Student-faculty ratio** 16:1 **Application deadline** Rolling (freshmen), rolling (transfer) **Freshmen** 73% were admitted **Housing** Yes **Expenses** Tuition $25,942; Room & Board $9998 **Undergraduates** 39% women, 11% part-time, 0.1% Native American, 3% Hispanic American, 3% African American, 2% Asian American/Pacific Islander **The most frequently chosen baccalaureate fields are** business/marketing, engineering, psychology **Academic program** Advanced placement, accelerated degree program, self-designed majors, honors program, summer session, adult/continuing education programs, internships **Contact** Dr. Charles R. Pollock, Vice President of Enrollment Management, Western New England College, 1215 Wilbraham Road, Springfield, MA 01119. Phone: 413-782-1321 or toll-free 800-325-1122 Ext. 1321. Fax: 413-782-1777. E-mail: ugradmis@wnec.edu. Web site: http://www.wnec.edu/.

WESTFIELD STATE COLLEGE
WESTFIELD, MASSACHUSETTS

General State-supported, comprehensive, coed **Entrance** Moderately difficult **Setting** 227-acre small-town campus **Total enrollment** 5,392 **Student-faculty ratio** 18:1 **Application deadline** 3/1 (freshmen), 4/1 (transfer) **Freshmen** 56% were admitted **Housing** Yes **Expenses** Tuition $6210; Room & Board $6458 **Undergraduates** 54% women, 11% part-time, 9% 25 or older, 0.3% Native American, 4% Hispanic American, 3% African American, 1% Asian American/Pacific Islander **The most frequently chosen baccalaureate fields are** business/marketing, education, security and protective services **Academic program** Advanced placement, self-designed majors, honors program, summer session, adult/continuing education programs, internships **Contact** Ms. Emily Gibbings, Associate Director of Admissions, Westfield State College, Western Avenue, Westfield, MA 01086. Phone: 413-572-5218 or toll-free 800-322-8401. Fax: 413-572-0520. E-mail: admission@wsc.ma.edu. Web site: http://www.wsc.ma.edu/.

WHEATON COLLEGE
NORTON, MASSACHUSETTS

General Independent, 4-year, coed **Entrance** Very difficult **Setting** 385-acre small-town campus **Total enrollment** 1,552 **Student-faculty ratio** 10:1 **Application deadline** 1/15 (freshmen), 4/1 (transfer) **Freshmen** 37% were admitted **Housing** Yes **Expenses** Tuition $36,690; Room & Board $8640 **Undergraduates** 60% women, 0.2% part-time, 0.3% Native American, 3% Hispanic American, 5% African American, 3% Asian American/Pacific Islander **The most frequently chosen baccalaureate fields are** psychology, social sciences, visual and performing arts **Academic program** Advanced placement, accelerated degree program, self-designed majors, honors program, internships **Contact** Ms. Gail Berson, Vice President For Enrollment and Dean of Admission and Student Aid, Wheaton College, 26 East Main Street, Norton, MA 02766. Phone: 508-286-8251 or toll-free 800-394-6003. Fax: 508-286-8271. E-mail: admission@wheatoncollege.edu. Web site: http://www.wheatoncollege.edu/.

WHEELOCK COLLEGE
BOSTON, MASSACHUSETTS

General Independent, comprehensive, coed, primarily women **Entrance** Moderately difficult **Setting** 7-acre urban campus **Total enrollment** 1,086 **Student-faculty ratio** 10:1 **Application deadline** 3/1 (freshmen), 4/15 (transfer) **Freshmen** 63% were admitted **Housing** Yes **Expenses** Tuition $26,080; Room & Board $10,400 **Undergraduates** 93% women, 7% part-time, 1% Native American, 7% Hispanic American, 9% African American, 3% Asian American/Pacific Islander **The most frequently chosen baccalaureate fields are** education, family and consumer sciences, public administration and social services **Academic program** Advanced placement, internships **Contact** Ms. Lisa Slavin, Dean of Enrollment, Wheelock College, 200 The Riverway, Boston, MA 02215. Phone: 617-879-2209 or toll-free 800-734-5212. Fax: 617-879-2449. E-mail: undergrad@wheelock.edu. Web site: http://www.wheelock.edu/.

WILLIAMS COLLEGE
WILLIAMSTOWN, MASSACHUSETTS

General Independent, comprehensive, coed **Entrance** Most difficult **Setting** 450-acre small-town campus **Total enrollment** 2,046 **Student-faculty ratio** 7:1 **Application deadline** 1/1 (freshmen), 3/15 (transfer) **Freshmen** 18% were admitted **Housing** Yes **Expenses** Tuition $35,670; Room & Board $9470 **Undergraduates** 50% women, 2% part-time, 1% 25 or older, 0.4% Native American, 9% Hispanic American, 10% African American, 11% Asian American/Pacific Islander **The most frequently chosen baccalaureate fields are** English, social sciences, visual and performing arts **Academic program** Advanced placement, accelerated degree program, self-designed majors, honors program, internships **Contact** Mr. Richard L. Nesbitt, Director of Admission, Williams College, 33 Stetson Court, Williamstown, MA 01267. Phone: 413-597-2211. Fax: 413-597-4052. E-mail: admission@williams.edu. Web site: http://www.williams.edu/.

WORCESTER POLYTECHNIC INSTITUTE
WORCESTER, MASSACHUSETTS

General Independent, university, coed **Entrance** Very difficult **Setting** 80-acre suburban campus **Total enrollment** 4,157 **Student-faculty ratio** 13:1 **Application deadline** 2/1 (freshmen), 4/15 (transfer) **Freshmen** 66% were admitted **Housing** Yes **Expenses** Tuition $34,830; Room & Board $10,410 **Undergraduates** 26% women, 1% part-time, 2% 25 or older, 0.5% Native American, 4% Hispanic American, 3% African American, 6% Asian American/Pacific Islander **The most frequently chosen baccalaureate fields are** computer and information sciences, biological/life sciences, engineering **Academic program** English as a second language, advanced placement, accelerated degree program, self-designed majors, summer session, internships **Contact** Mr. Edward J. Connor, Director of Admissions, Worcester Polytechnic Institute, 100 Institute Road, Worcester, MA 01609-2280. Phone: 508-831-5286. Fax: 508-831-5875. E-mail: admissions@wpi.edu. Web site: http://www.wpi.edu/.

WORCESTER STATE COLLEGE
WORCESTER, MASSACHUSETTS

General State-supported, comprehensive, coed **Entrance** Moderately difficult **Setting** 58-acre urban campus **Total enrollment** 5,358 **Student-faculty ratio** 15:1 **Application deadline** 6/1 (freshmen), 6/1 (transfer) **Freshmen** 53% were admitted **Housing** Yes **Expenses** Tuition $5864; Room & Board $7958 **Undergraduates** 59% women, 27% part-time, 18% 25 or older, 0.5% Native American, 5% Hispanic American, 4% African American, 3% Asian American/Pacific Islander **The most frequently chosen baccalaureate fields are** business/marketing, health professions and related sciences, psychology **Academic program** English as a second language, advanced placement, accelerated degree program, self-designed majors, honors program, summer session, adult/continuing education programs, internships **Contact** Ms. Golda Guella, Clerk of Admissions, Worcester State College, 486 Chandler Street, Administration Building, Worcester, MA 01602-2597. Phone: 508-929-8040 or toll-free 866-WSC-CALL. Fax: 508-929-8183. E-mail: admissions@worcester.edu. Web site: http://www.worcester.edu/.

MICHIGAN

ADRIAN COLLEGE
ADRIAN, MICHIGAN

General Independent, 4-year, coed, affiliated with United Methodist Church **Entrance** Moderately difficult **Setting** 100-acre small-town campus **Total enrollment** 1,308 **Student-faculty ratio** 14:1 **Application deadline** 3/15 (freshmen), 3/15 (transfer) **Freshmen** 64% were admitted **Housing** Yes **Expenses** Tuition $23,390; Room & Board $7600 **Undergraduates** 47% women, 3% part-time, 2% 25 or older, 0.2% Native American, 2% Hispanic American, 4% African American, 1% Asian American/Pacific Islander **The most frequently chosen baccalaureate fields are** business/marketing, health professions and related sciences, visual and performing arts **Academic program** English as a second language, advanced placement, self-designed majors, honors program, summer session, adult/continuing education programs, internships **Contact** Ms. Carolyn Quinlan, Director of Admissions, Adrian College, 110 South Madison Street, Adrian, MI 49221. Phone: 517-265-5161 Ext. 4326 or toll-free 800-877-2246. Fax: 517-264-3331. E-mail: admissions@adrian.edu. Web site: http://www.adrian.edu/.

ALBION COLLEGE
ALBION, MICHIGAN

General Independent Methodist, 4-year, coed **Entrance** Moderately difficult **Setting** 565-acre small-town campus **Total enrollment** 1,938 **Student-faculty ratio** 14:1 **Application deadline** 3/1 (freshmen), 6/1 (transfer) **Freshmen** 81% were admitted **Housing** Yes **Expenses** Tuition $27,530; Room & Board $7806 **Undergraduates** 55% women, 1% part-time, 1% 25 or older, 0.3% Native American, 1% Hispanic American, 3% African American, 2% Asian American/Pacific Islander **The most frequently chosen baccalaureate fields are** biological/life sciences, business/marketing, social sciences **Academic program** Advanced placement, self-designed majors, honors program, summer session, intern-

Albion College *(continued)*

ships **Contact** Mr. Doug Kellar, Associate Vice President for Enrollment, Albion College, 611 East Porter Street, Albion, MI 49224-1831. Phone: 517-629-0600 or toll-free 800-858-6770. Fax: 517-629-0569. E-mail: admissions@albion.edu. Web site: http://www.albion.edu/.

ALMA COLLEGE
ALMA, MICHIGAN

General Independent Presbyterian, 4-year, coed **Entrance** Moderately difficult **Setting** 125-acre small-town campus **Total enrollment** 1,355 **Student-faculty ratio** 13:1 **Application deadline** Rolling (freshmen), rolling (transfer) **Freshmen** 78% were admitted **Housing** Yes **Expenses** Tuition $23,688; Room & Board $7774 **Undergraduates** 57% women, 5% part-time, 1% 25 or older, 0.4% Native American, 2% Hispanic American, 1% African American, 2% Asian American/Pacific Islander **The most frequently chosen baccalaureate fields are** business/marketing, biological/life sciences, social sciences **Academic program** Advanced placement, self-designed majors, honors program, summer session, internships **Contact** Mr. Evan Montague, Director of Admissions, Alma College, Admissions Office, Alma, MI 48801-1599. Phone: toll-free 800-321-ALMA. Fax: 989-463-7057. E-mail: admissions@alma.edu. Web site: http://www.alma.edu/.

ANDREWS UNIVERSITY
BERRIEN SPRINGS, MICHIGAN

General Independent Seventh-day Adventist, university, coed **Entrance** Moderately difficult **Setting** 1,650-acre small-town campus **Total enrollment** 3,221 **Student-faculty ratio** 10:1 **Application deadline** Rolling (freshmen), rolling (transfer) **Freshmen** 57% were admitted **Housing** Yes **Expenses** Tuition $19,930; Room & Board $6330 **Undergraduates** 56% women, 14% part-time, 14% 25 or older, 0.5% Native American, 11% Hispanic American, 22% African American, 9% Asian American/Pacific Islander **The most frequently chosen baccalaureate fields are** business/marketing, biological/life sciences, health professions and related sciences **Academic program** English as a second language, advanced placement, accelerated degree program, self-designed majors, honors program, summer session, adult/continuing education programs, internships **Contact** Shanna Leak, Undergraduate Admissions Coordinator, Andrews University, Berrien Springs, MI 49104. Phone: 800-253-2874 or toll-free 800-253-2874. Fax: 269-471-3228. E-mail: enroll@andrews.edu. Web site: http://www.andrews.edu/.

AQUINAS COLLEGE
GRAND RAPIDS, MICHIGAN

General Independent Roman Catholic, comprehensive, coed **Entrance** Moderately difficult **Setting** 107-acre suburban campus **Total enrollment** 2,107 **Student-faculty ratio** 14:1 **Application deadline** Rolling (freshmen), rolling (transfer) **Freshmen** 81% were admitted **Housing** Yes **Expenses** Tuition $21,150; Room & Board $6678 **Undergraduates** 64% women, 17% part-time, 18% 25 or older, 1% Native American, 3% Hispanic American, 4% African American, 2% Asian American/Pacific Islander **The most frequently chosen baccalaureate fields are** business/marketing, education, social sciences **Academic program** Advanced placement, accelerated degree program, self-designed majors, honors program, summer session, adult/continuing education programs, internships **Contact** Ms. Erika Davis, Applications Specialist, Aquinas College, 1607 Robinson Road, SE, Grand Rapids, MI 49506-1799. Phone: 616-632-2851 or toll-free 800-678-9593. Fax: 616-732-4469. E-mail: admissions@aquinas.edu. Web site: http://www.aquinas.edu/.

THE ART INSTITUTE OF MICHIGAN
NOVI, MICHIGAN

General Proprietary, 4-year, coed **Housing** No **Contact** Ms. Melanie L. Gibson, Senior Director of Admissions, The Art Institute of Michigan, 28125 Cabot Drive, Suite 120, Novi, MI 48377. Phone: 248-675-3801 or toll-free 800-479-0087. Fax: 248-675-3830. E-mail: mgibson@aii.edu. Web site: http://www.artinstitutes.edu/detroit/.

AVE MARIA COLLEGE
YPSILANTI, MICHIGAN

Contact Ms. Nicole Myshak, Admissions Counselor, Ave Maria College, 300 West Forest Avenue, Ypsilanti, MI 48197. Phone: 734-337-4528 or toll-free 866-866-3030. Fax: 734-337-4140. E-mail: admissions@avemaria.edu. Web site: http://www.avemaria.edu/.

BAKER COLLEGE OF ALLEN PARK
ALLEN PARK, MICHIGAN

General Independent, 4-year, coed, primarily women **Setting** 13-acre suburban campus **Total enrollment** 2,204 **Student-faculty ratio** 34:1 **Application deadline** 9/24 (freshmen) **Freshmen** 100% were admitted **Housing** No **Expenses** Tuition $6840 **Undergraduates** 75% women, 47% part-time, 1% Native American, 5% Hispanic American, 33% African American, 1% Asian American/Pacific Islander **Contact** Mr. Steve Peterson, Vice President of Admissions, Baker

College of Allen Park, 4500 Enterprise Drive, Allen Park, MI 48101. Phone: 313-425-3700 or toll-free 800-767-4120. E-mail: steve.peterson@baker.edu. Web site: http://www.baker.edu/.

BAKER COLLEGE OF AUBURN HILLS

AUBURN HILLS, MICHIGAN

General Independent, 4-year, coed **Entrance** Noncompetitive **Setting** 7-acre urban campus **Total enrollment** 3,702 **Student-faculty ratio** 41:1 **Application deadline** Rolling (freshmen), rolling (transfer) **Freshmen** 100% were admitted **Housing** No **Expenses** Tuition $6840 **Undergraduates** 72% women, 51% part-time, 41% 25 or older, 1% Native American, 3% Hispanic American, 18% African American, 3% Asian American/Pacific Islander **Academic program** Advanced placement, accelerated degree program, summer session, internships **Contact** Ms. Jan Bohlen, Vice President for Admissions, Baker College of Auburn Hills, 1500 University Drive, Auburn Hills, MI 48326-1586. Phone: 248-340-0600 or toll-free 888-429-0410. Fax: 248-340-0608. E-mail: jan.bohlen@baker.edu. Web site: http://www.baker.edu/.

BAKER COLLEGE OF CADILLAC

CADILLAC, MICHIGAN

General Independent, 4-year, coed **Entrance** Noncompetitive **Setting** 40-acre small-town campus **Total enrollment** 1,806 **Student-faculty ratio** 42:1 **Application deadline** Rolling (freshmen), rolling (transfer) **Freshmen** 100% were admitted **Housing** No **Expenses** Tuition $6840 **Undergraduates** 74% women, 45% part-time, 56% 25 or older, 0.1% Native American, 0.1% Hispanic American, 0.2% African American, 0.1% Asian American/Pacific Islander **Academic program** Advanced placement, summer session, internships **Contact** Mr. Mike Tisdale, Director of Admissions, Baker College of Cadillac, 9600 East 13th Street, Cadillac, MI 49601. Phone: 231-876-3100 or toll-free 888-313-3463. Fax: 231-775-8505. E-mail: mike.tisdale@baker.edu. Web site: http://www.baker.edu/.

BAKER COLLEGE OF CLINTON TOWNSHIP

CLINTON TOWNSHIP, MICHIGAN

General Independent, 4-year, coed **Entrance** Noncompetitive **Setting** 25-acre urban campus **Total enrollment** 5,608 **Student-faculty ratio** 45:1 **Application deadline** Rolling (freshmen), rolling (transfer) **Freshmen** 100% were admitted **Housing** No **Expenses** Tuition $6840 **Undergraduates** 76% women, 50% part-time, 42% 25 or older, 1% Native American, 2% Hispanic American, 20% African American, 2% Asian American/Pacific Islander **Academic program** Advanced placement, summer session, internships **Contact** Ms. Annette Looser, Vice President for Admissions, Baker College of Clinton Township, 34401 South Gratiot Avenue, Clinton Township, MI 48035. Phone: 586-790-3000 or toll-free 888-272-2842. Fax: 586-791-6811. E-mail: annette.looser@baker.edu. Web site: http://www.baker.edu/.

BAKER COLLEGE OF FLINT

FLINT, MICHIGAN

General Independent, 4-year, coed **Entrance** Noncompetitive **Setting** 30-acre urban campus **Total enrollment** 5,808 **Student-faculty ratio** 31:1 **Application deadline** 9/20 (freshmen), 9/20 (transfer) **Freshmen** 100% were admitted **Housing** Yes **Expenses** Tuition $6840; Room only $2650 **Undergraduates** 71% women, 45% part-time, 1% Native American, 2% Hispanic American, 20% African American, 1% Asian American/Pacific Islander **Academic program** Advanced placement, accelerated degree program, summer session, internships **Contact** Ms. Jodi Cunelz, Director of Admissions, Baker College of Flint, 1050 West Bristol Road, Flint, MI 48507-5508. Phone: 810-766-4008 or toll-free 800-964-4299. Fax: 810-766-4049. Web site: http://www.baker.edu/.

BAKER COLLEGE OF JACKSON

JACKSON, MICHIGAN

General Independent, 4-year, coed **Entrance** Noncompetitive **Setting** 42-acre urban campus **Total enrollment** 1,813 **Student-faculty ratio** 36:1 **Application deadline** 9/19 (freshmen), rolling (transfer) **Freshmen** 100% were admitted **Housing** No **Expenses** Tuition $6840 **Undergraduates** 77% women, 49% part-time, 56% 25 or older, 0.2% Native American, 2% Hispanic American, 6% African American, 1% Asian American/Pacific Islander **Academic program** Advanced placement, accelerated degree program, summer session, internships **Contact** Ms. Kelli Stepka, Vice President for Admissions, Baker College of Jackson, 2800 Springport Road, Jackson, MI 49202. Phone: 517-788-7800 or toll-free 888-343-3683. Fax: 517-789-7331. E-mail: kelli.stepka@baker.edu. Web site: http://www.baker.edu/.

BAKER COLLEGE OF MUSKEGON

MUSKEGON, MICHIGAN

General Independent, 4-year, coed **Entrance** Noncompetitive **Setting** 40-acre suburban campus **Total enrollment** 5,010 **Student-faculty ratio** 55:1 **Application deadline** 9/24 (freshmen), rolling (transfer) **Freshmen** 100% were admitted

Baker College of Muskegon *(continued)*

Housing Yes **Expenses** Tuition $6840; Room only $2600 **Undergraduates** 71% women, 37% part-time, 45% 25 or older, 1% Native American, 4% Hispanic American, 14% African American, 0.4% Asian American/Pacific Islander **Academic program** Advanced placement, accelerated degree program, summer session, adult/continuing education programs, internships **Contact** Ms. Kathy Jacobson, Vice President of Admissions, Baker College of Muskegon, 1903 Marquette Avenue, Muskegon, MI 49442-3497. Phone: 231-777-5207 or toll-free 800-937-0337. Fax: 231-777-5201. E-mail: kathy.jacobson@baker.edu. Web site: http://www.baker.edu/.

BAKER COLLEGE OF OWOSSO
OWOSSO, MICHIGAN

General Independent, 4-year, coed **Entrance** Noncompetitive **Setting** 32-acre small-town campus **Total enrollment** 2,911 **Student-faculty ratio** 40:1 **Application deadline** Rolling (freshmen), rolling (transfer) **Freshmen** 100% were admitted **Housing** Yes **Expenses** Tuition $6840; Room only $2500 **Undergraduates** 69% women, 33% part-time, 41% 25 or older, 1% Native American, 2% Hispanic American, 4% African American, 0.3% Asian American/Pacific Islander **Academic program** Advanced placement, accelerated degree program, summer session, adult/continuing education programs, internships **Contact** Mr. Michael Konopacke, Vice President for Admissions, Baker College of Owosso, 1020 South Washington Street, Owosso, MI 48867. Phone: 989-729-3350 or toll-free 800-879-3797. Fax: 517-729-3359. E-mail: mike.konopacke@baker.edu. Web site: http://www.baker.edu/.

BAKER COLLEGE OF PORT HURON
PORT HURON, MICHIGAN

General Independent, 4-year, coed **Entrance** Noncompetitive **Setting** 10-acre urban campus **Total enrollment** 1,642 **Student-faculty ratio** 28:1 **Application deadline** 9/24 (freshmen), rolling (transfer) **Freshmen** 100% were admitted **Housing** No **Expenses** Tuition $6840 **Undergraduates** 75% women, 35% part-time, 51% 25 or older, 0.5% Native American, 2% Hispanic American, 4% African American, 0.3% Asian American/Pacific Islander **Academic program** Advanced placement, accelerated degree program, summer session, internships **Contact** Mr. Daniel Kenny, Vice President for Admissions, Baker College of Port Huron, 3403 Lapeer Road, Port Huron, MI 48060-2597. Phone: 810-985-7000 or toll-free 888-262-2442. Fax: 810-985-7066. E-mail: kenny_d@porthuron.baker.edu. Web site: http://www.baker.edu/.

CALVIN COLLEGE
GRAND RAPIDS, MICHIGAN

General Independent, comprehensive, coed, affiliated with Christian Reformed Church **Entrance** Moderately difficult **Setting** 370-acre suburban campus **Total enrollment** 4,224 **Student-faculty ratio** 12:1 **Application deadline** 8/15 (freshmen), rolling (transfer) **Freshmen** 95% were admitted **Housing** Yes **Expenses** Tuition $21,685; Room & Board $7460 **Undergraduates** 54% women, 3% part-time, 1% 25 or older, 0.1% Native American, 2% Hispanic American, 1% African American, 3% Asian American/Pacific Islander **The most frequently chosen baccalaureate fields are** business/marketing, health professions and related sciences, social sciences **Academic program** Advanced placement, accelerated degree program, self-designed majors, honors program, summer session, adult/continuing education programs, internships **Contact** Mr. Dale D. Kuiper, Director of Admissions, Calvin College, 3201 Burton Street, SE, Grand Rapids, MI 49546. Phone: 616-526-6106 or toll-free 800-688-0122. Fax: 616-526-6777. E-mail: admissions@calvin.edu. Web site: http://www.calvin.edu/.

CENTRAL MICHIGAN UNIVERSITY
MOUNT PLEASANT, MICHIGAN

General State-supported, university, coed **Entrance** Moderately difficult **Setting** 854-acre small-town campus **Total enrollment** 26,611 **Student-faculty ratio** 21:1 **Application deadline** Rolling (freshmen), rolling (transfer) **Freshmen** 73% were admitted **Housing** Yes **Expenses** Tuition $9120; Room & Board $7236 **Undergraduates** 56% women, 11% part-time, 6% 25 or older, 1% Native American, 2% Hispanic American, 6% African American, 1% Asian American/Pacific Islander **The most frequently chosen baccalaureate fields are** business/marketing, communications/journalism, education **Academic program** English as a second language, advanced placement, accelerated degree program, self-designed majors, honors program, summer session, adult/continuing education programs, internships **Contact** Ms. Betty J. Wagner, Director of Admissions, Central Michigan University, Warriner Hall 102, Mt. Pleasant, MI 48859. Phone: 989-774-3076 or toll-free 888-292-5366. Fax: 989-774-7267. E-mail: cmuadmit@cmich.edu. Web site: http://www.cmich.edu/.

CLEARY UNIVERSITY
ANN ARBOR, MICHIGAN

General Independent, comprehensive, coed **Entrance** Moderately difficult **Setting** 32-acre suburban campus **Total enrollment** 818 **Student-**

faculty ratio 10:1 **Application deadline** 8/15 (freshmen), 8/15 (transfer) **Freshmen** 90% were admitted **Housing** No **Expenses** Tuition $14,880 **Undergraduates** 51% women, 43% part-time, 76% 25 or older, 1% Native American, 2% Hispanic American, 7% African American, 1% Asian American/Pacific Islander **The most frequently chosen baccalaureate field is** business/marketing **Academic program** Advanced placement, accelerated degree program, summer session, adult/continuing education programs, internships **Contact** Ms. Charlotte Paquette, Admissions Representative, Cleary University, 3750 Cleary Drive, Howell, MI 48843. Phone: 517-548-3670 Ext. 2249 or toll-free 888-5-CLEARY Ext. 2249. Fax: 517-552-7805. E-mail: admissions@cleary.edu. Web site: http://www.cleary.edu/.

COLLEGE FOR CREATIVE STUDIES
DETROIT, MICHIGAN

General Independent, 4-year, coed **Entrance** Moderately difficult **Setting** 11-acre urban campus **Total enrollment** 1,307 **Student-faculty ratio** 8:1 **Application deadline** 8/1 (freshmen), rolling (transfer) **Freshmen** 39% were admitted **Housing** Yes **Expenses** Tuition $28,275; Room only $4300 **Undergraduates** 42% women, 15% part-time, 22% 25 or older, 1% Native American, 5% Hispanic American, 6% African American, 4% Asian American/Pacific Islander **Academic program** English as a second language, advanced placement, summer session, internships **Contact** Office of Admissions, College for Creative Studies, 201 East Kirby, Detroit, MI 48202-4034. Phone: 800-952-2787 or toll-free 800-952-ARTS. Fax: 313-872-2739. E-mail: admissions@ccscad.edu. Web site: http://www.ccscad.edu/.

CONCORDIA UNIVERSITY
ANN ARBOR, MICHIGAN

General Independent, comprehensive, coed, affiliated with Lutheran Church–Missouri Synod **Entrance** Moderately difficult **Setting** 187-acre suburban campus **Total enrollment** 1,075 **Student-faculty ratio** 17:1 **Application deadline** Rolling (freshmen), rolling (transfer) **Freshmen** 66% were admitted **Housing** Yes **Expenses** Tuition $19,770; Room & Board $7350 **Undergraduates** 54% women, 18% part-time, 17% 25 or older, 2% Native American, 2% Hispanic American, 8% African American, 2% Asian American/Pacific Islander **The most frequently chosen baccalaureate fields are** business/marketing, communications/journalism, education **Academic program** Advanced placement, accelerated degree program, self-designed majors, summer session, adult/continuing education programs, internships **Contact** Amy Becher, Executive Director of Enrollment Services, Concordia University, 4090 Geddes Road, Ann Arbor, MI 48105. Phone: 734-995-7450 or toll-free 800-253-0680. Fax: 734-995-4610. E-mail: admissions@cuaa.edu or bechea@cuaa.edu. Web site: http://www.cuaa.edu/.

CORNERSTONE UNIVERSITY
GRAND RAPIDS, MICHIGAN

General Independent nondenominational, comprehensive, coed **Entrance** Minimally difficult **Setting** 132-acre suburban campus **Total enrollment** 2,466 **Student-faculty ratio** 13:1 **Application deadline** Rolling (freshmen), rolling (transfer) **Freshmen** 62% were admitted **Housing** Yes **Expenses** Tuition $18,360; Room & Board $6300 **Undergraduates** 59% women, 21% part-time, 5% 25 or older, 1% Native American, 3% Hispanic American, 12% African American, 1% Asian American/Pacific Islander **The most frequently chosen baccalaureate fields are** business/marketing, education, theology and religious vocations **Academic program** English as a second language, advanced placement, accelerated degree program, honors program, summer session, adult/continuing education programs, internships **Contact** Mr. Brent Rudin, Dean of Admissions, Cornerstone University, 1001 East Beltline Avenue, NE, Grand Rapids, MI 49525. Phone: 616-222-1426 or toll-free 800-787-9778. Fax: 616-222-1400. E-mail: admissions@cornerstone.edu. Web site: http://www.cornerstone.edu/.

DAVENPORT UNIVERSITY
GRAND RAPIDS, MICHIGAN

General Independent, comprehensive, coed **Entrance** Minimally difficult **Setting** urban campus **Total enrollment** 11,606 **Student-faculty ratio** 13:1 **Application deadline** Rolling (freshmen), rolling (transfer) **Freshmen** 91% were admitted **Housing** Yes **Expenses** Tuition $9956; Room only $4750 **Undergraduates** 73% women, 70% part-time, 66% 25 or older, 0.4% Native American, 3% Hispanic American, 19% African American, 2% Asian American/Pacific Islander **The most frequently chosen baccalaureate fields are** business/marketing, computer and information sciences, health professions and related sciences **Academic program** English as a second language, advanced placement, accelerated degree program, self-designed majors, summer session, adult/continuing education programs, internships **Contact** Ms. Heather Knechtel, Director of Admissions, Davenport University, 415 East Fulton, Grand Rapids, MI 49503. Phone: 616-451-3511 or toll-free 800-632-9569. E-mail: heather.knechtel@davenport.edu. Web site: http://www.davenport.edu/.

DEVRY UNIVERSITY SOUTHFIELD CENTER
SOUTHFIELD, MICHIGAN

General Proprietary, comprehensive, coed **Total enrollment** 6 **Student-faculty ratio** 10:1 **Application deadline** Rolling (freshmen), rolling (transfer) **Expenses** Tuition $13,890 **Undergraduates** 67% women, 67% part-time, 83% 25 or older, 50% African American, 17% Asian American/Pacific Islander **Contact** Admissions Office, DeVry University Southfield Center, 26999 Central Park Boulevard, Suite 125, Southfield, MI 48076-4174. Web site: http://www.devry.edu/.

EASTERN MICHIGAN UNIVERSITY
YPSILANTI, MICHIGAN

General State-supported, comprehensive, coed **Entrance** Moderately difficult **Setting** 460-acre suburban campus **Total enrollment** 22,638 **Student-faculty ratio** 18:1 **Application deadline** Rolling (freshmen), rolling (transfer) **Freshmen** 75% were admitted **Housing** Yes **Expenses** Tuition $7490; Room & Board $6942 **Undergraduates** 59% women, 31% part-time, 28% 25 or older, 1% Native American, 3% Hispanic American, 18% African American, 2% Asian American/Pacific Islander **The most frequently chosen baccalaureate fields are** business/marketing, education, social sciences **Academic program** English as a second language, advanced placement, accelerated degree program, self-designed majors, honors program, summer session, adult/continuing education programs, internships **Contact** Kathy Orscheln, Interim Director of Admissions, Eastern Michigan University, 400 Pierce Hall, Ypsilanti, MI 48197. Phone: 734-487-3060 or toll-free 800-GO TO EMU. Fax: 734-487-1484. E-mail: admissions@emich.edu. Web site: http://www.emich.edu/.

FERRIS STATE UNIVERSITY
BIG RAPIDS, MICHIGAN

General State-supported, comprehensive, coed **Entrance** Minimally difficult **Setting** 880-acre small-town campus **Total enrollment** 13,087 **Student-faculty ratio** 15:1 **Application deadline** 8/1 (freshmen), 7/1 (transfer) **Housing** Yes **Expenses** Tuition $8862; Room & Board $7646 **Undergraduates** 47% women, 25% part-time, 21% 25 or older, 1% Native American, 2% Hispanic American, 7% African American, 2% Asian American/Pacific Islander **The most frequently chosen baccalaureate fields are** business/marketing, engineering technologies, security and protective services **Academic program** English as a second language, advanced placement, accelerated degree program, honors program, summer session, adult/continuing education programs, internships **Contact** Troy Tissue, Associate Director of Admissions, Ferris State University, 1201 South State Street, CSS201, Big Rapids, MI 49307-2742. Phone: 231-591-3801 or toll-free 800-433-7747. Fax: 231-591-3944. E-mail: admissions@ferris.edu. Web site: http://www.ferris.edu/.

FINLANDIA UNIVERSITY
HANCOCK, MICHIGAN

General Independent, 4-year, coed, affiliated with Evangelical Lutheran Church in America **Entrance** Minimally difficult **Setting** 25-acre small-town campus **Total enrollment** 545 **Student-faculty ratio** 10:1 **Application deadline** 8/25 (freshmen), 8/25 (transfer) **Freshmen** 67% were admitted **Housing** Yes **Expenses** Tuition $17,914; Room & Board $5800 **Undergraduates** 65% women, 11% part-time, 26% 25 or older, 2% Native American, 1% Hispanic American, 1% African American, 3% Asian American/Pacific Islander **The most frequently chosen baccalaureate fields are** business/marketing, health professions and related sciences, visual and performing arts **Academic program** English as a second language, advanced placement, accelerated degree program, summer session, adult/continuing education programs, internships **Contact** Martin Kinard, Finlandia University, 601 Quincy Street, Hancock, MI 49930. Phone: 906-487-7352 or toll-free 877-202-5491. Fax: 906-487-7383. E-mail: admissions@finlandia.edu. Web site: http://www.finlandia.edu/.

GRACE BIBLE COLLEGE
GRAND RAPIDS, MICHIGAN

General Independent, 4-year, coed, affiliated with Grace Gospel Fellowship **Entrance** Minimally difficult **Setting** 16-acre suburban campus **Total enrollment** 173 **Student-faculty ratio** 11:1 **Application deadline** 7/15 (freshmen) **Freshmen** 62% were admitted **Housing** Yes **Expenses** Tuition $11,620; Room & Board $6400 **Undergraduates** 46% women, 7% part-time, 9% 25 or older, 1% Native American, 2% Hispanic American, 4% African American, 1% Asian American/Pacific Islander **The most frequently chosen baccalaureate fields are** education, communication technologies, visual and performing arts **Academic program** English as a second language, advanced placement, internships **Contact** Mr. Kevin Gilliam, Director of Enrollment, Grace Bible College, 1101 Aldon Street, SW, PO Box 910, Grand Rapids, MI 49509. Phone: 616-538-2330 Ext. 239 or toll-free 800-968-1887. Fax: 616-538-0599. E-mail: gbc@gbcol.edu. Web site: http://www.gbcol.edu/.

GRAND VALLEY STATE UNIVERSITY
ALLENDALE, MICHIGAN

General State-supported, comprehensive, coed **Entrance** Moderately difficult **Setting** 900-acre small-town campus **Total enrollment** 23,464 **Student-faculty ratio** 18:1 **Application deadline** 5/1 (freshmen), 7/28 (transfer) **Freshmen** 69% were admitted **Housing** Yes **Expenses** Tuition $7240; Room & Board $6880 **Undergraduates** 60% women, 13% part-time, 11% 25 or older, 1% Native American, 3% Hispanic American, 5% African American, 3% Asian American/Pacific Islander **The most frequently chosen baccalaureate fields are** business/marketing, English, health professions and related sciences **Academic program** English as a second language, advanced placement, accelerated degree program, honors program, summer session, adult/continuing education programs, internships **Contact** Ms. Jodi Chycinski, Director of Admissions, Grand Valley State University, 1 Campus Drive, Allendale, MI 49401. Phone: 616-331-2025 or toll-free 800-748-0246. Fax: 616-331-2000. E-mail: go2gvsu@gvsu.edu. Web site: http://www.gvsu.edu/.

GREAT LAKES CHRISTIAN COLLEGE
LANSING, MICHIGAN

General Independent, 4-year, coed, affiliated with Christian Churches and Churches of Christ **Entrance** Moderately difficult **Setting** 50-acre suburban campus **Total enrollment** 260 **Student-faculty ratio** 14:1 **Application deadline** 8/1 (freshmen), 8/1 (transfer) **Housing** Yes **Expenses** Tuition $11,727; Room & Board $6600 **Undergraduates** 49% women, 29% part-time, 28% 25 or older, 1% Hispanic American, 11% African American, 1% Asian American/Pacific Islander **The most frequently chosen baccalaureate field is** theology and religious vocations **Academic program** Advanced placement, adult/continuing education programs, internships **Contact** Mr. Lloyd Scharer, Director of Admissions, Great Lakes Christian College, 6211 West Willow Highway, Lansing, MI 48917-1299. Phone: 517-321-0242 or toll-free 800-YES-GLCC. Fax: 517-321-5902. E-mail: lscharer@glcc.edu. Web site: http://www.glcc.edu/.

HILLSDALE COLLEGE
HILLSDALE, MICHIGAN

General Independent, 4-year, coed **Entrance** Very difficult **Setting** 200-acre small-town campus **Total enrollment** 1,326 **Student-faculty ratio** 10:1 **Application deadline** 2/15 (freshmen), 2/15 (transfer) **Freshmen** 64% were admitted **Housing** Yes **Expenses** Tuition $19,090; Room & Board $7340 **Undergraduates** 52% women, 3% part-time, 1% 25 or older **The most frequently chosen baccalaureate fields are** business/marketing, history, social sciences **Academic program** Advanced placement, accelerated degree program, honors program, summer session, internships **Contact** Mr. Jeffrey S. Lantis, Director of Admissions, Hillsdale College, 33 East College Street, Hillsdale, MI 49242-1298. Phone: 517-607-2327 Ext. 2327. Fax: 517-607-2223. E-mail: admissions@hillsdale.edu. Web site: http://www.hillsdale.edu/.

HOPE COLLEGE
HOLLAND, MICHIGAN

General Independent, 4-year, coed, affiliated with Reformed Church in America **Entrance** Moderately difficult **Setting** 45-acre suburban campus **Total enrollment** 3,226 **Student-faculty ratio** 12:1 **Application deadline** Rolling (freshmen), rolling (transfer) **Freshmen** 83% were admitted **Housing** Yes **Expenses** Tuition $23,800; Room & Board $7300 **Undergraduates** 59% women, 4% part-time, 1% 25 or older, 0.4% Native American, 3% Hispanic American, 2% African American, 2% Asian American/Pacific Islander **The most frequently chosen baccalaureate fields are** business/marketing, education, psychology **Academic program** English as a second language, advanced placement, self-designed majors, summer session, internships **Contact** Hope College Admissions, Hope College, 69 East 10th Street, P.O. Box 9000, Holland, MI 49422-9000. Phone: 616-395-7850 or toll-free 800-968-7850. Fax: 616-395-7130. E-mail: admissions@hope.edu. Web site: http://www.hope.edu/.

KALAMAZOO COLLEGE
KALAMAZOO, MICHIGAN

General Independent, 4-year, coed, affiliated with American Baptist Churches in the U.S.A. **Entrance** Very difficult **Setting** 60-acre suburban campus **Total enrollment** 1,340 **Student-faculty ratio** 11:1 **Application deadline** 2/1 (freshmen), 5/1 (transfer) **Freshmen** 63% were admitted **Housing** Yes **Expenses** Tuition $28,716; Room & Board $7122 **Undergraduates** 58% women, 1% 25 or older, 0.2% Native American, 4% Hispanic American, 4% African American, 6% Asian American/Pacific Islander **The most frequently chosen baccalaureate fields are** biological/life sciences, English, social sciences **Academic program** Advanced placement, internships **Contact** Mrs. Linda Wirgau, Records Manager, Kalamazoo College, Mandelle Hall, 1200 Academy Street, Kalamazoo, MI 49006-3295. Phone: 269-337-7166 or toll-free 800-253-3602. Fax: 269-337-7190. E-mail: admissions@kzoo.edu. Web site: http://www.kzoo.edu/.

KETTERING UNIVERSITY
FLINT, MICHIGAN

General Independent, comprehensive, coed, primarily men **Entrance** Very difficult **Setting** 85-acre urban campus **Total enrollment** 2,675 **Student-faculty ratio** 9:1 **Application deadline** Rolling (freshmen), rolling (transfer) **Freshmen** 72% were admitted **Housing** Yes **Expenses** Tuition $25,658; Room & Board $5798 **Undergraduates** 15% women, 6% 25 or older, 0.4% Native American, 2% Hispanic American, 5% African American, 5% Asian American/Pacific Islander **The most frequently chosen baccalaureate fields are** business/marketing, engineering, physical sciences **Academic program** Advanced placement, accelerated degree program, internships **Contact** Ms. Barbara Sosin, Director of Admissions, Kettering University, 1700 West Third Avenue, Flint, MI 48504-4898. Phone: 810-762-7865 or toll-free 800-955-4464 Ext. 7865 (in-state); 800-955-4464 (out-of-state). Fax: 810-762-9837. E-mail: admissions@kettering.edu. Web site: http://www.kettering.edu/.

KUYPER COLLEGE
GRAND RAPIDS, MICHIGAN

General Independent religious, 4-year, coed **Entrance** Moderately difficult **Setting** 34-acre suburban campus **Total enrollment** 300 **Student-faculty ratio** 15:1 **Application deadline** Rolling (freshmen) **Freshmen** 93% were admitted **Housing** Yes **Expenses** Tuition $13,909; Room & Board $5700 **Undergraduates** 51% women, 15% part-time, 33% 25 or older, 0.3% Native American, 4% Hispanic American, 3% African American, 2% Asian American/Pacific Islander **The most frequently chosen baccalaureate fields are** public administration and social services, education, theology and religious vocations **Academic program** English as a second language, advanced placement, summer session, internships **Contact** Admissions Office, Kuyper College, 3333 East Beltline Avenue, NE, Grand Rapids, MI 49525. Phone: 616-988-3632 or toll-free 800-511-3749. Fax: 616-222-3045. E-mail: admissions@kuyper.edu. Web site: http://www.kuyper.edu/.

LAKE SUPERIOR STATE UNIVERSITY
SAULT SAINTE MARIE, MICHIGAN

General State-supported, 4-year, coed **Entrance** Moderately difficult **Setting** 115-acre small-town campus **Total enrollment** 2,897 **Student-faculty ratio** 17:1 **Application deadline** 8/15 (freshmen), rolling (transfer) **Freshmen** 91% were admitted **Housing** Yes **Expenses** Tuition $7316; Room & Board $7172 **Undergraduates** 53% women, 29% part-time, 20% 25 or older, 7% Native American, 1% Hispanic American, 2% African American, 0.3% Asian American/Pacific Islander **The most frequently chosen baccalaureate fields are** business/marketing, education, security and protective services **Academic program** Advanced placement, self-designed majors, honors program, summer session, adult/continuing education programs, internships **Contact** Ms. Susan Camp, Director of Admissions, Lake Superior State University, 650 West Easterday Avenue, Sault Saint Marie, MI 49783-1699. Phone: 906-635-2231 or toll-free 888-800-LSSU Ext. 2231. Fax: 906-635-6669. E-mail: admissions@lssu.edu. Web site: http://www.lssu.edu/.

LAWRENCE TECHNOLOGICAL UNIVERSITY
SOUTHFIELD, MICHIGAN

General Independent, university, coed **Entrance** Moderately difficult **Setting** 115-acre suburban campus **Total enrollment** 4,609 **Student-faculty ratio** 13:1 **Application deadline** 8/15 (freshmen), 8/15 (transfer) **Freshmen** 60% were admitted **Housing** Yes **Expenses** Tuition $20,496; Room & Board $7872 **Undergraduates** 20% women, 45% part-time, 24% 25 or older, 0.3% Native American, 2% Hispanic American, 10% African American, 2% Asian American/Pacific Islander **The most frequently chosen baccalaureate fields are** architecture, engineering, engineering technologies **Academic program** English as a second language, advanced placement, summer session, adult/continuing education programs, internships **Contact** Ms. Jane Rohrback, Director of Admissions, Lawrence Technological University, 21000 West Ten Mile Road, Southfield, MI 48075. Phone: 248-204-3160 or toll-free 800-225-5588. Fax: 248-204-3188. E-mail: admissions@ltu.edu. Web site: http://www.ltu.edu/.

MADONNA UNIVERSITY
LIVONIA, MICHIGAN

General Independent Roman Catholic, comprehensive, coed **Entrance** Moderately difficult **Setting** 49-acre suburban campus **Total enrollment** 4,022 **Student-faculty ratio** 13:1 **Application deadline** Rolling (freshmen), rolling (transfer) **Freshmen** 77% were admitted **Housing** Yes **Expenses** Tuition $11,680; Room & Board $6092 **Undergraduates** 75% women, 49% part-time, 51% 25 or older, 0.4% Native American, 3% Hispanic American, 15% African American, 2% Asian American/Pacific Islander **The most frequently chosen baccalaureate fields are** health professions and related sciences, business/marketing, security and protective services **Academic program** English as a second language, advanced placement, accelerated degree program, self-designed majors, summer session, adult/continuing education programs, internships **Contact** Mr. Mike Quattro, Director of Enrollment Management, Madonna University, 36600 Schoolcraft Road, Livonia, MI 48150-1173. Phone: 734-432-5317 or toll-free 800-852-4951. Fax: 734-432-5393. E-mail: muinfo@madonna.edu. Web site: http://www.madonna.edu/.

MARYGROVE COLLEGE
DETROIT, MICHIGAN

General Independent Roman Catholic, comprehensive, coed, primarily women **Contact** Mr. John Ambrose, Director of Undergraduate Admissions, Marygrove College, Admissions Office, Detroit, MI 48221-2599. Phone: 313-927-1236 or toll-free 866-313-1297. Fax: 313-927-1345. E-mail: info@marygrove.edu. Web site: http://www.marygrove.edu/.

MICHIGAN JEWISH INSTITUTE
OAK PARK, MICHIGAN

General Independent, 4-year, coed **Entrance** Minimally difficult **Total enrollment** 256 **Application deadline** Rolling (freshmen), rolling (transfer) **Housing** No **Expenses** Tuition $10,180 **The most frequently chosen baccalaureate fields are** computer and information sciences, business/marketing, philosophy and religious studies **Academic program** English as a second language, advanced placement, accelerated degree program, summer session, adult/continuing education programs, internships **Contact** Mr. Dov Stein, Michigan Jewish Institute, 25401 Coolidge Highway, Oak Park, MI 48237-1304. Phone: 248-414-6900 Ext. 101. Fax: 248-414-6907. E-mail: dstein@mji.edu. Web site: http://www.mji.edu/.

MICHIGAN STATE UNIVERSITY
EAST LANSING, MICHIGAN

General State-supported, university, coed **Entrance** Moderately difficult **Setting** 5,192-acre suburban campus **Total enrollment** 46,045 **Student-faculty ratio** 17:1 **Application deadline** Rolling (freshmen), rolling (transfer) **Freshmen** 74% were admitted **Housing** Yes **Expenses** Tuition $9640; Room & Board $6676 **Undergraduates** 53% women, 8% part-time, 4% 25 or older, 1% Native American, 3% Hispanic American, 8% African American, 5% Asian American/Pacific Islander **The most frequently chosen baccalaureate fields are** business/marketing, communications/journalism, social sciences **Academic program** English as a second language, advanced placement, accelerated degree program, self-designed majors, honors program, summer session, adult/continuing education programs, internships **Contact** James Cotter, Acting Director of Admissions, Michigan State University, 250 Administration Building, East Lansing, MI 48824. Phone: 517-355-8332. Fax: 517-353-1647. E-mail: admis@msu.edu. Web site: http://www.msu.edu/.

MICHIGAN TECHNOLOGICAL UNIVERSITY
HOUGHTON, MICHIGAN

General State-supported, university, coed **Entrance** Moderately difficult **Setting** 925-acre small-town campus **Total enrollment** 6,758 **Student-faculty ratio** 11:1 **Application deadline** Rolling (freshmen), rolling (transfer) **Freshmen** 84% were admitted **Housing** Yes **Expenses** Tuition $9829; Room & Board $7315 **Undergraduates** 23% women, 9% part-time, 5% 25 or older, 1% Native American, 1% Hispanic American, 2% African American, 1% Asian American/Pacific Islander **The most frequently chosen baccalaureate fields are** business/marketing, engineering, engineering technologies **Academic program** English as a second language, advanced placement, self-designed majors, honors program, summer session, internships **Contact** Ms. Allison Carter, Director of Admissions, Michigan Technological University, 1400 Townsend Drive, Houghton, MI 49931-1295. Phone: 906-487-1888 or toll-free 888-MTU-1885. Fax: 906-487-2125. E-mail: mtu4u@mtu.edu. Web site: http://www.mtu.edu/.

NORTHERN MICHIGAN UNIVERSITY
MARQUETTE, MICHIGAN

General State-supported, comprehensive, coed **Entrance** Minimally difficult **Setting** 300-acre small-town campus **Total enrollment** 9,111 **Student-faculty ratio** 23:1 **Application deadline** Rolling (freshmen), rolling (transfer) **Freshmen** 78% were admitted **Housing** Yes **Expenses** Tuition $6709; Room & Board $7220 **Undergraduates** 53% women, 10% part-time, 15% 25 or older, 2% Native American, 1% Hispanic American, 1% African American, 1% Asian American/Pacific Islander **The most frequently chosen baccalaureate fields are** business/marketing, education, health professions and related sciences **Academic program** Advanced placement, self-designed majors, honors program, summer session, adult/continuing education programs, internships **Contact** Ms. Gerri Daniels, Director of Admissions, Northern Michigan University, 1401 Preque Isle Avenue, Marquette, MI 49855. Phone: 906-227-2650 or toll-free 800-682-9797. Fax: 906-227-1747. E-mail: admiss@nmu.edu. Web site: http://www.nmu.edu/.

NORTHWOOD UNIVERSITY
MIDLAND, MICHIGAN

General Independent, comprehensive, coed **Entrance** Moderately difficult **Setting** 434-acre small-town campus **Total enrollment** 2,352 **Student-faculty ratio** 29:1 **Application deadline** Rolling (freshmen), rolling (transfer) **Freshmen** 80% were admitted **Housing** Yes **Expenses** Tuition $16,455; Room & Board $7194 **Undergraduates** 35% women, 4% part-time, 4% 25 or older, 0.3% Native American, 2% Hispanic American, 12% African American, 1% Asian American/Pacific Islander **The most frequently chosen baccalaureate fields are** business/marketing, communications/journalism, parks and recreation **Academic program** English as a second language, advanced placement, accelerated degree program, honors program, summer session, adult/continuing education programs, internships **Contact** Mr. Daniel F. Toland, Dean of Admission, Northwood University, 4000 Whiting Drive, Midland, MI 48640. Phone: 989-837-4237 or toll-free 800-457-7878. Fax: 989-837-4490. E-mail: miadmit@northwood.edu. Web site: http://www.northwood.edu/.

OAKLAND UNIVERSITY
ROCHESTER, MICHIGAN

General State-supported, university, coed **Entrance** Moderately difficult **Setting** 1,444-acre suburban campus **Total enrollment** 18,081 **Student-faculty ratio** 21:1 **Application deadline** Rolling (freshmen), rolling (transfer) **Freshmen** 81% were admitted **Housing** Yes **Expenses** Tuition $7575; Room & Board $6670 **Undergraduates** 62% women, 28% part-time, 21% 25 or older, 0.4% Native American, 2% Hispanic American, 8% African American, 4% Asian American/Pacific Islander **The most frequently chosen baccalaureate fields are** business/marketing, education, health professions and related sciences **Academic program** English as a second language, advanced placement, accelerated degree program, self-designed majors, honors program, summer session, internships **Contact** Ms. Eleanor Reynolds, Interim Assistant Vice President, Student Affairs, Oakland University, 101 North Foundation Hall, Rochester, MI 48309-4401. Phone: 248-370-3364 or toll-free 800-OAK-UNIV. Fax: 248-370-4462. E-mail: ouinfo@oakland.edu. Web site: http://www.oakland.edu/.

OLIVET COLLEGE
OLIVET, MICHIGAN

Contact Mr. Bernie McConnell, Assistant Vice President for Enrollment Management, Olivet College, 320 South Main Street, Olivet, MI 49076-9701. Phone: 269-749-7500 or toll-free 800-456-7189. Fax: 269-749-6617. E-mail: bmcconnell@olivetcollege.edu. Web site: http://www.olivetcollege.edu/.

ROCHESTER COLLEGE
ROCHESTER HILLS, MICHIGAN

General Independent, 4-year, coed, affiliated with Church of Christ **Entrance** Minimally difficult **Setting** 83-acre suburban campus **Total enrollment** 980 **Student-faculty ratio** 6:1 **Application deadline** Rolling (freshmen), rolling (transfer) **Freshmen** 80% were admitted **Housing** Yes **Expenses** Tuition $14,860; Room & Board $6920 **Undergraduates** 62% women, 34% part-time, 47% 25 or older, 1% Native American, 2% Hispanic American, 20% African American, 1% Asian American/Pacific Islander **The most frequently chosen baccalaureate fields are** business/marketing, family and consumer sciences, psychology **Academic program** Advanced placement, accelerated degree program, summer session, adult/continuing education programs, internships **Contact** Mr. Larry Norman, Dean of Admissions, Rochester College, 800 West Avon Road, Rochester Hills, MI 48307-2764. Phone: 248-218-2190 or toll-free 800-521-6010. Fax: 248-218-2035. E-mail: admissions@rc.edu. Web site: http://www.rc.edu/.

SACRED HEART MAJOR SEMINARY
DETROIT, MICHIGAN

General Independent Roman Catholic, comprehensive, coed **Entrance** Moderately difficult **Setting** 24-acre urban campus **Total enrollment** 448 **Student-faculty ratio** 6:1 **Application deadline** 7/31 (freshmen), 7/31 (transfer) **Freshmen** 100% were admitted **Housing** Yes **Expenses** Tuition $12,530; Room & Board $7000 **Undergraduates** 42% women, 85% part-time, 56% 25 or older **The most frequently chosen baccalaureate fields are** liberal arts/general studies, philosophy and religious studies **Academic program** Advanced placement **Contact** Fr. Michael Byrnes, Vice Rector, Sacred Heart Major Seminary, 2701 Chicago Boulevard, Detroit, MI 48206. Phone: 313-883-8710. Fax: 313-868-6400. Web site: http://www.archdioceseofdetroit.org/shms/shms.htm.

SAGINAW VALLEY STATE UNIVERSITY
UNIVERSITY CENTER, MICHIGAN

General State-supported, comprehensive, coed **Entrance** Moderately difficult **Setting** 782-acre rural campus **Total enrollment** 9,662 **Student-faculty ratio** 20:1 **Application deadline** Rolling (freshmen), rolling (transfer) **Freshmen** 89% were admitted **Housing** Yes **Expenses** Tuition $6258;

Room & Board $6630 **Undergraduates** 59% women, 20% part-time, 22% 25 or older, 0.4% Native American, 2% Hispanic American, 7% African American, 1% Asian American/Pacific Islander **The most frequently chosen baccalaureate fields are** business/marketing, education, health professions and related sciences **Academic program** English as a second language, advanced placement, accelerated degree program, self-designed majors, honors program, summer session, adult/continuing education programs, internships **Contact** Mr. James P. Dwyer, Director of Admissions, Saginaw Valley State University, 7400 Bay Road, University Center, MI 48710-0001. Phone: 989-964-4200 or toll-free 800-968-9500. Fax: 989-790-0180. E-mail: admissions@svsu.edu. Web site: http://www.svsu.edu/.

SIENA HEIGHTS UNIVERSITY
ADRIAN, MICHIGAN

General Independent Roman Catholic, comprehensive, coed **Entrance** Moderately difficult **Setting** 140-acre small-town campus **Total enrollment** 2,161 **Student-faculty ratio** 14:1 **Application deadline** Rolling (freshmen), rolling (transfer) **Freshmen** 64% were admitted **Housing** Yes **Expenses** Tuition $9247; Room & Board $3145 **Undergraduates** 58% women, 59% part-time, 51% 25 or older, 1% Native American, 3% Hispanic American, 10% African American, 0.5% Asian American/Pacific Islander **The most frequently chosen baccalaureate fields are** business/marketing, health professions and related sciences, liberal arts/general studies **Academic program** Advanced placement, accelerated degree program, self-designed majors, summer session, adult/continuing education programs, internships **Contact** Mr. Frank Hribar, Vice President of Enrollment Management, Siena Heights University, 1247 East Siena Heights Drive, Adrian, MI 49221-1796. Phone: 517-264-7180 or toll-free 800-521-0009. Fax: 517-264-7745. E-mail: admissions@sienahts.edu. Web site: http://www.sienaheights.edu/.

SPRING ARBOR UNIVERSITY
SPRING ARBOR, MICHIGAN

General Independent Free Methodist, comprehensive, coed **Entrance** Moderately difficult **Setting** 123-acre small-town campus **Total enrollment** 3,970 **Student-faculty ratio** 15:1 **Application deadline** 8/1 (freshmen), rolling (transfer) **Freshmen** 78% were admitted **Housing** Yes **Expenses** Tuition $18,360; Room & Board $6370 **Undergraduates** 68% women, 27% part-time, 1% Native American, 2% Hispanic American, 9% African American, 1% Asian American/Pacific Islander **The most frequently chosen baccalaureate fields are** business/marketing, education, family and consumer sciences **Academic program** English as a second language, advanced placement, accelerated degree program, self-designed majors, honors program, summer session, adult/continuing education programs, internships **Contact** Mr. Randy Comfort, Director of Admissions, Spring Arbor University, 106 East Main Street, Spring Arbor, MI 49283-9799. Phone: 517-750-1200 Ext. 1468 or toll-free 800-968-0011. Fax: 517-750-6620. E-mail: admissions@arbor.edu. Web site: http://www.arbor.edu/.

UNIVERSITY OF DETROIT MERCY
DETROIT, MICHIGAN

Contact Ms. Denise Williams, Dean of Admissions, University of Detroit Mercy, 4001 West McNichols Road, detroit, MI 48221-3038. Phone: 313-993-1245 or toll-free 800-635-5020. Fax: 313-993-3326. E-mail: admissions@udmercy.edu. Web site: http://www.udmercy.edu/.

UNIVERSITY OF MICHIGAN
ANN ARBOR, MICHIGAN

General State-supported, university, coed **Entrance** Very difficult **Setting** 8,070-acre suburban campus **Total enrollment** 41,042 **Student-faculty ratio** 15:1 **Application deadline** 2/1 (freshmen), 2/1 (transfer) **Freshmen** 50% were admitted **Housing** Yes **Expenses** Tuition $10,447; Room & Board $8190 **Undergraduates** 50% women, 3% part-time, 2% 25 or older, 1% Native American, 5% Hispanic American, 6% African American, 12% Asian American/Pacific Islander **The most frequently chosen baccalaureate fields are** engineering, psychology, social sciences **Academic program** English as a second language, advanced placement, accelerated degree program, self-designed majors, honors program, summer session, adult/continuing education programs, internships **Contact** Mr. Ted Spencer, Director of Undergraduate Admissions, University of Michigan, 1220 Student Activities Building, 515 East Jefferson, Ann Arbor, MI 48109-1316. Phone: 734-764-7433. Fax: 734-936-0740. E-mail: ugadmiss@umich.edu. Web site: http://www.umich.edu/.

UNIVERSITY OF MICHIGAN–DEARBORN
DEARBORN, MICHIGAN

General State-supported, comprehensive, coed **Entrance** Moderately difficult **Setting** 210-acre suburban campus **Total enrollment** 8,336 **Student-faculty ratio** 16:1 **Application deadline** Rolling (freshmen), rolling (transfer) **Freshmen** 66% were admitted **Housing** No **Expenses** Tuition $7976 **Undergraduates** 52% women, 34% part-time, 29% 25 or older, 1% Native American, 3% Hispanic American, 10%

University of Michigan–Dearborn *(continued)*

African American, 6% Asian American/Pacific Islander **The most frequently chosen baccalaureate fields are** business/marketing, education, engineering **Academic program** Advanced placement, accelerated degree program, self-designed majors, honors program, summer session, adult/continuing education programs, internships **Contact** Mr. Christopher Tremblay, Director of Admissions and Orientation, University of Michigan–Dearborn, 4901 Eevergreen Road, Dearborn, MI 48128-1491. Phone: 313-593-5100. Fax: 313-436-9167. E-mail: admissions@umd.umich.edu. Web site: http://www.umd.umich.edu/.

UNIVERSITY OF MICHIGAN–FLINT
FLINT, MICHIGAN

General State-supported, comprehensive, coed **Entrance** Moderately difficult **Setting** 72-acre urban campus **Total enrollment** 6,883 **Student-faculty ratio** 15:1 **Application deadline** 8/19 (transfer) **Freshmen** 82% were admitted **Housing** No **Expenses** Tuition $7342 **Undergraduates** 62% women, 38% part-time, 40% 25 or older, 1% Native American, 3% Hispanic American, 12% African American, 2% Asian American/Pacific Islander **The most frequently chosen baccalaureate fields are** education, business/marketing, health professions and related sciences **Academic program** Advanced placement, self-designed majors, honors program, summer session, adult/continuing education programs, internships **Contact** Ms. Kimberley Buster-Williams, Director of Admissions, University of Michigan–Flint, 303 East Kearsley Street, 245 UPAV, Flint, MI 48502-1950. Phone: 810-762-3300 or toll-free 800-942-5636. Fax: 810-762-3272. E-mail: admissions@umflint.edu. Web site: http://www.umflint.edu/.

UNIVERSITY OF PHOENIX–METRO DETROIT CAMPUS
TROY, MICHIGAN

General Proprietary, comprehensive, coed **Contact** Ms. Evelyn Gaskin, Registrar/Executive Director, University of Phoenix–Metro Detroit Campus, 4615 East Elwood Street, Mail Stop AA-K101, Phoenix, AZ 85040-1958. Phone: 480-557-3301 or toll-free 800-776-4867 (in-state); 800-228-7240 (out-of-state). Fax: 480-643-1020. E-mail: evelyn.gaskin@phoenix.edu. Web site: http://www.phoenix.edu/.

UNIVERSITY OF PHOENIX–WEST MICHIGAN CAMPUS
WALKER, MICHIGAN

General Proprietary, comprehensive, coed **Contact** Ms. Evelyn Gaskin, Registrar/Executive Director, University of Phoenix–West Michigan Campus, 4615 East Elwood Street, Mail Stop AA-K101, Phoenix, AZ 85040-1958. Phone: 480-557-3301 or toll-free 800-776-4867 (in-state); 800-228-7240 (out-of-state). Fax: 480-643-1020. E-mail: evelyn.gaskin@phoenix.edu. Web site: http://www.phoenix.edu/.

WALSH COLLEGE OF ACCOUNTANCY AND BUSINESS ADMINISTRATION
TROY, MICHIGAN

Contact Ms. Victoria R. Scavone, Assistant Vice President for Enrollment and Student Services, Walsh College of Accountancy and Business Administration, 3838 Livernois Road, PO Box 7006, Troy, MI 48007-7006. Phone: 248-823-1209 or toll-free 800-925-7401. Fax: 248-823-1611. E-mail: admissions@walshcollege.edu. Web site: http://www.walshcollege.edu/.

WAYNE STATE UNIVERSITY
DETROIT, MICHIGAN

General State-supported, university, coed **Entrance** Moderately difficult **Setting** 203-acre urban campus **Total enrollment** 33,240 **Student-faculty ratio** 17:1 **Application deadline** 8/1 (freshmen), 8/1 (transfer) **Freshmen** 83% were admitted **Housing** Yes **Expenses** Tuition $7844; Room & Board $6702 **Undergraduates** 59% women, 40% part-time, 30% 25 or older, 0.5% Native American, 3% Hispanic American, 32% African American, 6% Asian American/Pacific Islander **The most frequently chosen baccalaureate fields are** business/marketing, education, health professions and related sciences **Academic program** English as a second language, advanced placement, accelerated degree program, self-designed majors, honors program, summer session, adult/continuing education programs, internships **Contact** Ms. Susan Zwieg, Director, Undergraduate Admissions, Wayne State University, The Welcome Center, WSU Main Campus, 42, W Warren, Detroit, MI 48202. Phone: 313-577-3577 or toll-free 877-978 Ext. 4636 (in-state); 800-WSU-INFO (out-of-state). Fax: 313-577-7536. E-mail: admissions@wayne.edu. Web site: http://www.wayne.edu/.

WESTERN MICHIGAN UNIVERSITY
KALAMAZOO, MICHIGAN

General State-supported, university, coed **Entrance** Moderately difficult **Setting** 1,200-acre urban campus **Total enrollment** 24,433 **Student-faculty ratio** 19:1 **Application deadline** Rolling (freshmen), 8/1 (transfer) **Freshmen** 86% were admitted **Housing** Yes **Expenses** Tuition $7260; Room & Board $7042 **Undergraduates** 50% women, 12% part-time, 9% 25 or older, 1% Native American, 2% Hispanic American, 6% African American, 2% Asian American/Pacific Islander **The most frequently chosen baccalaureate fields are** business/ marketing, communications/journalism, education **Academic program** English as a second language, advanced placement, accelerated degree program, self-designed majors, honors program, summer session, adult/continuing education programs, internships **Contact** Ms. Penny Bundy, Director, Office of Admissions, Western Michigan University, 1903 West Michigan Avenue, Kalamazoo, MI 49008-5211. Phone: 269-387-2000. Fax: 269-387-2096. E-mail: ask-wmu@wmich.edu. Web site: http://www.wmich.edu/.

YESHIVA GEDDOLAH OF GREATER DETROIT RABBINICAL COLLEGE
OAK PARK, MICHIGAN

Contact Mr. Eric Krohner, Executive Director, Yeshiva Geddolah of Greater Detroit Rabbinical College, 24600 Greenfield, Oak Park, MI 48237-1544.

MINNESOTA

ACADEMY COLLEGE
MINNEAPOLIS, MINNESOTA

General Proprietary, 4-year, coed **Entrance** Minimally difficult **Setting** urban campus **Total enrollment** 150 **Student-faculty ratio** 7:1 **Housing** No **Expenses** Tuition $19,777 **Undergraduates** 41% women, 6% part-time, 65% 25 or older, 1% Native American, 4% Hispanic American, 21% African American, 7% Asian American/Pacific Islander **The most frequently chosen baccalaureate fields are** business/marketing, computer and information sciences, visual and performing arts **Academic program** English as a second language, advanced placement, accelerated degree program, honors program, summer session, adult/continuing education programs, internships **Contact** Ms. Tracey Schantz, Director, Academy College, 1101 East 78th Street, Suite 100, Bloomington, MN 55420. Phone: 952-851-0066 Ext. 202 or toll-free 800-292-9149. Fax: 952-851-0094. E-mail: admissions@academycollege.edu. Web site: http://www.academycollege.edu/.

ARGOSY UNIVERSITY, TWIN CITIES
EAGAN, MINNESOTA

General Proprietary, university, coed **Setting** suburban campus **Contact** Admissions Director, Argosy University, Twin Cities, 1515 Central Parkway, Eagan, MN 55121. Phone: 651-846-2882 or toll-free 888-844-2004. Web site: http://www.argosy.edu/locations/twin-cities/.

THE ART INSTITUTES INTERNATIONAL MINNESOTA
MINNEAPOLIS, MINNESOTA

General Proprietary, 4-year, coed **Setting** urban campus **Contact** Director of Admissions, The Art Institutes International Minnesota, 15 South 9th Street, Minneapolis, MN 55402. Phone: 612-332-3361 Ext. 6820 or toll-free 800-777-3643. E-mail: aimadm@aii.edu. Web site: http://www.artinstitutes.edu/minneapolis/.

AUGSBURG COLLEGE
MINNEAPOLIS, MINNESOTA

General Independent Lutheran, comprehensive, coed **Entrance** Moderately difficult **Setting** 23-acre urban campus **Total enrollment** 3,732 **Student-faculty ratio** 14:1 **Application deadline** 8/15 (freshmen), 8/15 (transfer) **Freshmen** 61% were admitted **Housing** Yes **Expenses** Tuition $24,539; Room & Board $6902 **Undergraduates** 57% women, 19% part-time, 10% 25 or older, 1% Native American, 2% Hispanic American, 5% African American, 4% Asian American/Pacific Islander **The most frequently chosen baccalaureate fields are** business/ marketing, education, social sciences **Academic program** English as a second language, advanced placement, self-designed majors, honors program, summer session, adult/continuing education programs, internships **Contact** Ms. Carrie Carroll, Director of Undergraduate Day Admissions, Augsburg College, 2211 Riverside Avenue, Minneapolis, MN 55454-1351. Phone: 612-330-1001 or toll-free 800-788-5678. Fax: 612-330-1590. E-mail: admissions@augsburg.edu. Web site: http://www.augsburg.edu/.

BEMIDJI STATE UNIVERSITY
BEMIDJI, MINNESOTA

General State-supported, comprehensive, coed **Entrance** Moderately difficult **Setting** 89-acre small-town campus **Total enrollment** 4,898 **Student-faculty ratio** 19:1 **Application deadline** Rolling (freshmen), rolling (transfer) **Freshmen** 86% were admitted **Housing** Yes **Expenses** Tuition $6977; Room & Board $5874 **Undergraduates** 52% women, 25% part-time, 8% 25 or older, 4% Native American, 0.3% Hispanic American, 1% African American, 1% Asian American/Pacific Islander **The most frequently chosen baccalaureate fields are** business/marketing, education, psychology **Academic program** English as a second language, advanced placement, honors program, summer session, adult/continuing education programs, internships

Bemidji State University *(continued)*

Contact Mr. Russ Kreager, Director of Admissions, Bemidji State University, Deputy 102, 1500 Birchmont Drive NE, Bemidji, MN 56601. Phone: 218-755-2040 or toll-free 800-475-2001 (in-state); 800-652-9747 (out-of-state). Fax: 218-755-2074. E-mail: admissions@bemidjistate.edu. Web site: http://www.bemidjistate.edu/.

BETHANY LUTHERAN COLLEGE
MANKATO, MINNESOTA

General Independent Lutheran, 4-year, coed **Entrance** Moderately difficult **Setting** 50-acre small-town campus **Total enrollment** 617 **Student-faculty ratio** 11:1 **Application deadline** 7/1 (freshmen) **Freshmen** 83% were admitted **Housing** Yes **Expenses** Tuition $17,760; Room & Board $5278 **Undergraduates** 58% women, 4% part-time, 5% 25 or older, 0.3% Native American, 1% Hispanic American, 2% African American, 2% Asian American/Pacific Islander **The most frequently chosen baccalaureate fields are** business/marketing, communications/journalism, visual and performing arts **Academic program** Advanced placement, honors program, internships **Contact** Mr. Donald Westphal, Dean of Admissions, Bethany Lutheran College, 700 Luther Drive, Mankato, MN 56001. Phone: 507-344-7320 or toll-free 800-944-3066 Ext. 331. Fax: 507-344-7376. E-mail: dwestpha@blc.edu. Web site: http://www.blc.edu/.

BETHEL UNIVERSITY
ST. PAUL, MINNESOTA

General Independent, comprehensive, coed, affiliated with Baptist General Conference **Entrance** Moderately difficult **Setting** 248-acre suburban campus **Total enrollment** 4,162 **Student-faculty ratio** 14:1 **Application deadline** 8/1 (transfer) **Freshmen** 88% were admitted **Housing** Yes **Expenses** Tuition $24,510; Room & Board $7380 **Undergraduates** 63% women, 18% part-time, 22% 25 or older, 0.3% Native American, 2% Hispanic American, 3% African American, 3% Asian American/Pacific Islander **The most frequently chosen baccalaureate fields are** business/marketing, education, health professions and related sciences **Academic program** Advanced placement, accelerated degree program, self-designed majors, honors program, summer session, adult/continuing education programs, internships **Contact** Mr. Jay Fedje, Director of Admissions, Bethel University, 3900 Bethel Drive, St. Paul, MN 55112. Phone: 651-638-6371 or toll-free 800-255-8706 Ext. 6242. Fax: 651-635-1490. E-mail: buadmissions-cas@bethel.edu. Web site: http://www.bethel.edu/.

▶**For more information, see page 442.**

CAPELLA UNIVERSITY
MINNEAPOLIS, MINNESOTA

General Proprietary, upper-level, coed **Contact** Learner Support, Capella University, 225 South Sixth Street, 9th Floor, Minneapolis, MN 55402. Phone: 612-977-4222 or toll-free 888-CAPELLA. Fax: 612-977-5060. E-mail: info@capella.edu. Web site: http://www.capella.edu/.

CARLETON COLLEGE
NORTHFIELD, MINNESOTA

General Independent, 4-year, coed **Entrance** Very difficult **Setting** 955-acre small-town campus **Total enrollment** 2,005 **Student-faculty ratio** 9:1 **Application deadline** 1/15 (freshmen), 3/31 (transfer) **Freshmen** 30% were admitted **Housing** Yes **Expenses** Tuition $38,046; Room & Board $5223 **Undergraduates** 52% women, 1% part-time, 1% Native American, 6% Hispanic American, 5% African American, 10% Asian American/Pacific Islander **The most frequently chosen baccalaureate fields are** physical sciences, biological/life sciences, social sciences **Academic program** Advanced placement, accelerated degree program, self-designed majors, internships **Contact** Mr. Paul Thiboutot, Dean of Admissions, Carleton College, One North College Street, Northfield, MN 55057-4001. Phone: 507-222-4190 or toll-free 800-995-2275. Fax: 507-646-4526. E-mail: admissions@acs.carleton.edu. Web site: http://www.carleton.edu/.

COLLEGE OF SAINT BENEDICT
SAINT JOSEPH, MINNESOTA

General Independent Roman Catholic, 4-year, coed, primarily women, coordinate institution with Saint John's University (MN) **Entrance** Moderately difficult **Setting** 315-acre small-town campus **Total enrollment** 2,087 **Student-faculty ratio** 12:1 **Application deadline** Rolling (freshmen), rolling (transfer) **Freshmen** 76% were admitted **Housing** Yes **Expenses** Tuition $26,530; Room & Board $7430 **Undergraduates** 100% women, 2% part-time, 1% 25 or older, 0.3% Native American, 2% Hispanic American, 1% African American, 3% Asian American/Pacific Islander **The most frequently chosen baccalaureate fields are** English, health professions and related sciences, psychology **Academic program** English as a second language, advanced placement, accelerated degree program, self-designed majors, honors program, internships **Contact** Ms. Karen Backes, Associate Dean of Admissions, College of Saint Benedict, 37 South College Avenue, St. Joseph, MN 56374. Phone: 320-363-2196 or toll-free 800-544-1489. Fax: 320-363-2750. E-mail: admissions@csbsju.edu. Web site: http://www.csbsju.edu/.

COLLEGE OF ST. CATHERINE

ST. PAUL, MINNESOTA

General Independent Roman Catholic, comprehensive, undergraduate: women only; graduate: coed **Entrance** Moderately difficult **Setting** 110-acre urban campus **Total enrollment** 5,246 **Student-faculty ratio** 11:1 **Application deadline** Rolling (freshmen), rolling (transfer) **Freshmen** 81% were admitted **Housing** Yes **Expenses** Tuition $25,922; Room & Board $6788 **Undergraduates** 36% part-time, 15% 25 or older, 1% Native American, 3% Hispanic American, 11% African American, 7% Asian American/ Pacific Islander **The most frequently chosen baccalaureate fields are** business/marketing, education, health professions and related sciences **Academic program** Advanced placement, self-designed majors, honors program, summer session, adult/continuing education programs, internships **Contact** Ms. Cory Piper-Hauswirth, Associate Director of Admission and Financial Aid, College of St. Catherine, 2004 Randolph Avenue, St. Paul, MN 55105-1789. Phone: 651-690-6047 or toll-free 800-656-5283. Fax: 651-690-8824. E-mail: stkate@stkate.edu. Web site: http://www.stkate.edu/.

THE COLLEGE OF ST. SCHOLASTICA

DULUTH, MINNESOTA

General Independent, comprehensive, coed, affiliated with Roman Catholic Church **Entrance** Moderately difficult **Setting** 186-acre suburban campus **Total enrollment** 3,259 **Student-faculty ratio** 13:1 **Application deadline** Rolling (freshmen), rolling (transfer) **Freshmen** 88% were admitted **Housing** Yes **Expenses** Tuition $24,990; Room & Board $6684 **Undergraduates** 70% women, 10% part-time, 22% 25 or older, 2% Native American, 1% Hispanic American, 2% African American, 2% Asian American/Pacific Islander **The most frequently chosen baccalaureate fields are** business/marketing, biological/ life sciences, health professions and related sciences **Academic program** Advanced placement, accelerated degree program, self-designed majors, honors program, summer session, adult/ continuing education programs, internships **Contact** Mr. Brian Dalton, Vice President for Enrollment Management, The College of St. Scholastica, 1200 Kenwood Avenue, Duluth, MN 55811-4199. Phone: 218-723-6053 or toll-free 800-249-6412. Fax: 218-723-5991. E-mail: admissions@css.edu. Web site: http://www.css.edu/.

COLLEGE OF VISUAL ARTS

ST. PAUL, MINNESOTA

General Independent, 4-year, coed **Entrance** Moderately difficult **Setting** 2-acre urban campus **Total enrollment** 178 **Student-faculty ratio** 12:1 **Application deadline** Rolling (freshmen), rolling (transfer) **Freshmen** 98% were admitted **Housing** No **Expenses** Tuition $22,426 **Undergraduates** 58% women, 4% part-time, 16% 25 or older, 1% Native American, 2% Hispanic American, 3% African American, 3% Asian American/Pacific Islander **The most frequently chosen baccalaureate field is** visual and performing arts **Academic program** Advanced placement, honors program, summer session, internships **Contact** Mr. Paul Gaines, Director of Student Life, College of Visual Arts, 344 Summit Avenue, St. Paul, MN 55102-2124. Phone: 651-224-3416 or toll-free 800-224-1536. Fax: 651-224-8854. E-mail: pgaines@cva.edu. Web site: http://www.cva.edu/.

CONCORDIA COLLEGE

MOORHEAD, MINNESOTA

General Independent, comprehensive, coed, affiliated with Evangelical Lutheran Church in America **Entrance** Moderately difficult **Setting** 120-acre suburban campus **Total enrollment** 2,815 **Student-faculty ratio** 15:1 **Application deadline** Rolling (freshmen), rolling (transfer) **Freshmen** 85% were admitted **Housing** Yes **Expenses** Tuition $24,120; Room & Board $6160 **Undergraduates** 61% women, 2% part-time, 2% 25 or older, 0.3% Native American, 1% Hispanic American, 1% African American, 2% Asian American/Pacific Islander **The most frequently chosen baccalaureate fields are** business/ marketing, education, social sciences **Academic program** English as a second language, advanced placement, honors program, summer session, adult/continuing education programs, internships **Contact** Mr. Scott E. Ellingson, Director of Admissions, Concordia College, 901 8th Street South, Moorhead, MN 56562. Phone: 218-299-3004 or toll-free 800-699-9897. Fax: 218-299-3947. E-mail: admissions@cord.edu. Web site: http://www.concordiacollege.edu/.

CONCORDIA UNIVERSITY, ST. PAUL

ST. PAUL, MINNESOTA

General Independent, comprehensive, coed, affiliated with Lutheran Church–Missouri Synod **Entrance** Minimally difficult **Setting** 37-acre urban campus **Total enrollment** 2,260 **Student-faculty ratio** 12:1 **Application deadline** 8/1 (freshmen), 8/1 (transfer) **Freshmen** 57% were admitted **Housing** Yes **Expenses** Tuition $24,900; Room & Board $6900 **Undergraduates** 60% women, 16% part-time, 42% 25 or older, 0.5% Native American, 1% Hispanic American, 9% African American, 6% Asian American/Pacific Islander **The most frequently chosen baccalaureate fields are** business/marketing, education, family and consumer sciences **Academic**

Concordia University, St. Paul *(continued)*

program Advanced placement, accelerated degree program, self-designed majors, honors program, summer session, adult/continuing education programs, internships **Contact** Kristin Schoon, Director of Undergraduate Admission, Concordia University, St. Paul, 275 Syndicate North, St. Paul, MN 55104-5494. Phone: 651-641-8230 or toll-free 800-333-4705. Fax: 651-603-6320. E-mail: admission@csp.edu. Web site: http://www.csp.edu/.

CROSSROADS COLLEGE
ROCHESTER, MINNESOTA

General Independent, 4-year, coed, affiliated with Christian Churches and Churches of Christ **Entrance** Noncompetitive **Setting** 40-acre urban campus **Total enrollment** 184 **Student-faculty ratio** 9:1 **Application deadline** 8/15 (freshmen), 8/15 (transfer) **Housing** Yes **Expenses** Tuition $13,210; Room only $3900 **Undergraduates** 52% women, 19% part-time, 32% 25 or older, 1% Hispanic American, 8% African American, 3% Asian American/Pacific Islander **The most frequently chosen baccalaureate field is** theology and religious vocations **Academic program** Advanced placement, self-designed majors, adult/continuing education programs, internships **Contact** Mr. Scott Klaehn, Director of Admissions, Crossroads College, 920 Mayowood Road, SW, Rochester, MN 55902-2382. Phone: 507-288-4563 Ext. 304 or toll-free 800-456-7651. Fax: 507-288-9046. E-mail: admissions@crossroadscollege.edu. Web site: http://www.crossroadscollege.edu/.

CROWN COLLEGE
ST. BONIFACIUS, MINNESOTA

General Independent, comprehensive, coed, affiliated with The Christian and Missionary Alliance **Entrance** Minimally difficult **Setting** 215-acre suburban campus **Total enrollment** 1,270 **Student-faculty ratio** 19:1 **Application deadline** Rolling (freshmen), rolling (transfer) **Freshmen** 38% were admitted **Housing** Yes **Expenses** Tuition $19,198; Room & Board $7366 **Undergraduates** 62% women, 38% part-time, 35% 25 or older, 0.2% Native American, 1% Hispanic American, 2% African American, 6% Asian American/Pacific Islander **The most frequently chosen baccalaureate fields are** education, business/marketing, philosophy and religious studies **Academic program** English as a second language, advanced placement, accelerated degree program, honors program, summer session, adult/continuing education programs, internships **Contact** Ms. Jill Pautz, Director of Admissions, Crown College, 8700 College View Drive, St. Bonifacius, MN 55375-9001. Phone: 952-446-4144 or toll-free 800-68-CROWN. Fax: 952-446-4149. E-mail: info@crown.edu. Web site: http://www.crown.edu/.

DeVRY UNIVERSITY
EDINA, MINNESOTA

General Proprietary, comprehensive, coed **Total enrollment** 211 **Student-faculty ratio** 120:1 **Application deadline** Rolling (freshmen), rolling (transfer) **Expenses** Tuition $13,890 **Undergraduates** 39% women, 60% part-time, 78% 25 or older, 1% Native American, 4% Hispanic American, 10% African American, 5% Asian American/Pacific Islander **The most frequently chosen baccalaureate fields are** business/marketing, computer and information sciences **Academic program** Accelerated degree program **Contact** Admissions Office, DeVry University, 7700 France Avenue South, Suite 575, Edina, MN 55435. Web site: http://www.devry.edu/.

GUSTAVUS ADOLPHUS COLLEGE
ST. PETER, MINNESOTA

General Independent, 4-year, coed, affiliated with Evangelical Lutheran Church in America **Entrance** Very difficult **Setting** 340-acre small-town campus **Total enrollment** 2,628 **Student-faculty ratio** 13:1 **Application deadline** 4/1 (freshmen), 4/1 (transfer) **Freshmen** 80% were admitted **Housing** Yes **Expenses** Tuition $28,515; Room & Board $6775 **Undergraduates** 57% women, 2% part-time, 1% 25 or older, 0.2% Native American, 2% Hispanic American, 2% African American, 4% Asian American/Pacific Islander **The most frequently chosen baccalaureate fields are** business/marketing, biological/life sciences, social sciences **Academic program** Advanced placement, accelerated degree program, self-designed majors, honors program, summer session, internships **Contact** Mr. Mark Anderson, Vice President for Admission and Student Financial Aid, Gustavus Adolphus College, 800 West College Ave., St. Peter, MN 56082-1498. Phone: 507-933-7676 or toll-free 800-GUSTAVU(S). Fax: 507-933-7474. E-mail: admission@gac.edu. Web site: http://www.gustavus.edu/.

HAMLINE UNIVERSITY
ST. PAUL, MINNESOTA

General Independent, comprehensive, coed, affiliated with United Methodist Church **Entrance** Moderately difficult **Setting** 50-acre urban campus **Total enrollment** 4,803 **Student-faculty ratio** 14:1 **Application deadline** Rolling (freshmen), rolling (transfer) **Freshmen** 78% were admitted **Housing** Yes **Expenses** Tuition $26,533; Room & Board $7392 **Undergraduates** 59% women, 6% part-time, 1% Native American, 2% Hispanic

American, 5% African American, 6% Asian American/Pacific Islander **The most frequently chosen baccalaureate fields are** psychology, business/marketing, social sciences **Academic program** English as a second language, advanced placement, self-designed majors, honors program, summer session, adult/continuing education programs, internships **Contact** Ms. Ann Kjorstad, Director of Undergraduate Admission, Hamline University, 1536 Hewitt Avenue, C1930, St. Paul, MN 55104-2458. Phone: 651-523-2207 or toll-free 800-753-9753. Fax: 651-523-2458. E-mail: cla-admis@hamline.edu. Web site: http://www.hamline.edu/.

MACALESTER COLLEGE

ST. PAUL, MINNESOTA

General Independent Presbyterian, 4-year, coed **Entrance** Very difficult **Setting** 53-acre urban campus **Total enrollment** 1,920 **Student-faculty ratio** 10:1 **Application deadline** 1/15 (freshmen), 4/15 (transfer) **Freshmen** 41% were admitted **Housing** Yes **Expenses** Tuition $34,704; Room & Board $8472 **Undergraduates** 58% women, 2% part-time, 0.3% 25 or older, 1% Native American, 4% Hispanic American, 5% African American, 9% Asian American/Pacific Islander **The most frequently chosen baccalaureate fields are** foreign languages and literature, interdisciplinary studies, social sciences **Academic program** Self-designed majors, honors program, internships **Contact** Mr. Lorne T. Robinson, Dean of Admissions and Financial Aid, Macalester College, 1600 Grand Avenue, St. Paul, MN 55105-1899. Phone: 651-696-6357 or toll-free 800-231-7974. Fax: 651-696-6724. E-mail: admissions@macalester.edu. Web site: http://www.macalester.edu/.

MARTIN LUTHER COLLEGE

NEW ULM, MINNESOTA

General Independent, 4-year, coed, affiliated with Wisconsin Evangelical Lutheran Synod **Contact** Prof. Ronald B. Brutlag, Associate Director of Admissions, Martin Luther College, 1995 Luther Court, New Ulm, MN 56073. Phone: 507-354-8221 Ext. 211. Fax: 507-354-8225. E-mail: brutlaro@mlc-wels.edu. Web site: http://www.mlc-wels.edu/.

McNALLY SMITH COLLEGE OF MUSIC

SAINT PAUL, MINNESOTA

General Proprietary, 4-year, coed **Entrance** Noncompetitive **Setting** urban campus **Total enrollment** 542 **Student-faculty ratio** 10:1 **Application deadline** 8/1 (freshmen) **Housing** No **Expenses** Tuition $20,260 **Undergraduates** 18% women, 10% part-time, 11% 25 or older, 1% Native American, 4% Hispanic American, 9% African American, 1% Asian American/Pacific Islander **The most frequently chosen baccalaureate fields are** business/marketing, visual and performing arts **Academic program** Advanced placement, summer session, internships **Contact** Mrs. Kathy Hawks, Director of Admissions, McNally Smith College of Music, 19 Exchange Street East, St. Paul, MN 55101. Phone: 651-291-0177 Ext. 2373 or toll-free 800-594-9500. Fax: 651-291-0366. E-mail: khawks@mcnallysmith.edu. Web site: http://www.mcnallysmith.edu/.

METROPOLITAN STATE UNIVERSITY

ST. PAUL, MINNESOTA

General State-supported, comprehensive, coed **Entrance** Minimally difficult **Setting** urban campus **Total enrollment** 6,801 **Student-faculty ratio** 15:1 **Application deadline** 6/15 (freshmen), 6/15 (transfer) **Freshmen** 53% were admitted **Housing** No **Expenses** Tuition $5473 **Undergraduates** 59% women, 65% part-time, 1% 25 or older, 1% Native American, 2% Hispanic American, 12% African American, 9% Asian American/Pacific Islander **The most frequently chosen baccalaureate fields are** business/marketing, health professions and related sciences, liberal arts/general studies **Academic program** English as a second language, advanced placement, self-designed majors, summer session, adult/continuing education programs, internships **Contact** Ms. Monir Johnson, Director, Metropolitan State University, 700 East 7th Street, St. Paul, MN 55106. Phone: 651-793-1303. Fax: 651-793-1310. E-mail: monir.johnson@metrostate.edu. Web site: http://www.metrostate.edu/.

MINNEAPOLIS COLLEGE OF ART AND DESIGN

MINNEAPOLIS, MINNESOTA

General Independent, comprehensive, coed **Contact** Mr. William Mullen, Director of Admissions, Minneapolis College of Art and Design, 2501 Stevens Avenue South, Minneapolis, MN 55404. Phone: 612-874-3762 or toll-free 800-874-6223. E-mail: admissions@mn.mcad.edu. Web site: http://www.mcad.edu/.

MINNESOTA SCHOOL OF BUSINESS–BLAINE

BLAINE, MINNESOTA

General Proprietary, 4-year, coed, primarily women **Entrance** Moderately difficult **Total enrollment** 386 **Student-faculty ratio** 12:1 **Application deadline** 10/1 (freshmen), 10/1

Minnesota School of Business–Blaine *(continued)*

(transfer) **Freshmen** 100% were admitted **Housing** No **Expenses** Tuition $18,720 **Undergraduates** 75% women, 38% 25 or older, 1% Native American, 1% Hispanic American, 1% African American, 2% Asian American/Pacific Islander **Contact** Ms. Kristen Swanson, Director of Admissions, Minnesota School of Business–Blaine, 3680 Pheasant Ridge Drive NE, Blaine, MN 55449. Phone: 763-225-8003. Fax: 763-225-8001. E-mail: kswanson@msbcollege.edu. Web site: http://www.msbcollege.edu/oncampus/blaine/.

MINNESOTA SCHOOL OF BUSINESS–ROCHESTER
ROCHESTER, MINNESOTA

General Proprietary, 4-year, coed **Setting** small-town campus **Total enrollment** 535 **Student-faculty ratio** 13:1 **Application deadline** 10/6 (freshmen) **Freshmen** 82% were admitted **Housing** No **Expenses** Tuition $17,550 **Undergraduates** 76% women, 34% part-time, 47% 25 or older, 0.4% Native American, 1% African American, 2% Asian American/Pacific Islander **Academic program** Advanced placement, summer session, internships **Contact** Mr. Shan Pollitt, Director of Admissions, Minnesota School of Business–Rochester, 2521 Pennington Drive NW, Rochester, MN 55901. Phone: 507-586-9500 or toll-free 888-662-8772. Fax: 507-535-8011. E-mail: spollitt@msbcollege.edu. Web site: http://www.msbcollege.edu/.

MINNESOTA STATE UNIVERSITY MANKATO
MANKATO, MINNESOTA

General State-supported, comprehensive, coed **Entrance** Moderately difficult **Setting** 303-acre small-town campus **Total enrollment** 14,148 **Student-faculty ratio** 22:1 **Application deadline** Rolling (freshmen), rolling (transfer) **Freshmen** 90% were admitted **Housing** Yes **Expenses** Tuition $6050; Room & Board $5354 **Undergraduates** 53% women, 11% part-time, 11% 25 or older, 1% Native American, 1% Hispanic American, 3% African American, 2% Asian American/Pacific Islander **The most frequently chosen baccalaureate fields are** business/marketing, education, health professions and related sciences **Academic program** English as a second language, advanced placement, self-designed majors, honors program, summer session, adult/continuing education programs, internships **Contact** Office of Admissions, Minnesota State University Mankato, 122 Taylor Center, Mankato, MN 56001. Phone: 507-389-6670 or toll-free 800-722-0544. Fax: 507-389-1511. E-mail: admissions@mnsu.edu. Web site: http://www.mnsu.edu/.

MINNESOTA STATE UNIVERSITY MOORHEAD
MOORHEAD, MINNESOTA

Contact Ms. Gina Monson, Director of Admissions, Minnesota State University Moorhead, Owens Hall, Moorhead, MN 56563-0002. Phone: 218-477-2161 or toll-free 800-593-7246. Fax: 218-477-4374. E-mail: dragon@mnstate.edu. Web site: http://www.mnstate.edu/.

NATIONAL AMERICAN UNIVERSITY
ROSEVILLE, MINNESOTA

Contact Mr. Steve Grunlan, Director of Admissions, National American University, 1500 West Highway 36, Roseville, MN 55113-4035. Phone: 651-644-1265. Web site: http://www.national.edu/.

NORTH CENTRAL UNIVERSITY
MINNEAPOLIS, MINNESOTA

Contact Ms. Amber Stumph, Admissions Secretary, North Central University, 910 Elliot Avenue, Minneapolis, MN 55404-1322. Phone: 612-343-4460 or toll-free 800-289-6222. Fax: 612-343-4146. E-mail: admissions@northcentral.edu. Web site: http://www.northcentral.edu/.

NORTHWESTERN COLLEGE
ST. PAUL, MINNESOTA

General Independent nondenominational, 4-year, coed **Entrance** Moderately difficult **Setting** 107-acre suburban campus **Total enrollment** 1,925 **Student-faculty ratio** 15:1 **Application deadline** 8/1 (freshmen), 8/1 (transfer) **Freshmen** 93% were admitted **Housing** Yes **Expenses** Tuition $22,420; Room & Board $7050 **Undergraduates** 59% women, 3% part-time, 2% 25 or older, 1% Native American, 2% Hispanic American, 3% African American, 4% Asian American/Pacific Islander **The most frequently chosen baccalaureate fields are** education, communications/journalism, theology and religious vocations **Academic program** Advanced placement, self-designed majors, honors program, summer session, adult/continuing education programs, internships **Contact** Mr. Kenneth K. Faffler, Director of Admissions, Northwestern College, Officer of Admissions, 3003 Snelling Avenue North, 212 Nazareth Hall, St. Paul, MN 55113-1598. Phone: 651-631-5111 or toll-free 800-827-6827. Fax: 651-631-5680. E-mail: admissions@nwc.edu. Web site: http://www.nwc.edu/.

OAK HILLS CHRISTIAN COLLEGE
BEMIDJI, MINNESOTA

General Independent interdenominational, 4-year, coed **Entrance** Minimally difficult **Setting** 180-acre rural campus **Total enrollment** 163 **Student-faculty ratio** 7:1 **Application deadline** Rolling (freshmen), rolling (transfer) **Freshmen** 95% were admitted **Housing** Yes **Expenses** Tuition $12,820; Room & Board $4720 **Undergraduates** 45% women, 11% part-time, 22% 25 or older, 4% Native American, 2% Hispanic American, 2% African American, 2% Asian American/Pacific Islander **The most frequently chosen baccalaureate field is** theology and religious vocations **Academic program** Advanced placement, honors program, internships **Contact** Mr. Daniel Hovestol, Admissions Director, Oak Hills Christian College, 1600 Oak Hills Road, SW, Bemidji, MN 56601. Phone: 218-751-8670 Ext. 1220 or toll-free 888-751-8670 Ext. 285. Fax: 218-751-8825. E-mail: admissions@oakhills.edu. Web site: http://www.oakhills.edu/.

PILLSBURY BAPTIST BIBLE COLLEGE
OWATONNA, MINNESOTA

General Independent Baptist, 4-year, coed **Entrance** Noncompetitive **Setting** 14-acre small-town campus **Total enrollment** 164 **Student-faculty ratio** 7:1 **Application deadline** 8/20 (freshmen), 8/20 (transfer) **Housing** Yes **Expenses** Tuition $10,208; Room & Board $4996 **Undergraduates** 60% women, 13% part-time, 7% 25 or older, 1% Hispanic American, 1% African American, 1% Asian American/Pacific Islander **The most frequently chosen baccalaureate fields are** education, health professions and related sciences, theology and religious vocations **Academic program** Advanced placement, accelerated degree program, summer session, internships **Contact** Mr. Jason Nicholson, Admissions Counselor, Pillsbury Baptist Bible College, 315 South Grove Avenue, Owatonna, MN 55060-3097. Phone: 507-451-2710 Ext. 279 or toll-free 800-747-4557. Fax: 507-451-6459. E-mail: pbbc@pillsbury.edu. Web site: http://www.pillsbury.edu/.

RASMUSSEN COLLEGE MANKATO
MANKATO, MINNESOTA

Contact Ms. Kathy Clifford, Director of Admissions, Rasmussen College Mankato, 501 Holly Lane, Mankato, MN 56001-6803. Phone: 507-625-6556 or toll-free 800-657-6767. Fax: 507-625-6557. E-mail: rascoll@ic.mankato.mn.us. Web site: http://www.rasmussen.edu/.

ST. CLOUD STATE UNIVERSITY
ST. CLOUD, MINNESOTA

General State-supported, comprehensive, coed **Entrance** Moderately difficult **Setting** 922-acre suburban campus **Total enrollment** 15,808 **Student-faculty ratio** 20:1 **Application deadline** 6/1 (freshmen), 8/15 (transfer) **Freshmen** 76% were admitted **Housing** Yes **Expenses** Tuition $5955; Room & Board $5592 **Undergraduates** 53% women, 15% part-time, 12% 25 or older, 1% Native American, 1% Hispanic American, 3% African American, 2% Asian American/Pacific Islander **The most frequently chosen baccalaureate fields are** business/marketing, communications/journalism, education **Academic program** English as a second language, advanced placement, accelerated degree program, self-designed majors, honors program, summer session, adult/continuing education programs, internships **Contact** Mr. Jeff Rhodes, Director of Admissions, St. Cloud State University, 115 AS Building, 720 4th Avenue South, St. Cloud, MN 56301-4498. Phone: 320-308-3981 or toll-free 877-654-7278. Fax: 320-308-2243. E-mail: scsu4u@stcloudstate.edu. Web site: http://www.stcloudstate.edu/.

SAINT JOHN'S UNIVERSITY
COLLEGEVILLE, MINNESOTA

General Independent Roman Catholic, comprehensive, coed, primarily men, coordinate institution with College of Saint Benedict **Entrance** Moderately difficult **Setting** 2,400-acre rural campus **Total enrollment** 2,080 **Student-faculty ratio** 12:1 **Application deadline** Rolling (freshmen), rolling (transfer) **Freshmen** 74% were admitted **Housing** Yes **Expenses** Tuition $26,530; Room & Board $6870 **Undergraduates** 2% part-time, 1% 25 or older, 0.2% Native American, 1% Hispanic American, 1% African American, 2% Asian American/Pacific Islander **The most frequently chosen baccalaureate fields are** business/marketing, English, social sciences **Academic program** English as a second language, advanced placement, accelerated degree program, self-designed majors, honors program, internships **Contact** Mr. Matt Beirne, Director of Admission, Saint John's University, PO Box 7155, Collegeville, MN 56321-7155. Phone: 320-363-3036 or toll-free 800-544-1489. Fax: 320-363-2750. E-mail: admissions@csbsju.edu. Web site: http://www.csbsju.edu/.

SAINT MARY'S UNIVERSITY OF MINNESOTA
WINONA, MINNESOTA

General Independent Roman Catholic, comprehensive, coed **Entrance** Moderately difficult

Saint Mary's University of Minnesota *(continued)*

Setting 350-acre small-town campus **Total enrollment** 5,960 **Student-faculty ratio** 12:1 **Application deadline** 5/1 (freshmen), rolling (transfer) **Freshmen** 83% were admitted **Housing** Yes **Expenses** Tuition $24,150; Room & Board $6380 **Undergraduates** 53% women, 30% part-time, 2% 25 or older, 1% Native American, 3% Hispanic American, 4% African American, 3% Asian American/Pacific Islander **The most frequently chosen baccalaureate fields are** business/marketing, education, security and protective services **Academic program** English as a second language, advanced placement, accelerated degree program, self-designed majors, honors program, summer session, adult/continuing education programs, internships **Contact** Mr. Anthony M. Piscitiello, Vice President for Admission, Saint Mary's University of Minnesota, 700 Terrace Heights, Winona, MN 55987-1399. Phone: 507-457-1700 or toll-free 800-635-5987. Fax: 507-457-1722. E-mail: admissions@smumn.edu. Web site: http://www.smumn.edu/.

ST. OLAF COLLEGE
NORTHFIELD, MINNESOTA

General Independent Lutheran, 4-year, coed **Entrance** Very difficult **Setting** 300-acre small-town campus **Total enrollment** 3,040 **Student-faculty ratio** 13:1 **Application deadline** Rolling (freshmen), rolling (transfer) **Freshmen** 54% were admitted **Housing** Yes **Expenses** Tuition $34,300; Room & Board $7900 **Undergraduates** 55% women, 2% part-time, 1% 25 or older, 0.2% Native American, 1% Hispanic American, 1% African American, 5% Asian American/Pacific Islander **The most frequently chosen baccalaureate fields are** social sciences, English, visual and performing arts **Academic program** Advanced placement, self-designed majors, summer session, internships **Contact** Derek Gueldenzoph, Dean of Admissions, St. Olaf College, 1520 St. Olaf Avenue, Northfield, MN 55057. Phone: 507-786-3025 or toll-free 800-800-3025. Fax: 507-786-3832. E-mail: admissions@stolaf.edu. Web site: http://www.stolaf.edu/.

SOUTHWEST MINNESOTA STATE UNIVERSITY
MARSHALL, MINNESOTA

General State-supported, comprehensive, coed **Entrance** Minimally difficult **Setting** 216-acre small-town campus **Total enrollment** 6,073 **Student-faculty ratio** 23:1 **Application deadline** Rolling (freshmen), rolling (transfer) **Freshmen** 78% were admitted **Housing** Yes **Expenses** Tuition $6750; Room & Board $5900 **Undergraduates** 58% women, 59% part-time, 5% 25 or older, 0.5% Native American, 2% Hispanic American, 4% African American, 2% Asian American/Pacific Islander **The most frequently chosen baccalaureate fields are** business/marketing, education, psychology **Academic program** English as a second language, advanced placement, accelerated degree program, self-designed majors, honors program, summer session, adult/continuing education programs, internships **Contact** Mr. Richard Shearer, Director of Enrollment Services, Southwest Minnesota State University, 1501 State Street, Marshall, MN 56258. Phone: 507-537-6286 or toll-free 800-642-0684. Fax: 507-537-7145. E-mail: shearerr@southwestmsu.edu. Web site: http://www.southwest.msus.edu/.

UNIVERSITY OF MINNESOTA, CROOKSTON
CROOKSTON, MINNESOTA

General State-supported, 4-year, coed **Entrance** Moderately difficult **Setting** 237-acre rural campus **Total enrollment** 2,346 **Student-faculty ratio** 16:1 **Application deadline** Rolling (freshmen), rolling (transfer) **Freshmen** 83% were admitted **Housing** Yes **Expenses** Tuition $8821; Room & Board $5342 **Undergraduates** 50% women, 53% part-time, 22% 25 or older, 1% Native American, 2% Hispanic American, 5% African American, 2% Asian American/Pacific Islander **The most frequently chosen baccalaureate fields are** agriculture, business/marketing, natural resources/environmental science **Academic program** English as a second language, advanced placement, self-designed majors, summer session, adult/continuing education programs, internships **Contact** Ms. Amber Evans-Dailey, Director of Admissions, University of Minnesota, Crookston, 2900 University Avenue, Crookston, MN 56716-5001. Phone: 218-281-8569 or toll-free 800-862-6466. Fax: 218-281-8575. E-mail: info@UMCrookston.edu. Web site: http://www.umcrookston.edu/.

UNIVERSITY OF MINNESOTA, DULUTH
DULUTH, MINNESOTA

General State-supported, comprehensive, coed **Entrance** Moderately difficult **Setting** 250-acre suburban campus **Total enrollment** 11,184 **Student-faculty ratio** 22:1 **Application deadline** 2/1 (freshmen), 8/1 (transfer) **Freshmen** 70% were admitted **Housing** Yes **Expenses** Tuition $9600; Room & Board $5904 **Undergraduates** 48% women, 12% part-time, 7% 25 or older, 1% Native American, 1% Hispanic American, 1% African American, 3% Asian American/Pacific Islander **The most frequently chosen baccalaureate fields are** business/marketing, education, social sciences **Academic program** English as a second language, advanced placement, self-designed majors, honors program, summer session, adult/continuing education programs, internships **Contact** Admissions, University of Minnesota, Duluth, 23 Solon Campus Center, 1117 University Drive, Duluth, MN 55812-3000. Phone: 218-726-7171 or toll-free 800-232-1339. Fax: 218-726-7040. E-mail: umdadmis@d.umn.edu. Web site: http://www.d.umn.edu/.

UNIVERSITY OF MINNESOTA, MORRIS

MORRIS, MINNESOTA

General State-supported, 4-year, coed **Contact** Ms. Jaime Moquin, Director of Admissions, University of Minnesota, Morris, 600 East 4th Street, Morris, MN 56267-2199. Phone: 320-539-6035 or toll-free 800-992-8863. Fax: 320-589-1673. E-mail: admissions@morris.umn.edu. Web site: http://www.mrs.umn.edu/.

UNIVERSITY OF MINNESOTA, TWIN CITIES CAMPUS

MINNEAPOLIS, MINNESOTA

General State-supported, university, coed **Entrance** Moderately difficult **Setting** 2,000-acre urban campus **Total enrollment** 50,883 **Application deadline** Rolling (freshmen), rolling (transfer) **Freshmen** 57% were admitted **Housing** Yes **Expenses** Tuition $7950; Room & Board $7062 **Undergraduates** 53% women, 16% part-time, 10% 25 or older, 1% Native American, 2% Hispanic American, 5% African American, 10% Asian American/Pacific Islander **The most frequently chosen baccalaureate fields are** engineering, business/marketing, social sciences **Academic program** English as a second language, advanced placement, accelerated degree program, self-designed majors, honors program, summer session, adult/continuing education programs, internships **Contact** Rachelle Hernandez, Associate Director of Admissions, University of Minnesota, Twin Cities Campus, 240 Williamson, Minneapolis, MN 55455-0213. Phone: 612-625-2008 or toll-free 800-752-1000. Fax: 612-626-1693. E-mail: admissions@tc.umn.edu. Web site: http://www.umn.edu/tc/.

UNIVERSITY OF ST. THOMAS

ST. PAUL, MINNESOTA

General Independent Roman Catholic, university, coed **Entrance** Moderately difficult **Setting** 78-acre urban campus **Total enrollment** 10,984 **Student-faculty ratio** 15:1 **Application deadline** Rolling (freshmen), rolling (transfer) **Freshmen** 74% were admitted **Housing** Yes **Expenses** Tuition $27,822; Room & Board $7614 **Undergraduates** 49% women, 6% part-time, 5% 25 or older, 0.5% Native American, 3% Hispanic American, 3% African American, 4% Asian American/Pacific Islander **The most frequently chosen baccalaureate fields are** business/marketing, communications/journalism, social sciences **Academic program** English as a second language, advanced placement, self-designed majors, honors program, summer session, internships **Contact** Ms. Marla Friederichs, Associate Vice President of Enrollment Management, University of St. Thomas, 2115 Summit Avenue, St. Paul, MN 55105-1096. Phone: 651-962-6150 or toll-free 800-328-6819 Ext. 26150. Fax: 651-962-6160. E-mail: admissions@stthomas.edu. Web site: http://www.stthomas.edu/.

WALDEN UNIVERSITY

MINNEAPOLIS, MINNESOTA

General Proprietary, upper-level, coed **Total enrollment** 29,456 **Student-faculty ratio** 33:1 **Expenses** Tuition $11,250 **Undergraduates** 58% women, 94% part-time, 60% 25 or older, 0.1% Native American, 3% Hispanic American, 13% African American, 1% Asian American/Pacific Islander **The most frequently chosen baccalaureate fields are** business/marketing, computer and information sciences **Contact** Ms. Dawn Wolff, Director of Admissions, Walden University, 155 Fifth Avenue South, Minneapolis, MN 55401. Phone: 800-925-3368 or toll-free 866-492-5336. Fax: 410-843-8780. E-mail: request@waldenu.edu. Web site: http://www.waldenu.edu/.

WINONA STATE UNIVERSITY

WINONA, MINNESOTA

General State-supported, comprehensive, coed **Entrance** Moderately difficult **Setting** 40-acre small-town campus **Total enrollment** 8,220 **Student-faculty ratio** 21:1 **Application deadline** Rolling (freshmen), 8/1 (transfer) **Freshmen** 79% were admitted **Housing** Yes **Expenses** Tuition $7324; Room & Board $6110 **Undergraduates** 62% women, 8% part-time, 11% 25 or older, 0.3% Native American, 1% Hispanic American, 1% African American, 2% Asian American/Pacific Islander **Academic program** English as a second language, advanced placement, accelerated degree program, self-designed majors, honors program, summer session, adult/continuing education programs, internships **Contact** Carl Stange, Director of Admissions, Winona State University, PO Box 5838, Winona, MN 55987-5838. Phone: 507-457-5100 or toll-free 800-DIAL WSU. Fax: 507-457-5620. E-mail: admissions@winona.edu. Web site: http://www.winona.edu/.

MISSISSIPPI

ALCORN STATE UNIVERSITY
ALCORN STATE, MISSISSIPPI

General State-supported, comprehensive, coed **Entrance** Minimally difficult **Setting** 1,756-acre rural campus **Total enrollment** 3,668 **Student-faculty ratio** 17:1 **Application deadline** Rolling (freshmen), rolling (transfer) **Freshmen** 59% were admitted **Housing** Yes **Expenses** Tuition $4323; Room & Board $4879 **Undergraduates** 65% women, 10% part-time, 29% 25 or older, 0.03% Native American, 0.4% Hispanic American, 91% African American, 0.3% Asian American/Pacific Islander **The most frequently chosen baccalaureate fields are** health professions and related sciences, biological/life sciences, liberal arts/general studies **Academic program** Advanced placement, honors program, summer session, adult/continuing education programs, internships **Contact** Mr. Emanuel Barnes, Director of Admissions, Alcorn State University, 1000 ASU Drive #300, Alcorn State, MS 39096-7500. Phone: 601-877-6147 or toll-free 800-222-6790. Fax: 601-877-6347. E-mail: ebarnes@alcorn.edu. Web site: http://www.alcorn.edu/.

BELHAVEN COLLEGE
JACKSON, MISSISSIPPI

General Independent Presbyterian, comprehensive, coed **Entrance** Moderately difficult **Setting** 42-acre urban campus **Total enrollment** 2,485 **Student-faculty ratio** 18:1 **Application deadline** Rolling (freshmen), rolling (transfer) **Freshmen** 64% were admitted **Housing** Yes **Expenses** Tuition $16,360; Room & Board $6120 **Undergraduates** 66% women, 5% part-time, 54% 25 or older, 0.1% Native American, 3% Hispanic American, 35% African American, 0.4% Asian American/Pacific Islander **The most frequently chosen baccalaureate fields are** business/marketing, social sciences, visual and performing arts **Academic program** English as a second language, advanced placement, accelerated degree program, self-designed majors, honors program, summer session, adult/continuing education programs, internships **Contact** Mrs. Suzanne T. Sullivan, Director of Admission, Belhaven College, 150 Peachtree Street, Jackson, MS 39202. Phone: 601-968-5940 or toll-free 800-960-5940. Fax: 601-968-8946. E-mail: admission@belhaven.edu. Web site: http://www.belhaven.edu/.

BLUE MOUNTAIN COLLEGE
BLUE MOUNTAIN, MISSISSIPPI

Contact Ms. Maria Teel, Director of Admissions, Blue Mountain College, PO Box 160, Blue Mountain, MS 38610-0160. Phone: 662-685-4161 Ext. 176 or toll-free 800-235-0136. Fax: 662-685-4776. E-mail: eteel@bmc.edu. Web site: http://www.bmc.edu/.

DELTA STATE UNIVERSITY
CLEVELAND, MISSISSIPPI

General State-supported, comprehensive, coed **Entrance** Minimally difficult **Setting** 332-acre small-town campus **Total enrollment** 4,091 **Student-faculty ratio** 16:1 **Application deadline** 8/1 (freshmen), 8/1 (transfer) **Freshmen** 29% were admitted **Housing** Yes **Expenses** Tuition $4248; Room & Board $4876 **Undergraduates** 62% women, 18% part-time, 25% 25 or older, 0.2% Native American, 1% Hispanic American, 38% African American, 1% Asian American/Pacific Islander **The most frequently chosen baccalaureate fields are** business/marketing, education, health professions and related sciences **Academic program** Advanced placement, honors program, summer session, internships **Contact** Dr. Debbie Heslep, Dean of Enrollment Management, Delta State University, Kent Wyatt Hall 117, Cleveland, MS 38733. Phone: 662-846-4655 or toll-free 800-468-6378. Fax: 662-846-4684. E-mail: dheslep@deltastate.edu. Web site: http://www.deltastate.edu/.

JACKSON STATE UNIVERSITY
JACKSON, MISSISSIPPI

General State-supported, university, coed **Entrance** Minimally difficult **Setting** 250-acre urban campus **Total enrollment** 8,698 **Student-faculty ratio** 17:1 **Application deadline** 8/1 (freshmen), rolling (transfer) **Freshmen** 36% were admitted **Housing** Yes **Expenses** Tuition $4432; Room & Board $5600 **Undergraduates** 62% women, 13% part-time, 32% 25 or older, 0.1% Native American, 0.3% Hispanic American, 96% African American, 0.2% Asian American/Pacific Islander **The most frequently chosen baccalaureate fields are** business/marketing, education, security and protective services **Academic program** English as a second language, advanced placement, honors program, summer session, adult/continuing education programs, internships **Contact** Mrs. Linda Rush, Director, Marketing and Recruitment, Jackson State University, PO Box 17330, 1400 John R. Lynch Street, Jackson, MS 39217. Phone: 601-979-2100 or toll-free 800-682-5390 (in-state); 800-848-6817 (out-of-state). E-mail: schatman@ccaix.jsums.edu. Web site: http://www.jsums.edu/.

MAGNOLIA BIBLE COLLEGE
KOSCIUSKO, MISSISSIPPI

General Independent, 4-year, coed, primarily men, affiliated with Church of Christ **Entrance**

Noncompetitive **Setting** 5-acre small-town campus **Total enrollment** 35 **Student-faculty ratio** 7:1 **Application deadline** 8/31 (freshmen), 8/31 (transfer) **Freshmen** 100% were admitted **Housing** Yes **Expenses** Tuition $6540; Room only $1500 **Undergraduates** 23% women, 34% part-time, 80% 25 or older, 31% African American **The most frequently chosen baccalaureate field is** theology and religious vocations **Academic program** Summer session, internships **Contact** Mr. Travis Brown, Director of Admissions, Magnolia Bible College, PO Box 1109, Kosciusko, MS 39090. Phone: 662-289-2896 Ext. 109 or toll-free 800-748-8655. Fax: 662-289-1850. E-mail: tbrown@magnolia.edu. Web site: http://www.magnolia.edu/.

MILLSAPS COLLEGE
JACKSON, MISSISSIPPI

General Independent United Methodist, comprehensive, coed **Entrance** Moderately difficult **Setting** 100-acre urban campus **Total enrollment** 1,151 **Student-faculty ratio** 11:1 **Application deadline** Rolling (freshmen), rolling (transfer) **Freshmen** 77% were admitted **Housing** Yes **Expenses** Tuition $24,754; Room & Board $8800 **Undergraduates** 51% women, 2% part-time, 3% 25 or older, 0.1% Native American, 1% Hispanic American, 11% African American, 4% Asian American/Pacific Islander **The most frequently chosen baccalaureate fields are** biological/life sciences, business/marketing, psychology **Academic program** Advanced placement, accelerated degree program, self-designed majors, honors program, summer session, adult/continuing education programs, internships **Contact** Mr. Mathew Cox, Dean of Enrollment Management, Millsaps College, 1701 North State Street, Jackson, MS 39210-0001. Phone: 601-974-1050 or toll-free 800-352-1050. Fax: 601-974-1059. E-mail: admissions@millsaps.edu. Web site: http://www.millsaps.edu/.

MISSISSIPPI COLLEGE
CLINTON, MISSISSIPPI

General Independent Southern Baptist, comprehensive, coed **Entrance** Moderately difficult **Setting** 320-acre suburban campus **Total enrollment** 4,467 **Student-faculty ratio** 16:1 **Application deadline** Rolling (freshmen), rolling (transfer) **Freshmen** 65% were admitted **Housing** Yes **Expenses** Tuition $12,800; Room & Board $5800 **Undergraduates** 60% women, 14% part-time, 23% 25 or older, 0.4% Native American, 1% Hispanic American, 24% African American, 1% Asian American/Pacific Islander **The most frequently chosen baccalaureate fields are** business/marketing, education, health professions and related sciences **Academic program** English as a second language, advanced placement, accelerated degree program, honors program, summer session, adult/continuing education programs, internships **Contact** Mr. Chad Phillips, Director of Admissions, Mississippi College, PO Box 4026, 200 South Capitol Street, Clinton, MS 39058. Phone: 601-925-3315 or toll-free 800-738-1236. Fax: 601-925-3804. E-mail: enrollment-services@mc.edu. Web site: http://www.mc.edu/.

MISSISSIPPI STATE UNIVERSITY
MISSISSIPPI STATE, MISSISSIPPI

General State-supported, university, coed **Entrance** Moderately difficult **Setting** 4,200-acre small-town campus **Total enrollment** 17,039 **Student-faculty ratio** 15:1 **Application deadline** 8/1 (freshmen), 8/1 (transfer) **Freshmen** 70% were admitted **Housing** Yes **Expenses** Tuition $4978; Room & Board $6951 **Undergraduates** 47% women, 11% part-time, 15% 25 or older, 1% Native American, 1% Hispanic American, 21% African American, 1% Asian American/Pacific Islander **The most frequently chosen baccalaureate fields are** business/marketing, education, engineering **Academic program** English as a second language, advanced placement, accelerated degree program, self-designed majors, honors program, summer session, adult/continuing education programs, internships **Contact** Ms. Cheryl Dill, Associate Director of Admissions and Scholarships, Mississippi State University, PO Box 6334, Mississippi State, MS 39762. Phone: 662-325-2224. Fax: 662-325-1MSU. E-mail: admit@msstate.edu. Web site: http://www.msstate.edu/.

MISSISSIPPI UNIVERSITY FOR WOMEN
COLUMBUS, MISSISSIPPI

General State-supported, comprehensive, coed, primarily women **Entrance** Moderately difficult **Setting** 110-acre small-town campus **Total enrollment** 2,379 **Student-faculty ratio** 12:1 **Application deadline** Rolling (freshmen), rolling (transfer) **Freshmen** 46% were admitted **Housing** Yes **Expenses** Tuition $4209; Room & Board $4740 **Undergraduates** 84% women, 25% part-time, 32% 25 or older, 0.4% Native American, 1% Hispanic American, 34% African American, 2% Asian American/Pacific Islander **The most frequently chosen baccalaureate fields are** education, business/marketing, health professions and related sciences **Academic program** English as a second language, advanced placement, accelerated degree program, honors program, summer session, adult/continuing education programs, internships **Contact** Ms. Cassie Derden, Manager of Admissions, Mississippi University for Women, 1100 College Street, MUW-1600, Columbus, MS 39701-9998. Phone:

Mississippi University for Women *(continued)*

601-329-7106 or toll-free 877-GO 2 THE W. Fax: 601-241-7481. E-mail: admissions@muw.edu. Web site: http://www.muw.edu/.

MISSISSIPPI VALLEY STATE UNIVERSITY

ITTA BENA, MISSISSIPPI

General State-supported, comprehensive, coed **Entrance** Minimally difficult **Setting** 450-acre small-town campus **Total enrollment** 3,009 **Student-faculty ratio** 17:1 **Application deadline** Rolling (freshmen), rolling (transfer) **Freshmen** 25% were admitted **Housing** Yes **Expenses** Tuition $8834; Room & Board $4542 **Undergraduates** 65% women, 10% part-time, 37% 25 or older, 0.03% Native American, 0.4% Hispanic American, 94% African American, 0.2% Asian American/Pacific Islander **The most frequently chosen baccalaureate fields are** business/marketing, education, public administration and social services **Academic program** Honors program, summer session, internships **Contact** Ms. Nora Taylor, Director of Admissions and Recruitment, Mississippi Valley State University, 14000 Highway 82 West, Itta Bena, MS 38941-1400. Phone: 662-254-3344 or toll-free 800-844-6885. Fax: 662-254-7900. E-mail: nbtaylor@mvsu.edu. Web site: http://www.mvsu.edu/.

RUST COLLEGE

HOLLY SPRINGS, MISSISSIPPI

General Independent United Methodist, 4-year, coed **Entrance** Moderately difficult **Setting** 126-acre rural campus **Total enrollment** 979 **Student-faculty ratio** 20:1 **Application deadline** 7/15 (freshmen), 7/15 (transfer) **Freshmen** 40% were admitted **Housing** Yes **Expenses** Tuition $6600; Room & Board $3100 **Undergraduates** 63% women, 18% part-time, 27% 25 or older, 93% African American **The most frequently chosen baccalaureate fields are** biological/life sciences, business/marketing, family and consumer sciences **Academic program** Accelerated degree program, honors program, summer session, adult/continuing education programs, internships **Contact** Mr. Johnny McDonald, Director of Enrollment Services, Rust College, 150 Rust Avenue, Holly Springs, MS 38635-2328. Phone: 601-252-8000 Ext. 4065 or toll-free 888-886-8492 Ext. 4065. Fax: 662-252-8895. E-mail: admissions@rustcollege.edu. Web site: http://www.rustcollege.edu/.

SOUTHEASTERN BAPTIST COLLEGE

LAUREL, MISSISSIPPI

Contact Mrs. Emma Bond, Director of Admissions, Southeastern Baptist College, 4229 Highway 15 North, Laurel, MS 39440-1096. Phone: 601-426-6346.

TOUGALOO COLLEGE

TOUGALOO, MISSISSIPPI

General Independent, 4-year, coed, affiliated with United Church of Christ **Entrance** Minimally difficult **Setting** 500-acre suburban campus **Total enrollment** 856 **Student-faculty ratio** 13:1 **Application deadline** Rolling (freshmen), rolling (transfer) **Freshmen** 99% were admitted **Housing** Yes **Expenses** Tuition $9717; Room & Board $6330 **Undergraduates** 68% women, 5% part-time, 4% 25 or older, 0.2% Hispanic American, 99% African American, 0.1% Asian American/Pacific Islander **The most frequently chosen baccalaureate fields are** English, psychology, social sciences **Academic program** Accelerated degree program, self-designed majors, honors program, adult/continuing education programs, internships **Contact** Ms. Juno Jacobs, Director of Admissions, Tougaloo College, 500 West County Line Road, Tougaloo, MS 39174. Phone: 601-977-7765 or toll-free 888-42GALOO. Fax: 601-977-4501. E-mail: jjacobs@tougaloo.edu. Web site: http://www.tougaloo.edu/.

UNIVERSITY OF MISSISSIPPI

OXFORD, MISSISSIPPI

General State-supported, university, coed **Entrance** Moderately difficult **Setting** 2,500-acre small-town campus **Total enrollment** 15,129 **Student-faculty ratio** 20:1 **Freshmen** 90% were admitted **Housing** Yes **Expenses** Tuition $4932; Room & Board $6578 **Undergraduates** 53% women, 9% part-time, 11% 25 or older, 0.3% Native American, 1% Hispanic American, 13% African American, 1% Asian American/Pacific Islander **The most frequently chosen baccalaureate fields are** business/marketing, education, psychology **Academic program** English as a second language, advanced placement, accelerated degree program, honors program, summer session, adult/continuing education programs, internships **Contact** Mr. Jody Lowe, Associate Director of Admissions, University of Mississippi, 145 Martindale Student Services Center, University, MS 38677. Phone: 662-915-7226 or toll-free 800-653-6477. Fax: 662-915-5869. E-mail: admissions@olemiss.edu. Web site: http://www.olemiss.edu/.

UNIVERSITY OF MISSISSIPPI MEDICAL CENTER

JACKSON, MISSISSIPPI

General State-supported, upper-level, coed **Setting** 164-acre urban campus **Total enrollment** 2,092 **Student-faculty ratio** 2:1 **Application deadline** 2/15 (transfer) **Housing** Yes **Undergraduates** 80% women, 25% part-time, 0.4% Native American, 1% Hispanic American,

22% African American, 2% Asian American/Pacific Islander **The most frequently chosen baccalaureate field is** health professions and related sciences **Academic program** Internships **Contact** Ms. Barbara Westerfield, Director of Student Records and Registrar, University of Mississippi Medical Center, 2500 North State Street, Jackson, MS 39216-4505. Phone: 601-984-1080. Fax: 601-984-1079. Web site: http://www.umc.edu/.

UNIVERSITY OF SOUTHERN MISSISSIPPI

HATTIESBURG, MISSISSIPPI

General State-supported, university, coed **Entrance** Moderately difficult **Setting** 1,090-acre suburban campus **Total enrollment** 14,592 **Student-faculty ratio** 17:1 **Application deadline** 7/1 (freshmen), 7/1 (transfer) **Freshmen** 58% were admitted **Housing** Yes **Expenses** Tuition $4914; Room & Board $5040 **Undergraduates** 60% women, 14% part-time, 22% 25 or older, 0.4% Native American, 1% Hispanic American, 29% African American, 1% Asian American/Pacific Islander **The most frequently chosen baccalaureate fields are** business/marketing, education, health professions and related sciences **Academic program** English as a second language, advanced placement, accelerated degree program, honors program, summer session, adult/continuing education programs **Contact** Mr. Jason Beverly, Senior Admissions Counselor, University of Southern Mississippi, 118 College Drive, #5166, Hattiesburg, MS 39406-1000. Phone: 601-266-5000. Fax: 601-266-5148. E-mail: admissions@usm.edu. Web site: http://www.usm.edu/.

WESLEY COLLEGE

FLORENCE, MISSISSIPPI

General Independent Congregational Methodist, 4-year, coed **Contact** Mr. Chris Garcia, Director of Admissions, Wesley College, PO Box 1070, Florence, MS 39073-1070. Phone: 601-845-2265 or toll-free 800-748-9972. Fax: 601-845-2266. E-mail: cgarcia@admin.wesleycollege.edu. Web site: http://www.wesleycollege.com/.

WILLIAM CAREY UNIVERSITY

HATTIESBURG, MISSISSIPPI

General Independent Southern Baptist, comprehensive, coed **Contact** Mr. William N. Curry, Dean of Enrollment Management, William Carey University, 498 Tuscan Avenue, Hattiesburg, MS 39401-5499. Phone: 601-318-6051 Ext. 103 or toll-free 800-962-5991. Fax: 601-318-6154. E-mail: admissions@wmcarey.edu. Web site: http://www.wmcarey.edu/.

MISSOURI

AVILA UNIVERSITY

KANSAS CITY, MISSOURI

General Independent Roman Catholic, 4-year, coed **Entrance** Minimally difficult **Setting** 50-acre suburban campus **Total enrollment** 1,831 **Student-faculty ratio** 12:1 **Application deadline** 8/15 (freshmen), 8/15 (transfer) **Freshmen** 54% were admitted **Housing** Yes **Expenses** Tuition $20,150; Room & Board $5900 **Undergraduates** 66% women, 18% part-time, 21% 25 or older, 1% Native American, 6% Hispanic American, 15% African American, 2% Asian American/Pacific Islander **The most frequently chosen baccalaureate fields are** business/marketing, health professions and related sciences, psychology **Academic program** English as a second language, advanced placement, accelerated degree program, summer session, adult/continuing education programs, internships **Contact** Ms. Patricia Harper, Director of Admission, Avila University, 11901 Wornall Road, Kansas City, MO 64145. Phone: 816-501-3627 or toll-free 800-GO-AVILA. Fax: 816-501-2453. E-mail: patti.harper@avila.edu. Web site: http://www.avila.edu/.

BAPTIST BIBLE COLLEGE

SPRINGFIELD, MISSOURI

General Independent Baptist, comprehensive, coed **Entrance** Noncompetitive **Setting** 38-acre suburban campus **Total enrollment** 636 **Application deadline** Rolling (freshmen), rolling (transfer) **Freshmen** 76% were admitted **Housing** Yes **Expenses** Tuition $13,610; Room & Board $5500 **Undergraduates** 47% women, 18% part-time, 17% 25 or older, 1% Native American, 3% Hispanic American, 1% African American, 1% Asian American/Pacific Islander **Academic program** Summer session, internships **Contact** Mr. Terry Allcorn, Director of Admissions, Baptist Bible College, 628 East Kearney, Springfield, MO 65803-3498. Phone: 417-268-6000. Fax: 417-268-6694. Web site: http://www.baptist.edu/.

CALVARY BIBLE COLLEGE AND THEOLOGICAL SEMINARY

KANSAS CITY, MISSOURI

General Independent nondenominational, comprehensive, coed **Contact** Rev. Robert Reinsch, Director of Admissions, Calvary Bible College and Theological Seminary, 15800 Calvary Road, Kansas City, MO 64147-1341. Phone: 816-322-0110 Ext. 1326 or toll-free 800-326-3960. Fax: 816-331-4474. E-mail: admissions@calvary.edu. Web site: http://www.calvary.edu/.

CENTRAL BIBLE COLLEGE
SPRINGFIELD, MISSOURI

Contact Mrs. Eunice A. Bruegman, Director of Admissions and Records, Central Bible College, 3000 North Grant Avenue, Springfield, MO 65803-1096. Phone: 417-833-2551 Ext. 1184 or toll-free 800-831-4222 Ext. 1184. Fax: 417-833-5141. E-mail: info@cbcag.edu. Web site: http://www.cbcag.edu/.

CENTRAL CHRISTIAN COLLEGE OF THE BIBLE
MOBERLY, MISSOURI

Contact Mr. Jason Rodenbeck, Director of Admissions, Central Christian College of the Bible, 911 Urbandale Drive East, Moberly, MO 65270-1997. Phone: 660-263-3900 or toll-free 888-263-3900. Fax: 660-263-3936. E-mail: iwant2be@cccb.edu. Web site: http://www.cccb.edu/.

CENTRAL METHODIST UNIVERSITY
FAYETTE, MISSOURI

General Independent Methodist, comprehensive, coed **Contact** Mr. Larry Anderson, Director of Admissions, Central Methodist University, 411 Central Methodist Square, Fayette, MO 65248-1198. Phone: 660-248-6247 or toll-free 888-CMU-1854. Fax: 660-248-1872. E-mail: admissions@centralmethodist.edu. Web site: http://www.centralmethodist.edu/.

CHAMBERLAIN COLLEGE OF NURSING
ST. LOUIS, MISSOURI

Contact Ms. Michelle McGrail, Dean of Enrollment and Marketing, Chamberlain College of Nursing, 6150 Oakland Avenue, St. Louis, MO 63139-3215. Phone: 314-768-7528 or toll-free 800-942-4310. Fax: 314-768-5673. Web site: http://www.chamberlain.edu/.

COLLEGE OF THE OZARKS
POINT LOOKOUT, MISSOURI

General Independent Presbyterian, 4-year, coed **Entrance** Moderately difficult **Setting** 1,000-acre small-town campus **Total enrollment** 1,351 **Student-faculty ratio** 13:1 **Application deadline** 3/15 (freshmen), 3/15 (transfer) **Freshmen** 12% were admitted **Housing** Yes **Expenses** Room & Board $4700 **Undergraduates** 56% women, 3% part-time, 4% 25 or older, 1% Native American, 1% Hispanic American, 1% African American, 1% Asian American/Pacific Islander **The most frequently chosen baccalaureate fields are** business/marketing, education, security and protective services **Academic program** English as a second language, advanced placement, accelerated degree program, self-designed majors, honors program, internships **Contact** Mrs. Gayle Groves, Admissions Secretary, College of the Ozarks, PO Box 17, Point Lookout, MO 65726. Phone: 417-334-6411 Ext. 4217 or toll-free 800-222-0525. Fax: 417-335-2618. E-mail: admiss4@cofo.edu. Web site: http://www.cofo.edu/.

COLUMBIA COLLEGE
COLUMBIA, MISSOURI

General Independent, comprehensive, coed, affiliated with Christian Church (Disciples of Christ) **Contact** Ms. Regina Morin, Director of Admissions, Columbia College, 1001 Rogers Street, Columbia, MO 65216. Phone: 573-875-7354 or toll-free 800-231-2391 Ext. 7366. Fax: 573-875-7508. E-mail: admissions@ccis.edu. Web site: http://www.ccis.edu/.

CONCEPTION SEMINARY COLLEGE
CONCEPTION, MISSOURI

General Independent Roman Catholic, 4-year, men only **Contact** Br. Victor Schinstock OSB, Director of Recruitment and Admissions, Conception Seminary College, PO Box 502, Conception, MO 64433-0502. Phone: 660-944-2886. Fax: 660-944-2829. E-mail: vocations@conception.edu. Web site: http://www.conceptionabbey.org/.

COX COLLEGE OF NURSING AND HEALTH SCIENCES
SPRINGFIELD, MISSOURI

Contact Ms. Stacy Danaher, Admission Coordinator, Cox College of Nursing and Health Sciences, 1423 North Jefferson, Springfield, MO 65802. Phone: 417-269-3038 or toll-free 866-898-5355. Fax: 417-269-3581. E-mail: admissions@coxcollege.edu. Web site: http://www.coxcollege.edu/.

CULVER-STOCKTON COLLEGE
CANTON, MISSOURI

General Independent, 4-year, coed, affiliated with Christian Church (Disciples of Christ) **Entrance** Moderately difficult **Setting** 143-acre rural campus **Total enrollment** 849 **Student-faculty ratio** 15:1 **Application deadline** Rolling (freshmen), rolling (transfer) **Freshmen** 76% were admitted **Housing** Yes **Expenses** Tuition $16,600; Room & Board $6850 **Undergraduates** 60% women, 10% part-time, 10% 25 or older, 0.5% Native American, 1% Hispanic American, 6% African American, 1% Asian American/Pacific Islander **The most frequently chosen baccalaureate fields are** business/marketing, education, psychology **Academic program** Advanced placement, self-designed majors, honors program, summer session, internships **Contact** Mr. Jim Lynes, Director of Admissions, Culver-Stockton College, One College Hill, Canton, MO 63435-1299. Phone: 573-288-6467 or toll-free 800-537-1883. Fax: 573-288-6618. E-mail: enrollment@culver.edu. Web site: http://www.culver.edu/.

DeVRY UNIVERSITY
KANSAS CITY, MISSOURI

General Proprietary, comprehensive, coed **Entrance** Minimally difficult **Setting** 12-acre urban campus **Total enrollment** 1,086 **Student-faculty ratio** 15:1 **Application deadline** Rolling (freshmen), rolling (transfer) **Housing** No **Expenses** Tuition $13,990 **Undergraduates** 29% women, 46% part-time, 57% 25 or older, 2% Native American, 3% Hispanic American, 19% African American, 3% Asian American/Pacific Islander **The most frequently chosen baccalaureate fields are** business/marketing, computer and information sciences, engineering technologies **Academic program** Advanced placement, accelerated degree program, summer session, adult/continuing education programs **Contact** Admissions Office, DeVry University, 11224 Holmes Road, Kansas City, MO 64131-3698. Web site: http://www.devry.edu/.

DeVRY UNIVERSITY
KANSAS CITY, MISSOURI

Contact DeVry University, City Center Square, 1100 Main Street, Suite 118, Kansas City, MO 64105-2112. Web site: http://www.devry.edu/.

DeVRY UNIVERSITY
ST. LOUIS, MISSOURI

Contact DeVry University, 1801 Park 270 Drive, Suite 260, St. Louis, MO 63146-4020. Web site: http://www.devry.edu/.

DRURY UNIVERSITY
SPRINGFIELD, MISSOURI

General Independent, comprehensive, coed **Entrance** Moderately difficult **Setting** 80-acre urban campus **Total enrollment** 2,084 **Student-faculty ratio** 13:1 **Application deadline** 8/1 (freshmen), rolling (transfer) **Freshmen** 76% were admitted **Housing** Yes **Expenses** Tuition $18,409; Room & Board $6384 **Undergraduates** 53% women, 2% part-time, 4% 25 or older, 1% Native American, 2% Hispanic American, 2% African American, 2% Asian American/Pacific Islander **The most frequently chosen baccalaureate fields are** business/marketing, communications/journalism, visual and performing arts **Academic program** English as a second language, advanced placement, accelerated degree program, self-designed majors, honors program, summer session, adult/continuing education programs, internships **Contact** Mr. Chip Parker, Director of Admission, Drury University, 900 North Benton, Bay Hall, Springfield, MO 65802. Phone: 417-873-7205 or toll-free 800-922-2274. Fax: 417-866-3873. E-mail: druryad@drury.edu. Web site: http://www.drury.edu/.

EVANGEL UNIVERSITY
SPRINGFIELD, MISSOURI

General Independent, comprehensive, coed, affiliated with Assemblies of God **Entrance** Moderately difficult **Setting** 80-acre urban campus **Total enrollment** 1,657 **Student-faculty ratio** 16:1 **Application deadline** 8/1 (freshmen), 8/1 (transfer) **Freshmen** 76% were admitted **Housing** Yes **Expenses** Tuition $14,300; Room & Board $5120 **Undergraduates** 60% women, 5% part-time, 4% 25 or older, 0.5% Native American, 4% Hispanic American, 3% African American, 2% Asian American/Pacific Islander **The most frequently chosen baccalaureate fields are** business/marketing, communications/journalism, education **Academic program** Advanced placement, accelerated degree program, summer session, adult/continuing education programs, internships **Contact** Ms. Cheri Meyer, Director of Admissions, Evangel University, 1111 North Glenstone, Springfield, MO 65802. Phone: 417-865-2811 Ext. 7262 or toll-free 800-382-6435. Fax: 417-865-9599. E-mail: admissions@evangel.edu. Web site: http://www.evangel.edu/.

FONTBONNE UNIVERSITY
ST. LOUIS, MISSOURI

General Independent Roman Catholic, comprehensive, coed **Entrance** Moderately difficult **Setting** 13-acre suburban campus **Total enrollment** 2,969 **Student-faculty ratio** 16:1 **Application deadline** 8/1 (freshmen), rolling (transfer) **Freshmen** 75% were admitted **Housing** Yes **Expenses** Tuition $19,320; Room & Board $7207 **Undergraduates** 70% women, 26% part-time, 51% 25 or older, 0.3% Native American, 1% Hispanic American, 34% African American, 1% Asian American/Pacific Islander **The most frequently chosen baccalaureate fields are** business/marketing, education, visual and performing arts **Academic program** English as a second language, advanced placement, accelerated degree program, self-designed majors, honors program, summer session, adult/continuing education programs, internships **Contact** Ms. Peggy Musen, Vice President for Enrollment Management, Fontbonne University, 6800 Wydown Boulevard, St. Louis, MO 63105-3098. Phone: 314-889-

Fontbonne University *(continued)*

1400. Fax: 314-889-1451. E-mail: pmusen@fontbonne.edu. Web site: http://www.fontbonne.edu/.

GLOBAL UNIVERSITY
SPRINGFIELD, MISSOURI

General Independent, comprehensive, coed, affiliated with Assemblies of God **Entrance** Noncompetitive **Setting** small-town campus **Total enrollment** 7,096 **Student-faculty ratio** 11:1 **Application deadline** Rolling (freshmen), rolling (transfer) **Housing** No **Expenses** Tuition $3020 **Undergraduates** 32% women, 72% part-time, 91% 25 or older **The most frequently chosen baccalaureate field is** theology and religious vocations **Academic program** Honors program, adult/continuing education programs, internships **Contact** Rev. Todd Waggoner, Enrollment and International Student Services Director, Global University, 1211 South Glenstone Avenue, Springfield, MO 65804. Phone: 417-862-9533 Ext. 2335 or toll-free 800-443-1083. Fax: 417-863-9621. E-mail: twaggoner@globaluniversity.edu. Web site: http://www.globaluniversity.edu/.

GOLDFARB SCHOOL OF NURSING AT BARNES-JEWISH COLLEGE
ST. LOUIS, MISSOURI

General Independent, comprehensive, coed **Setting** urban campus **Total enrollment** 637 **Student-faculty ratio** 10:1 **Application deadline** Rolling (transfer) **Freshmen** 63% were admitted **Housing** No **Expenses** Tuition $19,878 **Undergraduates** 84% women, 19% part-time, 87% 25 or older **Academic program** Advanced placement, summer session **Contact** Office of Admissions, Goldfarb School of Nursing at Barnes-Jewish College, 4483 Duncan Ave., St. Louis, MO 63110. Phone: 314-454-7057 or toll-free 800-832-9009. Fax: 314-454-5239. E-mail: jhcollegeinquiry@bjc.org. Web site: http://www.barnesjewishcollege.edu/.

GRANTHAM UNIVERSITY
KANSAS CITY, MISSOURI

General Proprietary, 4-year, coed **Entrance** Noncompetitive **Setting** urban campus **Total enrollment** 8,500 **Application deadline** Rolling (freshmen), rolling (transfer) **Housing** No **Expenses** Tuition $7950 **Academic program** Advanced placement, accelerated degree program, adult/continuing education programs **Contact** Ms. DeAnn Wandler, Director of Admissions, Grantham University, 7200 NW 86th Street, Kansas City, MO 64153. Phone: 800-955-2527 or toll-free 800-955-2527. Fax: 816-595-5757. E-mail: admissions@grantham.edu. Web site: http://www.grantham.edu/.

HANNIBAL-LAGRANGE COLLEGE
HANNIBAL, MISSOURI

General Independent Southern Baptist, 4-year, coed **Entrance** Moderately difficult **Setting** 110-acre small-town campus **Total enrollment** 1,170 **Student-faculty ratio** 12:1 **Application deadline** Rolling (freshmen), rolling (transfer) **Freshmen** 96% were admitted **Housing** Yes **Expenses** Tuition $13,480; Room & Board $4930 **Undergraduates** 65% women, 28% part-time, 23% 25 or older, 1% Native American, 1% Hispanic American, 3% African American, 0.2% Asian American/Pacific Islander **The most frequently chosen baccalaureate fields are** business/marketing, education, social sciences **Academic program** Advanced placement, accelerated degree program, honors program, summer session, adult/continuing education programs, internships **Contact** Dr. Raymond Carty, Vice President for Enrollment Management, Hannibal-LaGrange College, 2800 Palmyra Road, Hannibal, MO 63401-1999. Phone: 573-629-2278 or toll-free 800-HLG-1119. E-mail: admissio@hlg.edu. Web site: http://www.hlg.edu/.

HARRIS-STOWE STATE UNIVERSITY
ST. LOUIS, MISSOURI

General State-supported, 4-year, coed **Entrance** Noncompetitive **Setting** 22-acre urban campus **Total enrollment** 1,882 **Student-faculty ratio** 25:1 **Application deadline** Rolling (freshmen), rolling (transfer) **Freshmen** 76% were admitted **Housing** Yes **Expenses** Tuition $5090; Room & Board $7200 **Undergraduates** 69% women, 34% part-time, 39% 25 or older, 0.1% Native American, 0.4% Hispanic American, 90% African American, 0.1% Asian American/Pacific Islander **The most frequently chosen baccalaureate fields are** business/marketing, education, interdisciplinary studies **Academic program** Advanced placement, self-designed majors, summer session, internships **Contact** Ms. LaShanda Boone, Executive Director of Enrollment Management, Harris-Stowe State University, 3026 Laclede Avenue, St. Louis, MO 63103. Phone: 314-340-3300. Fax: 314-340-3555. E-mail: admissions@hssu.edu. Web site: http://www.hssu.edu/.

KANSAS CITY ART INSTITUTE
KANSAS CITY, MISSOURI

General Independent, 4-year, coed **Entrance** Moderately difficult **Setting** 18-acre urban campus **Total enrollment** 676 **Student-faculty ratio** 12:1 **Application deadline** Rolling (freshmen), rolling (transfer) **Freshmen** 63% were admitted **Housing**

Yes **Expenses** Tuition $27,220; Room & Board $8260 **Undergraduates** 55% women, 1% part-time, 12% 25 or older, 1% Native American, 5% Hispanic American, 3% African American, 4% Asian American/Pacific Islander **The most frequently chosen baccalaureate field is** visual and performing arts **Academic program** English as a second language, advanced placement, summer session, adult/continuing education programs, internships **Contact** Mr. Gerald Valet, Director of Admission Technology, Kansas City Art Institute, 4415 Warwick Boulevard, Kansas City, MO 64111-1874. Phone: 816-474-5224 or toll-free 800-522-5224. Fax: 816-802-3309. E-mail: admiss@kcai.edu. Web site: http://www.kcai.edu/.

LINCOLN UNIVERSITY

JEFFERSON CITY, MISSOURI

General State-supported, comprehensive, coed **Entrance** Noncompetitive **Setting** 165-acre small-town campus **Total enrollment** 3,156 **Student-faculty ratio** 15:1 **Application deadline** 7/15 (freshmen), 6/15 (transfer) **Freshmen** 95% were admitted **Housing** Yes **Expenses** Tuition $6010; Room & Board $4590 **Undergraduates** 60% women, 32% part-time, 25% 25 or older, 0.4% Native American, 1% Hispanic American, 45% African American, 1% Asian American/Pacific Islander **The most frequently chosen baccalaureate fields are** business/marketing, computer and information sciences, education **Academic program** Advanced placement, accelerated degree program, honors program, summer session, adult/continuing education programs, internships **Contact** Mr. Mike Kosher, Director of Admissions, Lincoln University, Office of Admissions, 820 Chestnut Street, B-7 Young Hall, Jefferson City, MO 65102-0029. Phone: 573-681-5599 or toll-free 800-521-5052. Fax: 573-681-5889. E-mail: enroll@lincolnu.edu. Web site: http://www.lincolnu.edu/.

LINDENWOOD UNIVERSITY

ST. CHARLES, MISSOURI

General Independent Presbyterian, comprehensive, coed **Entrance** Moderately difficult **Setting** 420-acre suburban campus **Total enrollment** 9,633 **Student-faculty ratio** 18:1 **Application deadline** Rolling (freshmen), rolling (transfer) **Freshmen** 58% were admitted **Housing** Yes **Expenses** Tuition $13,000; Room & Board $6500 **Undergraduates** 57% women, 4% part-time, 30% 25 or older, 0.3% Native American, 1% Hispanic American, 12% African American, 1% Asian American/Pacific Islander **The most frequently chosen baccalaureate fields are** business/marketing, education, social sciences **Academic program** Advanced placement, accelerated degree program, self-designed majors, honors program, summer session, adult/continuing education programs, internships **Contact** Mr. Joseph Parisi, Dean of Undergraduate Day Admissions, Lindenwood University, 209 South Kingshighway, St. Charles, MO 63301-1695. Phone: 636-949-4949. Fax: 636-949-4989. E-mail: admissions@lindenwood.edu. Web site: http://www.lindenwood.edu/.

LOGAN UNIVERSITY–COLLEGE OF CHIROPRACTIC

CHESTERFIELD, MISSOURI

General Independent, upper-level, coed **Entrance** Moderately difficult **Setting** 111-acre suburban campus **Total enrollment** 1,133 **Application deadline** Rolling (transfer) **Housing** No **Expenses** Tuition $4830 **Undergraduates** 37% women, 40% part-time, 44% 25 or older, 3% Hispanic American, 8% African American, 2% Asian American/Pacific Islander **The most frequently chosen baccalaureate field is** biological/life sciences **Academic program** Advanced placement, adult/continuing education programs, internships **Contact** Robert Smith, Associate Director of Admissions, Logan University–College of Chiropractic, 1851 Schoettler Road, Chesterfield, MO 63006-1065. Phone: 636-227-2100 Ext. 1749 or toll-free 800-533-9210. Fax: 636-207-2425. E-mail: loganadm@logan.edu. Web site: http://www.logan.edu/.

MARYVILLE UNIVERSITY OF SAINT LOUIS

ST. LOUIS, MISSOURI

General Independent, comprehensive, coed **Entrance** Moderately difficult **Setting** 130-acre suburban campus **Total enrollment** 3,422 **Student-faculty ratio** 12:1 **Application deadline** 8/15 (freshmen), rolling (transfer) **Freshmen** 65% were admitted **Housing** Yes **Expenses** Tuition $19,050; Room & Board $7500 **Undergraduates** 77% women, 40% part-time, 37% 25 or older, 1% Native American, 1% Hispanic American, 7% African American, 2% Asian American/Pacific Islander **The most frequently chosen baccalaureate fields are** business/marketing, health professions and related sciences, psychology **Academic program** Advanced placement, accelerated degree program, self-designed majors, honors program, summer session, adult/continuing education programs, internships **Contact** Ms. Shani Lenore, Admissions Director, Maryville University of Saint Louis, 650 Maryville University Drive, St. Louis, MO 63141-7299. Phone: 314-529-9350 or toll-free 800-627-9855. Fax: 314-529-9927. E-mail: admissions@maryville.edu. Web site: http://www.maryville.edu/.

MESSENGER COLLEGE
JOPLIN, MISSOURI

General Independent Pentecostal, 4-year, coed **Contact** Ron Cannon, Vice President of Academic Affairs, Messenger College, PO Box 4050, Joplin, MO 64803. Phone: 417-624-7070 Ext. 108 or toll-free 800-385-8940. Fax: 417-624-5070. E-mail: info@messengercollege.edu. Web site: http://www.messengercollege.edu/.

MIDWEST UNIVERSITY
WENTZVILLE, MISSOURI

Contact Midwest University, PO Box 365, 851 Parr Road, Wentzville, MO 63385. Web site: http://www.midwest.edu/.

MISSOURI BAPTIST UNIVERSITY
ST. LOUIS, MISSOURI

General Independent Southern Baptist, comprehensive, coed **Entrance** Moderately difficult **Setting** 65-acre suburban campus **Total enrollment** 4,598 **Student-faculty ratio** 14:1 **Application deadline** Rolling (freshmen), rolling (transfer) **Freshmen** 72% were admitted **Housing** Yes **Expenses** Tuition $15,778; Room & Board $6350 **Undergraduates** 60% women, 67% part-time, 30% 25 or older, 1% Native American, 2% Hispanic American, 9% African American, 0.5% Asian American/Pacific Islander **The most frequently chosen baccalaureate fields are** business/marketing, education, psychology **Academic program** Advanced placement, accelerated degree program, self-designed majors, summer session, adult/continuing education programs, internships **Contact** Mr. Terry Dale Cruse, Director of Admissions, Missouri Baptist University, One College Park Drive, St. Louis, MO 63141-8660. Phone: 877-434-1115 or toll-free 877-434-1115 Ext. 2290. Fax: 314-434-7596. E-mail: admissions@mobap.edu. Web site: http://www.mobap.edu/.

MISSOURI SOUTHERN STATE UNIVERSITY
JOPLIN, MISSOURI

General State-supported, comprehensive, coed **Entrance** Moderately difficult **Setting** 350-acre small-town campus **Total enrollment** 5,593 **Student-faculty ratio** 16:1 **Application deadline** 8/1 (freshmen), 8/1 (transfer) **Freshmen** 99% were admitted **Housing** Yes **Expenses** Tuition $4816; Room & Board $5440 **Undergraduates** 60% women, 29% part-time, 34% 25 or older, 2% Native American, 2% Hispanic American, 3% African American, 1% Asian American/Pacific Islander **The most frequently chosen baccalaureate fields are** education, health professions and related sciences, security and protective services **Academic program** English as a second language, advanced placement, accelerated degree program, honors program, summer session, adult/continuing education programs, internships **Contact** Mr. Derek Skaggs, Director of Enrollment Services, Missouri Southern State University, 3950 East Newman Road, Joplin, MO 64801-1595. Phone: 417-625-9537 or toll-free 866-818-MSSU. Fax: 417-659-4429. E-mail: admissions@mssu.edu. Web site: http://www.mssu.edu/.

MISSOURI STATE UNIVERSITY
SPRINGFIELD, MISSOURI

General State-supported, comprehensive, coed **Entrance** Moderately difficult **Setting** 225-acre suburban campus **Total enrollment** 19,348 **Student-faculty ratio** 19:1 **Application deadline** 7/20 (freshmen), 7/20 (transfer) **Freshmen** 75% were admitted **Housing** Yes **Expenses** Tuition $6606; Room & Board $5312 **Undergraduates** 56% women, 22% part-time, 13% 25 or older, 1% Native American, 2% Hispanic American, 3% African American, 2% Asian American/Pacific Islander **The most frequently chosen baccalaureate fields are** business/marketing, education, social sciences **Academic program** English as a second language, advanced placement, accelerated degree program, self-designed majors, honors program, summer session, internships **Contact** Ms. Jill Duncan, Associate Director of Admissions, Missouri State University, 901 South National, Springfield, MO 65804-0094. Phone: 417-836-5521 or toll-free 800-492-7900. Fax: 417-836-6334. E-mail: info@missouristate.edu. Web site: http://www.missouristate.edu/.

MISSOURI TECH
ST. LOUIS, MISSOURI

Contact Mr. Bob Honaker, Director of Admissions, Missouri Tech, 1167 Corporate Lake Drive, St. Louis, MO 63132. Phone: 314-569-3600 Ext. 363. Fax: 314-569-1167. Web site: http://www.motech.edu/.

MISSOURI UNIVERSITY OF SCIENCE AND TECHNOLOGY
ROLLA, MISSOURI

General State-supported, university, coed, primarily men **Entrance** Very difficult **Setting** 284-acre small-town campus **Total enrollment** 6,167 **Student-faculty ratio** 15:1 **Application deadline** 7/1 (freshmen), 7/1 (transfer) **Freshmen** 67% were admitted **Housing** Yes **Expenses** Tuition $8172; Room & Board $6660 **Undergraduates** 22% women, 8% part-time, 8% 25 or older, 1% Native American, 2% Hispanic American, 5%

African American, 2% Asian American/Pacific Islander **The most frequently chosen baccalaureate fields are** computer and information sciences, biological/life sciences, engineering **Academic program** English as a second language, advanced placement, accelerated degree program, honors program, summer session, adult/continuing education programs, internships **Contact** Ms. Lynn Stichnote, Director of Admissions, Missouri University of Science and Technology, 1870 Miner Circle, Rolla, MO 65409. Phone: 573-341-4164 or toll-free 800-522-0938. Fax: 573-341-4082. E-mail: admissions@umr.edu. Web site: http://www.mst.edu/.

MISSOURI VALLEY COLLEGE
MARSHALL, MISSOURI

General Independent, 4-year, coed, affiliated with Presbyterian Church **Entrance** Minimally difficult **Setting** 140-acre small-town campus **Total enrollment** 1,639 **Student-faculty ratio** 18:1 **Application deadline** Rolling (freshmen), rolling (transfer) **Freshmen** 57% were admitted **Housing** Yes **Expenses** Tuition $15,950; Room & Board $6050 **Undergraduates** 43% women, 15% part-time, 9% 25 or older, 0.3% Native American, 6% Hispanic American, 17% African American, 4% Asian American/Pacific Islander **The most frequently chosen baccalaureate fields are** business/marketing, health professions and related sciences, security and protective services **Academic program** English as a second language, advanced placement, self-designed majors, summer session, adult/continuing education programs, internships **Contact** Ms. Debi Bultmann, Admissions Office Manager, Missouri Valley College, 500 East College, Marshall, MO 65340-3197. Phone: 660-831-4157. Fax: 660-831-4233. E-mail: admissions@moval.edu. Web site: http://www.moval.edu/.

MISSOURI WESTERN STATE UNIVERSITY
ST. JOSEPH, MISSOURI

General State-supported, 4-year, coed **Contact** Mr. Howard McCauley, Director of Admissions, Missouri Western State University, 4525 Downs Drive, St. Joseph, MO 64507-2294. Phone: 816-271-4267 or toll-free 800-662-7041 Ext. 60. Fax: 816-271-5833. E-mail: admission@missouriwestern.edu. Web site: http://www.missouriwestern.edu/.

NATIONAL AMERICAN UNIVERSITY
KANSAS CITY, MISSOURI

Contact Chuck Wolfe, Vice President, National American University, 4200 Blue Ridge Boulevard, Kansas City, MO 64133-1612. Phone: 816-353-4554. Fax: 816-353-1176. E-mail: jjoy@national.edu. Web site: http://www.national.edu/.

NORTHWEST MISSOURI STATE UNIVERSITY
MARYVILLE, MISSOURI

General State-supported, comprehensive, coed **Entrance** Moderately difficult **Setting** 240-acre small-town campus **Total enrollment** 6,613 **Student-faculty ratio** 21:1 **Application deadline** Rolling (freshmen), rolling (transfer) **Freshmen** 75% were admitted **Housing** Yes **Expenses** Tuition $6438; Room & Board $6276 **Undergraduates** 56% women, 11% part-time, 5% 25 or older, 0.5% Native American, 2% Hispanic American, 4% African American, 1% Asian American/Pacific Islander **The most frequently chosen baccalaureate fields are** business/marketing, education, psychology **Academic program** English as a second language, advanced placement, accelerated degree program, honors program, summer session, internships **Contact** Ms. Tami Grow, Associate Director of Admission, Northwest Missouri State University, 800 University Drive, Maryville, MO 64468. Phone: 660-562-1562 or toll-free 800-633-1175. Fax: 660-562-1121. E-mail: admissions@nwmissouri.edu. Web site: http://www.nwmissouri.edu/.

OZARK CHRISTIAN COLLEGE
JOPLIN, MISSOURI

General Independent Christian, 4-year, coed **Entrance** Noncompetitive **Setting** 110-acre small-town campus **Student-faculty ratio** 19:1 **Application deadline** 8/5 (freshmen), rolling (transfer) **Housing** Yes **Expenses** Tuition $8320; Room & Board $4550 **Academic program** English as a second language, summer session, adult/continuing education programs, internships **Contact** Mr. Troy B. Nelson, Executive Director of Admissions, Ozark Christian College, 1111 North Main Street, Joplin, MO 64801-4804. Phone: 417-624-2518 Ext. 2006 or toll-free 800-299-4622. Fax: 417-624-0090. E-mail: occadmin@occ.edu. Web site: http://www.occ.edu/.

PARK UNIVERSITY
PARKVILLE, MISSOURI

General Independent, comprehensive, coed **Entrance** Moderately difficult **Setting** 800-acre suburban campus **Total enrollment** 13,259 **Student-faculty ratio** 15:1 **Application deadline** 8/1 (freshmen), 8/1 (transfer) **Freshmen** 73% were admitted **Housing** Yes **Expenses** Tuition $7340; Room & Board $5322 **Undergraduates** 49% women, 91% part-time, 75% 25 or older, 1% Native American, 16% Hispanic American, 20% African American, 3% Asian American/

Park University *(continued)*

Pacific Islander **The most frequently chosen baccalaureate fields are** business/marketing, psychology, security and protective services **Academic program** English as a second language, advanced placement, self-designed majors, honors program, summer session, adult/continuing education programs, internships **Contact** Cathy Colapietro, Director of Admissions and Student Financial Services, Park University, 8700 NW River Park Drive, Campus Box 1, Parkville, MO 64152. Phone: 816-584-6728 or toll-free 800-745-7275. Fax: 816-741-4462. E-mail: admissions@mail.park.edu. Web site: http://www.park.edu/.

PATRICIA STEVENS COLLEGE
ST. LOUIS, MISSOURI

General Proprietary, 4-year, coed **Entrance** Moderately difficult **Setting** urban campus **Total enrollment** 145 **Student-faculty ratio** 9:1 **Application deadline** Rolling (freshmen) **Freshmen** 61% were admitted **Housing** No **Expenses** Tuition $15,120 **Undergraduates** 90% women, 36% part-time, 45% 25 or older, 1% Hispanic American, 45% African American, 1% Asian American/Pacific Islander **Academic program** Advanced placement, honors program, summer session, adult/continuing education programs, internships **Contact** Mr. John Willmon, Director of Admissions, Patricia Stevens College, 330 North Fourth Street, Suite 306, St. Louis, MO 63102. Phone: 314-421-0949 Ext. 12 or toll-free 800-871-0949. Fax: 314-421-0304. E-mail: admission@patriciastevenscollege.com. Web site: http://www.patriciastevenscollege.edu/.

RESEARCH COLLEGE OF NURSING
KANSAS CITY, MISSOURI

General Independent, comprehensive, coed, primarily women **Entrance** Moderately difficult **Setting** 66-acre urban campus **Total enrollment** 371 **Student-faculty ratio** 7:1 **Application deadline** 6/30 (freshmen), 2/15 (transfer) **Freshmen** 68% were admitted **Housing** Yes **Expenses** Tuition $22,720; Room & Board $6400 **Undergraduates** 93% women, 1% part-time, 30% 25 or older, 0.4% Native American, 5% Hispanic American, 6% African American, 5% Asian American/Pacific Islander **The most frequently chosen baccalaureate field is** health professions and related sciences **Academic program** Advanced placement, accelerated degree program, honors program, summer session **Contact** Mr. Lane Ramey, Director of Transfer Admission, Research College of Nursing, 2252 East Meyer Boulevard, Kansas City, MO 64132. Phone: 816-995-2820 or toll-free 800-842-6776. Fax: 816-501-4588. E-mail: lane.ramey@rockhurst.edu. Web site: http://www.researchcollege.edu/.

ROCKHURST UNIVERSITY
KANSAS CITY, MISSOURI

General Independent Roman Catholic (Jesuit), comprehensive, coed **Entrance** Moderately difficult **Setting** 35-acre urban campus **Total enrollment** 3,124 **Student-faculty ratio** 13:1 **Application deadline** 6/30 (freshmen), rolling (transfer) **Freshmen** 76% were admitted **Housing** Yes **Expenses** Tuition $22,840; Room & Board $6200 **Undergraduates** 60% women, 37% part-time, 10% 25 or older **The most frequently chosen baccalaureate fields are** business/marketing, health professions and related sciences, psychology **Academic program** Advanced placement, accelerated degree program, honors program, summer session, adult/continuing education programs, internships **Contact** Mr. Lane Ramey, Director of Freshman Admissions, Rockhurst University, 1100 Rockhurst Road, Kansas City, MO 64110-2561. Phone: 816-501-4100 or toll-free 800-842-6776. Fax: 816-501-4142. E-mail: admission@rockhurst.edu. Web site: http://www.rockhurst.edu/.

ST. LOUIS CHRISTIAN COLLEGE
FLORISSANT, MISSOURI

General Independent Christian, 4-year, coed **Entrance** Minimally difficult **Setting** 20-acre suburban campus **Total enrollment** 321 **Student-faculty ratio** 12:1 **Application deadline** 8/15 (freshmen), 8/15 (transfer) **Housing** Yes **Expenses** Tuition $9500; Room & Board $3300 **Undergraduates** 39% women, 15% part-time, 50% 25 or older, 1% Native American, 1% Hispanic American, 31% African American, 1% Asian American/Pacific Islander **The most frequently chosen baccalaureate field is** theology and religious vocations **Academic program** Advanced placement, accelerated degree program, adult/continuing education programs, internships **Contact** Carrie Chapman, Admissions Director, St. Louis Christian College, 1360 Grandview Drive, Florissant, MO 63033. Phone: 314-837-6777 Ext. 1500 or toll-free 800-887-SLCC. Fax: 314-837-8291. E-mail: cchapman@slcconline.edu. Web site: http://www.slcconline.edu/.

ST. LOUIS COLLEGE OF PHARMACY
ST. LOUIS, MISSOURI

General Independent, comprehensive, coed **Entrance** Moderately difficult **Setting** 5-acre urban campus **Total enrollment** 1,156 **Student-faculty ratio** 18:1 **Application deadline** 2/1 (freshmen), 2/1 (transfer) **Freshmen** 53% were admitted **Housing** Yes **Expenses** Tuition $20,825; Room & Board $8030 **Undergraduates** 55% women, 1% Hispanic American, 2% African American, 17% Asian American/Pacific Islander

The most frequently chosen baccalaureate field is health professions and related sciences **Academic program** Advanced placement, summer session, internships **Contact** Connie Horrall, Administrative Assistant, St. Louis College of Pharmacy, 4588 Parkview Place, St. Louis, MO 63110-1088. Phone: 314-446-8313 or toll-free 800-278-5267. Fax: 314-446-8310. E-mail: chorrall@stlcop.edu. Web site: http://www.stlcop.edu/.

SAINT LOUIS UNIVERSITY
ST. LOUIS, MISSOURI

General Independent Roman Catholic (Jesuit), university, coed **Entrance** Moderately difficult **Setting** 244-acre urban campus **Total enrollment** 12,309 **Student-faculty ratio** 13:1 **Application deadline** 8/1 (freshmen), rolling (transfer) **Freshmen** 80% were admitted **Housing** Yes **Expenses** Tuition $28,878; Room & Board $8550 **Undergraduates** 58% women, 7% part-time, 5% 25 or older, 0.3% Native American, 3% Hispanic American, 7% African American, 6% Asian American/Pacific Islander **The most frequently chosen baccalaureate fields are** business/marketing, health professions and related sciences, psychology **Academic program** English as a second language, advanced placement, accelerated degree program, self-designed majors, honors program, summer session, adult/continuing education programs, internships **Contact** Director, Saint Louis University, 221 North Grand Boulevard, St. Louis, MO 63103-2097. Phone: 314-977-3415 or toll-free 800-758-3678. Fax: 314-977-7136. E-mail: admitme@slu.edu. Web site: http://www.slu.edu/.

SAINT LUKE'S COLLEGE
KANSAS CITY, MISSOURI

General Independent Episcopal, upper-level, coed **Entrance** Very difficult **Setting** 3-acre urban campus **Total enrollment** 113 **Student-faculty ratio** 8:1 **Application deadline** 12/31 (transfer) **Housing** No **Expenses** Tuition $9520 **Undergraduates** 90% women, 11% part-time, 51% 25 or older, 1% Native American, 3% Hispanic American, 5% African American, 6% Asian American/Pacific Islander **Academic program** Summer session **Contact** Assistant Director of Admissions, Saint Luke's College, 4426 Wornall Road, Kansas City, MO 64111. Phone: 816-932-3372. Fax: 816-932-9064. E-mail: slc-admissions@saint-lukes.org. Web site: http://www.saintlukescollege.edu/.

SOUTHEAST MISSOURI STATE UNIVERSITY
CAPE GIRARDEAU, MISSOURI

General State-supported, comprehensive, coed **Entrance** Moderately difficult **Setting** 400-acre small-town campus **Total enrollment** 10,665 **Student-faculty ratio** 17:1 **Application deadline** 5/1 (freshmen), 5/1 (transfer) **Freshmen** 88% were admitted **Housing** Yes **Expenses** Tuition $5925; Room & Board $5923 **Undergraduates** 60% women, 25% part-time, 20% 25 or older, 1% Native American, 1% Hispanic American, 9% African American, 1% Asian American/Pacific Islander **The most frequently chosen baccalaureate fields are** business/marketing, education, liberal arts/general studies **Academic program** English as a second language, advanced placement, accelerated degree program, self-designed majors, honors program, summer session, adult/continuing education programs, internships **Contact** Dr. Deborah Below, Director of Admissions, Southeast Missouri State University, MS 3550, Cape Girardeau, MO 63701. Phone: 573-651-2590. Fax: 573-651-5936. E-mail: admissions@semo.edu. Web site: http://www.semo.edu/.

SOUTHWEST BAPTIST UNIVERSITY
BOLIVAR, MISSOURI

General Independent Southern Baptist, comprehensive, coed **Entrance** Moderately difficult **Setting** 152-acre small-town campus **Total enrollment** 3,539 **Student-faculty ratio** 13:1 **Application deadline** Rolling (freshmen), rolling (transfer) **Freshmen** 65% were admitted **Housing** Yes **Expenses** Tuition $15,870; Room & Board $5000 **Undergraduates** 66% women, 34% part-time, 5% 25 or older, 1% Native American, 1% Hispanic American, 4% African American, 1% Asian American/Pacific Islander **The most frequently chosen baccalaureate fields are** business/marketing, education, psychology **Academic program** Advanced placement, self-designed majors, honors program, summer session, internships **Contact** Mr. Darren Crowder, Director of Admissions, Southwest Baptist University, 1600 University Avenue, Bolivar, MO 65613-2597. Phone: 417-328-1817 or toll-free 800-526-5859. Fax: 417-328-1808. E-mail: dcrowder@sbuniv.edu. Web site: http://www.sbuniv.edu/.

STEPHENS COLLEGE
COLUMBIA, MISSOURI

General Independent, comprehensive, undergraduate: women only; graduate: coed **Entrance** Moderately difficult **Setting** 86-acre urban campus **Total enrollment** 1,050 **Student-faculty ratio** 12:1 **Application deadline** 8/1 (freshmen) **Freshmen** 71% were admitted **Housing** Yes **Expenses** Tuition $23,000; Room & Board $8730 **Undergraduates** 22% part-time, 26% 25 or older, 1% Native American, 3% Hispanic American, 9% African American, 2% Asian American/Pacific Islander **The most frequently chosen**

Stephens College *(continued)*

baccalaureate fields are business/marketing, health professions and related sciences, visual and performing arts **Academic program** English as a second language, advanced placement, accelerated degree program, self-designed majors, honors program, adult/continuing education programs, internships **Contact** Mr. David Adams, Director of Enrollment, Stephens College, 1200 East Broadway, Box 2121, Columbia, MO 65215-0002. Phone: 573-876-7207 or toll-free 800-876-7207. Fax: 573-876-7237. E-mail: apply@stephens.edu. Web site: http://www.stephens.edu/.

TRUMAN STATE UNIVERSITY

KIRKSVILLE, MISSOURI

General State-supported, comprehensive, coed **Entrance** Moderately difficult **Setting** 140-acre small-town campus **Total enrollment** 5,866 **Student-faculty ratio** 16:1 **Application deadline** 3/1 (freshmen), rolling (transfer) **Freshmen** 81% were admitted **Housing** Yes **Expenses** Tuition $6432; Room & Board $5815 **Undergraduates** 57% women, 2% part-time, 2% 25 or older, 1% Native American, 2% Hispanic American, 4% African American, 2% Asian American/Pacific Islander **The most frequently chosen baccalaureate fields are** business/marketing, English, parks and recreation **Academic program** Advanced placement, self-designed majors, honors program, summer session, internships **Contact** Mr. Brad Chambers, Director of Admissions, Truman State University, 205 McClain Hall, 100 East Normal Street, Kirksville, MO 63501-4221. Phone: 660-785-4114 or toll-free 800-892-7792. Fax: 660-785-7456. E-mail: admissions@truman.edu. Web site: http://www.truman.edu/.

UNIVERSITY OF CENTRAL MISSOURI

WARRENSBURG, MISSOURI

General State-supported, comprehensive, coed **Entrance** Moderately difficult **Setting** 1,561-acre small-town campus **Total enrollment** 10,918 **Student-faculty ratio** 17:1 **Application deadline** Rolling (freshmen), rolling (transfer) **Freshmen** 81% were admitted **Housing** Yes **Expenses** Tuition $6829; Room & Board $5846 **Undergraduates** 55% women, 21% part-time, 16% 25 or older, 1% Native American, 2% Hispanic American, 6% African American, 1% Asian American/Pacific Islander **The most frequently chosen baccalaureate fields are** business/marketing, education, engineering technologies **Academic program** English as a second language, advanced placement, self-designed majors, honors program, summer session, adult/continuing education programs, internships **Contact** Ms. Ann Nordyke, Chief Admission Officer, University of Central Missouri, 1401 Ward Edwards, Warrensburg, MO 64093. Phone: 660-543-4290 or toll-free 800-729-2678. Fax: 660-543-8517. E-mail: admit@ucmovmb.cmsu.edu. Web site: http://www.ucmo.edu/.

UNIVERSITY OF MISSOURI–COLUMBIA

COLUMBIA, MISSOURI

General State-supported, university, coed **Entrance** Moderately difficult **Setting** 1,358-acre suburban campus **Total enrollment** 28,477 **Student-faculty ratio** 17:1 **Application deadline** Rolling (freshmen), rolling (transfer) **Freshmen** 86% were admitted **Housing** Yes **Expenses** Tuition $8099; Room & Board $7002 **Undergraduates** 52% women, 6% part-time, 4% 25 or older, 1% Native American, 2% Hispanic American, 6% African American, 3% Asian American/Pacific Islander **The most frequently chosen baccalaureate fields are** business/marketing, communications/journalism, education **Academic program** English as a second language, advanced placement, accelerated degree program, self-designed majors, honors program, summer session, adult/continuing education programs, internships **Contact** Ms. Barbara Rupp, Director of Admissions, University of Missouri–Columbia, 230 Jesse Hall, Columbia, MO 65211. Phone: 573-882-7786 or toll-free 800-225-6075. Fax: 573-882-7887. E-mail: mu4u@missouri.edu. Web site: http://www.missouri.edu/.

UNIVERSITY OF MISSOURI–KANSAS CITY

KANSAS CITY, MISSOURI

General State-supported, university, coed **Entrance** Moderately difficult **Setting** 191-acre urban campus **Total enrollment** 14,442 **Student-faculty ratio** 9:1 **Application deadline** Rolling (freshmen), rolling (transfer) **Freshmen** 60% were admitted **Housing** Yes **Expenses** Tuition $8396; Room & Board $7841 **Undergraduates** 58% women, 39% part-time, 28% 25 or older, 1% Native American, 4% Hispanic American, 12% African American, 5% Asian American/Pacific Islander **The most frequently chosen baccalaureate fields are** business/marketing, education, liberal arts/general studies **Academic program** English as a second language, advanced placement, accelerated degree program, self-designed majors, honors program, summer session, adult/continuing education programs, internships **Contact** Ms. Jennifer DeHaemers, Director of Admissions, University of Missouri–Kansas City, Office of Admissions, 5100 Rockhill Road, Kansas City, MO 64110-2499. Phone: 816-235-1111 or toll-free 800-775-8652. Fax: 816-235-5544. E-mail: admit@umkc.edu. Web site: http://www.umkc.edu/.

UNIVERSITY OF MISSOURI–ST. LOUIS

ST. LOUIS, MISSOURI

General State-supported, university, coed **Entrance** Moderately difficult **Setting** 350-acre suburban campus **Total enrollment** 15,543 **Student-faculty ratio** 17:1 **Application deadline** Rolling (freshmen), rolling (transfer) **Freshmen** 46% were admitted **Housing** Yes **Expenses** Tuition $8264; Room & Board $7394 **Undergraduates** 59% women, 52% part-time, 39% 25 or older, 0.3% Native American, 2% Hispanic American, 18% African American, 3% Asian American/Pacific Islander **The most frequently chosen baccalaureate fields are** business/marketing, education, social sciences **Academic program** English as a second language, advanced placement, accelerated degree program, self-designed majors, honors program, summer session, adult/continuing education programs, internships **Contact** Mr. Dennis Saunders, Associate Director of Admissions, University of Missouri–St. Louis, 351 Millennium Student Center, One University Boulevard, St. Louis, MO 63121-4400. Phone: 314-516-5451 or toll-free 888-GO2-UMSL. Fax: 314-516-5310. E-mail: admissions@umsl.edu. Web site: http://www.umsl.edu/.

UNIVERSITY OF PHOENIX–KANSAS CITY CAMPUS

KANSAS CITY, MISSOURI

General Proprietary, comprehensive, coed **Contact** Ms. Evelyn Gaskin, Registrar/Executive Director, University of Phoenix–Kansas City Campus, 4615 East Elwood Street, Mail Stop AA-K101, Phoenix, AZ 85040-1958. Phone: 480-557-3301 or toll-free 800-776-4867 (in-state); 800-228-7240 (out-of-state). Fax: 480-643-1020. E-mail: evelyn@gaskin@phoenix.edu. Web site: http://www.phoenix.edu/.

UNIVERSITY OF PHOENIX–ST. LOUIS CAMPUS

ST. LOUIS, MISSOURI

General Proprietary, comprehensive, coed **Contact** Ms. Evelyn Gaskin, Registrar/Executive Director, University of Phoenix–St. Louis Campus, 4615 East Elwood Street, Mail Stop AA-K101, Phoenix, AZ 85040-1958. Phone: 480-557-3301 or toll-free 800-776-4867 (in-state); 800-228-7240 (out-of-state). Fax: 480-643-1020. E-mail: evelyn.gaskin@phoenix.edu. Web site: http://www.phoenix.edu/.

UNIVERSITY OF PHOENIX–SPRINGFIELD CAMPUS

SPRINGFIELD, MISSOURI

General Proprietary, comprehensive, coed **Contact** Ms. Evelyn Gaskin, Registrar/Executive Director, University of Phoenix–Springfield Campus, 4615 East Elwood Street, Phoenix, AZ 58040-1958. Phone: 480-557-3301 or toll-free 800-776-4867 (in-state); 800-228-7240 (out-of-state). Fax: 480-643-1020. E-mail: evelyn.gaskin@phoenix.edu. Web site: http://www.phoenix.edu/.

WASHINGTON UNIVERSITY IN ST. LOUIS

ST. LOUIS, MISSOURI

General Independent, university, coed **Entrance** Most difficult **Setting** 169-acre suburban campus **Total enrollment** 13,382 **Student-faculty ratio** 7:1 **Application deadline** 1/15 (freshmen), 4/15 (transfer) **Freshmen** 17% were admitted **Housing** Yes **Expenses** Tuition $37,248; Room & Board $11,636 **Undergraduates** 51% women, 15% part-time, 5% 25 or older, 0.1% Native American, 3% Hispanic American, 10% African American, 13% Asian American/Pacific Islander **The most frequently chosen baccalaureate fields are** business/marketing, engineering, social sciences **Academic program** English as a second language, advanced placement, accelerated degree program, self-designed majors, summer session, adult/continuing education programs, internships **Contact** Ms. Nanette Tarbouni, Director of Admissions, Washington University in St. Louis, Campus Box 1089, One Brookings Drive, St. Louis, MO 63130-4899. Phone: 314-935-6000 or toll-free 800-638-0700. Fax: 314-935-4290. E-mail: admissions@wustl.edu. Web site: http://www.wustl.edu/.

WEBSTER UNIVERSITY

ST. LOUIS, MISSOURI

General Independent, comprehensive, coed **Entrance** Moderately difficult **Setting** 47-acre suburban campus **Total enrollment** 8,430 **Student-faculty ratio** 10:1 **Application deadline** 6/1 (freshmen), 8/1 (transfer) **Freshmen** 56% were admitted **Housing** Yes **Expenses** Tuition $19,330; Room & Board $8220 **Undergraduates** 58% women, 27% part-time, 28% 25 or older, 0.2% Native American, 2% Hispanic American, 11% African American, 2% Asian American/Pacific Islander **The most frequently chosen baccalaureate fields are** business/marketing, communications/journalism, visual and performing arts **Academic program** English as a second language, advanced placement, accelerated degree program, self-designed majors, summer session, adult/continuing education

Webster University *(continued)*

programs, internships **Contact** Mr. Andrew Laue, Associate Director of Undergraduate Admission, Webster University, 470 East Lockwood Avenue, St. Louis, MO 63119-3194. Phone: 314-968-6991 or toll-free 800-75-ENROL. Fax: 314-968-7115. E-mail: admit@webster.edu. Web site: http://www.webster.edu/.

WESTMINSTER COLLEGE
FULTON, MISSOURI

General Independent, 4-year, coed, affiliated with Presbyterian Church **Entrance** Moderately difficult **Setting** 80-acre small-town campus **Total enrollment** 972 **Student-faculty ratio** 14:1 **Freshmen** 80% were admitted **Housing** Yes **Expenses** Tuition $17,250; Room & Board $6720 **Undergraduates** 44% women, 2% part-time, 1% 25 or older, 1% Native American, 2% Hispanic American, 4% African American, 2% Asian American/Pacific Islander **The most frequently chosen baccalaureate fields are** business/marketing, education, liberal arts/general studies **Academic program** Advanced placement, self-designed majors, honors program, summer session, internships **Contact** Dr. George Wolf, Vice President and Dean of Enrollment Services, Westminster College, 501 Westminster Avenue, Fulton, MO 65251-1299. Phone: 573-592-5251 or toll-free 800-475-3361. Fax: 573-592-5255. E-mail: admissions@westminster-mo.edu. Web site: http://www.westminster-mo.edu/.

WILLIAM JEWELL COLLEGE
LIBERTY, MISSOURI

General Independent Baptist, 4-year, coed **Entrance** Moderately difficult **Setting** 200-acre small-town campus **Total enrollment** 1,329 **Student-faculty ratio** 11:1 **Application deadline** 8/15 (freshmen), rolling (transfer) **Freshmen** 92% were admitted **Housing** Yes **Expenses** Tuition $23,300; Room & Board $6130 **Undergraduates** 60% women, 17% part-time, 5% 25 or older, 2% Native American, 3% Hispanic American, 4% African American, 1% Asian American/Pacific Islander **The most frequently chosen baccalaureate fields are** business/marketing, health professions and related sciences, psychology **Academic program** Advanced placement, self-designed majors, honors program, summer session, adult/continuing education programs, internships **Contact** Ms. Bridget Gramling, Dean of Admission, William Jewell College, 500 College Hill, Liberty, MO 64068-1843. Phone: 816-781-7700 Ext. 5263 or toll-free 888-2JEWELL. Fax: 816-415-5040. E-mail: gramblingb@william.jewell.edu. Web site: http://www.jewell.edu/.

WILLIAM WOODS UNIVERSITY
FULTON, MISSOURI

General Independent, comprehensive, coed, affiliated with Christian Church (Disciples of Christ) **Entrance** Moderately difficult **Setting** 170-acre small-town campus **Total enrollment** 2,185 **Student-faculty ratio** 14:1 **Application deadline** Rolling (freshmen), rolling (transfer) **Freshmen** 85% were admitted **Housing** Yes **Expenses** Tuition $16,080; Room & Board $6400 **Undergraduates** 73% women, 19% part-time, 18% 25 or older, 1% Native American, 1% Hispanic American, 3% African American, 0.1% Asian American/Pacific Islander **The most frequently chosen baccalaureate fields are** agriculture, business/marketing, law/legal studies **Academic program** Advanced placement, accelerated degree program, self-designed majors, honors program, summer session, adult/continuing education programs, internships **Contact** Ms. Sharon Horn, Admissions Data Analyst, William Woods University, One University Avenue, Fulton, MO 65251. Phone: 573-592-4221 or toll-free 800-995-3159 Ext. 4221. Fax: 573-592-1146. E-mail: admissions@williamwoods.edu. Web site: http://www.williamwoods.edu/.

MONTANA

CARROLL COLLEGE
HELENA, MONTANA

Contact Ms. Cynthia Thornquist, Director of Admissions and Enrollment, Carroll College, 1601 North Benton Avenue, Helena, MT 59625-0002. Phone: 406-447-4384 or toll-free 800-992-3648. Fax: 406-447-4533. E-mail: enroll@carroll.edu. Web site: http://www.carroll.edu/.

MONTANA STATE UNIVERSITY
BOZEMAN, MONTANA

General State-supported, university, coed **Entrance** Moderately difficult **Setting** 1,170-acre small-town campus **Total enrollment** 12,170 **Student-faculty ratio** 16:1 **Application deadline** Rolling (freshmen), rolling (transfer) **Freshmen** 64% were admitted **Housing** Yes **Expenses** Tuition $5749; Room & Board $6780 **Undergraduates** 46% women, 15% part-time, 15% 25 or older, 2% Native American, 1% Hispanic American, 0.5% African American, 1% Asian American/Pacific Islander **The most frequently chosen baccalaureate fields are** business/marketing, engineering, health professions and related sciences **Academic program** English as a second language, advanced placement, self-designed majors, honors program, summer session, adult/continuing education programs, internships **Contact** Ms. Ronda Russell, Director of New Student Services, Montana State University, PO Box 172190, Bozeman, MT 59717-2190. Phone: 406-994-2601 or toll-free 888-MSU-CATS. Fax: 406-994-1923. E-mail: admissions@montana.edu. Web site: http://www.montana.edu/.

MONTANA STATE UNIVERSITY–BILLINGS

BILLINGS, MONTANA

General State-supported, comprehensive, coed **Entrance** Moderately difficult **Setting** 92-acre urban campus **Total enrollment** 4,912 **Student-faculty ratio** 21:1 **Application deadline** 7/1 (freshmen), rolling (transfer) **Freshmen** 100% were admitted **Housing** Yes **Expenses** Tuition $5132; Room & Board $4882 **Undergraduates** 63% women, 26% part-time, 35% 25 or older, 5% Native American, 4% Hispanic American, 1% African American, 1% Asian American/Pacific Islander **The most frequently chosen baccalaureate fields are** business/marketing, education, liberal arts/general studies **Academic program** English as a second language, advanced placement, accelerated degree program, honors program, summer session, adult/continuing education programs, internships **Contact** Ms. Shelly Andersen, Associate Director of Admissions, Montana State University–Billings, 1500 University Drive, Billings, MT 59101. Phone: 406-657-2158 or toll-free 800-565-6782. Fax: 406-657-2302. E-mail: sandersen@msubillings.edu. Web site: http://www.msubillings.edu/.

MONTANA STATE UNIVERSITY–NORTHERN

HAVRE, MONTANA

Contact Ms. Rosalie Spinler, Director of Admissions, Montana State University–Northern, PO Box 7751, Havre, MT 59501-7751. Phone: 406-265-3704 or toll-free 800-662-6132. Fax: 406-265-3777. E-mail: msunadmit@nmcl.nmclites.edu. Web site: http://www.msun.edu/.

MONTANA TECH OF THE UNIVERSITY OF MONTANA

BUTTE, MONTANA

General State-supported, comprehensive, coed **Entrance** Moderately difficult **Setting** 56-acre small-town campus **Total enrollment** 2,347 **Student-faculty ratio** 16:1 **Application deadline** Rolling (freshmen), rolling (transfer) **Housing** Yes **Expenses** Tuition $5644; Room & Board $5860 **Undergraduates** 23% 25 or older **The most frequently chosen baccalaureate fields are** engineering, business/marketing, health professions and related sciences **Academic program** Advanced placement, self-designed majors, summer session, adult/continuing education programs, internships **Contact** Mr. Tony Campeau, Director of Admissions, Montana Tech of The University of Montana, 1300 West Park Street, Butte, MT 59701-8997. Phone: 406-496-4632 or toll-free 800-445-TECH Ext. 1. Fax: 406-496-4170. E-mail: admissions@mtech.edu. Web site: http://www.mtech.edu/.

ROCKY MOUNTAIN COLLEGE

BILLINGS, MONTANA

General Independent interdenominational, comprehensive, coed **Contact** Ms. Laurie Rodriguez, Director of Admissions, Rocky Mountain College, 1511 Poly Drive, Billings, MT 59102. Phone: 406-657-1026 or toll-free 800-877-6259. Fax: 406-259-9751. E-mail: admissions@rocky.edu. Web site: http://www.rocky.edu/.

UNIVERSITY OF GREAT FALLS

GREAT FALLS, MONTANA

General Independent Roman Catholic, comprehensive, coed **Entrance** Noncompetitive **Setting** 40-acre urban campus **Total enrollment** 723 **Student-faculty ratio** 11:1 **Application deadline** 8/1 (freshmen), 8/1 (transfer) **Freshmen** 57% were admitted **Housing** Yes **Expenses** Tuition $15,500; Room & Board $6490 **Undergraduates** 64% women, 25% part-time, 40% 25 or older, 5% Native American, 6% Hispanic American, 4% African American, 2% Asian American/Pacific Islander **The most frequently chosen baccalaureate fields are** education, psychology, security and protective services **Academic program** Advanced placement, summer session, adult/continuing education programs, internships **Contact** April Clutter, Director of Admissions, University of Great Falls, 1301 20th Street South, Great Falls, MT 59405. Phone: 406-791-5200 or toll-free 800-856-9544. Fax: 406-791-5209. E-mail: enroll@ugf.edu. Web site: http://www.ugf.edu/.

THE UNIVERSITY OF MONTANA

MISSOULA, MONTANA

General State-supported, university, coed **Entrance** Moderately difficult **Setting** 220-acre urban campus **Total enrollment** 13,858 **Student-faculty ratio** 19:1 **Application deadline** Rolling (freshmen), rolling (transfer) **Freshmen** 95% were admitted **Housing** Yes **Expenses** Tuition $5180; Room & Board $6258 **Undergraduates** 54% women, 16% part-time, 24% 25 or older, 4% Native American, 2% Hispanic American, 1%

The University of Montana *(continued)*

African American, 1% Asian American/Pacific Islander **The most frequently chosen baccalaureate fields are** business/marketing, natural resources/environmental science, social sciences **Academic program** English as a second language, advanced placement, honors program, summer session, adult/continuing education programs, internships **Contact** Ms. Juana Alcala, Manager, Enrollment Services, The University of Montana, Missoula, MT 59812-0002. Phone: 406-243-2361 or toll-free 800-462-8636. Fax: 406-243-5711. E-mail: admiss@umontana.edu. Web site: http://www.umt.edu/.

THE UNIVERSITY OF MONTANA–WESTERN
DILLON, MONTANA

General State-supported, 4-year, coed **Entrance** Minimally difficult **Setting** 36-acre small-town campus **Total enrollment** 1,148 **Student-faculty ratio** 17:1 **Application deadline** Rolling (freshmen), rolling (transfer) **Freshmen** 97% were admitted **Housing** Yes **Expenses** Tuition $4228; Room & Board $5350 **Undergraduates** 54% women, 16% part-time, 21% 25 or older, 4% Native American, 1% Hispanic American, 1% African American, 3% Asian American/Pacific Islander **The most frequently chosen baccalaureate fields are** business/marketing, education, liberal arts/general studies **Academic program** Advanced placement, accelerated degree program, self-designed majors, honors program, summer session, adult/continuing education programs, internships **Contact** Admissions, The University of Montana–Western, 710 South Atlantic, Dillon, MT 59725. Phone: 406-683-7331 or toll-free 866-869-6668 (in-state); 877-683-7493 (out-of-state). Fax: 406-683-7493. E-mail: admissions@umwestern.edu. Web site: http://www.umwestern.edu/.

NEBRASKA

BELLEVUE UNIVERSITY
BELLEVUE, NEBRASKA

General Independent, comprehensive, coed **Contact** Michelle Eppler, Dean of Students/Dean of Academic Services, Bellevue University, 1000 Galvin Road South, Bellevue, NE 68005-3098. Phone: 402-557-7010 or toll-free 800-756-7920. Fax: 402-557-5404. E-mail: michelle.eppler@bellevue.edu. Web site: http://www.bellevue.edu/.

CHADRON STATE COLLEGE
CHADRON, NEBRASKA

Contact Ms. Tena Cook Gould, Director of Admissions, Chadron State College, 1000 Main Street, Chadron, NE 69337-2690. Phone: 308-432-6263 or toll-free 800-242-3766. Fax: 308-432-6229. E-mail: inquire@csc1.csc.edu. Web site: http://www.csc.edu/.

CLARKSON COLLEGE
OMAHA, NEBRASKA

General Independent, comprehensive, coed, primarily women **Entrance** Moderately difficult **Setting** 3-acre urban campus **Total enrollment** 841 **Student-faculty ratio** 12:1 **Application deadline** Rolling (freshmen), rolling (transfer) **Freshmen** 60% were admitted **Housing** Yes **Expenses** Tuition $11,070; Room & Board $6200 **Undergraduates** 40% 25 or older, 1% Native American, 2% Hispanic American, 4% African American, 2% Asian American/Pacific Islander **The most frequently chosen baccalaureate field is** health professions and related sciences **Academic program** Advanced placement, accelerated degree program, summer session, adult/continuing education programs, internships **Contact** Ms. Denise Work, Director of Admissions, Clarkson College, 101 South 42nd Street, Omaha, NE 68131-2739. Phone: 402-552-3100 or toll-free 800-647-5500. Fax: 402-552-6057. E-mail: admiss@clarksoncollege.edu. Web site: http://www.clarksoncollege.edu/.

COLLEGE OF SAINT MARY
OMAHA, NEBRASKA

General Independent Roman Catholic, comprehensive, women only **Entrance** Minimally difficult **Setting** 25-acre suburban campus **Total enrollment** 973 **Student-faculty ratio** 9:1 **Application deadline** Rolling (freshmen), rolling (transfer) **Freshmen** 42% were admitted **Housing** Yes **Expenses** Tuition $20,220; Room & Board $6300 **Undergraduates** 24% part-time, 49% 25 or older, 1% Native American, 8% Hispanic American, 10% African American, 1% Asian American/Pacific Islander **The most frequently chosen baccalaureate fields are** business/marketing, education, health professions and related sciences **Academic program** Advanced placement, accelerated degree program, summer session, adult/continuing education programs, internships **Contact** Ms. Erika Pritchard, College of Saint Mary, 7000 Mercy Road, Omaha, NE 68106. Phone: 402-399-2407 or toll-free 800-926-5534. Fax: 402-399-2412. E-mail: enroll@csm.edu. Web site: http://www.csm.edu/.

CONCORDIA UNIVERSITY, NEBRASKA

SEWARD, NEBRASKA

General Independent, comprehensive, coed, affiliated with Lutheran Church–Missouri Synod **Entrance** Moderately difficult **Setting** 120-acre small-town campus **Total enrollment** 1,279 **Student-faculty ratio** 14:1 **Application deadline** 8/1 (freshmen) **Freshmen** 77% were admitted **Housing** Yes **Expenses** Tuition $20,700; Room & Board $5280 **Undergraduates** 55% women, 3% part-time, 5% 25 or older, 0.3% Native American, 1% Hispanic American, 1% African American, 0.5% Asian American/Pacific Islander **The most frequently chosen baccalaureate fields are** education, business/marketing, theology and religious vocations **Academic program** English as a second language, advanced placement, accelerated degree program, summer session, adult/continuing education programs, internships **Contact** Ms. Helen Schnell, Director of Undergraduate and Graduate Recruitment, Concordia University, Nebraska, 800 North Columbia Avenue, Seward, NE 68434-1599. Phone: 800-535-5494 Ext. 7233 or toll-free 800-535-5494. Fax: 402-643-4073. E-mail: admiss@cune.edu. Web site: http://www.cune.edu/.

CREIGHTON UNIVERSITY

OMAHA, NEBRASKA

General Independent Roman Catholic (Jesuit), university, coed **Entrance** Moderately difficult **Setting** 110-acre urban campus **Total enrollment** 6,992 **Student-faculty ratio** 12:1 **Application deadline** 2/15 (freshmen), 8/1 (transfer) **Freshmen** 81% were admitted **Housing** Yes **Expenses** Tuition $26,634; Room & Board $8180 **Undergraduates** 60% women, 7% part-time, 1% 25 or older, 1% Native American, 4% Hispanic American, 3% African American, 8% Asian American/Pacific Islander **The most frequently chosen baccalaureate fields are** business/marketing, biological/life sciences, health professions and related sciences **Academic program** English as a second language, advanced placement, accelerated degree program, honors program, summer session, adult/continuing education programs, internships **Contact** Ms. Mary Chase, Assistant Vice President for Enrollment Management and Director of Admissions and Scholarships, Creighton University, 2500 California Plaza, Omaha, NE 68178-0001. Phone: 402-280-2162 or toll-free 800-282-5835. Fax: 402-280-2685. E-mail: admissions@creighton.edu. Web site: http://www.creighton.edu/.

DANA COLLEGE

BLAIR, NEBRASKA

General Independent, 4-year, coed, affiliated with Evangelical Lutheran Church in America **Entrance** Moderately difficult **Setting** 150-acre small-town campus **Total enrollment** 634 **Student-faculty ratio** 13:1 **Application deadline** Rolling (freshmen) **Freshmen** 72% were admitted **Housing** Yes **Expenses** Tuition $19,370; Room & Board $5560 **Undergraduates** 47% women, 5% part-time, 3% 25 or older, 0.5% Native American, 4% Hispanic American, 3% African American, 1% Asian American/Pacific Islander **The most frequently chosen baccalaureate fields are** business/marketing, education, security and protective services **Academic program** English as a second language, advanced placement, accelerated degree program, self-designed majors, honors program, summer session, adult/continuing education programs, internships **Contact** Gretchen Foster, Dean of Enrollment Management, Dana College, 2848 College Drive, Blair, NE 68008-1099. Phone: 402-426-7220 or toll-free 800-444-3262. Fax: 402-426-7386. E-mail: admissions@dana.edu. Web site: http://www.dana.edu/.

DOANE COLLEGE

CRETE, NEBRASKA

General Independent, comprehensive, coed, affiliated with United Church of Christ **Entrance** Moderately difficult **Setting** 300-acre small-town campus **Total enrollment** 921 **Student-faculty ratio** 10:1 **Application deadline** Rolling (freshmen), rolling (transfer) **Freshmen** 75% were admitted **Housing** Yes **Expenses** Tuition $19,150; Room & Board $5410 **Undergraduates** 53% women, 1% part-time, 2% 25 or older, 0.1% Native American, 3% Hispanic American, 4% African American, 1% Asian American/Pacific Islander **The most frequently chosen baccalaureate fields are** business/marketing, biological/life sciences, education **Academic program** English as a second language, advanced placement, self-designed majors, honors program, summer session, internships **Contact** Mr. Cezar Mesquita, Director of Admission, Doane College, 1014 Boswell Avenue, Crete, NE 68333-2430. Phone: 402-826-8222 or toll-free 800-333-6263. Fax: 402-826-8600. E-mail: admissions@doane.edu. Web site: http://www.doane.edu/.

GRACE UNIVERSITY

OMAHA, NEBRASKA

General Independent interdenominational, comprehensive, coed **Entrance** Moderately difficult **Setting** 15-acre urban campus **Total enrollment** 431 **Student-faculty ratio** 18:1 **Application**

Grace University *(continued)*

deadline Rolling (freshmen), rolling (transfer) **Freshmen** 64% were admitted **Housing** Yes **Expenses** Tuition $14,490; Room & Board $5650 **Undergraduates** 56% women, 16% part-time, 34% 25 or older, 0.3% Native American, 2% Hispanic American, 7% African American, 2% Asian American/Pacific Islander **The most frequently chosen baccalaureate fields are** education, psychology, theology and religious vocations **Academic program** Advanced placement, accelerated degree program, self-designed majors, summer session, adult/continuing education programs, internships **Contact** Angela Wayman, Director of Admissions, Grace University, 1311 South Ninth Street, Omaha, NE 68108. Phone: 402-449-2831 or toll-free 800-383-1422. Fax: 402-341-9587. E-mail: admissions@graceuniversity.com. Web site: http://www.graceuniversity.edu/.

HASTINGS COLLEGE

HASTINGS, NEBRASKA

General Independent Presbyterian, comprehensive, coed **Entrance** Moderately difficult **Setting** 109-acre small-town campus **Total enrollment** 1,138 **Student-faculty ratio** 12:1 **Application deadline** 8/1 (freshmen), 8/1 (transfer) **Freshmen** 78% were admitted **Housing** Yes **Expenses** Tuition $19,604; Room & Board $5432 **Undergraduates** 46% women, 2% part-time, 3% 25 or older, 0.4% Native American, 3% Hispanic American, 2% African American, 1% Asian American/Pacific Islander **The most frequently chosen baccalaureate fields are** business/marketing, education, visual and performing arts **Academic program** Advanced placement, self-designed majors, summer session, adult/continuing education programs, internships **Contact** Ms. Mary Molliconi, Director of Admissions, Hastings College, 710 North Turner Avenue, Hastings, NE 68901-7621. Phone: 402-461-7320 or toll-free 800-532-7642. Fax: 402-461-7490. E-mail: mmolliconi@hastings.edu. Web site: http://www.hastings.edu/.

MIDLAND LUTHERAN COLLEGE

FREMONT, NEBRASKA

General Independent Lutheran, 4-year, coed **Entrance** Moderately difficult **Setting** 27-acre small-town campus **Total enrollment** 827 **Student-faculty ratio** 14:1 **Application deadline** Rolling (freshmen), rolling (transfer) **Freshmen** 88% were admitted **Housing** Yes **Expenses** Tuition $20,525; Room & Board $5150 **Undergraduates** 56% women, 2% part-time, 5% 25 or older, 0.3% Native American, 2% Hispanic American, 3% African American, 1% Asian American/Pacific Islander **Academic program** English as a second language, advanced placement, accelerated degree program, self-designed majors, honors program, summer session, internships **Contact** Mr. Todd Hansen, Associate Director of Admissions, Midland Lutheran College, 900 North Clarkson Street, Fremont, NE 68025-4200. Phone: 402-941-6521 or toll-free 800-642-8382 Ext. 6501. Fax: 402-941-6513. E-mail: admissions@mlc.edu. Web site: http://www.mlc.edu/.

NEBRASKA CHRISTIAN COLLEGE

PAPILLON, NEBRASKA

General Independent, 4-year, coed, affiliated with Christian Churches and Churches of Christ **Entrance** Minimally difficult **Setting** 85-acre small-town campus **Total enrollment** 146 **Student-faculty ratio** 7:1 **Application deadline** Rolling (freshmen), rolling (transfer) **Housing** Yes **Undergraduates** 43% women, 4% part-time, 3% 25 or older, 1% Hispanic American, 1% Asian American/Pacific Islander **Academic program** Internships **Contact** Ms. Alisha Livengood, Associate Director of Admissions, Nebraska Christian College, 12550 114th Steet, Papillon, NE 68046. Phone: 402-935-9407. Fax: 402-379-5100. E-mail: admissions@nechristian.edu. Web site: http://www.nechristian.edu/.

NEBRASKA METHODIST COLLEGE

OMAHA, NEBRASKA

General Independent, comprehensive, coed, primarily women, affiliated with United Methodist Church **Entrance** Moderately difficult **Setting** 5-acre urban campus **Total enrollment** 512 **Student-faculty ratio** 10:1 **Application deadline** 4/1 (freshmen), 4/1 (transfer) **Freshmen** 39% were admitted **Housing** Yes **Expenses** Tuition $14,040; Room only $6150 **Undergraduates** 89% women, 31% part-time, 27% 25 or older, 0.4% Native American, 1% Hispanic American, 4% African American, 2% Asian American/Pacific Islander **The most frequently chosen baccalaureate field is** health professions and related sciences **Academic program** Advanced placement, accelerated degree program, summer session, internships **Contact** Ms. Deann Sterner, Director of Admissions, Nebraska Methodist College, 720 North 87th Street, Omaha, NE 68114. Phone: 402-354-7205 or toll-free 800-335-5510. Fax: 402-354-7020. E-mail: deann.sterner@methodistcollege.edu. Web site: http://www.methodistcollege.edu/.

NEBRASKA WESLEYAN UNIVERSITY

LINCOLN, NEBRASKA

General Independent United Methodist, comprehensive, coed **Entrance** Moderately difficult

Setting 50-acre suburban campus **Total enrollment** 2,107 **Student-faculty ratio** 13:1 **Application deadline** 8/15 (freshmen), 8/15 (transfer) **Freshmen** 80% were admitted **Housing** Yes **Expenses** Tuition $20,252; Room & Board $5340 **Undergraduates** 57% women, 11% part-time, 3% 25 or older, 0.2% Native American, 1% Hispanic American, 2% African American, 1% Asian American/Pacific Islander **The most frequently chosen baccalaureate fields are** business/marketing, health professions and related sciences, parks and recreation **Academic program** Advanced placement, summer session, adult/continuing education programs, internships **Contact** Ms. Tara Sintek, Nebraska Wesleyan University, 5000 Saint Paul Avenue, Lincoln, NE 68504-2796. Phone: 402-465-2218 or toll-free 800-541-3818. Fax: 402-465-2177. E-mail: admissions@nebrwesleyan.edu. Web site: http://www.nebrwesleyan.edu/.

PERU STATE COLLEGE

PERU, NEBRASKA

General State-supported, comprehensive, coed **Entrance** Noncompetitive **Setting** 104-acre rural campus **Total enrollment** 2,307 **Student-faculty ratio** 20:1 **Application deadline** Rolling (freshmen), rolling (transfer) **Freshmen** 42% were admitted **Housing** Yes **Expenses** Room & Board $4816 **Undergraduates** 55% women, 40% part-time, 31% 25 or older, 1% Native American, 2% Hispanic American, 5% African American, 1% Asian American/Pacific Islander **The most frequently chosen baccalaureate fields are** business/marketing, education, security and protective services **Academic program** Advanced placement, accelerated degree program, honors program, summer session, adult/continuing education programs, internships **Contact** Ms. Micki Willis, Director of Recruitment and Admissions, Peru State College, PO Box 10, Peru, NE 68421. Phone: 402-872-2221 or toll-free 800-742-4412. Fax: 402-872-2296. E-mail: mwillis@oakmail.peru.edu. Web site: http://www.peru.edu/.

UNION COLLEGE

LINCOLN, NEBRASKA

General Independent Seventh-day Adventist, comprehensive, coed **Entrance** Moderately difficult **Setting** 26-acre suburban campus **Total enrollment** 1,015 **Student-faculty ratio** 13:1 **Application deadline** Rolling (freshmen), rolling (transfer) **Freshmen** 43% were admitted **Housing** Yes **Expenses** Tuition $16,130; Room & Board $5270 **Undergraduates** 56% women, 19% part-time, 11% 25 or older, 1% Native American, 6% Hispanic American, 2% African American, 3% Asian American/Pacific Islander **The most frequently chosen baccalaureate fields are** business/marketing, education, health professions and related sciences **Academic program** English as a second language, advanced placement, accelerated degree program, self-designed majors, honors program, summer session, adult/continuing education programs, internships **Contact** Huda McClelland, Director of Admissions, Union College, 3800 South 48th Street, Lincoln, NE 68506. Phone: 402-486-2504 or toll-free 800-228-4600. Fax: 402-486-2895. E-mail: ucenroll@ucollege.edu. Web site: http://www.ucollege.edu/.

UNIVERSITY OF NEBRASKA AT KEARNEY

KEARNEY, NEBRASKA

General State-supported, comprehensive, coed **Entrance** Moderately difficult **Setting** 235-acre small-town campus **Total enrollment** 6,478 **Student-faculty ratio** 16:1 **Application deadline** Rolling (freshmen), rolling (transfer) **Freshmen** 79% were admitted **Housing** Yes **Expenses** Tuition $5021; Room & Board $6000 **Undergraduates** 53% women, 11% part-time, 9% 25 or older, 0.3% Native American, 4% Hispanic American, 1% African American, 1% Asian American/Pacific Islander **The most frequently chosen baccalaureate fields are** business/marketing, education, security and protective services **Academic program** English as a second language, advanced placement, honors program, summer session, internships **Contact** Mr. Dusty Newton, Director of Admissions, University of Nebraska at Kearney, 905 West 25th Street, Kearney, NE 68849-0001. Phone: 308-865-8702 or toll-free 800-532-7639. Fax: 308-865-8987. E-mail: admissionsug@unk.edu. Web site: http://www.unk.edu/.

UNIVERSITY OF NEBRASKA AT OMAHA

OMAHA, NEBRASKA

General State-supported, university, coed **Entrance** Minimally difficult **Setting** 158-acre urban campus **Total enrollment** 14,156 **Student-faculty ratio** 18:1 **Application deadline** 8/1 (freshmen), 8/1 (transfer) **Freshmen** 86% were admitted **Housing** Yes **Expenses** Tuition $5531; Room & Board $6810 **Undergraduates** 52% women, 24% part-time, 21% 25 or older, 1% Native American, 4% Hispanic American, 6% African American, 3% Asian American/Pacific Islander **The most frequently chosen baccalaureate fields are** business/marketing, education, security and protective services **Academic program** English as a second language, advanced placement, self-designed majors, honors program, summer session, adult/continuing education programs, internships **Contact** Ms. Jolene Adams, Associate Director of Admissions, University of Nebraska at Omaha, 6001 Dodge Street, Omaha,

University of Nebraska at Omaha *(continued)*

NE 68182. Phone: 402-554-2416 or toll-free 800-858-8648. Fax: 402-554-3472. E-mail: jadams@mail.unomaha.edu. Web site: http://www.unomaha.edu/.

UNIVERSITY OF NEBRASKA–LINCOLN

LINCOLN, NEBRASKA

General State-supported, university, coed **Entrance** Moderately difficult **Setting** 623-acre urban campus **Total enrollment** 22,973 **Student-faculty ratio** 19:1 **Application deadline** 5/1 (freshmen), 6/30 (transfer) **Freshmen** 62% were admitted **Housing** Yes **Expenses** Tuition $6215; Room & Board $6523 **Undergraduates** 46% women, 7% part-time, 7% 25 or older, 1% Native American, 3% Hispanic American, 2% African American, 3% Asian American/Pacific Islander **The most frequently chosen baccalaureate fields are** business/marketing, education, engineering **Academic program** English as a second language, advanced placement, accelerated degree program, self-designed majors, honors program, summer session, adult/continuing education programs, internships **Contact** Pat McBride, Director, New Student Enrollment, University of Nebraska–Lincoln, 1410 Q Street, Lincoln, NE 68588-0256. Phone: 402-472-2030 or toll-free 800-742-8800. Fax: 402-472-0670. E-mail: admissions@unl.edu. Web site: http://www.unl.edu/.

UNIVERSITY OF NEBRASKA MEDICAL CENTER

OMAHA, NEBRASKA

General State-supported, upper-level, coed **Entrance** Moderately difficult **Setting** 51-acre urban campus **Total enrollment** 3,128 **Application deadline** Rolling (transfer) **Housing** No **Expenses** Tuition $5165 **Undergraduates** 88% women, 8% part-time, 30% 25 or older, 1% Native American, 3% Hispanic American, 1% African American, 2% Asian American/Pacific Islander **The most frequently chosen baccalaureate field is** health professions and related sciences **Academic program** Accelerated degree program, honors program, summer session, internships **Contact** Ms. Tymaree Tonjes, Administrative Technician, University of Nebraska Medical Center, 084230 Nebraska Medical Center, Omaha, NE 68198-4230. Phone: 402-559-6468 or toll-free 800-626-8431 Ext. 6468. Fax: 402-559-6796. E-mail: ttonjes@unmc.edu. Web site: http://www.unmc.edu/.

WAYNE STATE COLLEGE

WAYNE, NEBRASKA

General State-supported, comprehensive, coed **Entrance** Noncompetitive **Setting** 128-acre small-town campus **Total enrollment** 3,527 **Student-faculty ratio** 19:1 **Application deadline** Rolling (freshmen), rolling (transfer) **Freshmen** 100% were admitted **Housing** Yes **Expenses** Tuition $4322; Room & Board $4800 **Undergraduates** 54% women, 8% part-time, 11% 25 or older, 1% Native American, 2% Hispanic American, 3% African American, 1% Asian American/Pacific Islander **The most frequently chosen baccalaureate fields are** business/marketing, education, security and protective services **Academic program** Advanced placement, self-designed majors, honors program, summer session, adult/continuing education programs, internships **Contact** Ms. Tammy Young, Director of Admissions, Wayne State College, 1111 Main Street, Wayne, NE 68787. Phone: 402-375-7234 or toll-free 800-228-9972. Fax: 402-375-7204. E-mail: admit1@wsc.edu. Web site: http://www.wsc.edu/.

YORK COLLEGE

YORK, NEBRASKA

General Independent, 4-year, coed, affiliated with Church of Christ **Entrance** Moderately difficult **Setting** 44-acre small-town campus **Total enrollment** 402 **Student-faculty ratio** 9:1 **Application deadline** Rolling (freshmen), rolling (transfer) **Freshmen** 57% were admitted **Housing** Yes **Expenses** Tuition $14,000; Room & Board $4500 **Undergraduates** 51% women, 10% part-time, 6% 25 or older, 4% Hispanic American, 4% African American, 2% Asian American/Pacific Islander **The most frequently chosen baccalaureate fields are** business/marketing, education, liberal arts/general studies **Academic program** Advanced placement, honors program, summer session, adult/continuing education programs, internships **Contact** Ms. Judy Rinard, York College, 1125 East 8th Street, York, NE 68467-2699. Phone: 402-363-5627 or toll-free 800-950-9675. Fax: 402-363-5623. E-mail: enroll@york.edu. Web site: http://www.york.edu/.

NEVADA

THE ART INSTITUTE OF LAS VEGAS

HENDERSON, NEVADA

General Proprietary, 4-year, coed **Setting** suburban campus **Contact** Director of Admissions, The Art Institute of Las Vegas, 2350 Corporate Circle, Henderson, NV 89074. Phone: 702-369-9944. Fax: 702-992-8494. Web site: http://www.ailv.artinstitutes.edu/.

DeVRY UNIVERSITY
HENDERSON, NEVADA

General Proprietary, comprehensive, coed **Entrance** Minimally difficult **Total enrollment** 176 **Student-faculty ratio** 52:1 **Application deadline** Rolling (freshmen), rolling (transfer) **Housing** No **Expenses** Tuition $13,890 **Undergraduates** 43% women, 55% part-time, 61% 25 or older, 22% Hispanic American, 20% African American, 14% Asian American/Pacific Islander **The most frequently chosen baccalaureate field is** business/marketing **Academic program** Advanced placement, accelerated degree program, summer session, adult/continuing education programs **Contact** Admissions Office, DeVry University, 2490 Paseo Verde Parkway, Suite 150, Henderson, NV 89074-7120. Web site: http://www.devry.edu/.

MORRISON UNIVERSITY
RENO, NEVADA

General Proprietary, comprehensive, coed **Contact** Mr. Charles Timinsky, Director of Enrollment, Morrison University, 10315 Professional Circle, Suite 201, Reno, NV 89521. Phone: 775-850-0700 Ext. 101 or toll-free 800-369-6144. Fax: 775-850-0711. E-mail: ctiminsky@morrison.neumont.edu. Web site: http://www.morrison.neumont.edu/.

NEVADA STATE COLLEGE AT HENDERSON
HENDERSON, NEVADA

General State-supported, 4-year, coed **Contact** Ms. Patricia Ring, Registrar, Nevada State College at Henderson, 1125 Nevada State Drive, Henderson, NV 89015. Phone: 702-992-2024. Fax: 702-992-2111. E-mail: patricia.ring@nsc.nevada.edu. Web site: http://www.nsc.nevada.edu/.

SIERRA NEVADA COLLEGE
INCLINE VILLAGE, NEVADA

General Independent, comprehensive, coed **Contact** Matt Delekta, James McMaster, Dean of Enrollment Services and Registrar, Sierra Nevada College, 999 Tahoe Boulevard, Incline Village, NV 89451. Phone: 775-831-1314 Ext. 7440 or toll-free 775-831-1314. Fax: 775-831-6223. E-mail: admissions@sierranevada.edu. Web site: http://www.sierranevada.edu/.

UNIVERSITY OF NEVADA, LAS VEGAS
LAS VEGAS, NEVADA

General State-supported, university, coed **Entrance** Moderately difficult **Setting** 358-acre urban campus **Total enrollment** 28,008 **Student-faculty ratio** 18:1 **Application deadline** 7/20 (freshmen) **Freshmen** 68% were admitted **Housing** Yes **Expenses** Tuition $4583; Room & Board $9808 **Undergraduates** 56% women, 29% part-time, 27% 25 or older, 1% Native American, 13% Hispanic American, 9% African American, 17% Asian American/Pacific Islander **The most frequently chosen baccalaureate fields are** business/marketing, education, psychology **Academic program** English as a second language, advanced placement, accelerated degree program, self-designed majors, honors program, summer session, adult/continuing education programs, internships **Contact** Ms. Kristi Rodriguez, Director for Undergraduate Recruitment, University of Nevada, Las Vegas, 4505 Maryland Parkway, Box 451021, Las Vegas, NV 89154-1021. Phone: 702-895-1862. Fax: 702-774-8008. E-mail: undergraduate.recruitment@unlv.edu. Web site: http://www.unlv.edu/.

UNIVERSITY OF NEVADA, RENO
RENO, NEVADA

General State-supported, university, coed **Entrance** Moderately difficult **Setting** 200-acre urban campus **Total enrollment** 16,681 **Student-faculty ratio** 19:1 **Application deadline** Rolling (freshmen), rolling (transfer) **Freshmen** 88% were admitted **Housing** Yes **Expenses** Tuition $4411; Room & Board $9989 **Undergraduates** 53% women, 22% part-time, 15% 25 or older, 1% Native American, 8% Hispanic American, 3% African American, 7% Asian American/Pacific Islander **The most frequently chosen baccalaureate fields are** business/marketing, health professions and related sciences, social sciences **Academic program** English as a second language, advanced placement, honors program, summer session, adult/continuing education programs, internships **Contact** Dr. Melissa Choroszy, Associate Vice President of Enrollment Services, University of Nevada, Reno, Mail Stop 120, Reno, NV 89557. Phone: 775-784-4700 Ext. 2006 or toll-free 866-263-8232. Fax: 775-784-4283. E-mail: asknevada@unr.edu. Web site: http://www.unr.edu/.

UNIVERSITY OF PHOENIX–LAS VEGAS CAMPUS
LAS VEGAS, NEVADA

General Proprietary, comprehensive, coed **Contact** Ms. Evelyn Gaskin, Registrar/Executive Director, University of Phoenix–Las Vegas Campus, 4615 East Elwood Street, Mail Stop AA-K101, Phoenix, AZ 85040-1958. Phone: 480-557-3301 or toll-free 800-776-4867 (in-state); 800-228-7240 (out-of-state). Fax: 480-643-1020.

University of Phoenix–Las Vegas Campus *(continued)*

E-mail: evelyn.gaskin@phoenix.edu. Web site: http://www.phoenix.edu/.

UNIVERSITY OF PHOENIX–NORTHERN NEVADA CAMPUS
RENO, NEVADA

Contact Ms. Evelyn Gaskin, Registrar/Executive Director, University of Phoenix–Northern Nevada Campus, 4615 East Elwood Street, Mail Stop AA-K101, Phoenix, AZ 85040-1958. Phone: 480-557-3301. Fax: 480-643-1020. E-mail: evelyn.gaskin@phoenix.edu. Web site: http://www.phoenix.edu/.

NEW HAMPSHIRE

CHESTER COLLEGE OF NEW ENGLAND
CHESTER, NEW HAMPSHIRE

General Independent, 4-year, coed **Contact** Mrs. Pamela Adie, Director of Admissions, Chester College of New England, 40 Chester Street, Chester, NH 03036. Phone: 603-887-7400 or toll-free 800-974-6372. Fax: 603-887-1777. E-mail: admissions@chestercollege.edu. Web site: http://www.chestercollege.edu/.

COLBY-SAWYER COLLEGE
NEW LONDON, NEW HAMPSHIRE

General Independent, 4-year, coed **Entrance** Moderately difficult **Setting** 200-acre small-town campus **Total enrollment** 948 **Student-faculty ratio** 11:1 **Application deadline** 4/1 (freshmen), 8/1 (transfer) **Freshmen** 87% were admitted **Housing** Yes **Expenses** Tuition $29,620; Room & Board $10,340 **Undergraduates** 65% women, 2% part-time, 2% 25 or older, 0.4% Native American, 1% Hispanic American, 1% African American, 1% Asian American/Pacific Islander **The most frequently chosen baccalaureate fields are** health professions and related sciences, business/marketing, psychology **Academic program** English as a second language, advanced placement, accelerated degree program, honors program, internships **Contact** Director of Admissions and Financial Aid, Colby-Sawyer College, 541 Main Street, New London, NH 03257-4648. Phone: 603-526-3700 or toll-free 800-272-1015. Fax: 603-526-3452. E-mail: admissions@colby-sawyer.edu. Web site: http://www.colby-sawyer.edu/.

DANIEL WEBSTER COLLEGE
NASHUA, NEW HAMPSHIRE

General Independent, comprehensive, coed **Entrance** Moderately difficult **Setting** 50-acre suburban campus **Total enrollment** 930 **Student-faculty ratio** 14:1 **Application deadline** Rolling (freshmen), rolling (transfer) **Freshmen** 77% were admitted **Housing** Yes **Expenses** Tuition $27,282; Room & Board $9369 **Undergraduates** 24% women, 14% part-time, 3% Hispanic American, 4% African American, 1% Asian American/Pacific Islander **Academic program** Advanced placement, accelerated degree program, summer session, adult/continuing education programs, internships **Contact** Mr. Daniel Monahan, Dean of Admissions and Financial Assistance, Daniel Webster College, 20 University Drive, Nashua, NH 03063. Phone: 603-577-6600 or toll-free 800-325-6876. Fax: 603-577-6001. E-mail: admissions@dwc.edu. Web site: http://www.dwc.edu/.

DANIEL WEBSTER COLLEGE–PORTSMOUTH CAMPUS
PORTSMOUTH, NEW HAMPSHIRE

Contact Daniel Webster College–Portsmouth Campus, 119 International Drive, Pease International Tradeport, Portsmouth, NH 03801. Phone: toll-free 800-794-6188. Web site: http://www.dwc.edu/gcde/portsmouth/.

DARTMOUTH COLLEGE
HANOVER, NEW HAMPSHIRE

General Independent, university, coed **Entrance** Most difficult **Setting** 265-acre small-town campus **Total enrollment** 5,849 **Student-faculty ratio** 8:1 **Application deadline** 1/1 (freshmen), 3/1 (transfer) **Freshmen** 15% were admitted **Housing** Yes **Expenses** Tuition $35,178; Room & Board $10,305 **Undergraduates** 50% women, 1% part-time, 4% Native American, 6% Hispanic American, 7% African American, 14% Asian American/Pacific Islander **The most frequently chosen baccalaureate fields are** history, psychology, social sciences **Academic program** Advanced placement, self-designed majors, honors program, summer session, internships **Contact** Maria Laskaris, Dean of Admissions and Financial Aid, Dartmouth College, 6016 McNutt Hall, Hanover, NH 03755. Phone: 603-646-2875 or toll-free 603-646-2875. E-mail: admissions.office@dartmouth.edu. Web site: http://www.dartmouth.edu/.

FRANKLIN PIERCE UNIVERSITY
RINDGE, NEW HAMPSHIRE

General Independent, comprehensive, coed **Contact** Office of Admissions, Franklin Pierce

University, 20 College Road, Rindge, NH 03461. Phone: 603-899-4050 or toll-free 800-437-0048. Fax: 603-899-4394. E-mail: admissions@fpc.edu. Web site: http://www.franklinpierce.edu/.

GRANITE STATE COLLEGE
CONCORD, NEW HAMPSHIRE

General State and locally supported, 4-year, coed **Entrance** Noncompetitive **Setting** small-town campus **Total enrollment** 1,550 **Student-faculty ratio** 10:1 **Application deadline** Rolling (freshmen), rolling (transfer) **Freshmen** 100% were admitted **Housing** No **Expenses** Tuition $5523 **Undergraduates** 77% women, 62% part-time, 81% 25 or older, 1% Native American, 1% Hispanic American, 1% African American, 1% Asian American/Pacific Islander **The most frequently chosen baccalaureate fields are** business/marketing, interdisciplinary studies, liberal arts/general studies **Academic program** Advanced placement, accelerated degree program, self-designed majors, summer session, adult/continuing education programs, internships **Contact** Ms. Tessa McDonnell, Dean of Learner Services, Granite State College, 8 Old Suncook Road, Concord, NH 03301. Phone: 603-513-1391 or toll-free 800-582-7248 Ext. 313. Fax: 603-513-1386. E-mail: tessa.mcdonnell@granite.edu. Web site: http://www.granite.edu/.

KEENE STATE COLLEGE
KEENE, NEW HAMPSHIRE

General State-supported, comprehensive, coed **Entrance** Moderately difficult **Setting** 160-acre small-town campus **Total enrollment** 5,135 **Student-faculty ratio** 18:1 **Application deadline** 4/1 (freshmen), rolling (transfer) **Freshmen** 73% were admitted **Housing** Yes **Expenses** Tuition $8298; Room & Board $7460 **Undergraduates** 57% women, 9% part-time, 8% 25 or older, 0.04% Native American, 1% Hispanic American, 1% African American, 0.5% Asian American/Pacific Islander **The most frequently chosen baccalaureate fields are** education, engineering technologies, psychology **Academic program** English as a second language, advanced placement, self-designed majors, honors program, summer session, internships **Contact** Ms. Margaret Richmond, Director of Admissions, Keene State College, 229 Main Street, Keene, NH 03435-2604. Phone: 603-358-2273 or toll-free 800-KSC-1909. Fax: 603-358-2767. E-mail: admissions@keene.edu. Web site: http://www.keene.edu/.

MAGDALEN COLLEGE
WARNER, NEW HAMPSHIRE

Contact Mr. Justin Fout, Admissions Counselor, Magdalen College, 511 Kearsarge Mountain Road, Warner, NH 03278. Phone: 603-456-2656 or toll-free 877-498-1723. Fax: 603-456-2660. E-mail: admissions@magdalen.edu. Web site: http://www.magdalen.edu/.

NEW ENGLAND COLLEGE
HENNIKER, NEW HAMPSHIRE

General Independent, comprehensive, coed **Entrance** Moderately difficult **Setting** 225-acre small-town campus **Total enrollment** 1,460 **Student-faculty ratio** 13:1 **Application deadline** Rolling (freshmen), rolling (transfer) **Freshmen** 70% were admitted **Housing** Yes **Expenses** Tuition $26,470; Room & Board $9278 **Undergraduates** 47% women, 3% part-time, 5% 25 or older, 0.2% Native American, 2% Hispanic American, 3% African American, 1% Asian American/Pacific Islander **The most frequently chosen baccalaureate fields are** business/marketing, parks and recreation, psychology **Academic program** English as a second language, advanced placement, self-designed majors, honors program, summer session, adult/continuing education programs, internships **Contact** Diane Raymond, Director of Admissions, New England College, 24 Bridge Street, Henniker, NH 03242. Phone: 603-428-2223 or toll-free 800-521-7642. Fax: 603-428-7230. E-mail: admission@nec.edu. Web site: http://www.nec.edu/.

NEW HAMPSHIRE INSTITUTE OF ART
MANCHESTER, NEW HAMPSHIRE

General Proprietary, 4-year, coed **Contact** Ms. Amanda Abbott, Admissions Administrator, New Hampshire Institute of Art, 148 Concord Street, Manchester, NH 03104-4158. Phone: 866-241-4918 Ext. 575 or toll-free 866-241-4918. E-mail: admissions@nhia.edu. Web site: http://www.nhia.edu/.

PLYMOUTH STATE UNIVERSITY
PLYMOUTH, NEW HAMPSHIRE

General State-supported, comprehensive, coed **Entrance** Moderately difficult **Setting** 170-acre small-town campus **Total enrollment** 6,290 **Student-faculty ratio** 17:1 **Application deadline** 4/1 (freshmen), 4/1 (transfer) **Freshmen** 66% were admitted **Housing** Yes **Expenses** Tuition $8424; Room & Board $8150 **Undergraduates** 47% women, 5% part-time, 4% 25 or older, 0.2% Native American, 1% Hispanic American, 1% African American, 1% Asian American/Pacific Islander **The most frequently chosen baccalaureate fields are** business/marketing, education, visual and performing arts **Academic program** Advanced placement, accelerated degree program, self-designed majors, honors program, summer session, internships **Contact** Mr. Eugene Fahey,

Plymouth State University *(continued)*

Senior Associate Director of Admission, Plymouth State University, 17 High Street, MSC #52, Plymouth, NH 03264-1595. Phone: toll-free 800-842-6900. Fax: 603-535-2714. E-mail: plymouthadmit@plymouth.edu. Web site: http://www.plymouth.edu/.

RIVIER COLLEGE

NASHUA, NEW HAMPSHIRE

General Independent Roman Catholic, comprehensive, coed **Contact** David A. Boisvert, Vice President of Enrollment, Rivier College, 420 South Main Street, Nashua, NH 03060. Phone: 603-897-8507 or toll-free 800-44RIVIER. Fax: 603-891-1799. E-mail: rivadmit@rivier.edu. Web site: http://www.rivier.edu/.

SAINT ANSELM COLLEGE

MANCHESTER, NEW HAMPSHIRE

Contact Ms. Nancy Davis Griffin, Director of Admission, Saint Anselm College, 100 Saint Anselm Drive, Manchester, NH 03102-1310. Phone: 603-641-7500 or toll-free 888-4ANSELM. Fax: 603-641-7550. E-mail: admission@anselm.edu. Web site: http://www.anselm.edu/.

SOUTHERN NEW HAMPSHIRE UNIVERSITY

MANCHESTER, NEW HAMPSHIRE

General Independent, comprehensive, coed **Entrance** Moderately difficult **Setting** 288-acre suburban campus **Total enrollment** 4,340 **Student-faculty ratio** 15:1 **Application deadline** Rolling (freshmen), rolling (transfer) **Freshmen** 65% were admitted **Housing** Yes **Expenses** Tuition $23,346; Room & Board $8970 **Undergraduates** 55% women, 2% part-time, 3% 25 or older, 0.4% Native American, 2% Hispanic American, 1% African American, 1% Asian American/Pacific Islander **The most frequently chosen baccalaureate fields are** business/marketing, education, psychology **Academic program** English as a second language, advanced placement, accelerated degree program, honors program, summer session, adult/continuing education programs, internships **Contact** Mr. Steve Soba, Director of Admission, Southern New Hampshire University, 2500 North River Road, Manchester, NH 03106-1045. Phone: 603-645-9611 Ext. 9633 or toll-free 800-642-4968. Fax: 603-645-9693. E-mail: admission@snhu.edu. Web site: http://www.snhu.edu/.

THOMAS MORE COLLEGE OF LIBERAL ARTS

MERRIMACK, NEW HAMPSHIRE

General Independent, 4-year, coed, affiliated with Roman Catholic Church **Entrance** Moderately difficult **Setting** 14-acre small-town campus **Total enrollment** 99 **Student-faculty ratio** 14:1 **Application deadline** Rolling (freshmen), rolling (transfer) **Housing** Yes **Expenses** Tuition $13,200; Room & Board $8800 **Undergraduates** 49% women, 3% 25 or older **The most frequently chosen baccalaureate fields are** English, philosophy and religious studies, social sciences **Contact** Teddy Sifert, Director of Admissions, Thomas More College of Liberal Arts, 6 Manchester Street, Merrimack, NH 03054-4818. Phone: toll-free 800-880-8308. Fax: 603-880-9280. E-mail: admissions@thomasmorecollege.edu. Web site: http://www.thomasmorecollege.edu/.

UNIVERSITY OF NEW HAMPSHIRE

DURHAM, NEW HAMPSHIRE

General State-supported, university, coed **Entrance** Moderately difficult **Setting** 2,600-acre small-town campus **Total enrollment** 15,053 **Student-faculty ratio** 18:1 **Application deadline** 2/1 (freshmen), 3/1 (transfer) **Freshmen** 59% were admitted **Housing** Yes **Expenses** Tuition $11,070; Room & Board $8168 **Undergraduates** 56% women, 5% part-time, 3% 25 or older, 0.3% Native American, 2% Hispanic American, 1% African American, 2% Asian American/Pacific Islander **The most frequently chosen baccalaureate fields are** business/marketing, health professions and related sciences, social sciences **Academic program** English as a second language, advanced placement, self-designed majors, honors program, summer session, adult/continuing education programs, internships **Contact** Mr. Robert McGann, Director of Admissions, University of New Hampshire, Durham, NH 03824. Phone: 603-862-1360. Fax: 603-862-0077. E-mail: admissions@unh.edu. Web site: http://www.unh.edu/.

UNIVERSITY OF NEW HAMPSHIRE AT MANCHESTER

MANCHESTER, NEW HAMPSHIRE

General State-supported, comprehensive, coed **Entrance** Moderately difficult **Setting** 800-acre urban campus **Total enrollment** 998 **Student-faculty ratio** 12:1 **Application deadline** 6/15 (freshmen), 6/15 (transfer) **Freshmen** 66% were admitted **Housing** No **Expenses** Tuition $8595 **Undergraduates** 53% women, 44% part-time, 0.1% Native American, 3% Hispanic American, 1% African American, 2% Asian American/

Pacific Islander **The most frequently chosen baccalaureate fields are** business/marketing, communications/journalism, engineering technologies **Academic program** Advanced placement, self-designed majors, summer session, adult/continuing education programs, internships **Contact** Ms. Susan Miller, Administrative Assistant, University of New Hampshire at Manchester, 400 Commercial Street, Manchester, NH 03101. Phone: 603-641-4150. Fax: 603-641-4125. E-mail: unhm@unh.edu. Web site: http://www.unhm.unh.edu/.

NEW JERSEY

BETH MEDRASH GOVOHA
LAKEWOOD, NEW JERSEY

Contact Rabbi Yehuda Jacobs, Director of Admissions, Beth Medrash Govoha, 617 Sixth Street, Lakewood, NJ 08701-2797. Phone: 908-367-1060.

BLOOMFIELD COLLEGE
BLOOMFIELD, NEW JERSEY

General Independent, 4-year, coed, affiliated with Presbyterian Church (U.S.A.) **Entrance** Moderately difficult **Setting** 12-acre suburban campus **Total enrollment** 2,056 **Student-faculty ratio** 14:1 **Application deadline** 7/1 (freshmen), 8/1 (transfer) **Freshmen** 41% were admitted **Housing** Yes **Expenses** Tuition $18,000; Room & Board $8650 **Undergraduates** 66% women, 23% part-time, 34% 25 or older, 0.1% Native American, 20% Hispanic American, 49% African American, 4% Asian American/Pacific Islander **The most frequently chosen baccalaureate fields are** business/marketing, psychology, social sciences **Academic program** English as a second language, advanced placement, accelerated degree program, self-designed majors, honors program, summer session, internships **Contact** Mr. Adam Castro, Director of Admissions, Bloomfield College, Office of Enrollment Management and Admission, Bloomfield, NJ 07003-9981. Phone: 973-748-9000 or toll-free 800-848-4555 Ext. 230. Fax: 973-748-0916. E-mail: admission@bloomfield.edu. Web site: http://www.bloomfield.edu/.

CALDWELL COLLEGE
CALDWELL, NEW JERSEY

General Independent Roman Catholic, comprehensive, coed **Contact** Ms. Kathryn Reilly, Director of Admissions, Caldwell College, 9 Ryerson Avenue, Caldwell, NJ 07006. Phone: 973-618-3226 or toll-free 888-864-9516. Fax: 973-618-3600. E-mail: admissions@caldwell.edu. Web site: http://www.caldwell.edu/.

CENTENARY COLLEGE
HACKETTSTOWN, NEW JERSEY

General Independent, comprehensive, coed, affiliated with United Methodist Church **Entrance** Moderately difficult **Setting** 42-acre suburban campus **Total enrollment** 3,028 **Student-faculty ratio** 16:1 **Application deadline** Rolling (freshmen), rolling (transfer) **Freshmen** 70% were admitted **Housing** Yes **Expenses** Tuition $24,100; Room & Board $8900 **Undergraduates** 66% women, 12% part-time, 27% 25 or older, 0.2% Native American, 7% Hispanic American, 9% African American, 2% Asian American/Pacific Islander **The most frequently chosen baccalaureate fields are** business/marketing, security and protective services, social sciences **Academic program** English as a second language, advanced placement, accelerated degree program, self-designed majors, honors program, summer session, adult/continuing education programs, internships **Contact** Ms. Diane Finnan, Vice President for Enrollment Management and Strategic Branding, Centenary College, 400 Jefferson Street, Hackettstown, NJ 07840-2100. Phone: 908-852-1400 Ext. 2217 or toll-free 800-236-8679. Fax: 908-852-3454. E-mail: admissions@centenarycollege.edu. Web site: http://www.centenarycollege.edu/.

THE COLLEGE OF NEW JERSEY
EWING, NEW JERSEY

General State-supported, comprehensive, coed **Entrance** Very difficult **Setting** 255-acre suburban campus **Total enrollment** 6,964 **Student-faculty ratio** 13:1 **Application deadline** 2/15 (freshmen), 2/15 (transfer) **Freshmen** 47% were admitted **Housing** Yes **Expenses** Tuition $11,307; Room & Board $9242 **Undergraduates** 58% women, 3% part-time, 4% 25 or older, 0.1% Native American, 8% Hispanic American, 6% African American, 8% Asian American/Pacific Islander **The most frequently chosen baccalaureate fields are** business/marketing, education, psychology **Academic program** Advanced placement, self-designed majors, honors program, summer session, internships **Contact** Ms. Lisa Angeloni, Dean of Admissions, The College of New Jersey, PO Box 7718, Ewing, NJ 08628. Phone: 609-771-2131 or toll-free 800-624-0967. Fax: 609-637-5174. E-mail: admiss@tcnj.edu. Web site: http://www.tcnj.edu/.

COLLEGE OF SAINT ELIZABETH
MORRISTOWN, NEW JERSEY

General Independent Roman Catholic, comprehensive, undergraduate: women only; graduate:

College of Saint Elizabeth *(continued)*

coed **Entrance** Moderately difficult **Setting** 188-acre suburban campus **Total enrollment** 2,044 **Student-faculty ratio** 12:1 **Application deadline** 8/15 (freshmen), rolling (transfer) **Freshmen** 82% were admitted **Housing** Yes **Expenses** Tuition $22,547; Room & Board $9990 **Undergraduates** 41% part-time, 40% 25 or older, 0.3% Native American, 17% Hispanic American, 15% African American, 4% Asian American/Pacific Islander **The most frequently chosen baccalaureate fields are** health professions and related sciences, business/marketing, psychology **Academic program** English as a second language, advanced placement, accelerated degree program, self-designed majors, honors program, summer session, internships **Contact** Ms. Donna Tatarka, Dean of Admissions, College of Saint Elizabeth, 2 Convent Road, Morristown, NJ 07960-6989. Phone: 973-290-4700 or toll-free 800-210-7900. Fax: 973-290-4710. E-mail: apply@csa.edu. Web site: http://www.cse.edu/.

DeVRY UNIVERSITY
NORTH BRUNSWICK, NEW JERSEY

General Proprietary, 4-year, coed **Entrance** Minimally difficult **Setting** 10-acre urban campus **Total enrollment** 1,382 **Student-faculty ratio** 14:1 **Application deadline** Rolling (freshmen), rolling (transfer) **Housing** No **Expenses** Tuition $14,660 **Undergraduates** 26% women, 36% part-time, 39% 25 or older, 0.4% Native American, 20% Hispanic American, 24% African American, 8% Asian American/Pacific Islander **The most frequently chosen baccalaureate fields are** business/marketing, computer and information sciences, engineering technologies **Academic program** Advanced placement, accelerated degree program, summer session, adult/continuing education programs **Contact** Admissions Office, DeVry University, 630 US Highway 1, North Brunswick, NJ 08902-3362. Web site: http://www.devry.edu/.

DREW UNIVERSITY
MADISON, NEW JERSEY

General Independent, university, coed, affiliated with United Methodist Church **Entrance** Moderately difficult **Setting** 186-acre suburban campus **Total enrollment** 2,640 **Student-faculty ratio** 11:1 **Application deadline** 2/15 (freshmen), 8/1 (transfer) **Freshmen** 77% were admitted **Housing** Yes **Expenses** Tuition $34,790; Room & Board $9476 **Undergraduates** 61% women, 4% part-time, 2% 25 or older, 0.3% Native American, 7% Hispanic American, 6% African American, 5% Asian American/Pacific Islander **The most frequently chosen baccalaureate fields are** psychology, social sciences, visual and performing arts **Academic program** Advanced placement, accelerated degree program, self-designed majors, honors program, summer session, adult/continuing education programs, internships **Contact** Ms. Mary Beth Carey, Dean of Admissions and Financial Assistance, Drew University, 36 Madison Avenue, Madison, NJ 07940-1493. Phone: 973-408-3739. Fax: 973-408-3068. E-mail: cadm@drew.edu. Web site: http://www.drew.edu/.

FAIRLEIGH DICKINSON UNIVERSITY, COLLEGE AT FLORHAM
MADISON, NEW JERSEY

General Independent, comprehensive, coed **Entrance** Moderately difficult **Setting** 178-acre suburban campus **Total enrollment** 3,463 **Application deadline** Rolling (freshmen) **Freshmen** 63% were admitted **Housing** Yes **Expenses** Tuition $28,228; Room & Board $9982 **Undergraduates** 53% women, 10% part-time, 8% 25 or older, 0.4% Native American, 7% Hispanic American, 8% African American, 3% Asian American/Pacific Islander **The most frequently chosen baccalaureate fields are** business/marketing, psychology, visual and performing arts **Academic program** Advanced placement, accelerated degree program, honors program, summer session, adult/continuing education programs, internships **Contact** Mr. Jonathan Wexler, Fairleigh Dickinson University, College at Florham, 285 Madison Avenue, M-MS1-03, Madison, NJ 07940. Phone: 201-692-7304 or toll-free 800-338-8803. Fax: 201-692-7319. E-mail: globaleducation@fdu.edu. Web site: http://www.fdu.edu/.

FAIRLEIGH DICKINSON UNIVERSITY, METROPOLITAN CAMPUS
TEANECK, NEW JERSEY

General Independent, comprehensive, coed **Entrance** Moderately difficult **Setting** 88-acre suburban campus **Total enrollment** 8,658 **Application deadline** Rolling (freshmen) **Freshmen** 49% were admitted **Housing** Yes **Expenses** Tuition $26,232; Room & Board $10,328 **Undergraduates** 52% women, 63% part-time, 39% 25 or older, 0.3% Native American, 18% Hispanic American, 16% African American, 6% Asian American/Pacific Islander **The most frequently chosen baccalaureate fields are** business/marketing, health professions and related sciences, liberal arts/general studies **Academic program** English as a second language, advanced placement, accelerated degree program, self-designed majors, honors program, summer session, adult/continuing education programs, internships **Contact** Mr. Jonathan Wexler, Associate Vice President of Enrollment Management, Fairleigh

Dickinson University, Metropolitan Campus, 1000 River Road, H-DH3-10, Teaneck, NJ 07666. Phone: 201-692-7304 or toll-free 800-338-8803. Fax: 201-692-7319. E-mail: globaleducation@fdu.edu. Web site: http://www.fdu.edu/.

FELICIAN COLLEGE
LODI, NEW JERSEY

General Independent Roman Catholic, comprehensive, coed **Entrance** Moderately difficult **Setting** 37-acre suburban campus **Total enrollment** 1,980 **Student-faculty ratio** 11:1 **Application deadline** Rolling (freshmen), rolling (transfer) **Freshmen** 61% were admitted **Housing** Yes **Expenses** Tuition $23,500; Room & Board $8200 **Undergraduates** 78% women, 22% part-time, 32% 25 or older, 0.5% Native American, 17% Hispanic American, 15% African American, 11% Asian American/Pacific Islander **The most frequently chosen baccalaureate fields are** health professions and related sciences, personal and culinary services, science technologies **Academic program** English as a second language, advanced placement, accelerated degree program, self-designed majors, honors program, summer session, adult/continuing education programs, internships **Contact** College Admissions Office, Felician College, 262 South Main Street, Lodi, NJ 07644-2117. Phone: 201-559-6187. Fax: 201-559-6188. E-mail: admissions@felician.edu. Web site: http://www.felician.edu/.

GEORGIAN COURT UNIVERSITY
LAKEWOOD, NEW JERSEY

General Independent Roman Catholic, comprehensive, undergraduate: women only; graduate: coed **Entrance** Moderately difficult **Setting** 150-acre suburban campus **Total enrollment** 3,045 **Student-faculty ratio** 14:1 **Application deadline** 8/1 (freshmen), 8/1 (transfer) **Freshmen** 77% were admitted **Housing** Yes **Expenses** Tuition $22,078; Room & Board $8136 **Undergraduates** 28% part-time, 32% 25 or older, 0.2% Native American, 7% Hispanic American, 7% African American, 1% Asian American/Pacific Islander **The most frequently chosen baccalaureate fields are** education, business/marketing, psychology **Academic program** English as a second language, advanced placement, accelerated degree program, honors program, summer session, adult/continuing education programs, internships **Contact** Ms. Kathie Gallant, Director of Admissions, Georgian Court University, 900 Lakewood Avenue, Lakewood, NJ 08701-2697. Phone: 732-987-2760 or toll-free 800-458-8422. Fax: 732-987-2000. E-mail: admissions@georgian.edu. Web site: http://www.georgian.edu/.

KEAN UNIVERSITY
UNION, NEW JERSEY

General State-supported, comprehensive, coed **Entrance** Moderately difficult **Setting** 150-acre suburban campus **Total enrollment** 13,394 **Student-faculty ratio** 15:1 **Application deadline** 5/31 (freshmen), 8/1 (transfer) **Freshmen** 67% were admitted **Housing** Yes **Expenses** Tuition $8505; Room & Board $9190 **Undergraduates** 63% women, 24% part-time, 28% 25 or older, 0.2% Native American, 20% Hispanic American, 20% African American, 6% Asian American/Pacific Islander **The most frequently chosen baccalaureate fields are** business/marketing, education, psychology **Academic program** English as a second language, advanced placement, accelerated degree program, honors program, summer session, adult/continuing education programs, internships **Contact** Mr. Audley Bridges, Director of Undergraduate Admissions, Kean University, 1000 Morris Avenue, Union, NJ 07083. Phone: 908-737-7100. Fax: 908-737-7105. E-mail: admitme@kean.edu. Web site: http://www.kean.edu/.

MONMOUTH UNIVERSITY
WEST LONG BRANCH, NEW JERSEY

General Independent, comprehensive, coed **Entrance** Moderately difficult **Setting** 156-acre suburban campus **Total enrollment** 6,494 **Student-faculty ratio** 15:1 **Application deadline** 3/1 (freshmen), 7/15 (transfer) **Freshmen** 57% were admitted **Housing** Yes **Expenses** Tuition $23,034; Room & Board $8904 **Undergraduates** 58% women, 9% part-time, 9% 25 or older, 0.2% Native American, 5% Hispanic American, 4% African American, 2% Asian American/Pacific Islander **The most frequently chosen baccalaureate fields are** business/marketing, communications/journalism, education **Academic program** Advanced placement, accelerated degree program, self-designed majors, honors program, summer session, internships **Contact** Ms. Lauren Cifelli, Director of Undergraduate Admission, Monmouth University, 400 Cedar Avenue, West Long Branch, NJ 07764-1898. Phone: 732-571-3456 or toll-free 800-543-9671. Fax: 732-263-5166. E-mail: admission@monmouth.edu. Web site: http://www.monmouth.edu/.

MONTCLAIR STATE UNIVERSITY
MONTCLAIR, NEW JERSEY

General State-supported, comprehensive, coed **Entrance** Moderately difficult **Setting** 275-acre suburban campus **Total enrollment** 16,736 **Student-faculty ratio** 17:1 **Application deadline** 3/1 (freshmen), 6/15 (transfer) **Freshmen**

Montclair State University *(continued)*

57% were admitted **Housing** Yes **Expenses** Tuition $8895; Room & Board $9500 **Undergraduates** 62% women, 16% part-time, 17% 25 or older, 0.2% Native American, 19% Hispanic American, 10% African American, 6% Asian American/Pacific Islander **The most frequently chosen baccalaureate fields are** business/marketing, family and consumer sciences, psychology **Academic program** English as a second language, advanced placement, accelerated degree program, honors program, summer session, adult/continuing education programs, internships **Contact** Director of Admissions, Montclair State University, One Normal Avenue, Montclair, NJ 07043-1624. Phone: 973-655-5116 or toll-free 800-331-9205. Fax: 973-655-7700. E-mail: undergraduate.admissions@montclair.edu. Web site: http://www.montclair.edu/.

NEW JERSEY CITY UNIVERSITY
JERSEY CITY, NEW JERSEY

General State-supported, comprehensive, coed **Entrance** Moderately difficult **Setting** 46-acre urban campus **Total enrollment** 8,437 **Student-faculty ratio** 13:1 **Application deadline** 4/1 (freshmen), rolling (transfer) **Freshmen** 48% were admitted **Housing** Yes **Expenses** Tuition $8154; Room & Board $8558 **Undergraduates** 62% women, 29% part-time, 34% 25 or older, 0.1% Native American, 35% Hispanic American, 19% African American, 7% Asian American/Pacific Islander **The most frequently chosen baccalaureate fields are** business/marketing, psychology, security and protective services **Academic program** English as a second language, advanced placement, accelerated degree program, honors program, summer session, adult/continuing education programs, internships **Contact** Ms. Carmen Panlilio, New Jersey City University, 2039 Kennedy Boulevard, Jersey City, NJ 07305-1597. Phone: 201-200-3234 or toll-free 888-441-NJCU. E-mail: admissions@nicu.edu. Web site: http://www.njcu.edu/.

NEW JERSEY INSTITUTE OF TECHNOLOGY
NEWARK, NEW JERSEY

General State-supported, university, coed **Entrance** Moderately difficult **Setting** 45-acre urban campus **Total enrollment** 8,288 **Student-faculty ratio** 12:1 **Application deadline** 4/1 (freshmen), 6/1 (transfer) **Freshmen** 64% were admitted **Housing** Yes **Expenses** Tuition $11,350; Room & Board $9108 **Undergraduates** 20% women, 22% part-time, 17% 25 or older, 1% Native American, 17% Hispanic American, 10% African American, 20% Asian American/Pacific Islander **The most frequently chosen baccalaureate fields are** computer and information sciences, engineering, engineering technologies **Academic program** English as a second language, advanced placement, accelerated degree program, honors program, summer session, adult/continuing education programs, internships **Contact** Ms. Kathy Kelly, Director of Admissions, New Jersey Institute of Technology, University Heights, Newark, NJ 07102-1982. Phone: 973-596-3300 or toll-free 800-925-NJIT. Fax: 973-596-3461. E-mail: admissions@njit.edu. Web site: http://www.njit.edu/.

PRINCETON UNIVERSITY
PRINCETON, NEW JERSEY

General Independent, university, coed **Entrance** Most difficult **Setting** 600-acre suburban campus **Total enrollment** 7,334 **Student-faculty ratio** 8:1 **Application deadline** 1/1 (freshmen) **Freshmen** 10% were admitted **Housing** Yes **Expenses** Tuition $34,290; Room & Board $11,405 **Undergraduates** 47% women, 1% part-time, 1% Native American, 8% Hispanic American, 9% African American, 14% Asian American/Pacific Islander **The most frequently chosen baccalaureate fields are** engineering, history, social sciences **Academic program** Advanced placement, self-designed majors, adult/continuing education programs **Contact** Ms. Janet Rapelye, Dean of Admission, Princeton University, PO Box 430, Princeton, NJ 08542-0430. Phone: 609-258-0881. Fax: 609-258-6743. E-mail: uaoffice@princeton.edu. Web site: http://www.princeton.edu/.

RABBI JACOB JOSEPH SCHOOL
EDISON, NEW JERSEY

Contact Rabbi Jacob Joseph School, One Plainfield Ave, Edison, NJ 08817.

RABBINICAL COLLEGE OF AMERICA
MORRISTOWN, NEW JERSEY

General Independent Jewish, 4-year, men only **Entrance** Minimally difficult **Setting** 81-acre small-town campus **Total enrollment** 259 **Student-faculty ratio** 12:1 **Application deadline** Rolling (freshmen) **Freshmen** 100% were admitted **Housing** Yes **Expenses** Tuition $9700; Room & Board $6800 **Academic program** Accelerated degree program, summer session, internships **Contact** Sharon Miller, Registrar, Rabbinical College of America, 226 Sussex Avenue, PO Box 1996, Morristown, NJ 07962-1996. Phone: 973-267-9404. E-mail: rca079@aol.com.

RAMAPO COLLEGE OF NEW JERSEY
MAHWAH, NEW JERSEY

General State-supported, comprehensive, coed **Entrance** Moderately difficult **Setting** 300-acre suburban campus **Total enrollment** 5,702 **Student-faculty ratio** 18:1 **Application deadline** 3/1 (freshmen), 5/1 (transfer) **Freshmen** 49% were admitted **Housing** Yes **Expenses** Tuition $9965; Room & Board $10,310 **Undergraduates** 48% women, 11% part-time, 12% 25 or older, 0.3% Native American, 9% Hispanic American, 6% African American, 4% Asian American/Pacific Islander **The most frequently chosen baccalaureate fields are** business/marketing, communications/journalism, psychology **Academic program** English as a second language, advanced placement, accelerated degree program, self-designed majors, honors program, summer session, adult/continuing education programs, internships **Contact** Mr. Michael DiBartolomeo, Associate Director for Freshmen Admissions, Ramapo College of New Jersey, Office of Admissions, 505 Ramapo Valley Road, Mahwah, NJ 07430-1680. Phone: 201-684-7300 Ext. 7601 or toll-free 800-9RAMAPO. Fax: 201-684-7964. E-mail: admissions@ramapo.edu. Web site: http://www.ramapo.edu/.

THE RICHARD STOCKTON COLLEGE OF NEW JERSEY
POMONA, NEW JERSEY

General State-supported, comprehensive, coed **Entrance** Very difficult **Setting** 1,600-acre suburban campus **Total enrollment** 7,355 **Student-faculty ratio** 18:1 **Application deadline** 5/1 (freshmen), 6/1 (transfer) **Freshmen** 54% were admitted **Housing** Yes **Expenses** Tuition $9697; Room & Board $9077 **Undergraduates** 59% women, 13% part-time, 22% 25 or older, 0.4% Native American, 6% Hispanic American, 8% African American, 5% Asian American/Pacific Islander **The most frequently chosen baccalaureate fields are** business/marketing, psychology, social sciences **Academic program** Advanced placement, self-designed majors, honors program, summer session, adult/continuing education programs, internships **Contact** Mr. John Iacovelli, Dean of Admissions, The Richard Stockton College of New Jersey, PO Box 195, Pomona, NJ 08240-0195. Phone: 609-652-4261. Fax: 609-626-5541. E-mail: admissions@stockton.edu. Web site: http://www.stockton.edu/.

▶**For more information, see page 482.**

RIDER UNIVERSITY
LAWRENCEVILLE, NEW JERSEY

General Independent, comprehensive, coed **Entrance** Moderately difficult **Setting** 280-acre suburban campus **Total enrollment** 5,982 **Student-faculty ratio** 14:1 **Application deadline** Rolling (freshmen), rolling (transfer) **Freshmen** 75% were admitted **Housing** Yes **Expenses** Tuition $26,230; Room & Board $9780 **Undergraduates** 60% women, 18% part-time, 3% 25 or older, 0.2% Native American, 5% Hispanic American, 9% African American, 3% Asian American/Pacific Islander **The most frequently chosen baccalaureate fields are** business/marketing, education, English **Academic program** English as a second language, advanced placement, honors program, summer session, adult/continuing education programs, internships **Contact** William Larrousse, Director of Admissions, Rider University, 2083 Lawrenceville Road, Lawrenceville, NJ 08648. Phone: 609-895-5768 or toll-free 800-257-9026. Fax: 609-895-6645. E-mail: wlarrousse@rider.edu. Web site: http://www.rider.edu/.

ROWAN UNIVERSITY
GLASSBORO, NEW JERSEY

General State-supported, comprehensive, coed **Entrance** Moderately difficult **Setting** 200-acre suburban campus **Total enrollment** 10,091 **Student-faculty ratio** 15:1 **Application deadline** 3/1 (freshmen), 3/1 (transfer) **Freshmen** 52% were admitted **Housing** Yes **Expenses** Tuition $10,068; Room & Board $9242 **Undergraduates** 53% women, 14% part-time, 12% 25 or older, 0.4% Native American, 7% Hispanic American, 8% African American, 3% Asian American/Pacific Islander **The most frequently chosen baccalaureate fields are** communications/journalism, business/marketing, education **Academic program** English as a second language, advanced placement, honors program, summer session, adult/continuing education programs, internships **Contact** Mr. Albert Betts, Director of Admissions, Rowan University, 201 Mullica Hill Road, Glassboro, NJ 08028. Phone: 856-256-4200 or toll-free 800-447-1165. Fax: 856-256-4430. E-mail: admissions@rowan.edu. Web site: http://www.rowan.edu/.

RUTGERS, THE STATE UNIVERSITY OF NEW JERSEY, CAMDEN
CAMDEN, NEW JERSEY

General State-supported, university, coed **Entrance** Moderately difficult **Total enrollment** 5,159 **Student-faculty ratio** 11:1 **Application deadline** Rolling (freshmen) **Freshmen** 51% were admitted **Housing** Yes **Expenses** Tuition $10,532; Room & Board $9024 **Undergraduates** 56% women, 21% part-time, 29% 25 or older, 0.3% Native American, 7% Hispanic American, 17% African American, 8% Asian American/Pacific Islander **The most frequently chosen baccalau-**

Rutgers, The State University of New Jersey, Camden *(continued)*

reate fields are business/marketing, psychology, social sciences **Academic program** English as a second language, advanced placement, accelerated degree program, self-designed majors, honors program, summer session, internships **Contact** Ms. Diane Williams Harris, Associate Director of University Undergraduate Admissions, Rutgers, The State University of New Jersey, Camden, 311 North Fifth Street, Camden, NJ 08102-1401. Phone: 732-932-4636. E-mail: admissions@ugadm.rutgers.edu. Web site: http://camden-www.rutgers.edu/.

►**For more information, see page 484.**

RUTGERS, THE STATE UNIVERSITY OF NEW JERSEY, NEWARK

NEWARK, NEW JERSEY

General State-supported, university, coed **Entrance** Moderately difficult **Setting** 38-acre urban campus **Total enrollment** 10,553 **Student-faculty ratio** 12:1 **Application deadline** Rolling (freshmen), rolling (transfer) **Freshmen** 49% were admitted **Housing** Yes **Expenses** Tuition $10,267; Room & Board $10,034 **Undergraduates** 55% women, 22% part-time, 22% 25 or older, 0.2% Native American, 19% Hispanic American, 20% African American, 24% Asian American/Pacific Islander **The most frequently chosen baccalaureate fields are** business/marketing, health professions and related sciences, security and protective services **Academic program** English as a second language, advanced placement, accelerated degree program, self-designed majors, honors program, summer session, adult/continuing education programs **Contact** Mr. Jason Hand, Director of Admissions, Rutgers, The State University of New Jersey, Newark, Newark, NJ 07102. Phone: 973-353-1640. Fax: 973-353-1440. E-mail: admissions@ugadm.rutgers.edu. Web site: http://www.newark.rutgers.edu/.

RUTGERS, THE STATE UNIVERSITY OF NEW JERSEY, NEW BRUNSWICK

NEW BRUNSWICK, NEW JERSEY

General State-supported, university, coed **Entrance** Moderately difficult **Setting** 2,682-acre urban campus **Total enrollment** 34,804 **Student-faculty ratio** 14:1 **Application deadline** Rolling (freshmen), rolling (transfer) **Freshmen** 56% were admitted **Housing** Yes **Expenses** Tuition $10,686; Room & Board $9762 **Undergraduates** 49% women, 7% part-time, 29% 25 or older, 0.2% Native American, 8% Hispanic American, 9% African American, 24% Asian American/Pacific Islander **The most frequently chosen baccalaureate fields are** biological/life sciences, communications/journalism, social sciences **Academic program** English as a second language, advanced placement, accelerated degree program, self-designed majors, honors program **Contact** Ms. Diane Williams Harris, Associate Director of University Undergraduate Admissions, Rutgers, The State University of New Jersey, New Brunswick, New Brunswick, NJ 08901-1281. Phone: 732-932-4636. Fax: 732-445-0237. E-mail: admissions@ugadm.rutgers.edu. Web site: http://www.rutgers.edu/.

►**For more information, see page 485.**

SAINT PETER'S COLLEGE

JERSEY CITY, NEW JERSEY

General Independent Roman Catholic (Jesuit), comprehensive, coed **Entrance** Moderately difficult **Setting** 15-acre urban campus **Total enrollment** 3,081 **Student-faculty ratio** 16:1 **Application deadline** Rolling (freshmen), 8/1 (transfer) **Freshmen** 54% were admitted **Housing** Yes **Expenses** Tuition $24,026; Room & Board $9750 **Undergraduates** 57% women, 16% part-time, 2% 25 or older, 0.2% Native American, 27% Hispanic American, 22% African American, 9% Asian American/Pacific Islander **The most frequently chosen baccalaureate fields are** business/marketing, security and protective services, social sciences **Academic program** Advanced placement, accelerated degree program, self-designed majors, honors program, summer session, adult/continuing education programs, internships **Contact** Mr. Joe Giglio, Director of Admissions, Saint Peter's College, 2641 Kennedy Boulevard, Jersey City, NJ 07306-5997. Phone: 201-761-7106 or toll-free 888-SPC-9933. Fax: 201-432-5860. E-mail: admissions@spc.edu. Web site: http://www.spc.edu/.

SETON HALL UNIVERSITY

SOUTH ORANGE, NEW JERSEY

Contact Mr. Robert Herr, Director of Admissions, Seton Hall University, Enrollment Services, Bayley Hall, South Orange, NJ 07079-2697. Phone: 973-761-9688 or toll-free 800-THE HALL. Fax: 973-275-2040. E-mail: thehall@shu.edu. Web site: http://www.shu.edu/.

SOMERSET CHRISTIAN COLLEGE

ZAREPHATH, NEW JERSEY

General Independent Pillar of Fire International, 4-year, coed **Contact** Ms. Coleen Klein, Director of Recruitment, Somerset Christian College, 10 College Way, PO Box 9035, Zarephath, NJ 08890-9035. Phone: 732-356-1595 Ext. 1108 or toll-free 800-234-9305. Fax: 732-356-4846. E-mail: info@somerset.edu. Web site: http://www.somerset.edu/.

STEVENS INSTITUTE OF TECHNOLOGY
HOBOKEN, NEW JERSEY

General Independent, university, coed **Entrance** Very difficult **Setting** 55-acre urban campus **Total enrollment** 5,406 **Student-faculty ratio** 8:1 **Application deadline** 2/1 (freshmen), 7/1 (transfer) **Freshmen** 51% were admitted **Housing** Yes **Expenses** Tuition $36,500; Room & Board $11,200 **Undergraduates** 26% women, 0.2% part-time, 1% 25 or older, 0.2% Native American, 9% Hispanic American, 4% African American, 11% Asian American/Pacific Islander **The most frequently chosen baccalaureate fields are** business/marketing, computer and information sciences, engineering **Academic program** Advanced placement, accelerated degree program, honors program, summer session, internships **Contact** Mr. Daniel Gallagher, Dean of University Admissions, Stevens Institute of Technology, Castle Point on Hudson, Hoboken, NJ 07030. Phone: 201-216-5194 or toll-free 800-458-5323. Fax: 201-216-8348. E-mail: admissions@stevens.edu. Web site: http://www.stevens.edu/.

TALMUDICAL ACADEMY OF NEW JERSEY
ADELPHIA, NEW JERSEY

Contact Rabbi G. Finkel, Director of Admissions, Talmudical Academy of New Jersey, Route 524, Adelphia, NJ 07710. Phone: 201-431-1600.

THOMAS EDISON STATE COLLEGE
TRENTON, NEW JERSEY

General State-supported, comprehensive, coed **Entrance** Noncompetitive **Setting** 2-acre urban campus **Total enrollment** 16,423 **Application deadline** Rolling (transfer) **Housing** No **Expenses** Tuition $4300 **Undergraduates** 38% women, 100% part-time, 88% 25 or older, 1% Native American, 7% Hispanic American, 15% African American, 2% Asian American/Pacific Islander **The most frequently chosen baccalaureate fields are** engineering technologies, business/marketing, liberal arts/general studies **Academic program** Advanced placement, self-designed majors, summer session, adult/continuing education programs **Contact** Mr. David Hoftiezer, Acting Director of Admissions, Thomas Edison State College, 101 West State Street, Trenton, NJ 08608-1176. Phone: 888-442-8372 or toll-free 888-442-8372. Fax: 609-984-8447. E-mail: info@tesc.edu. Web site: http://www.tesc.edu/.

WILLIAM PATERSON UNIVERSITY OF NEW JERSEY
WAYNE, NEW JERSEY

General State-supported, comprehensive, coed **Entrance** Moderately difficult **Setting** 300-acre suburban campus **Total enrollment** 10,443 **Application deadline** 5/1 (freshmen), 6/1 (transfer) **Freshmen** 70% were admitted **Housing** Yes **Expenses** Tuition $9996; Room & Board $9650 **Undergraduates** 56% women, 17% part-time, 18% 25 or older, 0.2% Native American, 17% Hispanic American, 14% African American, 6% Asian American/Pacific Islander **The most frequently chosen baccalaureate fields are** business/marketing, communications/journalism, social sciences **Academic program** English as a second language, advanced placement, accelerated degree program, honors program, summer session, adult/continuing education programs, internships **Contact** Mr. Anthony Leckey, Acting Director of Admissions, William Paterson University of New Jersey, 300 Pompton Road, Wayne, NJ 07470-8420. Phone: 973-720-2900 or toll-free 877-WPU-EXCEL. Fax: 973-720-2910. E-mail: admissions@wpunj.edu. Web site: http://ww2.wpunj.edu/.

►**For more information, see page 502.**

NEW MEXICO

COLLEGE OF SANTA FE
SANTA FE, NEW MEXICO

General Independent, comprehensive, coed **Entrance** Moderately difficult **Setting** 100-acre suburban campus **Total enrollment** 672 **Student-faculty ratio** 7:1 **Application deadline** Rolling (freshmen), rolling (transfer) **Freshmen** 83% were admitted **Housing** Yes **Expenses** Tuition $28,558; Room & Board $8458 **Undergraduates** 49% women, 9% part-time, 14% 25 or older, 1% Native American, 12% Hispanic American, 2% African American, 3% Asian American/Pacific Islander **The most frequently chosen baccalaureate fields are** English, psychology, visual and performing arts **Academic program** Advanced placement, accelerated degree program, self-designed majors, summer session, adult/continuing education programs, internships **Contact** Mr. Joseph Fitzpatrick, College of Santa Fe, 1600 Saint Michael's Drive, Santa Fe, NM 87505-7634. Phone: 505-473-6133 or toll-free 800-456-2673. Fax: 505-473-6129. E-mail: admissions@csf.edu. Web site: http://www.csf.edu.

COLLEGE OF THE SOUTHWEST
HOBBS, NEW MEXICO

General Independent, comprehensive, coed **Entrance** Moderately difficult **Setting** 162-acre small-town campus **Total enrollment** 741 **Student-faculty ratio** 12:1 **Application deadline** Rolling (freshmen), rolling (transfer)

College of the Southwest *(continued)*

Freshmen 46% were admitted **Housing** Yes **Expenses** Tuition $11,700; Room & Board $6590 **Undergraduates** 62% women, 30% part-time, 42% 25 or older, 3% Native American, 30% Hispanic American, 3% African American, 0.5% Asian American/Pacific Islander **Academic program** Advanced placement, summer session, adult/continuing education programs, internships **Contact** Dr. Steve Hill, Dean of Recruitment, College of the Southwest, 6610 Lovington Highway, Hobbs, NM 88240-9129. Phone: 505-392-6563 or toll-free 800-530-4400. Fax: 505-392-6006. E-mail: shill@csw.edu. Web site: http://www.csw.edu/.

EASTERN NEW MEXICO UNIVERSITY

PORTALES, NEW MEXICO

General State-supported, comprehensive, coed **Entrance** Minimally difficult **Setting** 240-acre rural campus **Total enrollment** 4,173 **Student-faculty ratio** 15:1 **Application deadline** Rolling (freshmen), rolling (transfer) **Freshmen** 70% were admitted **Housing** Yes **Expenses** Tuition $3156; Room & Board $4888 **Undergraduates** 54% women, 31% part-time, 28% 25 or older, 3% Native American, 31% Hispanic American, 6% African American, 1% Asian American/Pacific Islander **The most frequently chosen baccalaureate fields are** education, business/marketing, liberal arts/general studies **Academic program** English as a second language, advanced placement, accelerated degree program, self-designed majors, honors program, summer session, adult/continuing education programs, internships **Contact** Ms. Donna Kittrell, Director, Eastern New Mexico University, Station #7 ENMU, Portales, NM 88130. Phone: 505-562-2178 or toll-free 800-367-3668. Fax: 505-562-2118. E-mail: donna.kittrell@enmu.edu. Web site: http://www.enmu.edu/.

NATIONAL AMERICAN UNIVERSITY

ALBUQUERQUE, NEW MEXICO

Contact Ms. Kim Hauser, Executive Admissions Representative, National American University, 4775 Indian School, NE, Suite 200, Albuquerque, NM 87110. Phone: 505-265-7517 or toll-free 800-843-8892. Fax: 505-265-7542. Web site: http://www.national.edu/.

NATIONAL COLLEGE OF MIDWIFERY

TAOS, NEW MEXICO

Contact Ms. Beth Enson, Dean of Students, National College of Midwifery, 209 State Road 240, Taos, NM 87571. Phone: 505-758-8914. Fax: 505-758-0302. Web site: http://www.midwiferycollege.org/.

NEW MEXICO HIGHLANDS UNIVERSITY

LAS VEGAS, NEW MEXICO

General State-supported, comprehensive, coed **Entrance** Minimally difficult **Setting** 120-acre small-town campus **Total enrollment** 3,457 **Application deadline** Rolling (freshmen), rolling (transfer) **Freshmen** 79% were admitted **Housing** Yes **Expenses** Tuition $2516; Room & Board $3431 **Undergraduates** 60% women, 30% part-time, 39% 25 or older, 7% Native American, 58% Hispanic American, 6% African American, 2% Asian American/Pacific Islander **The most frequently chosen baccalaureate fields are** education, business/marketing, health professions and related sciences **Academic program** Advanced placement, accelerated degree program, honors program, summer session, internships **Contact** Ms. Judy Cordova, Vice President for Student Affairs, New Mexico Highlands University, Box 9000, Las Vegas, NM 87701. Phone: 505-454-3405 or toll-free 800-338-6648. Fax: 505-454-3552. E-mail: judycordova@nmhu.edu. Web site: http://www.nmhu.edu/.

NEW MEXICO INSTITUTE OF MINING AND TECHNOLOGY

SOCORRO, NEW MEXICO

General State-supported, university, coed **Entrance** Moderately difficult **Setting** 320-acre small-town campus **Total enrollment** 1,882 **Student-faculty ratio** 11:1 **Application deadline** 8/1 (freshmen), 8/1 (transfer) **Freshmen** 55% were admitted **Housing** Yes **Expenses** Tuition $4105; Room & Board $5300 **Undergraduates** 33% women, 18% part-time, 8% 25 or older, 3% Native American, 25% Hispanic American, 1% African American, 3% Asian American/Pacific Islander **The most frequently chosen baccalaureate fields are** engineering, computer and information sciences, physical sciences **Academic program** Advanced placement, accelerated degree program, self-designed majors, summer session, internships **Contact** Mr. Mike Kloeppel, Director of Admissions, New Mexico Institute of Mining and Technology, 801 Leroy Place, Socorro, NM 87801. Phone: 575-835-5424 or toll-free 800-428-TECH. Fax: 575-835-5989. E-mail: admission@admin.nmt.edu. Web site: http://www.nmt.edu/.

NEW MEXICO STATE UNIVERSITY

LAS CRUCES, NEW MEXICO

General State-supported, university, coed **Entrance** Moderately difficult **Setting** 900-acre suburban campus **Total enrollment** 16,726

Student-faculty ratio 19:1 **Application deadline** 8/19 (freshmen), 8/14 (transfer) **Freshmen** 85% were admitted **Housing** Yes **Expenses** Tuition $4452; Room & Board $5766 **Undergraduates** 56% women, 15% part-time, 23% 25 or older, 3% Native American, 43% Hispanic American, 3% African American, 1% Asian American/Pacific Islander **The most frequently chosen baccalaureate fields are** business/marketing, education, engineering **Academic program** Advanced placement, accelerated degree program, self-designed majors, honors program, summer session, adult/continuing education programs, internships **Contact** Mr. Tyler Pruett, Director of Admissions, New Mexico State University, Box 30001, MSC 3A, Las Cruces, NM 88003-8001. Phone: 505-646-3121 or toll-free 800-662-6678. Fax: 505-646-6330. E-mail: admssions@nmsu.edu. Web site: http://www.nmsu.edu/.

ST. JOHN'S COLLEGE

SANTA FE, NEW MEXICO

General Independent, comprehensive, coed **Entrance** Very difficult **Setting** 250-acre suburban campus **Total enrollment** 538 **Student-faculty ratio** 8:1 **Application deadline** Rolling (freshmen), rolling (transfer) **Freshmen** 79% were admitted **Housing** Yes **Expenses** Tuition $36,596; Room & Board $8684 **Undergraduates** 40% women, 0.5% part-time, 5% 25 or older, 1% Native American, 6% Hispanic American, 1% African American, 3% Asian American/Pacific Islander **The most frequently chosen baccalaureate field is** liberal arts/general studies **Academic program** Summer session, internships **Contact** Mr. Larry Clendenin, Director of Admissions, St. John's College, 1160 Camino Cruz Blanca, Santa Fe, NM 87505. Phone: 505-984-6060 or toll-free 800-331-5232. Fax: 505-984-6162. E-mail: admissions@stjohnscollege.edu. Web site: http://www.stjohnscollege.edu/.

UNIVERSITY OF NEW MEXICO

ALBUQUERQUE, NEW MEXICO

General State-supported, university, coed **Entrance** Moderately difficult **Setting** 875-acre urban campus **Student-faculty ratio** 19:1 **Application deadline** 6/15 (freshmen), 6/15 (transfer) **Freshmen** 71% were admitted **Housing** Yes **Expenses** Tuition $4571; Room & Board $7020 **Undergraduates** 25% 25 or older **The most frequently chosen baccalaureate fields are** business/marketing, education, health professions and related sciences **Academic program** English as a second language, advanced placement, accelerated degree program, self-designed majors, honors program, summer session, adult/continuing education programs, internships **Contact** Ms. Kathleen Roberts, Coordinator of Freshmen Admissions, University of New Mexico, Office of Admissions, PO Box 4895, Albuquerque, NM 87196-4895. Phone: 505-277-2446 or toll-free 800-CALLUNM. Fax: 505-277-6686. E-mail: apply@unm.edu. Web site: http://www.unm.edu/.

UNIVERSITY OF PHOENIX–NEW MEXICO CAMPUS

ALBUQUERQUE, NEW MEXICO

General Proprietary, comprehensive, coed **Contact** Ms. Evelyn Gaskin, Registrar/Executive Director, University of Phoenix–New Mexico Campus, 4615 East Elwood Street, Mail Stop AA-K101, Phoenix, AZ 85040-1958. Phone: 480-557-3301 or toll-free 800-776-4867 (in-state); 800-228-7240 (out-of-state). Fax: 480-643-1020. E-mail: evelyn.gaskin@phoenix.edu. Web site: http://www.phoenix.edu/.

WESTERN NEW MEXICO UNIVERSITY

SILVER CITY, NEW MEXICO

General State-supported, comprehensive, coed **Entrance** Noncompetitive **Setting** 83-acre rural campus **Total enrollment** 2,697 **Student-faculty ratio** 17:1 **Application deadline** 8/1 (freshmen), 8/1 (transfer) **Freshmen** 100% were admitted **Housing** Yes **Expenses** Tuition $3431; Room & Board $5060 **Undergraduates** 63% women, 39% part-time, 46% 25 or older, 2% Native American, 46% Hispanic American, 4% African American, 1% Asian American/Pacific Islander **The most frequently chosen baccalaureate fields are** business/marketing, education, liberal arts/general studies **Academic program** Advanced placement, accelerated degree program, self-designed majors, summer session, adult/continuing education programs, internships **Contact** Mr. Dan Tressler, Director of Admissions, Western New Mexico University, PO Box 680, Silver City, NM 88062-0680. Phone: 505-538-6106 or toll-free 800-872-WNMU. Fax: 505-538-6127. E-mail: tresslerd@wnmu.edu. Web site: http://www.wnmu.edu/.

NEW YORK

ADELPHI UNIVERSITY

GARDEN CITY, NEW YORK

General Independent, university, coed **Entrance** Moderately difficult **Setting** 75-acre suburban campus **Total enrollment** 8,354 **Student-faculty ratio** 9:1 **Application deadline** Rolling (freshmen), rolling (transfer) **Freshmen** 69% were

Adelphi University *(continued)*

admitted **Housing** Yes **Expenses** Tuition $23,255; Room & Board $9900 **Undergraduates** 72% women, 18% part-time, 23% 25 or older, 0.2% Native American, 8% Hispanic American, 14% African American, 7% Asian American/Pacific Islander **The most frequently chosen baccalaureate fields are** business/marketing, health professions and related sciences, social sciences **Academic program** English as a second language, advanced placement, accelerated degree program, self-designed majors, honors program, summer session, internships **Contact** Ms. Christine Murphy, Director of Admissions, Adelphi University, Levermore Hall 110, 1 South Avenue, PO Box 701, Garden City, NY 11530-0701. Phone: 516-877-3050 or toll-free 800-ADELPHI. Fax: 516-877-3039. E-mail: admissions@adelphi.edu. Web site: http://www.adelphi.edu/.

ALBANY COLLEGE OF PHARMACY OF UNION UNIVERSITY

ALBANY, NEW YORK

General Independent, comprehensive, coed **Setting** 1-acre urban campus **Total enrollment** 1,423 **Student-faculty ratio** 16:1 **Application deadline** 2/1 (freshmen), 2/1 (transfer) **Freshmen** 54% were admitted **Housing** Yes **Expenses** Tuition $21,150; Room & Board $7300 **Undergraduates** 58% women, 0.3% part-time, 6% 25 or older, 0.1% Native American, 1% Hispanic American, 2% African American, 13% Asian American/Pacific Islander **The most frequently chosen baccalaureate field is** health professions and related sciences **Academic program** Advanced placement, accelerated degree program, summer session, internships **Contact** Ms. Carly Connors, Director of Admissions, Albany College of Pharmacy of Union University, 106 New Scotland Avenue, Albany, NY 12208-3492. Phone: 518-694-7221 or toll-free 888-203-8010. Fax: 518-694-7322. E-mail: admissions@acp.edu. Web site: http://www.acp.edu/.

ALFRED UNIVERSITY

ALFRED, NEW YORK

General Independent, university, coed **Entrance** Moderately difficult **Setting** 232-acre rural campus **Total enrollment** 2,436 **Student-faculty ratio** 12:1 **Application deadline** 2/1 (freshmen), 8/1 (transfer) **Freshmen** 74% were admitted **Housing** Yes **Expenses** Tuition $24,278; Room & Board $10,796 **Undergraduates** 51% women, 5% part-time, 5% 25 or older, 0.4% Native American, 2% Hispanic American, 4% African American, 2% Asian American/Pacific Islander **The most frequently chosen baccalaureate fields are** engineering, business/marketing, visual and performing arts **Academic program** Advanced placement, accelerated degree program, self-designed majors, honors program, summer session, internships **Contact** Mr. Jeremy Spencer, Director of Admissions, Alfred University, Alumni Hall, Alfred, NY 14802-1205. Phone: 607-871-2115 or toll-free 800-541-9229. Fax: 607-871-2198. E-mail: admissions@alfred.edu. Web site: http://www.alfred.edu/.

BARD COLLEGE

ANNANDALE-ON-HUDSON, NEW YORK

General Independent, comprehensive, coed **Entrance** Very difficult **Setting** 600-acre rural campus **Total enrollment** 2,062 **Student-faculty ratio** 9:1 **Application deadline** 1/15 (freshmen), 3/15 (transfer) **Freshmen** 27% were admitted **Housing** Yes **Expenses** Tuition $36,534; Room & Board $10,346 **Undergraduates** 56% women, 5% part-time, 1% 25 or older, 1% Native American, 3% Hispanic American, 2% African American, 3% Asian American/Pacific Islander **The most frequently chosen baccalaureate fields are** social sciences, English, visual and performing arts **Academic program** Advanced placement, self-designed majors, adult/continuing education programs, internships **Contact** Ms. Mary Backlund, Director of Admissions, Bard College, PO Box 5000, 51 Ravine Road, Annandale-on-Hudson, NY 12504-5000. Phone: 845-758-7472. Fax: 845-758-5208. E-mail: admission@bard.edu. Web site: http://www.bard.edu/.

BARNARD COLLEGE

NEW YORK, NEW YORK

General Independent, 4-year, women only **Entrance** Most difficult **Setting** 4-acre urban campus **Total enrollment** 2,346 **Student-faculty ratio** 10:1 **Application deadline** 1/1 (freshmen), 4/1 (transfer) **Freshmen** 29% were admitted **Housing** Yes **Expenses** Tuition $35,190; Room & Board $11,546 **Undergraduates** 2% part-time, 0.2% 25 or older, 0.3% Native American, 9% Hispanic American, 5% African American, 16% Asian American/Pacific Islander **The most frequently chosen baccalaureate fields are** psychology, area and ethnic studies, social sciences **Academic program** Advanced placement, accelerated degree program, self-designed majors, internships **Contact** Ms. Jennifer Gill Fondiller, Dean of Admissions, Barnard College, 3009 Broadway, New York, NY 10027-6598. Phone: 212-854-2014. Fax: 212-854-6220. E-mail: admissions@barnard.edu. Web site: http://www.barnard.edu/.

BEIS MEDRASH HEICHAL DOVID

FAR ROCKAWAY, NEW YORK

Contact Beis Medrash Heichal Dovid, 257 Beach 17th Street, Far Rockaway, NY 11691.

BERNARD M. BARUCH COLLEGE OF THE CITY UNIVERSITY OF NEW YORK
NEW YORK, NEW YORK

General State and locally supported, comprehensive, coed **Entrance** Very difficult **Setting** urban campus **Total enrollment** 16,097 **Student-faculty ratio** 19:1 **Application deadline** 2/1 (freshmen), 3/1 (transfer) **Freshmen** 26% were admitted **Housing** No **Expenses** Tuition $4320 **Undergraduates** 52% women, 25% part-time, 25% 25 or older, 0.1% Native American, 16% Hispanic American, 11% African American, 30% Asian American/Pacific Islander **The most frequently chosen baccalaureate fields are** business/marketing, communications/journalism, psychology **Academic program** English as a second language, advanced placement, accelerated degree program, self-designed majors, honors program, summer session, adult/continuing education programs, internships **Contact** Ms. Marybeth Murphy, Assistant Vice President for Undergraduate Admissions and Financial Aid, Bernard M. Baruch College of the City University of New York, 1 Bernard Baruch Way, New York, NY 10010-5585. Phone: 646-312-1400. E-mail: admissions@baruch.cuny.edu. Web site: http://www.baruch.cuny.edu/.

BETH HAMEDRASH SHAAREI YOSHER INSTITUTE
BROOKLYN, NEW YORK

Contact Mr. Menachem Steinberg, Director of Admissions, Beth HaMedrash Shaarei Yosher Institute, 4102-10 Sixteenth Avenue, Brooklyn, NY 11204. Phone: 718-854-2290.

BETH HATALMUD RABBINICAL COLLEGE
BROOKLYN, NEW YORK

Contact Rabbi Osina, Director of Admissions, Beth Hatalmud Rabbinical College, 2127 Eighty-second Street, Brooklyn, NY 11214. Phone: 718-259-2525.

BORICUA COLLEGE
NEW YORK, NEW YORK

General Independent, comprehensive, coed **Entrance** Moderately difficult **Setting** urban campus **Total enrollment** 1,058 **Student-faculty ratio** 20:1 **Application deadline** Rolling (freshmen), rolling (transfer) **Freshmen** 40% were admitted **Housing** No **Expenses** Tuition $9200 **Undergraduates** 79% women, 89% 25 or older, 0.1% Native American, 80% Hispanic American, 12% African American, 0.5% Asian American/Pacific Islander **Academic program** Accelerated degree program, honors program, summer session, adult/continuing education programs, internships **Contact** Mrs. Miriam Pfeffer, Director of Student Services, Boricua College, 186 North 6th Street, Brooklyn, NY 11211. Phone: 718-782-2200. Fax: 718-782-2025. E-mail: mpfeffer@boricuacollege.edu. Web site: http://www.boricuacollege.edu/.

BRIARCLIFFE COLLEGE
BETHPAGE, NEW YORK

General Proprietary, 4-year, coed **Contact** Ms. Theresa Donohue, Vice President of Marketing and Admissions, Briarcliffe College, 1055 Stewart Avenue, Bethpage, NY 11714. Phone: 516-918-3705 or toll-free 888-333-1150. Fax: 516-470-6020. E-mail: info@bcl.edu. Web site: http://www.bcl.edu/.

BROOKLYN COLLEGE OF THE CITY UNIVERSITY OF NEW YORK
BROOKLYN, NEW YORK

General State and locally supported, comprehensive, coed **Contact** Admissions Information Center, Brooklyn College of the City University of New York, 2900 Bedford Avenue, 1103 James Hall, Brooklyn, NY 11210-2889. Phone: 718-951-5001. Fax: 718-951-4506. E-mail: adminqry@brooklyn.cuny.edu. Web site: http://www.brooklyn.cuny.edu/.

►**For more information, see page 444.**

BUFFALO STATE COLLEGE, STATE UNIVERSITY OF NEW YORK
BUFFALO, NEW YORK

General State-supported, comprehensive, coed **Entrance** Moderately difficult **Setting** 115-acre urban campus **Total enrollment** 10,993 **Student-faculty ratio** 17:1 **Application deadline** Rolling (freshmen), rolling (transfer) **Freshmen** 47% were admitted **Housing** Yes **Expenses** Tuition $5375; Room & Board $8314 **Undergraduates** 59% women, 12% part-time, 19% 25 or older, 1% Native American, 5% Hispanic American, 14% African American, 2% Asian American/Pacific Islander **The most frequently chosen baccalaureate fields are** business/marketing, communications/journalism, education **Academic program** English as a second language, advanced placement, honors program, summer session, adult/continuing education programs, internships **Contact** Ms. Lesa Loritts, Director of Admissions, Buffalo State College, State University of New York, 110 Moot Hall, Buffalo, NY 14222. Phone: 716-878-4017. Fax: 716-878-6100. E-mail: admissions@buffalostate.edu. Web site: http://www.buffalostate.edu/.

CANISIUS COLLEGE
BUFFALO, NEW YORK

General Independent Roman Catholic (Jesuit), comprehensive, coed **Entrance** Moderately difficult **Setting** 36-acre urban campus **Total enrollment** 4,984 **Student-faculty ratio** 13:1 **Application deadline** 5/1 (freshmen), rolling (transfer) **Freshmen** 79% were admitted **Housing** Yes **Expenses** Tuition $26,427; Room & Board $9770 **Undergraduates** 55% women, 7% part-time, 4% 25 or older, 0.3% Native American, 2% Hispanic American, 6% African American, 1% Asian American/Pacific Islander **The most frequently chosen baccalaureate fields are** business/marketing, communications/journalism, education **Academic program** English as a second language, advanced placement, honors program, summer session, internships **Contact** Ms. Ann Marie Moscovic, Director of Admissions, Canisius College, 2001 Main Street, Buffalo, NY 14208-1098. Phone: 716-888-2200 or toll-free 800-843-1517. Fax: 716-888-3230. E-mail: admissions@canisius.edu. Web site: http://www.canisius.edu/.

CAZENOVIA COLLEGE
CAZENOVIA, NEW YORK

General Independent, 4-year, coed **Entrance** Minimally difficult **Setting** 40-acre small-town campus **Total enrollment** 1,006 **Student-faculty ratio** 11:1 **Application deadline** Rolling (freshmen), rolling (transfer) **Freshmen** 80% were admitted **Housing** Yes **Expenses** Tuition $21,500; Room & Board $8940 **Undergraduates** 78% women, 19% part-time, 10% 25 or older, 1% Native American, 2% Hispanic American, 5% African American, 1% Asian American/Pacific Islander **The most frequently chosen baccalaureate fields are** business/marketing, public administration and social services, visual and performing arts **Academic program** Advanced placement, accelerated degree program, honors program, summer session, adult/continuing education programs, internships **Contact** Office of Admission and Enrollment Services, Cazenovia College, 3 Sullivan Street, Cazenovia, NY 13035. Phone: 315-655-7208 or toll-free 800-654-3210. Fax: 315-655-4860. E-mail: admission@cazenovia.edu. Web site: http://www.cazenovia.edu/.

CENTRAL YESHIVA TOMCHEI TMIMIM-LUBAVITCH
BROOKLYN, NEW YORK

Contact Moses Gluckowsky, Director of Admissions, Central Yeshiva Tomchei Tmimim-Lubavitch, 841-853 Ocean Parkway, Brooklyn, NY 11230. Phone: 718-859-7600.

CITY COLLEGE OF THE CITY UNIVERSITY OF NEW YORK
NEW YORK, NEW YORK

General State and locally supported, university, coed **Entrance** Moderately difficult **Setting** 35-acre urban campus **Total enrollment** 14,536 **Student-faculty ratio** 13:1 **Application deadline** 3/1 (freshmen), 3/1 (transfer) **Freshmen** 40% were admitted **Housing** Yes **Expenses** Tuition $4359; Room only $8250 **Undergraduates** 29% 25 or older, 0.1% Native American, 33% Hispanic American, 24% African American, 20% Asian American/Pacific Islander **Academic program** English as a second language, advanced placement, accelerated degree program, self-designed majors, honors program, summer session, adult/continuing education programs, internships **Contact** Joseph A. Fantozzi, Director of Admissions, City College of the City University of New York, 160 Convent Avenue, New York, NY 10031-9198. Phone: 212-650-6977. Fax: 212-650-6417. E-mail: admissions@ccny.cuny.edu. Web site: http://www.ccny.cuny.edu/.

CLARKSON UNIVERSITY
POTSDAM, NEW YORK

General Independent, university, coed **Entrance** Very difficult **Setting** 640-acre small-town campus **Total enrollment** 2,949 **Student-faculty ratio** 15:1 **Application deadline** 1/15 (freshmen) **Freshmen** 82% were admitted **Housing** Yes **Expenses** Tuition $29,160; Room & Board $10,130 **Undergraduates** 26% women, 1% part-time, 1% 25 or older, 0.3% Native American, 2% Hispanic American, 3% African American, 3% Asian American/Pacific Islander **Academic program** English as a second language, advanced placement, accelerated degree program, self-designed majors, honors program, summer session, internships **Contact** Mr. Brian Grant, Director of Admission, Clarkson University, Holcroft House, Potsdam, NY 13699-5605. Phone: 315-268-6480 or toll-free 800-527-6577. Fax: 315-268-7647. E-mail: admission@clarkson.edu. Web site: http://www.clarkson.edu/.

COLGATE UNIVERSITY
HAMILTON, NEW YORK

General Independent, comprehensive, coed **Entrance** Most difficult **Setting** 515-acre rural campus **Total enrollment** 2,790 **Student-faculty ratio** 10:1 **Application deadline** 1/15 (freshmen), 3/15 (transfer) **Freshmen** 26% were admitted **Housing** Yes **Expenses** Tuition $37,660; Room & Board $9170 **Undergraduates** 53% women, 1% part-time **The most frequently chosen baccalaureate fields are** English, biological/life sciences, social sciences **Academic**

program Advanced placement, self-designed majors, honors program, internships **Contact** Mr. Gary L. Ross, Dean of Admission, Colgate University, 13 Oak Drive, Hamilton, NY 13346-1383. Phone: 315-228-7401. Fax: 315-228-7544. E-mail: admission@mail.colgate.edu. Web site: http://www.colgate.edu/.

THE COLLEGE AT BROCKPORT, STATE UNIVERSITY OF NEW YORK

BROCKPORT, NEW YORK

General State-supported, comprehensive, coed **Entrance** Moderately difficult **Setting** 435-acre small-town campus **Total enrollment** 8,303 **Student-faculty ratio** 18:1 **Application deadline** Rolling (freshmen), 8/1 (transfer) **Freshmen** 42% were admitted **Housing** Yes **Expenses** Tuition $5442; Room & Board $8597 **Undergraduates** 57% women, 10% part-time, 15% 25 or older, 0.4% Native American, 3% Hispanic American, 6% African American, 1% Asian American/Pacific Islander **The most frequently chosen baccalaureate fields are** business/marketing, education, health professions and related sciences **Academic program** Advanced placement, accelerated degree program, self-designed majors, honors program, summer session, internships **Contact** Mr. Bernard Valento, Director of Undergraduate Admissions, The College at Brockport, State University of New York, 350 New Campus Drive, Brockport, NY 14420-2997. Phone: 585-395-2751. Fax: 585-395-5452. E-mail: admit@brockport.edu. Web site: http://www.brockport.edu/.

COLLEGE OF MOUNT SAINT VINCENT

RIVERDALE, NEW YORK

General Independent, comprehensive, coed **Entrance** Moderately difficult **Setting** 70-acre suburban campus **Total enrollment** 1,742 **Student-faculty ratio** 14:1 **Application deadline** Rolling (freshmen), rolling (transfer) **Freshmen** 71% were admitted **Housing** Yes **Expenses** Tuition $24,480; Room & Board $9370 **Undergraduates** 73% women, 14% part-time, 8% 25 or older, 0.1% Native American, 30% Hispanic American, 11% African American, 11% Asian American/Pacific Islander **The most frequently chosen baccalaureate fields are** health professions and related sciences, business/marketing, liberal arts/general studies **Academic program** English as a second language, advanced placement, accelerated degree program, self-designed majors, honors program, summer session, adult/continuing education programs, internships **Contact** Mr. Roland Pinzon, Director of Admissions, College of Mount Saint Vincent, 6301 Riverdale Avenue, Riverdale, NY 10471-1093. Phone: 718-405-3268 or toll-free 800-665-CMSV. Fax: 718-549-7945. E-mail: roland.pinzon@mountsaintvincent.edu. Web site: http://www.mountsaintvincent.edu/.

THE COLLEGE OF NEW ROCHELLE

NEW ROCHELLE, NEW YORK

General Independent, comprehensive, coed, primarily women **Entrance** Moderately difficult **Setting** 20-acre suburban campus **Total enrollment** 2,030 **Student-faculty ratio** 12:1 **Application deadline** Rolling (freshmen), rolling (transfer) **Freshmen** 43% were admitted **Housing** Yes **Expenses** Tuition $23,700; Room & Board $8700 **Undergraduates** 92% women, 38% part-time, 40% 25 or older, 1% Native American, 14% Hispanic American, 33% African American, 4% Asian American/Pacific Islander **Academic program** Advanced placement, accelerated degree program, self-designed majors, honors program, summer session, adult/continuing education programs, internships **Contact** Ms. Stephanie Decker, Director of Admission, The College of New Rochelle, 29 Castle Place, New Rochelle, NY 10805-2339. Phone: 914-654-5452 or toll-free 800-933-5923. Fax: 914-654-5464. E-mail: admission@cnr.edu. Web site: http://cnr.edu/.

THE COLLEGE OF SAINT ROSE

ALBANY, NEW YORK

General Independent, comprehensive, coed **Entrance** Moderately difficult **Setting** 28-acre urban campus **Total enrollment** 4,949 **Student-faculty ratio** 14:1 **Application deadline** 5/1 (freshmen), 5/1 (transfer) **Freshmen** 67% were admitted **Housing** Yes **Expenses** Tuition $19,960; Room & Board $8558 **Undergraduates** 71% women, 7% part-time, 10% 25 or older, 0.3% Native American, 4% Hispanic American, 3% African American, 1% Asian American/Pacific Islander **The most frequently chosen baccalaureate fields are** business/marketing, education, visual and performing arts **Academic program** Advanced placement, accelerated degree program, self-designed majors, summer session, adult/continuing education programs, internships **Contact** Ms. Mary Elizabeth Amico, Director of Undergraduate Admissions, The College of Saint Rose, 432 Western Avenue, Albany, NY 12203-1419. Phone: 518-454-5150 or toll-free 800-637-8556. Fax: 518-454-2013. E-mail: admit@strose.edu. Web site: http://www.strose.edu/.

COLLEGE OF STATEN ISLAND OF THE CITY UNIVERSITY OF NEW YORK

STATEN ISLAND, NEW YORK

General State and locally supported, comprehensive, coed **Entrance** Moderately difficult **Setting** 204-acre urban campus **Total enrollment** 12,517

College of Staten Island of the City University of New York *(continued)*

Student-faculty ratio 18:1 **Application deadline** Rolling (freshmen), rolling (transfer) **Freshmen** 100% were admitted **Housing** No **Expenses** Tuition $4328 **Undergraduates** 60% women, 30% part-time, 24% 25 or older, 0.1% Native American, 11% Hispanic American, 8% African American, 8% Asian American/Pacific Islander **The most frequently chosen baccalaureate fields are** business/marketing, liberal arts/general studies, social sciences **Academic program** English as a second language, advanced placement, accelerated degree program, self-designed majors, honors program, summer session, adult/continuing education programs, internships **Contact** Ms. Mary Beth Reilly, Director of Recruitment and Admissions, College of Staten Island of the City University of New York, 2800 Victory Boulevard, Building 2A Room 103, Staten Island, NY 10314. Phone: 718-982-2010. Fax: 713-982-2500. E-mail: admissions@mail.cuny.csi.edu. Web site: http://www.csi.cuny.edu/.

COLUMBIA UNIVERSITY
NEW YORK, NEW YORK

General Independent, university, coed **Entrance** Most difficult **Total enrollment** 5,602 **Student-faculty ratio** 6:1 **Application deadline** 1/2 (freshmen), 3/15 (transfer) **Freshmen** 11% were admitted **Housing** Yes **Expenses** Tuition $37,216; Room & Board $9937 **Undergraduates** 46% women, 1% Native American, 10% Hispanic American, 9% African American, 18% Asian American/Pacific Islander **The most frequently chosen baccalaureate fields are** engineering, English, social sciences **Contact** Ms. Jessica Marinaccio, Dean of Undergraduate Admissions, Columbia University, 116th Street and Broadway, New York, NY 10027. Web site: http://www.columbia.edu/.

COLUMBIA UNIVERSITY, SCHOOL OF GENERAL STUDIES
NEW YORK, NEW YORK

General Independent, 4-year, coed **Contact** Mr. Curtis M. Rodgers, Dean of Admissions, Enrollment Management, and Communications, Columbia University, School of General Studies, Mail Code 4101, Lewisohn Hall, New York, NY 10027-9829. Phone: 212-854-2772 or toll-free 800-895-1169. Fax: 212-854-6316. E-mail: gsdegree@columbia.edu. Web site: http://www.gs.columbia.edu/.

►**For more information, see page 453.**

CONCORDIA COLLEGE–NEW YORK
BRONXVILLE, NEW YORK

General Independent Lutheran, 4-year, coed **Entrance** Moderately difficult **Setting** 33-acre suburban campus **Total enrollment** 748 **Student-faculty ratio** 12:1 **Application deadline** 3/15 (freshmen), 7/15 (transfer) **Freshmen** 67% were admitted **Housing** Yes **Expenses** Tuition $22,450; Room & Board $8520 **Undergraduates** 62% women, 14% part-time, 13% 25 or older, 0.4% Native American, 8% Hispanic American, 11% African American, 0.4% Asian American/Pacific Islander **The most frequently chosen baccalaureate fields are** business/marketing, liberal arts/general studies, social sciences **Academic program** English as a second language, advanced placement, accelerated degree program, self-designed majors, honors program, adult/continuing education programs, internships **Contact** Ms. Donna J. Hoyt, Dean of Enrollment, Concordia College–New York, 171 White Plains Road, Bronxville, NY 10708. Phone: 914-337-9300 Ext. 2149 or toll-free 800-YES-COLLEGE. Fax: 914-395-4636. E-mail: admission@concordia-ny.edu. Web site: http://www.concordia-ny.edu/.

COOPER UNION FOR THE ADVANCEMENT OF SCIENCE AND ART
NEW YORK, NEW YORK

General Independent, comprehensive, coed **Entrance** Most difficult **Setting** urban campus **Total enrollment** 957 **Student-faculty ratio** 8:1 **Application deadline** 1/1 (freshmen), 1/1 (transfer) **Freshmen** 11% were admitted **Housing** Yes **Expenses** Tuition $1450; Room & Board $13,700 **Undergraduates** 37% women, 0.1% part-time, 10% 25 or older, 0.4% Native American, 8% Hispanic American, 5% African American, 17% Asian American/Pacific Islander **The most frequently chosen baccalaureate fields are** education, architecture, visual and performing arts **Academic program** Advanced placement, self-designed majors, honors program, summer session, internships **Contact** Mr. Mitchell L. Lipton, Dean of Admissions and Records and Registrar, Cooper Union for the Advancement of Science and Art, 30 Cooper Square, New York, NY 10003. Phone: 212-353-4120. Fax: 212-353-4342. E-mail: admissions@cooper.edu. Web site: http://www.cooper.edu/.

CORNELL UNIVERSITY
ITHACA, NEW YORK

General Independent, university, coed **Entrance** Most difficult **Setting** 745-acre small-town campus **Total enrollment** 19,800 **Student-faculty ratio** 9:1 **Application deadline** 1/1 (freshmen), 3/15 (transfer) **Freshmen** 21% were admitted **Housing** Yes **Expenses** Tuition $34,781; Room & Board $11,190 **Undergraduates** 49% women, 1% 25 or older, 1% Native American, 6% Hispanic American, 5% African American, 16% Asian American/Pacific Islander **The most frequently chosen baccalaureate fields are** agriculture, business/marketing, engineering **Academic program** English as a second language, advanced placement, accelerated degree program, self-designed majors, honors program, summer session, internships **Contact** Mr. Jason Locke, Director of Undergraduate Admissions, Cornell University, Ithaca, NY 14853-0001. Phone: 607-255-3316. Fax: 607-255-0659. E-mail: admissions@cornell.edu. Web site: http://www.cornell.edu/.

THE CULINARY INSTITUTE OF AMERICA
HYDE PARK, NEW YORK

General Independent, 4-year, coed **Entrance** Moderately difficult **Setting** 170-acre suburban campus **Total enrollment** 2,823 **Student-faculty ratio** 18:1 **Application deadline** Rolling (freshmen) **Freshmen** 75% were admitted **Housing** Yes **Expenses** Tuition $22,270; Room & Board $9490 **Undergraduates** 42% women, 22% 25 or older, 1% Native American, 6% Hispanic American, 4% African American, 5% Asian American/Pacific Islander **Academic program** Adult/continuing education programs, internships **Contact** Ms. Rachel Birchwood, Director of Admissions, The Culinary Institute of America, 1946 Campus Drive, Hudson Hall, Hyde Park, NY 12538. Phone: 845-451-1302 or toll-free 800-CULINARY. Fax: 845-451-1068. E-mail: admissions@culinary.edu. Web site: http://www.ciachef.edu/.

DAEMEN COLLEGE
AMHERST, NEW YORK

General Independent, comprehensive, coed **Entrance** Moderately difficult **Setting** 35-acre suburban campus **Total enrollment** 2,511 **Student-faculty ratio** 13:1 **Application deadline** Rolling (freshmen), rolling (transfer) **Freshmen** 68% were admitted **Housing** Yes **Expenses** Tuition $18,750; Room & Board $8610 **Undergraduates** 73% women, 19% part-time, 19% 25 or older, 0.4% Native American, 2% Hispanic American, 10% African American, 1% Asian American/Pacific Islander **The most frequently chosen baccalaureate fields are** biological/life sciences, education, health professions and related sciences **Academic program** Advanced placement, accelerated degree program, self-designed majors, honors program, summer session, adult/continuing education programs, internships **Contact** Mr. Frank Williams, Associate Director of Admissions, Daemen College, 4380 Main Street, Amherst, NY 14226-3592. Phone: 716-839-8225 or toll-free 800-462-7652. Fax: 716-839-8229. E-mail: admissions@daemen.edu. Web site: http://www.daemen.edu/.

DARKEI NOAM RABBINICAL COLLEGE
BROOKLYN, NEW YORK

Contact Rabbi Pinchas Horowitz, Director of Admissions, Darkei Noam Rabbinical College, 2822 Avenue J, Brooklyn, NY 11210. Phone: 718-338-6464.

DAVIS COLLEGE
JOHNSON CITY, NEW YORK

General Independent nondenominational, 4-year, coed **Entrance** Minimally difficult **Setting** 22-acre suburban campus **Total enrollment** 323 **Student-faculty ratio** 14:1 **Application deadline** Rolling (freshmen), rolling (transfer) **Freshmen** 68% were admitted **Housing** Yes **Expenses** Tuition $10,250; Room & Board $5820 **Undergraduates** 54% women, 37% part-time, 29% 25 or older, 0.3% Native American, 2% Hispanic American, 6% African American, 2% Asian American/Pacific Islander **The most frequently chosen baccalaureate field is** theology and religious vocations **Academic program** English as a second language, advanced placement, summer session, adult/continuing education programs, internships **Contact** Director of Admissions, Davis College, PO Box 601, Bible School Park, NY 13737-0601. Phone: 607-729-1581 Ext. 406 or toll-free 800-331-4137 Ext. 406. Fax: 607-729-2962. E-mail: admissions@davisny.edu. Web site: http://www.davisny.edu/.

DeVRY COLLEGE OF NEW YORK
LONG ISLAND CITY, NEW YORK

General Proprietary, 4-year, coed **Entrance** Minimally difficult **Setting** 4-acre urban campus **Total enrollment** 1,042 **Student-faculty ratio** 14:1 **Application deadline** Rolling (freshmen), rolling (transfer) **Housing** No **Expenses** Tuition $14,660 **Undergraduates** 25% women, 29% part-time, 49% 25 or older, 1% Native American, 29% Hispanic American, 34% African American, 10% Asian American/Pacific Islander **The most frequently chosen baccalaureate fields are** business/marketing, computer and information sciences, engineering technologies **Academic program** Advanced placement, accelerated degree program, summer session, adult/continuing education programs **Contact** Admissions Office, DeVry College of New York, 30-20 Thomson Avenue, Long Island City, NY 11101. Web site: http://www.devry.edu/.

DOMINICAN COLLEGE
ORANGEBURG, NEW YORK

General Independent, comprehensive, coed **Entrance** Noncompetitive **Setting** 62-acre suburban campus **Total enrollment** 1,933 **Student-faculty ratio** 14:1 **Application deadline** Rolling (freshmen), rolling (transfer) **Freshmen** 75% were admitted **Housing** Yes **Expenses** Tuition $19,510; Room & Board $9357 **Undergraduates** 68% women, 27% part-time, 33% 25 or older, 0.3% Native American, 18% Hispanic American, 18% African American, 8% Asian American/Pacific Islander **The most frequently chosen baccalaureate fields are** business/marketing, health professions and related sciences, social sciences **Academic program** Advanced placement, accelerated degree program, honors program, summer session, adult/continuing education programs, internships **Contact** Ms. Joyce Elbe, Director of Admissions, Dominican College, 470 Western Highway, Orangeburg, NY 10962-1210. Phone: 845-848-7900 or toll-free 866-432-4636. Fax: 845-365-3150. E-mail: admissions@dc.edu. Web site: http://www.dc.edu/.

DOWLING COLLEGE
OAKDALE, NEW YORK

General Independent, comprehensive, coed **Entrance** Moderately difficult **Setting** 157-acre suburban campus **Total enrollment** 5,833 **Student-faculty ratio** 15:1 **Application deadline** Rolling (freshmen), rolling (transfer) **Freshmen** 76% were admitted **Housing** Yes **Expenses** Tuition $19,270; Room & Board $8907 **Undergraduates** 58% women, 36% part-time, 22% 25 or older, 0.3% Native American, 10% Hispanic American, 10% African American, 2% Asian American/Pacific Islander **The most frequently chosen baccalaureate fields are** business/marketing, education, liberal arts/general studies **Academic program** English as a second language, advanced placement, accelerated degree program, self-designed majors, honors program, summer session, internships **Contact** Ms. Ronnie Lee MacDonald, Assistant Vice President for Student Affairs, Dowling College, 150 Idle Hour Boulevard, Oakdale, NY 11769. Phone: 631-244-3030 or toll-free 800-DOWLING. Fax: 631-244-1078. E-mail: admissions@dowling.edu. Web site: http://www.dowling.edu/.

D'YOUVILLE COLLEGE
BUFFALO, NEW YORK

General Independent, comprehensive, coed **Entrance** Moderately difficult **Setting** 7-acre urban campus **Total enrollment** 3,018 **Student-faculty ratio** 13:1 **Application deadline** Rolling (freshmen), rolling (transfer) **Freshmen** 64% were admitted **Housing** Yes **Expenses** Tuition $17,800; Room & Board $8750 **Undergraduates** 75% women, 19% part-time, 34% 25 or older, 1% Native American, 5% Hispanic American, 15% African American, 1% Asian American/Pacific Islander **The most frequently chosen baccalaureate fields are** business/marketing, health professions and related sciences, interdisciplinary studies **Academic program** Accelerated degree program, summer session, adult/continuing education programs, internships **Contact** Mr. Ronald Dannecker, Director of Admissions, D'Youville College, 320 Porter Avenue, Buffalo, NY 14201-1084. Phone: 716-829-7600 or toll-free 800-777-3921. Fax: 716-829-7790. E-mail: admissions@dyc.edu. Web site: http://www.dyc.edu/.

ELMIRA COLLEGE
ELMIRA, NEW YORK

Contact Mr. Gary Fallis, Dean of Admissions, Elmira College, Office of Admissions, Elmira, NY 14901. Phone: 607-735-1724 or toll-free 800-935-6472. Fax: 607-735-1718. E-mail: admissions@elmira.edu. Web site: http://www.elmira.edu/.

►**For more information, see page 457.**

EUGENE LANG COLLEGE THE NEW SCHOOL FOR LIBERAL ARTS
NEW YORK, NEW YORK

General Independent, 4-year, coed **Entrance** Moderately difficult **Setting** 5-acre urban campus **Total enrollment** 1,294 **Student-faculty ratio** 15:1 **Application deadline** 2/1 (freshmen), 5/15 (transfer) **Freshmen** 63% were admitted **Housing** Yes **Expenses** Tuition $31,310; Room & Board $11,750 **Undergraduates** 69% women, 5% part-time, 3% 25 or older, 1% Native American, 6% Hispanic American, 4% African American, 5% Asian American/Pacific Islander **The most frequently chosen baccalaureate field is** liberal arts/general studies **Academic program** English as a second language, advanced placement, accelerated degree program, self-designed majors, summer session, adult/continuing education programs, internships **Contact** Nicole Curvin, Director of Admissions, Eugene Lang College The New School for Liberal Arts, 65 West 11th Street, New York, NY 10011-8601. Phone: 212-229-5665 or toll-free 877-528-3321. Fax: 212-229-5166. E-mail: lang@newschool.edu. Web site: http://www.lang.edu/.

EXCELSIOR COLLEGE
ALBANY, NEW YORK

General Independent, comprehensive, coed **Entrance** Noncompetitive **Setting** urban campus

Total enrollment 34,653 **Application deadline** Rolling (freshmen), rolling (transfer) **Housing** No **Undergraduates** 60% women, 100% part-time, 97% 25 or older, 1% Native American, 5% Hispanic American, 16% African American, 4% Asian American/Pacific Islander **The most frequently chosen baccalaureate fields are** business/marketing, computer and information sciences, liberal arts/general studies **Academic program** Advanced placement, accelerated degree program, self-designed majors, honors program, adult/continuing education programs **Contact** Admissions, Excelsior College, 7 Columbia Circle, Albany, NY 12203-5159. Phone: 518-464-8500 or toll-free 888-647-2388. Fax: 518-464-8777. E-mail: admissions@excelsior.edu. Web site: http://www.excelsior.edu/.

FARMINGDALE STATE COLLEGE
FARMINGDALE, NEW YORK

General State-supported, 4-year, coed **Entrance** Moderately difficult **Setting** 380-acre small-town campus **Total enrollment** 6,447 **Student-faculty ratio** 18:1 **Application deadline** Rolling (freshmen), rolling (transfer) **Freshmen** 52% were admitted **Housing** Yes **Expenses** Tuition $5345; Room & Board $11,410 **Undergraduates** 44% women, 31% part-time, 23% 25 or older, 0.2% Native American, 9% Hispanic American, 10% African American, 4% Asian American/Pacific Islander **The most frequently chosen baccalaureate fields are** business/marketing, computer and information sciences, engineering technologies **Academic program** Advanced placement, summer session, internships **Contact** Mr. Jim Hall, Director of Admissions, Farmingdale State College, 2350 Broadhollow Road, Farmingdale, NY 11735-1021. Phone: 631-420-2457 or toll-free 877-4-FARMINGDALE. Fax: 631-420-2633. E-mail: admissions@farmingdale.edu. Web site: http://www.farmingdale.edu/.

FASHION INSTITUTE OF TECHNOLOGY
NEW YORK, NEW YORK

General State and locally supported, comprehensive, coed, primarily women **Entrance** Moderately difficult **Setting** 5-acre urban campus **Total enrollment** 9,938 **Student-faculty ratio** 17:1 **Application deadline** 2/1 (freshmen), 1/1 (transfer) **Freshmen** 42% were admitted **Housing** Yes **Expenses** Tuition $5007; Room & Board $10,095 **Undergraduates** 85% women, 31% part-time, 23% 25 or older, 0.2% Native American, 11% Hispanic American, 6% African American, 9% Asian American/Pacific Islander **The most frequently chosen baccalaureate fields are** business/marketing, communications/journalism, visual and performing arts **Academic program** English as a second language, advanced placement, honors program, summer session, adult/continuing education programs, internships **Contact** Ms. Dolores Lombardi, Director of Admissions, Fashion Institute of Technology, Seventh Avenue at 27th Street, New York, NY 10001-5992. Phone: 212-217-3760 or toll-free 800-GOTOFIT. Fax: 212-217-3761. E-mail: fitinfo@fitnyc.edu. Web site: http://www.fitnyc.edu/.

FIVE TOWNS COLLEGE
DIX HILLS, NEW YORK

General Independent, comprehensive, coed **Entrance** Moderately difficult **Setting** 40-acre suburban campus **Total enrollment** 1,151 **Student-faculty ratio** 13:1 **Application deadline** Rolling (freshmen), rolling (transfer) **Freshmen** 71% were admitted **Housing** Yes **Expenses** Tuition $18,125; Room & Board $11,750 **Undergraduates** 38% women, 8% part-time, 1% 25 or older, 0.1% Native American, 11% Hispanic American, 19% African American, 1% Asian American/Pacific Islander **Academic program** Advanced placement, summer session, internships **Contact** Mr. Jerry Cohen, Dean of Enrollment, Five Towns College, 305 North Service Road, Dix Hills, NY 11746-6055. Phone: 631-424-7000 Ext. 2110. Fax: 631-656-2172. Web site: http://www.fivetowns.edu/.

►**For more information, see page 460.**

FORDHAM UNIVERSITY
NEW YORK, NEW YORK

General Independent Roman Catholic (Jesuit), university, coed **Entrance** Very difficult **Setting** 85-acre urban campus **Total enrollment** 14,448 **Student-faculty ratio** 12:1 **Application deadline** 1/15 (freshmen), 7/1 (transfer) **Freshmen** 42% were admitted **Housing** Yes **Expenses** Tuition $32,857; Room & Board $12,300 **Undergraduates** 57% women, 7% part-time, 7% 25 or older, 0.3% Native American, 12% Hispanic American, 6% African American, 6% Asian American/Pacific Islander **Academic program** English as a second language, advanced placement, accelerated degree program, self-designed majors, honors program, summer session, adult/continuing education programs, internships **Contact** Mr. Peter Farrell, Director of Admission, Fordham University, 441 East Fordham Road, New York, NY 10458. Phone: 718-817-4000 or toll-free 800-FORDHAM. Fax: 718-367-9404. E-mail: enroll@fordham.edu. Web site: http://www.fordham.edu/.

►**For more information, see page 461.**

GLOBAL COLLEGE OF LONG ISLAND UNIVERSITY
BROOKLYN, NEW YORK

General Independent, 4-year, coed **Entrance** Minimally difficult **Setting** urban campus **Total enrollment** 98 **Student-faculty ratio** 4:1 **Application deadline** Rolling (freshmen), rolling (transfer) **Freshmen** 73% were admitted **Housing** Yes **Expenses** Tuition $31,072; Room & Board $3800 **Undergraduates** 68% women, 10% 25 or older, 1% Native American, 8% Hispanic American, 8% African American, 6% Asian American/Pacific Islander **Academic program** Advanced placement, internships **Contact** Amy Greenstein, Director of Admissions, Global College of Long Island University, 9 Hanover Place, 4th Floor, Brooklyn, NY 11201. Phone: 718-780-4320. Fax: 718-780-4325. E-mail: fw@liu.edu. Web site: http://www.liu.edu/globalcollege/.

GLOBE INSTITUTE OF TECHNOLOGY
NEW YORK, NEW YORK

General Proprietary, 4-year, coed **Contact** Ms. Tanya Garelik, Admissions Director, Globe Institute of Technology, 291 Broadway, New York, NY 10007. Phone: 212-349-4330 Ext. 1624 or toll-free 877-394-5623. Fax: 212-227-5920. E-mail: admissions@globe.edu. Web site: http://www.globe.edu/.

HAMILTON COLLEGE
CLINTON, NEW YORK

General Independent, 4-year, coed **Entrance** Very difficult **Setting** 1,200-acre small-town campus **Total enrollment** 1,842 **Student-faculty ratio** 10:1 **Application deadline** 1/1 (freshmen), 4/15 (transfer) **Freshmen** 28% were admitted **Housing** Yes **Expenses** Tuition $36,860; Room & Board $9350 **Undergraduates** 52% women, 2% part-time, 1% 25 or older, 1% Native American, 5% Hispanic American, 4% African American, 7% Asian American/Pacific Islander **The most frequently chosen baccalaureate fields are** foreign languages and literature, social sciences, visual and performing arts **Academic program** English as a second language, advanced placement, accelerated degree program, self-designed majors, adult/continuing education programs, internships **Contact** Ms. Monica Inzer, Dean of Admission and Financial Aid, Hamilton College, 198 College Hill Road, Clinton, NY 13323-1296. Phone: 315-859-4421 or toll-free 800-843-2655. Fax: 315-859-4457. E-mail: admission@hamilton.edu. Web site: http://www.hamilton.edu/.

HARTWICK COLLEGE
ONEONTA, NEW YORK

General Independent, 4-year, coed **Entrance** Moderately difficult **Setting** 425-acre small-town campus **Total enrollment** 1,537 **Student-faculty ratio** 11:1 **Application deadline** 2/15 (freshmen), 8/1 (transfer) **Freshmen** 84% were admitted **Housing** Yes **Expenses** Tuition $30,730; Room & Board $8370 **Undergraduates** 56% women, 4% part-time, 2% 25 or older, 0.4% Native American, 5% Hispanic American, 5% African American, 2% Asian American/Pacific Islander **The most frequently chosen baccalaureate fields are** business/marketing, English, social sciences **Academic program** Advanced placement, accelerated degree program, self-designed majors, honors program, internships **Contact** Ms. Jacqueline Gregory, Director of Admissions, Hartwick College, PO Box 4022, Oneonta, NY 13820-4022. Phone: 607-431-4150 or toll-free 888-HARTWICK. Fax: 607-431-4102. E-mail: admissions@hartwick.edu. Web site: http://www.hartwick.edu/.

HILBERT COLLEGE
HAMBURG, NEW YORK

General Independent, 4-year, coed **Entrance** Minimally difficult **Setting** 40-acre small-town campus **Total enrollment** 1,046 **Student-faculty ratio** 12:1 **Application deadline** 9/1 (freshmen), 8/1 (transfer) **Freshmen** 85% were admitted **Housing** Yes **Expenses** Tuition $16,600; Room & Board $6600 **Undergraduates** 61% women, 24% part-time, 30% 25 or older, 2% Native American, 2% Hispanic American, 6% African American, 0.1% Asian American/Pacific Islander **The most frequently chosen baccalaureate fields are** business/marketing, liberal arts/general studies, security and protective services **Academic program** Advanced placement, honors program, summer session, internships **Contact** Mr. Timothy Lee, Director of Admissions, Hilbert College, 5200 South Park Avenue, Hamburg, NY 14075-1597. Phone: 716-649-7900 Ext. 244. Fax: 716-649-0702. E-mail: tlee@hilbert.edu. Web site: http://www.hilbert.edu/.

HOBART AND WILLIAM SMITH COLLEGES
GENEVA, NEW YORK

General Independent, 4-year, coed **Entrance** Very difficult **Setting** 200-acre small-town campus **Total enrollment** 2,009 **Student-faculty ratio** 11:1 **Application deadline** 2/1 (freshmen), 7/1 (transfer) **Freshmen** 55% were admitted **Housing** Yes **Expenses** Tuition $38,860; Room & Board $9686 **Undergraduates** 54% women, 0.2% part-time, 0.4% Native American, 3% Hispanic

American, 4% African American, 3% Asian American/Pacific Islander **The most frequently chosen baccalaureate fields are** English, history, social sciences **Academic program** English as a second language, advanced placement, accelerated degree program, self-designed majors, honors program, adult/continuing education programs, internships **Contact** Don W. Emmons, Dean of Admissions and Vice President of Enrollment, Hobart and William Smith Colleges, Geneva, NY 14456-3397. Phone: 315-781-3622 or toll-free 800-245-0100. Fax: 315-781-5471. E-mail: admissions@hws.edu. Web site: http://www.hws.edu/.

HOFSTRA UNIVERSITY
HEMPSTEAD, NEW YORK

General Independent, university, coed **Entrance** Moderately difficult **Setting** 240-acre suburban campus **Total enrollment** 12,490 **Student-faculty ratio** 14:1 **Application deadline** Rolling (freshmen) **Freshmen** 54% were admitted **Housing** Yes **Expenses** Tuition $26,730; Room & Board $10,300 **Undergraduates** 53% women, 9% part-time, 7% 25 or older, 1% Native American, 7% Hispanic American, 9% African American, 5% Asian American/Pacific Islander **The most frequently chosen baccalaureate fields are** business/marketing, communications/journalism, psychology **Academic program** English as a second language, advanced placement, accelerated degree program, self-designed majors, honors program, summer session, adult/continuing education programs, internships **Contact** Mr. Sunil Samuel, Senior Associate Dean of Admissions, Hofstra University, 100 Hofstra University, Hempstead, NY 11549. Phone: 516-463-6700 or toll-free 800-HOFSTRA. Fax: 516-463-5100. E-mail: admitme@hofstra.edu. Web site: http://www.hofstra.edu/.

►**For more information, see page 467.**

HOLY TRINITY ORTHODOX SEMINARY
JORDANVILLE, NEW YORK

General Independent Russian Orthodox, 5-year, men only **Entrance** Noncompetitive **Setting** 900-acre rural campus **Total enrollment** 28 **Student-faculty ratio** 2:1 **Application deadline** 5/1 (freshmen), 5/1 (transfer) **Freshmen** 80% were admitted **Housing** Yes **Expenses** Tuition $3025; Room & Board $2500 **Undergraduates** 11% part-time, 75% 25 or older, 4% Hispanic American **The most frequently chosen baccalaureate field is** theology and religious vocations **Academic program** English as a second language, accelerated degree program **Contact** Fr. Vladimir Tsurikov, Assistant Dean, Holy Trinity Orthodox Seminary, PO Box 36, Jordanville, NY 13361. Phone: 315-858-0945. Fax: 315-858-0945. E-mail: info@hts.edu. Web site: http://www.hts.edu/.

HOUGHTON COLLEGE
HOUGHTON, NEW YORK

General Independent Wesleyan, comprehensive, coed **Entrance** Moderately difficult **Setting** 1,300-acre rural campus **Total enrollment** 1,382 **Student-faculty ratio** 14:1 **Application deadline** Rolling (freshmen), rolling (transfer) **Freshmen** 84% were admitted **Housing** Yes **Expenses** Tuition $21,620; Room & Board $6860 **Undergraduates** 64% women, 5% part-time, 13% 25 or older, 0.4% Native American, 1% Hispanic American, 2% African American, 2% Asian American/Pacific Islander **The most frequently chosen baccalaureate fields are** business/marketing, education, theology and religious vocations **Academic program** Advanced placement, honors program, summer session, adult/continuing education programs, internships **Contact** Mr. Wayne MacBeth, Vice President for Enrollment Management and Market Relations, Houghton College, PO Box 128, Houghton, NY 14744. Phone: 585-567-9353 or toll-free 800-777-2556. Fax: 585-567-9522. E-mail: admission@houghton.edu. Web site: http://www.houghton.edu/.

HUNTER COLLEGE OF THE CITY UNIVERSITY OF NEW YORK
NEW YORK, NEW YORK

General State and locally supported, comprehensive, coed **Entrance** Moderately difficult **Setting** urban campus **Total enrollment** 20,845 **Student-faculty ratio** 15:1 **Application deadline** 3/15 (freshmen), 3/15 (transfer) **Freshmen** 30% were admitted **Housing** Yes **Expenses** Tuition $4349; Room only $5311 **Undergraduates** 68% women, 32% part-time, 28% 25 or older, 0.2% Native American, 19% Hispanic American, 12% African American, 18% Asian American/Pacific Islander **The most frequently chosen baccalaureate fields are** English, psychology, social sciences **Academic program** English as a second language, advanced placement, self-designed majors, honors program, summer session, internships **Contact** Mr. William Zlata, Director of Admissions, Hunter College of the City University of New York, 695 Park Avenue, New York, NY 10021-5085. Phone: 212-772-4490. Fax: 212-650-3472. E-mail: bill.zlata@hunter.cuny.edu. Web site: http://www.hunter.cuny.edu/.

IONA COLLEGE
NEW ROCHELLE, NEW YORK

General Independent, comprehensive, coed, affiliated with Roman Catholic Church **Entrance** Moderately difficult **Setting** 35-acre suburban campus **Total enrollment** 4,323 **Student-faculty ratio** 13:1 **Application deadline** 2/15

Iona College *(continued)*

(freshmen), 8/15 (transfer) **Freshmen** 59% were admitted **Housing** Yes **Expenses** Tuition $24,724; Room & Board $10,500 **Undergraduates** 54% women, 5% part-time, 5% 25 or older, 0.2% Native American, 11% Hispanic American, 6% African American, 2% Asian American/Pacific Islander **The most frequently chosen baccalaureate fields are** business/marketing, communications/journalism, psychology **Academic program** Advanced placement, accelerated degree program, honors program, summer session, adult/continuing education programs, internships **Contact** Mr. Kevin Cavanagh, Assistant Vice President for College Admissions, Iona College, Admissions, 715 North Avenue, New Rochelle, NY 10801. Phone: 914-633-2502 or toll-free 800-231-IONA. Fax: 914-637-2778. E-mail: icad@iona.edu. Web site: http://www.iona.edu/.

ITHACA COLLEGE
ITHACA, NEW YORK

General Independent, comprehensive, coed **Entrance** Moderately difficult **Setting** 757-acre small-town campus **Total enrollment** 6,660 **Student-faculty ratio** 12:1 **Application deadline** 2/1 (freshmen), 3/1 (transfer) **Freshmen** 74% were admitted **Housing** Yes **Expenses** Tuition $28,670; Room & Board $10,728 **Undergraduates** 55% women, 2% part-time, 0.5% Native American, 4% Hispanic American, 3% African American, 4% Asian American/Pacific Islander **The most frequently chosen baccalaureate fields are** communications/journalism, health professions and related sciences, visual and performing arts **Academic program** Advanced placement, accelerated degree program, self-designed majors, honors program, summer session, adult/continuing education programs, internships **Contact** Gerard Turbide, Director of Admission, Ithaca College, 100 Job Hall, Ithaca, NY 14850-7020. Phone: 607-274-3124 or toll-free 800-429-4274. Fax: 607-274-1900. E-mail: admission@ithaca.edu. Web site: http://www.ithaca.edu/.

►**For more information, see page 468.**

JOHN JAY COLLEGE OF CRIMINAL JUSTICE OF THE CITY UNIVERSITY OF NEW YORK
NEW YORK, NEW YORK

Contact Richard Saulnier PhD, Dean for Enrollment Services, John Jay College of Criminal Justice of the City University of New York, 899 Tenth Avenue, New York, NY 10019-1093. Phone: 212-237-8878 or toll-free 877-JOHNJAY. Web site: http://www.jjay.cuny.edu/.

THE JUILLIARD SCHOOL
NEW YORK, NEW YORK

General Independent, comprehensive, coed **Entrance** Most difficult **Setting** urban campus **Total enrollment** 832 **Student-faculty ratio** 3:1 **Application deadline** 12/1 (freshmen), 12/1 (transfer) **Freshmen** 6% were admitted **Housing** Yes **Expenses** Tuition $27,150; Room & Board $10,740 **Undergraduates** 45% women, 0.4% part-time, 0.2% Native American, 5% Hispanic American, 9% African American, 16% Asian American/Pacific Islander **The most frequently chosen baccalaureate field is** visual and performing arts **Academic program** English as a second language, accelerated degree program, adult/continuing education programs **Contact** Ms. Lee Cioppa, Associate Dean for Admissions, The Juilliard School, 60 Lincoln Center Plaza, New York, NY 10023-6588. Phone: 212-799-5000 Ext. 223. Fax: 212-724-0263. E-mail: admissions@julliard.edu. Web site: http://www.juilliard.edu/.

KEHILATH YAKOV RABBINICAL SEMINARY
BROOKLYN, NEW YORK

Contact Rabbi Zalman Gombo, Admissions Officer, Kehilath Yakov Rabbinical Seminary, 206 Wilson Street, Brooklyn, NY 11211-7207. Phone: 718-963-1212.

KEUKA COLLEGE
KEUKA PARK, NEW YORK

General Independent, comprehensive, coed, affiliated with American Baptist Churches in the U.S.A. **Entrance** Moderately difficult **Setting** 173-acre rural campus **Total enrollment** 1,629 **Student-faculty ratio** 14:1 **Application deadline** Rolling (freshmen), rolling (transfer) **Freshmen** 75% were admitted **Housing** Yes **Expenses** Tuition $20,550; Room & Board $8530 **Undergraduates** 71% women, 22% part-time, 17% 25 or older, 1% Native American, 2% Hispanic American, 6% African American, 1% Asian American/Pacific Islander **The most frequently chosen baccalaureate fields are** business/marketing, education, health professions and related sciences **Academic program** Advanced placement, accelerated degree program, self-designed majors, summer session, adult/continuing education programs, internships **Contact** Fred Hoyle, Associate Vice President of Admissions, Keuka College, Wagner House, Keuka Park, NY 14478. Phone: 315-279-5254 or toll-free 800-33-KEUKA. Fax: 315-279-5386. E-mail: admissions@mail.keuka.edu. Web site: http://www.keuka.edu/.

THE KING'S COLLEGE
NEW YORK, NEW YORK

General Independent nondenominational, 4-year, coed **Entrance** Very difficult **Setting** urban campus **Total enrollment** 216 **Student-faculty ratio** 13:1 **Application deadline** 2/1 (freshmen), 2/1 (transfer) **Freshmen** 75% were admitted **Housing** Yes **Expenses** Tuition $22,850; Room only $8750 **Undergraduates** 63% women, 0.5% part-time, 6% 25 or older, 3% Hispanic American, 2% African American, 2% Asian American/Pacific Islander **The most frequently chosen baccalaureate fields are** education, business/marketing, interdisciplinary studies **Academic program** Advanced placement, summer session **Contact** Mr. Brian Parker, Vice President for Admissions, The King's College, 350 Fifth Avenue, 15th Floor Empire State Building, New York, NY 10118. Phone: 212-659-7217 or toll-free 888-969-7200 Ext. 3610. Fax: 212-659-3611. E-mail: info@tkc.edu. Web site: http://www.tkc.edu/.

KOL YAAKOV TORAH CENTER
MONSEY, NEW YORK

Contact Assistant Director of Admissions, Kol Yaakov Torah Center, 29 West Maple Avenue, Monsey, NY 10952-2954. Phone: 914-425-3863. E-mail: horizonss@aol.com. Web site: http://horizons.edu/.

LABORATORY INSTITUTE OF MERCHANDISING
NEW YORK, NEW YORK

General Proprietary, 4-year, coed, primarily women **Entrance** Moderately difficult **Setting** urban campus **Total enrollment** 1,107 **Student-faculty ratio** 17:1 **Application deadline** Rolling (freshmen), rolling (transfer) **Freshmen** 63% were admitted **Housing** Yes **Expenses** Tuition $18,625; Room & Board $15,800 **Undergraduates** 95% women, 4% part-time, 3% 25 or older, 0.3% Native American, 16% Hispanic American, 9% African American, 6% Asian American/Pacific Islander **The most frequently chosen baccalaureate fields are** business/marketing, family and consumer sciences, visual and performing arts **Academic program** Advanced placement, accelerated degree program, summer session, internships **Contact** Ms. Kristina Gibson, Director of Admissions, Laboratory Institute of Merchandising, 12 East 53rd Street, New York, NY 10022. Phone: 212-752-1530 Ext. 217 or toll-free 800-677-1323. Fax: 212-317-8602. E-mail: admissions@limcollege.edu. Web site: http://www.limcollege.edu/.

LEHMAN COLLEGE OF THE CITY UNIVERSITY OF NEW YORK
BRONX, NEW YORK

General State and locally supported, comprehensive, coed **Entrance** Moderately difficult **Setting** 37-acre urban campus **Total enrollment** 10,922 **Student-faculty ratio** 15:1 **Application deadline** Rolling (freshmen), rolling (transfer) **Freshmen** 32% were admitted **Housing** No **Expenses** Tuition $4290 **Undergraduates** 71% women, 37% part-time, 44% 25 or older, 0.1% Native American, 49% Hispanic American, 32% African American, 4% Asian American/Pacific Islander **The most frequently chosen baccalaureate fields are** education, health professions and related sciences, social sciences **Academic program** English as a second language, advanced placement, self-designed majors, honors program, summer session, adult/continuing education programs, internships **Contact** Mr. Clarence Wilkes, Director of Admissions, Lehman College of the City University of New York, 250 Bedford Park Boulevard West, Bronx, NY 10468. Phone: 718-960-8706 Ext. 8712 or toll-free 877-Lehman1. Fax: 718-960-8712. E-mail: enroll@lehman.cuny.edu. Web site: http://www.lehman.cuny.edu/.

LE MOYNE COLLEGE
SYRACUSE, NEW YORK

General Independent Roman Catholic (Jesuit), comprehensive, coed **Entrance** Moderately difficult **Setting** 161-acre suburban campus **Total enrollment** 3,508 **Student-faculty ratio** 13:1 **Application deadline** 2/1 (freshmen), 6/1 (transfer) **Freshmen** 69% were admitted **Housing** Yes **Expenses** Tuition $23,760; Room & Board $9030 **Undergraduates** 62% women, 18% part-time, 13% 25 or older, 0.5% Native American, 4% Hispanic American, 4% African American, 2% Asian American/Pacific Islander **The most frequently chosen baccalaureate fields are** business/marketing, psychology, social sciences **Academic program** Advanced placement, accelerated degree program, honors program, summer session, adult/continuing education programs, internships **Contact** Mr. Dennis J. Nicholson, Director of Admission, Le Moyne College, 1419 Salt Spring Road, Syracuse, NY 13214-1301. Phone: 315-445-4707 or toll-free 800-333-4733. Fax: 315-445-4711. E-mail: admission@lemoyne.edu. Web site: http://www.lemoyne.edu/.

LIST COLLEGE, THE JEWISH THEOLOGICAL SEMINARY
NEW YORK, NEW YORK

General Independent Jewish, university, coed **Entrance** Very difficult **Setting** 1-acre urban campus **Total enrollment** 580 **Student-faculty**

List College, The Jewish Theological Seminary *(continued)*

ratio 6:1 **Application deadline** 2/15 (freshmen), 5/1 (transfer) **Freshmen** 61% were admitted **Housing** Yes **Expenses** Tuition $15,000 **Undergraduates** 61% women, 6% part-time, 2% Hispanic American **Academic program** Advanced placement, self-designed majors, honors program, summer session, adult/continuing education programs, internships **Contact** Ms. Reina Cohen, Director List Collect Admissions, List College, The Jewish Theological Seminary, 3080 Broadway, New York, NY 10027. Phone: 212-678-8832. Fax: 212-280-6022. E-mail: lcadmissions@jtsa.edu. Web site: http://www.jtsa.edu/.

LONG ISLAND UNIVERSITY, BRENTWOOD CAMPUS

BRENTWOOD, NEW YORK

Contact Mr. John P. Metcalfe, Director of Admissions, Long Island University, Brentwood Campus, 100 Second Avenue, Brentwood, NY 11717. Phone: 631-273-5112 Ext. 26. E-mail: information@brentwood.liu.edu. Web site: http://www.liu.edu/.

LONG ISLAND UNIVERSITY, BROOKLYN CAMPUS

BROOKLYN, NEW YORK

General Independent, university, coed **Entrance** Minimally difficult **Setting** 10-acre urban campus **Total enrollment** 8,174 **Application deadline** Rolling (freshmen), rolling (transfer) **Freshmen** 61% were admitted **Housing** Yes **Expenses** Tuition $25,950; Room & Board $9410 **Undergraduates** 72% women, 16% part-time, 26% 25 or older, 0.3% Native American, 12% Hispanic American, 35% African American, 16% Asian American/Pacific Islander **The most frequently chosen baccalaureate fields are** business/marketing, health professions and related sciences, psychology **Academic program** English as a second language, advanced placement, self-designed majors, honors program, summer session, adult/continuing education programs, internships **Contact** Elizabeth Storinge, Dean of Admissions, Long Island University, Brooklyn Campus, 1 University Plaza, Brooklyn, NY 11201. Phone: 718-488-1011 or toll-free 800-LIU-PLAN. Fax: 718-797-2399. E-mail: admissions@brooklyn.liu.edu. Web site: http://www.liu.edu/.

LONG ISLAND UNIVERSITY, C.W. POST CAMPUS

BROOKVILLE, NEW YORK

General Independent, comprehensive, coed **Entrance** Moderately difficult **Setting** 308-acre suburban campus **Total enrollment** 8,361 **Application deadline** Rolling (freshmen), rolling (transfer) **Freshmen** 78% were admitted **Housing** Yes **Expenses** Tuition $25,950; Room & Board $9600 **Undergraduates** 63% women, 15% part-time, 14% 25 or older, 0.2% Native American, 8% Hispanic American, 9% African American, 5% Asian American/Pacific Islander **The most frequently chosen baccalaureate fields are** business/marketing, education, health professions and related sciences **Academic program** English as a second language, advanced placement, accelerated degree program, self-designed majors, honors program, summer session, adult/continuing education programs, internships **Contact** Mr. Gary Bergman, Associate Provost for Enrollment Services, Long Island University, C.W. Post Campus, 720 Northern Boulevard, Brookville, NY 11548-1300. Phone: 516-299-2900 or toll-free 800-LIU-PLAN. Fax: 516-299-2137. E-mail: enroll@cwpost.liu.edu. Web site: http://www.liu.edu/.

MACHZIKEI HADATH RABBINICAL COLLEGE

BROOKLYN, NEW YORK

Contact Rabbi Abraham M. Lezerowitz, Director of Admissions, Machzikei Hadath Rabbinical College, 5407 Sixteenth Avenue, Brooklyn, NY 11204-1805. Phone: 718-854-8777.

MANHATTAN COLLEGE

RIVERDALE, NEW YORK

General Independent, comprehensive, coed, affiliated with Roman Catholic Church **Contact** Mr. William Bisset, Assistant Vice President for Enrollment Management, Manhattan College, 4513 Manhattan College Parkway, Riverdale, NY 10471. Phone: 718-862-7200 or toll-free 800-622-9235. Fax: 718-862-8019. E-mail: admit@manhattan.edu. Web site: http://www.manhattan.edu/.

MANHATTAN SCHOOL OF MUSIC

NEW YORK, NEW YORK

General Independent, comprehensive, coed **Entrance** Very difficult **Setting** 1-acre urban campus **Total enrollment** 854 **Student-faculty ratio** 5:1 **Application deadline** 12/1 (freshmen), 12/1 (transfer) **Freshmen** 37% were admitted **Housing** Yes **Undergraduates** 50% women, 1% part-time, 4% 25 or older, 0.2% Native American, 4% Hispanic American, 4% African American, 9% Asian American/Pacific Islander **The most frequently chosen baccalaureate field is** visual and performing arts **Academic program** English as a second language, advanced placement **Contact** Mrs. Amy Anderson, Director of Admission and Financial Aid, Manhattan School of Music, 120 Claremont Avenue, New York, NY 10027. Phone: 212-749-2802 Ext. 4501. Fax: 212-749-3025. E-mail: admission@msmnyc.edu. Web site: http://www.msmnyc.edu/.

MANHATTANVILLE COLLEGE

PURCHASE, NEW YORK

General Independent, comprehensive, coed **Entrance** Moderately difficult **Setting** 100-acre suburban campus **Total enrollment** 3,023 **Student-faculty ratio** 11:1 **Application deadline** 3/1 (freshmen), 3/1 (transfer) **Freshmen** 50% were admitted **Housing** Yes **Expenses** Tuition $31,620; Room & Board $13,040 **Undergraduates** 67% women, 7% part-time, 2% 25 or older, 1% Native American, 15% Hispanic American, 7% African American, 2% Asian American/Pacific Islander **The most frequently chosen baccalaureate fields are** business/marketing, psychology, social sciences **Academic program** English as a second language, advanced placement, accelerated degree program, self-designed majors, honors program, summer session, adult/continuing education programs, internships **Contact** Ms. Erica Padilla, Director of Admissions, Manhattanville College, 2900 Purchase Street, Purchase, NY 10577. Phone: 914-323-5124 or toll-free 800-328-4553. Fax: 914-694-1732. E-mail: admissions@mville.edu. Web site: http://www.manhattanville.edu/.

MANNES COLLEGE THE NEW SCHOOL FOR MUSIC

NEW YORK, NEW YORK

General Independent, comprehensive, coed **Entrance** Very difficult **Setting** urban campus **Total enrollment** 379 **Student-faculty ratio** 6:1 **Application deadline** 12/1 (freshmen), 5/15 (transfer) **Freshmen** 34% were admitted **Housing** Yes **Expenses** Tuition $30,410; Room & Board $11,750 **Undergraduates** 57% women, 16% part-time, 22% 25 or older, 5% Hispanic American, 3% African American, 9% Asian American/Pacific Islander **The most frequently chosen baccalaureate field is** visual and performing arts **Academic program** English as a second language, advanced placement, summer session, adult/continuing education programs **Contact** Ms. Georgia Schmitt, Director of Admissions, Mannes College The New School for Music, 150 West 85th Street, New York, NY 10024-4402. Phone: 212-580-0210 Ext. 4862 or toll-free 800-292-3040. Fax: 212-580-1738. E-mail: mannesadmissions@newschool.edu. Web site: http://www.newschool.mannes.edu/.

MARIST COLLEGE

POUGHKEEPSIE, NEW YORK

General Independent, comprehensive, coed **Entrance** Very difficult **Setting** 180-acre small-town campus **Total enrollment** 5,727 **Student-faculty ratio** 15:1 **Application deadline** 2/15 (freshmen), 6/1 (transfer) **Freshmen** 42% were admitted **Housing** Yes **Expenses** Tuition $24,040; Room & Board $10,250 **Undergraduates** 57% women, 8% part-time, 9% 25 or older, 0.2% Native American, 5% Hispanic American, 3% African American, 2% Asian American/Pacific Islander **The most frequently chosen baccalaureate fields are** business/marketing, communications/journalism, education **Academic program** English as a second language, advanced placement, accelerated degree program, honors program, summer session, adult/continuing education programs, internships **Contact** Mr. Kenton Rinehart, Dean of Undergraduate Admissions, Marist College, 3399 North Road, Poughkeepsie, NY 12601. Phone: 845-575-3226 or toll-free 800-436-5483. Fax: 845-575-3215. E-mail: admission@marist.edu. Web site: http://www.marist.edu/.

MARYMOUNT MANHATTAN COLLEGE

NEW YORK, NEW YORK

General Independent, 4-year, coed **Entrance** Moderately difficult **Setting** 3-acre urban campus **Total enrollment** 1,895 **Student-faculty ratio** 11:1 **Application deadline** Rolling (freshmen), rolling (transfer) **Freshmen** 74% were admitted **Housing** Yes **Expenses** Tuition $20,600; Room & Board $12,250 **Undergraduates** 75% women, 17% part-time, 12% 25 or older, 0.5% Native American, 11% Hispanic American, 11% African American, 3% Asian American/Pacific Islander **The most frequently chosen baccalaureate fields are** communications/journalism, psychology, visual and performing arts **Academic program** English as a second language, advanced placement, accelerated degree program, honors program, summer session, adult/continuing education programs, internships **Contact** Mr. James Rogers, Dean of Admissions, Marymount Manhattan College, 221 East 71st Street, New York, NY 10021. Phone: 212-517-0430 or toll-free 800-MARYMOUNT. Fax: 212-517-0448. E-mail: admissions@mmm.edu. Web site: http://www.mmm.edu/.

MEDAILLE COLLEGE

BUFFALO, NEW YORK

General Independent, comprehensive, coed **Entrance** Moderately difficult **Setting** 13-acre urban campus **Total enrollment** 2,929 **Student-faculty ratio** 15:1 **Application deadline** 8/1

Medaille College *(continued)*

(freshmen), rolling (transfer) **Freshmen** 79% were admitted **Housing** Yes **Expenses** Tuition $16,590; Room & Board $8424 **Undergraduates** 63% women, 5% part-time, 48% 25 or older, 1% Native American, 2% Hispanic American, 13% African American, 0.5% Asian American/Pacific Islander **The most frequently chosen baccalaureate fields are** business/marketing, education, security and protective services **Academic program** Advanced placement, accelerated degree program, self-designed majors, honors program, summer session, adult/continuing education programs, internships **Contact** Mr. Greg Florczak, Director of Undergraduate Admissions, Medaille College, Medaille College, Office of Admissions, Buffalo, NY 14214. Phone: 716-880-2200 or toll-free 800-292-1582. Fax: 716-880-2007. E-mail: admissionsug@medaille.edu. Web site: http://www.medaille.edu/.

MEDGAR EVERS COLLEGE OF THE CITY UNIVERSITY OF NEW YORK
BROOKLYN, NEW YORK

General State and locally supported, 4-year, coed **Entrance** Noncompetitive **Setting** 1-acre urban campus **Total enrollment** 5,551 **Student-faculty ratio** 16:1 **Application deadline** Rolling (freshmen), rolling (transfer) **Freshmen** 100% were admitted **Housing** No **Expenses** Tuition $4126 **Undergraduates** 75% women, 36% part-time, 50% 25 or older, 0.1% Native American, 4% Hispanic American, 89% African American, 1% Asian American/Pacific Islander **The most frequently chosen baccalaureate fields are** business/marketing, biological/life sciences, psychology **Academic program** English as a second language, advanced placement, honors program, summer session, adult/continuing education programs, internships **Contact** Ms. Rose Banton, Director of Admissions, Medgar Evers College of the City University of New York, 1650 Bedford Avenue, Brooklyn, NY 11225-2298. Phone: 718-270-6048. Fax: 718-270-6411. E-mail: rosebanton@mec.cuny.edu. Web site: http://www.mec.cuny.edu/.

MERCY COLLEGE
DOBBS FERRY, NEW YORK

General Independent, comprehensive, coed **Entrance** Minimally difficult **Setting** 60-acre suburban campus **Total enrollment** 8,628 **Student-faculty ratio** 16:1 **Application deadline** Rolling (freshmen), rolling (transfer) **Freshmen** 39% were admitted **Housing** Yes **Expenses** Tuition $14,170; Room & Board $9820 **Undergraduates** 70% women, 34% part-time, 47% 25 or older, 1% Native American, 26% Hispanic American, 24% African American, 3% Asian American/Pacific Islander **The most frequently chosen baccalaureate fields are** business/marketing, health professions and related sciences, social sciences **Academic program** English as a second language, advanced placement, accelerated degree program, self-designed majors, honors program, summer session, adult/continuing education programs, internships **Contact** Ms. Kathleen Jackson, Director of Admissions, Mercy College, 555 Broadway, Dobbs Ferry, NY 10522-1189. Phone: 800-MERCY-GO or toll-free 800-MERCY-NY. Fax: 914-674-7382. E-mail: admissions@mercy.edu. Web site: http://www.mercy.edu/.

MESIVTA OF EASTERN PARKWAY RABBINICAL SEMINARY
BROOKLYN, NEW YORK

Contact Rabbi Joseph Halberstadt, Dean, Mesivta of Eastern Parkway Rabbinical Seminary, 510 Dahill Road, Brooklyn, NY 11218-5559. Phone: 718-438-1002.

MESIVTA TIFERETH JERUSALEM OF AMERICA
NEW YORK, NEW YORK

Contact Rabbi Fishellis, Director of Admissions, Mesivta Tifereth Jerusalem of America, 145 East Broadway, New York, NY 10002-6301. Phone: 212-964-2830.

MESIVTA TORAH VODAATH RABBINICAL SEMINARY
BROOKLYN, NEW YORK

Contact Rabbi Issac Braun, Administrator, Mesivta Torah Vodaath Rabbinical Seminary, 425 East Ninth Street, Brooklyn, NY 11218-5299. Phone: 718-941-8000. Fax: 718-941-8032.

METROPOLITAN COLLEGE OF NEW YORK
NEW YORK, NEW YORK

General Independent, comprehensive, coed, primarily women **Entrance** Moderately difficult **Setting** urban campus **Total enrollment** 990 **Student-faculty ratio** 11:1 **Application deadline** 8/15 (freshmen), 8/15 (transfer) **Freshmen** 37% were admitted **Housing** No **Expenses** Tuition $16,720 **Undergraduates** 73% women, 9% part-time, 76% 25 or older, 14% Hispanic American, 53% African American, 1% Asian American/Pacific Islander **The most frequently chosen baccalaureate fields are** business/marketing, liberal arts/general studies **Academic program** English as a second language, accelerated degree program, summer session, adult/continuing education programs, internships **Contact** Mr. Steven Lenhart, Dean of Enrollment, Metropolitan College of New York, 431 Canal Street, New York, NY 10013. Phone: 212-343-1234 or toll-free 800-33-THINK Ext. 5001. Fax: 212-343-8470. Web site: http://www.metropolitan.edu/.

MIRRER YESHIVA
BROOKLYN, NEW YORK

Contact Director of Admissions, Mirrer Yeshiva, 1795 Ocean Parkway, Brooklyn, NY 11223-2010. Phone: 718-645-0536.

MOLLOY COLLEGE
ROCKVILLE CENTRE, NEW YORK

General Independent, comprehensive, coed **Entrance** Moderately difficult **Setting** 30-acre suburban campus **Total enrollment** 3,831 **Student-faculty ratio** 11:1 **Application deadline** Rolling (freshmen), rolling (transfer) **Freshmen** 63% were admitted **Housing** No **Expenses** Tuition $18,570 **Undergraduates** 79% women, 28% part-time, 33% 25 or older, 0.3% Native American, 10% Hispanic American, 21% African American, 7% Asian American/Pacific Islander **The most frequently chosen baccalaureate fields are** education, business/marketing, health professions and related sciences **Academic program** English as a second language, advanced placement, honors program, summer session, adult/continuing education programs, internships **Contact** Ms. Marguerite Lane, Director of Admissions, Molloy College, 1000 Hempstead Avenue, PO Box 5002, Rockville Centre, NY 11571-5002. Phone: 516-678-5000 Ext. 6240 or toll-free 888-4MOLLOY. Fax: 516-256-2247. E-mail: admissions@molloy.edu. Web site: http://www.molloy.edu/.

►**For more information, see page 476.**

MONROE COLLEGE
BRONX, NEW YORK

General Proprietary, comprehensive, coed **Entrance** Moderately difficult **Setting** urban campus **Total enrollment** 4,677 **Student-faculty ratio** 21:1 **Application deadline** 8/26 (freshmen), 8/26 (transfer) **Freshmen** 58% were admitted **Housing** Yes **Expenses** Tuition $10,684; Room & Board $10,658 **Undergraduates** 73% women, 17% part-time, 56% 25 or older **The most frequently chosen baccalaureate fields are** business/marketing, health professions and related sciences, security and protective services **Academic program** English as a second language, summer session, adult/continuing education programs, internships **Contact** Mr. Evan Jerome, Director of Admissions, Monroe College, Monroe College Way, Bronx, NY 10468-5407. Phone: 718-933-6700 Ext. 8246 or toll-free 800-55MONROE. Web site: http://www.monroecollege.edu/.

MONROE COLLEGE
NEW ROCHELLE, NEW YORK

General Proprietary, 4-year, coed **Entrance** Moderately difficult **Setting** suburban campus **Total enrollment** 2,018 **Student-faculty ratio** 20:1 **Application deadline** 8/26 (freshmen), 8/26 (transfer) **Freshmen** 58% were admitted **Housing** Yes **Expenses** Tuition $10,684; Room & Board $8100 **Undergraduates** 66% women, 11% part-time, 31% 25 or older, 0.1% Native American, 19% Hispanic American, 56% African American, 1% Asian American/Pacific Islander **The most frequently chosen baccalaureate fields are** business/marketing, computer and information sciences, security and protective services **Academic program** English as a second language, summer session, adult/continuing education programs, internships **Contact** Ms. Lisa Scorca, High School Admissions, Monroe College, 434 Main Street, New Rochelle, NY 10801-6410. Phone: 914-654-3200 or toll-free 800-55MONROE. E-mail: lscora@monroecollege.edu. Web site: http://www.monroecollege.edu/.

MOUNT SAINT MARY COLLEGE
NEWBURGH, NEW YORK

General Independent, comprehensive, coed **Entrance** Moderately difficult **Setting** 72-acre suburban campus **Total enrollment** 2,588 **Student-faculty ratio** 17:1 **Application deadline** Rolling (freshmen), rolling (transfer) **Freshmen** 77% were admitted **Housing** Yes **Expenses** Tuition $19,520; Room & Board $10,400 **Undergraduates** 72% women, 19% part-time, 20% 25 or older, 0.1% Native American, 9% Hispanic American, 10% African American, 3% Asian American/Pacific Islander **The most frequently chosen baccalaureate fields are** business/marketing, English, history **Academic program** Advanced placement, accelerated degree program, self-designed majors, honors program, summer session, adult/continuing education programs, internships **Contact** Mr. J. Ognibene, Director of Admissions, Mount Saint Mary College, 330 Powell Avenue, Newburgh, NY 12550-3494. Phone: 845-569-3248 or toll-free 888-937-6762. Fax: 845-562-6762. E-mail: admissions@msmc.edu. Web site: http://www.msmc.edu/.

NAZARETH COLLEGE OF ROCHESTER
ROCHESTER, NEW YORK

General Independent, comprehensive, coed **Entrance** Moderately difficult **Setting** 150-acre

Nazareth College of Rochester *(continued)*

suburban campus **Total enrollment** 3,185 **Student-faculty ratio** 12:1 **Application deadline** 2/15 (freshmen), 5/15 (transfer) **Freshmen** 74% were admitted **Housing** Yes **Expenses** Tuition $22,880; Room & Board $9500 **Undergraduates** 75% women, 8% part-time, 10% 25 or older, 0.4% Native American, 3% Hispanic American, 5% African American, 2% Asian American/Pacific Islander **The most frequently chosen baccalaureate fields are** business/marketing, education, health professions and related sciences **Academic program** Advanced placement, honors program, summer session, adult/continuing education programs, internships **Contact** Thomas DaRin, Vice President for Enrollment Management, Nazareth College of Rochester, 4245 East Avenue, Rochester, NY 14618-3790. Phone: 585-389-2860 or toll-free 800-462-3944. Fax: 585-389-2826. E-mail: admissions@naz.edu. Web site: http://www.naz.edu/.

THE NEW SCHOOL FOR GENERAL STUDIES

NEW YORK, NEW YORK

General Independent, upper-level, coed **Entrance** Moderately difficult **Setting** urban campus **Total enrollment** 1,722 **Application deadline** 7/1 (freshmen), 7/1 (transfer) **Housing** Yes **Expenses** Tuition $22,572; Room & Board $11,750 **Undergraduates** 64% women, 50% part-time, 68% 25 or older, 0.3% Native American, 7% Hispanic American, 11% African American, 2% Asian American/Pacific Islander **The most frequently chosen baccalaureate field is** liberal arts/general studies **Academic program** English as a second language, advanced placement, accelerated degree program, self-designed majors, summer session, adult/continuing education programs, internships **Contact** Ms. Cory Meyers, Assistant Director of Admissions, The New School for General Studies, 66 West 12th Street, Room 401, New York, NY 10011. Phone: 212-229-5630 or toll-free 800-862-5039. Fax: 212-989-3887. E-mail: nsadmissions@newschool.edu. Web site: http://www.nsu.newschool.edu/.

THE NEW SCHOOL FOR JAZZ AND CONTEMPORARY MUSIC

NEW YORK, NEW YORK

General Independent, 4-year, coed **Entrance** Very difficult **Setting** urban campus **Total enrollment** 245 **Student-faculty ratio** 10:1 **Application deadline** 3/15 (freshmen), 3/15 (transfer) **Freshmen** 60% were admitted **Housing** Yes **Expenses** Tuition $30,450; Room & Board $11,750 **Undergraduates** 20% women, 7% part-time, 21% 25 or older, 4% Hispanic American, 8% African American, 1% Asian American/Pacific Islander **The most frequently chosen baccalaureate field is** visual and performing arts **Contact** Ms. Terri Lucas, Jazz Admissions, The New School for Jazz and Contemporary Music, 66 West 12th Street, New York, NY 10011. Phone: 212-229-5896 Ext. 4589. Fax: 212-229-8936. E-mail: jazzadm@newschool.edu. Web site: http://www.jazz.newschool.edu.

NEW YORK CITY COLLEGE OF TECHNOLOGY OF THE CITY UNIVERSITY OF NEW YORK

BROOKLYN, NEW YORK

General State and locally supported, 4-year, coed **Entrance** Noncompetitive **Setting** urban campus **Total enrollment** 13,502 **Student-faculty ratio** 17:1 **Application deadline** 3/15 (freshmen), 3/15 (transfer) **Housing** No **Expenses** Tuition $4289 **Undergraduates** 49% women, 43% part-time, 33% 25 or older, 0.1% Native American, 26% Hispanic American, 39% African American, 14% Asian American/Pacific Islander **Academic program** English as a second language, advanced placement, self-designed majors, honors program, summer session, internships **Contact** Alexis Chaconis, Director of Admissions, New York City College of Technology of the City University of New York, 300 Jay Street, Brooklyn, NY 11201-2983. Phone: 718-260-5500. E-mail: achaconis@citytech.cuny.edu. Web site: http://www.citytech.cuny.edu/.

NEW YORK INSTITUTE OF TECHNOLOGY

OLD WESTBURY, NEW YORK

General Independent, university, coed **Entrance** Moderately difficult **Setting** 1,050-acre suburban campus **Total enrollment** 11,126 **Student-faculty ratio** 16:1 **Application deadline** Rolling (freshmen), rolling (transfer) **Freshmen** 69% were admitted **Housing** Yes **Expenses** Tuition $21,498; Room & Board $10,014 **Undergraduates** 37% women, 25% part-time, 21% 25 or older, 0.1% Native American, 7% Hispanic American, 8% African American, 9% Asian American/Pacific Islander **The most frequently chosen baccalaureate fields are** architecture, business/marketing, interdisciplinary studies **Academic program** English as a second language, advanced placement, accelerated degree program, self-designed majors, honors program, summer session, adult/continuing education programs, internships **Contact** Ms. Doreen Meyer, Director of Financial Aid, New York Institute of Technology, PO Box 8000, Old Westbury, NY 11568. Phone: 516-686-7925 or toll-free 800-345-NYIT. Fax: 516-686-7613. E-mail: admissions@nyit.edu. Web site: http://www.nyit.edu/.

NEW YORK SCHOOL OF INTERIOR DESIGN
NEW YORK, NEW YORK

General Independent, comprehensive, coed, primarily women **Entrance** Moderately difficult **Setting** 1-acre urban campus **Total enrollment** 703 **Student-faculty ratio** 10:1 **Application deadline** 3/1 (freshmen), 3/1 (transfer) **Freshmen** 48% were admitted **Housing** No **Expenses** Tuition $19,790 **Undergraduates** 92% women, 75% part-time, 72% 25 or older, 0.1% Native American, 8% Hispanic American, 4% African American, 9% Asian American/Pacific Islander **Academic program** English as a second language, advanced placement, summer session, internships **Contact** Cassandra Ramirez, Admissions Associate, New York School of Interior Design, 170 East 70th Street, New York, NY 10021-5110. Phone: 212-472-1500 Ext. 204 or toll-free 800-336-9743 Ext. 204. Fax: 212-472-1867. E-mail: admissions@nysid.edu. Web site: http://www.nysid.edu/.

NEW YORK UNIVERSITY
NEW YORK, NEW YORK

General Independent, university, coed **Entrance** Most difficult **Setting** urban campus **Total enrollment** 41,783 **Student-faculty ratio** 12:1 **Application deadline** 1/15 (freshmen), 4/1 (transfer) **Freshmen** 37% were admitted **Housing** Yes **Expenses** Tuition $35,290; Room & Board $12,200 **Undergraduates** 62% women, 7% part-time, 8% 25 or older, 0.2% Native American, 8% Hispanic American, 4% African American, 19% Asian American/Pacific Islander **The most frequently chosen baccalaureate fields are** social sciences, business/marketing, visual and performing arts **Academic program** English as a second language, advanced placement, self-designed majors, honors program, summer session, adult/continuing education programs, internships **Contact** Ms. Barbara Hall, Associate Provost for Admissions and Financial Aid, New York University, 22 Washington Square North, New York, NY 10011. Phone: 212-998-4500. Fax: 212-995-4902. E-mail: nyuadmit@uccvm.nyu.edu. Web site: http://www.nyu.edu/.

▶**For more information, see page 478.**

NIAGARA UNIVERSITY
NIAGARA FALLS, NEW YORK

General Independent, comprehensive, coed, affiliated with Roman Catholic Church **Entrance** Moderately difficult **Setting** 160-acre suburban campus **Total enrollment** 4,116 **Student-faculty ratio** 14:1 **Application deadline** 8/1 (freshmen), 8/15 (transfer) **Freshmen** 77% were admitted **Housing** Yes **Expenses** Tuition $22,300; Room & Board $9300 **Undergraduates** 62% women, 4% part-time, 10% 25 or older, 0.4% Native American, 2% Hispanic American, 4% African American, 1% Asian American/Pacific Islander **The most frequently chosen baccalaureate fields are** business/marketing, education, security and protective services **Academic program** English as a second language, advanced placement, accelerated degree program, honors program, summer session, adult/continuing education programs, internships **Contact** Ms. Christine M. McDermott, Associate Director of Admissions, Niagara University, Office of Admissions, Niagara, NY 14109. Phone: 716-286-8700 or toll-free 800-462-2111. Fax: 716-286-8733. E-mail: admissions@niagara.edu. Web site: http://www.niagara.edu/.

NYACK COLLEGE
NYACK, NEW YORK

General Independent, 4-year, coed, affiliated with The Christian and Missionary Alliance **Entrance** Moderately difficult **Setting** 102-acre suburban campus **Total enrollment** 3,250 **Student-faculty ratio** 20:1 **Application deadline** 9/1 (freshmen), 9/1 (transfer) **Housing** Yes **Expenses** Tuition $17,125; Room & Board $3800 **Undergraduates** 57% women, 17% part-time, 1% Native American, 21% Hispanic American, 35% African American, 7% Asian American/Pacific Islander **Academic program** English as a second language, advanced placement, accelerated degree program, honors program, summer session, adult/continuing education programs, internships **Contact** Ms. Andrea Hennessey, Director of Admissions, Nyack College, 1 South Boulevard, Nyack, NY 10960-3698. Phone: 845-675-4415 or toll-free 800-33-NYACK. Fax: 845-353-1297. E-mail: admissions@nyack.edu. Web site: http://www.nyack.edu.

OHR HAMEIR THEOLOGICAL SEMINARY
PEEKSKILL, NEW YORK

Contact Rabbi M. Z. Weisverg, Director of Admissions, Ohr Hameir Theological Seminary, Furnace Woods Road, Peekskill, NY 10566. Phone: 914-736-1500.

OHR SOMAYACH/JOSEPH TANENBAUM EDUCATIONAL CENTER
MONSEY, NEW YORK

General Independent Jewish, 5-year, coed, primarily men **Entrance** Moderately difficult **Setting** 7-acre small-town campus **Total enrollment** 96 **Application deadline** Rolling (freshmen), rolling (transfer) **Freshmen** 65% were admitted **Housing** Yes **Expenses** Tuition $13,500 **Undergraduates** 75% 25 or older **Academic program** Honors

Ohr Somayach/Joseph Tanenbaum Educational Center *(continued)*

program, summer session, adult/continuing education programs, internships **Contact** Rabbi Avrohom Braun, Dean of Students, Ohr Somayach/Joseph Tanenbaum Educational Center, PO Box 334, 244 Route 306, Monsey, NY 10952-0334. Phone: 845-425-1370 Ext. 22. E-mail: ohr@os.edu. Web site: http://www.ohrsomayach.edu/.

PACE UNIVERSITY
NEW YORK, NEW YORK

General Independent, university, coed **Entrance** Moderately difficult **Setting** urban campus **Total enrollment** 12,912 **Student-faculty ratio** 9:1 **Application deadline** 3/1 (freshmen), rolling (transfer) **Freshmen** 78% were admitted **Housing** Yes **Expenses** Tuition $30,158; Room & Board $10,320 **Undergraduates** 60% women, 22% part-time, 22% 25 or older, 0.3% Native American, 11% Hispanic American, 10% African American, 9% Asian American/Pacific Islander **The most frequently chosen baccalaureate fields are** business/marketing, communications/journalism, health professions and related sciences **Academic program** English as a second language, advanced placement, accelerated degree program, honors program, summer session, adult/continuing education programs, internships **Contact** Ms. Joanna Broda, Director of Admission, NY and Westchester, Pace University, One Pace Plaza, New York, NY 10038. Phone: 212-346-1302 or toll-free 800-874-7223. Fax: 212-346-1040. E-mail: infoctr@pace.edu. Web site: http://www.pace.edu/.

PARSONS THE NEW SCHOOL FOR DESIGN
NEW YORK, NEW YORK

General Independent, comprehensive, coed **Entrance** Very difficult **Setting** 2-acre urban campus **Total enrollment** 3,948 **Student-faculty ratio** 9:1 **Application deadline** 2/1 (freshmen), 2/1 (transfer) **Freshmen** 50% were admitted **Housing** Yes **Expenses** Tuition $32,640; Room & Board $11,750 **Undergraduates** 79% women, 7% part-time, 22% 25 or older, 0.2% Native American, 7% Hispanic American, 4% African American, 17% Asian American/Pacific Islander **The most frequently chosen baccalaureate fields are** physical sciences, visual and performing arts **Academic program** English as a second language, advanced placement, accelerated degree program, self-designed majors, honors program, summer session, adult/continuing education programs, internships **Contact** Director of Admissions, Parsons The New School for Design, 66 Fifth Avenue, New York, NY 10011-8878. Phone: 212-229-8989 or toll-free 877-528-3321. Fax: 212-229-8975. E-mail: parsadm@newschool.edu. Web site: http://www.parsons.newschool.edu/.

PAUL SMITH'S COLLEGE
PAUL SMITHS, NEW YORK

General Independent, 4-year, coed, primarily men **Entrance** Minimally difficult **Setting** 14,200-acre rural campus **Total enrollment** 910 **Student-faculty ratio** 14:1 **Application deadline** Rolling (freshmen), rolling (transfer) **Freshmen** 86% were admitted **Housing** Yes **Expenses** Tuition $20,250; Room & Board $8350 **Academic program** Advanced placement, honors program, summer session, adult/continuing education programs, internships **Contact** Admissions Office, Paul Smith's College, Routes 86 and 30, PO Box 265, Paul Smiths, NY 12970. Phone: 518-327-6227 or toll-free 800-421-2605. Fax: 518-327-6016. E-mail: admissions@paulsmiths.edu. Web site: http://www.paulsmiths.edu/.

POLYTECHNIC UNIVERSITY, BROOKLYN CAMPUS
BROOKLYN, NEW YORK

General Independent, university, coed **Entrance** Very difficult **Setting** 3-acre urban campus **Total enrollment** 3,317 **Student-faculty ratio** 14:1 **Application deadline** 2/1 (freshmen), rolling (transfer) **Freshmen** 22% were admitted **Housing** Yes **Expenses** Tuition $30,972; Room & Board $8500 **Undergraduates** 19% women, 4% part-time, 6% 25 or older, 0.2% Native American, 12% Hispanic American, 12% African American, 30% Asian American/Pacific Islander **The most frequently chosen baccalaureate fields are** computer and information sciences, business/marketing, engineering **Academic program** English as a second language, advanced placement, accelerated degree program, honors program, summer session, internships **Contact** Joy Colelli, Dean of Admissions and New Students, Polytechnic University, Brooklyn Campus, Six Metrotech Center, Brooklyn, NY 11201-2990. Phone: 718-260-5917 or toll-free 800-POLYTECH. Fax: 718-260-3446. E-mail: uadmit@poly.edu. Web site: http://www.poly.edu/.

PRATT INSTITUTE
BROOKLYN, NEW YORK

General Independent, comprehensive, coed **Entrance** Very difficult **Setting** 25-acre urban campus **Total enrollment** 4,668 **Student-faculty ratio** 11:1 **Application deadline** 1/5 (freshmen), 2/1 (transfer) **Freshmen** 43% were admitted **Housing** Yes **Expenses** Tuition $32,990; Room & Board $9476 **Undergraduates** 60% women, 5% part-time, 11% 25 or older, 0.5% Native American, 8% Hispanic American, 7% African American, 13% Asian American/Pacific Islander **The most frequently chosen baccalaureate fields are** architecture, English, visual and performing arts **Academic program** English as a second language, advanced placement, summer session, internships **Contact** Ms. Olga Burger, Visit Coordinator, Pratt Institute, 200 Willoughby Avenue, DeKalb Hall, Brooklyn, NY 11205. Phone: 718-636-3669 Ext. 3743 or toll-free 800-331-0834. Fax: 718-636-3670. E-mail: admissions@pratt.edu. Web site: http://www.pratt.edu/.

►**For more information, see page 480.**

PURCHASE COLLEGE, STATE UNIVERSITY OF NEW YORK
PURCHASE, NEW YORK

General State-supported, comprehensive, coed **Entrance** Moderately difficult **Setting** 500-acre small-town campus **Total enrollment** 4,265 **Student-faculty ratio** 17:1 **Application deadline** 7/15 (freshmen), rolling (transfer) **Freshmen** 37% were admitted **Housing** Yes **Expenses** Tuition $5997; Room & Board $9484 **Undergraduates** 55% women, 11% part-time, 14% 25 or older, 0.4% Native American, 9% Hispanic American, 7% African American, 3% Asian American/Pacific Islander **The most frequently chosen baccalaureate fields are** liberal arts/general studies, English, visual and performing arts **Academic program** English as a second language, advanced placement, self-designed majors, summer session, adult/continuing education programs, internships **Contact** Stephanie McCaine, Director of Admissions, Purchase College, State University of New York, 735 Anderson Hill Road, Purchase, NY 10577-1400. Phone: 914-251-6300. Fax: 914-251-6314. E-mail: admission@purchase.edu. Web site: http://www.purchase.edu/.

QUEENS COLLEGE OF THE CITY UNIVERSITY OF NEW YORK
FLUSHING, NEW YORK

General State and locally supported, comprehensive, coed **Entrance** Very difficult **Setting** 77-acre urban campus **Total enrollment** 18,728 **Student-faculty ratio** 17:1 **Application deadline** Rolling (freshmen), rolling (transfer) **Freshmen** 40% were admitted **Housing** No **Expenses** Tuition $4377 **Undergraduates** 61% women, 30% part-time, 33% 25 or older, 0.1% Native American, 18% Hispanic American, 9% African American, 20% Asian American/Pacific Islander **The most frequently chosen baccalaureate fields are** business/marketing, psychology, social sciences **Academic program** English as a second language, advanced placement, accelerated degree program, self-designed majors, honors program, summer session, adult/continuing education programs, internships **Contact** Mr. Vincent Angrisani, Executive Director of Enrollment Management and Admissions, Queens College of the City University of New York, Undergraduate Admissions, Jefferson Hall, Rm 217, 65-30 Kissena Boulevard, Flushing, NY 11367. Phone: 718-997-5600. Fax: 718-997-5617. E-mail: vincent.angrisani@qc.edu. Web site: http://www.qc.cuny.edu/.

RABBINICAL ACADEMY MESIVTA RABBI CHAIM BERLIN
BROOKLYN, NEW YORK

Contact Mr. Mayer Weinberger, Executive Administrator, Office of Admissions, Rabbinical Academy Mesivta Rabbi Chaim Berlin, 1605 Coney Island Avenue, Brooklyn, NY 11230-4715. Phone: 718-377-0777. Fax: 718-338-5578.

RABBINICAL COLLEGE BETH SHRAGA
MONSEY, NEW YORK

Contact Rabbi Schiff, Director of Admissions, Rabbinical College Beth Shraga, 28 Saddle River Road, Monsey, NY 10952-3035.

RABBINICAL COLLEGE BOBOVER YESHIVA B'NEI ZION
BROOKLYN, NEW YORK

Contact Mr. Israel Licht, Director of Admissions, Rabbinical College Bobover Yeshiva B'nei Zion, 1577 Forty-eighth Street, Brooklyn, NY 11219. Phone: 718-438-2018.

RABBINICAL COLLEGE CH'SAN SOFER
BROOKLYN, NEW YORK

Contact Director of Admissions, Rabbinical College Ch'san Sofer, 1876 Fiftieth Street, Brooklyn, NY 11204. Phone: 718-236-1171.

RABBINICAL COLLEGE OF LONG ISLAND
LONG BEACH, NEW YORK

Contact Director of Admissions, Rabbinical College of Long Island, 201 Magnolia Boulevard, Long Beach, NY 11561-3305. Phone: 516-431-7414.

RABBINICAL COLLEGE OF OHR SHIMON YISROEL

BROOKLYN, NEW YORK

Contact Rabbinical College of Ohr Shimon Yisroel, 215-217 Hewes Street, Brooklyn, NY 11211.

RABBINICAL SEMINARY ADAS YEREIM

BROOKLYN, NEW YORK

Contact Mr. Hersch Greenschweig, Director of Admissions, Rabbinical Seminary Adas Yereim, 185 Wilson Street, Brooklyn, NY 11211-7206. Phone: 718-388-1751.

RABBINICAL SEMINARY M'KOR CHAIM

BROOKLYN, NEW YORK

Contact Rabbi Benjamin Paler, Director of Admissions, Rabbinical Seminary M'kor Chaim, 1571 Fifty-fifth Street, Brooklyn, NY 11219. Phone: 718-851-0183.

RABBINICAL SEMINARY OF AMERICA

FLUSHING, NEW YORK

Contact Rabbi Abraham Semmel, Director of Admissions, Rabbinical Seminary of America, 76-01 147th Street, Flushing, NY 11367. Phone: 718-268-4700.

RENSSELAER POLYTECHNIC INSTITUTE

TROY, NEW YORK

General Independent, university, coed **Entrance** Very difficult **Setting** 284-acre suburban campus **Total enrollment** 7,299 **Student-faculty ratio** 14:1 **Application deadline** 1/15 (freshmen) **Freshmen** 49% were admitted **Housing** Yes **Expenses** Tuition $37,990; Room & Board $10,730 **Undergraduates** 27% women, 1% part-time, 2% 25 or older, 0.4% Native American, 6% Hispanic American, 4% African American, 10% Asian American/Pacific Islander **The most frequently chosen baccalaureate fields are** computer and information sciences, business/marketing, engineering **Academic program** English as a second language, advanced placement, accelerated degree program, self-designed majors, honors program, summer session, adult/continuing education programs, internships **Contact** Mr. James Nondorf, Vice President for Enrollment, Rensselaer Polytechnic Institute, 110 8th Street, Troy, NY 12180. Phone: 518-276-6216 or toll-free 800-448-6562. Fax: 518-276-4072. E-mail: admissions@rpi.edu. Web site: http://www.rpi.edu/.

►**For more information, see page 481.**

ROBERTS WESLEYAN COLLEGE

ROCHESTER, NEW YORK

General Independent, comprehensive, coed, affiliated with Free Methodist Church of North America **Entrance** Moderately difficult **Setting** 75-acre suburban campus **Total enrollment** 1,871 **Student-faculty ratio** 14:1 **Application deadline** 2/1 (freshmen), rolling (transfer) **Freshmen** 63% were admitted **Housing** Yes **Expenses** Tuition $22,922; Room & Board $8228 **Undergraduates** 69% women, 10% part-time, 23% 25 or older, 1% Native American, 3% Hispanic American, 6% African American, 1% Asian American/Pacific Islander **The most frequently chosen baccalaureate fields are** business/marketing, education, health professions and related sciences **Academic program** English as a second language, advanced placement, honors program, summer session, adult/continuing education programs, internships **Contact** Ms. Linda Kurtz Hoffman, Vice President for Admissions and Marketing, Roberts Wesleyan College, 2301 Westside Drive, Rochester, NY 14624. Phone: 585-594-6400 or toll-free 800-777-4RWC. Fax: 585-594-6371. E-mail: admissions@roberts.edu. Web site: http://www.roberts.edu/.

ROCHESTER INSTITUTE OF TECHNOLOGY

ROCHESTER, NEW YORK

General Independent, comprehensive, coed **Entrance** Moderately difficult **Setting** 1,300-acre suburban campus **Total enrollment** 15,989 **Student-faculty ratio** 14:1 **Application deadline** 2/1 (freshmen) **Freshmen** 65% were admitted **Housing** Yes **Expenses** Tuition $26,481; Room & Board $9054 **Undergraduates** 32% women, 12% part-time, 15% 25 or older, 0.4% Native American, 4% Hispanic American, 4% African American, 5% Asian American/Pacific Islander **The most frequently chosen baccalaureate fields are** computer and information sciences, engineering, visual and performing arts **Academic program** English as a second language, advanced placement, accelerated degree program, self-designed majors, honors program, summer session, adult/continuing education programs, internships **Contact** Dr. Daniel Shelley, Assistant Vice President, Rochester Institute of Technology, 60 Lomb Memorial Drive, Rochester, NY 14623-5604. Phone: 585-475-6631. Fax: 585-475-7424. E-mail: admissions@rit.edu. Web site: http://www.rit.edu/.

RUSSELL SAGE COLLEGE

TROY, NEW YORK

General Independent, 4-year, undergraduate: women only; graduate: coed **Entrance** Moderately difficult **Setting** 8-acre urban campus **Total enrollment** 682 **Student-faculty ratio** 10:1 **Application deadline** Rolling (freshmen), rolling (transfer) **Freshmen** 76% were admitted **Housing** Yes **Expenses** Tuition $25,990; Room & Board $8800 **Undergraduates** 7% part-time, 14% 25 or older, 1% Native American, 3% Hispanic American, 5% African American, 4% Asian American/Pacific Islander **The most frequently chosen baccalaureate fields are** education, health professions and related sciences, psychology **Academic program** Advanced placement, accelerated degree program, self-designed majors, honors program, summer session, adult/continuing education programs, internships **Contact** Ms. Kathy Rusch, Director of Admission, Russell Sage College, 45 Ferry Street, Troy, NY 12180. Phone: 518-244-2018 or toll-free 888-VERY-SAGE (in-state); 888-VERY SAGE (out-of-state). Fax: 518-244-6880. E-mail: ruschk@sage.edu. Web site: http://www.sage.edu/rsc/index.php.

SAGE COLLEGE OF ALBANY
ALBANY, NEW YORK

General Independent, 4-year, coed **Entrance** Minimally difficult **Setting** 15-acre urban campus **Total enrollment** 989 **Student-faculty ratio** 13:1 **Application deadline** Rolling (freshmen), 8/1 (transfer) **Freshmen** 67% were admitted **Housing** Yes **Expenses** Tuition $18,640; Room & Board $8950 **Undergraduates** 71% women, 43% part-time, 44% 25 or older, 0.1% Native American, 3% Hispanic American, 9% African American, 2% Asian American/Pacific Islander **The most frequently chosen baccalaureate fields are** business/marketing, interdisciplinary studies, visual and performing arts **Academic program** Advanced placement, self-designed majors, honors program, summer session, adult/continuing education programs, internships **Contact** Ms. Amy Sullivan, Director of Admission, Sage College of Albany, 140 New Scotland Avenue, Albany, NY 12208. Phone: 518-292-1730 or toll-free 888-VERY-SAGE. Fax: 518-292-1912. E-mail: scaadm@sage.edu. Web site: http://www.sage.edu/sca/index.php.

ST. BONAVENTURE UNIVERSITY
ST. BONAVENTURE, NEW YORK

Contact Mr. James M. DiRisio, Director of Admissions, St. Bonaventure University, PO Box D, St. Bonaventure, NY 14778. Phone: 716-375-2400 or toll-free 800-462-5050. Fax: 716-375-4005. E-mail: jdirisio@sbu.edu. Web site: http://www.sbu.edu/.

ST. FRANCIS COLLEGE
BROOKLYN HEIGHTS, NEW YORK

General Independent Roman Catholic, 4-year, coed **Contact** Ms. Monica Michalski, St. Francis College, 180 Remsen Street, Brooklyn Heights, NY 11201-4398. Phone: 718-489-5200. Fax: 718-522-1274. E-mail: mmichalski@stfranciscollege.edu. Web site: http://www.stfranciscollege.edu/.

ST. JOHN FISHER COLLEGE
ROCHESTER, NEW YORK

General Independent, comprehensive, coed, affiliated with Roman Catholic Church **Entrance** Moderately difficult **Setting** 136-acre suburban campus **Total enrollment** 3,793 **Student-faculty ratio** 13:1 **Application deadline** Rolling (freshmen), rolling (transfer) **Freshmen** 61% were admitted **Housing** Yes **Expenses** Tuition $22,960; Room & Board $10,040 **Undergraduates** 60% women, 8% part-time, 12% 25 or older, 0.5% Native American, 3% Hispanic American, 5% African American, 2% Asian American/Pacific Islander **The most frequently chosen baccalaureate fields are** business/marketing, education, social sciences **Academic program** Advanced placement, accelerated degree program, self-designed majors, honors program, summer session, adult/continuing education programs, internships **Contact** Mrs. Stacy A. Ledermann, Director of Freshmen Admissions, St. John Fisher College, 3690 East Avenue, Rochester, NY 14618. Phone: 585-385-8064 or toll-free 800-444-4640. Fax: 585-385-8386. E-mail: admissions@sjfc.edu. Web site: http://www.sjfc.edu/.

ST. JOHN'S UNIVERSITY
QUEENS, NEW YORK

General Independent, university, coed, affiliated with Roman Catholic Church **Entrance** Moderately difficult **Setting** 98-acre urban campus **Total enrollment** 20,086 **Student-faculty ratio** 17:1 **Application deadline** Rolling (freshmen), rolling (transfer) **Freshmen** 56% were admitted **Housing** Yes **Expenses** Tuition $26,890; Room & Board $12,070 **Undergraduates** 56% women, 21% part-time, 4% 25 or older **The most frequently chosen baccalaureate fields are** business/marketing, communications/journalism, education **Academic program** English as a second language, advanced placement, accelerated degree program, honors program, summer session, adult/continuing education programs, internships **Contact** Mrs. Karem Vahey, Admission Director, St. John's University, 8000 Utopia Parkway, Queens, NY 11439. Phone: 718-990-2000 or toll-free 888-9STJOHNS (in-state); 888-9ST JOHNS (out-of-state). Fax:

St. John's University *(continued)*

718-990-2160. E-mail: admhelp@stjohns.edu. Web site: http://www.stjohns.edu/.

ST. JOSEPH'S COLLEGE, LONG ISLAND CAMPUS

PATCHOGUE, NEW YORK

General Independent, comprehensive, coed **Entrance** Moderately difficult **Setting** 28-acre small-town campus **Total enrollment** 3,794 **Student-faculty ratio** 17:1 **Application deadline** Rolling (freshmen), rolling (transfer) **Freshmen** 79% were admitted **Housing** No **Expenses** Tuition $14,532 **Undergraduates** 74% women, 21% part-time, 37% 25 or older, 0.03% Native American, 7% Hispanic American, 4% African American, 2% Asian American/Pacific Islander **The most frequently chosen baccalaureate fields are** business/marketing, education, health professions and related sciences **Academic program** Advanced placement, honors program, summer session, adult/continuing education programs, internships **Contact** Ms. Gigi Lamens, Director of Admissions and Enrollment Services, St. Joseph's College, Long Island Campus, 155 West Roe Boulevard, Patchogue, NY 11772. Phone: 631-447-3219 or toll-free 866-AT ST JOE. Fax: 631-447-3601. E-mail: longislandas@sjcny.edu. Web site: http://www.sjcny.edu/.

ST. JOSEPH'S COLLEGE, NEW YORK

BROOKLYN, NEW YORK

General Independent, comprehensive, coed **Entrance** Moderately difficult **Setting** urban campus **Total enrollment** 1,296 **Student-faculty ratio** 15:1 **Application deadline** 8/15 (freshmen), 8/15 (transfer) **Freshmen** 75% were admitted **Housing** Yes **Expenses** Tuition $14,382 **Undergraduates** 77% women, 32% part-time, 49% 25 or older, 0.2% Native American, 12% Hispanic American, 37% African American, 7% Asian American/Pacific Islander **The most frequently chosen baccalaureate fields are** business/marketing, education, health professions and related sciences **Academic program** Advanced placement, honors program, summer session, adult/continuing education programs, internships **Contact** Ms. Theresa LaRocca Meyer, Director of Admissions, St. Joseph's College, New York, 245 Clinton Avenue, Brooklyn, NY 11205-3688. Phone: 718-636-6868. E-mail: asinfob@sjcny.edu. Web site: http://www.sjcny.edu/.

►**For more information, see page 486.**

ST. LAWRENCE UNIVERSITY

CANTON, NEW YORK

General Independent, comprehensive, coed **Entrance** Very difficult **Setting** 1,000-acre small-town campus **Total enrollment** 2,319 **Student-faculty ratio** 11:1 **Application deadline** 2/1 (freshmen), 4/1 (transfer) **Freshmen** 44% were admitted **Housing** Yes **Expenses** Tuition $35,600; Room & Board $9060 **Undergraduates** 55% women, 1% part-time, 1% 25 or older, 1% Native American, 3% Hispanic American, 3% African American, 2% Asian American/Pacific Islander **The most frequently chosen baccalaureate fields are** psychology, social sciences, visual and performing arts **Academic program** Advanced placement, self-designed majors, summer session, internships **Contact** Ms. Terry Cowdrey, Dean of Admissions and Financial Aid, St. Lawrence University, Payson Hall, Canton, NY 13617-1455. Phone: 315-229-5261 or toll-free 800-285-1856. Fax: 315-229-5818. E-mail: admissions@stlawu.edu. Web site: http://www.stlawu.edu/.

ST. THOMAS AQUINAS COLLEGE

SPARKILL, NEW YORK

General Independent, comprehensive, coed **Entrance** Moderately difficult **Setting** 46-acre suburban campus **Total enrollment** 2,238 **Student-faculty ratio** 16:1 **Application deadline** Rolling (freshmen), rolling (transfer) **Freshmen** 80% were admitted **Housing** Yes **Expenses** Tuition $20,000; Room & Board $9730 **Undergraduates** 54% women, 33% part-time, 3% 25 or older, 0.1% Native American, 15% Hispanic American, 6% African American, 3% Asian American/Pacific Islander **The most frequently chosen baccalaureate fields are** business/marketing, education, social sciences **Academic program** Advanced placement, accelerated degree program, honors program, summer session, adult/continuing education programs, internships **Contact** Mr. Vincent Crapanzano, Dean of Enrollment Management and Marketing, St. Thomas Aquinas College, 125 Route 340, Sparkill, NY 10976. Phone: 845-398-4100 or toll-free 800-999-STAC. Fax: 845-398-4114. E-mail: vcrapanz@stac.edu. Web site: http://www.stac.edu/.

SARAH LAWRENCE COLLEGE

BRONXVILLE, NEW YORK

General Independent, comprehensive, coed **Entrance** Very difficult **Setting** 40-acre suburban campus **Total enrollment** 1,700 **Student-faculty ratio** 6:1 **Application deadline** 1/1 (freshmen), 3/1 (transfer) **Freshmen** 44% were admitted **Housing** Yes **Expenses** Tuition $38,090; Room & Board $12,720 **Undergraduates** 74% women, 4% part-time, 4% 25 or older, 1% Native American, 5% Hispanic American, 4% African American, 5% Asian American/Pacific Islander **The most frequently chosen baccalaureate field is** liberal arts/general studies **Academic program**

Advanced placement, self-designed majors, adult/continuing education programs, internships **Contact** Mr. Stephen M. Schierloh, Acting Dean of Admission, Sarah Lawrence College, 1 Mead Way, Bronxville, NY 10708-5999. Phone: 914-395-2510 or toll-free 800-888-2858. Fax: 914-395-2515. E-mail: slcadmit@sarahlawrence.edu. Web site: http://www.sarahlawrence.edu/.

SCHOOL OF VISUAL ARTS
NEW YORK, NEW YORK

General Proprietary, comprehensive, coed **Entrance** Moderately difficult **Setting** 1-acre urban campus **Total enrollment** 3,946 **Student-faculty ratio** 4:1 **Application deadline** Rolling (freshmen), rolling (transfer) **Freshmen** 72% were admitted **Housing** Yes **Expenses** Tuition $23,520; Room only $11,350 **Undergraduates** 54% women, 7% part-time, 8% 25 or older, 0.5% Native American, 10% Hispanic American, 4% African American, 13% Asian American/Pacific Islander **The most frequently chosen baccalaureate field is** visual and performing arts **Academic program** English as a second language, advanced placement, honors program, summer session, adult/continuing education programs, internships **Contact** Admissions Office, School of Visual Arts, 209 East 23rd Street, New York, NY 10010. Phone: 212-592-2100 or toll-free 800-436-4204. Fax: 212-592-2116. E-mail: admissions@sva.edu. Web site: http://www.schoolofvisualarts.edu/.

SH'OR YOSHUV RABBINICAL COLLEGE
LAWRENCE, NEW YORK

Contact Rabbi Avrohom Halpern, Executive Director, Sh'or Yoshuv Rabbinical College, 1 Cedarlawn Avenue, Lawrence, NY 11559-1714. Phone: 718-327-7244. Web site: http://www.shoryoshuv.org/.

SIENA COLLEGE
LOUDONVILLE, NEW YORK

General Independent Roman Catholic, 4-year, coed **Entrance** Moderately difficult **Setting** 164-acre suburban campus **Total enrollment** 3,217 **Student-faculty ratio** 13:1 **Application deadline** 3/1 (freshmen), 8/15 (transfer) **Freshmen** 54% were admitted **Housing** Yes **Expenses** Tuition $22,685; Room & Board $8875 **Undergraduates** 55% women, 6% part-time, 5% 25 or older, 0.1% Native American, 4% Hispanic American, 2% African American, 4% Asian American/Pacific Islander **The most frequently chosen baccalaureate fields are** business/marketing, biological/life sciences, psychology **Academic program** English as a second language, advanced placement, accelerated degree program, honors program, summer session, adult/continuing education programs, internships **Contact** Ms. Heather Renault, Director of Admissions, Siena College, 515 Loudon Road, Loudonville, NY 12211-1462. Phone: 518-783-2426 or toll-free 888-AT-SIENA. Fax: 518-783-2436. E-mail: admit@siena.edu. Web site: http://www.siena.edu/.

SKIDMORE COLLEGE
SARATOGA SPRINGS, NEW YORK

General Independent, comprehensive, coed **Entrance** Very difficult **Setting** 800-acre small-town campus **Total enrollment** 2,863 **Student-faculty ratio** 9:1 **Application deadline** 1/15 (freshmen), 4/1 (transfer) **Freshmen** 37% were admitted **Housing** Yes **Expenses** Tuition $36,860; Room & Board $9836 **Undergraduates** 60% women, 7% part-time, 0.3% 25 or older, 1% Native American, 5% Hispanic American, 4% African American, 7% Asian American/Pacific Islander **The most frequently chosen baccalaureate fields are** social sciences, business/marketing, visual and performing arts **Academic program** Advanced placement, accelerated degree program, self-designed majors, honors program, summer session, adult/continuing education programs, internships **Contact** Ms. Mary Lou Bates, Dean of Admissions and Financial Aid, Skidmore College, 815 North Broadway, Saratoga Springs, NY 12866-1632. Phone: 518-580-5570 or toll-free 800-867-6007. Fax: 518-580-5584. E-mail: admissions@skidmore.edu. Web site: http://www.skidmore.edu/.

STATE UNIVERSITY OF NEW YORK AT BINGHAMTON
BINGHAMTON, NEW YORK

General State-supported, university, coed **Entrance** Very difficult **Setting** 930-acre suburban campus **Total enrollment** 14,435 **Student-faculty ratio** 20:1 **Application deadline** Rolling (freshmen), rolling (transfer) **Freshmen** 39% were admitted **Housing** Yes **Expenses** Tuition $6012; Room & Board $9188 **Undergraduates** 48% women, 4% part-time, 5% 25 or older, 0.2% Native American, 7% Hispanic American, 5% African American, 13% Asian American/Pacific Islander **The most frequently chosen baccalaureate fields are** business/marketing, psychology, social sciences **Academic program** English as a second language, advanced placement, accelerated degree program, self-designed majors, honors program, summer session, adult/continuing education programs, internships **Contact** Ms. Cheryl S. Brown, Director of Admissions, State University of New York at Binghamton, PO Box 6000, Binghamton, NY 13902-6000. Phone: 607-777-

State University of New York at Binghamton *(continued)*

2171. Fax: 607-777-4445. E-mail: admit@binghamton.edu. Web site: http://www.binghamton.edu/.

STATE UNIVERSITY OF NEW YORK AT FREDONIA

FREDONIA, NEW YORK

General State-supported, comprehensive, coed **Entrance** Moderately difficult **Setting** 249-acre small-town campus **Total enrollment** 5,404 **Student-faculty ratio** 16:1 **Application deadline** Rolling (freshmen), rolling (transfer) **Freshmen** 56% were admitted **Housing** Yes **Expenses** Tuition $5542; Room & Board $8380 **Undergraduates** 56% women, 4% part-time, 2% 25 or older, 1% Native American, 3% Hispanic American, 3% African American, 2% Asian American/Pacific Islander **The most frequently chosen baccalaureate fields are** business/marketing, education, visual and performing arts **Academic program** Advanced placement, accelerated degree program, self-designed majors, honors program, summer session, adult/continuing education programs, internships **Contact** Office of Admissions, State University of New York at Fredonia, 178 Central Ave, Fredonia, NY 14063. Phone: 716-673-3251 or toll-free 800-252-1212. Fax: 716-673-3249. E-mail: admissions.office@fredonia.edu. Web site: http://www.fredonia.edu/.

STATE UNIVERSITY OF NEW YORK AT NEW PALTZ

NEW PALTZ, NEW YORK

General State-supported, comprehensive, coed **Entrance** Very difficult **Setting** 216-acre small-town campus **Total enrollment** 7,690 **Student-faculty ratio** 14:1 **Application deadline** 4/1 (freshmen), 4/1 (transfer) **Freshmen** 36% were admitted **Housing** Yes **Expenses** Tuition $5390; Room & Board $8070 **Undergraduates** 68% women, 14% part-time, 14% 25 or older, 0.3% Native American, 10% Hispanic American, 7% African American, 3% Asian American/Pacific Islander **The most frequently chosen baccalaureate fields are** business/marketing, education, social sciences **Academic program** English as a second language, advanced placement, self-designed majors, honors program, summer session, adult/continuing education programs, internships **Contact** Ms. Kimberly A. Strano, Director of Freshmen Admissions, State University of New York at New Paltz, 1 Hawk Drive, New Paltz, NY 12561-2499. Phone: 845-257-3210 or toll-free 888-639-7589. Fax: 845-257-3209. E-mail: admissions@newpaltz.edu. Web site: http://www.newpaltz.edu/.

STATE UNIVERSITY OF NEW YORK AT OSWEGO

OSWEGO, NEW YORK

General State-supported, comprehensive, coed **Entrance** Moderately difficult **Setting** 696-acre small-town campus **Total enrollment** 8,660 **Student-faculty ratio** 18:1 **Application deadline** Rolling (freshmen), rolling (transfer) **Freshmen** 50% were admitted **Housing** Yes **Expenses** Tuition $5480; Room & Board $9470 **Undergraduates** 55% women, 14% part-time, 10% 25 or older, 0.5% Native American, 4% Hispanic American, 4% African American, 2% Asian American/Pacific Islander **The most frequently chosen baccalaureate fields are** business/marketing, communications/journalism, education **Academic program** English as a second language, advanced placement, accelerated degree program, self-designed majors, honors program, summer session, adult/continuing education programs, internships **Contact** Dr. Joseph Grant, Vice President for Student Affairs and Enrollment, State University of New York at Oswego, 7060 State Route 104, Oswego, NY 13126. Phone: 315-312-2250. Fax: 315-312-3260. E-mail: admiss@oswego.edu. Web site: http://www.oswego.edu/.

STATE UNIVERSITY OF NEW YORK AT PLATTSBURGH

PLATTSBURGH, NEW YORK

General State-supported, comprehensive, coed **Entrance** Very difficult **Setting** 265-acre small-town campus **Total enrollment** 6,259 **Student-faculty ratio** 17:1 **Application deadline** 3/1 (freshmen), rolling (transfer) **Freshmen** 46% were admitted **Housing** Yes **Expenses** Tuition $5416; Room & Board $7970 **Undergraduates** 56% women, 6% part-time, 10% 25 or older, 0.5% Native American, 4% Hispanic American, 5% African American, 2% Asian American/Pacific Islander **The most frequently chosen baccalaureate fields are** business/marketing, education, psychology **Academic program** English as a second language, advanced placement, accelerated degree program, self-designed majors, honors program, summer session, adult/continuing education programs, internships **Contact** Mr. Richard Higgins, Director of Admissions, State University of New York at Plattsburgh, 101 Broad Street, Plattsburgh, NY 12901-2681. Phone: 518-564-2040 or toll-free 888-673-0012. Fax: 518-564-2045. E-mail: admissions@plattsburgh.edu. Web site: http://www.plattsburgh.edu/.

STATE UNIVERSITY OF NEW YORK COLLEGE AT CORTLAND
CORTLAND, NEW YORK

General State-supported, comprehensive, coed **Entrance** Moderately difficult **Setting** 191-acre small-town campus **Total enrollment** 7,056 **Student-faculty ratio** 15:1 **Application deadline** Rolling (freshmen) **Freshmen** 44% were admitted **Housing** Yes **Expenses** Tuition $5439; Room & Board $8760 **Undergraduates** 56% women, 3% part-time, 6% 25 or older, 1% Native American, 5% Hispanic American, 3% African American, 2% Asian American/Pacific Islander **The most frequently chosen baccalaureate fields are** education, parks and recreation, social sciences **Academic program** Advanced placement, self-designed majors, honors program, summer session, adult/continuing education programs, internships **Contact** Mr. Mark Yacavone, Director of Admission, State University of New York College at Cortland, PO Box 2000, Cortland, NY 13045. Phone: 607-753-4711. Fax: 607-753-5998. E-mail: admissions@cortland.edu. Web site: http://www.cortland.edu/.

STATE UNIVERSITY OF NEW YORK COLLEGE AT GENESEO
GENESEO, NEW YORK

General State-supported, comprehensive, coed **Entrance** Very difficult **Setting** 220-acre small-town campus **Total enrollment** 5,548 **Student-faculty ratio** 19:1 **Application deadline** 1/1 (freshmen), 1/1 (transfer) **Freshmen** 36% were admitted **Housing** Yes **Expenses** Tuition $5616; Room & Board $8550 **Undergraduates** 58% women, 2% part-time, 3% 25 or older, 0.4% Native American, 3% Hispanic American, 2% African American, 6% Asian American/Pacific Islander **The most frequently chosen baccalaureate fields are** business/marketing, education, social sciences **Academic program** English as a second language, advanced placement, honors program, summer session, internships **Contact** Kris Shay, Director of Admissions, State University of New York College at Geneseo, 1 College Circle, Geneseo, NY 14454-1401. Phone: 585-245-5571 or toll-free 866-245-5211. Fax: 585-245-5550. E-mail: admissions@geneseo.edu. Web site: http://www.geneseo.edu/.

STATE UNIVERSITY OF NEW YORK COLLEGE AT OLD WESTBURY
OLD WESTBURY, NEW YORK

General State-supported, comprehensive, coed **Entrance** Moderately difficult **Setting** 605-acre suburban campus **Total enrollment** 3,565 **Student-faculty ratio** 18:1 **Application deadline** Rolling (freshmen), 12/15 (transfer) **Freshmen** 55% were admitted **Housing** Yes **Expenses** Tuition $5177; Room & Board $8800 **Undergraduates** 57% women, 17% part-time, 28% 25 or older, 0.2% Native American, 19% Hispanic American, 30% African American, 6% Asian American/Pacific Islander **The most frequently chosen baccalaureate fields are** business/marketing, education, social sciences **Academic program** English as a second language, advanced placement, honors program, summer session, internships **Contact** Ms. Mary Marquez Bell, Vice President Enrollment Services, State University of New York College at Old Westbury, PO Box 307, Old Westbury, NY 11568. Phone: 516-876-3073. Fax: 516-876-3307. E-mail: enroll@oldwestbury.edu. Web site: http://www.oldwestbury.edu/.

STATE UNIVERSITY OF NEW YORK COLLEGE AT ONEONTA
ONEONTA, NEW YORK

General State-supported, comprehensive, coed **Entrance** Very difficult **Setting** 250-acre small-town campus **Total enrollment** 5,893 **Student-faculty ratio** 17:1 **Application deadline** Rolling (freshmen), rolling (transfer) **Freshmen** 38% were admitted **Housing** Yes **Expenses** Tuition $5450; Room & Board $8306 **Undergraduates** 57% women, 3% part-time, 5% 25 or older, 0.2% Native American, 5% Hispanic American, 3% African American, 2% Asian American/Pacific Islander **The most frequently chosen baccalaureate fields are** education, family and consumer sciences, visual and performing arts **Academic program** English as a second language, advanced placement, honors program, summer session, adult/continuing education programs, internships **Contact** Ms. Karen Brown, Director of Admissions, State University of New York College at Oneonta, Alumni Hall 116, Oneonta, NY 13820-4015. Phone: 607-436-2524 or toll-free 800-SUNY-123. Fax: 607-436-3074. E-mail: admissions@oneonta.edu. Web site: http://www.oneonta.edu/.

STATE UNIVERSITY OF NEW YORK COLLEGE AT POTSDAM
POTSDAM, NEW YORK

General State-supported, comprehensive, coed **Entrance** Moderately difficult **Setting** 240-acre small-town campus **Total enrollment** 4,338 **Student-faculty ratio** 14:1 **Application deadline** Rolling (freshmen), rolling (transfer) **Freshmen** 66% were admitted **Housing** Yes **Expenses** Tuition $5406; Room & Board $8420 **Undergraduates** 56% women, 4% part-time, 9% 25 or older, 1% Native American, 3% Hispanic American, 2% African American, 1% Asian American/Pacific Islander **The most frequently**

State University of New York College at Potsdam *(continued)*

chosen baccalaureate fields are education, social sciences, visual and performing arts **Academic program** Advanced placement, self-designed majors, honors program, summer session, internships **Contact** Mr. Thomas Nesbitt, Director of Admissions, State University of New York College at Potsdam, 44 Pierrepont Avenue, Potsdam, NY 13676. Phone: 315-267-2180 or toll-free 877-POTSDAM. Fax: 315-267-2163. E-mail: admissions@potsdam.edu. Web site: http://www.potsdam.edu/.

STATE UNIVERSITY OF NEW YORK COLLEGE OF AGRICULTURE AND TECHNOLOGY AT COBLESKILL

COBLESKILL, NEW YORK

General State-supported, 4-year, coed **Entrance** Minimally difficult **Setting** 750-acre rural campus **Total enrollment** 2,601 **Student-faculty ratio** 18:1 **Application deadline** Rolling (freshmen), rolling (transfer) **Freshmen** 81% were admitted **Housing** Yes **Expenses** Tuition $5414; Room & Board $8650 **Undergraduates** 47% women, 5% part-time, 9% 25 or older, 0.2% Native American, 5% Hispanic American, 7% African American, 1% Asian American/Pacific Islander **The most frequently chosen baccalaureate fields are** agriculture, business/marketing, natural resources/environmental science **Academic program** English as a second language, advanced placement, honors program, summer session, adult/continuing education programs, internships **Contact** Christopher Tacea, Director of Admissions, State University of New York College of Agriculture and Technology at Cobleskill, Office of Admissions, Cobleskill, NY 12043. Phone: 518-255-5525 or toll-free 800-295-8988. Fax: 518-255-6769. E-mail: admissions@cobleskill.edu. Web site: http://www.cobleskill.edu/.

STATE UNIVERSITY OF NEW YORK COLLEGE OF ENVIRONMENTAL SCIENCE AND FORESTRY

SYRACUSE, NEW YORK

General State-supported, university, coed **Entrance** Moderately difficult **Setting** 12-acre urban campus **Total enrollment** 2,061 **Student-faculty ratio** 12:1 **Application deadline** 12/1 (freshmen), rolling (transfer) **Freshmen** 51% were admitted **Housing** Yes **Expenses** Tuition $5675; Room & Board $11,320 **Undergraduates** 38% women, 9% part-time, 8% 25 or older, 1% Native American, 4% Hispanic American, 1% African American, 3% Asian American/Pacific Islander **The most frequently chosen baccalaureate fields are** biological/life sciences, architecture, engineering **Academic program** English as a second language, advanced placement, accelerated degree program, honors program, adult/continuing education programs, internships **Contact** Ms. Susan Sanford, Director of Admissions, State University of New York College of Environmental Science and Forestry, Office of Undergraduate Admissions, 106 Bray Hall, 1 Forestry Lane, Syracuse, NY 13210-2779. Phone: 315-470-6600 or toll-free 800-777-7373. Fax: 315-470-6933. E-mail: esfinfo@esf.edu. Web site: http://www.esf.edu/.

STATE UNIVERSITY OF NEW YORK COLLEGE OF TECHNOLOGY AT CANTON

CANTON, NEW YORK

General State-supported, 4-year, coed **Contact** Mr. Jonathan Kent, Director of Admissions, State University of New York College of Technology at Canton, Cornell Drive, Canton, NY 13617. Phone: 315-386-7123 or toll-free 800-388-7123. Fax: 315-386-7929. E-mail: admissions@canton.edu. Web site: http://www.canton.edu/.

STATE UNIVERSITY OF NEW YORK DOWNSTATE MEDICAL CENTER

BROOKLYN, NEW YORK

General State-supported, upper-level, coed **Entrance** Moderately difficult **Setting** urban campus **Total enrollment** 1,598 **Application deadline** 5/1 (transfer) **Housing** Yes **Expenses** Tuition $7348; Room & Board $12,816 **Undergraduates** 83% women, 37% part-time, 6% Hispanic American, 41% African American, 11% Asian American/Pacific Islander **The most frequently chosen baccalaureate field is** health professions and related sciences **Academic program** Advanced placement, accelerated degree program, summer session, adult/continuing education programs, internships **Contact** SUNY Downstate Admissions Office, State University of New York Downstate Medical Center, 450 Clarkson Avenue, Box 60, Room 133, Basic Sciences Building, Brooklyn, NY 11203. Phone: 718-270-2446. Fax: 718-270-7592. E-mail: admissions@downstate.edu. Web site: http://www.downstate.edu/.

STATE UNIVERSITY OF NEW YORK EMPIRE STATE COLLEGE

SARATOGA SPRINGS, NEW YORK

General State-supported, comprehensive, coed **Entrance** Minimally difficult **Setting** small-town campus **Total enrollment** 12,914 **Student-faculty ratio** 10:1 **Application deadline** Rolling (freshmen), rolling (transfer) **Freshmen** 77% were admitted **Housing** No **Expenses** Tuition $4575

Undergraduates 60% women, 66% part-time, 80% 25 or older, 1% Native American, 7% Hispanic American, 12% African American, 1% Asian American/Pacific Islander **The most frequently chosen baccalaureate fields are** business/marketing, English, public administration and social services **Academic program** Advanced placement, self-designed majors, adult/continuing education programs **Contact** Ms. Jennifer Riley, Director of Admissions, State University of New York Empire State College, One Union Avenue, Saratoga Springs, NY 12866. Phone: 518-587-2100 Ext. 2214 or toll-free 800-847-3000. Fax: 518-587-9759. E-mail: jennifer.riley@esc.edu. Web site: http://www.esc.edu/.

STATE UNIVERSITY OF NEW YORK INSTITUTE OF TECHNOLOGY

UTICA, NEW YORK

General State-supported, comprehensive, coed **Entrance** Moderately difficult **Setting** 850-acre suburban campus **Total enrollment** 2,828 **Student-faculty ratio** 19:1 **Application deadline** Rolling (freshmen), rolling (transfer) **Freshmen** 39% were admitted **Housing** Yes **Expenses** Tuition $5405; Room & Board $7950 **Undergraduates** 49% women, 36% part-time, 42% 25 or older, 0.3% Native American, 3% Hispanic American, 8% African American, 3% Asian American/Pacific Islander **The most frequently chosen baccalaureate fields are** business/marketing, engineering technologies, health professions and related sciences **Academic program** English as a second language, advanced placement, accelerated degree program, summer session, internships **Contact** Amy stokes, State University of New York Institute of Technology, PO Box 3050, Utica, NY 13504-3050. Phone: 315-792-7500 or toll-free 800-SUNYTEC. Fax: 315-792-7837. E-mail: admissions@sunyit.edu. Web site: http://www.sunyit.edu/.

STATE UNIVERSITY OF NEW YORK MARITIME COLLEGE

THROGGS NECK, NEW YORK

General State-supported, comprehensive, coed, primarily men **Contact** Ms. Deirdre Whitman, Vice President of Enrollment and Campus Life, State University of New York Maritime College, 6 Pennyfield Avenue, Throggs Neck, NY 10465. Phone: 718-409-7220 or toll-free 800-654-1874 (in-state); 800-642-1874 (out-of-state). Fax: 718-409-7465. E-mail: admissions@sunymaritime.edu. Web site: http://www.sunymaritime.edu/.

STATE UNIVERSITY OF NEW YORK UPSTATE MEDICAL UNIVERSITY

SYRACUSE, NEW YORK

General State-supported, upper-level, coed **Entrance** Moderately difficult **Setting** 25-acre urban campus **Total enrollment** 1,277 **Student-faculty ratio** 2:1 **Application deadline** Rolling (transfer) **First-year students** 25% were admitted **Housing** Yes **Expenses** Tuition $9236; Room & Board $8800 **Undergraduates** 73% women, 38% part-time, 55% 25 or older, 0.4% Native American, 2% Hispanic American, 6% African American, 4% Asian American/Pacific Islander **The most frequently chosen baccalaureate field is** health professions and related sciences **Academic program** Advanced placement, summer session, internships **Contact** Ms. Donna L. Vavonese, Associate Director of Admissions, State University of New York Upstate Medical University, Weiskotten Hall, 766 Irving Avenue, Syracuse, NY 13210. Phone: 315-464-4570 or toll-free 800-736-2171. Fax: 315-464-8867. E-mail: admiss@upstate.edu. Web site: http://www.upstate.edu/.

STONY BROOK UNIVERSITY, STATE UNIVERSITY OF NEW YORK

STONY BROOK, NEW YORK

General State-supported, university, coed **Entrance** Very difficult **Setting** 1,100-acre small-town campus **Total enrollment** 23,347 **Student-faculty ratio** 18:1 **Application deadline** 3/1 (freshmen), 4/15 (transfer) **Freshmen** 43% were admitted **Housing** Yes **Expenses** Tuition $5760; Room & Board $8734 **Undergraduates** 50% women, 8% part-time, 10% 25 or older, 0.2% Native American, 8% Hispanic American, 9% African American, 22% Asian American/Pacific Islander **The most frequently chosen baccalaureate fields are** health professions and related sciences, biological/life sciences, social sciences **Academic program** English as a second language, advanced placement, self-designed majors, honors program, summer session, adult/continuing education programs, internships **Contact** Ms. Judith Burke-Berhanan, Stony Brook University, State University of New York, Nicolls Road, Stony Brook, NY 11794. Phone: 631-632-6868 or toll-free 800-872-7869. Fax: 631-632-9898. E-mail: ugadmissions@notes.cc.sunysb.edu. Web site: http://www.sunysb.edu/.

SWEDISH INSTITUTE, COLLEGE OF HEALTH SCIENCES

NEW YORK, NEW YORK

General Proprietary, comprehensive, coed **Contact** Admissions Advisor, Swedish Institute, College of Health Sciences, 226 West 26th Street,

Swedish Institute, College of Health Sciences *(continued)*

New York, NY 10001. Phone: 212-924-5900. E-mail: admissions@swedishinstitute.edu. Web site: http://www.swedishinstitute.org/.

SYRACUSE UNIVERSITY
SYRACUSE, NEW YORK

General Independent, university, coed **Entrance** Very difficult **Setting** 200-acre urban campus **Total enrollment** 17,677 **Student-faculty ratio** 15:1 **Application deadline** 1/1 (freshmen), 1/1 (transfer) **Freshmen** 51% were admitted **Housing** Yes **Expenses** Tuition $31,686; Room & Board $10,940 **Undergraduates** 55% women, 1% part-time, 1% 25 or older, 1% Native American, 6% Hispanic American, 7% African American, 9% Asian American/Pacific Islander **The most frequently chosen baccalaureate fields are** business/marketing, social sciences, visual and performing arts **Academic program** English as a second language, advanced placement, accelerated degree program, self-designed majors, honors program, summer session, adult/continuing education programs, internships **Contact** Office of Admissions, Syracuse University, 200 Crouse-Hinds Hall, South Crouse Avenue, Syracuse, NY 13244-2130. Phone: 315-443-3611. E-mail: orange@syr.edu. Web site: http://www.syracuse.edu/.

TALMUDICAL INSTITUTE OF UPSTATE NEW YORK
ROCHESTER, NEW YORK

Contact Rabbi Menachem Davidowitz, Director of Admissions, Talmudical Institute of Upstate New York, 769 Park Avenue, Rochester, NY 14607-3046. Phone: 716-473-2810. E-mail: tiuny@frontiernet.net. Web site: http://www.tiuny.org/.

TALMUDICAL SEMINARY OHOLEI TORAH
BROOKLYN, NEW YORK

Contact Rabbi E. Piekarski, Director of Academic Affairs, Talmudical Seminary Oholei Torah, 667 Eastern Parkway, Brooklyn, NY 11213-3310. Phone: 718-363-2034.

TORAH TEMIMAH TALMUDICAL SEMINARY
BROOKLYN, NEW YORK

Contact Rabbi I. Hisiger, Principal, Torah Temimah Talmudical Seminary, 507 Ocean Parkway, Brooklyn, NY 11218-5913. Phone: 718-853-8500.

TOURO COLLEGE
NEW YORK, NEW YORK

Contact Mr. Andre Baron, Director of Admissions, Touro College, 27-33 West 23rd Street, New York, NY 10010. Phone: 212-463-0400 Ext. 665. Web site: http://www.touro.edu/.

UNION COLLEGE
SCHENECTADY, NEW YORK

General Independent, 4-year, coed **Entrance** Very difficult **Setting** 120-acre urban campus **Total enrollment** 2,177 **Student-faculty ratio** 10:1 **Application deadline** 1/15 (freshmen), 5/1 (transfer) **Freshmen** 43% were admitted **Housing** Yes **Expenses** Tuition $46,245 **Undergraduates** 48% women, 1% part-time, 0.2% Native American, 4% Hispanic American, 3% African American, 6% Asian American/Pacific Islander **The most frequently chosen baccalaureate fields are** biological/life sciences, psychology, social sciences **Academic program** Advanced placement, accelerated degree program, self-designed majors, honors program, summer session, internships **Contact** Dean of Admissions, Union College, Grant Hall, Schenectady, NY 02308. Phone: 518-388-6112 or toll-free 888-843-6688. Fax: 518-388-6986. E-mail: admissions@union.edu. Web site: http://www.union.edu/.

UNITED STATES MERCHANT MARINE ACADEMY
KINGS POINT, NEW YORK

General Federally supported, 4-year, coed **Entrance** Very difficult **Setting** 82-acre suburban campus **Total enrollment** 925 **Student-faculty ratio** 11:1 **Application deadline** 3/1 (freshmen), 3/1 (transfer) **Freshmen** 16% were admitted **Housing** Yes **Undergraduates** 13% women, 1% Native American, 3% Hispanic American, 2% African American, 4% Asian American/Pacific Islander **Academic program** Honors program, internships **Contact** Capt. Robert E. Johnson, Director of Admissions and Financial Aid, United States Merchant Marine Academy, 300 Steamboat Road, Kings Point, NY 11024-1699. Phone: 516-773-5391 or toll-free 866-546-4778. Fax: 516-773-5390. E-mail: admissions@usmma.edu. Web site: http://www.usmma.edu/.

UNITED STATES MILITARY ACADEMY
WEST POINT, NEW YORK

Contact Col. Michael Jones, Director of Admissions, United States Military Academy, Building 606, West Point, NY 10996. Phone: 845-938-

4041. E-mail: 8dad@sunams.usma.army.mil. Web site: http://www.usma.edu/.

►For more information, see page 495.

UNITED TALMUDICAL SEMINARY
BROOKLYN, NEW YORK

Contact Director of Admissions, United Talmudical Seminary, 82 Lee Avenue, Brooklyn, NY 11211-7900. Phone: 718-963-9770.

UNIVERSITY AT ALBANY, STATE UNIVERSITY OF NEW YORK
ALBANY, NEW YORK

General State-supported, university, coed **Entrance** Moderately difficult **Setting** 560-acre suburban campus **Total enrollment** 17,684 **Student-faculty ratio** 19:1 **Application deadline** 3/1 (freshmen), 8/1 (transfer) **Freshmen** 52% were admitted **Housing** Yes **Expenses** Tuition $6018; Room & Board $9032 **Undergraduates** 50% women, 6% part-time, 7% 25 or older, 0.2% Native American, 7% Hispanic American, 9% African American, 6% Asian American/Pacific Islander **The most frequently chosen baccalaureate fields are** business/marketing, psychology, social sciences **Academic program** English as a second language, advanced placement, accelerated degree program, self-designed majors, honors program, summer session, internships **Contact** Mr. Robert Andrea, Director of Undergraduate Admissions, University at Albany, State University of New York, 1400 Washington Avenue, University Administration Building 101, Albany, NY 12222. Phone: 518-442-5435 or toll-free 800-293-7869. Fax: 518-442-5383. E-mail: ugadmissions@albany.edu. Web site: http://www.albany.edu/.

UNIVERSITY AT BUFFALO, THE STATE UNIVERSITY OF NEW YORK
BUFFALO, NEW YORK

General State-supported, university, coed **Entrance** Moderately difficult **Setting** 1,350-acre suburban campus **Total enrollment** 28,054 **Student-faculty ratio** 16:1 **Freshmen** 52% were admitted **Housing** Yes **Expenses** Tuition $6217; Room & Board $8620 **Undergraduates** 46% women, 7% part-time, 9% 25 or older, 0.4% Native American, 3% Hispanic American, 7% African American, 9% Asian American/Pacific Islander **The most frequently chosen baccalaureate fields are** business/marketing, engineering, psychology **Academic program** English as a second language, advanced placement, accelerated degree program, self-designed majors, honors program, summer session, adult/continuing education programs, internships **Contact** Ms. Patricia Armstrong, Director of Admissions, University at Buffalo, the State University of New York, 12 Capen Hall, North Campus, Buffalo, NY 14260-1660. Phone: 716-645-6900 or toll-free 888-UB-ADMIT. Fax: 716-645-6411. E-mail: ub-admissions@buffalo.edu. Web site: http://www.buffalo.edu/.

UNIVERSITY OF ROCHESTER
ROCHESTER, NEW YORK

General Independent, university, coed **Entrance** Very difficult **Setting** 534-acre suburban campus **Total enrollment** 9,334 **Student-faculty ratio** 9:1 **Application deadline** 1/1 (freshmen), 6/1 (transfer) **Freshmen** 41% were admitted **Housing** Yes **Expenses** Tuition $35,190; Room & Board $10,640 **Undergraduates** 51% women, 6% part-time, 0.2% Native American, 4% Hispanic American, 4% African American, 10% Asian American/Pacific Islander **The most frequently chosen baccalaureate fields are** social sciences, biological/life sciences, visual and performing arts **Academic program** English as a second language, advanced placement, accelerated degree program, self-designed majors, honors program, summer session, internships **Contact** Admissions Office, University of Rochester, PO Box 270251, 300 Wilson Boulevard, Rochester, NY 14627-0251. Phone: 585-275-3221 or toll-free 888-822-2256. Fax: 585-461-4595. E-mail: admit@admissions.rochester.edu. Web site: http://www.rochester.edu/.

►For more information, see page 498.

U.T.A. MESIVTA OF KIRYAS JOEL
MONROE, NEW YORK

Contact U.T.A. Mesivta of Kiryas Joel, 33 Forest Road, Suite 101, Monroe, NY 10950.

UTICA COLLEGE
UTICA, NEW YORK

General Independent, comprehensive, coed **Entrance** Moderately difficult **Setting** 128-acre suburban campus **Total enrollment** 3,010 **Student-faculty ratio** 12:1 **Application deadline** Rolling (freshmen), rolling (transfer) **Freshmen** 76% were admitted **Housing** Yes **Expenses** Tuition $24,584; Room & Board $10,294 **Undergraduates** 60% women, 19% part-time, 20% 25 or older, 1% Native American, 3% Hispanic American, 10% African American, 2% Asian American/Pacific Islander **The most frequently chosen baccalaureate fields are** business/marketing, health professions and related sciences, security and protective services **Academic program** Advanced placement, accelerated degree program, honors program, summer session, adult/continuing education programs,

Utica College *(continued)*

internships **Contact** Mr. Patrick Quinn, Vice President for Enrollment Management, Utica College, 1600 Burrstone Road, Utica, NY 13502. Phone: 315-792-3006 or toll-free 800-782-8884. Fax: 315-792-3003. E-mail: admiss@utica.edu. Web site: http://www.utica.edu/.

VASSAR COLLEGE
POUGHKEEPSIE, NEW YORK

General Independent, comprehensive, coed **Entrance** Very difficult **Setting** 1,000-acre suburban campus **Total enrollment** 2,451 **Student-faculty ratio** 8:1 **Application deadline** 1/1 (freshmen), 4/1 (transfer) **Freshmen** 29% were admitted **Housing** Yes **Expenses** Tuition $38,115; Room & Board $8570 **Undergraduates** 61% women, 2% part-time, 1% 25 or older, 0.2% Native American, 7% Hispanic American, 5% African American, 10% Asian American/Pacific Islander **The most frequently chosen baccalaureate fields are** English, social sciences, visual and performing arts **Academic program** Advanced placement, self-designed majors, internships **Contact** Dr. David M. Borus, Dean of Admission and Financial Aid, Vassar College, 124 Raymond Avenue, Poughkeepsie, NY 12604. Phone: 845-437-7300 or toll-free 800-827-7270. Fax: 845-437-7063. E-mail: admissions@vassar.edu. Web site: http://www.vassar.edu/.

VAUGHN COLLEGE OF AERONAUTICS AND TECHNOLOGY
FLUSHING, NEW YORK

General Independent, comprehensive, coed, primarily men **Contact** Mr. Vincent Papandrea, Director, Admissions, Vaughn College of Aeronautics and Technology, La Guardia Airport, 86-01 23rd Avenue, Flushing, NY 11369. Phone: 718-429-6600 Ext. 102 or toll-free 800-776-2376 Ext. 145. Fax: 718-779-2231. E-mail: admitme@vaughn.edu. Web site: http://www.vaughn.edu/.

WAGNER COLLEGE
STATEN ISLAND, NEW YORK

General Independent, comprehensive, coed **Entrance** Moderately difficult **Setting** 105-acre urban campus **Total enrollment** 2,294 **Student-faculty ratio** 13:1 **Application deadline** 2/15 (freshmen), 5/1 (transfer) **Freshmen** 60% were admitted **Housing** Yes **Expenses** Tuition $31,000; Room & Board $9250 **Undergraduates** 63% women, 2% part-time, 5% 25 or older, 0.5% Native American, 5% Hispanic American, 5% African American, 2% Asian American/Pacific Islander **The most frequently chosen baccalaureate fields are** business/marketing, health professions and related sciences, visual and performing arts **Academic program** Honors program, summer session, internships **Contact** Ms. Leigh-Ann Nowicki, Dean of Admissions, Wagner College, 1 Campus Road, Staten Island, NY 10301-4495. Phone: 718-420-4242 Ext. 3412 or toll-free 800-221-1010. Fax: 718-390-3105. E-mail: adm@wagner.edu. Web site: http://www.wagner.edu/.

WEBB INSTITUTE
GLEN COVE, NEW YORK

General Independent, 4-year, coed **Entrance** Most difficult **Setting** 26-acre suburban campus **Total enrollment** 91 **Student-faculty ratio** 12:1 **Application deadline** 2/15 (freshmen), 2/15 (transfer) **Freshmen** 31% were admitted **Housing** Yes **Expenses** Tuition $0; Room & Board $9500 **Undergraduates** 22% women, 1% 25 or older, 2% Hispanic American, 2% Asian American/Pacific Islander **The most frequently chosen baccalaureate field is** engineering **Academic program** Internships **Contact** Mr. William Murray, Director of Enrollment Management, Webb Institute, Crescent Beach Road, Glen Cove, NY 11542-1398. Phone: 516-671-2213. Fax: 516-674-9838. E-mail: admissions@webb-institute.edu. Web site: http://www.webb-institute.edu/.

WELLS COLLEGE
AURORA, NEW YORK

General Independent, 4-year, coed, primarily women **Entrance** Moderately difficult **Setting** 365-acre rural campus **Total enrollment** 557 **Student-faculty ratio** 9:1 **Application deadline** 3/1 (freshmen), rolling (transfer) **Freshmen** 64% were admitted **Housing** Yes **Expenses** Tuition $19,410; Room & Board $8420 **Undergraduates** 77% women, 3% part-time, 8% 25 or older, 1% Native American, 4% Hispanic American, 5% African American, 2% Asian American/Pacific Islander **The most frequently chosen baccalaureate fields are** psychology, social sciences, visual and performing arts **Academic program** English as a second language, advanced placement, accelerated degree program, self-designed majors, adult/continuing education programs, internships **Contact** Ms. Susan Raith Sloan, Wells College, 170 Main Street, Aurora, NY 13026. Phone: 315-364-3264 or toll-free 800-952-9355. Fax: 315-364-3227. E-mail: admissions@wells.edu. Web site: http://www.wells.edu/.

YESHIVA AND KOLEL BAIS MEDRASH ELYON

MONSEY, NEW YORK

Contact Yeshiva and Kolel Bais Medrash Elyon, 73 Main Street, Monsey, NY 10952.

YESHIVA AND KOLLEL HARBOTZAS TORAH

BROOKLYN, NEW YORK

Contact Yeshiva and Kollel Harbotzas Torah, 1049 East 15th Street, Brooklyn, NY 11230.

YESHIVA DERECH CHAIM

BROOKLYN, NEW YORK

Contact Mr. Y. Borchardt, Administrator, Yeshiva Derech Chaim, 1573 39th Street, Brooklyn, NY 11218. Phone: 718-438-5476.

YESHIVA D'MONSEY RABBINICAL COLLEGE

MONSEY, NEW YORK

Contact Yeshiva D'Monsey Rabbinical College, 2 Roman Boulevard, Monsey, NY 10952.

YESHIVA GEDOLAH IMREI YOSEF D'SPINKA

BROOKLYN, NEW YORK

Contact Yeshiva Gedolah Imrei Yosef D'Spinka, 1466 56th Street, Brooklyn, NY 11219.

YESHIVA KARLIN STOLIN RABBINICAL INSTITUTE

BROOKLYN, NEW YORK

Contact Mr. Aryeh L. Wolpin, Director of Admissions, Yeshiva Karlin Stolin Rabbinical Institute, 1818 Fifty-fourth Street, Brooklyn, NY 11204. Phone: 718-232-7800 Ext. 26. Fax: 718-331-4833.

YESHIVA OF NITRA RABBINICAL COLLEGE

MOUNT KISCO, NEW YORK

Contact Mr. Ernest Schwartz, Administrator, Yeshiva of Nitra Rabbinical College, Pines Bridge Road, Mount Kisco, NY 10549. Phone: 718-384-5460. Fax: 718-387-9400.

YESHIVA OF THE TELSHE ALUMNI

RIVERDALE, NEW YORK

Contact Yeshiva of the Telshe Alumni, 4904 Independence Avenue, Riverdale, NY 10471.

YESHIVA SHAAREI TORAH OF ROCKLAND

SUFFERN, NEW YORK

Contact Yeshiva Shaarei Torah of Rockland, 91 West Carlton Road, Suffern, NY 10901.

YESHIVA SHAAR HATORAH TALMUDIC RESEARCH INSTITUTE

KEW GARDENS, NEW YORK

Contact Rabbi Kalman Epstein, Assistant Dean, Yeshiva Shaar Hatorah Talmudic Research Institute, 117-06 84th Avenue, Kew Gardens, NY 11418-1469. Phone: 718-846-1940.

YESHIVAS NOVOMINSK

BROOKLYN, NEW YORK

Contact Yeshivas Novominsk, 1569 47th Street, Brooklyn, NY 11219.

YESHIVATH VIZNITZ

MONSEY, NEW YORK

Contact Rabbi Bernard Rosenfeld, Registrar, Yeshivath Viznitz, Phyllis Terrace, PO Box 446, Monsey, NY 10952. Phone: 914-356-1010.

YESHIVATH ZICHRON MOSHE

SOUTH FALLSBURG, NEW YORK

Contact Rabbi Abba Gorelick, Dean, Yeshivath Zichron Moshe, Laurel Park Road, South Fallsburg, NY 12779. Phone: 914-434-5240.

YESHIVAT MIKDASH MELECH

BROOKLYN, NEW YORK

Contact Rabbi S. Churba, Director of Admissions, Yeshivat Mikdash Melech, 1326 Ocean Parkway, Brooklyn, NY 11230-5601. Phone: 718-339-1090.

YESHIVA UNIVERSITY

NEW YORK, NEW YORK

Contact Mr. Michael Kranzler, Director of Undergraduate Admissions, Yeshiva University, 500 West 185th Street, New York, NY 10033-3201. Phone: 212-960-5277. Fax: 212-960-0086. E-mail: yuadmit@ymail.yu.edu. Web site: http://www.yu.edu/.

YORK COLLEGE OF THE CITY UNIVERSITY OF NEW YORK

JAMAICA, NEW YORK

General State and locally supported, 4-year, coed **Entrance** Moderately difficult **Setting** 50-acre

York College of the City University of New York *(continued)*

urban campus **Total enrollment** 6,727 **Student-faculty ratio** 17:1 **Application deadline** Rolling (freshmen), rolling (transfer) **Freshmen** 60% were admitted **Housing** No **Expenses** Tuition $4180 **Undergraduates** 67% women, 38% part-time, 35% 25 or older, 0.3% Native American, 17% Hispanic American, 45% African American, 11% Asian American/Pacific Islander **The most frequently chosen baccalaureate fields are** business/marketing, health professions and related sciences, psychology **Academic program** English as a second language, advanced placement, honors program, summer session, adult/continuing education programs, internships **Contact** Ms. Diane Warmsley, Director of Admissions, York College of the City University of New York, 94-20 Guy R. Brewer Boulevard, Jamaica, NY 11451. Phone: 718-262-2188. Fax: 718-262-2601. E-mail: warmsley@york.cuny.edu. Web site: http://www.york.cuny.edu/.

NORTH CAROLINA

APEX SCHOOL OF THEOLOGY
DURHAM, NORTH CAROLINA

General Independent interdenominational, comprehensive, coed **Contact** Dr. Henry D. Wells Jr., Registrar, Apex School of Theology, 5104 Revere Road, Durham, NC 27713. Phone: 919-572-1625. Fax: 919-572-1762. E-mail: registrar@apexsot.edu. Web site: http://www.apexsot.edu/.

APPALACHIAN STATE UNIVERSITY
BOONE, NORTH CAROLINA

General State-supported, comprehensive, coed **Entrance** Moderately difficult **Setting** 340-acre small-town campus **Total enrollment** 15,871 **Student-faculty ratio** 17:1 **Application deadline** Rolling (freshmen), rolling (transfer) **Freshmen** 65% were admitted **Housing** Yes **Expenses** Tuition $4241; Room & Board $5990 **Undergraduates** 51% women, 6% part-time, 9% 25 or older, 0.4% Native American, 2% Hispanic American, 4% African American, 1% Asian American/Pacific Islander **The most frequently chosen baccalaureate fields are** business/marketing, education, social sciences **Academic program** English as a second language, advanced placement, self-designed majors, honors program, summer session, adult/continuing education programs, internships **Contact** Mr. Paul Hiatt, Director of Admissions, Appalachian State University, Boone, NC 28608. Phone: 828-262-2120. Fax: 828-262-3296. E-mail: admissions@appstate.edu. Web site: http://www.appstate.edu/.

THE ART INSTITUTE OF CHARLOTTE
CHARLOTTE, NORTH CAROLINA

General Proprietary, 4-year, coed **Entrance** Minimally difficult **Setting** suburban campus **Total enrollment** 880 **Student-faculty ratio** 19:1 **Application deadline** Rolling (freshmen), rolling (transfer) **Freshmen** 39% were admitted **Housing** Yes **Expenses** Tuition $18,576; Room only $5780 **Undergraduates** 69% women, 29% part-time, 0.3% Native American, 5% Hispanic American, 33% African American, 2% Asian American/Pacific Islander **Academic program** Advanced placement, accelerated degree program, summer session, internships **Contact** Ms. Pamela Notemyer Rogers, Director of Admissions, The Art Institute of Charlotte, 2110 Water Ridge Parkway, Charlotte, NC 28217. Phone: 704-357-8020 or toll-free 800-872-4417. Fax: 704-357-1133. E-mail: pnotemyer@aii.edu. Web site: http://www.artinstitutes.edu/charlotte/.

THE ART INSTITUTE OF RALEIGH-DURHAM
DURHAM, NC, NORTH CAROLINA

Contact The Art Institute of Raleigh-Durham, 410 Blackwell Street, Durham, NC, NC 27701. Phone: toll-free 888-245-9593.

BARTON COLLEGE
WILSON, NORTH CAROLINA

General Independent, 4-year, coed, affiliated with Christian Church (Disciples of Christ) **Entrance** Minimally difficult **Setting** 76-acre small-town campus **Total enrollment** 1,130 **Student-faculty ratio** 11:1 **Application deadline** Rolling (freshmen), rolling (transfer) **Freshmen** 63% were admitted **Housing** Yes **Expenses** Tuition $19,938; Room & Board $6782 **Undergraduates** 71% women, 22% part-time, 28% 25 or older, 0.5% Native American, 3% Hispanic American, 23% African American, 1% Asian American/Pacific Islander **The most frequently chosen baccalaureate fields are** business/marketing, education, health professions and related sciences **Academic program** English as a second language, advanced placement, honors program, summer session, adult/continuing education programs, internships **Contact** Ms. Amanda Humphrey, Director of Admissions, Barton College, Box 5000, College Station, Wilson, NC 27893. Phone: 800-345-4973 or toll-free 800-345-4973. Fax: 252-399-6572. E-mail: enroll@barton.edu. Web site: http://www.barton.edu/.

BELMONT ABBEY COLLEGE
BELMONT, NORTH CAROLINA

General Independent Roman Catholic, 4-year, coed **Entrance** Moderately difficult **Setting** 650-acre small-town campus **Total enrollment** 1,337 **Student-faculty ratio** 16:1 **Application deadline** 8/1 (freshmen), 8/15 (transfer) **Freshmen** 70% were admitted **Housing** Yes **Expenses** Tuition $18,796; Room & Board $9713 **Undergraduates** 61% women, 8% part-time, 43% 25 or older, 0.4% Native American, 4% Hispanic American, 21% African American, 1% Asian American/Pacific Islander **The most frequently chosen baccalaureate fields are** business/marketing, education, philosophy and religious studies **Academic program** Advanced placement, accelerated degree program, honors program, summer session, adult/continuing education programs, internships **Contact** Roger L. Jones, Director of Admission, Belmont Abbey College, 100 Belmont-Mt. Holly Road, Belmont, NC 28012-1802. Phone: 704-825-6214 or toll-free 888-BAC-0110. Fax: 704-825-6220. E-mail: admissions@bac.edu. Web site: http://www.belmontabbeycollege.edu/.

BENNETT COLLEGE FOR WOMEN
GREENSBORO, NORTH CAROLINA

General Independent United Methodist, 4-year, women only **Contact** Ms. Ulisa Bowles, Director of Admissions, Bennett College For Women, Campus Box H, Greensboro, NC 27401. Phone: 336-517-8624. E-mail: admiss@bennett.edu. Web site: http://www.bennett.edu/.

BREVARD COLLEGE
BREVARD, NORTH CAROLINA

General Independent United Methodist, 4-year, coed **Entrance** Minimally difficult **Setting** 120-acre small-town campus **Total enrollment** 675 **Student-faculty ratio** 11:1 **Application deadline** Rolling (freshmen), rolling (transfer) **Freshmen** 63% were admitted **Housing** Yes **Expenses** Tuition $18,750; Room & Board $7050 **Undergraduates** 42% women, 4% part-time, 6% 25 or older, 1% Native American, 1% Hispanic American, 7% African American, 0.3% Asian American/Pacific Islander **The most frequently chosen baccalaureate fields are** business/marketing, parks and recreation, visual and performing arts **Academic program** Advanced placement, self-designed majors, honors program, adult/continuing education programs, internships **Contact** Mr. Ken Sigler, Vice President for Enrollment Management, Brevard College, One Brevard College Drive, Brevard, NC 28712. Phone: 828-884-8300 or toll-free 800-527-9090. Fax: 828-884-3790. E-mail: admissions@brevard.edu. Web site: http://www.brevard.edu/.

CABARRUS COLLEGE OF HEALTH SCIENCES
CONCORD, NORTH CAROLINA

General Independent, 4-year, coed, primarily women **Entrance** Moderately difficult **Setting** 5-acre suburban campus **Total enrollment** 358 **Student-faculty ratio** 7:1 **Application deadline** 3/1 (freshmen), 3/1 (transfer) **Freshmen** 62% were admitted **Housing** No **Expenses** Tuition $8750 **Undergraduates** 88% women, 37% part-time, 35% 25 or older, 2% Hispanic American, 6% African American, 1% Asian American/Pacific Islander **The most frequently chosen baccalaureate field is** health professions and related sciences **Academic program** Advanced placement **Contact** Mr. Mark Ellison, Director of Admissions, Cabarrus College of Health Sciences, 401 Medical Park Drive, Concord, NC 28025-2077. Phone: 704-403-1616. Fax: 704-403-2077. E-mail: mellison@cabarruscollege.edu. Web site: http://www.cabarruscollege.edu/.

CAMPBELL UNIVERSITY
BUIES CREEK, NORTH CAROLINA

General Independent, university, coed, affiliated with North Carolina Baptist State Convention **Entrance** Moderately difficult **Setting** 850-acre rural campus **Total enrollment** 4,743 **Student-faculty ratio** 14:1 **Application deadline** Rolling (freshmen), rolling (transfer) **Freshmen** 60% were admitted **Housing** Yes **Expenses** Tuition $20,050; Room & Board $6830 **Undergraduates** 51% women, 7% part-time, 12% 25 or older, 1% Native American, 3% Hispanic American, 12% African American, 1% Asian American/Pacific Islander **The most frequently chosen baccalaureate fields are** business/marketing, liberal arts/general studies, psychology **Academic program** Advanced placement, accelerated degree program, honors program, summer session, adult/continuing education programs, internships **Contact** Ms. Peggy Mason, Director of Admissions, Campbell University, PO Box 546, 450 Leslie Campbell Avenue, Buies Creek, NC 27506. Phone: 910-893-1291 or toll-free 800-334-4111. Fax: 910-893-1288. E-mail: adm@mailcenter.campbell.edu. Web site: http://www.campbell.edu/.

►**For more information, see page 447.**

CAROLINA CHRISTIAN COLLEGE
WINSTON-SALEM, NORTH CAROLINA

Contact Admissions Office, Carolina Christian College, 4117 Northampton Drive, PO Box 777,

Carolina Christian College *(continued)*

Winston-Salem, NC 27102-0777. Phone: 336-744-0900. Web site: http://www.wsbc.edu/.

CATAWBA COLLEGE
SALISBURY, NORTH CAROLINA

General Independent, comprehensive, coed, affiliated with United Church of Christ **Entrance** Moderately difficult **Setting** 210-acre small-town campus **Total enrollment** 1,323 **Student-faculty ratio** 15:1 **Application deadline** Rolling (freshmen), rolling (transfer) **Freshmen** 75% were admitted **Housing** Yes **Expenses** Tuition $22,290; Room & Board $7700 **Undergraduates** 50% women, 5% part-time, 27% 25 or older, 1% Native American, 1% Hispanic American, 16% African American, 1% Asian American/Pacific Islander **The most frequently chosen baccalaureate fields are** business/marketing, education, visual and performing arts **Academic program** Advanced placement, self-designed majors, honors program, summer session, adult/continuing education programs, internships **Contact** Dr. Michael Bitzer, Dean of Admissions, Catawba College, 2300 West Innes Street, Salisbury, NC 28144-2488. Phone: toll-free 800-CATAWBA. Fax: 704-637-4222. E-mail: admission@catawba.edu. Web site: http://www.catawba.edu/.

CHOWAN UNIVERSITY
MURFREESBORO, NORTH CAROLINA

Contact Mr. Jonathan Wirt, Vice President for Enrollment Management, Chowan University, 200 Jones Drive, Murfreesboro, NC 27855. Phone: 252-398-6314 or toll-free 800-488-4101. Fax: 252-398-1190. E-mail: admissions@chowan.edu. Web site: http://www.chowan.edu.

DAVIDSON COLLEGE
DAVIDSON, NORTH CAROLINA

General Independent Presbyterian, 4-year, coed **Entrance** Very difficult **Setting** 556-acre small-town campus **Total enrollment** 1,674 **Student-faculty ratio** 10:1 **Application deadline** 1/2 (freshmen), 3/15 (transfer) **Freshmen** 28% were admitted **Housing** Yes **Expenses** Tuition $31,794; Room & Board $9020 **Undergraduates** 51% women, 1% Native American, 4% Hispanic American, 7% African American, 3% Asian American/Pacific Islander **The most frequently chosen baccalaureate fields are** English, biological/life sciences, social sciences **Academic program** Advanced placement, self-designed majors, honors program **Contact** Mr. Christopher J. Gruber, Vice President and Dean of Admission and Financial Aid, Davidson College, Box 7156, Davidson, NC 28035-7156. Phone: 704-894-2230 or toll-free 800-768-0380. Fax: 704-894-2016. E-mail: admission@davidson.edu. Web site: http://www.davidson.edu/.

DEVRY UNIVERSITY
CHARLOTTE, NORTH CAROLINA

General Proprietary, comprehensive, coed **Entrance** Minimally difficult **Total enrollment** 224 **Student-faculty ratio** 21:1 **Application deadline** Rolling (freshmen), rolling (transfer) **Housing** No **Expenses** Tuition $13,890 **Undergraduates** 55% women, 53% part-time, 68% 25 or older, 7% Hispanic American, 61% African American, 3% Asian American/Pacific Islander **The most frequently chosen baccalaureate field is** business/marketing **Academic program** Advanced placement, accelerated degree program, summer session, adult/continuing education programs **Contact** Admissions Office, DeVry University, 4521 Sharon Road, Suite 145, Charlotte, NC 28211-3627. Web site: http://www.devry.edu/.

DUKE UNIVERSITY
DURHAM, NORTH CAROLINA

General Independent, university, coed, affiliated with United Methodist Church **Entrance** Most difficult **Setting** 8,500-acre suburban campus **Total enrollment** 13,598 **Student-faculty ratio** 8:1 **Application deadline** 1/2 (freshmen), 3/15 (transfer) **Freshmen** 23% were admitted **Housing** Yes **Expenses** Tuition $35,512; Room & Board $9609 **Undergraduates** 49% women, 1% part-time, 0.4% 25 or older, 0.2% Native American, 6% Hispanic American, 10% African American, 19% Asian American/Pacific Islander **The most frequently chosen baccalaureate fields are** engineering, psychology, social sciences **Academic program** English as a second language, advanced placement, accelerated degree program, self-designed majors, honors program, summer session, adult/continuing education programs, internships **Contact** Mr. Christoph Guttentag, Director of Admissions, Duke University, Durham, NC 27708-0586. Phone: 919-684-3214. Fax: 919-684-8941. E-mail: askduke@admiss.duke.edu. Web site: http://www.duke.edu/.

EAST CAROLINA UNIVERSITY
GREENVILLE, NORTH CAROLINA

General State-supported, university, coed **Entrance** Moderately difficult **Setting** 1,377-acre urban campus **Total enrollment** 25,990 **Student-faculty ratio** 20:1 **Application deadline** 3/15 (freshmen) **Freshmen** 84% were admitted **Housing** Yes **Expenses** Tuition $4368; Room & Board $7150 **Undergraduates** 59% women, 12% part-time, 16% 25 or older, 1%

Native American, 2% Hispanic American, 16% African American, 2% Asian American/Pacific Islander **The most frequently chosen baccalaureate fields are** business/marketing, education, health professions and related sciences **Academic program** Advanced placement, honors program, summer session, adult/continuing education programs, internships **Contact** Dr. Judith Bailey, Senior Executive Director of Enrollment Management, East Carolina University, Undergraduate Admission, Whichard Building 106, Greenville, NC 27858-4353. Phone: 252-328-6640. Fax: 252-328-6945. E-mail: admis@mail.ecu.edu. Web site: http://www.ecu.edu/.

ELIZABETH CITY STATE UNIVERSITY
ELIZABETH CITY, NORTH CAROLINA

Contact Mr. Grady Deese, Director of Admissions, Elizabeth City State University, 1704 Weeksville Road, Elizabeth City, NC 27909-7806. Phone: 252-335-3305 or toll-free 800-347-3278. Fax: 252-335-3537. E-mail: admissions@mail.ecsu.edu. Web site: http://www.ecsu.edu/.

ELON UNIVERSITY
ELON, NORTH CAROLINA

General Independent, comprehensive, coed, affiliated with United Church of Christ **Entrance** Moderately difficult **Setting** 580-acre suburban campus **Total enrollment** 5,456 **Student-faculty ratio** 14:1 **Application deadline** 1/10 (freshmen), rolling (transfer) **Freshmen** 41% were admitted **Housing** Yes **Expenses** Tuition $22,166; Room & Board $7296 **Undergraduates** 59% women, 2% part-time, 1% 25 or older, 0.2% Native American, 2% Hispanic American, 6% African American, 1% Asian American/Pacific Islander **Academic program** English as a second language, advanced placement, accelerated degree program, self-designed majors, honors program, summer session, internships **Contact** Ms. Melinda Wood, Associate Director of Admissions and Director of Application Review, Elon University, 100 Campus Box, Elon, NC 27244. Phone: 336-278-3566 or toll-free 800-334-8448. Fax: 336-278-7699. E-mail: admissions@elon.edu. Web site: http://www.elon.edu/.

FAYETTEVILLE STATE UNIVERSITY
FAYETTEVILLE, NORTH CAROLINA

General State-supported, comprehensive, coed **Entrance** Minimally difficult **Setting** 156-acre urban campus **Total enrollment** 6,692 **Student-faculty ratio** 21:1 **Application deadline** 7/1 (freshmen), 7/1 (transfer) **Freshmen** 78% were admitted **Housing** Yes **Expenses** Tuition $3382; Room & Board $4870 **Undergraduates** 69% women, 26% part-time, 32% 25 or older, 1% Native American, 4% Hispanic American, 74% African American, 1% Asian American/Pacific Islander **The most frequently chosen baccalaureate fields are** business/marketing, psychology, security and protective services **Academic program** Advanced placement, accelerated degree program, honors program, summer session, adult/continuing education programs, internships **Contact** Ms. Rozie Shabazz, Associate Vice Chancellor for Enrollment Management, Fayetteville State University, 100 Murchison Road, Fayetteville, NC 28301. Phone: 910-672-1784 or toll-free 800-222-2594. Fax: 910-672-2209. E-mail: rshabzz@uncfsu.edu. Web site: http://www.uncfsu.edu/.

GARDNER-WEBB UNIVERSITY
BOILING SPRINGS, NORTH CAROLINA

General Independent Baptist, comprehensive, coed **Entrance** Moderately difficult **Setting** 250-acre small-town campus **Total enrollment** 3,840 **Student-faculty ratio** 15:1 **Application deadline** Rolling (freshmen), rolling (transfer) **Freshmen** 70% were admitted **Housing** Yes **Expenses** Tuition $18,680; Room & Board $6060 **Undergraduates** 67% women, 16% part-time, 41% 25 or older, 1% Native American, 2% Hispanic American, 18% African American, 1% Asian American/Pacific Islander **The most frequently chosen baccalaureate fields are** business/marketing, health professions and related sciences, social sciences **Academic program** English as a second language, advanced placement, accelerated degree program, honors program, summer session, adult/continuing education programs, internships **Contact** Mr. Nathan Alexander, Assistant Vice President of Admissions, Gardner-Webb University, PO Box 817, 110 South Main Street, Boiling Springs, NC 28017. Phone: 704-406-4491 or toll-free 800-253-6472. Fax: 704-406-4488. E-mail: admissions@gardner-webb.edu. Web site: http://www.gardner-webb.edu/.

►**For more information, see page 462.**

GREENSBORO COLLEGE
GREENSBORO, NORTH CAROLINA

General Independent United Methodist, comprehensive, coed **Entrance** Moderately difficult **Setting** 75-acre urban campus **Total enrollment** 1,188 **Student-faculty ratio** 13:1 **Application deadline** Rolling (freshmen), rolling (transfer) **Freshmen** 64% were admitted **Housing** Yes **Expenses** Tuition $22,248; Room & Board $8420 **Undergraduates** 51% women, 17% part-time, 32% 25 or older, 0.1% Native American, 2% Hispanic American, 9% African American, 0.3% Asian American/Pacific Islander **The most frequently chosen baccalaureate fields are**

Greensboro College *(continued)*

education, social sciences, visual and performing arts **Academic program** English as a second language, advanced placement, accelerated degree program, self-designed majors, honors program, summer session, adult/continuing education programs, internships **Contact** Mr. Timothy L. Jackson, Dean of Enrollment Management, Greensboro College, 815 West Market Street, Greensboro, NC 27401-1875. Phone: 336-272-7102 Ext. 211 or toll-free 800-346-8226. Fax: 336-378-0154. E-mail: admissions@gborocollege.edu. Web site: http://www.gborocollege.edu/.

GUILFORD COLLEGE

GREENSBORO, NORTH CAROLINA

General Independent, 4-year, coed, affiliated with Society of Friends **Entrance** Moderately difficult **Setting** 340-acre suburban campus **Total enrollment** 2,688 **Student-faculty ratio** 16:1 **Application deadline** 2/15 (freshmen), 4/1 (transfer) **Freshmen** 58% were admitted **Housing** Yes **Expenses** Tuition $26,100; Room & Board $7140 **Undergraduates** 61% women, 16% part-time, 40% 25 or older, 1% Native American, 2% Hispanic American, 22% African American, 2% Asian American/Pacific Islander **The most frequently chosen baccalaureate fields are** biological/life sciences, business/marketing, psychology **Academic program** English as a second language, advanced placement, accelerated degree program, self-designed majors, honors program, summer session, adult/continuing education programs, internships **Contact** Ms. Tania Johnson, Associate Director of Admissions, Guilford College, 5800 West Friendly Avenue, Greensboro, NC 27410. Phone: 336-316-2100 or toll-free 800-992-7759. Fax: 336-316-2954. E-mail: admission@guilford.edu. Web site: http://www.guilford.edu/.

HERITAGE BIBLE COLLEGE

DUNN, NORTH CAROLINA

General Independent Pentecostal Free Will Baptist, 4-year, coed **Entrance** Minimally difficult **Setting** 82-acre small-town campus **Total enrollment** 84 **Student-faculty ratio** 20:1 **Application deadline** Rolling (freshmen), rolling (transfer) **Freshmen** 83% were admitted **Housing** Yes **Expenses** Tuition $5400; Room & Board $2400 **Undergraduates** 48% women, 27% part-time, 79% 25 or older, 4% Native American, 4% Hispanic American, 32% African American **The most frequently chosen baccalaureate field is** theology and religious vocations **Academic program** Summer session, adult/continuing education programs, internships **Contact** Mr. Jeff Nichols, Director of Admissions, Heritage Bible College, PO Box 1628, Dunn, NC 28335. Phone: 910-892-3178 Ext. 223 or toll-free 800-297-6351 Ext. 230. Fax: 910-892-1809. E-mail: jnichols@heritagebiblecollege.edu. Web site: http://www.heritagebiblecollege.org/.

HIGH POINT UNIVERSITY

HIGH POINT, NORTH CAROLINA

General Independent United Methodist, comprehensive, coed **Entrance** Moderately difficult **Setting** 130-acre suburban campus **Total enrollment** 3,061 **Student-faculty ratio** 15:1 **Application deadline** 8/15 (freshmen), 8/15 (transfer) **Freshmen** 73% were admitted **Housing** Yes **Expenses** Tuition $31,000 **Undergraduates** 62% women, 10% part-time, 3% 25 or older, 1% Native American, 3% Hispanic American, 17% African American, 3% Asian American/Pacific Islander **The most frequently chosen baccalaureate fields are** business/marketing, education, health professions and related sciences **Academic program** English as a second language, advanced placement, accelerated degree program, self-designed majors, honors program, summer session, adult/continuing education programs, internships **Contact** Ms. Jessie McIlrath-Carter, Director of Admissions, High Point University, Admissions Office, University Station 3187, High Point, NC 27262-3598. Phone: 336-841-9148 or toll-free 800-345-6993. Fax: 336-888-6382. E-mail: jmcilrat@highpoint.edu. Web site: http://www.highpoint.edu/.

JOHNSON & WALES UNIVERSITY

CHARLOTTE, NORTH CAROLINA

General Independent, 4-year, coed **Entrance** Minimally difficult **Total enrollment** 2,569 **Student-faculty ratio** 28:1 **Application deadline** Rolling (freshmen), rolling (transfer) **Freshmen** 63% were admitted **Housing** Yes **Expenses** Tuition $22,585; Room & Board $8892 **Undergraduates** 55% women, 2% part-time, 10% 25 or older, 0.5% Native American, 3% Hispanic American, 24% African American, 2% Asian American/Pacific Islander **The most frequently chosen baccalaureate fields are** business/marketing, family and consumer sciences, parks and recreation **Academic program** English as a second language, advanced placement, accelerated degree program, honors program **Contact** Director of Admissions, Johnson & Wales University, 801 West Trade Street, Charlotte, NC 28202. Phone: 866-598-2427 or toll-free 866-598-2427. Fax: 980-598-1111. E-mail: admissions.clt@jwu.edu. Web site: http://www.jwucharlotte.org/.

JOHNSON C. SMITH UNIVERSITY

CHARLOTTE, NORTH CAROLINA

General Independent, 4-year, coed **Entrance** Moderately difficult **Setting** 100-acre urban campus **Total enrollment** 1,463 **Student-faculty ratio** 14:1 **Freshmen** 46% were admitted **Housing** Yes **Expenses** Tuition $15,754; Room & Board $6132 **Undergraduates** 58% women, 3% part-time, 3% 25 or older, 0.1% Native American, 0.1% Hispanic American, 99% African American **The most frequently chosen baccalaureate fields are** business/marketing, communications/journalism, security and protective services **Academic program** Advanced placement, honors program, summer session, adult/continuing education programs, internships **Contact** Ms. Jocelyn Biggs, Director of Admissions, Johnson C. Smith University, 100 Beatties Ford Road, Charlotte, NC 28216. Phone: 704-378-1010 or toll-free 800-782-7303. Fax: 704-378-1242. E-mail: admissions@jcsu.edu. Web site: http://www.jcsu.edu/.

JOHN WESLEY COLLEGE
HIGH POINT, NORTH CAROLINA

General Independent interdenominational, 4-year, coed **Entrance** Minimally difficult **Setting** 24-acre urban campus **Total enrollment** 107 **Student-faculty ratio** 12:1 **Application deadline** 8/1 (freshmen), 8/1 (transfer) **Freshmen** 100% were admitted **Housing** Yes **Expenses** Tuition $10,844; Room only $2344 **Undergraduates** 33% women, 30% part-time, 70% 25 or older, 1% Native American, 3% Hispanic American, 25% African American, 2% Asian American/Pacific Islander **Academic program** Advanced placement, summer session, adult/continuing education programs, internships **Contact** Amanda Ziemba, Admissions Officer, John Wesley College, 2314 North Centennial Street, High Point, NC 27265-3197. Phone: 336-889-2262 Ext. 127. Fax: 336-889-2261. E-mail: admissions@johnwesley.edu. Web site: http://www.johnwesley.edu/.

LEES-McRAE COLLEGE
BANNER ELK, NORTH CAROLINA

General Independent, 4-year, coed, affiliated with Presbyterian Church (U.S.A.) **Entrance** Minimally difficult **Setting** 400-acre rural campus **Total enrollment** 882 **Application deadline** Rolling (freshmen), rolling (transfer) **Freshmen** 74% were admitted **Housing** Yes **Expenses** Tuition $19,500; Room & Board $6500 **Undergraduates** 60% women, 2% part-time, 20% 25 or older, 0.2% Native American, 3% Hispanic American, 5% African American, 1% Asian American/Pacific Islander **The most frequently chosen baccalaureate fields are** education, health professions and related sciences, visual and performing arts **Academic program** Advanced placement, self-designed majors, honors program, summer session, adult/continuing education programs, internships **Contact** Mr. Bill Sliwa, Lees-McRae College, PO Box 128, Banner Elk, NC 28604-0128. Phone: 828-898-8944 or toll-free 800-280-4562. Fax: 828-898-8707. E-mail: admissions@lmc.edu. Web site: http://www.lmc.edu/.

LENOIR-RHYNE COLLEGE
HICKORY, NORTH CAROLINA

General Independent Lutheran, comprehensive, coed **Entrance** Moderately difficult **Setting** 100-acre small-town campus **Total enrollment** 1,626 **Student-faculty ratio** 13:1 **Application deadline** 8/15 (freshmen), 8/15 (transfer) **Freshmen** 84% were admitted **Housing** Yes **Expenses** Tuition $23,070; Room & Board $8150 **Undergraduates** 63% women, 11% part-time, 12% 25 or older, 0.3% Native American, 1% Hispanic American, 8% African American, 3% Asian American/Pacific Islander **The most frequently chosen baccalaureate fields are** business/marketing, education, health professions and related sciences **Academic program** English as a second language, advanced placement, accelerated degree program, self-designed majors, honors program, summer session, adult/continuing education programs, internships **Contact** Karen Feezor, Lenoir-Rhyne College, 625 7th Avenue NE, Hickory, NC 28601. Phone: 828-328-7300 or toll-free 800-277-5721. Fax: 828-328-7378. E-mail: admission@lrc.edu. Web site: http://www.lrc.edu/.

LIVINGSTONE COLLEGE
SALISBURY, NORTH CAROLINA

General Independent, 4-year, coed, affiliated with African Methodist Episcopal Zion Church **Entrance** Minimally difficult **Setting** 45-acre small-town campus **Total enrollment** 960 **Student-faculty ratio** 16:1 **Application deadline** Rolling (freshmen), rolling (transfer) **Freshmen** 98% were admitted **Housing** Yes **Expenses** Tuition $12,474; Room & Board $5641 **Undergraduates** 44% women, 1% part-time, 11% 25 or older, 0.2% Native American, 0.3% Hispanic American, 94% African American, 0.2% Asian American/Pacific Islander **The most frequently chosen baccalaureate fields are** business/marketing, security and protective services, social sciences **Academic program** Advanced placement, honors program, adult/continuing education programs, internships **Contact** Ms. Nicole Daniels, Director of Admissions, Livingstone College, 701 West Monroe Street, Salifbury, NC 28144. Phone: 704-216-6001 or toll-free 800-835-3435. Fax: 704-216-6215. E-mail: admissions@livingstone.edu. Web site: http://www.livingstone.edu/.

MARS HILL COLLEGE

MARS HILL, NORTH CAROLINA

General Independent Baptist, 4-year, coed **Entrance** Moderately difficult **Setting** 194-acre small-town campus **Total enrollment** 1,250 **Student-faculty ratio** 12:1 **Application deadline** Rolling (freshmen), rolling (transfer) **Freshmen** 69% were admitted **Housing** Yes **Expenses** Tuition $19,894; Room & Board $6891 **Undergraduates** 20% 25 or older **Academic program** English as a second language, advanced placement, accelerated degree program, self-designed majors, honors program, summer session, adult/continuing education programs, internships **Contact** Ed Hoffmeyer, Director of Admissions, Mars Hill College, PO Box 370, Mars Hill, NC 28754. Phone: 828-689-1201 or toll-free 866-MHC-4-YOU. Fax: 828-689-1473. E-mail: ehoffmeyer@mhc.edu. Web site: http://www.mhc.edu/.

MEREDITH COLLEGE

RALEIGH, NORTH CAROLINA

General Independent, comprehensive, undergraduate: women only; graduate: coed **Entrance** Moderately difficult **Setting** 225-acre urban campus **Total enrollment** 2,202 **Student-faculty ratio** 10:1 **Application deadline** 2/15 (freshmen), 2/15 (transfer) **Freshmen** 88% were admitted **Housing** Yes **Expenses** Tuition $23,550; Room & Board $6740 **Undergraduates** 13% part-time, 12% 25 or older, 0.3% Native American, 2% Hispanic American, 11% African American, 2% Asian American/Pacific Islander **The most frequently chosen baccalaureate fields are** business/marketing, psychology, visual and performing arts **Academic program** Advanced placement, accelerated degree program, self-designed majors, honors program, summer session, adult/continuing education programs, internships **Contact** Ms. Heidi Fletcher, Director of Admissions, Meredith College, 3800 Hillsborough Street, Raleigh, NC 27807-5298. Phone: 919-760-8581 or toll-free 800-MEREDITH. Fax: 919-760-2348. E-mail: admissions@meredith.edu. Web site: http://www.meredith.edu/.

METHODIST UNIVERSITY

FAYETTEVILLE, NORTH CAROLINA

General Independent United Methodist, comprehensive, coed **Entrance** Moderately difficult **Setting** 600-acre suburban campus **Total enrollment** 2,118 **Student-faculty ratio** 12:1 **Application deadline** Rolling (freshmen), rolling (transfer) **Freshmen** 73% were admitted **Housing** Yes **Expenses** Tuition $21,944; Room & Board $7650 **Undergraduates** 46% women, 15% part-time, 26% 25 or older, 1% Native American, 5% Hispanic American, 19% African American, 2% Asian American/Pacific Islander **The most frequently chosen baccalaureate fields are** business/marketing, parks and recreation, public administration and social services **Academic program** English as a second language, advanced placement, accelerated degree program, honors program, summer session, adult/continuing education programs, internships **Contact** Mr. Jamie Legg, Director of Admissions, Methodist University, 5400 Ramset Street, Fayetteville, NC 28311-1496. Phone: 910-630-7027 or toll-free 800-488-7110 Ext. 7027. Fax: 910-630-7285. E-mail: admissions@methodist.edu. Web site: http://www.methodist.edu/.

MONTREAT COLLEGE

MONTREAT, NORTH CAROLINA

General Independent, comprehensive, coed, affiliated with Presbyterian Church (U.S.A.) **Contact** Kate Rogers, Director of Admissions, Montreat College, PO Box 1267, Montreat, NC 28757-1267. Phone: 828-669-8012 Ext. 3782 or toll-free 800-622-6968. Fax: 828-669-0120. E-mail: admissions@montreat.edu. Web site: http://www.montreat.edu/.

MOUNT OLIVE COLLEGE

MOUNT OLIVE, NORTH CAROLINA

General Independent Free Will Baptist, 4-year, coed **Entrance** Minimally difficult **Setting** 123-acre small-town campus **Total enrollment** 3,277 **Student-faculty ratio** 17:1 **Application deadline** Rolling (freshmen), rolling (transfer) **Freshmen** 67% were admitted **Housing** Yes **Expenses** Tuition $13,126; Room & Board $5300 **Undergraduates** 66% women, 23% part-time, 74% 25 or older **The most frequently chosen baccalaureate fields are** business/marketing, education, security and protective services **Academic program** Advanced placement, accelerated degree program, honors program, summer session, adult/continuing education programs, internships **Contact** Mr. Tim Woodard, Director of Admissions, Mount Olive College, 634 Henderson Street, Mount Olive, NC 28365. Phone: 919-658-2502 Ext. 3009 or toll-free 800-653-0854. Fax: 919-658-9816. E-mail: admissions@moc.edu. Web site: http://www.moc.edu/.

NEW LIFE THEOLOGICAL SEMINARY

CHARLOTTE, NORTH CAROLINA

Contact New Life Theological Seminary, PO Box 790106, Charlotte, NC 28206-7901. Web site: http://www.nlts.org/.

NORTH CAROLINA AGRICULTURAL AND TECHNICAL STATE UNIVERSITY
GREENSBORO, NORTH CAROLINA

General State-supported, university, coed **Entrance** Moderately difficult **Setting** 800-acre urban campus **Total enrollment** 11,098 **Application deadline** 6/1 (freshmen), rolling (transfer) **Freshmen** 77% were admitted **Housing** Yes **Expenses** Tuition $3500; Room only $2956 **Undergraduates** 53% women, 11% part-time, 0.2% Native American, 1% Hispanic American, 92% African American, 1% Asian American/ Pacific Islander **The most frequently chosen baccalaureate fields are** business/marketing, engineering, psychology **Academic program** Advanced placement, honors program, summer session, adult/continuing education programs, internships **Contact** Mr. Lee Young, Director of Admissions, North Carolina Agricultural and Technical State University, 1601 East Market Street, Greensboro, NC 27411. Phone: 336-334-7946 or toll-free 800-443-8964. Fax: 336-334-7478. E-mail: uadmit@ncat.edu. Web site: http://www.ncat.edu/.

NORTH CAROLINA CENTRAL UNIVERSITY
DURHAM, NORTH CAROLINA

General State-supported, comprehensive, coed **Entrance** Minimally difficult **Setting** 103-acre urban campus **Total enrollment** 8,383 **Student-faculty ratio** 15:1 **Application deadline** 8/1 (freshmen), 8/1 (transfer) **Freshmen** 74% were admitted **Housing** Yes **Expenses** Tuition $3670; Room & Board $6015 **Undergraduates** 65% women, 18% part-time, 25% 25 or older, 0.3% Native American, 1% Hispanic American, 88% African American, 1% Asian American/Pacific Islander **The most frequently chosen baccalaureate fields are** business/marketing, security and protective services, social sciences **Academic program** English as a second language, advanced placement, honors program, summer session, adult/continuing education programs, internships **Contact** Ms. Jocelyn Foy, Undergraduate Director of Admissions, North Carolina Central University, 1801 Fayetteville Street, McDougald House, Durham, NC 27707. Phone: 919-530-6298 or toll-free 877-667-7533. Fax: 919-530-7625. E-mail: admissions@nccu.edu. Web site: http://www.nccu.edu/.

NORTH CAROLINA SCHOOL OF THE ARTS
WINSTON-SALEM, NORTH CAROLINA

General State-supported, comprehensive, coed **Entrance** Very difficult **Setting** 57-acre urban campus **Total enrollment** 864 **Student-faculty ratio** 8:1 **Application deadline** 3/1 (freshmen), rolling (transfer) **Freshmen** 51% were admitted **Housing** Yes **Expenses** Tuition $5061; Room & Board $6431 **Undergraduates** 40% women, 1% part-time, 2% 25 or older, 1% Native American, 5% Hispanic American, 10% African American, 2% Asian American/Pacific Islander **The most frequently chosen baccalaureate field is** visual and performing arts **Academic program** Advanced placement **Contact** Ms. Sheeler Lawson, Director of Admissions, North Carolina School of the Arts, 1533 South Main Street, PO Box 12189, Winston-Salem, NC 27127-2188. Phone: 336-770-3290. Fax: 336-770-3370. E-mail: admissions@ncarts.edu. Web site: http://www.ncarts.edu/.

NORTH CAROLINA STATE UNIVERSITY
RALEIGH, NORTH CAROLINA

General State-supported, university, coed **Entrance** Very difficult **Setting** 2,110-acre urban campus **Total enrollment** 31,802 **Student-faculty ratio** 16:1 **Application deadline** 2/1 (freshmen), 4/1 (transfer) **Freshmen** 60% were admitted **Housing** Yes **Expenses** Tuition $5117; Room & Board $7373 **Undergraduates** 44% women, 14% part-time, 7% 25 or older, 1% Native American, 3% Hispanic American, 9% African American, 5% Asian American/Pacific Islander **The most frequently chosen baccalaureate fields are** business/marketing, biological/life sciences, engineering **Academic program** Advanced placement, accelerated degree program, self-designed majors, honors program, summer session, adult/continuing education programs, internships **Contact** Mr. Thomas Griffin, Director of Undergraduate Admissions, North Carolina State University, Box 7103, Raleigh, NC 27695. Phone: 919-515-2434. Fax: 919-515-5039. E-mail: undergrad_admissions@ncsu.edu. Web site: http://www.ncsu.edu/.

NORTH CAROLINA WESLEYAN COLLEGE
ROCKY MOUNT, NORTH CAROLINA

General Independent, 4-year, coed, affiliated with United Methodist Church **Entrance** Moderately difficult **Setting** 200-acre suburban campus **Total enrollment** 1,510 **Student-faculty ratio** 18:1 **Application deadline** Rolling (freshmen), 7/15 (transfer) **Freshmen** 63% were admitted **Housing** Yes **Expenses** Tuition $18,900; Room & Board $7100 **Undergraduates** 58% women, 23% part-time, 52% 25 or older, 1% Native American, 2% Hispanic American, 47% African American, 1% Asian American/Pacific Islander **Academic program** Advanced placement, accelerated degree program, honors program, summer session, adult/continuing education programs, internships **Contact** Ms. Cecelia Summers, Associate Director

North Carolina Wesleyan College *(continued)*

of Admissions, North Carolina Wesleyan College, 3400 North Wesleyan Boulevard, Rocky Mount, NC 27804. Phone: 252-985-5200 or toll-free 800-488-6292. Fax: 252-985-5295. E-mail: adm@ncwc.edu. Web site: http://www.ncwc.edu/.

PEACE COLLEGE

RALEIGH, NORTH CAROLINA

General Independent, 4-year, women only, affiliated with Presbyterian Church (U.S.A.) **Entrance** Moderately difficult **Setting** 19-acre urban campus **Total enrollment** 692 **Student-faculty ratio** 11:1 **Application deadline** Rolling (freshmen), rolling (transfer) **Freshmen** 75% were admitted **Housing** Yes **Expenses** Tuition $21,972; Room & Board $7518 **Undergraduates** 7% part-time, 8% 25 or older, 1% Native American, 3% Hispanic American, 15% African American, 2% Asian American/Pacific Islander **The most frequently chosen baccalaureate fields are** business/marketing, communications/journalism, psychology **Academic program** English as a second language, advanced placement, honors program, summer session, adult/continuing education programs, internships **Contact** Mr. Matt Green, Dean of Enrollment, Peace College, 15 East Peace Street, Raleigh, NC 27604-1194. Phone: 919-508-2016 or toll-free 800-PEACE-47. Fax: 919-508-2326. E-mail: mtgreen@peace.edu. Web site: http://www.peace.edu/.

PFEIFFER UNIVERSITY

MISENHEIMER, NORTH CAROLINA

General Independent United Methodist, comprehensive, coed **Entrance** Moderately difficult **Setting** 300-acre rural campus **Total enrollment** 2,053 **Student-faculty ratio** 14:1 **Application deadline** Rolling (freshmen), rolling (transfer) **Freshmen** 74% were admitted **Housing** Yes **Expenses** Tuition $18,570; Room & Board $7360 **Undergraduates** 57% women, 11% part-time, 10% 25 or older, 0.5% Native American, 3% Hispanic American, 21% African American, 1% Asian American/Pacific Islander **The most frequently chosen baccalaureate fields are** business/marketing, education, parks and recreation **Academic program** English as a second language, advanced placement, accelerated degree program, honors program, summer session, internships **Contact** Ms. Jennifer Pate, Assistant Director of Admissions, Pfeiffer University, PO Box 960, Highway 52 North, Misenheimer, NC 28109. Phone: 704-463-1360 Ext. 3057 or toll-free 800-338-2060. Fax: 704-463-1363. E-mail: admiss@pfeiffer.edu. Web site: http://www.pfeiffer.edu/.

PIEDMONT BAPTIST COLLEGE AND GRADUATE SCHOOL

WINSTON-SALEM, NORTH CAROLINA

Contact Ms. Kathy Holritz, Director of Admissions, Piedmont Baptist College and Graduate School, 420 South Broad Street, Winston-Salem, NC 27101-5197. Phone: 336-725-8344 Ext. 2322 or toll-free 800-937-5097. Fax: 336-725-5522. E-mail: admissions@pbc.edu. Web site: http://www.pbc.edu/.

QUEENS UNIVERSITY OF CHARLOTTE

CHARLOTTE, NORTH CAROLINA

General Independent Presbyterian, comprehensive, coed **Entrance** Moderately difficult **Setting** 30-acre suburban campus **Total enrollment** 2,243 **Student-faculty ratio** 12:1 **Application deadline** Rolling (freshmen), rolling (transfer) **Freshmen** 79% were admitted **Housing** Yes **Expenses** Tuition $22,068; Room & Board $7882 **Undergraduates** 76% women, 36% part-time, 1% Native American, 4% Hispanic American, 18% African American, 2% Asian American/Pacific Islander **The most frequently chosen baccalaureate fields are** business/marketing, communications/journalism, health professions and related sciences **Academic program** Advanced placement, honors program, summer session, adult/continuing education programs, internships **Contact** Mr. William Lee, Director of Admissions–Traditional Undergraduate, Queens University of Charlotte, 1900 Selwyn Avenue, Charlotte, NC 28274. Phone: 704-337-2362 or toll-free 800-849-0202. Fax: 704-337-2403. E-mail: admissions@queens.edu. Web site: http://www.queens.edu/.

ROANOKE BIBLE COLLEGE

ELIZABETH CITY, NORTH CAROLINA

General Independent Christian, 4-year, coed **Entrance** Minimally difficult **Setting** 19-acre small-town campus **Total enrollment** 146 **Student-faculty ratio** 7:1 **Application deadline** 8/1 (freshmen), 8/1 (transfer) **Freshmen** 55% were admitted **Housing** Yes **Expenses** Tuition $9915; Room & Board $5720 **Undergraduates** 45% women, 23% part-time, 32% 25 or older, 3% Hispanic American, 11% African American **The most frequently chosen baccalaureate field is** theology and religious vocations **Academic program** Advanced placement, internships **Contact** Mrs. Julie Fields, Roanoke Bible College, 715 North Poindexter Street, Elizabeth City, NC 27909-4054. Phone: 252-334-2005 or toll-free 800-RBC-8980. Fax: 252-334-2064. E-mail: admissions@roanokebible.edu. Web site: http://www.roanokebible.edu/.

ST. ANDREWS PRESBYTERIAN COLLEGE
LAURINBURG, NORTH CAROLINA

General Independent Presbyterian, 4-year, coed **Entrance** Moderately difficult **Setting** 600-acre small-town campus **Total enrollment** 747 **Student-faculty ratio** 12:1 **Application deadline** Rolling (freshmen), rolling (transfer) **Freshmen** 73% were admitted **Housing** Yes **Expenses** Tuition $18,192; Room & Board $7992 **Undergraduates** 60% women, 6% part-time, 11% 25 or older, 1% Native American, 3% Hispanic American, 9% African American, 1% Asian American/Pacific Islander **The most frequently chosen baccalaureate fields are** biological/life sciences, business/marketing, education **Academic program** Advanced placement, accelerated degree program, self-designed majors, honors program, summer session, adult/continuing education programs, internships **Contact** Rev. Glenn Batten, Dean for Student Affairs and Enrollment, St. Andrews Presbyterian College, 1700 Dogwood Mile, Laurinburg, NC 28352. Phone: 910-277-5555 or toll-free 800-763-0198. Fax: 910-277-5087. E-mail: admission@sapc.edu. Web site: http://www.sapc.edu/.

SAINT AUGUSTINE'S COLLEGE
RALEIGH, NORTH CAROLINA

Contact Mrs. Charlotte McKenzie-Hunter, Assistant Director, Admissions, Saint Augustine's College, 1315 Oakwood Avenue, Raleigh, NC 27604-2298. Phone: 919-516-4016 or toll-free 800-948-1126. Fax: 919-516-5805. E-mail: admissions@es.st-aug.edu. Web site: http://www.st-aug.edu/.

SALEM COLLEGE
WINSTON-SALEM, NORTH CAROLINA

General Independent Moravian, comprehensive, undergraduate: women only; graduate: coed **Entrance** Moderately difficult **Setting** 57-acre urban campus **Total enrollment** 992 **Student-faculty ratio** 12:1 **Application deadline** Rolling (freshmen), rolling (transfer) **Freshmen** 62% were admitted **Housing** Yes **Expenses** Tuition $19,190; Room & Board $10,050 **Undergraduates** 18% part-time, 40% 25 or older, 0.1% Native American, 3% Hispanic American, 19% African American, 1% Asian American/Pacific Islander **The most frequently chosen baccalaureate fields are** communications/journalism, business/marketing, social sciences **Academic program** Advanced placement, self-designed majors, honors program, summer session, adult/continuing education programs, internships **Contact** Katherine Knapp Watts, Chief Admissions Officer, Salem College, PO Box 10548, Shober House, Winston-Salem, NC 27108. Phone: 336-721-2621 or toll-free 800-327-2536. Fax: 336-724-7102. E-mail: admissions@salem.edu. Web site: http://www.salem.edu/.

SHAW UNIVERSITY
RALEIGH, NORTH CAROLINA

General Independent Baptist, comprehensive, coed **Entrance** Minimally difficult **Setting** 30-acre urban campus **Total enrollment** 2,866 **Student-faculty ratio** 16:1 **Application deadline** 7/30 (freshmen), 7/30 (transfer) **Freshmen** 45% were admitted **Housing** Yes **Expenses** Tuition $10,840; Room & Board $6800 **Undergraduates** 64% women, 11% part-time, 39% 25 or older, 0.1% Native American, 0.3% Hispanic American, 85% African American **The most frequently chosen baccalaureate fields are** business/marketing, security and protective services, social sciences **Academic program** Advanced placement, accelerated degree program, self-designed majors, honors program, summer session, adult/continuing education programs, internships **Contact** Ms. Sandy Clifton, Interim Director of Admissions and Recruitment, Shaw University, 118 East South Street, Raleigh, NC 27601-2399. Phone: 919-546-8275 or toll-free 800-214-6683. Fax: 919-546-8271. E-mail: sclifton@shawu.edu. Web site: http://www.shawuniversity.edu/.

SOUTHEASTERN BAPTIST THEOLOGICAL SEMINARY
WAKE FOREST, NORTH CAROLINA

Contact Mr. Jason Hall, Director of Admissions, Southeastern Baptist Theological Seminary, PO Box 1889, Wake Forest, NC 27588-1889. Phone: 919-761-2280 or toll-free 800-284-6317. E-mail: admissions@sebts.edu. Web site: http://www.sebts.edu/.

THE UNIVERSITY OF NORTH CAROLINA AT ASHEVILLE
ASHEVILLE, NORTH CAROLINA

General State-supported, comprehensive, coed **Entrance** Moderately difficult **Setting** 265-acre suburban campus **Total enrollment** 3,700 **Student-faculty ratio** 13:1 **Application deadline** 2/15 (freshmen), 3/15 (transfer) **Freshmen** 76% were admitted **Housing** Yes **Expenses** Tuition $4164; Room & Board $6230 **Undergraduates** 58% women, 20% part-time, 15% 25 or older, 0.3% Native American, 2% Hispanic American, 3% African American, 1% Asian American/Pacific Islander **The most frequently chosen baccalaureate fields are** business/marketing, psychology, social sciences **Academic program** Advanced placement, self-designed

The University of North Carolina at Asheville *(continued)*

majors, honors program, summer session, adult/continuing education programs, internships **Contact** Ms. Leigh McBride, Associate Director of Admissions, The University of North Carolina at Asheville, University Dining Hall, CPO # 1320, Asheville, NC 28804-8510. Phone: 828-251-6481 or toll-free 800-531-9842. Fax: 828-251-6482. E-mail: admissions@unca.edu. Web site: http://www.unca.edu/.

THE UNIVERSITY OF NORTH CAROLINA AT CHAPEL HILL

CHAPEL HILL, NORTH CAROLINA

General State-supported, university, coed **Entrance** Very difficult **Setting** 729-acre suburban campus **Total enrollment** 28,136 **Application deadline** 1/15 (freshmen), 3/1 (transfer) **Freshmen** 35% were admitted **Housing** Yes **Expenses** Tuition $5340; Room & Board $7696 **Undergraduates** 59% women, 5% part-time, 3% 25 or older, 1% Native American, 4% Hispanic American, 11% African American, 7% Asian American/Pacific Islander **The most frequently chosen baccalaureate fields are** communications/journalism, psychology, social sciences **Academic program** Advanced placement, self-designed majors, honors program, summer session, internships **Contact** Stephen Farmer, Assistant Provost and Director of Undergraduate Admissions, The University of North Carolina at Chapel Hill, Campus Box # 2200, Jackson Hill, Chapel Hill, NC 27599-2200. Phone: 919-966-3621. Fax: 919-962-3045. E-mail: uadm@email.unc.edu. Web site: http://www.unc.edu/.

THE UNIVERSITY OF NORTH CAROLINA AT CHARLOTTE

CHARLOTTE, NORTH CAROLINA

General State-supported, university, coed **Entrance** Moderately difficult **Setting** 1,000-acre suburban campus **Total enrollment** 22,388 **Student-faculty ratio** 15:1 **Application deadline** 7/1 (freshmen), 7/1 (transfer) **Freshmen** 75% were admitted **Housing** Yes **Expenses** Tuition $4152; Room & Board $6034 **Undergraduates** 52% women, 16% part-time, 19% 25 or older, 0.5% Native American, 4% Hispanic American, 14% African American, 5% Asian American/Pacific Islander **The most frequently chosen baccalaureate fields are** business/marketing, education, engineering **Academic program** English as a second language, advanced placement, honors program, summer session, adult/continuing education programs, internships **Contact** Tina McEntire, Director of Admissions, The University of North Carolina at Charlotte, 9201 University City Boulevard, 1st Floor, Cato Hall, Charlotte, NC 28223-0001. Phone: 704-687-2213. Fax: 704-687-6483. E-mail: unccadm@uncc.edu. Web site: http://www.uncc.edu/.

THE UNIVERSITY OF NORTH CAROLINA AT GREENSBORO

GREENSBORO, NORTH CAROLINA

General State-supported, university, coed **Entrance** Moderately difficult **Setting** 210-acre urban campus **Total enrollment** 17,157 **Student-faculty ratio** 16:1 **Application deadline** 3/1 (freshmen), 8/1 (transfer) **Freshmen** 71% were admitted **Housing** Yes **Expenses** Tuition $4029; Room & Board $6051 **Undergraduates** 68% women, 14% part-time, 23% 25 or older, 0.5% Native American, 3% Hispanic American, 21% African American, 3% Asian American/Pacific Islander **The most frequently chosen baccalaureate fields are** business/marketing, education, visual and performing arts **Academic program** Advanced placement, accelerated degree program, honors program, summer session, adult/continuing education programs, internships **Contact** Ms. Lise Keller, Director of Admissions, The University of North Carolina at Greensboro, 1400 Spring Garden Street, PO Box 26170, Greensboro, NC 27402. Phone: 336-334-5243. Fax: 336-334-4180. E-mail: undergrad_admissions@uncg.edu. Web site: http://www.uncg.edu/.

THE UNIVERSITY OF NORTH CAROLINA AT PEMBROKE

PEMBROKE, NORTH CAROLINA

General State-supported, comprehensive, coed **Entrance** Moderately difficult **Setting** 152-acre rural campus **Total enrollment** 5,937 **Student-faculty ratio** 14:1 **Application deadline** Rolling (freshmen), rolling (transfer) **Freshmen** 86% were admitted **Housing** Yes **Expenses** Tuition $3635; Room & Board $6190 **Undergraduates** 63% women, 21% part-time, 33% 25 or older, 18% Native American, 4% Hispanic American, 28% African American, 2% Asian American/Pacific Islander **The most frequently chosen baccalaureate fields are** business/marketing, biological/life sciences, education **Academic program** English as a second language, advanced placement, accelerated degree program, honors program, summer session, adult/continuing education programs, internships **Contact** Mrs. Natayla Freeman Locklear, Associate Director of Admissions, The University of North Carolina at Pembroke, PO Box 1510, Pembroke, NC 28372-1510. Phone: 910-521-6262 or toll-free 800-949-UNCP. Fax: 910-521-6497. Web site: http://www.uncp.edu/.

THE UNIVERSITY OF NORTH CAROLINA WILMINGTON

WILMINGTON, NORTH CAROLINA

General State-supported, comprehensive, coed **Entrance** Moderately difficult **Setting** 650-acre urban campus **Total enrollment** 11,840 **Student-faculty ratio** 17:1 **Application deadline** 2/1 (freshmen), 3/1 (transfer) **Freshmen** 58% were admitted **Housing** Yes **Expenses** Tuition $4398; Room & Board $6998 **Undergraduates** 58% women, 9% part-time, 11% 25 or older, 1% Native American, 3% Hispanic American, 5% African American, 2% Asian American/Pacific Islander **The most frequently chosen baccalaureate fields are** education, history, psychology **Academic program** English as a second language, advanced placement, accelerated degree program, honors program, summer session, adult/continuing education programs, internships **Contact** Dr. Terrence M. Curran, Associate Provost, The University of North Carolina Wilmington, 601 South College Road, Wilmington, NC 28403-3297. Phone: 910-962-3876 or toll-free 800-228-5571. Fax: 910-962-3038. E-mail: admissions@uncw.edu. Web site: http://www.uncw.edu/.

UNIVERSITY OF PHOENIX–CHARLOTTE CAMPUS

CHARLOTTE, NORTH CAROLINA

General Proprietary, comprehensive, coed **Contact** Ms. Evelyn Gaskin, Registrar/Executive Director, University of Phoenix–Charlotte Campus, 4615 East Elwood Street, Mail Stop AA-K101, Phoenix, AZ 58040-1958. Phone: 480-557-3301 or toll-free 800-776-4867 (in-state); 800-228-7240 (out-of-state). Fax: 480-643-1020. E-mail: evelyn.gaskin@phoenix.edu. Web site: http://www.phoenix.edu/.

UNIVERSITY OF PHOENIX–RALEIGH CAMPUS

RALEIGH, NORTH CAROLINA

General Proprietary, comprehensive, coed **Contact** Ms. Evelyn Gaskin, Registrar/Executive Director, University of Phoenix–Raleigh Campus, 4615 East Elwood Street, Mail Stop AA-K101, Phoenix, AZ 85040-1958. Phone: 480-557-3301 or toll-free 800-776-4867 (in-state); 800-228-7240 (out-of-state). Fax: 480-643-1020. E-mail: evelyn.gaskin@phoenix.edu. Web site: http://www.phoenix.edu/.

WAKE FOREST UNIVERSITY

WINSTON-SALEM, NORTH CAROLINA

General Independent, university, coed **Entrance** Very difficult **Setting** 340-acre suburban campus **Total enrollment** 6,788 **Student-faculty ratio** 10:1 **Application deadline** 1/15 (freshmen) **Freshmen** 42% were admitted **Housing** Yes **Expenses** Tuition $36,975; Room & Board $9867 **Undergraduates** 51% women, 1% part-time, 1% Native American, 2% Hispanic American, 7% African American, 5% Asian American/Pacific Islander **The most frequently chosen baccalaureate fields are** business/marketing, foreign languages and literature, social sciences **Academic program** Advanced placement, honors program, summer session, internships **Contact** Ms. Martha Allman, Director of Admissions, Wake Forest University, Reynolda Station, Winston-Salem, NC 27109. Phone: 336-758-5201. Fax: 336-758-5201. E-mail: admissions@wfu.edu. Web site: http://www.wfu.edu/.

WARREN WILSON COLLEGE

SWANNANOA, NORTH CAROLINA

General Independent, comprehensive, coed, affiliated with Presbyterian Church (U.S.A.) **Entrance** Moderately difficult **Setting** 1,135-acre small-town campus **Total enrollment** 953 **Student-faculty ratio** 13:1 **Application deadline** 3/15 (freshmen), 3/15 (transfer) **Freshmen** 81% were admitted **Housing** Yes **Expenses** Tuition $22,666; Room & Board $7116 **Undergraduates** 62% women, 1% part-time, 2% 25 or older, 0.3% Native American, 2% Hispanic American, 1% African American, 1% Asian American/Pacific Islander **The most frequently chosen baccalaureate fields are** natural resources/environmental science, biological/life sciences, social sciences **Academic program** English as a second language, advanced placement, self-designed majors, honors program, internships **Contact** Mr. Richard Blomgren, Dean of Admission, Warren Wilson College, PO Box 9000, Asheville, NC 28815-9000. Phone: 828-771-2073 or toll-free 800-934-3536. Fax: 828-298-1440. E-mail: admit@warren-wilson.edu. Web site: http://www.warren-wilson.edu/.

WESTERN CAROLINA UNIVERSITY

CULLOWHEE, NORTH CAROLINA

General State-supported, comprehensive, coed **Entrance** Moderately difficult **Setting** 260-acre rural campus **Total enrollment** 9,056 **Student-faculty ratio** 13:1 **Application deadline** 4/1 (freshmen), 6/1 (transfer) **Freshmen** 68% were admitted **Housing** Yes **Expenses** Tuition $4414; Room & Board $5626 **Undergraduates** 53% women, 15% part-time, 19% 25 or older, 1% Native American, 1% Hispanic American, 5% African American, 1% Asian American/Pacific Islander **The most frequently chosen baccalaureate fields are** business/marketing, education, health professions and related sciences **Academic**

Western Carolina University *(continued)*

program English as a second language, advanced placement, accelerated degree program, self-designed majors, honors program, summer session, adult/continuing education programs, internships **Contact** Mr. Alan Kines, Director of Admissions, Western Carolina University, Cullowhee, NC 28723. Phone: 828-227-7317 or toll-free 877-WCU4YOU. Fax: 828-277-7319. E-mail: admiss@email.wcu.edu. Web site: http://www.wcu.edu/.

WINGATE UNIVERSITY

WINGATE, NORTH CAROLINA

General Independent Baptist, comprehensive, coed **Entrance** Moderately difficult **Setting** 330-acre small-town campus **Total enrollment** 2,041 **Student-faculty ratio** 13:1 **Application deadline** Rolling (freshmen), rolling (transfer) **Freshmen** 50% were admitted **Housing** Yes **Expenses** Tuition $18,480; Room & Board $7100 **Undergraduates** 53% women, 4% part-time, 7% 25 or older, 1% Native American, 2% Hispanic American, 14% African American, 2% Asian American/Pacific Islander **The most frequently chosen baccalaureate fields are** business/marketing, education, visual and performing arts **Academic program** Advanced placement, honors program, summer session, adult/continuing education programs, internships **Contact** Mr. Rhett Brown, Dean of Enrollment Management, Wingate University, PO Box 159, Wingate, NC 28174. Phone: 704-233-8000 or toll-free 800-755-5550. Fax: 704-233-8110. E-mail: admit@wingate.edu. Web site: http://www.wingate.edu/.

WINSTON-SALEM STATE UNIVERSITY

WINSTON-SALEM, NORTH CAROLINA

General State-supported, comprehensive, coed **Entrance** Minimally difficult **Setting** 94-acre urban campus **Total enrollment** 5,870 **Student-faculty ratio** 15:1 **Application deadline** 7/15 (freshmen), rolling (transfer) **Freshmen** 68% were admitted **Housing** Yes **Expenses** Tuition $3299; Room & Board $5670 **Undergraduates** 71% women, 11% part-time, 29% 25 or older, 0.3% Native American, 1% Hispanic American, 82% African American, 1% Asian American/Pacific Islander **The most frequently chosen baccalaureate fields are** business/marketing, health professions and related sciences, social sciences **Academic program** Advanced placement, accelerated degree program, honors program, summer session, adult/continuing education programs, internships **Contact** Ms. Tomikia LeGrande, Director of Admissions, Winston-Salem State University, 601 Martin Luther King Jr. Drive, Thompson Center, Winston-Salem, NC 27110-0003. Phone: 336-750-2070 or toll-free 800-257-4052. Fax: 336-750-2079. E-mail: admissions@wssu.edu. Web site: http://www.wssu.edu/.

NORTH DAKOTA

DICKINSON STATE UNIVERSITY

DICKINSON, NORTH DAKOTA

General State-supported, 4-year, coed **Entrance** Minimally difficult **Setting** 100-acre small-town campus **Total enrollment** 2,572 **Student-faculty ratio** 19:1 **Application deadline** Rolling (freshmen), rolling (transfer) **Freshmen** 96% were admitted **Housing** Yes **Expenses** Tuition $4749; Room & Board $4076 **Undergraduates** 59% women, 33% part-time, 22% 25 or older, 3% Native American, 1% Hispanic American, 2% African American, 1% Asian American/Pacific Islander **The most frequently chosen baccalaureate fields are** business/marketing, education, liberal arts/general studies **Academic program** Advanced placement, accelerated degree program, self-designed majors, honors program, summer session, adult/continuing education programs, internships **Contact** Mr. Steve Glasser, Director of Enrollment Services, Dickinson State University, Campus Box 169, Dickinson, ND 58601. Phone: 701-483-2175 or toll-free 800-279-4295. Fax: 701-483-2409. E-mail: dsu.hawks@dsu.nodak.edu. Web site: http://www.dsu.nodak.edu/.

►**For more information, see page 454.**

JAMESTOWN COLLEGE

JAMESTOWN, NORTH DAKOTA

General Independent Presbyterian, 4-year, coed **Entrance** Minimally difficult **Setting** small-town campus **Total enrollment** 1,024 **Student-faculty ratio** 15:1 **Application deadline** Rolling (freshmen), rolling (transfer) **Freshmen** 79% were admitted **Housing** Yes **Expenses** Tuition $15,035; Room & Board $4850 **Undergraduates** 53% women, 8% part-time, 10% 25 or older, 1% Native American, 1% Hispanic American, 1% African American, 1% Asian American/Pacific Islander **The most frequently chosen baccalaureate fields are** business/marketing, education, health professions and related sciences **Academic program** Advanced placement, self-designed majors, honors program, summer session, internships **Contact** Mr. Dan Kunzman, Vice President Enrollment Management, Jamestown College, 6000 College Lane, Jamestown, ND 58405. Phone: 701-252-3467 Ext. 5512 or toll-free 800-336-2554. Fax: 701-253-4318. E-mail: admissions@jc.edu. Web site: http://www.jc.edu/.

MAYVILLE STATE UNIVERSITY
MAYVILLE, NORTH DAKOTA

General State-supported, 4-year, coed **Entrance** Noncompetitive **Setting** 60-acre rural campus **Total enrollment** 769 **Student-faculty ratio** 14:1 **Application deadline** Rolling (freshmen), rolling (transfer) **Freshmen** 70% were admitted **Housing** Yes **Expenses** Tuition $5438; Room & Board $4072 **Undergraduates** 58% women, 38% part-time, 7% 25 or older, 4% Native American, 1% Hispanic American, 5% African American, 1% Asian American/Pacific Islander **The most frequently chosen baccalaureate fields are** business/marketing, education, family and consumer sciences **Academic program** Advanced placement, accelerated degree program, self-designed majors, honors program, summer session, adult/continuing education programs, internships **Contact** Dr. Ray Gerszewski, Vice President, Student Affairs and International Research, Mayville State University, 330 3rd Street, NE, Mayville, ND 58257-1299. Phone: 701-788-4842 or toll-free 800-437-4104. Fax: 701-788-4748. E-mail: admit@mayvillestate.edu. Web site: http://www.mayvillestate.edu/.

MEDCENTER ONE COLLEGE OF NURSING
BISMARCK, NORTH DAKOTA

General Independent, upper-level, coed, primarily women **Entrance** Moderately difficult **Setting** 15-acre small-town campus **Total enrollment** 89 **Student-faculty ratio** 9:1 **Application deadline** 11/7 (transfer) **First-year students** 59% were admitted **Housing** No **Expenses** Tuition $10,017 **Undergraduates** 89% women, 2% part-time, 32% 25 or older, 1% Hispanic American **The most frequently chosen baccalaureate field is** health professions and related sciences **Academic program** Internships **Contact** Ms. Mary Smith, Director of Student Services, Medcenter One College of Nursing, 512 North 7th Street, Bismarck, ND 58501-4494. Phone: 701-323-6271. Fax: 701-323-6289. E-mail: msmith@mohs.org. Web site: http://medcenterone.com/college/nursing.htm.

MINOT STATE UNIVERSITY
MINOT, NORTH DAKOTA

General State-supported, comprehensive, coed **Entrance** Minimally difficult **Setting** 103-acre small-town campus **Total enrollment** 3,424 **Student-faculty ratio** 12:1 **Application deadline** Rolling (freshmen), rolling (transfer) **Freshmen** 80% were admitted **Housing** Yes **Expenses** Tuition $5766; Room & Board $3914 **Undergraduates** 63% women, 29% part-time, 33% 25 or older, 4% Native American, 2% Hispanic American, 3% African American, 1% Asian American/Pacific Islander **The most frequently chosen baccalaureate fields are** business/marketing, education, health professions and related sciences **Academic program** Advanced placement, accelerated degree program, self-designed majors, honors program, summer session, adult/continuing education programs, internships **Contact** Dr. John Girard, Director of Enrollment, Minot State University, 500 University Avenue West, Minot, ND 58707-0002. Phone: 701-858-3126 or toll-free 800-777-0750 Ext. 3350. Fax: 701-858-3825. E-mail: askmsu@minotstateu.edu. Web site: http://www.minotstateu.edu/.

NORTH DAKOTA STATE UNIVERSITY
FARGO, NORTH DAKOTA

General State-supported, university, coed **Entrance** Moderately difficult **Setting** 2,100-acre urban campus **Total enrollment** 12,527 **Student-faculty ratio** 19:1 **Application deadline** 8/15 (freshmen), 8/15 (transfer) **Freshmen** 85% were admitted **Housing** Yes **Expenses** Tuition $5975; Room & Board $5820 **Undergraduates** 45% women, 10% part-time, 12% 25 or older, 1% Native American, 1% Hispanic American, 1% African American, 1% Asian American/Pacific Islander **The most frequently chosen baccalaureate fields are** business/marketing, engineering, health professions and related sciences **Academic program** English as a second language, advanced placement, self-designed majors, honors program, summer session, internships **Contact** Jobey Lichtblau, Director of Admission, North Dakota State University, PO Box 5454, Fargo, ND 58105-5454. Phone: 701-231-8643 or toll-free 800-488-NDSU. Fax: 701-231-8802. E-mail: ndsu.admission@ndsu.edu. Web site: http://www.ndsu.edu/.

TRINITY BIBLE COLLEGE
ELLENDALE, NORTH DAKOTA

Contact Rev. Steve Tvedt, Vice President of College Relations, Trinity Bible College, 50 South 6th Avenue, Ellendale, ND 58436-7150. Phone: 701-349-3621 Ext. 2045 or toll-free 888-TBC-2DAY. Fax: 701-349-5443. E-mail: admissions@trinitybiblecollege.edu. Web site: http://www.trinitybiblecollege.edu/.

UNIVERSITY OF MARY
BISMARCK, NORTH DAKOTA

General Independent Roman Catholic, comprehensive, coed **Entrance** Moderately difficult **Setting** 107-acre suburban campus **Total enrollment** 2,590 **Student-faculty ratio** 17:1 **Application deadline** Rolling (freshmen), rolling

University of Mary *(continued)*

(transfer) **Freshmen** 85% were admitted **Housing** Yes **Expenses** Tuition $12,164; Room & Board $4820 **Undergraduates** 60% women, 20% part-time, 27% 25 or older, 5% Native American, 2% Hispanic American, 3% African American, 1% Asian American/Pacific Islander **The most frequently chosen baccalaureate fields are** business/marketing, education, health professions and related sciences **Academic program** Advanced placement, accelerated degree program, summer session, adult/continuing education programs, internships **Contact** Dr. Dave Heringer, Vice President for Enrollment Services, University of Mary, 7500 University Drive, Bismarck, ND 58504-9652. Phone: 701-355-8191 or toll-free 800-288-6279. Fax: 701-255-7687. E-mail: marauder@umary.edu. Web site: http://www.umary.edu/.

UNIVERSITY OF NORTH DAKOTA
GRAND FORKS, NORTH DAKOTA

General State-supported, university, coed **Entrance** Minimally difficult **Setting** 550-acre urban campus **Total enrollment** 12,559 **Student-faculty ratio** 19:1 **Application deadline** Rolling (transfer) **Freshmen** 70% were admitted **Housing** Yes **Expenses** Tuition $6130; Room & Board $5203 **Undergraduates** 45% women, 13% part-time, 14% 25 or older, 3% Native American, 1% Hispanic American, 1% African American, 1% Asian American/Pacific Islander **The most frequently chosen baccalaureate fields are** business/marketing, health professions and related sciences, transportation and materials moving **Academic program** English as a second language, advanced placement, accelerated degree program, self-designed majors, honors program, summer session, adult/continuing education programs, internships **Contact** Deborah Melby, Director of Admissions, University of North Dakota, Box 8382, Grand Forks, ND 58202. Phone: 701-777-3821 or toll-free 800-CALL UND. Fax: 701-777-2721. E-mail: enrollmentservices@mail.und.nodak.edu. Web site: http://www.und.nodak.edu/.

VALLEY CITY STATE UNIVERSITY
VALLEY CITY, NORTH DAKOTA

General State-supported, 4-year, coed **Entrance** Noncompetitive **Setting** 55-acre small-town campus **Total enrollment** 921 **Student-faculty ratio** 11:1 **Application deadline** Rolling (freshmen), rolling (transfer) **Freshmen** 93% were admitted **Housing** Yes **Expenses** Tuition $5584; Room & Board $3880 **Undergraduates** 55% women, 25% part-time, 27% 25 or older, 2% Native American, 1% Hispanic American, 4% African American, 0.3% Asian American/Pacific Islander **The most frequently chosen baccalaureate fields are** business/marketing, computer and information sciences, education **Academic program** Self-designed majors, summer session, internships **Contact** Ms. Charlene Stenson, Admission Counselor, Valley City State University, 101 College Street Southwest, Valley City, ND 58072. Phone: 701-845-7105 Ext. 7204 or toll-free 800-532-8641 Ext. 37101. Fax: 701-845-7299. E-mail: c.stenson@vcsu.edu. Web site: http://www.vcsu.edu/.

OHIO

ALLEGHENY WESLEYAN COLLEGE
SALEM, OHIO

Contact Admissions Office, Allegheny Wesleyan College, 2161 Woodsdale Road, Salem, OH 44460. Phone: 330-337-6403 or toll-free 800-292-3153. Web site: http://www.awc.edu/.

ANTIOCH COLLEGE
YELLOW SPRINGS, OHIO

General Independent, 4-year, coed **Contact** Ms. Cathy Paige, Information Manager, Antioch College, 795 Livermore Street, Yellow Springs, OH 45387-1697. Phone: 937-769-1100 Ext. 1107 or toll-free 800-543-9436. Fax: 937-769-1111. E-mail: admissions@college.antioch.edu. Web site: http://www.antioch-college.edu/.

ANTIOCH UNIVERSITY McGREGOR
YELLOW SPRINGS, OHIO

General Independent, upper-level, coed **Entrance** Noncompetitive **Setting** 100-acre small-town campus **Total enrollment** 681 **Student-faculty ratio** 8:1 **Application deadline** Rolling (transfer) **Housing** No **Expenses** Tuition $14,034 **Undergraduates** 72% women, 61% part-time, 92% 25 or older, 2% Native American, 4% Hispanic American, 21% African American, 1% Asian American/Pacific Islander **The most frequently chosen baccalaureate fields are** business/marketing, psychology, public administration and social services **Academic program** Advanced placement, accelerated degree program, summer session, adult/continuing education programs, internships **Contact** Mr. Oscar Robinson, Director of Admissions, Antioch University McGregor, Student and Alumni Services Division, Enrollment Services, Yellow Springs, OH 45387. Phone: 937-769-1823 or toll-free 937-769-1818. Fax: 937-769-1804. E-mail: sas@mcgregor.edu. Web site: http://www.mcgregor.edu/.

ART ACADEMY OF CINCINNATI

CINCINNATI, OHIO

General Independent, comprehensive, coed **Entrance** Moderately difficult **Setting** 184-acre urban campus **Total enrollment** 140 **Student-faculty ratio** 9:1 **Application deadline** 6/30 (freshmen), 6/30 (transfer) **Freshmen** 24% were admitted **Housing** Yes **Expenses** Tuition $21,300; Room only $5800 **Undergraduates** 65% women, 7% part-time, 12% 25 or older, 1% Native American, 3% Hispanic American, 6% African American, 3% Asian American/Pacific Islander **The most frequently chosen baccalaureate field is** visual and performing arts **Academic program** Advanced placement, self-designed majors, honors program, summer session, adult/continuing education programs, internships **Contact** Mr. John J. Wadell, Director of Admissions, Art Academy of Cincinnati, 1212 Jackson Street, Cincinnati, OH 45202-7106. Phone: 513-562-8744 or toll-free 800-323-5692. Fax: 513-562-8778. E-mail: admissions@artacademy.edu. Web site: http://www.artacademy.edu/.

ASHLAND UNIVERSITY

ASHLAND, OHIO

General Independent, comprehensive, coed, affiliated with Brethren Church **Entrance** Moderately difficult **Setting** 98-acre small-town campus **Total enrollment** 2,772 **Student-faculty ratio** 16:1 **Application deadline** Rolling (freshmen), rolling (transfer) **Freshmen** 83% were admitted **Housing** Yes **Expenses** Tuition $24,340; Room & Board $8876 **Undergraduates** 54% women, 10% part-time, 22% 25 or older, 0.4% Native American, 3% Hispanic American, 8% African American, 1% Asian American/Pacific Islander **The most frequently chosen baccalaureate fields are** business/marketing, education, visual and performing arts **Academic program** English as a second language, advanced placement, self-designed majors, honors program, summer session, adult/continuing education programs, internships **Contact** Mr. Thomas Mansperger, Director of Admission, Ashland University, 401 College Avenue, Ashland, OH 44805. Phone: 419-289-5052 or toll-free 800-882-1548. Fax: 419-289-5999. E-mail: enrollme@ashland.edu. Web site: http://www.exploreashland.com/.

BALDWIN-WALLACE COLLEGE

BEREA, OHIO

General Independent Methodist, comprehensive, coed **Entrance** Moderately difficult **Setting** 100-acre suburban campus **Total enrollment** 4,394 **Student-faculty ratio** 15:1 **Application deadline** Rolling (freshmen), rolling (transfer) **Freshmen** 66% were admitted **Housing** Yes **Expenses** Tuition $23,524; Room & Board $7728 **Undergraduates** 57% women, 17% part-time, 3% 25 or older, 0.1% Native American, 2% Hispanic American, 7% African American, 1% Asian American/Pacific Islander **The most frequently chosen baccalaureate fields are** business/marketing, education, visual and performing arts **Academic program** English as a second language, advanced placement, accelerated degree program, self-designed majors, honors program, summer session, adult/continuing education programs, internships **Contact** Ms. Grace B. Chalker, Interim Associate Director of Admissions, Baldwin-Wallace College, 275 Eastland Road, Berea, OH 44017-2088. Phone: 440-826-2222 or toll-free 877-BWAPPLY. Fax: 440-826-3830. E-mail: admission@baldwinw.edu. Web site: http://www.bw.edu/.

BLUFFTON UNIVERSITY

BLUFFTON, OHIO

General Independent Mennonite, comprehensive, coed **Entrance** Moderately difficult **Setting** 65-acre small-town campus **Total enrollment** 1,117 **Student-faculty ratio** 13:1 **Application deadline** 8/15 (freshmen), rolling (transfer) **Freshmen** 61% were admitted **Housing** Yes **Expenses** Tuition $21,780; Room & Board $7294 **Undergraduates** 57% women, 9% part-time, 13% 25 or older, 0.2% Native American, 2% Hispanic American, 4% African American, 1% Asian American/Pacific Islander **The most frequently chosen baccalaureate fields are** business/marketing, education, parks and recreation **Academic program** Advanced placement, self-designed majors, honors program, summer session, adult/continuing education programs, internships **Contact** Mr. Chris Jebsen, Director of Admissions, Bluffton University, 1 University Drive, Bluffton, OH 45817. Phone: 419-358-3254 or toll-free 800-488-3257. Fax: 419-358-3081. E-mail: admissions@bluffton.edu. Web site: http://www.bluffton.edu/.

BOWLING GREEN STATE UNIVERSITY

BOWLING GREEN, OHIO

General State-supported, university, coed **Entrance** Moderately difficult **Setting** 1,230-acre small-town campus **Total enrollment** 18,619 **Student-faculty ratio** 18:1 **Application deadline** 7/15 (freshmen), 7/15 (transfer) **Freshmen** 88% were admitted **Housing** Yes **Expenses** Tuition $9060; Room & Board $6878 **Undergraduates** 54% women, 7% part-time, 6% 25 or older, 1% Native American, 4% Hispanic American, 10% African American, 1% Asian American/Pacific Islander **The most frequently chosen baccalaureate fields are** business/marketing, education, visual and performing arts

Bowling Green State University *(continued)*

Academic program English as a second language, advanced placement, accelerated degree program, self-designed majors, honors program, summer session, adult/continuing education programs, internships **Contact** Mr. Gary Swegan, Assistant Vice Provost/Director of Admissions, Bowling Green State University, 110 McFall, Bowling Green, OH 43403. Phone: 419-372-BGSU. Fax: 419-372-6955. E-mail: admissions@bgsu.edu. Web site: http://www.bgsu.edu/.

BRYANT AND STRATTON COLLEGE
CLEVELAND, OHIO

General Proprietary, 4-year, coed **Contact** Ted Hanson, Director of Admissions, Bryant and Stratton College, 1700 East 13th Street, Cleveland, OH 44114-3203. Phone: 216-771-1700. Fax: 216-771-7787. E-mail: thanson@bryantstratton.edu. Web site: http://www.bryantstratton.edu/.

CAPITAL UNIVERSITY
COLUMBUS, OHIO

General Independent, comprehensive, coed, affiliated with Evangelical Lutheran Church in America **Entrance** Moderately difficult **Setting** 48-acre suburban campus **Total enrollment** 3,713 **Student-faculty ratio** 9:1 **Application deadline** 4/1 (freshmen), rolling (transfer) **Freshmen** 75% were admitted **Housing** Yes **Expenses** Tuition $26,360; Room & Board $6820 **Undergraduates** 62% women, 14% part-time, 18% 25 or older, 0.2% Native American, 2% Hispanic American, 9% African American, 1% Asian American/Pacific Islander **The most frequently chosen baccalaureate fields are** education, business/marketing, health professions and related sciences **Academic program** English as a second language, advanced placement, accelerated degree program, self-designed majors, honors program, summer session, adult/continuing education programs, internships **Contact** Dr. Amy Adams, Director of Institutional Research and Assessment, Capital University, 1 College and Main, Columbus, OH 43209. Phone: 614-236-6101 or toll-free 800-289-6289. Fax: 614-236-6926. E-mail: admissions@capital.edu. Web site: http://www.capital.edu/.

CASE WESTERN RESERVE UNIVERSITY
CLEVELAND, OHIO

General Independent, university, coed **Entrance** Very difficult **Setting** 150-acre urban campus **Total enrollment** 9,844 **Student-faculty ratio** 9:1 **Application deadline** 1/15 (freshmen), 5/15 (transfer) **Freshmen** 75% were admitted **Housing** Yes **Expenses** Tuition $33,538; Room & Board $9938 **Undergraduates** 42% women, 5% part-time, 3% 25 or older, 0.2% Native American, 2% Hispanic American, 5% African American, 16% Asian American/Pacific Islander **The most frequently chosen baccalaureate fields are** engineering, biological/life sciences, social sciences **Academic program** English as a second language, advanced placement, accelerated degree program, self-designed majors, honors program, summer session, adult/continuing education programs, internships **Contact** Ms. Elizabeth Woyczynski, Director of Undergraduate Admission, Case Western Reserve University, 10900 Euclid Avenue, Cleveland, OH 44106. Phone: 216-368-4450. Fax: 216-368-5111. E-mail: admission@case.edu. Web site: http://www.case.edu/.

CEDARVILLE UNIVERSITY
CEDARVILLE, OHIO

General Independent Baptist, comprehensive, coed **Entrance** Moderately difficult **Setting** 400-acre rural campus **Total enrollment** 3,055 **Student-faculty ratio** 16:1 **Application deadline** Rolling (freshmen), rolling (transfer) **Freshmen** 76% were admitted **Housing** Yes **Expenses** Tuition $21,130; Room & Board $5010 **Undergraduates** 55% women, 4% part-time, 2% 25 or older, 0.3% Native American, 2% Hispanic American, 1% African American, 1% Asian American/Pacific Islander **The most frequently chosen baccalaureate fields are** business/marketing, education, health professions and related sciences **Academic program** Advanced placement, accelerated degree program, honors program, summer session, internships **Contact** Mr. Roscoe Smith, Director of Admissions, Cedarville University, 251 North Main Street, Cedarville, OH 45314-0601. Phone: 937-766-7700 or toll-free 800-CEDARVILLE. Fax: 937-766-7575. E-mail: admiss@cedarville.edu. Web site: http://www.cedarville.edu/.

CENTRAL STATE UNIVERSITY
WILBERFORCE, OHIO

General State-supported, comprehensive, coed **Entrance** Minimally difficult **Setting** 60-acre rural campus **Total enrollment** 2,022 **Student-faculty ratio** 14:1 **Application deadline** 6/15 (freshmen), 6/15 (transfer) **Freshmen** 38% were admitted **Housing** Yes **Expenses** Tuition $5294; Room & Board $7402 **Undergraduates** 50% women, 9% part-time, 13% 25 or older, 0.2% Native American, 1% Hispanic American, 92% African American, 0.2% Asian American/Pacific Islander **The most frequently chosen baccalaureate fields are** business/marketing, communications/journalism, education **Academic program** Honors program, summer session, adult/continuing education programs, internships **Contact**

Ms. Robin Rucker, Interim Associate Director, Admissions, Central State University, PO Box 1004, 1400 Blush Row Road, Wilberforce, OH 45384. Phone: 937-376-6580 or toll-free 800-388-CSU1. Fax: 937-376-6648. E-mail: admissions@centralstate.edu. Web site: http://www.centralstate.edu/.

CINCINNATI CHRISTIAN UNIVERSITY
CINCINNATI, OHIO

General Independent, comprehensive, coed, affiliated with Church of Christ **Contact** Ms. Rachel Kitterman, Office Manager of Undergraduate Admissions, Cincinnati Christian University, 2700 Glenway Avenue, PO Box 04320, Cincinnati, OH 45204-3200. Phone: 800-949-4222 Ext. 8610 or toll-free 800-949-4228. Fax: 513-244-8140. E-mail: admissions@cincybible.edu. Web site: http://www.ccuniversity.edu/.

THE CLEVELAND INSTITUTE OF ART
CLEVELAND, OHIO

General Independent, comprehensive, coed **Entrance** Moderately difficult **Setting** 488-acre urban campus **Total enrollment** 485 **Student-faculty ratio** 8:1 **Application deadline** Rolling (freshmen), rolling (transfer) **Freshmen** 71% were admitted **Housing** Yes **Expenses** Tuition $30,090; Room & Board $8769 **Undergraduates** 53% women, 4% part-time, 10% 25 or older, 0.2% Native American, 4% Hispanic American, 5% African American, 5% Asian American/Pacific Islander **The most frequently chosen baccalaureate field is** visual and performing arts **Academic program** Advanced placement, honors program, internships **Contact** Office of Admissions, The Cleveland Institute of Art, 11141 East Boulevard, Cleveland, OH 44106-1700. Phone: 216-421-7427 or toll-free 800-223-4700. Fax: 216-754-3634. E-mail: admissions@cia.edu. Web site: http://www.cia.edu/.

CLEVELAND INSTITUTE OF MUSIC
CLEVELAND, OHIO

General Independent, comprehensive, coed **Contact** Mr. William Fay, Director of Admission, Cleveland Institute of Music, 11021 East Boulevard, Cleveland, OH 44106-1776. Phone: 216-795-3107. Fax: 216-791-1530. E-mail: cimadmission@po.cwru.edu. Web site: http://www.cim.edu/.

CLEVELAND STATE UNIVERSITY
CLEVELAND, OHIO

General State-supported, university, coed **Entrance** Moderately difficult **Setting** 70-acre urban campus **Total enrollment** 15,383 **Student-faculty ratio** 16:1 **Application deadline** 8/15 (freshmen), 7/15 (transfer) **Freshmen** 73% were admitted **Housing** Yes **Expenses** Tuition $7920; Room & Board $8100 **Undergraduates** 56% women, 29% part-time, 40% 25 or older, 0.3% Native American, 3% Hispanic American, 22% African American, 3% Asian American/Pacific Islander **The most frequently chosen baccalaureate fields are** business/marketing, health professions and related sciences, social sciences **Academic program** English as a second language, advanced placement, accelerated degree program, self-designed majors, honors program, summer session, adult/continuing education programs, internships **Contact** Undergraduate Admissions Office, Cleveland State University, 204 RTW, 1806 East 22nd Street, Cleveland, OH 44114. Phone: 216-687-2100 or toll-free 888-CSU-OHIO. Fax: 216-687-9210. E-mail: admissions@csuohio.edu. Web site: http://www.csuohio.edu/.

COLLEGE OF MOUNT ST. JOSEPH
CINCINNATI, OHIO

General Independent Roman Catholic, comprehensive, coed **Entrance** Moderately difficult **Setting** 92-acre suburban campus **Total enrollment** 2,282 **Student-faculty ratio** 11:1 **Application deadline** 8/15 (freshmen), 8/1 (transfer) **Freshmen** 72% were admitted **Housing** Yes **Expenses** Tuition $21,200; Room & Board $6500 **Undergraduates** 68% women, 30% part-time, 32% 25 or older, 0.4% Native American, 1% Hispanic American, 9% African American, 1% Asian American/Pacific Islander **The most frequently chosen baccalaureate fields are** business/marketing, health professions and related sciences, visual and performing arts **Academic program** Advanced placement, accelerated degree program, honors program, summer session, adult/continuing education programs, internships **Contact** Ms. Peggy Minnich, Director of Admission, College of Mount St. Joseph, 5701 Delhi Road, Cincinnati, OH 45233-1670. Phone: 513-244-4531 or toll-free 800-654-9314. Fax: 513-244-4629. E-mail: admissions@mail.msj.edu. Web site: http://www.msj.edu/.

THE COLLEGE OF WOOSTER
WOOSTER, OHIO

General Independent, 4-year, coed, affiliated with Presbyterian Church (U.S.A.) **Entrance** Moderately difficult **Setting** 240-acre small-town campus **Total enrollment** 1,777 **Student-faculty ratio** 12:1 **Application deadline** 2/15 (freshmen), 6/1 (transfer) **Freshmen** 74% were admitted **Housing** Yes **Expenses** Tuition $33,770; Room & Board $8650 **Undergraduates** 52% women, 1% part-time, 0.2% 25 or older, 0.5% Native American, 2% Hispanic American, 4% African American,

The College of Wooster *(continued)*

3% Asian American/Pacific Islander **The most frequently chosen baccalaureate fields are** history, philosophy and religious studies, social sciences **Academic program** Advanced placement, self-designed majors, summer session, internships **Contact** Ms. Mary Karen Vellines, Vice President for Enrollment, The College of Wooster, 1189 Beall Avenue, Wooster, OH 44691-2363. Phone: 330-263-2270 Ext. 2118 or toll-free 800-877-9905. Fax: 330-263-2621. E-mail: admissions@wooster.edu. Web site: http://www.wooster.edu/.

COLUMBUS COLLEGE OF ART & DESIGN
COLUMBUS, OHIO

General Independent, 4-year, coed **Entrance** Moderately difficult **Setting** 10-acre urban campus **Total enrollment** 1,623 **Student-faculty ratio** 12:1 **Application deadline** Rolling (freshmen), rolling (transfer) **Freshmen** 76% were admitted **Housing** Yes **Expenses** Tuition $22,412; Room & Board $6650 **Undergraduates** 59% women, 19% part-time, 9% 25 or older, 1% Native American, 3% Hispanic American, 8% African American, 2% Asian American/Pacific Islander **The most frequently chosen baccalaureate field is** visual and performing arts **Academic program** English as a second language, advanced placement, summer session, internships **Contact** Mr. Thomas E. Green, Director of Admissions, Columbus College of Art & Design, 107 North Ninth Street, Columbus, OH 43215-1758. Phone: 614-222-3261 Ext. 3263 or toll-free 877-997-2223. Fax: 614-232-8344. E-mail: admissions@ccad.edu. Web site: http://www.ccad.edu/.

DEFIANCE COLLEGE
DEFIANCE, OHIO

General Independent, comprehensive, coed, affiliated with United Church of Christ **Entrance** Moderately difficult **Setting** 150-acre small-town campus **Total enrollment** 973 **Student-faculty ratio** 12:1 **Application deadline** 8/15 (freshmen), 8/15 (transfer) **Freshmen** 80% were admitted **Housing** Yes **Expenses** Tuition $21,830; Room & Board $7150 **Undergraduates** 53% women, 19% part-time, 4% 25 or older, 0.2% Native American, 4% Hispanic American, 7% African American, 0.1% Asian American/Pacific Islander **Academic program** Advanced placement, self-designed majors, honors program, summer session, adult/continuing education programs, internships **Contact** Mr. Brad Harsha, Director of Admissions, Defiance College, 701 North Clinton Street, Defiance, OH 43512-1610. Phone: 419-783-2365 or toll-free 800-520-4632 Ext. 2359. Fax: 419-783-2468. E-mail: admissions@defiance.edu. Web site: http://www.defiance.edu/.

DENISON UNIVERSITY
GRANVILLE, OHIO

General Independent, 4-year, coed **Entrance** Very difficult **Setting** 900-acre small-town campus **Total enrollment** 2,242 **Student-faculty ratio** 10:1 **Application deadline** 1/15 (freshmen), 7/1 (transfer) **Freshmen** 39% were admitted **Housing** Yes **Expenses** Tuition $33,010; Room & Board $8570 **Undergraduates** 57% women, 1% part-time, 1% 25 or older, 0.4% Native American, 2% Hispanic American, 5% African American, 3% Asian American/Pacific Islander **The most frequently chosen baccalaureate fields are** communications/journalism, psychology, social sciences **Academic program** Advanced placement, self-designed majors, honors program, internships **Contact** Mr. Perry Robinson, Director of Admissions, Denison University, Granville, OH 43023. Phone: 740-587-6276 or toll-free 800-DENISON. E-mail: admissions@denison.edu. Web site: http://www.denison.edu/.

DeVRY UNIVERSITY
CLEVELAND, OHIO

Contact DeVry University, 200 Public Square, Suite 150, Cleveland, OH 44114-2301. Web site: http://www.devry.edu/.

DeVRY UNIVERSITY
COLUMBUS, OHIO

General Proprietary, comprehensive, coed **Entrance** Minimally difficult **Setting** 21-acre urban campus **Total enrollment** 2,624 **Student-faculty ratio** 28:1 **Application deadline** Rolling (freshmen), rolling (transfer) **Housing** No **Expenses** Tuition $13,990 **Undergraduates** 38% women, 39% part-time, 53% 25 or older, 0.3% Native American, 1% Hispanic American, 24% African American, 2% Asian American/Pacific Islander **The most frequently chosen baccalaureate fields are** business/marketing, computer and information sciences, engineering technologies **Academic program** Advanced placement, accelerated degree program, summer session, adult/continuing education programs **Contact** Admissions Office, DeVry University, 1350 Alum Creek Drive, Columbus, OH 43209-2705. Web site: http://www.devry.edu/.

DeVRY UNIVERSITY
SEVEN HILLS, OHIO

Contact DeVry University, The Genesis Building, 6000 Lombardo Center, Seven Hills, OH 44131-6907. Phone: toll-free 866-453-3879. Web site: http://www.devry.edu/.

FRANCISCAN UNIVERSITY OF STEUBENVILLE
STEUBENVILLE, OHIO

General Independent Roman Catholic, comprehensive, coed **Entrance** Moderately difficult **Setting** 124-acre suburban campus **Total enrollment** 2,434 **Student-faculty ratio** 15:1 **Application deadline** Rolling (freshmen), rolling (transfer) **Freshmen** 81% were admitted **Housing** Yes **Expenses** Tuition $18,180; Room & Board $6300 **Undergraduates** 60% women, 7% part-time, 6% 25 or older, 1% Native American, 1% Hispanic American, 1% African American, 1% Asian American/Pacific Islander **The most frequently chosen baccalaureate fields are** health professions and related sciences, business/marketing, theology and religious vocations **Academic program** Advanced placement, accelerated degree program, honors program, summer session, adult/continuing education programs, internships **Contact** Mrs. Margaret Weber, Director of Admissions, Franciscan University of Steubenville, 1235 University Boulevard, Steubenville, OH 43952-1763. Phone: 740-283-6226 or toll-free 800-783-6220. Fax: 740-284-5456. E-mail: admissions@franciscan.edu. Web site: http://www.franciscan.edu/.

FRANKLIN UNIVERSITY
COLUMBUS, OHIO

Contact Mr. Tracy Austin, Chief Student Officer, Franklin University, 201 South Grant Avenue, Columbus, OH 43215-5399. Phone: 614-797-4700 Ext. 7501 or toll-free 877-341-6300. Fax: 614-224-8027. E-mail: info@franklin.edu. Web site: http://www.franklin.edu/.

GOD'S BIBLE SCHOOL AND COLLEGE
CINCINNATI, OHIO

General Independent interdenominational, 4-year, coed **Contact** Mrs. Lisa Profitt, Director of Admissions, God's Bible School and College, 1810 Young Street, Cincinnati, OH 45202-6838. Phone: 513-721-7944 Ext. 205 or toll-free 800-486-4637. Fax: 513-721-3971. E-mail: lprofitt@gbs.edu. Web site: http://www.gbs.edu/.

HEIDELBERG COLLEGE
TIFFIN, OHIO

General Independent, comprehensive, coed, affiliated with United Church of Christ **Entrance** Moderately difficult **Setting** 115-acre small-town campus **Total enrollment** 1,584 **Student-faculty ratio** 14:1 **Application deadline** 8/15 (freshmen), 8/15 (transfer) **Freshmen** 73% were admitted **Housing** Yes **Expenses** Tuition $19,922; Room & Board $8138 **Undergraduates** 50% women, 16% part-time, 12% 25 or older, 2% Hispanic American, 7% African American, 0.5% Asian American/Pacific Islander **The most frequently chosen baccalaureate fields are** business/marketing, education, parks and recreation **Academic program** English as a second language, advanced placement, accelerated degree program, honors program, summer session, adult/continuing education programs, internships **Contact** Ms. Lindsay Sooy, Director of Admission, Heidelberg College, 310 East Market Street, Tiffin, OH 44883. Phone: 419-448-2330 or toll-free 800-434-3352. Fax: 419-448-2334. E-mail: adminfo@heidelberg.edu. Web site: http://www.heidelberg.edu/.

HIRAM COLLEGE
HIRAM, OHIO

General Independent, 4-year, coed, affiliated with Christian Church (Disciples of Christ) **Entrance** Moderately difficult **Setting** 110-acre rural campus **Total enrollment** 1,271 **Student-faculty ratio** 12:1 **Application deadline** 4/1 (freshmen), 7/15 (transfer) **Freshmen** 77% were admitted **Housing** Yes **Expenses** Tuition $25,160; Room & Board $8380 **Undergraduates** 56% women, 16% part-time, 0.5% Native American, 2% Hispanic American, 10% African American, 1% Asian American/Pacific Islander **The most frequently chosen baccalaureate fields are** business/marketing, biological/life sciences, social sciences **Academic program** English as a second language, advanced placement, self-designed majors, summer session, adult/continuing education programs, internships **Contact** Mr. Sherman C. Dean II, Director of Admission, Hiram College, PO Box 96, Hiram, OH 44234. Phone: 330-569-5169 or toll-free 800-362-5280. Fax: 330-569-5944. E-mail: admission@hiram.edu. Web site: http://www.hiram.edu/.

JOHN CARROLL UNIVERSITY
UNIVERSITY HEIGHTS, OHIO

General Independent Roman Catholic (Jesuit), comprehensive, coed **Entrance** Moderately difficult **Setting** 60-acre suburban campus **Total enrollment** 3,766 **Student-faculty ratio** 14:1 **Application deadline** 2/1 (freshmen), rolling (transfer) **Freshmen** 86% were admitted **Housing** Yes **Expenses** Tuition $28,090; Room & Board $7934 **Undergraduates** 54% women, 4% part-time, 3% 25 or older, 0.3% Native American, 3% Hispanic American, 5% African American, 2% Asian American/Pacific Islander **The most frequently chosen baccalaureate fields are** business/marketing, biological/life sciences, public administration and social services **Academic program** Advanced placement, accelerated degree program, self-designed majors, honors program,

John Carroll University *(continued)*

summer session, adult/continuing education programs, internships **Contact** Mr. Thomas P. Fanning, Director of Admission, John Carroll University, 20700 North Park Blvd, University Heights, OH 44118. Phone: 216-397-4294. Fax: 216-397-4981. E-mail: tfanning@jcu.edu. Web site: http://www.jcu.edu/.

KENT STATE UNIVERSITY

KENT, OHIO

General State-supported, university, coed **Entrance** Moderately difficult **Setting** 1,347-acre suburban campus **Total enrollment** 22,819 **Student-faculty ratio** 17:1 **Application deadline** 5/1 (freshmen) **Freshmen** 80% were admitted **Housing** Yes **Expenses** Tuition $8430; Room & Board $7200 **Undergraduates** 59% women, 15% part-time, 11% 25 or older, 0.4% Native American, 1% Hispanic American, 8% African American, 1% Asian American/Pacific Islander **The most frequently chosen baccalaureate fields are** business/marketing, education, health professions and related sciences **Academic program** English as a second language, advanced placement, accelerated degree program, self-designed majors, honors program, summer session, adult/continuing education programs, internships **Contact** Mr. Christopher Buttenschon, Assistant Director of Admissions, Kent State University, 161 Michael Schwartz Center, Kent, OH 44242-0001. Phone: 330-672-2444 or toll-free 800-988-KENT. Fax: 330-672-2499. E-mail: admissions@kent.edu. Web site: http://www.kent.edu/.

KENYON COLLEGE

GAMBIER, OHIO

General Independent, 4-year, coed **Entrance** Very difficult **Setting** 1,200-acre rural campus **Total enrollment** 1,663 **Student-faculty ratio** 10:1 **Application deadline** 1/15 (freshmen), 4/1 (transfer) **Freshmen** 29% were admitted **Housing** Yes **Expenses** Tuition $40,240; Room & Board $6590 **Undergraduates** 52% women, 1% part-time, 1% Native American, 3% Hispanic American, 4% African American, 5% Asian American/Pacific Islander **The most frequently chosen baccalaureate fields are** English, social sciences, visual and performing arts **Academic program** Advanced placement, accelerated degree program, self-designed majors, honors program, internships **Contact** Ms. Jennifer Delahunty, Dean of Admissions, Kenyon College, Ransom Hall, Gambier, OH 43022. Phone: 740-427-5778 or toll-free 800-848-2468. Fax: 740-427-5770. E-mail: admissions@kenyon.edu. Web site: http://www.kenyon.edu/.

KETTERING COLLEGE OF MEDICAL ARTS

KETTERING, OHIO

General Independent Seventh-day Adventist, 4-year, coed, primarily women **Entrance** Moderately difficult **Setting** 35-acre suburban campus **Total enrollment** 808 **Student-faculty ratio** 10:1 **Application deadline** Rolling (freshmen), rolling (transfer) **Freshmen** 50% were admitted **Housing** Yes **Expenses** Tuition $8130; Room & Board $5800 **Undergraduates** 81% women, 47% part-time, 48% 25 or older, 0.1% Native American, 2% Hispanic American, 9% African American, 2% Asian American/Pacific Islander **The most frequently chosen baccalaureate field is** health professions and related sciences **Academic program** Advanced placement, honors program, summer session **Contact** Mrs. Becky McDonald, Director of Enrollment Services, Kettering College of Medical Arts, 3737 Southern Boulevard, Kettering, OH 45429-1299. Phone: 937-395-8601 or toll-free 800-433-5262. Fax: 937-296-4238. Web site: http://www.kcma.edu/.

LAKE ERIE COLLEGE

PAINESVILLE, OHIO

Contact Mr. Eric Felver, Director of Admissions, Lake Erie College, 391 West Washington Street, Painesville, OH 44077-3389. Phone: 440-375-7050 or toll-free 800-916-0904. Fax: 440-375-7005. E-mail: admissions@lec.edu. Web site: http://www.lec.edu/.

LAURA AND ALVIN SIEGAL COLLEGE OF JUDAIC STUDIES

BEACHWOOD, OHIO

Contact Ms. Ruth Kronick, Director of Student Services, Laura and Alvin Siegal College of Judaic Studies, 26500 Shaker Boulevard, Beachwood, OH 44122-7116. Phone: 216-464-4050 Ext. 101 or toll-free 888-336-2257. Fax: 216-464-5827. E-mail: admissions@siegalcollege.edu. Web site: http://www.siegalcollege.edu/.

LOURDES COLLEGE

SYLVANIA, OHIO

General Independent Roman Catholic, comprehensive, coed **Setting** 90-acre suburban campus **Total enrollment** 2,029 **Student-faculty ratio** 11:1 **Application deadline** Rolling (freshmen), rolling (transfer) **Freshmen** 80% were admitted **Housing** No **Expenses** Tuition $14,040 **Undergraduates** 82% women, 47% part-time, 57% 25 or older, 1% Native American, 3% Hispanic American, 13% African American, 1% Asian American/Pacific Islander **Academic program** Advanced placement, self-designed majors, summer session, adult/continuing education programs, internships **Contact** Ms. Amy Mergen, Office of Admissions, Lourdes College, 6832 Convent Boulevard, Sylvania, OH 43560-2898. Phone: 419-885-5291 or toll-free 800-878-3210 Ext. 1299. Fax: 419-882-3987. E-mail: lcadmits@lourdes.edu. Web site: http://www.lourdes.edu/.

MALONE COLLEGE
CANTON, OHIO

General Independent, comprehensive, coed, affiliated with Evangelical Friends Church–Eastern Region **Entrance** Moderately difficult **Setting** 78-acre suburban campus **Total enrollment** 2,371 **Student-faculty ratio** 14:1 **Application deadline** 7/1 (freshmen), 7/1 (transfer) **Freshmen** 76% were admitted **Housing** Yes **Expenses** Tuition $18,870; Room & Board $6600 **Undergraduates** 61% women, 12% part-time, 23% 25 or older, 0.2% Native American, 1% Hispanic American, 6% African American, 1% Asian American/Pacific Islander **The most frequently chosen baccalaureate fields are** business/marketing, education, health professions and related sciences **Academic program** Advanced placement, accelerated degree program, self-designed majors, honors program, summer session, adult/continuing education programs, internships **Contact** Mr. John Russell, Director of Admissions, Malone College, 515 25th Street, NW, Canton, OH 44709-3897. Phone: 330-471-8145 or toll-free 800-521-1146. Fax: 330-471-8149. E-mail: admissions@malone.edu. Web site: http://www.malone.edu/.

MARIETTA COLLEGE
MARIETTA, OHIO

General Independent, comprehensive, coed **Entrance** Moderately difficult **Setting** 120-acre small-town campus **Total enrollment** 1,606 **Student-faculty ratio** 12:1 **Application deadline** 5/1 (freshmen), rolling (transfer) **Freshmen** 75% were admitted **Housing** Yes **Expenses** Tuition $24,842; Room & Board $7390 **Undergraduates** 51% women, 5% part-time, 2% 25 or older, 0.3% Native American, 1% Hispanic American, 4% African American, 2% Asian American/Pacific Islander **The most frequently chosen baccalaureate fields are** business/marketing, communications/journalism, visual and performing arts **Academic program** English as a second language, advanced placement, accelerated degree program, self-designed majors, honors program, summer session, adult/continuing education programs, internships **Contact** Mr. Jason Turley, Director of Admission, Marietta College, 215 Fifth Street, Marietta, OH 45750. Phone: 740-376-4600 or toll-free 800-331-7896. Fax: 740-376-8888. E-mail: admit@marietta.edu. Web site: http://www.marietta.edu/.

MEDCENTRAL COLLEGE OF NURSING
MANSFIELD, OHIO

Contact Mrs. Wendi Snyder, Admissions Counselor, MedCentral College of Nursing, 335 Glessner Avenue, Mansfield, OH 44903. Phone: toll-free 877-656-4360. Fax: 419-520-2610. E-mail: admissions@medcentral.edu. Web site: http://www.medcentral.edu/.

MERCY COLLEGE OF NORTHWEST OHIO
TOLEDO, OHIO

General Independent, 4-year, coed, primarily women, affiliated with Roman Catholic Church **Entrance** Moderately difficult **Setting** urban campus **Total enrollment** 803 **Student-faculty ratio** 12:1 **Application deadline** Rolling (freshmen), rolling (transfer) **Freshmen** 81% were admitted **Housing** Yes **Expenses** Tuition $9546 **Undergraduates** 85% women, 49% part-time, 48% 25 or older, 0.4% Native American, 3% Hispanic American, 6% African American, 0.4% Asian American/Pacific Islander **The most frequently chosen baccalaureate field is** health professions and related sciences **Academic program** Advanced placement, summer session, internships **Contact** Admissions Counselor, Mercy College of Northwest Ohio, 2221 Madison Avenue, Toledo, OH 43604. Phone: 419-251-1313 Ext. 11203 or toll-free 888-80-Mercy. Fax: 419-251-1462. E-mail: admissions@mercycollege.edu. Web site: http://www.mercycollege.edu/.

MIAMI UNIVERSITY
OXFORD, OHIO

General State-related, university, coed **Entrance** Moderately difficult **Setting** 2,000-acre small-town campus **Total enrollment** 15,922 **Student-faculty ratio** 15:1 **Application deadline** 1/31 (freshmen), 5/1 (transfer) **Freshmen** 75% were admitted **Housing** Yes **Expenses** Tuition $11,925; Room & Board $8600 **Undergraduates** 54% women, 2% part-time, 2% 25 or older, 1% Native American, 2% Hispanic American, 3% African American, 3% Asian American/Pacific Islander **The most frequently chosen baccalaureate fields are** business/marketing, education, social sciences **Academic program** Advanced placement, self-designed majors, honors program, summer session, adult/continuing education programs, internships **Contact** Laurie Koehler, Interim Director of Undergraduate Admissions, Miami University, 301 South Campus Avenue, Oxford, OH 45056. Phone: 513-529-5040. Fax: 513-529-1550. E-mail: admissions@muohio.edu. Web site: http://www.muohio.edu/.

MIAMI UNIVERSITY HAMILTON
HAMILTON, OHIO

General State-supported, 4-year, coed **Entrance** Noncompetitive **Setting** 78-acre suburban campus **Total enrollment** 3,384 **Student-faculty ratio** 21:1 **Application deadline** Rolling (freshmen) **Housing** No **Expenses** Tuition $4350 **Undergraduates** 55% women, 25% part-time, 26% 25 or older, 0.5% Native American, 2% Hispanic American, 6% African American, 2% Asian American/Pacific Islander **Academic program** English as a second language, advanced placement, self-designed majors, honors program, summer session, adult/continuing education programs, internships **Contact** Mr. Archie Nelson, Director of Admission and Financial Aid, Miami University Hamilton, 1601 Peck Boulevard, Hamilton, OH 45011-3399. Phone: 513-785-3111. Fax: 513-785-1807. E-mail: nelsona3@muohio.edu. Web site: http://www.ham.muohio.edu/.

MOUNT CARMEL COLLEGE OF NURSING
COLUMBUS, OHIO

General Independent, comprehensive, coed, primarily women **Entrance** Moderately difficult **Setting** urban campus **Total enrollment** 680 **Student-faculty ratio** 13:1 **Application deadline** Rolling (freshmen), rolling (transfer) **Freshmen** 60% were admitted **Housing** Yes **Expenses** Tuition $15,762 **Undergraduates** 91% women, 18% part-time, 32% 25 or older **The most frequently chosen baccalaureate field is** health professions and related sciences **Contact** Kim Campbell, Director, Admissions and Recruitment, Mount Carmel College of Nursing, 127 South Davis Avenue, Columbus, OH 43222. Phone: 614-234-1085. Fax: 614-234-5427. E-mail: mccnadmissions@mchs.com. Web site: http://www.mccn.edu/.

MOUNT UNION COLLEGE
ALLIANCE, OHIO

General Independent United Methodist, 4-year, coed **Entrance** Moderately difficult **Setting** 115-acre suburban campus **Total enrollment** 2,193 **Student-faculty ratio** 13:1 **Application deadline** Rolling (freshmen), rolling (transfer) **Freshmen** 79% were admitted **Housing** Yes **Expenses** Tuition $22,050; Room & Board $6700 **Undergraduates** 50% women, 5% part-time, 1% 25 or older, 0.2% Native American, 1% Hispanic American, 4% African American, 0.4% Asian American/Pacific Islander **The most frequently chosen baccalaureate fields are** business/marketing, education, parks and recreation **Academic program** English as a second language, advanced placement, accelerated degree program, self-designed majors, honors program, summer session, adult/continuing education programs, internships **Contact** Mr. Vincent Heslop, Director of Enrollment Technology, Mount Union College, 1972 Clark Avenue, Alliance, OH 44601. Phone: 330-823-2590 or toll-free 800-334-6682 (in-state); 800-992-6682 (out-of-state). Fax: 330-823-5097. E-mail: admission@muc.edu. Web site: http://www.muc.edu/.

MOUNT VERNON NAZARENE UNIVERSITY
MOUNT VERNON, OHIO

General Independent Nazarene, comprehensive, coed **Entrance** Moderately difficult **Setting** 401-acre small-town campus **Total enrollment** 2,675 **Student-faculty ratio** 13:1 **Application deadline** 8/1 (freshmen) **Freshmen** 77% were admitted **Housing** Yes **Expenses** Tuition $19,330; Room & Board $5550 **Undergraduates** 58% women, 12% part-time, 32% 25 or older, 0.1% Native American, 2% Hispanic American, 5% African American, 1% Asian American/Pacific Islander **The most frequently chosen baccalaureate fields are** business/marketing, biological/life sciences, education **Academic program** Advanced placement, honors program, summer session, adult/continuing education programs, internships **Contact** Mr. Jay Mahan, Director of Traditional Undergraduate Admissions, Mount Vernon Nazarene University, 800 Martinsburg Road, Mount Vernon, OH 43050. Phone: 740-392-6868 Ext. 4516 or toll-free 866-462-6868. Fax: 740-393-0511. E-mail: admissions@mvnu.edu. Web site: http://www.mvnu.edu/.

MUSKINGUM COLLEGE
NEW CONCORD, OHIO

Contact Mrs. Beth DaLonzo, Director of Admission, Muskingum College, 163 Stormont Street, New Concord, OH 43762. Phone: 740-826-8137 or toll-free 800-752-6082. Fax: 740-826-8100. E-mail: adminfo@muskingum.edu. Web site: http://www.muskingum.edu/.

MYERS UNIVERSITY
CLEVELAND, OHIO

Contact Christina Johnson, Vice President for Enrollment Management, Myers University, 3921 Chester Avenue, Cleveland, OH 44114-4624. Phone: 216-523-3806 Ext. 805 or toll-free 877-366-9377. Fax: 216-696-6430. E-mail: cjohnson@myers.edu. Web site: http://www.myers.edu/.

NOTRE DAME COLLEGE
SOUTH EUCLID, OHIO

General Independent Roman Catholic, comprehensive, coed **Contact** Mr. David Armstrong,

Dean of Admissions, Notre Dame College, 4545 College Road, South Euclid, OH 44121-4293. Phone: 216-373-5214 or toll-free 800-632-1680. Fax: 216-381-3802. E-mail: admissinos@ndc.edu. Web site: http://www.notredamecollege.edu/.

OBERLIN COLLEGE
OBERLIN, OHIO

General Independent, comprehensive, coed **Entrance** Very difficult **Setting** 440-acre small-town campus **Total enrollment** 2,774 **Student-faculty ratio** 9:1 **Application deadline** 1/15 (freshmen), 3/15 (transfer) **Freshmen** 31% were admitted **Housing** Yes **Expenses** Tuition $36,282; Room & Board $10,080 **Undergraduates** 55% women, 2% part-time, 1% 25 or older, 1% Native American, 5% Hispanic American, 6% African American, 8% Asian American/Pacific Islander **Academic program** English as a second language, advanced placement, self-designed majors, honors program, internships **Contact** Ms. Debra Chermonte, Dean of Admissions and Financial Aid, Oberlin College, Admissions Office, Carnegie Building, Oberlin, OH 44074-1090. Phone: 440-775-8411 or toll-free 800-622-OBIE. Fax: 440-775-6905. E-mail: college.admissions@oberlin.edu. Web site: http://www.oberlin.edu/.

OHIO CHRISTIAN UNIVERSITY
CIRCLEVILLE, OHIO

Contact Mr. Scott Faughn, Acting Director of Enrollment, Ohio Christian University, 1476 Lancaster Pike, PO Box 458, Circleville, OH 43113-9487. Phone: 740-477-7741 or toll-free 800-701-0222. Fax: 740-477-7755. E-mail: enroll@biblecollege.edu. Web site: http://www.ohiochristian.edu/.

OHIO DOMINICAN UNIVERSITY
COLUMBUS, OHIO

General Independent Roman Catholic, comprehensive, coed **Entrance** Moderately difficult **Setting** 62-acre urban campus **Total enrollment** 3,082 **Student-faculty ratio** 14:1 **Application deadline** Rolling (freshmen), rolling (transfer) **Freshmen** 69% were admitted **Housing** Yes **Expenses** Tuition $21,794; Room & Board $7200 **Undergraduates** 61% women, 31% part-time, 37% 25 or older, 0.4% Native American, 2% Hispanic American, 21% African American, 1% Asian American/Pacific Islander **The most frequently chosen baccalaureate fields are** business/marketing, education, social sciences **Academic program** English as a second language, advanced placement, self-designed majors, honors program, summer session, adult/continuing education programs, internships **Contact** Ms. Nicole A. Evans, Director of Admissions, Ohio Dominican University, 1216 Sunbury Road, Columbus, OH 43219. Phone: 614-251-4588 or toll-free 800-854-2670. Fax: 614-251-0156. E-mail: admissions@ohiodominican.edu. Web site: http://www.ohiodominican.edu/.

OHIO NORTHERN UNIVERSITY
ADA, OHIO

General Independent, comprehensive, coed, affiliated with United Methodist Church **Entrance** Moderately difficult **Setting** 300-acre small-town campus **Total enrollment** 3,603 **Student-faculty ratio** 13:1 **Application deadline** 8/15 (freshmen), 9/1 (transfer) **Freshmen** 88% were admitted **Housing** Yes **Expenses** Tuition $30,765; Room & Board $7890 **Undergraduates** 46% women, 4% part-time, 2% 25 or older, 0.3% Native American, 1% Hispanic American, 3% African American, 1% Asian American/Pacific Islander **The most frequently chosen baccalaureate fields are** business/marketing, biological/life sciences, engineering **Academic program** English as a second language, advanced placement, honors program, summer session, internships **Contact** Ms. Deborah Miller, Director of Admission, Ohio Northern University, 525 South Main, Ada, OH 45810-1599. Phone: 419-772-2260 or toll-free 888-408-4ONU. Fax: 419-772-2821. E-mail: admissions-ug@onu.edu. Web site: http://www.onu.edu/.

THE OHIO STATE UNIVERSITY
COLUMBUS, OHIO

General State-supported, university, coed **Entrance** Moderately difficult **Setting** 6,191-acre urban campus **Total enrollment** 52,568 **Student-faculty ratio** 13:1 **Application deadline** 2/1 (freshmen) **Freshmen** 59% were admitted **Housing** Yes **Expenses** Tuition $8676; Room & Board $7365 **Undergraduates** 47% women, 9% part-time, 8% 25 or older, 0.4% Native American, 3% Hispanic American, 7% African American, 5% Asian American/Pacific Islander **Academic program** English as a second language, advanced placement, accelerated degree program, self-designed majors, honors program, summer session, adult/continuing education programs, internships **Contact** The Ohio State University, 110 Enarson Hall, 154 West 12th Avenue, Columbus, OH 43210. Phone: 614-247-3980. Fax: 614-292-4818. E-mail: professional@osu.edu. Web site: http://www.osu.edu/.

THE OHIO STATE UNIVERSITY AT LIMA
LIMA, OHIO

General State-supported, comprehensive, coed **Entrance** Noncompetitive **Setting** 565-acre small-

The Ohio State University at Lima *(continued)*

town campus **Total enrollment** 1,340 **Student-faculty ratio** 22:1 **Application deadline** 7/1 (freshmen) **Freshmen** 99% were admitted **Housing** No **Expenses** Tuition $5664 **Undergraduates** 50% women, 17% part-time, 16% 25 or older, 0.3% Native American, 2% Hispanic American, 4% African American, 1% Asian American/Pacific Islander **Academic program** English as a second language, advanced placement, accelerated degree program, honors program, summer session, adult/continuing education programs **Contact** Ms. Beth Keehn, Director of Admissions, The Ohio State University at Lima, 4240 Campus Drive, Lima, OH 45804. Phone: 419-995-8434. Fax: 419-995-8483. E-mail: admissions@lima.ohio-state.edu. Web site: http://www.lima.ohio-state.edu/.

THE OHIO STATE UNIVERSITY AT MARION

MARION, OHIO

General State-supported, comprehensive, coed **Entrance** Noncompetitive **Setting** 180-acre small-town campus **Total enrollment** 1,633 **Student-faculty ratio** 24:1 **Application deadline** 7/1 (freshmen) **Freshmen** 99% were admitted **Housing** No **Expenses** Tuition $5664 **Undergraduates** 54% women, 18% part-time, 17% 25 or older, 0.4% Native American, 2% Hispanic American, 6% African American, 4% Asian American/Pacific Islander **Academic program** English as a second language, advanced placement, accelerated degree program, honors program, summer session, adult/continuing education programs **Contact** Mr. Matthew Moreau, Admissions and Financial Aid Coordinator, The Ohio State University at Marion, 1465 Mount Vernon Avenue, Marion, OH 43302. Phone: 740-725-6337. Fax: 740-386-2439. E-mail: moreau.1@osu.edu. Web site: http://www.marion.ohio-state.edu/.

THE OHIO STATE UNIVERSITY–MANSFIELD CAMPUS

MANSFIELD, OHIO

General State-supported, comprehensive, coed **Entrance** Noncompetitive **Setting** 644-acre small-town campus **Total enrollment** 1,553 **Student-faculty ratio** 20:1 **Application deadline** 7/1 (freshmen), 6/25 (transfer) **Freshmen** 99% were admitted **Housing** Yes **Expenses** Tuition $5664; Room & Board $4275 **Undergraduates** 60% women, 29% part-time, 21% 25 or older, 0.3% Native American, 2% Hispanic American, 7% African American, 2% Asian American/Pacific Islander **Academic program** English as a second language, advanced placement, accelerated degree program, honors program, summer session, adult/continuing education programs **Contact** Mr. Henry D. Thomas, Coordinator of Admissions and Financial Aid, The Ohio State University–Mansfield Campus, 1760 University Drive, Mansfield, OH 44906. Phone: 419-755-4225. Fax: 419-755-4241. E-mail: admissions@mansfield.ohio-state.edu. Web site: http://www.mansfield.osu.edu/.

THE OHIO STATE UNIVERSITY–NEWARK CAMPUS

NEWARK, OHIO

General State-supported, comprehensive, coed **Entrance** Noncompetitive **Setting** 106-acre small-town campus **Total enrollment** 2,505 **Student-faculty ratio** 26:1 **Application deadline** 7/1 (freshmen) **Freshmen** 100% were admitted **Housing** Yes **Expenses** Tuition $5664; Room only $5265 **Undergraduates** 53% women, 14% part-time, 11% 25 or older, 1% Native American, 2% Hispanic American, 8% African American, 2% Asian American/Pacific Islander **Academic program** English as a second language, advanced placement, accelerated degree program, honors program, summer session, adult/continuing education programs **Contact** Ms. Ann Donahue, Director of Enrollment, The Ohio State University–Newark Campus, 1179 University Drive, Newark, OH 43055. Phone: 740-366-9333. Fax: 740-364-9645. E-mail: barclay.3@osu.edu. Web site: http://www.newark.osu.edu/.

OHIO UNIVERSITY

ATHENS, OHIO

General State-supported, university, coed **Entrance** Moderately difficult **Setting** 1,700-acre small-town campus **Total enrollment** 20,711 **Student-faculty ratio** 19:1 **Application deadline** 2/1 (freshmen), 5/15 (transfer) **Freshmen** 82% were admitted **Housing** Yes **Expenses** Tuition $8907; Room & Board $8427 **Undergraduates** 51% women, 6% part-time, 4% 25 or older, 0.3% Native American, 2% Hispanic American, 4% African American, 1% Asian American/Pacific Islander **The most frequently chosen baccalaureate fields are** communications/journalism, business/marketing, education **Academic program** English as a second language, advanced placement, accelerated degree program, self-designed majors, honors program, summer session, adult/continuing education programs, internships **Contact** Undergraduate Admissions, Ohio University, Athens, OH 45701-2979. Phone: 740-593-4100. Fax: 740-593-0560. E-mail: admissions@ohio.edu. Web site: http://www.ohio.edu/.

OHIO UNIVERSITY–CHILLICOTHE
CHILLICOTHE, OHIO

Contact TJ Eveland, Coordinator of Student Enrollment, Ohio University–Chillicothe, 571 West Fifth Street, PO Box 629, Chillicothe, OH 45601-0629. Phone: 740-774-7200 Ext. 242 or toll-free 877-462-6824. Fax: 740-774-7295. E-mail: lowej@ohio.edu. Web site: http://www.chillicothe.ohiou.edu/.

OHIO UNIVERSITY–EASTERN
ST. CLAIRSVILLE, OHIO

Contact Assistant Vice President for Enrollment Services/Director of Admissions, Ohio University–Eastern, 45425 National Road, St. Clairsville, OH 43950-9724. Phone: 740-593-4120 or toll-free 800-648-3331. E-mail: chenowet@ohio.edu. Web site: http://www.eastern.ohiou.edu/.

OHIO UNIVERSITY–LANCASTER
LANCASTER, OHIO

Contact Mr. Nathan Thomas, Admissions Officer, Ohio University–Lancaster, 1570 Granville Pike, Lancaster, OH 43130-1097. Phone: 740-654-6711 Ext. 215 or toll-free 888-446-4468 Ext. 215. Fax: 740-687-9497. E-mail: fox@ohio.edu. Web site: http://www.ohiou.edu/lancaster/.

OHIO UNIVERSITY–SOUTHERN CAMPUS
IRONTON, OHIO

Contact Dr. Kim K. Lawson, Coordinator of Admissions, Ohio University–Southern Campus, 1804 Liberty Avenue, Ironton, OH 45638-2214. Phone: 740-533-4612 or toll-free 800-626-0513. Fax: 740-593-4632. Web site: http://www.ohiou.edu/.

OHIO UNIVERSITY–ZANESVILLE
ZANESVILLE, OHIO

General State-supported, comprehensive, coed **Entrance** Noncompetitive **Setting** 179-acre rural campus **Total enrollment** 1,805 **Student-faculty ratio** 23:1 **Application deadline** Rolling (freshmen), rolling (transfer) **Freshmen** 92% were admitted **Expenses** Tuition $4596; Room & Board $8067 **Undergraduates** 73% women, 40% part-time, 43% 25 or older, 1% Native American, 1% Hispanic American, 3% African American, 0.3% Asian American/Pacific Islander **Academic program** Advanced placement, self-designed majors, summer session, adult/continuing education programs **Contact** Mrs. Karen Ragsdale, Student Services Secretary, Ohio University–Zanesville, Office of Student Services, 1425 Newark Road, Zanesville, OH 43701. Phone: 740-588-1439 Ext. 1446. Fax: 740-588-1444. E-mail: ouzservices@ohio.edu. Web site: http://www.zanesville.ohiou.edu/.

OHIO WESLEYAN UNIVERSITY
DELAWARE, OHIO

General Independent United Methodist, 4-year, coed **Entrance** Very difficult **Setting** 200-acre small-town campus **Total enrollment** 1,967 **Student-faculty ratio** 12:1 **Application deadline** 3/1 (freshmen), 5/15 (transfer) **Freshmen** 66% were admitted **Housing** Yes **Expenses** Tuition $31,930; Room & Board $8030 **Undergraduates** 52% women, 1% part-time, 1% 25 or older, 0.4% Native American, 1% Hispanic American, 5% African American, 2% Asian American/Pacific Islander **The most frequently chosen baccalaureate fields are** business/marketing, biological/life sciences, social sciences **Academic program** Advanced placement, self-designed majors, honors program, summer session, internships **Contact** Ms. Carol DelPropost, Assistant Vice President of Admission and Financial Aid, Ohio Wesleyan University, 61 South Sandusky Street, Delaware, OH 43015. Phone: 740-368-3025 or toll-free 800-922-8953. Fax: 740-368-3314. E-mail: cjdelpro@owu.edu. Web site: http://www.owu.edu/.

OTTERBEIN COLLEGE
WESTERVILLE, OHIO

General Independent United Methodist, comprehensive, coed **Entrance** Moderately difficult **Setting** 142-acre suburban campus **Total enrollment** 3,107 **Student-faculty ratio** 12:1 **Application deadline** 3/1 (freshmen), rolling (transfer) **Freshmen** 81% were admitted **Housing** Yes **Expenses** Tuition $25,065; Room & Board $7149 **Undergraduates** 65% women, 16% part-time, 1% 25 or older, 0.1% Native American, 2% Hispanic American, 5% African American, 1% Asian American/Pacific Islander **Academic program** Advanced placement, self-designed majors, honors program, summer session, adult/continuing education programs, internships **Contact** Dr. Cass Johnson, Director of Admissions, Otterbein College, One Otterbein College, Westerville, OH 43081-9924. Phone: 614-823-1500 or toll-free 800-488-8144. Fax: 614-823-1200. E-mail: uotterb@otterbein.edu. Web site: http://www.otterbein.edu/.

PONTIFICAL COLLEGE JOSEPHINUM
COLUMBUS, OHIO

General Independent Roman Catholic, comprehensive, coed, primarily men **Entrance** Minimally difficult **Setting** 100-acre suburban campus **Total enrollment** 166 **Student-faculty ratio** 7:1 **Application deadline** 7/31 (freshmen), rolling

Pontifical College Josephinum *(continued)*

(transfer) **Freshmen** 93% were admitted **Housing** Yes **Expenses** Tuition $15,680; Room & Board $7498 **Undergraduates** 35% 25 or older, 9% Hispanic American, 2% Asian American/Pacific Islander **The most frequently chosen baccalaureate fields are** English, area and ethnic studies, philosophy and religious studies **Academic program** English as a second language, advanced placement, honors program, internships **Contact** Mrs. Arminda Crawford, Secretary for Admissions, Pontifical College Josephinum, 7825 North High Street, Columbus, OH 43235. Phone: 614-547-1615 or toll-free 888-252-5812. Fax: 614-885-2307. E-mail: acrawford@pcj.edu. Web site: http://www.pcj.edu/.

RABBINICAL COLLEGE OF TELSHE

WICKLIFFE, OHIO

Contact Rabbinical College of Telshe, 28400 Euclid Avenue, Wickliffe, OH 44092-2523.

SHAWNEE STATE UNIVERSITY

PORTSMOUTH, OHIO

General State-supported, 4-year, coed **Entrance** Noncompetitive **Setting** 52-acre small-town campus **Total enrollment** 3,699 **Student-faculty ratio** 17:1 **Application deadline** Rolling (freshmen), rolling (transfer) **Freshmen** 100% were admitted **Housing** Yes **Expenses** Tuition $5832; Room & Board $7234 **Undergraduates** 60% women, 19% part-time, 27% 25 or older, 1% Native American, 0.4% Hispanic American, 3% African American, 0.3% Asian American/Pacific Islander **The most frequently chosen baccalaureate fields are** business/marketing, education, social sciences **Academic program** Advanced placement, honors program, summer session, adult/continuing education programs, internships **Contact** Mr. Bob Trusz, Director of Admission, Shawnee State University, 940 Second Street, Commons Building, Portsmouth, OH 45662. Phone: 740-351-3610 Ext. 610 or toll-free 800-959-2SSU. Fax: 740-351-3111. E-mail: to_ssu@shawnee.edu. Web site: http://www.shawnee.edu/.

TEMPLE BAPTIST COLLEGE

CINCINNATI, OHIO

Contact Temple Baptist College, 11965 Kenn Road, Cincinnati, OH 45240. Web site: http://www.templebaptistcollege.com/.

TIFFIN UNIVERSITY

TIFFIN, OHIO

General Independent, comprehensive, coed **Entrance** Minimally difficult **Setting** 110-acre small-town campus **Total enrollment** 2,353 **Student-faculty ratio** 19:1 **Application deadline** Rolling (freshmen) **Freshmen** 71% were admitted **Housing** Yes **Expenses** Tuition $17,220; Room & Board $7580 **Undergraduates** 54% women, 10% part-time, 27% 25 or older, 0.1% Native American, 2% Hispanic American, 16% African American, 0.4% Asian American/Pacific Islander **The most frequently chosen baccalaureate fields are** business/marketing, psychology, security and protective services **Academic program** English as a second language, advanced placement, accelerated degree program, honors program, summer session, adult/continuing education programs, internships **Contact** Mr. Jeremy Marinis, Director of Undergraduate Admissions, Tiffin University, 155 Miami Street, Tiffin, OH 44883. Phone: 419-448-3368 or toll-free 800-968-6446. Fax: 419-443-5006. E-mail: marinisjj@tiffin.edu. Web site: http://www.tiffin.edu/.

TRI-STATE BIBLE COLLEGE

SOUTH POINT, OHIO

Contact Mr. Dale Cook, Admissions Director, Tri-State Bible College, 506 Margaret Street, PO Box 445, South Point, OH 45680-8402. Phone: 740-377-2520. Fax: 740-377-0001. E-mail: tsbc@zoomnet.net. Web site: http://www.tsbc.edu/.

UNION INSTITUTE & UNIVERSITY

CINCINNATI, OHIO

Contact Dr. Emily Harbold, Associate Vice President, Academic Affairs, Union Institute & University, 440 East McMillan Street, Cincinnati, OH 45206. Phone: toll-free 800-486-3116. E-mail: admissions@tui.edu. Web site: http://www.tui.edu/.

THE UNIVERSITY OF AKRON

AKRON, OHIO

General State-supported, university, coed **Entrance** Moderately difficult **Setting** 218-acre urban campus **Total enrollment** 23,007 **Student-faculty ratio** 19:1 **Application deadline** 8/11 (freshmen), rolling (transfer) **Freshmen** 82% were admitted **Housing** Yes **Expenses** Tuition $8382; Room & Board $8003 **Undergraduates** 50% women, 23% part-time, 24% 25 or older, 0.3% Native American, 1% Hispanic American, 14% African American, 2% Asian American/Pacific Islander **The most frequently chosen baccalaureate fields are** business/marketing, education, health professions and related sciences **Academic program** English as a second language, advanced placement, accelerated degree program, self-designed majors, honors program, summer session, adult/continuing education programs, internships **Contact** Ms. Diane Raybuck, Director of Admissions, The University of Akron, The University of Akron, Akron, OH 44325-2001. Phone: 330-972-7100 or toll-free 800-655-4884. Fax: 330-972-7022. E-mail: admissions@uakron.edu. Web site: http://www.uakron.edu/.

UNIVERSITY OF CINCINNATI
CINCINNATI, OHIO

General State-supported, university, coed **Entrance** Moderately difficult **Setting** 137-acre urban campus **Total enrollment** 29,319 **Student-faculty ratio** 14:1 **Application deadline** 9/1 (freshmen), rolling (transfer) **Freshmen** 75% were admitted **Housing** Yes **Expenses** Tuition $9399; Room & Board $8799 **Undergraduates** 51% women, 17% part-time, 17% 25 or older, 0.3% Native American, 2% Hispanic American, 11% African American, 3% Asian American/Pacific Islander **The most frequently chosen baccalaureate fields are** business/marketing, engineering, health professions and related sciences **Academic program** English as a second language, advanced placement, accelerated degree program, honors program, summer session, adult/continuing education programs, internships **Contact** Mr. Thomas Canepa, Assistant Vice President, Admissions, University of Cincinnati, 2624 Clifton Avenue, Cincinnati, OH 45221. Phone: 513-556-1100. Fax: 513-556-1105. E-mail: admissions@uc.edu. Web site: http://www.uc.edu/.

UNIVERSITY OF DAYTON
DAYTON, OHIO

General Independent Roman Catholic, university, coed **Entrance** Moderately difficult **Setting** 259-acre suburban campus **Total enrollment** 10,395 **Student-faculty ratio** 16:1 **Application deadline** Rolling (freshmen), 6/15 (transfer) **Freshmen** 82% were admitted **Housing** Yes **Expenses** Tuition $25,950; Room & Board $7720 **Undergraduates** 50% women, 8% part-time, 1% 25 or older, 0.3% Native American, 2% Hispanic American, 3% African American, 1% Asian American/Pacific Islander **The most frequently chosen baccalaureate fields are** business/marketing, communications/journalism, education **Academic program** English as a second language, advanced placement, accelerated degree program, self-designed majors, honors program, summer session, adult/continuing education programs, internships **Contact** Mr. Robert Durkle, Director of Admission, University of Dayton, 300 College Park, Dayton, OH 45469-1300. Phone: 937-229-4411 or toll-free 800-837-7433. Fax: 937-229-4729. E-mail: admission@udayton.edu. Web site: http://www.udayton.edu/.

THE UNIVERSITY OF FINDLAY
FINDLAY, OHIO

General Independent, comprehensive, coed, affiliated with Church of God **Entrance** Moderately difficult **Setting** 200-acre small-town campus **Total enrollment** 5,630 **Student-faculty ratio** 17:1 **Application deadline** 6/1 (freshmen), rolling (transfer) **Freshmen** 70% were admitted **Housing** Yes **Expenses** Tuition $23,890; Room & Board $8026 **Undergraduates** 61% women, 28% part-time, 19% 25 or older, 0.3% Native American, 1% Hispanic American, 3% African American, 1% Asian American/Pacific Islander **The most frequently chosen baccalaureate fields are** business/marketing, education, health professions and related sciences **Academic program** English as a second language, advanced placement, accelerated degree program, self-designed majors, honors program, summer session, adult/continuing education programs, internships **Contact** Mr. Randall Langston, Executive Director of Enrollment Services, The University of Findlay, 1000 North Main Street, Findlay, OH 45840-3653. Phone: 419-434-4540 or toll-free 800-548-0932. Fax: 419-434-4898. E-mail: admissions@findlay.edu. Web site: http://www.findlay.edu/.

UNIVERSITY OF PHOENIX–CINCINNATI CAMPUS
WEST CHESTER, OHIO

General Proprietary, comprehensive, coed **Contact** Ms. Evelyn Gaskin, Registrar/Executive Director, University of Phoenix–Cincinnati Campus, 4615 East Elwood Street, Mail Stop AA-K101, Phoenix, AZ 85040-1958. Phone: 480-557-3301 or toll-free 800-776-4867 (in-state); 800-228-7240 (out-of-state). Fax: 480-643-1020. E-mail: evelyn.gaskin@phoenix.edu. Web site: http://www.phoenix.edu/.

UNIVERSITY OF PHOENIX–CLEVELAND CAMPUS
INDEPENDENCE, OHIO

General Proprietary, comprehensive, coed **Contact** Ms. Evelyn Gaskin, Registrar/Executive Director, University of Phoenix–Cleveland Campus, 4615 East Elwood Street, Mail Stop AA-K101, Phoenix, AZ 85040-1958. Phone: 480-557-3301 or toll-free 800-776-4867 (in-state); 800-228-7240 (out-of-state). Fax: 480-643-1020. E-mail: evelyn.gaskin@phoenix.edu. Web site: http://www.phoenix.edu/.

UNIVERSITY OF PHOENIX–COLUMBUS OHIO CAMPUS
COLUMBUS, OHIO

General Proprietary, comprehensive, coed **Contact** Ms. Evelyn Gaskin, Registrar/Execu-

University of Phoenix–Columbus Ohio Campus *(continued)*

tive Director, University of Phoenix–Columbus Ohio Campus, 8415 Pulsar Place, Columbus, OH 43240-4032. Phone: 480-557-3301 or toll-free 800-776-4867 (in-state); 800-228-7240 (out-of-state). Fax: 480-643-1020. E-mail: evelyn.gaskin@phoenix.edu. Web site: http://www.phoenix.edu/.

UNIVERSITY OF RIO GRANDE

RIO GRANDE, OHIO

General Independent, comprehensive, coed **Entrance** Noncompetitive **Setting** 170-acre rural campus **Total enrollment** 2,429 **Student-faculty ratio** 18:1 **Application deadline** Rolling (freshmen), rolling (transfer) **Freshmen** 63% were admitted **Housing** Yes **Expenses** Room & Board $6820 **Undergraduates** 59% women, 22% part-time, 12% 25 or older, 0.4% Native American, 1% Hispanic American, 3% African American, 0.4% Asian American/Pacific Islander **The most frequently chosen baccalaureate fields are** business/marketing, education, health professions and related sciences **Academic program** English as a second language, advanced placement, accelerated degree program, self-designed majors, honors program, summer session, adult/continuing education programs, internships **Contact** Ms. Tammy McCain, Admissions Officer, University of Rio Grande, PO Box 500, Rio Grande, OH 45674. Phone: 740-245-7208 or toll-free 800-282-7201. Fax: 740-245-7260. E-mail: admissions@rio.edu. Web site: http://www.rio.edu/.

THE UNIVERSITY OF TOLEDO

TOLEDO, OHIO

General State-supported, university, coed **Entrance** Noncompetitive **Setting** 407-acre suburban campus **Total enrollment** 19,768 **Student-faculty ratio** 17:1 **Application deadline** Rolling (freshmen), rolling (transfer) **Freshmen** 93% were admitted **Housing** Yes **Expenses** Tuition $7927; Room & Board $8446 **Undergraduates** 49% women, 19% part-time, 15% 25 or older, 0.3% Native American, 3% Hispanic American, 14% African American, 2% Asian American/Pacific Islander **The most frequently chosen baccalaureate fields are** business/marketing, education, engineering **Academic program** English as a second language, advanced placement, self-designed majors, honors program, summer session, adult/continuing education programs, internships **Contact** Mr. William Pierce, Director of Undergraduate Admissions, The University of Toledo, 2801 West Bancroft, Toledo, OH 43606-3390. Phone: 419-530-5742 or toll-free 800-5TOLEDO. Fax: 419-530-5713. E-mail: william.pierce@utoledo.edu. Web site: http://www.utoledo.edu/.

URBANA UNIVERSITY

URBANA, OHIO

Contact Ms. Paula Brown, Director of Admissions, Urbana University, 579 College Way, Urbana, OH 43078. Phone: 937-484-1356 or toll-free 800-7-URBANA. Fax: 937-652-6871. E-mail: admiss@urbana.edu. Web site: http://www.urbana.edu/.

URSULINE COLLEGE

PEPPER PIKE, OHIO

General Independent Roman Catholic, comprehensive, undergraduate: women only; graduate: coed **Entrance** Minimally difficult **Setting** 112-acre suburban campus **Total enrollment** 1,550 **Student-faculty ratio** 9:1 **Application deadline** Rolling (freshmen), rolling (transfer) **Freshmen** 66% were admitted **Housing** Yes **Expenses** Tuition $21,140; Room & Board $7036 **Undergraduates** 32% part-time, 46% 25 or older, 0.3% Native American, 2% Hispanic American, 25% African American, 3% Asian American/Pacific Islander **The most frequently chosen baccalaureate fields are** business/marketing, health professions and related sciences, psychology **Academic program** Advanced placement, accelerated degree program, summer session, adult/continuing education programs, internships **Contact** Director of Admissions, Ursuline College, 2550 Lander Road, Pepper Pike, OH 44124. Phone: 440-449-4203 or toll-free 888-URSULINE. Fax: 440-684-6138. E-mail: admission@ursuline.edu. Web site: http://www.ursuline.edu/.

WALSH UNIVERSITY

NORTH CANTON, OHIO

General Independent Roman Catholic, comprehensive, coed **Entrance** Moderately difficult **Setting** 134-acre small-town campus **Total enrollment** 2,546 **Student-faculty ratio** 14:1 **Application deadline** Rolling (freshmen), rolling (transfer) **Freshmen** 79% were admitted **Housing** Yes **Expenses** Tuition $20,050; Room & Board $7760 **Undergraduates** 65% women, 20% part-time, 22% 25 or older, 0.3% Native American, 1% Hispanic American, 5% African American, 1% Asian American/Pacific Islander **The most frequently chosen baccalaureate fields are** business/marketing, education, health professions and related sciences **Academic program** English as a second language, advanced placement, accelerated degree program, honors program, summer session, adult/continuing education programs, internships **Contact** Mr. Brett Freshour, Vice President for Enrollment Management, Walsh University, 2020 East Maple, North Canton, OH 44720. Phone: 330-490-7171 or toll-free 800-362-9846 (in-state); 800-362-8846 (out-of-state). Fax: 330-490-7165. E-mail: admissions@walsh.edu. Web site: http://www.walsh.edu/.

WILBERFORCE UNIVERSITY
WILBERFORCE, OHIO

Contact Ms. Kenya LeNoir Messer, Vice President for Student Development and Enrollment Management/Dean of Admissions, Wilberforce University, 1055 North Bickett Road, Wilberforce, OH 45384. Phone: 937-708-5721 or toll-free 800-367-8568. Fax: 937-376-4751. E-mail: kchristm@wilberforce.edu. Web site: http://www.wilberforce.edu/.

WILMINGTON COLLEGE
WILMINGTON, OHIO

General Independent Friends, comprehensive, coed **Entrance** Moderately difficult **Setting** 1,465-acre small-town campus **Total enrollment** 1,605 **Student-faculty ratio** 14:1 **Application deadline** Rolling (freshmen), rolling (transfer) **Freshmen** 98% were admitted **Housing** Yes **Expenses** Tuition $22,078; Room & Board $7706 **Undergraduates** 54% women, 17% part-time, 5% 25 or older **The most frequently chosen baccalaureate fields are** business/marketing, education, psychology **Academic program** Advanced placement, accelerated degree program, self-designed majors, honors program, summer session, adult/continuing education programs, internships **Contact** Ms. Tina Garland, Director of Admission and Financial Aid, Wilmington College, 1870 Quaker Way, Wilmington, OH 45177. Phone: 937-382-6661 Ext. 426 or toll-free 800-341-9318. Fax: 937-383-8542. E-mail: admissions@wilmington.edu. Web site: http://www.wilmington.edu/.

WITTENBERG UNIVERSITY
SPRINGFIELD, OHIO

General Independent, comprehensive, coed, affiliated with Evangelical Lutheran Church **Entrance** Moderately difficult **Setting** 71-acre suburban campus **Total enrollment** 2,078 **Student-faculty ratio** 12:1 **Application deadline** Rolling (transfer) **Freshmen** 73% were admitted **Housing** Yes **Expenses** Tuition $33,236; Room & Board $8314 **Undergraduates** 55% women, 6% part-time, 2% 25 or older, 0.2% Native American, 1% Hispanic American, 5% African American, 1% Asian American/Pacific Islander **The most frequently chosen baccalaureate fields are** biological/life sciences, business/marketing, social sciences **Academic program** English as a second language, advanced placement, self-designed majors, honors program, summer session, adult/continuing education programs, internships **Contact** Mr. Brad Pochard, Director of Admission, Wittenberg University, PO Box 720, Springfield, OH 45501-0720. Phone: 877-206-0332 Ext. 6377 or toll-free 800-677-7558 Ext. 6314. Fax: 937-327-6379. E-mail: admission@wittenberg.edu. Web site: http://www.wittenberg.edu/.

WRIGHT STATE UNIVERSITY
DAYTON, OHIO

General State-supported, university, coed **Entrance** Minimally difficult **Setting** 557-acre suburban campus **Total enrollment** 16,151 **Student-faculty ratio** 25:1 **Application deadline** Rolling (freshmen), rolling (transfer) **Freshmen** 83% were admitted **Housing** Yes **Expenses** Tuition $7278; Room & Board $7180 **Undergraduates** 55% women, 15% part-time, 16% 25 or older, 0.4% Native American, 2% Hispanic American, 13% African American, 3% Asian American/Pacific Islander **The most frequently chosen baccalaureate fields are** business/marketing, education, health professions and related sciences **Academic program** English as a second language, advanced placement, self-designed majors, honors program, summer session, adult/continuing education programs, internships **Contact** Ms. Cathy Davis, Director of Undergraduate Admissions, Wright State University, 3640 Colonel Glenn Highway, Dayton, OH 45435. Phone: 937-775-5700 or toll-free 800-247-1770. Fax: 937-775-5795. E-mail: admissions@wright.edu. Web site: http://www.wright.edu/.

XAVIER UNIVERSITY
CINCINNATI, OHIO

General Independent Roman Catholic, comprehensive, coed **Entrance** Moderately difficult **Setting** 140-acre urban campus **Total enrollment** 6,646 **Student-faculty ratio** 12:1 **Application deadline** 2/1 (freshmen), rolling (transfer) **Freshmen** 73% were admitted **Housing** Yes **Expenses** Tuition $26,860; Room & Board $9270 **Undergraduates** 56% women, 13% part-time, 14% 25 or older, 0.4% Native American, 3% Hispanic American, 11% African American, 3% Asian American/Pacific Islander **The most frequently chosen baccalaureate fields are** business/marketing, communications/journalism, liberal arts/general studies **Academic program** English as a second language, advanced placement, honors program, summer session, adult/continuing education programs, internships **Contact** Ms. Marianne Borgmann, Interim Director of Admission, Xavier University, 3800

Xavier University *(continued)*

Victory Parkway, Cincinnati, OH 45207-5311. Phone: 513-745-3301 or toll-free 800-344-4698. Fax: 513-745-4319. E-mail: xuadmit@xavier.edu. Web site: http://www.xu.edu/.

YOUNGSTOWN STATE UNIVERSITY

YOUNGSTOWN, OHIO

General State-supported, comprehensive, coed **Entrance** Noncompetitive **Setting** 200-acre urban campus **Total enrollment** 13,489 **Student-faculty ratio** 17:1 **Application deadline** 8/15 (freshmen), 8/15 (transfer) **Freshmen** 81% were admitted **Housing** Yes **Expenses** Tuition $6721; Room & Board $6740 **Undergraduates** 54% women, 21% part-time, 27% 25 or older, 0.4% Native American, 2% Hispanic American, 14% African American, 1% Asian American/Pacific Islander **The most frequently chosen baccalaureate fields are** business/marketing, education, health professions and related sciences **Academic program** English as a second language, advanced placement, accelerated degree program, self-designed majors, honors program, summer session, adult/continuing education programs, internships **Contact** Ms. Sue Davis, Director of Undergraduate Admissions, Youngstown State University, One University Plaza, Youngstown, OH 44555-0001. Phone: 330-941-2000 or toll-free 877-468-6978. Fax: 330-941-3674. E-mail: enroll@ysu.edu. Web site: http://www.ysu.edu/.

OKLAHOMA

BACONE COLLEGE

MUSKOGEE, OKLAHOMA

Contact Ms. Tina Sorick, Admissions Counselor, Bacone College, 2299 Old Bacone Road, Muskogee, OK 74403-1597. Phone: 918-781-7349 or toll-free 888-682-5514 Ext. 7340. Fax: 918-781-7416. E-mail: admissions@bacone.edu. Web site: http://www.bacone.edu/.

CAMERON UNIVERSITY

LAWTON, OKLAHOMA

General State-supported, comprehensive, coed **Entrance** Minimally difficult **Setting** 160-acre small-town campus **Total enrollment** 5,475 **Student-faculty ratio** 18:1 **Application deadline** Rolling (freshmen), rolling (transfer) **Freshmen** 100% were admitted **Housing** Yes **Expenses** Tuition $3756; Room & Board $3970 **Undergraduates** 60% women, 35% part-time, 43% 25 or older, 8% Native American, 8% Hispanic American, 16% African American, 3% Asian American/Pacific Islander **The most frequently chosen baccalaureate fields are** business/marketing, education, security and protective services **Academic program** English as a second language, advanced placement, accelerated degree program, honors program, summer session, adult/continuing education programs, internships **Contact** Ms. Brenda Dally, Assistant Director of Admissions, Cameron University, Admissions, 2800 West Gore Boulevard, Lawton, OK 73505. Phone: 580-581-2289 or toll-free 888-454-7600. Fax: 580-581-5514. E-mail: admiss@cua.cameron.edu. Web site: http://www.cameron.edu/.

DEVRY UNIVERSITY

OKLAHOMA CITY, OKLAHOMA

General Proprietary, comprehensive, coed **Total enrollment** 64 **Student-faculty ratio** 124:1 **Application deadline** Rolling (freshmen), rolling (transfer) **Expenses** Tuition $13,890 **Undergraduates** 27% women, 48% part-time, 57% 25 or older, 2% Native American, 2% Hispanic American, 18% African American **The most frequently chosen baccalaureate field is** business/marketing **Academic program** Accelerated degree program **Contact** Admissions Office, DeVry University, Lakepointe Towers, 4013 NW Expressway Street, Suite 100, Oklahoma City, OK 73116. Web site: http://www.devry.edu/.

EAST CENTRAL UNIVERSITY

ADA, OKLAHOMA

General State-supported, comprehensive, coed **Entrance** Minimally difficult **Setting** 140-acre small-town campus **Total enrollment** 4,463 **Student-faculty ratio** 18:1 **Freshmen** 96% were admitted **Housing** Yes **Expenses** Tuition $3796; Room & Board $3860 **Undergraduates** 59% women, 19% part-time, 31% 25 or older, 21% Native American, 3% Hispanic American, 4% African American, 1% Asian American/Pacific Islander **The most frequently chosen baccalaureate fields are** education, health professions and related sciences, public administration and social services **Academic program** Advanced placement, honors program, summer session, adult/continuing education programs, internships **Contact** Ms. Pam Denny, Freshman Admissions Officer, East Central University, PMBJ8, 1100 East 14th Street, Ada, OK 74820-6999. Phone: 580-310-5239 Ext. 239. Fax: 580-310-5432. E-mail: pdenny@ecok.edu. Web site: http://www.ecok.edu/.

HILLSDALE FREE WILL BAPTIST COLLEGE

MOORE, OKLAHOMA

General Independent Free Will Baptist, comprehensive, coed **Entrance** Noncompetitive **Setting**

41-acre suburban campus **Total enrollment** 262 **Housing** Yes **Expenses** Tuition $9260; Room & Board $4700 **Undergraduates** 37% women, 12% part-time, 17% 25 or older, 10% Native American, 4% Hispanic American, 10% African American **The most frequently chosen baccalaureate fields are** business/marketing, interdisciplinary studies, theology and religious vocations **Academic program** English as a second language, advanced placement, accelerated degree program, summer session, adult/continuing education programs, internships **Contact** Ryan Giles, Admission Officer, Hillsdale Free Will Baptist College, PO Box 7208, Moore, OK 73160. Phone: 405-912-9011. Fax: 405-912-9050. E-mail: recruitment@hc.edu. Web site: http://www.hc.edu/.

ITT TECHNICAL INSTITUTE
OKLAHOMA CITY, OKLAHOMA

General Proprietary, 4-year, coed **Contact** Mr. Ron Gross, Director of Recruitment, ITT Technical Institute, 50 Penn Place Office Tower, 1900 Northwest Expressway, Suite 305R, Oklahoma City, OK 73118. Phone: 405-810-4100 or toll-free 800-518-1612. Web site: http://www2.itt-tech.edu/dnm/campus/.

LANGSTON UNIVERSITY
LANGSTON, OKLAHOMA

General State-supported, comprehensive, coed **Contact** Maurice Osborne, Assistant Director of Admission, Langston University, PO Box 667, Langston, OK 73050. Phone: 405-466-2980 or toll-free 405-466-3428. Fax: 405-466-3391. Web site: http://www.lunet.edu/.

MID-AMERICA CHRISTIAN UNIVERSITY
OKLAHOMA CITY, OKLAHOMA

Contact Ms. Dani Brunet, Admissions Office Manager, Mid-America Christian University, 3500 Southwest 119th Street, Oklahoma City, OK 73170-4504. Phone: 405-392-3180. Fax: 405-692-3165. E-mail: mbcinfo@mabc.edu. Web site: http://www.macu.edu/.

NORTHEASTERN STATE UNIVERSITY
TAHLEQUAH, OKLAHOMA

General State-supported, comprehensive, coed **Entrance** Moderately difficult **Setting** 160-acre small-town campus **Total enrollment** 9,261 **Student-faculty ratio** 22:1 **Application deadline** 8/1 (freshmen), 8/1 (transfer) **Freshmen** 71% were admitted **Housing** Yes **Expenses** Tuition $3798; Room & Board $4544 **Undergraduates** 62% women, 25% part-time, 36% 25 or older, 30% Native American, 2% Hispanic American, 5% African American, 1% Asian American/Pacific Islander **The most frequently chosen baccalaureate fields are** business/marketing, education, psychology **Academic program** Advanced placement, self-designed majors, honors program, summer session, adult/continuing education programs, internships **Contact** Ms. Dawn Cain, Director of Admissions, Northeastern State University, 600 North Grand Avenue, Tahlequah, OK 74464. Phone: 918-444-2200 or toll-free 800-722-9614. Fax: 918-458-2342. E-mail: cain@nsuok.edu. Web site: http://www.nsuok.edu/.

NORTHWESTERN OKLAHOMA STATE UNIVERSITY
ALVA, OKLAHOMA

General State-supported, comprehensive, coed **Entrance** Moderately difficult **Setting** 70-acre small-town campus **Total enrollment** 2,030 **Student-faculty ratio** 16:1 **Application deadline** Rolling (freshmen), rolling (transfer) **Freshmen** 100% were admitted **Housing** Yes **Expenses** Tuition $3750; Room & Board $3400 **Undergraduates** 59% women, 22% part-time, 25% 25 or older, 5% Native American, 4% Hispanic American, 5% African American, 1% Asian American/Pacific Islander **The most frequently chosen baccalaureate fields are** business/marketing, agriculture, education **Academic program** Advanced placement, summer session, adult/continuing education programs, internships **Contact** Mr. Matt Adair, Director of Recruitment, Northwestern Oklahoma State University, 709 Oklahoma Boulevard, Alva, OK 73717-2799. Phone: 580-327-8550. Fax: 580-327-8699. E-mail: wmadair@nwosu.edu. Web site: http://www.nwosu.edu/.

OKLAHOMA BAPTIST UNIVERSITY
SHAWNEE, OKLAHOMA

Contact Mr. Trent Argo, Dean of Enrollment Management, Oklahoma Baptist University, 500 West University, Shawnee, OK 74804. Phone: 405-878-2033 or toll-free 800-654-3285. Fax: 405-878-2046. E-mail: admissions@mail.okbu.edu. Web site: http://www.okbu.edu/.

OKLAHOMA CHRISTIAN UNIVERSITY
OKLAHOMA CITY, OKLAHOMA

General Independent, comprehensive, coed, affiliated with Church of Christ **Entrance** Noncompetitive **Setting** 200-acre suburban campus **Total enrollment** 2,258 **Student-faculty ratio** 14:1 **Application deadline** Rolling (freshmen), rolling (transfer) **Freshmen** 74% were admitted **Housing** Yes **Expenses** Tuition $16,566; Room & Board $6390 **Undergraduates** 51% women, 3% part-time, 4% Native American, 3% Hispanic

Oklahoma Christian University *(continued)*

American, 5% African American, 2% Asian American/Pacific Islander **The most frequently chosen baccalaureate fields are** business/ marketing, education, liberal arts/general studies **Academic program** English as a second language, advanced placement, accelerated degree program, honors program, summer session, internships **Contact** Ms. Risa Forrester, Dean of Admissions and Marketing, Oklahoma Christian University, Box 11000, Oklahoma City, OK 73136-1100. Phone: 405-425-5050 or toll-free 800-877-5010. Fax: 405-425-5208. E-mail: info@oc.edu. Web site: http://www.oc.edu/.

OKLAHOMA CITY UNIVERSITY
OKLAHOMA CITY, OKLAHOMA

General Independent United Methodist, comprehensive, coed **Entrance** Moderately difficult **Setting** 75-acre urban campus **Total enrollment** 3,865 **Student-faculty ratio** 11:1 **Application deadline** 8/20 (freshmen), rolling (transfer) **Freshmen** 81% were admitted **Housing** Yes **Expenses** Tuition $21,000; Room & Board $8400 **Undergraduates** 62% women, 16% part-time, 7% 25 or older, 5% Native American, 5% Hispanic American, 8% African American, 4% Asian American/Pacific Islander **The most frequently chosen baccalaureate fields are** liberal arts/ general studies, health professions and related sciences, visual and performing arts **Academic program** English as a second language, advanced placement, accelerated degree program, self-designed majors, honors program, summer session, adult/continuing education programs, internships **Contact** Ms. Michelle Lockhart, Associate Director, Undergraduate Admissions, Oklahoma City University, 2501 North Blackwelder, Oklahoma City, OK 73106. Phone: 405-208-5600 or toll-free 800-633-7242. Fax: 405-208-5916. E-mail: mlockhart@okcu.edu. Web site: http://www.okcu.edu/.

OKLAHOMA PANHANDLE STATE UNIVERSITY
GOODWELL, OKLAHOMA

General State-supported, 4-year, coed **Entrance** Noncompetitive **Setting** 40-acre rural campus **Total enrollment** 1,152 **Student-faculty ratio** 14:1 **Application deadline** Rolling (freshmen), rolling (transfer) **Freshmen** 96% were admitted **Housing** Yes **Expenses** Tuition $3820; Room & Board $3300 **Undergraduates** 51% women, 17% part-time, 23% 25 or older, 3% Native American, 13% Hispanic American, 7% African American, 1% Asian American/Pacific Islander **The most frequently chosen baccalaureate fields are** agriculture, education, psychology **Academic program** English as a second language, advanced placement, summer session, internships **Contact** Mr. Bobby Jenkins, Registrar and Director of Admissions, Oklahoma Panhandle State University, PO Box 430, 323 Eagle Boulevard, Goodwell, OK 73939-0430. Phone: 580-349-1376 or toll-free 800-664-6778. Fax: 580-349-1371. E-mail: opsu@opsu.edu. Web site: http://www.opsu.edu/.

OKLAHOMA STATE UNIVERSITY
STILLWATER, OKLAHOMA

General State-supported, university, coed **Entrance** Moderately difficult **Setting** 840-acre small-town campus **Total enrollment** 23,005 **Student-faculty ratio** 19:1 **Application deadline** Rolling (freshmen), rolling (transfer) **Freshmen** 88% were admitted **Housing** Yes **Expenses** Tuition $5491; Room & Board $6267 **Undergraduates** 49% women, 13% part-time, 13% 25 or older, 10% Native American, 2% Hispanic American, 4% African American, 2% Asian American/Pacific Islander **The most frequently chosen baccalaureate fields are** agriculture, business/marketing, education **Academic program** English as a second language, advanced placement, accelerated degree program, self-designed majors, honors program, summer session, adult/continuing education programs, internships **Contact** Karen Lucas, Director of Undergraduate Admissions, Oklahoma State University, 219 Student Union, Stillwater, OK 74078. Phone: 405-744-3087 or toll-free 800-233-5019 Ext. 1 (in-state); 800-852-1255 (out-of-state). Fax: 405-744-7092. E-mail: admissions@okstate.edu. Web site: http://osu.okstate.edu/.

OKLAHOMA WESLEYAN UNIVERSITY
BARTLESVILLE, OKLAHOMA

General Independent, comprehensive, coed, affiliated with Wesleyan Church **Entrance** Minimally difficult **Setting** 127-acre small-town campus **Total enrollment** 1,159 **Student-faculty ratio** 14:1 **Application deadline** Rolling (freshmen), rolling (transfer) **Freshmen** 48% were admitted **Housing** Yes **Expenses** Tuition $16,585; Room & Board $6050 **Undergraduates** 11% Native American, 2% Hispanic American, 5% African American, 0.5% Asian American/Pacific Islander **Academic program** English as a second language, advanced placement, accelerated degree program, self-designed majors, summer session, adult/ continuing education programs, internships **Contact** Mark Molder, Assistant Director of Enrollment Services, Oklahoma Wesleyan University, 2201 Silver Lake Drive, Bartlesville, OK 74006. Phone: 866-222-8226 or toll-free 866-222-8226. Fax: 918-335-6229. E-mail: admissions@okwu.edu. Web site: http://www.okwu.edu/.

ORAL ROBERTS UNIVERSITY
TULSA, OKLAHOMA

General Independent interdenominational, comprehensive, coed **Entrance** Moderately difficult **Setting** 263-acre urban campus **Total enrollment** 3,170 **Student-faculty ratio** 13:1 **Application deadline** Rolling (freshmen), rolling (transfer) **Freshmen** 75% were admitted **Housing** Yes **Expenses** Tuition $17,400; Room & Board $7350 **Undergraduates** 59% women, 9% part-time, 11% 25 or older, 2% Native American, 6% Hispanic American, 17% African American, 2% Asian American/Pacific Islander **The most frequently chosen baccalaureate fields are** business/marketing, communications/journalism, theology and religious vocations **Academic program** English as a second language, advanced placement, self-designed majors, honors program, summer session, adult/continuing education programs, internships **Contact** Chris Belcher, Director of Admissions, Oral Roberts University, 7777 South Lewis Avenue, Tulsa, OK 74171-0001. Phone: 918-495-6529 or toll-free 800-678-8876. Fax: 918-495-6222. E-mail: cbelcher@oru.edu. Web site: http://www.oru.edu/.

ROGERS STATE UNIVERSITY
CLAREMORE, OKLAHOMA

General State-supported, 4-year, coed **Entrance** Noncompetitive **Setting** 40-acre small-town campus **Total enrollment** 3,855 **Student-faculty ratio** 20:1 **Application deadline** Rolling (freshmen), rolling (transfer) **Freshmen** 64% were admitted **Housing** Yes **Expenses** Tuition $4966; Room & Board $6615 **Undergraduates** 64% women, 42% part-time, 35% 25 or older, 28% Native American, 3% Hispanic American, 3% African American, 1% Asian American/Pacific Islander **The most frequently chosen baccalaureate fields are** business/marketing, engineering technologies, social sciences **Academic program** Advanced placement, honors program, summer session, adult/continuing education programs, internships **Contact** Ms. Lindsay Fields, Director of Enrollment Management, Rogers State University, 1701 W. Will Rogers Blvd., Claremore, OK 74017. Phone: 918-343-7545 or toll-free 800-256-7511. Fax: 918-343-7595. E-mail: info@rsu.edu. Web site: http://www.rsu.edu/.

ST. GREGORY'S UNIVERSITY
SHAWNEE, OKLAHOMA

General Independent Roman Catholic, 4-year, coed **Entrance** Minimally difficult **Setting** 640-acre small-town campus **Total enrollment** 799 **Student-faculty ratio** 10:1 **Application deadline** Rolling (freshmen), rolling (transfer) **Freshmen** 72% were admitted **Housing** Yes **Expenses** Tuition $15,560; Room & Board $5994 **Undergraduates** 63% women, 47% part-time, 57% 25 or older, 8% Native American, 7% Hispanic American, 7% African American, 0.4% Asian American/Pacific Islander **The most frequently chosen baccalaureate fields are** business/marketing, parks and recreation, social sciences **Academic program** English as a second language, advanced placement, accelerated degree program, self-designed majors, honors program, summer session, adult/continuing education programs, internships **Contact** Mr. Bill Halbach, Director of Admissions, St. Gregory's University, 1900 West MacArthur Drive, Shawnee, OK 74804. Phone: 405-878-5447 or toll-free 888-STGREGS. Fax: 405-878-5198. E-mail: admissions@stgregorys.edu. Web site: http://www.stgregorys.edu/.

SOUTHEASTERN OKLAHOMA STATE UNIVERSITY
DURANT, OKLAHOMA

General State-supported, comprehensive, coed **Entrance** Moderately difficult **Setting** 177-acre small-town campus **Total enrollment** 4,002 **Student-faculty ratio** 19:1 **Application deadline** Rolling (freshmen), rolling (transfer) **Freshmen** 72% were admitted **Housing** Yes **Expenses** Tuition $3926; Room & Board $4284 **Undergraduates** 56% women, 22% part-time, 24% 25 or older, 30% Native American, 3% Hispanic American, 6% African American, 1% Asian American/Pacific Islander **The most frequently chosen baccalaureate fields are** education, engineering technologies, liberal arts/general studies **Academic program** Advanced placement, accelerated degree program, honors program, summer session, adult/continuing education programs, internships **Contact** Ms. Kristie Luke, Associate Dean of Admissions and Records/Registrar, Southeastern Oklahoma State University, 1405 North 4th Avenue, Durant, OK 74701-0609. Phone: 580-745-2060 or toll-free 800-435-1327. Fax: 580-745-7502. E-mail: admissions@sosu.edu. Web site: http://www.sosu.edu/.

SOUTHERN NAZARENE UNIVERSITY
BETHANY, OKLAHOMA

General Independent Nazarene, comprehensive, coed **Entrance** Noncompetitive **Setting** 40-acre suburban campus **Total enrollment** 2,090 **Student-faculty ratio** 14:1 **Application deadline** 8/15 (freshmen), 8/15 (transfer) **Freshmen** 50% were admitted **Housing** Yes **Expenses** Tuition $17,224; Room & Board $5770 **Undergraduates** 49% women, 3% part-time, 31% 25 or older, 5% Native American, 4% Hispanic American, 10% African American, 2% Asian American/Pacific Islander **The most frequently**

Southern Nazarene University *(continued)*

chosen baccalaureate fields are business/marketing, family and consumer sciences, health professions and related sciences **Academic program** Advanced placement, accelerated degree program, self-designed majors, honors program, summer session, adult/continuing education programs, internships **Contact** Mr. Warren W. Rogers III, Director of Admissions, Southern Nazarene University, 6729 Northwest 39th Expressway, Bethany, OK 73008. Phone: 405-491-6324 or toll-free 800-648-9899. Fax: 405-491-6320. E-mail: admiss@snu.edu. Web site: http://www.snu.edu/.

SOUTHWESTERN CHRISTIAN UNIVERSITY
BETHANY, OKLAHOMA

Contact Megan Miles, Director of Admissions, Southwestern Christian University, PO Box 340, Bethany, OK 73008-0340. Phone: 405-789-7661 Ext. 3442. Fax: 405-495-0078. E-mail: admissions@swcu.edu. Web site: http://www.swcu.edu/.

SOUTHWESTERN OKLAHOMA STATE UNIVERSITY
WEATHERFORD, OKLAHOMA

General State-supported, comprehensive, coed **Entrance** Minimally difficult **Setting** 73-acre small-town campus **Total enrollment** 5,017 **Student-faculty ratio** 20:1 **Application deadline** Rolling (freshmen), rolling (transfer) **Freshmen** 90% were admitted **Housing** Yes **Expenses** Tuition $3750; Room & Board $3800 **Undergraduates** 59% women, 15% part-time, 18% 25 or older, 7% Native American, 5% Hispanic American, 5% African American, 1% Asian American/Pacific Islander **The most frequently chosen baccalaureate fields are** business/marketing, education, health professions and related sciences **Academic program** Advanced placement, accelerated degree program, self-designed majors, summer session, adult/continuing education programs, internships **Contact** Ms. Connie Phillips, Admission Counselor, Southwestern Oklahoma State University, 100 Campus Drive, Weatherford, OK 73096-3098. Phone: 580-774-3009. Fax: 580-774-3795. E-mail: ropers@swosu.edu. Web site: http://www.swosu.edu/.

UNIVERSITY OF CENTRAL OKLAHOMA
EDMOND, OKLAHOMA

General State-supported, comprehensive, coed **Entrance** Minimally difficult **Setting** 200-acre suburban campus **Total enrollment** 15,753 **Student-faculty ratio** 22:1 **Application deadline** Rolling (freshmen), rolling (transfer) **Freshmen** 72% were admitted **Housing** Yes **Expenses** Tuition $3857; Room & Board $6380 **Undergraduates** 58% women, 30% part-time, 26% 25 or older, 5% Native American, 4% Hispanic American, 10% African American, 3% Asian American/Pacific Islander **The most frequently chosen baccalaureate fields are** business/marketing, education, liberal arts/general studies **Academic program** English as a second language, advanced placement, accelerated degree program, honors program, summer session, adult/continuing education programs, internships **Contact** Ms. Linda Lofton, Director, Admissions and Records Processing, University of Central Oklahoma, Office of Enrollment Services, 100 North University Drive, Box 151, Edmond, OK 73034-5209. Phone: 405-974-2338 Ext. 2338 or toll-free 800-254-4215. Fax: 405-341-4964. E-mail: admituco@ucok.edu. Web site: http://www.ucok.edu/.

UNIVERSITY OF OKLAHOMA
NORMAN, OKLAHOMA

General State-supported, university, coed **Entrance** Moderately difficult **Setting** 3,762-acre suburban campus **Total enrollment** 26,205 **Student-faculty ratio** 19:1 **Application deadline** 4/1 (freshmen), 4/1 (transfer) **Freshmen** 89% were admitted **Housing** Yes **Expenses** Tuition $4534; Room & Board $7058 **Undergraduates** 49% women, 14% part-time, 12% 25 or older, 8% Native American, 4% Hispanic American, 6% African American, 6% Asian American/Pacific Islander **The most frequently chosen baccalaureate fields are** business/marketing, communications/journalism, social sciences **Academic program** English as a second language, advanced placement, accelerated degree program, self-designed majors, honors program, summer session, adult/continuing education programs, internships **Contact** Mr. Craig Hayes, Executive Director of Recruitment Services, University of Oklahoma, 550 Parrington Oval, L-1, Norman, OK 73019-3032. Phone: 405-325-2151 or toll-free 800-234-6868. Fax: 405-325-7478. E-mail: ou-pss@ou.edu. Web site: http://www.ou.edu/.

UNIVERSITY OF OKLAHOMA HEALTH SCIENCES CENTER
OKLAHOMA CITY, OKLAHOMA

General State-supported, upper-level, coed **Setting** 200-acre urban campus **Total enrollment** 3,736 **Student-faculty ratio** 8:1 **Application deadline** Rolling (transfer) **Housing** No **Expenses** Tuition $4765 **Undergraduates** 88% women, 10% part-time, 39% 25 or older, 9% Native American, 3% Hispanic American, 4%

African American, 7% Asian American/Pacific Islander **The most frequently chosen baccalaureate fields are** health professions and related sciences, interdisciplinary studies **Academic program** Advanced placement, honors program, summer session, internships **Contact** Mr. Heath Burge, Director of Admissions, University of Oklahoma Health Sciences Center, BSE-200, PO Box 26901, Oklahoma City, OK 73190-0901. Phone: 405-271-2359 Ext. 48902. Fax: 405-271-2480. E-mail: admissions@ouhsc.edu. Web site: http://www.ouhsc.edu/.

UNIVERSITY OF PHOENIX–OKLAHOMA CITY CAMPUS
OKLAHOMA CITY, OKLAHOMA

General Proprietary, comprehensive, coed **Contact** Ms. Evelyn Gaskin, Registrar/Executive Director, University of Phoenix–Oklahoma City Campus, 4615 East Elwood Street, Mail Stop AA-K101, Phoenix, AZ 85040-1958. Phone: 480-557-3301 or toll-free 800-776-4867 (in-state); 800-228-7240 (out-of-state). Fax: 480-643-1020. E-mail: evelyn.gaskin@phoenix.edu. Web site: http://www.phoenix.edu/.

UNIVERSITY OF PHOENIX–TULSA CAMPUS
TULSA, OKLAHOMA

General Proprietary, comprehensive, coed **Contact** Ms. Evelyn Gaskin, Registrar/Executive Director, University of Phoenix–Tulsa Campus, 4615 East Elwood Street, Mail Stop AA-K101, Phoenix, AZ 85040-1958. Phone: 480-557-3301 or toll-free 800-776-4867 (in-state); 800-228-7240 (out-of-state). Fax: 480-643-1020. E-mail: evelyn.gaskin@phoenix.edu. Web site: http://www.phoenix.edu/.

UNIVERSITY OF SCIENCE AND ARTS OF OKLAHOMA
CHICKASHA, OKLAHOMA

General State-supported, 4-year, coed **Entrance** Moderately difficult **Setting** 75-acre small-town campus **Total enrollment** 1,254 **Student-faculty ratio** 14:1 **Application deadline** 8/31 (freshmen), 8/31 (transfer) **Freshmen** 94% were admitted **Housing** Yes **Expenses** Tuition $4050; Room & Board $4540 **Undergraduates** 63% women, 23% part-time, 22% 25 or older, 13% Native American, 4% Hispanic American, 4% African American, 1% Asian American/Pacific Islander **The most frequently chosen baccalaureate fields are** business/marketing, education, psychology **Academic program** Advanced placement, accelerated degree program, self-designed majors, summer session, adult/continuing education programs, internships **Contact** Office of Admissions, University of Science and Arts of Oklahoma, 1727 West Alabama, Chickasha, OK 73018-5322. Phone: 405-574-1357 or toll-free 800-933-8726 Ext. 1212. Fax: 405-574-1220. E-mail: usao-admissions@usao.edu. Web site: http://www.usao.edu/.

UNIVERSITY OF TULSA
TULSA, OKLAHOMA

General Independent, university, coed, affiliated with Presbyterian Church (U.S.A.) **Entrance** Very difficult **Setting** 2,090-acre urban campus **Total enrollment** 4,165 **Student-faculty ratio** 10:1 **Application deadline** Rolling (freshmen), rolling (transfer) **Freshmen** 51% were admitted **Housing** Yes **Expenses** Tuition $21,780; Room & Board $7404 **Undergraduates** 48% women, 6% part-time, 7% 25 or older, 3% Native American, 4% Hispanic American, 6% African American, 3% Asian American/Pacific Islander **The most frequently chosen baccalaureate fields are** business/marketing, engineering, visual and performing arts **Academic program** English as a second language, advanced placement, accelerated degree program, self-designed majors, honors program, summer session, adult/continuing education programs, internships **Contact** Mr. Earl Johnson, Dean of Admission, University of Tulsa, 600 South College Avenue, Tulsa, OK 74104. Phone: 918-631-2307 or toll-free 800-331-3050. Fax: 918-631-5003. E-mail: admission@utulsa.edu. Web site: http://www.utulsa.edu/.

OREGON

THE ART INSTITUTE OF PORTLAND
PORTLAND, OREGON

General Proprietary, 4-year, coed **Setting** urban campus **Contact** Director of Admissions, The Art Institute of Portland, 1122 NW Davis Street, Portland, OR 97209. Phone: 503-228-6528 Ext. 4794 or toll-free 888-228-6528. Fax: 503-227-1945. E-mail: aipdadm@aii.edu. Web site: http://www.artinstitutes.edu/portland/.

BIRTHINGWAY COLLEGE OF MIDWIFERY
PORTLAND, OREGON

Contact Birthingway College of Midwifery, 12113 SE Foster Road, Portland, OR 97299. Web site: http://www.birthingway.edu/.

CASCADE COLLEGE
PORTLAND, OREGON

General Independent, 4-year, coed, affiliated with Church of Christ **Entrance** Noncompetitive **Setting** 13-acre urban campus **Total enrollment** 265 **Student-faculty ratio** 12:1 **Application deadline** Rolling (freshmen), rolling (transfer) **Freshmen** 60% were admitted **Housing** Yes **Expenses** Tuition $14,250; Room & Board $6700 **Undergraduates** 58% women, 2% part-time, 7% 25 or older, 1% Native American, 11% Hispanic American, 8% African American, 4% Asian American/Pacific Islander **The most frequently chosen baccalaureate fields are** business/marketing, interdisciplinary studies, psychology **Academic program** Advanced placement, accelerated degree program, summer session, internships **Contact** Ms. Carrie Rude, Office Manager, Cascade College, 9101 East Burnside, Portland, OR 97216-1515. Phone: 503-257-1202 or toll-free 800-550-7678. Fax: 503-257-1222. E-mail: cmrude@cascade.edu. Web site: http://www.cascade.edu/.

CONCORDIA UNIVERSITY
PORTLAND, OREGON

General Independent, comprehensive, coed, affiliated with Lutheran Church–Missouri Synod **Entrance** Moderately difficult **Setting** 13-acre urban campus **Total enrollment** 1,642 **Student-faculty ratio** 17:1 **Application deadline** Rolling (freshmen), rolling (transfer) **Freshmen** 65% were admitted **Housing** Yes **Expenses** Tuition $22,100; Room & Board $6400 **Undergraduates** 66% women, 16% part-time, 30% 25 or older, 1% Native American, 5% Hispanic American, 7% African American, 5% Asian American/Pacific Islander **The most frequently chosen baccalaureate fields are** business/marketing, education, psychology **Academic program** English as a second language, advanced placement, accelerated degree program, self-designed majors, summer session, adult/continuing education programs, internships **Contact** Ms. Bobi Swan, Dean of Admission, Concordia University, 2811 Northeast Holman, Portland, OR 97211-6099. Phone: 503-493-6526 or toll-free 800-321-9371. Fax: 503-280-8531. E-mail: admissions@cu-portland.edu. Web site: http://www.cu-portland.edu/.

CORBAN COLLEGE
SALEM, OREGON

General Independent religious, 4-year, coed **Contact** Ms. Heidi Stowman, Director of Admissions, Corban College, 5000 Deer Park Drive, SE, Salem, OR 97301-9392. Phone: 503-375-7115 or toll-free 800-845-3005. Fax: 503-585-4316. E-mail: admissions@corban.edu. Web site: http://www.corban.edu/.

DeVRY UNIVERSITY
PORTLAND, OREGON

General Proprietary, comprehensive, coed **Entrance** Minimally difficult **Total enrollment** 117 **Student-faculty ratio** 53:1 **Application deadline** Rolling (freshmen), rolling (transfer) **Housing** No **Expenses** Tuition $13,890 **Undergraduates** 45% women, 41% part-time, 61% 25 or older, 8% Hispanic American, 12% African American, 3% Asian American/Pacific Islander **The most frequently chosen baccalaureate field is** business/marketing **Academic program** Advanced placement, accelerated degree program, summer session, adult/continuing education programs **Contact** Admissions Office, DeVry University, Peterkort Center II, 9755 SW Barnes Road, Suite 150, Portland, OR 97225-6651. Web site: http://www.devry.edu/.

EASTERN OREGON UNIVERSITY
LA GRANDE, OREGON

General State-supported, comprehensive, coed **Contact** Mr. Jaime Contraras, Director, Admissions, Eastern Oregon University, 1 University Boulevard, La Grande, OR 97850-2899. Phone: 541-962-3393 or toll-free 800-452-8639 (in-state); 800-452-3393 (out-of-state). Fax: 541-962-3418. E-mail: admissions@eou.edu. Web site: http://www.eou.edu/.

EUGENE BIBLE COLLEGE
EUGENE, OREGON

General Independent, 4-year, coed, affiliated with Open Bible Standard Churches **Entrance** Minimally difficult **Setting** 40-acre suburban campus **Total enrollment** 222 **Student-faculty ratio** 10:1 **Application deadline** 9/1 (freshmen), 9/1 (transfer) **Freshmen** 46% were admitted **Housing** Yes **Undergraduates** 44% women, 32% part-time, 25% 25 or older **The most frequently chosen baccalaureate field is** theology and religious vocations **Academic program** Advanced placement, summer session, internships **Contact** Scott Thomas, Director of Admissions, Eugene Bible College, 2155 Bailey Hill Road, Eugene, OR 97405. Phone: 541-485-1780 Ext. 3106 or toll-free 800-322-2638. Fax: 541-343-5801. E-mail: scottthomas@ebc.edu. Web site: http://www.ebc.edu/.

GEORGE FOX UNIVERSITY
NEWBERG, OREGON

General Independent Friends, university, coed **Entrance** Moderately difficult **Setting** 85-acre small-town campus **Total enrollment** 3,293 **Student-faculty ratio** 11:1 **Application deadline** 2/1 (freshmen), 6/1 (transfer) **Freshmen** 83% were admitted **Housing** Yes **Expenses** Tuition $23,790; Room & Board $7600 **Undergraduates** 63% women, 13% part-time, 14% 25 or older, 2% Native American, 4% Hispanic American, 1% African American, 5% Asian American/Pacific Islander **The most frequently chosen baccalaureate fields are** business/marketing, interdisciplinary studies, visual and performing arts **Academic program** English as a second language, advanced placement, accelerated degree program, self-designed majors, honors program, summer session, adult/continuing education programs, internships **Contact** Mr. Ryan Dougherty, Director of Undergraduate Admissions, George Fox University, 414 North Meridian Street, Newberg, OR 97132. Phone: 503-554-2240 or toll-free 800-765-4369. Fax: 503-554-3110. E-mail: admissions@georgefox.edu. Web site: http://www.georgefox.edu/.

GUTENBERG COLLEGE

EUGENE, OREGON

General Independent religious, 4-year, coed **Entrance** Moderately difficult **Setting** urban campus **Total enrollment** 51 **Student-faculty ratio** 6:1 **Application deadline** 3/1 (freshmen) **Freshmen** 76% were admitted **Housing** Yes **Expenses** Tuition $11,852; Room & Board $4725 **Undergraduates** 45% women, 10% 25 or older, 2% Hispanic American **The most frequently chosen baccalaureate field is** liberal arts/general studies **Contact** Mr. Terry Stollar, Director of Admissions and Development, Gutenberg College, 1883 University Street, Eugene, OR 97403. Phone: 541-736-9071. Fax: 541-683-6997. E-mail: tstollar@gutenberg.edu. Web site: http://www.gutenberg.edu/.

LEWIS & CLARK COLLEGE

PORTLAND, OREGON

General Independent, comprehensive, coed **Entrance** Very difficult **Setting** 137-acre suburban campus **Total enrollment** 3,562 **Student-faculty ratio** 12:1 **Application deadline** 2/1 (freshmen), 7/1 (transfer) **Freshmen** 56% were admitted **Housing** Yes **Expenses** Tuition $33,726; Room & Board $8820 **Undergraduates** 61% women, 1% part-time, 1% 25 or older, 1% Native American, 5% Hispanic American, 2% African American, 6% Asian American/Pacific Islander **The most frequently chosen baccalaureate fields are** psychology, social sciences, visual and performing arts **Academic program** English as a second language, advanced placement, accelerated degree program, self-designed majors, honors program, summer session, internships **Contact** Mr. Michael Sexton, Dean of Admissions, Lewis & Clark College, 0615 SW Palatine Hill Road, Portland, OR 97219-7899. Phone: 503-768-7040 or toll-free 800-444-4111. Fax: 503-768-7055. E-mail: admissions@lclark.edu. Web site: http://www.lclark.edu/.

LINFIELD COLLEGE

MCMINNVILLE, OREGON

General Independent American Baptist Churches in the USA, 4-year, coed **Entrance** Moderately difficult **Setting** 193-acre small-town campus **Total enrollment** 1,693 **Student-faculty ratio** 12:1 **Application deadline** 2/15 (freshmen), 4/15 (transfer) **Freshmen** 80% were admitted **Housing** Yes **Expenses** Tuition $25,644; Room & Board $7400 **Undergraduates** 54% women, 3% part-time, 2% 25 or older, 1% Native American, 4% Hispanic American, 2% African American, 8% Asian American/Pacific Islander **The most frequently chosen baccalaureate fields are** business/marketing, parks and recreation, social sciences **Academic program** English as a second language, advanced placement, self-designed majors, summer session, adult/continuing education programs, internships **Contact** Ms. Lisa Knodle-Bragiel, Director of Admission, Linfield College, 900 SE Baker Street, McMinnville, OR 97128. Phone: 503-883-2213 or toll-free 800-640-2287. Fax: 503-883-2472. E-mail: admission@linfield.edu. Web site: http://www.linfield.edu/.

MARYLHURST UNIVERSITY

MARYLHURST, OREGON

General Independent Roman Catholic, comprehensive, coed **Entrance** Noncompetitive **Setting** 73-acre suburban campus **Total enrollment** 1,433 **Application deadline** Rolling (freshmen), rolling (transfer) **Housing** No **Expenses** Tuition $15,570 **Undergraduates** 72% women, 77% part-time, 81% 25 or older, 0.1% Native American, 1% Hispanic American, 1% African American, 1% Asian American/Pacific Islander **The most frequently chosen baccalaureate fields are** business/marketing, interdisciplinary studies, visual and performing arts **Academic program** English as a second language, advanced placement, accelerated degree program, self-designed majors, summer session, adult/continuing education programs, internships **Contact** Admissions, Marylhurst University, 17600 Pacific Highway (Highway 43), PO Box 261, Marylhurst, OR 97036. Phone: 503-636-8141 or toll-free 800-634-9982. Fax: 503-635-6585. E-mail: admissions@marylhurst.edu. Web site: http://www.marylhurst.edu/.

MOUNT ANGEL SEMINARY
SAINT BENEDICT, OREGON

Contact Registrar/Admissions Officer, Mount Angel Seminary, Saint Benedict, OR 97373. Phone: 503-845-3951 Ext. 14. Web site: http://www.mtangel.edu/seminary/index.html.

MULTNOMAH BIBLE COLLEGE AND BIBLICAL SEMINARY
PORTLAND, OREGON

General Independent interdenominational, comprehensive, coed **Entrance** Moderately difficult **Setting** 22-acre urban campus **Total enrollment** 819 **Student-faculty ratio** 16:1 **Application deadline** 7/15 (freshmen), 7/15 (transfer) **Freshmen** 81% were admitted **Housing** Yes **Expenses** Tuition $13,480; Room & Board $5600 **Undergraduates** 45% women, 8% part-time, 17% 25 or older, 1% Native American, 2% Hispanic American, 1% African American, 4% Asian American/Pacific Islander **The most frequently chosen baccalaureate field is** theology and religious vocations **Academic program** Advanced placement, summer session, adult/continuing education programs, internships **Contact** Ms. Nancy Gerecz, Admissions Assistant, Multnomah Bible College and Biblical Seminary, 8435 Northeast Glisan Street, Portland, OR 97220-5898. Phone: 503-255-0332 Ext. 371 or toll-free 800-275-4672. Fax: 503-254-1268. E-mail: admiss@multnomah.edu. Web site: http://www.multnomah.edu/.

NORTHWEST CHRISTIAN COLLEGE
EUGENE, OREGON

General Independent Christian, comprehensive, coed **Entrance** Moderately difficult **Setting** 8-acre urban campus **Total enrollment** 485 **Student-faculty ratio** 8:1 **Application deadline** Rolling (freshmen), rolling (transfer) **Freshmen** 45% were admitted **Housing** Yes **Expenses** Tuition $21,481; Room & Board $6770 **Undergraduates** 59% women, 23% part-time, 3% 25 or older, 2% Native American, 2% Hispanic American, 2% African American, 3% Asian American/Pacific Islander **The most frequently chosen baccalaureate fields are** business/marketing, education, interdisciplinary studies **Academic program** English as a second language, advanced placement, accelerated degree program, self-designed majors, summer session, adult/continuing education programs, internships **Contact** Director of Admissions, Northwest Christian College, 828 East 11th Avenue, Eugene, OR 97401-3745. Phone: 541-684-7201 or toll-free 877-463-6622. Fax: 541-684-7317. E-mail: admissions@nwcc.edu. Web site: http://www.nwcc.edu/.

OREGON COLLEGE OF ART & CRAFT
PORTLAND, OREGON

General Independent, 4-year, coed **Contact** Ms. Debrah Spencer, Interim Director of Admissions, Oregon College of Art & Craft, 8245 Southwest Barnes Road, Portland, OR 97225-6349. Phone: 503-297-5544 Ext. 129 or toll-free 800-390-0632 Ext. 129. Fax: 503-297-9651. E-mail: admissions@ocac.edu. Web site: http://www.ocac.edu/.

OREGON HEALTH & SCIENCE UNIVERSITY
PORTLAND, OREGON

General State-related, upper-level, coed **Contact** Jennifer Anderson, Registrar and Director of Financial Aid, Oregon Health & Science University, 3181 Southwest Sam Jackson Park Road, Mail Code: 337A/SNADM, Portland, OR 97201-3098. Phone: 503-494-7800. Fax: 503-494-4350. E-mail: andersje@ohsu.edu. Web site: http://www.ohsu.edu/.

OREGON INSTITUTE OF TECHNOLOGY
KLAMATH FALLS, OREGON

General State-supported, 4-year, coed **Entrance** Moderately difficult **Setting** 173-acre small-town campus **Total enrollment** 3,146 **Student-faculty ratio** 14:1 **Application deadline** 10/1 (freshmen), 2/1 (transfer) **Freshmen** 88% were admitted **Housing** Yes **Expenses** Tuition $7140; Room & Board $7452 **Undergraduates** 49% women, 42% part-time, 38% 25 or older, 2% Native American, 4% Hispanic American, 1% African American, 5% Asian American/Pacific Islander **Academic program** Advanced placement, summer session, internships **Contact** Mr. John Duarte, Director of Admissions, Oregon Institute of Technology, 3201 Campus Drive, Klamath Falls, OR 97601-8801. Phone: 541-885-1150 or toll-free 800-422-2017 (in-state); 800-343-6653 (out-of-state). Fax: 541-885-1115. E-mail: oit@oit.edu. Web site: http://www.oit.edu/.

OREGON STATE UNIVERSITY
CORVALLIS, OREGON

General State-supported, university, coed **Entrance** Moderately difficult **Setting** 422-acre small-town campus **Total enrollment** 19,753 **Application deadline** 9/1 (freshmen), 5/1 (transfer) **Freshmen** 86% were admitted **Housing** Yes **Expenses** Tuition $5911; Room & Board $7566 **Undergraduates** 47% women, 14% part-time, 11% 25 or older, 1% Native American, 4% Hispanic American, 2% African American, 9% Asian American/Pacific Islander **The most frequently chosen baccalaureate fields are** business/marketing, engineering, family and consumer sciences **Academic program** English as a second language, advanced placement, accelerated degree program, self-designed majors, honors program, summer session, internships **Contact** Ms. Michele Sandlin, Director of Admissions, Oregon State University, Corvallis, OR 97331. Phone: 541-737-4411 or toll-free 800-291-4192. E-mail: osuadmit@orst.edu. Web site: http://oregonstate.edu/.

►**For more information, see page 479.**

OREGON STATE UNIVERSITY–CASCADES
BEND, OREGON

Contact Oregon State University–Cascades, 2600 NW College Way, Bend, OR 97701. Web site: http://www.osucascades.edu.

PACIFIC NORTHWEST COLLEGE OF ART
PORTLAND, OREGON

General Independent, 4-year, coed **Entrance** Moderately difficult **Setting** 2-acre urban campus **Total enrollment** 432 **Student-faculty ratio** 11:1 **Freshmen** 59% were admitted **Housing** Yes **Expenses** Tuition $23,722; Room & Board $7550 **Undergraduates** 63% women, 10% part-time, 29% 25 or older, 1% Native American, 5% Hispanic American, 1% African American, 4% Asian American/Pacific Islander **Academic program** Advanced placement, self-designed majors, adult/continuing education programs, internships **Contact** Mr. Chris Sweet Jr., Director of Admissions, Pacific Northwest College of Art, 1241 NW Johnson Street, Portland, OR 97209. Phone: 503-821-8972. Fax: 503-821-8978. E-mail: admissions@pnca.edu. Web site: http://www.pnca.edu/.

PACIFIC UNIVERSITY
FOREST GROVE, OREGON

General Independent, comprehensive, coed **Entrance** Moderately difficult **Setting** 60-acre small-town campus **Total enrollment** 2,976 **Student-faculty ratio** 12:1 **Application deadline** 8/15 (freshmen), rolling (transfer) **Freshmen** 83% were admitted **Housing** Yes **Expenses** Tuition $26,670; Room & Board $7170 **Undergraduates** 63% women, 5% part-time, 10% 25 or older, 1% Native American, 4% Hispanic American, 1% African American, 24% Asian American/Pacific Islander **The most frequently chosen baccalaureate fields are** parks and recreation, business/marketing, social sciences **Academic program** English as a second language, advanced placement, summer session, internships **Contact** Ms. Karen Dunston, Director of Undergraduate Admission, Pacific University, 2043 College Way, Forest Grove, OR 97116-1797. Phone: 503-352-2218 or toll-free 877-722-8648. Fax: 503-352-2975. E-mail: admissions@pacificu.edu. Web site: http://www.pacificu.edu/.

PIONEER PACIFIC COLLEGE–EUGENE/SPRINGFIELD BRANCH
SPRINGFIELD, OREGON

Contact Pioneer Pacific College–Eugene/Springfield Branch, 3800 Sports Way, Springfield, OR 97477. Web site: http://www.pioneerpacificcollege.com/.

PORTLAND STATE UNIVERSITY
PORTLAND, OREGON

General State-supported, university, coed **Entrance** Moderately difficult **Setting** 49-acre urban campus **Total enrollment** 24,963 **Student-faculty ratio** 19:1 **Application deadline** Rolling (freshmen), rolling (transfer) **Freshmen** 91% were admitted **Housing** Yes **Expenses** Tuition $5765; Room & Board $9207 **Undergraduates** 54% women, 39% part-time, 36% 25 or older, 1% Native American, 5% Hispanic American, 4% African American, 10% Asian American/Pacific Islander **The most frequently chosen baccalaureate fields are** business/marketing, liberal arts/general studies, social sciences **Academic program** English as a second language, advanced placement, accelerated degree program, honors program, summer session, adult/continuing education programs, internships **Contact** Ms. Agnes A. Hoffman, Associate Vice Provost for Enrollment Management & Student Affairs, Portland State University, PO Box 751, Portland, OR 97207-0751. Phone: 503-725-5502 or toll-free 800-547-8887. Fax: 503-725-5525. E-mail: admissions@pdx.edu. Web site: http://www.pdx.edu/.

REED COLLEGE
PORTLAND, OREGON

General Independent, comprehensive, coed **Entrance** Most difficult **Setting** 110-acre urban campus **Total enrollment** 1,492 **Student-faculty ratio** 10:1 **Application deadline** 1/15 (freshmen), 3/1 (transfer) **Freshmen** 34% were admitted **Housing** Yes **Expenses** Tuition $36,420; Room & Board $9460 **Undergraduates** 55% women, 3% part-time, 2% 25 or older, 1% Native American, 6% Hispanic American, 3% African American, 8% Asian American/Pacific Islander **The most frequently chosen baccalaureate fields are** philosophy and religious studies, biological/life sciences, social sciences **Academic program** Advanced placement, internships **Contact** Mr. Paul Marthers, Dean of Admission, Reed College, 3203 Southeast Woodstock Boulevard, Portland, OR 97202-8199. Phone: 503-777-

Reed College *(continued)*

7511 or toll-free 800-547-4750. Fax: 503-777-7553. E-mail: admission@reed.edu. Web site: http://www.reed.edu/.

SOUTHERN OREGON UNIVERSITY
ASHLAND, OREGON

General State-supported, comprehensive, coed **Entrance** Moderately difficult **Setting** 175-acre small-town campus **Total enrollment** 4,801 **Student-faculty ratio** 22:1 **Application deadline** Rolling (freshmen), rolling (transfer) **Freshmen** 83% were admitted **Housing** Yes **Expenses** Tuition $5409; Room & Board $7941 **Undergraduates** 57% women, 25% part-time, 21% 25 or older, 2% Native American, 4% Hispanic American, 2% African American, 4% Asian American/Pacific Islander **The most frequently chosen baccalaureate fields are** business/marketing, communications/journalism, social sciences **Academic program** English as a second language, advanced placement, accelerated degree program, self-designed majors, honors program, summer session, adult/continuing education programs, internships **Contact** Mr. Mark Bottorff, Director of Admissions, Southern Oregon University, 1250 Siskiyou Boulevard, Ashland, OR 97520. Phone: 541-552-6411 or toll-free 800-482-7672. Fax: 541-552-6614. E-mail: admissions@sou.edu. Web site: http://www.sou.edu/.

UNIVERSITY OF OREGON
EUGENE, OREGON

General State-supported, university, coed **Entrance** Moderately difficult **Setting** 295-acre urban campus **Total enrollment** 20,332 **Student-faculty ratio** 18:1 **Application deadline** 1/15 (freshmen), 5/15 (transfer) **Freshmen** 87% were admitted **Housing** Yes **Expenses** Tuition $6036; Room & Board $7849 **Undergraduates** 52% women, 10% part-time, 10% 25 or older, 1% Native American, 4% Hispanic American, 2% African American, 6% Asian American/Pacific Islander **The most frequently chosen baccalaureate fields are** business/marketing, communications/journalism, social sciences **Academic program** English as a second language, advanced placement, accelerated degree program, self-designed majors, honors program, summer session, adult/continuing education programs, internships **Contact** Brian Henley, Interim Director of Admissions, University of Oregon, Eugene, OR 97403. Phone: 541-346-3201 or toll-free 800-232-3825. Fax: 541-346-5815. E-mail: uoadmit@uoregon.edu. Web site: http://www.uoregon.edu/.

UNIVERSITY OF PHOENIX–OREGON CAMPUS
TIGARD, OREGON

General Proprietary, comprehensive, coed **Contact** Ms. Evelyn Gaskin, Registrar/Executive Director, University of Phoenix–Oregon Campus, 4615 East Elwood Street, Mail Stop AA-K101, Phoenix, AZ 85040-1958. Phone: 480-557-3301 or toll-free 800-776-4867 (in-state); 800-228-7240 (out-of-state). Fax: 480-643-1020. E-mail: evelyn.gaskin@phoenix.edu. Web site: http://www.phoenix.edu/.

UNIVERSITY OF PORTLAND
PORTLAND, OREGON

General Independent Roman Catholic, comprehensive, coed **Entrance** Moderately difficult **Setting** 125-acre urban campus **Total enrollment** 3,667 **Student-faculty ratio** 13:1 **Application deadline** 6/1 (freshmen), 6/1 (transfer) **Freshmen** 59% were admitted **Housing** Yes **Expenses** Tuition $28,854; Room & Board $8300 **Undergraduates** 62% women, 3% part-time, 3% 25 or older, 1% Native American, 4% Hispanic American, 1% African American, 10% Asian American/Pacific Islander **The most frequently chosen baccalaureate fields are** business/marketing, biological/life sciences, health professions and related sciences **Academic program** Advanced placement, honors program, summer session, adult/continuing education programs, internships **Contact** Mr. Jason McDonald, Dean of Admissions, University of Portland, 5000 North Willamette Boulevard, Portland, OR 97203-5798. Phone: 503-943-7147 or toll-free 888-627-5601. Fax: 503-943-7315. E-mail: admissions@up.edu. Web site: http://www.up.edu/.

WARNER PACIFIC COLLEGE
PORTLAND, OREGON

General Independent, comprehensive, coed, affiliated with Church of God **Entrance** Moderately difficult **Setting** 15-acre urban campus **Total enrollment** 797 **Student-faculty ratio** 14:1 **Application deadline** Rolling (freshmen), rolling (transfer) **Freshmen** 48% were admitted **Housing** Yes **Expenses** Tuition $23,717; Room & Board $6028 **Undergraduates** 0.3% Native American, 5% Hispanic American, 5% African American, 3% Asian American/Pacific Islander **Academic program** Advanced placement, accelerated degree program, self-designed majors, honors program, summer session, adult/continuing education programs, internships **Contact** Mrs. Shannon Mackey, Executive Director of Enrollment Management, Warner Pacific College, 2219 Southeast 68th Avenue, Portland, OR 97215. Phone: 503-517-1020 or toll-free 800-582-7885 (in-state);

800-804-1510 (out-of-state). Fax: 503-517-1352. E-mail: admiss@warnerpacific.edu. Web site: http://www.warnerpacific.edu/.

WESTERN OREGON UNIVERSITY

MONMOUTH, OREGON

General State-supported, comprehensive, coed **Entrance** Moderately difficult **Setting** 157-acre rural campus **Total enrollment** 5,009 **Student-faculty ratio** 19:1 **Application deadline** Rolling (freshmen), rolling (transfer) **Freshmen** 73% were admitted **Housing** Yes **Expenses** Tuition $6275; Room & Board $7600 **Undergraduates** 58% women, 13% part-time, 15% 25 or older, 3% Native American, 8% Hispanic American, 2% African American, 6% Asian American/Pacific Islander **The most frequently chosen baccalaureate fields are** business/marketing, education, interdisciplinary studies **Academic program** English as a second language, advanced placement, self-designed majors, honors program, summer session, adult/continuing education programs, internships **Contact** Mr. Rob Findtner, Assistant Director of Admissions, Western Oregon University, 345 North Monmouth Avenue, Monmouth, OR 97361. Phone: 503-838-8211 or toll-free 877-877-1593. Fax: 503-838-8067. E-mail: wolfgram@wou.edu. Web site: http://www.wou.edu/.

WILLAMETTE UNIVERSITY

SALEM, OREGON

General Independent United Methodist, comprehensive, coed **Entrance** Very difficult **Setting** 72-acre urban campus **Total enrollment** 2,720 **Student-faculty ratio** 11:1 **Application deadline** 2/1 (freshmen), 2/1 (transfer) **Freshmen** 77% were admitted **Housing** Yes **Expenses** Tuition $31,968; Room & Board $7570 **Undergraduates** 55% women, 6% part-time, 2% 25 or older, 0.5% Native American, 3% Hispanic American, 1% African American, 5% Asian American/Pacific Islander **The most frequently chosen baccalaureate fields are** English, business/marketing, social sciences **Academic program** Advanced placement, accelerated degree program, self-designed majors, internships **Contact** Dr. Robin Brown, Vice President for Enrollment, Willamette University, 900 State Street, Salem, OR 97301. Phone: 503-370-6303 or toll-free 877-542-2787. Fax: 503-375-5363. E-mail: libarts@williamette.edu. Web site: http://www.willamette.edu/.

PENNSYLVANIA

ALBRIGHT COLLEGE

READING, PENNSYLVANIA

General Independent, comprehensive, coed, affiliated with United Methodist Church **Entrance** Moderately difficult **Setting** 118-acre suburban campus **Total enrollment** 2,233 **Student-faculty ratio** 13:1 **Application deadline** Rolling (freshmen), rolling (transfer) **Freshmen** 77% were admitted **Housing** Yes **Expenses** Tuition $28,884; Room & Board $8484 **Undergraduates** 59% women, 2% part-time, 1% 25 or older, 0.4% Native American, 5% Hispanic American, 8% African American, 2% Asian American/Pacific Islander **The most frequently chosen baccalaureate fields are** business/marketing, psychology, social sciences **Academic program** English as a second language, advanced placement, accelerated degree program, self-designed majors, honors program, summer session, internships **Contact** Mr. Gregory Eichhorn, Vice President for Enrollment Management, Albright College, PO Box 15234, 13th and Bern Streets, Reading, PA 19612-5234. Phone: 610-921-7260 or toll-free 800-252-1856. Fax: 610-921-7294. E-mail: admission@albright.edu. Web site: http://www.albright.edu/.

ALLEGHENY COLLEGE

MEADVILLE, PENNSYLVANIA

General Independent, 4-year, coed **Entrance** Very difficult **Setting** 259-acre small-town campus **Total enrollment** 2,193 **Student-faculty ratio** 14:1 **Application deadline** 2/15 (freshmen), 7/1 (transfer) **Freshmen** 57% were admitted **Housing** Yes **Expenses** Tuition $32,000; Room & Board $8000 **Undergraduates** 56% women, 2% part-time, 1% 25 or older, 0.2% Native American, 2% Hispanic American, 2% African American, 3% Asian American/Pacific Islander **The most frequently chosen baccalaureate fields are** psychology, biological/life sciences, social sciences **Academic program** English as a second language, advanced placement, self-designed majors, internships **Contact** Ms. Jennifer Winge, Director of Admissions, Allegheny College, 520 North Main Street, Box 5, Meadville, PA 16335. Phone: 814-332-4351 or toll-free 800-521-5293. Fax: 814-337-0431. E-mail: admissions@allegheny.edu. Web site: http://www.allegheny.edu/.

ALVERNIA COLLEGE

READING, PENNSYLVANIA

General Independent Roman Catholic, comprehensive, coed **Entrance** Moderately difficult **Setting** 85-acre suburban campus **Total enroll-**

Alvernia College *(continued)*

ment 2,761 **Student-faculty ratio** 14:1 **Application deadline** Rolling (freshmen), rolling (transfer) **Freshmen** 76% were admitted **Housing** Yes **Expenses** Tuition $21,614; Room & Board $8530 **Undergraduates** 69% women, 22% part-time, 34% 25 or older, 1% Native American, 6% Hispanic American, 11% African American, 1% Asian American/Pacific Islander **The most frequently chosen baccalaureate fields are** health professions and related sciences, business/marketing, security and protective services **Academic program** Advanced placement, accelerated degree program, honors program, summer session, adult/continuing education programs, internships **Contact** Mr. Jeff Dittman, Vice President for Enrollment Management, Alvernia College, 400 Saint Bernardine Street, Reading, PA 19607-1799. Phone: 610-796-3005 or toll-free 888-ALVERNIA. Fax: 610-796-2873. E-mail: admissions@alvernia.edu. Web site: http://www.alvernia.edu/.

ARCADIA UNIVERSITY
GLENSIDE, PENNSYLVANIA

General Independent, comprehensive, coed, affiliated with Presbyterian Church (U.S.A.) **Entrance** Moderately difficult **Setting** 71-acre suburban campus **Total enrollment** 3,592 **Student-faculty ratio** 13:1 **Application deadline** 3/1 (freshmen), 6/15 (transfer) **Freshmen** 75% were admitted **Housing** Yes **Expenses** Tuition $29,700; Room & Board $10,280 **Undergraduates** 74% women, 8% part-time, 19% 25 or older, 0.1% Native American, 3% Hispanic American, 7% African American, 3% Asian American/Pacific Islander **The most frequently chosen baccalaureate fields are** business/marketing, education, visual and performing arts **Academic program** English as a second language, advanced placement, self-designed majors, honors program, summer session, adult/continuing education programs, internships **Contact** Mr. Mark Lapreziosa, Assistant Vice President of Enrollment Management, Arcadia University, 450 South Easton Road, Glenside, PA 19038. Phone: 215-572-2910 or toll-free 877-ARCADIA. Fax: 215-572-4049. E-mail: admiss@arcadia.edu. Web site: http://www.arcadia.edu/.

THE ART INSTITUTE OF PHILADELPHIA
PHILADELPHIA, PENNSYLVANIA

General Proprietary, 4-year, coed **Entrance** Moderately difficult **Setting** urban campus **Total enrollment** 3,749 **Student-faculty ratio** 22:1 **Application deadline** Rolling (freshmen), rolling (transfer) **Freshmen** 53% were admitted **Housing** Yes **Undergraduates** 58% women, 31% part-time, 20% 25 or older, 0.4% Native American, 4% Hispanic American, 16% African American, 4% Asian American/Pacific Islander **Academic program** Advanced placement, summer session, adult/continuing education programs, internships **Contact** Admissions Office, The Art Institute of Philadelphia, 1622 Chestnut Street, Philadelphia, PA 19103. Phone: 215-405-6777 or toll-free 800-275-2474. Fax: 215-405-6399. E-mail: aiphinfo@aii.edu. Web site: http://www.artinstitutes.edu/philadelphia/.

THE ART INSTITUTE OF PITTSBURGH
PITTSBURGH, PENNSYLVANIA

General Proprietary, 4-year, coed **Entrance** Minimally difficult **Setting** urban campus **Total enrollment** 10,975 **Student-faculty ratio** 20:1 **Application deadline** Rolling (freshmen), rolling (transfer) **Freshmen** 51% were admitted **Housing** Yes **Expenses** Tuition $20,405; Room & Board $6555 **Undergraduates** 62% women, 71% part-time, 36% 25 or older, 0.2% Native American, 1% Hispanic American, 2% African American, 0.3% Asian American/Pacific Islander **The most frequently chosen baccalaureate fields are** computer and information sciences, personal and culinary services, visual and performing arts **Academic program** English as a second language, advanced placement, summer session, adult/continuing education programs, internships **Contact** Mr. Jeffrey A. Bucklew, Director of Admissions, The Art Institute of Pittsburgh, 420 Boulevard of the Allies, Pittsburgh, PA 15219. Phone: 800-275-2470 or toll-free 800-275-2470. Fax: 412-263-6667. E-mail: admissions@aii.edu. Web site: http://www.artinstitutes.edu/pittsburgh/.

BAPTIST BIBLE COLLEGE OF PENNSYLVANIA
CLARKS SUMMIT, PENNSYLVANIA

General Independent Baptist, comprehensive, coed **Entrance** Minimally difficult **Setting** 124-acre suburban campus **Total enrollment** 872 **Student-faculty ratio** 16:1 **Application deadline** 8/15 (freshmen), rolling (transfer) **Freshmen** 76% were admitted **Housing** Yes **Expenses** Tuition $15,080; Room & Board $5600 **Undergraduates** 59% women, 6% part-time, 5% 25 or older, 0.1% Native American, 2% Hispanic American, 1% African American, 1% Asian American/Pacific Islander **The most frequently chosen baccalaureate fields are** education, psychology, theology and religious vocations **Academic program** Advanced placement, summer session, internships **Contact** Ms. Becki Scouten, Admissions Counselor, Baptist Bible College of Pennsylvania, 538 Venard Road, Clarks Summit, PA 18411-1297. Phone: 570-586-2400 Ext. 9291 or toll-free 800-451-7664. Fax:

570-585-9400. E-mail: bscouten@bbc.edu. Web site: http://www.bbc.edu/.

BLOOMSBURG UNIVERSITY OF PENNSYLVANIA
BLOOMSBURG, PENNSYLVANIA

General State-supported, comprehensive, coed **Entrance** Moderately difficult **Setting** 282-acre small-town campus **Total enrollment** 8,745 **Student-faculty ratio** 20:1 **Application deadline** Rolling (freshmen), rolling (transfer) **Freshmen** 61% were admitted **Housing** Yes **Expenses** Tuition $6623; Room & Board $6030 **Undergraduates** 59% women, 7% part-time, 6% 25 or older, 0.2% Native American, 2% Hispanic American, 7% African American, 1% Asian American/Pacific Islander **The most frequently chosen baccalaureate fields are** business/marketing, education, social sciences **Academic program** Advanced placement, honors program, summer session, adult/continuing education programs, internships **Contact** Mr. Christopher Keller, Director of Admissions, Bloomsburg University of Pennsylvania, 104 Student Services Center, Bloomsburg, PA 17815-1905. Phone: 570-389-4316. Fax: 570-389-4741. E-mail: buadmiss@bloomu.edu. Web site: http://www.bloomu.edu/.

BRYN ATHYN COLLEGE OF THE NEW CHURCH
BRYN ATHYN, PENNSYLVANIA

General Independent Swedenborgian, comprehensive, coed **Entrance** Minimally difficult **Setting** 130-acre suburban campus **Total enrollment** 139 **Student-faculty ratio** 5:1 **Application deadline** 7/1 (freshmen), 7/1 (transfer) **Freshmen** 97% were admitted **Housing** Yes **Expenses** Tuition $10,114; Room & Board $5574 **Undergraduates** 55% women, 3% part-time, 8% 25 or older, 2% African American, 3% Asian American/Pacific Islander **The most frequently chosen baccalaureate fields are** education, English, interdisciplinary studies **Academic program** English as a second language, advanced placement, accelerated degree program, self-designed majors, internships **Contact** Admissions Office, Bryn Athyn College of the New Church, Box 717, Bryn Athyn, PA 19009. Phone: 267-502-2593. Fax: 267-502-2658. E-mail: admissions@brynathyn.edu. Web site: http://www.brynathyn.edu/.

BRYN MAWR COLLEGE
BRYN MAWR, PENNSYLVANIA

General Independent, university, undergraduate: women only; graduate: coed **Entrance** Most difficult **Setting** 135-acre suburban campus **Total enrollment** 1,790 **Student-faculty ratio** 8:1 **Application deadline** 1/15 (freshmen), 3/15 (transfer) **Freshmen** 45% were admitted **Housing** Yes **Expenses** Tuition $34,650; Room & Board $11,024 **Undergraduates** 2% part-time, 4% 25 or older, 0.1% Native American, 3% Hispanic American, 6% African American, 12% Asian American/Pacific Islander **The most frequently chosen baccalaureate fields are** foreign languages and literature, English, social sciences **Academic program** Advanced placement, accelerated degree program, self-designed majors, summer session, adult/continuing education programs, internships **Contact** Ms. Jody Sanford Sweeney, Director of Admissions, Bryn Mawr College, 101 North Merion Avenue, Bryn Mawr, PA 19010. Phone: 610-526-5152 or toll-free 800-BMC-1885. Fax: 610-526-7471. E-mail: admissions@brynmawr.edu. Web site: http://www.brynmawr.edu/.

BUCKNELL UNIVERSITY
LEWISBURG, PENNSYLVANIA

General Independent, comprehensive, coed **Entrance** Most difficult **Setting** 445-acre small-town campus **Total enrollment** 3,677 **Student-faculty ratio** 11:1 **Application deadline** 1/15 (freshmen), 3/15 (transfer) **Freshmen** 30% were admitted **Housing** Yes **Expenses** Tuition $39,652; Room & Board $8728 **Undergraduates** 51% women, 1% part-time, 1% 25 or older, 0.5% Native American, 3% Hispanic American, 3% African American, 7% Asian American/Pacific Islander **The most frequently chosen baccalaureate fields are** engineering, business/marketing, social sciences **Academic program** Advanced placement, self-designed majors, honors program, summer session, internships **Contact** Mr. Kurt M. Thiede, Vice President, Enrollment Management and Dean of Admissions, Bucknell University, Lewisburg, PA 17837. Phone: 570-577-1101. Fax: 570-577-3538. E-mail: admissions@bucknell.edu. Web site: http://www.bucknell.edu/.

CABRINI COLLEGE
RADNOR, PENNSYLVANIA

General Independent Roman Catholic, comprehensive, coed **Entrance** Moderately difficult **Setting** 112-acre suburban campus **Total enrollment** 3,108 **Student-faculty ratio** 16:1 **Application deadline** Rolling (freshmen), rolling (transfer) **Freshmen** 75% were admitted **Housing** Yes **Expenses** Tuition $28,030; Room & Board $10,290 **Undergraduates** 65% women, 10% part-time, 9% 25 or older, 0.4% Native American, 3% Hispanic American, 6% African American, 2% Asian American/Pacific Islander **The most**

Cabrini College *(continued)*

frequently chosen baccalaureate fields are business/marketing, communications/journalism, education **Academic program** Advanced placement, accelerated degree program, self-designed majors, honors program, summer session, adult/continuing education programs, internships **Contact** Mr. Mark Osborn, Vice President for Enrollment Services, Cabrini College, 610 King of Prussia Road, Radnor, PA 19087-3698. Phone: 610-902-8552 or toll-free 800-848-1003. Fax: 610-902-8508. E-mail: admit@cabrini.edu. Web site: http://www.cabrini.edu/.

CALIFORNIA UNIVERSITY OF PENNSYLVANIA
CALIFORNIA, PENNSYLVANIA

General State-supported, comprehensive, coed **Contact** Mr. William Edmonds, Dean of Enrollment Management and Academic Services, California University of Pennsylvania, 250 University Avenue, California, PA 15419. Phone: 724-938-4404. Fax: 724-938-4564. E-mail: inquiry@cup.edu. Web site: http://www.cup.edu/.

CARLOW UNIVERSITY
PITTSBURGH, PENNSYLVANIA

General Independent Roman Catholic, comprehensive, coed, primarily women **Entrance** Moderately difficult **Setting** 14-acre urban campus **Total enrollment** 2,178 **Student-faculty ratio** 12:1 **Application deadline** 7/1 (freshmen), rolling (transfer) **Freshmen** 60% were admitted **Housing** Yes **Expenses** Tuition $19,514; Room & Board $7684 **Undergraduates** 94% women, 26% part-time, 34% 25 or older, 1% Native American, 1% Hispanic American, 16% African American, 1% Asian American/Pacific Islander **The most frequently chosen baccalaureate fields are** education, business/marketing, health professions and related sciences **Academic program** Advanced placement, accelerated degree program, self-designed majors, honors program, summer session, adult/continuing education programs, internships **Contact** Office of Admissions, Carlow University, 3333 Fifth Avenue, Pittsburgh, PA 15213. Phone: 412-578-6059 or toll-free 800-333-CARLOW. Fax: 412-578-6668. E-mail: admissions@carlow.edu. Web site: http://www.carlow.edu/.

CARNEGIE MELLON UNIVERSITY
PITTSBURGH, PENNSYLVANIA

General Independent, university, coed **Entrance** Most difficult **Setting** 144-acre urban campus **Total enrollment** 10,493 **Student-faculty ratio** 11:1 **Application deadline** 1/1 (freshmen), 3/1 (transfer) **Freshmen** 28% were admitted **Housing** Yes **Expenses** Tuition $39,564; Room & Board $10,050 **Undergraduates** 39% women, 3% part-time, 1% 25 or older, 0.4% Native American, 5% Hispanic American, 5% African American, 24% Asian American/Pacific Islander **The most frequently chosen baccalaureate fields are** business/marketing, engineering, visual and performing arts **Academic program** Advanced placement, self-designed majors, summer session, internships **Contact** Mr. Michael Steidel, Director of Admissions, Carnegie Mellon University, 5000 Forbes Avenue, Pittsburgh, PA 15213. Phone: 412-268-2082. Fax: 412-268-7838. E-mail: undergraduate-admissions@andrew.cmu.edu. Web site: http://www.cmu.edu/.

CEDAR CREST COLLEGE
ALLENTOWN, PENNSYLVANIA

General Independent, comprehensive, women only, affiliated with United Church of Christ **Entrance** Moderately difficult **Setting** 84-acre suburban campus **Total enrollment** 1,901 **Student-faculty ratio** 11:1 **Application deadline** Rolling (freshmen), rolling (transfer) **Freshmen** 62% were admitted **Housing** Yes **Expenses** Tuition $25,340; Room & Board $8624 **Undergraduates** 46% part-time, 43% 25 or older, 1% Native American, 7% Hispanic American, 6% African American, 2% Asian American/Pacific Islander **The most frequently chosen baccalaureate fields are** health professions and related sciences, business/marketing, psychology **Academic program** Advanced placement, accelerated degree program, self-designed majors, honors program, summer session, adult/continuing education programs, internships **Contact** Ms. Judith A. Neyhart, Vice President for Enrollment, Cedar Crest College, 100 College Drive, Allentown, PA 18104-6196. Phone: 610-740-3780 or toll-free 800-360-1222. Fax: 610-606-4647. E-mail: cccadmis@cedarcrest.edu. Web site: http://www.cedarcrest.edu/.

►**For more information, see page 448.**

CENTRAL PENNSYLVANIA COLLEGE
SUMMERDALE, PENNSYLVANIA

General Proprietary, 4-year, coed **Entrance** Minimally difficult **Setting** 35-acre small-town campus **Total enrollment** 1,103 **Student-faculty ratio** 16:1 **Application deadline** 9/20 (freshmen), 9/20 (transfer) **Freshmen** 41% were admitted **Housing** Yes **Expenses** Tuition $13,275; Room & Board $6015 **Undergraduates** 67% women, 35% part-time, 38% 25 or older, 1% Native American, 5% Hispanic American, 20% African American, 1% Asian American/Pacific Islander **The most frequently chosen baccalaureate fields are** business/marketing, computer and information sciences, security and protective services **Academic program** Advanced placement, honors program, summer session, adult/continuing education programs, internships **Contact** Ms. Katie Borrelli, Director of Admissions, Central Pennsylvania College, Campus on College Hill and Valley Roads, Summerdale, PA 17093. Phone: 717-728-2213 or toll-free 800-759-2727 Ext. 2201. Fax: 717-732-5254. E-mail: admissions@centralpenn.edu. Web site: http://www.centralpenn.edu/.

CHATHAM UNIVERSITY
PITTSBURGH, PENNSYLVANIA

General Independent, comprehensive, undergraduate: women only; graduate: coed **Entrance** Moderately difficult **Setting** 32-acre urban campus **Total enrollment** 1,860 **Student-faculty ratio** 8:1 **Application deadline** Rolling (freshmen), rolling (transfer) **Freshmen** 76% were admitted **Housing** Yes **Expenses** Tuition $26,116; Room & Board $7892 **Undergraduates** 32% part-time, 13% 25 or older, 0.5% Native American, 2% Hispanic American, 10% African American, 2% Asian American/Pacific Islander **The most frequently chosen baccalaureate fields are** psychology, biological/life sciences, visual and performing arts **Academic program** English as a second language, advanced placement, accelerated degree program, self-designed majors, honors program, summer session, adult/continuing education programs, internships **Contact** Ms. Lisa D. Zandier, Director of Admissions, Chatham University, Woodland Road, Pittsburgh, PA 15232. Phone: 800-837-1290 or toll-free 800-837-1290. Fax: 412-365-1609. E-mail: lzandier@chatham.edu. Web site: http://www.chatham.edu/.

CHESTNUT HILL COLLEGE
PHILADELPHIA, PENNSYLVANIA

General Independent Roman Catholic, comprehensive, coed, primarily women **Entrance** Moderately difficult **Setting** 75-acre suburban campus **Total enrollment** 2,062 **Student-faculty ratio** 11:1 **Application deadline** Rolling (freshmen), rolling (transfer) **Freshmen** 74% were admitted **Housing** Yes **Expenses** Tuition $26,000; Room & Board $8550 **Undergraduates** 67% women, 24% part-time, 7% 25 or older, 6% Hispanic American, 36% African American, 2% Asian American/Pacific Islander **The most frequently chosen baccalaureate fields are** business/marketing, public administration and social services, security and protective services **Academic program** English as a second language, advanced placement, self-designed majors, honors program, summer session, adult/continuing education programs, internships **Contact** Mr. William Fritz, Director of Admissions, Chestnut Hill College, 9601 Germantown Avenue, Philiadelphia, PA 19118-2693. Phone: 215-248-7001 or toll-free 800-248-0052. Fax: 215-248-7082. E-mail: chcapply@chc.edu. Web site: http://www.chc.edu/.

►**For more information, see page 450.**

CHEYNEY UNIVERSITY OF PENNSYLVANIA
CHEYNEY, PENNSYLVANIA

General State-supported, comprehensive, coed **Entrance** Minimally difficult **Setting** 275-acre suburban campus **Total enrollment** 1,436 **Student-faculty ratio** 13:1 **Application deadline** 3/31 (freshmen), rolling (transfer) **Freshmen** 47% were admitted **Housing** Yes **Expenses** Tuition $6412; Room & Board $6586 **Undergraduates** 55% women, 5% part-time, 10% 25 or older, 1% Hispanic American, 94% African American, 0.1% Asian American/Pacific Islander **The most frequently chosen baccalaureate fields are** business/marketing, communications/journalism, social sciences **Academic program** Honors program, summer session, adult/continuing education programs, internships **Contact** Ms. Gemma Stemley, Director of Admissions, Cheyney University of Pennsylvania, 1837 University Circle, Cheyney, PA 19319. Phone: 610-399-2275 or toll-free 800-CHEYNEY. Fax: 610-399-2099. E-mail: gstemley@cheyney.edu. Web site: http://www.cheyney.edu/.

CLARION UNIVERSITY OF PENNSYLVANIA
CLARION, PENNSYLVANIA

General State-supported, comprehensive, coed **Entrance** Minimally difficult **Setting** 100-acre rural campus **Total enrollment** 6,795 **Student-faculty ratio** 19:1 **Application deadline** Rolling (freshmen), rolling (transfer) **Freshmen** 69% were admitted **Housing** Yes **Expenses** Tuition $6866; Room & Board $5808 **Undergraduates** 60% women, 12% part-time, 16% 25 or older, 0.2% Native American, 1% Hispanic American, 5% African American, 1% Asian American/Pacific Islander **The most frequently chosen baccalaureate fields are** business/marketing, communications/journalism, education **Academic program** Advanced placement, accelerated degree program, honors program, summer session, adult/continuing education programs, internships **Contact** Mr. William Bailey, Dean of Enrollment Management, Clarion University of Pennsylvania, 890 Wood Street, Clarion, PA 16214. Phone: 814-393-2306 or toll-free 800-672-7171. Fax: 814-393-2030. E-mail: mdunlap@clarion.edu. Web site: http://www.clarion.edu/.

THE CURTIS INSTITUTE OF MUSIC
PHILADELPHIA, PENNSYLVANIA

Contact Mr. Christopher Hodges, Admissions Officer, The Curtis Institute of Music, 1726 Locust Street, Philadelphia, PA 19103-6107. Phone: 215-893-5262. Fax: 215-893-7900. Web site: http://www.curtis.edu/.

DELAWARE VALLEY COLLEGE
DOYLESTOWN, PENNSYLVANIA

General Independent, comprehensive, coed **Entrance** Moderately difficult **Setting** 600-acre suburban campus **Total enrollment** 2,081 **Student-faculty ratio** 15:1 **Application deadline** 5/1 (freshmen), rolling (transfer) **Freshmen** 66% were admitted **Housing** Yes **Expenses** Tuition $26,328; Room & Board $9502 **Undergraduates** 58% women, 15% part-time, 11% 25 or older, 0.3% Native American, 2% Hispanic American, 3% African American, 1% Asian American/Pacific Islander **The most frequently chosen baccalaureate fields are** agriculture, biological/life sciences, business/marketing **Academic program** Advanced placement, honors program, summer session, adult/continuing education programs, internships **Contact** Mr. Stephen Zenko, Director of Admissions, Delaware Valley College, 700 East Butler Avenue, Doylestown, PA 18901-2697. Phone: 215-489-2211 Ext. 2211 or toll-free 800-2DELVAL. Fax: 215-230-2968. E-mail: admitme@devalcol.edu. Web site: http://www.delval.edu/.

DESALES UNIVERSITY
CENTER VALLEY, PENNSYLVANIA

General Independent Roman Catholic, comprehensive, coed **Entrance** Moderately difficult **Setting** 400-acre suburban campus **Total enrollment** 2,966 **Student-faculty ratio** 13:1 **Application deadline** 8/1 (freshmen), 8/1 (transfer) **Freshmen** 77% were admitted **Housing** Yes **Expenses** Tuition $23,900; Room & Board $8750 **Undergraduates** 58% women, 25% part-time, 22% 25 or older, 0.1% Native American, 2% Hispanic American, 1% African American, 1% Asian American/Pacific Islander **The most frequently chosen baccalaureate fields are** business/marketing, health professions and related sciences, visual and performing arts **Academic program** Advanced placement, accelerated degree program, honors program, summer session, adult/continuing education programs, internships **Contact** Mrs. Mary Birkhead, Executive Director of Admissions, DeSales University, 2755 Station Avenue, Center Valley, PA 18034-9568. Phone: 610-282-1100 Ext. 1532 or toll-free 877-4DESALES. Fax: 610-282-0131. E-mail: admiss@desales.edu. Web site: http://www.desales.edu.

DEVRY UNIVERSITY
CHESTERBROOK, PENNSYLVANIA

Contact DeVry University, 701 Lee Road, Suite 103, Chesterbrook, PA 19087-5612. Web site: http://www.devry.edu/.

DEVRY UNIVERSITY
FORT WASHINGTON, PENNSYLVANIA

General Proprietary, comprehensive, coed **Entrance** Minimally difficult **Total enrollment** 930 **Student-faculty ratio** 11:1 **Application deadline** Rolling (freshmen), rolling (transfer) **Housing** No **Expenses** Tuition $14,660 **Undergraduates** 33% women, 45% part-time, 47% 25 or older, 0.5% Native American, 6% Hispanic American, 35% African American, 4% Asian American/Pacific Islander **The most frequently chosen baccalaureate fields are** business/marketing, computer and information sciences, engineering technologies **Academic program** Advanced placement, accelerated degree program, summer session, adult/continuing education programs **Contact** Admissions Office, DeVry University, 1140 Virginia Drive, Fort Washington, PA 19034. Web site: http://www.devry.edu/.

DEVRY UNIVERSITY
PHILADELPHIA, PENNSYLVANIA

Contact DeVry University, Philadelphia Downtown Center, 1800 JFK Boulevard, Suite 104, Philadelphia, PA 19103-7421. Web site: http://www.devry.edu/.

DEVRY UNIVERSITY
PITTSBURGH, PENNSYLVANIA

Contact DeVry University, FreeMarkets Center, 210 Sixth Avenue, Suite 200, Pittsburgh, PA 15222-9123. Phone: toll-free 866-77DEVRY. Web site: http://www.devry.edu/.

DICKINSON COLLEGE
CARLISLE, PENNSYLVANIA

General Independent, 4-year, coed **Entrance** Very difficult **Setting** 120-acre suburban campus **Total enrollment** 2,381 **Student-faculty ratio** 11:1 **Application deadline** 2/1 (freshmen), 4/1 (transfer) **Freshmen** 42% were admitted **Housing** Yes **Expenses** Tuition $38,234; Room & Board $9600 **Undergraduates** 55% women, 1% part-time, 1% 25 or older, 0.3% Native American, 5% Hispanic American, 4% African American, 5% Asian American/Pacific Islander **The most frequently chosen baccalaureate fields are** foreign languages and literature, English, social sciences **Academic program** English as a second language, advanced placement, accelerated degree program, self-designed majors, summer session, adult/continuing education programs, internships **Contact** Catherine Davenport, Acting Dean of Admissions, Dickinson College, PO Box 1773, Carlisle, PA 17013-2896. Phone: toll-free 800-644-1773. Fax: 717-245-1442. E-mail: admit@dickinson.edu. Web site: http://www.dickinson.edu/.

DREXEL UNIVERSITY
PHILADELPHIA, PENNSYLVANIA

General Independent, university, coed **Entrance** Moderately difficult **Setting** 42-acre urban campus **Total enrollment** 20,682 **Student-faculty ratio** 10:1 **Application deadline** 3/1 (freshmen), rolling (transfer) **Freshmen** 72% were admitted **Housing** Yes **Expenses** Tuition $30,440; Room & Board $12,135 **Undergraduates** 44% women, 20% part-time, 18% 25 or older, 0.3% Native American, 3% Hispanic American, 8% African American, 12% Asian American/Pacific Islander **The most frequently chosen baccalaureate fields are** business/marketing, engineering, health professions and related sciences **Academic program** English as a second language, advanced placement, accelerated degree program, honors program, summer session, adult/continuing education programs, internships **Contact** Ms. Joan MacDonald, Vice President of Enrollment Management, Drexel University, 3141 Chestnut Street, Philadelphia, PA 19104-2875. Phone: 215-895-2400 or toll-free 800-2-DREXEL. Fax: 215-895-5939. E-mail: enroll@drexel.edu. Web site: http://www.drexel.edu/.

►**For more information, see page 456.**

DUQUESNE UNIVERSITY
PITTSBURGH, PENNSYLVANIA

General Independent Roman Catholic, university, coed **Entrance** Moderately difficult **Setting** 50-acre urban campus **Total enrollment** 10,296 **Student-faculty ratio** 15:1 **Application deadline** 7/1 (freshmen), 7/1 (transfer) **Freshmen** 74% were admitted **Housing** Yes **Expenses** Tuition $23,950; Room & Board $8546 **Undergraduates** 58% women, 10% part-time, 5% 25 or older, 0.1% Native American, 1% Hispanic American, 3% African American, 2% Asian American/Pacific Islander **The most frequently chosen baccalaureate fields are** business/marketing, education, health professions and related sciences **Academic program** English as a second language, advanced placement, accelerated degree program, self-designed majors, honors program, summer session, adult/continuing education programs, internships **Contact** Mr. Paul-James Cukanna, Associate Vice President for Enrollment Management and Director of Admissions, Duquesne University, 1st Floor Administration Building, 600 Forbes Avenue, Pittsburgh, PA 15282-0201. Phone: 412-396-5002 or toll-free 800-456-0590. Fax: 412-396-5644. E-mail: admissions@duq.edu. Web site: http://www.duq.edu/.

EASTERN UNIVERSITY
ST. DAVIDS, PENNSYLVANIA

General Independent American Baptist Churches in the USA, comprehensive, coed **Contact** Mr. Michael Dziedziak, Director of Undergraduate Admissions, Eastern University, 1300 Eagle Road, St. Davids, PA 19087-3696. Phone: 610-341-5967 or toll-free 800-452-0996. Fax: 610-341-1723. E-mail: ugadm@eastern.edu. Web site: http://www.eastern.edu/.

EAST STROUDSBURG UNIVERSITY OF PENNSYLVANIA
EAST STROUDSBURG, PENNSYLVANIA

General State-supported, comprehensive, coed **Entrance** Moderately difficult **Setting** 213-acre small-town campus **Total enrollment** 7,053 **Student-faculty ratio** 19:1 **Application deadline** 4/1 (freshmen), 5/1 (transfer) **Freshmen** 66% were admitted **Housing** Yes **Expenses** Tuition $6809; Room & Board $5686 **Undergraduates** 56% women, 8% part-time, 10% 25 or older, 0.3% Native American, 5% Hispanic American, 5% African American, 1% Asian American/Pacific Islander **The most frequently chosen baccalaureate fields are** business/marketing, education, parks and recreation **Academic program** Advanced placement, accelerated degree program, self-designed majors, honors program, summer session, adult/continuing education programs, internships **Contact** Mr. Jeff Jones, East Stroudsburg University of Pennsylvania, 200 Prospect Street, East Stroudsburg, PA 18301. Phone: 570-422-3542 or toll-free 877-230-5547. Fax: 570-422-3933. E-mail: undergrads@po-box.esu.edu. Web site: http://www4.esu.edu/.

EDINBORO UNIVERSITY OF PENNSYLVANIA
EDINBORO, PENNSYLVANIA

General State-supported, comprehensive, coed **Entrance** Moderately difficult **Setting** 585-acre small-town campus **Total enrollment** 7,686 **Student-faculty ratio** 17:1 **Application deadline** Rolling (transfer) **Freshmen** 82% were admitted **Housing** Yes **Expenses** Tuition $6686; Room & Board $5718 **Undergraduates** 57% women, 13% part-time, 18% 25 or older, 0.3% Native American, 1% Hispanic American, 10% African American, 1% Asian American/Pacific Islander **The most frequently chosen baccalau-**

Edinboro University of Pennsylvania *(continued)*

reate fields are education, security and protective services, visual and performing arts **Academic program** Advanced placement, self-designed majors, honors program, summer session, adult/continuing education programs, internships **Contact** Mr. J. P. Cooney, Director of Undergraduate Admissions, Edinboro University of Pennsylvania, Academy Hall, Edinboro, PA 16444. Phone: 814-732-2761 or toll-free 888-846-2676 (in-state); 800-626-2203 (out-of-state). Fax: 814-732-2420. E-mail: eup_admissions@edinboro.edu. Web site: http://www.edinboro.edu/.

ELIZABETHTOWN COLLEGE

ELIZABETHTOWN, PENNSYLVANIA

General Independent, comprehensive, coed, affiliated with Church of the Brethren **Entrance** Moderately difficult **Setting** 193-acre small-town campus **Total enrollment** 2,360 **Student-faculty ratio** 12:1 **Application deadline** 3/1 (freshmen), 8/1 (transfer) **Freshmen** 58% were admitted **Housing** Yes **Expenses** Tuition $30,650; Room & Board $7950 **Undergraduates** 65% women, 17% part-time, 15% 25 or older, 0.2% Native American, 2% Hispanic American, 3% African American, 2% Asian American/Pacific Islander **The most frequently chosen baccalaureate fields are** business/marketing, education, social sciences **Academic program** English as a second language, advanced placement, honors program, summer session, adult/continuing education programs, internships **Contact** Ms. Debra Murray, Director of Admissions, Elizabethtown College, One Alpha Drive, Elizabethtown, PA 17022. Phone: 717-361-1400. Fax: 717-361-1365. E-mail: admissions@etown.edu. Web site: http://www.etown.edu/.

FRANKLIN & MARSHALL COLLEGE

LANCASTER, PENNSYLVANIA

General Independent, 4-year, coed **Entrance** Very difficult **Setting** 125-acre suburban campus **Total enrollment** 2,104 **Student-faculty ratio** 10:1 **Application deadline** 2/1 (freshmen), 5/1 (transfer) **Freshmen** 37% were admitted **Housing** Yes **Expenses** Tuition $36,480; Room & Board $9174 **Undergraduates** 49% women, 2% part-time, 0.3% Native American, 4% Hispanic American, 4% African American, 4% Asian American/Pacific Islander **The most frequently chosen baccalaureate fields are** health professions and related sciences, biological/life sciences, social sciences **Academic program** Advanced placement, accelerated degree program, self-designed majors, honors program, summer session, internships **Contact** Sara Harberson, Vice President for Enrollment Management, Franklin & Marshall College, PO Box 3003, Lancaster, PA 17604-3003. Phone: 717-291-3953. Fax: 717-291-4389. E-mail: admission@fandm.edu. Web site: http://www.fandm.edu/.

GANNON UNIVERSITY

ERIE, PENNSYLVANIA

General Independent Roman Catholic, comprehensive, coed **Entrance** Moderately difficult **Setting** 13-acre urban campus **Total enrollment** 4,134 **Student-faculty ratio** 14:1 **Application deadline** Rolling (freshmen), rolling (transfer) **Freshmen** 83% were admitted **Housing** Yes **Expenses** Tuition $21,346; Room & Board $8300 **Undergraduates** 60% women, 16% part-time, 10% 25 or older, 0.3% Native American, 2% Hispanic American, 5% African American, 2% Asian American/Pacific Islander **The most frequently chosen baccalaureate fields are** business/marketing, health professions and related sciences, security and protective services **Academic program** English as a second language, accelerated degree program, honors program, summer session, adult/continuing education programs, internships **Contact** Office of Admissions, Gannon University, 109 University Square, Erie, PA 16541. Phone: 814-871-7240 or toll-free 800-GANNONU. Fax: 814-871-5803. E-mail: admissions@gannon.edu. Web site: http://www.gannon.edu/.

GENEVA COLLEGE

BEAVER FALLS, PENNSYLVANIA

General Independent, comprehensive, coed, affiliated with Reformed Presbyterian Church of North America **Entrance** Moderately difficult **Setting** 55-acre small-town campus **Total enrollment** 1,880 **Student-faculty ratio** 13:1 **Application deadline** Rolling (freshmen), rolling (transfer) **Freshmen** 84% were admitted **Housing** Yes **Expenses** Tuition $20,400; Room & Board $7450 **Undergraduates** 55% women, 8% part-time, 21% 25 or older, 0.1% Native American, 1% Hispanic American, 11% African American, 1% Asian American/Pacific Islander **The most frequently chosen baccalaureate fields are** business/marketing, education, theology and religious vocations **Academic program** English as a second language, advanced placement, accelerated degree program, self-designed majors, honors program, summer session, adult/continuing education programs, internships **Contact** Mr. David Layton, Dean for Undergraduate Enrollment, Geneva College, 3200 College Avenue, Beaver Falls, PA 15010. Phone: 724-847-6500 or toll-free 800-847-8255. Fax: 724-847-6776. E-mail: admissions@geneva.edu. Web site: http://www.geneva.edu/.

GETTYSBURG COLLEGE
GETTYSBURG, PENNSYLVANIA

General Independent, 4-year, coed, affiliated with Evangelical Lutheran Church in America **Entrance** Most difficult **Setting** 200-acre small-town campus **Total enrollment** 2,497 **Student-faculty ratio** 11:1 **Application deadline** 2/1 (freshmen), rolling (transfer) **Freshmen** 36% were admitted **Housing** Yes **Expenses** Tuition $35,990; Room & Board $8630 **Undergraduates** 53% women, 1% part-time, 1% 25 or older, 0.04% Native American, 2% Hispanic American, 4% African American, 2% Asian American/Pacific Islander **The most frequently chosen baccalaureate fields are** business/marketing, biological/life sciences, social sciences **Academic program** Advanced placement, self-designed majors, adult/continuing education programs, internships **Contact** Ms. Gail Sweezey, Director of Admissions, Gettysburg College, 300 North Washington Street, Gettysburg, PA 17325. Phone: 717-337-6100 or toll-free 800-431-0803. Fax: 717-337-6145. E-mail: admiss@gettysburg.edu. Web site: http://www.gettysburg.edu/.

GRATZ COLLEGE
MELROSE PARK, PENNSYLVANIA

General Independent Jewish, comprehensive, coed **Contact** Ms. Ruthann Crosby, Director of Student Life, Gratz College, 7605 Old York Road, Melrose Park, PA 19027. Phone: 215-635-7300 Ext. 140 or toll-free 800-475-4635 Ext. 140. Fax: 215-635-7399. E-mail: admissions@gratz.edu. Web site: http://www.gratzcollege.edu/.

GROVE CITY COLLEGE
GROVE CITY, PENNSYLVANIA

General Independent Presbyterian, 4-year, coed **Entrance** Most difficult **Setting** 150-acre small-town campus **Total enrollment** 2,504 **Student-faculty ratio** 15:1 **Application deadline** 2/1 (freshmen), 8/15 (transfer) **Freshmen** 55% were admitted **Housing** Yes **Expenses** Tuition $11,500; Room & Board $6134 **Undergraduates** 50% women, 1% part-time, 0.1% Native American, 1% Hispanic American, 1% African American, 2% Asian American/Pacific Islander **The most frequently chosen baccalaureate fields are** business/marketing, biological/life sciences, education **Academic program** Advanced placement, self-designed majors, summer session, internships **Contact** Mr. Jeffrey Mincey, Director of Admissions, Grove City College, 100 Campus Drive, Grove City, PA 16127-2104. Phone: 724-458-2100. Fax: 724-458-3395. E-mail: admissions@gcc.edu. Web site: http://www.gcc.edu/.

►**For more information, see page 464.**

GWYNEDD-MERCY COLLEGE
GWYNEDD VALLEY, PENNSYLVANIA

General Independent Roman Catholic, comprehensive, coed **Entrance** Moderately difficult **Setting** 170-acre suburban campus **Total enrollment** 2,644 **Student-faculty ratio** 11:1 **Application deadline** Rolling (freshmen), 8/20 (transfer) **Freshmen** 57% were admitted **Housing** Yes **Expenses** Tuition $22,790; Room & Board $8990 **Undergraduates** 74% women, 34% part-time, 25% 25 or older, 0.3% Native American, 1% Hispanic American, 16% African American, 3% Asian American/Pacific Islander **The most frequently chosen baccalaureate fields are** business/marketing, education, health professions and related sciences **Academic program** English as a second language, advanced placement, accelerated degree program, honors program, summer session, adult/continuing education programs, internships **Contact** Ms. Michelle Diehl, Director of Admissions, Gwynedd-Mercy College, 1325 Sumneytown Pike, Gwynedd Valley, PA 19437-0901. Phone: 215-646-7300 or toll-free 800-DIAL-GMC. Fax: 215-641-5556. E-mail: admissions@gmc.edu. Web site: http://www.gmc.edu/.

HARRISBURG UNIVERSITY OF SCIENCE AND TECHNOLOGY
HARRISBURG, PENNSYLVANIA

General Independent, comprehensive, coed **Entrance** Minimally difficult **Setting** urban campus **Total enrollment** 162 **Student-faculty ratio** 5:1 **Freshmen** 86% were admitted **Housing** No **Expenses** Tuition $14,750 **Undergraduates** 52% women, 54% part-time, 20% 25 or older, 14% Hispanic American, 42% African American, 4% Asian American/Pacific Islander **Academic program** Advanced placement, self-designed majors, summer session, adult/continuing education programs, internships **Contact** Office of Admissions, Harrisburg University of Science and Technology, 304 Market Street, Harrisburg, PA 17101. Phone: 717-901-5128 or toll-free 866-HBG-UNIV. Fax: 717-901-3160. E-mail: admissions@harrisburgu.net. Web site: http://www.harrisburgu.net/.

HAVERFORD COLLEGE
HAVERFORD, PENNSYLVANIA

General Independent, 4-year, coed **Entrance** Most difficult **Setting** 200-acre suburban campus **Total enrollment** 1,169 **Student-faculty ratio** 8:1 **Application deadline** 1/15 (freshmen), 3/31 (transfer) **Freshmen** 25% were admitted **Housing** Yes **Expenses** Tuition $35,380; Room & Board $10,880 **Undergraduates** 54% women, 1% Native American, 8% Hispanic American, 8%

Haverford College *(continued)*

African American, 11% Asian American/Pacific Islander **The most frequently chosen baccalaureate fields are** biological/life sciences, physical sciences, social sciences **Academic program** Advanced placement, self-designed majors, internships **Contact** Mr. Jess Lord, Dean of Admissions and Financial Aid, Haverford College, 370 Lancaster Avenue, Haverford, PA 19041-1392. Phone: 610-896-1350. Fax: 610-896-1338. E-mail: admitme@haverford.edu. Web site: http://www.haverford.edu/.

►**For more information, see page 465.**

HOLY FAMILY UNIVERSITY

PHILADELPHIA, PENNSYLVANIA

General Independent Roman Catholic, comprehensive, coed **Entrance** Moderately difficult **Setting** 47-acre suburban campus **Total enrollment** 3,487 **Student-faculty ratio** 15:1 **Application deadline** Rolling (freshmen), rolling (transfer) **Freshmen** 63% were admitted **Housing** Yes **Expenses** Tuition $21,590; Room & Board $9400 **Undergraduates** 75% women, 38% part-time, 31% 25 or older, 0.3% Native American, 3% Hispanic American, 7% African American, 5% Asian American/Pacific Islander **The most frequently chosen baccalaureate fields are** education, business/marketing, health professions and related sciences **Academic program** Advanced placement, accelerated degree program, honors program, summer session, adult/continuing education programs, internships **Contact** Ms. Lauren McDermott-Campbell, Director of Admissions, Holy Family University, 9801 Frankford Avenue, Philadelphia, PA 19114-2009. Phone: 215-637-3050 or toll-free 800-637-1191. Fax: 215-281-1022. E-mail: admissions@holyfamily.edu. Web site: http://www.holyfamily.edu/.

HUSSIAN SCHOOL OF ART

PHILADELPHIA, PENNSYLVANIA

General Proprietary, 4-year, coed **Entrance** Minimally difficult **Setting** 1-acre urban campus **Total enrollment** 142 **Student-faculty ratio** 18:1 **Application deadline** Rolling (freshmen), rolling (transfer) **Freshmen** 95% were admitted **Housing** No **Expenses** Tuition $11,825 **Undergraduates** 30% women, 2% 25 or older, 6% Hispanic American, 13% African American **Academic program** Internships **Contact** Ms. Lynne Wartman, Director of Admissions, Hussian School of Art, 1118 Market Street, Philadelphia, PA 19107. Phone: 215-981-0900. Fax: 215-864-9115. E-mail: info@hussianart.edu. Web site: http://www.hussianart.edu/.

IMMACULATA UNIVERSITY

IMMACULATA, PENNSYLVANIA

General Independent Roman Catholic, comprehensive, coed, primarily women **Entrance** Moderately difficult **Setting** 400-acre suburban campus **Total enrollment** 4,038 **Student-faculty ratio** 10:1 **Application deadline** Rolling (freshmen), rolling (transfer) **Freshmen** 80% were admitted **Housing** Yes **Expenses** Tuition $22,650; Room & Board $9800 **Undergraduates** 77% women, 64% part-time, 0.1% Native American, 2% Hispanic American, 10% African American, 2% Asian American/Pacific Islander **The most frequently chosen baccalaureate fields are** business/marketing, health professions and related sciences, psychology **Academic program** English as a second language, advanced placement, accelerated degree program, honors program, summer session, adult/continuing education programs, internships **Contact** Ms. Rebecca Bowlby, Director of Admissions, Immaculata University, PO Box 642, Immaculata, PA 19345-0702. Phone: 610-647-4400 Ext. 3046 or toll-free 877-428-6328. Fax: 610-640-0836. E-mail: admiss@immaculata.edu. Web site: http://www.immaculata.edu/.

INDIANA UNIVERSITY OF PENNSYLVANIA

INDIANA, PENNSYLVANIA

General State-supported, university, coed **Entrance** Moderately difficult **Setting** 350-acre small-town campus **Total enrollment** 14,018 **Student-faculty ratio** 16:1 **Application deadline** Rolling (freshmen), rolling (transfer) **Freshmen** 65% were admitted **Housing** Yes **Expenses** Tuition $6695; Room & Board $5436 **Undergraduates** 55% women, 8% part-time, 11% 25 or older, 0.3% Native American, 2% Hispanic American, 11% African American, 1% Asian American/Pacific Islander **The most frequently chosen baccalaureate fields are** business/marketing, social sciences, visual and performing arts **Academic program** English as a second language, advanced placement, accelerated degree program, honors program, summer session, adult/continuing education programs, internships **Contact** Office of Admissions, Indiana University of Pennsylvania, 1011 South Drive, Sutton Hall 214, Indiana, PA 15705. Phone: 724-357-2230 or toll-free 800-442-6830. Fax: 724-357-6281. E-mail: admissions-inquiry@iup.edu. Web site: http://www.iup.edu/.

JUNIATA COLLEGE

HUNTINGDON, PENNSYLVANIA

General Independent, 4-year, coed, affiliated with Church of the Brethren **Entrance** Moderately difficult **Setting** 110-acre small-town campus **Total enrollment** 1,506 **Student-faculty ratio** 13:1 **Application deadline** 3/1 (freshmen), 6/15 (transfer) **Freshmen** 67% were admitted **Housing** Yes **Expenses** Tuition $30,280; Room & Board $8420 **Undergraduates** 54% women, 5% part-time, 2% 25 or older, 0.1% Native American, 1% Hispanic American, 1% African American, 1% Asian American/Pacific Islander **The most frequently chosen baccalaureate fields are** biological/life sciences, business/marketing, social sciences **Academic program** English as a second language, advanced placement, accelerated degree program, self-designed majors, honors program, summer session, adult/continuing education programs, internships **Contact** Terry Bollman-Dalansky, Director of Admissions, Juniata College, 1700 Moore Street, Huntingdon, PA 16652-2119. Phone: 814-641-3432 or toll-free 877-JUNIATA. Fax: 814-641-3100. E-mail: admissions@juniata.edu. Web site: http://www.juniata.edu/.

KEYSTONE COLLEGE
LA PLUME, PENNSYLVANIA

General Independent, 4-year, coed **Entrance** Minimally difficult **Setting** 270-acre rural campus **Total enrollment** 1,796 **Student-faculty ratio** 12:1 **Application deadline** 7/1 (freshmen), 8/1 (transfer) **Freshmen** 95% were admitted **Housing** Yes **Expenses** Tuition $17,805; Room & Board $8580 **Undergraduates** 62% women, 26% part-time, 26% 25 or older, 0.1% Native American, 1% Hispanic American, 2% African American, 0.5% Asian American/Pacific Islander **The most frequently chosen baccalaureate fields are** business/marketing, education, security and protective services **Academic program** Advanced placement, self-designed majors, honors program, summer session, adult/continuing education programs, internships **Contact** Ms. Sarah Keating, Assistant Vice President for Enrollment, Keystone College, One College Green, La Plume, PA 18440-1099. Phone: 570-945-8112 or toll-free 877-4COLLEGE Ext. 1. Fax: 570-945-7916. E-mail: admissions@keystone.edu. Web site: http://www.keystone.edu/.

KING'S COLLEGE
WILKES-BARRE, PENNSYLVANIA

General Independent Roman Catholic, comprehensive, coed **Entrance** Moderately difficult **Setting** 48-acre urban campus **Total enrollment** 2,583 **Student-faculty ratio** 13:1 **Application deadline** Rolling (freshmen), rolling (transfer) **Freshmen** 78% were admitted **Housing** Yes **Expenses** Tuition $23,450; Room & Board $8930 **Undergraduates** 49% women, 15% part-time, 6% 25 or older, 0.1% Native American, 3% Hispanic American, 2% African American, 1% Asian American/Pacific Islander **The most frequently chosen baccalaureate fields are** business/marketing, communications/journalism, education **Academic program** English as a second language, advanced placement, accelerated degree program, self-designed majors, honors program, summer session, adult/continuing education programs, internships **Contact** Ms. Michelle Lawrence-Schmude, Director of Admissions, King's College, 133 North River Street, Wilkes-Barre, PA 18711-0801. Phone: 570-208-5858 or toll-free 888-KINGSPA. Fax: 570-208-5971. E-mail: admissions@kings.edu. Web site: http://www.kings.edu/.

KUTZTOWN UNIVERSITY OF PENNSYLVANIA
KUTZTOWN, PENNSYLVANIA

General State-supported, comprehensive, coed **Entrance** Moderately difficult **Setting** 326-acre rural campus **Total enrollment** 10,295 **Student-faculty ratio** 19:1 **Application deadline** Rolling (freshmen), rolling (transfer) **Freshmen** 65% were admitted **Housing** Yes **Expenses** Tuition $6873; Room & Board $6960 **Undergraduates** 59% women, 10% part-time, 7% 25 or older, 0.3% Native American, 4% Hispanic American, 7% African American, 1% Asian American/Pacific Islander **The most frequently chosen baccalaureate fields are** business/marketing, education, visual and performing arts **Academic program** Advanced placement, accelerated degree program, self-designed majors, honors program, summer session, adult/continuing education programs, internships **Contact** Dr. William Stahler, Director of Admissions, Kutztown University of Pennsylvania, 15200 Kutztown Road, Kutztown, PA 19530-0730. Phone: 610-683-4060 Ext. 4153 or toll-free 877-628-1915. Fax: 610-683-1375. E-mail: admission@kutztown.edu. Web site: http://www.kutztown.edu/.

LAFAYETTE COLLEGE
EASTON, PENNSYLVANIA

General Independent, 4-year, coed, affiliated with Presbyterian Church (U.S.A.) **Entrance** Most difficult **Setting** 340-acre suburban campus **Total enrollment** 2,403 **Student-faculty ratio** 11:1 **Application deadline** 1/1 (freshmen), 6/1 (transfer) **Freshmen** 35% were admitted **Housing** Yes **Expenses** Tuition $36,200; Room & Board $11,200 **Undergraduates** 48% women, 2% part-time, 0.1% Native American, 5% Hispanic American, 5% African American, 3% Asian American/Pacific Islander **The most frequently chosen baccalaureate fields are** engineering, English, social sciences **Academic program** Advanced placement, accelerated degree program, self-designed majors, honors program, summer

Lafayette College *(continued)*

session, adult/continuing education programs, internships **Contact** Ms. Carol Rowlands, Director of Admissions, Lafayette College, Easton, PA 18042-1798. Phone: 610-330-5100. Fax: 610-330-5355. E-mail: admissions@lafayette.edu. Web site: http://www.lafayette.edu/.

LANCASTER BIBLE COLLEGE
LANCASTER, PENNSYLVANIA

General Independent nondenominational, comprehensive, coed **Contact** Mrs. Joanne M. Roper, Associate Vice President for Admissions, Lancaster Bible College, PO Box 83403, Lancaster, PA 17608. Phone: 717-560-8271 or toll-free 866-LBC4YOU. Fax: 717-560-8213. E-mail: admissions@lbc.edu. Web site: http://www.lbc.edu/.

LA ROCHE COLLEGE
PITTSBURGH, PENNSYLVANIA

General Independent, comprehensive, coed, affiliated with Roman Catholic Church **Entrance** Minimally difficult **Setting** 80-acre suburban campus **Total enrollment** 1,499 **Student-faculty ratio** 12:1 **Application deadline** Rolling (freshmen), rolling (transfer) **Freshmen** 73% were admitted **Housing** Yes **Expenses** Tuition $19,470; Room & Board $7942 **Undergraduates** 67% women, 16% part-time, 16% 25 or older, 1% Native American, 1% Hispanic American, 5% African American, 1% Asian American/Pacific Islander **The most frequently chosen baccalaureate fields are** business/marketing, education, health professions and related sciences **Academic program** English as a second language, advanced placement, accelerated degree program, self-designed majors, summer session, adult/continuing education programs, internships **Contact** Mr. Thomas Hassett, Director of Admissions, La Roche College, 9000 Babcock Boulevard, Pittsburgh, PA 15237. Phone: 412-536-1198 or toll-free 800-838-4LRC. Fax: 412-536-1048. E-mail: admissions@laroche.edu. Web site: http://www.laroche.edu/.

LA SALLE UNIVERSITY
PHILADELPHIA, PENNSYLVANIA

General Independent Roman Catholic, comprehensive, coed **Entrance** Moderately difficult **Setting** 100-acre urban campus **Total enrollment** 6,012 **Student-faculty ratio** 13:1 **Application deadline** 8/15 (transfer) **Freshmen** 68% were admitted **Housing** Yes **Expenses** Tuition $29,400; Room & Board $10,300 **Undergraduates** 62% women, 24% part-time, 4% 25 or older, 0.1% Native American, 8% Hispanic American, 16% African American, 4% Asian American/Pacific Islander **The most frequently chosen baccalaureate fields are** business/marketing, communications/journalism, health professions and related sciences **Academic program** Advanced placement, accelerated degree program, self-designed majors, honors program, summer session, adult/continuing education programs, internships **Contact** Mr. Robert G. Voss, Dean of Admission and Financial Aid, La Salle University, 1900 West Olney Avenue, Philadelphia, PA 19141-1199. Phone: 215-951-1500 or toll-free 800-328-1910. Fax: 215-951-1656. E-mail: admiss@lasalle.edu. Web site: http://www.lasalle.edu/.

LEBANON VALLEY COLLEGE
ANNVILLE, PENNSYLVANIA

General Independent United Methodist, comprehensive, coed **Entrance** Moderately difficult **Setting** 340-acre small-town campus **Total enrollment** 1,936 **Student-faculty ratio** 13:1 **Application deadline** Rolling (freshmen), rolling (transfer) **Freshmen** 71% were admitted **Housing** Yes **Expenses** Tuition $27,800; Room & Board $7430 **Undergraduates** 55% women, 9% part-time, 4% 25 or older, 0.3% Native American, 2% Hispanic American, 1% African American, 2% Asian American/Pacific Islander **The most frequently chosen baccalaureate fields are** business/marketing, education, psychology **Academic program** Advanced placement, self-designed majors, summer session, adult/continuing education programs, internships **Contact** Ms. Susan Sarisky, Director of Admission, Lebanon Valley College, 101 North College Avenue, Annville, PA 17003. Phone: toll-free 866-LVC-4ADM. Fax: 717-867-6026. E-mail: admission@lvc.edu. Web site: http://www.lvc.edu/.

►**For more information, see page 471.**

LEHIGH UNIVERSITY
BETHLEHEM, PENNSYLVANIA

General Independent, university, coed **Entrance** Most difficult **Setting** 1,600-acre suburban campus **Total enrollment** 6,845 **Student-faculty ratio** 9:1 **Application deadline** 1/1 (freshmen), 4/1 (transfer) **Freshmen** 32% were admitted **Housing** Yes **Expenses** Tuition $37,550; Room & Board $9770 **Undergraduates** 41% women, 2% part-time, 1% 25 or older, 0.1% Native American, 4% Hispanic American, 3% African American, 6% Asian American/Pacific Islander **The most frequently chosen baccalaureate fields are** business/marketing, engineering, social sciences **Academic program** English as a second language, advanced placement, accelerated degree program, honors program, summer session, adult/continuing education programs, internships **Contact**

J. Bruce Gardiner, Director of Admissions, Lehigh University, 27 Memorial Drive West, Bethlehem, PA 18015. Phone: 610-758-3100. Fax: 610-758-4361. E-mail: admissions@lehigh.edu. Web site: http://www.lehigh.edu/.

LINCOLN UNIVERSITY
LINCOLN UNIVERSITY, PENNSYLVANIA

General State-related, comprehensive, coed **Entrance** Moderately difficult **Setting** 422-acre rural campus **Total enrollment** 2,449 **Student-faculty ratio** 18:1 **Application deadline** Rolling (freshmen), rolling (transfer) **Freshmen** 38% were admitted **Housing** Yes **Expenses** Tuition $7894; Room & Board $7392 **Undergraduates** 60% women, 2% part-time, 3% 25 or older, 1% Hispanic American, 96% African American **The most frequently chosen baccalaureate fields are** education, business/marketing, social sciences **Academic program** Advanced placement, accelerated degree program, self-designed majors, honors program, summer session, adult/continuing education programs, internships **Contact** Mr. Michael Taylor, Director of Admissions, Lincoln University, PO Box 179, MSC 147, Lincoln University, PA 19352-0999. Phone: 484-365-7206 or toll-free 800-790-0191. Fax: 484-365-8109. E-mail: admiss@lincoln.edu. Web site: http://www.lincoln.edu/.

LOCK HAVEN UNIVERSITY OF PENNSYLVANIA
LOCK HAVEN, PENNSYLVANIA

General State-supported, comprehensive, coed **Entrance** Moderately difficult **Setting** 165-acre rural campus **Total enrollment** 5,241 **Student-faculty ratio** 20:1 **Application deadline** Rolling (freshmen), rolling (transfer) **Freshmen** 74% were admitted **Housing** Yes **Expenses** Tuition $6678; Room & Board $5900 **Undergraduates** 56% women, 8% part-time, 8% 25 or older, 0.2% Native American, 2% Hispanic American, 7% African American, 1% Asian American/Pacific Islander **The most frequently chosen baccalaureate fields are** education, business/marketing, parks and recreation **Academic program** English as a second language, advanced placement, self-designed majors, honors program, summer session, adult/continuing education programs, internships **Contact** Mr. Steven Lee, Director of Admissions, Lock Haven University of Pennsylvania, Office of Admission, Akeley Hall, Lock Haven, PA 17745. Phone: 570-484-2027 or toll-free 800-332-8900 (in-state); 800-233-8978 (out-of-state). Fax: 570-484-2201. E-mail: admissions@lhup.edu. Web site: http://www.lhup.edu/.

LYCOMING COLLEGE
WILLIAMSPORT, PENNSYLVANIA

General Independent United Methodist, 4-year, coed **Entrance** Moderately difficult **Setting** 35-acre small-town campus **Total enrollment** 1,431 **Student-faculty ratio** 14:1 **Application deadline** 5/1 (freshmen), rolling (transfer) **Freshmen** 78% were admitted **Housing** Yes **Expenses** Tuition $27,129; Room & Board $7238 **Undergraduates** 55% women, 2% part-time, 2% 25 or older, 0.5% Native American, 2% Hispanic American, 3% African American, 1% Asian American/Pacific Islander **The most frequently chosen baccalaureate fields are** business/marketing, psychology, social sciences **Academic program** Advanced placement, accelerated degree program, self-designed majors, honors program, summer session, internships **Contact** Mr. James Spencer, Vice President of Admissions and Financial Aid, Lycoming College, 700 College Place, Williamsport, PA 17701. Phone: 570-321-4026 or toll-free 800-345-3920 Ext. 4026. Fax: 570-321-4317. E-mail: admissions@lycoming.edu. Web site: http://www.lycoming.edu/.

MANSFIELD UNIVERSITY OF PENNSYLVANIA
MANSFIELD, PENNSYLVANIA

General State-supported, comprehensive, coed **Entrance** Moderately difficult **Setting** 205-acre small-town campus **Total enrollment** 3,338 **Student-faculty ratio** 16:1 **Application deadline** Rolling (freshmen), rolling (transfer) **Freshmen** 70% were admitted **Housing** Yes **Expenses** Tuition $7004; Room & Board $6236 **Undergraduates** 62% women, 9% part-time, 13% 25 or older, 1% Native American, 2% Hispanic American, 5% African American, 1% Asian American/Pacific Islander **The most frequently chosen baccalaureate fields are** education, business/marketing, security and protective services **Academic program** Advanced placement, accelerated degree program, self-designed majors, honors program, summer session, adult/continuing education programs, internships **Contact** Mr. Brian Barden, Director of Admissions, Mansfield University of Pennsylvania, Academy Street, Mansfield, PA 16933. Phone: 570-662-4813 or toll-free 800-577-6826. Fax: 570-662-4121. E-mail: admissions@mnsfld.edu. Web site: http://www.mansfield.edu/.

MARYWOOD UNIVERSITY
SCRANTON, PENNSYLVANIA

General Independent Roman Catholic, comprehensive, coed **Entrance** Moderately difficult **Setting** 115-acre suburban campus **Total enrollment** 3,316 **Student-faculty ratio** 13:1 **Appli-**

Marywood University *(continued)*

cation deadline Rolling (freshmen), rolling (transfer) **Housing** Yes **Expenses** Tuition $24,090; Room & Board $10,410 **Undergraduates** 71% women, 8% part-time, 13% 25 or older, 0.4% Native American, 3% Hispanic American, 1% African American, 2% Asian American/Pacific Islander **Academic program** English as a second language, advanced placement, accelerated degree program, self-designed majors, honors program, summer session, adult/continuing education programs, internships **Contact** Mr. Robert W. Reese, Director of University Admissions, Marywood University, 2300 Adams Avenue, Scranton, PA 18509-1598. Phone: 570-348-6234 or toll-free 800-346-5014. Fax: 570-961-4763. E-mail: yourfuture@marywood.edu. Web site: http://www.marywood.edu/.

MERCYHURST COLLEGE
ERIE, PENNSYLVANIA

General Independent Roman Catholic, comprehensive, coed **Entrance** Moderately difficult **Setting** 88-acre suburban campus **Total enrollment** 4,253 **Student-faculty ratio** 17:1 **Application deadline** Rolling (freshmen), rolling (transfer) **Freshmen** 66% were admitted **Housing** Yes **Expenses** Tuition $21,175; Room & Board $7458 **Undergraduates** 58% women, 11% part-time, 14% 25 or older, 0.4% Native American, 2% Hispanic American, 5% African American, 1% Asian American/Pacific Islander **The most frequently chosen baccalaureate fields are** business/marketing, education, security and protective services **Academic program** Advanced placement, accelerated degree program, self-designed majors, honors program, summer session, adult/continuing education programs, internships **Contact** Emily Crawford, Director of Undergraduate Admissions, Mercyhurst College, 501 East 38th Street, Erie, PA 16546-0001. Phone: 814-824-2576 or toll-free 800-825-1926 Ext. 2202. Fax: 814-824-2071. E-mail: ecrawford@mercyhurst.edu. Web site: http://www.mercyhurst.edu/.

MESSIAH COLLEGE
GRANTHAM, PENNSYLVANIA

General Independent interdenominational, 4-year, coed **Entrance** Moderately difficult **Setting** 485-acre small-town campus **Total enrollment** 2,837 **Student-faculty ratio** 13:1 **Application deadline** Rolling (freshmen) **Freshmen** 79% were admitted **Housing** Yes **Expenses** Tuition $24,420; Room & Board $7340 **Undergraduates** 63% women, 2% part-time, 3% 25 or older, 0.1% Native American, 1% Hispanic American, 2% African American, 2% Asian American/Pacific Islander **The most frequently chosen baccalaureate fields are** business/marketing, education, health professions and related sciences **Academic program** English as a second language, advanced placement, accelerated degree program, self-designed majors, honors program, summer session, adult/continuing education programs, internships **Contact** Mr. John Chopka, Dean for Enrollment Management, Messiah College, PO Box 3005, One College Avenue, Grantham, PA 17027. Phone: 717-691-6000 or toll-free 800-233-4220. Fax: 717-796-5374. E-mail: admiss@messiah.edu. Web site: http://www.messiah.edu/.

MILLERSVILLE UNIVERSITY OF PENNSYLVANIA
MILLERSVILLE, PENNSYLVANIA

General State-supported, comprehensive, coed **Entrance** Moderately difficult **Setting** 220-acre small-town campus **Total enrollment** 8,306 **Student-faculty ratio** 19:1 **Application deadline** Rolling (freshmen), rolling (transfer) **Freshmen** 57% were admitted **Housing** Yes **Expenses** Tuition $10,354; Room & Board $6876 **Undergraduates** 56% women, 9% part-time, 9% 25 or older, 0.2% Native American, 4% Hispanic American, 7% African American, 2% Asian American/Pacific Islander **The most frequently chosen baccalaureate fields are** business/marketing, education, social sciences **Academic program** Advanced placement, accelerated degree program, honors program, summer session, adult/continuing education programs, internships **Contact** Mr. Douglas Zander, Director of Admissions, Millersville University of Pennsylvania, PO Box 1002, Millersville, PA 17551-0302. Phone: 717-872-3371 or toll-free 800-MU-ADMIT. Fax: 717-871-2147. E-mail: admissions@millersville.edu. Web site: http://www.millersville.edu/.

MISERICORDIA UNIVERSITY
DALLAS, PENNSYLVANIA

General Independent Roman Catholic, comprehensive, coed, primarily women **Entrance** Moderately difficult **Setting** 100-acre small-town campus **Total enrollment** 2,355 **Student-faculty ratio** 12:1 **Application deadline** Rolling (freshmen), rolling (transfer) **Freshmen** 74% were admitted **Housing** Yes **Expenses** Tuition $21,950; Room & Board $9100 **Undergraduates** 73% women, 29% part-time, 26% 25 or older, 1% Native American, 1% Hispanic American, 1% African American, 1% Asian American/Pacific Islander **The most frequently chosen baccalaureate fields are** education, business/marketing, health professions and related sciences **Academic program** English as a second language, advanced placement, accelerated degree program, self-designed majors, honors program, summer session, adult/continuing education programs, internships **Contact** Mr. Glenn Bozinski, Director of Admissions, Misericordia University, 301 Lake Street, Dallas, PA 18612-1098. Phone: 570-675-6264 or toll-free 866-262-6363. Fax: 570-674-6232. E-mail: admiss@misericordia.edu. Web site: http://www.misericordia.edu/.

MOORE COLLEGE OF ART & DESIGN
PHILADELPHIA, PENNSYLVANIA

General Independent, 4-year, women only **Entrance** Moderately difficult **Setting** 3-acre urban campus **Total enrollment** 557 **Student-faculty ratio** 8:1 **Application deadline** 8/15 (freshmen), rolling (transfer) **Freshmen** 62% were admitted **Housing** Yes **Expenses** Tuition $27,848; Room & Board $10,502 **Undergraduates** 6% part-time, 17% 25 or older, 1% Native American, 5% Hispanic American, 11% African American, 3% Asian American/Pacific Islander **The most frequently chosen baccalaureate fields are** education, visual and performing arts **Academic program** Advanced placement, summer session, adult/continuing education programs, internships **Contact** Ms. Heesung Lee, Director of Admissions, Moore College of Art & Design, 20th Street and The Parkway, Philadelphia, PA 19103-1179. Phone: 215-568-4515 Ext. 1108 or toll-free 800-523-2025. Fax: 215-965-8544. E-mail: enroll@moore.edu. Web site: http://www.moore.edu/.

MORAVIAN COLLEGE
BETHLEHEM, PENNSYLVANIA

General Independent, comprehensive, coed, affiliated with Moravian Church **Entrance** Moderately difficult **Setting** 60-acre suburban campus **Total enrollment** 1,917 **Student-faculty ratio** 11:1 **Application deadline** 3/1 (freshmen), 3/1 (transfer) **Freshmen** 64% were admitted **Housing** Yes **Expenses** Tuition $28,388; Room & Board $7993 **Undergraduates** 58% women, 11% part-time, 0.2% Native American, 3% Hispanic American, 2% African American, 2% Asian American/Pacific Islander **The most frequently chosen baccalaureate fields are** business/marketing, psychology, social sciences **Academic program** Advanced placement, self-designed majors, honors program, summer session, adult/continuing education programs, internships **Contact** Mr. James Mackin, Director of Admission, Moravian College, 1200 Main Street, Bethlehem, PA 18018. Phone: 610-861-1320 or toll-free 800-441-3191. Fax: 610-625-7930. E-mail: admissions@moravian.edu. Web site: http://www.moravian.edu/.

MOUNT ALOYSIUS COLLEGE
CRESSON, PENNSYLVANIA

General Independent Roman Catholic, comprehensive, coed **Entrance** Minimally difficult **Setting** 165-acre small-town campus **Total enrollment** 1,595 **Student-faculty ratio** 14:1 **Application deadline** Rolling (freshmen), rolling (transfer) **Freshmen** 87% were admitted **Housing** Yes **Expenses** Tuition $16,580; Room & Board $6950 **Undergraduates** 72% women, 26% part-time, 33% 25 or older, 0.1% Native American, 1% Hispanic American, 2% African American, 0.3% Asian American/Pacific Islander **The most frequently chosen baccalaureate fields are** business/marketing, health professions and related sciences, liberal arts/general studies **Academic program** Advanced placement, accelerated degree program, self-designed majors, honors program, summer session, adult/continuing education programs, internships **Contact** Mr. Francis C. Crouse Jr., Vice President for Enrollment, Mount Aloysius College, 7373 Admiral Peary Highway, Cresson, PA 16630-1999. Phone: 814-886-6383 or toll-free 888-823-2220. Fax: 814-886-6441. E-mail: admissions@mtaloy.edu. Web site: http://www.mtaloy.edu/.

MUHLENBERG COLLEGE
ALLENTOWN, PENNSYLVANIA

General Independent, 4-year, coed, affiliated with Lutheran Church **Entrance** Very difficult **Setting** 75-acre suburban campus **Total enrollment** 2,457 **Student-faculty ratio** 12:1 **Application deadline** 2/15 (freshmen), 6/15 (transfer) **Freshmen** 37% were admitted **Housing** Yes **Expenses** Tuition $33,090; Room & Board $7790 **Undergraduates** 59% women, 7% part-time, 5% 25 or older, 0.2% Native American, 4% Hispanic American, 2% African American, 2% Asian American/Pacific Islander **The most frequently chosen baccalaureate fields are** business/marketing, social sciences, visual and performing arts **Academic program** Advanced placement, accelerated degree program, self-designed majors, honors program, summer session, adult/continuing education programs, internships **Contact** Mr. Christopher Hooker-Haring, Director of Undergraduate Admissions, Muhlenberg College, 2400 Chew Street, Allentown, PA 18104. Phone: 484-664-3245. Fax: 484-664-3234. E-mail: adm@muhlenberg.edu. Web site: http://www.muhlenberg.edu/.

►**For more information, see page 477.**

NEUMANN COLLEGE
ASTON, PENNSYLVANIA

General Independent Roman Catholic, comprehensive, coed **Entrance** Moderately difficult

Neumann College *(continued)*

Setting 50-acre suburban campus **Total enrollment** 3,084 **Student-faculty ratio** 14:1 **Application deadline** 4/1 (freshmen), rolling (transfer) **Freshmen** 95% were admitted **Housing** Yes **Expenses** Tuition $19,486; Room & Board $8838 **Undergraduates** 65% women, 21% part-time, 26% 25 or older, 0.2% Native American, 2% Hispanic American, 13% African American, 1% Asian American/Pacific Islander **The most frequently chosen baccalaureate fields are** health professions and related sciences, education, liberal arts/general studies **Academic program** Advanced placement, accelerated degree program, self-designed majors, honors program, summer session, adult/continuing education programs, internships **Contact** Mr. Dennis J. Murphy, Vice President for Enrollment Management, Neumann College, One Neumann Drive, Aston, PA 19014-1298. Phone: 610-361-2448 or toll-free 800-963-8626. Fax: 610-558-5652. E-mail: neumann@neumann.edu. Web site: http://www.neumann.edu/.

PEIRCE COLLEGE
PHILADELPHIA, PENNSYLVANIA

General Independent, 4-year, coed **Entrance** Noncompetitive **Setting** 1-acre urban campus **Total enrollment** 2,181 **Student-faculty ratio** 17:1 **Application deadline** Rolling (freshmen), rolling (transfer) **Housing** No **Expenses** Tuition $13,750 **Undergraduates** 73% women, 59% part-time, 83% 25 or older, 0.3% Native American, 6% Hispanic American, 55% African American, 1% Asian American/Pacific Islander **The most frequently chosen baccalaureate fields are** business/marketing, computer and information sciences, law/legal studies **Academic program** Advanced placement, accelerated degree program, summer session, internships **Contact** Mr. Steve W. Bird, Supervisor, Admissions, Peirce College, 1420 Pine Street, Philadelphia, PA 19102. Phone: 215-670-9236 or toll-free 888-467-3472. Fax: 215-670-9366. E-mail: info@peirce.edu. Web site: http://www.peirce.edu/.

PENN STATE ABINGTON
ABINGTON, PENNSYLVANIA

General State-related, 4-year, coed **Entrance** Very difficult **Setting** 45-acre small-town campus **Total enrollment** 3,352 **Student-faculty ratio** 21:1 **Application deadline** Rolling (freshmen), rolling (transfer) **Freshmen** 80% were admitted **Expenses** Tuition $11,006 **Undergraduates** 50% women, 21% part-time, 12% 25 or older, 0.2% Native American, 6% Hispanic American, 13% African American, 15% Asian American/Pacific Islander **The most frequently chosen baccalaureate fields are** business/marketing, psychology, security and protective services **Academic program** English as a second language, advanced placement, accelerated degree program, self-designed majors, honors program, summer session, adult/continuing education programs, internships **Contact** Anne L. Rohrbach, Executive Director for Undergraduate Admissions, Penn State Abington, 201 Shields Building, Box 3000, University Park, PA 16804-3000. Phone: 814-865-5471. Fax: 814-863-7590. E-mail: admissions@psu.edu. Web site: http://www.abington.psu.edu/.

PENN STATE ALTOONA
ALTOONA, PENNSYLVANIA

General State-related, 4-year, coed **Entrance** Very difficult **Setting** 150-acre suburban campus **Total enrollment** 4,034 **Student-faculty ratio** 19:1 **Application deadline** Rolling (freshmen), rolling (transfer) **Freshmen** 70% were admitted **Housing** Yes **Expenses** Tuition $11,464; Room & Board $7180 **Undergraduates** 49% women, 7% part-time, 9% 25 or older, 0.1% Native American, 2% Hispanic American, 6% African American, 2% Asian American/Pacific Islander **The most frequently chosen baccalaureate fields are** business/marketing, education, security and protective services **Academic program** English as a second language, advanced placement, self-designed majors, honors program, summer session, adult/continuing education programs, internships **Contact** Anne L. Rohrbach, Executive Director for Undergraduate Admissions, Penn State Altoona, 201 Shields Building, Box 3000, University Park, PA 16804-3000. Phone: 814-865-5471 or toll-free 800-848-9843. Fax: 814-863-7590. E-mail: admissions@psu.edu. Web site: http://www.aa.psu.edu/.

PENN STATE BERKS
READING, PENNSYLVANIA

General State-related, 4-year, coed **Entrance** Very difficult **Setting** 258-acre suburban campus **Total enrollment** 2,824 **Student-faculty ratio** 19:1 **Application deadline** Rolling (freshmen), rolling (transfer) **Freshmen** 75% were admitted **Housing** Yes **Expenses** Tuition $11,464; Room & Board $7850 **Undergraduates** 43% women, 11% part-time, 8% 25 or older, 0.04% Native American, 4% Hispanic American, 8% African American, 4% Asian American/Pacific Islander **The most frequently chosen baccalaureate fields are** business/marketing, computer and information sciences, interdisciplinary studies **Academic program** Advanced placement, accelerated degree program, honors program, summer session, adult/continuing education programs, internships **Contact** Anne L. Rohrbach, Executive Director for Undergraduate Admissions, Penn State Berks, 201 Shields Building, Box 3000, University Park,

PA 16804-3000. Phone: 814-865-5471. Fax: 814-863-7590. E-mail: admissions@psu.edu. Web site: http://www.bk.psu.edu/.

PENN STATE ERIE, THE BEHREND COLLEGE
ERIE, PENNSYLVANIA

General State-related, comprehensive, coed **Entrance** Very difficult **Setting** 725-acre suburban campus **Total enrollment** 4,171 **Student-faculty ratio** 17:1 **Application deadline** Rolling (freshmen), rolling (transfer) **Freshmen** 79% were admitted **Housing** Yes **Expenses** Tuition $11,464; Room & Board $7180 **Undergraduates** 35% women, 7% part-time, 7% 25 or older, 0.1% Native American, 2% Hispanic American, 3% African American, 2% Asian American/Pacific Islander **The most frequently chosen baccalaureate fields are** business/marketing, engineering, engineering technologies **Academic program** Advanced placement, accelerated degree program, honors program, summer session, adult/continuing education programs, internships **Contact** Anne L. Rohrbach, Executive Director for Undergraduate Admissions, Penn State Erie, The Behrend College, 201 Shields Building, Box 3000, University Park, PA 16804-3000. Phone: 814-865-5471 or toll-free 866-374-3378. Fax: 814-863-7590. E-mail: admissions@psu.edu. Web site: http://www.pserie.psu.edu/.

PENN STATE HARRISBURG
MIDDLETOWN, PENNSYLVANIA

General State-related, comprehensive, coed **Entrance** Very difficult **Setting** 218-acre small-town campus **Total enrollment** 3,907 **Student-faculty ratio** 12:1 **Application deadline** Rolling (freshmen), rolling (transfer) **Freshmen** 70% were admitted **Housing** Yes **Expenses** Tuition $11,454; Room & Board $8610 **Undergraduates** 46% women, 20% part-time, 24% 25 or older, 0.2% Native American, 4% Hispanic American, 9% African American, 7% Asian American/Pacific Islander **The most frequently chosen baccalaureate fields are** business/marketing, education, engineering **Academic program** Advanced placement, accelerated degree program, self-designed majors, honors program, summer session, adult/continuing education programs, internships **Contact** Anne L. Rohrbach, Executive Director for Undergraduate Admissions, Penn State Harrisburg, 201 Shields Building, Box 3000, University Park, PA 16804-3000. Phone: 814-865-5471 or toll-free 800-222-2056. Fax: 814-863-7590. E-mail: admissions@psu.edu. Web site: http://www.hbg.psu.edu/.

PENN STATE UNIVERSITY PARK
STATE COLLEGE, PENNSYLVANIA

General State-related, university, coed **Entrance** Very difficult **Setting** 15,984-acre small-town campus **Total enrollment** 43,252 **Student-faculty ratio** 17:1 **Application deadline** Rolling (freshmen), rolling (transfer) **Freshmen** 51% were admitted **Housing** Yes **Expenses** Tuition $12,844; Room & Board $7180 **Undergraduates** 45% women, 4% part-time, 3% 25 or older, 0.1% Native American, 4% Hispanic American, 4% African American, 5% Asian American/Pacific Islander **The most frequently chosen baccalaureate fields are** business/marketing, communications/journalism, engineering **Academic program** English as a second language, advanced placement, accelerated degree program, self-designed majors, honors program, summer session, adult/continuing education programs, internships **Contact** Anne L. Rohrbach, Director for Undergraduate Admissions, Penn State University Park, 201 Shields Building, Box 3000, University Park, PA 16804-3000. Phone: 814-865-5471. Fax: 814-863-7590. E-mail: admissions@psu.edu. Web site: http://www.psu.edu/.

PENNSYLVANIA COLLEGE OF ART & DESIGN
LANCASTER, PENNSYLVANIA

General Independent, 4-year, coed **Entrance** Moderately difficult **Setting** urban campus **Total enrollment** 253 **Student-faculty ratio** 9:1 **Application deadline** Rolling (freshmen), rolling (transfer) **Freshmen** 56% were admitted **Housing** No **Expenses** Tuition $15,205 **Undergraduates** 60% women, 7% part-time, 5% 25 or older, 1% Native American, 3% Hispanic American, 4% African American, 3% Asian American/Pacific Islander **The most frequently chosen baccalaureate field is** visual and performing arts **Academic program** Advanced placement, internships **Contact** Director of Admissions and Marketing, Pennsylvania College of Art & Design, 204 North Prince Street, PO Box 59, Lancaster, PA 17608. Phone: 717-396-7833. Fax: 717-396-1339. E-mail: admissions@pcad.edu. Web site: http://www.pcad.edu/.

PENNSYLVANIA COLLEGE OF TECHNOLOGY
WILLIAMSPORT, PENNSYLVANIA

General State-related, 4-year, coed **Entrance** Noncompetitive **Setting** 981-acre small-town campus **Total enrollment** 6,682 **Student-faculty ratio** 19:1 **Application deadline** 7/1 (freshmen), rolling (transfer) **Freshmen** 95% were admitted **Housing** Yes **Expenses** Tuition $11,250; Room & Board $7700 **Undergraduates** 34%

Pennsylvania College of Technology *(continued)*

women, 15% part-time, 17% 25 or older, 1% Native American, 1% Hispanic American, 3% African American, 1% Asian American/Pacific Islander **The most frequently chosen baccalaureate fields are** business/marketing, computer and information sciences, engineering technologies **Academic program** English as a second language, advanced placement, self-designed majors, summer session, internships **Contact** Mr. Chester Schuman, Director of Admissions, Pennsylvania College of Technology, One College Avenue, DIF #119, Williamsport, PA 17701. Phone: 570-327-4761 or toll-free 800-367-9222. Fax: 570-321-5551. E-mail: cschuman@pct.edu. Web site: http://www.pct.edu/.

PHILADELPHIA BIBLICAL UNIVERSITY

LANGHORNE, PENNSYLVANIA

General Independent nondenominational, comprehensive, coed **Entrance** Moderately difficult **Setting** 105-acre suburban campus **Total enrollment** 1,388 **Student-faculty ratio** 14:1 **Application deadline** Rolling (freshmen), rolling (transfer) **Freshmen** 98% were admitted **Housing** Yes **Expenses** Tuition $17,785; Room & Board $7150 **Undergraduates** 54% women, 7% part-time, 18% 25 or older, 0.2% Native American, 2% Hispanic American, 12% African American, 3% Asian American/Pacific Islander **The most frequently chosen baccalaureate fields are** education, business/marketing, philosophy and religious studies **Academic program** Advanced placement, accelerated degree program, honors program, summer session, adult/continuing education programs, internships **Contact** Ms. Lisa Yoder, Director of Undergraduate Admissions, Philadelphia Biblical University, 200 Manor Avenue, Langhorne, PA 19047. Phone: 215-702-4550 or toll-free 800-366-0049. Fax: 215-702-4248. E-mail: admissions@pbu.edu. Web site: http://www.pbu.edu/.

PHILADELPHIA UNIVERSITY

PHILADELPHIA, PENNSYLVANIA

General Independent, comprehensive, coed **Entrance** Moderately difficult **Setting** 100-acre suburban campus **Total enrollment** 3,349 **Student-faculty ratio** 13:1 **Application deadline** Rolling (freshmen), rolling (transfer) **Freshmen** 64% were admitted **Housing** Yes **Expenses** Tuition $25,456; Room & Board $8358 **Undergraduates** 69% women, 9% part-time, 9% 25 or older, 0.2% Native American, 3% Hispanic American, 10% African American, 4% Asian American/Pacific Islander **The most frequently chosen baccalaureate fields are** business/marketing, architecture, visual and performing arts **Academic program** English as a second language, advanced placement, accelerated degree program, honors program, summer session, adult/continuing education programs, internships **Contact** Ms. Christine Greb, Director of Admissions, Philadelphia University, School House Lane and Henry Avenue, Philadelphia, PA 19144-5497. Phone: 215-951-2800. Fax: 215-951-2907. E-mail: admissions@philau.edu. Web site: http://www.philau.edu/.

POINT PARK UNIVERSITY

PITTSBURGH, PENNSYLVANIA

General Independent, comprehensive, coed **Entrance** Moderately difficult **Setting** urban campus **Total enrollment** 3,592 **Student-faculty ratio** 17:1 **Application deadline** Rolling (freshmen), rolling (transfer) **Freshmen** 75% were admitted **Housing** Yes **Expenses** Tuition $18,990; Room & Board $8440 **Undergraduates** 60% women, 21% part-time, 32% 25 or older, 0.4% Native American, 2% Hispanic American, 19% African American, 1% Asian American/Pacific Islander **The most frequently chosen baccalaureate fields are** business/marketing, security and protective services, visual and performing arts **Academic program** Advanced placement, accelerated degree program, self-designed majors, honors program, summer session, adult/continuing education programs, internships **Contact** Ms. Joell Minford, Director, Full-Time Admissions, Point Park University, 201 Wood Street, Pittsburgh, PA 15222. Phone: 412-392-3430 or toll-free 800-321-0129. Fax: 412-392-3902. E-mail: enroll@pointpark.edu. Web site: http://www.pointpark.edu/.

ROBERT MORRIS UNIVERSITY

MOON TOWNSHIP, PENNSYLVANIA

General Independent, university, coed **Entrance** Moderately difficult **Setting** 230-acre suburban campus **Total enrollment** 5,055 **Student-faculty ratio** 16:1 **Application deadline** 7/1 (freshmen), 7/1 (transfer) **Freshmen** 76% were admitted **Housing** Yes **Expenses** Tuition $17,900; Room & Board $8520 **Undergraduates** 47% women, 20% part-time, 22% 25 or older, 0.1% Native American, 1% Hispanic American, 8% African American, 1% Asian American/Pacific Islander **The most frequently chosen baccalaureate fields are** business/marketing, communications/journalism, education **Academic program** Advanced placement, accelerated degree program, honors program, summer session, adult/continuing education programs, internships **Contact** Enrollment Services Department, Robert Morris University, 6001 University Boulevard, Moon Township, PA 15108-1189. Phone: 412-397-

5200 or toll-free 800-762-0097. Fax: 412-397-2425. E-mail: admissions@rmu.edu. Web site: http://www.rmu.edu/.

ROSEMONT COLLEGE
ROSEMONT, PENNSYLVANIA

General Independent Roman Catholic, comprehensive, undergraduate: women only; graduate: coed **Entrance** Moderately difficult **Setting** 56-acre suburban campus **Total enrollment** 940 **Student-faculty ratio** 8:1 **Application deadline** Rolling (freshmen), rolling (transfer) **Freshmen** 60% were admitted **Housing** Yes **Expenses** Tuition $22,835; Room & Board $9200 **Undergraduates** 28% part-time, 35% 25 or older, 8% Hispanic American, 36% African American, 6% Asian American/Pacific Islander **The most frequently chosen baccalaureate fields are** business/marketing, English, visual and performing arts **Academic program** English as a second language, advanced placement, accelerated degree program, self-designed majors, honors program, summer session, adult/continuing education programs, internships **Contact** Ms. Rennie Andrews, Dean, Undergraduate Women's College Admissions, Rosemont College, 1400 Montgomery Avenue, Main Building, Rosemont, PA 19010. Phone: 610-527-0200 Ext. 2952 or toll-free 800-331-0708. Fax: 610-520-4399. E-mail: admissions@rosemont.edu. Web site: http://www.rosemont.edu/.

ST. CHARLES BORROMEO SEMINARY, OVERBROOK
WYNNEWOOD, PENNSYLVANIA

General Independent Roman Catholic, comprehensive, undergraduate: men only; graduate: coed **Entrance** Moderately difficult **Setting** 77-acre suburban campus **Total enrollment** 240 **Student-faculty ratio** 7:1 **Application deadline** 7/15 (freshmen), 7/15 (transfer) **Freshmen** 100% were admitted **Housing** Yes **Expenses** Tuition $12,321; Room & Board $8269 **Undergraduates** 32% part-time, 17% 25 or older, 4% Hispanic American, 1% African American **The most frequently chosen baccalaureate field is** philosophy and religious studies **Academic program** English as a second language, advanced placement, accelerated degree program, summer session, adult/continuing education programs **Contact** Rev. David E. Diamond, Vice Rector, St. Charles Borromeo Seminary, Overbrook, 100 East Wynnewood Road, Wynnewood, PA 19096. Phone: 610-785-6271 Ext. 271. Fax: 610-617-9267. E-mail: cao@adphila.org. Web site: http://www.scs.edu/.

SAINT FRANCIS UNIVERSITY
LORETTO, PENNSYLVANIA

General Independent Roman Catholic, comprehensive, coed **Entrance** Moderately difficult **Setting** 600-acre rural campus **Total enrollment** 2,163 **Student-faculty ratio** 16:1 **Application deadline** Rolling (freshmen), rolling (transfer) **Freshmen** 85% were admitted **Housing** Yes **Expenses** Tuition $23,494; Room & Board $7984 **Undergraduates** 64% women, 11% part-time, 3% 25 or older, 0.3% Native American, 1% Hispanic American, 5% African American, 1% Asian American/Pacific Islander **Academic program** Advanced placement, accelerated degree program, self-designed majors, honors program, summer session, adult/continuing education programs, internships **Contact** Robert Beener, Associate Dean for Enrollment Management, Saint Francis University, PO Box 600, 117 Evergreen Drive, Loretto, PA 15940-0600. Phone: 814-472-3100 or toll-free 800-342-5732. Fax: 814-472-3335. E-mail: rbeener@francis.edu. Web site: http://www.francis.edu/.

SAINT JOSEPH'S UNIVERSITY
PHILADELPHIA, PENNSYLVANIA

General Independent Roman Catholic (Jesuit), comprehensive, coed **Entrance** Moderately difficult **Setting** 65-acre suburban campus **Total enrollment** 7,542 **Student-faculty ratio** 12:1 **Application deadline** 2/1 (freshmen), 3/1 (transfer) **Freshmen** 62% were admitted **Housing** Yes **Expenses** Tuition $30,985; Room & Board $10,550 **Undergraduates** 52% women, 17% part-time, 10% 25 or older, 0.2% Native American, 3% Hispanic American, 8% African American, 3% Asian American/Pacific Islander **The most frequently chosen baccalaureate fields are** business/marketing, education, social sciences **Academic program** English as a second language, advanced placement, accelerated degree program, self-designed majors, honors program, summer session, adult/continuing education programs, internships **Contact** John G. Haller, Associate Provost of Enrollment Management, Saint Joseph's University, 5600 City Avenue, Philadelphia, PA 19131-1395. Phone: 610-660-1300 or toll-free 888-BEAHAWK. Fax: 610-660-1314. E-mail: admit@sju.edu. Web site: http://www.sju.edu/.

SAINT VINCENT COLLEGE
LATROBE, PENNSYLVANIA

General Independent Roman Catholic, comprehensive, coed **Entrance** Moderately difficult **Setting** 200-acre suburban campus **Total enrollment** 1,924 **Student-faculty ratio** 13:1 **Application deadline** 5/1 (freshmen), 7/1 (transfer)

Saint Vincent College *(continued)*

Freshmen 62% were admitted **Housing** Yes **Expenses** Tuition $24,106; Room & Board $7580 **Undergraduates** 50% women, 6% part-time, 5% 25 or older, 0.2% Native American, 2% Hispanic American, 3% African American, 1% Asian American/Pacific Islander **The most frequently chosen baccalaureate fields are** business/marketing, history, psychology **Academic program** Advanced placement, accelerated degree program, honors program, summer session, adult/continuing education programs, internships **Contact** Mr. David A. Collins, Assistant Vice President of Admission and Financial Aid, Saint Vincent College, 300 Fraser Purchase Road, Latrobe, PA 15650. Phone: 724-532-5089 or toll-free 800-782-5549. Fax: 724-532-5069. E-mail: admission@stvincent.edu. Web site: http://www.stvincent.edu/.

SETON HILL UNIVERSITY

GREENSBURG, PENNSYLVANIA

General Independent Roman Catholic, comprehensive, coed **Entrance** Moderately difficult **Setting** 200-acre small-town campus **Total enrollment** 1,967 **Student-faculty ratio** 14:1 **Application deadline** 8/15 (freshmen), rolling (transfer) **Freshmen** 63% were admitted **Housing** Yes **Expenses** Tuition $25,006; Room & Board $7740 **Undergraduates** 63% women, 20% part-time, 10% 25 or older, 0.4% Native American, 2% Hispanic American, 8% African American, 0.5% Asian American/Pacific Islander **The most frequently chosen baccalaureate fields are** business/marketing, psychology, visual and performing arts **Academic program** English as a second language, advanced placement, accelerated degree program, self-designed majors, honors program, summer session, adult/continuing education programs, internships **Contact** Ms. Sherri Bett, Director of Admissions, Seton Hill University, Seton Hill Drive, Greensburg, PA 15601. Phone: 724-838-4255 or toll-free 800-826-6234. Fax: 724-830-1294. E-mail: admit@setonhill.edu. Web site: http://www.setonhill.edu/.

SHIPPENSBURG UNIVERSITY OF PENNSYLVANIA

SHIPPENSBURG, PENNSYLVANIA

General State-supported, comprehensive, coed **Entrance** Moderately difficult **Setting** 200-acre rural campus **Total enrollment** 7,765 **Student-faculty ratio** 19:1 **Application deadline** Rolling (freshmen), rolling (transfer) **Freshmen** 75% were admitted **Housing** Yes **Expenses** Tuition $6849; Room & Board $6272 **Undergraduates** 53% women, 5% part-time, 6% 25 or older, 0.3% Native American, 2% Hispanic American, 6% African American, 1% Asian American/Pacific Islander **The most frequently chosen baccalaureate fields are** business/marketing, education, security and protective services **Academic program** Advanced placement, accelerated degree program, honors program, summer session, internships **Contact** Dr. Thomas Speakman, Dean of Enrollment Services, Shippensburg University of Pennsylvania, 1871 Old Main Drive, Shippensburg, PA 17257-2299. Phone: 717-477-1231 or toll-free 800-822-8028. Fax: 717-477-4016. E-mail: admiss@ship.edu. Web site: http://www.ship.edu/.

SLIPPERY ROCK UNIVERSITY OF PENNSYLVANIA

SLIPPERY ROCK, PENNSYLVANIA

General State-supported, comprehensive, coed **Entrance** Moderately difficult **Setting** 650-acre rural campus **Total enrollment** 8,325 **Student-faculty ratio** 20:1 **Freshmen** 58% were admitted **Housing** Yes **Expenses** Tuition $6671; Room & Board $7862 **Undergraduates** 56% women, 7% part-time, 10% 25 or older, 0.2% Native American, 1% Hispanic American, 5% African American, 1% Asian American/Pacific Islander **The most frequently chosen baccalaureate fields are** business/marketing, education, health professions and related sciences **Academic program** Advanced placement, honors program, summer session, adult/continuing education programs, internships **Contact** Mr. W. C. Vance, Director of Admissions, Slippery Rock University of Pennsylvania, 1 Morrow Way, 146 North Hall, Slippery Rock, PA 16057. Phone: 724-738-2015 or toll-free 800-SRU-9111. Fax: 724-738-2913. E-mail: asktherock@sru.edu. Web site: http://www.sru.edu/.

SUSQUEHANNA UNIVERSITY

SELINSGROVE, PENNSYLVANIA

General Independent, 4-year, coed, affiliated with Evangelical Lutheran Church in America **Entrance** Moderately difficult **Setting** 220-acre suburban campus **Total enrollment** 2,039 **Student-faculty ratio** 14:1 **Application deadline** 3/1 (freshmen), 7/1 (transfer) **Freshmen** 86% were admitted **Housing** Yes **Expenses** Tuition $31,080; Room & Board $8400 **Undergraduates** 54% women, 3% part-time, 1% 25 or older, 0.1% Native American, 2% Hispanic American, 3% African American, 2% Asian American/Pacific Islander **The most frequently chosen baccalaureate fields are** business/marketing, communications/journalism, education **Academic program** Advanced placement, accelerated degree program, self-designed majors, honors program, summer session, adult/continuing education programs, internships **Contact** Mr. Chris Markle,

Director of Admissions, Susquehanna University, 514 University Avenue, Selinsgrove, PA 17870. Phone: 570-372-4260 or toll-free 800-326-9672. Fax: 570-372-2722. E-mail: suadmiss@susqu.edu. Web site: http://www.susqu.edu/.

SWARTHMORE COLLEGE

SWARTHMORE, PENNSYLVANIA

General Independent, 4-year, coed **Entrance** Most difficult **Setting** 357-acre suburban campus **Total enrollment** 1,491 **Student-faculty ratio** 8:1 **Application deadline** 1/2 (freshmen), 4/1 (transfer) **Freshmen** 18% were admitted **Housing** Yes **Expenses** Tuition $34,884; Room only $5544 **Undergraduates** 52% women, 0.4% part-time, 1% Native American, 10% Hispanic American, 8% African American, 17% Asian American/Pacific Islander **The most frequently chosen baccalaureate fields are** biological/life sciences, foreign languages and literature, social sciences **Academic program** Advanced placement, self-designed majors, honors program, internships **Contact** Mr. Jim Bock, Dean of Admissions and Financial Aid, Swarthmore College, 500 College Avenue, Swarthmore, PA 19081. Phone: 610-328-8300 or toll-free 800-667-3110. Fax: 610-328-8580. E-mail: admissions@swarthmore.edu. Web site: http://www.swarthmore.edu/.

TALMUDICAL YESHIVA OF PHILADELPHIA

PHILADELPHIA, PENNSYLVANIA

Contact Rabbi Shmuel Kamenetsky, Co-Dean, Talmudical Yeshiva of Philadelphia, 6063 Drexel Road, Philadelphia, PA 19131-1296. Phone: 215-473-1212.

TEMPLE UNIVERSITY

PHILADELPHIA, PENNSYLVANIA

General State-related, university, coed **Setting** 110-acre urban campus **Total enrollment** 34,696 **Student-faculty ratio** 17:1 **Application deadline** 4/1 (freshmen), 6/15 (transfer) **Freshmen** 63% were admitted **Housing** Yes **Expenses** Tuition $10,802; Room & Board $8518 **Undergraduates** 55% women, 13% part-time, 12% 25 or older, 0.3% Native American, 3% Hispanic American, 17% African American, 10% Asian American/Pacific Islander **The most frequently chosen baccalaureate fields are** business/marketing, communications/journalism, visual and performing arts **Academic program** English as a second language, advanced placement, self-designed majors, honors program, summer session, adult/continuing education programs, internships **Contact** Dr. Timm Rinehart, Associate Vice President Enrollment Management, Temple University, 1801 North Broad Street, Philadelphia, PA 19122-6096. Phone: 215-204-7200 or toll-free 888-340-2222. Fax: 215-204-5694. E-mail: tuadm@temple.edu. Web site: http://www.temple.edu/.

THIEL COLLEGE

GREENVILLE, PENNSYLVANIA

General Independent, 4-year, coed, affiliated with Evangelical Lutheran Church in America **Entrance** Moderately difficult **Setting** 135-acre rural campus **Total enrollment** 1,219 **Student-faculty ratio** 16:1 **Application deadline** 6/30 (freshmen), rolling (transfer) **Freshmen** 75% were admitted **Housing** Yes **Expenses** Tuition $20,214; Room & Board $7840 **Undergraduates** 46% women, 6% part-time, 6% 25 or older, 0.3% Native American, 1% Hispanic American, 6% African American, 1% Asian American/Pacific Islander **The most frequently chosen baccalaureate fields are** business/marketing, education, psychology **Academic program** English as a second language, advanced placement, honors program, summer session, adult/continuing education programs, internships **Contact** Sonya Lapikas, Chief Admissions Officer, Thiel College, 75 College Avenue, Greenville, PA 16125. Phone: 724-589-2172 or toll-free 800-248-4435. Fax: 724-589-2013. E-mail: admissions@thiel.edu. Web site: http://www.thiel.edu/.

THOMAS JEFFERSON UNIVERSITY

PHILADELPHIA, PENNSYLVANIA

General Independent, university, coed **Contact** Ms. Karen Jacobs, Director of Admissions, Thomas Jefferson University, Edison Building, 130 South Ninth Street, Philadelphia, PA 19107. Phone: 215-503-1040 or toll-free 877-533-3247. Fax: 215-503-7241. E-mail: chpadmissions@mail.tju.edu. Web site: http://www.jefferson.edu/.

UNIVERSITY OF PENNSYLVANIA

PHILADELPHIA, PENNSYLVANIA

General Independent, university, coed **Entrance** Most difficult **Setting** 269-acre urban campus **Total enrollment** 18,916 **Student-faculty ratio** 6:1 **Application deadline** 1/1 (freshmen), 3/15 (transfer) **Freshmen** 16% were admitted **Housing** Yes **Expenses** Tuition $35,916; Room & Board $10,208 **Undergraduates** 49% women, 3% part-time, 1% 25 or older, 0.4% Native American, 6% Hispanic American, 8% African American, 17% Asian American/Pacific Islander **The most frequently chosen baccalaureate fields are** business/marketing, engineering, social sciences **Academic program** English as a second language, advanced placement, accelerated degree program, self-designed majors, honors program, summer session, adult/continuing education programs,

University of Pennsylvania *(continued)*

internships **Contact** Eric J. Kaplan, Interim Dean of Admissions, University of Pennsylvania, 1 College Hall, Levy Park, Philadelphia, PA 19104. Phone: 215-898-7507. E-mail: info@admissions.ugao.upenn.edu. Web site: http://www.upenn.edu/.

UNIVERSITY OF PHOENIX–PHILADELPHIA CAMPUS
WAYNE, PENNSYLVANIA

General Proprietary, comprehensive, coed **Contact** Ms. Evelyn Gaskin, Registrar/Executive Director, University of Phoenix–Philadelphia Campus, 4615 East Elwood Street, Mail Stop AA-K101, Phoenix, AZ 85040-1958. Phone: 480-557-3301 or toll-free 800-776-4867 (in-state); 800-228-7240 (out-of-state). Fax: 480-643-1020. E-mail: evelyn.gaskin@phoenix.edu. Web site: http://www.phoenix.edu/.

UNIVERSITY OF PHOENIX–PITTSBURGH CAMPUS
PITTSBURGH, PENNSYLVANIA

General Proprietary, comprehensive, coed **Contact** Ms. Evelyn Gaskin, Registrar/Executive Director, University of Phoenix–Pittsburgh Campus, 4615 East Elwood Street, Mail Stop AA-K101, Phoenix, AZ 85040-1958. Phone: 480-557-3301 or toll-free 800-776-4867 (in-state); 800-228-7240 (out-of-state). Fax: 480-643-1020. E-mail: evelyn.gaskin@phoenix.edu. Web site: http://www.phoenix.edu/.

UNIVERSITY OF PITTSBURGH
PITTSBURGH, PENNSYLVANIA

General State-related, university, coed **Entrance** Moderately difficult **Setting** 132-acre urban campus **Total enrollment** 27,020 **Student-faculty ratio** 16:1 **Application deadline** Rolling (freshmen), rolling (transfer) **Freshmen** 56% were admitted **Housing** Yes **Expenses** Tuition $12,876; Room & Board $8300 **Undergraduates** 51% women, 9% part-time, 12% 25 or older, 0.2% Native American, 1% Hispanic American, 8% African American, 5% Asian American/Pacific Islander **The most frequently chosen baccalaureate fields are** business/marketing, engineering, social sciences **Academic program** English as a second language, advanced placement, accelerated degree program, self-designed majors, honors program, summer session, adult/continuing education programs, internships **Contact** Dr. Betsy A. Porter, Director of Office of Admissions and Financial Aid, University of Pittsburgh, 4227 Fifth Avenue, First Floor, Alumni Hall, Pittsburgh, PA 15260. Phone: 412-624-7488. Fax: 412-648-8815. E-mail: oafa@pitt.edu. Web site: http://www.pitt.edu/.

UNIVERSITY OF PITTSBURGH AT BRADFORD
BRADFORD, PENNSYLVANIA

General State-related, 4-year, coed **Entrance** Minimally difficult **Setting** 317-acre small-town campus **Total enrollment** 1,407 **Student-faculty ratio** 14:1 **Application deadline** Rolling (freshmen), rolling (transfer) **Freshmen** 84% were admitted **Housing** Yes **Expenses** Tuition $11,300; Room & Board $6850 **Undergraduates** 58% women, 15% part-time, 20% 25 or older, 0.3% Native American, 1% Hispanic American, 4% African American, 2% Asian American/Pacific Islander **The most frequently chosen baccalaureate fields are** business/marketing, health professions and related sciences, social sciences **Academic program** Advanced placement, accelerated degree program, summer session, adult/continuing education programs, internships **Contact** Ms. Vicky Pingie, Associate Director of Admissions, University of Pittsburgh at Bradford, 300 Campus Drive, Bradford, PA 16701. Phone: 814-362-7677 or toll-free 800-872-1787. Fax: 814-362-5150. E-mail: monti@upb.pitt.edu. Web site: http://www.upb.pitt.edu/.

UNIVERSITY OF PITTSBURGH AT GREENSBURG
GREENSBURG, PENNSYLVANIA

General State-related, 4-year, coed **Entrance** Moderately difficult **Setting** 219-acre small-town campus **Total enrollment** 1,777 **Student-faculty ratio** 18:1 **Application deadline** 8/1 (freshmen), 8/1 (transfer) **Freshmen** 85% were admitted **Housing** Yes **Expenses** Tuition $11,320; Room & Board $7000 **Undergraduates** 50% women, 8% part-time, 7% 25 or older, 0.1% Native American, 1% Hispanic American, 5% African American, 2% Asian American/Pacific Islander **The most frequently chosen baccalaureate fields are** business/marketing, English, psychology **Academic program** Advanced placement, accelerated degree program, self-designed majors, summer session, adult/continuing education programs, internships **Contact** Ms. Heather Kabala, Director of Admissions, University of Pittsburgh at Greensburg, 1150 Mount Pleasant Road, Greensburg, PA 15601-5860. Phone: 724-836-9880. Fax: 724-836-7160. E-mail: upgadmit@pitt.edu. Web site: http://www.upg.pitt.edu/.

UNIVERSITY OF PITTSBURGH AT JOHNSTOWN

JOHNSTOWN, PENNSYLVANIA

General State-related, 4-year, coed **Entrance** Moderately difficult **Setting** 650-acre suburban campus **Total enrollment** 3,121 **Student-faculty ratio** 19:1 **Application deadline** Rolling (freshmen), rolling (transfer) **Freshmen** 88% were admitted **Housing** Yes **Expenses** Tuition $11,332; Room & Board $6400 **Undergraduates** 47% women, 6% part-time, 7% 25 or older, 0.03% Native American, 1% Hispanic American, 2% African American, 1% Asian American/Pacific Islander **The most frequently chosen baccalaureate fields are** business/marketing, education, engineering technologies **Academic program** Advanced placement, accelerated degree program, self-designed majors, summer session, adult/continuing education programs, internships **Contact** Office of Admissions, University of Pittsburgh at Johnstown, 157 Blackington Hall, Johnstown, PA 15904. Phone: 814-269-7050 or toll-free 800-765-4875. Fax: 814-269-7044. E-mail: upjadmit@pitt.edu. Web site: http://www.upj.pitt.edu/.

THE UNIVERSITY OF SCRANTON

SCRANTON, PENNSYLVANIA

General Independent Roman Catholic (Jesuit), comprehensive, coed **Entrance** Moderately difficult **Setting** 50-acre urban campus **Total enrollment** 5,612 **Student-faculty ratio** 11:1 **Application deadline** 3/1 (freshmen), rolling (transfer) **Freshmen** 66% were admitted **Housing** Yes **Expenses** Tuition $28,758; Room & Board $10,610 **Undergraduates** 57% women, 6% part-time, 4% 25 or older, 0.2% Native American, 5% Hispanic American, 1% African American, 2% Asian American/Pacific Islander **The most frequently chosen baccalaureate fields are** business/marketing, education, health professions and related sciences **Academic program** Advanced placement, accelerated degree program, self-designed majors, honors program, summer session, adult/continuing education programs, internships **Contact** Mr. Joseph Roback, Associate Vice President, Undergraduate Admissions and Enrollment, The University of Scranton, St. Thomas Hall, Room 409, Scranton, PA 18510-4501. Phone: 570-941-7540 or toll-free 888-SCRANTON. Fax: 570-941-4370. E-mail: admissions@scranton.edu. Web site: http://www.scranton.edu/.

THE UNIVERSITY OF THE ARTS

PHILADELPHIA, PENNSYLVANIA

General Independent, comprehensive, coed **Entrance** Moderately difficult **Setting** 18-acre urban campus **Total enrollment** 2,396 **Student-faculty ratio** 10:1 **Application deadline** Rolling (freshmen), rolling (transfer) **Freshmen** 48% were admitted **Housing** Yes **Expenses** Tuition $30,600; Room only $7047 **Undergraduates** 55% women, 2% part-time, 5% 25 or older, 0.4% Native American, 5% Hispanic American, 10% African American, 3% Asian American/Pacific Islander **The most frequently chosen baccalaureate fields are** communications/journalism, education, visual and performing arts **Academic program** English as a second language, advanced placement, internships **Contact** Ms. Susan Gandy, Director of Admission, The University of the Arts, 320 South Broad Street, Philadelphia, PA 19102-4944. Phone: 215-717-6039 or toll-free 800-616-ARTS. Fax: 215-717-6045. E-mail: admissions@uarts.edu. Web site: http://www.uarts.edu/.

UNIVERSITY OF THE SCIENCES IN PHILADELPHIA

PHILADELPHIA, PENNSYLVANIA

General Independent, university, coed **Entrance** Moderately difficult **Setting** 35-acre urban campus **Total enrollment** 2,969 **Student-faculty ratio** 13:1 **Application deadline** Rolling (freshmen) **Freshmen** 58% were admitted **Housing** Yes **Expenses** Tuition $26,930; Room & Board $10,524 **Undergraduates** 59% women, 2% part-time, 3% 25 or older, 0.4% Native American, 2% Hispanic American, 5% African American, 34% Asian American/Pacific Islander **The most frequently chosen baccalaureate fields are** biological/life sciences, business/marketing, health professions and related sciences **Academic program** English as a second language, advanced placement, honors program, summer session, adult/continuing education programs, internships **Contact** Mr. Louis Hegyes, Director of Admission, University of the Sciences in Philadelphia, 600 South 43rd Street, Philadelphia, PA 19104-4495. Phone: 215-596-8810 or toll-free 888-996-8747. Fax: 215-596-8821. E-mail: admit@usip.edu. Web site: http://www.usip.edu/.

URSINUS COLLEGE

COLLEGEVILLE, PENNSYLVANIA

General Independent, 4-year, coed **Entrance** Very difficult **Setting** 168-acre suburban campus **Total enrollment** 1,583 **Student-faculty ratio** 12:1 **Application deadline** 2/15 (freshmen), 8/15 (transfer) **Freshmen** 53% were admitted **Housing** Yes **Expenses** Tuition $35,160; Room & Board $8000 **Undergraduates** 52% women, 1% part-time, 0.2% Native American, 3% Hispanic American, 6% African American, 5% Asian American/Pacific Islander **The most frequently chosen baccalaureate fields are** biological/life sciences, psychology, social sciences **Academic**

Ursinus College *(continued)*

program English as a second language, advanced placement, self-designed majors, honors program, adult/continuing education programs, internships **Contact** Mr. Robert McCullough, Dean of Admissions, Ursinus College, Ursinus College, PO Box 1000, Main Street, Collegeville, PA 19426. Phone: 610-409-3200. Fax: 610-409-3662. E-mail: admissions@ursinus.edu. Web site: http://www.ursinus.edu/.

VALLEY FORGE CHRISTIAN COLLEGE
PHOENIXVILLE, PENNSYLVANIA

General Independent Assemblies of God, 4-year, coed **Contact** Rev. William Chenco, Director of Admissions, Valley Forge Christian College, 1401 Charlestown Road, Phoenixville, PA 19460. Phone: 610-935-0450 Ext. 1430 or toll-free 800-432-8322. Fax: 610-935-9353. E-mail: admissions@vfcc.edu. Web site: http://www.vfcc.edu/.

VILLANOVA UNIVERSITY
VILLANOVA, PENNSYLVANIA

General Independent Roman Catholic, comprehensive, coed **Entrance** Very difficult **Setting** 254-acre suburban campus **Total enrollment** 10,430 **Student-faculty ratio** 14:1 **Application deadline** 1/7 (freshmen), 6/1 (transfer) **Freshmen** 42% were admitted **Housing** Yes **Expenses** Tuition $34,900; Room & Board $9810 **Undergraduates** 51% women, 9% part-time, 5% 25 or older, 0.2% Native American, 6% Hispanic American, 4% African American, 6% Asian American/Pacific Islander **The most frequently chosen baccalaureate fields are** business/marketing, engineering, social sciences **Academic program** English as a second language, advanced placement, accelerated degree program, honors program, summer session, adult/continuing education programs, internships **Contact** Mr. Michael Gaynor, Director of University Admission, Villanova University, 800 Lancaster Avenue, Villanova, PA 19085-1672. Phone: 610-519-4000. Fax: 610-519-6450. E-mail: gotovu@villanova.edu. Web site: http://www.villanova.edu/.

WASHINGTON & JEFFERSON COLLEGE
WASHINGTON, PENNSYLVANIA

General Independent, 4-year, coed **Entrance** Very difficult **Setting** 51-acre small-town campus **Total enrollment** 1,531 **Student-faculty ratio** 12:1 **Application deadline** 3/1 (freshmen), rolling (transfer) **Freshmen** 34% were admitted **Housing** Yes **Expenses** Tuition $29,532; Room & Board $8030 **Undergraduates** 47% women, 1% part-time, 1% 25 or older, 0.1% Native American, 1% Hispanic American, 2% African American, 1% Asian American/Pacific Islander **The most frequently chosen baccalaureate fields are** biological/life sciences, business/marketing, psychology **Academic program** Advanced placement, accelerated degree program, self-designed majors, honors program, summer session, internships **Contact** Mr. Alton E. Newell, Vice President for Enrollment Management, Washington & Jefferson College, 60 South Lincoln Street, Washington, PA 15301. Phone: 724-223-6025 or toll-free 888-WANDJAY. Fax: 724-223-6534. E-mail: admission@washjeff.edu. Web site: http://www.washjeff.edu/.

WAYNESBURG UNIVERSITY
WAYNESBURG, PENNSYLVANIA

General Independent, comprehensive, coed, affiliated with Presbyterian Church (U.S.A.) **Entrance** Moderately difficult **Setting** 30-acre small-town campus **Total enrollment** 2,159 **Student-faculty ratio** 13:1 **Application deadline** Rolling (freshmen), rolling (transfer) **Freshmen** 74% were admitted **Housing** Yes **Expenses** Tuition $17,080; Room & Board $7050 **Undergraduates** 62% women, 18% part-time, 19% 25 or older, 0.1% Native American, 1% Hispanic American, 3% African American, 0.2% Asian American/Pacific Islander **The most frequently chosen baccalaureate fields are** business/marketing, education, health professions and related sciences **Academic program** Advanced placement, accelerated degree program, honors program, adult/continuing education programs, internships **Contact** Ms. Robin L. King, Dean of Admissions, Waynesburg University, 51 West College Street, Waynesburg, PA 15370. Phone: 724-852-3333 or toll-free 800-225-7393. Fax: 724-627-8124. E-mail: admissions@waynesburg.edu. Web site: http://www.waynesburg.edu/.

WEST CHESTER UNIVERSITY OF PENNSYLVANIA
WEST CHESTER, PENNSYLVANIA

General State-supported, comprehensive, coed **Entrance** Moderately difficult **Setting** 547-acre suburban campus **Total enrollment** 13,219 **Student-faculty ratio** 17:1 **Application deadline** Rolling (freshmen), rolling (transfer) **Freshmen** 48% were admitted **Housing** Yes **Expenses** Tuition $6676; Room & Board $6590 **Undergraduates** 61% women, 10% part-time, 9% 25 or older, 0.3% Native American, 3% Hispanic American, 9% African American, 2% Asian American/Pacific Islander **The most frequently chosen baccalaureate fields are** business/marketing, education, health professions and related sciences **Academic program** English as a second language, advanced placement, accelerated degree program, self-designed majors, honors program, summer session, adult/continuing education programs, internships **Contact** Ms. Marsha Haug, Vice President of Enrollment Services and Admissions, West Chester University of Pennsylvania, Messikomer Hall, Rosedale Avenue, West Chester, PA 19383. Phone: 610-436-3414 or toll-free 877-315-2165. Fax: 610-436-2907. E-mail: ugadmiss@wcupa.edu. Web site: http://www.wcupa.edu/.

WESTMINSTER COLLEGE
NEW WILMINGTON, PENNSYLVANIA

Contact Bradley Tokar, Director of Admissions, Westminster College, 319 South Market Street, New Wilmington, PA 16172-0001. Phone: 724-946-7109 or toll-free 800-942-8033. Fax: 724-946-7171. E-mail: tokarbp@westminster.edu. Web site: http://www.westminster.edu/.

WIDENER UNIVERSITY
CHESTER, PENNSYLVANIA

General Independent, comprehensive, coed **Entrance** Moderately difficult **Setting** 110-acre suburban campus **Total enrollment** 6,571 **Student-faculty ratio** 12:1 **Application deadline** Rolling (freshmen), rolling (transfer) **Freshmen** 66% were admitted **Housing** Yes **Expenses** Tuition $28,630; Room & Board $10,240 **Undergraduates** 58% women, 23% part-time, 19% 25 or older, 0.3% Native American, 3% Hispanic American, 13% African American, 3% Asian American/Pacific Islander **The most frequently chosen baccalaureate fields are** business/marketing, health professions and related sciences, psychology **Academic program** English as a second language, advanced placement, accelerated degree program, self-designed majors, honors program, summer session, adult/continuing education programs, internships **Contact** Office of Admissions, Widener University, One University Place, Chester, PA 19013. Phone: 610-499-4126 or toll-free 888-WIDENER. Fax: 610-499-4676. E-mail: admissions.office@widener.edu. Web site: http://www.widener.edu/.

WILKES UNIVERSITY
WILKES-BARRE, PENNSYLVANIA

General Independent, comprehensive, coed **Entrance** Moderately difficult **Setting** 25-acre urban campus **Total enrollment** 5,114 **Student-faculty ratio** 15:1 **Application deadline** Rolling (freshmen), rolling (transfer) **Freshmen** 79% were admitted **Housing** Yes **Expenses** Tuition $24,080; Room & Board $10,310 **Undergraduates** 50% women, 10% part-time, 7% 25 or older, 0.3% Native American, 2% Hispanic American, 3% African American, 2% Asian American/Pacific Islander **The most frequently chosen baccalaureate fields are** business/marketing, health professions and related sciences, liberal arts/general studies **Academic program** English as a second language, advanced placement, accelerated degree program, self-designed majors, honors program, summer session, adult/continuing education programs, internships **Contact** Mr. Michael Frantz, Vice President of Enrollment Services, Wilkes University, 84 West South Street, Wilkes-Barre, PA 18766. Phone: 570-408-4400 or toll-free 800-945-5378 Ext. 4400. Fax: 570-408-4904. E-mail: admissions@wilkes.edu. Web site: http://www.wilkes.edu/.

WILSON COLLEGE
CHAMBERSBURG, PENNSYLVANIA

General Independent, 4-year, women only, affiliated with Presbyterian Church (U.S.A.) **Entrance** Moderately difficult **Setting** 300-acre small-town campus **Total enrollment** 727 **Student-faculty ratio** 9:1 **Application deadline** Rolling (freshmen), rolling (transfer) **Freshmen** 48% were admitted **Housing** Yes **Expenses** Tuition $25,900; Room & Board $8630 **Undergraduates** 49% part-time, 35% 25 or older **The most frequently chosen baccalaureate fields are** education, business/marketing, health professions and related sciences **Academic program** English as a second language, advanced placement, self-designed majors, honors program, summer session, adult/continuing education programs, internships **Contact** Deborah Arthur, Admissions Administrator, Wilson College, 1015 Philadelphia Avenue, Chambersburg, PA 17201. Phone: 717-262-2002 Ext. 3269 or toll-free 800-421-8402. Fax: 717-262-2546. E-mail: admissions@wilson.edu. Web site: http://www.wilson.edu/.

YESHIVA BETH MOSHE
SCRANTON, PENNSYLVANIA

Contact Rabbi I. Bressler, Dean, Yeshiva Beth Moshe, 930 Hickory Street, PO Box 1141, Scranton, PA 18505-2124. Phone: 717-346-1747.

YORK COLLEGE OF PENNSYLVANIA
YORK, PENNSYLVANIA

General Independent, comprehensive, coed **Entrance** Moderately difficult **Setting** 118-acre suburban campus **Total enrollment** 5,721 **Student-faculty ratio** 15:1 **Application deadline** 8/1 (freshmen), rolling (transfer) **Freshmen** 64% were admitted **Housing** Yes **Expenses** Tuition $12,750; Room & Board $7410 **Undergraduates** 56% women, 15% part-time, 13% 25 or older, 0.2% Native American, 2% Hispanic American, 2% African American, 1% Asian American/Pacific Islander **The most frequently**

York College of Pennsylvania *(continued)*

chosen baccalaureate fields are business/marketing, education, health professions and related sciences **Academic program** Advanced placement, accelerated degree program, self-designed majors, honors program, summer session, adult/continuing education programs, internships **Contact** Mrs. Nancy L. Spataro, Director of Admissions, York College of Pennsylvania, York, PA 17405-7199. Phone: 717-849-1600 or toll-free 800-455-8018. Fax: 717-849-1607. E-mail: admissions@ycp.edu. Web site: http://www.ycp.edu/.

RHODE ISLAND

BROWN UNIVERSITY
PROVIDENCE, RHODE ISLAND

General Independent, university, coed **Entrance** Most difficult **Setting** 140-acre urban campus **Total enrollment** 8,167 **Student-faculty ratio** 9:1 **Application deadline** 1/1 (freshmen), 3/1 (transfer) **Freshmen** 14% were admitted **Housing** Yes **Expenses** Tuition $36,342; Room & Board $9606 **Undergraduates** 52% women, 4% part-time, 1% 25 or older, 1% Native American, 8% Hispanic American, 7% African American, 15% Asian American/Pacific Islander **The most frequently chosen baccalaureate fields are** biological/life sciences, physical sciences, social sciences **Academic program** Advanced placement, accelerated degree program, self-designed majors, honors program, summer session, adult/continuing education programs, internships **Contact** Mr. James Miller, Dean of Admission, Brown University, Box 1876, Providence, RI 02912. Phone: 401-863-2378. Fax: 401-863-9300. E-mail: admission_undergraduate@brown.edu. Web site: http://www.brown.edu/.

BRYANT UNIVERSITY
SMITHFIELD, RHODE ISLAND

General Independent, comprehensive, coed **Contact** Ms. Michelle Beauregard, Director of Admission, Bryant University, 1150 Douglas Pike, Smithfield, RI 02917. Phone: 401-232-6100 or toll-free 800-622-7001. Fax: 401-232-6741. E-mail: admission@bryant.edu. Web site: http://www.bryant.edu/.

►**For more information, see page 445.**

JOHNSON & WALES UNIVERSITY
PROVIDENCE, RHODE ISLAND

General Independent, comprehensive, coed **Entrance** Minimally difficult **Setting** 47-acre urban campus **Total enrollment** 10,105 **Student-faculty ratio** 27:1 **Application deadline** Rolling (freshmen), rolling (transfer) **Freshmen** 72% were admitted **Housing** Yes **Expenses** Tuition $22,585; Room & Board $8892 **Undergraduates** 53% women, 10% part-time, 11% 25 or older, 0.4% Native American, 7% Hispanic American, 8% African American, 3% Asian American/Pacific Islander **The most frequently chosen baccalaureate fields are** business/marketing, family and consumer sciences, personal and culinary services **Academic program** English as a second language, advanced placement, accelerated degree program, honors program, summer session, adult/continuing education programs, internships **Contact** Ms. Maureen Dumas, Dean of Admissions, Johnson & Wales University, 8 Abbott Park Place, Providence, RI 02903-3703. Phone: 401-598-2310 or toll-free 800-598-1000 (in-state); 800-342-5598 (out-of-state). Fax: 401-598-2948. E-mail: admissions.pvd@jwu.edu. Web site: http://www.jwu.edu/.

PROVIDENCE COLLEGE
PROVIDENCE, RHODE ISLAND

General Independent Roman Catholic, comprehensive, coed **Entrance** Very difficult **Setting** 105-acre suburban campus **Total enrollment** 4,759 **Student-faculty ratio** 12:1 **Application deadline** 1/15 (freshmen), 4/1 (transfer) **Freshmen** 41% were admitted **Housing** Yes **Expenses** Tuition $29,499; Room & Board $10,335 **Undergraduates** 56% women, 0.4% part-time, 0.1% Native American, 2% Hispanic American, 2% African American, 2% Asian American/Pacific Islander **The most frequently chosen baccalaureate fields are** business/marketing, education, social sciences **Academic program** Advanced placement, self-designed majors, honors program, summer session, adult/continuing education programs, internships **Contact** Mr. Christopher Lydon, Associate Vice President for Admission and Enrollment Planning, Providence College, 549 River Avenue, Providence, RI 02918. Phone: 401-865-2535 or toll-free 800-721-6444. Fax: 401-865-2826. E-mail: pcadmiss@providence.edu. Web site: http://www.providence.edu/.

RHODE ISLAND COLLEGE
PROVIDENCE, RHODE ISLAND

General State-supported, comprehensive, coed **Entrance** Moderately difficult **Setting** 180-acre suburban campus **Total enrollment** 9,042 **Student-faculty ratio** 16:1 **Application deadline** 5/1 (freshmen), 6/1 (transfer) **Freshmen** 72% were admitted **Housing** Yes **Expenses** Tuition $5552; Room & Board $8250 **Undergraduates** 68% women, 29% part-time, 23% 25 or older,

0.3% Native American, 6% Hispanic American, 6% African American, 2% Asian American/ Pacific Islander **The most frequently chosen baccalaureate fields are** education, health professions and related sciences, psychology **Academic program** Advanced placement, self-designed majors, honors program, summer session, adult/ continuing education programs, internships **Contact** Dr. Holly Shadoian, Director of Admissions, Rhode Island College, 600 Mount Pleasant Avenue, Providence, RI 02908-1927. Phone: 401-456-8234 or toll-free 800-669-5760. Fax: 401-456-8817. E-mail: admissions@ric.edu. Web site: http://www.ric.edu/.

RHODE ISLAND SCHOOL OF DESIGN
PROVIDENCE, RHODE ISLAND

General Independent, comprehensive, coed **Contact** Mr. Edward Newhall, Director of Admissions, Rhode Island School of Design, 2 College Street, Providence, RI 02905-2791. Phone: 401-454-6307 or toll-free 800-364-7473. Fax: 401-454-6309. E-mail: admissions@risd.edu. Web site: http://www.risd.edu/.

ROGER WILLIAMS UNIVERSITY
BRISTOL, RHODE ISLAND

General Independent, comprehensive, coed **Entrance** Moderately difficult **Setting** 140-acre small-town campus **Total enrollment** 5,166 **Student-faculty ratio** 13:1 **Application deadline** 2/1 (freshmen), rolling (transfer) **Freshmen** 68% were admitted **Housing** Yes **Expenses** Tuition $25,942; Room & Board $11,490 **Undergraduates** 49% women, 12% part-time, 11% 25 or older, 0.3% Native American, 2% Hispanic American, 1% African American, 1% Asian American/Pacific Islander **The most frequently chosen baccalaureate fields are** business/ marketing, psychology, security and protective services **Academic program** English as a second language, advanced placement, self-designed majors, honors program, summer session, adult/ continuing education programs, internships **Contact** Mr. Didier Bouvet, Director of Freshman Admission, Roger Williams University, 1 Old Ferry Road, Bristol, RI 02809. Phone: 401-254-3500 or toll-free 800-458-7144. Fax: 401-254-3557. E-mail: admit@rwu.edu. Web site: http://www.rwu.edu/.

▶**For more information, see page 483.**

SALVE REGINA UNIVERSITY
NEWPORT, RHODE ISLAND

General Independent Roman Catholic, comprehensive, coed **Entrance** Moderately difficult **Setting** 70-acre suburban campus **Total enrollment** 2,686 **Student-faculty ratio** 14:1 **Application deadline** 3/1 (freshmen), rolling (transfer) **Freshmen** 54% were admitted **Housing** Yes **Expenses** Tuition $26,950; Room & Board $10,200 **Undergraduates** 69% women, 4% part-time, 4% 25 or older, 0.4% Native American, 3% Hispanic American, 2% African American, 1% Asian American/Pacific Islander **The most frequently chosen baccalaureate fields are** business/marketing, education, health professions and related sciences **Academic program** English as a second language, advanced placement, accelerated degree program, honors program, summer session, adult/continuing education programs, internships **Contact** Ms. Colleen Emerson, Dean of Undergraduate Admissions, Salve Regina University, 100 Ochre Point Avenue, Newport, RI 02840-4192. Phone: 401-847-6650 Ext. 2908 or toll-free 888-GO SALVE. Fax: 401-848-2823. E-mail: sruadmis@salve.edu. Web site: http://www.salve.edu/.

UNIVERSITY OF RHODE ISLAND
KINGSTON, RHODE ISLAND

General State-supported, university, coed **Entrance** Moderately difficult **Setting** 1,200-acre small-town campus **Total enrollment** 15,650 **Student-faculty ratio** 19:1 **Application deadline** 2/1 (freshmen), 5/1 (transfer) **Freshmen** 79% were admitted **Housing** Yes **Expenses** Tuition $8184; Room & Board $8732 **Undergraduates** 56% women, 13% part-time, 11% 25 or older, 0.5% Native American, 5% Hispanic American, 5% African American, 2% Asian American/ Pacific Islander **The most frequently chosen baccalaureate fields are** business/marketing, communications/journalism, health professions and related sciences **Academic program** Advanced placement, honors program, summer session, adult/continuing education programs, internships **Contact** Ms. Joanne Hood, Assistant Dean of Admissions, University of Rhode Island, Undergrad Admission Office, Newman Hall, 14 Upper College Rd., Kingston, RI 02881. Phone: 401-874-7100. Fax: 401-874-5523. E-mail: jhood@uri.edu. Web site: http://www.uri.edu.

ZION BIBLE COLLEGE
BARRINGTON, RHODE ISLAND

Contact Zion Bible College, 27 Middle Highway, Barrington, RI 02806. Phone: toll-free 800-356-4014. Web site: http://www.zbc.edu/.

SOUTH CAROLINA

ALLEN UNIVERSITY
COLUMBIA, SOUTH CAROLINA

Contact Ms. Constants Adams, Admissions Representative, Allen University, 1530 Harden

Allen University *(continued)*

Street, Columbia, SC 29204. Phone: 803-376-5789 or toll-free 877-625-5368. Fax: 803-376-5731. E-mail: admissions@allenuniversity.edu. Web site: http://www.allenuniversity.edu/.

ANDERSON UNIVERSITY
ANDERSON, SOUTH CAROLINA

General Independent Baptist, 4-year, coed **Entrance** Minimally difficult **Setting** 44-acre suburban campus **Total enrollment** 1,902 **Student-faculty ratio** 16:1 **Application deadline** 7/1 (freshmen), 8/1 (transfer) **Housing** Yes **Expenses** Tuition $17,400; Room & Board $7050 **Undergraduates** 66% women, 24% part-time, 20% 25 or older, 0.3% Native American, 2% Hispanic American, 10% African American, 1% Asian American/Pacific Islander **The most frequently chosen baccalaureate fields are** business/marketing, education, visual and performing arts **Academic program** Advanced placement, accelerated degree program, honors program, summer session, adult/continuing education programs, internships **Contact** Ms. Pam Bryant, Director of Admissions, Anderson University, 316 Boulevard, Anderson, SC 29621. Phone: 864-231-2030 or toll-free 800-542-3594. Fax: 864-231-3033. E-mail: admissions@ac.edu. Web site: http://www.ac.edu/.

THE ART INSTITUTE OF CHARLESTON
CHARLESTON, SOUTH CAROLINA

General Proprietary, 4-year, coed **Entrance** Noncompetitive **Setting** urban campus **Total enrollment** 224 **Student-faculty ratio** 17:1 **Freshmen** 63% were admitted **Housing** Yes **Undergraduates** 62% women, 11% part-time, 21% 25 or older, 1% Native American, 4% Hispanic American, 15% African American, 2% Asian American/Pacific Islander **Academic program** Advanced placement, accelerated degree program, summer session, adult/continuing education programs, internships **Contact** Mr. Brian Stanley, The Art Institute of Charleston, The Carroll Building, 24 North Market Street, Charleston, SC 29401. Phone: 843-727-3500 Ext. 3442 or toll-free 866-211-0107. Fax: 843-727-3440. E-mail: mdearsman@aii.edu. Web site: http://www.artinstitutes.edu/charleston/.

BENEDICT COLLEGE
COLUMBIA, SOUTH CAROLINA

Contact Mr. Gary Knight, Vice President, Institutional Effectiveness, Benedict College, 1600 Harden Street, Columbia, SC 29204. Phone: 803-253-5275 or toll-free 800-868-6598. Fax: 803-253-5215. E-mail: knightg@benedict.edu. Web site: http://www.benedict.edu/.

BOB JONES UNIVERSITY
GREENVILLE, SOUTH CAROLINA

General Independent religious, university, coed **Entrance** Minimally difficult **Setting** 225-acre urban campus **Total enrollment** 4,159 **Student-faculty ratio** 15:1 **Application deadline** 8/1 (freshmen), 8/1 (transfer) **Housing** Yes **Expenses** Tuition $11,730; Room & Board $5100 **Undergraduates** 54% women, 1% part-time, 3% 25 or older **The most frequently chosen baccalaureate fields are** education, business/marketing, theology and religious vocations **Academic program** English as a second language, advanced placement, summer session, adult/continuing education programs, internships **Contact** Mr. Gary Deedrick, Director of Admissions, Bob Jones University, 1700 Wade Hampton Boulevard, Greenville, SC 29614. Phone: 864-242-5100 or toll-free 800-BJANDME. Fax: 800-232-9258. E-mail: admissions@bju.edu. Web site: http://www.bju.edu/.

CHARLESTON SOUTHERN UNIVERSITY
CHARLESTON, SOUTH CAROLINA

General Independent Baptist, comprehensive, coed **Entrance** Moderately difficult **Setting** 500-acre suburban campus **Total enrollment** 3,286 **Student-faculty ratio** 18:1 **Application deadline** Rolling (freshmen), rolling (transfer) **Housing** Yes **Expenses** Tuition $18,678; Room & Board $7178 **Undergraduates** 62% women, 14% part-time, 12% 25 or older, 0.5% Native American, 2% Hispanic American, 29% African American, 1% Asian American/Pacific Islander **The most frequently chosen baccalaureate fields are** business/marketing, education, psychology **Academic program** Advanced placement, accelerated degree program, honors program, summer session, internships **Contact** Mr. Jim Rhoden, Director of Enrollment Management, Charleston Southern University, PO Box 118087, Charleston, SC 19423-8087. Phone: 843-863-7050 or toll-free 800-947-7474. E-mail: enroll@csuniv.edu. Web site: http://www.charlestonsouthern.edu/.

THE CITADEL, THE MILITARY COLLEGE OF SOUTH CAROLINA
CHARLESTON, SOUTH CAROLINA

General State-supported, comprehensive, coed **Entrance** Moderately difficult **Setting** 130-acre urban campus **Total enrollment** 3,300 **Student-faculty ratio** 15:1 **Application deadline** Rolling (freshmen), rolling (transfer) **Freshmen** 78% were admitted **Housing** Yes **Expenses** Tuition $8735;

Room & Board $5390 **Undergraduates** 8% women, 5% part-time, 5% 25 or older, 0.5% Native American, 5% Hispanic American, 7% African American, 3% Asian American/Pacific Islander **The most frequently chosen baccalaureate fields are** business/marketing, engineering, security and protective services **Academic program** English as a second language, summer session, internships **Contact** Lt. Col. John Powell, Director of Admissions, The Citadel, The Military College of South Carolina, 171 Moultrie Street, Charleston, SC 29409. Phone: 843-953-5230 or toll-free 800-868-1842. Fax: 843-953-7036. E-mail: admissions@citadel.edu. Web site: http://www.citadel.edu.

CLAFLIN UNIVERSITY

ORANGEBURG, SOUTH CAROLINA

General Independent United Methodist, comprehensive, coed **Entrance** Minimally difficult **Setting** 32-acre small-town campus **Total enrollment** 1,763 **Student-faculty ratio** 13:1 **Application deadline** Rolling (freshmen), rolling (transfer) **Freshmen** 45% were admitted **Housing** Yes **Expenses** Tuition $12,358; Room & Board $6640 **Undergraduates** 68% women, 6% part-time, 5% 25 or older, 0.1% Native American, 0.2% Hispanic American, 94% African American, 0.2% Asian American/Pacific Islander **The most frequently chosen baccalaureate fields are** business/marketing, security and protective services, social sciences **Academic program** Advanced placement, honors program, summer session, adult/continuing education programs, internships **Contact** Mr. Michael Zeigler, Director of Admissions, Claflin University, 400 Magnolia Street, Orangeburg, SC 29115. Phone: 803-535-5747 or toll-free 800-922-1276. Fax: 803-535-5387. E-mail: mzeigler@claflin.edu. Web site: http://www.claflin.edu/.

CLEMSON UNIVERSITY

CLEMSON, SOUTH CAROLINA

General State-supported, university, coed **Entrance** Moderately difficult **Setting** 1,400-acre small-town campus **Total enrollment** 17,165 **Student-faculty ratio** 14:1 **Application deadline** 5/1 (freshmen), 8/1 (transfer) **Freshmen** 50% were admitted **Housing** Yes **Expenses** Tuition $10,370; Room & Board $6170 **Undergraduates** 46% women, 6% part-time, 5% 25 or older, 0.4% Native American, 1% Hispanic American, 7% African American, 2% Asian American/Pacific Islander **The most frequently chosen baccalaureate fields are** business/marketing, education, engineering **Academic program** Advanced placement, accelerated degree program, honors program, summer session, internships **Contact** Ms. Audrey R. Bodell, Associate Director of Admissions, Clemson University, PO Box 345124, 105 Sikes Hall, Clemson, SC 29634. Phone: 864-656-2287. Fax: 864-656-2464. E-mail: cuadmissions@clemson.edu. Web site: http://www.clemson.edu/.

COASTAL CAROLINA UNIVERSITY

CONWAY, SOUTH CAROLINA

General State-supported, comprehensive, coed **Entrance** Moderately difficult **Setting** 302-acre suburban campus **Total enrollment** 7,872 **Student-faculty ratio** 18:1 **Application deadline** 8/15 (freshmen), 8/15 (transfer) **Freshmen** 68% were admitted **Housing** Yes **Expenses** Tuition $7600; Room & Board $6680 **Undergraduates** 53% women, 9% part-time, 8% 25 or older, 0.5% Native American, 2% Hispanic American, 12% African American, 1% Asian American/Pacific Islander **The most frequently chosen baccalaureate fields are** biological/life sciences, business/marketing, education **Academic program** Advanced placement, accelerated degree program, self-designed majors, honors program, summer session, adult/continuing education programs, internships **Contact** Dr. Judy Vogt, Vice President, Enrollment Services, Coastal Carolina University, PO Box 261954, Conway, SC 29528. Phone: 843-349-2037 or toll-free 800-277-7000. Fax: 843-349-2127. E-mail: admissions@coastal.edu. Web site: http://www.coastal.edu/.

COKER COLLEGE

HARTSVILLE, SOUTH CAROLINA

General Independent, 4-year, coed **Entrance** Moderately difficult **Setting** 30-acre small-town campus **Total enrollment** 634 **Student-faculty ratio** 10:1 **Application deadline** 8/1 (freshmen), rolling (transfer) **Freshmen** 55% were admitted **Housing** Yes **Expenses** Tuition $18,602; Room & Board $5920 **Undergraduates** 61% women, 2% part-time, 5% 25 or older, 0.2% Native American, 2% Hispanic American, 21% African American, 1% Asian American/Pacific Islander **The most frequently chosen baccalaureate fields are** business/marketing, communications/journalism, history **Academic program** English as a second language, advanced placement, self-designed majors, honors program, summer session, adult/continuing education programs, internships **Contact** Mrs. Perry Wilson, Director of Admissions, Coker College, 300 East College Avenue, Hartsville, SC 29550. Phone: 843-383-8050 or toll-free 800-950-1908. Fax: 843-383-8056. E-mail: admissions@coker.edu. Web site: http://www.coker.edu/.

COLLEGE OF CHARLESTON

CHARLESTON, SOUTH CAROLINA

General State-supported, comprehensive, coed **Entrance** Moderately difficult **Setting** 52-acre

College of Charleston *(continued)*

urban campus **Total enrollment** 11,316 **Student-faculty ratio** 13:1 **Application deadline** 4/1 (freshmen), 4/1 (transfer) **Freshmen** 65% were admitted **Housing** Yes **Expenses** Tuition $7778; Room & Board $8495 **Undergraduates** 64% women, 9% part-time, 7% 25 or older, 0.3% Native American, 2% Hispanic American, 6% African American, 2% Asian American/Pacific Islander **The most frequently chosen baccalaureate fields are** business/marketing, communications/journalism, social sciences **Academic program** English as a second language, advanced placement, accelerated degree program, honors program, summer session, adult/continuing education programs, internships **Contact** Ms. Suzette Stille, Director of Undergraduate Admissions, College of Charleston, 66 George Street, Charleston, SC 29424-0001. Phone: 843-953-5670 or toll-free 843-953-5670. Fax: 843-953-6322. E-mail: admissions@cofc.edu. Web site: http://www.cofc.edu/.

COLUMBIA COLLEGE
COLUMBIA, SOUTH CAROLINA

General Independent United Methodist, comprehensive, undergraduate: women only; graduate: coed **Entrance** Moderately difficult **Setting** 33-acre suburban campus **Total enrollment** 1,510 **Student-faculty ratio** 12:1 **Application deadline** 8/1 (freshmen), 8/1 (transfer) **Freshmen** 71% were admitted **Housing** Yes **Expenses** Tuition $21,650; Room & Board $6232 **Undergraduates** 21% part-time, 27% 25 or older, 0.5% Native American, 2% Hispanic American, 44% African American, 1% Asian American/Pacific Islander **The most frequently chosen baccalaureate fields are** business/marketing, education, visual and performing arts **Academic program** Advanced placement, self-designed majors, honors program, summer session, adult/continuing education programs, internships **Contact** Ms. Julie King, Director of Admissions, Columbia College, 1301 Columbia College Drive, Columbia, SC 29203. Phone: 803-786-3091 or toll-free 800-277-1301. Fax: 803-786-3674. E-mail: admissions@colacoll.edu. Web site: http://www.columbiacollegesc.edu/.

COLUMBIA INTERNATIONAL UNIVERSITY
COLUMBIA, SOUTH CAROLINA

General Independent nondenominational, comprehensive, coed **Contact** Ms. Michelle MacGregor, Director of College Admissions, Columbia International University, PO Box 3122, Columbia, SC 29230-3122. Phone: 803-754-4100 Ext. 3024 or toll-free 800-777-2227 Ext. 3024. Fax: 803-786-4041. E-mail: yesciu@ciu.edu. Web site: http://www.ciu.edu/.

CONVERSE COLLEGE
SPARTANBURG, SOUTH CAROLINA

General Independent, comprehensive, undergraduate: women only; graduate: coed **Entrance** Moderately difficult **Setting** 70-acre urban campus **Total enrollment** 1,881 **Application deadline** 7/1 (transfer) **Freshmen** 47% were admitted **Housing** Yes **Expenses** Tuition $24,500; Room & Board $7550 **Undergraduates** 14% part-time, 22% 25 or older, 1% Native American, 2% Hispanic American, 12% African American, 1% Asian American/Pacific Islander **The most frequently chosen baccalaureate fields are** education, business/marketing, visual and performing arts **Academic program** English as a second language, advanced placement, self-designed majors, honors program, summer session, adult/continuing education programs, internships **Contact** Mr. Aaron Meis, Dean of Admission, Converse College, 580 East Main Street, Spartanburg, SC 29302. Phone: 864-596-9040 Ext. 9746 or toll-free 800-766-1125. Fax: 864-596-9225. E-mail: admissions@converse.edu. Web site: http://www.converse.edu/.

ERSKINE COLLEGE
DUE WEST, SOUTH CAROLINA

General Independent, 4-year, coed, affiliated with Associate Reformed Presbyterian Church **Entrance** Moderately difficult **Setting** 85-acre rural campus **Total enrollment** 892 **Student-faculty ratio** 12:1 **Application deadline** Rolling (freshmen), rolling (transfer) **Freshmen** 66% were admitted **Housing** Yes **Expenses** Tuition $21,680; Room & Board $7426 **Undergraduates** 56% women, 2% part-time, 1% 25 or older, 1% Hispanic American, 7% African American, 1% Asian American/Pacific Islander **The most frequently chosen baccalaureate fields are** biological/life sciences, business/marketing, education **Academic program** Advanced placement, summer session, internships **Contact** Mr. Bart Walker, Director of Admissions, Erskine College, PO Box 176, Due West, SC 29639. Phone: 864-379-8830 or toll-free 800-241-8721. Fax: 864-379-8759. E-mail: admissions@erskine.edu. Web site: http://www.erskine.edu/.

FRANCIS MARION UNIVERSITY
FLORENCE, SOUTH CAROLINA

General State-supported, comprehensive, coed **Entrance** Moderately difficult **Setting** 309-acre rural campus **Total enrollment** 3,864 **Student-faculty ratio** 15:1 **Application deadline** Rolling (freshmen), rolling (transfer) **Freshmen** 65% were admitted **Housing** Yes **Expenses** Tuition $7632; Room & Board $6024 **Undergraduates** 67% women, 10% part-time, 9% 25 or older, 1% Native

American, 1% Hispanic American, 43% African American, 1% Asian American/Pacific Islander **The most frequently chosen baccalaureate fields are** biological/life sciences, business/marketing, social sciences **Academic program** Advanced placement, accelerated degree program, honors program, summer session, adult/continuing education programs, internships **Contact** Mr. James Schlimmer, Director of Admissions, Francis Marion University, PO Box 100547, Florence, SC 29501-0547. Phone: 843-661-1231 or toll-free 800-368-7551. Fax: 843-661-4635. E-mail: admission@fmarion.edu. Web site: http://www.fmarion.edu/.

FURMAN UNIVERSITY
GREENVILLE, SOUTH CAROLINA

General Independent, comprehensive, coed **Entrance** Very difficult **Setting** 750-acre suburban campus **Total enrollment** 2,951 **Student-faculty ratio** 11:1 **Application deadline** 1/15 (freshmen), 6/1 (transfer) **Freshmen** 56% were admitted **Housing** Yes **Expenses** Tuition $31,560; Room & Board $8064 **Undergraduates** 56% women, 5% part-time, 0.2% Native American, 1% Hispanic American, 7% African American, 2% Asian American/Pacific Islander **The most frequently chosen baccalaureate fields are** business/marketing, history, social sciences **Academic program** Advanced placement, accelerated degree program, self-designed majors, summer session, adult/continuing education programs, internships **Contact** Mr. David R. O'Cain, Director of Admissions, Furman University, 3300 Poinsett Highway, Greenville, SC 29613. Phone: 864-294-2034. Fax: 864-294-2018. E-mail: admissions@furman.edu. Web site: http://www.furman.edu/.

LANDER UNIVERSITY
GREENWOOD, SOUTH CAROLINA

General State-supported, comprehensive, coed, primarily women **Entrance** Moderately difficult **Setting** 100-acre small-town campus **Total enrollment** 2,408 **Student-faculty ratio** 14:1 **Application deadline** 8/1 (freshmen), rolling (transfer) **Freshmen** 42% were admitted **Housing** Yes **Expenses** Tuition $8278; Room & Board $5940 **Undergraduates** 66% women, 11% part-time, 14% 25 or older, 1% Native American, 1% Hispanic American, 24% African American, 1% Asian American/Pacific Islander **The most frequently chosen baccalaureate fields are** business/marketing, education, social sciences **Academic program** Advanced placement, accelerated degree program, self-designed majors, honors program, summer session, adult/continuing education programs, internships **Contact** Dr. Bettie R. Horne, Director of Admissions, Lander University, 320 Stanley Avenue, Greenwood, SC 29649. Phone: 864-388-8307 or toll-free 888-452-6337. Fax: 864-388-8125. E-mail: admissions@lander.edu. Web site: http://www.lander.edu/.

LIMESTONE COLLEGE
GAFFNEY, SOUTH CAROLINA

General Independent, 4-year, coed **Entrance** Moderately difficult **Setting** 115-acre suburban campus **Total enrollment** 780 **Student-faculty ratio** 13:1 **Application deadline** Rolling (freshmen), rolling (transfer) **Freshmen** 59% were admitted **Housing** Yes **Expenses** Tuition $17,300; Room & Board $6400 **Undergraduates** 43% women, 2% part-time, 9% 25 or older, 0.3% Native American, 2% Hispanic American, 15% African American, 0.4% Asian American/Pacific Islander **The most frequently chosen baccalaureate fields are** business/marketing, education, parks and recreation **Academic program** Advanced placement, accelerated degree program, self-designed majors, honors program, summer session, adult/continuing education programs, internships **Contact** Ms. Sharon Chery, Admissions Office Manager, Limestone College, 1115 College Drive, Gaffney, SC 29340-3799. Phone: 864-488-4549 or toll-free 800-795-7151 Ext. 554. Fax: 864-487-8706. E-mail: cphenicie@limestone.edu. Web site: http://www.limestone.edu/.

MEDICAL UNIVERSITY OF SOUTH CAROLINA
CHARLESTON, SOUTH CAROLINA

Contact Mr. George W. Ohlandt, Director of Admissions, Medical University of South Carolina, 171 Ashley Avenue, Charleston, SC 29425-0002. Phone: 843-792-3813. Fax: 843-792-6615. E-mail: oesadmis@musc.edu. Web site: http://www.musc.edu/.

MORRIS COLLEGE
SUMTER, SOUTH CAROLINA

General Independent, 4-year, coed, affiliated with Baptist Educational and Missionary Convention of South Carolina **Entrance** Noncompetitive **Setting** 34-acre small-town campus **Total enrollment** 871 **Student-faculty ratio** 16:1 **Application deadline** Rolling (freshmen), rolling (transfer) **Freshmen** 90% were admitted **Housing** Yes **Expenses** Tuition $9250; Room & Board $4134 **Undergraduates** 57% women, 3% part-time, 14% 25 or older, 100% African American **The most frequently chosen baccalaureate fields are** business/marketing, security and protective services, social sciences **Academic program** Advanced placement, accelerated degree program, honors program, summer session, adult/continuing education programs, internships **Contact**

Morris College *(continued)*

Ms. Deborah C. Calhoun, Director of Admissions and Records, Morris College, 100 West College Street, Sumter, SC 29150-3599. Phone: 803-934-3225 or toll-free 866-853-1345. Fax: 803-773-8241. E-mail: dcalhoun@morris.edu. Web site: http://www.morris.edu/.

NEWBERRY COLLEGE
NEWBERRY, SOUTH CAROLINA

General Independent Evangelical Lutheran, 4-year, coed **Entrance** Moderately difficult **Setting** 60-acre small-town campus **Total enrollment** 918 **Student-faculty ratio** 14:1 **Application deadline** Rolling (freshmen), rolling (transfer) **Freshmen** 73% were admitted **Housing** Yes **Expenses** Tuition $21,600; Room & Board $7360 **Undergraduates** 41% women, 2% part-time, 10% 25 or older, 0.3% Native American, 2% Hispanic American, 25% African American, 1% Asian American/Pacific Islander **The most frequently chosen baccalaureate fields are** biological/life sciences, business/marketing, communications/journalism **Academic program** Advanced placement, self-designed majors, honors program, summer session, adult/continuing education programs, internships **Contact** Mr. Mike Ryan, Director of Admissions, Newberry College, 2100 College Street, Holland Hall, Newberry, SC 29108. Phone: 803-321-5129 or toll-free 800-845-4955 Ext. 5127. Fax: 803-321-5138. E-mail: admissions@newberry.edu. Web site: http://www.newberry.edu/.

NORTH GREENVILLE UNIVERSITY
TIGERVILLE, SOUTH CAROLINA

General Independent Southern Baptist, comprehensive, coed **Entrance** Minimally difficult **Setting** 500-acre rural campus **Total enrollment** 2,094 **Student-faculty ratio** 16:1 **Application deadline** 8/18 (freshmen), 8/21 (transfer) **Freshmen** 37% were admitted **Housing** Yes **Expenses** Tuition $11,680; Room & Board $6720 **Undergraduates** 51% women, 12% part-time, 6% 25 or older, 0.2% Native American, 1% Hispanic American, 5% African American, 0.2% Asian American/Pacific Islander **The most frequently chosen baccalaureate fields are** business/marketing, education, liberal arts/general studies **Academic program** English as a second language, advanced placement, accelerated degree program, self-designed majors, honors program, summer session, internships **Contact** Ms. Keli Sewell, Vice President of Admissions and Financial Aid, North Greenville University, PO Box 1892, Tigerville, SC 29688-1892. Phone: 864-977-7052 or toll-free 800-468-6642 Ext. 7001. Fax: 864-977-7177. E-mail: bfreeman@ngc.edu. Web site: http://www.ngu.edu/.

PRESBYTERIAN COLLEGE
CLINTON, SOUTH CAROLINA

General Independent, 4-year, coed, affiliated with Presbyterian Church (U.S.A.) **Entrance** Very difficult **Setting** 215-acre small-town campus **Total enrollment** 1,181 **Student-faculty ratio** 12:1 **Application deadline** 6/1 (freshmen), 7/1 (transfer) **Freshmen** 71% were admitted **Housing** Yes **Expenses** Tuition $27,902; Room & Board $8064 **Undergraduates** 51% women, 5% part-time, 0.3% Native American, 1% Hispanic American, 7% African American, 1% Asian American/Pacific Islander **The most frequently chosen baccalaureate fields are** business/marketing, history, social sciences **Academic program** Advanced placement, accelerated degree program, honors program, summer session, internships **Contact** Mrs. Leni Patterson, Dean of Admissions and Financial Aid, Presbyterian College, South Broad Street, Clinto, SC 29325. Phone: 864-833-8229 or toll-free 800-476-7272. Fax: 864-833-8481. E-mail: lpatters@presby.edu. Web site: http://www.presby.edu/.

SOUTH CAROLINA STATE UNIVERSITY
ORANGEBURG, SOUTH CAROLINA

General State-supported, comprehensive, coed **Entrance** Minimally difficult **Setting** 160-acre small-town campus **Total enrollment** 4,933 **Student-faculty ratio** 18:1 **Application deadline** 7/31 (freshmen), 7/31 (transfer) **Freshmen** 88% were admitted **Housing** Yes **Expenses** Tuition $7318; Room & Board $8040 **Undergraduates** 55% women, 7% part-time, 9% 25 or older, 0.3% Hispanic American, 97% African American, 0.3% Asian American/Pacific Islander **The most frequently chosen baccalaureate fields are** business/marketing, biological/life sciences, family and consumer sciences **Academic program** Advanced placement, honors program, summer session, adult/continuing education programs, internships **Contact** Mr. Antonio Boyle, Assistant Vice President of Enrollment Management, South Carolina State University, 300 College Street Northeast, Orangeburg, SC 29117-0001. Phone: 803-536-7186 or toll-free 800-260-5956. Fax: 803-536-8990. E-mail: admissions@scsu.edu. Web site: http://www.scsu.edu/.

SOUTHERN METHODIST COLLEGE
ORANGEBURG, SOUTH CAROLINA

Contact Ms. Juanta Webb, Recruitment Officer, Southern Methodist College, PO Box 1027, Orangeburg, SC 29116-7827. Phone: 803-534-7826 or toll-free 800-360-1503. Fax: 803-534-7827. E-mail: jwebb@smcollege.edu. Web site: http://www.smcollege.edu/.

SOUTHERN WESLEYAN UNIVERSITY
CENTRAL, SOUTH CAROLINA

General Independent, comprehensive, coed, affiliated with Wesleyan Church **Entrance** Minimally difficult **Setting** 230-acre small-town campus **Total enrollment** 2,445 **Student-faculty ratio** 24:1 **Application deadline** 8/1 (freshmen), 8/1 (transfer) **Freshmen** 95% were admitted **Housing** Yes **Expenses** Tuition $17,200; Room & Board $6200 **Undergraduates** 63% women, 2% part-time, 64% 25 or older, 0.3% Native American, 2% Hispanic American, 30% African American, 0.5% Asian American/Pacific Islander **The most frequently chosen baccalaureate fields are** business/marketing, education, philosophy and religious studies **Academic program** English as a second language, advanced placement, accelerated degree program, self-designed majors, honors program, summer session, adult/continuing education programs, internships **Contact** Mrs. Beth Roe, Director of First Year Experience, Southern Wesleyan University, PO Box 1020, 907 Wesleyan Drive, Central, SC 29630-1020. Phone: 864-644-5550 Ext. 5558 or toll-free 800-289-1292 Ext. 5550. Fax: 864-644-5901. E-mail: broe@swu.edu. Web site: http://www.swu.edu/.

SOUTH UNIVERSITY
COLUMBIA, SOUTH CAROLINA

General Proprietary, comprehensive, coed **Setting** urban campus **Contact** Admissions Office, South University, 9 Science Court, Columbia, SC 29203. Phone: 803-935-4299 or toll-free 866-688-0932. Fax: 803-935-4382. Web site: http://www.southuniversity.edu/.

UNIVERSITY OF SOUTH CAROLINA
COLUMBIA, SOUTH CAROLINA

General State-supported, university, coed **Entrance** Moderately difficult **Setting** 315-acre urban campus **Total enrollment** 27,272 **Student-faculty ratio** 16:1 **Application deadline** 12/1 (freshmen), 6/1 (transfer) **Freshmen** 59% were admitted **Housing** Yes **Expenses** Tuition $8346; Room & Board $6946 **Undergraduates** 55% women, 8% part-time, 8% 25 or older, 0.4% Native American, 2% Hispanic American, 12% African American, 3% Asian American/Pacific Islander **The most frequently chosen baccalaureate fields are** business/marketing, communication technologies, social sciences **Academic program** English as a second language, advanced placement, accelerated degree program, self-designed majors, honors program, summer session, adult/continuing education programs, internships **Contact** Mr. Scott Verzyl, Director of Undergraduate Admissions, University of South Carolina, Columbia, SC 29208. Phone: 803-777-7700 or toll-free 800-868-5872. Fax: 803-777-0101. E-mail: admissions-ugrad@sc.edu. Web site: http://www.sc.edu/.

UNIVERSITY OF SOUTH CAROLINA AIKEN
AIKEN, SOUTH CAROLINA

General State-supported, comprehensive, coed **Entrance** Moderately difficult **Setting** 453-acre suburban campus **Total enrollment** 3,267 **Student-faculty ratio** 14:1 **Application deadline** 8/1 (freshmen), 8/1 (transfer) **Freshmen** 51% were admitted **Housing** Yes **Expenses** Tuition $7036; Room & Board $5870 **Undergraduates** 66% women, 26% part-time, 13% 25 or older, 0.2% Native American, 2% Hispanic American, 27% African American, 1% Asian American/Pacific Islander **The most frequently chosen baccalaureate fields are** business/marketing, education, health professions and related sciences **Academic program** Advanced placement, accelerated degree program, honors program, summer session, adult/continuing education programs, internships **Contact** Mr. Andrew Hendrix, Director of Admissions, University of South Carolina Aiken, 471 University Parkway, Aiken, SC 29801-6309. Phone: 803-648-6851 Ext. 3366 or toll-free 888-WOW-USCA. Fax: 803-641-3727. E-mail: admit@usca.edu. Web site: http://www.usca.edu/.

UNIVERSITY OF SOUTH CAROLINA BEAUFORT
BEAUFORT, SOUTH CAROLINA

General State-supported, 4-year, coed **Entrance** Minimally difficult **Setting** 5-acre small-town campus **Total enrollment** 1,461 **Student-faculty ratio** 15:1 **Application deadline** Rolling (freshmen), rolling (transfer) **Freshmen** 61% were admitted **Housing** Yes **Expenses** Tuition $6340; Room only $5176 **Undergraduates** 61% women, 38% part-time, 24% 25 or older, 1% Native American, 3% Hispanic American, 17% African American, 1% Asian American/Pacific Islander **The most frequently chosen baccalaureate fields are** business/marketing, education, social sciences **Academic program** Advanced placement, summer session, adult/continuing education programs, internships **Contact** Ms. Monica Williams, University of South Carolina Beaufort, 1 University Boulevard, Bluffton, SC 29909. Phone: 843-208-8118. Fax: 843-208-8015. E-mail: mrwilli5@gwm.sc.edu. Web site: http://www.sc.edu/beaufort/.

UNIVERSITY OF SOUTH CAROLINA UPSTATE

SPARTANBURG, SOUTH CAROLINA

General State-supported, comprehensive, coed **Entrance** Moderately difficult **Setting** 300-acre urban campus **Total enrollment** 4,918 **Student-faculty ratio** 17:1 **Freshmen** 54% were admitted **Housing** Yes **Expenses** Tuition $7900; Room & Board $6000 **Undergraduates** 65% women, 18% part-time, 23% 25 or older, 0.4% Native American, 2% Hispanic American, 25% African American, 2% Asian American/Pacific Islander **The most frequently chosen baccalaureate fields are** business/marketing, education, health professions and related sciences **Academic program** English as a second language, advanced placement, accelerated degree program, self-designed majors, honors program, summer session, adult/continuing education programs, internships **Contact** Ms. Donette Stewart, Assistant Vice Chancellor for Enrollment Services, University of South Carolina Upstate, 800 University Way, Spartanburg, SC 29303. Phone: 864-503-5280 or toll-free 800-277-8727. Fax: 864-503-5727. E-mail: dstewart@uscupstate.edu. Web site: http://www.uscupstate.edu/.

VOORHEES COLLEGE

DENMARK, SOUTH CAROLINA

General Independent Episcopal, 4-year, coed **Entrance** Moderately difficult **Setting** 350-acre rural campus **Total enrollment** 587 **Student-faculty ratio** 11:1 **Application deadline** Rolling (freshmen), rolling (transfer) **Freshmen** 89% were admitted **Housing** Yes **Expenses** Tuition $8984; Room & Board $5342 **Undergraduates** 60% women, 5% part-time, 7% 25 or older, 99% African American **Academic program** Advanced placement, honors program, summer session, adult/continuing education programs, internships **Contact** Dr. Willie Jefferson, Dean of Enrollment Management, Voorhees College, P.O. Box 678, Denmark, SC 29042. Phone: 803-780-1030 or toll-free 866-685-9904. Fax: 803-793-1117. E-mail: williej@voorhees.edu. Web site: http://www.voorhees.edu/.

WINTHROP UNIVERSITY

ROCK HILL, SOUTH CAROLINA

General State-supported, comprehensive, coed **Entrance** Moderately difficult **Setting** 418-acre suburban campus **Total enrollment** 6,382 **Student-faculty ratio** 14:1 **Application deadline** 5/1 (freshmen) **Freshmen** 70% were admitted **Housing** Yes **Expenses** Tuition $10,210; Room & Board $5800 **Undergraduates** 69% women, 11% part-time, 9% 25 or older, 0.4% Native American, 2% Hispanic American, 27% African American, 2% Asian American/Pacific Islander **The most frequently chosen baccalaureate fields are** business/marketing, education, visual and performing arts **Academic program** Advanced placement, honors program, summer session, adult/continuing education programs, internships **Contact** Ms. Deborah Barber, Director of Admissions, Winthrop University, 701 Oakland Avenue, Rock Hill, SC 29733. Phone: 803-323-2191 or toll-free 800-763-0230. Fax: 803-323-2137. E-mail: admissions@winthrop.edu. Web site: http://www.winthrop.edu/.

WOFFORD COLLEGE

SPARTANBURG, SOUTH CAROLINA

General Independent, 4-year, coed, affiliated with United Methodist Church **Entrance** Very difficult **Setting** 200-acre urban campus **Total enrollment** 1,327 **Student-faculty ratio** 11:1 **Application deadline** 2/1 (freshmen), rolling (transfer) **Freshmen** 53% were admitted **Housing** Yes **Expenses** Tuition $27,830; Room & Board $7705 **Undergraduates** 47% women, 2% part-time, 0.3% Native American, 2% Hispanic American, 6% African American, 2% Asian American/Pacific Islander **The most frequently chosen baccalaureate fields are** biological/life sciences, business/marketing, social sciences **Academic program** Advanced placement, accelerated degree program, self-designed majors, summer session, internships **Contact** Ms. Jennifer B. Page, Director of Admissions, Wofford College, 429 North Church Street, Spartanburg, SC 29303-3663. Phone: 864-597-4130. Fax: 864-597-4147. E-mail: admission@wofford.edu. Web site: http://www.wofford.edu/.

SOUTH DAKOTA

AUGUSTANA COLLEGE

SIOUX FALLS, SOUTH DAKOTA

General Independent, comprehensive, coed, affiliated with Evangelical Lutheran Church in America **Entrance** Moderately difficult **Setting** 100-acre urban campus **Total enrollment** 1,745 **Student-faculty ratio** 12:1 **Application deadline** 8/1 (freshmen), rolling (transfer) **Freshmen** 82% were admitted **Housing** Yes **Expenses** Tuition $21,182; Room & Board $5640 **Undergraduates** 62% women, 6% part-time, 3% 25 or older, 0.5% Native American, 0.4% Hispanic American, 2% African American, 2% Asian American/Pacific Islander **The most frequently chosen baccalaureate fields are** business/marketing, education, health professions and related sciences **Academic program** Advanced placement, accelerated degree program, self-designed majors, honors program, summer session, internships **Contact** Ms. Nancy Davidson, Vice President for Enrollment, Augustana College, 2001 S. Summit Avenue, Sioux Falls, SD 57197. Phone: 605-274-5516 or toll-free 800-727-2844 Ext. 5516 (in-state); 800-727-2844 (out-of-state). Fax: 605-274-5518. E-mail: admission@augie.edu. Web site: http://www.augie.edu/.

BLACK HILLS STATE UNIVERSITY
SPEARFISH, SOUTH DAKOTA

General State-supported, comprehensive, coed **Contact** Ms. Lisa Jenner, Black Hills State University, 1200 University ST USB 9502, Spearfish, SD 57799-9502. Phone: 605-642-6343 or toll-free 800-255-2478. Fax: 605-642-6254. E-mail: admissions@bhsu.edu. Web site: http://www.bhsu.edu/.

COLORADO TECHNICAL UNIVERSITY SIOUX FALLS
SIOUX FALLS, SOUTH DAKOTA

General Proprietary, comprehensive, coed **Entrance** Minimally difficult **Setting** 3-acre urban campus **Total enrollment** 26,375 **Application deadline** Rolling (freshmen), rolling (transfer) **Housing** No **Academic program** Accelerated degree program, summer session, adult/continuing education programs, internships **Contact** Director of Admissions, Colorado Technical University Sioux Falls, 3901 West 59th Street, Sioux Falls, SD 57108. Phone: 605-361-0200. Fax: 605-361-5954. Web site: http://www.ctusiouxfalls.com/.

DAKOTA STATE UNIVERSITY
MADISON, SOUTH DAKOTA

General State-supported, comprehensive, coed **Entrance** Minimally difficult **Setting** 40-acre rural campus **Total enrollment** 2,546 **Student-faculty ratio** 15:1 **Application deadline** Rolling (freshmen), rolling (transfer) **Freshmen** 97% were admitted **Housing** Yes **Expenses** Tuition $6045; Room & Board $4308 **Undergraduates** 56% women, 49% part-time, 19% 25 or older, 1% Native American, 1% Hispanic American, 1% African American, 1% Asian American/Pacific Islander **The most frequently chosen baccalaureate fields are** computer and information sciences, business/marketing, education **Academic program** English as a second language, advanced placement, honors program, summer session, adult/continuing education programs, internships **Contact** Ms. Dana Hoff, Admissions Secretary, Dakota State University, 820 North Washington, Madison, SD 57042-1799. Phone: 605-256-5696 or toll-free 888-DSU-9988. Fax: 605-256-5020. E-mail: yourfuture@dsu.edu. Web site: http://www.dsu.edu/.

DAKOTA WESLEYAN UNIVERSITY
MITCHELL, SOUTH DAKOTA

General Independent United Methodist, comprehensive, coed **Entrance** Moderately difficult **Setting** 50-acre small-town campus **Total enrollment** 788 **Student-faculty ratio** 13:1 **Application deadline** 8/27 (freshmen), 8/27 (transfer) **Freshmen** 68% were admitted **Housing** Yes **Expenses** Tuition $17,600; Room & Board $5400 **Undergraduates** 56% women, 4% part-time, 22% 25 or older, 3% Native American, 4% Hispanic American, 4% African American, 1% Asian American/Pacific Islander **The most frequently chosen baccalaureate fields are** business/marketing, education, security and protective services **Academic program** Advanced placement, self-designed majors, honors program, summer session, adult/continuing education programs, internships **Contact** Mrs. Amy Novak, Vice President for Enrollment Management, Dakota Wesleyan University, 1200 West University Avenue, Mitchell, SD 57301-4398. Phone: 605-995-2600 Ext. 2661 or toll-free 800-333-8506. Fax: 605-995-2699. E-mail: admissions@dwu.edu. Web site: http://www.dwu.edu/.

MOUNT MARTY COLLEGE
YANKTON, SOUTH DAKOTA

General Independent Roman Catholic, comprehensive, coed **Entrance** Minimally difficult **Setting** 80-acre small-town campus **Total enrollment** 1,224 **Student-faculty ratio** 11:1 **Application deadline** Rolling (freshmen), rolling (transfer) **Freshmen** 68% were admitted **Housing** Yes **Expenses** Tuition $17,468; Room & Board $5058 **Undergraduates** 63% women, 43% part-time, 31% 25 or older, 2% Native American, 2% Hispanic American, 1% African American, 1% Asian American/Pacific Islander **The most frequently chosen baccalaureate fields are** education, business/marketing, health professions and related sciences **Academic program** Advanced placement, accelerated degree program, self-designed majors, honors program, summer session, adult/continuing education programs, internships **Contact** Ms. Brandi DeFries, Vice President for Enrollment Management, Mount Marty College, 1105 West 8th Street, Yankton, SD 57078. Phone: 605-668-1545 or toll-free 800-658-4552. Fax: 605-668-1607. E-mail: mmcadmit@mtmc.edu. Web site: http://www.mtmc.edu/.

NATIONAL AMERICAN UNIVERSITY
RAPID CITY, SOUTH DAKOTA

General Proprietary, comprehensive, coed **Entrance** Noncompetitive **Setting** 8-acre urban campus **Total enrollment** 518 **Student-faculty ratio** 26:1 **Application deadline** Rolling (freshmen), rolling (transfer) **Housing** Yes **Expenses** Room & Board $4230 **Undergraduates** 64% women, 27% part-time, 55% 25 or older, 8% Native American, 2% Hispanic American, 2% African American, 5% Asian American/Pacific Islander **The most frequently chosen baccalaureate fields are** business/marketing, computer and information sciences, health professions and related sciences **Academic program** English as a second language, advanced placement, accelerated degree program, summer session, adult/continuing education programs, internships **Contact** Ms. Angela Beck, Director of Enrollment Management, National American University, 321 Kansas City Street, Rapid City, SD 57701. Phone: 605-394-4902 or toll-free 800-843-8892. Fax: 605-394-4871. E-mail: abeck@national.edu. Web site: http://www.rapid.national.edu/.

NATIONAL AMERICAN UNIVERSITY–SIOUX FALLS BRANCH
SIOUX FALLS, SOUTH DAKOTA

General Proprietary, 4-year, coed **Entrance** Noncompetitive **Setting** urban campus **Total enrollment** 375 **Application deadline** Rolling (freshmen), rolling (transfer) **Freshmen** 100% were admitted **Housing** No **Undergraduates** 76% 25 or older, 1% Native American, 1% African American **Academic program** English as a second language, advanced placement, accelerated degree program, summer session, adult/continuing education programs, internships **Contact** Ms. Lisa Houtsma, Director of Admissions, National American University–Sioux Falls Branch, 2801 South Kiwanis Avenue, Suite 100, Sioux Falls, SD 57105-4293. Phone: 605-336-4600 or toll-free 800-388-5430. Fax: 605-336-4605. E-mail: lhoutsma@national.edu. Web site: http://www.national.edu/.

NORTHERN STATE UNIVERSITY
ABERDEEN, SOUTH DAKOTA

General State-supported, comprehensive, coed **Entrance** Minimally difficult **Setting** 52-acre small-town campus **Total enrollment** 2,578 **Student-faculty ratio** 19:1 **Application deadline** 9/1 (freshmen), 9/1 (transfer) **Freshmen** 89% were admitted **Housing** Yes **Expenses** Tuition $5280; Room & Board $4499 **Undergraduates** 59% women, 32% part-time, 21% 25 or older **The most frequently chosen baccalaureate fields are** business/marketing, education, social sciences **Academic program** English as a second language, advanced placement, accelerated degree program, self-designed majors, honors program, summer session, adult/continuing education programs, internships **Contact** Mr. Allan Vogel, Director of Admissions-Campus, Northern State University, 1200 South Jay Street, Aberdeen, SD 57401. Phone: 605-626-2544 or toll-free 800-678-5330. Fax: 605-626-2587. E-mail: admissions1@northern.edu. Web site: http://www.northern.edu/.

OGLALA LAKOTA COLLEGE
KYLE, SOUTH DAKOTA

General State and locally supported, comprehensive, coed **Contact** Director of Admissions, Oglala Lakota College, 490 Piya Wiconi Road, Kyle, SD 57752-0490. Phone: 605-455-2321 Ext. 236. E-mail: lmeseteth@olc.edu. Web site: http://www.olc.edu/.

PRESENTATION COLLEGE
ABERDEEN, SOUTH DAKOTA

General Independent Roman Catholic, 4-year, coed, primarily women **Entrance** Noncompetitive **Setting** 100-acre small-town campus **Total enrollment** 773 **Student-faculty ratio** 9:1 **Application deadline** Rolling (freshmen), rolling (transfer) **Freshmen** 32% were admitted **Housing** Yes **Expenses** Tuition $13,150; Room & Board $4875 **Undergraduates** 81% women, 36% part-time, 37% 25 or older, 8% Native American, 1% Hispanic American, 1% African American, 0.4% Asian American/Pacific Islander **The most frequently chosen baccalaureate fields are** biological/life sciences, business/marketing, health professions and related sciences **Academic program** Advanced placement, accelerated degree program, summer session, adult/continuing education programs, internships **Contact** Ms. Jo Ellen Lindner, Vice President for Enrollment and Student Retention, Presentation College, 1500 North Main Street, Aberdeen, SD 57401. Phone: 605-229-8492 or toll-free 800-437-6060. Fax: 605-229-8425. E-mail: admit@presentation.edu. Web site: http://www.presentation.edu/.

SINTE GLESKA UNIVERSITY
MISSION, SOUTH DAKOTA

Contact Mr. Jack Herman, Registrar and Director of Admissions, Sinte Gleska University, 101 Antelope Lake Circle, P.O. Box 105, Mission, SD 57555. Phone: 605-856-8100 Ext. 8479. Fax: 605-747-2098. Web site: http://www.sintegleska.edu/.

SOUTH DAKOTA SCHOOL OF MINES AND TECHNOLOGY
RAPID CITY, SOUTH DAKOTA

General State-supported, university, coed, primarily men **Entrance** Moderately difficult **Setting** 120-acre suburban campus **Total enrollment** 2,070 **Student-faculty ratio** 14:1 **Application deadline** Rolling (freshmen), rolling (transfer) **Freshmen** 88% were admitted **Housing** Yes **Expenses** Tuition $5670; Room & Board $4600 **Undergraduates** 29% women, 22% part-time, 15% 25 or older, 3% Native American, 1% Hispanic American, 1% African American, 1% Asian American/Pacific Islander **The most frequently chosen baccalaureate fields are** engineering, computer and information sciences, interdisciplinary studies **Academic program** English as a second language, advanced placement, summer session, adult/continuing education programs, internships **Contact** Mr. Tex Claymore, Director of Admissions, South Dakota School of Mines and Technology, 501 East Saint Joseph, Rapid City, SD 57701-3995. Phone: 605-394-2414 Ext. 1266 or toll-free 800-544-8162 Ext. 2414. Fax: 605-394-1268. E-mail: admissions@sdsmt.edu. Web site: http://www.sdsmt.edu/.

SOUTH DAKOTA STATE UNIVERSITY
BROOKINGS, SOUTH DAKOTA

General State-supported, university, coed **Entrance** Minimally difficult **Setting** 272-acre small-town campus **Total enrollment** 11,645 **Student-faculty ratio** 17:1 **Application deadline** Rolling (freshmen), rolling (transfer) **Freshmen** 94% were admitted **Housing** Yes **Expenses** Tuition $5373; Room & Board $5240 **Undergraduates** 52% women, 20% part-time, 13% 25 or older, 2% Native American, 1% Hispanic American, 1% African American, 1% Asian American/Pacific Islander **The most frequently chosen baccalaureate fields are** agriculture, health professions and related sciences, social sciences **Academic program** English as a second language, advanced placement, accelerated degree program, honors program, summer session, adult/continuing education programs, internships **Contact** Ms. Michelle Kuebler, Assistant Director of Admissions, South Dakota State University, PO Box 2201, Brookings, SD 57007. Phone: 605-688-4121 or toll-free 800-952-3541. Fax: 605-688-6891. E-mail: sdsu.admissions@sdstate.edu. Web site: http://www.sdstate.edu/.

UNIVERSITY OF SIOUX FALLS
SIOUX FALLS, SOUTH DAKOTA

General Independent American Baptist Churches in the USA, comprehensive, coed **Entrance** Moderately difficult **Setting** 22-acre suburban campus **Total enrollment** 1,628 **Student-faculty ratio** 15:1 **Application deadline** Rolling (freshmen), rolling (transfer) **Freshmen** 97% were admitted **Housing** Yes **Expenses** Tuition $19,326; Room & Board $5640 **Undergraduates** 53% women, 18% part-time, 15% 25 or older, 0.4% Native American, 1% Hispanic American, 3% African American, 0.2% Asian American/Pacific Islander **The most frequently chosen baccalaureate fields are** business/marketing, biological/life sciences, health professions and related sciences **Academic program** Advanced placement, accelerated degree program, self-designed majors, honors program, summer session, adult/continuing education programs, internships **Contact** Ms. Amanda Anderson, Director of Recruitment and Retention, University of Sioux Falls, 1101 West 22nd Street, Sioux Falls, SD 57105. Phone: 605-331-6600 Ext. 6602 or toll-free 800-888-1047. Fax: 605-331-6615. E-mail: admissions@usiouxfalls.edu. Web site: http://www.usiouxfalls.edu/.

THE UNIVERSITY OF SOUTH DAKOTA
VERMILLION, SOUTH DAKOTA

General State-supported, university, coed **Entrance** Moderately difficult **Setting** 216-acre small-town campus **Total enrollment** 9,243 **Student-faculty ratio** 17:1 **Application deadline** Rolling (freshmen), rolling (transfer) **Freshmen** 80% were admitted **Housing** Yes **Expenses** Tuition $5392; Room & Board $5174 **Undergraduates** 63% women, 35% part-time, 21% 25 or older, 2% Native American, 1% Hispanic American, 1% African American, 1% Asian American/Pacific Islander **The most frequently chosen baccalaureate fields are** business/marketing, education, psychology **Academic program** English as a second language, advanced placement, honors program, summer session, internships **Contact** Ms. Stephanie Moser, Director of Admissions, The University of South Dakota, 414 East Clark Street, Vermillion, SD 57069. Phone: 605-677-5434 or toll-free 877-269-6837. Fax: 605-677-6753. E-mail: admiss@usd.edu. Web site: http://www.usd.edu/.

TENNESSEE

AMERICAN BAPTIST COLLEGE OF AMERICAN BAPTIST THEOLOGICAL SEMINARY
NASHVILLE, TENNESSEE

General Independent Baptist, 4-year, coed **Entrance** Noncompetitive **Setting** 52-acre urban

American Baptist College of American Baptist Theological Seminary *(continued)*

campus **Total enrollment** 107 **Student-faculty ratio** 14:1 **Application deadline** 7/12 (freshmen), 7/12 (transfer) **Freshmen** 69% were admitted **Housing** Yes **Expenses** Tuition $4700; Room & Board $3300 **Undergraduates** 32% women, 27% part-time, 90% 25 or older, 94% African American **The most frequently chosen baccalaureate field is** theology and religious vocations **Academic program** Advanced placement, summer session, adult/continuing education programs **Contact** Ms. Marcella Lockhart, Director of Enrollment Management, American Baptist College of American Baptist Theological Seminary, 1800 Baptist World Center Drive, Nashville, TN 37207. Phone: 615-256-1463 Ext. 2227. Fax: 615-226-7855. E-mail: mlockhart@abcnash.edu. Web site: http://www.abcnash.edu/.

AQUINAS COLLEGE
NASHVILLE, TENNESSEE

General Independent Roman Catholic, 4-year, coed **Entrance** Minimally difficult **Setting** 92-acre urban campus **Total enrollment** 836 **Student-faculty ratio** 14:1 **Application deadline** Rolling (freshmen), rolling (transfer) **Freshmen** 73% were admitted **Housing** No **Expenses** Tuition $12,234 **Undergraduates** 72% 25 or older **Academic program** Advanced placement, accelerated degree program, summer session, adult/continuing education programs, internships **Contact** Ms. Connie Hansom, Director of Admission, Aquinas College, 4210 Harding Road, Nashville, TN 37205-2005. Phone: 615-297-7545 Ext. 411 or toll-free 800-649-9956. Fax: 615-279-3893. Web site: http://www.aquinascollege.edu/.

ARGOSY UNIVERSITY, NASHVILLE
NASHVILLE, TENNESSEE

General Proprietary, university, coed **Contact** Director of Admissions, Argosy University, Nashville, 100 Centerview Drive, Suite 225, Nashville, TN 37214. Phone: 615-525-2800 or toll-free 866-833-6598. Fax: 615-525-2900. Web site: http://www.argosy.edu/locations/nashville/.

THE ART INSTITUTE OF TENNESSEE–NASHVILLE
NASHVILLE, TENNESSEE

General Proprietary, 4-year, coed **Setting** urban campus **Total enrollment** 266 **Student-faculty ratio** 10:1 **Application deadline** Rolling (freshmen) **Housing** Yes **Expenses** Tuition $21,936; Room only $5433 **Undergraduates** 45% women, 11% part-time, 18% 25 or older, 1% Native American, 4% Hispanic American, 23% African American, 2% Asian American/Pacific Islander **Academic program** Advanced placement, summer session, internships **Contact** Mrs. Leslie Starks, The Art Institute of Tennessee–Nashville, 100 CNA Drive, Nashville, TN 37214. Phone: 615-847-1067 or toll-free 866-747-5770. Fax: 615-874-3530. E-mail: lstarks@aii.edu. Web site: http://www.artinstitutes.edu/nashville/.

AUSTIN PEAY STATE UNIVERSITY
CLARKSVILLE, TENNESSEE

General State-supported, comprehensive, coed **Entrance** Moderately difficult **Setting** 200-acre suburban campus **Total enrollment** 9,094 **Student-faculty ratio** 20:1 **Application deadline** 7/25 (freshmen), rolling (transfer) **Freshmen** 91% were admitted **Housing** Yes **Expenses** Tuition $5238; Room & Board $5510 **Undergraduates** 62% women, 28% part-time, 40% 25 or older, 1% Native American, 4% Hispanic American, 16% African American, 2% Asian American/Pacific Islander **The most frequently chosen baccalaureate fields are** business/marketing, health professions and related sciences, interdisciplinary studies **Academic program** English as a second language, advanced placement, accelerated degree program, honors program, summer session, adult/continuing education programs, internships **Contact** Mr. Ryan Forsythe, Director of Admissions, Austin Peay State University, PO Box 4548, Clarksville, TN 37044-4548. Phone: 931-221-7661 or toll-free 800-844-2778. Fax: 931-221-6168. E-mail: admissions@apsu.apsu.edu. Web site: http://www.apsu.edu/.

BAPTIST COLLEGE OF HEALTH SCIENCES
MEMPHIS, TENNESSEE

General Independent Southern Baptist, 4-year, coed, primarily women **Entrance** Moderately difficult **Setting** urban campus **Total enrollment** 925 **Application deadline** 6/1 (freshmen), 6/1 (transfer) **Freshmen** 38% were admitted **Housing** Yes **Expenses** Tuition $8150; Room only $2700 **Undergraduates** 88% women, 32% part-time, 0.3% Native American, 2% Hispanic American, 30% African American, 2% Asian American/Pacific Islander **The most frequently chosen baccalaureate field is** health professions and related sciences **Academic program** Advanced placement **Contact** Ms. Lissa Morgan, Manager of Admissions/Retention, Baptist College of Health Sciences, 1003 Monroe Avenue, Memphis, TN 38104. Phone: 901-572-2441 or toll-free 866-575-2247. Fax: 901-572-2461. E-mail: admissions@bchs.edu. Web site: http://www.bchs.edu/.

BELHAVEN COLLEGE
MEMPHIS, TENNESSEE

Contact Belhaven College, 5100 Poplar Avenue, Suite 200, Memphis, TN 38137. Web site: http://www.belhaven.edu/.

BELMONT UNIVERSITY
NASHVILLE, TENNESSEE

General Independent Baptist, comprehensive, coed **Entrance** Moderately difficult **Setting** 34-acre urban campus **Total enrollment** 4,756 **Student-faculty ratio** 12:1 **Application deadline** 8/1 (freshmen), 8/1 (transfer) **Freshmen** 62% were admitted **Housing** Yes **Expenses** Tuition $21,110; Room & Board $10,000 **Undergraduates** 59% women, 9% part-time, 7% 25 or older, 0.4% Native American, 2% Hispanic American, 4% African American, 2% Asian American/Pacific Islander **The most frequently chosen baccalaureate fields are** business/marketing, health professions and related sciences, visual and performing arts **Academic program** Advanced placement, accelerated degree program, self-designed majors, honors program, summer session, adult/continuing education programs, internships **Contact** Dr. Kathryn Baugher, Dean of Enrollment Services, Belmont University, 1900 Belmont Boulevard, Nashville, TN 37212-3757. Phone: 615-460-6785 or toll-free 800-56E-NROL. Fax: 615-460-5434. E-mail: buadmission@mail.belmont.edu. Web site: http://www.belmont.edu/.

►**For more information, see page 440.**

BETHEL COLLEGE
MCKENZIE, TENNESSEE

General Independent Cumberland Presbyterian, comprehensive, coed **Entrance** Minimally difficult **Setting** 100-acre small-town campus **Total enrollment** 2,155 **Student-faculty ratio** 15:1 **Application deadline** Rolling (freshmen), rolling (transfer) **Freshmen** 57% were admitted **Housing** Yes **Expenses** Tuition $12,242; Room & Board $6926 **Undergraduates** 59% women, 21% part-time, 55% 25 or older, 0.4% Native American, 2% Hispanic American, 29% African American, 0.5% Asian American/Pacific Islander **The most frequently chosen baccalaureate fields are** business/marketing, biological/life sciences, education **Academic program** Advanced placement, accelerated degree program, self-designed majors, honors program, summer session, adult/continuing education programs, internships **Contact** Mrs. Tina Hodges, Director of Admissions and Marketing, Bethel College, 325 Cherry Avenue, McKenzie, TN 38201. Phone: 731-352-4030. Fax: 731-352-4069. E-mail: admissions@bethel-college.edu. Web site: http://www.bethel-college.edu/.

BRYAN COLLEGE
DAYTON, TENNESSEE

General Independent interdenominational, 4-year, coed **Entrance** Moderately difficult **Setting** 100-acre small-town campus **Total enrollment** 1,044 **Student-faculty ratio** 13:1 **Application deadline** Rolling (freshmen), rolling (transfer) **Freshmen** 71% were admitted **Housing** Yes **Expenses** Tuition $17,020; Room & Board $5095 **Undergraduates** 52% women, 6% part-time, 1% 25 or older, 0.3% Native American, 1% Hispanic American, 4% African American, 1% Asian American/Pacific Islander **The most frequently chosen baccalaureate fields are** business/marketing, communications/journalism, education **Academic program** Advanced placement, honors program, summer session, adult/continuing education programs, internships **Contact** Michael Sapienza, Director of Admissions, Bryan College, PO Box 7000, Dayton, TN 37321-7000. Phone: 423-775-2041 or toll-free 800-277-9522. Fax: 423-775-7199. E-mail: admissions@bryan.edu. Web site: http://www.bryan.edu/.

CARSON-NEWMAN COLLEGE
JEFFERSON CITY, TENNESSEE

General Independent Southern Baptist, comprehensive, coed **Entrance** Moderately difficult **Setting** 90-acre small-town campus **Total enrollment** 2,012 **Student-faculty ratio** 13:1 **Application deadline** 8/1 (freshmen), 8/1 (transfer) **Freshmen** 62% were admitted **Housing** Yes **Expenses** Tuition $16,980; Room & Board $5360 **Undergraduates** 58% women, 5% part-time, 10% 25 or older, 0.5% Native American, 1% Hispanic American, 9% African American, 1% Asian American/Pacific Islander **The most frequently chosen baccalaureate fields are** education, business/marketing, health professions and related sciences **Academic program** English as a second language, advanced placement, accelerated degree program, self-designed majors, honors program, summer session, adult/continuing education programs, internships **Contact** Mr. Tom Huebner, Dean of Admissions, Carson-Newman College, PO Box 72025, Jefferson City, TN 37760. Phone: 865-471-3223 or toll-free 800-678-9061. Fax: 865-471-3502. E-mail: cnadmiss@cn.edu. Web site: http://www.cn.edu/.

CHRISTIAN BROTHERS UNIVERSITY
MEMPHIS, TENNESSEE

General Independent Roman Catholic, comprehensive, coed **Entrance** Moderately difficult **Setting** 75-acre urban campus **Total enrollment** 1,874 **Student-faculty ratio** 14:1 **Application deadline** 8/1 (freshmen), 8/23 (transfer) **Freshmen** 69% were admitted **Housing** Yes

Christian Brothers University *(continued)*

Expenses Tuition $22,600; Room & Board $5880 **Undergraduates** 55% women, 17% part-time, 25% 25 or older, 2% Hispanic American, 33% African American, 5% Asian American/Pacific Islander **The most frequently chosen baccalaureate fields are** business/marketing, engineering, psychology **Academic program** Advanced placement, accelerated degree program, honors program, summer session, internships **Contact** Ms. Tracey Dysart-Ford, Dean of Admissions, Christian Brothers University, 650 East Parkway South, Memphis, TN 38104. Phone: 901-321-3205 or toll-free 800-288-7576. Fax: 901-321-3202. E-mail: admissions@cbu.edu. Web site: http://www.cbu.edu/.

CRICHTON COLLEGE
MEMPHIS, TENNESSEE

General Independent, 4-year, coed **Entrance** Minimally difficult **Setting** 7-acre urban campus **Total enrollment** 1,090 **Student-faculty ratio** 14:1 **Application deadline** Rolling (freshmen), 8/15 (transfer) **Housing** Yes **Expenses** Tuition $11,256; Room & Board $7982 **Undergraduates** 67% women, 47% part-time, 63% 25 or older, 0.1% Native American, 1% Hispanic American, 53% African American, 0.3% Asian American/Pacific Islander **Academic program** Advanced placement, accelerated degree program, self-designed majors, honors program, summer session, adult/continuing education programs, internships **Contact** Mrs. Shelly Luttrell, Dean of Day Admissions, Crichton College, 255 North Highland, Memphis, TN 38111-1375. Phone: 901-320-9791 or toll-free 800-960-9777. Fax: 901-320-9791. E-mail: info@crichton.edu. Web site: http://www.crichton.edu/.

CUMBERLAND UNIVERSITY
LEBANON, TENNESSEE

General Independent, comprehensive, coed **Entrance** Moderately difficult **Setting** 44-acre small-town campus **Total enrollment** 1,335 **Student-faculty ratio** 16:1 **Application deadline** Rolling (freshmen), rolling (transfer) **Freshmen** 61% were admitted **Housing** Yes **Expenses** Tuition $16,720; Room & Board $6070 **Undergraduates** 52% women, 15% part-time, 16% 25 or older, 1% Native American, 2% Hispanic American, 11% African American, 1% Asian American/Pacific Islander **The most frequently chosen baccalaureate fields are** business/marketing, education, health professions and related sciences **Academic program** Advanced placement, accelerated degree program, honors program, summer session, adult/continuing education programs, internships **Contact** Mr. Jason A. Brewer, Assistant Dean of Students, Cumberland University, One Cumberland Square, Lebanon, TN 37087. Phone: 615-547-1225 or toll-free 800-467-0562. Fax: 615-444-2569. E-mail: admissions@cumberland.edu. Web site: http://www.cumberland.edu/.

DEVRY UNIVERSITY
MEMPHIS, TENNESSEE

General Proprietary, comprehensive, coed **Total enrollment** 57 **Application deadline** Rolling (freshmen), rolling (transfer) **Expenses** Tuition $13,890 **Undergraduates** 69% women, 44% part-time, 68% 25 or older, 79% African American, 3% Asian American/Pacific Islander **Contact** DeVry University, PennMarc Centre, 6401 Poplar Avenue, Suite 600, Memphis, TN 38119. Phone: toll-free 888-563-3879. Web site: http://www.devry.edu/locations/campuses/loc_memphis.jsp.

EAST TENNESSEE STATE UNIVERSITY
JOHNSON CITY, TENNESSEE

General State-supported, university, coed **Entrance** Moderately difficult **Setting** 366-acre small-town campus **Total enrollment** 13,119 **Student-faculty ratio** 18:1 **Freshmen** 97% were admitted **Housing** Yes **Expenses** Tuition $4887; Room & Board $5166 **Undergraduates** 57% women, 16% part-time, 26% 25 or older, 0.5% Native American, 1% Hispanic American, 4% African American, 2% Asian American/Pacific Islander **The most frequently chosen baccalaureate fields are** business/marketing, health professions and related sciences, liberal arts/general studies **Academic program** Advanced placement, accelerated degree program, honors program, summer session, adult/continuing education programs, internships **Contact** Mr. Mike Pitts, Director of Admissions, East Tennessee State University, PO Box 70731, Johnson City, TN 37614-0734. Phone: 423-439-4213 or toll-free 800-462-3878. Fax: 423-439-4630. E-mail: go2etsu@etsu.edu. Web site: http://www.etsu.edu/.

FISK UNIVERSITY
NASHVILLE, TENNESSEE

Contact Director of Admissions, Fisk University, 1000 17th Avenue North, Nashville, TN 37208-3051. Phone: 615-329-8819 or toll-free 800-443-FISK. Fax: 615-329-8774. E-mail: admit@fisk.edu. Web site: http://www.fisk.edu/.

FREED-HARDEMAN UNIVERSITY
HENDERSON, TENNESSEE

General Independent, comprehensive, coed, affiliated with Church of Christ **Entrance** Moderately difficult **Setting** 96-acre small-town campus **Total**

enrollment 2,011 **Student-faculty ratio** 14:1 **Application deadline** Rolling (freshmen), rolling (transfer) **Freshmen** 55% were admitted **Housing** Yes **Expenses** Tuition $13,860; Room & Board $6970 **Undergraduates** 55% women, 8% part-time, 5% 25 or older, 0.5% Native American, 1% Hispanic American, 4% African American, 0.4% Asian American/Pacific Islander **The most frequently chosen baccalaureate fields are** business/marketing, communications/journalism, theology and religious vocations **Academic program** Advanced placement, accelerated degree program, self-designed majors, honors program, summer session, internships **Contact** Dr. Belinda Anderson, Director of Admissions, Freed-Hardeman University, 158 East Main Street, Henderson, TN 38340-2399. Phone: 731-989-6651 or toll-free 800-630-3480. Fax: 731-989-6047. E-mail: admissions@fhu.edu. Web site: http://www.fhu.edu/.

FREE WILL BAPTIST BIBLE COLLEGE

NASHVILLE, TENNESSEE

General Independent Free Will Baptist, 4-year, coed **Entrance** Noncompetitive **Setting** 10-acre urban campus **Total enrollment** 324 **Student-faculty ratio** 11:1 **Application deadline** Rolling (freshmen) **Freshmen** 75% were admitted **Housing** Yes **Expenses** Tuition $12,382; Room & Board $4866 **Undergraduates** 51% women, 26% part-time, 15% 25 or older, 3% African American, 0.3% Asian American/Pacific Islander **The most frequently chosen baccalaureate fields are** business/marketing, education, theology and religious vocations **Academic program** Advanced placement, self-designed majors, summer session, internships **Contact** Mr. Heath Hubbard, Director of Recruitment, Free Will Baptist Bible College, 3606 West End Avenue, Nashville, TN 37205. Phone: 615-844-5197 or toll-free 800-763-9222. Fax: 615-269-6028. E-mail: hhubbard@fwbbc.edu. Web site: http://www.fwbbc.edu/.

HUNTINGTON COLLEGE OF HEALTH SCIENCES

KNOXVILLE, TENNESSEE

General Proprietary, comprehensive, coed, primarily women **Entrance** Noncompetitive **Setting** suburban campus **Total enrollment** 460 **Student-faculty ratio** 29:1 **Application deadline** Rolling (freshmen), rolling (transfer) **Freshmen** 100% were admitted **Undergraduates** 64% women, 90% 25 or older **Academic program** Self-designed majors, summer session, adult/continuing education programs **Contact** Ms. Cheryl Freeman, Director/Registrar, Huntington College of Health Sciences, Huntington College of Health Sciences, 1204 Kenesaw Avenue, Suite D, Knoxville, TN 37919. Phone: 800-290-4226 or toll-free 800-290-4226. Fax: 865-524-8339. E-mail: cfreeman@hchs.edu. Web site: http://www.hchs.edu/.

JOHNSON BIBLE COLLEGE

KNOXVILLE, TENNESSEE

General Independent, comprehensive, coed, affiliated with Christian Churches and Churches of Christ **Entrance** Moderately difficult **Setting** 75-acre rural campus **Total enrollment** 890 **Student-faculty ratio** 17:1 **Application deadline** 7/1 (freshmen), 7/1 (transfer) **Freshmen** 85% were admitted **Housing** Yes **Expenses** Tuition $7180; Room & Board $4890 **Undergraduates** 51% women, 3% part-time, 15% 25 or older **The most frequently chosen baccalaureate fields are** education, communication technologies, theology and religious vocations **Academic program** English as a second language, advanced placement, accelerated degree program, honors program, summer session, adult/continuing education programs, internships **Contact** Mr. Tim Wingfield, Director of Admissions, Johnson Bible College, 7900 Johnson Drive, Knoxville, TN 37998-1001. Phone: 865-251-2346 or toll-free 800-827-2122. Fax: 865-251-2336. E-mail: twingfield@jbc.edu. Web site: http://www.jbc.edu/.

KING COLLEGE

BRISTOL, TENNESSEE

General Independent, comprehensive, coed, affiliated with Presbyterian Church (U.S.A.) **Entrance** Moderately difficult **Setting** 135-acre suburban campus **Total enrollment** 1,515 **Student-faculty ratio** 14:1 **Application deadline** Rolling (freshmen), rolling (transfer) **Freshmen** 22% were admitted **Housing** Yes **Expenses** Tuition $20,582; Room & Board $6900 **Undergraduates** 63% women, 7% part-time, 27% 25 or older, 0.2% Native American, 2% Hispanic American, 2% African American, 1% Asian American/Pacific Islander **The most frequently chosen baccalaureate fields are** business/marketing, health professions and related sciences, psychology **Academic program** English as a second language, advanced placement, self-designed majors, honors program, summer session, adult/continuing education programs, internships **Contact** Ms. Mandy Butterworth, Director of Recruitment, King College, 1350 King College Road, Bristol, TN 37620-2699. Phone: 423-652-4861 or toll-free 800-362-0014. Fax: 423-652-4727. E-mail: admissions@king.edu. Web site: http://www.king.edu/.

LAMBUTH UNIVERSITY

JACKSON, TENNESSEE

General Independent United Methodist, 4-year, coed **Entrance** Moderately difficult **Setting**

Lambuth University *(continued)*

50-acre urban campus **Total enrollment** 751 **Student-faculty ratio** 9:1 **Application deadline** Rolling (freshmen), rolling (transfer) **Freshmen** 49% were admitted **Housing** Yes **Expenses** Tuition $17,400; Room & Board $7160 **Undergraduates** 52% women, 6% part-time, 11% 25 or older, 0.1% Native American, 2% Hispanic American, 19% African American, 2% Asian American/Pacific Islander **The most frequently chosen baccalaureate fields are** business/marketing, parks and recreation, social sciences **Academic program** English as a second language, advanced placement, accelerated degree program, self-designed majors, honors program, summer session, adult/continuing education programs, internships **Contact** Ms. Melissa Boyd, Director of Financial Aid, Lambuth University, 705 Lambuth Boulevard, Jackson, TN 38301. Phone: 731-425-3240 or toll-free 800-526-2884. Fax: 731-425-3496. E-mail: boyd-m@lambuth.edu. Web site: http://www.lambuth.edu/.

LANE COLLEGE
JACKSON, TENNESSEE

General Independent, 4-year, coed, affiliated with Christian Methodist Episcopal Church **Contact** Ms. Sherrill Berry Scott, Vice President for Student Affairs, Lane College, 545 Lane Avenue, Jackson, TN 38301-4598. Phone: 731-426-7533 or toll-free 800-960-7533. Fax: 731-426-7559. E-mail: sbscott@lanecollege.edu. Web site: http://www.lanecollege.edu/.

LEE UNIVERSITY
CLEVELAND, TENNESSEE

General Independent, comprehensive, coed, affiliated with Church of God **Entrance** Minimally difficult **Setting** 115-acre small-town campus **Total enrollment** 4,086 **Student-faculty ratio** 16:1 **Application deadline** 9/1 (freshmen), 9/1 (transfer) **Freshmen** 51% were admitted **Housing** Yes **Expenses** Tuition $10,782; Room & Board $5276 **Undergraduates** 56% women, 12% part-time, 14% 25 or older, 0.5% Native American, 3% Hispanic American, 4% African American, 1% Asian American/Pacific Islander **The most frequently chosen baccalaureate fields are** education, business/marketing, physical sciences **Academic program** English as a second language, advanced placement, honors program, summer session, adult/continuing education programs, internships **Contact** Mr. Phillip Cook, Assistant Vice President for Enrollment, Lee University, PO Box 3450, Cleveland, TN 37320-3450. Phone: 423-614-8500 or toll-free 800-533-9930. Fax: 423-614-8533. E-mail: admissions@leeuniversity.edu. Web site: http://www.leeuniversity.edu/.

LEMOYNE-OWEN COLLEGE
MEMPHIS, TENNESSEE

General Independent, 4-year, coed, affiliated with United Church of Christ **Entrance** Minimally difficult **Setting** 15-acre urban campus **Total enrollment** 592 **Student-faculty ratio** 8:1 **Application deadline** 4/1 (freshmen), rolling (transfer) **Freshmen** 51% were admitted **Housing** Yes **Expenses** Tuition $10,318; Room & Board $4852 **Undergraduates** 65% women, 15% part-time, 40% 25 or older, 0.2% Hispanic American, 98% African American **The most frequently chosen baccalaureate fields are** business/marketing, education, security and protective services **Academic program** Advanced placement, accelerated degree program, honors program, summer session, adult/continuing education programs, internships **Contact** Samuel King, Interim Director of Admissions and Recruitment, LeMoyne-Owen College, 807 Walker Avenue, Memphis, TN 38126. Phone: 901-435-1500. Fax: 901-435-1524. E-mail: admissions@loc.edu. Web site: http://www.loc.edu/.

LINCOLN MEMORIAL UNIVERSITY
HARROGATE, TENNESSEE

General Independent, comprehensive, coed **Contact** Mr. Conrad Daniels, Dean of Admissions and Recruitment, Lincoln Memorial University, 6965 Cumberland Gap Parkway, Harrogate, TN 37752-1901. Phone: 423-869-6280 or toll-free 800-325-0900. Fax: 423-869-6444. E-mail: admissions@lmunet.edu. Web site: http://www.lmunet.edu/.

LIPSCOMB UNIVERSITY
NASHVILLE, TENNESSEE

General Independent, comprehensive, coed, affiliated with Church of Christ **Entrance** Moderately difficult **Setting** 65-acre suburban campus **Total enrollment** 2,744 **Student-faculty ratio** 15:1 **Application deadline** Rolling (freshmen), rolling (transfer) **Freshmen** 57% were admitted **Housing** Yes **Expenses** Tuition $16,811; Room & Board $7070 **Undergraduates** 57% women, 10% part-time, 5% 25 or older, 0.5% Native American, 2% Hispanic American, 5% African American, 2% Asian American/Pacific Islander **The most frequently chosen baccalaureate fields are** business/marketing, education, health professions and related sciences **Academic program** Advanced placement, accelerated degree program, honors program, summer session, adult/continuing education programs, internships **Contact** Corey Patterson, Senior Director of Enrollment, Lipscomb University, 3901 Granny White Pike, Nashville, TN 37204-3951. Phone: 615-966-1000 or toll-free 877-582-4766. Fax: 615-966-

1804. E-mail: admissions@lipscomb.edu. Web site: http://www.lipscomb.edu/.

MARTIN METHODIST COLLEGE
PULASKI, TENNESSEE

Contact Michael Kelley, Director of Admissions, Martin Methodist College, 433 West Madison Street, Pulaski, TN 38478-2716. Phone: 931-363-9804 or toll-free 800-467-1273. Fax: 931-363-9818. E-mail: admissions@martinmethodist.edu. Web site: http://www.martinmethodist.edu/.

MARYVILLE COLLEGE
MARYVILLE, TENNESSEE

General Independent Presbyterian, 4-year, coed **Entrance** Moderately difficult **Setting** 350-acre suburban campus **Total enrollment** 1,176 **Student-faculty ratio** 12:1 **Application deadline** 3/1 (freshmen), rolling (transfer) **Freshmen** 76% were admitted **Housing** Yes **Expenses** Tuition $25,350; Room & Board $7800 **Undergraduates** 55% women, 1% part-time, 6% 25 or older, 1% Native American, 2% Hispanic American, 6% African American, 1% Asian American/Pacific Islander **The most frequently chosen baccalaureate fields are** business/marketing, education, social sciences **Academic program** English as a second language, advanced placement, self-designed majors, honors program, summer session, adult/continuing education programs, internships **Contact** Ms. Linda L. Moore, Administrative Assistant of Admissions, Maryville College, 502 East Lamar Alexander Parkway, Maryville, TN 37804-5907. Phone: 865-981-8092 or toll-free 800-597-2687. Fax: 865-981-8005. E-mail: admissions@maryvillecollege.edu. Web site: http://www.maryvillecollege.edu/.

MEMPHIS COLLEGE OF ART
MEMPHIS, TENNESSEE

General Independent, comprehensive, coed **Entrance** Moderately difficult **Setting** 200-acre urban campus **Total enrollment** 341 **Student-faculty ratio** 10:1 **Application deadline** Rolling (freshmen), rolling (transfer) **Freshmen** 46% were admitted **Housing** Yes **Expenses** Tuition $21,560; Room only $5760 **Undergraduates** 55% women, 10% part-time, 14% 25 or older, 2% Hispanic American, 16% African American, 2% Asian American/Pacific Islander **The most frequently chosen baccalaureate field is** visual and performing arts **Academic program** Advanced placement, summer session, adult/continuing education programs, internships **Contact** Ms. Annette Moore, Director of Admission, Memphis College of Art, 1930 Poplar Avenue, Memphis, TN 38104. Phone: 901-272-5153 or toll-free 800-727-1088. Fax: 901-272-5158. E-mail: info@mca.edu. Web site: http://www.mca.edu/.

MIDDLE TENNESSEE STATE UNIVERSITY
MURFREESBORO, TENNESSEE

General State-supported, university, coed **Entrance** Moderately difficult **Setting** 500-acre urban campus **Total enrollment** 23,246 **Student-faculty ratio** 21:1 **Application deadline** 7/1 (freshmen), rolling (transfer) **Freshmen** 39% were admitted **Housing** Yes **Expenses** Tuition $5278; Room & Board $6204 **Undergraduates** 53% women, 15% part-time, 27% 25 or older, 0.5% Native American, 2% Hispanic American, 14% African American, 3% Asian American/Pacific Islander **The most frequently chosen baccalaureate fields are** business/marketing, interdisciplinary studies, visual and performing arts **Academic program** English as a second language, advanced placement, accelerated degree program, self-designed majors, honors program, summer session, adult/continuing education programs, internships **Contact** Ms. Lynn Palmer, Director of Admissions, Middle Tennessee State University, 1301 East Main Street, Murfreesboro, TN 37132. Phone: 615-898-2111 or toll-free 800-331-MTSU (in-state); 800-433-MTSU (out-of-state). Fax: 615-898-5478. E-mail: admissions@mtsu.edu. Web site: http://www.mtsu.edu/.

MILLIGAN COLLEGE
MILLIGAN COLLEGE, TENNESSEE

General Independent Christian, comprehensive, coed **Entrance** Moderately difficult **Setting** 181-acre suburban campus **Total enrollment** 1,006 **Student-faculty ratio** 11:1 **Application deadline** 8/1 (freshmen), rolling (transfer) **Freshmen** 78% were admitted **Housing** Yes **Expenses** Tuition $19,510; Room & Board $5350 **Undergraduates** 61% women, 5% part-time, 13% 25 or older, 0.3% Native American, 2% Hispanic American, 3% African American, 1% Asian American/Pacific Islander **The most frequently chosen baccalaureate fields are** business/marketing, education, health professions and related sciences **Academic program** Advanced placement, summer session, adult/continuing education programs, internships **Contact** Ms. Tracy Brinn, Director of Enrollment Management, Milligan College, PO Box 210, Milligan College, TN 37682. Phone: 423-461-8730 or toll-free 800-262-8337. Fax: 423-461-8982. E-mail: admissions@milligan.edu. Web site: http://www.milligan.edu/.

O'MORE COLLEGE OF DESIGN
FRANKLIN, TENNESSEE

General Independent, 4-year, coed, primarily women **Entrance** Moderately difficult **Setting**

O'More College of Design *(continued)*

6-acre small-town campus **Total enrollment** 219 **Student-faculty ratio** 8:1 **Application deadline** 8/1 (freshmen), 8/1 (transfer) **Housing** No **Expenses** Tuition $14,884 **Undergraduates** 91% women, 14% part-time, 60% 25 or older, 1% Hispanic American, 3% African American, 2% Asian American/Pacific Islander **The most frequently chosen baccalaureate field is** visual and performing arts **Academic program** Advanced placement, summer session, internships **Contact** Mr. Chris Lee, Dean of Enrollment, O'More College of Design, 423 South Margin Street, Franklin, TN 37064-2816. Phone: 615-794-4254 Ext. 232. Fax: 615-790-1662. E-mail: dee@omorecollege.edu. Web site: http://www.omorecollege.edu/.

RHODES COLLEGE
MEMPHIS, TENNESSEE

General Independent Presbyterian, comprehensive, coed **Entrance** Very difficult **Setting** 100-acre suburban campus **Total enrollment** 1,698 **Student-faculty ratio** 11:1 **Application deadline** 1/15 (freshmen), 1/15 (transfer) **Freshmen** 51% were admitted **Housing** Yes **Expenses** Tuition $30,652; Room & Board $7468 **Undergraduates** 58% women, 1% part-time, 0.2% Native American, 2% Hispanic American, 6% African American, 5% Asian American/Pacific Islander **The most frequently chosen baccalaureate fields are** biological/life sciences, liberal arts/general studies, social sciences **Academic program** Advanced placement, self-designed majors, honors program, internships **Contact** Mr. David J. Wottle, Dean of Admissions and Financial Aid, Rhodes College, 2000 North Parkway, Memphis, TN 38112-1690. Phone: 901-843-3700 or toll-free 800-844-5969. Fax: 901-843-3631. E-mail: adminfo@rhodes.edu. Web site: http://www.rhodes.edu/.

SEWANEE: THE UNIVERSITY OF THE SOUTH
SEWANEE, TENNESSEE

General Independent Episcopal, comprehensive, coed **Entrance** Very difficult **Setting** 10,000-acre small-town campus **Total enrollment** 1,561 **Student-faculty ratio** 11:1 **Application deadline** 2/1 (freshmen), 4/1 (transfer) **Freshmen** 64% were admitted **Housing** Yes **Expenses** Tuition $30,660; Room & Board $8780 **Undergraduates** 53% women, 1% part-time, 1% Native American, 2% Hispanic American, 4% African American, 2% Asian American/Pacific Islander **The most frequently chosen baccalaureate fields are** English, social sciences, visual and performing arts **Academic program** Advanced placement, self-designed majors, summer session, internships **Contact** Mr. David Lesesne, Dean of Admission, Sewanee: The University of the South, 735 University Avenue, Sewanee, TN 37383-1000. Phone: 931-598-1238 or toll-free 800-522-2234. Fax: 931-598-3248. E-mail: admiss@sewanee.edu. Web site: http://www.sewanee.edu/.

SOUTHERN ADVENTIST UNIVERSITY
COLLEGEDALE, TENNESSEE

General Independent Seventh-day Adventist, comprehensive, coed **Entrance** Moderately difficult **Setting** 1,000-acre small-town campus **Total enrollment** 2,640 **Student-faculty ratio** 16:1 **Application deadline** Rolling (freshmen), rolling (transfer) **Freshmen** 68% were admitted **Housing** Yes **Expenses** Tuition $16,560; Room & Board $4900 **Undergraduates** 55% women, 14% part-time, 10% 25 or older, 0.5% Native American, 13% Hispanic American, 11% African American, 5% Asian American/Pacific Islander **The most frequently chosen baccalaureate fields are** business/marketing, health professions and related sciences, visual and performing arts **Academic program** English as a second language, advanced placement, honors program, summer session, internships **Contact** Mr. Marc Grundy, Associate Vice President, Marketing and Enrollment Services, Southern Adventist University, PO Box 370, Collegedale, TN 37315-0370. Phone: 423-236-2844 or toll-free 800-768-8437. Fax: 423-236-1844. E-mail: admissions@southern.edu. Web site: http://www.southern.edu/.

TENNESSEE STATE UNIVERSITY
NASHVILLE, TENNESSEE

General State-supported, comprehensive, coed **Entrance** Minimally difficult **Setting** 450-acre urban campus **Total enrollment** 9,065 **Student-faculty ratio** 14:1 **Application deadline** 8/1 (freshmen), 8/1 (transfer) **Freshmen** 80% were admitted **Housing** Yes **Expenses** Tuition $4886; Room & Board $5202 **Undergraduates** 64% women, 19% part-time, 26% 25 or older, 0.1% Native American, 1% Hispanic American, 80% African American, 1% Asian American/Pacific Islander **The most frequently chosen baccalaureate fields are** health professions and related sciences, business/marketing, liberal arts/general studies **Academic program** Accelerated degree program, honors program, summer session, adult/continuing education programs, internships **Contact** Ms. Vernella Smith, Admissions Coordinator, Tennessee State University, 3500 John A Merritt Boulevard, Nashville, TN 37209-1561. Phone: 615-963-5101. Fax: 615-963-5108. E-mail: vsmith@tnstate.edu. Web site: http://www.tnstate.edu/.

TENNESSEE TECHNOLOGICAL UNIVERSITY

COOKEVILLE, TENNESSEE

General State-supported, university, coed **Entrance** Moderately difficult **Setting** 235-acre small-town campus **Total enrollment** 10,321 **Student-faculty ratio** 18:1 **Application deadline** 8/1 (freshmen), 8/1 (transfer) **Freshmen** 88% were admitted **Housing** Yes **Expenses** Tuition $4980; Room & Board $6330 **Undergraduates** 46% women, 11% part-time, 15% 25 or older, 0.3% Native American, 1% Hispanic American, 4% African American, 1% Asian American/ Pacific Islander **The most frequently chosen baccalaureate fields are** business/marketing, education, engineering **Academic program** English as a second language, advanced placement, accelerated degree program, honors program, summer session, adult/continuing education programs, internships **Contact** Ms. Vanessa Palmer, Interim Director of Admissions, Tennessee Technological University, PO Box 5006, Cookeville, TN 38505. Phone: 931-372-3888 or toll-free 800-255-8881. Fax: 931-372-6250. E-mail: admissions@tntech.edu. Web site: http://www.tntech.edu/.

TENNESSEE TEMPLE UNIVERSITY

CHATTANOOGA, TENNESSEE

Contact Mr. Chris Dooley, Director of Enrollment Services, Tennessee Temple University, 1815 Union Avenue, Chattanooga, TN 37404-3587. Phone: 423-493-4371 or toll-free 800-553-4050. Fax: 423-492-4497. E-mail: ttuinfo@tntemple.edu. Web site: http://www.tntemple.edu/.

TENNESSEE WESLEYAN COLLEGE

ATHENS, TENNESSEE

General Independent United Methodist, 4-year, coed **Entrance** Minimally difficult **Setting** 40-acre small-town campus **Total enrollment** 861 **Student-faculty ratio** 12:1 **Application deadline** 8/31 (freshmen), 8/31 (transfer) **Freshmen** 79% were admitted **Housing** Yes **Expenses** Tuition $17,050; Room & Board $5830 **Undergraduates** 63% women, 14% part-time, 23% 25 or older, 0.1% Native American, 2% Hispanic American, 3% African American, 0.5% Asian American/Pacific Islander **The most frequently chosen baccalaureate fields are** business/ marketing, education, health professions and related sciences **Academic program** Advanced placement, accelerated degree program, self-designed majors, honors program, summer session, adult/continuing education programs, internships **Contact** Stan Harrison, Vice President of Enrollment Services and Director of Athletics, Tennessee Wesleyan College, 204 East College Street, Athens, TN 37303. Phone: 423-746-7504 Ext. 5310 or toll-free 800-PICK-TWC. Fax: 423-745-9335. E-mail: sharrison@twcnet.edu. Web site: http://www.twcnet.edu/.

TREVECCA NAZARENE UNIVERSITY

NASHVILLE, TENNESSEE

General Independent Nazarene, comprehensive, coed **Entrance** Moderately difficult **Setting** 65-acre urban campus **Total enrollment** 2,286 **Student-faculty ratio** 17:1 **Application deadline** 4/1 (freshmen), rolling (transfer) **Freshmen** 68% were admitted **Housing** Yes **Expenses** Tuition $15,512; Room & Board $6874 **Undergraduates** 56% women, 13% part-time, 26% 25 or older, 1% Native American, 1% Hispanic American, 8% African American, 1% Asian American/Pacific Islander **The most frequently chosen baccalaureate fields are** business/ marketing, education, visual and performing arts **Academic program** Advanced placement, summer session, adult/continuing education programs, internships **Contact** Mr. Michael, Director of Undergraduate Admissions, Trevecca Nazarene University, 333 Murfreesboro Road, Nashville, TN 37210-2834. Phone: 615-248-1320 or toll-free 888-210-4TNU. Fax: 615-248-7406. E-mail: admissions_und@trevecca.edu. Web site: http://www.trevecca.edu/.

TUSCULUM COLLEGE

GREENEVILLE, TENNESSEE

General Independent Presbyterian, comprehensive, coed **Entrance** Moderately difficult **Setting** 140-acre small-town campus **Total enrollment** 2,605 **Student-faculty ratio** 16:1 **Application deadline** Rolling (freshmen), rolling (transfer) **Freshmen** 68% were admitted **Housing** Yes **Expenses** Tuition $17,385; Room & Board $6910 **Undergraduates** 61% women, 3% part-time, 6% 25 or older, 0.1% Native American, 2% Hispanic American, 11% African American, 0.3% Asian American/Pacific Islander **The most frequently chosen baccalaureate fields are** business/ marketing, education, parks and recreation **Academic program** English as a second language, advanced placement, self-designed majors, honors program, summer session, adult/continuing education programs, internships **Contact** Ms. Melissa Ripley, Director of Operations, Tusculum College, PO Box 5047, Greeneville, TN 37743-9997. Phone: 423-636-7300 Ext. 5631 or toll-free 800-729-0256. Fax: 423-798-1622. E-mail: admissions@tusculum.edu. Web site: http://www.tusculum.edu/.

UNION UNIVERSITY

JACKSON, TENNESSEE

General Independent Southern Baptist, comprehensive, coed **Entrance** Moderately difficult

Union University *(continued)*

Setting 290-acre small-town campus **Total enrollment** 3,229 **Student-faculty ratio** 12:1 **Application deadline** Rolling (freshmen), rolling (transfer) **Freshmen** 81% were admitted **Housing** Yes **Expenses** Tuition $18,620; Room & Board $6500 **Undergraduates** 60% women, 20% part-time, 24% 25 or older, 0.2% Native American, 2% Hispanic American, 11% African American, 1% Asian American/Pacific Islander **The most frequently chosen baccalaureate fields are** health professions and related sciences, business/marketing, interdisciplinary studies **Academic program** English as a second language, advanced placement, accelerated degree program, honors program, summer session, adult/continuing education programs, internships **Contact** Mr. Robbie Graves, Director of Enrollment Services, Union University, 1050 Union University Drive, Jackson, TN 38305-3697. Phone: 731-661-5102 or toll-free 800-33-UNION. Fax: 731-661-5017. E-mail: cgraves@uu.edu. Web site: http://www.uu.edu/.

UNIVERSITY OF MEMPHIS
MEMPHIS, TENNESSEE

General State-supported, university, coed **Entrance** Moderately difficult **Setting** 1,100-acre urban campus **Total enrollment** 20,379 **Student-faculty ratio** 20:1 **Application deadline** 7/1 (freshmen), 7/1 (transfer) **Freshmen** 66% were admitted **Housing** Yes **Expenses** Tuition $5802; Room & Board $5433 **Undergraduates** 62% women, 26% part-time, 31% 25 or older, 0.3% Native American, 2% Hispanic American, 38% African American, 2% Asian American/Pacific Islander **The most frequently chosen baccalaureate fields are** business/marketing, interdisciplinary studies, liberal arts/general studies **Academic program** English as a second language, advanced placement, accelerated degree program, self-designed majors, honors program, summer session, adult/continuing education programs, internships **Contact** Mr. David Wallace, Director of Admissions, University of Memphis, Memphis, TN 38152. Phone: 901-678-2101 or toll-free 800-669-2678. Fax: 901-678-3053. E-mail: dwallace@memphis.edu. Web site: http://www.memphis.edu/.

UNIVERSITY OF PHOENIX–NASHVILLE CAMPUS
NASHVILLE, TENNESSEE

General Proprietary, comprehensive, coed **Contact** Ms. Evelyn Gaskin, Registrar/Executive Director, University of Phoenix–Nashville Campus, 4615 East Elwood Street, Mail Stop AA-K101, Phoenix, AZ 85040-1958. Phone: 480-557-3301 or toll-free 800-776-4867 (in-state); 800-228-7240 (out-of-state). Fax: 480-643-1020. E-mail: evelyn.gaskin@phoenix.edu. Web site: http://www.phoenix.edu/.

THE UNIVERSITY OF TENNESSEE
KNOXVILLE, TENNESSEE

General State-supported, university, coed **Entrance** Moderately difficult **Setting** 533-acre urban campus **Total enrollment** 29,937 **Student-faculty ratio** 15:1 **Application deadline** 2/1 (freshmen), 6/1 (transfer) **Freshmen** 71% were admitted **Housing** Yes **Expenses** Tuition $6188; Room & Board $6676 **Undergraduates** 51% women, 7% part-time, 8% 25 or older, 0.3% Native American, 2% Hispanic American, 9% African American, 3% Asian American/Pacific Islander **The most frequently chosen baccalaureate fields are** business/marketing, psychology, social sciences **Academic program** English as a second language, advanced placement, accelerated degree program, self-designed majors, honors program, summer session, adult/continuing education programs, internships **Contact** Mr. Richard Bayer, Dean of Admissions, The University of Tennessee, 305 Student Services Building, 1331 Circle Park, Knoxville, TN 37996-0230. Phone: 865-974-2184 or toll-free 800-221-8657. Fax: 865-974-6341. E-mail: admissions@tennessee.edu. Web site: http://www.tennessee.edu/.

THE UNIVERSITY OF TENNESSEE AT CHATTANOOGA
CHATTANOOGA, TENNESSEE

General State-supported, comprehensive, coed **Entrance** Moderately difficult **Setting** 120-acre urban campus **Total enrollment** 9,558 **Student-faculty ratio** 17:1 **Freshmen** 83% were admitted **Housing** Yes **Expenses** Tuition $5062; Room & Board $7555 **Undergraduates** 56% women, 13% part-time, 16% 25 or older, 0.4% Native American, 2% Hispanic American, 19% African American, 2% Asian American/Pacific Islander **The most frequently chosen baccalaureate fields are** business/marketing, family and consumer sciences, psychology **Academic program** English as a second language, advanced placement, honors program, summer session, adult/continuing education programs, internships **Contact** Mr. Yancy Freeman, Director, Admissions and Recruitment, The University of Tennessee at Chattanooga, 615 McCallie Avenue, Guerry Hall, Chattanooga, TN 37403. Phone: 423-425-4662 or toll-free 800-UTC-MOCS. Fax: 423-425-4157. E-mail: yancy-freeman@utc.edu. Web site: http://www.utc.edu/.

THE UNIVERSITY OF TENNESSEE AT MARTIN

MARTIN, TENNESSEE

General State-supported, comprehensive, coed **Entrance** Moderately difficult **Setting** 250-acre small-town campus **Total enrollment** 7,173 **Student-faculty ratio** 18:1 **Application deadline** Rolling (freshmen), rolling (transfer) **Freshmen** 77% were admitted **Housing** Yes **Expenses** Tuition $5005; Room & Board $4446 **Undergraduates** 57% women, 22% part-time, 19% 25 or older, 0.3% Native American, 1% Hispanic American, 16% African American, 1% Asian American/Pacific Islander **The most frequently chosen baccalaureate fields are** business/marketing, agriculture, interdisciplinary studies **Academic program** English as a second language, advanced placement, accelerated degree program, self-designed majors, honors program, summer session, adult/continuing education programs, internships **Contact** Ms. Judy Rayburn, Director of Admissions, The University of Tennessee at Martin, 200 Hall-Moody Administration Building, Martin, TN 38238. Phone: 731-881-7032 or toll-free 800-829-8861. Fax: 731-881-7029. E-mail: jrayburn@utm.edu. Web site: http://www.utm.edu/.

VANDERBILT UNIVERSITY

NASHVILLE, TENNESSEE

General Independent, university, coed **Entrance** Very difficult **Setting** 330-acre urban campus **Total enrollment** 11,847 **Application deadline** 1/3 (freshmen), 3/1 (transfer) **Freshmen** 33% were admitted **Housing** Yes **Expenses** Tuition $35,276; Room & Board $11,446 **Undergraduates** 53% women, 1% part-time, 1% 25 or older, 0.3% Native American, 6% Hispanic American, 9% African American, 7% Asian American/Pacific Islander **The most frequently chosen baccalaureate fields are** engineering, foreign languages and literature, social sciences **Academic program** English as a second language, advanced placement, accelerated degree program, self-designed majors, honors program, summer session, internships **Contact** Mr. Douglas Christiansen, Dean of Undergraduate Admissions, Vanderbilt University, Nashville, TN 37240-1001. Phone: toll-free 800-288-0432. Fax: 615-343-7765. E-mail: admissions@vanderbilt.edu. Web site: http://www.vanderbilt.edu/.

WATKINS COLLEGE OF ART AND DESIGN

NASHVILLE, TENNESSEE

General Independent, 4-year, coed **Entrance** Moderately difficult **Setting** 13-acre urban campus **Total enrollment** 393 **Student-faculty ratio** 10:1 **Application deadline** 6/1 (freshmen), 6/1 (transfer) **Freshmen** 79% were admitted **Housing** Yes **Expenses** Tuition $14,160; Room only $6000 **Undergraduates** 63% women, 43% part-time, 28% 25 or older, 3% Hispanic American, 5% African American, 2% Asian American/Pacific Islander **The most frequently chosen baccalaureate field is** visual and performing arts **Academic program** Advanced placement, summer session, adult/continuing education programs, internships **Contact** Ms. Jenna Maurice, Recruitment Officer, Watkins College of Art and Design, 2298 Metro Center Boulevard, Nashville, TN 37228. Phone: 615-383-4848. Fax: 615-383-4849. E-mail: admissions@watkins.edu. Web site: http://www.watkins.edu/.

WILLIAMSON CHRISTIAN COLLEGE

FRANKLIN, TENNESSEE

General Independent interdenominational, 4-year, coed **Entrance** Noncompetitive **Setting** 1-acre suburban campus **Total enrollment** 64 **Student-faculty ratio** 5:1 **Application deadline** 9/1 (freshmen), 9/1 (transfer) **Housing** No **Expenses** Tuition $8605 **Undergraduates** 58% women, 14% part-time, 76% 25 or older, 3% Hispanic American, 11% African American **The most frequently chosen baccalaureate fields are** business/marketing, theology and religious vocations **Academic program** Accelerated degree program, adult/continuing education programs, internships **Contact** Ms. Mary Newby, Recruiter, Williamson Christian College, 200 Seaboard Lane, Franklin, TN 37067. Phone: 615-771-7821. Fax: 615-771-7810. E-mail: mary@williamsoncc.edu. Web site: http://www.williamsoncc.edu/.

TEXAS

ABILENE CHRISTIAN UNIVERSITY

ABILENE, TEXAS

General Independent, comprehensive, coed, affiliated with Church of Christ **Entrance** Moderately difficult **Setting** 208-acre urban campus **Total enrollment** 4,675 **Student-faculty ratio** 15:1 **Application deadline** 8/1 (freshmen), rolling (transfer) **Freshmen** 47% were admitted **Housing** Yes **Expenses** Tuition $17,410; Room & Board $6350 **Undergraduates** 55% women, 7% part-time, 6% 25 or older, 1% Native American, 6% Hispanic American, 8% African American, 1% Asian American/Pacific Islander **The most frequently chosen baccalaureate fields are** business/marketing, education, interdisciplinary studies **Academic program** English as a second language, advanced placement, self-designed majors, honors program, summer session, adult/

Abilene Christian University *(continued)*

continuing education programs, internships **Contact** Hayley Webb, Director of Admissions, Abilene Christian University, Zellner Hall Room 200A, ACU Box 29000, Abilene, TX 79699-9000. Phone: 325-674-2650 or toll-free 877-APPLYUB. Fax: 325-674-2130. E-mail: info@admissions.acu.edu. Web site: http://www.acu.edu/.

AMBERTON UNIVERSITY
GARLAND, TEXAS

General Independent nondenominational, upper-level, coed **Entrance** Minimally difficult **Setting** 5-acre suburban campus **Total enrollment** 1,586 **Student-faculty ratio** 25:1 **Application deadline** Rolling (transfer) **Housing** No **Expenses** Tuition $6750 **Undergraduates** 62% women, 48% part-time, 98% 25 or older, 1% Native American, 7% Hispanic American, 31% African American, 2% Asian American/Pacific Islander **Academic program** Self-designed majors, summer session, adult/continuing education programs, internships **Contact** Dr. Don Hebbard, Academic Dean, Amberton University, 1700 Eastgate Drive, Garland, TX 75041-5595. Phone: 972-279-6511 Ext. 153. Fax: 972-279-9773. E-mail: advisor@amberton.edu. Web site: http://www.amberton.edu/.

AMERICAN INTERCONTINENTAL UNIVERSITY
HOUSTON, TEXAS

General Proprietary, comprehensive, coed **Entrance** Minimally difficult **Total enrollment** 26,686 **Application deadline** Rolling (freshmen), rolling (transfer) **Contact** Director of Admissions, American InterContinental University, 9999 Richmond Avenue, Houston, TX 77042. Phone: 832-201-3600 or toll-free 888-607-9888. Web site: http://www.aiuniv.edu/.

ANGELO STATE UNIVERSITY
SAN ANGELO, TEXAS

General State-supported, comprehensive, coed **Entrance** Moderately difficult **Setting** 268-acre urban campus **Total enrollment** 6,265 **Student-faculty ratio** 20:1 **Application deadline** 8/15 (freshmen), 8/15 (transfer) **Freshmen** 99% were admitted **Housing** Yes **Expenses** Tuition $4343; Room & Board $5518 **Undergraduates** 55% women, 16% part-time, 15% 25 or older, 1% Native American, 24% Hispanic American, 7% African American, 1% Asian American/Pacific Islander **The most frequently chosen baccalaureate fields are** business/marketing, education, psychology **Academic program** Advanced placement, honors program, summer session, internships **Contact** Ms. Amanda Taylor, Coordinator of Recruiting, Angelo State University, ASU Station #11014, Hardeman Building, San Angelo, TX 76909-1014. Phone: 325-942-2185 or toll-free 800-946-8627. Fax: 325-942-2128. E-mail: admissions@angelo.edu. Web site: http://www.angelo.edu/.

ARGOSY UNIVERSITY, DALLAS
DALLAS, TEXAS

General Proprietary, university, coed **Setting** urban campus **Contact** Director of Admissions, Argosy University, Dallas, 8080 Park Lane, Suite 400A, Dallas, TX 75231. Phone: 214-890-9900 or toll-free 866-954-9900. Fax: 214-696-3900. E-mail: 8080 Parklane, Suite 400A. Web site: http://www.argosy.edu/locations/dallas/.

ARLINGTON BAPTIST COLLEGE
ARLINGTON, TEXAS

General Independent Baptist, 4-year, coed **Entrance** Noncompetitive **Setting** 32-acre urban campus **Total enrollment** 144 **Student-faculty ratio** 11:1 **Application deadline** Rolling (freshmen), rolling (transfer) **Freshmen** 100% were admitted **Housing** Yes **Expenses** Tuition $6090; Room & Board $4100 **Undergraduates** 47% women, 26% part-time, 31% 25 or older, 3% Hispanic American, 4% African American **The most frequently chosen baccalaureate fields are** education, theology and religious vocations **Academic program** Advanced placement, summer session, internships **Contact** Ms. Janie Taylor, Registrar/Admissions, Arlington Baptist College, 3001 West Division, Arlington, TX 76012-3425. Phone: 817-461-8741 Ext. 105. Fax: 817-274-1138. E-mail: jhall@abconline.org. Web site: http://www.abconline.edu/.

THE ART INSTITUTE OF AUSTIN
AUSTIN, TEXAS

Contact Director of Admissions, The Art Institute of Austin, 100 Farmers Circle, Suite 100, Austin, TX 78728. Phone: 512-691-1707 or toll-free 866-583-7952. Fax: 512-691-1790. Web site: http://www.artinstitutes.edu/austin.

THE ART INSTITUTE OF DALLAS
DALLAS, TEXAS

General Proprietary, 4-year, coed **Setting** 2-acre urban campus **Contact** Director of Admissions, The Art Institute of Dallas, 8080 Park Lane, Suite 100, Dallas, TX 75231-5993. Phone: 214-692-8080 or toll-free 800-275-4243. Fax: 214-750-9460. E-mail: aidadm@aii.edu. Web site: http://www.artinstitutes.edu/dallas.

THE ART INSTITUTE OF HOUSTON
HOUSTON, TEXAS

General Proprietary, 4-year, coed **Setting** urban campus **Contact** Director of Admissions, The Art Institute of Houston, 1900 Yorktown, Houston, TX 77056-4115. Phone: 713-623-2040 or toll-free 800-275-4244. Fax: 713-966-2797. Web site: http://www.artinstitutes.edu/houston.

AUSTIN COLLEGE
SHERMAN, TEXAS

General Independent Presbyterian, comprehensive, coed **Entrance** Very difficult **Setting** 60-acre suburban campus **Total enrollment** 1,339 **Student-faculty ratio** 12:1 **Application deadline** 5/1 (freshmen), 5/1 (transfer) **Freshmen** 71% were admitted **Housing** Yes **Expenses** Tuition $26,530; Room & Board $8304 **Undergraduates** 52% women, 1% part-time, 1% 25 or older, 1% Native American, 8% Hispanic American, 3% African American, 14% Asian American/Pacific Islander **The most frequently chosen baccalaureate fields are** psychology, business/marketing, social sciences **Academic program** Advanced placement, self-designed majors, honors program, summer session, adult/continuing education programs, internships **Contact** Ms. Nan Davis, Vice President for Institutional Enrollment, Austin College, 900 North Grand Avenue, Suite 6N, Sherman, TX 75090-4400. Phone: 903-813-3000 or toll-free 800-442-5363. Fax: 903-813-3198. E-mail: admission@austincollege.edu. Web site: http://www.austincollege.edu/.

AUSTIN GRADUATE SCHOOL OF THEOLOGY
AUSTIN, TEXAS

Contact Celeste Scarbrough, Director of Admissions, Austin Graduate School of Theology, 1909 University Avenue, Austin, TX 78705. Phone: 512-476-2772 Ext. 203 or toll-free 866-AUS-GRAD. Fax: 512-476-3919. E-mail: registrar@austingrad.edu. Web site: http://www.austingrad.edu/.

BAPTIST MISSIONARY ASSOCIATION THEOLOGICAL SEMINARY
JACKSONVILLE, TEXAS

Contact Dr. Philip Attebery, Dean and Registrar, Baptist Missionary Association Theological Seminary, 1530 East Pine Street, Jacksonville, TX 75766-5407. Phone: 903-586-2501 Ext. 229. Fax: 903-586-0378. E-mail: bmatsem@fbmats.edu. Web site: http://www.bmats.edu/.

BAPTIST UNIVERSITY OF THE AMERICAS
SAN ANTONIO, TEXAS

Contact Abraham Garcia, Student Council President, Baptist University of the Americas, 8019 South Pan Am Expressway, San Antonio, TX 78224. Phone: 210-924-4338 Ext. 202 or toll-free 800-721-1396. Fax: 210-924-2701. E-mail: agarcia@bua.edu. Web site: http://www.bua.edu/.

BAYLOR UNIVERSITY
WACO, TEXAS

General Independent Baptist, university, coed **Entrance** Moderately difficult **Setting** 508-acre urban campus **Total enrollment** 14,174 **Student-faculty ratio** 15:1 **Application deadline** 2/1 (freshmen), rolling (transfer) **Freshmen** 44% were admitted **Expenses** Tuition $26,234; Room & Board $8230 **Undergraduates** 58% women, 2% part-time, 2% 25 or older, 1% Native American, 10% Hispanic American, 8% African American, 7% Asian American/Pacific Islander **The most frequently chosen baccalaureate fields are** business/marketing, communications/journalism, health professions and related sciences **Academic program** Advanced placement, accelerated degree program, self-designed majors, honors program, summer session, internships **Contact** Ms. Jennifer Carron, Director of Admissions, Baylor University, PO Box 97056, Waco, TX 76798. Phone: 254-710-3435 or toll-free 800-BAYLORU. Fax: 254-710-3436. E-mail: admissions@baylor.edu. Web site: http://www.baylor.edu/.

COLLEGE OF BIBLICAL STUDIES–HOUSTON
HOUSTON, TEXAS

General Independent nondenominational, 4-year, coed **Entrance** Noncompetitive **Setting** 10-acre urban campus **Total enrollment** 1,399 **Expenses** Tuition $5114 **Undergraduates** 0.2% Native American, 26% Hispanic American, 47% African American, 3% Asian American/Pacific Islander **The most frequently chosen baccalaureate field is** philosophy and religious studies **Academic program** English as a second language, accelerated degree program, honors program, summer session, adult/continuing education programs **Contact** Admissions, College of Biblical Studies–Houston, 6000 Dale Carnegie Drive, Houston, TX 77036. Phone: 832-252-3377. Fax: 713-532-8150. E-mail: admissions@cbshouston.edu. Web site: http://www.cbshouston.edu/.

THE COLLEGE OF SAINT THOMAS MORE
FORT WORTH, TEXAS

General Independent, 4-year, coed, affiliated with Roman Catholic Church **Contact** Dr. James A.

The College of Saint Thomas More *(continued)*

Patrick, The College of Saint Thomas More, 3020 Lubbock Avenue, Fort Worth, TX 76109-2323. Phone: 817-923-8459 or toll-free 800-583-6489. Fax: 817-924-3206. E-mail: more-info@cstm.edu. Web site: http://www.cstm.edu/.

CONCORDIA UNIVERSITY TEXAS
AUSTIN, TEXAS

General Independent, comprehensive, coed, affiliated with Lutheran Church–Missouri Synod **Entrance** Moderately difficult **Setting** 20-acre urban campus **Total enrollment** 1,826 **Student-faculty ratio** 17:1 **Application deadline** 8/15 (freshmen), rolling (transfer) **Freshmen** 62% were admitted **Housing** Yes **Expenses** Tuition $18,910; Room & Board $7300 **Undergraduates** 57% women, 29% part-time, 0.1% Native American, 20% Hispanic American, 10% African American, 1% Asian American/Pacific Islander **The most frequently chosen baccalaureate fields are** business/marketing, education, theology and religious vocations **Academic program** Advanced placement, accelerated degree program, honors program, summer session, adult/continuing education programs, internships **Contact** Kristi Kirk, Director of Enrollment Services, Concordia University Texas, 3400 Interstate 35 North, Austin, TX 78705. Phone: 512-486-2000 Ext. 1156 or toll-free 800-285-4252. Fax: 512-459-8517. E-mail: ctxadmis@crf.cuis.edu. Web site: http://www.concordia.edu/.

THE CRISWELL COLLEGE
DALLAS, TEXAS

Contact Mr. W. Danny Blair, Vice President for Enrollment and Academic Services, The Criswell College, 4010 Gaston Avenue, Dallas, TX 75246-1537. Phone: 214-818-1305 or toll-free 800-899-0012. Fax: 214-818-1310. E-mail: wdblair@criswell.edu. Web site: http://www.criswell.edu/.

DALLAS BAPTIST UNIVERSITY
DALLAS, TEXAS

General Independent, comprehensive, coed, affiliated with Baptist General Convention of Texas **Entrance** Moderately difficult **Setting** 293-acre urban campus **Total enrollment** 5,244 **Student-faculty ratio** 15:1 **Application deadline** Rolling (freshmen), rolling (transfer) **Freshmen** 52% were admitted **Housing** Yes **Expenses** Tuition $14,940; Room & Board $5148 **Undergraduates** 59% women, 39% part-time, 43% 25 or older, 1% Native American, 9% Hispanic American, 18% African American, 2% Asian American/Pacific Islander **Academic program** English as a second language, advanced placement, honors program, summer session, adult/continuing education programs, internships **Contact** Ms. Erin Dennis, Associate Director of Freshman Recruitment/ Undergraduate Admissions, Dallas Baptist University, 3000 Mountain Creek Parkway, Dallas, TX 75211-9299. Phone: 214-333-5360 or toll-free 800-460-1328. Fax: 214-333-5447. E-mail: admiss@dbu.edu. Web site: http://www.dbu.edu/.

DALLAS CHRISTIAN COLLEGE
DALLAS, TEXAS

General Independent, 4-year, coed, affiliated with Christian Churches and Churches of Christ **Entrance** Minimally difficult **Setting** 22-acre urban campus **Total enrollment** 358 **Student-faculty ratio** 16:1 **Application deadline** Rolling (freshmen), rolling (transfer) **Freshmen** 47% were admitted **Housing** Yes **Expenses** Tuition $10,170; Room & Board $6250 **Undergraduates** 44% women, 32% part-time, 40% 25 or older, 3% Native American, 11% Hispanic American, 15% African American, 2% Asian American/Pacific Islander **Academic program** Advanced placement, accelerated degree program, summer session, adult/continuing education programs, internships **Contact** Mr. Eric Hinton, Director of Admissions, Dallas Christian College, 2700 Christian Parkway, Dallas, TX 75234-7299. Phone: 972-241-3371 Ext. 113. Fax: 972-241-8021. E-mail: ehinton@dallas.edu. Web site: http://www.dallas.edu/.

DeVRY UNIVERSITY
HOUSTON, TEXAS

General Proprietary, comprehensive, coed **Total enrollment** 1,079 **Student-faculty ratio** 21:1 **Application deadline** Rolling (freshmen), rolling (transfer) **Expenses** Tuition $13,990 **Undergraduates** 43% women, 36% part-time, 54% 25 or older, 0.2% Native American, 35% Hispanic American, 35% African American, 5% Asian American/Pacific Islander **The most frequently chosen baccalaureate fields are** business/marketing, computer and information sciences, engineering technologies **Academic program** Advanced placement, accelerated degree program, summer session **Contact** Admissions Office, DeVry University, 11125 Equity Drive, Houston, TX 77041. Phone: toll-free 866-703-3879. Web site: http://www.devry.edu/.

DeVRY UNIVERSITY
IRVING, TEXAS

General Proprietary, comprehensive, coed **Entrance** Minimally difficult **Setting** 13-acre suburban campus **Total enrollment** 1,706

Student-faculty ratio 19:1 **Application deadline** Rolling (freshmen), rolling (transfer) **Housing** No **Expenses** Tuition $13,990 **Undergraduates** 31% women, 52% part-time, 56% 25 or older, 1% Native American, 20% Hispanic American, 32% African American, 4% Asian American/Pacific Islander **The most frequently chosen baccalaureate fields are** business/marketing, computer and information sciences, engineering technologies **Academic program** Advanced placement, accelerated degree program, summer session, adult/continuing education programs **Contact** Admissions Office, DeVry University, 4800 Regent Boulevard, Irving, TX 75063-2439. Web site: http://www.devry.edu/.

DeVRY UNIVERSITY
RICHARDSON, TEXAS

Contact DeVry University, Richardson Center, 2201 N. Central Expressway, Richardson, TX 75080. Web site: http://www.devry.edu/.

EAST TEXAS BAPTIST UNIVERSITY
MARSHALL, TEXAS

General Independent Baptist, 4-year, coed **Entrance** Moderately difficult **Setting** 200-acre small-town campus **Total enrollment** 1,308 **Student-faculty ratio** 15:1 **Application deadline** 8/14 (freshmen), 8/14 (transfer) **Freshmen** 75% were admitted **Housing** Yes **Expenses** Tuition $14,680; Room & Board $4663 **Undergraduates** 53% women, 12% part-time, 8% 25 or older, 1% Native American, 4% Hispanic American, 16% African American, 1% Asian American/Pacific Islander **The most frequently chosen baccalaureate fields are** business/marketing, education, health professions and related sciences **Academic program** Advanced placement, honors program, summer session, adult/continuing education programs, internships **Contact** Ms. Melissa Fitts, Director of Admissions, East Texas Baptist University, 1209 North Grove, Marshall, TX 75670-1498. Phone: 903-923-2000 or toll-free 800-804-ETBU. Fax: 903-923-2001. E-mail: admissions@etbu.edu. Web site: http://www.etbu.edu/.

HARDIN-SIMMONS UNIVERSITY
ABILENE, TEXAS

General Independent Baptist, comprehensive, coed **Entrance** Moderately difficult **Setting** 120-acre urban campus **Total enrollment** 2,435 **Student-faculty ratio** 14:1 **Application deadline** Rolling (freshmen), rolling (transfer) **Freshmen** 36% were admitted **Housing** Yes **Expenses** Tuition $18,380; Room & Board $5180 **Undergraduates** 57% women, 13% part-time, 9% 25 or older, 1% Native American, 10% Hispanic American, 5% African American, 1% Asian American/Pacific Islander **The most frequently chosen baccalaureate fields are** business/marketing, communications/journalism, education **Academic program** Advanced placement, accelerated degree program, honors program, summer session, adult/continuing education programs, internships **Contact** Ms. Brynn Reynolds, Visitor Coordinator, Hardin-Simmons University, Box 16050, Abilene, TX 79698-6050. Phone: 325-670-1207 or toll-free 877-464-7889. Fax: 325-671-2115. E-mail: breynolds@hsutx.edu. Web site: http://www.hsutx.edu/.

HOUSTON BAPTIST UNIVERSITY
HOUSTON, TEXAS

General Independent Baptist, comprehensive, coed **Entrance** Moderately difficult **Setting** 100-acre urban campus **Total enrollment** 2,339 **Student-faculty ratio** 15:1 **Application deadline** Rolling (freshmen), rolling (transfer) **Freshmen** 48% were admitted **Housing** Yes **Expenses** Tuition $18,820; Room & Board $4995 **Undergraduates** 67% women, 10% part-time, 18% 25 or older, 0.4% Native American, 17% Hispanic American, 19% African American, 16% Asian American/Pacific Islander **The most frequently chosen baccalaureate fields are** biological/life sciences, business/marketing, education **Academic program** English as a second language, advanced placement, accelerated degree program, honors program, summer session, adult/continuing education programs, internships **Contact** Eduardo Borges, Director of Admissions, Houston Baptist University, 7502 Fondren Road, Houston, TX 77074-3298. Phone: 281-649-3299 or toll-free 800-696-3210. Fax: 281-649-3217. E-mail: eborges@hbu.edu. Web site: http://www.hbu.edu/.

HOWARD PAYNE UNIVERSITY
BROWNWOOD, TEXAS

General Independent, 4-year, coed, affiliated with Baptist General Convention of Texas **Entrance** Moderately difficult **Setting** 30-acre small-town campus **Total enrollment** 1,385 **Student-faculty ratio** 11:1 **Application deadline** 8/1 (freshmen), 8/1 (transfer) **Freshmen** 62% were admitted **Housing** Yes **Expenses** Tuition $17,400; Room & Board $4460 **Undergraduates** 48% women, 24% part-time, 16% 25 or older, 1% Native American, 15% Hispanic American, 7% African American, 1% Asian American/Pacific Islander **The most frequently chosen baccalaureate fields are** business/marketing, education, theology and religious vocations **Academic program** English as a second language, advanced placement, honors program, summer session, adult/continuing education programs, internships

Howard Payne University *(continued)*

Contact Ms. Cheryl Mangrum, Associate Director of Admission, Howard Payne University, 1000 Fisk Street, Brownwood, TX 76801. Phone: 325-649-8020 or toll-free 800-880-4478. Fax: 325-649-8901. E-mail: enroll@hputx.edu. Web site: http://www.hputx.edu/.

HUSTON-TILLOTSON UNIVERSITY
AUSTIN, TEXAS

General Independent interdenominational, 4-year, coed **Entrance** Moderately difficult **Setting** 23-acre urban campus **Total enrollment** 768 **Student-faculty ratio** 16:1 **Application deadline** 7/1 (freshmen), 7/1 (transfer) **Freshmen** 41% were admitted **Housing** Yes **Expenses** Tuition $10,038; Room & Board $5892 **Undergraduates** 50% women, 6% part-time, 19% 25 or older, 12% Hispanic American, 76% African American, 1% Asian American/Pacific Islander **The most frequently chosen baccalaureate fields are** business/marketing, interdisciplinary studies, social sciences **Academic program** English as a second language, advanced placement, accelerated degree program, summer session, internships **Contact** Mrs. Shakitha Stinson, Huston-Tillotson University, 900 Chicon Street, Austin, TX 78702. Phone: 512-505-3031. Fax: 512-505-3192. E-mail: slstinson@htu.edu. Web site: http://www.htu.edu/.

JARVIS CHRISTIAN COLLEGE
HAWKINS, TEXAS

General Independent, 4-year, coed, affiliated with Christian Church (Disciples of Christ) **Entrance** Minimally difficult **Setting** 465-acre rural campus **Total enrollment** 712 **Student-faculty ratio** 13:1 **Application deadline** 8/1 (freshmen), rolling (transfer) **Freshmen** 21% were admitted **Housing** Yes **Expenses** Tuition $8208; Room & Board $4954 **Undergraduates** 50% women, 8% part-time, 7% 25 or older, 5% Hispanic American, 94% African American **The most frequently chosen baccalaureate fields are** business/marketing, computer and information sciences, security and protective services **Academic program** Advanced placement, honors program, summer session, adult/continuing education programs, internships **Contact** Mr. Christopher Wooten, Admissions Counselor, Jarvis Christian College, PO Box 1470, Hawkins, TX 75765-9989. Phone: 903-769-5745. Fax: 903-769-4842. E-mail: chris_wooten@jarvis.edu. Web site: http://www.jarvis.edu/.

LAMAR UNIVERSITY
BEAUMONT, TEXAS

Contact Ms. Melissa Chesser, Director of Recruitment, Lamar University, PO Box 10009, Beaumont, TX 77710. Phone: 409-880-8354. Fax: 409-880-8463. E-mail: admissions@hal.lamar.edu. Web site: http://www.lamar.edu/.

LeTOURNEAU UNIVERSITY
LONGVIEW, TEXAS

General Independent nondenominational, comprehensive, coed **Setting** 162-acre suburban campus **Total enrollment** 3,921 **Student-faculty ratio** 19:1 **Application deadline** 8/1 (freshmen), 8/1 (transfer) **Freshmen** 70% were admitted **Housing** Yes **Expenses** Tuition $17,910; Room & Board $6950 **Undergraduates** 58% women, 13% part-time, 7% 25 or older, 0.4% Native American, 8% Hispanic American, 22% African American, 2% Asian American/Pacific Islander **The most frequently chosen baccalaureate fields are** business/marketing, education, engineering **Academic program** Advanced placement, accelerated degree program, honors program, summer session, adult/continuing education programs, internships **Contact** Mr. James Townsend, Director of Admissions, LeTourneau University, PO Box 7001, Longview, TX 75607-7001. Phone: 903-233-3400 or toll-free 800-759-8811. Fax: 903-233-3411. E-mail: admissions@letu.edu. Web site: http://www.letu.edu/.

LUBBOCK CHRISTIAN UNIVERSITY
LUBBOCK, TEXAS

General Independent, comprehensive, coed, affiliated with Church of Christ **Entrance** Moderately difficult **Setting** 120-acre suburban campus **Total enrollment** 1,960 **Student-faculty ratio** 14:1 **Application deadline** 8/1 (freshmen), rolling (transfer) **Freshmen** 73% were admitted **Housing** Yes **Expenses** Tuition $14,290; Room & Board $4750 **Undergraduates** 57% women, 19% part-time, 33% 25 or older, 0.2% Native American, 16% Hispanic American, 5% African American, 1% Asian American/Pacific Islander **The most frequently chosen baccalaureate fields are** business/marketing, education, health professions and related sciences **Academic program** Advanced placement, accelerated degree program, self-designed majors, honors program, summer session, adult/continuing education programs, internships **Contact** Mr. Mondy Brewer, Director of Admissions, Lubbock Christian University, 5601 19th Street, Lubbock, TX 79407. Phone: 806-720-7803 or toll-free 800-933-7601. Fax: 806-720-7162. E-mail: admissions@lcu.edu. Web site: http://www.lcu.edu/.

McMURRY UNIVERSITY
ABILENE, TEXAS

General Independent United Methodist, 4-year, coed **Entrance** Moderately difficult **Setting**

41-acre urban campus **Total enrollment** 1,462 **Student-faculty ratio** 14:1 **Application deadline** 8/15 (freshmen), 8/15 (transfer) **Freshmen** 53% were admitted **Housing** Yes **Expenses** Tuition $18,175; Room & Board $6689 **Undergraduates** 50% women, 19% part-time, 19% 25 or older, 1% Native American, 16% Hispanic American, 14% African American, 1% Asian American/Pacific Islander **The most frequently chosen baccalaureate fields are** business/marketing, education, health professions and related sciences **Academic program** Advanced placement, accelerated degree program, honors program, summer session, adult/continuing education programs, internships **Contact** Mr. Scott Smiley, Director of Admissions, McMurry University, McMurry Station 278, Abilene, TX 79697. Phone: 325-793-4720 or toll-free 800-477-0077. Fax: 325-793-4701. E-mail: admissions@mcm.edu. Web site: http://www.mcm.edu/.

MIDLAND COLLEGE
MIDLAND, TEXAS

Contact Mr. Ryan Gibbs, Director of Admissions, Midland College, 3600 North Garfield, Midland, TX 79705-6399. Phone: 432-685-5502 or toll-free 432-685-5502. Fax: 432-685-6401. E-mail: rgibbs@midland.edu. Web site: http://www.midland.edu/.

MIDWESTERN STATE UNIVERSITY
WICHITA FALLS, TEXAS

General State-supported, comprehensive, coed **Entrance** Minimally difficult **Setting** 255-acre urban campus **Total enrollment** 6,027 **Student-faculty ratio** 19:1 **Application deadline** 8/7 (freshmen), 8/7 (transfer) **Freshmen** 69% were admitted **Housing** Yes **Expenses** Tuition $4716; Room & Board $5220 **Undergraduates** 58% women, 27% part-time, 30% 25 or older, 1% Native American, 9% Hispanic American, 13% African American, 4% Asian American/Pacific Islander **The most frequently chosen baccalaureate fields are** business/marketing, health professions and related sciences, interdisciplinary studies **Academic program** English as a second language, advanced placement, honors program, summer session, adult/continuing education programs, internships **Contact** Ms. Barbara Merkle, Director of Admissions, Midwestern State University, 3410 Taft Boulevard, Wichita Falls, TX 76308. Phone: 940-397-4334 or toll-free 800-842-1922. Fax: 940-397-4672. E-mail: admissions@mwsu.edu. Web site: http://www.mwsu.edu/.

NORTHWOOD UNIVERSITY, TEXAS CAMPUS
CEDAR HILL, TEXAS

General Independent, 4-year, coed **Entrance** Moderately difficult **Setting** 360-acre small-town campus **Total enrollment** 526 **Student-faculty ratio** 20:1 **Application deadline** Rolling (freshmen), rolling (transfer) **Freshmen** 60% were admitted **Housing** Yes **Expenses** Tuition $16,455; Room & Board $6888 **Undergraduates** 48% women, 5% part-time, 5% 25 or older, 1% Native American, 30% Hispanic American, 15% African American, 4% Asian American/Pacific Islander **The most frequently chosen baccalaureate fields are** business/marketing, communications/journalism, parks and recreation **Academic program** Advanced placement, accelerated degree program, honors program, summer session, adult/continuing education programs, internships **Contact** Ms. Sylvia Correa, Director of Admissions, Northwood University, Texas Campus, 1114 West FM 1382, Cedar Hil, TX 75104. Phone: 989-837-4237 or toll-free 800-927-9663. Fax: 972-291-3824. E-mail: txadmit@northwood.edu. Web site: http://www.northwood.edu/.

OUR LADY OF THE LAKE UNIVERSITY OF SAN ANTONIO
SAN ANTONIO, TEXAS

General Independent Roman Catholic, comprehensive, coed **Entrance** Moderately difficult **Setting** 75-acre urban campus **Total enrollment** 2,608 **Student-faculty ratio** 13:1 **Application deadline** 7/15 (freshmen), 7/15 (transfer) **Freshmen** 49% were admitted **Housing** Yes **Expenses** Tuition $19,116; Room & Board $5838 **Undergraduates** 76% women, 28% part-time, 62% 25 or older, 0.3% Native American, 74% Hispanic American, 7% African American, 1% Asian American/Pacific Islander **The most frequently chosen baccalaureate fields are** business/marketing, education, science technologies **Academic program** English as a second language, advanced placement, summer session, adult/continuing education programs, internships **Contact** Ms. Rhonda Moses, Retention Office, Our Lady of the Lake University of San Antonio, 411 Southwest 24th Street, San Antonio, TX 78207-4689. Phone: 210-434-6711 Ext. 314 or toll-free 800-436-6558. Fax: 210-431-4036. E-mail: admission@lake.ollusa.edu. Web site: http://www.ollusa.edu/.

PAUL QUINN COLLEGE
DALLAS, TEXAS

General Independent African Methodist Episcopal, 4-year, coed **Entrance** Moderately difficult **Setting** 132-acre suburban campus **Total enrollment** 567 **Student-faculty ratio** 5:1 **Application deadline** 6/1 (freshmen), 6/1 (transfer) **Freshmen** 9% were admitted **Housing** Yes **Expenses** Tuition $7800; Room & Board $4750 **Undergraduates** 47% women, 15% part-time, 38% 25 or older, 4% Hispanic American, 88%

Paul Quinn College *(continued)*

African American **The most frequently chosen baccalaureate fields are** business/marketing, biological/life sciences, education **Academic program** Advanced placement, accelerated degree program, honors program, summer session, adult/continuing education programs, internships **Contact** Ms. Nena Taylor-Richey, Director of Admissions and Recruitment, Paul Quinn College, 3837 Simpson-Stuart Road, Dallas, TX 75241-4331. Phone: 214-302-3575 or toll-free 800-237-2648. Fax: 214-302-3520. Web site: http://www.pqc.edu/.

PRAIRIE VIEW A&M UNIVERSITY
PRAIRIE VIEW, TEXAS

General State-supported, comprehensive, coed **Entrance** Moderately difficult **Setting** 1,440-acre small-town campus **Total enrollment** 8,382 **Student-faculty ratio** 17:1 **Application deadline** 6/1 (freshmen), 6/1 (transfer) **Freshmen** 40% were admitted **Housing** Yes **Expenses** Tuition $8700; Room & Board $6477 **Undergraduates** 57% women, 11% part-time, 39% 25 or older, 0.1% Native American, 4% Hispanic American, 90% African American, 2% Asian American/Pacific Islander **The most frequently chosen baccalaureate fields are** business/marketing, engineering, health professions and related sciences **Academic program** English as a second language, advanced placement, accelerated degree program, honors program, summer session, internships **Contact** Ms. Mary Gooch, Director of Admissions, Prairie View A&M University, PO Box 519, MS #1009, Prarie View, TX 77446-0188. Phone: 936-261-1066. Fax: 936-857-2699. E-mail: megooch@pvamu.edu. Web site: http://www.pvamu.edu/.

RICE UNIVERSITY
HOUSTON, TEXAS

General Independent, university, coed **Entrance** Most difficult **Setting** 300-acre urban campus **Total enrollment** 5,243 **Student-faculty ratio** 5:1 **Application deadline** 1/2 (freshmen), 3/15 (transfer) **Freshmen** 25% were admitted **Housing** Yes **Expenses** Tuition $30,479; Room & Board $10,750 **Undergraduates** 48% women, 2% part-time, 1% 25 or older, 1% Native American, 12% Hispanic American, 7% African American, 19% Asian American/Pacific Islander **The most frequently chosen baccalaureate fields are** engineering, biological/life sciences, social sciences **Academic program** English as a second language, advanced placement, accelerated degree program, self-designed majors, honors program, summer session, internships **Contact** Office of Admission, Rice University, Office of Admission, PO Box 1892, MS 17, Houston, TX 77251-1892. Phone: 713-348-RICE or toll-free 800-527-OWLS. E-mail: admi@rice.edu. Web site: http://www.rice.edu/.

ST. EDWARD'S UNIVERSITY
AUSTIN, TEXAS

General Independent Roman Catholic, comprehensive, coed **Entrance** Moderately difficult **Setting** 160-acre urban campus **Total enrollment** 5,317 **Student-faculty ratio** 15:1 **Application deadline** 5/1 (freshmen), 7/1 (transfer) **Freshmen** 65% were admitted **Housing** Yes **Expenses** Tuition $22,150; Room & Board $8158 **Undergraduates** 60% women, 23% part-time, 5% 25 or older, 1% Native American, 31% Hispanic American, 5% African American, 2% Asian American/Pacific Islander **The most frequently chosen baccalaureate fields are** business/marketing, communications/journalism, social sciences **Academic program** Advanced placement, honors program, summer session, adult/continuing education programs, internships **Contact** Ms. Karen Gregg, Inquiry Coordinator, St. Edward's University, 3001 South Congress Avenue, Austin, TX 78704. Phone: 512-448-8602 or toll-free 800-555-0164. Fax: 512-464-8877. E-mail: seu.admit@stedwards.edu. Web site: http://www.stedwards.edu/.

ST. MARY'S UNIVERSITY
SAN ANTONIO, TEXAS

General Independent Roman Catholic, comprehensive, coed **Entrance** Moderately difficult **Setting** 135-acre urban campus **Total enrollment** 3,920 **Student-faculty ratio** 13:1 **Application deadline** Rolling (freshmen), rolling (transfer) **Freshmen** 62% were admitted **Housing** Yes **Expenses** Tuition $21,500; Room & Board $6986 **Undergraduates** 59% women, 8% part-time, 11% 25 or older, 0.1% Native American, 70% Hispanic American, 4% African American, 3% Asian American/Pacific Islander **The most frequently chosen baccalaureate fields are** business/marketing, biological/life sciences, social sciences **Academic program** English as a second language, advanced placement, honors program, summer session, adult/continuing education programs, internships **Contact** Mr. Chad Bridwell, Director of Undergraduate Admission, St. Mary's University, One Camino Santa Maria, San Antonio, TX 78228. Phone: 210-436-3126 or toll-free 800-FOR-STMU. Fax: 210-431-6742. E-mail: uadm@stmarytx.edu. Web site: http://www.stmarytx.edu/.

SAM HOUSTON STATE UNIVERSITY
HUNTSVILLE, TEXAS

General State-supported, university, coed **Entrance** Moderately difficult **Setting** 1,256-

acre small-town campus **Total enrollment** 16,454 **Student-faculty ratio** 20:1 **Application deadline** 8/1 (freshmen), rolling (transfer) **Freshmen** 61% were admitted **Housing** Yes **Expenses** Tuition $5566; Room & Board $6046 **Undergraduates** 57% women, 16% part-time, 14% 25 or older, 1% Native American, 12% Hispanic American, 15% African American, 1% Asian American/Pacific Islander **The most frequently chosen baccalaureate fields are** business/marketing, agriculture, law/legal studies **Academic program** English as a second language, advanced placement, honors program, summer session, adult/continuing education programs, internships **Contact** Mr. Trevor B. Thorn, Director of Admissions and Recruitment, Sam Houston State University, PO Box 2418, Huntsville, TX 77341. Phone: 936-294-1828 or toll-free 866-232-7528 Ext. 1828. Fax: 936-294-3758. E-mail: admissions@shsu.edu. Web site: http://www.shsu.edu/.

SCHREINER UNIVERSITY
KERRVILLE, TEXAS

General Independent Presbyterian, comprehensive, coed **Entrance** Moderately difficult **Setting** 175-acre small-town campus **Total enrollment** 982 **Student-faculty ratio** 13:1 **Application deadline** 8/1 (freshmen), 8/1 (transfer) **Freshmen** 58% were admitted **Housing** Yes **Expenses** Tuition $17,008; Room & Board $7910 **Undergraduates** 57% women, 7% part-time, 14% 25 or older, 1% Native American, 20% Hispanic American, 3% African American, 1% Asian American/Pacific Islander **The most frequently chosen baccalaureate fields are** business/marketing, biological/life sciences, education **Academic program** Advanced placement, accelerated degree program, self-designed majors, honors program, summer session, internships **Contact** Ms. Sandy Speed, Dean of Admission and Financial Aid, Schreiner University, 2100 Memorial Boulevard, Kerrville, TX 78028. Phone: 830-792-7217 or toll-free 800-343-4919. Fax: 830-792-7226. E-mail: admissions@schreiner.edu. Web site: http://www.schreiner.edu/.

SOUTHERN METHODIST UNIVERSITY
DALLAS, TEXAS

General Independent, university, coed, affiliated with United Methodist Church **Entrance** Moderately difficult **Setting** 210-acre suburban campus **Total enrollment** 10,829 **Student-faculty ratio** 12:1 **Application deadline** 1/15 (freshmen), 7/1 (transfer) **Freshmen** 50% were admitted **Housing** Yes **Expenses** Tuition $33,198; Room & Board $11,875 **Undergraduates** 54% women, 5% part-time, 5% 25 or older, 1% Native American, 8% Hispanic American, 5% African American, 6% Asian American/Pacific Islander **The most frequently chosen baccalaureate fields are** business/marketing, communications/journalism, social sciences **Academic program** English as a second language, advanced placement, accelerated degree program, self-designed majors, honors program, summer session, adult/continuing education programs, internships **Contact** Mr. Ron Moss, Director of Admission and Enrollment Management, Southern Methodist University, PO Box 750181, Dallas, TX 75275-0181. Phone: 214-768-1101 or toll-free 800-323-0672. Fax: 214-768-0202. E-mail: enrol_serv@smu.edu. Web site: http://www.smu.edu/.

SOUTHWESTERN ADVENTIST UNIVERSITY
KEENE, TEXAS

General Independent Seventh-day Adventist, comprehensive, coed **Entrance** Minimally difficult **Setting** 150-acre rural campus **Total enrollment** 889 **Student-faculty ratio** 15:1 **Application deadline** 8/31 (freshmen), 8/31 (transfer) **Freshmen** 48% were admitted **Housing** Yes **Expenses** Tuition $14,284; Room & Board $6424 **Undergraduates** 60% women, 16% part-time, 28% 25 or older, 1% Native American, 28% Hispanic American, 13% African American, 9% Asian American/Pacific Islander **The most frequently chosen baccalaureate fields are** business/marketing, education, theology and religious vocations **Academic program** English as a second language, accelerated degree program, self-designed majors, honors program, summer session, internships **Contact** Ms. Charlotte Coy, Director of Admissions, Southwestern Adventist University, PO Box 567, Keene, TX 76059. Phone: 817-645-3921 Ext. 6252 or toll-free 800-433-2240. Fax: 817-556-4744. E-mail: ccoy@swau.edu. Web site: http://www.swau.edu/.

SOUTHWESTERN ASSEMBLIES OF GOD UNIVERSITY
WAXAHACHIE, TEXAS

Contact Mr. Pat Thompson, Admissions Counselor, Southwestern Assemblies of God University, 1200 Sycamore Street, Waxahachie, TX 75165-5735. Phone: 972-937-4010 or toll-free 888-937-7248. Fax: 972-923-0006. E-mail: info@sagu.edu. Web site: http://www.sagu.edu/.

SOUTHWESTERN CHRISTIAN COLLEGE
TERRELL, TEXAS

Contact Admissions Department, Southwestern Christian College, Box 10, 200 Bowser Street, Terrell, TX 75160. Phone: 214-524-3341 Ext. 155. Fax: 972-563-7133. Web site: http://www.swcc.edu/.

SOUTHWESTERN UNIVERSITY
GEORGETOWN, TEXAS

General Independent Methodist, 4-year, coed **Entrance** Very difficult **Setting** 700-acre suburban campus **Total enrollment** 1,294 **Student-faculty ratio** 10:1 **Application deadline** 2/15 (freshmen), 4/1 (transfer) **Freshmen** 67% were admitted **Housing** Yes **Expenses** Tuition $25,740; Room & Board $8130 **Undergraduates** 61% women, 2% part-time, 2% 25 or older, 1% Native American, 14% Hispanic American, 3% African American, 5% Asian American/Pacific Islander **The most frequently chosen baccalaureate fields are** communications/journalism, biological/life sciences, social sciences **Academic program** Advanced placement, self-designed majors, summer session, internships **Contact** Mr. Tom Oliver, Vice President for Enrollment Services, Southwestern University, 1001 East University Avenue, Georgetown, TX 78626. Phone: 512-863-1200 or toll-free 800-252-3166. Fax: 512-863-9601. E-mail: admission@southwestern.edu. Web site: http://www.southwestern.edu/.

STEPHEN F. AUSTIN STATE UNIVERSITY
NACOGDOCHES, TEXAS

General State-supported, comprehensive, coed **Entrance** Moderately difficult **Setting** 400-acre small-town campus **Total enrollment** 11,607 **Student-faculty ratio** 21:1 **Application deadline** Rolling (freshmen) **Freshmen** 74% were admitted **Housing** Yes **Expenses** Tuition $6162; Room & Board $6885 **Undergraduates** 59% women, 13% part-time, 22% 25 or older, 1% Native American, 9% Hispanic American, 19% African American, 1% Asian American/Pacific Islander **The most frequently chosen baccalaureate fields are** business/marketing, health professions and related sciences, interdisciplinary studies **Academic program** Advanced placement, accelerated degree program, self-designed majors, honors program, summer session, adult/continuing education programs, internships **Contact** Ms. Beth Smith, Associate Director of Admissions, Stephen F. Austin State University, PO Box 13051, SFA Station, Nacogdoches, TX 75962. Phone: 936-468-2504 or toll-free 800-731-2902. Fax: 936-468-3849. E-mail: admissions@sfasu.edu. Web site: http://www.sfasu.edu/.

SUL ROSS STATE UNIVERSITY
ALPINE, TEXAS

General State-supported, comprehensive, coed **Contact** Robert Cullins, Registrar, Sul Ross State University, East Highway 90, Alpine, TX 79832. Phone: 432-837-8050 or toll-free 888-722-7778. Fax: 432-837-8186. E-mail: rcullins@sulross.edu. Web site: http://www.sulross.edu/.

TARLETON STATE UNIVERSITY
STEPHENVILLE, TEXAS

General State-supported, comprehensive, coed **Entrance** Moderately difficult **Setting** 125-acre small-town campus **Total enrollment** 9,460 **Student-faculty ratio** 18:1 **Application deadline** 8/1 (freshmen), 7/1 (transfer) **Freshmen** 55% were admitted **Housing** Yes **Expenses** Tuition $6492; Room & Board $5944 **Undergraduates** 57% women, 23% part-time, 25% 25 or older, 1% Native American, 9% Hispanic American, 8% African American, 1% Asian American/Pacific Islander **The most frequently chosen baccalaureate fields are** agriculture, business/marketing, interdisciplinary studies **Academic program** Advanced placement, accelerated degree program, honors program, summer session, adult/continuing education programs, internships **Contact** Ms. Cindy Hess, Director of Undergraduate Admissions, Tarleton State University, Box T-0030, Tarleton Station, Stephenville, TX 76402. Phone: 254-968-9123 or toll-free 800-687-8236. Fax: 254-968-9951. E-mail: uadm@tarleton.edu. Web site: http://www.tarleton.edu/.

TEXAS A&M HEALTH SCIENCE CENTER
COLLEGE STATION, TEXAS

General State-supported, upper-level, coed **Setting** urban campus **Total enrollment** 544 **Application deadline** Rolling (transfer) **Housing** No **Undergraduates** 100% women, 19% 25 or older, 2% Native American, 10% Hispanic American, 2% African American, 20% Asian American/Pacific Islander **The most frequently chosen baccalaureate field is** health professions and related sciences **Contact** Dr. Jack L. Long, Associate Dean for Student Services, Texas A&M Health Science Center, PO Box 660677, 3302 Gaston Avenue, Dallas, TX 75266-0677. Phone: 214-828-8230. Fax: 214-874-4567. Web site: http://www.tamhsc.edu/.

TEXAS A&M INTERNATIONAL UNIVERSITY
LAREDO, TEXAS

General State-supported, comprehensive, coed **Entrance** Moderately difficult **Setting** 300-acre urban campus **Total enrollment** 5,188 **Student-faculty ratio** 17:1 **Application deadline** 7/1 (freshmen), 7/1 (transfer) **Freshmen** 54% were admitted **Housing** Yes **Expenses** Tuition $5038; Room & Board $6630 **Undergraduates** 63% women, 34% part-time, 28% 25 or older, 0.05% Native American, 92% Hispanic American, 1% African American, 1% Asian American/Pacific Islander **The most frequently chosen baccalaureate fields are** business/marketing, interdisciplinary studies, security and protective services

Academic program English as a second language, advanced placement, honors program, summer session, internships **Contact** Ms. Gina Gonzalez, Director of Recruitment and School Relations, Texas A&M International University, 5201 University Boulevard, Laredo, TX 78041-1900. Phone: 956-326-2200 or toll-free 888-489-2648. Fax: 956-326-2199. E-mail: enroll@tamiu.edu. Web site: http://www.tamiu.edu/.

TEXAS A&M UNIVERSITY
COLLEGE STATION, TEXAS

General State-supported, university, coed **Entrance** Moderately difficult **Setting** 5,200-acre suburban campus **Total enrollment** 46,542 **Student-faculty ratio** 19:1 **Application deadline** 2/1 (freshmen), 3/15 (transfer) **Freshmen** 76% were admitted **Housing** Yes **Expenses** Tuition $7335; Room & Board $7660 **Undergraduates** 48% women, 9% part-time, 2% 25 or older, 1% Native American, 12% Hispanic American, 3% African American, 4% Asian American/Pacific Islander **The most frequently chosen baccalaureate fields are** agriculture, business/marketing, engineering **Academic program** English as a second language, advanced placement, accelerated degree program, honors program, summer session, internships **Contact** Mr. Scott McDonald, Director of Admissions, Texas A&M University, 217 John J. Koldus Building, College Station, TX 77843-1265. Phone: 979-845-3741. Fax: 979-845-8737. E-mail: admissions@tamu.edu. Web site: http://www.tamu.edu/.

TEXAS A&M UNIVERSITY AT GALVESTON
GALVESTON, TEXAS

General State-supported, comprehensive, coed **Entrance** Moderately difficult **Setting** 122-acre suburban campus **Total enrollment** 1,614 **Student-faculty ratio** 15:1 **Application deadline** Rolling (freshmen), rolling (transfer) **Freshmen** 78% were admitted **Housing** Yes **Expenses** Tuition $6055; Room & Board $5203 **Undergraduates** 41% women, 7% part-time, 6% 25 or older, 1% Native American, 11% Hispanic American, 2% African American, 1% Asian American/Pacific Islander **The most frequently chosen baccalaureate fields are** biological/life sciences, business/marketing, transportation and materials moving **Academic program** English as a second language, advanced placement, accelerated degree program, summer session, internships **Contact** Ms. Sarah Trombley, Associate Director of Admissions and Records, Texas A&M University at Galveston, PO Box 1675, Galveston, TX 77553-1675. Phone: 409-740-4448 or toll-free 87—SEAAGGIE. Fax: 409-740-4731. E-mail: seaaggie@tamug.edu. Web site: http://www.tamug.edu/.

TEXAS A&M UNIVERSITY–COMMERCE
COMMERCE, TEXAS

General State-supported, university, coed **Entrance** Moderately difficult **Setting** 1,883-acre small-town campus **Total enrollment** 8,882 **Student-faculty ratio** 17:1 **Application deadline** 8/11 (freshmen), rolling (transfer) **Freshmen** 55% were admitted **Housing** Yes **Expenses** Tuition $5126; Room & Board $6484 **Undergraduates** 62% women, 26% part-time, 33% 25 or older, 1% Native American, 10% Hispanic American, 18% African American, 2% Asian American/Pacific Islander **The most frequently chosen baccalaureate fields are** business/marketing, interdisciplinary studies, parks and recreation **Academic program** Advanced placement, honors program, summer session, adult/continuing education programs, internships **Contact** Hope Young, Director of Admissions, Texas A&M University–Commerce, PO Box 3011, Commerce, TX 75429. Phone: 903-886-5103 or toll-free 800-331-3878. Fax: 903-886-5888. E-mail: admissions@tamu-commerce.edu. Web site: http://www.tamu-commerce.edu/.

TEXAS A&M UNIVERSITY–CORPUS CHRISTI
CORPUS CHRISTI, TEXAS

General State-supported, comprehensive, coed **Contact** Ms. Margaret Dechant, Director of Admissions, Texas A&M University–Corpus Christi, 6300 Ocean Drive, Corpus Christi, TX 78412-5503. Phone: 361-825-2414 or toll-free 800-482-6822. Fax: 361-825-5887. E-mail: judith.perales@mail.tamucc.edu. Web site: http://www.tamucc.edu/.

►**For more information, see page 493.**

TEXAS A&M UNIVERSITY–KINGSVILLE
KINGSVILLE, TEXAS

Contact Ms. Maggie Williams, Director of Admissions, Texas A&M University–Kingsville, West Santa Gertrudis, Kingsville, TX 78363. Phone: 361-593-2811 or toll-free 800-687-6000. Fax: 361-593-2195. Web site: http://www.tamuk.edu/.

TEXAS A&M UNIVERSITY–TEXARKANA
TEXARKANA, TEXAS

General State-supported, upper-level, coed **Contact** Mrs. Patricia Black, Director of Admissions and Registrar, Texas A&M University–Texarkana, PO Box 5518, Texarkana, TX 75505-

Texas A&M University–Texarkana *(continued)*

5518. Phone: 903-223-3068. Fax: 903-223-3140. E-mail: admissions@tamut.edu. Web site: http://www.tamut.edu/.

TEXAS CHIROPRACTIC COLLEGE
PASADENA, TEXAS

General Independent, upper-level, coed **Contact** Dr. Sandra Hughes, Director of Admissions, Texas Chiropractic College, 5912 Spencer Highway, Pasadena, TX 77505-1699. Phone: 281-998-6098 or toll-free 800-468-6839. Fax: 281-991-5237. E-mail: shughes@txchiro.edu. Web site: http://www.txchiro.edu/.

TEXAS CHRISTIAN UNIVERSITY
FORT WORTH, TEXAS

General Independent, university, coed, affiliated with Christian Church (Disciples of Christ) **Entrance** Moderately difficult **Setting** 260-acre suburban campus **Total enrollment** 8,668 **Student-faculty ratio** 14:1 **Application deadline** 2/15 (freshmen), 4/15 (transfer) **Freshmen** 49% were admitted **Housing** Yes **Expenses** Tuition $24,868; Room & Board $8200 **Undergraduates** 59% women, 5% part-time, 5% 25 or older, 0.5% Native American, 7% Hispanic American, 5% African American, 3% Asian American/Pacific Islander **The most frequently chosen baccalaureate fields are** business/marketing, communications/journalism, health professions and related sciences **Academic program** English as a second language, advanced placement, accelerated degree program, honors program, summer session, adult/continuing education programs, internships **Contact** Mr. Wes Waggoner, Director of Freshman Admissions, Texas Christian University, 2800 South University Drive, Fort Worth, TX 76129-0002. Phone: 817-257-7490 or toll-free 800-828-3764. Fax: 817-257-7268. E-mail: frogmail@tcu.edu. Web site: http://www.tcu.edu/.

TEXAS COLLEGE
TYLER, TEXAS

General Independent, 4-year, coed, affiliated with Christian Methodist Episcopal Church **Entrance** Noncompetitive **Setting** 25-acre urban campus **Total enrollment** 774 **Student-faculty ratio** 15:1 **Application deadline** Rolling (freshmen), rolling (transfer) **Housing** Yes **Expenses** Tuition $8746; Room & Board $5600 **Undergraduates** 42% women, 3% part-time, 23% 25 or older, 9% Hispanic American, 87% African American **The most frequently chosen baccalaureate fields are** biological/life sciences, business/marketing, public administration and social services **Academic program** Accelerated degree program, summer session, adult/continuing education programs, internships **Contact** Dr. Reggie Brazzle, Dean of Enrollment Services, Texas College, 2404 North Grand Avenue, PO Box 4500, Tyler, TX 75712-4500. Phone: 903-593-8311 Ext. 2277 or toll-free 800-306-6299. Fax: 903-596-0001. E-mail: rbrazzle@texascollege.edu. Web site: http://www.texascollege.edu/.

TEXAS LUTHERAN UNIVERSITY
SEGUIN, TEXAS

General Independent, 4-year, coed, affiliated with Evangelical Lutheran Church **Entrance** Moderately difficult **Setting** 196-acre suburban campus **Total enrollment** 1,375 **Student-faculty ratio** 14:1 **Application deadline** Rolling (freshmen), rolling (transfer) **Freshmen** 71% were admitted **Housing** Yes **Expenses** Tuition $20,060; Room & Board $5860 **Undergraduates** 52% women, 5% part-time, 7% 25 or older, 0.4% Native American, 19% Hispanic American, 9% African American, 1% Asian American/Pacific Islander **The most frequently chosen baccalaureate fields are** business/marketing, education, parks and recreation **Academic program** Advanced placement, honors program, summer session, adult/continuing education programs, internships **Contact** Mr. E. Jones, Vice President for Enrollment Services, Texas Lutheran University, 1000 West Court Street, Seguin, TX 78155-5999. Phone: 830-372-8050 or toll-free 800-771-8521. Fax: 830-372-8096. E-mail: admissions@tlu.edu. Web site: http://www.tlu.edu/.

TEXAS SOUTHERN UNIVERSITY
HOUSTON, TEXAS

General State-supported, university, coed **Entrance** Noncompetitive **Setting** 147-acre urban campus **Total enrollment** 9,540 **Student-faculty ratio** 20:1 **Application deadline** 8/15 (freshmen), 8/13 (transfer) **Freshmen** 98% were admitted **Housing** Yes **Expenses** Tuition $5428; Room & Board $6664 **Undergraduates** 59% women, 20% part-time, 27% 25 or older, 0.1% Native American, 4% Hispanic American, 90% African American, 3% Asian American/Pacific Islander **The most frequently chosen baccalaureate fields are** business/marketing, biological/life sciences, health professions and related sciences **Academic program** English as a second language, accelerated degree program, honors program, summer session, adult/continuing education programs, internships **Contact** Enrollment Services Customer Service Center, Texas Southern University, 3100 Cleburne Street, Houston, TX 77004-4598. Phone: 713-313-6861. Fax: 713-313-7851. E-mail: eservices@em.tsu.edu. Web site: http://www.tsu.edu/.

TEXAS STATE UNIVERSITY–SAN MARCOS
SAN MARCOS, TEXAS

General State-supported, university, coed **Entrance** Moderately difficult **Setting** 423-acre suburban campus **Total enrollment** 28,121 **Student-faculty ratio** 23:1 **Application deadline** 5/1 (freshmen), 7/1 (transfer) **Freshmen** 71% were admitted **Housing** Yes **Expenses** Tuition $6536; Room & Board $5878 **Undergraduates** 55% women, 18% part-time, 18% 25 or older, 1% Native American, 22% Hispanic American, 5% African American, 2% Asian American/Pacific Islander **The most frequently chosen baccalaureate fields are** business/marketing, interdisciplinary studies, visual and performing arts **Academic program** English as a second language, advanced placement, accelerated degree program, honors program, summer session, adult/continuing education programs, internships **Contact** Mrs. Christie Kangas, Director of Admissions, Texas State University–San Marcos, Admissions and Visitors Center, San Marcos, TX 78666-5709. Phone: 512-245-2364 Ext. 2803. Fax: 512-245-8044. E-mail: admissions@txstate.edu. Web site: http://www.txstate.edu/.

TEXAS TECH UNIVERSITY
LUBBOCK, TEXAS

General State-supported, university, coed **Entrance** Moderately difficult **Setting** 1,839-acre urban campus **Total enrollment** 28,257 **Student-faculty ratio** 18:1 **Application deadline** 5/1 (freshmen), rolling (transfer) **Freshmen** 77% were admitted **Housing** Yes **Expenses** Tuition $6783; Room & Board $7460 **Undergraduates** 44% women, 9% part-time, 8% 25 or older, 1% Native American, 13% Hispanic American, 4% African American, 3% Asian American/Pacific Islander **The most frequently chosen baccalaureate fields are** business/marketing, engineering, family and consumer sciences **Academic program** English as a second language, advanced placement, accelerated degree program, self-designed majors, honors program, summer session, internships **Contact** Dr. Robert M. Sweazy, Director, Office of Admissions, Texas Tech University, Box 45005, Lubbock, TX 79409-5005. Phone: 806-742-1480. Fax: 806-742-0062. E-mail: admissions@ttu.edu. Web site: http://www.ttu.edu/.

TEXAS WESLEYAN UNIVERSITY
FORT WORTH, TEXAS

General Independent United Methodist, comprehensive, coed **Entrance** Moderately difficult **Setting** 74-acre urban campus **Total enrollment** 3,087 **Student-faculty ratio** 15:1 **Application deadline** Rolling (freshmen), rolling (transfer) **Freshmen** 61% were admitted **Housing** Yes **Expenses** Tuition $15,775; Room & Board $5870 **Undergraduates** 64% women, 33% part-time, 1% 25 or older, 0.4% Native American, 20% Hispanic American, 19% African American, 2% Asian American/Pacific Islander **The most frequently chosen baccalaureate fields are** business/marketing, education, interdisciplinary studies **Academic program** English as a second language, advanced placement, summer session, adult/continuing education programs, internships **Contact** Holly Kiser, Director, Admissions, Texas Wesleyan University, 1201 Wesleyan Street, Fort Worth, TX 76105-1536. Phone: 817-531-4405 or toll-free 800-580-8980. Fax: 817-531-7515. E-mail: freshman@txwesleyan.edu. Web site: http://www.txwes.edu/.

TEXAS WOMAN'S UNIVERSITY
DENTON, TEXAS

General State-supported, university, coed, primarily women **Entrance** Minimally difficult **Setting** 270-acre suburban campus **Total enrollment** 12,168 **Student-faculty ratio** 14:1 **Application deadline** 7/1 (freshmen), 7/15 (transfer) **Freshmen** 88% were admitted **Housing** Yes **Expenses** Tuition $6540; Room & Board $5846 **Undergraduates** 93% women, 29% part-time, 37% 25 or older, 1% Native American, 17% Hispanic American, 21% African American, 7% Asian American/Pacific Islander **The most frequently chosen baccalaureate fields are** health professions and related sciences, business/marketing, interdisciplinary studies **Academic program** Advanced placement, accelerated degree program, honors program, summer session, adult/continuing education programs, internships **Contact** Ms. Erma Nieto-Brecht, Director of Admissions, Texas Woman's University, PO Box 425589, Denton, TX 76204-5589. Phone: 940-898-3188 or toll-free 888-948-9984. Fax: 940-898-3081. E-mail: admissions@twu.edu. Web site: http://www.twu.edu/.

TRINITY UNIVERSITY
SAN ANTONIO, TEXAS

General Independent, comprehensive, coed, affiliated with Presbyterian Church **Entrance** Very difficult **Setting** 113-acre urban campus **Total enrollment** 2,679 **Student-faculty ratio** 10:1 **Application deadline** 2/1 (freshmen), 3/1 (transfer) **Freshmen** 52% were admitted **Housing** Yes **Expenses** Tuition $27,699; Room & Board $8822 **Undergraduates** 54% women, 1% part-time, 1% 25 or older, 1% Native American, 11% Hispanic American, 4% African American, 6% Asian American/Pacific Islander **The most frequently chosen baccalaureate fields are**

Trinity University *(continued)*

health professions and related sciences, foreign languages and literature, social sciences **Academic program** Advanced placement, accelerated degree program, honors program, summer session, internships **Contact** Mr. Christopher Ellertson, Dean of Admissions and Financial Aid, Trinity University, One Trinity Place, San Antonio, TX 78212-7200. Phone: 210-999-7207 or toll-free 800-TRINITY. Fax: 210-999-8164. E-mail: admissions@trinity.edu. Web site: http://www.trinity.edu/.

UNIVERSITY OF DALLAS
IRVING, TEXAS

General Independent Roman Catholic, university, coed **Entrance** Moderately difficult **Setting** 750-acre suburban campus **Total enrollment** 2,972 **Student-faculty ratio** 13:1 **Application deadline** 8/1 (freshmen), 7/1 (transfer) **Freshmen** 75% were admitted **Housing** Yes **Expenses** Tuition $24,770; Room & Board $7885 **Undergraduates** 54% women, 3% part-time, 3% 25 or older, 0.4% Native American, 16% Hispanic American, 1% African American, 6% Asian American/Pacific Islander **The most frequently chosen baccalaureate fields are** business/marketing, biological/life sciences, English **Academic program** Advanced placement, self-designed majors, summer session, internships **Contact** Sr. Mary Brian Bole, Assistant Dean of Enrollment Management, University of Dallas, 1845 East Northgate Drive, Irving, TX 75062-4799. Phone: 972-721-5266 or toll-free 800-628-6999. Fax: 972-721-5017. E-mail: ugadmis@udallas.edu. Web site: http://www.udallas.edu/.

UNIVERSITY OF HOUSTON
HOUSTON, TEXAS

General State-supported, university, coed **Entrance** Moderately difficult **Setting** 550-acre urban campus **Total enrollment** 34,663 **Student-faculty ratio** 21:1 **Application deadline** 4/1 (freshmen), 5/1 (transfer) **Freshmen** 77% were admitted **Housing** Yes **Expenses** Tuition $7450; Room & Board $6651 **Undergraduates** 52% women, 29% part-time, 20% 25 or older, 0.3% Native American, 22% Hispanic American, 15% African American, 22% Asian American/Pacific Islander **The most frequently chosen baccalaureate fields are** business/marketing, psychology, social sciences **Academic program** English as a second language, advanced placement, accelerated degree program, honors program, summer session, adult/continuing education programs, internships **Contact** Mr. Jeff Fuller, Admissions, University of Houston, Room 122, Ezekiel Cullen Building, Houston, TX 77204-2023. Phone: 713-743-9562. Fax: 713-743-9633. E-mail: admissions@uh.edu. Web site: http://www.uh.edu/.

UNIVERSITY OF HOUSTON–CLEAR LAKE
HOUSTON, TEXAS

General State-supported, upper-level, coed **Entrance** Minimally difficult **Setting** 487-acre suburban campus **Total enrollment** 7,522 **Student-faculty ratio** 22:1 **Application deadline** Rolling (transfer) **First-year students** 49% were admitted **Housing** Yes **Expenses** Tuition $5619; Room only $7361 **Undergraduates** 64% 25 or older, 1% Native American, 20% Hispanic American, 8% African American, 6% Asian American/Pacific Islander **The most frequently chosen baccalaureate fields are** business/marketing, interdisciplinary studies, psychology **Academic program** English as a second language, accelerated degree program, self-designed majors, summer session, internships **Contact** Ms. Rauchelle Jones, Director of Admissions, University of Houston–Clear Lake, 2700 Bay Area Boulevard, Box 13, Houston, TX 77058-1098. Phone: 281-283-2518. Fax: 281-283-2530. E-mail: admissions@uhcl.edu. Web site: http://www.uhcl.edu/.

UNIVERSITY OF HOUSTON–DOWNTOWN
HOUSTON, TEXAS

General State-supported, comprehensive, coed **Entrance** Noncompetitive **Setting** 20-acre urban campus **Total enrollment** 11,793 **Student-faculty ratio** 21:1 **Application deadline** 7/15 (freshmen), 8/1 (transfer) **Freshmen** 99% were admitted **Housing** No **Expenses** Tuition $8100 **Undergraduates** 59% women, 48% part-time, 49% 25 or older, 0.2% Native American, 36% Hispanic American, 27% African American, 10% Asian American/Pacific Islander **The most frequently chosen baccalaureate fields are** business/marketing, interdisciplinary studies, liberal arts/general studies **Academic program** English as a second language, advanced placement, accelerated degree program, self-designed majors, honors program, summer session, adult/continuing education programs, internships **Contact** Jose Cantu, Director of Admissions, University of Houston–Downtown, One Main Street, Houston, TX 77002. Phone: 713-221-8522. Fax: 713-221-8157. E-mail: uhdadmit@uhd.edu. Web site: http://www.uhd.edu/.

UNIVERSITY OF HOUSTON–VICTORIA
VICTORIA, TEXAS

General State-supported, upper-level, coed **Entrance** Minimally difficult **Setting** 20-acre small-town campus **Total enrollment** 2,784 **Student-faculty ratio** 16:1 **Application dead-**

line Rolling (freshmen), rolling (transfer) **Housing** No **Expenses** Tuition $4965 **Undergraduates** 74% women, 64% part-time, 1% Native American, 22% Hispanic American, 9% African American, 4% Asian American/Pacific Islander **The most frequently chosen baccalaureate fields are** business/marketing, education, history **Academic program** Summer session, adult/continuing education programs, internships **Contact** Mrs. Trudy Wortham, Registrar, University of Houston–Victoria, 3007 North Ben Wilson Street, Victoria, TX 77901-4450. Phone: 361-570-4290 or toll-free 877-970-4848 Ext. 110. Fax: 361-570-4114. E-mail: admissions@uhv.edu. Web site: http://www.uhv.edu/.

UNIVERSITY OF MARY HARDIN-BAYLOR
BELTON, TEXAS

General Independent Southern Baptist, comprehensive, coed **Entrance** Moderately difficult **Setting** 100-acre small-town campus **Total enrollment** 2,651 **Student-faculty ratio** 14:1 **Application deadline** Rolling (freshmen), rolling (transfer) **Freshmen** 76% were admitted **Housing** Yes **Expenses** Tuition $17,760; Room & Board $4700 **Undergraduates** 63% women, 11% part-time, 18% 25 or older, 1% Native American, 12% Hispanic American, 12% African American, 2% Asian American/Pacific Islander **The most frequently chosen baccalaureate fields are** business/marketing, education, health professions and related sciences **Academic program** English as a second language, advanced placement, accelerated degree program, honors program, summer session, adult/continuing education programs, internships **Contact** Ms. Robbin Steen, Director of Admissions, University of Mary Hardin-Baylor, UMHB Station Box 8004, 900 College Street, Belton, TX 76513-2599. Phone: 254-295-4520 or toll-free 800-727-8642. Fax: 254-295-5049. E-mail: admission@umhb.edu. Web site: http://www.umhb.edu/.

UNIVERSITY OF NORTH TEXAS
DENTON, TEXAS

General State-supported, university, coed **Entrance** Moderately difficult **Setting** 744-acre suburban campus **Total enrollment** 34,153 **Student-faculty ratio** 19:1 **Application deadline** 6/16 (freshmen), 6/16 (transfer) **Freshmen** 65% were admitted **Housing** Yes **Expenses** Tuition $6320; Room & Board $5490 **Undergraduates** 55% women, 21% part-time, 18% 25 or older, 1% Native American, 12% Hispanic American, 13% African American, 5% Asian American/Pacific Islander **The most frequently chosen baccalaureate fields are** business/marketing, interdisciplinary studies, social sciences **Academic program** English as a second language, advanced placement, accelerated degree program, honors program, summer session, internships **Contact** Mr. Kent Marshall, Coordinator of New Student Mentoring Programs, University of North Texas, Box 311277, Denton, TX 76203-9988. Phone: 940-565-3921 or toll-free 800-868-8211. Fax: 940-565-2408. E-mail: undergradadm@unt.edu. Web site: http://www.unt.edu/.

UNIVERSITY OF PHOENIX–DALLAS CAMPUS
DALLAS, TEXAS

General Proprietary, comprehensive, coed **Contact** Ms. Evelyn Gaskin, Registrar/Executive Director, University of Phoenix–Dallas Campus, 4615 East Elwood Street, Mail Stop AA-K101, Phoenix, AZ 85040-1958. Phone: 480-557-3301 or toll-free 800-776-4867 (in-state); 800-228-7240 (out-of-state). Fax: 480-643-1020. E-mail: evelyn.gaskin@phoenix.edu. Web site: http://www.phoenix.edu/.

UNIVERSITY OF PHOENIX–HOUSTON CAMPUS
HOUSTON, TEXAS

General Proprietary, comprehensive, coed **Contact** Ms. Evelyn Gaskin, Associate Vice President, Student Admissions and Services, University of Phoenix–Houston Campus, 4615 East Elwood Street, Mail Stop AA-K101, Phoenix, AZ 85040-1958. Phone: 480-557-3301 or toll-free 800-776-4867 (in-state); 800-228-7240 (out-of-state). Fax: 480-894-1758. E-mail: beth.barilla@phoenix.edu. Web site: http://www.phoenix.edu/.

UNIVERSITY OF ST. THOMAS
HOUSTON, TEXAS

General Independent Roman Catholic, comprehensive, coed **Entrance** Moderately difficult **Setting** 21-acre urban campus **Total enrollment** 3,350 **Student-faculty ratio** 12:1 **Application deadline** Rolling (freshmen) **Freshmen** 84% were admitted **Housing** Yes **Expenses** Tuition $18,900; Room & Board $7300 **Undergraduates** 61% women, 24% part-time, 24% 25 or older, 1% Native American, 29% Hispanic American, 5% African American, 11% Asian American/Pacific Islander **The most frequently chosen baccalaureate fields are** business/marketing, liberal arts/general studies, social sciences **Academic program** Advanced placement, honors program, summer session, adult/continuing education programs, internships **Contact** Dr. David Melton, Assistant Vice President of University Admissions, University of St. Thomas, 3800 Montrose

University of St. Thomas *(continued)*

Boulevard, Houston, TX 77006-4696. Phone: 713-525-3833 or toll-free 800-856-8565. Fax: 713-525-3558. E-mail: admissions@stthom.edu. Web site: http://www.stthom.edu/.

THE UNIVERSITY OF TEXAS AT ARLINGTON

ARLINGTON, TEXAS

General State-supported, university, coed **Entrance** Moderately difficult **Setting** 395-acre urban campus **Total enrollment** 25,095 **Student-faculty ratio** 19:1 **Application deadline** 6/1 (freshmen), rolling (transfer) **Freshmen** 77% were admitted **Housing** Yes **Expenses** Tuition $7194; Room & Board $6180 **Undergraduates** 52% women, 32% part-time, 28% 25 or older, 1% Native American, 17% Hispanic American, 15% African American, 12% Asian American/Pacific Islander **The most frequently chosen baccalaureate fields are** business/marketing, biological/life sciences, interdisciplinary studies **Academic program** English as a second language, advanced placement, self-designed majors, honors program, summer session, adult/continuing education programs, internships **Contact** Dr. Hans Gatterdam, Director of Admissions and Records, The University of Texas at Arlington, Box 19111, 701 South Nedderman Drive, Arlington, TX 76019-0088. Phone: 817-272-6287. Fax: 817-272-3435. E-mail: admissions@uta.edu. Web site: http://www.uta.edu/.

THE UNIVERSITY OF TEXAS AT AUSTIN

AUSTIN, TEXAS

General State-supported, university, coed **Entrance** Very difficult **Setting** 350-acre urban campus **Total enrollment** 50,170 **Student-faculty ratio** 18:1 **Application deadline** 2/1 (freshmen), 3/1 (transfer) **Freshmen** 51% were admitted **Housing** Yes **Expenses** Tuition $7670; Room & Board $8576 **Undergraduates** 52% women, 8% part-time, 5% 25 or older, 0.4% Native American, 18% Hispanic American, 5% African American, 17% Asian American/Pacific Islander **The most frequently chosen baccalaureate fields are** communications/journalism, business/marketing, social sciences **Academic program** English as a second language, advanced placement, accelerated degree program, self-designed majors, honors program, summer session, adult/continuing education programs, internships **Contact** Dr. Bruce Walker, Vice Provost and Director of Admissions, The University of Texas at Austin, Office of Admissions, Freshman Admissions Center, PO Box 8058, Austin, TX 78713-8058. Phone: 512-475-7399. Fax: 512-475-7475. Web site: http://www.utexas.edu/.

THE UNIVERSITY OF TEXAS AT BROWNSVILLE

BROWNSVILLE, TEXAS

General State-supported, 4-year, coed **Entrance** Noncompetitive **Setting** 380-acre urban campus **Total enrollment** 17,215 **Student-faculty ratio** 21:1 **Application deadline** 7/1 (freshmen), 8/1 (transfer) **Freshmen** 100% were admitted **Housing** Yes **Expenses** Tuition $3874; Room only $2520 **Undergraduates** 59% women, 64% part-time, 36% 25 or older, 0.1% Native American, 89% Hispanic American, 0.3% African American, 0.5% Asian American/Pacific Islander **The most frequently chosen baccalaureate fields are** business/marketing, interdisciplinary studies, security and protective services **Academic program** English as a second language, advanced placement, summer session, internships **Contact** Carlo Tamayo, New Student Relations Coordinator, The University of Texas at Brownsville, 80 Fort Brown, Brownsville, TX 78520-4991. Phone: 956-882-8295 or toll-free 800-850-0160. Fax: 956-882-8959. E-mail: admissions@utb.edu. Web site: http://www.utb.edu/.

THE UNIVERSITY OF TEXAS AT DALLAS

RICHARDSON, TEXAS

General State-supported, university, coed **Entrance** Very difficult **Setting** 455-acre suburban campus **Total enrollment** 14,556 **Student-faculty ratio** 19:1 **Application deadline** 7/1 (freshmen) **Freshmen** 56% were admitted **Housing** Yes **Expenses** Tuition $8554; Room & Board $6671 **Undergraduates** 46% women, 27% part-time, 25% 25 or older, 1% Native American, 11% Hispanic American, 7% African American, 20% Asian American/Pacific Islander **The most frequently chosen baccalaureate fields are** business/marketing, interdisciplinary studies, psychology **Academic program** Advanced placement, accelerated degree program, self-designed majors, honors program, summer session, adult/continuing education programs, internships **Contact** Enrollment Services, The University of Texas at Dallas, PO Box 830688, Mail Station HH10, Richardson, TX 75083-0688. Phone: 972-883-2270 or toll-free 800-889-2443. Fax: 972-883-2599. E-mail: interest@utdallas.edu. Web site: http://www.utdallas.edu/.

THE UNIVERSITY OF TEXAS AT EL PASO

EL PASO, TEXAS

General State-supported, university, coed **Entrance** Minimally difficult **Setting** 360-acre urban campus **Total enrollment** 20,154 **Student-faculty ratio** 20:1 **Application deadline** 7/31 (freshmen), 7/31 (transfer) **Freshmen** 99% were admitted **Housing** Yes **Expenses** Tuition $5610;

Room only $4410 **Undergraduates** 55% women, 35% part-time, 28% 25 or older, 0.2% Native American, 76% Hispanic American, 3% African American, 1% Asian American/Pacific Islander **The most frequently chosen baccalaureate fields are** business/marketing, engineering technologies, interdisciplinary studies **Academic program** English as a second language, advanced placement, accelerated degree program, honors program, summer session, adult/continuing education programs, internships **Contact** Director of Admissions, The University of Texas at El Paso, 500 West University Avenue, El Paso, TX 79968-0001. Phone: 915-747-5588 or toll-free 877-746-4636. Fax: 915-747-8893. E-mail: futureminer@utep.edu. Web site: http://www.utep.edu/.

THE UNIVERSITY OF TEXAS AT SAN ANTONIO

SAN ANTONIO, TEXAS

General State-supported, university, coed **Entrance** Moderately difficult **Setting** 600-acre suburban campus **Total enrollment** 28,533 **Student-faculty ratio** 24:1 **Application deadline** 7/1 (freshmen), 7/1 (transfer) **Freshmen** 93% were admitted **Housing** Yes **Expenses** Tuition $6677; Room & Board $8169 **Undergraduates** 51% women, 24% part-time, 23% 25 or older, 0.5% Native American, 44% Hispanic American, 8% African American, 6% Asian American/Pacific Islander **The most frequently chosen baccalaureate fields are** business/marketing, biological/life sciences, interdisciplinary studies **Academic program** English as a second language, advanced placement, accelerated degree program, honors program, summer session, adult/continuing education programs, internships **Contact** Ms. Jennifer Ehlers, Director of Admissions, The University of Texas at San Antonio, 6900 North Loop 1604 West, San Antonio, TX 78249-0617. Phone: 210-458-4600 or toll-free 800-669-0919. Fax: 210-458-2001. E-mail: prospects@utsa.edu. Web site: http://www.utsa.edu/.

THE UNIVERSITY OF TEXAS AT TYLER

TYLER, TEXAS

General State-supported, comprehensive, coed **Entrance** Moderately difficult **Setting** 200-acre urban campus **Total enrollment** 6,137 **Student-faculty ratio** 17:1 **Application deadline** Rolling (freshmen), rolling (transfer) **Freshmen** 80% were admitted **Housing** Yes **Expenses** Tuition $5382; Room & Board $7338 **Undergraduates** 59% women, 22% part-time, 26% 25 or older, 1% Native American, 7% Hispanic American, 9% African American, 2% Asian American/Pacific Islander **The most frequently chosen baccalaureate fields are** business/marketing, health professions and related sciences, interdisciplinary studies **Academic program** English as a second language, advanced placement, self-designed majors, summer session, adult/continuing education programs, internships **Contact** Mr. Jim Hutto, Assistant Vice President, Enrollment Management, The University of Texas at Tyler, 3900 University Boulevard, Tyler, TX 75799-0001. Phone: 903-566-7195 or toll-free 800-UTTYLER. Fax: 903-566-7068. E-mail: admissions@uttyler.edu. Web site: http://www.uttyler.edu/.

THE UNIVERSITY OF TEXAS HEALTH SCIENCE CENTER AT HOUSTON

HOUSTON, TEXAS

Contact Mr. Robert L. Jenkins, Registrar, The University of Texas Health Science Center at Houston, PO Box 20036, Houston, TX 77225-0036. Phone: 713-500-3361. Fax: 713-500-3356. E-mail: registrar@uth.tmc.edu. Web site: http://www.uth.tmc.edu/.

THE UNIVERSITY OF TEXAS HEALTH SCIENCE CENTER AT SAN ANTONIO

SAN ANTONIO, TEXAS

Contact Ms. Debra Goode, Associate Registrar, The University of Texas Health Science Center at San Antonio, 7703 Floyd Curl Drive, San Antonio, TX 78229-3900. Phone: 210-567-2621. Fax: 210-567-2685. E-mail: registrars@uthscsa.edu. Web site: http://www.uthscsa.edu/.

THE UNIVERSITY OF TEXAS MEDICAL BRANCH

GALVESTON, TEXAS

General State-supported, upper-level, coed **Entrance** Very difficult **Setting** 85-acre small-town campus **Total enrollment** 2,422 **Housing** Yes **Expenses** Tuition $3872 **Undergraduates** 80% women, 46% part-time, 56% 25 or older, 0.2% Native American, 13% Hispanic American, 15% African American, 17% Asian American/Pacific Islander **Academic program** Advanced placement, summer session, internships **Contact** Ms. Vicki Brewer, Registrar, The University of Texas Medical Branch, 301 University Boulevard, Galveston, TX 77555-1305. Phone: 409-772-1215. Fax: 409-772-4466. E-mail: enrollment.services@utmb.edu. Web site: http://www.utmb.edu/.

THE UNIVERSITY OF TEXAS OF THE PERMIAN BASIN

ODESSA, TEXAS

General State-supported, comprehensive, coed **Entrance** Moderately difficult **Setting** 600-acre urban campus **Total enrollment** 3,559 **Student-**

The University of Texas of the Permian Basin *(continued)*

faculty ratio 18:1 **Application deadline** 8/15 (freshmen), rolling (transfer) **Freshmen** 98% were admitted **Housing** Yes **Expenses** Tuition $3902; Room & Board $4160 **Undergraduates** 61% women, 28% part-time, 33% 25 or older, 1% Native American, 40% Hispanic American, 5% African American, 2% Asian American/Pacific Islander **The most frequently chosen baccalaureate fields are** business/marketing, family and consumer sciences, history **Academic program** Advanced placement, accelerated degree program, summer session, internships **Contact** Trey Wetendorf, Director of Admissions, The University of Texas of the Permian Basin, 4901 East University Boulevard, Odessa, TX 79762-0001. Phone: 432-552-2605 or toll-free 866-552-UTPB. Fax: 432-552-3605. E-mail: admissions@utpb.edu. Web site: http://www.utpb.edu/.

THE UNIVERSITY OF TEXAS–PAN AMERICAN
EDINBURG, TEXAS

General State-supported, comprehensive, coed **Entrance** Noncompetitive **Setting** 289-acre small-town campus **Total enrollment** 17,435 **Student-faculty ratio** 20:1 **Application deadline** 8/11 (freshmen), 8/11 (transfer) **Freshmen** 62% were admitted **Housing** Yes **Expenses** Tuition $3899; Room & Board $4900 **Undergraduates** 58% women, 26% part-time, 24% 25 or older, 0.1% Native American, 88% Hispanic American, 1% African American, 1% Asian American/Pacific Islander **The most frequently chosen baccalaureate fields are** business/marketing, health professions and related sciences, interdisciplinary studies **Academic program** Advanced placement, honors program, summer session, adult/continuing education programs, internships **Contact** Dr. Magdalena Hinojosa, Dean of Admissions and Enrollment Services, The University of Texas–Pan American, Office of Admissions and Records, 1201 West University Drive, Edinburg, TX 78541. Phone: 956-381-2481. Fax: 956-381-2321. E-mail: recruitment@utpa.edu. Web site: http://www.utpa.edu/.

THE UNIVERSITY OF TEXAS SOUTHWESTERN MEDICAL CENTER AT DALLAS
DALLAS, TEXAS

General State-supported, upper-level, coed **Entrance** Moderately difficult **Setting** 98-acre urban campus **Total enrollment** 2,253 **Application deadline** Rolling (transfer) **First-year students** 43% were admitted **Housing** No **Expenses** Tuition $3300 **Undergraduates** 76% women, 13% part-time, 50% 25 or older, 1% Native American, 10% Hispanic American, 15% African American, 10% Asian American/Pacific Islander **The most frequently chosen baccalaureate field is** health professions and related sciences **Academic program** Advanced placement, internships **Contact** Anne Mclane, Associate Director of Admissions, The University of Texas Southwestern Medical Center at Dallas, 5323 Harry Hines Boulevard, Dallas, TX 75390. Phone: 214-648-5617. Fax: 214-648-3289. E-mail: admissions@utsouthwestern.edu. Web site: http://www.utsouthwestern.edu/.

UNIVERSITY OF THE INCARNATE WORD
SAN ANTONIO, TEXAS

General Independent Roman Catholic, comprehensive, coed **Entrance** Moderately difficult **Setting** 200-acre urban campus **Total enrollment** 5,752 **Student-faculty ratio** 13:1 **Application deadline** Rolling (freshmen), rolling (transfer) **Freshmen** 80% were admitted **Housing** Yes **Expenses** Tuition $20,260; Room & Board $7380 **Undergraduates** 68% women, 38% part-time, 42% 25 or older, 0.4% Native American, 58% Hispanic American, 7% African American, 2% Asian American/Pacific Islander **The most frequently chosen baccalaureate fields are** business/marketing, health professions and related sciences, visual and performing arts **Academic program** English as a second language, advanced placement, accelerated degree program, summer session, adult/continuing education programs, internships **Contact** Ms. Andrea Cyterski-Acosta, Dean of Enrollment, University of the Incarnate Word, 4301 Broadway, CPO 285, San Antonio, TX 78209. Phone: 210-829-6005 or toll-free 800-749-WORD. Fax: 210-829-3921. E-mail: admis@uiwtx.edu. Web site: http://www.uiw.edu/.

WAYLAND BAPTIST UNIVERSITY
PLAINVIEW, TEXAS

General Independent Baptist, comprehensive, coed **Entrance** Minimally difficult **Setting** 80-acre small-town campus **Total enrollment** 1,260 **Student-faculty ratio** 11:1 **Application deadline** 8/1 (freshmen), rolling (transfer) **Freshmen** 75% were admitted **Housing** Yes **Expenses** Tuition $11,250; Room & Board $3584 **Undergraduates** 55% women, 21% part-time, 18% 25 or older, 1% Native American, 24% Hispanic American, 4% African American, 1% Asian American/Pacific Islander **The most frequently chosen baccalaureate fields are** business/marketing, education, history **Academic program** Advanced placement, accelerated degree program, honors program, summer session, adult/continuing education programs, internships

Contact Ms. Debbie Stennett, Director of Student Admissions, Wayland Baptist University, 1900 West 7th Street, CMB 712, Plainview, TX 79072. Phone: 806-291-3500 or toll-free 800-588-1928. Fax: 806-291-1960. E-mail: admityou@wbu.edu. Web site: http://www.wbu.edu/.

WEST TEXAS A&M UNIVERSITY
CANYON, TEXAS

General State-supported, comprehensive, coed **Entrance** Moderately difficult **Setting** 128-acre small-town campus **Total enrollment** 7,502 **Student-faculty ratio** 20:1 **Application deadline** Rolling (freshmen), rolling (transfer) **Freshmen** 71% were admitted **Housing** Yes **Expenses** Room & Board $5627 **Undergraduates** 55% women, 24% part-time, 28% 25 or older, 1% Native American, 18% Hispanic American, 5% African American, 2% Asian American/Pacific Islander **The most frequently chosen baccalaureate fields are** business/marketing, interdisciplinary studies, liberal arts/general studies **Academic program** English as a second language, advanced placement, honors program, summer session, adult/continuing education programs, internships **Contact** Mr. Shawn Thomas, Director of Admissions, West Texas A&M University, WT Box 60907, Canyon, TX 79016-0001. Phone: 806-651-2020 or toll-free 800-99-WTAMU. Fax: 806-651-5285. E-mail: sthomas@mail.wtamu.edu. Web site: http://www.wtamu.edu/.

WILEY COLLEGE
MARSHALL, TEXAS

General Independent, 4-year, coed, affiliated with United Methodist Church **Entrance** Minimally difficult **Setting** 58-acre small-town campus **Total enrollment** 925 **Student-faculty ratio** 15:1 **Application deadline** 8/1 (freshmen), 8/1 (transfer) **Freshmen** 40% were admitted **Housing** Yes **Expenses** Tuition $8272; Room & Board $5300 **Undergraduates** 59% women, 13% part-time, 39% 25 or older, 0.2% Native American, 3% Hispanic American, 89% African American **The most frequently chosen baccalaureate fields are** business/marketing, education, social sciences **Academic program** Self-designed majors, summer session, adult/continuing education programs **Contact** Ms. Alvena Jones, Interim Director of Admissions/Recruitment, Wiley College, 711 Wiley Avenue, Marshall, TX 75670-5199. Phone: 903-927-3222 or toll-free 800-658-6889. Fax: 903-923-8878. E-mail: vvalentine@wileyc.edu. Web site: http://www.wileyc.edu/.

UTAH

THE ART INSTITUTE OF SALT LAKE CITY
DRAPER, UTAH

General Proprietary, 4-year, coed **Contact** Director of Admissions, The Art Institute of Salt Lake City, 121 West Election Road, Draper, UT 84020-9492. Phone: 801-601-4700 or toll-free 800-978-0096. Fax: 801-601-4724. Web site: http://www.artinstitutes.edu/SaltLakeCity/.

BRIGHAM YOUNG UNIVERSITY
PROVO, UTAH

General Independent, university, coed, affiliated with The Church of Jesus Christ of Latter-day Saints **Entrance** Moderately difficult **Setting** 557-acre suburban campus **Total enrollment** 34,174 **Student-faculty ratio** 21:1 **Application deadline** 2/1 (freshmen), 3/1 (transfer) **Freshmen** 74% were admitted **Housing** Yes **Expenses** Tuition $7680; Room & Board $6460 **Undergraduates** 49% women, 10% part-time, 14% 25 or older, 1% Native American, 3% Hispanic American, 0.4% African American, 3% Asian American/Pacific Islander **The most frequently chosen baccalaureate fields are** business/marketing, education, social sciences **Academic program** English as a second language, advanced placement, accelerated degree program, honors program, summer session, adult/continuing education programs, internships **Contact** Mr. Tom Gourley, Dean of Admissions and Records, Brigham Young University, A-153 Abraham Smoot Building, Provo, UT 84602. Phone: 801-422-2507. Fax: 801-422-0005. E-mail: admissions@byu.edu. Web site: http://www.byu.edu/.

DeVRY UNIVERSITY
SANDY, UTAH

General Proprietary, comprehensive, coed **Total enrollment** 55 **Student-faculty ratio** 8:1 **Application deadline** Rolling (freshmen), rolling (transfer) **Expenses** Tuition $13,890 **Undergraduates** 44% women, 77% part-time, 77% 25 or older, 10% Hispanic American, 3% African American **Contact** Admissions Office, DeVry University, 9350 S. 150 E., Suite 420, Sandy, UT 84070. Web site: http://www.devry.edu/keller/locations/centers/loc_sandy.jsp.

DIXIE STATE COLLEGE OF UTAH
ST. GEORGE, UTAH

General State-supported, 4-year, coed **Entrance** Noncompetitive **Setting** 117-acre small-town campus **Total enrollment** 5,598 **Student-faculty ratio** 22:1 **Application deadline** Rolling

Dixie State College of Utah *(continued)*

(freshmen) **Freshmen** 72% were admitted **Housing** Yes **Expenses** Tuition $2893; Room & Board $3498 **Undergraduates** 54% women, 44% part-time, 24% 25 or older **The most frequently chosen baccalaureate fields are** business/marketing, computer and information sciences, education **Academic program** English as a second language, advanced placement, honors program, summer session, adult/continuing education programs **Contact** Ms. Darla Rollins, Admissions Coordinator, Dixie State College of Utah, 225 South 700 East, St. George, UT 84770-3876. Phone: 435-652-7704 or toll-free 888-GO2DIXIE. Fax: 435-656-4005. E-mail: rollins@dixie.edu. Web site: http://www.dixie.edu/.

INDEPENDENCE UNIVERSITY
SALT LAKE CITY, UTAH

Contact Ms. Deborah Hopkins, Enrollment Manager, Independence University, 5295 South Commerce Drive, Salt Lake City, UT 84107. Phone: toll-free 800-791-7353. E-mail: info@cchs.edu. Web site: http://www.independence.edu/.

MIDWIVES COLLEGE OF UTAH
OREM, UTAH

General Independent, comprehensive, women only **Entrance** Noncompetitive **Setting** urban campus **Total enrollment** 73 **Application deadline** 7/29 (freshmen) **Freshmen** 76% were admitted **Housing** No **Undergraduates** 100% part-time **The most frequently chosen baccalaureate field is** health professions and related sciences **Contact** Kristy Ridd-Young, President, Midwives College of Utah, 1174 East 2700 South, Suite 8, Salt Lake City, UT 84106. Phone: 801-649-5230 or toll-free 866-764-9068. Fax: 866-207-2024. E-mail: office@midwifery.edu. Web site: http://www.midwifery.edu/.

NEUMONT UNIVERSITY
SOUTH JORDAN, UTAH

General Proprietary, 4-year, coed, primarily men **Entrance** Moderately difficult **Setting** suburban campus **Total enrollment** 295 **Student-faculty ratio** 9:1 **Application deadline** Rolling (freshmen), rolling (transfer) **Freshmen** 59% were admitted **Housing** Yes **Expenses** Tuition $36,000 **Undergraduates** 7% women **The most frequently chosen baccalaureate field is** computer and information sciences **Academic program** Accelerated degree program **Contact** Charlie Parker, Director of Admissions, Neumont University, 10701 S. River Front Parkway, Suite 300, South Jordan, UT 84095. Phone: 801-302-2800 or toll-free 866-622-3448. Fax: 801-302-2811. E-mail: charlie.parker@neumont.edu. Web site: http://www.neumont.edu/.

SOUTHERN UTAH UNIVERSITY
CEDAR CITY, UTAH

General State-supported, comprehensive, coed **Entrance** Moderately difficult **Setting** 113-acre small-town campus **Total enrollment** 7,057 **Student-faculty ratio** 23:1 **Application deadline** 8/1 (freshmen), rolling (transfer) **Freshmen** 84% were admitted **Housing** Yes **Expenses** Tuition $3796; Room only $1820 **Undergraduates** 56% women, 23% part-time, 17% 25 or older, 2% Native American, 4% Hispanic American, 1% African American, 2% Asian American/Pacific Islander **The most frequently chosen baccalaureate fields are** business/marketing, education, health professions and related sciences **Academic program** English as a second language, advanced placement, honors program, summer session, adult/continuing education programs, internships **Contact** Mr. Stephen Allen, Director of Admissions, Southern Utah University, 351 West University Boulevard, Cedar City, UT 84720-2498. Phone: 435-586-7740. Fax: 435-865-8223. E-mail: admininfo@suu.edu. Web site: http://www.suu.edu/.

UNIVERSITY OF PHOENIX–UTAH CAMPUS
SALT LAKE CITY, UTAH

General Proprietary, comprehensive, coed **Contact** Ms. Evelyn Gaskin, Registrar/Executive Director, University of Phoenix–Utah Campus, 4615 East Elwood Street, Mail Stop AA-K101, Phoenix, AZ 85040-1958. Phone: 480-557-3301 or toll-free 800-776-4867 (in-state); 800-228-7240 (out-of-state). Fax: 480-643-1020. E-mail: evelyn.gaskin@phoenix.edu. Web site: http://www.phoenix.edu/.

UNIVERSITY OF UTAH
SALT LAKE CITY, UTAH

General State-supported, university, coed **Entrance** Moderately difficult **Setting** 1,500-acre urban campus **Total enrollment** 28,025 **Student-faculty ratio** 13:1 **Application deadline** 4/1 (freshmen), 4/1 (transfer) **Freshmen** 82% were admitted **Housing** Yes **Expenses** Tuition $4986; Room & Board $5778 **Undergraduates** 45% women, 32% part-time, 33% 25 or older, 1% Native American, 5% Hispanic American, 1% African American, 5% Asian American/Pacific Islander **The most frequently chosen baccalaureate fields are** business/marketing, communications/journalism, social sciences **Academic program** English as a second language, advanced placement, accelerated degree program, self-designed majors, honors program, summer session, internships **Contact** Mateo Remsburg, Director of High School Services, University of Utah, 201 Presidents Circle Room 206, Salt Lake City, UT 84112. Phone: 801-581-7281 or toll-free 800-444-8638. Fax: 801-585-3257. E-mail: mremsburg@sa.utah.edu. Web site: http://www.utah.edu/.

UTAH STATE UNIVERSITY
LOGAN, UTAH

General State-supported, university, coed **Entrance** Moderately difficult **Setting** 456-acre urban campus **Total enrollment** 14,893 **Student-faculty ratio** 17:1 **Application deadline** Rolling (freshmen), rolling (transfer) **Freshmen** 98% were admitted **Housing** Yes **Expenses** Tuition $4200; Room & Board $4580 **Undergraduates** 49% women, 16% part-time, 18% 25 or older, 0.5% Native American, 2% Hispanic American, 1% African American, 1% Asian American/Pacific Islander **The most frequently chosen baccalaureate fields are** business/marketing, education, social sciences **Academic program** English as a second language, advanced placement, accelerated degree program, self-designed majors, honors program, summer session, adult/continuing education programs, internships **Contact** Ms. Jenn Putnam, Director, Admissions Office, Utah State University, 0160 Old Main Hill, Logan, UT 84322-0160. Phone: 435-797-1079 or toll-free 800-488-8108. Fax: 435-797-3708. E-mail: admit@usu.edu. Web site: http://www.usu.edu/.

UTAH VALLEY STATE COLLEGE
OREM, UTAH

General State-supported, 4-year, coed **Entrance** Noncompetitive **Setting** 200-acre suburban campus **Total enrollment** 23,840 **Student-faculty ratio** 20:1 **Application deadline** Rolling (freshmen), rolling (transfer) **Freshmen** 100% were admitted **Expenses** Tuition $3528; Room & Board $6212 **Undergraduates** 39% 25 or older **The most frequently chosen baccalaureate fields are** business/marketing, education, psychology **Academic program** English as a second language, advanced placement, accelerated degree program, self-designed majors, honors program, summer session, internships **Contact** Mrs. Liz Childs, Senior Director of Admissions, Utah Valley State College, 800 West University Parkway, Orem, UT 84058-5999. Phone: 801-863-8460. Fax: 801-225-4677. E-mail: info@uvsc.edu. Web site: http://www.uvsc.edu/.

WEBER STATE UNIVERSITY
OGDEN, UTAH

General State-supported, comprehensive, coed **Entrance** Noncompetitive **Setting** 526-acre urban campus **Total enrollment** 18,081 **Student-faculty ratio** 22:1 **Application deadline** 8/22 (freshmen), rolling (transfer) **Freshmen** 100% were admitted **Housing** Yes **Expenses** Tuition $3663; Room & Board $5328 **Undergraduates** 51% women, 46% part-time, 39% 25 or older, 1% Native American, 4% Hispanic American, 1% African American, 2% Asian American/Pacific Islander **The most frequently chosen baccalaureate fields are** business/marketing, education, health professions and related sciences **Academic program** English as a second language, advanced placement, accelerated degree program, self-designed majors, honors program, summer session, adult/continuing education programs, internships **Contact** Mr. Mark Simpson, Admissions Advisor, Weber State University, 1137 University Circle, Ogden, UT 84408-1137. Phone: 801-626-6047 or toll-free 800-634-6568 (in-state); 800-848-7770 (out-of-state). Fax: 801-626-6744. E-mail: admissions@weber.edu. Web site: http://weber.edu/.

WESTERN GOVERNORS UNIVERSITY
SALT LAKE CITY, UTAH

Contact Chris Mallett, Director of Enrollment, Western Governors University, 4001 South 700 East, Suite 700, Salt Lake City, UT 84107. Phone: 801-274-3280 Ext. 336 or toll-free 877-435-7948. Fax: 801-274-3305. E-mail: info@wgu.edu. Web site: http://www.wgu.edu/.

WESTMINSTER COLLEGE
SALT LAKE CITY, UTAH

General Independent, comprehensive, coed **Entrance** Moderately difficult **Setting** 27-acre suburban campus **Total enrollment** 2,661 **Student-faculty ratio** 10:1 **Application deadline** Rolling (freshmen), rolling (transfer) **Freshmen** 86% were admitted **Housing** Yes **Expenses** Tuition $22,374; Room & Board $6354 **Undergraduates** 58% women, 11% part-time, 21% 25 or older, 1% Native American, 6% Hispanic American, 1% African American, 3% Asian American/Pacific Islander **The most frequently chosen baccalaureate fields are** business/marketing, health professions and related sciences, psychology **Academic program** Advanced placement, accelerated degree program, self-designed majors, honors program, summer session, internships **Contact** Christina Twelves, Interim Director of Undergraduate Admissions, Westminster College, 1840 South 1300 East, Salt Lake City, UT 84105-3697. Phone: 801-832-2200 or toll-free 800-748-4753. Fax: 801-832-3101. E-mail: admission@westminstercollege.edu. Web site: http://www.westminstercollege.edu/.

VERMONT

BENNINGTON COLLEGE
BENNINGTON, VERMONT

General Independent, comprehensive, coed **Entrance** Very difficult **Setting** 470-acre small-town campus **Total enrollment** 723 **Student-faculty ratio** 8:1 **Application deadline** 1/3 (freshmen), 3/15 (transfer) **Freshmen** 63% were admitted **Housing** Yes **Expenses** Tuition $36,800; Room & Board $9380 **Undergraduates** 68% women, 0.3% part-time, 1% 25 or older, 0.2% Native American, 2% Hispanic American, 2% African American, 2% Asian American/Pacific Islander **The most frequently chosen baccalaureate fields are** English, foreign languages and literature, visual and performing arts **Academic program** English as a second language, accelerated degree program, self-designed majors, internships **Contact** Mr. Ken Himmelman, Dean of Admissions and Financial Aid, Bennington College, One College Drive, Bennington, VT 05201-6003. Phone: 802-440-4312 or toll-free 800-833-6845. Fax: 802-440-4320. E-mail: admissions@bennington.edu. Web site: http://www.bennington.edu/.

BURLINGTON COLLEGE
BURLINGTON, VERMONT

General Independent, 4-year, coed **Entrance** Moderately difficult **Setting** 1-acre urban campus **Total enrollment** 179 **Student-faculty ratio** 5:1 **Freshmen** 62% were admitted **Housing** Yes **Expenses** Tuition $19,640; Room only $6095 **Undergraduates** 45% women, 33% part-time, 45% 25 or older, 2% Native American, 1% Hispanic American, 3% African American, 1% Asian American/Pacific Islander **The most frequently chosen baccalaureate fields are** interdisciplinary studies, English, visual and performing arts **Academic program** Advanced placement, self-designed majors, honors program, summer session, adult/continuing education programs, internships **Contact** Admissions, Burlington College, 95 North Avenue, Burlington, VT 05401-2998. Phone: 802-862-9616 Ext. 104 or toll-free 800-862-9616. Fax: 802-660-4331. E-mail: admissions@burlington.edu. Web site: http://www.burlington.edu/.

CASTLETON STATE COLLEGE
CASTLETON, VERMONT

General State-supported, comprehensive, coed **Entrance** Moderately difficult **Setting** 160-acre rural campus **Total enrollment** 2,144 **Student-faculty ratio** 14:1 **Application deadline** Rolling (freshmen), rolling (transfer) **Freshmen** 71% were admitted **Housing** Yes **Expenses** Tuition $8284; Room & Board $7509 **Undergraduates** 55% women, 13% part-time, 13% 25 or older, 1% Native American, 2% Hispanic American, 1% African American, 1% Asian American/Pacific Islander **The most frequently chosen baccalaureate fields are** business/marketing, communications/journalism, psychology **Academic program** Advanced placement, self-designed majors, honors program, summer session, internships **Contact** Mr. Maurice Ouimet, Admissions Director, Castleton State College, 62 Seminary Street, Castleton, VT 05735. Phone: 802-468-1213 or toll-free 800-639-8521. Fax: 802-468-1476. E-mail: info@castleton.edu. Web site: http://www.castleton.edu/.

CHAMPLAIN COLLEGE
BURLINGTON, VERMONT

General Independent, comprehensive, coed **Entrance** Moderately difficult **Setting** 21-acre suburban campus **Total enrollment** 2,741 **Student-faculty ratio** 16:1 **Application deadline** 1/31 (freshmen), rolling (transfer) **Freshmen** 58% were admitted **Housing** Yes **Expenses** Tuition $22,550; Room & Board $10,910 **Undergraduates** 51% women, 27% part-time, 28% 25 or older, 0.5% Native American, 1% Hispanic American, 0.5% African American, 1% Asian American/Pacific Islander **The most frequently chosen baccalaureate fields are** business/marketing, computer and information sciences, education **Academic program** Advanced placement, honors program, summer session, internships **Contact** Dr. Laryn Runco, Director of Admissions, Champlain College, 163 South Willard Street, Burlington, VT 05401. Phone: 802-860-2727 or toll-free 800-570-5858. Fax: 802-860-2767. E-mail: admission@champlain.edu. Web site: http://www.champlain.edu/.

COLLEGE OF ST. JOSEPH
RUTLAND, VERMONT

General Independent Roman Catholic, comprehensive, coed **Entrance** Minimally difficult **Setting** 90-acre small-town campus **Total enrollment** 442 **Student-faculty ratio** 11:1 **Application deadline** Rolling (freshmen), rolling (transfer) **Freshmen** 88% were admitted **Housing** Yes **Expenses** Tuition $16,740; Room & Board $8150 **Undergraduates** 56% women, 38% part-time, 32% 25 or older, 1% Native American, 4% Hispanic American, 3% African American, 1% Asian American/Pacific Islander **The most frequently chosen baccalaureate fields are** business/marketing, education, psychology **Academic program** English as a second language, advanced placement, accelerated degree program, summer session, adult/continuing education programs, internships **Contact** Mrs. Tracy Gallipo, College of St. Joseph, 71 Clement Road, Rutland, VT 05701-3899. Phone: 802-773-5900 Ext. 3286 or toll-free 877-270-9998. Fax: 802-776-5258. E-mail: admissions@csj.edu. Web site: http://www.csj.edu/.

GODDARD COLLEGE
PLAINFIELD, VERMONT

General Independent, comprehensive, coed **Entrance** Moderately difficult **Setting** 250-acre rural campus **Total enrollment** 686 **Student-faculty ratio** 11:1 **Application deadline** Rolling (freshmen), rolling (transfer) **Freshmen** 100% were admitted **Housing** Yes **Expenses** Tuition $11,664; Room & Board $1088 **Undergraduates** 71% women, 2% part-time, 68% 25 or older, 2% Native American, 4% Hispanic American, 4% African American, 2% Asian American/Pacific Islander **Academic program** Advanced placement, self-designed majors, adult/continuing education programs, internships **Contact** Rachel Keach, Admissions Counselor, Goddard College, 123 Pitkin Road, Plainfield, VT 05667-9432. Phone: 802-454-8311 Ext. 240 or toll-free 800-906-8312 Ext. 243. Fax: 802-454-1029. E-mail: admissions@goddard.edu. Web site: http://www.goddard.edu/.

GREEN MOUNTAIN COLLEGE
POULTNEY, VERMONT

General Independent, comprehensive, coed **Entrance** Moderately difficult **Setting** 155-acre small-town campus **Total enrollment** 823 **Student-faculty ratio** 14:1 **Application deadline** Rolling (freshmen), rolling (transfer) **Freshmen** 79% were admitted **Housing** Yes **Expenses** Tuition $24,565; Room & Board $9064 **Undergraduates** 49% women, 2% part-time, 6% 25 or older, 1% Native American, 2% Hispanic American, 3% African American, 1% Asian American/Pacific Islander **The most frequently chosen baccalaureate fields are** natural resources/environmental science, business/marketing, parks and recreation **Academic program** English as a second language, advanced placement, accelerated degree program, self-designed majors, honors program, summer session, adult/continuing education programs, internships **Contact** Ms. Anne Lundquist, Dean of Student Life, Green Mountain College, One College Circle, Poultney, VT 05764. Phone: 802-287-8371 or toll-free 800-776-6675. Fax: 802-287-8098. E-mail: lundquista@greenmtn.edu. Web site: http://www.greenmtn.edu/.

JOHNSON STATE COLLEGE
JOHNSON, VERMONT

General State-supported, comprehensive, coed **Entrance** Moderately difficult **Setting** 350-acre rural campus **Total enrollment** 1,867 **Student-faculty ratio** 17:1 **Application deadline** Rolling (freshmen), rolling (transfer) **Freshmen** 80% were admitted **Housing** Yes **Expenses** Tuition $8000; Room & Board $7581 **Undergraduates** 60% women, 34% part-time, 13% 25 or older, 1% Native American, 2% Hispanic American, 2% African American, 1% Asian American/Pacific Islander **The most frequently chosen baccalaureate fields are** business/marketing, liberal arts/general studies, psychology **Academic program** English as a second language, advanced placement, accelerated degree program, honors program, summer session, internships **Contact** Patrick Rogers, Assistant Director of Admissions, Johnson State College, 337 College Hill, Johnson, VT 05656-9405. Phone: 802-635-1219 or toll-free 800-635-2356. Fax: 802-635-1230. E-mail: jscadmissions@jsc.edu. Web site: http://www.johnsonstatecollege.edu/.

LYNDON STATE COLLEGE
LYNDONVILLE, VERMONT

General State-supported, comprehensive, coed **Entrance** Moderately difficult **Setting** 175-acre rural campus **Total enrollment** 1,415 **Student-faculty ratio** 17:1 **Application deadline** Rolling (freshmen), rolling (transfer) **Freshmen** 89% were admitted **Housing** Yes **Expenses** Tuition $7244; Room & Board $7220 **Undergraduates** 47% women, 12% part-time, 1% Native American, 1% Hispanic American, 2% African American, 1% Asian American/Pacific Islander **The most frequently chosen baccalaureate fields are** business/marketing, health professions and related sciences, psychology **Academic program** Advanced placement, accelerated degree program, self-designed majors, honors program, summer session, adult/continuing education programs, internships **Contact** Ms. Donna "Dee" Gile, Admissions Assistant, Lyndon State College, 1001 College Road, PO Box 919, Lyndonville, VT 05851. Phone: 802-626-6413 or toll-free 800-225-1998. Fax: 802-626-6335. E-mail: admissions@lyndonstate.edu. Web site: http://www.lyndonstate.edu/.

MARLBORO COLLEGE
MARLBORO, VERMONT

General Independent, comprehensive, coed **Entrance** Moderately difficult **Setting** 350-acre rural campus **Total enrollment** 338 **Student-faculty ratio** 8:1 **Application deadline** 3/1 (freshmen), 4/15 (transfer) **Freshmen** 44% were admitted **Housing** Yes **Expenses** Tuition $30,680; Room & Board $8860 **Undergraduates** 51% women, 2% part-time, 1% 25 or older, 0.3% Native American, 3% Hispanic American, 1% African American, 4% Asian American/Pacific

Marlboro College *(continued)*

Islander **Academic program** Advanced placement, accelerated degree program, self-designed majors, internships **Contact** Ms. Amy VanTassel, Associate Director of Admission, Marlboro College, PO Box A, South Road, Marlboro, VT 05344-0300. Phone: toll-free 800-343-0049. Fax: 800-451-7555. E-mail: admissions@marlboro.edu. Web site: http://www.marlboro.edu/.

MIDDLEBURY COLLEGE
MIDDLEBURY, VERMONT

General Independent, comprehensive, coed **Entrance** Most difficult **Setting** 350-acre small-town campus **Total enrollment** 2,500 **Student-faculty ratio** 9:1 **Application deadline** 1/1 (freshmen), 3/1 (transfer) **Freshmen** 21% were admitted **Housing** Yes **Expenses** Tuition $46,910 **Undergraduates** 51% women, 1% part-time, 0.5% Native American, 6% Hispanic American, 3% African American, 8% Asian American/Pacific Islander **The most frequently chosen baccalaureate fields are** history, English, social sciences **Academic program** Advanced placement, accelerated degree program, self-designed majors, honors program, summer session, internships **Contact** Mr. Robert Clagett, Dean of Admissions, Middlebury College, Emma Willard House, Middlebury, VT 05753-6002. Phone: 802-443-3000. Fax: 802-443-2056. E-mail: admissions@middlebury.edu. Web site: http://www.middlebury.edu/.

NORWICH UNIVERSITY
NORTHFIELD, VERMONT

General Independent, comprehensive, coed, primarily men **Entrance** Moderately difficult **Setting** 1,125-acre small-town campus **Total enrollment** 3,104 **Student-faculty ratio** 14:1 **Application deadline** Rolling (freshmen), rolling (transfer) **Freshmen** 59% were admitted **Housing** Yes **Expenses** Tuition $24,430; Room & Board $8522 **Undergraduates** 27% women, 4% part-time, 3% 25 or older, 0.2% Native American, 4% Hispanic American, 3% African American, 2% Asian American/Pacific Islander **The most frequently chosen baccalaureate fields are** health professions and related sciences, architecture, security and protective services **Academic program** English as a second language, advanced placement, summer session, adult/continuing education programs, internships **Contact** Ms. Shelby Wallace, Director of Admissions, Norwich University, 158 Harmon Drive, Northfield, VT 05663. Phone: 802-485-2658 or toll-free 800-468-6679. Fax: 802-485-2032. E-mail: nuadm@norwich.edu. Web site: http://www.norwich.edu/.

SAINT MICHAEL'S COLLEGE
COLCHESTER, VERMONT

General Independent Roman Catholic, comprehensive, coed **Entrance** Moderately difficult **Setting** 440-acre suburban campus **Total enrollment** 2,449 **Student-faculty ratio** 13:1 **Application deadline** 2/1 (freshmen), 3/15 (transfer) **Freshmen** 69% were admitted **Housing** Yes **Expenses** Tuition $29,945; Room & Board $7460 **Undergraduates** 53% women, 2% part-time, 1% 25 or older, 0.4% Native American, 1% Hispanic American, 1% African American, 1% Asian American/Pacific Islander **The most frequently chosen baccalaureate fields are** business/marketing, psychology, social sciences **Academic program** English as a second language, advanced placement, self-designed majors, honors program, summer session, internships **Contact** Ms. Jacqueline Murphy, Director of Admission, Saint Michael's College, One Winooski Park, Colchester, VT 05452. Phone: 802-654-3000 or toll-free 800-762-8000. Fax: 802-654-2906. E-mail: admission@smcvt.edu. Web site: http://www.smcvt.edu/.

SOUTHERN VERMONT COLLEGE
BENNINGTON, VERMONT

General Independent, 4-year, coed **Entrance** Minimally difficult **Setting** 371-acre small-town campus **Total enrollment** 450 **Student-faculty ratio** 17:1 **Application deadline** Rolling (freshmen), rolling (transfer) **Freshmen** 94% were admitted **Housing** Yes **Expenses** Tuition $16,800; Room & Board $8100 **Undergraduates** 0.5% Native American, 2% Hispanic American, 6% African American, 1% Asian American/Pacific Islander **The most frequently chosen baccalaureate fields are** business/marketing, liberal arts/general studies, psychology **Academic program** Advanced placement, accelerated degree program, self-designed majors, honors program, summer session, adult/continuing education programs, internships **Contact** Mr. Joel Wincowski, Dean of Enrollment Management, Southern Vermont College, 982 Mansion Drive, Bennington, VT 05201. Phone: 802-447-6304 or toll-free 800-378-2782. Fax: 802-447-4695. E-mail: admis@svc.edu. Web site: http://www.svc.edu/.

STERLING COLLEGE
CRAFTSBURY COMMON, VERMONT

General Independent, 4-year, coed **Entrance** Moderately difficult **Setting** 430-acre rural campus **Total enrollment** 105 **Student-faculty ratio** 5:1 **Application deadline** 2/15 (freshmen), rolling (transfer) **Freshmen** 76% were admitted **Housing** Yes **Expenses** Tuition $21,655; Room & Board $7192 **Undergraduates** 45% women,

2% part-time, 8% 25 or older, 2% Hispanic American **The most frequently chosen baccalaureate fields are** area and ethnic studies, agriculture, liberal arts/general studies **Academic program** Advanced placement, self-designed majors, summer session, internships **Contact** Gwyn Harris, Director of Admissions, Sterling College, PO Box 72, Craftsbury Common, VT 05827. Phone: 802-586-7711 Ext. 100 or toll-free 800-648-3591 Ext. 100. Fax: 802-586-2596. E-mail: admissions@sterlingcollege.edu. Web site: http://www.sterlingcollege.edu/.

UNIVERSITY OF VERMONT
BURLINGTON, VERMONT

General State-supported, university, coed **Entrance** Moderately difficult **Setting** 425-acre suburban campus **Total enrollment** 12,239 **Student-faculty ratio** 16:1 **Application deadline** 1/15 (freshmen), 4/1 (transfer) **Freshmen** 70% were admitted **Housing** Yes **Expenses** Tuition $12,054; Room & Board $8024 **Undergraduates** 55% women, 11% part-time, 3% 25 or older, 0.3% Native American, 2% Hispanic American, 1% African American, 2% Asian American/Pacific Islander **The most frequently chosen baccalaureate fields are** business/ marketing, psychology, social sciences **Academic program** English as a second language, advanced placement, self-designed majors, honors program, summer session, internships **Contact** Susan Wertheimer, Interim Dean of Admissions, University of Vermont, Office of Admissions, 194 South Prospect Street, Burlington, VT 05401-3596. Phone: 802-656-3370. Fax: 802-656-8611. E-mail: admissions@uvm.edu. Web site: http://www.uvm.edu/.

VERMONT TECHNICAL COLLEGE
RANDOLPH CENTER, VERMONT

General State-supported, 4-year, coed **Entrance** Moderately difficult **Setting** 544-acre rural campus **Total enrollment** 1,556 **Student-faculty ratio** 12:1 **Application deadline** Rolling (freshmen), rolling (transfer) **Freshmen** 58% were admitted **Housing** Yes **Expenses** Tuition $13,766; Room & Board $7220 **Undergraduates** 41% women, 25% part-time, 32% 25 or older, 1% Native American, 1% Hispanic American, 1% African American, 2% Asian American/Pacific Islander **The most frequently chosen baccalaureate fields are** business/marketing, computer and information sciences, engineering technologies **Academic program** English as a second language, advanced placement, accelerated degree program, honors program, summer session, internships **Contact** Mr. Dwight A. Cross, Assistant Dean of Enrollment, Vermont Technical College, PO Box 500, Randolph Center, VT 05061. Phone: 802-728-1244 or toll-free 800-442-VTC1. Fax: 802-728-1390. E-mail: admissions@vtc.edu. Web site: http://www.vtc.edu/.

WOODBURY COLLEGE
MONTPELIER, VERMONT

General Independent, 4-year, coed **Entrance** Noncompetitive **Setting** 8-acre small-town campus **Total enrollment** 99 **Student-faculty ratio** 7:1 **Application deadline** Rolling (freshmen), rolling (transfer) **Freshmen** 40% were admitted **Housing** No **Expenses** Tuition $16,050 **Undergraduates** 96% women, 24% part-time, 80% 25 or older, 1% Hispanic American, 3% Asian American/Pacific Islander **The most frequently chosen baccalaureate fields are** law/legal studies, interdisciplinary studies, public administration and social services **Academic program** Self-designed majors, adult/continuing education programs, internships **Contact** Admissions Office, Woodbury College, 660 Elm Street, Montpelier, VT 05602. Phone: 802-229-0516 Ext. 270 or toll-free 800-639-6039. Fax: 802-229-2141. E-mail: admiss@woodbury-college.edu. Web site: http://www.woodbury-college.edu/.

VIRGINIA

ARGOSY UNIVERSITY, WASHINGTON DC
ARLINGTON, VIRGINIA

General Proprietary, university, coed **Setting** urban campus **Contact** Director of Admissions, Argosy University, Washington DC, 1550 Wilson Boulevard, Suite 600, Arlington, VA 22209. Phone: 703-526-5800 or toll-free 866-703-2777. Fax: 703-243-8973. Web site: http://www.argosy.edu/locations/washington-dc/.

THE ART INSTITUTE OF WASHINGTON
ARLINGTON, VIRGINIA

General Proprietary, 4-year, coed **Setting** urban campus **Total enrollment** 1,700 **Student-faculty ratio** 20:1 **Application deadline** Rolling (freshmen), rolling (transfer) **Housing** Yes **Expenses** Tuition $20,880; Room only $8385 **Academic program** Advanced placement, accelerated degree program, honors program, internships **Contact** Ms. Sara Cruley, Director of Admissions, The Art Institute of Washington, 1820 North Fort Meyer Drive, Ground Floor, Arlington, VA 22209. Phone: 703-358-9550 or toll-free 877-303-3771. Fax: 703-358-9759. E-mail: aiw_admin@aii.edu. Web site: http://www.artinstitutes.edu/arlington/.

AVERETT UNIVERSITY
DANVILLE, VIRGINIA

General Independent, comprehensive, coed, affiliated with Baptist General Association of Virginia **Entrance** Moderately difficult **Setting** 19-acre small-town campus **Total enrollment** 865 **Student-faculty ratio** 11:1 **Application deadline** 7/15 (freshmen), 8/15 (transfer) **Freshmen** 90% were admitted **Housing** Yes **Expenses** Tuition $20,512; Room & Board $7100 **Undergraduates** 45% women, 5% part-time, 10% 25 or older, 1% Native American, 4% Hispanic American, 28% African American, 1% Asian American/Pacific Islander **The most frequently chosen baccalaureate fields are** parks and recreation, business/marketing, security and protective services **Academic program** Advanced placement, accelerated degree program, self-designed majors, honors program, summer session, adult/continuing education programs, internships **Contact** Mr. Jerry McCombs, Director of Admissions, Averett University, Admissions Office, Danville, VA 24541. Phone: 434-791-7301 or toll-free 800-AVERETT. Fax: 434-797-2784. E-mail: jerry.mccombs@averett.edu. Web site: http://www.averett.edu/.

BLUEFIELD COLLEGE
BLUEFIELD, VIRGINIA

General Independent Southern Baptist, 4-year, coed **Entrance** Minimally difficult **Setting** 85-acre small-town campus **Total enrollment** 793 **Student-faculty ratio** 12:1 **Application deadline** Rolling (freshmen), rolling (transfer) **Freshmen** 52% were admitted **Housing** Yes **Expenses** Tuition $15,630; Room & Board $6584 **Undergraduates** 60% women, 19% part-time, 49% 25 or older, 0.1% Native American, 1% Hispanic American, 19% African American, 0.3% Asian American/Pacific Islander **The most frequently chosen baccalaureate fields are** business/marketing, psychology, security and protective services **Academic program** Advanced placement, accelerated degree program, honors program, summer session, adult/continuing education programs, internships **Contact** Mr. George Campbell, Bluefield College, 3000 College Drive, Bluefield, VA 24605-1799. Phone: 276-326-4217 or toll-free 800-872-0175. Fax: 276-326-4395. E-mail: admissions@bluefield.edu. Web site: http://www.bluefield.edu/.

BRIDGEWATER COLLEGE
BRIDGEWATER, VIRGINIA

General Independent, 4-year, coed, affiliated with Church of the Brethren **Entrance** Moderately difficult **Setting** 190-acre small-town campus **Total enrollment** 1,541 **Student-faculty ratio** 14:1 **Application deadline** Rolling (freshmen), rolling (transfer) **Freshmen** 84% were admitted **Housing** Yes **Expenses** Tuition $23,090; Room & Board $9900 **Undergraduates** 57% women, 1% part-time, 1% 25 or older, 1% Native American, 2% Hispanic American, 7% African American, 1% Asian American/Pacific Islander **The most frequently chosen baccalaureate fields are** business/marketing, biological/life sciences, parks and recreation **Academic program** Advanced placement, honors program, summer session, adult/continuing education programs, internships **Contact** Ms. Linda Stout, Director of Enrollment Operations, Bridgewater College, 402 East College Street, Bridgewater, VA 22812-1599. Phone: 540-828-5375 or toll-free 800-759-8328. Fax: 540-828-5481. E-mail: admissions@bridgewater.edu. Web site: http://www.bridgewater.edu/.

CHRISTENDOM COLLEGE
FRONT ROYAL, VIRGINIA

General Independent Roman Catholic, comprehensive, coed **Entrance** Very difficult **Setting** 100-acre rural campus **Total enrollment** 465 **Student-faculty ratio** 14:1 **Application deadline** 3/1 (freshmen), 3/1 (transfer) **Freshmen** 81% were admitted **Housing** Yes **Expenses** Tuition $18,756; Room & Board $6688 **Undergraduates** 54% women, 2% part-time, 3% 25 or older, 0.3% Native American, 3% Hispanic American, 2% Asian American/Pacific Islander **The most frequently chosen baccalaureate fields are** history, philosophy and religious studies, theology and religious vocations **Academic program** Advanced placement, accelerated degree program, summer session, internships **Contact** Mr. Tom McFadden, Director of Admissions, Christendom College, 134 Christendom Drive, Front Royal, VA 22630-5103. Phone: 540-636-2900 Ext. 290 or toll-free 800-877-5456 Ext. 290. Fax: 540-636-1655. E-mail: tmcfadden@christendom.edu. Web site: http://www.christendom.edu/.

CHRISTOPHER NEWPORT UNIVERSITY
NEWPORT NEWS, VIRGINIA

General State-supported, comprehensive, coed **Setting** 175-acre suburban campus **Total enrollment** 4,884 **Student-faculty ratio** 17:1 **Application deadline** 3/1 (freshmen), 3/1 (transfer) **Freshmen** 54% were admitted **Housing** Yes **Expenses** Tuition $10,138; Room & Board $8500 **Undergraduates** 55% women, 5% part-time, 4% 25 or older, 1% Native American, 3% Hispanic American, 7% African American, 3% Asian American/Pacific Islander **The most frequently chosen baccalaureate fields are** business/marketing, biological/life sciences, social sciences **Academic program** Advanced placement, accelerated degree program, self-designed majors, honors program, summer session, internships **Contact** Mr. Curtis Davidson, Senior Associate Director of Admissions, Christopher Newport University, 1 University Place, Newport News, VA 23606-2998. Phone: 757-594-7015 or toll-free 800-333-4268. Fax: 757-594-7333. E-mail: admit@cnu.edu. Web site: http://www.cnu.edu/.

THE COLLEGE OF WILLIAM AND MARY
WILLIAMSBURG, VIRGINIA

General State-supported, university, coed **Entrance** Very difficult **Setting** 1,200-acre small-town campus **Total enrollment** 7,795 **Student-faculty ratio** 11:1 **Application deadline** 1/1 (freshmen), 2/15 (transfer) **Freshmen** 34% were admitted **Housing** Yes **Expenses** Tuition $9164; Room & Board $7385 **Undergraduates** 54% women, 2% part-time, 2% 25 or older, 1% Native American, 6% Hispanic American, 7% African American, 7% Asian American/Pacific Islander **The most frequently chosen baccalaureate fields are** business/marketing, interdisciplinary studies, social sciences **Academic program** Advanced placement, accelerated degree program, self-designed majors, honors program, summer session **Contact** Henry Broaddus, Dean of Admissions, The College of William and Mary, PO Box 8795, Williamsburg, VA 23187-8795. Phone: 757-221-3980. Fax: 757-221-1242. E-mail: admiss@wm.edu. Web site: http://www.wm.edu/.

DeVRY UNIVERSITY
ARLINGTON, VIRGINIA

General Proprietary, comprehensive, coed **Entrance** Minimally difficult **Total enrollment** 681 **Student-faculty ratio** 20:1 **Application deadline** Rolling (freshmen), rolling (transfer) **Housing** No **Expenses** Tuition $14,250 **Undergraduates** 27% women, 40% part-time, 43% 25 or older, 1% Native American, 10% Hispanic American, 48% African American, 4% Asian American/Pacific Islander **The most frequently chosen baccalaureate fields are** business/marketing, computer and information sciences, engineering technologies **Academic program** Advanced placement, accelerated degree program, summer session, adult/continuing education programs **Contact** Admissions Office, DeVry University, 2450 Crystal Drive, Arlington, VA 22202. Web site: http://www.devry.edu/.

DeVRY UNIVERSITY
McLEAN, VIRGINIA

Contact DeVry University, 1751 Pinnacle Drive, Suite 250, McLean, VA 22102-3832. Web site: http://www.devry.edu/.

EASTERN MENNONITE UNIVERSITY
HARRISONBURG, VIRGINIA

General Independent Mennonite, comprehensive, coed **Entrance** Moderately difficult **Setting** 93-acre small-town campus **Total enrollment** 1,234 **Student-faculty ratio** 10:1 **Application deadline** Rolling (freshmen), 8/15 (transfer) **Freshmen** 71% were admitted **Housing** Yes **Expenses** Tuition $21,960; Room & Board $6900 **Undergraduates** 62% women, 3% part-time, 13% 25 or older, 0.2% Native American, 3% Hispanic American, 8% African American, 1% Asian American/Pacific Islander **The most frequently chosen baccalaureate fields are** business/marketing, health professions and related sciences, liberal arts/general studies **Academic program** English as a second language, advanced placement, honors program, summer session, adult/continuing education programs, internships **Contact** Mrs. Stephanie C. Shafer, Director of Admissions, Eastern Mennonite University, 1200 Park Road, Harrisonburg, VA 22802-2462. Phone: 540-432-4118 or toll-free 800-368-2665. Fax: 540-432-4444. E-mail: admiss@emu.edu. Web site: http://www.emu.edu/.

EMORY & HENRY COLLEGE
EMORY, VIRGINIA

General Independent United Methodist, comprehensive, coed **Entrance** Moderately difficult **Setting** 331-acre rural campus **Total enrollment** 977 **Student-faculty ratio** 10:1 **Application deadline** Rolling (freshmen), rolling (transfer) **Freshmen** 72% were admitted **Housing** Yes **Expenses** Tuition $23,860; Room & Board $7980 **Undergraduates** 49% women, 5% part-time, 1% 25 or older, 0.4% Native American, 1% Hispanic American, 6% African American, 1% Asian American/Pacific Islander **The most frequently chosen baccalaureate fields are** business/marketing, parks and recreation, social sciences **Academic program** Advanced placement, self-designed majors, honors program, summer session, internships **Contact** Ms. Liz Daniels, Dean of Admissions and Financial Aid, Emory & Henry College, 30479 Armbrister Drive, PO Box 10, Emory, VA 24327. Phone: 276-944-6133 or toll-free 800-848-5493. Fax: 276-944-6935. E-mail: ehadmiss@ehc.edu. Web site: http://www.ehc.edu/.

FERRUM COLLEGE
FERRUM, VIRGINIA

General Independent United Methodist, 4-year, coed **Entrance** Minimally difficult **Setting** 720-acre rural campus **Total enrollment** 1,240 **Student-faculty ratio** 15:1 **Application deadline** Rolling (freshmen), rolling (transfer)

Ferrum College *(continued)*

Freshmen 78% were admitted **Housing** Yes **Expenses** Tuition $20,885; Room & Board $6900 **Undergraduates** 44% women, 2% part-time, 2% 25 or older, 1% Native American, 2% Hispanic American, 27% African American, 1% Asian American/Pacific Islander **The most frequently chosen baccalaureate fields are** business/marketing, parks and recreation, security and protective services **Academic program** Advanced placement, self-designed majors, honors program, summer session, adult/continuing education programs, internships **Contact** Ms. Gilda Q. Woods, Director of Admissions, Ferrum College, Spilman-Daniel House, PO Box 1000, Ferrum, VA 24088-9001. Phone: 540-365-4290 or toll-free 800-868-9797. Fax: 540-365-4266. E-mail: admissions@ferrum.edu. Web site: http://www.ferrum.edu/.

GEORGE MASON UNIVERSITY

FAIRFAX, VIRGINIA

General State-supported, university, coed **Entrance** Moderately difficult **Setting** 677-acre suburban campus **Total enrollment** 30,332 **Student-faculty ratio** 15:1 **Application deadline** 1/15 (freshmen), 4/1 (transfer) **Freshmen** 56% were admitted **Housing** Yes **Expenses** Tuition $6840; Room & Board $7020 **Undergraduates** 53% women, 25% part-time, 23% 25 or older, 0.3% Native American, 7% Hispanic American, 8% African American, 16% Asian American/Pacific Islander **The most frequently chosen baccalaureate fields are** business/marketing, English, social sciences **Academic program** English as a second language, advanced placement, accelerated degree program, self-designed majors, honors program, summer session, adult/continuing education programs, internships **Contact** Mr. Eddie Tallent, Assistant Dean, Executive Director Undergraduate Admissions, George Mason University, Finley Building, Fairfax, VA 22030-4444. Phone: 703-993-2395. Fax: 703-993-2392. E-mail: etallent@gmu.edu. Web site: http://www.gmu.edu/.

HAMPDEN-SYDNEY COLLEGE

HAMPDEN-SYDNEY, VIRGINIA

General Independent, 4-year, men only, affiliated with Presbyterian Church (U.S.A.) **Entrance** Moderately difficult **Setting** 1,200-acre rural campus **Total enrollment** 1,122 **Student-faculty ratio** 10:1 **Application deadline** 3/1 (freshmen), 7/1 (transfer) **Freshmen** 67% were admitted **Housing** Yes **Expenses** Tuition $29,254; Room & Board $9148 **Undergraduates** 0.4% 25 or older, 0.2% Native American, 1% Hispanic American, 5% African American, 1% Asian American/Pacific Islander **The most frequently chosen baccalaureate fields are** business/marketing, history, social sciences **Academic program** Advanced placement, accelerated degree program, honors program, summer session, internships **Contact** Ms. Anita H. Garland, Dean of Admissions, Hampden-Sydney College, PO Box 667, Hampden-Sydney, VA 23943-0667. Phone: 434-223-6120 or toll-free 800-755-0733. Fax: 434-223-6346. E-mail: hsapp@hsc.edu. Web site: http://www.hsc.edu/.

HAMPTON UNIVERSITY

HAMPTON, VIRGINIA

General Independent, university, coed **Entrance** Moderately difficult **Setting** 210-acre urban campus **Total enrollment** 5,656 **Student-faculty ratio** 16:1 **Application deadline** 3/1 (freshmen) **Housing** Yes **Expenses** Tuition $15,610; Room & Board $7084 **Undergraduates** 64% women, 6% part-time, 9% 25 or older, 0.3% Native American, 1% Hispanic American, 95% African American, 1% Asian American/Pacific Islander **The most frequently chosen baccalaureate fields are** business/marketing, health professions and related sciences, psychology **Academic program** Advanced placement, accelerated degree program, honors program, summer session, adult/continuing education programs, internships **Contact** Mrs. Barbara Inman, Assistant Vice President of Student Affairs, Hampton University, Hampton, VA 23668. Phone: 757-727-5328 or toll-free 800-624-3328. Fax: 757-727-5095. E-mail: barbara.inman@hamptonu.edu. Web site: http://www.hamptonu.edu/.

HOLLINS UNIVERSITY

ROANOKE, VIRGINIA

General Independent, comprehensive, undergraduate: women only; graduate: coed **Entrance** Moderately difficult **Setting** 475-acre suburban campus **Total enrollment** 1,049 **Student-faculty ratio** 9:1 **Application deadline** Rolling (freshmen) **Freshmen** 88% were admitted **Housing** Yes **Expenses** Tuition $27,055; Room & Board $9650 **Undergraduates** 4% part-time, 12% 25 or older, 1% Native American, 3% Hispanic American, 8% African American, 2% Asian American/Pacific Islander **The most frequently chosen baccalaureate fields are** English, social sciences, visual and performing arts **Academic program** Advanced placement, accelerated degree program, self-designed majors, adult/continuing education programs, internships **Contact** Ms. Rebecca Eckstein, Dean of Admissions, Hollins University, PO Box 9707, Roanoke, VA 24020-1707. Phone: 540-362-6401 or toll-free 800-456-9595. Fax: 540-362-6218. E-mail: huadm@hollins.edu. Web site: http://www.hollins.edu/.

JAMES MADISON UNIVERSITY

HARRISONBURG, VIRGINIA

General State-supported, comprehensive, coed **Entrance** Very difficult **Setting** 655-acre small-town campus **Total enrollment** 17,918 **Student-faculty ratio** 16:1 **Application deadline** 1/15 (freshmen), 3/1 (transfer) **Freshmen** 64% were admitted **Housing** Yes **Expenses** Tuition $6666; Room & Board $7108 **Undergraduates** 60% women, 5% part-time, 2% 25 or older, 0.3% Native American, 2% Hispanic American, 4% African American, 5% Asian American/Pacific Islander **The most frequently chosen baccalaureate fields are** business/marketing, health professions and related sciences, social sciences **Academic program** Advanced placement, accelerated degree program, honors program, summer session, adult/continuing education programs, internships **Contact** Mr. Michael D. Walsh, Director of Admission, James Madison University, 800 South Main Street, Harrisonburg, VA 22807. Phone: 540-568-5681. Fax: 540-568-3332. E-mail: admissions@jmu.edu. Web site: http://www.jmu.edu/.

JEFFERSON COLLEGE OF HEALTH SCIENCES

ROANOKE, VIRGINIA

General Independent, comprehensive, coed **Entrance** Moderately difficult **Setting** 1-acre urban campus **Total enrollment** 971 **Student-faculty ratio** 11:1 **Application deadline** Rolling (freshmen) **Freshmen** 43% were admitted **Housing** Yes **Expenses** Tuition $15,500; Room & Board $6310 **Undergraduates** 83% women, 30% part-time, 50% 25 or older, 0.3% Native American, 1% Hispanic American, 13% African American, 1% Asian American/Pacific Islander **The most frequently chosen baccalaureate fields are** biological/life sciences, health professions and related sciences **Academic program** Advanced placement, accelerated degree program, summer session, adult/continuing education programs, internships **Contact** Ms. Judith McKeon, Director of Admissions, Jefferson College of Health Sciences, PO Box 13186, Roanoke, VA 24031-3186. Phone: 540-985-9083 or toll-free 888-985-8483. Fax: 540-985-9773. E-mail: jmckeon@chs.edu. Web site: http://www.jchs.edu/.

LIBERTY UNIVERSITY

LYNCHBURG, VIRGINIA

General Independent nondenominational, comprehensive, coed **Entrance** Minimally difficult **Setting** 4,400-acre suburban campus **Total enrollment** 27,063 **Student-faculty ratio** 24:1 **Application deadline** 6/30 (freshmen) **Freshmen** 95% were admitted **Housing** Yes **Expenses** Tuition $15,800; Room & Board $5400 **Undergraduates** 52% women, 30% part-time, 41% 25 or older, 1% Native American, 4% Hispanic American, 12% African American, 1% Asian American/Pacific Islander **The most frequently chosen baccalaureate fields are** business/marketing, interdisciplinary studies, philosophy and religious studies **Academic program** English as a second language, advanced placement, accelerated degree program, self-designed majors, honors program, summer session, internships **Contact** Mr. Richmond Plyter, Director of Admissions, Liberty University, 1971 University Boulevard, Lynchburg, VA 24502. Phone: 434-592-3015 or toll-free 800-543-5317. Fax: 800-542-2311. E-mail: admissions@liberty.edu. Web site: http://www.liberty.edu/.

LONGWOOD UNIVERSITY

FARMVILLE, VIRGINIA

General State-supported, comprehensive, coed **Entrance** Moderately difficult **Setting** 160-acre small-town campus **Total enrollment** 4,727 **Student-faculty ratio** 20:1 **Application deadline** 3/1 (freshmen), 3/1 (transfer) **Freshmen** 66% were admitted **Housing** Yes **Expenses** Tuition $8058; Room & Board $6740 **Undergraduates** 65% women, 4% part-time, 2% 25 or older, 0.4% Native American, 2% Hispanic American, 6% African American, 2% Asian American/Pacific Islander **The most frequently chosen baccalaureate fields are** business/marketing, liberal arts/general studies, social sciences **Academic program** Advanced placement, accelerated degree program, honors program, summer session, internships **Contact** Mr. Robert J. Chonko, Dean of Admissions, Longwood University, Longwood University, 201 High Street, Farmville, VA 23909. Phone: 434-395-2060 or toll-free 800-281-4677. Fax: 434-395-2332. E-mail: admissions@longwood.edu. Web site: http://www.longwood.edu/.

LYNCHBURG COLLEGE

LYNCHBURG, VIRGINIA

General Independent, comprehensive, coed, affiliated with Christian Church (Disciples of Christ) **Entrance** Moderately difficult **Setting** 214-acre suburban campus **Total enrollment** 2,489 **Student-faculty ratio** 12:1 **Application deadline** Rolling (freshmen), rolling (transfer) **Freshmen** 69% were admitted **Housing** Yes **Expenses** Tuition $26,765; Room & Board $7370 **Undergraduates** 59% women, 5% part-time, 7% 25 or older, 1% Native American, 2% Hispanic American, 7% African American, 2% Asian American/Pacific Islander **The most frequently chosen baccalaureate fields are** education, busi-

Lynchburg College *(continued)*

ness/marketing, social sciences **Academic program** Advanced placement, accelerated degree program, honors program, summer session, adult/continuing education programs, internships **Contact** Ms. Sharon Walters-Bower, Director of Admissions, Lynchburg College, 1501 Lakeside Drive, Lynchburg, VA 24501-3199. Phone: 434-544-8300 or toll-free 800-426-8101. Fax: 434-544-8653. E-mail: admissions@lynchburg.edu. Web site: http://www.lynchburg.edu/.

MARY BALDWIN COLLEGE
STAUNTON, VIRGINIA

General Independent, comprehensive, coed **Entrance** Moderately difficult **Setting** 54-acre small-town campus **Total enrollment** 1,685 **Student-faculty ratio** 10:1 **Application deadline** Rolling (freshmen), rolling (transfer) **Freshmen** 74% were admitted **Housing** Yes **Expenses** Tuition $22,730; Room & Board $6470 **Undergraduates** 94% women, 31% part-time, 2% 25 or older, 0.5% Native American, 4% Hispanic American, 18% African American, 2% Asian American/Pacific Islander **The most frequently chosen baccalaureate fields are** psychology, business/marketing, social sciences **Academic program** English as a second language, advanced placement, accelerated degree program, self-designed majors, honors program, adult/continuing education programs, internships **Contact** Ms. Lisa Branson, Associate Vice President for Enrollment Management, Mary Baldwin College, Frederick and New Streets, Staunton, VA 24401. Phone: 540-887-7019 Ext. 7220 or toll-free 800-468-2262. Fax: 540-887-7229. E-mail: lbranson@mbc.edu. Web site: http://www.mbc.edu/.

MARYMOUNT UNIVERSITY
ARLINGTON, VIRGINIA

General Independent, comprehensive, coed, affiliated with Roman Catholic Church **Entrance** Moderately difficult **Setting** 21-acre suburban campus **Total enrollment** 3,609 **Student-faculty ratio** 14:1 **Application deadline** Rolling (freshmen), rolling (transfer) **Freshmen** 81% were admitted **Housing** Yes **Expenses** Tuition $20,410; Room & Board $8705 **Undergraduates** 75% women, 14% part-time, 22% 25 or older, 1% Native American, 12% Hispanic American, 15% African American, 8% Asian American/Pacific Islander **The most frequently chosen baccalaureate fields are** health professions and related sciences, business/marketing, visual and performing arts **Academic program** English as a second language, advanced placement, self-designed majors, honors program, summer session, internships **Contact** Mr. Mike Canfield, Associate Director of Undergraduate Admissions, Marymount University, 2807 North Glebe Road, Arlington, VA 22207-4299. Phone: 703-284-1500 or toll-free 800-548-7638. Fax: 703-522-0349. E-mail: admissions@marymount.edu. Web site: http://www.marymount.edu/.

NORFOLK STATE UNIVERSITY
NORFOLK, VIRGINIA

General State-supported, comprehensive, coed **Contact** Ms. Michelle Marable, Director of Admissions, Norfolk State University, 700 Park Avenue, Norfolk, VA 23504. Phone: 757-823-8396. Fax: 757-823-2078. E-mail: admissions@nsu.edu. Web site: http://www.nsu.edu/.

OLD DOMINION UNIVERSITY
NORFOLK, VIRGINIA

General State-supported, university, coed **Setting** 188-acre urban campus **Total enrollment** 22,287 **Application deadline** 3/15 (freshmen), 5/1 (transfer) **Freshmen** 74% were admitted **Housing** Yes **Undergraduates** 58% women, 27% part-time, 28% 25 or older, 1% Native American, 4% Hispanic American, 22% African American, 6% Asian American/Pacific Islander **The most frequently chosen baccalaureate fields are** business/marketing, health professions and related sciences, social sciences **Academic program** English as a second language, advanced placement, accelerated degree program, self-designed majors, honors program, summer session, adult/continuing education programs, internships **Contact** Ms. Alice McAdory, Director of Admissions, Old Dominion University, 108 Rollins Hall, Norfolk, VA 23529-0050. Phone: 757-683-3648 or toll-free 800-348-7926. Fax: 757-683-3255. E-mail: admissions@odu.edu. Web site: http://www.odu.edu/.

PATRICK HENRY COLLEGE
PURCELLVILLE, VIRGINIA

General Independent nondenominational, 4-year, coed **Entrance** Very difficult **Setting** 106-acre small-town campus **Total enrollment** 461 **Student-faculty ratio** 17:1 **Freshmen** 56% were admitted **Housing** Yes **Expenses** Tuition $18,500; Room & Board $6600 **Undergraduates** 48% women, 30% part-time **The most frequently chosen baccalaureate fields are** English, liberal arts/general studies, social sciences **Academic program** Internships **Contact** Ms. Rebekah A. Knable, Director of Admissions, Patrick Henry College, PO Box 1776, One Patrick Henry Circle, Purcellville, VA 20134. Phone: 540-338-1776. Fax: 540-338-9808. E-mail: admissions@phc.edu. Web site: http://www.phc.edu/.

RADFORD UNIVERSITY
RADFORD, VIRGINIA

General State-supported, comprehensive, coed **Entrance** Moderately difficult **Setting** 177-acre small-town campus **Total enrollment** 9,122 **Student-faculty ratio** 18:1 **Application deadline** 2/1 (freshmen), 6/1 (transfer) **Freshmen** 78% were admitted **Housing** Yes **Expenses** Tuition $6176; Room & Board $6490 **Undergraduates** 58% women, 5% part-time, 9% 25 or older, 0.3% Native American, 2% Hispanic American, 6% African American, 2% Asian American/Pacific Islander **The most frequently chosen baccalaureate fields are** business/marketing, communications/journalism, interdisciplinary studies **Academic program** English as a second language, advanced placement, accelerated degree program, self-designed majors, honors program, summer session, internships **Contact** Mr. David W. Kraus, Director of Admissions, Radford University, PO Box 6903, Radford, VA 24142. Phone: 540-831-5371 or toll-free 800-890-4265. Fax: 540-831-5038. E-mail: ruadmiss@radford.edu. Web site: http://www.radford.edu/.

RANDOLPH COLLEGE
LYNCHBURG, VIRGINIA

General Independent Methodist, 4-year, coed **Entrance** Moderately difficult **Setting** 100-acre suburban campus **Total enrollment** 656 **Student-faculty ratio** 8:1 **Application deadline** 3/1 (freshmen), 6/1 (transfer) **Freshmen** 83% were admitted **Housing** Yes **Expenses** Tuition $25,860; Room & Board $9000 **Undergraduates** 88% women, 4% part-time, 6% 25 or older, 1% Native American, 6% Hispanic American, 9% African American, 3% Asian American/Pacific Islander **The most frequently chosen baccalaureate fields are** social sciences, biological/life sciences, visual and performing arts **Academic program** Advanced placement, accelerated degree program, self-designed majors, honors program, adult/continuing education programs, internships **Contact** Mr. Jim Duffy, Senior Associate Director of Admissions, Randolph College, 2500 Rivermont Avenue, Lynchburg, VA 24503-1526. Phone: 434-947-8100 or toll-free 800-745-7692. Fax: 434-947-8996. E-mail: admissions@randolphcollege.edu. Web site: http://www.randolphcollege.edu/.

RANDOLPH-MACON COLLEGE
ASHLAND, VIRGINIA

General Independent United Methodist, 4-year, coed **Entrance** Moderately difficult **Setting** 120-acre suburban campus **Total enrollment** 1,176 **Student-faculty ratio** 11:1 **Application deadline** 3/1 (freshmen), 4/1 (transfer) **Freshmen** 61% were admitted **Housing** Yes **Expenses** Tuition $26,830; Room & Board $8180 **Undergraduates** 54% women, 2% part-time, 1% 25 or older, 1% Native American, 2% Hispanic American, 9% African American, 2% Asian American/Pacific Islander **The most frequently chosen baccalaureate fields are** business/marketing, English, social sciences **Academic program** Advanced placement, accelerated degree program, honors program, summer session, internships **Contact** Dr. Steven W. Nape, Dean of Admissions and Financial Aid, Randolph-Macon College, PO Box 5005, Ashland, VA 23005-5505. Phone: 804-752-7305 or toll-free 800-888-1762. Fax: 804-752-4707. E-mail: admissions@rmc.edu. Web site: http://www.rmc.edu/.

REGENT UNIVERSITY
VIRGINIA BEACH, VIRGINIA

General Independent, comprehensive, coed **Entrance** Minimally difficult **Setting** suburban campus **Total enrollment** 4,494 **Student-faculty ratio** 10:1 **Application deadline** 8/1 (freshmen), 8/1 (transfer) **Freshmen** 53% were admitted **Housing** Yes **Expenses** Tuition $12,750 **Undergraduates** 69% women, 53% part-time, 71% 25 or older, 1% Native American, 5% Hispanic American, 25% African American, 2% Asian American/Pacific Islander **The most frequently chosen baccalaureate fields are** business/marketing, communications/journalism, psychology **Academic program** Summer session, adult/continuing education programs **Contact** Mr. Ken Baker, Director of Admissions, Regent University, 1000 Regent University Drive, Virginia Beach, VA 23464. Phone: 757-226-4826 or toll-free 800-373-5504. Fax: 757-226-4509. E-mail: kbaker@regent.edu. Web site: http://www.regent.edu/.

ROANOKE COLLEGE
SALEM, VIRGINIA

General Independent, 4-year, coed, affiliated with Evangelical Lutheran Church in America **Entrance** Moderately difficult **Setting** 68-acre suburban campus **Total enrollment** 2,006 **Student-faculty ratio** 14:1 **Application deadline** 3/15 (freshmen), 8/1 (transfer) **Freshmen** 73% were admitted **Housing** Yes **Expenses** Tuition $27,935; Room & Board $9285 **Undergraduates** 57% women, 5% part-time, 2% 25 or older, 0.4% Native American, 2% Hispanic American, 3% African American, 1% Asian American/Pacific Islander **The most frequently chosen baccalaureate fields are** business/marketing, history, social sciences **Academic program** English as a second language, advanced placement, accelerated degree program, honors program, summer session, adult/continuing educa-

Roanoke College *(continued)*

tion programs, internships **Contact** Ms. Brenda Poggendorf, Vice President of Enrollment, Roanoke College, 221 College Lane, Salem, VA 24153. Phone: 540-375-2270 or toll-free 800-388-2276. Fax: 540-375-2267. E-mail: admissions@roanoke.edu. Web site: http://www.roanoke.edu/.

SAINT PAUL'S COLLEGE

LAWRENCEVILLE, VIRGINIA

General Independent Episcopal, 4-year, coed **Entrance** Minimally difficult **Setting** 75-acre small-town campus **Total enrollment** 700 **Student-faculty ratio** 18:1 **Freshmen** 86% were admitted **Housing** Yes **Expenses** Tuition $13,210; Room & Board $6640 **Undergraduates** 52% women, 5% part-time, 22% 25 or older, 0.1% Hispanic American, 97% African American, 1% Asian American/Pacific Islander **The most frequently chosen baccalaureate fields are** business/marketing, liberal arts/general studies, public administration and social services **Academic program** Honors program, summer session, adult/continuing education programs, internships **Contact** Mrs. Rosemary Lewis, Vice President for Student Affairs, Saint Paul's College, 115 College Drive, Lawrenceville, VA 23868-1202. Phone: 434-848-6493 or toll-free 800-678-7071. Fax: 434-848-0229. E-mail: rlewis@saintpauls.edu. Web site: http://www.saintpauls.edu/.

SHENANDOAH UNIVERSITY

WINCHESTER, VIRGINIA

General Independent United Methodist, comprehensive, coed **Entrance** Moderately difficult **Setting** 100-acre small-town campus **Total enrollment** 3,393 **Student-faculty ratio** 8:1 **Application deadline** Rolling (freshmen), rolling (transfer) **Freshmen** 88% were admitted **Housing** Yes **Expenses** Tuition $23,340; Room & Board $8350 **Undergraduates** 57% women, 8% part-time, 18% 25 or older, 0.3% Native American, 1% Hispanic American, 7% African American, 2% Asian American/Pacific Islander **The most frequently chosen baccalaureate fields are** health professions and related sciences, biological/life sciences, visual and performing arts **Academic program** English as a second language, advanced placement, accelerated degree program, self-designed majors, summer session, adult/continuing education programs, internships **Contact** Mr. David Anthony, Dean of Admissions, Shenandoah University, 1460 University Drive, Winchester, VA 22601-5195. Phone: 540-665-4581 or toll-free 800-432-2266. Fax: 540-665-4627. E-mail: admit@su.edu. Web site: http://www.su.edu/.

SOUTHERN VIRGINIA UNIVERSITY

BUENA VISTA, VIRGINIA

General Independent Latter-day Saints, 4-year, coed **Contact** Mr. Tony Caputo, Dean of Admissions, Southern Virginia University, One University Hill Drive, Buena Vista, VA 24416. Phone: 540-261-2756 or toll-free 800-229-8420. Fax: 540-261-8559. E-mail: admissions@southernvirginia.edu. Web site: http://svu.edu/.

STRATFORD UNIVERSITY

FALLS CHURCH, VIRGINIA

Contact Kelly Martin, Director of High School Program, Stratford University, 7777 Leesburg Pike, Falls Church, VA 22043. Phone: 703-821-8570 or toll-free 800-444-0804. Fax: 703-734-5339. E-mail: kmartin@stratford.edu. Web site: http://www.stratford.edu/.

SWEET BRIAR COLLEGE

SWEET BRIAR, VIRGINIA

General Independent, comprehensive, women only **Entrance** Moderately difficult **Setting** 3,250-acre rural campus **Total enrollment** 815 **Student-faculty ratio** 9:1 **Application deadline** 2/1 (freshmen), 5/1 (transfer) **Freshmen** 81% were admitted **Housing** Yes **Expenses** Tuition $26,995; Room & Board $10,160 **Undergraduates** 6% part-time, 3% 25 or older, 1% Native American, 3% Hispanic American, 3% African American, 1% Asian American/Pacific Islander **The most frequently chosen baccalaureate fields are** business/marketing, social sciences, visual and performing arts **Academic program** Advanced placement, accelerated degree program, self-designed majors, honors program, summer session, adult/continuing education programs, internships **Contact** Mr. Ken Huus, Director of Admissions, Sweet Briar College, PO Box B, Sweet Briar, VA 24595. Phone: 434-381-6142 or toll-free 800-381-6142. Fax: 434-381-6152. E-mail: admissions@sbc.edu. Web site: http://www.sbc.edu/.

UNIVERSITY OF MANAGEMENT AND TECHNOLOGY

ARLINGTON, VIRGINIA

General Proprietary, comprehensive, coed **Setting** urban campus **Housing** No **Expenses** Tuition $10,890 **Contact** Dr. C. Kirkland, Vice President, University of Management and Technology, Suite 700, 1901 North Fort Meyers Drive, Arlington, VA 22209. Phone: 703-516-0035 or toll-free 800-924-4885. Fax: 703-516-0985. E-mail: admissions@umtweb.edu. Web site: http://www.umtweb.edu/.

UNIVERSITY OF MARY WASHINGTON
FREDERICKSBURG, VIRGINIA

General State-supported, comprehensive, coed **Entrance** Very difficult **Setting** 176-acre small-town campus **Total enrollment** 5,001 **Student-faculty ratio** 15:1 **Application deadline** 2/1 (freshmen), 3/1 (transfer) **Freshmen** 71% were admitted **Housing** Yes **Undergraduates** 66% women, 14% part-time, 10% 25 or older, 0.5% Native American, 3% Hispanic American, 3% African American, 4% Asian American/Pacific Islander **The most frequently chosen baccalaureate fields are** business/marketing, English, social sciences **Academic program** Advanced placement, accelerated degree program, self-designed majors, summer session, adult/continuing education programs, internships **Contact** Dr. Martin Wilder, Vice President for Enrollment and Communications, University of Mary Washington, 1301 College Avenue, Fredericksburg, VA 22401-5358. Phone: 540-654-2000 or toll-free 800-468-5614. Fax: 540-654-1857. E-mail: admit@umw.edu. Web site: http://www.umw.edu/.

UNIVERSITY OF NORTHERN VIRGINIA
MANASSAS, VIRGINIA

Contact Mr. Robert Frantz, Director of Admissions, University of Northern Virginia, 10021 Balls Ford Road, Manassas, VA 20109. Phone: 703-392-0771 Ext. 2402. E-mail: bfrantz@unva.edu. Web site: http://www.unva.edu/.

UNIVERSITY OF PHOENIX–NORTHERN VIRGINIA CAMPUS
RESTON, VIRGINIA

General Proprietary, comprehensive, coed **Contact** Ms. Evelyn Gaskin, Registrar/Executive Director, University of Phoenix–Northern Virginia Campus, 4615 East Elwood Street, Mail Stop AA-K101, Phoenix, AZ 85040-1958. Phone: 480-557-3301 or toll-free 800-776-4867 (in-state); 800-228-7240 (out-of-state). Fax: 480-643-1020. E-mail: evelyn.gaskin@phoenix.edu. Web site: http://www.phoenix.edu/.

UNIVERSITY OF PHOENIX–RICHMOND CAMPUS
RICHMOND, VIRGINIA

General Proprietary, comprehensive, coed **Contact** Ms. Evelyn Gaskin, Registrar/Executive Director, University of Phoenix–Richmond Campus, 4615 East Elwood Street, Phoenix, AZ 85040-1958. Phone: 480-557-3301 or toll-free 800-776-4867 (in-state); 800-228-7240 (out-of-state). Fax: 480-643-1020. E-mail: evelyn.gaskin@phoenix.edu. Web site: http://www.phoenix.edu/.

UNIVERSITY OF RICHMOND
RICHMOND, VIRGINIA

General Independent, comprehensive, coed **Entrance** Very difficult **Setting** 350-acre suburban campus **Total enrollment** 3,448 **Student-faculty ratio** 9:1 **Application deadline** 1/15 (freshmen), 2/15 (transfer) **Freshmen** 40% were admitted **Housing** Yes **Expenses** Tuition $38,850; Room & Board $8200 **Undergraduates** 49% women, 1% part-time, 0.3% Native American, 3% Hispanic American, 6% African American, 4% Asian American/Pacific Islander **The most frequently chosen baccalaureate fields are** business/marketing, English, social sciences **Academic program** English as a second language, advanced placement, accelerated degree program, self-designed majors, honors program, summer session, adult/continuing education programs, internships **Contact** Ms. Pamela Spence, Dean of Admission, University of Richmond, 28 Westhampton Way, University of Richmond, VA 23173. Phone: 804-289-8640 or toll-free 800-700-1662. Fax: 804-287-6003. E-mail: admissions@richmond.edu. Web site: http://www.richmond.edu/.

UNIVERSITY OF VIRGINIA
CHARLOTTESVILLE, VIRGINIA

General State-supported, university, coed **Entrance** Very difficult **Setting** 1,160-acre suburban campus **Total enrollment** 24,257 **Student-faculty ratio** 15:1 **Application deadline** 1/2 (freshmen), 3/1 (transfer) **Freshmen** 35% were admitted **Housing** Yes **Expenses** Tuition $8500; Room & Board $7435 **Undergraduates** 56% women, 5% part-time, 3% 25 or older, 0.2% Native American, 4% Hispanic American, 9% African American, 11% Asian American/Pacific Islander **The most frequently chosen baccalaureate fields are** engineering, business/marketing, social sciences **Academic program** English as a second language, advanced placement, accelerated degree program, self-designed majors, honors program, summer session, adult/continuing education programs, internships **Contact** Mr. John A. Blackburn, Dean of Admission, University of Virginia, PO Box 400160, Charlottesville, VA 22904-4727. Phone: 434-982-3200. Fax: 434-954-3587. E-mail: undergrad-admission@virginia.edu. Web site: http://www.virginia.edu/.

THE UNIVERSITY OF VIRGINIA'S COLLEGE AT WISE
WISE, VIRGINIA

General State-supported, 4-year, coed **Entrance** Moderately difficult **Setting** 396-acre small-town campus **Total enrollment** 1,803 **Student-faculty ratio** 17:1 **Application deadline** 8/1 (freshmen), 8/15 (transfer) **Freshmen** 80% were admitted **Housing** Yes **Expenses** Tuition $6439; Room & Board $6912 **Undergraduates** 52% women, 16% part-time, 11% 25 or older, 0.3% Native American, 2% Hispanic American, 7% African American, 1% Asian American/Pacific Islander **The most frequently chosen baccalaureate fields are** business/marketing, liberal arts/general studies, social sciences **Academic program** Advanced placement, accelerated degree program, self-designed majors, honors program, summer session, adult/continuing education programs, internships **Contact** Mr. Russell D. Necessary, Vice Chancellor for Enrollment Management, The University of Virginia's College at Wise, 1 College Avenue, Wise, VA 24293. Phone: 276-328-0322 or toll-free 888-282-9324. Fax: 276-328-0251. E-mail: admissions@uvawise.edu. Web site: http://www.uvawise.edu/.

VIRGINIA COMMONWEALTH UNIVERSITY
RICHMOND, VIRGINIA

General State-supported, university, coed **Setting** 140-acre urban campus **Total enrollment** 31,907 **Student-faculty ratio** 18:1 **Freshmen** 62% were admitted **Housing** Yes **Expenses** Tuition $6196; Room & Board $7567 **Undergraduates** 59% women, 20% part-time, 14% 25 or older, 1% Native American, 4% Hispanic American, 21% African American, 11% Asian American/Pacific Islander **The most frequently chosen baccalaureate fields are** business/marketing, psychology, visual and performing arts **Academic program** English as a second language, advanced placement, accelerated degree program, self-designed majors, honors program, summer session, adult/continuing education programs, internships **Contact** Ms. Sybil Halloran, Director of Undergraduate Admissions, Virginia Commonwealth University, 821 West Franklin Street, Box 842526, Richmond, VA 23284-2526. Phone: 804-828-6125 or toll-free 800-841-3638. Fax: 804-828-1899. E-mail: ugrad@vcu.edu. Web site: http://www.vcu.edu/.

VIRGINIA INTERMONT COLLEGE
BRISTOL, VIRGINIA

General Independent, 4-year, coed, affiliated with Baptist Church **Entrance** Minimally difficult **Setting** 13-acre small-town campus **Total enrollment** 635 **Student-faculty ratio** 10:1 **Application deadline** Rolling (freshmen), rolling (transfer) **Freshmen** 69% were admitted **Housing** Yes **Expenses** Tuition $22,150; Room & Board $6495 **Undergraduates** 74% women, 17% part-time, 12% 25 or older, 0.3% Native American, 1% Hispanic American, 5% African American, 0.3% Asian American/Pacific Islander **The most frequently chosen baccalaureate fields are** agriculture, business/marketing, education **Academic program** English as a second language, advanced placement, accelerated degree program, honors program, summer session, adult/continuing education programs, internships **Contact** Mr. Tony England, Director of Admissions, Virginia Intermont College, 1013 Moore Street, Campus Box D-460, Bristol, VA 24201. Phone: 276-466-7856 or toll-free 800-451-1842. Fax: 276-466-7885. E-mail: viadmit@vic.edu. Web site: http://www.vic.edu/.

VIRGINIA MILITARY INSTITUTE
LEXINGTON, VIRGINIA

General State-supported, 4-year, coed, primarily men **Entrance** Moderately difficult **Setting** 134-acre small-town campus **Total enrollment** 1,378 **Student-faculty ratio** 10:1 **Application deadline** 3/1 (freshmen), 2/15 (transfer) **Freshmen** 54% were admitted **Housing** Yes **Expenses** Tuition $8043; Room & Board $6108 **Undergraduates** 8% women, 1% 25 or older, 0.4% Native American, 3% Hispanic American, 6% African American, 4% Asian American/Pacific Islander **Academic program** Advanced placement, accelerated degree program, honors program, summer session, internships **Contact** Lt. Col. Tom Mortenson, Associate Director of Admissions, Virginia Military Institute, Admissions Office, Lexington, VA 24450. Phone: 540-464-7211 or toll-free 800-767-4207. Fax: 540-464-7746. E-mail: admissions@vmi.edu. Web site: http://www.vmi.edu/.

VIRGINIA POLYTECHNIC INSTITUTE AND STATE UNIVERSITY
BLACKSBURG, VIRGINIA

General State-supported, university, coed **Entrance** Moderately difficult **Setting** 2,600-acre small-town campus **Total enrollment** 29,898 **Student-faculty ratio** 17:1 **Application deadline** 1/15 (freshmen), 2/15 (transfer) **Freshmen** 67% were admitted **Housing** Yes **Expenses** Tuition $7397; Room & Board $5106 **Undergraduates** 42% women, 2% part-time, 3% 25 or older, 0.3% Native American, 3% Hispanic American, 4% African American, 7% Asian American/Pacific Islander **The most frequently chosen baccalaureate fields are** business/marketing, engineering, family and consumer sciences **Academic program** English as a second language, advanced placement, accelerated degree program, honors program, summer session, adult/continuing education programs, internships **Contact** Ms. Mildred Johnson, Senior Associate Director for Undergraduate Admissions, Virginia Polytechnic Institute and State University, 201 Burruss Hall, Blacksburg, VA 24061-0202. Phone: 540-231-6267. Fax: 540-231-3242. E-mail: vtadmiss@vt.edu. Web site: http://www.vt.edu/.

VIRGINIA STATE UNIVERSITY

PETERSBURG, VIRGINIA

General State-supported, comprehensive, coed **Entrance** Minimally difficult **Setting** 236-acre suburban campus **Total enrollment** 4,720 **Student-faculty ratio** 14:1 **Application deadline** 5/1 (freshmen), 5/1 (transfer) **Freshmen** 58% were admitted **Housing** Yes **Expenses** Tuition $5655; Room & Board $7340 **Undergraduates** 61% women, 7% part-time, 9% 25 or older, 0.1% Native American, 1% Hispanic American, 95% African American, 0.3% Asian American/Pacific Islander **The most frequently chosen baccalaureate fields are** business/marketing, education, interdisciplinary studies **Academic program** Advanced placement, self-designed majors, honors program, summer session, adult/continuing education programs, internships **Contact** Mrs. Irene Logan, Director of Admissions, Virginia State University, Office of Admissions, Petersburg, VA 23806-2096. Phone: 804-524-5902 or toll-free 800-871-7611. Fax: 804-524-5055. E-mail: ilogan@vsu.edu. Web site: http://www.vsu.edu/.

VIRGINIA UNION UNIVERSITY

RICHMOND, VIRGINIA

Contact Mr. Gil Powell, Director of Admissions, Virginia Union University, 1500 North Lombardy Street, Richmond, VA 23220-1170. Phone: 804-257-5881 or toll-free 800-368-3227. Fax: 804-329-8477. E-mail: gpowell@vuu.edu. Web site: http://www.vuu.edu/.

VIRGINIA UNIVERSITY OF LYNCHBURG

LYNCHBURG, VIRGINIA

General Independent religious, comprehensive, coed **Entrance** Noncompetitive **Setting** urban campus **Total enrollment** 215 **Student-faculty ratio** 7:1 **Application deadline** Rolling (freshmen) **Freshmen** 100% were admitted **Housing** Yes **Expenses** Tuition $5300; Room & Board $3600 **Undergraduates** 61% women, 69% part-time, 86% 25 or older, 96% African American, 1% Asian American/Pacific Islander **The most frequently chosen baccalaureate fields are** philosophy and religious studies, social sciences **Academic program** Advanced placement, summer session, adult/continuing education programs **Contact** Ms. Debbie Smith, Registrar, Virginia University of Lynchburg, 2058 Garfield Avenue, Lynchburg, VA 24501-6417. Phone: 434-528-5276. Fax: 434-528-2705. E-mail: dsmith@vul.edu. Web site: http://www.vul.edu/.

VIRGINIA WESLEYAN COLLEGE

NORFOLK, VIRGINIA

General Independent United Methodist, 4-year, coed **Entrance** Moderately difficult **Setting** 300-acre urban campus **Total enrollment** 1,444 **Student-faculty ratio** 13:1 **Application deadline** Rolling (freshmen), rolling (transfer) **Freshmen** 90% were admitted **Housing** Yes **Expenses** Tuition $26,438; Room & Board $7100 **Undergraduates** 63% women, 17% part-time, 20% 25 or older, 0.1% Native American, 4% Hispanic American, 19% African American, 2% Asian American/Pacific Islander **The most frequently chosen baccalaureate fields are** business/marketing, interdisciplinary studies, social sciences **Academic program** Advanced placement, self-designed majors, honors program, summer session, adult/continuing education programs, internships **Contact** Mrs. Sara Gastler, Director of Admissions, Virginia Wesleyan College, 1584 Wesleyan Drive, Norfolk, VA 23502-5599. Phone: 757-455-3208 or toll-free 800-737-8684. Fax: 757-461-5238. E-mail: admissions@vwc.edu. Web site: http://www.vwc.edu/.

WASHINGTON AND LEE UNIVERSITY

LEXINGTON, VIRGINIA

General Independent, comprehensive, coed **Entrance** Most difficult **Setting** 322-acre small-town campus **Total enrollment** 2,181 **Student-faculty ratio** 10:1 **Application deadline** 1/15 (freshmen), 4/1 (transfer) **Freshmen** 27% were admitted **Housing** Yes **Expenses** Tuition $35,445; Room & Board $8725 **Undergraduates** 50% women, 0.2% part-time, 0.3% Native American, 1% Hispanic American, 4% African American, 3% Asian American/Pacific Islander **The most frequently chosen baccalaureate fields are** business/marketing, history, social sciences **Academic program** Advanced placement, self-designed majors, honors program, internships **Contact** Mr. William M. Hartog, Dean of Admissions and Financial Aid, Washington and Lee University, 204 West Washington Street, Lexington, VA 24450-2116. Phone: 540-458-8710. Fax: 540-458-8062. E-mail: admissions@wlu.edu. Web site: http://www.wlu.edu/.

WESTWOOD COLLEGE–ANNANDALE CAMPUS

ANNANDALE, VIRGINIA

General Proprietary, 4-year, coed **Contact** Ms. Amy McPherson, Westwood College–Annandale

Westwood College–Annandale Campus *(continued)*

Campus, 7619 Little River Turnpike, Suite 500, Annandale, VA 22203. Phone: 703-462-6505 or toll-free 800-281-2978. Fax: 703-642-3772. E-mail: amcpherson@westwood.edu. Web site: http://www.westwood.edu/locations/virginia-colleges/annandale-college.asp.

WESTWOOD COLLEGE–ARLINGTON BALLSTON CAMPUS

ARLINGTON, VIRGINIA

General Proprietary, 4-year, coed **Contact** Shebony Corbin, Westwood College–Arlington Ballston Campus, 4300 Wilson Boulevard, Suite 200, Arlington, VA 22203. Phone: 703-243-3900. Fax: 703-243-3992. E-mail: scorbin@westwood.edu. Web site: http://www.westwood.edu/.

WORLD COLLEGE

VIRGINIA BEACH, VIRGINIA

General Proprietary, 4-year, coed **Entrance** Noncompetitive **Setting** suburban campus **Total enrollment** 445 **Application deadline** Rolling (freshmen) **Housing** No **Expenses** Tuition $3540 **Undergraduates** 94% 25 or older **The most frequently chosen baccalaureate fields are** computer and information sciences, engineering technologies **Academic program** Accelerated degree program, adult/continuing education programs **Contact** Mrs. Audre Piratsky, Admissions Counselor, World College, 5193 Shore Drive, Suite 105, Virginia Beach, VA 23455. Phone: 757-464-4600 or toll-free 800-696-7532. Fax: 757-464-3687. E-mail: instruct@cie-wc.edu. Web site: http://www.worldcollege.edu/.

WASHINGTON

ANTIOCH UNIVERSITY SEATTLE

SEATTLE, WASHINGTON

Contact Ms. Vickie Lopez, Admissions Associate, Antioch University Seattle, 2326 Sixth Avenue, Seattle, WA 98121-1814. Phone: 206-441-5352. E-mail: admissions@antiochsea.edu. Web site: http://www.antiochsea.edu/.

ARGOSY UNIVERSITY, SEATTLE

SEATTLE, WASHINGTON

General Proprietary, university, coed **Setting** urban campus **Contact** Director of Admissions, Argosy University, Seattle, 2601-A Elliott Avenue, Seattle, WA 98121. Phone: 206-283-4500 or toll-free 866-283-2777. Fax: 206-283-5777. Web site: http://www.argosy.edu/locations/seattle/.

THE ART INSTITUTE OF SEATTLE

SEATTLE, WASHINGTON

General Proprietary, 4-year, coed **Entrance** Moderately difficult **Setting** urban campus **Total enrollment** 2,352 **Student-faculty ratio** 20:1 **Application deadline** Rolling (freshmen), rolling (transfer) **Freshmen** 94% were admitted **Housing** Yes **Expenses** Tuition $19,968; Room & Board $10,684 **Undergraduates** 51% women, 35% part-time, 40% 25 or older, 2% Native American, 6% Hispanic American, 4% African American, 12% Asian American/Pacific Islander **Academic program** Advanced placement, honors program, summer session, adult/continuing education programs, internships **Contact** Mr. Michael Reese, Registrar, The Art Institute of Seattle, 2323 Elliott Avenue, Seattle, WA 98121. Phone: 206-448-0900 or toll-free 800-275-2471. Fax: 206-269-0275. E-mail: mreese@aii.edu. Web site: http://www.artinstitutes.edu/seattle/.

BASTYR UNIVERSITY

KENMORE, WASHINGTON

General Independent, upper-level, coed **Setting** 50-acre suburban campus **Total enrollment** 1,086 **Student-faculty ratio** 13:1 **Application deadline** 3/15 (transfer) **First-year students** 77% were admitted **Housing** Yes **Expenses** Tuition $18,780; Room only $4100 **Undergraduates** 83% women, 9% part-time, 85% 25 or older, 2% Native American, 5% Hispanic American, 0.5% African American, 6% Asian American/Pacific Islander **The most frequently chosen baccalaureate fields are** health professions and related sciences, psychology **Academic program** Summer session, internships **Contact** Mr. Ted Olsen, Director of Admissions, Bastyr University, 14500 Juanita Drive NE, Kenmore, WA 98028-4966. Phone: 425-602-3101. Fax: 425-602-3090. E-mail: admissions@bastyr.edu. Web site: http://www.bastyr.edu/.

CENTRAL WASHINGTON UNIVERSITY

ELLENSBURG, WASHINGTON

General State-supported, comprehensive, coed **Entrance** Moderately difficult **Setting** 380-acre small-town campus **Total enrollment** 10,505 **Student-faculty ratio** 21:1 **Application deadline** 4/1 (freshmen), 4/1 (transfer) **Freshmen** 80% were admitted **Housing** Yes **Expenses** Tuition $5723; Room & Board $8052 **Undergraduates** 53% women, 13% part-time, 18% 25 or older, 2% Native American, 8% Hispanic American, 3% African American, 7% Asian American/

Pacific Islander **The most frequently chosen baccalaureate fields are** business/marketing, education, security and protective services **Academic program** English as a second language, advanced placement, self-designed majors, honors program, summer session, adult/continuing education programs, internships **Contact** Ms. Lisa Garcia-Hanson, Director of Admissions, Central Washington University, 400 East University Way, Ellensburg, WA 98926-7463. Phone: 509-963-1211 or toll-free 866-298-4968. Fax: 509-963-3022. E-mail: cwuadmis@cwu.edu. Web site: http://www.cwu.edu/.

CITY UNIVERSITY OF SEATTLE
BELLEVUE, WASHINGTON

General Independent, comprehensive, coed **Entrance** Noncompetitive **Setting** suburban campus **Total enrollment** 3,107 **Student-faculty ratio** 7:1 **Application deadline** Rolling (freshmen), rolling (transfer) **Housing** No **Expenses** Tuition $13,275 **Undergraduates** 61% women, 44% part-time, 81% 25 or older, 1% Native American, 3% Hispanic American, 3% African American, 5% Asian American/Pacific Islander **The most frequently chosen baccalaureate fields are** business/marketing, computer and information sciences, education **Academic program** English as a second language, advanced placement, accelerated degree program, self-designed majors, summer session, adult/continuing education programs, internships **Contact** Student Services Center, City University of Seattle, 11900 NE First Street, Bellvue, WA 98005. Phone: 588-422-4898 or toll-free 888-42-CITYU. Fax: 425-709-5361. E-mail: info@cityu.edu. Web site: http://www.cityu.edu/.

►**For more information, see page 451.**

CORNISH COLLEGE OF THE ARTS
SEATTLE, WASHINGTON

Contact Ms. Sharron Starling, Associate Director of Admissions, Cornish College of the Arts, 1000 Lenora Street, Seattle, WA 98121. Phone: 206-726-5018 or toll-free 800-726-ARTS. Fax: 206-720-1011. E-mail: admissions@cornish.edu. Web site: http://www.cornish.edu/.

DeVRY UNIVERSITY
BELLEVUE, WASHINGTON

Contact DeVry University, 500 108th Avenue NE, Suite 320, Bellevue, WA 98004-5519. Web site: http://www.devry.edu/.

DeVRY UNIVERSITY
FEDERAL WAY, WASHINGTON

General Proprietary, comprehensive, coed **Entrance** Minimally difficult **Setting** 12-acre suburban campus **Total enrollment** 769 **Student-faculty ratio** 17:1 **Application deadline** Rolling (freshmen), rolling (transfer) **Housing** No **Expenses** Tuition $14,660 **Undergraduates** 27% women, 32% part-time, 48% 25 or older, 1% Native American, 7% Hispanic American, 9% African American, 11% Asian American/Pacific Islander **The most frequently chosen baccalaureate fields are** business/marketing, computer and information sciences, engineering technologies **Academic program** Advanced placement, accelerated degree program, summer session, adult/continuing education programs **Contact** Admissions Department, DeVry University, 3600 South 344th Way, Federal Way, WA 98001. Fax: 253-943-2800. Web site: http://www.devry.edu/.

DIGIPEN INSTITUTE OF TECHNOLOGY
REDMOND, WASHINGTON

General Proprietary, comprehensive, coed **Entrance** Moderately difficult **Setting** 1-acre suburban campus **Total enrollment** 873 **Student-faculty ratio** 14:1 **Application deadline** Rolling (freshmen), rolling (transfer) **Freshmen** 36% were admitted **Housing** Yes **Expenses** Tuition $19,200 **The most frequently chosen baccalaureate field is** computer and information sciences **Academic program** Advanced placement, summer session, internships **Contact** Ms. Angela Kugler, Admissions Director, DigiPen Institute of Technology, 5001 150th Avenue NE, Redmond, WA 98052. Phone: 425-895-4438. Fax: 425-558-0378. E-mail: akugler@digipen.edu. Web site: http://www.digipen.edu/.

EASTERN WASHINGTON UNIVERSITY
CHENEY, WASHINGTON

General State-supported, comprehensive, coed **Contact** Ms. Shannon Carr, Director of Admissions, Eastern Washington University, 526 Fifth Street, SUT 101, Cheney, WA 99004-2447. Phone: 509-359-6582. Fax: 509-359-6692. E-mail: admissions@mail.ewu.edu. Web site: http://www.ewu.edu/.

THE EVERGREEN STATE COLLEGE
OLYMPIA, WASHINGTON

General State-supported, comprehensive, coed **Entrance** Moderately difficult **Setting** 1,000-acre rural campus **Total enrollment** 4,586 **Student-faculty ratio** 23:1 **Application deadline** Rolling (freshmen), rolling (transfer) **Freshmen** 97% were admitted **Housing** Yes **Expenses** Tuition $5127; Room & Board $7842 **Undergraduates** 56% women, 11% part-time, 30% 25 or older, 4% Native American, 5% Hispanic American, 4% African American, 5% Asian American/Pacific Islander **The most**

The Evergreen State College *(continued)*

frequently chosen baccalaureate fields are interdisciplinary studies, liberal arts/general studies **Academic program** Advanced placement, accelerated degree program, self-designed majors, summer session, internships **Contact** Mr. Doug Scrima, Director of Admissions, The Evergreen State College, 2700 Evergreen Parkway NW, Olympia, WA 98505. Phone: 360-867-6170. Fax: 360-867-5114. E-mail: admissions@evergreen.edu. Web site: http://www.evergreen.edu/.

GONZAGA UNIVERSITY
SPOKANE, WASHINGTON

General Independent Roman Catholic, comprehensive, coed **Entrance** Moderately difficult **Setting** 94-acre urban campus **Total enrollment** 6,873 **Student-faculty ratio** 11:1 **Application deadline** 2/1 (freshmen), 6/1 (transfer) **Freshmen** 69% were admitted **Housing** Yes **Expenses** Tuition $28,262; Room & Board $7860 **Undergraduates** 53% women, 3% part-time, 5% 25 or older, 1% Native American, 4% Hispanic American, 1% African American, 5% Asian American/Pacific Islander **The most frequently chosen baccalaureate fields are** business/marketing, communications/journalism, social sciences **Academic program** English as a second language, advanced placement, accelerated degree program, honors program, summer session, adult/continuing education programs, internships **Contact** Ms. Julie McCulloh, Dean of Admission, Gonzaga University, 502 East Boone Avenue, Spokane, WA 99258-0102. Phone: 509-323-6591 or toll-free 800-322-2584 Ext. 6572. Fax: 509-323-5780. E-mail: admissions@gonzaga.edu. Web site: http://www.gonzaga.edu/.

►**For more information, see page 463.**

HERITAGE UNIVERSITY
TOPPENISH, WASHINGTON

Contact Ms. Leticia Garcia, Director of Admissions and Recruitment, Heritage University, 3240 Fort Road, Toppenish, WA 98948-9599. Phone: 509-865-8508 or toll-free 888-272-6190. Fax: 509-865-4469. E-mail: garcia_l@heritage.edu. Web site: http://www.heritage.edu/.

NORTHWEST COLLEGE OF ART
POULSBO, WASHINGTON

General Proprietary, 4-year, coed **Contact** Mr. Mark Stoddard, Admissions, Northwest College of Art, 16464 State Highway 305, Poulsbo, WA 98370. Phone: 360-779-9993 or toll-free 800-769-ARTS. Fax: 360-779-9933. E-mail: mstoddard@nca.edu. Web site: http://www.nca.edu/.

NORTHWEST UNIVERSITY
KIRKLAND, WASHINGTON

General Independent, comprehensive, coed, affiliated with Assemblies of God **Entrance** Moderately difficult **Setting** 56-acre suburban campus **Total enrollment** 1,196 **Student-faculty ratio** 17:1 **Application deadline** 8/1 (freshmen), 8/1 (transfer) **Freshmen** 79% were admitted **Housing** Yes **Expenses** Tuition $20,790; Room & Board $6578 **Undergraduates** 60% women, 6% part-time, 24% 25 or older, 1% Native American, 4% Hispanic American, 3% African American, 6% Asian American/Pacific Islander **The most frequently chosen baccalaureate fields are** business/marketing, health professions and related sciences, theology and religious vocations **Academic program** English as a second language, advanced placement, accelerated degree program, summer session, adult/continuing education programs, internships **Contact** Mr. Ben Thomas, Director of Admissions, Northwest University, PO Box 579, Kirkland, WA 98083-0579. Phone: 425-889-5598 or toll-free 800-669-3781. Fax: 425-889-5224. E-mail: admissions@northwestu.edu. Web site: http://www.northwestu.edu/.

PACIFIC LUTHERAN UNIVERSITY
TACOMA, WASHINGTON

General Independent, comprehensive, coed, affiliated with Evangelical Lutheran Church in America **Entrance** Moderately difficult **Setting** 126-acre suburban campus **Total enrollment** 3,661 **Student-faculty ratio** 14:1 **Application deadline** Rolling (freshmen), rolling (transfer) **Freshmen** 76% were admitted **Housing** Yes **Expenses** Tuition $25,088; Room & Board $7712 **Undergraduates** 63% women, 7% part-time, 10% 25 or older, 1% Native American, 2% Hispanic American, 2% African American, 7% Asian American/Pacific Islander **The most frequently chosen baccalaureate fields are** business/marketing, health professions and related sciences, social sciences **Academic program** English as a second language, advanced placement, self-designed majors, summer session, adult/continuing education programs, internships **Contact** Dr. Laura Majovski, Vice President for Admissions and Student Life, Pacific Lutheran University, Tacoma, WA 98447. Phone: 253-535-7151 or toll-free 800-274-6758. Fax: 253-536-5136. E-mail: admission@plu.edu. Web site: http://www.plu.edu/.

SAINT MARTIN'S UNIVERSITY
LACEY, WASHINGTON

General Independent Roman Catholic, comprehensive, coed **Entrance** Moderately difficult **Setting** 300-acre suburban campus **Total enroll-**

ment 1,605 **Student-faculty ratio** 11:1 **Application deadline** 8/1 (transfer) **Freshmen** 93% were admitted **Housing** Yes **Expenses** Tuition $23,810; Room & Board $8040 **Undergraduates** 54% women, 19% part-time, 37% 25 or older, 2% Native American, 6% Hispanic American, 7% African American, 10% Asian American/Pacific Islander **The most frequently chosen baccalaureate fields are** business/marketing, engineering, psychology **Academic program** English as a second language, advanced placement, accelerated degree program, summer session, adult/continuing education programs, internships **Contact** Mr. Eric Pedersen, Dean of Enrollment, Saint Martin's University, 5300 Pacific Avenue, SE, Lacey, WA 98503-1297. Phone: 360-438-4590 or toll-free 800-368-8803. Fax: 360-412-6189. E-mail: admissions@stmartin.edu. Web site: http://www.stmartin.edu/.

SEATTLE PACIFIC UNIVERSITY
SEATTLE, WASHINGTON

General Independent Free Methodist, comprehensive, coed **Entrance** Moderately difficult **Setting** 35-acre urban campus **Total enrollment** 3,842 **Student-faculty ratio** 14:1 **Application deadline** 2/1 (freshmen), 8/1 (transfer) **Freshmen** 85% were admitted **Housing** Yes **Expenses** Tuition $25,128; Room & Board $8082 **Undergraduates** 67% women, 5% part-time, 6% 25 or older, 1% Native American, 3% Hispanic American, 2% African American, 7% Asian American/Pacific Islander **The most frequently chosen baccalaureate fields are** business/marketing, family and consumer sciences, social sciences **Academic program** English as a second language, advanced placement, self-designed majors, honors program, summer session, adult/continuing education programs, internships **Contact** Mr. Jobe Nice, Acting Director of Admissions, Seattle Pacific University, 3307 3rd Avenue, W, Seattle, WA 98119-1997. Phone: 206-281-2517 or toll-free 800-366-3344. Fax: 206-281-2669. E-mail: admissions@spu.edu. Web site: http://www.spu.edu/.

►**For more information, see page 490.**

SEATTLE UNIVERSITY
SEATTLE, WASHINGTON

General Independent Roman Catholic, comprehensive, coed **Entrance** Moderately difficult **Setting** 46-acre urban campus **Total enrollment** 7,529 **Student-faculty ratio** 13:1 **Application deadline** Rolling (freshmen), 8/15 (transfer) **Freshmen** 64% were admitted **Housing** Yes **Expenses** Tuition $28,260; Room & Board $8340 **Undergraduates** 61% women, 7% part-time, 12% 25 or older, 1% Native American, 7% Hispanic American, 5% African American, 20% Asian American/Pacific Islander **The most frequently chosen baccalaureate fields are** business/marketing, health professions and related sciences, social sciences **Academic program** English as a second language, advanced placement, accelerated degree program, self-designed majors, honors program, summer session, adult/continuing education programs, internships **Contact** Mr. Michael K. McKeon, Dean of Admissions, Seattle University, 902 12th Avenue, PO Box 222000, Seattle, WA 98122-1090. Phone: 206-296-2000 or toll-free 800-542-0833 (in-state); 800-426-7123 (out-of-state). Fax: 206-296-5656. E-mail: admissions@seattleu.edu. Web site: http://www.seattleu.edu/.

TRINITY LUTHERAN COLLEGE
ISSAQUAH, WASHINGTON

General Independent Lutheran, 4-year, coed **Entrance** Minimally difficult **Setting** 46-acre suburban campus **Total enrollment** 115 **Application deadline** 9/15 (freshmen), 9/15 (transfer) **Freshmen** 51% were admitted **Housing** Yes **Expenses** Tuition $14,170; Room & Board $6078 **Undergraduates** 22% 25 or older **Academic program** English as a second language, advanced placement, internships **Contact** Mr. Sean Lacy, Director of Admissions, Trinity Lutheran College, 4221 228th Avenue, SE, Issaquah, WA 98029-9299. Phone: 425-961-5512 or toll-free 800-843-5659. Fax: 425-392-0404. E-mail: admission@tlc.edu. Web site: http://www.tlc.edu/.

UNIVERSITY OF PHOENIX–EASTERN WASHINGTON CAMPUS
SPOKANE VALLEY, WASHINGTON

General Proprietary, comprehensive, coed **Contact** Ms. Evelyn Gaskin, Registrar/Executive Director, University of Phoenix–Eastern Washington Campus, 4615 East Elwood Street, Mail Stop AA-K101, Phoenix, AZ 85040-1958. Phone: 480-557-3301 or toll-free 800-697-8223 (in-state); 800-228-7240 (out-of-state). Fax: 480-643-1020. E-mail: evelyn.gaskin@phoenix.edu. Web site: http://www.phoenix.edu/.

UNIVERSITY OF PHOENIX–WASHINGTON CAMPUS
SEATTLE, WASHINGTON

General Proprietary, comprehensive, coed **Contact** Ms. Evelyn Gaskin, Registrar/Executive Director, University of Phoenix–Washington Campus, 4615 East Elwood Street, Mail Stop AA-K101, Phoenix, AZ 85040-1958. Phone: 480-557-3301 or toll-free 800-776-4867 (in-state); 800-228-7240 (out-of-state). Fax: 480-643-1020.

University of Phoenix–Washington Campus *(continued)*

E-mail: evelyn.gaskin.phoenix.edu. Web site: http://www.phoenix.edu/.

UNIVERSITY OF PUGET SOUND

TACOMA, WASHINGTON

General Independent, comprehensive, coed **Entrance** Moderately difficult **Setting** 97-acre suburban campus **Total enrollment** 2,799 **Student-faculty ratio** 11:1 **Application deadline** 2/1 (freshmen), 7/1 (transfer) **Freshmen** 66% were admitted **Housing** Yes **Expenses** Tuition $31,895; Room & Board $8265 **Undergraduates** 59% women, 2% part-time, 2% 25 or older, 1% Native American, 4% Hispanic American, 3% African American, 9% Asian American/Pacific Islander **The most frequently chosen baccalaureate fields are** business/marketing, social sciences, visual and performing arts **Academic program** Advanced placement, self-designed majors, honors program, summer session, internships **Contact** Dr. George Mills, Vice President for Enrollment, University of Puget Sound, 1500 North Warner Street, Tacoma, WA 98416-1062. Phone: 253-879-3211 or toll-free 800-396-7191. Fax: 253-879-3993. E-mail: admission@ups.edu. Web site: http://www.ups.edu/.

UNIVERSITY OF WASHINGTON

SEATTLE, WASHINGTON

General State-supported, comprehensive, coed **Entrance** Moderately difficult **Setting** 703-acre urban campus **Total enrollment** 40,218 **Student-faculty ratio** 12:1 **Application deadline** 1/15 (freshmen), 2/15 (transfer) **Freshmen** 65% were admitted **Housing** Yes **Expenses** Tuition $6385; Room & Board $8337 **Undergraduates** 52% women, 15% part-time, 10% 25 or older, 1% Native American, 5% Hispanic American, 3% African American, 26% Asian American/Pacific Islander **The most frequently chosen baccalaureate fields are** biological/life sciences, business/marketing, social sciences **Academic program** English as a second language, advanced placement, accelerated degree program, self-designed majors, honors program, summer session, adult/continuing education programs, internships **Contact** Admissions Office, University of Washington, Seattle, WA 98195. Phone: 206-543-9686. Fax: 206-685-3655. Web site: http://www.washington.edu/.

UNIVERSITY OF WASHINGTON, BOTHELL

BOTHELL, WASHINGTON

General State-supported, upper-level, coed **Entrance** Moderately difficult **Setting** 128-acre suburban campus **Total enrollment** 1,871 **Student-faculty ratio** 14:1 **Application deadline** 1/15 (freshmen) **First-year students** 72% were admitted **Housing** No **Expenses** Tuition $6247 **Undergraduates** 57% women, 37% part-time, 49% 25 or older, 1% Native American, 5% Hispanic American, 3% African American, 17% Asian American/Pacific Islander **The most frequently chosen baccalaureate fields are** business/marketing, health professions and related sciences, interdisciplinary studies **Academic program** Advanced placement, honors program, summer session, adult/continuing education programs, internships **Contact** Lindsey Kattenhorn, Assistant Director of Admissions, University of Washington, Bothell, 18115 Campus Way NE, Bothell, WA 98011-8246. Phone: 425-352-5317. Fax: 425-352-5455. E-mail: freshmen@uwb.edu. Web site: http://www.uwb.edu.

UNIVERSITY OF WASHINGTON, TACOMA

TACOMA, WASHINGTON

General State-supported, upper-level, coed **Entrance** Minimally difficult **Setting** 46-acre urban campus **Total enrollment** 2,653 **Student-faculty ratio** 15:1 **Application deadline** 3/1 (freshmen) **First-year students** 82% were admitted **Housing** No **Undergraduates** 59% women, 31% part-time, 44% 25 or older, 1% Native American, 6% Hispanic American, 6% African American, 16% Asian American/Pacific Islander **The most frequently chosen baccalaureate fields are** business/marketing, health professions and related sciences, interdisciplinary studies **Academic program** Advanced placement, accelerated degree program, honors program, summer session, adult/continuing education programs, internships **Contact** Fiona Johnson, Admissions Advising and Outreach, University of Washington, Tacoma, 1900 Commerce Street, Tacoma, WA 98402-3100. Phone: 253-692-4400 or toll-free 800-736-7750. Fax: 253-692-4788. E-mail: bobbe@u.washington.edu. Web site: http://www.tacoma.washington.edu/.

WALLA WALLA UNIVERSITY

COLLEGE PLACE, WASHINGTON

General Independent Seventh-day Adventist, comprehensive, coed **Entrance** Moderately difficult **Setting** 77-acre small-town campus **Total enrollment** 1,829 **Student-faculty ratio** 8:1 **Application deadline** Rolling (freshmen), rolling (transfer) **Freshmen** 93% were admitted **Housing** Yes **Expenses** Tuition $21,945; Room & Board $5055 **Undergraduates** 48% women, 7% part-time, 10% 25 or older, 1% Native American, 9% Hispanic American, 4% African American, 6% Asian American/Pacific Islander **Academic program** English as a second language, advanced placement, honors program, summer session, internships **Contact** Mr. Dallas Weis, Interim Vice President for Admissions and Marketing, Walla Walla University, 204 South College Avenue, College Place, WA 99324. Phone: 509-527-2327 or toll-free 800-541-8900. Fax: 509-527-2397. E-mail: info@wallawalla.edu. Web site: http://www.wallawalla.edu/.

WASHINGTON STATE UNIVERSITY
PULLMAN, WASHINGTON

General State-supported, university, coed **Entrance** Moderately difficult **Setting** 620-acre rural campus **Total enrollment** 24,396 **Student-faculty ratio** 14:1 **Freshmen** 76% were admitted **Housing** Yes **Expenses** Tuition $6866; Room & Board $7316 **Undergraduates** 52% women, 15% part-time, 8% 25 or older, 1% Native American, 5% Hispanic American, 2% African American, 6% Asian American/Pacific Islander **The most frequently chosen baccalaureate fields are** business/marketing, communications/journalism, social sciences **Academic program** English as a second language, advanced placement, accelerated degree program, self-designed majors, honors program, summer session, internships **Contact** Ms. Wendy Peterson, Director of Admissions, Washington State University, PO Box 641067, Pullman, WA 99164-1067. Phone: 509-335-5586 or toll-free 888-468-6978. Fax: 509-335-4902. E-mail: admiss2@wsu.edu. Web site: http://www.wsu.edu/.

WESTERN WASHINGTON UNIVERSITY
BELLINGHAM, WASHINGTON

General State-supported, comprehensive, coed **Entrance** Moderately difficult **Setting** 223-acre small-town campus **Total enrollment** 14,276 **Student-faculty ratio** 19:1 **Application deadline** 3/1 (freshmen), 4/1 (transfer) **Freshmen** 73% were admitted **Housing** Yes **Expenses** Tuition $5291; Room & Board $7090 **Undergraduates** 55% women, 8% part-time, 10% 25 or older, 2% Native American, 4% Hispanic American, 3% African American, 9% Asian American/Pacific Islander **The most frequently chosen baccalaureate fields are** business/marketing, English, social sciences **Academic program** English as a second language, advanced placement, accelerated degree program, self-designed majors, honors program, summer session, internships **Contact** Ms. Karen Copetas, Director of Admissions, Western Washington University, 516 High Street, Bellingham, WA 98225-9009. Phone: 360-650-3440. Fax: 360-650-7369. E-mail: admit@wwu.edu. Web site: http://www.wwu.edu/.

WHITMAN COLLEGE
WALLA WALLA, WASHINGTON

General Independent, 4-year, coed **Entrance** Very difficult **Setting** 117-acre small-town campus **Total enrollment** 1,489 **Student-faculty ratio** 10:1 **Application deadline** 1/15 (freshmen), 3/1 (transfer) **Freshmen** 49% were admitted **Housing** Yes **Expenses** Tuition $32,980; Room & Board $8310 **Undergraduates** 56% women, 2% part-time, 1% 25 or older, 1% Native American, 5% Hispanic American, 2% African American, 10% Asian American/Pacific Islander **The most frequently chosen baccalaureate fields are** biological/life sciences, social sciences, visual and performing arts **Academic program** Advanced placement, accelerated degree program, self-designed majors, honors program **Contact** Mr. Tony Cabasco, Dean of Admission and Financial Aid, Whitman College, 515 Boyer Avenue, Walla Walla, WA 99362-2083. Phone: 509-527-5176 or toll-free 877-462-9448. Fax: 509-527-4967. E-mail: admission@whitman.edu. Web site: http://www.whitman.edu/.

WHITWORTH UNIVERSITY
SPOKANE, WASHINGTON

General Independent Presbyterian, comprehensive, coed **Entrance** Very difficult **Setting** 200-acre suburban campus **Total enrollment** 2,607 **Student-faculty ratio** 13:1 **Application deadline** 3/1 (freshmen), 7/1 (transfer) **Freshmen** 49% were admitted **Housing** Yes **Expenses** Tuition $25,692; Room & Board $7294 **Undergraduates** 59% women, 12% part-time, 2% 25 or older, 1% Native American, 3% Hispanic American, 2% African American, 3% Asian American/Pacific Islander **The most frequently chosen baccalaureate fields are** business/marketing, education, social sciences **Academic program** English as a second language, advanced placement, self-designed majors, summer session, adult/continuing education programs, internships **Contact** Ms. Marianne Hansen, Director of Admission, Whitworth University, 300 West, Hawthorne Road, Spokane, WA 99251. Phone: 509-777-4348 or toll-free 800-533-4668. Fax: 509-777-3758. E-mail: admission@whitworth.edu. Web site: http://www.whitworth.edu/.

WEST VIRGINIA

ALDERSON-BROADDUS COLLEGE
PHILIPPI, WEST VIRGINIA

General Independent, comprehensive, coed, affiliated with American Baptist Churches in the U.S.A.

Alderson-Broaddus College *(continued)*

Entrance Moderately difficult **Setting** 170-acre rural campus **Total enrollment** 751 **Student-faculty ratio** 10:1 **Application deadline** Rolling (freshmen), rolling (transfer) **Freshmen** 70% were admitted **Housing** Yes **Expenses** Tuition $20,030; Room & Board $6470 **Undergraduates** 67% women, 7% part-time, 14% 25 or older, 0.2% Native American, 1% Hispanic American, 5% African American, 2% Asian American/Pacific Islander **The most frequently chosen baccalaureate fields are** business/marketing, education, health professions and related sciences **Academic program** Advanced placement, accelerated degree program, honors program, summer session, internships **Contact** Ms. Kimberly N. Klaus, Director of Admissions, Alderson-Broaddus College, PO Box 2003, College Hill, Philippi, WV 26416. Phone: 304-457-1700 or toll-free 800-263-1549. Fax: 304-457-6239. E-mail: admissions@ab.edu. Web site: http://www.ab.edu/.

AMERICAN PUBLIC UNIVERSITY SYSTEM
CHARLES TOWN, WEST VIRGINIA

General Proprietary, comprehensive, coed **Entrance** Noncompetitive **Total enrollment** 14,694 **Student-faculty ratio** 16:1 **Application deadline** Rolling (freshmen), rolling (transfer) **Freshmen** 49% were admitted **Housing** No **Expenses** Tuition $6000 **Undergraduates** 23% women, 92% part-time, 79% 25 or older, 1% Native American, 8% Hispanic American, 12% African American, 2% Asian American/Pacific Islander **The most frequently chosen baccalaureate fields are** business/marketing, military science and technologies, security and protective services **Academic program** Adult/continuing education programs **Contact** Student Advisor, American Public University System, 322-C West Washington Street, Charles Town, WV 25414. Phone: 877-468-6268 Option 2 or toll-free 877-468-6268. Fax: 304-724-3788. E-mail: admissions@apus.edu. Web site: http://www.apus.edu/.

APPALACHIAN BIBLE COLLEGE
BRADLEY, WEST VIRGINIA

General Independent nondenominational, 4-year, coed **Entrance** Noncompetitive **Setting** 110-acre small-town campus **Total enrollment** 273 **Student-faculty ratio** 17:1 **Application deadline** Rolling (freshmen), rolling (transfer) **Freshmen** 62% were admitted **Housing** Yes **Expenses** Tuition $9270; Room & Board $4920 **Undergraduates** 47% women, 19% part-time **The most frequently chosen baccalaureate field is** theology and religious vocations **Academic program** Advanced placement, honors program, summer session, adult/continuing education programs, internships **Contact** Miss Ashley Siders, Admissions Assistant, Appalachian Bible College, PO Box ABC, Bradley, WV 25818. Phone: 304-877-6428 Ext. 3202 or toll-free 800-678-9ABC Ext. 3213. Fax: 304-877-5082. E-mail: admissions2@abc.edu. Web site: http://www.abc.edu/.

BETHANY COLLEGE
BETHANY, WEST VIRGINIA

General Independent, 4-year, coed, affiliated with Christian Church (Disciples of Christ) **Entrance** Moderately difficult **Setting** 1,600-acre rural campus **Total enrollment** 815 **Student-faculty ratio** 14:1 **Application deadline** Rolling (freshmen), rolling (transfer) **Freshmen** 60% were admitted **Housing** Yes **Expenses** Tuition $18,205; Room & Board $7770 **Undergraduates** 54% women, 1% part-time, 2% 25 or older, 1% Native American, 1% Hispanic American, 4% African American, 1% Asian American/Pacific Islander **The most frequently chosen baccalaureate fields are** communications/journalism, education, psychology **Academic program** Advanced placement, self-designed majors, internships **Contact** Mr. Kevin Wilson, Director of Admission, Bethany College, Office of Admission, Bethany, WV 26032. Phone: 304-829-7611 or toll-free 800-922-7611. Fax: 304-829-7142. E-mail: admission@bethanywv.edu. Web site: http://www.bethanywv.edu/.

BLUEFIELD STATE COLLEGE
BLUEFIELD, WEST VIRGINIA

General State-supported, 4-year, coed **Entrance** Noncompetitive **Setting** 45-acre small-town campus **Total enrollment** 1,804 **Student-faculty ratio** 14:1 **Application deadline** Rolling (freshmen), rolling (transfer) **Freshmen** 91% were admitted **Housing** No **Expenses** Tuition $3984 **Undergraduates** 59% women, 19% part-time, 43% 25 or older, 0.3% Native American, 0.4% Hispanic American, 12% African American, 1% Asian American/Pacific Islander **Academic program** Advanced placement, self-designed majors, honors program, summer session, adult/continuing education programs, internships **Contact** Mr. Kenneth Mandeville, Director of Student Recruitment, Bluefield State College, 219 Rock Street, Bluefield, WV 24701-2198. Phone: 304-327-4567 or toll-free 800-344-8892 Ext. 4065 (in-state); 800-654-7798 Ext. 4065 (out-of-state). Fax: 304-325-7747. E-mail: bscadmit@bluefieldstate.edu. Web site: http://www.bluefieldstate.edu/.

CONCORD UNIVERSITY
ATHENS, WEST VIRGINIA

General State-supported, 4-year, coed **Entrance** Minimally difficult **Setting** 100-acre rural campus

Total enrollment 2,752 **Student-faculty ratio** 20:1 **Application deadline** Rolling (freshmen), rolling (transfer) **Freshmen** 69% were admitted **Housing** Yes **Expenses** Tuition $4414; Room & Board $6280 **Undergraduates** 59% women, 18% part-time, 18% 25 or older, 0.1% Native American, 1% Hispanic American, 6% African American, 1% Asian American/Pacific Islander **The most frequently chosen baccalaureate fields are** business/marketing, education, liberal arts/general studies **Academic program** English as a second language, advanced placement, accelerated degree program, self-designed majors, honors program, summer session, internships **Contact** Mr. Michael Curry, Vice President of Admissions and Financial Aid, Concord University, 1000 Vermillion Street, Athens, WV 24712. Phone: 304-384-5248 or toll-free 888-384-5249. Fax: 304-384-9044. E-mail: admissions@concord.edu. Web site: http://www.concord.edu/.

DAVIS & ELKINS COLLEGE
ELKINS, WEST VIRGINIA

General Independent Presbyterian, 4-year, coed **Entrance** Moderately difficult **Setting** 170-acre small-town campus **Total enrollment** 640 **Student-faculty ratio** 10:1 **Application deadline** Rolling (freshmen), rolling (transfer) **Freshmen** 75% were admitted **Housing** Yes **Expenses** Tuition $18,746; Room & Board $6350 **Undergraduates** 65% women, 11% part-time, 24% 25 or older, 1% Native American, 2% Hispanic American, 4% African American, 1% Asian American/Pacific Islander **The most frequently chosen baccalaureate fields are** business/marketing, education, parks and recreation **Academic program** English as a second language, advanced placement, accelerated degree program, self-designed majors, honors program, summer session, adult/continuing education programs, internships **Contact** Ms. Reneé Heckel, Director of Enrollment Management, Davis & Elkins College, 100 Campus Drive, Elkins, WV 26241. Phone: 304-637-1974 or toll-free 800-624-3157 Ext. 1230. Fax: 304-637-1800. E-mail: admiss@davisandelkins.edu. Web site: http://www.davisandelkins.edu/.

FAIRMONT STATE UNIVERSITY
FAIRMONT, WEST VIRGINIA

General State-supported, comprehensive, coed **Entrance** Minimally difficult **Setting** 80-acre small-town campus **Total enrollment** 7,320 **Student-faculty ratio** 18:1 **Application deadline** 6/15 (freshmen), 6/15 (transfer) **Freshmen** 79% were admitted **Housing** Yes **Expenses** Tuition $4856; Room & Board $5990 **Undergraduates** 57% women, 26% part-time, 30% 25 or older, 0.3% Native American, 1% Hispanic American, 4% African American, 1% Asian American/Pacific Islander **The most frequently chosen baccalaureate fields are** business/marketing, education, engineering technologies **Academic program** English as a second language, advanced placement, accelerated degree program, honors program, summer session, adult/continuing education programs, internships **Contact** Mr. Steve Leadman, Director of Admissions and Recruiting, Fairmont State University, 1201 Locust Avenue, Fairmont, WV 26554. Phone: 304-367-4892 or toll-free 800-641-5678. Fax: 304-367-4789. E-mail: admit@fairmontstate.edu. Web site: http://www.fairmontstate.edu/.

GLENVILLE STATE COLLEGE
GLENVILLE, WEST VIRGINIA

General State-supported, 4-year, coed **Entrance** Noncompetitive **Setting** 331-acre rural campus **Total enrollment** 1,441 **Student-faculty ratio** 19:1 **Application deadline** Rolling (freshmen), 8/27 (transfer) **Freshmen** 100% were admitted **Housing** Yes **Expenses** Tuition $4174; Room & Board $5800 **Undergraduates** 49% women, 25% part-time, 19% 25 or older, 0.3% Native American, 1% Hispanic American, 13% African American, 0.3% Asian American/Pacific Islander **The most frequently chosen baccalaureate fields are** business/marketing, education, social sciences **Academic program** English as a second language, advanced placement, accelerated degree program, self-designed majors, summer session, adult/continuing education programs, internships **Contact** Lucinda Patrick, Glenville State College, 200 High Street, Glenville, WV 26351-1200. Phone: 304-462-4128 or toll-free 800-924-2010. Fax: 304-462-8619. E-mail: admissions@glenville.edu. Web site: http://www.glenville.edu/.

MARSHALL UNIVERSITY
HUNTINGTON, WEST VIRGINIA

General State-supported, university, coed **Entrance** Moderately difficult **Setting** 70-acre urban campus **Total enrollment** 13,808 **Student-faculty ratio** 20:1 **Application deadline** Rolling (freshmen), rolling (transfer) **Freshmen** 86% were admitted **Housing** Yes **Expenses** Tuition $4560; Room & Board $6818 **Undergraduates** 56% women, 18% part-time, 20% 25 or older, 0.4% Native American, 1% Hispanic American, 5% African American, 1% Asian American/Pacific Islander **The most frequently chosen baccalaureate fields are** business/marketing, education, liberal arts/general studies **Academic program** English as a second language, advanced placement, accelerated degree program, honors program, summer session, adult/continuing education programs, internships **Contact** Dr. Tammy

Marshall University *(continued)*

Johnson, Director of Admissions, Marshall University, 1 John Marshall Drive, Huntington, WV 25755. Phone: 304-696-3160 or toll-free 800-642-3499. Fax: 304-696-3135. E-mail: admissions@marshall.edu. Web site: http://www.marshall.edu/.

MOUNTAIN STATE UNIVERSITY

BECKLEY, WEST VIRGINIA

General Independent, comprehensive, coed **Entrance** Noncompetitive **Setting** 24-acre small-town campus **Total enrollment** 4,847 **Student-faculty ratio** 22:1 **Application deadline** Rolling (freshmen), rolling (transfer) **Freshmen** 100% were admitted **Housing** Yes **Expenses** Tuition $8100; Room & Board $5854 **Undergraduates** 64% women, 27% part-time, 63% 25 or older, 1% Native American, 2% Hispanic American, 8% African American, 3% Asian American/Pacific Islander **The most frequently chosen baccalaureate fields are** business/marketing, health professions and related sciences, security and protective services **Academic program** English as a second language, advanced placement, accelerated degree program, self-designed majors, summer session, adult/continuing education programs, internships **Contact** Ms. Darlene Brown, Administrative Assistant for Recruiting Services, Mountain State University, PO Box 9003, Beckley, WV 25802-9003. Phone: 304-929-1668 or toll-free 800-766-6067 Ext. 1433. Fax: 304-253-5072. E-mail: gomsu@mountainstate.edu. Web site: http://www.mountainstate.edu/.

OHIO VALLEY UNIVERSITY

VIENNA, WEST VIRGINIA

General Independent, 4-year, coed, affiliated with Church of Christ **Entrance** Minimally difficult **Setting** 299-acre small-town campus **Total enrollment** 546 **Student-faculty ratio** 12:1 **Application deadline** 8/15 (freshmen), rolling (transfer) **Freshmen** 56% were admitted **Housing** Yes **Expenses** Tuition $13,510; Room & Board $6140 **Undergraduates** 54% women, 7% part-time, 23% 25 or older, 0.4% Native American, 3% Hispanic American, 6% African American, 0.2% Asian American/Pacific Islander **The most frequently chosen baccalaureate fields are** business/marketing, education, interdisciplinary studies **Academic program** English as a second language, advanced placement, honors program, summer session, adult/continuing education programs, internships **Contact** Mrs. Valerie Wright, Admissions Office Manager, Ohio Valley University, 1 Campus View Drive, Vienna, WV 26105. Phone: 304-865-6203 or toll-free 877-446-8668 Ext. 6200. Fax: 304-865-6001. E-mail: admissions@ovu.edu. Web site: http://www.ovu.edu/.

SALEM INTERNATIONAL UNIVERSITY

SALEM, WEST VIRGINIA

General Independent, comprehensive, coed **Entrance** Minimally difficult **Setting** 300-acre rural campus **Student-faculty ratio** 13:1 **Application deadline** Rolling (freshmen), rolling (transfer) **Housing** Yes **Expenses** Tuition $12,750 **Undergraduates** 30% 25 or older **The most frequently chosen baccalaureate fields are** business/marketing, computer and information sciences, education **Academic program** English as a second language, advanced placement, accelerated degree program, internships **Contact** Ms. Gina Cossey, Vice President, Recruiting and Admissions, Salem International University, PO Box 500, Salem, WV 26426-0500. Phone: 304-326-1359 or toll-free 800-283-4562. Fax: 304-326-1592. E-mail: admissions@salemiu.edu. Web site: http://www.salemu.edu/.

SHEPHERD UNIVERSITY

SHEPHERDSTOWN, WEST VIRGINIA

General State-supported, comprehensive, coed **Entrance** Moderately difficult **Setting** 320-acre small-town campus **Total enrollment** 4,119 **Student-faculty ratio** 19:1 **Application deadline** Rolling (freshmen), rolling (transfer) **Freshmen** 88% were admitted **Housing** Yes **Expenses** Tuition $4564; Room & Board $6714 **Undergraduates** 58% women, 21% part-time, 19% 25 or older, 0.3% Native American, 3% Hispanic American, 6% African American, 1% Asian American/Pacific Islander **The most frequently chosen baccalaureate fields are** business/marketing, education, liberal arts/general studies **Academic program** Advanced placement, accelerated degree program, honors program, summer session, adult/continuing education programs, internships **Contact** Mr. Randall Friend, Acting Director of Admissions, Shepherd University, PO Box 3210, Shepherdstown, WV 25443-3210. Phone: 304-876-5212 or toll-free 800-344-5231. Fax: 304-876-5165. E-mail: admissions@shepherd.edu. Web site: http://www.shepherd.edu/.

UNIVERSITY OF CHARLESTON

CHARLESTON, WEST VIRGINIA

General Independent, comprehensive, coed **Entrance** Moderately difficult **Setting** 40-acre urban campus **Total enrollment** 1,398 **Student-faculty ratio** 13:1 **Application deadline** Rolling (freshmen), rolling (transfer) **Freshmen** 67% were admitted **Housing** Yes **Expenses** Tuition $22,050; Room & Board $7930 **Undergraduates** 60% women, 7% part-time, 13% 25 or older, 0.2% Native American, 1% Hispanic American, 5% African American, 1% Asian American/Pacific

Islander **The most frequently chosen baccalaureate fields are** business/marketing, health professions and related sciences, visual and performing arts **Academic program** English as a second language, advanced placement, accelerated degree program, self-designed majors, summer session, adult/continuing education programs, internships **Contact** Mr. Brad Parrish, Vice President for Enrollment, University of Charleston, 2300 MacCorkle Avenue, SE, Charleston, WV 25304. Phone: 304-357-4750 or toll-free 800-995-GOUC. Fax: 304-357-4781. E-mail: admissions@ucwv.edu. Web site: http://www.ucwv.edu/.

WEST LIBERTY STATE COLLEGE
WEST LIBERTY, WEST VIRGINIA

General State-supported, 4-year, coed **Entrance** Minimally difficult **Setting** 290-acre rural campus **Total enrollment** 2,405 **Student-faculty ratio** 18:1 **Freshmen** 83% were admitted **Housing** Yes **Expenses** Tuition $4312; Room & Board $5984 **Undergraduates** 57% women, 14% part-time, 11% 25 or older, 0.3% Native American, 1% Hispanic American, 4% African American, 0.5% Asian American/Pacific Islander **The most frequently chosen baccalaureate fields are** business/marketing, education, liberal arts/general studies **Academic program** Advanced placement, accelerated degree program, self-designed majors, honors program, summer session, adult/continuing education programs, internships **Contact** Ms. Stephanie North, Admissions Counselor, West Liberty State College, PO Box 295, West Liberty, WV 26074. Phone: 304-336-8078 or toll-free 800-732-6204 Ext. 8076. Fax: 304-336-8403. E-mail: wladmsn1@westliberty.edu. Web site: http://www.westliberty.edu/.

WEST VIRGINIA STATE UNIVERSITY
INSTITUTE, WEST VIRGINIA

General State-supported, comprehensive, coed **Contact** Ms. Trina Sweeney, Admission Assistant, West Virginia State University, Campus Box 197, PO Box 1000, Ferrell Hall, Room 106, Institute, WV 25112-1000. Phone: 304-766-3221 Ext. 3033 or toll-free 800-987-2112. Fax: 304-766-4158. E-mail: sweeneyt@wvstateu.edu. Web site: http://www.wvstateu.edu/.

WEST VIRGINIA UNIVERSITY
MORGANTOWN, WEST VIRGINIA

General State-supported, university, coed **Entrance** Moderately difficult **Setting** 913-acre small-town campus **Total enrollment** 28,113 **Student-faculty ratio** 23:1 **Application deadline** 8/1 (freshmen), 8/1 (transfer) **Freshmen** 89% were admitted **Housing** Yes **Expenses** Tuition $4722; Room & Board $7046 **Undergraduates** 46% women, 7% part-time, 7% 25 or older, 0.4% Native American, 2% Hispanic American, 3% African American, 2% Asian American/Pacific Islander **The most frequently chosen baccalaureate fields are** business/marketing, communications/journalism, engineering **Academic program** English as a second language, advanced placement, accelerated degree program, self-designed majors, honors program, summer session, adult/continuing education programs, internships **Contact** Ms. Kim Guynn, Admissions Supervisor, West Virginia University, PO Box 6009, Morgantown, WV 26506-6009. Phone: 304-293-2121 Ext. 1511 or toll-free 800-344-9881. Fax: 304-293-3080. E-mail: go2wvu@mail.wvu.edu. Web site: http://www.wvu.edu/.

WEST VIRGINIA UNIVERSITY INSTITUTE OF TECHNOLOGY
MONTGOMERY, WEST VIRGINIA

Contact Ms. Lisa Graham, Director of Admissions, West Virginia University Institute of Technology, 405 Fayette Pike, Montgomery, WV 25136. Phone: 304-442-3167 or toll-free 888-554-8324. Fax: 304-442-3097. E-mail: wvutech@wvit.wvnet.edu. Web site: http://www.wvutech.edu/.

WEST VIRGINIA WESLEYAN COLLEGE
BUCKHANNON, WEST VIRGINIA

General Independent, comprehensive, coed, affiliated with United Methodist Church **Entrance** Moderately difficult **Setting** 80-acre small-town campus **Total enrollment** 1,276 **Student-faculty ratio** 13:1 **Freshmen** 77% were admitted **Housing** Yes **Expenses** Tuition $20,980; Room & Board $6160 **Undergraduates** 54% women, 3% part-time, 4% 25 or older, 0.1% Native American, 1% Hispanic American, 3% African American, 0.5% Asian American/Pacific Islander **The most frequently chosen baccalaureate fields are** business/marketing, education, social sciences **Academic program** English as a second language, advanced placement, self-designed majors, honors program, summer session, adult/continuing education programs, internships **Contact** Director of Admission, West Virginia Wesleyan College, 59 College Avenue, Buckhannon, WV 26201. Phone: 304-473-8510 or toll-free 800-722-9933. Fax: 304-473-8108. E-mail: admissions@wvwc.edu. Web site: http://www.wvwc.edu/.

WHEELING JESUIT UNIVERSITY
WHEELING, WEST VIRGINIA

General Independent Roman Catholic (Jesuit), comprehensive, coed **Entrance** Moderately difficult **Setting** 65-acre suburban campus **Total**

Wheeling Jesuit University *(continued)*

enrollment 1,420 **Student-faculty ratio** 12:1 **Application deadline** Rolling (freshmen), rolling (transfer) **Freshmen** 69% were admitted **Housing** Yes **Expenses** Tuition $24,390; Room & Board $8640 **Undergraduates** 62% women, 20% part-time, 17% 25 or older, 0.2% Native American, 1% Hispanic American, 2% African American, 1% Asian American/Pacific Islander **The most frequently chosen baccalaureate fields are** business/marketing, health professions and related sciences, liberal arts/general studies **Academic program** English as a second language, advanced placement, accelerated degree program, self-designed majors, honors program, summer session, adult/continuing education programs, internships **Contact** Mr. Denny Bardos, Dean of Enrollment, Wheeling Jesuit University, 316 Washington Avenue, Wheeling, WV 26003-6295. Phone: 304-243-2359 or toll-free 800-624-6992 Ext. 2359. Fax: 304-243-2397. E-mail: admiss@wju.edu. Web site: http://www.wju.edu/.

WISCONSIN

ALVERNO COLLEGE
MILWAUKEE, WISCONSIN

General Independent Roman Catholic, comprehensive, undergraduate: women only; graduate: coed **Contact** Ms. Mary Kay Farrell, Director of Admissions, Alverno College, 3400 South 43 Street, PO Box 343922, Milwaukee, WI 53234-3922. Phone: 414-382-6031 or toll-free 800-933-3401. Fax: 414-382-6354. E-mail: admissions@alverno.edu. Web site: http://www.alverno.edu/.

BELLIN COLLEGE OF NURSING
GREEN BAY, WISCONSIN

Contact Dr. Penny Croghan, Admissions Director, Bellin College of Nursing, 725 South Webster Ave, PO Box 23400, Green Bay, WI 54305-3400. Phone: 920-433-5803 or toll-free 800-236-8707. Fax: 920-433-7416. E-mail: admissio@bcon.edu. Web site: http://www.bcon.edu/.

BELOIT COLLEGE
BELOIT, WISCONSIN

General Independent, 4-year, coed **Entrance** Very difficult **Setting** 65-acre small-town campus **Total enrollment** 1,352 **Student-faculty ratio** 11:1 **Application deadline** 1/15 (freshmen), rolling (transfer) **Freshmen** 60% were admitted **Housing** Yes **Expenses** Tuition $29,908; Room & Board $6408 **Undergraduates** 58% women, 3% part-time, 3% 25 or older, 1% Native American, 3% Hispanic American, 3% African American, 4% Asian American/Pacific Islander **The most frequently chosen baccalaureate fields are** social sciences, foreign languages and literature, visual and performing arts **Academic program** English as a second language, advanced placement, self-designed majors, summer session, adult/continuing education programs, internships **Contact** Mr. James S. Zielinski, Director of Admissions, Beloit College, 700 College Street, Beloit, WI 53511-5596. Phone: 608-363-2380 or toll-free 800-9-BELOIT. Fax: 608-363-2075. E-mail: admiss@beloit.edu. Web site: http://www.beloit.edu/.

BRYANT AND STRATTON COLLEGE, WAUWATOSA CAMPUS
WAUWATOSA, WISCONSIN

Contact Mr. Cori Prohaska, Campus Director, Bryant and Stratton College, Wauwatosa Campus, 10950 W. Potter Road, Wauwatosa, WI 53226. Phone: 414-302-7000. Web site: http://www.bryantstratton.edu/.

CARDINAL STRITCH UNIVERSITY
MILWAUKEE, WISCONSIN

General Independent Roman Catholic, comprehensive, coed **Entrance** Moderately difficult **Setting** 40-acre suburban campus **Total enrollment** 6,255 **Student-faculty ratio** 16:1 **Application deadline** 8/1 (freshmen), rolling (transfer) **Freshmen** 93% were admitted **Housing** Yes **Expenses** Tuition $20,510; Room & Board $5920 **Undergraduates** 67% women, 7% part-time, 75% 25 or older, 1% Native American, 3% Hispanic American, 23% African American, 2% Asian American/Pacific Islander **The most frequently chosen baccalaureate fields are** business/marketing, education, health professions and related sciences **Academic program** English as a second language, advanced placement, accelerated degree program, self-designed majors, honors program, summer session, adult/continuing education programs, internships **Contact** Ms. Kristine Bueno, Associate Director of Admissions, Cardinal Stritch University, 6801 North Yates Road, Milwaukee, WI 53217-3985. Phone: 414-410-4040 or toll-free 800-347-8822 Ext. 4040. Fax: 414-410-4058. E-mail: admityou@stritch.edu. Web site: http://www.stritch.edu/.

CARROLL COLLEGE
WAUKESHA, WISCONSIN

General Independent Presbyterian, comprehensive, coed **Entrance** Moderately difficult **Setting** 52-acre suburban campus **Total enrollment** 3,325 **Student-faculty ratio** 16:1 **Application dead-**

line Rolling (freshmen), rolling (transfer) **Freshmen** 72% were admitted **Housing** Yes **Expenses** Tuition $20,830; Room & Board $6350 **Undergraduates** 68% women, 18% part-time, 14% 25 or older, 0.4% Native American, 3% Hispanic American, 2% African American, 1% Asian American/Pacific Islander **The most frequently chosen baccalaureate fields are** business/marketing, education, health professions and related sciences **Academic program** Advanced placement, self-designed majors, honors program, summer session, adult/continuing education programs, internships **Contact** Mr. James Wiseman, Vice President of Enrollment, Carroll College, 100 North East Avenue, Waukesha, WI 53186-5593. Phone: 262-524-7221 or toll-free 800-CARROLL. Fax: 262-524-7139. E-mail: cc.info@ccadmin.cc.edu. Web site: http://www.cc.edu/.

CARTHAGE COLLEGE
KENOSHA, WISCONSIN

General Independent, comprehensive, coed, affiliated with Evangelical Lutheran Church in America **Entrance** Moderately difficult **Setting** 72-acre suburban campus **Total enrollment** 2,778 **Student-faculty ratio** 15:1 **Application deadline** Rolling (freshmen), rolling (transfer) **Freshmen** 77% were admitted **Housing** Yes **Expenses** Tuition $26,500; Room & Board $7500 **Undergraduates** 58% women, 16% part-time, 12% 25 or older, 0.1% Native American, 4% Hispanic American, 4% African American, 2% Asian American/Pacific Islander **The most frequently chosen baccalaureate fields are** business/marketing, education, social sciences **Academic program** Advanced placement, accelerated degree program, self-designed majors, honors program, summer session, adult/continuing education programs, internships **Contact** Mr. Bradley J. Andrews, Vice President for Enrollment & Student Life, Carthage College, 2001 Alford Park Drive, Kenosha, WI 53140. Phone: 262-551-6000 or toll-free 800-351-4058. Fax: 262-551-5762. E-mail: admissions@carthage.edu. Web site: http://www.carthage.edu/.

COLUMBIA COLLEGE OF NURSING
MILWAUKEE, WISCONSIN

General Independent, 4-year, coed **Entrance** Moderately difficult **Setting** urban campus **Total enrollment** 260 **Student-faculty ratio** 15:1 **Application deadline** 8/1 (freshmen), rolling (transfer) **Freshmen** 46% were admitted **Housing** Yes **Expenses** Tuition $20,195; Room & Board $4200 **Undergraduates** 97% women, 7% part-time, 2% Hispanic American, 13% African American, 3% Asian American/Pacific Islander **Academic program** Advanced placement, honors program, summer session **Contact** Ms. Amy Dobson, Dean of Admissions, Columbia College of Nursing, 2121 East Newport Avenue, Milwaukee, WI 53211-2952. Phone: 414-256-1219 or toll-free 800-321-6265. Fax: 414-256-0180. E-mail: admiss@mtmary.edu. Web site: http://www.ccon.edu/.

CONCORDIA UNIVERSITY WISCONSIN
MEQUON, WISCONSIN

General Independent, comprehensive, coed, affiliated with Lutheran Church–Missouri Synod **Entrance** Moderately difficult **Setting** 192-acre suburban campus **Total enrollment** 5,933 **Student-faculty ratio** 13:1 **Application deadline** 8/15 (freshmen), rolling (transfer) **Freshmen** 66% were admitted **Housing** Yes **Expenses** Tuition $19,040; Room & Board $7200 **Undergraduates** 62% women, 45% part-time, 4% 25 or older, 1% Native American, 2% Hispanic American, 12% African American, 1% Asian American/Pacific Islander **The most frequently chosen baccalaureate fields are** business/marketing, education, health professions and related sciences **Academic program** English as a second language, advanced placement, accelerated degree program, self-designed majors, honors program, summer session, adult/continuing education programs, internships **Contact** Ms. Julie Schroeder, Concordia University Wisconsin, Admissions Office, 12800 N. Lake Drive, Mequon, WI 53097. Phone: 262-243-4305 Ext. 4305 or toll-free 888-628-9472. Fax: 262-243-4351. E-mail: admission@cuw.edu. Web site: http://www.cuw.edu/.

DeVRY UNIVERSITY
MILWAUKEE, WISCONSIN

General Proprietary, comprehensive, coed **Entrance** Minimally difficult **Total enrollment** 206 **Student-faculty ratio** 79:1 **Application deadline** Rolling (freshmen), rolling (transfer) **Housing** No **Expenses** Tuition $13,890 **Undergraduates** 65% women, 61% part-time, 66% 25 or older, 10% Hispanic American, 48% African American, 3% Asian American/Pacific Islander **The most frequently chosen baccalaureate field is** business/marketing **Academic program** Advanced placement, accelerated degree program, summer session, adult/continuing education programs **Contact** Admissions Office, DeVry University, 100 East Wisconsin Avenue, Suite 2550, Milwaukee, WI 53202-4107. Web site: http://www.devry.edu/.

DeVRY UNIVERSITY
WAUKESHA, WISCONSIN

Contact DeVry University, 20935 Swenson Drive, Suite 450, Waukesha, WI 53186-4047. Web site: http://www.devry.edu/.

EDGEWOOD COLLEGE
MADISON, WISCONSIN

General Independent Roman Catholic, comprehensive, coed **Entrance** Moderately difficult **Setting** 55-acre urban campus **Total enrollment** 2,582 **Student-faculty ratio** 12:1 **Application deadline** 8/26 (freshmen), 8/26 (transfer) **Freshmen** 80% were admitted **Housing** Yes **Expenses** Tuition $20,040; Room & Board $6826 **Undergraduates** 70% women, 23% part-time, 23% 25 or older, 1% Native American, 3% Hispanic American, 3% African American, 2% Asian American/Pacific Islander **Academic program** Advanced placement, summer session, adult/continuing education programs **Contact** Ms. Christine Benedict, Director of Admission, Edgewood College, 1000 Edgewood College Drive, Madison, WI 53711-1997. Phone: 608-663-2328 or toll-free 800-444-4861 Ext. 2294. Fax: 608-663-2214. E-mail: admissions@edgewood.edu. Web site: http://www.edgewood.edu/.

LAKELAND COLLEGE
SHEBOYGAN, WISCONSIN

General Independent, comprehensive, coed, affiliated with United Church of Christ **Contact** Mr. Nathan Dehne, Director of Admissions, Lakeland College, PO Box 359, Nash Visitors Center, Sheboygan, WI 53082-0359. Phone: 920-565-1588 or toll-free 800-242-3347. Fax: 920-565-1206. E-mail: admissions@lakeland.edu. Web site: http://www.lakeland.edu/.

LAWRENCE UNIVERSITY
APPLETON, WISCONSIN

General Independent, 4-year, coed **Entrance** Very difficult **Setting** 84-acre small-town campus **Total enrollment** 1,451 **Student-faculty ratio** 9:1 **Application deadline** 1/15 (freshmen), 5/1 (transfer) **Freshmen** 56% were admitted **Housing** Yes **Expenses** Tuition $31,080; Room & Board $6690 **Undergraduates** 54% women, 4% part-time, 1% 25 or older, 0.2% Native American, 2% Hispanic American, 2% African American, 3% Asian American/Pacific Islander **The most frequently chosen baccalaureate fields are** social sciences, biological/life sciences, visual and performing arts **Academic program** Advanced placement, self-designed majors, internships **Contact** Mr. Steven T. Syverson, Vice President for Enrollment Management, Lawrence University, PO Box 599, Appleton, WI 54912-0599. Phone: 920-832-6500 or toll-free 800-227-0982. Fax: 920-832-6782. E-mail: excel@lawrence.edu. Web site: http://www.lawrence.edu/.

MARANATHA BAPTIST BIBLE COLLEGE
WATERTOWN, WISCONSIN

General Independent Baptist, comprehensive, coed **Entrance** Noncompetitive **Setting** 60-acre small-town campus **Total enrollment** 895 **Student-faculty ratio** 16:1 **Application deadline** Rolling (freshmen), rolling (transfer) **Freshmen** 63% were admitted **Housing** Yes **Expenses** Tuition $9486; Room & Board $5500 **Undergraduates** 55% women, 7% part-time, 3% 25 or older, 1% Hispanic American, 1% African American, 1% Asian American/Pacific Islander **The most frequently chosen baccalaureate fields are** education, interdisciplinary studies, theology and religious vocations **Academic program** Accelerated degree program, summer session, internships **Contact** Dr. James Harrison, Director of Admissions, Maranatha Baptist Bible College, 745 West Main Street, Watertown, WI 53094. Phone: 920-206-2327 or toll-free 800-622-2947. Fax: 920-261-9109. E-mail: admissions@mbbc.edu. Web site: http://www.mbbc.edu/.

MARIAN COLLEGE OF FOND DU LAC
FOND DU LAC, WISCONSIN

General Independent Roman Catholic, comprehensive, coed **Entrance** Moderately difficult **Setting** 77-acre small-town campus **Total enrollment** 2,957 **Student-faculty ratio** 12:1 **Application deadline** Rolling (freshmen), rolling (transfer) **Freshmen** 85% were admitted **Housing** Yes **Expenses** Tuition $18,680; Room & Board $5220 **Undergraduates** 74% women, 30% part-time, 38% 25 or older, 1% Native American, 2% Hispanic American, 3% African American, 1% Asian American/Pacific Islander **The most frequently chosen baccalaureate fields are** business/marketing, health professions and related sciences, security and protective services **Academic program** English as a second language, advanced placement, accelerated degree program, self-designed majors, honors program, summer session, adult/continuing education programs, internships **Contact** Ms. Stacey Akey, Vice President for Enrollment and Marketing, Marian College of Fond du Lac, 45 South National Avenue, Fond du Lac, WI 54935-4699. Phone: 920-923-7650 or toll-free 800-2-MARIAN Ext. 7652. Fax: 920-923-8755. E-mail: admit@mariancollege.edu. Web site: http://www.mariancollege.edu/.

MARQUETTE UNIVERSITY
MILWAUKEE, WISCONSIN

General Independent Roman Catholic (Jesuit), university, coed **Entrance** Moderately difficult **Setting** 80-acre urban campus **Total enrollment** 11,516 **Student-faculty ratio** 15:1 **Application**

deadline 12/1 (freshmen), 12/1 (transfer) **Freshmen** 67% were admitted **Housing** Yes **Expenses** Tuition $28,128 **Undergraduates** 54% women, 6% part-time, 4% 25 or older, 0.3% Native American, 5% Hispanic American, 5% African American, 5% Asian American/Pacific Islander **The most frequently chosen baccalaureate fields are** business/marketing, communications/journalism, social sciences **Academic program** English as a second language, advanced placement, honors program, summer session, adult/continuing education programs, internships **Contact** Mr. Robert Blust, Dean of Undergraduate Admissions, Marquette University, PO Box 1881, Milwaukee, WI 53201-1881. Phone: 414-288-7004 or toll-free 800-222-6544. Fax: 414-288-3764. E-mail: admissions@marquette.edu. Web site: http://www.marquette.edu/.

MILWAUKEE INSTITUTE OF ART AND DESIGN

MILWAUKEE, WISCONSIN

Contact Mr. Mark Fetherston, Director of Admissions, Milwaukee Institute of Art and Design, 273 East Erie Street, Milwaukee, WI 53202. Phone: 414-847-3259 or toll-free 888-749-MIAD. Fax: 414-291-8077. E-mail: admissions@miad.edu. Web site: http://www.miad.edu/.

MILWAUKEE SCHOOL OF ENGINEERING

MILWAUKEE, WISCONSIN

General Independent, comprehensive, coed, primarily men **Entrance** Moderately difficult **Setting** 15-acre urban campus **Total enrollment** 2,516 **Student-faculty ratio** 14:1 **Application deadline** Rolling (freshmen), rolling (transfer) **Freshmen** 65% were admitted **Housing** Yes **Expenses** Tuition $25,980; Room & Board $6501 **Undergraduates** 19% women, 11% part-time, 15% 25 or older, 1% Native American, 3% Hispanic American, 4% African American, 3% Asian American/Pacific Islander **The most frequently chosen baccalaureate fields are** business/marketing, engineering, engineering technologies **Academic program** English as a second language, advanced placement, summer session, adult/continuing education programs, internships **Contact** Paul Borens, Director of Admissions, Milwaukee School of Engineering, 1025 North Broadway, Milwaukee, WI 53202-3109. Phone: 414-277-7150 or toll-free 800-332-6763. Fax: 414-277-7475. E-mail: borens@msoe.edu. Web site: http://www.msoe.edu/.

MOUNT MARY COLLEGE

MILWAUKEE, WISCONSIN

General Independent Roman Catholic, comprehensive, undergraduate: women only; graduate: coed **Entrance** Moderately difficult **Setting** 80-acre urban campus **Total enrollment** 1,702 **Student-faculty ratio** 9:1 **Application deadline** Rolling (freshmen), rolling (transfer) **Freshmen** 59% were admitted **Housing** Yes **Expenses** Tuition $20,350; Room & Board $6994 **Undergraduates** 40% part-time, 41% 25 or older, 2% Native American, 6% Hispanic American, 19% African American, 4% Asian American/Pacific Islander **The most frequently chosen baccalaureate fields are** health professions and related sciences, business/marketing, visual and performing arts **Academic program** Advanced placement, accelerated degree program, self-designed majors, honors program, summer session, internships **Contact** Ms. Mary Ellen Stepanski, Admission Counselor Assistant/Receptionist, Mount Mary College, 2900 North Menomonee River Parkway, Milwaukee, WI 53222-4597. Phone: 414-258-4810 Ext. 219. Fax: 414-256-0180. E-mail: admiss@mtmary.edu. Web site: http://www.mtmary.edu/.

NORTHLAND COLLEGE

ASHLAND, WISCONSIN

General Independent, 4-year, coed, affiliated with United Church of Christ **Entrance** Moderately difficult **Setting** 130-acre small-town campus **Total enrollment** 676 **Student-faculty ratio** 15:1 **Application deadline** 5/1 (freshmen), 5/1 (transfer) **Freshmen** 71% were admitted **Housing** Yes **Expenses** Tuition $23,101; Room & Board $6440 **Undergraduates** 55% women, 9% part-time, 11% 25 or older, 2% Native American, 3% Hispanic American, 1% African American, 1% Asian American/Pacific Islander **The most frequently chosen baccalaureate fields are** biological/life sciences, education, interdisciplinary studies **Academic program** Advanced placement, accelerated degree program, self-designed majors, honors program, summer session, adult/continuing education programs, internships **Contact** Susan Greenwald, Director of Admission, Northland College, 1411 Ellis Avenue, Ashland, WI 54806. Phone: 715-682-1224 or toll-free 800-753-1840 (in-state); 800-753-1040 (out-of-state). Fax: 715-682-1258. E-mail: admit@northland.edu. Web site: http://www.northland.edu/.

RIPON COLLEGE

RIPON, WISCONSIN

General Independent, 4-year, coed **Entrance** Moderately difficult **Setting** 250-acre small-town campus **Total enrollment** 1,000 **Student-faculty ratio** 15:1 **Application deadline** Rolling (freshmen), rolling (transfer) **Freshmen** 80% were admitted **Housing** Yes **Expenses** Tuition $23,298; Room & Board $6410 **Undergraduates** 53%

Ripon College *(continued)*

women, 2% part-time, 1% 25 or older, 1% Native American, 3% Hispanic American, 2% African American, 1% Asian American/Pacific Islander **The most frequently chosen baccalaureate fields are** biological/life sciences, business/marketing, social sciences **Academic program** Advanced placement, accelerated degree program, self-designed majors, internships **Contact** Office of Admission, Ripon College, 300 Seward Street, PO Box 248, Ripon, WI 54971. Phone: 920-748-8185 or toll-free 800-947-4766. Fax: 920-748-8335. E-mail: adminfo@ripon.edu. Web site: http://www.ripon.edu/.

ST. NORBERT COLLEGE
DE PERE, WISCONSIN

General Independent Roman Catholic, comprehensive, coed **Entrance** Moderately difficult **Setting** 92-acre suburban campus **Total enrollment** 2,169 **Student-faculty ratio** 14:1 **Application deadline** Rolling (freshmen), rolling (transfer) **Freshmen** 87% were admitted **Housing** Yes **Expenses** Tuition $24,653; Room & Board $6579 **Undergraduates** 57% women, 3% part-time, 1% 25 or older, 1% Native American, 3% Hispanic American, 1% African American, 1% Asian American/Pacific Islander **The most frequently chosen baccalaureate fields are** business/marketing, education, social sciences **Academic program** English as a second language, advanced placement, self-designed majors, honors program, summer session, internships **Contact** Ms. Bridget O'Connor, Interim Vice President for Enrollment Management and Communications, St. Norbert College, 100 Grant Street, De Pere, WI 54115-2099. Phone: 920-403-3005 or toll-free 800-236-4878. Fax: 920-403-4072. E-mail: admit@snc.edu. Web site: http://www.snc.edu/.

SILVER LAKE COLLEGE
MANITOWOC, WISCONSIN

General Independent Roman Catholic, comprehensive, coed **Entrance** Minimally difficult **Setting** 30-acre rural campus **Total enrollment** 832 **Student-faculty ratio** 5:1 **Application deadline** 8/1 (freshmen), 8/1 (transfer) **Freshmen** 65% were admitted **Housing** Yes **Expenses** Tuition $19,194; Room & Board $5450 **Undergraduates** 72% women, 66% part-time, 63% 25 or older, 6% Native American, 1% Hispanic American, 1% African American, 0.3% Asian American/Pacific Islander **The most frequently chosen baccalaureate fields are** business/marketing, education, psychology **Academic program** English as a second language, advanced placement, accelerated degree program, self-designed majors, summer session, adult/continuing education programs, internships **Contact** Matthew Thielen, Student Life and Dean of Students, Silver Lake College, 2406 South Alverno Road, Manitowoc, WI 54220. Phone: 920-686-6208 Ext. 208 or toll-free 800-236-4752 Ext. 175. Fax: 920-684-7082. E-mail: admslc@silver.sl.edu. Web site: http://www.sl.edu/.

UNIVERSITY OF PHOENIX–WISCONSIN CAMPUS
BROOKFIELD, WISCONSIN

General Proprietary, comprehensive, coed **Contact** Ms. Evelyn Gaskin, Registrar/Executive Director, University of Phoenix–Wisconsin Campus, 4615 East Elwood Street, Mail Stop AA-K101, Phoenix, AZ 85040-1958. Phone: 480-557-3301 or toll-free 800-776-4867 (in-state); 800-228-7240 (out-of-state). Fax: 480-643-1020. E-mail: evelyn.gaskin@phoenix.edu. Web site: http://www.phoenix.edu/.

UNIVERSITY OF WISCONSIN–EAU CLAIRE
EAU CLAIRE, WISCONSIN

General State-supported, comprehensive, coed **Entrance** Moderately difficult **Setting** 333-acre urban campus **Total enrollment** 10,593 **Student-faculty ratio** 19:1 **Application deadline** Rolling (freshmen), 7/1 (transfer) **Freshmen** 69% were admitted **Housing** Yes **Expenses** Tuition $5845; Room & Board $5150 **Undergraduates** 59% women, 7% part-time, 7% 25 or older, 1% Native American, 1% Hispanic American, 0.5% African American, 3% Asian American/Pacific Islander **The most frequently chosen baccalaureate fields are** business/marketing, education, health professions and related sciences **Academic program** English as a second language, advanced placement, honors program, summer session, adult/continuing education programs, internships **Contact** Ms. Kristina Anderson, Executive Director of Enrollment Management and Director of Admissions, University of Wisconsin–Eau Claire, PO Box 4004, Eau Claire, WI 54702-4004. Phone: 715-836-5415. Fax: 715-836-2409. E-mail: admissions@uwec.edu. Web site: http://www.uwec.edu/.

UNIVERSITY OF WISCONSIN–GREEN BAY
GREEN BAY, WISCONSIN

General State-supported, comprehensive, coed **Entrance** Moderately difficult **Setting** 700-acre suburban campus **Total enrollment** 6,083 **Student-faculty ratio** 24:1 **Freshmen** 71% were admitted **Housing** Yes **Expenses** Tuition $5959; Room & Board $5200 **Undergraduates** 65% women, 21% part-time, 19% 25 or older, 2%

Native American, 1% Hispanic American, 1% African American, 3% Asian American/Pacific Islander **The most frequently chosen baccalaureate fields are** business/marketing, biological/life sciences, psychology **Academic program** Advanced placement, self-designed majors, summer session, adult/continuing education programs, internships **Contact** Ms. Pam Harvey-Jacobs, Director of Admissions, University of Wisconsin–Green Bay, 2420 Nicolet Drive, Green Bay, WI 54311-7001. Phone: 920-465-2111 or toll-free 888-367-8942. Fax: 920-465-5754. E-mail: uwgb@uwgb.edu. Web site: http://www.uwgb.edu/.

UNIVERSITY OF WISCONSIN–LA CROSSE
LA CROSSE, WISCONSIN

General State-supported, comprehensive, coed **Entrance** Moderately difficult **Setting** 121-acre suburban campus **Total enrollment** 9,975 **Student-faculty ratio** 23:1 **Application deadline** Rolling (freshmen), rolling (transfer) **Freshmen** 65% were admitted **Housing** Yes **Expenses** Tuition $4876; Room & Board $5130 **Undergraduates** 58% women, 5% part-time, 4% 25 or older, 1% Native American, 1% Hispanic American, 1% African American, 3% Asian American/Pacific Islander **The most frequently chosen baccalaureate fields are** business/marketing, education, social sciences **Academic program** English as a second language, advanced placement, honors program, summer session, adult/continuing education programs, internships **Contact** Ms. Kathryn Kiefer, Director of Admissions, University of Wisconsin–La Crosse, 1725 State Street, La Crosse, WI 54601-3742. Phone: 608-785-8939. Fax: 608-785-8940. E-mail: admissions@uwlax.edu. Web site: http://www.uwlax.edu/.

UNIVERSITY OF WISCONSIN–MADISON
MADISON, WISCONSIN

General State-supported, university, coed **Entrance** Very difficult **Setting** 1,050-acre urban campus **Total enrollment** 42,041 **Student-faculty ratio** 13:1 **Application deadline** 2/1 (freshmen), 2/1 (transfer) **Freshmen** 56% were admitted **Housing** Yes **Expenses** Tuition $8047 **Undergraduates** 53% women, 9% part-time, 5% 25 or older, 1% Native American, 3% Hispanic American, 3% African American, 6% Asian American/Pacific Islander **The most frequently chosen baccalaureate fields are** biological/life sciences, engineering, social sciences **Academic program** English as a second language, advanced placement, accelerated degree program, self-designed majors, honors program, summer session, adult/continuing education programs, internships **Contact** Office of Undergraduate Admissions, University of Wisconsin–Madison, 716 Langdon Street, Madison, WI 53706-1481. Phone: 608-262-3961. Fax: 608-262-7706. E-mail: onwisconsin@admissions.wisc.edu. Web site: http://www.wisc.edu/.

UNIVERSITY OF WISCONSIN–MILWAUKEE
MILWAUKEE, WISCONSIN

General State-supported, university, coed **Entrance** Moderately difficult **Setting** 90-acre urban campus **Total enrollment** 29,338 **Student-faculty ratio** 33:1 **Application deadline** 7/1 (freshmen), 8/1 (transfer) **Freshmen** 83% were admitted **Housing** Yes **Expenses** Tuition $7727; Room only $3620 **Undergraduates** 52% women, 17% part-time, 16% 25 or older, 1% Native American, 4% Hispanic American, 7% African American, 4% Asian American/Pacific Islander **The most frequently chosen baccalaureate fields are** business/marketing, education, health professions and related sciences **Academic program** English as a second language, advanced placement, accelerated degree program, self-designed majors, honors program, summer session, adult/continuing education programs, internships **Contact** Ms. Jan Ford, Director, Recruitment and Outreach, University of Wisconsin–Milwaukee, PO Box 413, Milwaukee, WI 53201-0413. Phone: 414-229-3800. Fax: 414-229-6940. E-mail: uwmlook@uwm.edu. Web site: http://www.uwm.edu/.

UNIVERSITY OF WISCONSIN–OSHKOSH
OSHKOSH, WISCONSIN

General State-supported, comprehensive, coed **Entrance** Moderately difficult **Setting** 192-acre suburban campus **Total enrollment** 12,693 **Student-faculty ratio** 22:1 **Application deadline** Rolling (freshmen), rolling (transfer) **Freshmen** 79% were admitted **Housing** Yes **Expenses** Tuition $5693; Room & Board $5746 **Undergraduates** 59% women, 21% part-time, 17% 25 or older, 1% Native American, 2% Hispanic American, 1% African American, 3% Asian American/Pacific Islander **The most frequently chosen baccalaureate fields are** business/marketing, education, health professions and related sciences **Academic program** English as a second language, advanced placement, accelerated degree program, self-designed majors, honors program, summer session, adult/continuing education programs, internships **Contact** Mr. Richard Hillman, Associate Director of Admissions, University of Wisconsin–Oshkosh, 800 Algoma Boulevard, Oshkosh, WI 54901. Phone: 920-424-0202. E-mail: oshadmuw@uwosh.edu. Web site: http://www.uwosh.edu/.

UNIVERSITY OF WISCONSIN–PARKSIDE
KENOSHA, WISCONSIN

General State-supported, comprehensive, coed **Entrance** Moderately difficult **Setting** 700-acre suburban campus **Total enrollment** 5,013 **Student-faculty ratio** 20:1 **Application deadline** 8/1 (freshmen), 8/1 (transfer) **Freshmen** 76% were admitted **Housing** Yes **Expenses** Tuition $9638; Room & Board $5610 **Undergraduates** 55% women, 27% part-time, 20% 25 or older, 1% Native American, 7% Hispanic American, 11% African American, 3% Asian American/Pacific Islander **The most frequently chosen baccalaureate fields are** business/marketing, communications/journalism, public administration and social services **Academic program** English as a second language, advanced placement, accelerated degree program, honors program, summer session, internships **Contact** Mr. Matthew Jensen, Director of Admissions, University of Wisconsin–Parkside, PO Box 2000, 900 Wood Road, Kenosha, WI 53141-2000. Phone: 262-595-2784. Fax: 262-595-2008. E-mail: matthew.jensen@uwp.edu. Web site: http://www.uwp.edu/.

UNIVERSITY OF WISCONSIN–PLATTEVILLE
PLATTEVILLE, WISCONSIN

General State-supported, comprehensive, coed **Entrance** Moderately difficult **Setting** 380-acre small-town campus **Total enrollment** 7,086 **Student-faculty ratio** 20:1 **Application deadline** Rolling (freshmen), rolling (transfer) **Freshmen** 85% were admitted **Housing** Yes **Expenses** Tuition $6065; Room & Board $5440 **Undergraduates** 36% women, 10% part-time, 10% 25 or older, 0.5% Native American, 1% Hispanic American, 2% African American, 1% Asian American/Pacific Islander **The most frequently chosen baccalaureate fields are** business/marketing, education, engineering **Academic program** English as a second language, advanced placement, self-designed majors, honors program, summer session, adult/continuing education programs, internships **Contact** Ms. Angela Udelhofen, Director of Admissions and Enrollment Management, University of Wisconsin–Platteville, 1 University Plaza, 120 Brigham Hall, Platteville, WI 53818-3099. Phone: 608-342-1125 or toll-free 800-362-5515. Fax: 608-342-1122. E-mail: admit@uwplatt.edu. Web site: http://www.uwplatt.edu/.

UNIVERSITY OF WISCONSIN–RIVER FALLS
RIVER FALLS, WISCONSIN

General State-supported, comprehensive, coed **Contact** Dr. Alan Tuchtenhagen, Director of Admissions, University of Wisconsin–River Falls, 410 South Third Street, River Falls, WI 54022-5001. Phone: 715-425-3500. Fax: 715-425-0676. E-mail: admit@uwrf.edu. Web site: http://www.uwrf.edu/.

UNIVERSITY OF WISCONSIN–STEVENS POINT
STEVENS POINT, WISCONSIN

General State-supported, comprehensive, coed **Entrance** Moderately difficult **Setting** 335-acre small-town campus **Total enrollment** 8,888 **Student-faculty ratio** 21:1 **Application deadline** Rolling (freshmen), rolling (transfer) **Freshmen** 74% were admitted **Housing** Yes **Expenses** Tuition $5834; Room & Board $4832 **Undergraduates** 53% women, 7% part-time, 11% 25 or older, 1% Native American, 1% Hispanic American, 1% African American, 2% Asian American/Pacific Islander **The most frequently chosen baccalaureate fields are** natural resources/environmental science, biological/life sciences, social sciences **Academic program** English as a second language, advanced placement, accelerated degree program, self-designed majors, summer session, adult/continuing education programs, internships **Contact** Ms. Catherine Glennon, Director of Admissions, University of Wisconsin–Stevens Point, 2100 Main Street, Stevens Point, WI 54481. Phone: 715-346-2441. Fax: 715-346-3296. E-mail: admiss@uwsp.edu. Web site: http://www.uwsp.edu/.

UNIVERSITY OF WISCONSIN–STOUT
MENOMONIE, WISCONSIN

General State-supported, comprehensive, coed **Entrance** Moderately difficult **Setting** 120-acre small-town campus **Total enrollment** 8,327 **Student-faculty ratio** 19:1 **Application deadline** Rolling (transfer) **Freshmen** 78% were admitted **Housing** Yes **Expenses** Tuition $7272; Room & Board $4994 **Undergraduates** 49% women, 12% part-time, 11% 25 or older, 1% Native American, 1% Hispanic American, 1% African American, 2% Asian American/Pacific Islander **The most frequently chosen baccalaureate fields are** business/marketing, education, visual and performing arts **Academic program** Accelerated degree program, honors program, adult/continuing education programs, internships **Contact** Dr. Cynthia S. Gilberts, Executive Director of Enrollment Services, University of Wisconsin–Stout, Admissions UW-Stout, Bowman Hall, Menomonie, WI 54751. Phone: 715-232-2639 or toll-free 800-HI-STOUT. Fax: 715-232-2639. E-mail: admissions@uwstout.edu. Web site: http://www.uwstout.edu/.

UNIVERSITY OF WISCONSIN–SUPERIOR
SUPERIOR, WISCONSIN

General State-supported, comprehensive, coed **Entrance** Moderately difficult **Setting** 230-acre suburban campus **Total enrollment** 2,753 **Student-faculty ratio** 17:1 **Application deadline** Rolling (freshmen), rolling (transfer) **Freshmen** 74% were admitted **Housing** Yes **Expenses** Tuition $5907; Room & Board $4720 **Undergraduates** 57% women, 18% part-time, 29% 25 or older, 3% Native American, 1% Hispanic American, 2% African American, 1% Asian American/Pacific Islander **The most frequently chosen baccalaureate fields are** business/marketing, communications/journalism, education **Academic program** English as a second language, advanced placement, self-designed majors, honors program, summer session, adult/continuing education programs, internships **Contact** Lee Parker, Admissions Advisor, University of Wisconsin–Superior, Belknap and Catlin, PO Box 2000, Superior, WI 54880-4500. Phone: 715-394-8230 or toll-free 715-394-8230. Fax: 715-394-8407. E-mail: admissions@uwsuper.edu. Web site: http://www.uwsuper.edu/.

UNIVERSITY OF WISCONSIN–WHITEWATER
WHITEWATER, WISCONSIN

General State-supported, comprehensive, coed **Entrance** Moderately difficult **Setting** 385-acre small-town campus **Total enrollment** 10,737 **Student-faculty ratio** 22:1 **Application deadline** Rolling (freshmen), rolling (transfer) **Freshmen** 75% were admitted **Housing** Yes **Expenses** Tuition $6730; Room & Board $4474 **Undergraduates** 50% women, 8% part-time, 10% 25 or older, 0.5% Native American, 3% Hispanic American, 5% African American, 2% Asian American/Pacific Islander **The most frequently chosen baccalaureate fields are** business/marketing, communications/journalism, education **Academic program** English as a second language, advanced placement, accelerated degree program, self-designed majors, honors program, summer session, adult/continuing education programs, internships **Contact** Mr. Stephen J. McKellips, Director of Admissions, University of Wisconsin–Whitewater, 800 West Main Street, Whitewater, WI 53190-1790. Phone: 262-472-1440 Ext. 1512. Fax: 262-472-1515. E-mail: uwwadmit@uww.edu. Web site: http://www.uww.edu/.

VITERBO UNIVERSITY
LA CROSSE, WISCONSIN

General Independent Roman Catholic, comprehensive, coed **Entrance** Moderately difficult **Setting** 72-acre suburban campus **Total enrollment** 3,088 **Student-faculty ratio** 12:1 **Application deadline** Rolling (freshmen), rolling (transfer) **Freshmen** 88% were admitted **Housing** Yes **Expenses** Tuition $19,490; Room & Board $6380 **Undergraduates** 71% women, 25% part-time, 29% 25 or older, 1% Native American, 1% Hispanic American, 1% African American, 1% Asian American/Pacific Islander **The most frequently chosen baccalaureate fields are** business/marketing, education, health professions and related sciences **Academic program** Advanced placement, accelerated degree program, self-designed majors, honors program, summer session, adult/continuing education programs, internships **Contact** Mr. Wayne Wojciechowski, Assistant Academic Vice President, Viterbo University, 900 Viterbo Drive, LaCrosse, WI 54601. Phone: 608-796-3010 or toll-free 800-VITERBO Ext. 3010. Fax: 608-796-3020. E-mail: admission@viterbo.edu. Web site: http://www.viterbo.edu/.

WISCONSIN LUTHERAN COLLEGE
MILWAUKEE, WISCONSIN

General Independent, 4-year, coed, affiliated with Wisconsin Evangelical Lutheran Synod **Entrance** Moderately difficult **Setting** 48-acre suburban campus **Total enrollment** 720 **Student-faculty ratio** 9:1 **Freshmen** 82% were admitted **Housing** Yes **Expenses** Tuition $20,560; Room & Board $6990 **Undergraduates** 56% women, 6% part-time, 3% 25 or older, 0.1% Native American, 2% Hispanic American, 2% African American, 2% Asian American/Pacific Islander **The most frequently chosen baccalaureate fields are** communications/journalism, education, psychology **Academic program** Advanced placement, self-designed majors, summer session, internships **Contact** Ms. Amanda Delaney, Wisconsin Lutheran College, 8800 West Bluemound Road, Milwaukee, WI 53226-9942. Phone: 414-443-8811 or toll-free 888-WIS LUTH. Fax: 414-443-8514. E-mail: amanda.delaney@wlc.edu. Web site: http://www.wlc.edu/.

WYOMING

UNIVERSITY OF WYOMING
LARAMIE, WYOMING

General State-supported, university, coed **Entrance** Moderately difficult **Setting** 785-acre small-town campus **Total enrollment** 12,875 **Student-faculty ratio** 15:1 **Application deadline** 8/10 (freshmen), 8/10 (transfer) **Freshmen** 96% were admitted **Housing** Yes **Expenses**

University of Wyoming *(continued)*

Tuition $3554; Room & Board $7274 **Undergraduates** 53% women, 18% part-time, 22% 25 or older, 1% Native American, 3% Hispanic American, 1% African American, 1% Asian American/Pacific Islander **The most frequently chosen baccalaureate fields are** business/marketing, education, engineering **Academic program** English as a second language, advanced placement, accelerated degree program, self-designed majors, honors program, summer session, internships **Contact** Aaron Appelhans, Assistant Director of Admissions, University of Wyoming, 1000 East University Avenue, Department 3435, Laramie, WY 82071. Phone: 307-766-5160 or toll-free 800-342-5996. Fax: 307-766-4042. E-mail: why-wyo@uwyo.edu. Web site: http://www.uwyo.edu/.

COLLEGE CLOSE-UPS

AMERICAN UNIVERSITY

■ WASHINGTON, D.C.

THE UNIVERSITY

American University (AU) is for academically distinctive and engaged students who want to turn ideas into action and action into service. AU's thorough curriculum enables students to combine serious theoretical study with meaningful real-world learning experiences. American's unique core curriculum; Washington, D.C., location; and emphasis on the practical application of knowledge prepare students to be major contributors in their fields.

For an application and more information, students should contact:

Undergraduate Admissions
American University
4400 Massachusetts Avenue, NW
Washington, D.C. 20016-8001
Phone: 202-885-6000
E-mail: admissions@american.edu
Web site:
http://admissions.american.edu

AU's more than 5,000 undergraduates are a microcosm of the world's diversity. From across the United States and more than 140 countries, they share a desire to shape tomorrow's world. AU actively promotes international understanding, and this is reflected in its curriculum offerings, its faculty research, and the regular presence of world leaders on campus.

Almost all first-year students and about 65 percent of all students live in on-campus housing. The University's six smoke-free residence halls offer a choice of single-sex or coed floors and special interest options. Nonresidential fraternities and sororities, more than 160 student-run organizations, NCAA Division I athletics, and intramural and club sports offer students a range of opportunities.

ACADEMIC PROGRAMS

Students can choose from more than seventy programs in the arts and humanities, business, education, international studies, public affairs, sciences, social sciences, or preprofessional programs in law and medicine. Students may double major or construct their own interdisciplinary major. Students may major in one AU school and minor in another school or college. Most majors offer the option of pursuing a combined bachelor's/master's program. Students do not need to formally declare a major until the end of their sophomore year.

The educational goals of the College of Arts and Sciences include teaching students to examine Western and non-Western cultures, appreciate scientific inquiry, master written and oral expression, develop the ability to analyze and synthesize information, and build an understanding of the moral and ethical dimensions that underlie decision making. Students select internships and develop courses of study in more than forty majors in the arts, education, humanities, mathematics, performing arts, sciences, and social sciences.

American's School of International Service (SIS) is the largest of its kind in the United States and is able to offer serious students a breadth of study in international relations. Students select an area of specialization from among Africa, the Americas, Asia, Europe, the Middle East, or Russia and Central Eurasia and also select a functional field of concentration.

Students in the School of Public Affairs are engaged in learning about local, national, and international politics, with a focus on public institutions; public policy; crime; justice; and law. These areas frame a comprehensive program that incorporates classroom learning, individualized research projects, relevant field studies, and professional training.

The goal of the School of Communication (SOC) is to develop professionally trained communicators who are equipped intellectually and ethically to convey the issues of contemporary society. The curriculum benefits from the environment of Washington, D.C., one of the world's major communications centers. The school emphasizes involving students with Washington's communicators and communication facilities.

The Kogod School of Business provides students with a solid foundation in business, including the preparation to be responsible citizens and assume leadership roles in a global business economy. Kogod is entrepreneurial, relevant to today's markets, and flexible in its strategies. The Washington, D.C., area provides Kogod students with limitless opportunities to enhance classroom learning through internship experiences.

FINANCIAL AID

AU offers merit scholarships to approximately 25 percent of each freshman class. These scholarships are not based on financial need, and no separate application forms are required. The scholarships include awards of up to full tuition.

APPLICATION AND INFORMATION

The deadline for early decision freshmen is November 15, and notification is made by December 31. The regular decision deadline is January 15.

BELMONT UNIVERSITY

■ NASHVILLE, TENNESSEE

THE UNIVERSITY

Nationally recognized programs thrive on the Belmont University campus, which is located in the heart of the state capital, known both as Music City, U.S.A., and the Athens of the South (for its many educational institutions). Nashville offers big-city advantages with small-town charm.

Belmont's vision is to be a leader among teaching universities, bringing together the best of liberal arts and professional education in a Christian community of learning and service. Central to the fulfillment of that vision are faculty members who have a passion for teaching and the belief that premier teaching is interactive, technology-supported, motivational, creative, and exciting.

For an application and more information, students should contact:

Office of Admissions
Belmont University
1900 Belmont Boulevard
Nashville, Tennessee 37212
Phone: 615-460-6785
800-56ENROLL (toll-free)
E-mail: buadmission@mail.belmont.edu
Web site: http://www.belmont.edu

With an enrollment of approximately 4,700 students, Belmont is the second-largest of Tennessee's private colleges and universities. In addition to the twenty-five countries represented in the student body, Belmont University attracts students from almost every state in the United States. This culturally diverse institution is committed to listening and learning from everyone. Students of today are helping shape the way students of tomorrow will be educated.

Belmont's beautiful, antebellum campus reflects a long, rich history that dates back to the nineteenth century, when the grounds were Adelicia Acklen's Belle Monte estate. University buildings that were erected over the past 110 years flank the Italianate mansion, which is still used by the campus. On the way to classes that prepare them for the twenty-first century, students enjoy Victorian gardens, statuary, and gazebos that recall a treasured past.

In addition to seven baccalaureate degrees, Belmont University offers twelve graduate degrees: the Master of Accountancy, the Master of Arts in Teaching, the Master of Business Administration, the Master of Sport Administration, the Master of English, the Master of Music, the Master of Education, the Master of Science in Nursing, the Master of Science in Occupational Therapy, the Doctor of Occupational Therapy, the Doctor of Pharmacy, and the Doctor of Physical Therapy.

ACADEMIC PROGRAMS

Uniquely positioned to provide the best of liberal arts and professional education, Belmont University offers celebrated professional programs structured to provide an academically well-rounded education. Belmont University operates on a two-semester schedule with classes beginning in late August and ending in early May. Two summer sessions are also offered. The academic program is arranged by school: the College of Arts and Sciences, the College of Business Administration, the Gordon E. Inman College of Health Sciences and Nursing, the College of Visual and Performing Arts, the Mike Curb College of Entertainment and Music Business, and the School of Religion.

In addition to the degrees offered through the schools, Belmont University offers an honors program, which was created to provide an enrichment opportunity for students who have potential for superior academic performance and who seek added challenge and breadth to their studies. Students enrolled in the honors program are led in designing and working through a flexible, individual curriculum and interdisciplinary general education curriculum by a private tutor who is an honors faculty member.

The University's advancements in undergraduate research are credited to a faculty committed to helping students practice their disciplines. The annual Belmont Undergraduate Research Symposium puts Belmont at the forefront of this national movement by providing a public forum for in-depth research at the undergraduate level.

FINANCIAL AID

More than 75 percent of Belmont's students receive some type of financial assistance. The financial aid program at Belmont combines merit-based assistance with need-based assistance to make the University program affordable. Institutional merit awards range from full-tuition Presidential Scholarships to performance scholarships. Also included are many levels of academic merit awards. Belmont University also administers traditional state and federal programs. Campus employment is available. Parents may arrange monthly tuition payments through an outside vendor. To apply for assistance, the student must complete the Free Application for Federal Student Aid (FAFSA).

BENEDICTINE UNIVERSITY

■ LISLE, ILLINOIS

THE UNIVERSITY

Benedictine University was founded in 1887 as St. Procopius College. One hundred twenty-one years later, the University remains committed to providing a high-quality, Catholic, liberal education for men and women. The undergraduate enrollment is nearly 3,000 students. The student body comprises students of diverse ages, religions, races, and national origins. Twenty-five percent of the full-time students reside on campus.

Benedictine University is situated on a rolling, tree-covered 108-acre campus of twenty major buildings with air-conditioned classrooms and modern, well-equipped laboratories. A student athletic center features three full-size basketball courts, a competition-size swimming pool, three tennis courts, and training facilities. All of the residence halls are comfortable and spacious and have access to the Internet. On-campus apartments offer one-, two-, and four-bedroom residences. Other features include a scenic lake; a student center with dining halls, lounges, a chapel, a bookstore, and meeting rooms; and the Village of Lisle–Benedictine University Sports Complex, featuring a lighted multipurpose football/soccer stadium with a nine-lane track and lighted baseball and softball fields.

For an application and more information, students should contact:

Enrollment Center
Benedictine University
5700 College Road
Lisle, Illinois 60532
Phone: 630-829-6300
888-829-6363 (toll-free outside Illinois)
E-mail: admissions@ben.edu
Web site: http://www.ben.edu

Benedictine University is highly competitive in varsity sports with a total of nineteen sports. Men's varsity sports are baseball, basketball, cross-country, football, golf, soccer, swimming and diving, and track and field (indoor and outdoor). Women's varsity sports are basketball, cross-country, golf, soccer, softball, swimming and diving, tennis, track and field (indoor and outdoor), and volleyball. Aside from varsity and intramural athletic programs, forty organizations and clubs exist on campus, including student government, a student newspaper, an orchestra, a jazz group, an African-American Student Union, a Muslim Student Association, the Association of Latin American Students, campus ministry, and various other extracurricular and academic organizations.

At Benedictine University, the environment is strengthened by success, not size. Renowned faculty members know students by name and care as much about each student's progress as they do about their own research. Those personal relationships have produced superb results. Benedictine graduates are accepted into some of the most prestigious graduate programs in the country. Approximately two thirds of Benedictine graduates who apply to medical school are accepted, in addition to similar ratios for other health-related professional schools (optometry, pharmacy, physical therapy, and podiatry). The liberal arts curriculum has helped place the University among some of the finest small private schools in the nation. *U.S. News & World Report's* 2008 rankings listed Benedictine University as a Top School in the Midwest and sixth in Illinois for campus diversity.

ACADEMIC PROGRAMS

For graduation, a student must earn at least 120 semester hours, 55 of which must be completed at a four-year regionally accredited college. At least the final 45 semester hours must be completed at Benedictine University.

Each year, a select number of talented and motivated prospective students are invited to participate in the Scholars Program. The program is designed to enhance the college experience by developing students' international awareness and strengthening their leadership ability.

FINANCIAL AID

In 2006–07, Benedictine University freshmen received approximately $4.5 million from financial aid sources that included loans, scholarship and grants, tuition remission, and employment opportunities. Ninety-two percent of the freshman class received financial aid. The average package was $14,762. Benedictine University has dedicated more than $8.2 million of the annual budget to providing grants and scholarships to its students. Students who wish to apply for aid must complete the FAFSA, the Benedictine University application for financial aid, and the Benedictine University application for admission.

APPLICATION AND INFORMATION

Applications are reviewed on a rolling basis. Students are encouraged to apply for admission at any time after completing their junior year of high school. Transfer students may apply for admission during their last semester or quarter before anticipated transfer to Benedictine University. Earlier applications are encouraged for scholarship and financial aid opportunities.

BETHEL UNIVERSITY

■ ST. PAUL, MINNESOTA

THE UNIVERSITY

Bethel University began its Christian liberal arts program in 1945 but traces its roots to Bethel Seminary, founded in 1871. The University encourages growth and learning in a distinctly Christian environment, continually striving to help students discover and develop the skills God has given them. Campus lifestyle expectations have been designed to build unity within diversity. All Bethel students, faculty members, and staff members are expected to follow those expectations during their time as members of the Bethel community. Bethel's approximately 6,000 students represent a range of national and international cultures. Most of Bethel's undergraduate students are between 18 and 22 years of age, but older and younger students bring a welcome variety to campus life. Bethel students are involved in a wealth of cocurricular activities, from music to ministry, Bible study to broadcasting, theater to tennis, and art to athletics. Bethel sports teams compete in NCAA Division III and the Minnesota Intercollegiate Athletic Conference. The Sports and Recreation Center is used almost continuously for intercollegiate and intramural sports events as well as personal recreation, and the Community Life Center provides a 1,700-seat performance hall and chapel.

For an application and more information, students should contact:

Office of Admissions
Bethel University
3900 Bethel Drive
St. Paul, Minnesota 55112
Phone: 651-638-6242
800-255-8706 Ext. 6242 (toll-free)
E-mail: BUadmissions-cas@bethel.edu
Web site: http://www.bethel.edu

The campus, built in the 1970s, is the newest among Minnesota colleges and universities. Versatile buildings are centers for the sciences, humanities, physical education, learning resources, and fine arts. A series of skyways and breezeways connect the facilities and make getting to and from class a pleasure—even in the heart of winter. Residence life at Bethel takes many forms. Traditional college dorm rooms, spacious suites, town houses—whatever their preference, Bethel students find a warm, family atmosphere in the living areas. All freshman and sophomore students, except those who are married or living with their parents while in attendance, are required to live in University housing.

ACADEMIC PROGRAMS

Bethel was named among the top Midwestern universities by *U.S. News & World Report* for 2007. Students are required to take classes that will give them a broad view of the world and their role in it as Christians. General education classes are grouped around the following themes: personal development; biblical foundations; math, science, and technology; and global perspectives. In addition, in order to graduate, all Bethel students must partake in an off-campus cross-cultural experience and a capstone course in contemporary Christian issues.

Bethel University follows a semester calendar consisting of two 15-week semesters and a three-week interim in January. A full-time academic load for each semester is 12 to 18 credits. To graduate, students must complete a minimum of 122 credits with a cumulative grade point average of at least 2.0 and a minimum 2.25 grade point average in their majors. Also required are 51–52 credits of general education. Bethel awards advanced placement credit in recognition of learning that has been achieved apart from a college or university classroom situation. A maximum of 30 advanced placement credits can be applied toward a degree program. Students may also individualize their academic programs through directed studies with faculty members and through academic internships with off-campus institutions.

FINANCIAL AID

Bethel University strives to make it financially possible for every qualified student to attend. Each year, more than 90 percent of the students receive some kind of financial aid, including scholarships, grants, loans, and assistance in the form of on-campus employment. Students who wish to be considered for financial aid must first be admitted to the University and then submit both the FAFSA and a Bethel University Financial Aid Application. Bethel's priority deadline is April 15 of each year. Students who have completed and mailed all necessary forms by this date receive first consideration.

APPLICATION AND INFORMATION

Students wishing to apply for admission to Bethel must send the following: a completed Bethel application form with a $25 nonrefundable application fee (waived before November 1); test scores from the PSAT, SAT, or ACT; essay; transcripts of all course work completed at the high school and college levels; and references from a pastor and a school official. Students considering Bethel should apply in the fall of their senior year. The Office of Admissions reviews applications throughout the year. Early action decisions are made for students who submit applications by November 1.

BOWIE STATE UNIVERSITY

■ BOWIE, MARYLAND

THE UNIVERSITY

Bowie State University began as a normal school in the city of Baltimore in 1865, and it has evolved over the years into a four-year, coeducational, liberal arts institution. It is currently situated on a beautiful 500-acre campus in Prince Georges County, Maryland, and offers both graduate and undergraduate programs of study.

Bowie State University's physical plant is valued at more than $22.5 million, and its current enrollment is approximately 5,400 students. The University has twenty-two buildings on campus including the $21-million state-of-the-art Center for Learning and Technology that opened in 2000 and the $11.8-million Computer Science Center that opened in 2002. In addition, the new $19-million Center for Business and Graduate Studies opened in 2007. Seven residence halls house approximately 850 students. In addition, a 460-bed apartment-style residence hall, Christa McAuliffe, was completed in 2004. The $2.6-million physical education complex houses a 3,000-seat basketball arena, an Olympic-size swimming pool with underwater viewing windows and facilities for 200 spectators, an apparatus gymnasium, a dance studio, a wrestling room, a weight-training room, eight handball/squash courts, a therapy room, and offices for instructors and coaches. The $5.5-million University Activities Center includes a cafeteria.

Bowie State University considers the student activities program a vital part of the total educational program. Students have access to more than forty different activities. These include student government, the student union, intercollegiate athletics, eight fraternities and sororities, numerous departmental clubs and preprofessional organizations, and music and drama organizations.

For an application and more information, students should contact:

Admissions Office
Bowie State University
Bowie, Maryland 20715-9465
Phone: 301-860-3415
410-880-4100 Ext. 3415 (from the Baltimore-Columbia area)
877-77-BOWIE (toll-free)
E-mail: undergradadmissions@bowiestate.edu
Web site: http://www.bowiestate.edu

ACADEMIC PROGRAMS

Academic offerings are housed under four schools (School of Arts and Sciences, School of Education, School of Professional Studies, and the School of Business) and can be divided into four main areas: humanities, science and mathematics, social sciences, and education.

The Honors Program is designed for students with outstanding academic records and potential and provides a special educational opportunity for young adults with exceptional talent. The program is comprehensive and multidisciplinary in structure and interdisciplinary in application.

The Special Services Project is a federally funded program designed to retain and graduate first-generation, low-income, and disabled students who have been admitted to Bowie State University. The purpose of the project is to help students overcome academic and nonacademic barriers to academic success through participation in specially designed activities, including counseling, tutoring, and workshops on test-taking and study skills.

Through the Cooperative Education Program, a student may choose either the alternate or parallel programs of study and work in business, industry, government, or a social-service agency.

The University participates in the College-Level Examination Program (CLEP), administered by the Educational Testing Service for the College Board, and in the Defense Activity for Non-Traditional Education Support (DANTES) program. The University also has a program for awarding students credit for learning acquired through life and work experience. In addition, the University offers an Army ROTC program.

FINANCIAL AID

Federal grants, loans, and Work-Study are are available. University scholarships, tuition waivers, and diversity grants are awarded. Most awards are based on need. Academic scholarships could be offered to students with required minimum GPAs and SAT scores. In addition, merit awards are given for athletics, music and fine arts, and ROTC. More than 74 percent of all undergraduate students receive some form of financial aid. Scholarships and assistantships are offered through the Model Institutions for Excellence Program for Science, Engineering, and Mathematics. Deadlines are March 1 for the fall semester and November 15 for the spring semester.

APPLICATION AND INFORMATION

The application deadline is April 1 for the fall semester and November 1 for spring.

BROOKLYN COLLEGE OF THE CITY UNIVERSITY OF NEW YORK

■ BROOKLYN, NEW YORK

THE COLLEGE

Founded in 1930, Brooklyn College is a premier, four-year liberal arts college where students are given the knowledge, awareness, and experience to succeed. The College is situated on a 26-acre campus in the most dynamic New York City borough.

Brooklyn College enrolls nearly 16,000 undergraduate and graduate students, offering more than 130 programs in the humanities, education, the arts, business, sciences, and social sciences leading to bachelor's and master's degrees and advanced certificates. As one of the eleven senior colleges of the City University of New York, it shares the mission of the University, whose primary goals are access and excellence.

For an application and more information, students should contact:

Office of Admissions
1103 James Hall
Brooklyn College
The City University of New York
2900 Bedford Avenue
Brooklyn, New York 11210
Phone: 718-951-5001
E-mail: adminqry@brooklyn.cuny.edu
Web site: http://www.brooklyn.cuny.edu

The College has an ambitious program of expansion and renewal. In 2002 the College completed an extensive renovation and expansion of its library, now the most technologically advanced facility in the CUNY system. The College's West Quad Building is scheduled to open its doors in 2008. The building is designed to consolidate under one roof all student services—admissions, financial aid, scholarships, registration, and the bursar. Its plans also include state-of-the-art physical education and athletic facilities, including a swimming pool, competition and practice gymnasiums, racquetball courts, a fitness center, and teaching and research labs.

Brooklyn College's students participate in more than 140 chartered campus groups, including academic clubs, service and honor societies, athletics groups, special interest groups, and performing arts organizations. Special lectures, concerts, and events are scheduled throughout the year. On the campus quad and in the Student Center, fraternities and sororities provide social and community service activities.

ACADEMIC PROGRAMS

The liberal arts education at Brooklyn College consists of three kinds of study: the College-wide core curriculum, which provides a diverse educational experience in the liberal arts for all students; major studies, which comprise specialized, intensive study in one discipline or an interdisciplinary program; and elective courses, selected from more than seventy-five areas. The undergraduate curriculum aims to prepare students to make rational career and personal choices by developing their critical and independent thinking skills, their ability to acquire and organize knowledge, and their proficiency with both verbal and written communication.

The Honors Academy comprises eight units: the Scholars Program; the Coordinated B.A./M.D. Program; the William E. Macaulay Honors College Program; the Mellon Mays Undergraduate Fellowship; the Honors Academy Research Colloquium; the Dean's List Honors Research Program; the Engineering Honors Program; and the Special Baccalaureate Degree Program. Applications for all eight programs are available in the Office of Admissions.

FINANCIAL AID

Admission decisions and financial aid and scholarship decisions are made independently of each other, and an application for aid does not hinder a student's opportunity for admission. Financial assistance is available for eligible students through state and federal grant, loan, and work-study programs.

New and continuing students, especially those with strong high school or college academic records and SAT scores, are encouraged to apply for annual scholarships. The requirements vary for each award, but recipients are chosen based on academic performance, financial need, and various other criteria that may be stipulated by the donors. Scholarships range from $100 to $4000 per year.

APPLICATION AND INFORMATION

Application for admission to the undergraduate program for the fall or spring semester should be made on a standard CUNY application form, available from the Office of Admissions at any CUNY college or online at http://www.brooklyn.cuny.edu. For some honors programs, fellowships, and coordinated programs, applications are available only through the Brooklyn College Office of Admissions. Although applications are processed on a rolling basis, applicants who apply before January 15 for fall admission and before October 15 for spring admission have the best opportunity for comprehensive advisement and course registration. The CUNY Honors College Program applicants are required to apply by November 1 (early decision) and December 15 (regular decision) for fall admission.

BRYANT UNIVERSITY

■ SMITHFIELD, RHODE ISLAND

THE UNIVERSITY

Founded in 1863, Bryant is a four-year, private university in New England where students build knowledge, develop character, and achieve success—as *they* define it. Throughout its 144-year history, Bryant has empowered students to achieve their personal best in life and their chosen careers. The University is the choice for individuals seeking the best integration of business and liberal arts and state-of-the-art technology. Its cross-disciplinary approach provides a well-rounded education that teaches students the creative problem-solving and communication skills they need to successfully compete in a complex, global environment.

Bryant's 3,268 full-time undergraduate students represent thirty-two states and thirty-four countries. They enjoy all the advantages of small classes and the close relationships among students, faculty members, and administrators. In this environment, students come to understand the interaction among various academic disciplines and their practical applications in the global community.

For an application and more information, students should contact:

For admission information:
Director of Admission
Bryant University
1150 Douglas Pike
Smithfield, Rhode Island 02917-1285
Phone: 401-232-6100
800-622-7001 (toll-free)
E-mail: admission@bryant.edu
Web site: http://admission.bryant.edu

For financial aid information:
Director of Financial Aid
Phone: 401-232-6020
800-248-4036 (toll-free)
E-mail: finaid@bryant.edu
Web site: http://admission.bryant.edu

Sports and recreation play an integral role at Bryant. Students can balance their academic pursuits with overall well-being at the Elizabeth and Malcolm Chace Wellness and Athletic Center. This impressive facility features a fully equipped fitness center, a six-lane swimming pool, circuit-training equipment and free weights, and a group exercise room. Students can participate in any of Bryant's twenty-two intercollegiate varsity sports teams as well as club and intramural sports.

Bryant has close to eighty student clubs and organizations that benefit many social causes, provide recreational enjoyment, promote intellectual exploration, and offer opportunities to develop new talents and passions. The Student Programming Board, the Intercultural Center, the Arts and Culture Club, the Marketing Association, and the Student Senate are just a few of the organizations where students can get involved in campus life. There are many places on and off campus for students to gather and enjoy music, comedy, and other kinds of entertainment.

ACADEMIC PROGRAMS

Academic programs focus on the intellectual and professional development of each student, in preparation for leadership positions in a wide range of careers. Students must complete a core curriculum that integrates business, liberal arts, and technology.

Entering students may receive credit through the Advanced Placement (AP) Program or the College-Level Examination Program (CLEP) administered by the College Board. Credit is also awarded for International Baccalaureate (IB) higher-level exams. The Honors Program is an excellent vehicle for highly motivated students to stretch their intellectual limits and experience stimulating academic challenges. Bryant also participates in the Army ROTC Program.

FINANCIAL AID

Bryant has a comprehensive program of merit- and need-based financial aid. More than $63 million in financial aid to cover educational expenses was processed for Bryant students in 2007–08. The majority of freshmen receive financial aid through a combination of scholarships, loans, grants, and part-time jobs. Students interested in applying for financial assistance in the form of need-based grants, work-study, and education loans need to file the FAFSA, which can be found online at http://www.fafsa.ed.gov. The FAFSA can be submitted as early as January 1, and February 15 is the deadline.

APPLICATION AND INFORMATION

Applications must be submitted to the Office of Admission with a nonrefundable fee of $50 by November 15 (early decision) or February 1 (regular decision). It is the responsibility of the applicant to request that the secondary school guidance office send a copy of the student's school record directly to Bryant and also have SAT or ACT scores sent. International applicants must also submit TOEFL scores and a completed Certification of Finances form.

CALIFORNIA COLLEGE OF THE ARTS

■ OAKLAND AND SAN FRANCISCO, CALIFORNIA

THE COLLEGE

For an application and more information, students should contact:

Office of Enrollment Services
California College of the Arts
1111 Eighth Street
San Francisco, California 94107-2247
Phone: 800-447-1ART (toll-free)
Web site: http://www.cca.edu

Founded in 1907, California College of the Arts (CCA) is the largest regionally accredited, independent school of art and design in the western United States. CCA offers twenty undergraduate majors in the areas of art, architecture, design, and writing. The College provides world-class facilities on two dynamic campuses in Oakland and San Francisco. CCA students regularly win major recognition in their fields; in 2005, 12 graphic design students had work in the *Graphis New Talent Design Annual,* and in 2006, products by industrial design students were shown at the Milan Furniture Fair. At CCA, students make art that makes a difference.

Students and faculty members create a supportive community of friends, colleagues, and mentors in an intimate, private-college environment. CCA has approximately 1,300 undergraduate and 300 graduate students. In the undergraduate population, 59 percent are women, 41 percent are men; 24 percent are from underrepresented populations, and 7 percent are international students. First-time freshmen comprise 50 percent of the entering class; 50 percent are transfer and second-degree students. About 35 percent come from out of state. CCA offers a well-rounded first-year program, with a residence hall housing 75 percent of the first-time freshmen.

Campus life includes exhibitions at the CCA Wattis Institute for Contemporary Arts, lectures by visiting artists and scholars, film screenings, literary readings, and more. Through the CCA Center for Art and Public Life, students may teach or create art in the community. CCA's undergraduate exhibition program presents shows throughout the year. The Student Affairs Office sponsors a variety of campus events. Student organizations include preprofessional groups affiliated with local chapters of AIA, AIGA, and other associations.

The Oakland campus offers a traditional college atmosphere and campus housing in a residence hall and CCA-owned apartments. Housing is also available at a residence hall in downtown Oakland. Students are not required to live on campus. CCA offers no meal plan; all residences have kitchens, and each campus has a café. CCA maintains a local housing list to assist students in finding off-campus housing.

ACADEMIC PROGRAMS

The B.F.A. requires completion of a minimum of 126 semester units (75 in studio work and 51 in humanities and sciences). The B.A. requires completion of 126 semester units (51 in humanities and sciences, 36 in the major, and 39 in studio work). The B.Arch. requires completion of a minimum of 162 semester units, including the core program and a nine-semester major program.

The core program defines students' first-year experience, emphasizing skill building, experimentation, and critical thinking within a year of cross-disciplinary study, with exposure to a variety of media. The core curriculum includes studio courses and seminars in writing and visual studies.

CCA's humanities and sciences curriculum is based on the belief that visual arts are guided as much by the mind as by the hand. Students acquire oral and written communication skills, tools of critical thinking, and cultural literacy.

FINANCIAL AID

Scholarships, grants, loans, and work-study awards are available on the basis of merit and financial need. Students applying for aid should submit the FAFSA by March 1 for priority consideration. CCA continues to fund students after the priority deadline as long as funds remain available. Applications for Federal Pell Grants and Federal Direct Student Loans may be submitted throughout the school year. CCA is approved for veterans attending under the Veterans Administration Educational Benefits Program. Approximately 75 percent of students attending CCA during 2006–07 received some type of financial aid. CCA offers an extended interest-free payment plan.

APPLICATION AND INFORMATION

CCA has two priority deadlines for fall admission: February 1 for merit scholarship consideration, and March 1 for all other applicants. For spring applicants, the priority deadline is October 1. Students who meet these deadlines are given priority consideration regarding admission, housing, and financial aid. CCA reviews undergraduate applications on a rolling admission basis; applications are reviewed in the order in which they are received, and students are accepted and awarded financial aid after the priority dates. The application fee is $50. CCA encourages students to apply online.

CAMPBELL UNIVERSITY

■ BUIES CREEK, NORTH CAROLINA

THE UNIVERSITY

Founded in 1887, Campbell University has had the distinction of being North Carolina's second-largest private undergraduate institution. Its current enrollment is about 6,500 students at all campuses. There are more than 4,200 students at the main campus in Buies Creek. In an average year, the student body comes from all 100 North Carolina counties, all fifty states, and fifty countries. Seventy-five percent of the students come from North Carolina. Members of minority groups make up 25 percent of the student body.

For an application and more information, students should contact:

Office of Admissions
Campbell University
P.O. Box 546
Buies Creek, North Carolina 27506
Phone: 910-893-1320
910-893-1417 (international)
800-334-4111 (toll-free)
E-mail: adm@mailcenter.campbell.edu
Web site: http://www.campbell.edu/

Campbell University is nonsectarian. Approximately 48 percent of its students are Baptist, but young people of twenty-two other faiths complete its student body. It is concerned with maintaining, for living and learning, an environment consistent with Christian ideals. Among the extracurricular activities available at Campbell are band, choir, and drama groups; religious, political, professional, social, and academic groups; and intercollegiate and intramural sports organizations.

In athletics, the University is a member of NCAA Division I (Sun Athletic Conference) for men and women (except wrestling, which is in the Colonial Conference). Men's sports include baseball, basketball, cross-country, golf, soccer, tennis, track, wrestling, and NCAA Division II football. Women's sports include basketball, cheerleading, cross-country, golf, soccer, softball, swimming, tennis, track, and volleyball.

A $30-million convocation center for athletic events and special concerts is scheduled to be completed in 2008. A stadium to accommodate the return of football to Campbell University is also scheduled for completion in 2008.

The University also has campuses offering a variety of undergraduate and graduate courses at Fort Bragg, Raleigh/Morrisville, Rocky Mount, and Jacksonville, North Carolina.

ACADEMIC PROGRAMS

The curriculum of Campbell University is designed to meet individual needs and interests. During the first two years, students follow a general course of study, the General College Curriculum, to broaden their backgrounds in the basic fields of knowledge. By the end of the sophomore year, they should have selected a major subject for specialized study during the final two years.

Campbell offers the nation's first undergraduate program in trust and wealth management and since 1968 has been training prospective trust officers for the banks and trust companies of the region.

Campbell's School of Pharmacy has served the health-care needs of North Carolina and beyond for more than twenty years, paving the path for minority student recruitment and education enhancement through the Advancement for Underrepresented Minority Pharmacists Program. The school's curriculum is designed to focus on Pharmacy College Admission Test preparation, educational seminars, and a mentoring program in order to better prepare students for a career in pharmacy. Campbell's pharmacy students have maintained a 99 percent passage rate on the national board exams and 99 percent on state board exams.

Campbell's School of Education was established in 1985 in response to the need for fully qualified educators for the educational system of North Carolina and the country. School of Education students continue their history of academic excellence, posting a passage rate for the Praxis II exam of 96 percent in 2007. The School of Education has also been selected to participate in the North Carolina Teaching Fellows, joining thirteen public and four private institutions across the state.

The Military Science Department offers Army Reserve Officer Training Corps (ROTC) classes, leading to a commission as an officer in the Active, Reserve, or National Guard component of the United States Army. Campbell's ROTC program is one of the best in the nation, earning the MacArthur Award seven times since 1989 as the premier leadership-training program in the nation.

FINANCIAL AID

Campbell University has private and institutional scholarships, federal grants, loans, and Federal Work-Study Program awards. Needs analysis forms (Free Application for Federal Student Aid) are available January 1 and are due in the Financial Aid Office by March 15 if the applicant wishes to be considered for a maximum award. Ninety-one percent of the student body received financial assistance in 2007–08. All assistance is offered without regard to race, creed, or national origin.

APPLICATION AND INFORMATION

An application for admission, accompanied by a $35 nonrefundable application fee, must be filed. Students may also apply online. When all records are on file, the Admissions Committee notifies the student of its decision.

CEDAR CREST COLLEGE

■ ALLENTOWN, PENNSYLVANIA

THE COLLEGE

Since its founding in 1867 as an independent liberal arts college for women, Cedar Crest has educated women for leadership in a changing world. Approximately 1,900 students come to the College annually from thirty-two states and twenty other countries. The 11:1 student-faculty ratio provides for small classes, individual advising, and independent work in an environment that emphasizes interdisciplinary, values-oriented education. The Honor Philosophy is a most compelling statement of each student's rights and responsibilities for her own academic and cocurricular performance.

For an application and more information, students should contact:

Vice President for Enrollment
Cedar Crest College
100 College Drive
Allentown, Pennsylvania 18104-6196
Phone: 800-360-1222 (toll-free)
E-mail: cccadmis@cedarcrest.edu
Web site: http://www.cedarcrest.edu

Cedar Crest's science programs, including conservation biology, forensic science, genetic engineering, neuroscience, nuclear medicine, nursing, and nutrition, generate the largest student enrollment. Business and marketing, psychology, and education generate the next largest enrollments. The genetic engineering major was the first such program at a women's college and the second at an undergraduate institution.

Cedar Crest has a national Gold Award program for health and wellness that includes personal sports training, nutrition counseling, and a full schedule of dance classes plus yoga and aerobics. The Rodale Aquatic Center for Civic Health, a state-of-the-art two-pool complex, offers health and fitness opportunities for the entire campus community. The campus also includes tennis courts and regulation fields for field hockey, lacrosse, soccer, and softball.

Student Affairs sponsors workshops and retreats on leadership and service throughout the year. More than forty-five campus organizations offer opportunities in the performing arts, preprofessional areas, environmental awareness, cultural diversity, and much more. An active community service program is made up of student and faculty volunteers with many groups, from Habitat for Humanity to the Girls Club. Healthy lifestyle, community building, and innovative quality-of-life programs are held regularly in the four residence halls.

The Office of Career Planning offers placement opportunities, internships at nearly 350 companies worldwide, and four-year guidance in preparing resumes and interviewing for employment and graduate schools.

The Cedar Crest Falcons compete in eight NCAA Division III intercollegiate sports: basketball, cross-country, field hockey, lacrosse, soccer, softball, tennis, and volleyball. Intramural activities include badminton, basketball, soccer, softball, and tennis. The Equestrian Club competes in collegiate horse shows.

ACADEMIC PROGRAMS

Self-designed majors, double majors, minors, independent-study programs, and individual and group research projects support serious concentration at the undergraduate level. Working with her adviser, each student designs a program of study that meets the major requirements as well as her personal interests and professional goals. The College's curriculum is structured to provide course work in the areas that define a liberal arts education. The Ethical Life Course integrates applied ethics and service-learning opportunities. Science majors begin conducting advanced research at the freshman level, opening opportunities that often lead to internships at major research institutions.

Each major has a Capstone experience that reflects on previous learning and experience and explores issues emerging in the present and expected in the future. The academic program emphasizes independent and faculty-supported student research.

FINANCIAL AID

Cedar Crest offers a generous program of financial aid based on academic achievement and financial need, including scholarships, grants, loans, and employment. The size of an award varies with need. More than 90 percent of the students at Cedar Crest receive aid. Students applying for financial aid should file the FAFSA. Outstanding international students may also qualify for financial aid.

Applicants who rank in the top 25 percent of their class and score 1100 or higher on the critical reading and math sections of the SAT (24 on the ACT) can qualify for a scholarship of up to one-half tuition per year. Sibling grants are awarded to students when 2 siblings are attending Cedar Crest full-time, concurrently. Recipients of Girl Scout Gold awards, graduates of Governor's School of Excellence programs, and HOBY alumnae are also eligible for scholarship recognition. Students can receive an early estimate of aid eligibility by completing a Cedar Crest financial aid application/planner.

APPLICATION AND INFORMATION

Cedar Crest has a rolling admission policy; applications are reviewed on a continuing basis. Students are encouraged to apply early in their senior year of high school. Admission is awarded for the fall or spring semester.

CHAPMAN UNIVERSITY

■ ORANGE, CALIFORNIA

THE UNIVERSITY

During its 146-year history, Chapman has evolved from a small, traditional liberal arts college founded in 1861 by members of the First Christian Church (Disciples of Christ) into a midsized comprehensive liberal arts and sciences university distinguished for its nationally recognized programs in film and television production, business and economics, theater, dance, music, education, and the natural and applied sciences. The mission of Chapman University is to provide personalized education of distinction that leads to inquiring, ethical, and productive lives as global citizens.

For an application and more information, students should contact:

Office of Admission
Chapman University
One University Drive
Orange, California 92866
Phone: 714-997-6711
888-CUAPPLY (toll-free)
E-mail: admit@chapman.edu
Web site: http://www.chapman.edu

Chapman's parklike ivy-covered, tree-lined campus features a blending of fully refurbished historic structures with the newest in state-of-the-art Internet and satellite-connected learning environments. Five residence halls and six on-campus apartment buildings are conveniently located on the edge of the campus.

Chapman University's academic structure includes the Wilkinson College of Letters and Sciences, the CILECT-accredited Dodge College of Film and Media Arts, the AACSB International–accredited Argyros School of Business and Economics, the CTC-approved School of Education, the ABA-accredited School of Law, and the College of Performing Arts, which includes the NASM-accredited School of Music. Other nationally accredited programs include the IFT-accredited program in food sciences and the APTA-accredited program in physical therapy. Chapman has been recognized by the Templeton Foundation as one of only 100 colleges to be designated as a Templeton Foundation "Character-Building College" for its emphasis on global citizenry and student involvement in community action and stewardship activities.

The University environment is electric, involving, and outdoor-oriented. Chapman students enjoy a dynamic and involving student activities program. Although predominantly from California, Chapman students come from more than forty states and thirty-four other countries. Chapman's long and distinguished heritage in intercollegiate athletics includes five NCAA national championships in baseball, tennis, and softball. Chapman competes as an independent in the NCAA Division III level and fields teams in baseball, basketball (m/w), crew (m/w), cross-country (m/w), football, golf, lacrosse, soccer (m/w), softball, swimming (w), tennis (m/w), track and field (m/w), volleyball (w), and water polo (m/w).

More than seventy clubs and organizations are available, many with commitments to a wide range of community service efforts. Chapman's Greek system includes six nationally chartered fraternities for men and five nationally chartered sororities for women. A comprehensive intramural sports program involves myriad sports activities for all campus community members throughout the school year. On-campus intercollegiate athletic events as well as music, art, and theater productions provide students with extensive extracurricular activity options.

ACADEMIC PROGRAMS

Possibly unique to Chapman is the University's relationship with the professional mentoring program, Inside Track. In addition to traditionally assigned academic advisers, each freshman is also assigned a life coach with whom they meet once weekly to develop critical skills, set goals, and address the many challenges that might interfere with their success.

The requirements for graduation are commensurate with the liberal arts philosophy of education maintained by Chapman. The program of studies is designed to ensure a breadth of subject matter selection in the liberal arts as well as depth of preparation in the student's major field. Ample opportunities are available for alternative learning experiences. Internships and cooperative education programs are recommended. Students may also undertake in-depth individual study or research in conjunction with a faculty member.

FINANCIAL AID

More than 85 percent of Chapman students benefit from some form of financial aid or scholarship assistance. Need-based financial awards include a combination of grants, scholarships, loans, and work-study jobs on campus. Merit and talent scholarship awards are awarded regardless of financial need. Chapman offers an Early Aid Estimator service that gives students an up-front picture of what their prospective aid/scholarship eligibility is.

APPLICATION AND INFORMATION

Students are strongly encouraged to visit and tour the campus. Freshman applicants can choose a nonbinding November 15 early action application deadline or the January 15 regular application deadline. Candidates who apply after the deadlines are considered on a space-available basis.

CHESTNUT HILL COLLEGE

■ PHILADELPHIA, PENNSYLVANIA

THE COLLEGE

Chestnut Hill College is a four-year, coeducational, Catholic liberal arts college. Founded in 1924 by the Sisters of St. Joseph, it is situated on a 75-acre campus overlooking the Wissahickon Creek. Enrolling more than 1,500 students, Chestnut Hill College is a diverse community of learners. Working adults are enrolled in the accelerated evening and weekend undergraduate program (School of Continuing and Professional Studies). In addition to its undergraduate degrees, Chestnut Hill awards the M.Ed., M.A., and M.S. (School of Graduate Studies) in six fields, including administration of human services, applied technology, counseling psychology and human services, education, holistic spirituality, and holistic spirituality and health care. The College also awards a doctoral degree in clinical psychology (Psy.D.).

For an application and more information, students should contact:

Office of Admissions
School of Undergraduate Studies
Chestnut Hill College
9601 Germantown Avenue
Philadelphia, Pennsylvania 19118
Phone: 215-248-7001
800-248-0052 (toll-free)
E-mail: chcapply@chc.edu
Web site: http://www.chc.edu

When it comes to student activities, students enthusiastically engage in the many clubs and organizations available and participate in everything from aerobics and horseback riding to golf and archery. The College is an NCAA Division II provisional member and competes in baseball (men), basketball (men and women), cross-country (men and women), golf (men and women), lacrosse (women), soccer (men and women), softball (women), tennis (men and women), and volleyball (women). A swimming pool, a gymnasium, a fitness room, and outdoor basketball and tennis courts provide excellent athletic facilities for Chestnut Hill's students.

ACADEMIC PROGRAMS

The academic year consists of two 15-week semesters. There are also two 6-week summer sessions.

As a liberal arts college, Chestnut Hill offers courses of study that provide the student with a broad background in the fine arts and humanities, a knowledge of science, and a keen awareness of the social problems of the day, as well as intensive, in-depth study in a major field.

Chestnut Hill College confers a B.S. or B.A. degree to students who earn 120 semester hours of credit and satisfy specific requirements set by the faculty. Core seminars are interdisciplinary and provide opportunities for experiential learning. In addition, students must take 6 semester hours of religious studies, 6 hours beyond the elementary level in a classical or modern foreign language, and 3 hours in a writing course (unless exempted by the English department). Focused on six perspectives (historical, literary, artistic, scientific, behavior, and problem solving and analysis), the Ways of Knowing component of the core curriculum is designed to introduce students to different learning methodologies and strategies.

A student with the ability and proper motivation may be permitted to major in two departments. The student must consult with the chair of each department to determine the feasibility of the proposal and then submit it to the dean of the college for approval. It is understood that the student will satisfy the requirements of both departments.

Each year, selected first-year students and sophomores are invited into an interdepartmental honors program that challenges intellectual initiative and provides the opportunity for independent study and seminar discussion. The completion of the four honors courses and an honors paper satisfies all distributional requirements. Students may apply for admission at the beginning of their first year or sophomore year.

Sophomores of high scholastic standing are invited by their major departments to engage in a program of independent study during their junior and senior years. This opportunity for independent study and original research culminates in an honors thesis, which is a prerequisite for the conferring of honors at graduation.

FINANCIAL AID

Financial aid is available in the form of academic scholarships, loans, work-study programs, federal grants, and Chestnut Hill College grants. Most of these are based on financial need and are awarded in financial aid packages that combine various forms of aid and are tailored to each student's need. More than 75 percent of Chestnut Hill College students receive financial aid to meet college costs. All applicants for aid should file a copy of the Free Application for Federal Student Aid (FAFSA). Merit-based scholarships and awards are granted for academic achievement.

APPLICATION AND INFORMATION

Applications are processed on a rolling admission system.

CITY UNIVERSITY OF SEATTLE

■ BELLEVUE, WASHINGTON

THE UNIVERSITY

City University of Seattle opened its doors in 1973 with one primary purpose: to provide educational opportunities for those segments of the population not being fully served through traditional means. City University believes that education is a lifelong process, and it is a pioneer in the concept of education unhindered by time, format, or location. City University is a private, not-for-profit institution of higher learning, open to anyone with the desire to achieve. Classes are offered in the day, evening, on weekends, or online in order to meet student needs without interrupting established lifestyles and associations.

For an application and more information, students should contact:

Office of Admissions and Student Services
City University of Seattle
11900 NE First Street
Bellevue, Washington 98005
Phone: 888-42-CITYU (24898) (toll-free)
425-450-4660 (TTY)
E-mail: info@cityu.edu
Web site: http://www.cityu.edu

City University's students are primarily working adults, drawn from all walks of life. In the 2006–07 school year, the University enrolled more than 4,000 undergraduate students worldwide. Of those, more than 56 percent were women and, for those reporting, 11 percent were members of minority groups. Although the majority of students attend classes near their homes in the Pacific Northwest, many live and study at locations around the globe. Often programs are available at the student's workplace through cooperative arrangements with progressive employers or professional associations.

City University of Seattle is accredited by the Northwest Commission on Colleges and Universities.

Most City University students are already established in either a job or career and have chosen a path they are preparing to follow. As alumni, they are able to realize their career goals in business, in public administration, or in one of several professions.

ACADEMIC PROGRAMS

Candidates for the bachelor's degree must complete 180 hours of credit by completing regular or distance learning classes or through recognized transfer credits or prior learning experience. Lower-division requirements total 90 credits, including a total of 55 general education credits in the broad areas of writing, mathematics, humanities, natural sciences/mathematics, and social sciences. For most bachelor's degree programs, upper-division course work consists of a series of common core courses respective to their degrees, followed by a series of elective courses. Most undergraduate programs are designed to allow students to satisfy certain general education requirements through upper-division course work.

For the Associate of Science degree, students complete 90 credit hours, 35 of which are in general education. Each of these programs is wholly compatible with and transferable to baccalaureate degree study. Depending on the particular choice of program, students can complete an undergraduate certificate program with 24 to 45 credits.

The academic year is divided into four quarters. City University offers day, evening, weekend, and distance learning courses.

FINANCIAL AID

To help qualified students achieve their educational and professional goals, City University participates in several financial aid programs. Federal Pell Grants, Federal Supplemental Educational Opportunity Grants, Federal Stafford Student Loans, Federal PLUS loans, and Federal Work-Study are available.

In addition, the University awards scholarships on the basis of financial need, demonstrated academic ability, and other criteria. Employer reimbursement programs and military tuition assistance programs are also recognized, and all programs are approved for veterans' education benefits.

Students interested in financial aid should contact City University's Financial Aid Office at the toll-free number listed below for more information.

APPLICATION AND INFORMATION

Because of City University's rolling admissions policy, applications for admission may be submitted at any time.

COLUMBIA COLLEGE CHICAGO

■ CHICAGO, ILLINOIS

THE COLLEGE

Columbia College Chicago is the nation's largest and most diverse visual, performing, media, and communication arts college. The foundation of a Columbia education features small class sizes that ensure close interaction with a faculty of working professionals, abundant internship opportunities with major employers in the Chicago and national marketplaces, and outstanding professional facilities that foster learning by doing. All students are encouraged to begin course work in their chosen fields during their freshman year, allowing them four full years in which to master their craft and build professional portfolios, audition tapes, resumes, and clip books. The College provides a strong liberal arts background and supports student employment goals through a full range of career services.

For an application and more information, students should contact:

Office of Undergraduate Admissions
Columbia College Chicago
600 South Michigan Avenue
Chicago, Illinois 60605
Phone: 312-344-7130
E-mail: admissions@colum.edu
Web site: http://www.colum.edu

Columbia's enrollment of more than 12,000 students is drawn from Chicago and its suburbs, across the United States, and more than forty-six other countries. The student body is almost equally divided between men and women. Creative students who enjoy a supportive but challenging environment thrive at Columbia. The College's six residence halls extend the supportive philosophy of the College. There are a variety of available housing options with amenities that may include computer and study rooms, drawing and painting studio space, music practice space, fitness rooms, an indoor heated pool, lake views, and a laundry room. Apartments, suites, and rooms are fully furnished. All facilities are conveniently located steps from the main campus buildings and close to public transportation, all in the heart of downtown Chicago. Columbia College students are immersed in a creative environment both in and out of the classroom.

Outside the classroom, students participate in activities that include the College's award-winning student newspaper, radio station, electronic newsletter, two student magazines, cable television soap opera, three theaters, dance center, photography and art museums, and film and video festival. Many of the more than seventy-five student clubs on campus are linked to an academic discipline and offer opportunities to expand social and professional networking experiences. Several gallery/café environments allow students to relax or study between classes. These centers feature a variety of activities, including art exhibits, film screenings, lectures, and live performances of music, comedy, readings, or dance.

ACADEMIC PROGRAMS

Columbia supports creative and integrated approaches to education and encourages interdisciplinary study. The B.A. degree is awarded to students who successfully complete 120 semester hours, and the B.F.A. degree is awarded to students who successfully complete 128 semester hours of study in designated programs. Of the required 120 hours toward the completion of the B.A., 48 (36 for B.F.A. candidates) are distributed among courses in the humanities and literature, science and mathematics, English composition, oral communications, social sciences, and computer applications.

Columbia College Chicago's Portfolio Center is uniquely geared to provide students with professional-grade portfolio development. The Portfolio Center links industry professionals and alumni with current students through workshops, portfolio development sessions, and networking events. The center also maintains an online Portfolio Archive that serves as an invaluable resource and inspiration for students.

FINANCIAL AID

Columbia College makes every effort to help students obtain financial assistance, including grants, on-campus work, and loans. The Office of Student Financial Services administers federal and state grant and loan programs. The College also provides information for students seeking part-time employment both on and off campus. Columbia offers institution-based scholarships, such as Presidential Scholarships for freshmen, scholarships for transfer students, academic excellence awards, leadership awards, and housing grants. The Fischetti Scholarships support the efforts of outstanding Columbia journalism students, and the Weisman Scholarships support special communication-related projects.

APPLICATION AND INFORMATION

Students are strongly advised to apply early. The priority date is May 1 for the fall semester, November 15 for the spring semester, and April 15 for the summer term. Applicants are notified of their acceptance within two to four weeks after the College receives all the required information and documents. Students who want to live in campus housing are strongly advised to apply early. Housing assignments are offered on a first-come, first-served basis until full occupancy is achieved. To arrange for a tour or an appointment with an admissions counselor, students should call the Office of Undergraduate Admissions.

COLUMBIA UNIVERSITY, SCHOOL OF GENERAL STUDIES

■ NEW YORK, NEW YORK

THE UNIVERSITY AND THE SCHOOL

The School of General Studies (GS) of Columbia University is one of the finest liberal arts colleges in the country dedicated specifically to students with nontraditional backgrounds seeking a traditional education at an Ivy League university. Most students at GS have, for personal or professional reasons, interrupted their education, never attended college, or are only able to attend part-time. GS is unique among colleges of its type, because its students are fully integrated into the Columbia undergraduate curriculum: they take the same courses with the same faculty members and earn the same degree as all other Columbia undergraduates.

GS students come from varied backgrounds and all walks of life. They have the option to study either full- or part-time. Many students work full-time while pursuing a degree, and many have family responsibilities; others attend classes full-time and experience Columbia's more traditional college life. In the classroom, the diversity and varied personal experience of the student body promote discussion and debate, fostering an environment of academic rigor and intellectual development. GS has approximately 1,200 undergraduate degree candidates and close to 400 postbaccalaureate premedical students. The average age of a GS student is 29. More than 60 percent of GS students attend classes full-time.

In addition to its bachelor's degree program, GS offers combined undergraduate/graduate degree programs with Columbia's Schools of Social Work, International and Public Affairs, Law, Business, Dental Medicine, Teachers College, and the College of Physicians and Surgeons. Between 80 and 85 percent of the School's students continue on to graduate and professional study after graduation. The acceptance rate for GS postbaccalaureate premedical students applying to U.S. medical schools is more than 90 percent.

For an application and more information, students should contact:

Curtis M. Rodgers, Dean of Admissions
Office of Admissions and Financial Aid
School of General Studies
408 Lewisohn Hall
2970 Broadway
Columbia University, Mail Code 4101
New York, New York 10027

Phone: 212-854-2772
E-mail: gsdegree@columbia.edu
Web site: http://www.gs.columbia.edu

ACADEMIC PROGRAMS

The School of General Studies offers a traditional liberal arts education designed to provide students with the broad knowledge and intellectual skills that foster continued education and growth in the years after college as well as providing a sound foundation for positions of responsibility in the professional world.

Requirements for the bachelor's degree comprise three elements: (1) core requirements, intended to develop in students the ability to write and communicate clearly; to understand the modes of thought that characterize the humanities, social sciences, and sciences; to gain familiarity with central cultural ideas through literature, fine arts, and music; and to acquire a working proficiency in a foreign language; (2) major requirements, designed to give students sustained and coherent exposure to a particular discipline in an area of strong intellectual interest; and (3) elective courses, in which students pursue particular interests and skills for their own personal growth or for their relationship to future professional or personal objectives. Students are required to complete a minimum of 124 credits for the bachelor's degree; 60 of these may be in transfer credit, but at least 64 credits (including the last 30 credits) must be completed at Columbia. In addition to the usual graduation honors (cum laude, magna cum laude, and summa cum laude), honors programs for superior students are available in a majority of the University's departments.

FINANCIAL AID

The School of General Studies awards financial aid based upon need and academic ability. Approximately 70 percent of GS degree candidates receive some form of financial aid, including Federal Pell Grants, New York State TAP Grants, Federal Stafford and unsubsidized Stafford Loans, Federal Perkins Loans, General Studies Scholarships, and Federal Work-Study Program awards. Priority application deadlines for new students are June 1 for the fall semester and October 15 for the spring semester.

APPLICATION AND INFORMATION

Application deadlines are March 1 for early action (nonbinding), June 1 for the fall semester, and October 15 for the spring semester. Applicants from countries outside the U.S. are urged to apply by August 15 for the spring semester and April 1 for the fall semester. Applications are reviewed as they are completed, and applicants are notified of decisions shortly thereafter.

DICKINSON STATE UNIVERSITY

■ DICKINSON, NORTH DAKOTA

THE UNIVERSITY

Student success, both inside and outside the classroom, has been the focus of Dickinson State University since 1918. The tradition continues today, allowing easy access to and meaningful relationships with qualified professors, supportive and comfortable living arrangements on campus, and student activities that provide something for everyone.

Dickinson State, with an enrollment of approximately 2,670 students, is the only comprehensive, four-year public university in West River North Dakota. The University is proud of its safe campus. Its location offers students a secure environment in which to pursue their educational and social interests.

For an application and more information, students should contact:

Office of Enrollment Services
Dickinson State University
Dickinson, North Dakota 58601-4896
Phone: 701-483-2175
800-279-HAWK Ext. 2175 (toll-free)
E-mail: dsu.hawks@dickinsonstate.edu
Web site: http://www.dickinsonstate.edu

The University's mission is to provide high-quality, accessible programs; to promote excellence in teaching and learning; to support scholarly and creative activities; and to provide service that is relevant to the economy, health, and quality of life of the citizens of North Dakota. With a wide range of academic programs, Dickinson State University prepares students to live, learn, and lead in the twenty-first century.

At Dickinson State, there are approximately forty-five different organizations to help every student find a niche. Students choose from intramural sports, band, chorus, drama, art, student government, honorary societies, academic clubs, and cheerleading, to name just a few.

Living in a residence hall at Dickinson State offers many conveniences and countless opportunities to build friendships in an exciting environment that is close to classes and University activities. Meal plans are available on campus for five or seven days per week. For added ease, students can also opt to purchase meals at the snack bar. Rooms have free access to the campus computer network and cable television. Features in each hall include a game room, exercise equipment, computer stations, free laundry facilities, and a kitchenette. Students can select to live in women's, men's, or coed halls or student apartments. Family student housing complexes provide apartments at reasonable housing rates to nontraditional students.

ACADEMIC PROGRAMS

While many of the majors that Dickinson State University offers have unique academic requirements, the basic baccalaureate degree academic curriculum consists of approximately 39 semester hours of general education courses from the areas of communications, scientific inquiry, expression of human civilization, understanding human civilization, multicultural studies, and physical education; a specific major core curriculum of 32 to 60 or more semester hours; approximately 24 semester hours of credit in a minor field of study (when a minor is required); and professional education course work for those students entering the teaching profession. Students seeking a Bachelor of Arts degree must also complete a minimum of 16 semester hours of a foreign language. A minimum of 128 semester hours is required for graduation in a baccalaureate degree program. Associate degree programs require 64 credit hours for graduation.

FINANCIAL AID

College is a valuable investment in the future, and Dickinson State realizes financing it can be challenging. One of the best college buys in the region, Dickinson State's tuition and housing rates are among the lowest in the upper Midwest. In addition, attractive tuition rates are offered for students living in states and provinces bordering on North Dakota. Special rates also exist for students who live in those states participating in the Western Undergraduate Exchange (WUE) and the Midwest Student Exchange Program (MSEP). These include Alaska, Arizona, California, Colorado, Hawaii, Idaho, Kansas, Michigan, Missouri, Nebraska, Nevada, New Mexico, Oregon, Utah, Washington, and Wyoming.

The Office of Financial Aid is ready to help ease the cost of a college education through a number of financial aid programs, including scholarships, grants, loans, student employment opportunities, cultural diversity awards, and international awards. Approximately 80 percent of Dickinson State's students received financial assistance last year.

APPLICATION AND INFORMATION

The enrollment services staff is anxious to discuss the variety of programs the University has to offer and give a tour of the beautiful campus and its classrooms, facilities, and residence halls. When students are on campus, they should meet with the financial aid staff to discuss concerns about financing an education. Enrollment counselors are available Monday through Friday, 8 a.m. to 4:30 p.m., Mountain Time.

DOMINICAN UNIVERSITY OF CALIFORNIA

■ SAN RAFAEL, CALIFORNIA

THE UNIVERSITY

Dominican University of California is an independent, international, learner-centered university of Dominican heritage. It offers a beautiful setting, a close-knit community of approximately 2,000 students, and an intimate social environment that is an important context for academic goals and personal development.

The University offers many services that support the University's educational programs. It provides tutoring, life-planning, career, and personal counseling without charge to Dominican students; offers housing, health, and job placement services; and helps students make the most of their college experience by its readiness to assist them in resolving problems.

For an application and more information, students should contact:

Office of Admissions
Dominican University of California
50 Acacia Avenue
San Rafael, California 94901-2298
Phone: 415-485-3204
888-323-6763 (toll-free)
E-mail: enroll@dominican.edu
Web site: http://www.dominican.edu

The University and the Associated Students of Dominican University sponsor a number of campus activities each year for both resident and nonresident students. Dominican supports ten intercollegiate teams that compete in the NAIA California Pacific Conference: men's and women's basketball, golf, and soccer; men's lacrosse; and women's softball, tennis, and volleyball. Students can participate in the chorus, drama group, the literary magazine, campus newspaper, campus ministry activities, special interest clubs, dances, and other social events.

Campus Ministry responds to the spiritual needs of Catholic and non-Catholic members of the University community. Catholic liturgies, ecumenical activities for students of all faiths, and community service projects are scheduled throughout the year.

The University is approved by the California Commission on Teacher Credentialing to prepare and recommend candidates for credentials in elementary, secondary, and special education.

Four residence halls of varied architecture accommodate more than 600 students; there is a dining hall for resident students and others who wish to purchase meals on campus. Forest Meadows, which comprises approximately 25 acres, is the site of the Conlan Recreation Center, a soccer field, tennis courts, and an outdoor amphitheater where commencement exercises are held. The Recreation Center features regulation basketball and volleyball courts, two cross-courts for volleyball and basketball, and 1,285 spectator seats. It also features a weight-training and fitness room, a multipurpose room, lockers, athletic department offices, and conference rooms. Outside is a six-lane, recreational swimming pool and grassy patio area.

ACADEMIC PROGRAMS

The General Education Program offers more than a brief exposure to the major areas of knowledge in the humanities, arts, and natural and social sciences. It is designed to provide a sequence of courses with a thematic focus that integrates the wisdom and perspectives of several disciplines. The focus assists students in discovering relationships between areas of knowledge, beliefs, cultures, and peoples that differ globally and historically, as well as in acquiring an awareness of tradition, a love of discovery, a respect for the diversity of the human condition, and a realization of human interdependence. Courses within the General Education Program also expose students to a variety of learning experiences that include discussion, lectures, seminars, simulations, practicums, and quiet reflection.

A strong internship program offers students job experience in areas of their choice.

FINANCIAL AID

Financial aid is awarded on the basis of need and merit. Merit awards are available for both freshmen and transfer students based on academic achievement. Dominican University of California participates in various federal and state need-based financial aid programs and also has its own financial aid funds.

Need-based financial aid comes in the form of scholarships, grants, part-time employment, and loans. Eligibility for need-based aid is determined after the student, who must be a citizen or permanent resident of the United States, files the FAFSA and the Dominican Financial Aid Application. The need-based financial aid deadline for first priority consideration is March 2, although late applications are accepted. Student assistantship positions are also available for graduate students.

APPLICATION AND INFORMATION

The Admissions Office makes its decision on each freshman candidate after receiving his or her completed application form with a $40 nonrefundable fee; an official high school transcript to date; one recommendation from a teacher, administrator, or counselor; scores from either the SAT or the ACT; and a personal essay as described in the application. An interview with a member of the admission staff is strongly recommended to enable the candidate and the University to become acquainted with one another.

DREXEL UNIVERSITY

■ PHILADELPHIA, PENNSYLVANIA

THE UNIVERSITY

Drexel, a private, nonsectarian, coeducational university, has maintained a reputation for academic excellence since its founding in 1891. Its technologically focused academic programs prepare undergraduates for graduate school and a variety of careers. Full-time professional experience through Drexel's cooperative education program is a vital part of a Drexel education. Students gain professional experience in jobs related to their career interests by alternating classroom study with periods of professional experience.

Drexel University grants bachelor's, master's, and doctoral degrees. Last year's undergraduate enrollment numbered 12,906 full-time students representing forty states and fifty-three countries.

In 2006, Drexel admitted 181 students to the new College of Law. The College of Law is the first law school to be founded by a major research university in thirty years. Traditionally, Drexel University has great strength in the areas of engineering, science, business, and health care. The J.D. program has been designed around these innovative fields to prepare law students for the challenges of twenty-first-century practice.

Eight residential halls house more than 2,600 students on campus. In conjunction with Drexel's fourteen fraternities and ten sororities, the Campus Activities Board sponsors events such as dances, lectures, excursions, and films. Students take part in a variety of extracurricular activities, including musical groups, a recording studio, Mad Dragon Records, a dance ensemble, theatrical productions, a student-run newspaper, a radio station, and a cable TV station. Drexel offers sixteen NCAA Division I varsity athletic programs, competes in the Colonial Athletic Association Conference, and produces some of the nation's top student athletes in both the academic and athletic arenas. The University sponsors intramural and club sports.

For an application and more information, students should contact:

Undergraduate Admissions
Drexel University
3141 Chestnut Street
Philadelphia, Pennsylvania 19104-2876
Phone: 215-895-2400
800-2-DREXEL (toll-free)
Web site: http://www.drexel.edu/em

Ms. Joan McDonald
Vice President of Enrollment Management
Drexel University
Phone: 800-2-DREXEL (toll-free)
Fax: 215-895-5939
E-mail: enroll@drexel.edu

ACADEMIC PROGRAMS

Students with high ability can apply to the Pennoni Honors College, which is open to students in every major. Honors sections of general and required courses and honors colloquia and seminars are available. Special living communities designed for the exceptional student and independent projects characterize the program.

At Drexel, students have opportunities to conduct research. Students Tackling Advanced Research (STAR) allows students to participate in research projects in their field as early as the freshman year. Students who take part in these research opportunities may be eligible for stipends or academic credit for their work.

FINANCIAL AID

Approximately 90 percent of all freshmen receive financial aid. The aid package may contain academic, athletic, or performing arts scholarships; grants; loans; or part-time employment. Federal programs are also included. All students applying for aid must submit the Free Application for Federal Student Aid (FAFSA) by March 1. Notification to incoming freshmen and transfer students begins mid-March. Drexel offers a unique achievement-based award, the A. J. Drexel Scholarship, to all qualified incoming freshmen and transfer students. With an annual award value of up to $26,000, the A. J. Drexel Scholarship is renewable on a yearly basis, provided the student maintains at least a 3.0 GPA and full-time status. Criteria include a strong academic record and involvement in extracurricular and community service activities.

APPLICATION AND INFORMATION

Applications to Drexel are available online (http://www.drexel.edu/apply) or from the address listed. Each application must be accompanied by a nonrefundable application fee of $75; however, the fee is waived for online applications or if submitted during a campus visit. Applications for regular full-time undergraduate status are accepted throughout the senior year until March 1. Applications for Drexel's premier scholarship program—the A. J. Drexel scholarship—are due on January 15. Applications for accelerated degree options are due on December 1. Drexel subscribes to the College Board's Candidates Reply Date of May 1. Transfer students should apply at least three months before the beginning of the term in which they wish to enroll.

An essay or personal statement is required, with its subject dependent on the major and program. Interviews are optional.

ELMIRA COLLEGE

■ ELMIRA, NEW YORK

THE COLLEGE

Elmira College is a small, private, coeducational college that is recognized for its emphasis on education of high quality in the liberal arts and preprofessional programs. One of the oldest colleges in the United States, Elmira was founded in 1855. The College has always produced graduates interested in both community service and successful careers. Friendliness, personal attention, strong college spirit, and support for learning beyond the classroom help to make Elmira a special place. Elmira College is one of only 270 colleges in the nation to be granted a chapter of the prestigious Phi Beta Kappa honor society.

For an application and more information, students should contact:

Dean of Admissions
Elmira College
Elmira, New York 14901
Phone: 800-935-6472 (toll-free)
E-mail: admissions@elmira.edu
Web site: http://www.elmira.edu

The full-time undergraduate enrollment is about 1,200 men and women. The students at Elmira represent more than thirty-five states, primarily those in the Northeast, with the highest representation coming from New York, New Jersey, Massachusetts, Connecticut, Maine, and Pennsylvania. International students from more than thirty countries were enrolled in 2007. Ninety percent of the full-time undergraduates live in College residence halls, and dormitory rooms are equipped to provide direct access to the Internet. Wireless access is also available in the Library and Campus Center.

The intercollegiate sports program includes men's and women's basketball, golf, ice hockey, lacrosse, soccer, and tennis and women's cheerleading, field hockey, softball, and volleyball. An intramural program is also available. Emerson Hall houses the student fitness center, a pool, and a gym capable of seating 1,000, as well as the Gibson Theatre, which has a state-of-the-art sound and lighting system. Professional societies; clubs; music, dance, and drama groups; a student-operated FM radio station; and the student newspaper, yearbook, and literary magazine also provide numerous opportunities for extracurricular activity.

ACADEMIC PROGRAMS

The College's calendar is composed of two 12-week terms followed by a six-week spring term. Students enroll for four subjects during the twelve-week terms, completing the first term by mid-December and the second during the first week of April. The six-week term, from mid-April through May, may be devoted to a particular project involving travel, internship, research, or independent study. Students are required to participate in internships in order to gain practical and meaningful experience related to their program of study. Credit is awarded for these projects. Forty percent of Elmira College students study abroad at some point during their four years of study.

Special opportunities for outstanding students include participation in thirteen national honorary societies on campus and a chance to assist faculty members in teaching and research. The College also offers an accelerated three-year graduation option for outstanding students, and an Advanced Placement Program is available.

Army ROTC and Air Force ROTC are available.

FINANCIAL AID

Financial aid is available for both freshmen and transfer students. Awards are based upon the Free Application for Federal Student Aid (FAFSA) as well as the student's past academic performance. Types of aid include grants, scholarships, loans, and work opportunities. Sources of aid include college, federal, state, and private dollars. In addition, superior students may qualify for non-need Elmira College Honors Scholarships, which are available to both freshmen and transfer students and range from $4000 to full tuition per year. For 2006–07, the average freshman aid package (including all types of aid) amounted to more than $23,500. About 76 percent of the full-time undergraduates receive need-based financial aid. Twenty-one percent of students receive non-need merit aid.

EMBRY–RIDDLE AERONAUTICAL UNIVERSITY

■ DAYTONA BEACH, FLORIDA

THE UNIVERSITY

Embry-Riddle's history, legacy, and reputation date back almost to the time of the Wright brothers. The University prides itself on being the leader in aviation and aerospace education, provided through its residential campuses in Daytona Beach, Florida, and Prescott, Arizona, and its many Worldwide Campus locations, serving the continuing education needs of the aviation industry.

Approximately 4,800 undergraduate students and 400 graduate students are currently enrolled at the Daytona Beach residential campus. Students come from all fifty states and nearly 100 countries, which makes Embry-Riddle truly an international university.

For an application and more information, students should contact:

University Admissions
Embry-Riddle Aeronautical University
P.O. Box 11767
Daytona Beach, Florida 32120-1767
Phone: 386-226-6100
800-862-2416 (toll-free nationwide)
E-mail: univadm@erau.edu
Web site: http://www.embryriddle.edu

More than twenty bachelor's degree programs and six graduate programs are offered at the Daytona Beach campus. Embry-Riddle's premier aeronautical science (professional pilot) program and award-winning aerospace engineering program are the largest on campus and the largest of their type in the nation.

Students at the Daytona Beach campus enjoy a wide array of activities and clubs, many focused on aviation and aerospace, as well as fraternities, sororities, and recreational opportunities. Forty-three percent of students live on campus.

Embry-Riddle's award-winning precision flight demonstration teams offer students the opportunity to compete nationally in air and ground events. Embry-Riddle also has the largest all-volunteer Air Force ROTC detachment in the country and among the fastest-growing Navy ROTC units and Army ROTC battalions. Embry-Riddle athletes participate in intercollegiate and intramural competitions in many sports, including baseball, basketball, crew, cross-country, golf, soccer, tennis, volleyball, and ice hockey.

The 68,000-square-foot ICI Center contains two full-size NCAA basketball courts, a fitness center, and a weight room. The ICI Center provides a place to host sporting events and assemblies. The University sports complex also includes a soccer field, the Sliwa Stadium ballpark, the Ambassador William Crotty Tennis Center, and the Track and Field Complex. New in 2007, the Tine Davis Fitness Center is adjacent to the Olympic-size pool and features comprehensive fitness services and wellness programs.

The 5,300-square-foot interfaith chapel accommodates the variety of faiths represented by the student body of Embry-Riddle. It consists of a 140-seat nondenominational worship area, four prayer rooms (Catholic, Jewish, Muslim, and Protestant), and administrative spaces for Campus Ministry's 2 chaplains and student assistants.

ACADEMIC PROGRAMS

Even a field as specialized as aviation requires a broad background. General education courses required of all students who are pursuing a baccalaureate program include communication skills, such as English composition, literature, and technical report writing; humanities; social sciences; mathematics; physical science; economics; and computer science. To ensure academic success, Embry-Riddle provides free tutorial services.

The calendar year is divided into two semesters of fifteen weeks each, with the summer session divided into two terms. The average course load for each fall or spring semester is 15 credit hours.

FINANCIAL AID

Applicants for financial aid are required to complete the Department of Education's Free Application for Federal Student Aid (FAFSA) and any other documents requested by the University. Students are encouraged to apply early if they wish to be considered for all types of programs. Florida residents may also apply for several additional programs that are available through the state.

APPLICATION AND INFORMATION

Embry-Riddle requires each applicant to submit an application form and fee, SAT or ACT scores, two letters of recommendation, and an official high school/college transcript. Flight students must provide an FAA Class I or Class II medical certificate. When a student is accepted for admission, tuition and housing deposits are required by May 1.

EMERSON COLLEGE

■ BOSTON, MASSACHUSETTS

THE COLLEGE

Founded in 1880, Emerson is one of the premier colleges in the United States for the study of communication and the arts. Students may choose from more than two dozen undergraduate and graduate programs supported by state-of-the-art facilities and a nationally renowned faculty. The campus is home to WERS-FM, the oldest noncommercial radio station in Boston; the historic 1,200-seat Cutler Majestic Theatre; and *Ploughshares,* the award-winning literary journal for new writing.

For an application and more information, students should contact:

Office of Undergraduate Admission
Emerson College
120 Bolyston Street
Boston, Massachusetts 02116-4624
Phone: 617-824-8600
E-mail: admission@emerson.edu
Web site: http://www.emerson.edu

A pioneer in the fields of communication and performing arts, Emerson was one of the first colleges in the nation to establish a program in children's theater (1919), an undergraduate program in broadcasting (1937), professional-level training in speech pathology and audiology (1935), educational FM radio (1949), closed-circuit television (1955), and a B.F.A. degree program in film as early as 1972. In 1980, the College created the country's first graduate program in professional writing and publishing.

Today, Emerson's 3,000 undergraduate and 900 graduate students come from across the country and more than forty other countries. Approximately 1,200 students live on campus, some in special learning communities, such as the Writers' Block and Digital Culture Floor. Emerson's residence halls are air conditioned with cable television and Internet access. Wireless service is available in several campus locations. There is a fitness center, athletic field, and a new fourteen-story campus center and residence hall that houses a gymnasium, student-services offices, and meeting space for student organizations.

Emerson College is fully accredited by the New England Association of Schools and Colleges.

In addition to its undergraduate programs, Emerson College offers more than a dozen master's degree programs for its graduate students.

ACADEMIC PROGRAMS

Emerson's academic calendar consists of two fifteen-week semesters, plus two six-week sessions during the summer months. The requirements for graduation combine general education and liberal arts courses with advanced, specialized classes that are specific to individual departments and majors. Internships for academic credit are available in almost every major and the Institute for Liberal Arts & Interdisciplinary Studies offers exciting first-year seminars, independent study options, and innovative courses that cut across academic disciplines.

FINANCIAL AID

Each year, more than two thirds of Emerson's student body receive some form of financial assistance, packaged in awards that typically combine grant and scholarship, loan, and College work-study. Academic scholarships ranging from $8000 to half-tuition are awarded on a limited basis to students who meet high academic standards. Special performance-based scholarships, averaging $4000, are available to exceptional students in the performing arts.

In order to apply for financial assistance, students must complete the Free Application for Federal Student Assistance (FAFSA) and CSS PROFILE form. Deadlines are March 1 for September admission or November 15 for January admission. More information about financial assistance at Emerson can be found online at http://www.emerson.edu/financial_services or by contacting the Office of Student Financial Services at 617-824-8655 or finaid@emerson.edu.

APPLICATION AND INFORMATION

First-year candidates for September admission should file their application by January 5. Early Action applications are due November 1. The regular admission deadline for January admission is November 1.

Transfer students should submit their applications and supporting credentials by March 15 for September admission or November 1 for January admission.

FIVE TOWNS COLLEGE

■ DIX HILLS, NEW YORK

THE COLLEGE

Located on Long Island's North Shore, Five Towns College offers students the opportunity to study in a suburban environment that is close to New York City. Founded in 1972, Five Towns College is an independent, nonsectarian, coeducational institution that places its emphasis on the student as an individual. Many students are drawn to the College because of its strong reputation in music, media, and the performing arts. The College offers associate, bachelor's, master's, and doctoral degrees.

For an application and more information, students should contact:

Director of Admissions
Five Towns College
305 North Service Road
Dix Hills, New York 11746-5871
Phone: 631-424-7000 Ext. 2110
E-mail: admissions@ftc.edu
Web site: http://www.ftc.edu

From as far away as England and Japan and from as close as Long Island and New York City, the 1,000 full-time students reflect a rich cultural diversity. The College's enrollment is 60 percent men and 40 percent women, with a minority population of approximately 30 percent. The College's music programs are contemporary jazz in nature, although classical musicians are also part of this creative community. The most popular programs are audio recording technology, broadcasting, journalism, music performance, music business, music and elementary teacher education, theater, and film/video production.

Coeducational living accommodations are available on campus. The Five Towns College Living/Learning Center is a brand-new complex containing modern dormitories. Each residence hall contains single- and double-occupancy rooms equipped with private bathrooms, broadband Internet access, cable television, and other amenities.

ACADEMIC PROGRAMS

The following describes some of the more popular programs at Five Towns College. For a complete description of the College's academic program, students should visit the Five Towns College Web site at http://www.ftc.edu.

The music education program is designed for students interested in a career as a teacher of music in a public or private school. The undergraduate program leads to New York State provisional certification. The course work provides professional training and includes a student-teaching experience. The audio recording technology concentration is designed to provide students with the tools needed to succeed as professional studio engineers and producers in the music industry. The music business concentration is designed for students interested in a career in entertainment-related business fields. The course work includes the technical, legal, production, management, and merchandising aspects of the music business. The composition/songwriting concentration provides intensive instruction in a core of technical studies in harmony, orchestration, counterpoint, MIDI, songwriting, form and analysis, arranging, and composition for those who intend to pursue careers as composers, arrangers, and songwriters. The performance concentration includes a common core of technical studies and a foundation of specialized courses, such as music history, harmony, counterpoint, improvisation, ensemble performance, and private instruction. The theater arts program is designed for students interested in careers as actors, entertainers, scenic designers, directors, stage managers, and lighting or sound directors. The film/video program includes extensive technical preparation in videography, filmmaking, linear and nonlinear editing, storyboarding, scriptwriting, producing, and directing for filmmakers and videographers. Elementary education students are prepared as teachers for grades 1–6, while those interested in journalism and broadcasting are prepared for careers in radio, television, newspaper, and editorial writing.

FINANCIAL AID

The annual tuition at Five Towns College is among the lowest of all the private colleges in the region. Nevertheless, approximately 72 percent of all students receive some form of financial assistance. Need-based and/or merit-based grants, scholarships, loans, and work-study programs are available to qualified recipients, including transfer students. Prospective students are urged to contact the Financial Aid Office as early as possible.

APPLICATION AND INFORMATION

Admission into any music program is contingent upon passing an audition demonstrating skill in performance on a major instrument or vocally. Admission into any theater program is also contingent upon passing an audition. In some cases, the Admissions Committee may request an on-campus interview with an applicant. Music, theater, and film/video students are encouraged to submit a portfolio tape or reel, if available.

Except for applicants applying on an early decision basis, new students are accepted on a rolling basis, with decisions for the fall and spring semesters mailed starting February 15 and October 15, respectively. There is an application fee of $35.

FORDHAM UNIVERSITY

■ NEW YORK, NEW YORK

THE UNIVERSITY

Fordham, the Jesuit University of New York, offers a distinctive educational experience that is rooted in the 450-year-old Jesuit tradition of intellectual rigor and personal respect for the individual. The University enrolls approximately 14,700 students, of whom 7,652 are undergraduates.

Fordham has four undergraduate colleges and six graduate schools. In addition to its full-time undergraduate programs, the University offers part-time undergraduate study at Fordham College of Liberal Studies and during two summer sessions.

Fordham College at Rose Hill and the College of Business Administration, located on the Rose Hill campus, are adjacent to the New York Botanical Garden and the Bronx Zoo. Rose Hill is a self-contained 85-acre campus with residential facilities for more than 3,100 students and ample parking for commuters. It is easily accessible by public and private transportation. Fordham also provides an intercampus van service to transport students to and from Manhattan. Fordham College at Lincoln Center is located on Manhattan's Upper West Side, overlooking the famous Lincoln Center for the Performing Arts complex. The Lincoln Center campus has an 850-bed apartment-style residence, McMahon Hall, and is accessible via the West Side Highway and major subway lines.

For an application and more information, students should contact:

Peter Farrell
Director of Admission
Duane Library
Fordham University
441 East Fordham Road
Bronx, New York 10458
Phone: 800-FORDHAM (367-3426) (toll-free)
E-mail: enroll@fordham.edu
Web site: http://www.fordham.edu

The University has an extensive athletics program consisting of twenty-three varsity sports and numerous club and intramural sports. The recently renovated Murphy Field is the heart of intramural and recreational sports at Fordham, hosting softball, soccer, and flag football games. The Vincent T. Lombardi Memorial Center provides facilities for basketball, squash, swimming and diving, tennis, track, and water polo.

ACADEMIC PROGRAMS

Students in all undergraduate colleges pursue a common core curriculum designed to provide them with the breadth of knowledge that marks the educated person. Drawn from nine disciplines, the core includes the study of philosophy, English composition and literature, history, theology, mathematical reasoning, natural science, social sciences, the fine arts, and foreign language. Business students benefit from the core curriculum as well as from required business core courses.

FINANCIAL AID

More than 85 percent of the entering students enroll with aid from Fordham as well as from outside sources. Among the major aid programs are Federal Pell Grants, Federal Supplemental Educational Opportunity Grants, Federal Perkins Loans, work grants sponsored by both the government and the University, and University grants-in-aid. Outside sources of aid include state scholarships, the New York State Tuition Assistance Program (TAP), privately sponsored scholarships, state government loan programs, and deferred-payment programs. The University also offers academic scholarships ranging from $10,000 to the full cost of tuition and room.

Applicants for aid must submit the Free Application for Federal Student Aid (FAFSA) and the College Scholarship Service (CSS) PROFILE. Inquiries should be directed to Fordham's Office of Undergraduate Admission or Office of Student Financial Services.

APPLICATION AND INFORMATION

Application may be made for either September or January enrollment. The application deadline is January 15 for fall admission. The completed application, the secondary school report, the results of the SAT or ACT, all financial aid forms, and an application fee of $50 (check or money order made payable to Fordham University) should be submitted by this date. Students are notified on or about April 1. Candidates for Early Action should apply by November 1 and receive notification by December 25. Transfer students must apply by December 1 for spring admission or by July 1 for fall admission.

GARDNER-WEBB UNIVERSITY

■ BOILING SPRINGS, NORTH CAROLINA

For an application and more information, students should contact:

Director of Undergraduate Admissions and Enrollment Management
Gardner-Webb University
Boiling Springs, North Carolina 28017
Phone: 704-406-4GWU
800-253-6472 (toll-free)
Web site:
http://www.gardner-webb.edu

THE UNIVERSITY

Gardner-Webb's mission is to provide a high-quality liberal arts education in a Christian environment with the personal touch. The most outstanding characteristics of the University are its Christian environment, sense of community, and proven record of academic distinction. Its origins are obviously deep in Christian tradition, which is exemplified in the lives of staff and faculty members. Because the University is small, students can be well known by a large percentage of the faculty and administration members. The cosmopolitan student body (more than 3,800 men and women, of whom nearly 2,700 are undergraduates) represents thirty states and thirty other countries and gives an added, valuable dimension to a student's educational experience.

The heritage of the University is reflected in its beautiful landscape and stately brick buildings. However, the University is constantly forging ahead with advanced technology and state-of-the-art facilities. There are several social and service clubs on campus, including the Drama Club, Fellowship of Christian Athletes (FCA), Campus Ministries United, student government, and various University and student committees. There are many extracurricular activities for those who are interested. An Army ROTC program; the Gardner-Webb Student YMCA (GWSY), which trains students for leadership positions at YMCAs; and the GWU Marching Band provide strong outlets for student involvement on campus. The Student Entertainment Association offers a full program of social events and entertainment. The Gardner-Webb Theatre offers a full season of plays. There are a student newspaper, a literary magazine, a television studio, and a campus radio station. Students may also participate in community projects or in various kinds of off-campus ministries, including those to the deaf and to prison inmates.

There are over twenty intramural sports, including basketball, racquetball, softball, tennis, touch football, and volleyball. Intercollegiate sports include baseball, basketball, cross-country running, football, golf, soccer, softball, swimming, tennis, track and field, volleyball, and wrestling. A modern physical education building, an indoor heated pool, and an athletic field amply accommodate these programs. A new wellness center and an Alpine Tower are available for student use.

The Program for the Blind at Gardner-Webb University has been developed to allow students with visual handicaps to receive a liberal arts education. Special support services and job opportunities are provided for every entering student who is visually impaired.

The Degree Program for the Deaf provides interpreters, note takers, and tutors who are skilled in sign language so that hearing-impaired students have full access to all University programs.

ACADEMIC PROGRAMS

The total program is marked by flexibility for the student but encourages, through active faculty advisement, choosing a substantial course of study. Elements of the humanities, the social and physical sciences, and mathematics or related disciplines must be taken. A typical bachelor's degree program requires 128 semester hours for graduation: 59 to 63 in the core (humanities and social and physical sciences), 30 in the major, and 39 to 42 in supporting subjects and free electives. Requirements for science curricula vary somewhat. The associate degree requires the completion of 64 semester hours.

FINANCIAL AID

Gardner-Webb University makes available to its students a variety of scholarships, loans, grants-in-aid, and work-study awards. Prospective applicants with financial need should contact the financial aid director early in their senior year of high school for a financial need estimate. Applications received after April 1 can be considered only in terms of available funds. An applicant must be accepted for admission before being awarded aid. Students must file the FAFSA. Scholarships and other types of aid include academic awards, Christian service awards, endowed scholarships, and annual scholarships. There are several Gardner-Webb loan funds. The University also administers aid from the full range of federal programs. North Carolina students have access to state grant funds administered by the University. Scholarships based on academic promise are also granted each year. Of all students, 90 percent receive aid in some form. The two criteria for receiving financial aid are financial need and academic promise.

APPLICATION AND INFORMATION

Applications, together with a nonrefundable $40 application fee, may be submitted for either semester. Students may also apply online at http://www.gardner-webb.edu. Early application is advised. Notification of the admission decision is given on a rolling basis upon receipt of all application data.

GONZAGA UNIVERSITY

■ SPOKANE, WASHINGTON

THE UNIVERSITY

Founded in 1887, Gonzaga is an independent, comprehensive university with a distinguished background in the Catholic, Jesuit, and humanistic tradition. Gonzaga emphasizes the moral and ethical implications of learning, living, and working in today's global society. As a testament to this educational approach, Gonzaga's first-to-second-year retention rate tops 90 percent. Through the University Core Curriculum, each student develops a strong liberal arts foundation, which many alumni cite as a most valuable asset. In addition, students specialize in any of more than seventy-five academic areas of study.

For an application and more information, students should contact:

Julie McCulloh
Dean of Admission
Gonzaga University
Spokane, Washington 99258-0102
Phone: 800-322-2584 (toll-free)
E-mail: admissions@gonzaga.edu
Web site: http://www.gonzaga.edu

Gonzaga's 110-acre campus is characterized by sprawling green lawns and majestic evergreen trees. Towering above the campus are the stately spires of St. Aloysius Church, the well-recognized landmark featured in the University logo.

Because personal growth is as important as intellectual development, Gonzaga places great emphasis on student life outside of class. Ranging in population size from 35 to 361 students and offering both coed and single-sex living, Gonzaga's seventeen residence halls and seven apartment complexes offer an intimate atmosphere and a lively campus experience. Each hall has one or more Residence Assistants and a chaplain or a resident Jesuit. While freshmen and sophomores are required to live on campus, 40 percent of the upperclass students also reside in Gonzaga's halls and apartments. Campus-based activities ranging from residence hall government to current affairs symposiums to intramural sports keep students informed and entertained. Students in all academic majors integrate with the Spokane community through a variety of activities, such as volunteer opportunities and internships at numerous businesses and agencies. Gonzaga provides both career and counseling centers.

Gonzaga enrolls approximately 6,600 students, of whom about 4,275 are undergraduates. About 45 percent of the students come from Washington State, with forty-three other states and forty-two other countries also represented.

ACADEMIC PROGRAMS

Gonzaga University believes that all students, regardless of their chosen major or profession, benefit from attaining an education that goes beyond specialization. Therefore, all students receive a strong liberal arts background as well as depth in their majors.

The Honors Program challenges exceptional students with an integrated curriculum that is compatible with any major and most double majors. Motivated and imaginative students in all majors create new ventures and seek to make a difference in the world through the Hogan Entrepreneurial Leadership Program. The Comprehensive Leadership Program, which is also open to students from all majors, allows students to fine-tune their leadership skills and knowledge while completing an academic leadership concentration. All three programs require separate applications. Gonzaga University Summer Term (GUST) offers motivated high school students intensive course work in a variety of academic disciplines. Academic and cocurricular activities are included in the six-week session.

FINANCIAL AID

Gonzaga University offers many different types of financial aid to qualified students, including scholarships, federal aid programs, and on- and off-campus employment. In order to apply for financial aid awards, a student must first be accepted by the University and must submit the FAFSA by February 1. After this date, awards are made on a funds-available basis. Approximately 95 percent of the students at Gonzaga receive financial assistance, and the average award for this group is $19,181 (includes all types of aid).

APPLICATION AND INFORMATION

Gonzaga University's nonbinding Early Action deadline for admission applications is November 15. Students who meet this deadline with a complete application are notified of an admission decision by January 15. The final deadline for freshmen to apply for admission under Regular Decision is February 1. Regular Decision applicants receive an admission decision by the middle of March. Transfer students are admitted on a rolling admission basis. Transfer students seeking financial aid are encouraged to apply for admission by March 1. Otherwise, to ensure a smooth transition to Gonzaga, transfer students should apply by June 1. After June 1, the University accepts transfer applicants only if space is available. Students may apply by using the Common Application, APPLY!, CollegeLink, and the Catholic College Common Application. For priority financial aid, all students are encouraged to submit the FAFSA by February 1.

GROVE CITY COLLEGE

■ GROVE CITY, PENNSYLVANIA

THE COLLEGE

For an application and more information, students should contact:

Jeffrey C. Mincey
Director of Admissions
Grove City College
100 Campus Drive
Grove City, Pennsylvania 16127-2104
Phone: 724-458-2100
E-mail: admissions@gcc.edu
Web site: http://www.gcc.edu

The beautifully landscaped campus of Grove City College (GCC) stretches across more than 150 acres and includes twenty-seven neo-Gothic buildings valued at more than $100 million. The campus is considered one of the loveliest in the nation. While the College has changed to meet the needs of the society it serves, its basic philosophy has remained unchanged since its founding in 1876. It is a Christian liberal arts and sciences institution of ideal size and dedicated to the principle of providing the highest-quality education at the lowest possible cost. Wishing to remain truly independent and to retain its distinctive qualities as a private school governed by private citizens (trustees), it is one of the very few colleges in the country that does not accept any state or federal monies. Affiliated with the Presbyterian Church (U.S.A.) but not narrowly denominational, the College believes that to be well educated a student should be exposed to the central ideas of the Judeo-Christian tradition. Sixteen chapel services per semester are required out of fifty opportunities. Religious organizations and activities exist to provide fellowship and spiritual growth.

Grove City students generally come from middle-income families. The greatest number comes from Pennsylvania, Ohio, New Jersey, Virginia, and New York, although forty-one states and twelve other countries were represented in 2006–07. Eighty-eight percent of the women and 71 percent of the men in the most recent freshman class ranked in the top fifth of their high school class.

Ninety-three percent of the 2,500 students live in separate men's and women's residence halls. A full program of cultural, professional, athletic, and social activities is offered. An arena, Crawford Auditorium, and the J. Howard Pew Fine Arts Center are used for athletics, concerts, movies, plays, and lectures. The Physical Learning Center includes an eight-lane bowling alley, two swimming pools, handball/racquetball courts, playing surfaces, fitness rooms with free weights, aerobic equipment and Cybex machines, an indoor three-lane running track, and the basketball arena. The Student Union includes an eatery, mailroom, bookstore, and commuters' lounge. There are more than 100 organizations and special interest groups, including local fraternities and sororities. No alcohol or drugs are permitted on campus. The athletic activities include an extensive intramural, club, and varsity sports program that provides nineteen intercollegiate teams that compete at the NCAA Division III level for men and women.

One of Grove City's strengths is placing students in business, industrial, and teaching positions, as well as in professional institutions such as medical schools.

ACADEMIC PROGRAMS

Grove City College's goal is to assist young men and women in developing as complete individuals—academically, spiritually, and physically. The general education requirements include courses with emphases in the humanities, social sciences, and natural sciences and in quantitative and logical reasoning, as well as a language requirement for nonengineering and science majors. Degree candidates must also complete the requirements in their field of concentration, physical education, electives, and convocation.

A distinctive liberal arts–engineering program includes engineering courses plus courses in the humanities to provide students with a well-grounded preparation for entering the engineering field, as well as the civic and cultural life of society. The economics program exposes students to all economic philosophies, yet strongly advocates economic freedoms and free markets. Honors courses, independent study, seminars, and the opportunity for juniors to study abroad for credit are also offered.

FINANCIAL AID

Because the College's tuition charges are low, every student, in effect, receives significant financial assistance. Sixty-two percent of the freshmen receive additional aid from GCC. Students applying for financial assistance must complete Grove City College's financial aid form. Job opportunities are available on and off campus.

APPLICATION AND INFORMATION

The application should include scores on the SAT (preferred) or the ACT, a high school transcript, references, a recommendation from the student's principal or counselor, and a nonrefundable application fee of $50. An early decision applicant should take the entrance test in the eleventh grade, visit the College for an interview, and submit the application by November 15. Applicants seeking regular decision must submit the completed application and supporting documents by February 1 of their senior year. Applications received after February 1 are considered as space permits. The College receives three applications for every freshman vacancy.

HAVERFORD COLLEGE

■ HAVERFORD, PENNSYLVANIA

THE COLLEGE

Founded in 1833 as the first college established by members of the Society of Friends (Quakers), Haverford College has chosen to remain small, undergraduate, and residential in order to offer students remarkable classroom and research opportunities while maintaining a strong sense of community. Haverford's Honor Code, created and implemented by students, is an important part of the College's identity. It allows students to directly confront academic and social issues in a spirit of cooperation and mutual respect.

Haverford's 1,169 students represent forty-six states, Puerto Rico, the District of Columbia, and forty-four countries. Thirty-one percent of the students are students of color, while an additional 6 percent are international students.

For an application and more information, students should contact:

Office of Admission and Financial Aid
Haverford College
370 Lancaster Avenue
Haverford, Pennsylvania 19041-1392
Phone: 610-896-1350
610-896-1436 (TTY/TDD)
E-mail: admission@haverford.edu (Admission)
finaid@haverford.edu (Financial Aid)
Web site: http://www.haverford.edu

Haverford is a residential campus with 99 percent of the students and 50 percent of the faculty living on campus. Housing on Haverford's campus is single-sex or coed, and residence halls vary in accommodations from 4-person apartments to suites and singles. Other choices of residence facilities include the Ira De A. Reid House (Black Cultural Center), La Casa Hispanica, and an environmental house.

Haverford's athletic teams participate in Division III of the NCAA. Intercollegiate sports include baseball, basketball, cricket, cross-country, fencing, field hockey, lacrosse, soccer, softball, squash, tennis, track and field, and volleyball. Haverford also sponsors several junior varsity, club, and intramural sports teams. Athletic facilities include the Alumni Field House, the Ryan Gymnasium, and the new Douglas B. Gardner Integrated Athletic Center.

ACADEMIC PROGRAMS

The academic experience at Haverford is centered around a deep commitment to the core values of a liberal arts education and its emphasis on the dual pursuit of a breadth of study and in-depth work. While the College mandates that all students take classes across the academic spectrum, there is no core curriculum of specific required courses. Instead, Haverford's system of distribution requirements ensures that students will take at least three classes in each of the divisions of the College (humanities, natural sciences, and social sciences) while allowing them the flexibility to choose courses they find truly interesting. In addition, students must fulfill requirements in foreign language, social justice, writing, and quantitative course work. Majors are selected at the end of the sophomore year.

Haverford's small size and exclusive focus on undergraduate education allow students to count on discussion-based classes and research opportunities that students at most colleges would not be able to experience until graduate school. It is common for Haverford students to pursue independent study, and approximately half study abroad, typically during the junior year.

Haverford's three academic centers—the John B. Hurford Humanities Center, the Marian E. Koshland Integrated Natural Sciences Center, and the Center for Peace and Global Citizenship—provide opportunities for integrated learning, bringing students and faculty in related fields together and promoting conversation and collaboration across disciplines. The centers also help to bring an outward view to students' education by sponsoring speaker series, artists in residence, and colloquia on campus.

One of Haverford's distinctive features is its extensive academic and social cooperation with Bryn Mawr College. Students may take courses or major at either school, live on either campus, and eat on either campus. There are more than 3,500 cross-registrations annually. Both colleges jointly operate a weekly newspaper, a drama club, a radio station, an orchestra, social action groups, and intramural sports. A free bus service between the two campuses, which are a mile apart, facilitates cooperative arrangements. Haverford and Bryn Mawr also share library resources with and are linked electronically to nearby Swarthmore College.

FINANCIAL AID

Fifty-four percent of Haverford's students receive financial aid, which is awarded solely based on need. Candidates must file the College Board PROFILE application and the FAFSA, along with other forms. Complete information is available at http://www.haverford.edu/financialaid.

APPLICATION AND INFORMATION

The application deadlines for admission are November 15 for early decision candidates, January 15 for regular decision candidates, and March 31 for transfer candidates. Haverford uses the Common Application, which is available in school guidance offices and online.

HAWAI'I PACIFIC UNIVERSITY

■ HONOLULU, HAWAI'I

THE UNIVERSITY

Hawai'i Pacific University (HPU) is a private, nonprofit, nonsectarian university founded in 1965. HPU offers more than fifty undergraduate programs as well as twelve graduate programs. HUP prides itself on maintaining strong academic programs, small class sizes, individual attention to students, and a diverse faculty and student population. HPU is accredited by the Western Association of Schools and Colleges, the National League for Nursing Accrediting Commission, and the Council on Social Work Education to name a few.

For an application and more information, students should contact:

Office of Admissions
Hawai'i Pacific University
1164 Bishop Street, Suite 200
Honolulu, Hawai'i 96813
Phone: 808-544-0238
866-CALL-HPU (toll-free in the U.S. and Canada)
Fax: 808-544-1136
E-mail: admissions@hpu.edu
Web site: http://www.hpu.edu

HPU is the largest private university in Hawai'i, with 8,200 students from every state in the United States and more than 100 countries. The diversity of the student body stimulates learning about other cultures firsthand, both inside and outside of the classroom. There is no majority population at HPU. Students are encouraged to examine the values, customs, traditions, and principles of others to gain a clearer understanding of their own perspectives. HPU students develop friendships with students from throughout the United States and the world and form important connections for success in the global economy of the twenty-first century.

In addition to the undergraduate programs, HPU offers twelve graduate programs. The Master of Arts (M.A.) is offered in communications, diplomacy and military studies, global leadership and sustainable development, human resource management, organizational change, and teaching English as a second language. The Master of Business Administration (M.B.A.) is available in accounting, e-business, economics, finance, human resource management, information systems, international business, management, marketing, and travel industry management. The Master of Education in secondary education (M.Ed.), the Master of Science in Information Systems (M.S.I.S.), the Master of Science in Marine Science (M.S.M.S.), the Master of Science in Nursing (M.S.N.), as well as the Master of Social Work (M.S.W.) are also offered.

HPU has NCAA Division II intercollegiate sports. Men's athletic programs include baseball, basketball, cross-country, golf, soccer, and tennis. Women's athletics include basketball, cross-country, soccer, softball, tennis, and volleyball.

The housing office at HPU offers many services and living options for students. Residence halls with cafeteria service are available on the windward Hawai'i Loa campus, while off-campus apartments are available in the Honolulu and Waikiki areas for those seeking more independent living arrangements.

ACADEMIC PROGRAM

The baccalaureate student must complete at least 124 semester hours of credit. Forty-five of these credits provide the student with a strong foundation in the liberal arts, with the remaining credits composed of appropriate upper-division classes in the student's major and related areas. The academic year operates on a semester system, with regular fall and spring semesters as well as shorter sessions, including one winter and four summer sessions. A student can earn up to 15 semester hours of credit during these summer sessions. By attending the supplemental summer and winter sessions, a student may complete the baccalaureate degree program in three years. A five-year B.S.B.A./M.B.A. program is also available.

FINANCIAL AID

HPU participates in most forms of federal financial aid, including student grant and loan programs as well as loans for parents of dependent students. Over 60 percent of the University's students benefit from federal financial aid programs or a wide range of institutional scholarships. Students should complete the Free Application for Federal Student Aid (FAFSA) to be considered for federal aid programs. While aid can be awarded throughout the academic year, students should submit the application prior to the March 1 priority deadline to be considered for all available funding. Students should visit http://www.hpu.edu/financialaid for current financial aid and scholarship information.

APPLICATION AND INFORMATION

Candidates are notified of admission decisions on a rolling basis, usually within two weeks of receipt of application materials. Early entrance and deferred entrance are available.

HOFSTRA UNIVERSITY

■ HEMPSTEAD, NEW YORK

THE UNIVERSITY

Hofstra University is a dynamic, private University where students find their edge to succeed in 145 undergraduate and 155 graduate programs of study. With an outstanding faculty, advanced technological resources, and state-of-the-art facilities, Hofstra has a growing national reputation. Yet the average class size is just 22, and the student-to-faculty ratio is 14:1. Professors teach small classes that emphasize interaction, critical thinking, and analysis.

For an application and more information, students should contact:

Hofstra University
100 Hofstra University
Hempstead, New York 11549-1000
Phone: 516-463-6700
800-HOFSTRA Ext. 618
(toll-free)
Fax: 516-463-5100
Web site: http://www.hofstra.edu

Six undergraduate colleges at Hofstra offer students a broad array of academic offerings. Major University divisions are the Hofstra College of Liberal Arts and Sciences, the School of Communication, the Frank G. Zarb School of Business, the School of Education and Allied Human Services, Honors College, and New College.

Hofstra's student body is diverse, with students on the main campus representing fifty-one states and territories and sixty-five countries. Total enrollment at Hofstra is about 12,600, with 7,718 full-time undergraduates.

Residential facilities accommodate more than 4,000 students in thirty-seven modern residence halls. Hofstra is 100 percent program accessible to persons with disabilities. Necessary services are provided for students with physical, learning, and/or psychological disabilities who meet all academic requirements for admission.

Hofstra has a vibrant campus life, with more than 150 clubs and organizations, about thirty local and national fraternities and sororities, eighteen NCAA Division I athletic teams for men and women, and more than 500 cultural events on campus each year.

Recreational and athletic facilities include a 15,000-seat stadium, a 5,000-seat arena, a 1,600-seat field turf soccer stadium, and a new field hockey stadium. Students can also take advantage of a physical fitness center, a swim center with an indoor Olympic-size swimming pool and high-dive area, a softball stadium, a recreation center offering a multipurpose gymnasium, an indoor track, a fully equipped weight room, spacious locker rooms, a cardio area, and mirrored aerobics/martial arts room. Extensive recreational and intramural sports are also available.

ACADEMIC PROGRAMS

Requirements for graduation vary among schools and majors. A liberal arts core curriculum is an integral part of all areas of concentration. The University calendar is organized on a traditional semester system, including one January session and three summer sessions. Some divisions offer part-time programs during the day and evening and on weekends.

Hofstra offers many innovative programs designed to meet the needs of its diverse student body. These include Honors College, New College, Legal Education Accelerated Program, and First Year Connections.

Honors College provides a rich academic and social experience for students who show both the potential and the desire to excel. Honors students can elect to study in any of the University's 145 undergraduate programs; these students are involved in all fields of advanced study, including premedicine, prelaw, engineering, business, communication and media arts, humanities, and social sciences.

New College offers interdisciplinary study and innovative block scheduling. The Legal Education Accelerated Program allows students to earn both a B.A. and a J.D. in just six years. First Year Connections, an integrated academic and social program, helps first-year students connect to all of the resources and opportunities of the University.

FINANCIAL AID

To help students achieve their education goals, Hofstra University offers several financial aid options. Hofstra awarded more than $55 million in financial assistance in 2007–08, and 81 percent of all Hofstra students received some type of financial aid. For more detailed information, students should visit http://www.hofstra.edu/FinancialAid.

ITHACA COLLEGE

■ ITHACA, NEW YORK

THE COLLEGE

Coeducational and nonsectarian since its founding in 1892, Ithaca College enrolls approximately 6,400 students. The College community is a diverse one; virtually every state is represented in the student population, as are sixty-one other countries. Students come to Ithaca College to get active, hands-on learning that brings together the best of liberal arts and professional studies. Academic programs are offered in five schools—the School of Humanities and Sciences (2,350 students), School of Business (600 students), Roy H. Park School of Communications (1,250 students), School of Health Sciences and Human Performance (1,200 students), and School of Music (500 students)—and the Division of Interdisciplinary and International Studies (100 students). There are approximately 400 graduate students.

For an application and more information, students should contact:

Gerard Turbide
Director of Admission
Office of Admission
Ithaca College
100 Job Hall
Ithaca, New York 14850-7020
Phone: 607-274-3124
800-429-4274 (toll-free)
E-mail: admission@ithaca.edu
Web site: http://www.ithaca.edu/admission

Freshmen and most upperclassmen (with some exceptions) are expected to live on campus. There are fifty-two residence halls, which range from garden apartments to fourteen-story towers. Extracurricular life abounds at Ithaca. There are approximately 150 student organizations, a strong Division III intercollegiate athletic program (twenty-five teams), extensive intramural and club sports programs, and dramatic and musical ensembles. A wide range of services is available, beginning with summer orientation for new students and including career planning and placement assistance, a counseling center, and a health center that is staffed by 4 physicians as well as numerous physician assistants, nurses, and lab technologists.

According to College surveys completed in the past three years, 97 percent of first-year graduates are employed and/or are full-time graduate students.

ACADEMIC PROGRAMS

Undergraduate programs of study address two primary needs: the need for rigorous academic preparation in highly specialized professional fields and the need for students to prepare for the complex demands of society by acquiring an intellectual breadth that extends beyond their chosen profession. Each degree offered requires a minimum of 120 credit hours and a specified number of liberal arts credits. Minors, academic concentrations, and numerous teacher certification programs are available. Exceptionally qualified applicants to the School of Humanities and Sciences will be invited to apply to the honors program, an intensive four-year program of interdisciplinary seminars. The Writing Center offers assistance to students at any stage of the writing process, and Information Technology Services aids students in the use of personal and College computers. The Center for the Study of Culture, Race, and Ethnicity serves as a multidisciplinary clearinghouse for studying the experiences of groups that traditionally have been marginalized, underrepresented, or misrepresented in the United States as well as in college curricula. The Gerontology Institute provides opportunities for students to work with the elderly in a variety of community settings. The Department of Education coordinates the courses of study leading to a teaching certificate.

ROTC programs are offered in conjunction with Cornell University.

FINANCIAL AID

Financial aid totaling more than $125 million from all sources is extended to approximately 85 percent of Ithaca students. To apply for financial aid, students should check the proper space on the Common Application, and if seeking federal aid, complete the FAFSA online by February 1. All accepted applicants are considered for merit aid in recognition of their academic and personal achievement.

APPLICATION AND INFORMATION

For fall enrollment, prospective students should apply early in their senior year and no later than February 1; applicants are notified of a decision on a rolling basis no later than April 15 and must confirm their enrollment by May 1. Freshman applicants seeking institutional and federal aid should file the FAFSA by February 1 with the federal processor.

Ithaca accepts the Common Application. An overview of the application process, a list of special requirements, and Ithaca's Common Application supplement form may be found online at http://www.ithaca.edu/admission/apply.php.

JOHN CABOT UNIVERSITY

■ ROME, ITALY

THE UNIVERSITY

John Cabot University, founded in 1972, concentrates on the liberal arts and social sciences using the American system, with a distinctive European and international character. It is strategically located in one of the world centers of diplomacy and international organizations. That, coupled with its unique relationship with leading multinational corporations, embassies, media, and other organizations, gives degree-seeking students the opportunity to participate in exclusive internship programs and become first-run candidates for job openings around the world. The University has a truly international student body—about a quarter of the students are Italian, half are American, and a quarter are from more than sixty other countries. The average class size is 20 students, and there are approximately 100 full- and part-time faculty members holding advanced degrees from major universities in the U.S. and Europe. Working closely with professors and classmates in a small-class setting, students receive the individual attention needed to fully develop their talents and abilities. With a student-centered approach to both education and human relationships, the University offers an active learning environment while also teaching the ethical standards that are essential in dealing with social pressures and in deciding how best to fulfill one's goals in life.

For an application and more information, students should contact:

Admissions Office
John Cabot University
Via della Lungara, 233
00165 Rome
Italy
Phone: 39-06-681-9121
E-mail: admissions@johncabot.edu
Web site: http://www.johncabot.edu

The Housing Office places students in off-campus apartments and in a residential hotel close to the University. Along with various campus activities, the Student Services and Activities Office organizes a wide variety of off-campus events, including educational travel throughout Italy.

The University is licensed by the Delaware Department of Education to award its degrees and is authorized by the Italian Ministry of Research and Instruction to operate as an institution of American higher education in Rome. John Cabot University is accredited by the Commission on Higher Education of the Middle States Association of Colleges and Schools (215-662-5606).

ACADEMIC PROGRAMS

The curricula of the University's programs are divided into two basic categories: the general distribution requirements of the first two years of study, which give the student a broad exposure to the basic disciplines of the liberal arts educational experience, and the specified, additional requirements of each degree awarded by the University.

The general distribution and other introductory courses equip the student to select an area of specialization as a degree candidate in the junior and senior years. Within each degree program, there are specific requirements that must be met by the student who wishes to earn a degree at John Cabot. These requirements include ten to twelve core courses deemed by faculty members to be essential to the discipline of the degree and comparable to the requirements for the same degree at recognized and accredited colleges and universities in the American system of higher education. In addition to the core requirements, other requisites include electives that support the core program and offer opportunities to take courses in other discipline areas of particular interest or need.

Special programs include the Honors Program, internships, and the American Language Program (ALP).

FINANCIAL AID

U.S. citizens attending a college or university outside the United States are eligible to apply for the Federal Family Education Loans (FFEL), including the Stafford Student Loan and PLUS loans. The FAFSA must be completed to apply for a Stafford Student Loan. Academic scholarships are awarded each year based on merit and need. John Cabot University is proud to participate in the Secchia Family Foundation's Secchia Scholars program, which awards four types of scholarships, and institutional scholarships are available, as well. A number of work-study assistantships are available for full-time, degree-seeking students who are interested in and capable of assisting the various administrative offices and academic departments of the University.

APPLICATION AND INFORMATION

Admissions decisions are based on the review of official transcripts, results of standardized tests, the student's GPA, final examination results, a personal statement, and letters of recommendation from teachers or university professors. An application form completed in its entirety must be accompanied by two recent passport-size photographs and a nonrefundable application fee of $50 or €50. Students may complete the application online or use the printable application. The University deadline is July 15 for fall admission and November 15 for the spring semester. Candidates are urged to submit their application and supporting documents as early as possible.

LAGRANGE COLLEGE

■ LAGRANGE, GEORGIA

THE COLLEGE

Founded in 1831, LaGrange College is the oldest private college in Georgia. A four-year liberal arts and sciences institution affiliated with the United Methodist Church, LaGrange holds fast to its longstanding mission of challenging students' minds, inspiring their souls—and changing their lives. The College is ranked in the top five and as a "best value" among ninety-three Southern baccalaureate schools by *U.S. News & World Report* and has an enrollment of about 1,100 men and women. LaGrange College students come from twenty-one states and twelve countries, and they enjoy a student-faculty ratio of 12:1. Fully accredited, LaGrange provides a challenging and supportive academic environment. The Bachelor of Arts (B.A.), Bachelor of Science (B.S.), Bachelor of Science in Nursing (B.S.N.), and Bachelor of Music (B.M.) degrees are offered in addition to the Master of Education (M.Ed.) degree and the Master of Arts in Teaching (M.A.T.) degree

For an application and more information, students should contact:

Office of Admission
LaGrange College
601 Broad Street
LaGrange, Georgia 30240
Phone: 706-880-8005
800-593-2885 (toll-free)
E-mail: admission@lagrange.edu
Web site: http://www.lagrange.edu

LaGrange College students can start their own special-interest group or join one of more than forty clubs and organizations, including student government, honor societies, service clubs, sororities and fraternities, performance groups, religious organizations, and student publications. Students also can get involved in service efforts, such as building homes through Habitat for Humanity, or traveling to Costa Rica or the Czech Republic on a mission trip. On-campus activities include intramural sports tournaments, theater performances, karaoke and open mike competitions, art exhibitions, "Vegas on the Hill," and Greek Week. Off-campus excursions are planned each semester, such as snow-skiing trips to North Carolina or visits to Atlanta Braves games.

LaGrange College's athletic facilities include an indoor competition swimming pool, an outdoor recreational swimming pool, a fully equipped fitness center, a $2-million baseball facility, two gymnasiums, two lighted softball fields, a lighted soccer field, and a training facility. Intercollegiate athletic teams for men include baseball, basketball, cross-country, football, golf, soccer, swimming, and tennis. Women's teams include basketball, cross-country, fast-pitch softball, soccer, swimming, tennis, and volleyball.

More than 60 percent of students live on campus in residence halls that include apartment-style facilities. Meal plan options are offered for the College's dining hall and student grill.

ACADEMIC PROGRAMS

Each program of study contains a substantial interdisciplinary core component. Providing a background in the natural and social sciences, arts, and humanities, the core helps students see how subjects interrelate, while developing the research and problem-solving skills employers and graduate schools seek most. A minimum of 120 semester hours is required to earn a bachelor's degree; 46 semester hours of liberal studies core courses are required for all bachelor's degrees. Most majors require an additional 36 to 56 semester hours of credit beyond the liberal studies curriculum. Students may be eligible for credit and/or exemption in certain areas through Advanced Placement (AP) tests or the College-Level Examination Program (CLEP).

The College operates on the 4-1-4 academic calendar, a schedule which allows for a one-month January interim term between fall and spring semesters. During January term, students focus on unique subject areas or participate in classes incorporating domestic and international travel.

FINANCIAL AID

Approximately 90 percent of LaGrange students receive some combination of financial awards. These awards may include grants, loans, scholarships, and employment opportunities. Federal financial aid and institutional funds are available to all students who qualify. The state of Georgia provides additional funding for Georgia residents. All Georgia residents who enroll as full-time students receive the Georgia Tuition Equalization Grant in the amount of $1000 per year. The HOPE Scholarship, which totals $3000 per year, is awarded to all Georgia residents who have graduated from high school with a B average and who enter as freshmen. Georgia residents who do not qualify for the HOPE Scholarship as freshmen may be able to obtain the HOPE Scholarship by earning a 3.0 cumulative grade point average. Academic scholarships that range from $1000 to full scholarships are also awarded. All accepted students are considered for scholarships; a separate application is not required.

APPLICATION AND INFORMATION

Applications for admission are evaluated on a rolling basis and should be submitted at least one month prior to the beginning of the semester in which entrance is desired. Weekday campus visits are encouraged, and appointments can be arranged by contacting the Admission Office.

LEBANON VALLEY COLLEGE

■ ANNVILLE, PENNSYLVANIA

THE COLLEGE

With 141 years of tradition, an outstanding student body and faculty, and exceptional facilities, this private liberal arts college stands out among other schools. Founded in 1866, Lebanon Valley College (LVC) is steeped in a tradition of providing students with an educational foundation that transcends time and embraces new technology. The College has instilled in its graduates the desire and ability to think, ask questions, solve problems, and communicate effectively. These qualities, combined with a love for education and learning, prepare students to be competitive in a world that is constantly changing. A supportive community provides the final ingredient students need to achieve success in the job market and professional or graduate school.

For an application and more information, students should contact:

Susan Sarisky
Director of Admission
Lebanon Valley College
101 North College Avenue
Annville, Pennsylvania 17003-1400
Phone: 866-LVC-4ADM (toll-free)
E-mail: admission@lvc.edu
Web site: http://www.lvc.edu

Students' efforts and accomplishments are being recognized. Few other small colleges have received more Fulbright awards than Lebanon Valley College—fourteen awards in the past thirty-seven years—with mathematics majors receiving five during that period. For the thirteenth consecutive year, *U.S. News & World Report* rated Lebanon Valley College among the top-tier schools in the Northern Universities–Master's: Top Schools category. LVC also ranked eighth on its list of Great Schools at Great Prices.

The Lebanon Valley College family of 1,660 students represents twenty-one states and five countries. Students enjoy state-of-the-art facilities whether they are studying in the atrium of the Bishop Library, using a workstation in the molecular modeling lab, or performing student-faculty research in the science center that is scheduled for an $18-million transformation. The College's forty-five buildings provide for every facet of college life with thirty-two residence halls, including four apartment-style halls; classroom buildings, including a revitalized academic center with all of the latest technology for teaching and learning; a physical therapy facility; two student centers; a recreational sports center; a new varsity gymnasium; a music center; an art gallery and recital hall; an art studio; and a chapel. One of the keys to providing students with a rich, well-rounded experience is to offer a wealth of opportunities for learning and growth beyond the classroom. Each student's academic program is fully complemented by a wide range of extracurricular activities, including guest lectures; concerts; Division III athletics; trips to New York and Washington, D.C.; and a variety of cultural activities.

ACADEMIC PROGRAMS

Lebanon Valley has long been known for the strength of its academic programs and the achievement of its faculty members and alumni. The science program is particularly strong, with exceptionally well-equipped laboratories. In the latest numbers released by the National Science Foundation, the College ranked among the top 15 percent in the nation for Ph.D.'s produced at "Private, Predominantly Undergraduate Institutions" for biology, biochemistry, and chemistry in the past ten years. Lebanon Valley's mission arises directly from its historical traditions and a relationship with the United Methodist Church. The College's aim is to enable its students to become people of broad vision capable of making informed decisions and prepared for a life of service to others. To that end, the College provides an education that helps students to acquire the knowledge, skills, attitudes, and values necessary to live and work in a changing, diverse, and fragile world. The general education core provides students with the breadth of knowledge and experience across the curriculum, in addition to their major course work.

FINANCIAL AID

Lebanon Valley is committed to helping families finance a college education and has received national recognition for its outstanding merit-based scholarship program. Students who graduate in the top 30 percent of their high school class automatically receive one of the College's academic scholarships for up to half of the cost of tuition. Additional need-based financial aid is available, and 98 percent of students receive some form of financial aid. The College committed more than $17.8 million last year to institutional aid. The FAFSA and the LVC Undergraduate Financial Aid Application must be completed to determine eligibility. The priority deadline for filing for financial aid is March 1.

APPLICATION AND INFORMATION

To apply, students should submit a completed application, a $30 application fee, and official copies of their high school transcript. Lebanon Valley has a rolling admission process, but students are encouraged to apply during the fall of their senior year. Careful consideration is given to scholastic credentials as well as to the nonacademic qualities of each applicant. Personal visits to the campus are encouraged.

LOYOLA UNIVERSITY NEW ORLEANS

■ NEW ORLEANS, LOUISIANA

THE UNIVERSITY

Founded by the Jesuits in 1912, Loyola University's more than 35,000 graduates have excelled in innumerable professional fields for over ninety years. More than 3,000 undergraduate students (5,000 students total) enjoy the individual attention of a caring faculty in a university dedicated to creating community and fostering individualism while educating the whole person, not only intellectually, but spiritually, socially, and athletically. Loyola students represent all fifty states and forty-eight countries. This diversity is found in a setting where the average class size is 17–24 students. Almost 70 percent of the students permanently reside outside Louisiana, and 36 percent are members of minority groups.

For an application and more information, students should contact:

Office of Admissions
Loyola University New Orleans
6363 St. Charles Avenue, Box 18
New Orleans, Louisiana 70118
Phone: 504-865-3240
800-4-LOYOLA (toll-free)
E-mail: admit@loyno.edu
Web site: http://www.loyno.edu

Loyola's 20-acre main campus and 4-acre Broadway campus are located in the historic uptown area of New Orleans and are hubs of student activity. The University's residence halls are home to nearly 75 percent of the freshmen who reside on campus. The Joseph A. Danna Center, the student center, houses six food venues, including the Orleans Room, Godfather's Pizza, Smoothie King, the Underground, and a gourmet coffee shop. An art gallery, concierge desk, and post office can also be found in the Danna Center. Nationally affiliated fraternities and sororities are among Loyola's more than 120 student organizations. Students can join the 2006 Pacemaker Award–winning newspaper, the Loyola University Community Action Program (a volunteer community service organization, the largest organization on campus), or one of the many special interest groups. About a third of the student body participates in club sports such as cheerleading, crew, cycling, dance, golf, swimming, and volleyball as well as in men's lacrosse, rugby, and soccer. Loyola participates in the National Association of Intercollegiate Athletics (NAIA) men's baseball, basketball, cross-country, and track (distance) and women's basketball, cross-country, and volleyball. The Recreational Sports Complex offers six multipurpose courts, an elevated running track, an Olympic-size swimming pool, weight rooms, and aerobics and combat-sports facilities.

The Joseph A. Butt, S.J., College of Business is fully accredited at both the undergraduate and graduate levels by the AACSB International, and houses the Mildred Soule and Clarence A. Lengendre Chair in Business Ethics. The College of Music and Fine Arts offers students opportunities in music industry studies and music performance areas as well as visual and theater arts. This college also hosts the Thelonious Monk Institute of Jazz Performance. Students in the College of Humanities and Natural Sciences might choose premed preparation, psychology, or areas in the humanities, such as history or modern foreign languages. The College of Social Sciences houses a School of Mass Communication that offers award-winning programs in advertising, journalism, and public relations.

ACADEMIC PROGRAMS

Once enrolled at Loyola, students are introduced to the Common Curriculum, designed to give them a well-rounded preparation in their major field of concentration as well as the ability to understand and reflect on disciplines allied to or outside their major. The curriculum is divided into four categories: major, minor, Common Curriculum, and elective courses. Students must meet the requirements of their degree program as specified by their particular college. Common Curriculum courses include seven introductory courses in English composition, math, science, philosophy, religion, literature, and history and nine upper-division courses in humanities, social science, and natural science. The College of Business requires that all students with junior or senior standing complete a 3-credit-hour internship. Internships provide professional-level experience along with college credit for semester-long participation. The College of Humanities and Natural Sciences also requires a minimum of one year of study in a modern foreign language. The honors program and independent studies provide special opportunities for qualified students.

FINANCIAL AID

Loyola University's endowment provides money for financial aid in addition to that provided by federal funding. Assistance in the forms of merit- and talent-based scholarships, loans, work-study, and grants is awarded on the basis of academic achievement and need. More than 450 scholarships are awarded annually to students with competitive grades and test scores. To apply for one of the scholarships, students must have a GPA of at least 3.2 and competitive standardized test scores. Offers of financial aid are not made until after admission. Notifications of awards are sent in early February. Awards of need-based financial aid packages are made on a first-come, first-served basis and are announced in mid-March. Eighty-four percent of Loyola students receive some form of financial aid.

LUTHER COLLEGE

■ DECORAH, IOWA

THE COLLEGE

Luther College, founded in 1861 by Norwegian immigrants, is a four-year residential liberal arts college of the Evangelical Lutheran Church in America. The College is an academic community of faith and learning where students of promise from all beliefs and backgrounds have the freedom to learn, to express themselves, to perform, to compete, and to grow. The College is home to 2,550 students from thirty-five states and thirty-three countries. Thirty-six percent of the students are from Iowa; 89 percent come from the four-state area of Iowa, Minnesota, Wisconsin, and Illinois. Each year, over 100 international students choose to study at Luther.

For an application and more information, students should contact:

Admissions Office
Luther College
Decorah, Iowa 52101-1042
Phone: 563-387-1287
800-458-8437 (toll-free)
E-mail: admissions@luther.edu
finaid@luther.edu
Web site: http://www.luther.edu

In keeping with its liberal arts tradition, the College requires students to develop a depth of knowledge in their chosen major and a breadth of knowledge through exposure to a wide range of subjects and intellectual approaches (general requirements). Learning at Luther is about engagement: faculty members who are passionate in their teaching and scholarship, students who are active and involved, and a College community characterized by personal attention, hands-on experiences, academic challenge, and community support. At Luther, all students become immersed in the liberal arts through the College's common year-long course for first-year students called Paideia. The course, which is uncommon in its approach, helps train students' minds and develop their research and writing skills as they explore human cultures and history. In addition, Luther offers a Phi Beta Kappa chapter and several departmental honor societies, evidence of the quality of teaching and learning on campus.

At Luther, students are encouraged to seek out connections between their lives in the classroom and their lives outside the classroom. The College provides a stimulating cultural and educational atmosphere by bringing distinguished public figures, theater groups, musicians, and educators to the campus. Cocurricular activities are an important part of College life. The College sponsors seven choirs, three orchestras, three bands, two jazz bands, and a full theater and dance program. Numerous student organizations and societies provide ample opportunities for student involvement in meaningful activities. As a community of faith, students can participate in daily chapel, weekly Sunday worship, outreach teams, and midweek Eucharist.

Nineteen intercollegiate sports are offered. Men may participate in ten sports: baseball, basketball, cross-country, football, golf, soccer, swimming, tennis, track and field, and wrestling. Women compete in nine intercollegiate sports: basketball, cross-country, golf, soccer, softball, swimming, tennis, track and field, and volleyball. Club sports include Ultimate Frisbee, rugby, and men's volleyball. Sixty-four percent of the student body is involved in an extensive intramural and recreational sports program. Available for recreational use and for the physical education program are twelve outdoor tennis courts, an eight-lane polyurethane 400-meter track, numerous cross-country running and ski trails, and 15 acres of intramural fields. The well-equipped field house contains a 25-yard indoor pool, three racquetball courts, four hardwood basketball courts, a wrestling complex, and a 3,000-seat gymnasium. A sports forum houses a six-lane, 200-meter indoor track; six indoor tennis courts; locker rooms; and athletic training facilities. The Legends Fitness for Life Center provides the latest fitness equipment and a 30-foot-high rock-climbing wall.

ACADEMIC PROGRAMS

Each candidate is required to complete a total of 128 semester hours of credit with a C average or better. At least 76 of the required 128 semester hours must be earned outside the major discipline. Each senior writes a research paper in his or her major. Students are required to complete 12 hours of Paideia, an interdisciplinary course; 9–12 of religion/philosophy; 7–8 of natural science; 6–8 of social science; 3–9 of foreign language (proficiency based); 3–4 of fine arts; 3–4 of global studies; 3–4 of quantitative or symbolic reasoning; and 2 of physical education. Advanced placement and credit by examination are available. A qualified student may develop an interdisciplinary major with a faculty adviser.

FINANCIAL AID

More than 97 percent of all Luther students receive financial aid in the form of grants, such as the Federal Pell Grant; scholarships from Luther and other sources; loans; and jobs on campus. Luther awards Regent and Presidential Scholarships to those demonstrating superior academic achievement. The amount of aid given is determined by the College's analysis of the Free Application for Federal Student Aid (FAFSA). The priority deadline for a financial aid application is March 1.

APPLICATION AND INFORMATION

An application, SAT or ACT scores, an educator's reference, a transcript of previous academic work, and a $25 application fee are required for admission. On-campus interviews are recommended but not required.

LYNN UNIVERSITY

■ BOCA RATON, FLORIDA

THE UNIVERSITY

Lynn University is a private, coeducational, liberal arts university awarding bachelor's, master's, and doctoral degrees in the liberal arts and sciences and professional education. Founded in 1962 and accredited by the Southern Association of Colleges and Schools, Lynn offers a distinctive, innovative, and individualized approach to learning within an international community. The University currently enrolls more than 2,600 students representing forty-three states and ninety-three nations. Its specialty programs include a Conservatory of Music, a School of Aeronautics, and the Institute for Achievement and Learning, an international pioneer in developing successful teaching strategies for students with learning differences.

For an application and more information, students should contact:

Office of Admissions
Lynn University
3601 North Military Trail
Boca Raton, Florida 33431-5598
Phone: 561-237-7900
800-888-5966 (toll-free)
E-mail: admission@lynn.edu
Web site: http://www.lynn.edu/admission

The University's five colleges and two schools offer twenty-one undergraduate majors and thirty specializations as well as seven master's degrees and a doctoral degree program. Every major includes opportunities for hands-on learning through projects and internships, giving students the opportunity to acquire the skills and knowledge essential for successful careers in the twenty-first century and for informed and effective citizenship in a global society.

More than 60 percent of Lynn's undergraduate students live in one of its five air-conditioned residence halls. Residence halls include study and computer lounges and recreation areas as well as health and fitness facilities with free weights, exercise machines, and cardiovascular equipment. The Lynn Student Center is a campus hub, housing the dining room, an auditorium, comfortable lounge areas, and the popular Knight's Court snack bar. Right next door is the campus' newest hangout spot, Christine's, which serves a full menu of Starbucks coffee drinks, smoothies, snacks, salads, sandwiches, and desserts.

Students develop and strengthen their leadership talents through Lynn's student involvement program, which consists of more than thirty campus organizations and activities covering a wide variety of special interests, including student government, multicultural organizations, Greek life, and a leadership academy.

Lynn also has a top-ranked NCAA athletic program, which has brought home eighteen national championships and twenty-one Sunshine State Conference championships and has been honored with the selection of two NCAA coaches of the year. The Fighting Knights intercollegiate athletic program includes men's and women's basketball, golf, soccer, and tennis; men's baseball; and women's softball and volleyball.

ACADEMIC PROGRAMS

Lynn University is a learning-centered community, with faculty members who love teaching and who challenge students to become active, intentional, and purposeful learners. The University embraces students who have varying levels of academic abilities and learning styles coupled with a strong motivation to excel. Classes are small by design, with an average 15:1 student-faculty ratio.

The entire Lynn University curriculum is innovative, challenging students to build increasing competencies not only in their chosen field of study, but in every area of their life. Students put theory into practice through internships, partnerships with business, and community service projects. Students benefit from an exceptionally strong advising program that pairs each incoming student with a faculty member in the student's chosen major field. Faculty advisers become a mentor throughout each student's academic career and beyond. The Honors Program's innovative curriculum stimulates creative discovery among students with particularly strong academic promise.

Lynn University's Institute for Achievement and Learning is a model for all of higher education. Led by a nationally recognized learning specialist, the institute brings together an array of services and professionals that help support every student, regardless of his or her learning style. The Institute for Achievement and Learning's Metamorphosis Program uses a naturalist, experiential coaching model to help students with AD/HD adapt their behavior to transition from seemingly unorganized study skills to patterned, creative living and learning environments.

FINANCIAL AID

Lynn is committed to making the University affordable for every student. The University's broad program of student financial aid includes grants, work-study, loans, and academic, athletic, and need-based scholarships. For complete information, students should visit http://www.lynn.edu/scholarships.

APPLICATION AND INFORMATION

Applications are processed and applicants are notified on a rolling basis upon receipt of all credentials.

MILLS COLLEGE

■ OAKLAND, CALIFORNIA

THE COLLEGE

For more than 150 years, Mills College has shaped women's lives. Offering a progressive liberal arts curriculum taught by a nationally renowned faculty, Mills gives students the personal attention that leads to extraordinary learning. Through intensive, collaborative study in a community of forward-thinking individuals, students gain the ability to make their voices heard, the strength to risk bold visions, an eagerness to experiment, and a desire to change the world.

For an application and more information, students should contact:

Office of Admission
Mills College
5000 MacArthur Boulevard
Oakland, California 94613
Phone: 510-430-2135
800-87-MILLS (toll-free)
E-mail: admission@mills.edu
Web site: http://www.mills.edu

Historically a college for women only, Mills continues that proud tradition today at the undergraduate level. To provide enhanced professional opportunities for all students, Mills also offers renowned graduate programs that are open to both women and men. Ranked one of the top colleges in the West by *U.S. News & World Report,* Mills is also one of the top 50 colleges for African Americans according to *Black Enterprise* magazine.

The faculty of nationally and internationally respected scholars and artists is dedicated to developing the strengths of every student, preparing them for lifelong intellectual, personal, and professional growth. With an impressive student-teacher ratio of 11:1, Mills women are assured of access to and support from these inspiring and committed professors. The hallmark of a Mills education is the collaboration between dedicated students and distinguished faculty members that goes beyond the classroom and into meaningful work and innovative research.

In addition to exercising their minds, Mills students also compete in seven intercollegiate sports—cross-country, rowing, soccer, swimming, tennis, track and field, and volleyball—as members of the National Collegiate Athletic Association (NCAA) Division III. Students may also participate in recreational activity courses for credit or take advantage of the on-campus fitness facilities and off-campus activity excursions.

ACADEMIC PROGRAMS

The innovative general education program is guided by a set of learning outcomes, not a generic list of required courses. Each student designs her own program with the guidance of her faculty adviser, ensuring that a Mills education is tailored to the student's specific needs and interests. The program places the work a student does in her major in a larger context and ensures that she explores and appreciates realms of knowledge beyond her field. The general education requirements fall into three outcome categories: skills (written communication, quantitative and computational reasoning, and information literacy/information technology skills), perspectives (interdisciplinary, women and gender, and multicultural), and disciplinary experiences (creation and criticism in the arts, historical perspectives, natural sciences, and human institutions and behavior).

Career Services offers a four-year counseling program to assist students in clarifying their career and life goals. Workshops, individual counseling sessions, an extensive internship program, a strong alumnae network, and special opportunities to meet Bay Area business leaders and top professional women in every field all help students to focus their interests and plan career goals.

FINANCIAL AID

In fall 2007, more than 80 percent of undergraduates at the College received some type of financial assistance. Awards are based on need and academic merit and include grants and scholarships, loans, and student employment. Some are funded by Mills directly, and others are state and federal programs. Scholarship grants range from $1000 per year to full tuition. Financial aid applicants must complete the FAFSA. California residents must also file the Cal Grant GPA Verification Form to determine eligibility for a Cal Grant. Students who seek Mills need-based scholarship funds must also file the Mills Financial Aid Form. Priority is given to applicants who meet the published deadlines.

APPLICATION AND INFORMATION

The priority scholarship deadline for admission applications is February 1 for first-year students. All students are encouraged to meet this deadline; however, merit scholarship applicants (including international students) must apply by February 1. The regular decision deadline date is March 1 for first-year applicants. For admission to the spring term, the deadline is November 1.

MOLLOY COLLEGE

■ ROCKVILLE CENTRE, NEW YORK

THE COLLEGE

For an application and more information, students should contact:

Director of Admissions
Molloy College
1000 Hempstead Avenue
P.O. Box 5002
Rockville Centre, New York 11571-5002
Phone: 888-4-MOLLOY (toll-free)
Web site: http://www.molloy.edu

In 1955, 44 students became part of an exciting new tradition in higher education on Long Island. As the first freshman class of Molloy College, these young students made a commitment to academic excellence. Today, Molloy College has become one of the most respected four-year private coeducational institutions of higher learning in the area. It provides academic programs in both day and evening divisions. The Molloy population consists of recent high school graduates, transfer students, and graduate students. Molloy College is accredited by the Board of Regents of the University of the State of New York and the Middle States Association of Colleges and Schools, and its programs in nursing, social work, and education are accredited by the National League for Nursing Accrediting Commission, the Council on Social Work Education, and NCATE.

Molloy College provides an intimate and personal atmosphere; it encourages the 3,700 students to develop close working relationships with the faculty. The student body represents many ethnic and socioeconomic groups; to meet their varied needs, the College offers more than fifty undergraduate majors and programs.

The key word at the College is involvement. Student-run clubs and organizations offer a variety of planned activities. Student publications provide an outlet for students who want to share their literary and journalistic talents. Molloy College offers opportunities for students to exercise their leadership abilities, contribute their special talents, utilize their initiative, and expand their social horizons through the variety of activities made conveniently available to them. Athletics, an integral part of student life, are represented at Molloy College on the varsity level. Women's teams are offered in basketball, lacrosse, soccer, softball, tennis, and volleyball. Men's teams include baseball, basketball, lacrosse, and soccer. Cross-country is offered for men and women. These teams compete in the NCAA Division II, the ECAC, and the NYCAC. The equestrian team holds membership in the Intercollegiate Horse Show Association.

Student services include the Career and Counseling Center, Campus Ministry, the Siena Women's Center, and health services.

ACADEMIC PROGRAMS

Molloy College, dedicated to the total development of the student, offers a strong liberal arts core curriculum as an integral part of all major fields of study. A minimum of 128 credits is required for a baccalaureate degree. Double majors can be chosen, and numerous minors are available.

Advanced placement credit is granted for a score of 3 or better on the AP exam. CLEP and CPE credit is also given. Qualified full-time students may participate in the Army ROTC program at Hofstra University or St. John's University on a cross-enrolled basis. Molloy students may also elect Air Force ROTC on a cross-enrolled basis with New York Institute of Technology.

FINANCIAL AID

More than 85 percent of the student body of Molloy College is awarded financial aid in the form of scholarships, grants, loans, and Federal Work-Study Program employment. Financial aid awards are based on academic achievement and financial need. Completion of the Molloy College Application for Financial Aid/Scholarship and the FAFSA is required. Non-need scholarships and grants are also available.

Students who have attained a 95 percent or better high school average and a minimum combined score of 1250 on the SAT (composite math and verbal scores) are considered for the Molloy Scholars' Program, which awards full-tuition scholarships. Partial scholarships are available under Dominican, Community Service, and Performing Arts Scholarships. The Transfer Scholarship Program grants partial-tuition scholarships to students transferring into Molloy College with at least a 3.0 cumulative average. Athletic grants (Division II only) are awarded to full-time students based on athletic ability in baseball, basketball, cross-country, equestrian, lacrosse, soccer, softball, tennis, and volleyball. The Community Service Award is awarded to full-time freshmen demonstrating a commitment to their community and their school.

APPLICATION AND INFORMATION

To apply to Molloy College, students should submit a completed application for admission, a nonrefundable $30 application fee, an official high school transcript or GED score report, official results of the SAT or ACT, and official college transcripts (transfer students only). The College uses a rolling admission system.

MUHLENBERG COLLEGE

■ ALLENTOWN, PENNSYLVANIA

THE COLLEGE

Founded in 1848, Muhlenberg College aims to develop independent critical thinkers who are intellectually agile, characterized by a zeal for reasoned and civil debate, knowledgeable about the achievements and traditions of diverse civilizations and cultures, able to express ideas with clarity and grace, committed to lifelong learning, equipped with ethical values, and prepared for lives of leadership and service.

For an application and more information, students should contact:

Christopher Hooker-Haring
Dean of Admission and Financial Aid
Muhlenberg College
Allentown, Pennsylvania 18104-5586
Phone: 484-664-3200
E-mail: admissions@muhlenberg.edu
Web site: http://www.muhlenberg.edu

Muhlenberg students achieve the College's goals by assuming strong individual responsibility for intense involvement in vigorous academic work and for personal involvement within the College community. The more than 100 student organizations provide outlets for the diversified cultural, athletic, religious, social, leadership, and service interests of the students. The campus is primarily residential; more than 90 percent of the 2,150 students live on campus. A close sense of community develops naturally, one in which their diversified academic and personal interests enable students to contribute positively to the intellectual and personal growth of their peers.

Students are aided by an active Career Planning and Placement Service in relating academic and personal knowledge and skills to appropriate career goals and in obtaining positions upon graduation. About one third of a typical graduating class proceeds immediately to graduate or professional school.

ACADEMIC PROGRAMS

The A.B. and B.S. programs emphasize breadth of study in the liberal arts as well as in-depth study of a particular academic major. All students must fulfill requirements in foreign culture, the humanities, social sciences, and natural sciences. Strong achievement on Advanced Placement examinations may enable a student to receive advanced placement, possibly with credit. Scores of 4 or 5 earn automatic credit. Scores of 3 are evaluated by the appropriate department.

Students work closely with academic advisers to formulate programs well suited to their individual interests, abilities, needs, and goals. Generally, students are expected to declare their major at the end of the freshman year; however, many students later change their academic major with no difficulty. A double major is possible, and several fields are available as minor programs. These minor fields are accounting, African American studies, anthropology, business, chemistry, computer science, economics, English, French, German, history, Jewish studies, mathematics, music, philosophy, physics, political science, public health, religion, sociology, Spanish, and women's studies. In addition, independent study and research are available. The College also enriches the freshman-year experience through more than thirty special-focus Freshman Seminars.

FINANCIAL AID

Muhlenberg College endeavors to make its educational opportunities available to all qualified students regardless of their financial circumstances. While most financial aid at Muhlenberg is based on financial need as demonstrated by the College Scholarship Service Financial Aid PROFILE, there is also significant merit aid available. Typically, about 65 percent of Muhlenberg's students qualify for and receive financial aid.

APPLICATION AND INFORMATION

Students who wish to be considered for admission should submit a completed application form as early as possible during their senior year of secondary school and no later than February 15. Candidates receive notice of admission decisions in late March. Early decision plans and transfer admission are possible.

NEW YORK UNIVERSITY

■ NEW YORK, NEW YORK

THE UNIVERSITY

For an application and more information, students should contact:

Office of Undergraduate Admissions
New York University
22 Washington Square North
New York, New York 10011

Phone: 212-998-4500
Web site: http://admissions.nyu.edu

New York University (NYU) was founded in 1831 by Albert Gallatin, Secretary of the Treasury under Thomas Jefferson; he believed that the place for a university was not in "the seclusion of cloistered halls but in the throbbing heart of a great city." NYU draws top students from every state and more than 133 other countries. The distinguished academic atmosphere attracts the teachers, and the teachers and the atmosphere together attract students who are capable of benefiting from both. Eighty-seven percent of recent NYU graduates say they are either enrolled in a postbaccalaureate program or are planning to do so within the next five years. The faculty includes world-famous scholars, researchers, and artists, among them Nobel laureates, Pulitzer Prize winners, and National Science Foundation members. NYU is a member of the prestigious Association of American Universities. Full professors teach on both the graduate and undergraduate levels. Eight undergraduate schools and colleges provide extensive offerings in a wide range of subjects: more than 2,500 courses in more than 160 major fields are available to NYU's full-time undergraduates. The average class size is under 30, and the faculty-student ratio is 1:11—benefits generally associated with a much smaller institution.

NYU's residence hall program is an important aspect of the total educational experience. Approximately 12,500 undergraduate students live in twenty-one University residence halls, seven of which are reserved exclusively for freshmen. All freshmen who request housing on their admission application and meet all deadlines are guaranteed housing accommodations during all their years of undergraduate study. Freshmen are not required to live on campus, and many students live in private apartments off campus.

The traditions of campus life—nearly 400 clubs, fourteen fraternities and six sororities, and athletics and other activities—are very much a part of the University. Students have the opportunity to write for the campus newspaper and to work with the University's radio station, WNYU-FM. The Jerome S. Coles Sports and Recreation Center and the Palladium Athletic Facility serve the recreational needs of all students. Coles provides the setting for seventy-five intramural sports teams and is the home of NYU's twenty intercollegiate teams. NYU and eight other private, urban research universities have formed a varsity league, the University Athletic Association. The athletic program includes men's basketball, fencing, golf, soccer, swimming and diving, tennis, track and cross-country, volleyball, and wrestling and women's basketball, cross-country, fencing, golf, soccer, swimming and diving, tennis, track, and volleyball.

ACADEMIC PROGRAMS

Requirements for graduation vary among departments and schools. A liberal arts core curriculum is an integral part of all areas of concentration. The baccalaureate degree requires completion of at least 128 credits. The University calendar is organized on the traditional semester system, including two 6-week summer sessions. Some divisions offer part-time programs during the day and evening and on weekends.

FINANCIAL AID

Financial aid at NYU comes from many sources. All students are encouraged to apply for financial assistance or one of NYU's innovative financing plans. Seventy-seven percent of NYU's full-time undergraduates receive financial assistance. Each year, approximately 2,500 entering freshmen are awarded scholarships based on academic promise and/or financial need. The University may offer a package of aid that includes scholarships or grants, loans, or work-study programs. NYU requires the submission of the Free Application for Federal Student Aid (FAFSA). The deadline for filing this financial aid form is February 15 for the fall semester and November 1 for the spring semester. An estimated financial aid package is available to early decision admitted students. The early decision financial aid application is included in the admissions packet or online at http://www.nyu.edu/financial.aid.

APPLICATION AND INFORMATION

For entrance in the fall term, the application for admission—including all supporting credentials—must be received by November 1 (early decision freshman candidates), January 15 (freshmen), or April 1 (transfer students). For entrance in the spring term (transfer students only), the application materials must be received by November 1. Applications for admission received after these dates are considered only if space remains. Official notification of fall admission is made on April 1 and on a rolling basis thereafter. A campus tour or an appointment for an information session can be arranged online at http://admissions.nyu.edu or by calling 212-998-4524.

OREGON STATE UNIVERSITY

■ CORVALLIS, OREGON

For an application and more information, students should contact:

Office of Admissions
Oregon State University
104 Kerr Administration Building
Corvallis, Oregon 97331-2106
Phone: 800-291-4192 (toll-free)
E-mail: osuadmit@oregonstate.edu
Web site: http://oregonstate.edu

THE UNIVERSITY

Exceptional students, an outstanding faculty, and a challenging curriculum combine to make Oregon State University (OSU) a nationally and internationally recognized comprehensive university. Widely recognized research programs add to the quality of teaching by bringing new knowledge into the classroom and by encouraging undergraduate students to work with faculty members on research projects.

The University's 19,700 students come from all fifty states and more than ninety-three countries to pursue a wide choice of undergraduate programs that prepare them for careers and leadership positions in science, engineering and computer-related fields, natural resources, government, teaching and social service, pharmacy, and other professions. Employers from across the nation recognize the value of an OSU degree, and more of them recruit at Oregon State University each year than at any other university in the state.

OSU is committed to offering students the resources they need to be successful in their education. In addition to utilizing Blackboard™ as an electronic tool to assist students with class materials, interactive topic conversations, and resources, OSU continues to innovate by systematically adding wireless networks to classrooms, libraries, and common areas on campus. Students also have access to one of the largest open-source software labs in the world, where new shareware is developed, housed, and distributed.

Students also benefit from more than 300 cocurricular activities on campus. These include student government, student media, theater and music, intramural and club sports, and numerous social, academic, cultural, and professional clubs and organizations. In addition, Dixon Recreation Center offers opportunities for swimming and diving, weight training, aerobic exercise, and the largest collegiate rock-climbing center in the Northwest.

OSU offers a wide range of housing and dining options. Many apartments and houses are available within biking or walking distance of OSU for students who choose to live off campus. There are more than fifteen restaurants on campus.

ACADEMIC PROGRAMS

OSU has more majors, minors, and special programs than any other college in Oregon and offers a University Exploratory Studies Program for students who want to try various options before choosing a major field. All undergraduate students at Oregon State complete the Baccalaureate Core, which helps develop skills and knowledge in writing, critical thinking, cultural diversity, the arts, science, literature, lifelong fitness, and global awareness, ensuring that as graduates they will be well prepared for life as well as a career. Many students take advantage of OSU's first-year experience program, called Odyssey, which offers opportunities for new students to interact with faculty members and other students throughout the year, thus easing the transition to college life.

The Academic Success Center helps OSU students deal with problems and develop the skills they need in college and beyond. The Center for Writing and Learning, the Math Learning Center, and departmental resource centers assist students in preparing for assignments in specific areas, while the African American, Hispanic American, Asian American, and Native American education offices, along with the Educational Opportunities Program, help mentor students throughout their college careers. University Counseling and Psychological Services offers learning resource materials and professional assistance to help students deal with problems, both in and out of the classroom. Career Services assists students in locating internships and in finding jobs when they graduate.

FINANCIAL AID

OSU offers the full range of scholarships, grants, work-study, and loans from federal, state, and University sources, investing more than $108 million in student aid annually. Some form of financial assistance is received by 80 percent of the students at OSU. To qualify, students must have applied for admission and must submit the FAFSA, listing OSU as one of their top six choices. Some students help meet educational expenses with one of the many part-time jobs available on or near the campus. For financial aid information, interested students should contact the Office of Financial Aid and Scholarships (541-737-2241; http://oregonstate.edu/admin/finaid/).

Through the University Scholars Program, OSU offers a variety of scholarships and additional scholarship search assistance for new students who have strong academic records. In addition, most OSU colleges offer scholarships to new students, and the OSU Foundation has a number of University-wide scholarships.

APPLICATION AND INFORMATION

Applicants are encouraged to complete OSU's online application. Prospective students are encouraged to visit OSU to determine in person whether the University meets their needs.

PRATT INSTITUTE

■ BROOKLYN, NEW YORK

THE INSTITUTE

For an application and more information, students should contact:

Office of Admissions
Pratt Institute
200 Willoughby Avenue
Brooklyn, New York 11205
Phone: 718-636-3514
800-331-0834 (toll-free)
E-mail: admissions@pratt.edu
Web site: http://www.pratt.edu

Founded in 1887 on its present site in Brooklyn by industrialist and philanthropist Charles Pratt, Pratt Institute educated on nonbaccalaureate levels for its first half-century. As the educational preparation necessary for various professions expanded, Pratt Institute moved with the times. It granted its first baccalaureate degree in 1938 and started its first graduate program in 1950. With a wide variety of programs in art, design, and architecture, Pratt has continued to add programs at all educational levels, including undergraduate programs in creative writing and critical and visual studies, undergraduate and graduate programs in art history, and graduate programs in art education, arts and cultural management, historic preservation, and design management. Although the characteristics and educational requirements of the professions for which Pratt prepares people have changed over the course of a century, the Institute has succeeded in pursuing its abiding purpose—to blend theoretical learning with professional and humanistic development.

Pratt offers four-year bachelor's, two-year associate, and master's degrees. In educating more than four generations of students to be creative, technically skilled, and adaptable professionals as well as responsible citizens, Pratt has gained a national and international reputation that attracts undergraduate and graduate students from more than forty-six states, the District of Columbia, Puerto Rico, the Virgin Islands, and seventy countries. Unlike the typical American college student, most of those who choose Pratt already have career objectives, or at least they know they want to study art, design, architecture, or creative writing.

A short bus or subway ride from the museum, gallery, and design centers of both Manhattan and Brooklyn, Pratt Institute has twenty-four buildings of differing architectural styles spread about a 25-acre campus. Eighteen of the buildings house studios, classrooms, laboratories, administrative offices, auditoria, sports facilities, food services, and student centers. Six buildings are student residences, including the new Stabile Hall freshman residence, which provides studio space on each floor. There are adequate parking facilities for residents and commuters. Student services include career planning and placement, health and counseling, and student development. The more than sixty student organizations include fraternities and sororities, honorary societies, professional societies, and clubs.

ACADEMIC PROGRAMS

Educating artists and creative professionals to be responsible contributors to society has been the mission of Pratt Institute since it assembled its first group of students in 1887. Within the structure of that professional education, Pratt students are encouraged to acquire the diverse knowledge that is necessary for them to succeed in their chosen fields. In addition to the professional studies, the curriculum in each of Pratt's schools includes a broad range of liberal arts courses. Students from all schools take these courses together and have the opportunity to examine the interrelationships of art, science, technology, and human need.

At the time of graduation, students in the associate degree programs have completed 67 credit hours of course work. In the bachelor's programs, credit-hour requirements range from 132 to 135 credits, depending on the particular program. For the Bachelor of Architecture degree, 170 credits are required.

Pratt's academic calendar consists of two semesters plus optional summer terms that allow students to choose alternative courses or various options usually not offered during the fall or spring semester. Two summer sessions are offered.

FINANCIAL AID

Pratt Institute offers a large number of grants, scholarships, loans, and awards on the basis of academic achievement, talent, financial need, or all three. More than 75 percent of Pratt students receive aid in one or more of these kinds of aid. Through funds from the federal and state governments, contributions from Pratt alumni, and industry scholarships, Pratt is able to maintain an effective aid program in a time of escalating costs. Pratt attempts to ensure that no student is prevented by lack of funds from completing his or her education.

APPLICATION AND INFORMATION

Pratt has two admissions deadlines: November 1 for early action and January 15 for regular admissions. To receive full consideration, students must submit applications by January 15 for anticipated entrance in the fall semester and by October 1 for anticipated entrance in the spring semester.

RENSSELAER POLYTECHNIC INSTITUTE

■ TROY, NEW YORK

THE INSTITUTE

For an application and more information, students should contact:

Rensselaer Admissions
Undergraduate Programs
Rensselaer Polytechnic Institute
Troy, New York 12180-3590

Phone: 518-276-6216
E-mail: admissions@rpi.edu
Web site: http://admissions.rpi.edu

The oldest degree-granting technological university in North America, Rensselaer Polytechnic Institute (RPI) was founded in 1824 "for the purpose of instructing persons in the application of science to the common purposes of life." Rensselaer has become one of the world's premier technological research universities, offering more than 144 programs and 1,000 courses that lead to bachelor's, master's, and doctoral degrees. Undergraduates pursue their studies in the Schools of Architecture, Engineering, Humanities and Social Sciences, Management and Technology, and Science and in the multidisciplinary area of information technology (IT). As a pioneer in interactive learning, Rensselaer has a long tradition of providing real-world, hands-on educational experiences to its students. Many of the courses cut across academic disciplines. Students have ready access to laboratories and often work in teams on research projects. Classes involve lively discussion, problem solving, and faculty mentoring, which encourages students to formulate new ideas and new discoveries. Rensselaer's approach to education has created generations of graduates who are known for their ability to solve some of the world's most challenging technical problems.

Rensselaer's 5,000 undergraduate and 1,200 graduate students are a bright, ambitious, and technologically savvy group who come from forty-eight states, the District of Columbia, Puerto Rico, the Virgin Islands, and sixty-seven other countries. A wide variety of nonacademic activities, virtually all of which are run by the students, is available. There are thirty-three fraternities and sororities, a weekly newspaper, a progressive 10,000-watt FM stereo station, dramatics groups, musical ensembles, and more than 160 clubs, special-interest groups, professional societies, sports, and organizations. More than 5,000 students participate in twenty-four intramural sports. Rensselaer is a member of the NCAA. Varsity sports include Division I men's and women's ice-hockey teams and twenty-one Division III men's and women's teams in twelve sports. Recreational facilities include the Mueller Fitness Center, an indoor track, all-weather track and field facilities, handball and squash courts, weight rooms, several indoor tennis courts, and two swimming pools. The Student Union, Chapel and Cultural Center, and Houston Field House bring many forms of entertainment and nationally known performing groups and lecturers to the campus.

The Office of the First-Year Experience offers a comprehensive array of programs and initiatives for both students and their primary support team that begins before students arrive on campus and continues well beyond their first year. This office sponsors the Navigating Rensselaer & Beyond orientation program, family programs, community service, and the Information and Personal Assistance Center (IPAC), along with many other programming initiatives for students and families.

Rensselaer continually upgrades residence halls and dining facilities across the campus. The Institute also is pursuing the development of several new athletic facilities, including a new field house, basketball arena, and natatorium as well as new administrative space, locker rooms, and weight rooms.

ACADEMIC PROGRAMS

While each of Rensselaer's schools has its own sequence requirements, the following minimums apply to all students: 124 credit hours and a 1.8 quality point average in all courses; 24 credit hours in physical, life, and engineering sciences; 24 in humanities and social sciences; 30 in a selected discipline; and 24 in electives. Students are strongly encouraged to learn outside the classroom through independent projects, study abroad, cooperative education, internships, and partnering with faculty members on specific research projects. The Undergraduate Research Program offers hands-on experience to students in hundreds of areas where a full-time undergraduate may participate for credit or pay during the academic year or the summer. Co-op assignments give students the opportunity to add practical experience to their academic study. Air Force, Army, and Naval/Marine ROTC programs are available on an elective basis. Computing is integrated into the curriculum at Rensselaer, and all incoming undergraduates are required to have a laptop computer. Rensselaer's Mobile Computing Program provides students with the latest computing technology choices. Students may bring their own laptops to the campus, but they must comply with Rensselaer's computing requirements.

FINANCIAL AID

Nearly all freshmen who have financial need are offered assistance under a comprehensive program of scholarships, loans, and part-time employment that provides annual assistance ranging from $100 up to full tuition, room, and board. Available federal funds include student loans, Federal Work-Study Program awards, and ROTC scholarships.

THE RICHARD STOCKTON COLLEGE OF NEW JERSEY

■ POMONA, NEW JERSEY

THE COLLEGE

The Richard Stockton College of New Jersey (RSCNJ) is a selective, medium-sized, highly-ranked, public liberal arts college within the New Jersey system of higher education, offering programs in the arts and humanities, business, professional studies, and social, behavioral, and natural sciences. Founded in 1969, the College was named for Richard Stockton, one of the New Jersey signers of the Declaration of Independence.

Stockton enrolls more than 7,000 students from New Jersey and the surrounding mid-Atlantic states, providing distinctive traditional educational programs and alternative educational experiences that extend learning beyond the classroom. Stockton seeks to develop the analytic and creative capabilities of its students and encourages them to undertake individually planned courses of study that promote self-reliance, acceptance of change, and an educated response to change.

For an application and more information, students should contact:

Dean of Enrollment Management
The Richard Stockton College of New Jersey
P.O. Box 195
Pomona, New Jersey 08240-0195
Phone: 609-652-4261
866-RSC-2885 (toll-free)
E-mail: admissions@stockton.edu
Web site: http://www.stockton.edu

The College's campus provides an excellent natural setting for a wide range of outdoor recreational activities, including sailing, canoeing, hiking, jogging, and fishing. Students and faculty and staff members join together in an extensive intramural and club sports program that includes aikido, crew, flag football, golf, ice hockey, soccer, softball, street hockey, swimming, and volleyball. At the intercollegiate level, Stockton fields NCAA Division III sports teams in men's baseball, basketball, lacrosse, and soccer; women's basketball, crew, field hockey, soccer, softball, tennis, and volleyball; and men's and women's cross-country and track and field. The new multipurpose Sports and Recreation Center has fitness facilities, a glass-enclosed indoor swimming pool, racquetball courts, weight rooms, a gymnasium, and outdoor recreational facilities that include a field house, NCAA track, field-event venues, and four playing fields for soccer and lacrosse.

College Center I is the hub for social, recreational, cultural, and leisure activities. More than eighty clubs and organizations have their offices in the center: social clubs, such as the Film Committee, Concert Committee, and Performing Arts Committee; service clubs, including the Social Work Club, Speech and Hearing Association, and Unified Black Students' Society; special interest clubs, such as the Accounting and Finance Society, Dance Club, and Photography Club; and independent organizations, including the Jewish Student Union, New Life Christian Fellowship, and twenty-one sororities and fraternities.

College Center II, which is connected to the main academic complex, is an open living room–type area featuring a dining facility for students and staff members, a wide-screen television, a game room, lounge areas, and several conference rooms.

Stockton provides on-campus housing for almost 2,500 students in traditional residence hall–style arrangements and apartment-style living. All complexes are completely furnished and air conditioned, with cable TV, telephone service, and Internet access (port-per-pillow) provided. Students choosing to live off campus can find a number of nearby complexes as well as summer shore homes not used during the academic year that are rented to Stockton students.

ACADEMIC PROGRAMS

Degree programs include a combination of general studies and program (major field) studies. General studies courses are broad cross-disciplinary courses designed to introduce students to all major areas of the curriculum and to the broadly applicable intellectual skills necessary for success in college.

Stockton students have special opportunities to influence what and how they learn by participating in the major decisions that shape their academic lives. The opportunities of the preceptorial system enable students to work on a personalized basis with an assigned faculty-staff preceptor in planning and evaluating individual courses of study and in exploring various career alternatives. Stockton's academic programs emphasize curricular organization and methods of instruction that promote independent learning and research, cross-disciplinary study, problem solving, and decision making through analysis and synthesis.

FINANCIAL AID

Financial aid is available in the form of scholarships, grants, loans, and work-study. Need-based financial aid is awarded according to student and family need. Students seeking financial aid should file the FAFSA by March 1. Merit-based aid is awarded to recognize academic excellence. Stockton offers aggressive and generous scholarship opportunities for academically talented freshmen and transfer students based on standardized test scores, grade point average, high school class rank, and college-level performance.

ROGER WILLIAMS UNIVERSITY

■ BRISTOL, RHODE ISLAND

THE UNIVERSITY

Roger Williams University (RWU), which has been ranked in the top tier of Best Comprehensive Colleges in its region and category by *U.S. News & World Report*'s "America's Best Colleges," has experienced tremendous growth with new facilities and an increasingly diverse and vigorous academic curriculum. During the last decade, Roger Williams has moved ahead by expanding undergraduate programs and creating master's degree programs to meet students' needs. As a leading liberal arts university, Roger Williams exemplifies core values that represent higher education at its best: a love for learning, preparation for the future, applied research, service to others and the community as a whole, a global perspective, and respect for the individual. The University enrolls approximately 3,775 full-time undergraduate students in thirty-eight majors. Roger Williams University's dedicated faculty members, who are noted experts in their fields, take a genuine interest in students, ensuring an engaging learning environment.

For an application and more information, students should contact:

Office of Undergraduate Admission
Roger Williams University
One Old Ferry Road
Bristol, Rhode Island 02809-2921
Phone: 401-254-3500
800-458-7144 Ext. 3500
E-mail: admit@rwu.edu
Web site: http://www.rwu.edu

The main campus, overlooking beautiful Mt. Hope Bay in Bristol, Rhode Island, opened in 1969 and features modern academic and recreational facilities, including a waterfront Marine and Natural Sciences Building; an $8-million Main Library; the award-winning Architecture Building and Architecture Library; and the Performing Arts Center. In 2003, the University opened a multimillion-dollar addition to the Campus Recreation Center, which includes an eight-lane swimming pool, racquetball courts, and a state-of-the-art workout facility. Outdoor recreational facilities include softball and baseball diamonds, three rugby/lacrosse/soccer fields, six tennis courts, and a jogging track. Roger Williams University teams compete in Division III of the NCAA, the ECAC, and the CCC; the University sponsors eighteen varsity sports for men and women as well as clubs in men's and women's rugby, coed crew, and coed track and field. In addition, an extensive program of intramural and recreational activities is offered all year long.

A variety of other comfortable residences located on the main campus offer students a choice of residential living in facilities directly on Mt. Hope Bay. Residential units include 24-hour quiet areas for study and some specialized living/learning units grouped by major or areas of interest, including honors and wellness initiatives.

The University sponsors many social, cultural, and academic activities. Students may choose from a variety of structured and informal activities, including Socrates Café, which is held in the Mary Tefft White Cultural Center; the Alive! Arts Series; Main Season theater and dance productions; Penny Arcade Film Series; visiting speakers forum; and lectures by distinguished speakers, visiting novelists, and poets. The student radio station, WQRI, provides opportunities to gain broadcasting experience; students gain journalism and publishing experience working on the yearbook, newspaper, literary magazine, and new weekly produced news media program, *The Feed.* Additional opportunities include participation in campus and community choruses, service projects both on and off campus, numerous student clubs and organizations, and student government. Also of note are national honor societies, Alpha Chi and Beta Gamma Sigma; numerous departmental honor societies; continuing education opportunities; and a strong Career Services department.

ACADEMIC PROGRAMS

The fall semester begins in September and ends in December; the spring semester begins in late January and ends in May. During the month of January, special on- and off-campus intersession programs, including opportunities for travel and service, are open to students at other institutions of higher learning. The University Honors Program invites applicants who have demonstrated academic excellence.

FINANCIAL AID

The University offers merit scholarships to recognize students with superior academic achievement. Merit scholarship recipients are determined by high school or prior college record, GPA, and SAT or ACT scores. There is no separate application for these scholarships. The vast majority of the funds and programs administered by the Office of Student Financial Aid and Financial Planning at the University require the demonstration of financial need as an essential consideration. The University requires the submission of the FAFSA and the CSS Financial Aid PROFILE to the respective processors by January 1. The FAFSA must be received at the federal processor no later than February 1 to be considered for maximum financial aid.

APPLICATION AND INFORMATION

The deadline for early decision is November 1; for early action, November 15; and for regular decision, February 1. A nonrefundable fee of $50 must accompany the application.

RUTGERS, THE STATE UNIVERSITY OF NEW JERSEY, CAMDEN

■ CAMDEN, NEW JERSEY

THE UNIVERSITY

Located in the heart of the University District on the exciting Camden Waterfront, Rutgers-Camden is a vibrant academic community of 5,383 undergraduate and graduate students who work closely with professors who are among the top scholars in their fields. These students enjoy strong success with national employers and in gaining admission to the nation's most prestigious graduate programs.

For an application and more information, students should contact:

Office of University Undergraduate Admissions
Rutgers, The State University of New Jersey
406 Penn Street
Camden, New Jersey 08102-1400
Phone: 856-225-6104
Web site: http://camden.rutgers.edu

Rutgers-Camden is the southernmost of the three campuses that comprise New Jersey's flagship public research university: Rutgers, The State University of New Jersey. Faculty members at Rutgers-Camden are selected and promoted based on the same high standards as their peers across every Rutgers campus, and Camden students enjoy the same access to Rutgers' system-wide research library and state-of-the-art computing network.

Students seeking the opportunity to work closely with world-class scholars select Rutgers-Camden for its unique combination of "small college" ambience, with day and evening classes offered during the traditional fall and spring semesters and a smaller schedule of offerings during winter and summer sessions.

Located at the foot of the Benjamin Franklin Bridge, Rutgers-Camden is directly across the Delaware River from Philadelphia; in fact, Rutgers-Camden is the four-year college closest to the Liberty Bell. On-campus housing is available for 550 students on a first-come basis. Some students choose to live in the comfortable southern New Jersey communities located along the PATCO Speedline, which has a station located one block from campus and offers a very convenient option for commuting. A light-rail system stops on campus and is an easy commuting option for residents of northern counties. The campus is accessible by all major regional transportation arteries.

A spacious Campus Center offers dining areas as well as offices for student organizations. A University District bookstore offers comprehensive service directly adjacent to the campus. The gymnasium offers a complete health club experience, including squash and racquetball courts and strength and cardio conditioning.

On-campus dining is available through a dining hall and the Courtyard Café restaurant. An on-campus Starbucks provides a relaxing gathering spot for students. In addition, a number of small eateries surround the campus.

The Rutgers-Camden Center for the Arts brings established and emerging performers to the campus and offers a series of intriguing exhibitions in the Stedman Gallery and the Gordon Theater. The Office of Student Affairs works with students to provide a diverse schedule of activities throughout the year. The Rutgers-Camden Scarlet Raptors compete in NCAA Division III sports, with thirteen competitive men's and women's teams. The women's softball team won the NCAA Division III championship in 2006.

ACADEMIC PROGRAMS

Each college or school establishes its own admission, scholastic standing, and graduation requirements, and each offers specific academic programs that reflect the mission and philosophy of the college or school. Highly qualified students are invited to participate in the Honors College, a college within a college. Special academic programs include honors courses, tracks, and programs; ROTC; national honors societies; undergraduate research; graduate course work; internships; cooperative education; and service learning. Students are encouraged to participate in independent research under the guidance of a faculty member and may qualify for grants to support their research.

FINANCIAL AID

University-wide, undergraduate students received more than $292 million in federal and state grants and loans, work/study jobs, and university scholarships in 2006–07. Seventy-three percent of Rutgers-Camden undergraduates receive financial assistance. Merit and need-based scholarships are offered by the University and by individual colleges and schools.

APPLICATION AND INFORMATION

Candidates for admission submit a single application for consideration at any three Rutgers colleges or schools. Applying online to meet priority application dates is strongly urged. Priority dates are October 15 for spring admission for first-year and transfer students, December 1 for fall admission for first-year students, and January 15 for fall admission for transfer students. Letters of recommendation are not required. Personal interviews are not required and are not granted. Campus tours are encouraged.

RUTGERS, THE STATE UNIVERSITY OF NEW JERSEY, NEW BRUNSWICK

■ NEW BRUNSWICK, NEW JERSEY

THE UNIVERSITY

Chartered in 1766 as Queen's College, Rutgers is one of the original nine colonial colleges and the eighth-oldest institution of higher education in the nation. Today, seven (Brown, Columbia, Dartmouth, Harvard, Princeton, the University of Pennsylvania, and Yale) of the nine colonial colleges are private and two (Rutgers and the College of William and Mary) are public. Rutgers is New Jersey's flagship public research university, is a member of the prestigious Association of American Universities (a group comprising the top research universities in North America), and is accredited by the Middle States Association of Colleges and Schools.

For an application and more information, students should contact:

Office of University Undergraduate Admissions
Room 202
Rutgers, The State University of New Jersey
65 Davidson Road
Piscataway, New Jersey 08854-8097
Phone: 732-932-INFO
Web site: http://admissions.rutgers.edu

With ten schools offering more than 100 undergraduate majors and five residential campus communities, students choose Rutgers for all the advantages of a small school and the resources of a leading research university. The liberal arts college is the School of Arts and Sciences. The professional schools are the School of Environmental and Biological Sciences, Mason Gross School of the Arts, Ernest Mario School of Pharmacy, Rutgers Business School, School of Engineering, Edward J. Bloustein School of Planning and Public Policy, School of Social Work, College of Nursing, and School of Communication, Information, and Library Studies. Each school has a unique culture, personality, and undergraduate enrollment, which ranges from about 600 at Mason Gross School of the Arts to 20,000 at the School of Arts and Sciences, where students are served by five smaller residential campus communities.

In fall 2007, 24,878 full-time undergraduates were enrolled at the New Brunswick campus, including 12,156 women and 12,722 men, 54 percent of whom were between the ages of 18 and 21. University-wide, 92 percent of Rutgers undergraduates are New Jersey residents. Residents of all twenty-one New Jersey counties, forty-six states, and 119 nations of the world are enrolled at Rutgers.

Rutgers has an extensive network of housing, restaurants, museums, student centers, cultural centers, student clubs and organizations, parks, hiking trails, recreational facilities, and more. The Division of Housing in New Brunswick houses approximately 14,000 undergraduate and graduate students on five residential campuses. Campus housing is allocated on a first-come, first-served basis and is generally assigned according to the undergraduate school in which one enrolls. On-campus housing is complemented by a lively fraternity and sorority scene and by off-campus housing in privately owned apartments and houses. The campus offers a wide array of dining options that include meal-plan dining halls, food courts, snack bars, cafés, and concessions. Meal plan options include location, menu, and the number of meals.

The birthplace of college football, Rutgers has a proud past in producing outstanding scholar-athletes and is the alma mater of dozens of athletes who have distinguished themselves on America's national, Olympic, and professional sports teams. Rutgers–New Brunswick participates in the NCAA Division I Big East Conference with twenty-five competitive men's and women's teams.

ACADEMIC PROGRAMS

Each college or school offers specific academic programs that reflect its mission and philosophy. Special academic programs include honors courses, tracks, and programs; ROTC; national honor societies; undergraduate research; graduate course work; internships; cooperative education; and service learning.

FINANCIAL AID

A wide variety of merit- and need-based financial aid is available to students at Rutgers, offered by the University and its individual colleges and schools. University-wide, undergraduate students received more than $308 million in federal and state grants and loans, work-study jobs, and University scholarships in 2006–07, with an average first-year award of $11,800. More than 85 percent of Rutgers undergraduates receive financial assistance.

APPLICATION AND INFORMATION

Candidates for admission submit a single application for consideration at any three Rutgers colleges or schools. Applying online to meet priority application dates is strongly urged. Priority dates are October 15 for spring first-year and transfer students, December 1 for fall first-year students, and January 15 for fall transfer students. Letters of recommendation are not required. Personal interviews are not required and are not granted, except for Mason Gross School of the Arts, which requires a portfolio review or talent assessment. Candidates may apply online.

ST. JOSEPH'S COLLEGE

■ BROOKLYN AND PATCHOGUE, NEW YORK

THE COLLEGE

Since 1916, St. Joseph's College has been inspiring students to transform their lives. A private coeducational institution with campuses in Brooklyn and Patchogue, Long Island, the College enrolls 4,885 undergraduates and 508 graduate students in its School of Arts and Sciences and School of Professional and Graduate Studies.

St. Joseph's helps students turn aspirations into accomplishments. In addition to a liberal arts education of the highest quality, St. Joseph's offers students an unrivaled degree of personal attention, encouraging them to lead lives characterized by integrity, a commitment to upholding intellectual and spiritual values, social responsibility, and service to others.

St. Joseph's students immerse themselves in learning in ways that go far beyond the classroom, through independent projects, team-building assignments, internships, community service opportunities, and study-abroad programs designed to suit every schedule. And, with just 15 students for every professor on campus, St. Joseph's students easily find mentors to guide them in everything from academics to focusing on future career and life goals.

For an application and more information, students should contact:

Brooklyn Campus:
Director of Admissions
St. Joseph's College
245 Clinton Avenue
Brooklyn, New York 11205
Phone: 718-636-6868

Long Island Campus:
Director of Admissions
St. Joseph's College
155 West Roe Boulevard
Patchogue, New York 11772
Phone: 631-447-3219
Web site: http://www.sjcny.edu

Although most of St. Joseph's students live off campus, the Brooklyn campus offers student housing at the nearby St. George Residence. Each of the campuses offers a lively atmosphere enriched by social events, athletic competitions, and a Common Hour to encourage students to explore new possibilities for fun, leadership, and connections. On any given day at St. Joseph's, students might come to campus to hear a Pulitzer Prize–winning author, enjoy a jazz concert, join a community service effort, view an art exhibit, attend an athletic event, or engage in a political debate over dinner with other students and professors. Each campus supports over thirty student clubs and activities, including intercollegiate basketball; women's softball, tennis, and volleyball; men's basketball; and coed cross-country. The Long Island campus also offers men's soccer, a women's swim team, and a coed equestrian team.

For undergraduates, St. Joseph's offers fast tracks to advanced degrees through special affiliated programs in accounting, podiatry, and computer science. The School of Professional and Graduate Studies at St. Joseph's College offers a wide range of graduate programs in education, management, and nursing.

ACADEMIC PROGRAMS

The School of Arts and Sciences at each campus operates on the semester system, with additional courses offered in January and during the summer. St. Joseph's students take a core curriculum of 128 credits to graduate; a wide range of choices allows students to tailor their academic programs to their personal and professional needs. The College recognizes the Advanced Placement (AP) Program and offers credit and placement for scores of 3 or above on AP tests. In each case, the score is reviewed by the registrar and/or department chairperson to determine credit and placement.

The School of Professional and Graduate Studies on each campus offers flexible schedules, summer programs, and online courses to meet the needs of working students. Courses may meet for a semester or for six- or twelve-week sessions.

FINANCIAL AID

St. Joseph's offers scholarships and grants-in-aid. Students who wish to apply for either form of assistance must file the Free Application for Federal Student Aid (FAFSA) and a state aid form. After a student has been accepted to the College and all financial aid forms are processed, the Financial Aid Office prepares aid packages that usually consist of federal, state, and College funds. St. Joseph's is fully approved for veterans. Campus work-study programs are also available.

APPLICATION AND INFORMATION

Admission is offered on a rolling basis. Applications and supporting documents should be submitted online or to the appropriate school. The College reviews each application carefully and usually sends a decision one month after receiving all necessary credentials. For more information and an online application, students can access the Web site at http://www.sjcny.edu.

ST. MARY'S COLLEGE OF MARYLAND
The Public Honors College

■ ST. MARY'S CITY, MARYLAND

THE COLLEGE

St. Mary's College of Maryland is a public, state-supported, coeducational college dedicated to providing an excellent education in the liberal arts and sciences. There are 1,909 full-time students, of whom 817 are men and 1,092 are women. Almost 83 percent of the students live on campus, where housing is guaranteed for eight semesters.

For an application and more information, students should contact:

Admissions
St. Mary's College of Maryland
18952 East Fisher Road
St. Mary's City, Maryland 20686
Phone: 240-895-5000
800-492-7181 (toll-free)
E-mail: admissions@smcm.edu
Web site: http://www.smcm.edu

Designated the State of Maryland's Public Honors College in 1992 in recognition of the academic excellence of its faculty and students, every St. Mary's student participates in the intellectual and social life of the College. St. Mary's combines the educational and personal advantages of a small private college with the affordability of a public institution. Active learning and the development of critical thinking are encouraged in the discussion-oriented format made possible by modest class sizes. Student leadership in academic, cultural, and social spheres is aided by the community atmosphere; opportunities are greater than at larger schools, and involvement is easier.

The campus covers 319 acres, including riverfront, open space, and woodland. Among the waterfront facilities are a boat house, ocean kayaks, rowing shells, and a fleet of sailboats. Other facilities include a field house, lighted tennis courts, a baseball field, an outdoor track, and a stadium for field hockey, soccer, and lacrosse. The new athletic facility includes an aquatic center with an Olympic-sized indoor pool, a basketball stadium, a fitness center, an aerobic center, additional team rooms, and a rock-climbing wall. The College's teams compete in NCAA Division III and the Intercollegiate Sailing Association. Varsity sports for men are baseball, basketball, lacrosse, sailing, soccer, swimming, and tennis; for women, basketball, field hockey, lacrosse, sailing, soccer, swimming, tennis, and volleyball. The College's sailing teams are especially noted for their national recognitions. Club sports include cross-country and track, equestrian, fencing, golf, rowing, rugby, sailing, soccer, and Ultimate Frisbee.

ACADEMIC PROGRAMS

The undergraduate course of study at the College provides both diversity and depth, leading to a broad understanding of the liberal arts and sciences and a specific competence in at least one major field. All students must complete the requirements for a major and the general education requirements. The general education requirements are designed to develop skills in communication and analysis, acquaint students with the legacy of the modern world, confront students with the forces and insights that are shaping the modern world, and promote the capacity for integration and synthesis of knowledge.

History, anthropology, and archaeology students can take advantage of the College's location on the site of colonial St. Mary's City, the fourth permanent English settlement in the New World and Maryland's first capital. Many experts consider this area to contain the most abundant and earliest undisturbed artifacts of any American seventeenth-century town.

St. Mary's College offers several courses in aquatic biology as an option within the major program in biology. The College's location on the St. Mary's River, a tributary of the Potomac near the mouth of the Chesapeake Bay, is ideal for the study of estuarine ecology.

A strong music program provides advanced training in composition and piano performance and a jazz ensemble, percussion ensemble, choir, chamber vocal group, wind ensemble, and chamber orchestra.

Independent study for credit is possible in every major, allowing students to investigate subjects not covered in normal course offerings. There is also an opportunity for students to design their own majors using components from several majors to create an interdisciplinary, individualized program of study.

FINANCIAL AID

The Office of Financial Aid provides advice and assistance to students in need of financial aid and joins other College offices in awarding scholarships and loans and in offering part-time employment under the work-study program. Various scholarships are awarded on a merit basis, and other scholarships, loans, and grants are awarded on the basis of ability and need as determined by the FAFSA, which should be filed no later than March 1.

SAMFORD UNIVERSITY

■ BIRMINGHAM, ALABAMA

THE UNIVERSITY

Samford University is a private, comprehensive liberal arts university with high-academic standards. The University's academic reputation is due to well-prepared, accessible faculty members who take time to know and interact with students. Samford, which has some 4,500 students, offers a wide range of extracurricular activities diverse enough to satisfy the social, cultural, physical, and spiritual needs of all of its students. A lively Greek system; an honors program; men's and women's intramural and varsity athletics, including seventeen NCAA Division I sports; music and drama groups; an award-winning debate program; and other interest groups bond the students and faculty members into a community of friends and scholars. Students come from forty-four states and thirty-three countries. A large number of students live on campus, enhancing the sense of school spirit and involvement. Students enjoy modern recreational facilities, including a concert hall, a theater, an indoor pool, racquetball and tennis courts, and an indoor track. Comfortable housing, including modern apartment-style units and fraternity/sorority residence facilities, is available.

For an application and more information, students should contact:

Phil Kimrey, Ed.D.
Dean of Admission and Financial Aid
Samford University
Birmingham, Alabama 35229
Phone: 205-726-3673
800-888-7218 (toll-free)
Web site: http://www.samford.edu

Samford University has ranked third among 130 regional universities in the South, as published by *U.S. News & World Report*; marked as "very competitive" by *Barron's Profiles of American Colleges*; and has been selected for *Peterson's Competitive Colleges*. Samford programs are included in *The Templeton Guide: Colleges that Encourage Character Development*.

Special student services include an active and successful Career Development Center, which offers guidance in career exploration as well as ample opportunities for placement interviews. Co-op programs add work experience and business contacts to the rewards of achievement and income for the participants. The co-op program is an excellent source of financial assistance that complements the significant scholarship and federal aid programs available to Samford students.

ACADEMIC PROGRAMS

In order to graduate, students must complete a minimum of 128 semester credits with an average grade of C or better. The core curriculum consists of the following six courses: Cultural Perspectives I and II, Communication Arts I and II, Biblical Perspectives, and Concepts of Fitness and Health. The curriculum is designed to address ideas and issues that cross the usual disciplinary boundaries and to help students actively engage in learning rather than simply memorizing notes for an exam. The core is also designed to promote a global perspective, recognizing the influence and achievement of many cultures.

In addition, students complete several education courses designed to prepare them for work in a major field and/or to help them experience the sciences, the social sciences, the humanities, and the fine arts.

At least 40 credits must be earned in junior- and senior-level courses. At least 50 percent of credits must be earned at Samford University. Between the end of the sophomore year and graduation, undergraduate students (including transfer students) must pass a writing proficiency test.

FINANCIAL AID

At Samford University, a student's educational costs are frequently offset by scholarship and other financial assistance programs, which annually total more than $30 million. The application for admission also serves as the application for merit-based scholarships. Students interested in need-based opportunities should complete the Free Application for Federal Student Aid (FAFSA) by the March 1 priority filing date. In addition, non-need-based scholarship awards, usually based on academic merit, range up to full tuition.

APPLICATION AND INFORMATION

Applications are received and notification is processed on a monthly rolling basis beginning in November. Students may also apply online by visiting the University's Web site. Applications are accepted until the class is filled.

SAVANNAH COLLEGE OF ART AND DESIGN

■ SAVANNAH, GEORGIA

THE COLLEGE

The Savannah College of Art and Design (SCAD) was founded in Savannah, Georgia, in 1978 with a curriculum designed to provide an excellent arts education and effective career preparation for students. Today, with two locations as well as online programs, the College continues to adhere to this mission, attracting students from all fifty states and from more than ninety countries. The College exists to prepare talented students for professional careers, emphasizing learning through individual attention in a positively oriented university environment. The goal of the College is to nurture and cultivate the unique qualities of each student through an interesting curriculum in an inspiring environment under the leadership of involved professors.

SCAD is a private, nonprofit institution accredited by the Commission on Colleges of the Southern Association of Colleges and Schools (1866 Southern Lane, Decatur, Georgia 30033-4097; telephone: 404-679-4501) to award bachelor's and master's degrees. The College offers Bachelor of Arts, Bachelor of Fine Arts, Master of Architecture, Master of Arts, Master of Arts in Teaching, Master of Fine Arts, and Master of Urban Design degrees, as well as undergraduate and graduate certificates. The five-year professional M.Arch. degree is accredited by the National Architectural Accrediting Board. Online degree programs are offered through SCAD-eLearning (http://www.scad.edu/elearning).

For an application and more information, students should contact:

Savannah and eLearning Admissions:
Admission Department
Savannah College of Art and Design
P.O. Box 2072
Savannah, Georgia 31402-2072
Phone: 912-525-5100
800-869-7223 (toll-free)
E-mail: admission@scad.edu
Web site: http://www.scad.edu

Atlanta Admissions:
Admission Department
Savannah College of Art and Design–Atlanta
P.O. Box 77300
Atlanta, Georgia 30357-77300
Phone: 404-253-2700
877-722-3285 (toll-free)
E-mail: scadatl@scad.edu
Web site: http://www.scad.edu

The Savannah College of Art and Design offers both intercollegiate and intramural athletic programs. The College competes in the Florida Sun Conference of the National Association of Intercollegiate Athletics. SCAD offers men's and women's basketball, cross-country, equestrian, golf, soccer, swimming, and tennis; women's softball and volleyball; and men's baseball and men's and women's lacrosse.

ACADEMIC PROGRAMS

The College operates on the quarter system. Fall, winter, and spring sessions extend from mid-September through May. Summer sessions run from late June through August.

A balanced curriculum offers a well-rounded liberal arts education, the traditional components of a fine arts education, the opportunity to acquire contemporary high-tech skills through the use of state-of-the-art facilities, and the option of pursuing double majors and multidisciplinary explorations. Total course of study for the B.F.A. degree consists of 180 quarter credit hours (36 courses). Of these, students take 30 to 50 hours in the foundation studies program, 55 to 65 hours in the liberal arts program (with a concentration on art history classes), 60 to 70 hours in the major area of study, and 10 to 15 hours in electives.

FINANCIAL AID

Approximately 50 percent of undergraduates and 53 percent of freshmen receive financial assistance. The Savannah College of Art and Design has a number of financial aid programs, which may consist of scholarships, grants, loans, or any combination of these, from federal (including the Federal Direct Loan Program), state, and college sources. Students also help finance educational expenses by jobs secured through the Federal Work-Study Program and the College's Student Placement Service. A detailed listing of financial aid programs may be obtained from the admission office.

APPLICATION AND INFORMATION

As a general rule, applications for fall quarter should be completed no later than March 1 in order for admission decisions to be rendered by April 1. Scholarships for fall quarter are awarded by May 1 and students are requested to indicate their acceptance of admission and of institutional scholarship offers by June 1 through payment of a one-time matriculation fee. This same time frame applies with corresponding dates for students entering winter, spring, or summer quarters. Applications received less than one month prior to the intended entry date are considered only on a space available basis.

Files are reviewed as soon as they are complete, and applicants are notified immediately of their admission status. Only accepted students are eligible for scholarship consideration and federal/state aid.

SEATTLE PACIFIC UNIVERSITY

■ SEATTLE, WASHINGTON

THE UNIVERSITY

With a long and distinguished history in Christian higher education, Seattle Pacific University (SPU) entered the new century positioned to engage the culture and influence the world for good. At a time when the legacy of the secularized modern university is under scrutiny, Seattle Pacific provides more than 3,800 students with a high-quality, comprehensive education grounded on the gospel of Jesus Christ.

Founded in 1891, SPU has been designated one of "America's Best Colleges" by *U.S. News & World Report* and has been acknowledged as one of the country's character-building institutions. Located just minutes from downtown Seattle, the leading urban center in the Pacific Northwest, SPU is committed to engaging and serving in the modern city, cultivating a global consciousness, supporting the church, and addressing the crisis of meaning in modern culture. SPU believes these are some of the Christian university's most important contributions in this century. The University's unique leadership program encourages students to cultivate their individual talents through opportunities in student government, ministries, performing groups, publications, clubs, and organizations.

For an application and more information, students should contact:

Jobe Nice, Director of Undergraduate Admissions
Seattle Pacific University
3307 Third Avenue West, Suite 115
Seattle, Washington 98119-1922
Phone: 206-281-2021
800-366-3344 (toll-free)
E-mail: admissions@spu.edu
Web site: http://www.spu.edu

SPU students come from forty-four states and twenty-four countries, representing more than forty-two different Christian denominations. More than half of the undergraduate students live on the campus. All Seattle Pacific residence facilities are wired to allow students dedicated online connections.

Seattle Pacific University celebrates diversity and learning to live together in Christian community. In 2004, civil rights leader John Perkins and SPU President Philip Eaton founded the John Perkins Center on campus. The first of its kind in the nation, the Perkins Center helps SPU become a more diverse campus, practice reconciliation, build new relationships in the city, and bring about positive change in the world. The Ames Minority Leadership Scholarships support high school graduates who are members of minority groups and have leadership potential.

Seattle Pacific's intercollegiate athletic program fields NCAA Division II teams in men's and women's basketball, crew, cross-country, soccer, and track and field and women's gymnastics and volleyball. All students have access to forty-seven intramural sports as well as other health and fitness activities.

ACADEMIC PROGRAMS

Seattle Pacific's academic disciplines set high standards for students. Undergraduate students are taught not by graduate assistants but by experienced professors who are recognized locally and nationally for the quality of their scholarship. Small classes mean students actively participate in their own education, gaining the confidence to achieve their goals.

The Common Curriculum, which includes seven required courses spread out over four years, is at the heart of an undergraduate liberal arts education at Seattle Pacific. Students begin in the first quarter of their freshman year with University Seminar, a focused exploration of a special interdisciplinary topic. The fewer than 25 students enrolled in each course form a "cohort" and attend other freshman classes in the Common Curriculum together, with their University Seminar professor serving as their academic adviser. In their first three years, students participate in two parallel sequences of required courses that address key human questions from the perspective of various disciplines and the foundations of Christian faith.

FINANCIAL AID

Seattle Pacific expects to award nearly $60 million in scholarships and financial aid in 2008–09. Need-based financial aid is available in the form of scholarships, grants, loans, and employment. To be considered for maximum aid, students must submit the FAFSA as soon as possible after January 1 and be admitted to the University by March 1. Merit-based University scholarships, ranging from $1500 to full tuition, are given annually to students who exhibit academic excellence and exemplify the ideals of the institution. The Division of Fine Arts and the Athletic Department also award scholarships.

APPLICATION AND INFORMATION

Prospective students may visit SPU's Web site to apply online or request application materials. High school students should request these materials early in their senior year. While applications for autumn quarter are accepted until June 1, prospective students must be admitted by March 1 to be considered for scholarships and the best financial aid, housing, and course registration opportunities. Applications are reviewed in the order they are received.

SIMPSON COLLEGE

■ INDIANOLA, IOWA

THE COLLEGE

Simpson College was founded in 1860. The institution was named Simpson College to honor Bishop Matthew Simpson (1811–1884), one of the best-known and most influential religious leaders of his day. The College is coeducational; although it is affiliated with the United Methodist Church, it is nonsectarian in spirit and accepts students without regard to race, color, creed, national origin, religion, sex, age, disability, veteran status, sexual orientation, or gender identity.

For more than a century, Simpson has played a vital role in the educational, cultural, intellectual, political, and religious life of the nation. The College has thirty-five buildings on 85 acres of beautiful campus and enrolls more than 2,000 students.

For an application and more information, students should contact:

Office of Admissions
Simpson College
701 North C Street
Indianola, Iowa 50125
Phone: 515-961-1624
800-362-2454 Ext. 1624 (toll-free)
E-mail: admiss@simpson.edu
Web site: http://www.simpson.edu

Extracurricular activities at Simpson are designed to supplement and reinforce the academic program and contribute toward a total learning experience. Students may participate in student government, publications, music, theater, and social groups. Simpson competes in eighteen intercollegiate sports and has an extensive intramural program for both men and women. Men's and women's athletics at Simpson are governed by the NCAA. Simpson also has chapters of three national fraternities, one local fraternity, and three national sororities.

ACADEMIC PROGRAMS

Simpson College operates on a 4-4-1 academic calendar. The first semester starts in late August and ends in mid-December; the second semester starts in mid-January and ends in late April. A three-week session takes place during the month of May. During this period, students have the opportunity to take one class that focuses on a single subject, to study abroad, or to participate in a field experience or internship.

Students must participate in one May Term class or program for each year of full-time study at Simpson College. All students must complete the requirements of the cornerstone studies in liberal arts and competencies in foreign language, math, and writing. To earn the Bachelor of Arts degree, students may take no more than 42 hours in the major department, excluding May Term programs, and 84 hours in the division of the major, including May Term programs. At least 128 semester hours of course work must be accumulated with a grade point average of C (2.0) or better.

For a Bachelor of Music degree, the same requirements apply, except that 84 hours must be earned in the major, excluding May Terms, and the candidate is limited to 12 additional hours in the division of fine arts. A minimum of 132 hours of course work must be completed with a cumulative grade point average of C (2.0) or better.

The First Year Program is a broadly inclusive program of orientation, group-building, mentoring, community service, advising, and classroom work structured to help new students adapt to their first year of college. The program begins with summer registration and extends throughout the full year.

The academic component of the First Year Program is the Liberal Arts Seminar, a joint classroom and advising concept that is unique among first-year programs. The seminars are small in size—no more than 18 first-year students each—and all are taught by students' faculty advisers.

FINANCIAL AID

Simpson College seeks to make it financially possible for qualified students to experience the advantages of a Simpson education. Generous gifts from alumni, trustees, and friends of the College—in addition to state and federal student aid programs—make this opportunity possible. Simpson offers financial aid on both a need and non-need basis. Need is determined by filing the Free Application for Federal Student Aid.

Financial aid granted on a non-need basis includes academic scholarships, which are awarded on the basis of prior academic records, and talent scholarships, which are available in theater, music, and art. The talent scholarships are determined by audition/portfolio.

APPLICATION AND INFORMATION

Simpson's rolling admission policy allows flexibility; however, early application is recommended. Transfer and international students are welcome. Students are strongly encouraged to visit the campus.

SPRINGFIELD COLLEGE

■ SPRINGFIELD, MASSACHUSETTS

THE COLLEGE

Springfield College graduates enter the workforce or advanced education with a competitive advantage—top-quality academic preparation and real-world experience. Founded in 1885 to train leaders for the YMCA, Springfield College now offers forty undergraduate major fields of study and has an international reputation for educating leaders in health sciences, human and social services, sports and movement studies, education, and the arts and sciences. Students perform fieldwork, internships, or service learning as early as their freshman year. It is a learning advantage based on the College's mission—education in spirit, mind, and body for leadership in service to others. Springfield College has been named one of the twenty-five "best neighbor" urban colleges and has received the Jostens/NADIIIAA Award of Merit for community service by student athletes. The Institute for International Sport named it one of the fifteen most influential educators through sport in America.

For an application and more information, students should contact:

Office of Admissions
Springfield College
263 Alden Street
Springfield, Massachusetts 01109
Phone: 413-748-3136
800-343-1257 (toll-free)
E-mail: admissions@spfldcol.edu
Web site:
http://www.springfieldcollege.edu

Springfield College is a vibrant living and learning environment. An ethnically diverse student body of 3,000 undergraduate and graduate students at the main campus comes from many U.S. states and abroad, with the majority from the Northeast. The picturesque, 150-acre lakeside campus is technologically up to date. Ten campus residence halls provide guaranteed on-campus housing. Options include traditional residence halls and suite-style accommodations with private rooms for 2 to 4 students sharing a lounge, kitchen, and bathrooms. There are single-sex and coeducational residences. Seniors may elect to live off campus. The main student dining facility features a range of fresh food options, and there are snack and other light-fare services around the campus.

Enriching the undergraduate experience is a wide array of cocurricular activities, health and wellness programs, and arts and cultural events; an extensive campus recreation program; and one of the largest athletics programs in the nation for a midsized college. There are more than 100 organizations and opportunities for involvement. More than 80 percent of undergraduates participate in some form of athletics, including varsity teams, intramurals, or club sports. There are teams in men's and women's basketball, cross-country, gymnastics, lacrosse, soccer, swimming, tennis, track, and volleyball; women's field hockey and softball; and men's baseball, football, golf, and wrestling.

ACADEMIC PROGRAMS

Consistent with Springfield College's humanics philosophy, undergraduate education is designed to promote an understanding of how the spirit, mind, and body work together in preparing students for a life of leadership in service to others.

To graduate, students must complete 130 credits, including required courses for the major field of study, electives, and required courses for all students (writing, computer applications, arts and humanities, analytical and natural sciences, social sciences, international/multicultural studies, social justice, and physical education). Students may also earn credit for successful completion of Advanced Placement (AP) high school courses, the DANTES subject standard test, and the College-Level Examination Program (CLEP) administered by the College Board. Springfield College has agreements with several medical schools that guarantee acceptance of its qualified students. In addition, many Springfield College programs allow undergraduates to take graduate-level courses. There are campus chapters of the following honor societies: Beta Beta Beta (biology), Kappa Delta Pi (education), Phi Alpha (social work), Phi Epsilon Kappa (health, physical education, recreation, and safety), and Psi Chi (psychology).

FINANCIAL AID

Students are encouraged to apply for grants, loans, and student employment. Springfield College financial aid is based on need, intellectual promise, leadership, and character. The College gives full consideration to students who submit the Free Application for Federal Student Aid and the College Scholarship Service Financial Aid PROFILE by March 15, 2008, for first-year students and May 1, 2008, for transfer students. Students not eligible for financial aid may be considered for campus employment.

APPLICATION AND INFORMATION

Application due dates for the 2008–09 academic year are April 1, 2008, for undergraduate applicants and August 1, 2008, for transfer students; students in athletic training and physical therapy, physician assistant studies, and occupational therapy have earlier deadlines. Students should contact the Office of Admissions for more information. Applications are reviewed as they are received.

TEXAS A&M UNIVERSITY–CORPUS CHRISTI

■ CORPUS CHRISTI, TEXAS

THE UNIVERSITY

Texas A&M University–Corpus Christi, a public institution of higher education, awards bachelor's, master's, and doctoral degrees. Situated on a coastal island along Corpus Christi Bay, Texas A&M–Corpus Christi's modern campus serves a diverse, growing student population of more than 8,600 students.

The University is driven by a desire to achieve. The Texas A&M University System Board of Regents has called Texas A&M University–Corpus Christi "the gem of the A&M System." *U.S. News & World Report* has included the University many times in its list of best colleges and universities, and the University is the only senior-level institution to twice receive the prestigious Texas Higher Education Coordinating Board Star Award.

For an application and more information, students should contact:

Office of Admissions and Records
Texas A&M University–Corpus Christi
6300 Ocean Drive
Corpus Christi, Texas 78412
Phone: 361-825-2624
800-4TAMUCC (toll-free)
E-mail: admiss@tamucc.edu
Web site: http://www.tamucc.edu

On-campus housing provides students with the opportunity to develop friendships, participate in group activities, and enjoy the unique island setting of the University. University apartments and residence halls have several floor plans available, accommodating 1, 2, or 4 residents. The University hosts a broad array of academic, community service, cultural, Greek, honors, religious, and special-interest organizations. As an NCAA Division I institution, the "Islanders" provide top-flight game action, and intramural sports, fitness and wellness classes, informal recreation, sport clubs, outdoor adventure, and special events are also available.

New Student Orientation is an action-packed and informative program designed especially for incoming freshman students. This two-day program reflects the University's collective effort to provide care and instruction to students to facilitate their transition into Texas A&M–Corpus Christi. In addition, New Student Orientation prepares students for the University's educational opportunities, builds awareness about student services, familiarizes students with their environment, and helps students form friendships that may last a lifetime. At New Student Orientation, students register for classes for the upcoming semester, meet representatives from the academic colleges, discuss the multitude of services and resources available, learn about opportunities to become involved in on-campus student activities and organizations, tour the campus, and interact with other new and current students.

In 2006, more than 6,500 undergraduates attended Texas A&M University–Corpus Christi, 61 percent of who were women. International students came from more than twenty countries.

ACADEMIC PROGRAMS

For the bachelor's degree, students must complete 120 semester hours, at least 45 of which must be upper-division course work. The University core curriculum is a 45- to 48-semester-hour program of study that is required of undergraduates to provide them with a foundation for further study and learning. Students are involved with core curriculum course work through the junior year. A broad range of disciplines are covered, including English composition, U.S. history, political science, natural science, mathematics, public speaking, social science, literature, fine arts, and philosophy.

In each of their first two semesters, full-time students are expected to enroll in specially selected groups of three or four classes known as Triads and Tetrads. The students and teachers within each Triad or Tetrad form a learning community; they take all the classes within a given Triad or Tetrad together and have many opportunities to collaborate, get to know each other, and learn. The teachers in each learning community work with each other to develop connections among the classes. All Triads and Tetrads include the First-Year Seminar (FYS) and the First-Year Writing class, both of which have 25 or fewer students. FYS immerses students in an active learning environment to help them develop their ability to learn through study, discussion, cooperation, and collaboration.

FINANCIAL AID

Students may apply for financial assistance through scholarship, grant, work-study, and loan programs. Academically competitive scholarships offered through the University include Academic Achievement Scholarships of $2000 per year for four academic years and the President's Council Scholarship, which provides $6000 per year for four years to an outstanding individual. Application forms and detailed instructions on applying for financial aid can be found at http://www.tamucc.edu/~faoweb.

APPLICATION AND INFORMATION

Completed applications for first-time freshmen are processed as they are received, and applicants are usually informed of their admission status within three to four weeks. Applications are due July 1, November 1, and April 1 for the fall, spring, and summer semesters, respectively.

TULANE UNIVERSITY

■ NEW ORLEANS, LOUISIANA

THE UNIVERSITY

Tulane University in New Orleans is known nationally and internationally for its teaching and research. At Tulane a student can get an international education in a European city without leaving America. The University is comprehensive by nature, with more than 10,000 students enrolled in nine schools and colleges ranging from the liberal arts and sciences through a full spectrum of professional schools: law, medicine, business, engineering, architecture, social work, and public health and tropical medicine. Tulane's 5,500 full-time undergraduates choose from more than seventy majors in colleges of liberal arts, sciences and engineering, architecture, business, and public health and continuing studies and may opt for joint-degree programs in Tulane's professional schools to earn undergraduate and graduate degrees in a shorter period of time. Tulane's distinctive arrangement of undergraduate schools gives every student the personal attention and teaching excellence of a small college while providing the interdisciplinary opportunities and research resources of a university that *U.S. News & World Report* ranks in the nation's top quartile. The average class size is 23. Senior faculty members are in the classroom at all levels, and the 8:1 student-teacher ratio ensures individual attention.

For an application and more information, students should contact:

Earl Retif
Vice President for Enrollment Management
210 Gibson Hall
Tulane University
6823 St. Charles Avenue
New Orleans, Louisiana 70118-5680
Phone: 504-865-5731
800-873-9283 (toll-free)
E-mail:
undergrad.admission@tulane.edu
Web site:
http://www.admission.tulane.edu

On its residential campus about 4 miles from downtown New Orleans, Tulane requires housing for freshmen and sophomores. Students may choose from several special interest floors in the residence halls, with areas for honors students, those interested in international and urban affairs, and women science majors, among others. Students participate in more than 300 campus organizations, including fraternities and sororities, intramural and intercollegiate club sports, and Tulane's community volunteer organization. Tulane fields eight NCAA Division I sports, competing in Conference USA.

More than 80 percent of Tulane students plan to go on eventually to graduate or professional school. Tulane students are among the country's most likely to be selected for several prestigious fellowships, including the Fulbright, Marshall, Rhodes, Truman, and Watson scholarships, that support postgraduate study.

Recent additions to Tulane's campus have included a brand new, state-of-the-art student center; a new, larger baseball stadium on campus; an addition to the School of Business; a center for engineering and biotechnology; a law school building; a fine arts complex; residence halls; and a new science facility.

Tulane's programs are shaped by the University's direct experience with the unprecedented natural disaster of Hurricane Katrina. This experience is providing faculty and staff members and students with equally unprecedented research, learning, and community-service opportunities that will have a lasting and profound impact on them, the city of New Orleans, the Gulf Coast region, and other communities around the world.

ACADEMIC PROGRAMS

All freshmen enroll in the Undergraduate College that comprises all of the undergraduate programs in Liberal Arts, Science and Engineering, Business, Public Health and Tropical Medicine, and Architecture.

The Tulane Core Curriculum provides a common academic experience for undergraduates across all schools of the University, requiring course work in all areas of knowledge. Students are offered an integrative, themed first-year seminar experience known as TIDES. The prominent role of public service and leadership reflects the value Tulane places upon developing a lifelong commitment to public service and citizenship.

Every Tulane undergraduate must complete a Senior Capstone Experience related to his or her major, which allows students to demonstrate the capacity to bring information, skills, and ideas acquired from the major and other parts of their education to bear on one significant project.

FINANCIAL AID

The University operates a comprehensive aid program; 74 percent of new students receive some form of financial aid. Need, determined by family financial information on the FAFSA and the PROFILE from the College Scholarship Service, establishes the appropriate amount of assistance. Merit, based on academic record, determines the proportion of Tulane-funded scholarships in the aid package.

APPLICATION AND INFORMATION

Regular decision applications should be submitted by January 15 for admission to the fall semester. Deans' Honor Scholarship applicants must apply by December 15 and are notified by February 20. Early action candidates should have all credentials on file by November 1 for notification by December 15. The application fee has been eliminated.

UNITED STATES MILITARY ACADEMY

■ WEST POINT, NEW YORK

THE ACADEMY

The United States Military Academy at West Point, the nation's oldest service academy, offers young men and women the nation's premier education and leadership development programs. West Point advocates the "whole person" concept and provides a broadly structured undergraduate curriculum that balances the physical sciences and engineering with the behavioral and social sciences.

West Point's mission is to educate, train, and inspire the Corps of Cadets so that each graduate is a commissioned leader of character who is committed to the values of duty, honor, and country and prepared for a career of professional excellence and service to the nation as an officer in the United States Army. Upon graduation, cadets are commissioned as second lieutenants in the U.S. Army and are normally required to serve on active duty for at least five years.

For an application and more information, students should contact:

Director of Admissions
United States Military Academy
606 Thayer Road
West Point, New York 10996-1797
Phone: 845-938-4041
E-mail: admissions@usma.edu
Web site: http://admissions.usma.edu

There are more than 4,100 men and women enrolled at West Point. West Pointers who remain in the Army are normally selected to attend civilian graduate schools in the United States or abroad between their fourth and tenth years of service.

In addition to academic and military education, cadets participate in athletic and extracurricular activities. Cadets have distinguished themselves in twenty-six intercollegiate varsity sports: baseball, basketball, cross-country, football, golf, gymnastics, hockey, indoor track, lacrosse, outdoor track, rifle, soccer, sprint football, swimming, tennis, and wrestling for men and basketball, cross-country, indoor track, outdoor track, rifle, soccer, softball, swimming, tennis, and volleyball for women.

There are more than 100 organized extracurricular activities, including mountaineering, hunting, fishing, scuba diving, archery, team handball, and orienteering clubs as well as clubs that compete on a national or intercollegiate level in crew, orienteering, powerlifting, handball, rugby, sport parachuting, triathlon, horseback riding, sailing, judo, karate, bowling, and marathon running. There are academic clubs, including mathematics, language, and electronics clubs; the Cadet Fine Arts Forum; Model United Nations; and the Debate Council. The Student Conference on United States Affairs has met for more than thirty years.

ACADEMIC PROGRAMS

The academic program at the United States Military Academy provides cadets with a broad background in the arts and sciences and prepares them for future graduate study. The total curriculum is designed to develop essential character, competence, and intellectual ability in an officer. The core curriculum is the cornerstone of the academic program and provides a foundation in mathematics, basic sciences, engineering sciences, information technology, humanities, behavior sciences, and social sciences. The core curriculum, including twenty-six to thirty courses, depending upon the major, represents the essential broad base of knowledge that is necessary for success as a commissioned officer while also supporting each cadet's choice of academic specialization.

Classes at West Point are small, averaging 12 to 18 cadets per section. Cadets receive individual attention, and tutorial sessions are available upon request. Advanced and honors courses are available to cadets having exceptional ability. All cadets study military science and receive classroom instruction in the principles of small-unit tactics and leadership in eight semester-long courses. Concentrated summer field training provides each cadet with the opportunity to learn and practice individual military skills and to apply the principles of tactics and leadership studied in the classroom.

FINANCIAL AID

There are no financial aid programs because expenses are paid by the U.S. government.

APPLICATION AND INFORMATION

First, prospective candidates should visit the Directorate of Admissions Web site at http://admissions.usma.edu and read through the Prospectus prior to completing the Candidate Questionnaire, because it outlines the West Point entrance requirements. They should then complete the Candidate Questionnaire, which opens a candidate's admissions file, to begin the application process. All applicants are encouraged to start a candidate file at West Point during the spring semester of their junior year or as soon thereafter as possible.

UNIVERSITY OF ADVANCING TECHNOLOGY

■ TEMPE, ARIZONA

THE UNIVERSITY

The University of Advancing Technology (UAT) is a unique, technology-infused private college founded by a techno-geek for techno-geeks. Its mission is to educate students in the fields of advancing technology to become innovators of the future. UAT's campus culture is devoted to continually nurturing a thriving geek community where everyone's personal lives and professional aspirations revolve around technology. UAT offers students a well-rounded education in a nontraditional setting. Students who are seeking a strictly career-oriented technical college experience will not find it here. Because of UAT's dedication to both scholastic excellence and technological innovation, it stands apart in academia as an ideal destination for the geeks of the world who feel disenfranchised by conventional institutions of higher learning. For the student who is looking at the future of technology and wishes to become a vital part of it, UAT beckons.

For an application and more information, students should contact:

UAT Admissions
University of Advancing Technology
2625 West Baseline Road
Tempe, Arizona 85283-1056
Phone: 602-383-8228
800-658-5744 (toll-free)
E-mail: admission@uat.edu
Web site: http://www.uat.edu

The beginning of the twenty-first century is an exciting time to be in the technology community, and UAT is serious about technology. As the twenty-first century unfolds, it is becoming more and more apparent how technology in all its manifestations profoundly alters how people work, live, play, and interact with each other. UAT students benefit from their fundamental understanding of both theoretical and applied aspects of technology. As technologists, UAT students see that there will always be newer and newer tools created to address mankind's emergent needs and desires. Changing the world through technology is inherent in UAT's mission. Current subjects of ongoing research and scholarship at UAT include robotics and embedded systems, artificial life programming, network security, game development, and other areas of advanced technology.

UAT has always devoted all of its resources to creating a vital academic environment where students are challenged to achieve, explore new and traditional concepts, and practice what they learn in real-world situations. This combination of research, scholarship, and application creates technically adept graduates who are equally at home in academia and the working world and valued by both. UAT graduates thrive in the digital age and meet and surpass every expectation of their high-technology employers and peers. They enter the professional world with accredited associate and bachelor's degrees, and many return to pursue a master's degree in the Graduate College of Applied Technology.

UAT's 1,200 students (from all fifty states and many other countries) still find plenty of time to time to participate in clubs and other activities that enhance UAT's geek-friendly environment, such as ancient games, anime, technology philosophy, Yu-Gi-Oh, game developers, Web development, biking, C++, and photography. Special on-campus events include live-action games, Oktoberfest, LAN parties, Guitar Hero tournaments, and Thanksgiving dinner.

At any time, day or night, there are groups of students pounding coffee while working on course work and projects, looking to create the next big thing. It is not uncommon to see students burning the midnight oil, pulling all-nighters, exchanging ideas, and searching for solutions to perfect their creative innovations. There are also gatherings of students and instructors engaged in discussions of the latest technology developments and how they can make them better. UAT has an academic and social environment that integrates the contemporary and advancing principles of education and technology with its Year-Round Balanced Learning (YRBL) teaching model to create a unique collaborative educational environment.

ACADEMIC PROGRAMS

The Bachelor of Arts and Bachelor of Science programs require a minimum of 120 semester credits, including 84 core credits, forty 300/400–level credits, and 36 general education credits. The Associate of Arts and Associate of Science programs require a minimum of 60 semester credits: 45 core credits, and 15 general education credits.

FINANCIAL AID

Average aid per academic year for first-academic-year freshmen is $11,784. The percentage of freshmen who receive aid is 84 percent. The percentage of freshmen who receive UAT academic scholarships is 26 percent. The average amount of scholarships received per freshman student per academic year is $1200.

APPLICATION AND INFORMATION

Students may apply online at http://www.uat.edu/admissions. To request an application, students should either e-mail admissions@uat.edu or call 877-UAT-GEEK (toll-free).

UNIVERSITY OF MASSACHUSETTS DARTMOUTH

■ NORTH DARTMOUTH, MASSACHUSETTS

THE UNIVERSITY

For an application and more information, students should contact:

Office of Admissions
UMass Dartmouth
285 Old Westport Road
North Dartmouth, Massachusetts 02747-2300
Phone: 508-999-8605
E-mail: admissions@umassd.edu
Web site: http://explore.umassd.edu/

The University of Massachusetts Dartmouth traces its roots to 1895 when the Massachusetts legislature chartered the New Bedford Textile School and the Bradford Durfee Textile School in Fall River. As the region's economic base shifted from textiles to more diverse manufacturing and service industries, the program of the colleges changed. Courses were developed to respond to the needs of new generations of students, stimulated by the clear economic and social advantages of a well-educated citizenry. In 1962, Southeastern Massachusetts Technological Institute (SMTI) was created, and in 1969, out of a need and a clear demand for a comprehensive public university, SMTI became Southeastern Massachusetts University. Then, in 1988, the Swain School of Design merged with the University's College of Visual and Performing Arts.

In 1991, a new University of Massachusetts system was created, which combined the Amherst and Boston campuses with the University of Lowell, Southeastern Massachusetts University, and the Medical Center in Worcester. Today, UMass Dartmouth provides educational programs, research, extension, and continuing education and cyber education in the liberal and creative arts and sciences and in the professions. A broad range of bachelor's, master's, and doctoral degrees are offered.

UMass Dartmouth enrolls approximately 8,500 students; 90 percent are from Massachusetts, with a growing number from other states and countries outside the United States. A residential campus with a variety of student organizations, athletic programs, cultural opportunities, and interest groups, the University fosters personal development, diversity, and responsible citizenship.

ACADEMIC PROGRAMS

The University operates on a two-semester calendar. A five-week intersession is offered between semesters. Summer-term courses are offered in June, July, and early August. Undergraduate students usually enroll in four or five courses each semester, and a typical course earns 3 credits. An undergraduate degree requires a minimum of 120 credits (there are a few majors that require 135 credits); a student can complete degree requirements for a specified major within a department or an approved interdepartmental major (30 credits). Students must also complete requirements according to the degree being sought.

Other learning opportunities include independent study, contract learning, and directed study; study abroad; study at a nearby university through cross-registration; and credit by examination. UMass Dartmouth is a member of SACHEM (Southeastern Association for Cooperation in Higher Education in Massachusetts), allowing for cross-registration at Bridgewater State College, Bristol Community College, Cape Cod Community College, Dean College, Massachusetts Maritime Academy, Massasoit Community College, Stonehill College, and Wheaton College. The University has formal exchange agreements with, among others, the University of Grenoble (France), the Lycée du Grésivaudan at Meylan and the Lycée Aristide Berges, Nottingham Trent University (England), the Baden-Württemberg Universities (Germany), Centro de Arte e Comunicação (Portugal), Nova Scotia College of Art and Design, the École Nationale Supérieure des Industries Textiles, Université de Haute Alsace (France), and Minho University (Portugal). Students may also take initiative in finding other programs in addition to the exchange-agreement institutions.

The College of Engineering provides majors in any of the engineering fields and offers students work experience through cooperative education or internships.

FINANCIAL AID

Nearly all students are eligible for some type of financial aid. UMass Dartmouth awards financial aid based on federal, state, and institutional guidelines; students must submit the FAFSA. In determining need, the Financial Aid Services Office considers the total costs of attending the University (tuition, fees, books, room and board, the cost of commuting, and an allowance for living and personal expenses). The difference between total University cost and the estimate of expected family contribution is the amount that the financial aid staff considers to be financial need.

APPLICATION AND INFORMATION

Students are invited to visit the University for a campus tour and a meeting with an admissions officer; interviews are not required. Some majors, such as nursing, may close early due to enrollment capacity. Admission is rolling except for early decision (freshmen). The early decision deadline is November 15.

UNIVERSITY OF ROCHESTER

■ ROCHESTER, NEW YORK

THE UNIVERSITY

Founded in 1850, Rochester is one of the leading private universities in the country, one of sixty-two members of the prestigious Association of American Universities, and one of eight national private research institutions in the premier University Athletic Association. Including the Eastman School of Music, the University has a full-time enrollment of 4,608 undergraduates and 2,900 graduate students. Rochester's personal scale and the breadth of its research and academic programs permit both attention to the individual and unusual flexibility in planning undergraduate studies.

Located on a bend in the Genesee River, the River Campus is home to almost all undergraduates who live in a variety of residence halls, fraternity houses, and special-interest housing. Most of the campus is built in a consistent neoclassical architecture, yet all academic buildings are wireless, and all residence halls are wired for the Internet and cable television. Among the facilities are Wilson Commons, the student union; the multipurpose Athletic Center; and a brand-new research facility, the Goergen Hall of Biomedical Engineering and Optics.

Rochester students participate in more than 220 student organizations, including twenty-two varsity teams, thirty-six intramural and club sports, eighteen fraternities and thirteen sororities, performing arts groups, musical ensembles, WRUR radio, URTV, and various campus publications.

For an application and more information, students should contact:

Dean of Admissions and Financial Aid
University of Rochester
P.O. Box 270251
Rochester, New York 14627-0251
Phone: 585-275-3221
888-822-2256 (toll-free)
Web site: http://www.enrollment.rochester.edu/admissions

Director of Admissions
Eastman School of Music
26 Gibbs Street
Rochester, New York 14604
Phone: 585-274-1060
800-388-9695 (toll-free)
Web site:
http://www.rochester.edu/eastman

ACADEMIC PROGRAMS

The distinctive Rochester Curriculum allows students to select their major from one of the three branches of learning (the humanities, the natural sciences, and the social sciences). In each of the two branches outside their major, students choose a "cluster" of three courses that allows them to dig deeply in an area that particularly interests them. For most students, there are no other distribution requirements, except choosing one of seventy freshman writing classes.

The Quest program offers first-year students the advantages of small classes, student/teacher collaboration, and original research. As a result, Quest courses teach students how to learn, both as undergraduates and beyond.

Students may arrange independent study courses or pursue research in all departments. Those whose interests may not be fully realized through a traditional major, double major, or major/minor, may work with faculty advisers to design an interdepartmental concentration.

Undergraduates from any academic discipline may devote their senior year to a self-designed creative project in the form of scholarly research, a scientific experiment, or a literary or artistic work through the Senior Scholars Program.

Undergraduates enrolled in the College may take private instruction at the Eastman School of Music. A double-degree program leading to the Bachelor of Music degree from Eastman and a bachelor's degree from the College is also available.

The Rochester Early Medical Scholars program is an eight-year B.A. or B.S./M.D. program for exceptionally talented undergraduates. Students enrolled in this program enter the University of Rochester with assurance of admission to the University's medical school upon successful completion of their undergraduate degree program.

FINANCIAL AID

The University offers a strong program of financial assistance, including academic merit scholarships, grants, loans, tuition payment plans, and part-time jobs. Applicants for financial aid should submit the CSS PROFILE application and the FAFSA.

WASHINGTON COLLEGE

■ CHESTERTOWN, MARYLAND

THE COLLEGE

Founded in 1782, Washington College is the tenth-oldest college in the United States. George Washington, for whom the College was named, was an early benefactor and member of the College's Board of Visitors and Governors. Today, the College is one of the few nationally recognized selective liberal arts institutions with an enrollment of fewer than 1,350 students. The intimacy of a small-college environment, the tradition of a challenging liberal arts curriculum, and the relaxed informality characteristic of the Chesapeake Bay region continue to exert their influence on the College and all who come to it.

For an application and more information, students should contact:

Office of Admissions
Washington College
300 Washington Avenue
Chestertown, Maryland 21620-1197
Phone: 410-778-7700
800-422-1782 (toll-free)
E-mail: adm.off@washcoll.edu
Web site: http://www.washcoll.edu

The current enrollment is 1,300 men and women. Although most students come from the Northeast, international students and students from other regions of the country are enrolled in numbers sufficient to add geographic diversity to the student body. Eighty percent of all students live in residences located on the 120-acre campus; special interest housing is available for students interested in science, foreign languages, international studies, creative arts, and Greek organizations.

The College enjoys a high participation rate in intramural sports, in the performing arts, and in student publications, community service clubs, recreational activities, and social organizations. The Division III intercollegiate program offers fifteen varsity sports, including baseball, basketball, lacrosse, rowing, soccer, swimming, and tennis for men and basketball, field hockey, lacrosse, rowing, sailing, softball, swimming, tennis, and volleyball for women.

ACADEMIC PROGRAMS

The College's four-course plan is intended to broaden and deepen a student's education by providing for the intensive study of a limited number of subjects and by encouraging individual responsibility for learning. General education requirements include two freshman seminars and ten semester courses chosen from the following categories: social science, natural science, humanities, fine arts, quantitative studies, and foreign language. Candidates for a degree must satisfactorily complete thirty-two semester courses and must fulfill the senior obligation (for example, a comprehensive examination or thesis).

Washington College offers a nationally renowned creative writing program and awards the prestigious Sophie Kerr Prize every year to the graduating senior who shows the most promise for a career in literary endeavors.

With the aid of a faculty adviser, students can construct their own major fields of study in some areas or pursue independent study for course credit.

FINANCIAL AID

Washington College offers financial assistance to approximately 80 percent of its student body. Awards are based on need and academic performance. Financial aid includes scholarships, grants, loans, and jobs. The College participates in the Federal Perkins Loan Program, the Federal Stafford Student Loan Program, and the Federal Work-Study Program. Federal Pell Grants and Federal Supplemental Educational Opportunity Grants are applicable to Washington College. In addition, financial assistance from the Maryland scholarship program and other state programs can be applied to expenses at the College.

Members of the National Honor Society and Cum Laude Society who are admitted to Washington College are awarded $40,000 academic scholarships ($10,000 annually for four years). Other academic scholarships ranging in value from $5000 to $13,750 are offered without regard to financial need.

To be eligible for financial assistance, applicants should file the FAFSA by February 15. An application for admission, with all supporting credentials, should be received by February 15 to establish eligibility. Students interested in Federal Pell Grant assistance or in-state scholarship programs must apply directly to the program concerned.

APPLICATION AND INFORMATION

The application, a $45 fee, the high school transcript (and college transcript, for transfer applicants), scores on the SAT or ACT, and one teacher recommendation are required. Applications for early decision must be received by November 15. For regular admission, forms must be submitted prior to February 15.

WEBBER INTERNATIONAL UNIVERSITY

■ BABSON PARK, FLORIDA

THE UNIVERSITY

Webber International University was founded in 1927 by Roger Babson, who was an internationally known economist in the early 1900s. The four-year independent coeducational university is located on a beautiful 110-acre campus along the shoreline of Lake Caloosa, 45 minutes from Disney World, Cypress Gardens, and many other attractions. Built on a strong tradition that sets it apart, the University exemplifies integrity, high standards, and achievement. Webber International University provides an environment that encourages success through academic excellence and hard work. About 319 men and 200 women are enrolled as undergraduates at Webber. Seventy-nine percent are from Florida; the other 21 percent represent nineteen states and thirty-three different countries.

For an application and more information, students should contact:

Webber International University
1201 North Scenic Highway
P.O. Box 96
Babson Park, Florida 33827-9990
Phone: 863-638-2910
E-mail: admissions@webber.edu
Web site: http://www.webber.edu

Webber International University's off-campus internship programs provide a real-world business environment for Webber students. Field trips also supplement students' business education.

The University offers intercollegiate sports in baseball, basketball, cross-country, football, golf, soccer, tennis, and track and field for men and in basketball, cheerleading, cross-country, golf, soccer, softball, tennis, track and field, and volleyball for women. Intramural athletics are also available for all students. The University's physical education complex includes two gymnasiums, a fitness room, racquetball courts, a soccer field, a junior Olympic-size swimming pool, beach volleyball court, and tennis courts. Webber students also enjoy lakeside activities such as beach volleyball, canoeing, fishing, and kayaking. Among the wide variety of social organizations and clubs are Phi Beta Lambda, a student government association, an international club, Webber ambassadors, Eta Sigma Delta and the Society of Hosteurs, a marketing club, a tourism society, FCA, a sport management club, SIFE, and athletic boosters. These groups and others help to sponsor the various social functions at Webber.

ACADEMIC PROGRAMS

The University requires the completion of 60 credit hours for the Associate of Science degree and 120 credit hours for the Bachelor of Science degree with a minimum grade point average of 2.0. The average course load is 15 hours per semester. Students in the Bachelor of Science degree program are required to complete approximately 30 hours in the major, 36 hours in the business core, 36 hours in the general education core, and 18 hours of tailored electives. Students in the Associate of Science degree program are required to complete 27 hours in the business core, 18 hours in the general education core, and 15 hours in the major and tailored elective.

The Bachelor of Science degree in general business studies requires the completion of 45 hours in the general business studies core, 39 hours in the general education core, and 36 hours of tailored electives.

All students must complete 30 of the last 33 hours at Webber International University to receive a degree. Credit is awarded for successful scores on AP and CLEP general tests.

FINANCIAL AID

The Student Financial Aid Department offers students its counsel and assistance in meeting their educational expenses. Aid is awarded on the basis of an applicant's need, academic performance, and promise. Approximately 80 percent of the students at Webber International University receive financial assistance. To demonstrate need, applicants are required to file the FAFSA. Various types of aid, such as scholarships, grants, loans, and Federal Work-Study awards, are used to meet student needs. A limited number of no-need scholarships are available; these awards are based on academic performance, on community and college service, or on athletic ability in basketball, tennis, volleyball, golf, soccer, softball, cross-country, and track and field. Webber participates in the Federal Perkins Loan, Federal Supplemental Educational Opportunity Grant, and Federal Work-Study programs. All applicants are expected to apply for any entitlement grant for which they are eligible, such as the Federal Pell Grant; Florida residents must apply for a Florida Student Assistance Grant and the Florida Tuition Voucher Program. Federal Stafford Student Loans are also available. Financial aid applicants should submit their requests and forms before April 1.

APPLICATION AND INFORMATION

An application is ready for consideration by the Admissions Committee when it has been received with a $35 application fee for domestic students and $75 for international students, the required test scores and references, and transcripts from each school attended. The University uses a system of rolling admissions. It is recommended that applications be submitted as early as possible, since on-campus housing is limited. Freshmen are required to live in the dormitory unless they reside with a parent, guardian, or spouse.

WENTWORTH INSTITUTE OF TECHNOLOGY

■ BOSTON, MASSACHUSETTS

THE INSTITUTE

Wentworth Institute of Technology was founded in 1904 to provide education in the mechanical arts. Today, it is one of the nation's leading technical institutes, offering study in a variety of disciplines. Wentworth has a current undergraduate day enrollment of approximately 3,500 men and women (3,000 full-time) and graduates more engineering technicians and technologists each year than any other college in the United States. The technical education acquired at Wentworth enables graduates to assume creative and responsible careers in business and industry. Wentworth is located on a 35-acre campus on Huntington Avenue in Boston.

For an application and more information, students should contact:

Admissions Office
Wentworth Institute of Technology
550 Huntington Avenue
Boston, Massachusetts 02115
Phone: 617-989-4000
800-556-0610 (toll-free)
E-mail: admissions@wit.edu
Web site: http://www.wit.edu

Wentworth provides dormitory and suite-style residence halls on campus for men and women. Students residing in the residence halls are on a full meal plan. Upperclass students have the option of living in on-campus apartments. Students residing in the apartments may prepare their own meals. A cafeteria, snack bar, and new convenience store are available for those wishing to purchase their meals.

Career counseling and placement assistance are available to all alumni and to students who have completed at least one semester of study at the Institute. While many graduates of Wentworth are employed in the Boston area, alumni have secured positions throughout the United States and abroad.

ACADEMIC PROGRAMS

At Wentworth Institute of Technology, college-level study in technological fundamentals and principles is combined with appropriate laboratory, field, and studio experience. Students apply theory to practical problems, and they acquire skills and techniques by using, operating, and controlling equipment and instruments that are particular to their area of specialization. In addition, study in the social sciences and humanities provides a balanced understanding of the world in which graduates work. Wentworth's programs of study are more practical than theoretical in approach.

During the first two years of study in a degree program at Wentworth, students lay the foundation for more advanced study in the third and fourth (and fifth, where applicable) years. While nearly all majors allow continuous study from the freshman through the senior year, the architecture major requires a petition for acceptance to the baccalaureate program during the sophomore year.

All bachelor's degree programs are conducted as cooperative (co-op) education programs: upon entering their third year, students alternate semesters of academic study at Wentworth with semester-long periods of employment in industry. Two semesters of co-op employment are required; one additional (summer) semester of co-op is optional. Both students and the companies that hire them are enthusiastic about the co-op program and agree that it is a mutually valuable experience.

FINANCIAL AID

Scholarships are available to students who demonstrate need and academic promise. Merit-based scholarships are also available. Wentworth also provides federal and state financial assistance, such as Federal Pell and Federal Supplemental Educational Opportunity Grants, Federal Perkins Loans, Federal Work-Study Program awards, Gilbert Matching Grants, and Massachusetts No-Interest Loans, to students with financial need in accordance with federal and state guidelines. To apply for financial aid, new students should complete the FAFSA by March 1. Applications received after this date are considered as funds allow.

Wentworth participates in the Federal Direct Lending program. As a result, students are eligible to borrow under the Federal Direct Stafford Student Loan program and parents may borrow under the Federal Direct PLUS program. Individuals participating in these programs borrow money directly from the federal government rather than through lending institutions.

In addition to these need-based programs, Wentworth also participates in the MEFA loan program sponsored by the Massachusetts Educational Financing Authority. Wentworth offers several payment options through payment plans and alternative loan financing.

APPLICATION AND INFORMATION

Students are admitted to Wentworth for September and January enrollment. Notification of admission is made on a rolling basis. The preferred method for applying is online at http://www.wit.edu/apply. The online application fee is $10. An application form, the application fee, transcripts from the secondary school and any colleges previously attended, SAT or ACT scores, a personal statement, and a letter of recommendation should be sent to the Admissions Office.

WILLIAM PATERSON UNIVERSITY OF NEW JERSEY

■ WAYNE, NEW JERSEY

THE UNIVERSITY

Since its founding in 1855, William Paterson University has grown into a comprehensive state institution whose programs reflect the area's need for challenging, affordable educational options. Ideally midsized (the total enrollment is 10,443, of whom 8,863 are degree-seeking undergraduates), William Paterson offers a wider variety of academic programs than smaller universities, yet provides students with a more personalized atmosphere than larger institutions. Once the site of the family estate of Garret Hobart, the twenty-fourth vice president of the United States, William Paterson's 370-acre spacious campus, with its wooded areas and waterfalls, offers an environment in which students may develop both intellectually and socially. Although the majority of the University's students come from the New Jersey and New York vicinity, some international and out-of-state students enroll each year. Twenty-three percent of undergraduates reside on campus in ten residence halls or apartment-style facilities, which accommodate 2,700 students. On-campus housing is offered on a first-come, first-served basis. Portions of the residence halls are dedicated to dynamic "learning communities" centered around students' shared interests and themes, such as the University's Honors College and health and wellness.

For an application and more information, students should contact:

Office of Admissions
William Paterson University of New Jersey
Wayne, New Jersey 07470
Phone: 973-720-2125
877-WPU-EXCEL (toll-free)
E-mail: admissions@wpunj.edu
Web site: http://www.wpunj.edu

Social, cultural, and recreational activities complement the academic programs. Cultural events take place throughout the year, featuring both William Paterson's own talent as well as renowned professional artists. Among the programs are concerts presenting jazz, classical, and contemporary music; theater productions; gallery exhibits; and a distinguished-lecturer series. The brand new University Commons complex, including the redesigned John Victor Machuga Student Center, is the heart of the campus, where the entire University community gathers and interacts. This state-of-the-art campus center provides students with an exquisite setting for a vast array of social and extracurricular activities, dining venues, and student support services, all under one roof. The Student Activities Programming Board helps the more than fifty clubs and organizations to develop diverse activities for the entire student body. William Paterson has twenty-two social fraternities and sororities and sixteen honor societies. Students staff the campus radio station (WPSC) and the television station (WPC-TV), which develops a number of widely distributed television programs for local and statewide cable networks. The Recreation Center serves as the focal point for physical recreation. In addition to the main courts, which accommodate badminton, basketball, indoor tennis, and volleyball, the 4,000-seat facility has racquetball courts, an exercise room, saunas, and Jacuzzis. The University has twelve intercollegiate sports teams, five for men and seven for women, including successful NCAA teams in men's baseball and women's softball. In addition, bowling, dance, horseback riding, and ice hockey are organized as club sports. The University has a competition-size indoor pool, outdoor tennis courts, and a lighted athletics field complex.

ACADEMIC PROGRAMS

Students must complete a minimum of 128 credits to earn a baccalaureate degree. Degree programs include a 60-credit general education requirement, 30–60 credits in a major, and 20–40 credits in elective courses. (In specialized degree programs, such as the B.F.A. and the B.M., general education and major course requirements may differ.) Students uncertain of which career path to follow may take advantage of advisement and counseling programs. In addition, the general education requirements enable students to take up to 60 credits before declaring a major. Diagnostic testing and career seminars, provided by the Career Development Office, also ensure that students receive the guidance necessary to make wise course selections and career decisions.

William Paterson offers a variety of special programs, including its Honors College, which currently offers seven program tracks—biopsychology, cognitive science, humanities, life science and environmental ethics, music, performing and literary arts, and social sciences.

FINANCIAL AID

Financial aid is available through a number of federal and state grant, loan, scholarship, and work-study programs. To apply for need-based aid, students must file the FAFSA by the priority date of April 1. Both the University and the Alumni Association award a number of competitive scholarships, based solely on academic merit, to entering freshmen. Each year, more than 1,000 scholarships are awarded, which total more than $4.8 million.

APPLICATION AND INFORMATION

Application forms and transcripts from candidates for freshman status must be received by May 1 for fall admission and November 1 for spring admission. A $50 application fee is required. Applications are reviewed on a rolling basis. Campus tours are available on weekdays by appointment when classes are in session.

INDEX

Alphabetical Listing of Four-Year Colleges

Page numbers refer to each college's profile; page numbers in **bold-faced** text refer to **Close-Ups.**